A GREEK - ENGLISH LEXICON

OF THE SEPTUAGINT

A Greek - English Lexicon

of the Septuagint

Part II

Κ - Ω

Compiled by

J. Lust
E. Eynikel
K. Hauspie

Deutsche Bibelgesellschaft

1996

ISBN 3-438-05126-5
A Greek-English Lexicon of the Septuagint, Part II
© 1996 Deutsche Bibelgesellschaft, Stuttgart
All rights reserved
Printed in Germany

5. 2000

CONTENTS

CONTENTS

PREFACE

The second and final volume of this lexicon appears four years after the first. Like the first, it is the result of a team effort. At the end of this venture I wish to express my warmest gratitude to my assistant K. Hauspie for her sustained and outstanding work. She was responsible for the research on the Greek vocabulary of the second volume and for the coordination of the contributions of the other members of the team and of the external advisors. Together with my colleague E. Eynikel and myself, she was the engine behind the project. Several collaborators to the first volume also made valuable contributions to the second: A. Claes, D. D'huyvetters, B. Doyle, G. Hauspie, and E. Joris. Among the new collaborators we mention J. Philips and G. Sinnaeve. Special acknowledgement must be made of the generous efforts of our external advisors and correctors: the experts in matters of Greek language: W. Clarysse, C.C. Caragounis, and F. Van Segbroeck, and the specialists in Semitic languages: A. Schoors, M. Zipor, and J. Cook. With regard to the bibliography, the notes of P.-M. Bogaert and the careful supervision of F. Van Segbroeck were of a great help.

In the introduction to the first volume we announced the publication of a separate volume listing all the verb forms and their lemmata. Taylor's *Parsing Guide* published in 1994[1] made this work redundant. Meanwhile another supplement, treating the variants mentioned in the apparatuses of the critical editions, is in the planning stage. We are also working on a lexicon of Aquila, Theodotion, and Symmachus. The successful completion of these additional projects largely depends on the generosity of sponsors such as those who have supported us up to now: the "Onderzoeksfonds" of the K.U.Leuven, the Belgian "Nationaal Fonds voor Wetenschappelijk Onderzoek", the Abbey of Westmalle, and the German Bible Society. A special word of thanks is due to J. Lange, secretary to the administration of the German Bible Society, who kindly and smoothly handled any problems related to business and publication.

Leuven, October, 1996   J. Lust

---

1. B.A. TAYLOR, *The Analytical Lexicon to the Septuagint. A Complete Parsing Guide*, Grands Rapids, MI, 1994.

For the general principles of the lexicon the reader is referred to the Introduction of Volume I. The present Introduction is only concerned with the relatively minor changes that have been made in our policy in response to the useful suggestions and critiques made by users of the first volume, and as a consequence of our growing expertise.

1. Abbreviations

In Volume I, in the section *ABBREVIATIONS, II. Books of the Bible* we noted that some books, or parts of books, occur twice in the list of abbreviations. The reason for this is that Rahlfs' edition of the Septuagint comprises two versions of these texts. Some of the rather confusing implications, especially in connection with the statistics and the five references provided immediately after the lemma, should perhaps be explained more fully with the help of two (shortened) examples:

κατάβασις,-εως⁺   N3F 0-7-2-0-3-12

Jos 8,24; 10,11; Jgs 1,16; 1 Sm 23,20

descent, precipice Mi 1,4; *falling down* (of snow) Sir 43,18; *id.* (of hailstones) Sir 46,6

καταβιβάζω⁺   V 1-2-6-1-1-11

Dt 21,4; Jos 2,18; Jgsᴬ 7,5; Jer 28(51),40; Ez 26,20

A: *to make to go down to* [τινα εἴς τι] Jgsᴬ 7,5; *to bring down* [τινα] Ez 28,8; *id.* [τι] (of anim.) Dt 21,4; *to bring down to* [τινα πρός τινα] Ez 26,20; *to let down* [τινα] Jos 2,18

P: *to descend* Ez 31,18

With respect to the first lemma, "Jgs 1,16" indicates that the word in question occurs both in Ms A and in Ms B. The word is counted twice in the statistics. As a consequence, the list of the first five occurrences is limited to four passages since the passage in Jgs 1,16 is counted twice. With respect to the second lemma, "Jgsᴬ 7,5" indicates that the word in question occurs in the text of Ms A of Jgs (but not in Ms B). In the statistics it is counted only once. A similar procedure applies to Daniel (Dnᴸˣˣ and Dnᵀʰ), to Susannah (Susᴸˣˣ and Susᵀʰ), to Bel (Belᴸˣˣ and Belᵀʰ), and to Tobit (Tobᴮᴬ and Tobˢ).

The policy is somewhat different in Joshua where sections 15,22-62 and 18,22-19,45 only are represented twice in Rahlfs' edition. For these sections the respective abbreviations Josᴬ and Josᴮ indicate that the word occurs respectively in Ms A or in Ms B, whereas Josᴮᴬ means that it occurs both in Ms A and in Ms B. In the latter case, the word is counted twice.

2. Bibliography

An abbreviated list of references to commentaries providing lexicographical and text-critical information frequently used in the lexicon is given before the general bibliography. With the exception of the commentaries on the Septuagint (M. HARL et al., *La Bible d'Alexandrie*, J.W. WEVERS, *Notes on the Greek Text*) they are only exceptionally referred to at the lemmata. In the general bibliography the full reference to these works is marked by an asterisk.

For references to the lexicographical instruments that were regularly consulted we refer to the Introduction to Volume I, page I, note 3. T. Muraoka's Lexicon to the Twelve Prophets (1993) should now be added to the works listed there. Special mention should be made of the frequently overlooked Supplement to the Lexicon of Liddell-Scott-Jones, first published in 1968. With the help of Baars' review [*VT* 20 (1970) 371-379] we checked all the entries in the Supplement that give additional information about the use of a particular word in the Septuagint. In the second volume of our work, the entries in question are systematically signalled at the end of the discussion of the relevant lemmata. In as far as possible, the Revised Supplement, recently edited by P.G.W. Glare (1996), has also been taken into account. For full references, see the general bibliography in the present volume.

In order to facilitate the use of the general bibliography, the list of the first volume has been completed and reprinted. The lay-out has also been changed in order to avoid needless repetitions.

When publications are reprinted in collected essays, the reference given at the end of an entry is to the pagination of the more recent publication. Thus at κατάρχω, CAIRD 1969 = 1972, 133 refers to page 133 of G.B. Caird's contribution in the collected essays edited by R. Kraft in 1972, and not to the page of the original publication of 1969.

3. Lemmata

- Transliterations, signalled by an equals sign (=) are more clearly distinguished from loanwords (and homoeophonic words). Transliterations are Hebrew or Aramaic words that are not translated but simply written in Greek characters. They do not follow the Greek declension rules. Loanwords are Hebrew, Aramaic, or other Semitic words that are fully Hellenized, meaning that they received a Greek accentuation and declinable endings. (The name, definition, and existence of homoeophones is highly disputed. In our tentative definition, a homoeophonic word is a Greek word chosen as a translational equivalent of a Hebrew or Aramaic word because it sounds similar or looks similar. In our Lexicon, the number of words explicitly characterized as such is relatively small. In most of the disputed cases we simply refer to the bibliography on the subject.)
- Verbs of which the simple form does not exist are preceded by a hyphen (-) representing the prefix. Following the policy of LSJ, the lemma of a verb is in the active mood, even when the LXX uses it only in its passive or medial forms.
- In order to introduce more clarity into the data following the lemma, more subdivisions are employed: a first subdivision concerns the moods of the verbs: Active (A:); Medial (M:); Passive (P:); a second concerns the meanings.
- The lexicon offers translation equivalents rather than descriptions of meanings. For practical reasons this policy has been continued in the second volume. Descriptions or elements of description are added between brackets ( ) when the translation appears to be ambiguous. A word may also be added between brackets ( ) when it is needed for the translation although it is not directly included in the meaning of the Greek word.

παραλύω⁺   V 4-2-10-0-8-24
Gn 4,15; 19,11; Lv 13,45; Dt 32,36; 2 Sm 8,4
A: *to disband* [τι] 2 Sm 8,4; *to weaken, to
disable, to enfeeble* [τινα] Jdt 16,6; *id.* [τι] Ez
25,9; *to bring down* (the proud) [τι] Is 23,9; *to
pay* (penalty) [τι] Gn 4,15
P: *to be loosed* (of garments) Lv 13,45; *to be
weakened, to be feeble* (of limbs) Jer 6,24; *to be
paralysed* Wis 17,14; *to be exhausted* Gn 19,11
Cf. CAIRD 1969=1972, 139; HARL 1986ᵃ, 116-117.180-181;
→NIDNTT

παροιστράω   V 0-0-3-0-0-3
Ez 2,6; Hos 4,16(bis)
to rage madly, to be provoked, to be incited (of
anim. by e.g. a goad); neol.

παροράω⁺   V 5-1-1-3-9-19
Lv 5,21(bis); Nm 5,6(bis).12
A: *to overlook* [τι] Jb 11,11; *id.* [τινα] Is 57,11;
to disregard, to despise [τι] Sir 32,18
P: *to be overlooked* 1 Kgs 10,3

*Nm 5,12 παρίδῃ *she despises* -◊עלם‎ for MT
◊עמל‎ *act perfidiously*
Cf. LARCHER 1985, 691; WALTERS 1973, 262-264

παροργίζω⁺   V 4-23-13-7-10-57
Dt 4,25; 31,29; 32,21(bis); Jgsᴬ 2,12
to provoke to anger [τινα] Dt 4,25; *id.* Ez 32,9
*Ez 16,54 ἐν τῷ σε παροργίσαι με *in your
provoking me to anger* corr.?, ἐν τῷ σε
παρηγορεῦσαι for MT ב/נחמ/ך‎ *in your being a
consolation, when you become a consolation,* see
Syh
→NIDNTT

-πειρέω
(→ἐμ-)

χωμαριμ   N M 0-1-0-0-0-1
2 Kgs 23,5
= כמרים‎ (pl.) *idolatrous priests*, cpr. Hos 10,5 (see
παραπικραίνω) and Zph 1,4
Cf. SIMOTAS 1968, 149-150

- A hyphen before the lemma (-) signals that the simple form of the verb in question does not
exist.
- A supralinear ⁺ added to the lemma signals that the word occurs also in the New Testament.
- The lemma is always followed by a code indicating its grammatical form. It defines the "kind of
word" (e.g. N for noun), the class (1, 2, or 3), the gender (M, F, N, respectively for masculine,
feminine, or neuter). When the noun is a transliteration of the Hebrew, only the kind of word is
mentioned. See General Abbreviations. In addition, the genitive is indicated for nouns, and the
masculine, feminine, and neuter forms for adjectives.
- The same line gives the statistical information explained above. The figures are divided by a
hyphen. The sixth figure represents the total. For some biblical books - Judges, Tobit, Daniel with
its Greek appendices, and for parts of Joshua - Rahlfs' edition gives two versions based on
different manuscripts. A word occurring in both of these versions is counted twice in the statistics.
- The second line provides the references to the first five occurrences, when available.
- The text starting on the third line may exceptionally begin with an equals sign (=) followed by a
Hebrew word. This indicates that the Greek is a transliteration. As a rule, the third line renders
the translation of the lemma in *italics*. When the word in question has more than one meaning,
several translations are offered, each of them with a reference to an example.
- The asterisk (*) indicates that the following case deals with a passage in which the Greek differs
from the Hebrew and in which the difference can be explained on the level of the writing, reading,
or hearing of the Hebrew word, or as an error in the transmission of the Greek text.
- The slash (/) in Hebrew words indicates prefixed and attached elements. As a rule, prefixes and
suffixes are marked only when useful for the argument.

- The abbreviation "corr." suggests that the Greek word found in the manuscripts printed in Rahlfs should perhaps be corrected. It may have to be replaced by the following Greek word which gives a better rendition of the Hebrew.

- A hyphen before a Hebrew word (-) indicates that the translator probably read or wished to read that word instead of the term given by the MT.

- The diamond (◊) before a Hebrew word designates it as a "root" rather than the form in which it occurs in the text.

- The qualifier neol. at the end of a lemma indicates that the word in question is a neologism. Its earliest occurrence is in the LXX. When a question-mark is added (neol.?) the suggestion is that the word occurs also in the literature contemporary with the LXX.

The abbreviations in the bibliography are explained in the fuller bibliography given in the introduction to the lexicon.

I. MORPHOLOGICAL CODES

This list contains the codes used in the morphological tagging of each word. The information is given on the first line, immediately before the statistical data.

V = verb
N = noun   1 = first declension   M = masculine
          2 = second declension   F = feminine
          3 = third declension   N = neuter

A = adjective
M = numeral   C = cardinal
            O = ordinal
            D = adverbial

P = preposition
D = adverb
X = particle
I = interjection
C = conjunction
R = pronoun

II. BOOKS OF THE BIBLE

1.	Genesis	Gn	4. Psalms	Ps
	Exodus	Ex	Job	Jb
	Leviticus	Lv	Proverbs	Prv
	Numbers	Nm	Ruth	Ru
	Deuteronomy	Dt	Canticle (Song of Solom.)	Ct
2.	Joshua	Jos	Ecclesiastes (Preacher)	Eccl
	Joshua^B (15,22-62; 18,22-19,45)	Jos^B	Lamentations (Threni)	Lam
	Joshua^A (15,22-62; 18,22-19,45)	Jos^A	Esther	Est
	Judges^A	Jgs^A	Daniel^{LXX}	Dn^{LXX}
	Judges^B	Jgs^B	DanielTh	DnTh
	1 Samuel (1 Kingdoms)	1 Sm	Ezra (Esdras II)	Ezr
	2 Samuel (2 Kingdoms)	2 Sm	Nehemiah	Neh
	1 Kings (3 Kingdoms)	1 Kgs	5. Esdras a (Esdras I)	1 Ezr
	2 Kings (4 Kingdoms)	2 Kgs	Judith	Jdt
	1 Chronicles	1 Chr	Tobit^{BA}	Tob^{BA}
	2 Chronicles	2 Chr	Tobit^S	Tob^S
3.	Isaiah	Is	I Maccabees	1 Mc
	Jeremiah	Jer	II Maccabees	2 Mc
	Ezekiel	Ez	III Maccabees	3 Mc
	Hosea	Hos	IV Maccabees	4 Mc
	Joel	Jl	Psalm 151	Ps 151
	Amos	Am	Odes	Od
	Obadiah	Ob	Wisdom of Solomon	Wis
	Jonah	Jon	Wisdom of Sirach	Sir
	Micah	Mi	Psalms of Solomon	PSal
	Nahum	Na	Baruch	Bar
	Habakkuk	Hab	Epistle of Jeremiah	LtJ
	Zephaniah	Zph	Susannah^{LXX}	Sus^{LXX}
	Haggai	Hag	SusannahTh	SusTh
	Zechariah	Zech	Bel^{LXX}	Bel^{LXX}
	Malachi	Mal	BelTh	BelTh

III. General Abbreviations

A	active	Hebr.	Hebrew
abbrev.	abbreviation	hi.	hiphil
abs.	absolute	hist.	historical
abstr.	abstract	hoph.	hophal
acc.	accusative	id.	idem
Accad.	Accadic	i.e.	*id est*
act.	active	imper.	imperative
add.	addition	impers.	impersonal
adj.	adjective	impft.	imperfect
adv.	adverb	ind.	indicative
affirm.	affirmative	indir.	indirect
anim.	animal(s)	inf.	infinitive
aor.	aorist	instr.	instrumental
Arab.	Arabic	intrans.	intransitive
Aram.	Aramaic	introd.	introduces/introducing
archit.	architecture/architectural	l.	litre(s)
art.	article	L	Lucianic Recension of LXX
Att.	Attic	Lat.	Latin
augm.	augment	LH	Late Hebrew
c.	circa	lit.	literally
Cf.	Confer (bibl.)	Lk	Luke
class.	classical	LXX	Septuagint
cogn.	cognate	M	medium, middle
col.	column(s)	metaph.	metaphorical
coll.	collective	metath.	metathesis
comp.	comparative	meton.	metonymical
contr.	contraction	metonym.	metonymically
corr.	correction for	MH	Mishnaic Hebrew
correl.	correlative	mil.	military
cpr.	compare	(m)m	(milli)meter
dat.	dative	ms(s)	manuscript(s)
dim.	diminutive	Mt	Matthew
dir.	direct	MT	masoretic text
ed. Sexta	editio Sexta	MT^k	masoretic text ketib
Eg.	Egyptian	MT^q	masoretic text qere
e.g.	*exempli gratia*	n.	note
epith.	epitheton	neg.	negative or negation
esp.	especially	neol.	neologism
et al.	et alii	neutr.	neutral
etym.	etymological	nom.	nominative
euph.	euphemism	opp.	opposite or opposition
fem.	feminine	opt.	optative
fut.	future	P	passive
gen.	genitive	pap.	papyrus or papyri
gen. abs.	*genitivus absolutus*	part.	particle
geogr.	geographical	pass.	passive
haplogr.	haplography	pejor.	pejorative

pers.	person(s)	Semit.	Semitic
pft.	perfect tense	semit.	semitism
pi.	piel	sg.	singular
pl.	plural	sit.	situation
pos.	positive	st. cstr.	*status constructus*
pred.	predicate	sth	something
prep.	preposition	subj.	subjunctive
pres.	present (tense)	subst.	substantive
prob.	probably	sup.	superlative
prol.	prologue	Syh	Syrohexapla
pron.	pronoun	symb.	symbolically
ptc.	participle	syn.	synonymous or synonym
1QIsᵃ	cave 1, Qumran scroll, Isaiahᵃ	Syr.	Syriac
1QpHab	cave 1, Qumran scroll, pesher	T	Targum
	Habakkuk	Theod.	Theodotion
1QSm	cave 1, Qumran scroll, Samuel	tit.	title
4QpNa	cave 4, Qumran scroll, pesher	transl.	translation
	Nahum	translit.	transliteration
rel.	relative	usu.	usually
relig.	religious	V	Vulgate
Rom	Romans	var.	variant
Sam.(Pent.)	Samaritan (Pentateuch)	verb. (adj.)	verbal adjective
sb	somebody	v.l.	*varia lectio*
sc.	*scilicet*	voc.	vocative
semi-prep.	semi-preposition		

AASF	Annales academiae scientiarum fennicae
AEcR	*American Ecclesiastical Review*
Aeg	*Aegyptus*
AGJU	Arbeiten zur Geschichte des antiken Judentums und des Urchristentums
AJA	*American Journal of Archaeology*
AJBI	*Annual of the Japanese Biblical Institute*
AJSL	*American Journal of Semitic Languages and Literatures*
AmJPg	*American Journal of Philology*
AnBib	Analecta Biblica
AncB	Anchor Bible
AnCl	*Antiquité classique*
ANRW	Aufstieg und Niedergang der römischen Welt
AThR	*Anglican Theological Review*
BeO	*Bibbia e Oriente*
BETL	Bibliotheca Ephemeridum Theologicarum Lovaniensium
Bib	*Biblica*
BibOr	Biblica et orientalia
BIOSCS	*Bulletin of the International Organisation for Septuagint and Cognate Studies*
BiTr	*Bible Translator*
BJRL	*Bulletin of the John Rylants University Library of Manchester*
BKAT	Biblischer Kommentar Altes Testament
BWANT	Beiträge zur Wissenschaft vom Alten und Neuen Testament
BZ	*Biblische Zeitschrift*
BZAW	Beihefte zur *ZAW*
BZNW	Beihefte zur *ZNW*
CATSS	Computer Assisted Tools for Septuagint Studies
CB.NT	Coniectanea biblica New Testament
CB.OT	Coniectanea biblica Old Testament
CBLa	Collectanea biblica latina
CBQ MS	Catholic Biblical Quarterly. Monograph Series
CÉg	*Chronique d'Égypte*
DBS	Dictionnaire de la Bible. Supplément
DCH	Dictionary of Classical Hebrew (→ Clines)
DJD	Discoveries in the Judaean Desert
ÉeC	Études et commentaires
Est Bib	*Estudios Biblicos*
ET	*Expository Times*
ÉtB	Études bibliques
ETL	*Ephemerides Theologicae Lovanienses*
ÉTR	*Études théologiques et religieuses*
FzB	Forschung zur Bibel
GRBS	*Greek, Roman and Byzantine Studies*
HAT	Handkommentar zum Alten Testament
HSM	Harvard Semitic Monographs
HUBP	Hebrew University Bible Project (→ Goshen-Gottstein)
Hyp	Hypomnemata. Untersuchungen zur Antike und zu ihrem Nachleben

ICC	The International Critical Commentary
IEJ	*Israel Exploration Journal*
IF	Indogermanische Forschungen
IJT	*Indian Journal of Theology*
IP	Instrumenta patristica
JAC	*Jahrbuch für Antike und Christentum*
JAOS	*Journal of the American Oriental Society*
JBL	*Journal of Biblical Literature*
JBS	Jerusalem Biblical Studies
JEOL	*Jaarbericht ... Ex Oriente Lux*
JJP	*Journal of Juristic Papyrology*
JQR	*Jewish Quarterly Review*
JSJ	*Journal for the Study of Judaism in the Persian, Hellenistic and Roman Period*
JSNT	*Journal for the Study of the New Testament*
JSNT SS	Journal for the Study of the New Testament. Supplement Series
JSOT SS	Journal for the Study of the Old Testament. Supplement Series
JSS	*Journal of Semitic Studies*
JTS	*Journal of Theological Studies*
KAT	Kommentar zum Alten Testament
LeDiv	Lectio Divina
LSJ	Liddell-Scott-Jones (→ LIDDELL)
LSJ RSuppl	Liddell-Scott-Jones. Revised Supplement (→ LIDDELL)
LSJ Suppl	Liddell-Scott-Jones. Supplement (→ LIDDELL)
Mar	*Marianum*
MM	*The Vocabulary of the Greek Testament* (→ MOULTON 1914)
MSS	Münchener Studien zur Sprachwissenschaft
MSU	Mitteilungen des Septuaginta-Unternehmens
NIDNTT	The New Intern. Diction. of New Testament Theology (→ C. BROWN)
NIDOTT	The New Intern. Diction. of Old Testament Theology (→ VANGEMEREN)
Muséon	*Le Muséon. Revue d'études orientales*
NT	*Novum Testamentum*
NTS	*New Testament Studies*
NT Suppl	Supplements to Novum Testamentum
OBO	Orbis biblicus et orientalis
OLA	Orientalia lovaniensia analecta
Or	*Orientalia*
OTL	Old Testament Library
OTS	Oudtestamentische studiën
PEQ	*The Palestine Exploration Quarterly*
RAC	Reallexicon für Antike und Christentum
RB	*Revue biblique*
RdÉ	*Revue d'égyptologie*
RÉAug	*Revue des études augustiniennes*
RÉByz	*Revue des études byzantines*
RechSR	*Recherches de science religieuse*
RÉG	*Revue des études grecques*
RCatalana Teo	*Revista catalana de teologia*
RHPR	*Revue d'histoire et de philosophie religieuses*

RFIC	*Rivista di filologia e d'istruzione classica*
RPTK	Realencyklopädie für protestantische Theologie und Kirche
RSPhTh	*Revue des sciences philosophiques et théologiques*
RTP	*Revue de théologie et de philosophie*
SBFLA	*Studium biblicum franciscanum. Liber annuus*
SBL MS	Society of Biblical Literature. Monograph Series
SCS	Septuagint and Cognate Studies
SNTS MS	Society for New Testament Study. Monograph Series
SO	*Symbolae Osloenses*
SR	*Studies in Religion/Sciences Religieuses*
StHell	Studia hellenistica
SVT	Supplements to Vetus Testamentum
SVTG	Septuaginta. Vetus Testamentum Graecum
ThLZ	*Theologische Literaturzeitung*
TrinJ	*Trinity Journal*
TU	Texte und Untersuchungen zur Geschichte der altchristlichen Literatur
TWAT	Theologisches Wörterbuch zum Alten Testament (→ BOTTERWECK)
TWNT	Theologisches Wörterbuch zum Neuen Testament (→ KITTEL)
UF	Ugarit-Forschungen
UUA	Uppsala universitets arsskrift
VetChr	*Vetera Christianorum*
VT	*Vetus Testamentum*
WBC	Word Biblical Commentaries
WUNT	Wissenschaftliche Untersuchungen zum Neuen Testament
ZAW	*Zeitschrift für die alttestamentliche Wissenschaft*
ZDPV	*Zeitschrift des Deutschen Palästina-Vereins*
ZNW	*Zeitschrift für die neutestamentliche Wissenschaft*

The following list includes in alphabetical order the abbreviations and the full titles of all the works referred to in the description of the lemmata.

The asterisk refers to commentaries and studies providing lexicographical and text-critical information frequently used in the lexicon. With the exception of the commentaries to the Septuagint they are not, or only exceptionally, explicitly referred to at the lemmata. The following works have been systematically consulted: ABEL 1949, ALBREKTSON 1963, ALLEN 1974, BARUCQ 1964, BUTLER 1983, DHORME 1910/1926, DOGNIEZ 1992, DORIVAL 1994, DRIVER 1902, HARL 1986ᵃ, HARLÉ 1988, HOLLADAY 1986/1989, KOENIG 1982, LARCHER 1969/1983/1984/1985, LE BOULLUEC 1989, McKANE 1970/1986, MONTGOMERY 1951, MULDER 1987, OTTLEY 1906, PODECHARD 1949/1954, RUDOLPH 1962/1966/1971/1975/1976, SCHREINER 1957, SEELIGMANN 1948, SKEHAN 1987, WEVERS 1990/1993/1995, WILLIAMSON 1985, ZIEGLER 1934, ZIMMERLI 1969.

ABEL, F.-M.
1949 * *Les livres des Maccabées* (ÉtB), Paris, 1949.

ACKROYD, P.
1969 נצח - εἰς τέλος, in *ET* 80 (1968-69) 126.

AEJMELAEUS, A.
1982 *Parataxis in the Septuagint. A Study of the Renderings of the Hebrew Coordinate Clauses in the Greek Pentateuch* (AASF Diss. Hum. Litt., 31), Helsinki, 1982.
1985 Ὅτι *causale in Septuagintal Greek*, in N. FERNÁNDEZ MARCOS (ed.), *La Septuaginta en la investigación contemporanea (V Congreso de la IOSCS)*, Madrid, 1985, pp. 115-132; = A. AEJMELAEUS, *On the Trail of the Septuagint Translators*, 1993, pp. 17-36.
1987 *What Can We Know about the Hebrew Vorlage of the Septuagint?*, in *ZAW* 99 (1987) 58-89.
1990 Ὅτι *recitativum in Septuagintal Greek*, in D. FRAENKEL, U. QUAST & J.W. WEVERS a.o. (eds.), *Studien zur Septuaginta. FS R. Hanhart* (MSU, 20), Göttingen, 1990, pp. 74-82; = A. AEJMELAEUS, *On the Trail of the Septuagint Translators*, 1993, pp. 37-48.
1991 *Translation Technique and the Intention of the Translator*, in C.E. COX (ed.) 1991, pp. 23-36.
1993 *On the Trail of the Septuagint Translators. Collected Essays*, Kampen, 1993.

AERTS, W.J.
1965 *Periphrastica. An Investigation into the Use of* εἶναι *and* ἔχειν *as Auxiliaries or Pseudo-auxiliaries in Greek from Homer up to the Present Day* (Publications Issued under the Auspices of the Byzantine-New Greek Seminary of the University of Amsterdam, 2), Amsterdam, 1965, pp. 52-209.

ALAND, B. & K. → BAUER, W.

ALBREKTSON, B.
1963 * *Studies in the Text and Theology of the Book of Lamentations* (Stud. Theol. Lundensia, 21), Lund, 1963.

ALEXANDRE, M.
1988 *Le commencement du livre Genèse I-V. La version grecque de la Septante et sa réception* (Christianisme antique, 3), Paris, 1988.
→ HARL, M. 1986ᵃ

ALFRINK, B.

1959   L'idée de résurrection d'après Dan., XII,1.2, in Bib 40 (1959) 355-371.

ALLEN, L.C.

1970   The Old Testament Background of (προ)ὁρίζειν in the New Testament, in NTS 17 (1970-71) 104-108.

1974 * The Greek Chronicles. The Relation of I and II Chronicles to the Massoretic Text. Part I. The Translator's Craft. Part II. Textual Criticism (SVT, 25 and 27), 2 vols., Leiden, 1974.

ALLEN, W.C.

1894   On the Meaning of προσήλυτος in the Septuagint, in The Expositor IV/10 (1894) 264-275.

ALTHANN, R.

1985   Numbers 21,30b in the Light of the Ancient Versions and Ugaritic, in Bib 66 (1985) 568-571.

ALTINK, W.

1984   1 Chronicles 16:8-36 as Literary Source for Revelation 14:6-7, in Andrews University Seminary Studies 22 (1984) 187-196.

AMIGUES, S.

1980   Remarques sur la syntaxe de πρίν, in Les études classiques 48 (1980) 193-210.

AMSTUTZ, J.

1968   Ἁπλότης. Eine begriffsgeschichtliche Studie zum jüdisch-christlichen Griechisch (Theophaneia. Beiträge zur Religions- und Kirchengeschichte des Altertums, 19), Bonn, 1968.

AMUSIN, I.D.

1986   I termini designanti la schiavitù dell'Egitto ellenistico in base ai dati dei Settanta, in I. BIEZUNSKA MALOWIST (ed.), Schiavitù e produzione nella Roma repubblicana (Problemi e Ricerche di Storia Antica, 9), Roma, 1986, pp. 107-146.

ANDERSEN, J.G.

1980   Leprosy in Translations of the Bible, in BiTr 31 (1980) 207-212.

ARGYLE, A.W.

1956   O. Cullmann's Theory Concerning κωλύειν, in ET 67 (1955-56) 17.

AUBIN, P.

1963   Le problème de la "Conversion". Étude sur un terme commun à l'hellénisme et au christianisme des trois premiers siècles (Théologie historique, 1), Paris, 1963.

AVALOS, H.

1989   Δεῦρο/δεῦτε and the Imperatives of הלך New Criteria for the "Kaige" Recension of Reigns, in Est Bib 47 (1989) 165-176.

BANKS, R.

1987   "Walking" as a Metaphor of the Christian Life: the Origins of a Significant Pauline Usage, in E.W. CONRAD & E.G. NEWING (eds.), Perspectives on Language and Text. FS F.I. Andersen, Winona Lake, IN, 1987, pp. 303-313.

BARBER, E.A. → LIDDELL, H.G.

BARC, B. → DORIVAL, G.

BARDTKE, H.
1963   Das Buch Esther (KAT, 17/5), Gütersloh, 1963.

BARDY, G.
1910   Δεσπότης, in RechSR 1 (1910) 373-379.
1911   Le plus ancien usage de δεσπότης, in RechSR 2 (1911) 458-459.

BARR, J.
1961   The Semantics of Biblical Language, Oxford, 1961.
1968   Seeing the Wood for the Trees? An Enigmatic Ancient Translation, in JSS 13 (1968)
        11-20.
1969   Biblical Words for Time (SBT, 1/33), London, 1969².
1974ᵃ   Ἐρίζω and ἐρείδω in the Septuagint: A Note Principally on Gen. XLIX.6, in JSS 19
        (1974) 198-215.
1974ᵇ   Philology and Exegesis. Some General Remarks, with Illustrations from Job, in C.
        BREKELMANS (ed.), Questions disputées d'Ancient Testament (BETL, 33), Leuven,
        1974, 1989², pp. 39-61.
1975   באר‬ - μόλις: Prov. xi.31, I Pet. iv.18, in JSS 20 (1975) 149-164.
1979   The Typology of Literalism in Ancient Biblical Translations (Nachrichten Akademie
        Göttingen 1979/11) = (MSU, 15), Göttingen, 1979, pp. 279-325.
1980   The Meaning of ἐπακούω and Cognates in the LXX, in JTS 31 (1980) 67-72.
1985   Doubts about Homoeophony in the Septuagint, in Textus 12 (1985) 1-77.
1987   Words for Love in Biblical Greek, in L. D. HURST & N. T. WRIGHT (eds.), The Glory
        of Christ in the New Testament. FS G.B. Caird, Oxford, 1987, pp. 3-18.

BARRY, P
1904   On Luke xv.25, συμφωνία: Bagpipe, in JBL 23 (1904) 180-190.

BARTELINK, G.J.M.
1961   Zur Spiritualisierung eines Opferterminus, in Glotta 39 (1961) 43-48.

BARTH, G.
1982   Πίστις in hellenistischer Religiosität, in ZNW 73 (1982) 110-126.

BARTHÉLEMY, D.
1960   Quinta ou Version selon les Hébreux?, in Theologische Zeitschrift 16 (1960) 342-353.
1963   Les devanciers d'Aquila. Première publication intégrale du texte des fragments du
        Dodécaprophéton (SVT, 10), Leiden, 1963; = D. BARTHÉLEMY 1978, pp. 66-90 (pp.
        IX-XII, 126-127, 144-157, 266-270).
1971   Eusèbe, la Septante et "les autres", in La Bible et les Pères, Paris, 1971, pp. 51-65; =
        D. BARTHÉLEMY 1978, pp. 179-193.
1978   Études d'histoire du texte de l'Ancien Testament (OBO, 21), Fribourg/Suisse - Göttingen,
        1978.
1982   Critique textuelle de l'Ancien Testament (OBO, 50/1-3), 3 vols., Fribourg/Suisse -
        Göttingen, 1982/1986/1992.
1990   Les relations de la Complutensis avec le papyrus 967 pour Èz 40,42 à 46,24, in D.
        FRAENKEL, U. QUAST & J.W. WEVERS (eds.), Studien zur Septuaginta. FS R. Hanhart
        (MSU, 20), Göttingen, 1990, pp. 252-261.

BARTINA, S.

1965   Ὀθόνια ex papyrorum testimoniis linteamina, in Studia Papyrologica 4 (1965) 27-38.

BARUCQ, A.

1964 * Le livre des Proverbes (Sources bibliques), Paris, 1964.

BASSER, H.W.

1985   Derrett's 'Binding' Reopened, in JBL 104 (1985) 297-300.

BATTAGLIA, E.

1989   Ἄρτος: il lessico della panificazione nei papiri greci (Bibl. Aevum Antiquum, 2), Milano, 1989.

BAUDISSIN, W.W.G.

1929   Κύριος als Gottesname im Judentum und seine Stelle in der Religionsgeschichte. Vol 1. Der Gebrauch des Gottesnamens Kyrios in Septuaginta; Vol 2. Die Herkunft des Gottesnamens Kyrios in Septuaginta, Giessen, 1929.

BAUER, J.

1957   Πῶς in der griechischen Bibel, in NT 2 (1957) 81-91; = J. BAUER, Scholia biblica et patristica, Graz, 1972, pp. 27-39.

BAUER, W.

1988   ALAND, K. & ALAND, B., Griechisch-deutsches Wörterbuch zu den Schriften des Neuen Testaments und der frühchristlichen Literatur, 6. völlig neu bearbeitete Auflage, Berlin - New York, 1988.

BAUMGARTEN, J.M.

1984   On the Non-literal Use of Ma'aser/Dekatè, in JBL 103 (1984) 245-251.

BAUMGARTNER, W. → KOEHLER, L.

BEAUCAMP, É.

1978   Aux origines du mot «rédemption». Le mot «rachat» dans l'Ancien Testament, in Laval Théologique Philosophique 34 (1978) 49-56.

BEEK, M.A.

1950   Das Problem des aramäischen Stammvaters (Deut. XXVI 5), in OTS 8 (1950) 192-212.

BELL, H.I.

1949   Φιλανθρωπία in the Papyri of the Roman Period, in Hommages à Joseph Bidez et à Franz Cumont (Collection Latomus, 2), Bruxelles, [1949], pp. 31-37.

BENOIT, P.

1952   Prétoire, Lithostroton et Gabbatha, in RB 59 (1952) 531-550; = P. BENOIT, Exegese et théologie, 1, Paris, 1961, pp. 316-339.

BERENGUER SANCHEZ, J.A.

1989   Ἀρνόν en PGurob 22 y el empleo del término ἀρνίον en los papiros documentales, in Emerita 57 (1989) 277-288.

BERÉNYI, G.

1984   Gal 2,20: A Pre-Pauline or A Pauline Text?, in Bib 65 (1984) 490-537.

BERGMANS, M.

1979   Théores argiens au Fayoum (P. Lond. VII 1973), in CÉg 54 (1979) 127-130.

BERTHIAUME, G.

1982   Les rôles du μάγειρος (Mnemosyne, 70), Leiden, 1982.

BERTRAM, G.

1932   Der Begriff der Erziehung in der griechischen Bibel, in Imago Dei. Beiträge zur theologischen Anthropologie. FS Gustav Krüger, Giessen, 1932, pp. 33-51.

1952   Hebräischer und griechischer Qohelet. Ein Beitrag zur Theologie der hellenistischen Bibel, in ZAW 64 (1952) 26-49.

1958   Ἱκανός in den griechischen Übersetzungen des ATs als Wiedergabe von schaddaj, in ZAW 70 (1958) 20-31.

1964   'Hochmut' und verwandte Begriffe im griechischen und hebräischen Alten Testament, in Welt des Orients 3 (1964) 32-43.

BEWER, J.A.

1942   Notes on 1 Sam 13,21; 2 Sam 32,1; Psalm 48,8, in JBL 62 (1942) 45-49.

1953   Textual and Exegetical Notes on the Book of Ezekiel, in JBL 72 (1953) 158-168.

BI[C]KERMAN[N], E.J.

1930   Zur Datierung des Pseudo-Aristeas, in ZNW 29 (1930) 280-298; = E.J. BICKERMAN 1976, pp. 123-136.

1933   Ein jüdischer Festbrief vom Jahre 124 v. Chr (II Macc. 1,1-9), in ZNW 32 (1933) 233-254; = E.J. BICKERMAN 1980, pp. 136-158.

1935ᵃ   La Charte séleucide de Jérusalem, in Revue des études juives 100 (1935) 4-35; = E.J. BICKERMAN 1980, pp. 44-85.

1935ᵇ   Utilitas crucis. Observations sur les récits du procès de Jésus dans les évangiles canoniques, in Revue de l'histoire des religions 112 (1935) 169-241; = E.J. BICKERMAN 1986, pp. 82-138.

1938   Institutions des Séleucides, Paris, 1938.

1944   Héliodore au temple de Jérusalem, in Annuaire de l'Institut de philologie et d'histoire orientales et slaves 7 (1939-44); = E.J. BICKERMAN 1980, pp. 159-191.

1946   Une proclamation séleucide relative au temple de Jérusalem, in Syria 25 (1946-48) 67-85; = E.J. BICKERMAN 1980, pp. 86-104.

1947   The Warning Inscription of Herod's Temple, in JQR 37 (1946-47) 387-405; = E.J. BICKERMAN 1980, pp. 210-224.

1949   The Name of Christians, in HTR 42 (1949) 109-124; = E.J. BICKERMAN 1986, pp. 139-151.

1950   The Date of the Testaments of the Twelve Patriarchs, in JBL 69 (1950) 245-260; = E.J. BICKERMAN 1980, pp. 1-23.

1956   Two Legal Interpretations of the Septuagint, in Revue internationale des droits de l'Antiquité 3/3 (1956) 81-104; = E.J. BICKERMAN 1976, pp. 201-224.

1959   The Septuagint as a Translation, in Proceedings of the American Academy for Jewish Research 28 (1959); = E.J. BICKERMAN 1976, pp. 167-200.

1962ᵃ   The Civic Prayer for Jerusalem, in HTR 55 (1962) 163-185; = E.J. BICKERMAN 1980, pp. 290-312.

1962ᵇ   Bénédiction et prière, in RB 69 (1962) 524-532; = E.J. BICKERMAN 1980, pp. 313-323.

1965   Les deux erreurs du prophète Jonas, in RHPR 45 (1965) 232-264; = E.J. BICKERMAN 1976, pp. 33-71.

1968   Pliny, Trajan, Hadrian and the Christians, in Rivista di filologia e di istruzione classica 96 (1968) 290-315; = E.J. BICKERMAN 1986, pp. 152-171.

1976   Studies in Jewish and Christian History. Part One (AGJU, 9), Leiden, 1976.

1980   *Studies in Jewish and Christian History. Part Two* (AGJU, 9), Leiden, 1980.

1986   *Studies in Jewish and Christian History. Part Three* (AGJU, 9), Leiden, 1986.

BIRD, T.E.

1940   *Exegetical Notes: Self-control* (σωφροσύνη), in *CBQ* 2 (1940) 259-263.

BISCARDI, A.

1983   *Osservazioni critiche sulla terminologia* διαθήκη - διατίθημαι, in *Symposium 1979*,
        Köln - Wien, 1983, pp. 21-36.

BISSOLI, G.

1983   *MAKON -* ἕτοιμος. *A proposito di Esodo 15,17*, in *SBFLA* 33 (1983) 53-56.

BITTER, R.A.

1982   *Vreemdelingschap bij Philo van Alexandrië. Een onderzoek naar de betekenis van* πάροικος,
        Utrecht, 1982.

BJERKELUND, C.J.

1967   Παρακαλῶ: *Form, Funktion und Sinn der* παρακαλῶ-*Sätze in den paulinischen Briefen*
        (Bibliotheca Theologica Norvegica, 1), Oslo, 1967.

BLACK, M. → MARTINI, C.M.

BLAKENEY, E.

1944   *A Note on the Word* σιώπησις: *Canticles iv.1,3; vi.6*, in *ET* 55 (1943-44) 138.

BLANK, S.H.

1930   *LXX Renderings of Old Testament Terms for Law*, in *HUCA* 7 (1930) 259-283.

BLASS, F.

1990   & A. DEBRUNNER & F. REHKOPF, *Grammatik des neutestamentlichen Griechisch*,
        Göttingen, 1990[17].

BLAU, J.

1957   *Über homonyme und angeblich homonyme Wurzeln II*, in *VT* 7 (1957) 98-102.

BLOMQVIST, J.

1969   *Greek Particles in Hellenistic Prose*, Lund, 1969.

1974   *Juxtaposed* τε καί *in Post-Classical Prose*, in *Hermes* 102 (1974) 170-178.

1979   *Das sogenannte* καί *adversativum. Zur Semantik einer griechischen Partikel* (Acta
        Universitatis Upsaliensis. Studia Graeca Upsaliensia, 13), Uppsala, 1979.

BOGAERT, P.-M.

1981   *L'orientation du parvis du sanctuaire dans la version grecque de l'Exode (Ex., 27,9-13
        LXX)*, in *AnCl* 50 (1981) 79-85.

1984   *Relecture et refonte historicisantes du livre de Daniel attestées par la première version
        grecque (Papyrus 967)*, in R. KUNTZMANN & J. SCHLOSSER (eds.), *Études sur le judaïsme
        hellénistique. Congrès de Strasbourg 1983* (LeDiv, 119), Paris, 1984.

1986   *Les deux rédactions conservées (LXX et TM) d'Ézéchiel 7*, in J. LUST (ed.), *Ezekiel
        and his Book*, 1986, pp. 21-47.

BOGNER, H.

1941   *Was heisst* μοιχεύειν?, in *Hermes* 76 (1941) 318-320.

BOLKESTEIN, J.C.

1936   Ὅσιος *en* Εὐσεβής. *Bijdrage tot de godsdienstige en zedelijke terminologie van de Grieken.
        Avec un résumé en français*, Amsterdam, 1936.

BONNEAU, D.
1985   *Aigialos* (αἰγιαλός), *la "terre riveraine" en Egypte, d'après la documentation papyrologique*, in N. LEWIS (ed.), *Papyrology* (Yale Classical Studies, 28), Cambridge, MA, 1985, pp. 131-143.

BONS, E.
1994   Ἐλπίς, *l'espérance de la vie en l'au-delà, dans la littérature juive hellénistique*, in R. KUNTZMANN (ed.), *Le Dieu qui vient. FS Bernard Renaud*, Paris, 1994, pp. 345-370.

BOTTERWECK, G.J.
1970   & RINGGREN, H., *Theologisches Wörterbuch zum Alten Testament*, Stuttgart, 1970-; = *Theological Dictionary of the Old Testament*, Grand Rapids, MI, 1977-.

BOUSFIELD, G.
1929   *Resheph*, in *JTS* 31 (1929-30) 397-399.

BRATSIOTIS, N.P.
1966   בָּשָׂר - ψυχή. *Ein Beitrag zur Erforschung der Sprache und der Theologie der Septuaginta*, in *Volume du Congrès Genève 1965* (VTS, 15), Leiden, 1966, pp. 58-89.

BRAUNERT, H.
1971   Ἀγοραστής, in *ZPE* 8 (1971) 118-122.

BREYTENBACH, C.
1993   *Versöhnung, Stellvertretung und Sühne*, in *NTS* 39 (1993) 58-79.

BROCK, S.
1982   *A Fourteenth-Century Polyglot Psalter*, in G.E. KADISH & G.E. FREEMAN (eds.), *Studies in Philology. FS R.J. Williams*, Toronto, 1982, pp. 1-15.

BROCKINGTON, L.H.
1951   *The Greek Translator of Isaiah and His Interest in* δόξα, in *VT* 1 (1951) 23-32.
1954   *Septuagint and Targum*, in *ZAW* 66 (1954) 81-86.

BROOKE, C.J.
1992   & LINDARS, B. (eds.), *Septuagint, Scrolls and Cognate Writings. Papers Presented to the International Symposium on the Septuagint and its Relation to the Dead Sea Scrolls and other Writings Manchester 1990* (SCS, 33), Atlanta, GA, 1992.

BROWN, C.
1975   (ed.), *The New International Dictionary of New Testament Theology*, 3 vols., Exeter, 1975/1976/1978.
        → COENEN, L. 1967

BROWN, J.P.
1980   *The Sacrificial Cult and its Critique in Greek and Hebrew (II)*, in *JSS* 25 (1980) 1-21.

BROWN, R.
1958   *The Pre-Christian Semitic Concept of 'Mystery'*, in *CBQ* 20 (1958) 417-443.

BRUCE, F.F.
1979   *Prophetic Interpretation in the Septuagint*, in *BIOSCS* 12 (1979) 17-26.

BRUNEAU, P.
1967   *Deux noms antiques de pavement:* κατάκλυστον *et* λιθόστρωτον, in *Bulletin de correspondance hellénique* 91 (1967) 423-446.

BRUNET, G.
1966   La vision de l'étain: réinterprétation d'Amos VII 7-9, in VT 16 (1966) 387-395.

BRUNSCHWIG, J.
1973   Sur quelques emplois d'ὄψις, in Zetesis. FS E. de Strycker, Antwerpen, 1973, 24-39.

BUCHANAN, G.W.
1959   Mark 11.15-19: Brigands in the Temple, in HUCA 30 (1959) 169-177.

BURNS, A.L.
1953   Two Words for 'Time' in the New Testament, in Australian Biblical Review 3 (1953) 7-22.

BUSCEMI, M.
1979   Ἐξαιρέομαι, verbo di liberazione, in SBFLA 29 (1979) 293-314.

BUTLER, T.C.
1983 * Joshua (WBC, 7), Waco, TX, 1983.

CADELL, H.
1967   & RÉMONDON, R., Sens et emplois de τὸ ὄρος dans les documents papyrologiques, in RÉG 80 (1967) 343-349.
1973   Papyrologica: à propos de πυρός et de σῖτος, in CÉg 48 (1973) 329-338.
1984   Sur un hapax grec connu par le Code Théodosien, in Atti XVII Congr. Int. Pap., III, Napoli, 1984, pp. 1279-1285.

CAIRD, G.B.
1968ᵃ   The Glory of God in the Fourth Gospel: An Exercise in Biblical Semantics, in NTS 15 (1968-69) 265-277.
1968ᵇ   Towards a Lexicon of the Septuagint. I, in JTS 19 (1968) 453-475; = R.A. KRAFT (ed.) 1972, pp. 110-132.
1969   Towards a Lexicon of the Septuagint. II, in JTS 20 (1969) 21-40; = R.A. KRAFT (ed.) 1972, pp. 133-152.
1976   Homoeophony in the Septuagint, in R. HAMERTON-KELLY & R. SCROGGS (eds.), Jews, Greeks and Christians: Religious Cultures in Late Antiquity. FS W.D. Davies, Leiden, 1976, pp. 74-88.

CAMBE, M.
1963   La χάρις chez saint Luc. Remarques sur quelques textes, notamment le κεχαριτωμένη, in RB 70 (1963) 193-202.

CAPPELLUS, L.
1775   Critica Sacra, Magdeburgicae, 1775.

CAQUOT, A.
1980   Ben Porat (Genèse 49,22), in Semitica 30 (1980) 43-56.

CARAGOUNIS, C.C.
1974   Ὀψώνιον: A Reconsideration of its Meaning, in NT 16 (1974) 35-57.
1977   The Ephesian Mysterion. Meaning and Content (CB.NT, 8), Lund, 1977.
1986   The Son of Man. Vision and Interpretation (WUNT, 1/38), Tübingen, 1986.

1989   *Kingdom of God, Son of Man and Jesus' Self-Understanding*, in *Tyndale Bulletin* 40 (1989) 3-23.223-238.

1990   *Peter and the Rock* (BZNW, 58), Berlin - New York, 1990, pp. 9-16. 26-30.

1996ª   *'Fornication' and 'Concession'? Interpreting 1 Cor 7,1-7*, in R. BIERINGER (ed.), *The Corinthian Correspondence* (BETL, 125), Leuven, 1996, pp. 543-559.

1996ᵇ   בח - בן, in W.A. VANGEMEREN (ed.), *New International Dictionary*, Vol. 1, 1996 (forthcoming).

1997   *Stein*, in L. COENEN & K. HAACKER (eds.), *Theologisches Begriffslexikon zum Neuen Testament*, revised edition, vol. 3, 1997 (forthcoming).

CASANOVA, G.

1982   *Le parole dell'amore nei papiri: osservazioni su ἐράω e corradicali*, in *Anagennesis* 2 (1982) 213-226.

CASARICO, L.

1984   Ἑορτή e πανήγυρις *nei papiri*, in *Aeg* 64 (1984) 135-162.

CERESA-GASTALDO, A.

1953   Ἀγάπη *nei documenti estranei all' influsso biblico*, in *RFIC* 31 (1953) 347-355.

CERFAUX, L.

1931ª   *Le nom divin «Kyrios» dans la Bible grecque*, in *RSPhTh* 20 (1931) 27-51; = *Recueil Lucien Cerfaux*, I, 1954, pp. 113-136.

1931ᵇ   *'Adonai' et 'Kyrios'*, in *RSPhTh* 20 (1931) 417-452; = *Recueil Lucien Cerfaux*, I, 1954, pp. 137-172.

1954   *Recueil Lucien Cerfaux. Études d'exégèse et d'histoire religieuse de Monseigneur Cerfaux.* Tome I-II (BETL, 6-7), Gembloux, 1954.

1957   *Kurios*, in DBS 5 (1957) col. 200-228.

CERNUDA, A.V.

1975   *«Considerar», acepción axiológica de* καλέω *y su presencia en la Biblia*, in *Augustinianum* 15 (1975) 445-455.

CERVIN, R.S.

1989   *Does* κεφαλή *Mean "Source" or "Authority over" in Greek Literature? A Rebuttal*, in *Trinity Journal* 10 (1989) 85-112
        → GRUDEM, W.

CHANTRAINE, P.

1955   *Les noms de l'agneau*, in H. KRAHE a.o. (eds.), *Corolla Linguistica. FS F. Sommer*, Berlin, 1955, pp. 12-19.

1964   *Grec* αἴθριον, in *Rech. de Pap.* 3 (1964) 7-15.

1968   *Dictionnaire étymologique de la langue grecque. Histoire des mots*, Paris, 1968.

CHARLES, R.H.

1913   *The Apocrypha and Pseudepigrapha of the Old Testament in English with Introductions and Critical and Explanatory Notes to the Several Books*, Vol. 1. *Apocrypha*, Oxford, 1913; 1963².

CIFOLETTI, G.

1974   Ἀποδέχομαι *nella diplomazia imperiale (a proposito di P. Ned. 70. 01)*, in *Incontri linguistici* 1, Trieste, 1974, pp. 55-60.

CIMOSA, M.

1985   *Il vocabolario di preghiera nel pentateuco greco dei LXX* (Quaderni di Salesianum, 10), Roma, 1985.

1991   *Il vocabolario della preghiera nella traduzione greca (LXX) dei salmi*, in *Ephemerides Liturgicae* 105 (1991) 89-119.

CLARK, K.W.

1972   *The Meaning of* ἄρα, in E.H. BARTH & R.E. COCROFT (eds.), *Festschrift to honor F. Wilbur Gingrich*, Leiden, 1972, pp. 70-84.

1976   *The Meaning of* [κατα] κυριεύειν, in J.K. ELLIOTT (ed.), *Studies in New Testament Language and Text. FS G. Kilpatrick* (NT Suppl., 44), Leiden, 1976, pp. 100-105.

CLARYSSE, W.

1976   *Harmachis, Agent of the Oikonomos: an Archive from the Time of Philopator*, in *Ancient Society* 7 (1976) 185-207.

1989   & WINNICKI, J.K., *Documentary Papyri*, in E. VAN 'T DACK a.o. (eds.), *The Judean-Syrian-Egyptian Conflict of 103-101 B.C. A Multilingual Dossier Concerning a "War of Sceptres"* (Collectanea Hellenistica, I), Brussel, 1989, pp. 37-81.

1990   *Abbreviations and Lexicography*, in *Ancient Society* 21 (1990) 33-44.

CLERMONT-GANNEAU, C.

1905   *Recueil d'archéologie orientale, t. 6,* Paris, 1905, pp. 357-359.

CLINES, D.J.A.

1993   *The Dictionary of Classical Hebrew*, 2 vols., Sheffield, 1993.

COENEN, L.

1967   & HAACKER, K. (eds.), *Theologisches Begriffslexikon zum Neuen Testament*, 3 vols., Wuppertal, 1967-1971; revised edition, 1997.
      → BROWN, C.

COLEMAN, W.D.

1927   *Some Noteworthy Uses of* εἰ *or* εἰ *in Hellenistic Greek, with a Note on St. Mark viii 12*, in *JTS* 28 (1927) 159-167.

CONNOLLY, R.H.

1924   *The Meaning of* ἐπίκλησις: *A Reply*, in *JTS* 25 (1924) 337-364.

CONYBEARE, F.C.

1905   & STOCK, ST.-G., *Selections from the Septuagint according to the Text of Swete*, Boston, MA, 1905; reprint of pp. 25-100 in ID., *A Grammar of Septuagint Greek*, Grand Rapids, MI, 1980; reprint ID., *Grammar of Septuagint Greek. With Selected Readings from the Septuagint According to the Text of Swete*, Peabody, MA, 1988.

COOK, J.

1987   *Hellenistic Influence in the Book of Proverbs (Septuagint)?*, in *BIOSCS* 20 (1987) 30-42.

1991   *Hellenistic Influence in the Septuagint Book of Proverbs,* in C.E. COX (ed.) 1991, pp. 341-353.

1994   אִשָּׁה זָרָה *(Proverbs 1-9 Septuagint): A Metaphor for Foreign Wisdom?*, in *ZAW* 106 (1994) 458-476.

CORNILL, C.H.

1886   *Das Buch des Propheten Ezechiel*, Leipzig, 1886.

CORSSEN, P.

1918 *Über Bildung und Bedeutung der Komposita* ψευδοπροφήτης, ψευδόμαντις, ψευδόμαρτυς. *Eine Erwiderung*, in *Sokrates. Zeitschrift für das Gymnasialwesen* 6 (1918), 106-114.

COUROYER, B.

1984 *Tobie, VII,9. Problème de critique textuelle*, in *RB* 91 (1984) 351-361.

COX, C.E.

1981 Εἰσακούω *and* ἐπακούω *in the Greek Psalter*, in *Bib* 62 (1981) 251-258.

1987 (ed.), *VIth Congress of the IOSCS Jerusalem 1986* (SCS, 23), Atlanta, GA, 1987.

1990 *Vocabulary for Wrongdoing and Forgiveness in the Greek Translations of Job*, in *Textus* 15 (1990) 119-130.

1991 (ed.), *VIIth Congress of the IOSCS Leuven 1989* (SCS, 31), Atlanta, GA, 1991.
→ PIETERSMA, A. 1984

CUNEN, F.

1959 *Les pratiques divinatoires attribuées à Joseph d'Égypte*, in *RevSR* 33 (1959) 396-404.

CUSS, D.

1974 *Imperial Cult and Honorary Terms in the New Testament* (Paradosis, 23), Fribourg/Suisse, 1974.

DA FONSECA, L.G.

1927 Διαθήκη - *Foedus an Testamentum?*, in *Bib* 8 (1927) 31-50.161-181.290-319.418-441; 9 (1928) 26-40, 143-160.

DANIEL, C.

1971 *Trois noms égyptiens de chefs en grec:* βασιλεύς, ἥρος *et* τίταξ, in *Studia et acta orientalia* 8 (1971) 59-69.

DANIEL, S.

1966 *Recherches sur le vocabulaire du culte dans la Septante* (ÉeC, 61), Paris, 1966.

DANIÉLOU, J.

1966 *Études d'exégèse judéo-chrétienne. Les Testimonia* (Théologie historique, 5), Paris, 1966.

DARIS, S.

1983 *Ricerche di papirologia documentaria. II*, in *Aeg* 63 (1983) 117-169.

DAVID, M.

1943 *Deux anciens termes bibliques pour le gage*, in OTS 2 (1943) 79-86.

DAVISON, J.E.

1985 'Ανομία *and the Question of the Antinomian Polemic in Matthew*, in *JBL* 104 (1985) 617-635.

DEBRUNNER, A. → BLASS, F.

DEBUS, J.

1967 *Die Sünde Jerobeams. Studien zur Darstellung Jerobeams und der Geschichte des Nordreichs in der deuteronomistischen Geschichtsschreibung* (FRLANT, 93), Göttingen, 1967.

DEISSMANN, A.

1897   *Neue Bibelstudien. Sprachgeschichtliche Beiträge, zumeist aus den Papyri und Inschriften zur Erklärung des Neuen Testaments,* Marburg, 1897.

1899   *Hellenistic Greek with Special Consideration of the Greek Bible,* in RPTK³ 7 (1899) 627-639; = S.E. PORTER (ed.), *The Language of the New Testament. Classic Essays* (JSNT SS, 60), Sheffield, 1991, pp. 35-59.

1901   *Anathema,* in *ZNW* 2 (1901) 342.

1903   Ἱλαστήριος *und* ἱλαστήριον. *Eine lexikalische Studie,* in *ZNW* 4 (1903) 193-212.

1927   *Light from the Ancient East. The New Testament Illustrated by Recently Discovered Texts of the Graeco-Roman World,* London, 1927.

DE JONGE, M.

1966   *The Use of the Word "Anointed" in the Time of Jesus,* in *NT* 8 (1966) 132-148.

DE LA POTTERIE, I.

1974   *La parole de Jésus "Voici ta Mère" et l'accueil du disciple (Jn 19,27b),* in *Mar* 36 (1974) 1-39.

        → NEIRYNCK, F. 1979

DELCOR, M.

1967ᵃ   *Le livre de Judith et l'époque grecque,* in *Klio* 49 (1967) 151-179.

1967ᵇ   *Two Special Meanings of the Word* יד *in Biblical Hebrew,* in *JSS* 12 (1967) 230-240.

1974   *Astarté et la fécondité des troupeaux en Deut. 7,13 et parallèlles,* in *UF* 6 (1974) 7-14.

DELEKAT, L.

1964   *Probleme der Psalmenüberschrifte,* in *ZAW* 76 (1964) 280-297.

DELLING, G.

1952   Μόνος θεός, in *ThLZ* 77 (1952) 469-476.

1970   *Studien zum Neuen Testament und zum hellenistischen Judentum. Gesammelte Aufsätze 1950-1968.* Ed. F. HAHN, T. HOLTZ & N. WALTER, Göttingen, 1970.

1977   *Das* ἀγαθόν *der Hebräer bei den griechischen christlichen Schriftstellern,* in *TU* 120 (1977) 151-172.

DEMONT, P.

1978   *Remarques sur le sens de* τρέφω, in *RÉG* 91 (1978) 358-384.

DEPUYDT, L.

1985   *"Voir" et "regarder" en Copte: étude synchronique et diachronique,* in *RdÉ* 36 (1985) 35-42.

DESCAMPS, A.

1948   *La justice de Dieu dans la Bible grecque,* in *StHell* 5 (1948) 69-92.

DES PLACES, É.

1964ᵃ   *Syngeneia. La parenté de l'homme avec Dieu d'Homère à la patristique* (ÉeC, 51), Paris, 1964.

1964ᵇ   *Tempora vel momenta (Act. 1,7; cf. 17,26 et 30),* in *Mélanges Eugène Tisserant. Vol. I. Écriture Sainte - Ancien Orient* (Studi e testi, 231), Roma, 1964, pp. 105-117.

1975   *Un terme biblique et platonicien:* ἀκοινώνητος, in M. PELLEGRINO a.o. (eds.), *Forma Futuri. FS M. Pellegrino,* Torino, 1975, pp. 154-158.

DE TROYER, K.

1997   *On Crowns and Diadems from Kings, Queens, Horses and Men*, in B. TAYLOR (ed.), *Proceedings of the IOSCS Meeting Cambridge 1995* (SCS, ..), Atlanta, GA (forthcoming).

DE WAARD, J.

1979   *The Translator and Textual Criticism (with Particular Reference to Eccl 2,25)*, in *Bib* 60 (1979) 509-529.

1981   *'Homophony' in the Septuagint*, in *Bib* 62 (1981) 551-561.

DHORME, P.

1910 *   *Les livres de Samuel* (ÉtB), Paris, 1910.

1926 *   *Le livre de Job* (ÉtB), Paris, 1926.

DIJKSTRA, M.

1992   *The Altar of Ezekiel: Fact or Fiction?*, in *VT* 42 (1992) 22-36.

DION, P.E.

1981   *Did Cultic Prostitution Fall into Oblivion during the Postexilic Era? Some Evidence from Chronicles and the Septuagint*, in *CBQ* 43 (1981) 41-48.

DIETHART, J.M.

1982   Κύριε βοήθει *in byzantinischen Notarunterschriften*, in *ZPE* 49 (1982) 79-82.

DIHLE, A.

1988   *Heilig*, in *RAC* 14 (1988) 2-66.

DI LELLA, A.A. → SKEHAN, P.W.

DIMANT, D.

1981   *A Cultic Term in the Psalms of Solomon in the Light of the Septuagint*, in *Textus* 9 (1981) 136 [τὰ ἅγια].

DODD, C.H.

1930   Ἱλάσκεσθαι. *Its Cognates, Derivates, and Synonyms in the Septuagint*, in *JTS* 32 (1930-31) 352-360.

1935   *The Bible and the Greeks*, London, 1935, 1954².

1976   *New Testament Translation Problems*: παρθένος, in *BiTr* 27 (1976) 301-305.

DÖRRIE, H.

1955   Ὑπόστασις. *Wort und Bedeutungsgeschichte* (Nachrichten der Akademie der Wissenschaften in Göttingen. I. Philologisch-historische Klasse, 3), Göttingen, 1955, pp. 35-92.

DOGNIEZ, C.

1992 *   & HARL, M., *La Bible d'Alexandrie. V. Le Deutéronome*, Paris, 1992.
          → HARL, M. 1986⁰

DONAT, H.

1911   *Mich 2,6-9*, in *BZ* 9 (1911) 350-366.

DORIVAL, G.

1994 *   & BARC, B., FAVRELLE, G., PETIT, M. & TOLILA, J., *La Bible d'Alexandrie. IV. Les Nombres*, Paris, 1994.

1995   *Les phénomènes d'intertextualité dans le livre grec des Nombres*, in G. DORIVAL & O. MUNNICH (eds.), *Selon les Septante. FS Marguerite Harl*, Paris, 1995, pp. 253-285.
          → HARL, M. 1988

DOWNEY, G.

1937 *The Architectural Significance of the Use of the Words* στοά *and* βασιλική *in Classical Literature*, in *AJA* 41 (1937) 194-211.

DRAGUET, R.

1944 *Le chapître de l'Histoire Lausiaque sur les Tabennésiotes dérive-t-il d'une source copte?*, in *Muséon* 57 (1944) 53-145.

DRESCHER, J.

1969 *Graeco-coptica*, in *Muséon* 82 (1969) 85-100.
1970 *Graeco-coptica II*, in *Muséon* 83 (1970) 139-155.
1976 *Graeco-coptica. Postscript*, in *Muséon* 89 (1976) 307-321.

DRESSLER, H.

1947 *The Usage of* ἀσκέω *and its Cognates in Greek Documents to 200 A. D.* (Catholic University of America, 78), Washington, DC, 1947.

DREW-BEAR, T.

1972 *Some Greek Words:I & II*, in *Glotta* 50 (1972) 61-96.182-228.

DREXHAGE, H.-J.

1991 *Einige Bemerkungen zu den* ἔμποροι *und* κάπηλοι *im römischen Ägypten (1.-3.Jh.n.)*, in *Münstersche Beiträge zur antiken Handelsgeschichte* 10 (1991) 28-46.

DRIVER, G.R.

1940 *Hebrew Notes on Prophets and Proverbs*, in *JTS* 41 (1940) 162-175.
1954 *Problems and Solutions*, in *VT* 4 (1954) 225-245.
1955 *Birds in the Old Testament: II. Birds in Life*, in *PEQ* 87 (1955) 129-140.
1962 *Plurima mortis imago*, in M. BEN-HORIN, B. WEINRYB & S. ZEITLIN (eds.), *Studies and Essays in Honour of A.A. Newman*, Leiden, 1962, pp. 128-143.

DRIVER, S.R.

1902 * *A Critical and Exegetical Commentary on Deuteronomy* (ICC), Edinburgh, 1902.
1913 *Notes on the Hebrew Text and the Topography of the Books of Samuel. With an Introduction on Hebrew Palaeography and the Ancient Versions*, Oxford, 1913.

DRUCE, G.C.

1923 *An Account of the* Μυρμηκολέων *or Ant-lion*, in *The Antiquaries Journal* 8 (1923) 347-364.

DUBARLE, A.-M.

1955 Δράξασθε παιδείας *(Ps., II, 12)*, in *RB* 62 (1955) 511-512.
1978 *La conception virginale et la citation d'Is., VII,14 dans l'évangile de Matthieu*, in *RB* 85 (1978) 362-380.

DU PLESSIS, P.J.

1959 Τέλειος: *The Idea of Perfection in the New Testament*, Kampen, 1959.

DUPONT, J.

1948 Συνείδησις. *Aux origines de la notion chrétienne de conscience morale*, in *StHell* 5 (1948) 119-153.
1961 Τὰ ὅσια Δαυιδ τὰ πιστά *(Ac XIII 34 = Is LV 3)*, in *RB* 68 (1961) 91-114; = J. DUPONT, *Études sur les Actes des Apôtres* (LeDiv, 45), Paris, 1967, pp. 337-359.
1967 *Les «simples» (petâyim) dans la Bilbe et à Qumrân. A propos des* νήπιοι *de Mt. 11,25; Lc. 10,21*, in *Studi sull'Oriente e la Bibbia. FS G. Rinaldi*, Genova, 1967, pp. 329-336;

= J. DUPONT, *Études sur les évangiles synoptiques* (BETL, 70), vol. 2, Leuven, 1985, pp. 583-591.

EDWARDS, J.R.

1987   *The Use of προσέρχεσθαι in the Gospel of Matthew*, in *JBL* 106 (1987) 65-74.

EMERTON, J.A.

1969   *Notes on Jeremiah 12,9*, in *ZAW* 81 (1969) 182-188.

ENGEL, H.

1985   *Die Susanna-erzählung: Einleitung, Übersetzung und Kommentar zum Septuaginta-Text und zur Theodotion-Bearbeitung* (OBO, 61), Fribourg/Suisse - Göttingen, 1985.

EYNIKEL, E.

1991   & LUST, J., *The Use of δεῦρο and δεῦτε in the LXX*, in *ETL* 67 (1991) 57-68.

1997   & HAUSPIE, K., *The Use of καιρός and χρόνος in the LXX*, in *ETL* (1997) (forthcoming).

FASCHER, E.

1927   Προφήτης: *Eine sprach- und religionsgeschichtliche Untersuchung*, Giessen, 1927.

1954   *Theologische Beobachtungen zu δεῖ im Alten Testament*, in *ZNW* 45 (1954) 244-252.

1971   *Zum Begriff des Fremden*, in *TLZ* 96 (1971) 161-168.

FAVRELLE, G. → **DORIVAL, G.** 1994

FERNÁNDEZ MARCOS, M.

1980[a]   *Nueva acepcion de τέρας en las «Vidas de los profetas»*, in *Sefarad* 40 (1980) 27-39.

1980[b]   Ἐλπίζειν *or* ἐγγίζειν? *in Prophetarum Vitae Fabulosae 12,9 and in the Septuagint*, in *VT* 30 (1980) 357-360.

FIEDLER, M.J.

1970   Δικαιοσύνη *in der diaspora-jüdischen und intertestamentarischen Literatur*, in *JSJ* 1 (1970) 120-143.

FISCHER, J.B.

1958   *The Term δεσπότης in Josephus*, in *JQR* 49 (1958-59) 132-138.

FLASHAR, H.

1912   *Exegetische Studien zum Septuagintapsalter*, in *ZAW* 32 (1912) 241-268.

FLUSSER, D.

1962   *The Text of Isa. xlix,17 in the DSS*, in *Textus* 2 (1962) 140-142.

FORD, J.M.

1956   *The Meaning of 'Virgin'*, in *NTS* 2 (1955-56) 293-299.

FORSTER, A.H.

1929   *The Meaning of δόξα in the Greek Bible*, in *AThR* 12 (1929-30) 311-316.

FRAADE, S.D.

1984   *Enosh and His Generation. Pre-Israelite Hero and History in Postbiblical Interpretation* (SBL MS, 30), Chico, CA, 1984.

FRANKEL, Z.

1841   *Historisch-kritische Studien zu der Septuaginta. Vorstudien zu der Septuaginta I/1*, Leipzig, 1841.

FREY, J.-B.

1930   *La signification du terme* πρωτότοκος *d'après une inscription juive*, in *Bib* 11 (1930) 373-390.

1952   *Corpus Inscriptionum Iudaicarum*. II, Roma, 1952, pp. 218-219.

FRIDRICHSEN, A.

1916   *Hagios-qados. Ein Beitrag zu den Voruntersuchungen zur christlichen Begriffsgeschichte*, Kristiana, 1916.

1938   Ἰσόψυχος = *ebenbürtig, solidarisch*, in *SO* 18 (1938) 42-49.

FRIEDRICH, G. → KITTEL, G.

FRISK, H.

1973   *Griechisches etymologisches Wörterbuch*, Heidelberg, 1973².

FUCHS, E.

1977   *Gloire de Dieu, gloire de l'homme: Essai sur les termes* καυχᾶσθαι, καύχημα, καύχησις *dans la Septante*, in *RTP* 27 (1977) 321-332.

GARBINI, G.

1982   *Note linguistico-filologiche (Cantico VI, 9; Salmo XX,6; 1 Re VII,6)*, in *Henoch* 4 (1982) 163-173.

GASTON, L.

1984   *Works of Law as a Subjective Genitive*, in *SR* 13 (1984) 39-46.

GAVENTA, B.R.

1983   *'You Proclaim The Lord's Death': 1 Corinthians 11:26 and Paul's Understanding of Worship*, in *Review and Expositor* 80 (1983) 377-387.

GEHMAN, H.S.

1948   *A Note on I Samuel 21,13(14)*, in *JBL* 67 (1948) 241-243.

1951   *The Hebraic Character of Septuagint Greek*, in *VT* 1 (1951) 81-90; = R.A. KRAFT (ed.) 1972, pp. 92-101; = S.E. PORTER (ed.), *The Language of the New Testament. Classic Essays* (JSNT SS, 60), Sheffield, 1991, pp. 163-173.

1953   *Hebraisms of the Old Greek Version of Genesis*, in *VT* 3 (1953) 141-148.

1954   Ἅγιος *in the Septuagint, and Its Relation to the Hebrew Original*, in *VT* 4 (1954) 337-348.

1966   *Adventures in Septuagint Lexicography*, in *Textus* 5 (1966) 125-132; = R.A. KRAFT (ed.) 1972, pp. 102-109.

1972   Ἐπισκέπομαι (sic), ἐπίσκεψις, ἐπίσκοπος, *and* ἐπισκοπή *in the Septuagint in Relation to* פקד *and other Hebrew Roots - A Case of Semantic Development Similar to that of Hebrew*, in *VT* 22 (1972) 197-207.

1974   *Peregrinations in Septuagint Lexicography*, in H.N. BRAM, R.D. HEIM & C.A. MOORE (eds.), *A Light unto My Path. FS Jacob M. Myers*, Philadelphia, 1974, pp. 223-240. → JOHNSON, A.C.; MONTGOMERY, J.A. 1951

GENTRY, P.J.

1995   *The Asterisked Materials in the Greek Job* (SCS, 38), Atlanta, GA, 1995.

GERHARDT, M.
1965   *The Ant-lion*, in *Vivarium* 3 (1965) 1-23.

GERLEMAN, G.
1946ᵃ   *Studies in the Septuagint. I. Book of Job* (Lunds Universitets Årsskrift. N.F. 1/43.2), Lund, 1946.
1946ᵇ   *Studies in the Septuagint. II. Chronicles* (Lunds Universitets Årsskrift. N.F. 1/43.3), Lund, 1946.
        → ORLINSKY, H.M. 1948

GERMAIN, L.R.F.
1984   *Apothesis ou ekthesis. Problème de terminologie en matière d'exposition d'enfants*, in Μνήμη *Georges A. Petropoulos*, I, Athens, 1984, pp. 389-399.

GESE, H.
1971   *Natus ex Virgine*, in H.W. WOLFF (ed.), *Probleme biblischer Theologie, FS Gerhard von Rad*, München, 1971, pp. 73-89.

GHEDINI, G.
1935   *Note di sintassi greca*, in *Aeg* 15 (1935) 230-238.

GHIRON-BISTAGNE, P.
1983   *L'emploi du terme grec* πρόσωπον *dans l'Ancien et le Nouveau Testament*, in *Mélanges Édouard Delebecque*, Aix-en-Provence, 1983, pp. 155-174.

GILBERT, M.
1973   *La critique des dieux dans le Livre de la Sagesse (Sg 13-15)* (AnBib, 53), Roma, 1973.

GILMORE, G.W.
1890   ῞Εως *in Hellenistic Greek*, in *JBL* 9 (1890) 153-160.

GLARE, P.G.W. → LIDDELL, H.G.

GLOMBITZA, O.
1958   *Die Titel* διδάσκαλος *und* ἐπιστάτης *für Jesus bei Lukas,* in *ZNW* 49 (1958) 275-278.

GÖRG, M.
1988   & LANG, B. (eds.), *Neues Bibel-Lexikon*, Zürich, 1988-

GÖTTSBERGER, J.
1906   *Zu* εἰρήνη *bei Hatch-Redpath*, in *BZ* 4 (1906) 246.

GOLDSTEIN, J.
1976   *I Maccabees. A New Translation with Introduction and Commentary* (AncB, 41), Garden City, NY, 1976.
1983   *II Maccabees. A New Translation with Introduction and Commentary* (AncB, 41A), Garden City, NY, 1983.

GOODING, D.W.
1959   *The Account of the Tabernacle. Translation and Textual Problems of the Greek Exodus* (Texts and Studies NS, 6), Cambridge, 1959.
1976   *Relics of Ancient Exegesis. A Study of the Miscellanies in 3 Reigns 2* (SOTS MS, 4), Cambridge, 1976.
1981   *Review* of J.W. OLLEY, *'Righteousness' in the Septuagint of Isaiah: A Contextual Study*, by , in *JTS* 32 (1981) 204-212.

GOODWIN, D.R.

1881   *On the Use of* ψυχή *and* πνεῦμα, *and connected Words in the Sacred Writings,* in *Journal of the Society Biblical Literature and Exegesis* 1 (1881) 73-86.

GOSHEN-GOTTSTEIN, M.H.

1995   *The Book of Isaiah.* Vol.1 (1,1-22,10). Vol.2 (22,11-44,28). Vol.3 (45,1-66,24) (HUBP), Jerusalem, 1975/1981/1995.

GRAMBERG, K.P.C.A.

1960   *'Leprosy' and the Bible,* in *BiTr* 11 (1960) 10-23.

GRAYSTON, K

1981   Ἱλάσκεσθαι *and Related Words in LXX,* in *NTS* 27 (1980-81) 640-656.

GRIBOMONT, J.

1959   & THIBAUT, A., *Méthode et esprit des traducteurs du Psautier grec,* in P. SALMON (ed.), *Richesses et déficiences des anciens Psautiers Latins* (CBLa, 13), Roma, 1959, pp. 51-105.

GRINDEL, J.A.

1969   *Another Characteristic of the kaige Recension:* נצח / νῖκος, in *CBQ* 31 (1969) 499-513.

GROBE, K.

1954   Σῶμα *as 'Self, Person' in the Septuagint,* in W. ELTESTER (ed.), *Neutestamentliche Studien für Rudolf Bultmann* (BZNW, 21), Berlin, 1954, pp. 52-59.

GROSART, A.

1890   Χριστός *and* ὁ Χριστός *in the Septuagint,* in *ET* 1 (1889-1890) 275-276.

GROSSFELD, B.

1984   *The Translation of Biblical Hebrew* כפר *in the Targum, Peshitta, Vulgate and Septuagint,* in *ZAW* 96 (1984) 83-101.

GRUDEM, W.

1985   *Does* κεφαλή *Mean "Source" or "Authority over" in Greek Literature? A Survey of 2,336 Examples,* in *Trinity Journal* 6 NS (1985) 38-59.
        → CERVIN, R.S.

GRUNDMANN, W.

1932   *Der Begriff der Kraft in der neutestamentlichen Gedankenwelt* (BWANT, 60), Stuttgart, 1932.

GUÉRAUD, O.

1979   & NAUTIN, P., *Origène. Sur la pâque* (Christianisme antique, 2), Paris, 1979.

GUILLAMAUD, P.

1988   *L'essence du kairos,* in *RÉAnc* 90 (1988) 359-371.

GUILLAND, R.

1959   *Études sur l'histoire administrative de l'empire byzantin: le despote,* δεσπότης, in *RÉByz* 17 (1959) 52-89.

GUINOT, J.N.

1989   *Sur le vêtement du grand prêtre: le* δῆλος *était-il une pierre divinatoire?,* in *VetChr* 26 (1989) 23-48.

GUYOT, P.

1980   *Eunuchen als Sklaven und Freigelassene in der griechisch-römischen Antike,* Stuttgart, 1980.

HAAS, C.

1989   *Job's Perseverance in the Testament of Job*, in M.A. KNIBB & P.W. VAN DER HORST (eds.), *Studies on the Testament of Job* (SNTS MS, 66), Cambridge, 1989, pp. 117-154.

HABERMANN, W.

1988   *Lexikalische und semantische Untersuchung am griechischen Begriff* βύρσα, in *Glotta* 66 (1988) 93-99.

HADAS-LEBEL, M.

1972   *Le paganisme à travers les sources rabbiniques des IIe et IIIe siècles. Contribution à l'étude du syncrétisme dans l'empire romain*, in ANRW II.19.2 (1972), pp. 397-485.

HAERENS, H.

1948   Σωτήρ *et* σωτηρία, in *StHell* 5 (1948) 57-68.

HAGEDORN, D.

1980   & WORP, K.A., *Von* κύριος *zu* δεσπότης. *Eine Bemerkung zur Kaiserstitulatur im 3./4. Jhdt.*, in *ZPE* 39 (1980) 165-177.

HALLEUX, R.

1973   *Le sens d'*ἄσημος *dans le papyrus chimique de Leyde et dans l'alchimie gréco-égyptienne*, in *CÉg* 48 (1973) 370-380.

HAMM, W.

1969   *Der Septuaginta-Text des Buches Daniel Kap. 1-2 nach dem Kölner Teil der Papyrus 967* (Papyrologische Texte und Abhandlungen, 10), Bonn, 1969.

1977   *Der Septuaginta-Text des Buches Daniel Kap. 3-4 nach dem Kölner Teil der Papyrus 967* (Papyrologische Texte und Abhandlungen, 21), Bonn, 1977.

HANHART, R.

1967   *Drei Studien zum Judentum*, in *Theologische Existenz Heute NF* 140 (1967) 7-64.

1979   *Text und Textgeschichte des Buches Judith* (MSU, 14), Göttingen, 1979.

1992   *The Translation of the Septuagint in Light of Earlier Tradition and Subsequent Influences*, in C.J. BROOKE & B. LINDARS (eds.) 1992, pp. 339-379.

1993   *Esdrae liber II* (Septuaginta. Vetus Testamentum Graecum, Vol. VIII, 2), Göttingen, 1993.

1994   *Die Übersetzung der Septuaginta im Licht ihr vorgegebener und auf ihr gründender Tradition*, in S.E. BALENTINE & J. BARTON (eds.), *Language, Theology, and the Bible. FS James Barr*, Oxford, 1994, pp. 81-112.

HARL, M.

1960   *A propos des* logia de Jésus: *le sens du mot* μοναχός, in *RÉG* 73 (1960) 464-474; = M. HARL, *La langue de Japhet*, 1992ᵃ, pp. 203-214.

1961   *Le guetteur et la cible: les deux sens de* σκοπός *dans la langue des chrétiens*, in *RÉG* 74 (1961) 450-468; = M. HARL, *La langue de Japhet*, 1992ᵃ, pp. 215-234.

1963   *Remarques sur la langue des chrétiens, à propos de G.W.H. LAMPE, 'Patristic Greek Lexicon'*, in *JTS* 14 (1963) 406-420; = M. HARL, *La langue de Japhet*, 1992ᵃ, pp. 169-182.

1971   *Y a-t-il une influence du «grec biblique» sur la langue spirituelle des chrétiens?*, in *La Bible des Pères*, Paris, 1971, 243-262; = M. HARL, *La langue de Japhet*, 1992ᵃ, pp. 183-202.

1974   *Cadeaux de fiançailles et contrat de mariage pour l'épouse du «Cantique des Cantiques»* selon quelques commentateurs grecs, in *Mélanges d'histoire des religions. FS Henri-Charles Puech*, Paris, 1974, pp. 243-261.

1984ª   *Traduire la Septante en français: pourquoi et comment*, in *Lalies. Actes des sessions de linguistique et de littérature*, 3, Paris, 1984, pp. 83-93; = M. HARL, *La langue de Japhet*, 1992ª, pp. 33-42.

1984ᵇ   *Un groupe de mots grecs dans le judaïsme hellénistique: à propos d'ἐμπαιγμός dans le Psaume 37,8 de la Septante*, in E. LUCCHESI & H.D. SAFFREY (eds.), *Mémorial André-Jean Festugière. Antiquité païenne et chrétienne* (Cahiers d'Orientalisme, 10), Genève, 1984, pp. 89-105; = M. HARL, *La langue de Japhet* 1992ª, pp. 43-58.

1986ª *   & ALEXANDRE, M. & DOGNIEZ, C. E.A., *La Bible d'Alexandrie I. La Genèse*, Paris, 1986.

1986ᵇ   *Les origines grecques du mot et de la notion de "componction" dans la Septante et chez ses commentateurs* (Κατανύσσεσθαι), in *RÉAug* 32 (1986) 3-21; = M. HARL, *La langue de Japhet*, 1992ª, pp. 77-95.

1986ᶜ   *La "ligature" d'Isaac (Gen. 22,9) dans la Septante et chez les Pères grecs*, in A. CAQUOT, M. HADAS-LEBEL & J. RIAUD (eds.), *Hellenica et Judaica. FS V. Nikiprowetzky*, Leuven-Paris 1986, pp. 457-472; = M. HARL, *La langue de Japhet*, 1992ª , pp. 59-76.

1987   *Le nom de l'"arche" de Noé dans la Septante*, in C. MONDÉSERT a.o. (eds.), Αλεξανδρινα. *Hellénisme, judaïsme et christianisme à Alexandrie. FS C. Mondésert*, Paris, 1987, pp. 18. 15-43; = M. HARL, *La langue de Japhet*, 1992ª, pp. 97-125.

1988   & DORIVAL, G. & MUNNICH, O., *La bible grecque des Septante. Du judaïsme hellénistique au christianisme ancien* (Initiations au christianisme ancien), Paris, 1988

1990ª   *La place de la Septante dans les études bibliques*, in *ÉTR* (1990) 161-169; = M. HARL, *La langue de Japhet*, 1992ª, pp. 267-276.

1990ᵇ   *Références philosophiques et références bibliques du langage de Grégoire de Nysse dans «Orationes in Canticum canticorum»*, in H. EISENBERGER (ed.), Ἑρμηνεύματα. *FS H. Hörner*, Heidelberg, 1990, pp. 117-131; = M. HARL, *La langue de Japhet*, 1992ª, pp. 235-252.

1991   *Le renouvellement du lexique des Septante d'après le témoignage des recensions, révisions et commentaires grecs anciens*, in C.E. COX (ed.) 1991, pp. 239-259; = M. HARL, *La langue de Japhet*, 1992ª, pp. 145-168.

1992ª   *La langue de Japhet. Quinze études sur la Septante et le grec des chrétiens*, Paris, 1992.

1992ᵇ   *La Septante et la pluralité textuelle des Écritures: le témoignage des Pères grecs*, in *La langue de Japhet*, 1992ª, pp. 253-266; = *Naissance de la méthode critique Colloque du centenaire de l'École biblique et archéologique française de Jérusalem*, Paris, 1992, pp. 231-243.

1992ᶜ   *Le grand cantique de Moïse en Deutéronome 32: quelques traits originaux de la version grecque des Septante*, in *La langue de Japhet*, 1992ª, pp. 127-144; = in G. SED-RAJNA (ed.), *Rashi 1040-1990. Hommage à Ephraïm E. Urbach*, Paris, 1993, pp. 183-201.

HARLÉ, P.

1988 *   & PRALON, D., *La Bible d'Alexandrie III. Le Lévitique*, Paris, 1988.

HARRISVILLE, R.

1955   *The Concept of Newness in the New Testament*, in *JBL* 74 (1955) 69-79.

HATCH, E.

1889   *Essays in Biblical Greek*, Oxford, 1889.

1897   & REDPATH, H.A., *A Concordance to the Septuagint and the Other Greek Versions of the Old Testament*, 2 vols., Oxford, 1897; reprint Graz, 1954.

HAUDEBERT, P.

1987   *La métanoia, des Septante à Saint Luc*, in H. CAZELLES (ed.), *La vie de la parole. FS P. Grelot*, Paris, 1987, pp. 355-366.

HAUSHERR, I.

1966   *Hésychasme et prière* (Orientalia christiana analecta, 176), Roma, 1966.

HAUSPIE, K. → EYNIKEL, E. 1997

HEATER, H.

1982   *A Septuagint Translation Technique in the Book of Job* (CBQ MS, 11), Washington, 1982.

HEDLEY, P.L.

1933   Διαβουλία, in *JTS* 34 (1933) 270.

HEIDLAND, H.-W.

1936   *Die Anrechnung des Glaubens zur Gerechtigkeit. Untersuchungen zur Begriffsbestimmung von* חשב *und* λογίζεσθαι (BWANT 4/18), Stuttgart, 1936.

HEINEN, H.

1984   *Zur Terminologie der Sklaverei im ptolemäischen Ägypten.* Παῖς *und* παιδίσκη *in den Papyri und der Septuaginta*, in *Atti del XVII congresso internazionale di papirologia Napoli 1984*, III, Napoli, 1984, pp. 1287-1295.

HEITMÜLLER, W.

1903   *"Im Namen Jesu." Eine sprach- und religionsgeschichtliche Untersuchung, speziell zur altchristliche Taufe* (FRLANT, 1/2), Göttingen, 1903.

HELBING, R.

1907   *Grammatik der Septuaginta. Laut- und Wortlehre*, Göttingen, 1907.

1928   *Die Kasussyntax der Verba bei den Septuaginta. Ein Beitrag zur Hebraismenfrage und zur Syntax der* Κοινή, Göttingen, 1928.

HELTZER, M.

1988   Μισθωτός *im Buche Judith*, in M. WISSEMAN (ed.), *Roma renascens: Beiträge zur Spätantike und Rezeptions-geschichte*, Frankfurt aM - Bern - New York - Paris, 1988, pp. 118-124.

HERMANN, E.

1918   *Etymologisches*, in *Nachrichten von der Königlichen Gesellschaft der Wissenschaften zu Göttingen. Philologisch-historische Klasse*, Berlin, 1918, pp. 281-287.

HERTZBERG, H.W.

1963   *Der Prediger* (KAT, 17/4), Gütersloh, 1963.

HILHORST, A.

1982   *Darius' Pillow (1 Esdras III.8)*, in *JTS* 33 (1982) 161-163.

1989   *"Servir Dieu" dans la terminologie du judaïsme hellénistique et des premières générations chrétiennes de langue grecque* (IP, 19), Göttingen, 1989, pp. 176-192.

HILL, D.

1967   *Greek Words and Hebrew Meanings: Studies in the Semantics of Soteriological Terms* (SNTS MS, 5), Cambridge, 1967.

HINDLEY, J.C.

1961   *The Translation of Words for Covenant*, in *IJT* 10 (1961) 13-24.

HOFFMEIER, J.K.

1985   *"Sacred" in the Vocabulary of Ancient Egypt. The Term "dsr" with Special Reference to Dynasties I-XX* (OBO, 59), Fribourg/Suisse - Göttingen, 1985.

HOLLADAY, W.L.

1958   *The Root šûbh in the Old Testament with Particular Reference to Its Usages in Covenantal Contexts*, Leiden, 1958.

1986 *   *Jeremiah 1: A Commentary on the Book of the Prophet Jeremiah Chapters 1--25* (Hermeneia), Philadelphia, PA, 1986.

1989 *   *Jeremiah 2: A Commentary on the Book of the Prophet Jeremiah Chapters 26--52* (Hermeneia), Minneapolis, MN, 1989.

HOLLEAUX, M.

1942   *Ceux qui sont dans le bagage*, in Id. *Etudes d'épigraphie et d'histoire grecques. Tome III. Lagides et Séleucides*, Paris, 1942, pp. 15-26.

HOLM-NIELSEN, S.

1977   *Die Psalmen Salomos* (Jüdische Schriften aus hellenistisch-römischer Zeit, 4/2), Gütersloh, 1977, pp. 49-112.

HOLTZMANN, O.

1912   *Zwei Stellen zum Gottesbegriff des Philo*, in *ZNW* 13 (1912) 270-272.

HORSLEY, G.H.R.

1981   *New Documents Illustrating Early Christianity. Vol. 1. A Review of the Greek Inscriptions and Papyri Published in 1976*, Macquarie University, N.S.W., 1981.

1982   *New Documents Illustrating Early Christianity. Vol. 2. A Review of the Greek Inscriptions and Papyri Published in 1977*, Macquarie University, N.S.W., 1982.

1983   *New Documents Illustrating Early Christianity. Vol. 3. A Review of the Greek Inscriptions and Papyri Published in 1978*, Macquarie University, N.S.W., 1983.

1987   *New Documents Illustrating Early Christianity. Vol. 4. A Review of the Greek Inscriptions and Papyri Published in 1979*, Macquarie University, N.S.W., 1987.

1989   *New Documents Illustrating Early Christianity. Vol. 5. Linguistic Essays*, Macquarie University, N.S.W., 1989.

HORST, J.

1932   Προσκυνεῖν *zur Anbetung im Urchristentum nach ihrer religionsgeschichtlichen Eigenart* (Neutestamentliche Forschungen, 3/2), Gütersloh, 1932.

HULSE, E.V.

1975   *The Nature of Biblical 'Leprosy' and the Use of Alternative Medical Terms in Modern Translations of the Bible*, in *PEQ* 107 (1975) 86-105.

HULTSCH, F.

1882   *Griechische und römische Metrologie*, Berlin, 1882.

HUMBACH, H.

1968   *Die Feminina von* ἱερεύς, in *MSS*, 24, München, 1968, pp. 10-25.

HURST, L.D.

1983   *How 'Platonic' Are Heb. viii.5 and ix.23f.?*, in *JTS* 34 (1983) 156-165.

HUSSON, G.

1967   *Recherches sur le sens du mot* προάστιον *dans le grec d'Égypte*, in *Recherches de papyrologie IV*, Paris 1967, pp. 187-200.

1983ª   *Oikia. Le vocabulaire de la maison privée en Égypte d'après les papyrus grecs* (Papyrologie, 2), Paris, 1983.

1983ᵇ   *Un sens méconnu de* θυρίς *et de* fenestra, in *JJP* 19 (1983) 155-162.

1988   *Le paradis de délices (Genèse 3,23-24)*, in *RÉG* 101 (1988) 64-73.

1991   *Sur quelques termes du grec d'Égypte désignant des bâtiments agricoles*, in *Revue de philologie, de littérature et d'histoire anciennes* 65 (1991) 119-125.

HUYS, M.

1989   ῎Εκθεσις *and* ἀπόθεσις. *The Terminology of Infant Exposure in Greek Antiquity*, in *AnCl* 58 (1989) 190-197.

JACOBSON, H.

1976   *Wisdom XVIII 9*, in *JSJ* 7 (1976) 204.

JANZEN, J.G.

1973   *Studies in the Text of Jeremiah* (HSM, 6), Cambridge, MA, 1973.

JASTROW, M.

1926   *A Dictionary of the Targumim, the Talmud Babli and Yerushalmi, and the Midrashic Literature*, 2 vols., New York - Berlin - London, 1926; reprint New York, 1950.

JAUBERT, A.

1963   *La notion d'alliance dans le judaïsme aux abords de l'ère chrétienne* (Patristica Sorbonensia, 6), Parijs, 1963.

JEANSONNE, S.P.

1988   *The Old Greek Translation of Daniel 7-12* (CBQ MS, 19), Washington, 1988.

JEREMIAS, J.

1939   *Beobachtungen zu neutestamentlichen Stellen an Hand des neugefundenen griechischen Henoch-Textes*, in *ZNW* 38 (1939) 115-124.

JOBES, K.H.

1991   *Distinguishing the Meaning of Greek Verbs in the Semantic Domain for Worship*, in *Filologia Neotestamentaria* 4 (1991) 182-191.

JOHANNESSOHN, M.

1910   *Der Gebrauch der Präpositionen in der Septuaginta* (Diss.), Berlin, 1910.

1926   *Der Gebrauch der Präpositionen in der Septuaginta* (MSU, 3), Berlin, 1926, pp. 165-388.

JOHNSON, A.C.

1938   & GEHMAN, H.S. & KASE, E.H., *The John H. Scheide Biblical Papyri: Ezekiel* (Princeton University Studies in Papyrology, 3), Princeton, NJ, 1938.

JOLY, R.

1968   *Le vocabulaire chrétien de l'amour est-il original?* Φιλεῖν *et* ἀγαπᾶν *dans le grec antique*, Bruxelles, 1968.

JONES, C.P.

1987   Στίγμα: *Tattooing and Branding in Graeco-roman Antiquity*, in *Journal of Roman Studies* 77 (1987) 139-155.

JONES, D.

1955   Ἀνάμνησις *in the LXX and the Interpretation of I Cor. XI. 25*, in *JTS* 6 (1955) 183-191.

JONES, H.S. → LIDDELL, H.G.

JOÜON, P.

1925   *Notes de philologie paulinienne*, in *RechSR* 15 (1925) 531-535.

1937   Ὄχλος *au sens de «peuple, population» dans le grec du Nouveau Testament et dans la lettre d'Aristée*, in *RechSR* 27 (1937) 618-619.

KAHANE, H. & R.

1987   *Religious Key Terms in Hellenism and Byzantium. Three Facets*, in *Illinois Classical Studies* 12 (1987) 243-263.

KALLITSUNAKIS, J.

1926   Ὄψον *und* ὀψάριον. *Ein Beitrag zur griechischen Semasiologie*, in *Festschrift für Universitäts-professor Hofrat Dr. Paul Kretschmer. Beiträge zur griechischen und lateinischen Sprachforschung*, Wien-Leipzig-New York, 1926, pp. 96-106.

KASE, E.H.

1938   *The nomen sacrum of Ezekiel*, in JOHNSON, A.C., *The John H. Scheide Biblical Papyri*, Princeton, NJ., 1938, pp. 48-51.
        → JOHNSON 1938

KATZ, P.[= WALTERS P.]

1938   *Biblia Hebraica*, in *ThLZ* 63 (1938) col.32-34.

1939   Rec. E. SCHWYZER, *Griechische Grammatik*, 1934, in *ThLZ* 64 (1939) col.7-9.

1946ᵃ   Καταπαῦσαι *as a Corruption of* καταλῦσαι *in the LXX*, in *JBL* 65 (1946) 319-324.

1946ᵇ   *Notes on the Septuagint: IV.* Ἔα δέ *Let alone in Job*, in *JTS* 47 (1946) 168-169.

1950   *Philo's Bible. The Aberrant Text of Bible Quotations in Some Philonic Writings and Its Place in the Textual History of the Greek Bible*, Cambridge, 1950, esp. pp. 141-154.

1956   *Zur Übersetzungstechnik der Septuaginta*, in *Die Welt des Orients* II/3 (1956) 267-273.

1960   Rec. W. BAUER, *Wörterbuch*, 1958⁵, in *Kratylos* 5 (1960) 157-163.

KAUPEL, H.

1935   *'Sirenen' in der Septuaginta*, in *BZ* 23 (1935-36) 158-165.

KERR, A.J.

1988   Ἀρραβών, in *JTS* 39 (1988) 92-97.

KHIOK-KHNG, Y.

1991   *The Meaning and Usage of the Theology of 'Rest' (*Κατάπαυσις *and* σαββατισμός*) in Hebrews 3:7-4:13*, in *Asia Journal of Theology* 5 (1991) 2-33.

KIESSLING, E.

1927   *Die Aposkeuai und die prozessrechtliche Stellung der Ehefrauen im ptolemäischen Ägypten,*
        in *Archiv für Papyrusforschung und verwandte Gebiete* 8 (1927) 240-249.

1956   *Über den Rechtsbegriff der* παραθήκη, in *Akten des VII. internationalen Kongresses für
        Papyrologie Wien 1955,* Wien, 1956, pp. 69-77.
        → PREISIGKE, F.

KILPATRICK, G.D.

1942   *A Theme of the Lucan Passion Story and Luke xxiii,47,* in *JTS* 43 (1942) 34-36; =
        G.D. KILPATRICK 1990, pp. 327-329.

1943   Προσανοικοδομηθήσεται *Ecclus. 3,14,* in *JTS* 44 (1943) 147-148.

1947   Φρόνιμος, Σοφός *and* Συνετός *in Matthew and Luke,* in *JTS* 48 (1947) 63-64; = G.D.
        KILPATRICK 1990, pp. 225-226.

1961   *The Meaning of* θύειν *in the New Testament,* in *BiTr* 12 (1961) 130-132; = G.D.
        KILPATRICK 1990, pp. 201-204.

1963   *Atticism and the Text of the Greek New Testament,* in J. BLINZLER (ed.),
        Neutestamentliche Aufsätze. FS J.Schmid, Regensburg, 1963, pp. 125-137; = G.D.
        KILPATRICK 1990, pp. 14-32.

1967   *The Aorist of* γαμεῖν *in the New Testament,* in *JTS* 18 (1967) 139-140;= G.D.
        KILPATRICK 1990, pp. 187-188.

1968   Κύριος *in the Gospels,* in *L'Evangile, hier et aujourd'hui. FS Franz-J. Leenhardt,* Genève,
        1968, pp. 65-70; = G.D. KILPATRICK 1990, pp. 207-212.

1969   *Some Problems in New Testament Text and Language,* in E.E. ELLIS & M. WILCOX
        (eds.) *Neotestamentica et Semitica. FS M. Black,* Edinburgh, 1969, pp. 198-208; =
        G.D. KILPATRICK 1990, pp. 229-240.

1973   Κύριος *again,* in P. HOFFMANN (ed.), *Orientierung an Jesus. Zur Theologie der Synoptiker.
        FS Josef Schmid,* Freiburg-Basel-Wien, 1973, pp. 214-219; = G.D. KILPATRICK 1990,
        pp. 216-222.

1975   *Anamnesis,* in *Liturg. Review* 5 (1975) 35-40.

1977   *Eclecticism and Atticism,* in *ETL* 53 (1977) 107-112; = G.D. KILPATRICK 1990, pp.
        73-79.

1979   *Three Problems of New Testament Text,* in *NT* 21 (1979) 289-292; = G.D. KILPATRICK
        1990, pp. 241-244.

1983ᵃ   *Atticism and the Future of* Ζῆν, in *NT* 25 (1983) 146-151; = G.D. KILPATRICK 1990,
        pp. 195-200.

1983ᵇ   Ἐπιθύειν *and* ἐπικρίνειν *in the Greek Bible,* in *ZNW* 74 (1983) 151-153; = G.D.
        KILPATRICK 1990, pp. 191-194.

1990   *The Principles and Practice of New Testament Textual Criticism. Collected Essays.* Ed.
        J.K. ELLIOT (BETL, 96), Leuven, 1990.

KINDSTRAND, J.F.

1983   Θυροκόπος. *A Study of the Greek Compounds with* -κόπος, -κοπία *and* -κοπέω *in the
        Classical and Hellenistic Periods,* in *AnCl* 52 (1983) 86-109.

KITTEL, G.

1933   & FRIEDRICH, G., *Theologisches Wörterbuch zum Neuen Testament,* 11 vols., Stuttgart,
        1933-1979; = *Theological Dictionary of the New Testament,* 10 vols., Grand Rapids,
        MI, 1964-1976.

KLASSEN, W.

1993   *The Sacred Kiss in the New Testament,* in *NTS* 39 (1993) 122-135.

KLAUCK, H.-J.

1980   Θυσιαστήριον - *eine Berichtigung*, in *ZNW* 71 (1980) 274-277.

1989   *4. Makkabäerbuch* (Jüdische Schriften aus hellenistisch-römischer Zeit, 3/6), Gütersloh 1989.

KLEIN, F.-N.

1962   *Die Lichtterminologie bei Philon von Alexandrien und in den hermetischen Schriften. Untersuchungen zur Struktur der religiösen Sprache der hellenistischen Mystik*, Leiden, 1962.

KOEHLER, L.

1990   & BAUMGARTNER, W., *Hebräisches und aramäisches Lexikon zum Alten Testament*, Leiden, 1953; neu bearbeitet von J.J. STAMM, Leiden, 1990.

KOENIG, J.

1982 *   *L'herméneutique analogique du Judaïsme antique d'après les témoins textuels d'Isaïe*, Leiden, 1982.

KOLARI, E.

1947   *Musikinstrumente und ihre Verwendung im Alten Testament*, Helsinki, 1947.

KOONCE, K.

1988   Ἄγαλμα *and* εἰκών, in *AmJPg* 109 (1988) 108-110.

KORN, J.H.

1937   Πειρασμός. *Die Versuchung des Gläubigen in der griechischen Bibel* (BWANT, 72), Stuttgart, 1937.

KRAABEL, A.T.

1969   Ὕψιστος *and the Synagogue at Sardis*, in *GRBS* 10 (1969) 81-93.

KRAFT, R.A.

1972ᵃ   (ed.) *Septuagintal Lexicography* (SCS, 1), Missoula, MT, 1972.

1972ᵇ   *Prefatory Remarks to the Lexical "Probes". Towards a Lexicon of Jewish Translation Greek*, in R.A. KRAFT (ed.) 1972ᵃ, pp. 157-178.

1972ᶜ   *Approaches to Translation Greek Lexicography*, in R.A. KRAFT (ed.) 1972ᵃ, pp. 30-39.

1972ᵈ   Εἰς νίκος = *Permanently/Successfully: 1 Cor 15.54, Matt 12.20*, in R.A. KRAFT (ed.) 1972ᵃ, pp. 153-156.

KRASOVEC, J.

1988   *La justice (Sdp) de Dieu dans la Bible hébraïque et l'interprétation juive et chrétienne* (OBO, 76), Fribourg/Suisse - Göttingen, 1988.

KRISCHER, T.

1981   Σιγᾶν *und* σιωπᾶν, in *Glotta* 59 (1981) 93-107.

1984   Νόος, νοεῖν, νόημα, in *Glotta* 62 (1984) 141-149.

KUPISZEWSKI, H.

1958   & MODRZEJEWSKI, J., Ὑπηρέται, in *JJP* 11/12 (1957-58) 141-166.

LABERGE, L.

1978   *La Septante d'Isaïe 28--33. Étude de tradition textuelle*, Ottawa, 1978.

LACHS, S.T.

1978   *A Note on the Original Language of Susanna*, in *JQR* 69 (1978) 52-54.

LAMPE, G.

1976   *A Patristic Greek Lexicon*, Oxford, 1976.

LARCHER, C.

1969 * *   *Études sur le livre de la Sagesse* (ÉtB), Paris, 1969.
1983 *   *Le livre de la Sagesse ou la Sagesse de Salomon I* (ÉtB NS, 1), Paris, 1983.
1984 *   *Le livre de la Sagesse ou la Sagesse de Salomon II* (ÉtB NS, 3), Paris, 1984.
1985 *   *Le livre de la Sagesse ou la Sagesse de Salomon III* (ÉtB NS, 5), Paris, 1985.

LAUNEY, M.

1949   *Recherches sur les armées hellénistiques*. I. *Recherches ethniques*, Paris, 1949.
1950   *Recherches sur les armées hellénistiques*. II. *Recherches sociologiques*, Paris, 1950.

LAURENTIN, A.

1964   *We'attah - Kai nun. Formule caractéristique des textes juridiques et liturgiques*, in *Bib* 45 (1964) 168-197.

LE BOHEC, S.

1985   *Les φίλοι des rois Antigonides*, in *RÉG* 98 (1985) 93-124.

LE BOULLUEC, A.

1989 *   & SANDEVOIR, P., *La Bible d'Alexandrie II. L'Exode*, Paris, 1989.

LE DÉAUT, R.

1964   Φιλανθρωπία *dans la littérature grecque jusqu'au Nouveau Testament (Tite III,4)*, in *Mélanges Eugène Tisserant. Vol. I. Écriture sainte - Ancien Orient* (Studi e testi, 231), Roma, 1964, pp. 255-294.

1981   *Le thème de la circoncision du coeur (Dt. xxx 6; Jér. iv 4) dans les versions anciennes (LXX et Targum) et à Qumrân*, in J.A. EMERTON (ed.), *Congress Volume. Vienna 1980* (SVT, 32), Leiden, 1981, pp.178-205.

1984   *La Septante, un Targum?*, in R. KUNTZMANN & J. SCHLOSSER (eds.), *Études sur le judaïsme hellénistique. Congrès de Strasbourg 1983* (LeDiv, 119), Paris, pp. 1984, 147-195.

LEDOGAR, R.J.

1967   *Verbs of Praise in the LXX Translation of the Hebrew Canon*, in *Bib* 48 (1967) 29-56.

LEE, E.K.

1962   *Words Denoting 'Pattern' in the New Testament*, in *NTS* 8 (1961-62) 166-173.

LEE, G.M.

1970   *'Perhaps' in Greek and Coptic*, in *Muséon* 83 (1970) 137-138.

LEE, J.A.L.

1969   *A Note on Septuagint Material in the Supplement to Liddell and Scott*, in *Glotta* 47 (1969) 234-242.
1972   *A Neglected Sense of* μέρος, in *Antichton* 6 (1972) 39-42.
1980ᵃ   *The Future of* Ζῆν *in Late Greek*, in *NT* 22 (1980) 289-298.
1980ᵇ   *Equivocal and Stereotyped Renderings in the LXX*, in *RB* 87 (1980) 104-117.

1983   *A Lexical Study of the Septuagint Version of the Pentateuch* (SCS, 14), Chico, CA, 1983.

1985   *Some Features of the Speech of Jesus in Mark's Gospel*, in *NT* 27 (1985) 1-26.

1990   Συνίστημι· *A Sample Lexical Entry*, in T. MURAOKA (ed.) 1990, pp. 1-15.

LEFEBVRE, P.

1991   *Salomon et Bacchus*, in C.E. COX (ed.) 1991, pp. 312-323.

LEFORT, L.T.

1935   *Un passage obscur des hymnes à Chenoute*, in *Or* 4 (1935) 411-415.

LÉGASSE, S.

1960   *La révélation aux* νήπιοι, in *Bib* 67 (1960) 321-348.

LEIVESTAD, R.

1966   Ταπεινός - ταπεινόφρων, in *NT* 8 (1966) 36-47.

LEVIN, S.

1969   *Grassmann's 'Law' in the Early Semitic Loan-Word* χιτών, κιθών, in *Studi micenei ed egeo-anatolici* (Incunabula graeca, 38, 8), Roma, 1969, pp. 66-75.

LEWIS, N.

1960   Λειτουργία *and Related Terms*, in *GRBS* 3 (1960) 175-184.

1974   *Papyrus in Classical Antiquity*, Oxford, 1974.

1989   *The Documents from the Bar Kokhba Period in the Cave of Letters: Greek Papyri*, Jerusalem, 1989.

LIAÑO, J.M.

1966   *Los pobres en el Antiguo Testamento*, in *Est Bib* 25 (1966) 117-167.

LIDDELL, H.G.

1996   & SCOTT, R., *A Greek-English Lexicon*, Oxford, 1843; revised and augmented by H.S. JONES, with the assistance of R. MCKENZIE, 1925; with *A Supplement*, ed. E.A. BARBER with the assistance of P. MAAS, M. SCHELLER & M.L. WEST, 1968; *Revised Supplement*, ed. P.G.W. GLARE, with the assistance of A.A. THOMPSON, 1996.
→ RENEHAN, R.

LIEBERMAN, P.

1942   *Greek in Jewish Palestine*, New York, 1942.

LIEBERMAN, S.

1946   *Two Lexicographical Notes*, in *JBL* 65 (1946) 67-72.

1950   *Hellenism in Jewish Palestine*, New York, 1950, ²1962.

LIFSHITZ, B.

1961   *The Greek Documents from Nahal Seelim and Nahal Mishmar*, in *IEJ* 11 (1961) 52-63.

1962ᵃ   *Beiträge zur palästinischen Epigraphik*, in *ZDPV* 78 (1962) 65-88.

1962ᵇ   *Papyrus grecs du désert de Juda*, in *Aeg* 42 (1962) 240-256.

LIGHTSTONE, J.N.

1984   *Torah is nomos - Except When It Is Not: Prolegomena to the Study of the Law in Late Antique Judaism*, in *SR* 13 (1984) 29-38.

LINDBLOM, J.

1921   Σκάνδαλον. *Eine lexikalisch-exegetische Untersuchung* (UUA), Uppsala, 1921.

LINDHAGEN, C.

1950 Ἐργάζεσθαι. *Die Wurzel* σαπ *in NT und AT. Zwei Beiträge zur Lexikographie der Griechischen Bibel* (UUA, 5), Uppsala, 1950.

LINDSAY, D.

1993 *The Roots and Development of the* πιστ- *Word Group as Faith Terminology*, in *JSNT* 49 (1993) 103-118.

LIPIŃSKI, É.

1968 *Macarismes et psaumes de congratulation*, in *RB* 75 (1968) 321-367.
1970 *Recherches sur le livre de Zacharie*, in *VT* 20 (1970) 25-55.
1975 *Review of* J.A. SOGGIN, *Introduzione all' Antico Testamento*. Seconda edizione riveduta ed aggiornata, Brescia, 1974, in *VT* 25 (1975) 553-561.

LLEWELYN, S.R.

1992 *New Documents Illustrating Early Christianity. Vol. 6. A Review of the Greek Inscriptions and Papyri Published in 1980-81*, Macquarie University, NSW, 1992.
1994 *New Documents Illustrating Early Christianity. Vol. 7. A Review of the Greek Inscriptions and Papyri published in 1982-83*, Macquarie University, NSW, 1994.

LOADER, J.

1973 *An Explanation of the Term* προσήλυτος, in *NT* 15 (1973) 270-277.

LOEWE, R.

1952 *Jerome's Treatment of an Anthropopatism*, in *VT* 2 (1952) 261-272.

LOFTHOUSE, W.F.

1949 *Poneron and Kakon in Old and New Testaments*, in *ET* 60 (1948-49) 264-268.

LOMBARD, H.

1971 Κατάπαυσις *in the Letter to the Hebrews*, in *Neotestamentica* 5 (1971) 60-71.

LOWE, A.D.

1967 *The Origin of* οὐαί, in *Hermathena* 105 (1967) 34-39.

LOUW, P.

1988 & NIDA, A., *Greek-English Lexicon of the New Testament*, 2 vols., New York, 1988.

LUCCHESI, E.

1978[a] *Un 'hapax' grec retrouvé en copte (shenoutien)*, in *The Journal of Egyptian Archaelogy* 64 (1978) 141-142.
1978[b] *Un terme inconnu de l'Évangile de Vérité*, in *Or* 47 (1978) 483-484.

LUCIANI, F.

1973 *Camminare davanti a Dio*. II. *I Settanta*, in *Aevum* 47 (1973) 468-476.
1984 *La prima frase di Es. 12,16b: differenze tra testo Ebraico e versione dei LXX*, in *Rivista Biblica* 32 (1984) 425-429.

LÜHRMANN, D.

1971 Ἐπιφάνεια. *Zur Bedeutungsgeschichte eines griechischen Wortes*, in G. JEREMIAS, H-W. KUHN & H. STEGEMANN (eds.) *Tradition und Glaube. FS K.G. Kuhn*, Göttingen, 1971, pp. 185-199.
1973 Πίστις *in Judentum*, in *ZNW* 64 (1973) 19-38.

LUST, J.

1968   «Monseigneur Jahweh» dans le texte hébreu d' Ézéchiel, in *ETL* 44 (1968) 482-488.

1978   *Daniel 7,13 and the Septuagint*, in *ETL* 54 (1978), 62-69.

1985   *Messianism and Septuagint. Ez 21,30-32*, in J. EMERTON (ed.), *Congress Volume Salamanca 1983* (SVT, 36), Leiden, 1985, pp. 174-191.

1986   (ed.), *Ezekiel and His Book. Textual and Literary Criticism and their Interrelation* (BETL, 74), Leuven, 1986.

1987   *Exegesis and Theology in the Septuagint of Ezekiel. The longer 'Pluses' and Ezek 43:1-9*, in C.E. COX (ed.) 1987, pp. 201-232.

1990ᵃ   *J. F. Schleusner and the Lexicon of the Septuagint*, in *ZAW* 102 (1990) 256-262.

1990ᵇ   *Le messianisme et la Septante d'Ézéchiel*, in *Tsafon* 2/3 (1990) 3-14.

1991ᵃ   *Messianism and the Greek Version of Jeremiah*, in C.E. COX (ed.) 1991, pp. 87-122.

1991ᵇ   *Molek and* ἄρχων, in *Studia Phoenicia* 11 (OLA, 44), Leuven, 1991, pp. 193-208.

1992   Ἕδρα *and the Philistine Plague*, in C.J. BROOKE (ed.) 1992, pp. 569-597.

1993ᵃ   *Cult and Sacrifice in Daniel. The Tamid and the Abomination of Desolation*, in *Ritual and Sacrifice in the Ancient Near East* (OLA, 55), Leuven, 1993, pp. 283-299.

1993ᵇ   The Septuagint Version of Daniel 4-5, in A.S. VAN DER WOUDE (ed.), *The Book of Daniel in Light of New Findings* (BETL, 106), Leuven, 1993, pp. 39-53.

1993ᶜ   *Two New Lexica of the Septuagint and Related Remarks*, in *JNWSL* 19 (1993) 95-105.

1994   *For I lift up my Hand to Heaven and swear: Deut 32:40*, in F. GARCÍA MARTÍNEZ, A. HILHORST, J. VAN RUITEN & A. VAN DER WOUDE (eds.), *Studies in Deuteronomy. FS C.J. Labuschagne* (SVT, 53), Leiden, 1994, pp. 155-164.

1995   *The Greek Version of Balaam's Third and Forth Oracles. The* ἄνθρωπος *in Num 24:7 and 17. Messianism and Lexicography*, in L. GREENSPOON & O. MUNNICH (eds.), *VIIth Congres of the IOSCS Paris 1992* (SCS, 41), Atlanta, GA, 1995, pp. 233-257.

1996ᵃ   *The Septuagint of Ezekiel according to Papyrus 967 and the Pentateuch*, in *ETL* 72 (1996) 131-137.

1996ᵇ   ארני יהוה *in Ezekiel and Its Counterpart in the Old Greek*, in *ETL* 72 (1996) 138-145.

1996ᶜ   *A Lexicon of Hexaplaric Recensions. The Transliterations in Ezekiel* (forthcoming).

1997   *'And I Shall Hang Him on a Lofty Mountain.' Ezek 17,22-24 and Messianism in the Septuagint*, in B. TAYLOR (ed.), *Proceedings of the IOSCS Meeting Cambridge 1995* (SCS, ..), Atlanta, GA (forthcoming).
        → EYNIKEL, E. 1991

LYONNET, S.

1958   *Le sens de* πειράζειν *en sap 2,24 et la doctrine du péché originel*, in *Bib* 39 (1958) 27-36.

LYS, D.

1966   *The Israelite Soul according to the LXX*, in *VT* 16 (1966) 181-228.

1983   *L'arrière-plan et les connotations vétérotestamentaires de* σάρξ *et de* σῶμα (LeDiv, 114), Paris, 1983, pp. 47-70.

1986   *L'arrière-plan et les connotations vétérotestamentaires de* σάρξ *et de* σῶμα *(Étude préliminaire)*, in *VT* 36 (1986) 163-204.

MAAS, P. → LIDDELL, H.G.

MACLAURIN, E.C.B.

1973   *The Semitic Background of the Use of 'en splanchnois'*, in *PEQ* 103 (1973) 42-45.

MANSON, T.W.

1945   Ἱλαστήριον, in *JTS* 46 (1945) 1-10.
1946   *The Life of Jesus: a Survey of the Available Material. (4) The Gospel According to St. Matthew*, in *BJRL* 29 (1946) 392-428.

MARGOLIS, B.

1970   *The Psalm of Habakkuk: A Reconstruction and Interpretation*, in *ZAW* 82 (1970) 409-442.

MARGOLIS, M.L.

1905   *Specimen Article for a Revised Edition of the Hebrew-Aramaic Equivalents in the Oxford Concordance to the Septuagint and the Other Greek Versions of the Old Testament*, in *ZAW* 25 (1905) 311-319; = R.A. KRAFT (ed.) 1972, pp. 52-64.
1906ª   Λαμβάνειν *(Including Compounds and Derivatives) and its Hebrew-Aramaic Equivalents in Old Testament Greek*, in *AJSL* 22 (1906) 110-119; = R.A. KRAFT (ed.) 1972 pp. 70-79.
1906ᵇ   Καίειν *(einschliesslich der Komposita und Derivata) und seine hebräisch-aramäischen Äquivalente im Gräzismus des A.T.*, in *ZAW* 26 (1906) 85-90; = R.A. KRAFT (ed.) 1972, pp. 65-69.
1907   *Studien im griechischen Alten Testament*, in *ZAW* 27 (1907) 212-270.
1909   *The Particle* ἤ *in Old Testament Greek*, in *AJSL* 25 (1908-09) 257-275
1911   Ἡνία, χαλινός, in *ZAW* 31 (1911) 314.

MARSHALL, A.

1954   *A Note on* τε .... καὶ, in *BiTr* 5 (1954) 182-183.

MARTIN, R.A.

1960   *Some Syntactical Criteria of Translation Greek*, in *VT* 10 (1960) 295-310.
1965   *The Earliest Messianic Interpretation of Genesis 3,15*, in *JBL* 84 (1965) 425-427.
1974   *Syntactical Evidence of Semitic Sources in Greek Documents* (SCS, 3), Missoula, MT, 1974.

MARTINI, C.M.

1974   *Eclecticism and Atticism in the Textual Criticism of the Greek New Testament*, in M. BLACK & W.A. SMALLEY (eds.), *on Language, Culture and Religion. FS E.A. Nida*, Den Haag - Paris, 1974, pp. 149-156; = C.M. MARTINI, *La parola di Dio alle origini della Chiesa* (AnBib, 93), Roma, 1980, pp. 145-152.

MASSON, M.

1986   Σφαῖρα, σφαιρωτήρ: *problème d'étymologie grecque* (Bulletin de la Société de Linguistique de Paris, 81/1), Paris, 1986, pp. 231-252.

MATEOS, J.

1990   Σάββατα, σάββατον, προσάββατον, παρασκευή, in *Filologia Neotestamentaria* 3 (1990) 19-38.

MATTIOLI, U.

1983   Ἀσθένεια e ἀνδρεία; *aspetti della femminilità nella letteratura classica, biblica e cristiana antica*, in *Università di Parma. Istituto Latine*, vol. 9, Roma, 1983.

MAXWELL-STUART, P.G.

1981   *Studies in Greek Colour Terminology. II.* Χαροπός (Mnemosyne Suppl., 67), Leiden, 1981.

MAY, G.L.

1951   *Temple or Shrine*, in *ET* 62 (1950-51) 346-347.

MAYSER, E.

1970   & SCHMOLL, H., *Grammatik der Griechischen Papyri aus der Ptolemäerzeit. Mit Einschluß der gleichzeitigen Ostraka und der in Ägypten verfassten Inschriften.* Band I: *Laut- und Wortlehre.* I. Teil: *Einleitung und Lautlehre*, Berlin, 1970.

McCARTER, P.K.

1984   *II Samuel. A New Translation with Introduction, Notes and Commentary* (AncB, 9), New York, 1984.

McCARTHY, C.

1981   *The Apple of the Eye*, in P. CASETTI, O. KEEL & A. SCHENKER (eds.), *Mélanges Dominique Barthélemy* (OBO, 38), Fribourg/Suisse - Göttingen 1981, 289-295.

McKANE, W.

1970 *   *Proverbs* (OTL), London, 1970.
1986 *   *A Critical and Exegetical Commentary on Jeremiah. I* (ICC), Edinburgh, 1986.

McKENZIE, R. → LIDDELL, H.G.

MEALAND, D.L.

1990   *The Close of Acts and Its Hellenistic Greek Vocabulary*, in *NTS* 36 (1990) 583-597.

MEGAS, G.

1928   *Das* χειρόγραφον *Adams. Ein Beitrag zu Col 2:13-15*, in *ZNW* 27 (1928) 305-320.

MENESTRINA, G.

1978ᵃ   Ναῦς, in *BeO* 20 (1978) 134.
1978ᵇ   Κλείς, in *BeO* 20 (1978) 182.
1979   Κατάθεμα, in *BeO* 21 (1979) 12.

MERCATI, G.

1943   *Una singolare versione di Deut. XXVI, 17 e 18 e l'originale di essa*, in *Bib* 24 (1943) 201-204.

MERKELBACH, R.

1970   Σημεῖον *im Liebesepigramm*, in *ZPE* 6 (1970) 244-245
1971   Σωτήρ *'Artz'*, in *ZPE* 8 (1971) 14

METZLER, K.

1991   *Der griechische Begriff des Verzeihens: Untersucht am Wortstamm* συγγνώμη *von den ersten Belegen bis zum vierten Jahrhundert n. Chr.* (WUNT 2/44), Tübingen, 1991.

MEYERS, E.M.

1971   *Jewish Ossuaries: Reburial and Rebirth* (BibOr, 24), Roma, 1971.

MICHAELIS, W.

1954ᵃ   *Zelt und Hütte im biblischen Denken*, in *Evangelische Theologie* 14 (1954) 29-49.
1954ᵇ   *Der Beitrag der Septuaginta zur Bedeutungsgeschichte von* πρωτότοκος, in *Sprachgeschichte und Wortbedeutung. FS A. Debrunner*, Bern, 1954, pp. 313-320.

MICHIELS, R.

1965 *La conception lucanienne de la conversion*, in *ETL* 41 (1965) 42-78.

MILNE, M.J.

1941 *The Use of* τορεύω *and Related Words*, in *AJA* 45 (1941) 390-398.

MILLIGAN, G.

1910 *Selections from the Greek Papyri. Edited with Translations and Notes*, Cambridge, 1910; reprint Chicago, IL, 1980.
→ MOULTON, J.H. 1914

MIQUEL, P.

1986 *Lexique du désert. Étude de quelques mots-clés du vocabulaire monastique grec ancien* (Spiritualité orientale, 44), Bégrolles-en-Mauges, 1986.

1989 *Le vocabulaire de l'expérience spirituelle dans la tradition patristique grecque du IVe au XIVe siècle* (Théologie historique, 86), Paris, 1989.

MITCHELL, T.C.

1965 & JOYCE, R., *The Musical Instruments in Nebuchadnezzar's Orchestra*, in D.J. WISEMAN, T.C. MITCHELL, R. JOYCE, W.J. MARTIN & K.A. KITCHEN, *Notes on Some Problems in the Book of Daniel*, London, 1965, 1970².

MOHRMANN, C.

1953 *Epiphania*, in *RSPhTh* 37 (1953) 644-670.

1954 *Note sur doxa*, in *Sprachgeschichte und Wortbedeutung. FS A. Debrunner*, Bern, 1954, pp. 321-328.

MOLONEY, F.J.

1983 *John 1:18: "In the Bosom of" or "turned towards" the Father?*, in *Australian Biblical Review* 31 (1983) 63-71.

MONSENGWO PASINYA, L.

1973 *La notion de* νόμος *dans le pentateuque grec* (AnBib, 52; Recherches africaines de théologie, 5), Roma, 1973.

1980 *Deux textes messianiques de la Septante: Gn 49,10 et Ez 21,32*, in *Bib* 61 (1980) 357-376.

MONTEVECCHI, O.

1957ᵃ *Dal paganesimo al christianesimo: aspetti dell'evoluzione della lingua greca nei papiri dell'Egitto*, in *Aeg* 37 (1957) 41-59.

1957ᵇ Παντοκράτωρ, in *FS A. Calderini & S.R. Paribeni*, Milano, 1957, pp. 401-432.

1964 *Continuità ed evoluzione della lingua greca nella Settanta e nei papiri*, in J. WOLSKI (ed.), *Actes du Xᵒ Congrès International de Papyrologues. Varsovie-Cracovie 3-9 sept. 1961*, Wroclaw - Varsovie - Cracovie, 1964, pp. 39-49.

1979ᵃ *Nomen christianum*, in R. CANTALAMESSA & L.F. PIZZOLATO (eds.), *Paradoxos politeia. FS Giuseppe Lazzati* (Studia patristica mediolanensia, 10), Milano, 1979, pp. 485-500.

1979ᵇ *Laos. Linee di una ricerca storico-linguistica*, in *Actes du XVᵉ Congres International de Papyrologie. IV. Papyrologie documentaire* (Papyrologica Bruxellensia, 19), Bruxelles, 1979, pp. 51-67.

1988 *La papirologia*, Brescia, 1973; 1988².

MONTGOMERY, J.A.

1927 *A Critical and Exegetical Commentary on the Book of Daniel* (ICC), Edinburgh, 1927.

1938 *Hebraica*, in *JAOS* 58 (1938) 130-139.

1939   *Hebrew* Hesed *and Greek* Charis, in *Harvard Theological Review* 32 (1939) 97-102.
1951 *   & GEHMAN, H.S., *A Critical and Exegetical Commentary on the Books of Kings* (ICC), Edinburgh, 1951.

MOORE, C.A.
1977   *Daniel, Esther and Jeremiah: The Additions. A New Translation with Introduction and Commentary*, New York, 1977.
1985   *Judith. A New Translation with Introduction and Commentary* (AncB, 40), New York, 1985.

MOORE, G.F.
1905   Συμφωνία *not a Bagpipe*, in *JBL* 24 (1905) 166-175.

MOOREN, L.
1977   *La hiérarchie du cour ptolémaïque. Contribution à l'étude des institutions et des classes dirigeantes à l'époque hellénistique*, in *StHell* 23 (1977) 28-36

MORENZ, S.
1964   *Ägyptische Spuren in der Septuaginta*, in *JAC, Ergänzungsband* 1 (1964) 250-258.

MORRIS, L.
1955   *The Meaning of* ἱλαστήριον *in Romans III, 25*, in *NTS* 2 (1955-56) 33-43.

MOSÈS, A.
1970   *De specialibus legibus III et IV* (Les oeuvres de Philon d'Alexandrie, 25), Paris, 1970.

MOULTON, J.H.
1910   *A Grammar of the Septuagint*, in *JTS* 11 (1910) 293-300.
1914   & MILLIGAN, G., *The Vocabulary of the Greek Testament, Illustrated from the Papyri and Other Non-literary Sources*, London, 1914-29, 1949².
1915   *Contributions and Comments -* Σκάνδαλον, in *ET* 26 (1914-15) 331-332.

MOUSSY, C.
1969   *Recherches sur* τρέφω *et les verbes grecs signifiants «nourrir»*, Paris, 1969.

MOWINCKEL, S.
1965   אָשַׁרְנָא *Ezr. 5:3,9*, in *Studia Theologica* 19 (1965) 130-135.

MULDER, M.J.
1987 * *Koningen* (Commentaar op het Oude Testament), Deel 1, Kampen, 1987.

MUNNICH, O.
1983   *La Septante des Psaumes et le groupe* καίγε, in *VT* 33 (1983) 75-89.
1986   *Note sur la Bible de Philon:* κλοποφορεῖν/κλοποφρονεῖν *en Gen 31,26 et en Leg. All. II,20*, in A. CAQUOT, M. HADAS-LEBEL & J. RIAUD (eds.), *Hellenica et Judaica. FS V. Nikiprowetzky*, Leuven - Paris, 1986, pp. 43-51.
1995   *Les Nomina Sacra dans les versions grecques de Daniel et leurs suppléments deutérocanoniques*, in G. DORIVAL & O. MUNNICH (eds.), *Selon les Septante. FS M. Harl*, Paris, 1995, pp. 145-167.
        → HARL, M. 1988

MURAOKA, T.

1964   *The Use of* ὡς *in the Greek Bible*, in *NT* 7 (1964) 51-72.
1970   *Is the Septuagint Amos vii,12-ix,10 a Separate Unit?*, in *VT* 20 (1970) 496-500.
1973   *Purpose or Result?* Ὥστε *in Biblical Greek*, in *NT* 15 (1973) 205-219.
1983   *Hosea iv in the Septuagint Version*, in *AJBI* 9 (1983) 24-65.
1984   *On Septuagint Lexicography and Patristics*, in *JTS* 35 (1984) 441-448.
1986   *Hosea V in the Septuagint Version*, in *Abr-Nahrain* 29 (1986) 120-138.
1987   *Towards a Septuagint Lexicon*, in C.E. COX (ed.), 1987, pp. 255-276.
1990   (ed.), *Melbourne Symposium on Septuagint Lexicography* (SCS, 28), Atlanta, GA, 1990.
1991   *Hebrew Hapax Legomena and Septuagint Lexicography*, in C.E. COX (ed.), 1991, pp. 205-222.
1993   *A Greek-English Lexicon of the Septuagint. (Twelve Prophets)*, Leuven, 1993.

MURPHY, J.L.

1958   *"Ekklesia" and the Septuagint*, in *AEcR* 139 (1958) 381-390.

NAUCK, W.

1958   *Das* οὖν-*paräneticum*, in *ZNW* 49 (1958) 134-135.

NAUTIN, P. → GUÉRAUD, O.

NEIRYNCK, F.

1977   Παρακύψας βλέπει: *Lc 24,12 et Jn 20,5*, in *ETL* 53 (1977) 113-152. = ID., *Evangelica. Gospel Studies - Études d'Évangile. Collected Essays.* Ed. F. VAN SEGBROECK (BETL, 60), Leuven, 1982, pp. 401-440.
1979   Εἰς τὰ ἴδια: *Jn 19,27 (et 16,32)*, in *ETL* 55 (1979) 357-365; = *Evangelica* 1982, pp. 456-464.
        → DE LA POTTERIE, I.

NESTLE, E.

1895   חבר = ἔθνος, in *ZAW* 15 (1895) 288-290.
1900   *Neue Stoffe zu Doktorarbeiten*, in *ZAW* 20 (1900) 168-171.
1903   *Sykophantia im biblischen Griechisch*, in *ZNW* 4 (1903) 271-272.
1904   *Zur aramäischen Bezeichnung der Proselyten*, in *ZNW* 5 (1904) 263-264.

NEYREY, J.H.

1980   *The Lucan Redaction of Lk 22,39-46*, in *Bib* 61 (1980) 153-171.

NIDA, A. → LOUW, P.

NIEDDU, G.F.

1988   *Sulla nozione di 'leggere' in greco; decifrare* [ἀνανέμω, ἐπιλέγομαι, ἀναγιγνώσκω]. . *percorrere* [διέρχομαι], in *Giornale Italiano di Filologia* 40 (1988) 17-37.

NIKIPROWETZKY, V.

1976   *Rébecca, vertu de constance et constance de vertu chez Philon d'Alexandrie*, in *Semitica* 26 (1976) 109-136.

NOCK, A.D.

1951   *Soter and Euergetes,* in S.E. JOHNSON (ed.), *The Joy of Study. FS F.C. Grant*, 1951, pp. 127-148; = A.D. NOCK, *Essays on Religion and the Ancient World*. Ed. Z. STEWART, vol. 2, Oxford, 1972, pp. 720-735.

NORTH, J.L.

1973 'Ακηδία *and* ἀκηδιᾶν *in the Greek and Latin Biblical Tradition,* in TU 112 (1973) 387-392.

NORTON, F.O.

1908 *A Lexicographical and Historical Study of* διαθήκη, Chicago, IL, 1908.

NUCHELMANS, J.

1989 *A propos de Hagios avant l'époque hellénistique,* in A.R. BASTIAENSEN, A. HILHORST & C.H. KNEEPKENS (eds.), *Fructus centesimus, FS G.J.M. Bartelinck* (Instrumenta Patristica, 19), Steenbrugge - Dordrecht, 1989, pp. 239-258.

NÚÑEZ, H.M.

1966 'Ānî, πτωχός, *pobre (Métodos para el entronque del vocabulario griego-hebreo),* in *Est Bib* 25 (1966) 193-205.

O'CALLAGHAN, J.

1971 *El vocativo singular de* ἀδελφός *en el griego biblico,* in *Bib* 52 (1971) 217-225.

1980 *Il termine* θυσία *nei papiri,* in F. VATTIONI (ed.), *Sangue e antropologia biblica* (Centro Studi Sanguis Christi, 1), Roma, 1980, pp. 325-330.

1986 ¿'Αγάπη *como titulo de trato en el siglo V°?,* in *Aeg* 66 (1986) 169-173.

OLESON, J.P.

1984 *Greek and Roman Mechanical Water-Lifting Devices: The History of a Technology,* Dordrecht - Boston - Lancaster, 1984.

OLLEY, J.W.

1979 *'Righteousness' in the Septuagint of Isaiah: A Contextual Study* (SCS, 8), Missoula, MT, 1979.
→ GOODING, D.W., 1981

OLOFSSON, S.

1990ᵃ *The LXX Version. A Guide to the Translation Technique of the Septuagint* (CB.OT, 30), Stockholm, 1990.

1990ᵇ *God is My Rock. A Study of Translation Technique and Theological Exegesis of the Septuagint* (CB.OT, 31), Stockholm, 1990.

OPPENHEIM, A.L.

1956 *Sumerian: inim.gar, Akkadian: egirrû = Greek: kledon,* in *Archiv für Orientforschung* 17 (1954-56) 49-55.

ORLINSKY, H.M.

1935 *Some Corruptions in the Greek Text of Job,* in *JQR* 26 (1935-36) 133-145.

1937 'Αποβαίνω *and* ἐπιβαίνω *in the Septuagint of Job,* in *JBL* 56 (1937) 361-367.

1948 *Book Reviews:* G. GERLEMAN, *Studies in the Septuagint: I. Book of Job; II Chronicles,* in *JBL* 67 (1948) 381-390.

1962 *Studies in the Septuagint of the Book of Job,* in *HUCA* 33 (1962) 119-151.

ORRIEUX, C.

1985 *Zénon de Caunos, parépidèmos, et le destin grec* (Centre de recherches d'histoire ancienne, 64), Paris, 1985.

OTTLEY, R.R.

1906 * *The Book of Isaiah according to the Septuagint*, Cambridge, 1906.

OTTO, W.

1949 *Beiträge zur Hierodulie im hellenistischen Ägypten*, in *Bayerische Akademie der Wissenschaften* 1949) 9-12

OWEN, E.C.E.

1929 Ἀποτυμπανίζω, ἀποτυμπανισμός (τυμπανισμός), τυμπανίζω, τύμπανον (τύπανον), in *JTS* 30 (1929) 259-266.

1931 Δαίμων *and Cognate Words*, in *JTS* 32 (1931) 133-266.

PAESLACK, M.

1954 *Zur Bedeutungsgeschichte der Wörter* φιλεῖν *'lieben',* φιλία *'Liebe' 'Freundschaft',* φίλος *'Freund' in der Septuaginta und im Neuen Testament (unter Berücksichtigung ihrer Beziehungen zu* ἀγαπᾶν, ἀγάπη, ἀγαπητός), in *Theologia Viatorum, Jahrbuch der Kirchlichen Hochschule Berlin* 5 (1953-54) 51-142.

PARADISE, B.

1986 *Food for Thought: The Septuagint Translation of Genesis 1.11-12*, in J.D. MARTIN & P.R. DAVIES, *A Word in Season. FS W. McKane* (JSOT SS, 42), Sheffield, 1986, pp. 177-204.

PASSONI DELL'ACQUA, A.

1974 Σκύλμος, in *Aeg* 54 (1974) 197-202.

1976 *Euergetes*, in *Aeg* 56 (1976) 177-191.

1981 *Ricerche sulla versione dei LXX e i papiri. I Pastophorion*, in *Aeg* 61 (1981) 171-211.

1982ª *Ricerche sulla versione dei LXX e i papiri. II Nomós; III Andrizomai*, in *Aeg* 62 (1982) 173-194.

1982ᵇ *Precisazione sul valore di* δῆμος *nella versione dei LXX*, in *Rivista Biblica* 30 (1982) 197-214.

1983 *Indagine lessicale su* ἐρευνάω *e composti. Dall'età classica a quella moderna*, in *Anagennesis* 3 (1983) 201-326.

1984 Καταπάτησις: *storia del termine, con un papiro inedito (P Med. Inv. 63, Ispezione di un terreno)*, in *Atti del XVII congresso internazionale di papirologia Napoli 1984*, III Napoli, 1984, pp. 1309-1315.

1986 *L'immagine del «Calpestare» dall'A.T. ai Padri della chiesa*, in *Anagennesis* 4 (1986) 63-129.

1988 *La terminologia dei reati nei* προστάγματα *dei Tolemei e nella versione dei LXX*, in B.G. MANDILARAS (ed.), *Proceedings of the XVIII International Congress of Papyrology. Athens 25-31 May 1986*, II, Athens, 1988, pp. 335-350.

PAX, E.

1955 Ἐπιφάνεια: *Ein religionsgeschichtlicher Beitrag zur biblischen Theologie* (Münchener Theologische Studien, I/10), München, 1955.

PELLETIER, A.

1954 *L'attentat au droit du pauvre dans le Pentateuque des LXX*, in *RechSR* 42 (1954) 523-527.

1955 *Le «Voile» du temple de Jérusalem, est-il devenu la «Portière» du temple d'Olympie?*, in *Syria* 32 (1955) 289-307.

1960 *Pains de proposition*, in DBS 6 (1960) 965-976.

1962 *Flavius Josèphe adaptateur de la Lettre d'Aristée. Une réaction atticisante contre la Koinè*, Paris, 1962.

1967ᵃ *Une particularité du Rituel des "pains d'oblation" conservée par la Septante (Lev. xxiv 8 & Ex. xxv 30)*, in *VT* 17 (1967) 364-367.

1967ᵇ *Valeur évocatrice d'un démarquage chrétien de la Septante*, in *Bib* 48 (1967) 388-394.

1967ᶜ *Note sur les mots:* ἱερόν, διάθεσις *dans P. Gen., inv. 108*, in *Recherches de Papyrologie* 4 (1967) 175-186.

1972 Σαββατα. *Transcription grecque de l'araméen*, in *VT* 22 (1972) 436-447.

1975 *La nomenclature du calendrier juif à l'époque hellénistique*, in *RB* 82 (1975) 218-233.

1979 *Actes de l'association. La philantropia dans les livres de sagesse juifs* in *RÉG* 92 (1979), XIV-XV.

1980 *Ce n'est pas la sagesse mais le Dieu Sauveur qui aime l'humanité*, in *RB* 87 (1980) 397-403.

1982 *L'autorité divine d'après le Pentateuque grec*, in *VT* 32 (1982) 236-242.

1984 *De la culture sémitique à la culture hellénique: rencontre, affrontement, pénétration*, in *RÉG* 97 (1984) 403-418.

PENNA, A.

1965 Διαθήκη *e* συνθήκη *nei libri dei Maccabei*, in *Bib* 46 (1965) 149-180.

PÉPIN, J.

1987 *Le «conseiller» de Dieu*, in *Lectures anciennes de la Bible* (Cahiers de Biblia Patristica, 1), Strasbourg, 1987, 53-74.

PERI, I.

1989 *Ecclesia und synagoga in der lateinischen Übersetzung des Alten Testamentes*, in *BZ* 33 (1989) 245-251.

PERLITT, L.

1990 *Dtn 1,12LXX*, in D. FRAENKEL, U. QUAST & J.W. WEVERS (eds.), *Studien zur Septuaginta - FS R. Hanhart* (MSU, 20), Göttingen, 1990, pp. 299-311.

PERPILLOU-THOMAS, F.

1989 *P.Sorb. inv. 2381:* γρύλλος, καλαμαύλης, χορός, in *ZPE* 78 (1989) 153-155.

PETERSEN, H.

1986 *Wörter zusammengesetzt mit* ἀμφί, in *Glotta* 64 (1986) 193-213.

PETIT, M. → DORIVAL, G. 1994

PETIT, T.

1988 *L'évolution sémantique des termes hébreux et araméens phh et sgn et accadien pāhatu et šaknu*, in *JBL* 107 (1988) 53-67.

PIETERSMA, A.

1984 Κύριος *or Tetragram: A Renewed Quest for the Original LXX*, in A. PIETERSMA & C.E. COX (eds.), *De Septuaginta. FS J.W. Wevers*, Mississauga (Ontario), 1984, pp. 85-101.

1985 *Septuagint Research: A Plea for a Return to Basic Issues*, in *VT* 35 (1985) 296-311.

1990 *Ra 2110 (P. Bodmer XXIV) and the Text of the Greek Psalter*, in D. FRAENKEL, U. QUAST & J.W. WEVERS (eds.), *Studien zur Septuaginta. FS R. Hanhart* (MSU, 20), Göttingen, 1990, pp. 262-282.

PODECHARD, E.

1912   *L'Ecclésiaste* (ÉtB), Paris, 1912.

1949 *   *Le Psautier: notes critiques. Psaumes 1-75,* Lyon, 1949.

1954 *   *Le Psautier: traduction littérale, explication historique et notes critiques. Psaumes 76-100 et 110,* Lyon, 1954.

POHLMANN, K.-F.

1970   *Studien zum dritten Esra* (FRLANT, 104), Göttingen, 1970.

POLAND, F.

1932   Συμβίωσις, in G. WISSOWA, W. KROLL & K. MITTELHAUS (eds.), *Paulys Realencyclopädie der classischen Altertumswissenschaft* (IV A), Stuttgart, 1932, col. 1075-1082.

PONTHOT, J.

1986   *L'expression cultuelle du ministère paulinien selon Rm 15,16,* in A. VANHOYE (ed.), *L'Apôtre Paul: personnalité, style et conception du ministère* (BETL, 43), Leuven, 1986, pp. 254-262.

PRALON, D. → HARLÉ

PRÉAUX, C.

1931   Ὅτι *suivi d'un discours direct après un verbe dicendi,* in *CÉg* 6 (1931) 414-415.

PREISIGKE, F.

1925   & E. KIESSLING, *Wörterbuch der griechischen Papyrusurkunden, mit Einschluß der griechischen Inschriften, Ausschriften, Ostraka, Mumienschilder usw. aus Ägypten.* Band 1, Berlin, 1925; Band 2, 1927; Band 3, 1931; Band 4 (KIESSLING), Marburg, fasc. 1 ἀ-ἄρτος (1944), fasc. 2 ἄρτος-δένδρον (1958), fasc. 3 δένδρον-Εἰρήνης (1966), fasc. 4 Εἰρηνικός-ἐπικόπτω (1971).

PRIJS, L.

1948   *Jüdische Tradition in der Septuaginta,* Leiden, 1948.

QUAST, U.

1990   *Der rezensionelle Charakter einiger Wortvarianten im Buche Numeri,* in D. FRAENKEL, U. QUAST & J.W. WEVERS (eds.), *Studien zur Septuaginta. FS R. Hanhart* (MSU, 20), Göttingen, 1990, pp. 230-252.

RABIN, C.

1954   *The Zadokite Documents. I. The Admonition. II. The Laws,* Oxford, 1954; 1958².

RABINOWITZ, J.J.

1958   *Grecisms and Greek Terms in the Aramaic Papyri,* in *Bib* 39 (1958) 77-82.

RAHLFS, A.

1911   *Septuaginta-Studien: 3. Heft. Lucians Rezension der Königsbücher,* Göttingen, 1911.

1931   *Psalmi cum Odis* (Septuaginta Societatis Scientiarum Gottingensis, X), Göttingen, 1931.

1935   *Septuaginta. Id est Vetus Testamentum graece iuxta LXX interpretes,* 2 vols, Stuttgart, 1935, 1965⁸.

RAURELL, F.

1976   *"Archontes" en la interpretació midràshica d'Is-LXX*, in *RCatalana Teo* 1 (1976) 255-256.

1979   *The Religious Meaning of "Doxa" in the Book of Wisdom*, in M. GILBERT (ed.), *La Sagesse de l'Ancien Testament* (BETL, 51), Leuven, 1979, pp. 370-383.

1980   *"Doxa" i particularisme nacionalista en Ba 4,5-5,9*, in *RCatalana Teo* 5 (1980) 265-269.

1982   *LXX-Is 26: la "Doxa" com a participacio en la vida escatologica*, in *RCatalana Teo* 7 (1982) 57-89.

1984ª   *"Doxa Kyriou" in Ez-LXX: Between Nationalism and Universalism*, in *Estudios Franciscanos* 85 (1984) 287-311.

1984ᵇ   *Significat antropologic de "doxa" en Job-LXX*, in *RCatalana Teo* 9 (1984) 1-33.

1985   *Lloc i signifcat de "Doxa" en Jer-LXX*, in *RCatalana Teo* 10 (1985) 1-30.

1986   *The Polemical Role of the* ἄρχοντες *and* ἀφηγούμενοι *in Ez LXX*, in J. LUST (ed.) 1986, pp. 85-89.

REDDITT, P.L.

1983   *The Concept of* νόμος *in Fourth Maccabees*, in *CBQ* 45 (1983) 249-270.

REDPATH, H.A.

1906   *A Contribution towards Settling the Dates of the Translation of the Various Books of the Septuagint*, in *JTS* 7 (1906) 606-615.
        → HATCH, E. 1897

REEKMANS, T.

1975   *Treasure-Trove and Parapherna*, in J. BINGEN (ed.), *Le monde grec. FS Claire Préaux* (Université libre de Bruxelles. Faculté de Philosophie et Lettres, LXII), Wetteren, 1975, pp. 748-759.

1985   ᾿Αργός *and its Derivatives in the Papyri*, in *CÉg* 60 (1985) 275-291.

REHKOPF, F. → **BLASS, F.**

REHRL, S.

1961   *Das Problem der Demut in der Profan-Griechischen Literatur. Im Vergleich zu Septuaginta und Neuen Testament* (Aevum Christianum, 4), Münster, 1961.

REILING, J.

1971   *The Use of* ψευδοπροφήτης *in the Septuagint, Philo and Josephus*, in *NT* 13 (1971) 147-156.

RÉMONDON, R. → **CADELL, H.**

RENEHAN, R.

1972   *Greek Lexicographical Notes: Fifth Series*, in *Glotta* 50 (1972) 38-60.

1975   *Greek Lexicographical Notes. A Critical Supplement to the Greek-English Lexicon of Liddell-Scott-Jones* (Hyp, 45), Göttingen, 1975.

1982   *Greek Lexicographical Notes. A Critical Supplement to the Greek-English Lexicon of Liddell-Scott-Jones. Second Series* (Hyp, 74), Göttingen, 1982.

REPO, E.

1951   *Der Begriff 'Rhèma' im Biblisch-Griechischen. Eine traditionsgeschichtliche und semologische Untersuchung. I. 'Rhèma' in der Septuaginta* (AASF, B-75/2), Helsinki, 1951.

REUMANN, J.H.P.

1958   'Stewards of God'. Pre-christian Religious Application of οἰκονόμος in Greek, in JBL
         77 (1958) 339-349.
1978   The Use of οἰκονομία and Related Terms in Greek Sources to about A.D. 100 as a
         Background for Patristic Application. Part I. Previous Studies: Earlier Literature and
         the Problem of the Use of οἰκονομία and Related Terms, in Ekklesiastikos Pharos 60
         (1978) 482-579.
1979   The Use of οἰκονομία and Related Terms in Greek Sources to about A.D. 100. Part
         II. The Evidence, in Ekklesiastikos Pharos 61 (1979) 563-603.
1980   The Use of οἰκονομία and Related Terms in Greek Sources to about A.D. 100. Part
         II. The Evidence, in Ἐκκλησία καὶ Θεογονία Α' (1980) 368-430.
1981   The Use of οἰκονομία and Related Terms in Greek Sources to about A.D. 100, in
         Ἐκκλησία καὶ Θεογονία Β' (1981) 591-617.
1982   The Use of οἰκονομία and Related Terms in Greek Sources to about A.D. 100, in
         Ἐκκλησία καὶ Θεογονία Γ' (1982) 115-140.

RIESENFELD, H.

1941   Étude bibliographique sur la notion d'ἀγάπη, in Coniectanea Neotestamentica 5 (1941)
         1-27.
1963   Zu μακροθυμεῖν (Lk 18,7), in J. BLINZLER, O. KUSS & F. MUSSNER (eds.),
         Neutestamentliche Aufsätze. FS Josef Schmid, Regensburg, 1963, pp. 214-217.

RINALDI, G.

1968   Κατενώπιον, in BeO 10 (1968) 320.
1982   Ἀπογραφή censimento, in BeO 24 (1982) 206.

RINGGREN, H. → BOTTERWECK, G.J.

ROBERT, L.

1937   Études anatoliennes. Recherches sur les inscriptions grecques de l'Asie Mineure (Études
         orientales V), Paris, 1937.
1938   Études épigraphiques et philologiques (Bibliothèque de l'École des Hautes Études.
         Sciences historiques et philologiques, 272), Paris, 1938.
1940   Les gladiateurs dans l'Orient Grec (Bibliothèque de l'École des Hautes Études. Sciences
         historiques et philologiques, 278), Paris, 1940; = L. ROBERT, Les gladiateurs dans
         l'Orient Grec, Amsterdam, 1971.
1950   Ἀνεμοφθορία [dans le vocabulaire grec de la magie], in ID. (ed.), Hellenica. Recueil
         d'épigraphie, de numismatique et d'antiquités grecques, 9 (1950) 69, n.1.
1958   & ROBERT, J., Bulletin épigraphique, in RÉG 71 (1958) 208.
1960   Recherches épigraphiques, in RÉAnc 62 (1960) 276-361.
1961   & ROBERT, J., Bulletin épigraphique, in RÉG 74 (1961) 119-268.
1962   & ROBERT, J., Bulletin épigraphique, in RÉG 75 (1962) 130-226.
1972   & ROBERT, J., Bulletin épigraphique, in RÉG 85 (1972) 365-542.
1989   Le Serpent Glycon d'Abônouteichos à Athènes et Artémis d'Ephèse à Rome, in ID.
         Opera minora selecta. Épigraphie et antiquités grecques, Amsterdam, 1989, pp. 747-769.

ROCCO, B.

1969   La μάννα di Baruch 1,10, in BeO 11 (1969) 273-277.

RÖSEL, M.

1994   Übersetzung als Vollendung der Auslegung. Studien zur Genesis-Septuaginta (BZAW,
         223), Berlin, 1994.

ROFÉ, A.
1988   *The Prophetical Stories. The Narratives about the Prophets in the Hebrew Bible. Their Literary Types and History*, Jerusalem, 1988, pp. 165-167 [Dt 19,14 μετακινέω].

ROMEO, A.
1949   *Il termine* λειτουργία *nella grecità biblica*, in *Miscellanea Liturgica. FS L. Cuniberti Mohlberg* (Bibliotheca Ephemerides Liturgicae, 23), Roma, 1949, pp. 467-519.

RONCHI, G.
1975   *Lexicon theonymon rerumque sacrarum et divinarum ad Aegyptum pertinentium quae in papyris ostracis titulis graecis latinisque in Aegypto repertis laudantur.* I: Διοσκούρειον; II: Διοσκούρειος - Θεός; III Θεός - μέγας, 3 vols., Milano, 1975.

ROQUET, G.
1988   *Chenoute critique d'une étymologie du Cratyle:* δαιμόνιον, in *Zeitschrift für ägyptische Sprache und Altertumskunde* 115 (1988) 153-156.

ROSÉN, H.B.
1963   *Palestinian* κοινή *in Rabbinic Illustration*, in *JSS* 8 (1963) 56-72.

ROST, L.
1967   *Die Vorstufen von Kirche un Synagoge im Alten Testament. Eine wortgeschichtliche Untersuchung*, Darmstadt, 1967.

ROUSSEL, P.
1927   *Les mystères de Panamara*, in *Bulletin de correspondance hellénique* 51 (1927) 123-137.

ROUX, G.
1961   *Le sens de* τύπος, in *RÉAnc* 63 (1961) 5-14.

RUDOLPH, W.
1962 * *Das Buch Ruth, Das Hohe Lied, Die Klagelieder* (KAT, 17/1-3), Gütersloh, 1962.
1966 * *Hosea* (KAT, 13/1), Gütersloh, 1966.
1971 * *Joel, Amos, Obadja, Jona* (KAT, 13/2), Gütersloh, 1971.
1975 * *Micha, Nahum, Habakuk, Zephanja* (KAT, 13/3), Gütersloh, 1975.
1976 * *Haggai, Sacharja 1--8/9--14, Maleachi* (KAT, 13/4), Gütersloh, 1976.

RUIZ, G.
1984   *El clamor de las piedras (Lc 19,40 - Hab 2,11). El Reino choca con la ciudad injusta en la fiesta de Ramos*, in *Estudios eclesiásticos* 59 (1984) 297-312.

RUNDGREN, F.
1957   *Zur Bedeutung von* οἰκογενής *in 3. Esra 3,1*, in *Eranos* 55 (1957) 145-152.

RUOZZI SALA, S.M.
1974   *Lexicon nominum semiticorum quae in papyris graecis in Aegypto repertis ab anno 323 a. Chr. n. usque ad annum 70 p. Chr. n. laudata reperiuntur* (Testi e Documenti per lo studio dell' Antichità, 46), Milano, 1974.

SAMUEL, A.E.

1965   The Role of παραμονή Clauses in Ancient Documents, in JJP 15 (1965) 221-311.

1966   The Judicial Competence of the οἰκονόμος in the Third Century B.C., in Atti dell'XI Congresso Internazionale di Papirologia Milano 2-8 Settembre 1965, Milano, 1966, pp. 444-450.

SANDERS, T.K.

1990   A New Approach to 1 Corinthians 13.1, in NTS 36 (1990) 614-618.

SANDEVOIR, P. → LE BOULLUEC, A.

SANDY, D.B.

1984   Oil Specification in the Papyri: What is ἔλαιον, in Atti XVII Congr. Int. Pap., III, Napoli, 1984, pp. 1317-1323.

SANTI AMANTINI, L.

1979   Sulla terminologia relativa alla pace nelle epigrafi greche fino all'avvento della 'Koiné Eiréne', in Atti dell'Istituto Veneto di scienze, lettere ed arti. Classe di scienze morali, lettere ed arti, 138, Venezia, 1979-1980, pp. 467-495.

SASSON, J.M.

1990   Jonah. A New Translation with Introduction, Commentary and Interpretation (AncB, 24B), New York, 1990.

SCHAPER, J.L.W

1994   The Unicorn in the Messianic Imagery of the Greek Bible, in JTS 45 (1994) 117-136.

SCHARBERT, J.

1972   Fleisch, Geist und Seele in der Pentateuch-Septuaginta, in J. SCHREINER (ed.), Wort, Lied und Gottesspruch. Beiträge zur Septuaginta. FS J. Ziegler (FzB, 1), Würzburg, 1972, pp. 121-143.

SCHELLER, M. → LIDDELL, H.G.

SCHENKER, A.

1982ᵃ   «Köper» et expiation, in Bib 63 (1982) 32-46.

1982ᵇ   Substitution du châtiment ou prix de la paix? Le don de la vie du Fils de l'homme en Mc 10,45 et par. à la lumière de l'Ancien Testament, in M. BENZERATH, A. SCHMID & J. GUILLET (eds.), La pâque du Christ mystère du salut. FS F.-X. Durrwell (LeDiv, 111), Paris, 1982, pp. 75-90.

SCHERMANN, T.

1910   Εὐχαριστία und εὐχαριστέω in ihrem Bedeutungswandel bis 200 n. Chr., in Philologus 69 (1910) 375-410.

SCHLEUSNER, J.F.

1820   Novus Thesaurus Philologico-Criticus, sive Lexicon in LXX et reliquos interpretes graecos ac scriptores apocryphos Veteris Testamenti, 5 vols., Leipzig, 1820-21; reprint Turnhout, 1994.

SCHMIDT, K.L.

1927   Die Kirche des Urchristentums. Eine lexikographische und biblisch-theologische Studie, in ID. (ed.), FS A. Deissmann, Tübingen, 1927, pp. 258-319.

SCHMITT, A.

1974   Interpretation der Genesis aus hellenistischem Geist, in ZAW 86 (1974) 137-163.

SCHMOLL, H. → MAYSER, E.

SCHNEBEL, M.

1925   *Die Landwirtschaft im hellenistischen Ägypten*, München, 1925.

SCHOLL, R.

1983   *Sklaverei in den Zenonpapyri. Eine Untersuchung zu den Sklaventermini, zum Sklavenerwerb und zur Sklavenflucht* (Trierer Historische Forschungen, 4), Trier, 1983.

1984   *Zur Bezeichnung* ἱερόδουλος *im griechisch-römischen Ägypten*, in *Atti del XVII congresso internazionale di papirologia Napoli 1984, III*, Napoli, 1984, pp. 977-983.

1990   *Corpus der Ptolemäischen Sklaventexte*, 3 vols., Stuttgart, 1990.

SCHOONHEIM, P.L.

1966   *Der alttestamentliche Boden der Vokabel* ὑπερήφανος *Lukas I 51*, in *NT* 8 (1966) 235-246.

SCHREINER, J.

1957 * *Septuaginta-Massora des Buches der Richter. Eine textkritische Studie* (AnBib, 7), Rome, 1957.

1961   *Zum B-Text des griechischen Canticum Deborae*, in *Bib* 42 (1961) 333-358.

1972   'Αντί *in der Septuaginta*, in ID. (ed.), *Wort, Lied und Gottesspruch. Beiträge zur Septuaginta. FS J. Ziegler* (FzB, 1), Würzburg, 1972, pp. 171-176.

SCHUBERT, P.

1939   *Form and Function of the Pauline Thanksgivings* (BZNW, 20), Berlin, 1939, pp. 114-121.

SCHÜRER, E.

1890   *A History of the Jewish People in the Time of Jesus Christ*, 1, Edinburgh, 1890.

SCHWARTZ, D.R.

1983   *Non-Joining Sympathizers*, in *Bib* 64 (1983) 550-555.

SCHWYZER, E.

1935   *Altes und Neues zu (hebr.-)griech.* σάββατα, *(griech.-)lat. sabbata usw.*, in *Zeitschrift für vergleichende Sprachforschung* 62 (1935) 1-16.
        → KATZ, P.

SEELIGMANN, I.L.

1940   *Problemen en perspectieven in het moderne Septuaginta-onderzoek*, in *JEOL* 7 (1940) 359-390e, 763-766.

1948 * *The Septuagint Version of Isaiah: A Discussion of Its Problems* (Mededelingen en Verhandelingen van het Vooraziatisch-Egyptisch Genootschap "Ex Oriente Lux", 9), Leiden, 1948.

SEGAL, A.F.

1984   *Torah and nomos in Recent Scholarly Discussion*, in *SR* 13 (1984) 19-27.

SEGALLO, G.

1965   *La voluntà di Dio nei LXX in rapporto al TM:* θέλημα, *rasôn, hefes*, in *Rivista Biblica* 13 (1965) 121-143.

SETTIS, S.

1973   *'Esedra' e 'ninfeo' nella terminologia architettonica del mondo romano. Dall'età republicana alla tarda antichità*, in ANRW I,4 Text, Berlin, 1973, 661-745.

SHENKEL, J.D.
1968   *Chronology and Recensional Development in the Greek Text of Kings* (HSM, 1), Cambridge, MA, 1968.

SHIPP, G.P.
1979   *Modern Greek Evidence for the Ancient Greek Vocabulary*, Sydney, 1979.

SIDER, J.W.
1981   *The Meaning of* παραβολή *in the Usage of the Synoptic Evangelists*, in *Bib* 62 (1981) 453-470.

SIJPESTEIJN, P.J.
1987   *On the Meaning of* ὁ δεῖνα (δεύτερος), in *ZPE* 68 (1987) 138-141.

SILVA, M.
1980   *Bilingualism and the Character of Palestinian Greek*, in *Bib* 61 (1980) 198-219.

SIMON, M.
1972   *Theos Hypsistos*, in G. WIDENGREN (ed.), *Ex Orbe Religionum. Pars prior* (Studies in the History of Religions. Supplements to *Numen*, 21), Leiden, 1972, pp. 372-385.

SIMOTAS, P.N. = [Π.Ν. Σιμοτας]
1968   Αἱ ἀμετάφραστοι λέξεις ἐν τῷ κειμένῳ τῶν Ο', Thessaloniki, 1968.

SKEAT, T.C.
1979   *'Especially the Parchments': A Note on 2 Timothy IV.13*, in *JTS* 30 (1979) 173-177.

SKEHAN, P.W.
1987 * & DI LELLA, A.A., *The Wisdom of Ben Sira* (AncB, 39), Garden City, NY, 1987.

SMALLWOOD, M.E.
1976   *The Jews under Roman Rule: From Pompey to Diocletian*, Leiden, 1976.

SMEND, R.
1906   *Die Weisheit des Jesus Sirach*, Berlin, 1906.

SMITH, M.
1967   *Another Criterion for the* καίγε *Recension*, in *Bib* 48 (1967) 443-445.

SNAITH, N.H.
1944   *The Distinctive Ideas of the Old Testament*, London, 1944.

SOGGIN, J.A. → LIPIŃSKI, É.

SOISALON-SOININEN, I.
1951   *Die Textformen der Septuaginta-Übersetzung des Richterbuches* (AASF, B-72/1), Helsinki, 1951.
1975   *Septuaginta, Vetus Testamentum*, in *Theologische Revue* 71 (1975) col. 367-369.
1978   *Der Gebrauch des Verbes* ἔχειν *in der Septuaginta*, in *VT* 28 (1978) 92-99.
1982   Ἐν *für* εἰς *in der Septuaginta*, in *VT* 32 (1982) 190-200.

SOLLAMO, R.
1975   *Some "improper" Prepositions such as* ἐνώπιον, ἐναντίον, ἔναντι, *etc., in the Septuagint and Early Koinè Greek*, in *VT* 25 (1975) 773-782.
1979   *Renderings of Hebrew Semiprepositions in the Septuagint* (AASF, 19), Helsinki, 1979.
1991   *The Pleonastic Use of the Pronoun in Connection with the Relative Pronoun in the Greek Pentateuch*, in C.E. COX (ed.) 1991, pp. 75-85.

SOUTER, A.

1926   Ἀγαπητός, in *JTS* 28 (1926-27) 59-60.

SPARKS, I.A.

1972   *A Fragment of Sapientia Salomonis from Oxyrhynchus*, in *JSJ* 3 (1972) 149-152.

SPICQ, C.

1947   *Bénignité, mansuétude, douceur, clémence*, in *RB* 54 (1947) 321-339.

1953   *L'épître aux Hébreux: II. Commentaire* (ÉtB), Paris, 1953.

1957   Ἐπιποθεῖν, *désirer ou chérir?*, in *RB* 64 (1957) 184-195.

1973   *Note sur* μορφή *dans les papyrus et quelques inscriptions*, in *RB* 80 (1973) 37-45.

1978ᵃ   *Notes de lexicographie néo-testamentaire. Tome I/II* (OBO, 22/1 and 2), 2 vols., Fribourg/Suisse - Göttingen, 1978; = *Lexique Théologique du Nouveau Testament. Réédition en un volume*, Fribourg/Suisse, 1991 (our pagination refers to the first edition); = *Theological Lexicon of the New Testament*, 3 vols., Peabody, MA, 1994 (translation of the first edition).

1978ᵇ   *Le vocabulaire de l'esclavage dans le Nouveau Testament*, in *RB* 85 (1978) 201-226.

1981   *Religion (Vertu de)*, in DBS 10 (1981) 210-240.

1982   *Notes de lexicographie néo-testamentaire. Supplément* (OBO, 22/3), Fribourg/Suisse - Göttingen, 1982; = *Lexique Théologique du Nouveau Testament. Réédition en un volume*, Fribourg/Suisse, 1991 (our pagination refers to the first edition); = *Theological Lexicon of the New Testament*, 3 vols., Peabody, MA, 1994 (translation of the first edition).

STACHOWIAK, L.R.

1957   Χρηστότης, *ihre biblisch-theologische Entwicklung und Eigenart* (Studia Friburgensia, 17), Freiburg, 1957.

STÄHLIN, G.

1930   *Skandalon. Untersuchungen zur Geschichte eines biblischen Begriffs* (Beiträge zur Förderung christlicher Theologie, 2/24), Gütersloh, 1930.

STAMM, J.J. → KOEHLER, L.

STANTON, G.R.

1988   Τέκνον, παῖς *and Related Words in Koine Greek*, in B.G. MANDILARAS (ed.), *Proceedings of the XVIII International Congress of Papyrology Athens 25-31 May 1986*, I, Athens, 1988, pp. 463-480.

STARCKY, J.

1951   «*Obfirmavit faciem suam ut iret Jerusalem*». *Sens et portée de Luc, IX, 51* (Mélanges Lebreton, I), in *RechSR* 39 (1951-52) 197-202.

STEENBURG, D.

1988   *The Case against the Synonymity of* μορφή *and* εἰκών, in *JSNT* 34 (1988) 77-86.

STEINMUELLER, J.E.

1951   Ἐρᾶν, φιλεῖν, ἀγαπᾶν *in Extra-biblical and Biblical Sources*, in A. METZINGER (ed.), *Miscellanea Biblica et Orientalia R.P. Athanasio A. Miller oblata* (Studia Anselmiana, 27-28), Roma, 1951, pp. 404-423.

STERENBERG, J.

1908   *The Use of Conditional Sentences in the Alexandrian Version of the Pentateuch*, München, 1908.

STEUERNAGEL, C.
1898   *Das Deuteronomium* (HAT), Göttingen, 1898.
1899   *Das Buch Josua* (HAT), Göttingen, 1899.

STIEB, R.
1939   *Die Versdubletten des Psalters*, in *ZAW* 57 (1939) 102-110.

STOCK, ST.-G. → CONYBEARE, F.C.

STROBEL, A.
1965   *Der Begriff des 'Hauses' im Griechischen und Römischen Privatrecht*, in *ZNW* 56 (1965)
        91-100.

SUÑOL, I.
1965   «*Señor*» *y* «*amo*» *en la correspondencia cristiana de los siglos V y VI*, in *Studia Papyrologica*
        4 (1965) 39-54.

SWELLENGREBEL, J.L.
1960   *'Leprosy' and the Bible. The Translation of 'Tsara'ath' and 'Lepra'*, in *BiTr* 11 (1960)
        69-80.

SWETNAM, J.
1966   *Diatheke in the Septuagint Account of Sinai: A Suggestion*, in *Bib* 47 (1966) 438-444.

SWINN, S.P.
1990   'Αγαπᾶν *in the Septuagint*, in T. MURAOKA (ed.) 1990, pp. 49-81.

TABACHOVITZ, D.
1956   *Die Septuaginta und das Neue Testament*, Lund, 1956.

TAILLARDAT, J.
1978   *Le thème* ψαλ-, ψελ- *en grec* (ψάλιον, ψέλιον, ψαλίς, σπάλιων), in *RÉG* 91 (1978)
        1-11.

TALMON, S.
1960   *Double Readings in the Massoretic Text*, in *Textus* 1 (1960) 144-184.
1961   *Synonymous Readings in the Textual Traditions of the Old Testament*, in C. RABIN
        (ed.), *Studies in the Bible* (Scripta Hierosolymitana, VIII), Jerusalem, 1961, pp. 335-383.
1964   *Aspects of the Textual Transmission of the Bible in the Light of Qumran Manuscripts*,
        in *Textus* 4 (1964) 95-132.
1981   & TOV, E., *A Commentary on the Text of Jeremiah. I. The LXX of Jeremiah 1:1-7*,
        in *Textus* 9 (1981) 1-15.

TALSHIR, Z.
1984   *The Milieu of 1 Esdras in the Light of its Vocabulary*, in A. PIETERSMA & C.E. COX
        (eds.), *De Septuaginta. FS J.W. Wevers*, Ontario, 1984, pp. 129-147.
1987   *The Representation of the Divine Epithet* צבאות *in the Septuagint and the Accepted Division*
        of the Books of Kingdoms, in *JQR* 78 (1987) 57-75.

TARELLI, C.C.
1950   'Αγάπη, in *JTS* 1 (1950) 64-67.

THACKERAY, H.ST.J.

1909   *A Grammar of the Old Testament in Greek according to the Septuagint*, Cambridge, 1909.

1923   *The Septuagint and Jewish Worship* (The Schweich Lectures 1920), London, 1923.

THIBAUT, A.

1988   *L'infidélité du peuple élu: ἀπειθῶ entre la bible hébraïque et la bible latine* (CBLa, 17), Roma - Turnhout, 1988.
        → GRIBOMONT, J.

THOMAS, D.W.

1940   *A Note on the Meaning of מחתם in Gen xxvii, 42*, in *ET* 51 (1939-40) 252.

THOMPSON, A.A. → LIDDELL, H.G.

THOMPSON, E.

1908   Μετανοέω *and* Μεταμέλει *in Greek Literature until 100 A.D., Including Discussion of their Cognates and of their Hebrew Equivalents* (Historical and Linguistic Studies in Literature Related to the New Testament. 2. Series Linguistic and Exegetic Studies 1/5), Chicago, 1908, pp. 1-29.

THORNTON, T.C.G.

1972   *Trees, Gibbets, and Crosses*, in *JTS* 75 (1972) 130-131.

THRALL, M.E.

1962   *Greek Particles in the New Testament. Linguistic and Exegetical Studies* (New Testament Tools and Studies, 3) Leiden, 1962.

TOD, M.N.

1939   *The Scorpion in Graeco-Roman Egypt*, in *The Journal of Egyptian Archaeology* 25 (1939) 55-61.

TOLILA, J. → DORIVAL, G. 1994

TORIBIO CUADRADO, J.F.

1993   *«El viniente». Estudio exegético y teológico del verbo ἔρχεσθαι en la literatura joánica* (Pontifica Universitas Gregoriana, Facultas Theologiae), Marcilla, 1993.

TORM, F.

1934   *Der Pluralis οὐρανοί*, in *ZNW* 33 (1934) 48-50.

TOSATO, A.

1975   *Per una revisione degli studi sulla μετάνοια neotestamentaria*, in *Rivista Biblica* 23 (1975) 3-45.

1982   *Sulle origini del termine ἀκροβυστία (prepuzio, incirconcisione)*, in *BeO* 24 (1982) 43-49.

TOURNAY, R.

1960   *Le Psaume CX*, in *RB* 67 (1960) 5-41.

TOV, E.

1976ᵃ   *The Septuagint Translation of Jeremiah and Baruch* (HSM, 8), Missoula, MT, 1976.

1976ᵇ   *Three Dimensions of LXX Words*, in *RB* 83 (1976) 529-544.

1977   *Compound Words in the LXX Representing Two or More Hebrew Words*, in *Bib* 58 (1977) 189-212.

1978   *Midrash-Type Exegesis in the LXX of Joshua*, in *RB* 85 (1978) 50-61.

1979   *Loan-words, Homophony and Transliterations in the Septuagint*, in *Bib* 60 (1979)

1981   *The Text-critical Use of the Septuagint in Biblical Research* (JBS, 3), Jerusalem, 1981.
1984[a] *Did the Septuagint Translators always understand their Hebrew Text*, in A. PIETERSMA
         & C.E. COX (eds.) *De Septuaginta. FS J.W. Wevers*, Missisauga (Ontario), 1984, pp.
         53-70.
1984[b] *The Rabbinic Tradition Concerning the "Alterations" inserted into the Greek Pentateuch
         and Their Relation to the Original Text of the LXX*, in *JSJ* 15 (1984), 65-89.
1984[c] *The LXX Additions (Miscellanies) in 1 Kings 2 (3 Reigns 2)*, in *Textus* 11 (1984) 89-118.
1987   *Die griechischen Bibelübersetzungen*, in ANRW II.20.1 (1987), pp. 121-189.
1990   *Greek Words and Hebrew Meanings*, in T. MURAOKA (ed.) 1990, pp. 83-125.
         → TALMON, S. 1981

TREBOLLE BARRERA, J.
1989   *Centena in Libros Samuelis et Regum*, Madrid, 1989.
1991   *Posible substrato semitico del uso transitivo o intransitivo del verbo* ἐκάθισεν *en Jn 19,13*,
         in *Filologia Neotestamentaria* 4 (1991) 51-54.

TRÉDÉ, M.
1984   Καιρός: *problèmes d'étymologie*, in *RÉG* 97 (1984) xi-xvi.

TRÉHEUX, J.
1987   Κοινόν, in *RÉAnc* 89 (1987) 39-46.

TRENCH, R.C.
1890   *Synonyms of the New Testament*, London, 1890.

TURNER, C.H.
1926   Ὁ υἱός μου ὁ ἀγαπητός, in *JTS* 27 (1926) 113-129.

TURNER, P.D.M.
1977   Ἀνοικοδομεῖν *and Intra-septuagintal Borrowing*, in *VT* 27 (1977) 492-493.
1978   *Two Septuagintalisms with* στηρίζειν, in *VT* 28 (1978) 481-482.

TYRER, J.W.
1924   *The Meaning of* ἐπίκλησις, in *JTS* 25 (1924) 139-150.

ULRICH, E.C.
1978   *The Qumran Text of Samuel and Josephus* (HSM, 19), Missoula, MT, 1978.

VAN DAALEN, D.H.
1982   *The 'ēmunah*/ πίστις *of Habakkuk 2.4 and Romans 1.17*, in E.A. LIVINGSTONE (ed.),
         Studia Evangelica 7 (TU, 126), Berlin, 1982, pp. 523-527.

VAN DER KOOIJ, A.
1981   *Die alten Textzeugen des Jesajabuches: ein Beitrag zur Textgeschichte des Alten Testaments*
         (OBO, 35), Fribourg/Suisse - Göttingen, 1981.

VANDERSLEYEN, C.
1973   *Le mot* λαός *dans la langue des papyrus grecs*, in *CÉg* 48 (1973) 339-349.

VAN DER WAL, A.

1982   *Planten uit de Bijbel,* Amsterdam, 1982.

VANGEMEREN, W.A.

1996   (ed.), *New International Dictionary of Old Testament Theology,* 3 vols., Grand Rapids, MI, 1996/.../... (forthcoming).

VAN HOONACKER, A.

1905   *Un nom grec (ᾅδης) dans le livre de Jonas (II,7),* in *RB* NS 2 (1905) 398-399.

VAN LEEUWEN, W.S.

1940   *Eirene in het Nieuwe Testament. Een semasiologische, exegetische bijdrage op grond van de Septuaginta en de Joodsche Literatuur,* Wageningen, 1940.

VAN MENXEL, F.

1983   Ἐλπίς. *Espoir. Espérance. Études sémantiques et théologiques du vocabulaire de l'espérance dans l'Hellénisme et le Judaïsme avant le Nouveau Testament* (Europäische Hochschulschriften, 23/213), Frankfurt/M - Bern - New York, 1983.

VANNI, U.

1977   Ὁμοίωμα *in Paolo (Rm 1,23: 5,14: 6,5: 8,3: Fil 2,7). Un'interpretazione esegetico-teologica alla luce dell'uso dei LXX,* in *Gregorianum* 58 (1977) 321-345. 431-470.

1995   *La creazione in Paolo. Una prospettiva di teologia biblica,* in *Rassegna di teologia* 36 (1995) 285-325.

VAN ROMPAY, L.

1976   *The Rendering of* πρόσωπον λαμβάνειν *and Related Expressions in the Early Oriental Versions of the New Testament,* in *Orientalia Lovaniensia Periodica* 6/7 (1975/1976) 568-575.

VAN ROON, A.

1974   *The Authenticity of Ephesians,* (NT Suppl., 39), Leiden, 1974, pp. 275-293.

VAN RUITEN, J.T.A.G.M.

1990   *Een begin zonder einde. De doorwerking van Jesaja 65:17 in de intertestamentaire literatuur en het Nieuwe Testament,* Sliedrecht, 1990.

VAN 'T DACK, E.

1988   *Ptolemaïca Selecta,* in *StHell* 25 (1988) 96-102.

VAN UNNIK, W.C.

1962   *De semitische achtergrond van* παρρησία *in het Nieuwe Testament* (Mededelingen der Koninklijke Nederlandse Akademie van Wetenschappen, afd. Letterkunde, 25/11), Amsterdam, 1962.

1973   *Jesus: Anathema or Kurios (I Cor. 12:3),* in B. LINDARS (ed.), *Christ and Spirit in the New Testament. FS C.F.D. Moule,* London, 1973, pp. 113-126.

VASOJEVIĆ, A. & N.

1984   Νάφθα, in *Philologus* 128 (1984) 208-229.

VATIN, C.

1970   *Recherches sur le mariage et la condition de la femme mariée à l'époque hellénistique* (Biblioth. des écoles françaises d'Athènes et de Rome, 216), Paris, 1970.

VATTIONI, F.

1980   *La lessicografia dei LXX nei papiri,* in *Studia Papyrologica* 19 (1980) 39-59.

VAWTER, B.

1980   *Prov 8:22: Wisdom and Creation*, in *JBL* 99 (1980) 205-216.

1985   *Were the Prophets nābî's?*, in *Bib* 66 (1985) 206-219.

VERGOTE, J.

1938   *Grec biblique*, in DBS 3 (1938) 1321-1396.

VERMES, G.

1961   *Scripture and Tradition in Judaism. Hagadic Studies* (Studia Post-Biblica, 4), Leiden, 1961.

1975   *Post-Biblical Jewish Studies* (Studies in Judaism in Late Antiquity, 8), Leiden, 1975.

VERVENNE, M.

1987   *Hebrew šālîš - Ugaritic ṯlṯ*, in *UF* 19 (1987) 355-373.

VOIGT, C.

1989   *Einleitung*, in B.J. DIESSNER & R. KASSER, *Hamburger Papyrus Bil.1*, Genève, 1989, pp. 7-49.

VON SODEN, H.

1911   Μυστήριον *und Sacramentum in den ersten zwei Jahrhunderten der Kirche*, in *ZNW* 12 (1911) 188-227.

VYCICHL, W.

1983   *Dictionnaire étymologique de la langue copte*, Leuven, 1983.

WAANDERS, F.M.J.

1983   *The History of* τέλος *and* τελέω *in Ancient Greek*, Amsterdam, 1983.

WACKERNAGEL, J.

1969   *Lateinisch-Griechisches*, in ID., *Kleine Schriften*, 1969, pp. 1228-1248; = ID., *Lateinisch-Griechisches*, in K. BRUGMANN & W. STREITBERG (eds.), *Indogermanische Forschungen. FS B. Delbrück*, = *Zeitschrift für indogermanische Sprach- und Altertumskunde* 31 (1912-13) 251-271, esp. 262-267: "parabola".

WALLACE, D.H.

1966   *A Note on* μορφή, in *Theologische Zeitschrift* 22 (1966) 19-25 .

WALTERS, P. [= KATZ P.]

1973   *The Text of the Septuagint. Its Corruptions and Their Emendation*, Cambridge, 1973.

WAMBACQ, B.N.

1957   *Jeremias. Klaagliederen. Baruch. Brief van Jeremias* (De boeken van het Oude Testament, 10), Roermond - Maaseik, 1957.

1959   *L'unité littéraire de Bar. , I--III,8*, in J. COPPENS a.o. (eds.), *Sacra Pagina. Miscellanea Biblica Congressus Internationalis Catholici de Re Biblica, I* (BETL, 12), Leuven, 1959, pp. 455-460.

WEBER, R.

1950   *La traduction primitive de* βάρις *dans les anciens psautiers latins*, in *VetChr* 4 (1950) 20-32.

WEINFELD, M.

1980   *The Royal Guard according to the Temple Scroll*, in *RB* 87 (1980) 394-396.

WELCH, A.C.

1918 *The Septuagint Version of Leviticus,* in *ET* 30 (1918-19) 277-278.

WELLHAUSEN, J.

1871 *Der Text der Bücher Samuelis,* Göttingen, 1871.

WEST, M.L. → LIDDELL, H.G.

WEST, S.

1967 *Alleged Pagan Use of agape in P Oxy 1380,* in *JTS* 18 (1967) 142-143.
→ WITT, R.E. 1968

WESTERHOLM, S.

1986 *Torah, nomos, and Law: A Question of 'Meaning',* in *SR* 15 (1986) 327-336.

WESTERMANN, C.

1974 *Genesis 1--11* (BKAT, 1/1), Neukirchen-Vluyn, 1974.
1981 *Genesis 12--36* (BKAT, 1/2), Neukirchen-Vluyn, 1981.
1982 *Genesis 37--50* (BKAT, 1/3), Neukirchen-Vluyn, 1982.

WEVERS, J.W.

1950 *Exegetical Principles Underlying the Septuagint Text of 1 Kings ii 12 - xxi 43,* in *OTS* 8 (1950) 300-322.
1982 *Text History of the Greek Numbers* (MSU, 16), Göttingen, 1982.
1985 *An Apologia for Septuagint Studies,* in *BIOSCS* 18 (1985) 16-38.
1990 * *Notes on the Greek Text of Exodus* (SCS, 30), Atlanta, 1990.
1991 *The Göttingen Pentateuch: Some Post-partem Reflections,* in C.E. COX (ed.) 1991, pp. 51-60.
1992 *Text History of the Greek Exodus* (MSU, 21), Göttingen, 1992.
1993 * *Notes on the Greek Text of Genesis* (SCS, 35), Atlanta, 1993.
1995 * *Notes on the Greek Text of Deuteronomy* (SCS, 39), Atlanta, 1995.

WIFSTRAND, A.

1964 *Lukas 18,7,* in *NTS* 11 (1964-65) 72-74.

WIKENHAUSER, A.

1910 Ἐνώπιος-ἐνώπιον-κατενώπιον, in *BZ* 8 (1910) 263-270.

WILHELM, A.

1932 *Neue Beiträge zur griechischen Inschriftenkunde 5* (Akademie der Wissenschaften in Wien. Philosophisch-historische Klasse), Wien - Leipzig, 1932.

WILL, ÉDOUARD

1987 *Note sur* μισθός, in J. BINGEN, G. CAMBIER & G. NACHTERGAEL (eds.), *Le monde grec. FS Claire Préaux,* Bruxelles, 1975, pp. 578-584.

WILL, ERNEST

1987ᵃ *La Tour de Straton: mythes et réalités,* in *Syria* 64 (1987) 245-251.
1987ᵇ *Qu'est-ce qu'une* βᾶρις, in *Syria* 64 (1987) 253-259.

WILLIAMSON, H.G.M.

1977 *Eschatology in Chronicles,* in *Tyndale Bulletin* 28 (1977) 115-154.
1985 * *Ezra, Nehemiah* (WBC, 16), Waco, TX, 1985.

WILLIGER, E.

1922   "Αγιος. *Untersuchungen zur Terminologie des Heiligen in den hellenisch-hellenistischen Religionen* (Religionsgeschichtliche Versuche und Vorarbeiten, 19/1), Giessen, 1922.

WILLIS, J.T.

1970   *Micah 2:6-8 and the "People of God" in Micah*, in *BZ* 14 (1970) 72-87.

WILSON, J.R.

1980   Καιρός *as 'Due Measure'*, in *Glotta* 58 (1980) 177-204.

WINNICKI, J.K. → **CLARYSSE, W.** 1989

WISSEMANN, M.

1988   Κεφαλή = *'Schwadron, Schar'? Spätantike Übersetzungen als Hilfsmittel moderner Lexikologie*, in M. WISSEMAN (ed.), *Roma renascens: Beiträge zur Spätantike und Rezeptions-geschichte*, Frankfurt aM - Bern - New York - Paris, 1988, pp. 377-384.

WITHERINGTON, B.

1993   *Not so Idle Thoughts about* εἰδωλόθυτον, in *Tyndale Bulletin* 44 (1993) 237-254.

WITT, R.E.

1933   Ὑπόστασις, in H.G. WOOD (ed.), *Amicitæ corolla. FS James Rendel Harris*, London, 1933, pp. 319-343.

1968   *Use of H Agape in P Oxy 1380*, in *JTS* 19 (1968) 209-211.

→ WEST, S.

WODKE, W.

1977   Οἶκος *in der Septuaginta. Erste Grundlagen*, in O. RÖSSLER (ed.), *Hebraica* (Marburger Studien zur Afrika- und Asienkunde B/4), Berlin, 1977, pp. 57-140.

WOLFSON, H.A.

1947   *On the Septuagint Use of* τὸ ἅγιον *for the Temple*, in *JQR* 38 (1947) 109-110.

WOLLENTIN, U.

1961   Ὁ Κίνδυνος *in den Papyri*, Dissertation, Köln, 1961.

WORP, K.A. → **HAGEDORN, D.**

WOSCHITZ, K.M.

1979   Ἐλπίς *Hoffnung. Geschichte, Philosophie, Exegese, Theologie eines Schlüsselbegriffs*, Wien - Freiburg - Basel, 1979.

1988   Αἰών, in M. GÖRG & B. LANG (eds.), *Neues Bibel Lexikon*, 1 (1988) 52-54.

YOUTIE, H.C.

1970   Σημεῖον *in the Papyri and its Significance for Plato Epistle 13 (360 a-b)*, in *ZPE* 6 (1970) 105-116.

1975   *Commentary,* [Θεός, περιτέμνω, διαθήκη], in *ZPE* 18 (1975) 149-154.

1978   *Wörterbuch I, s. v.* βρέχω, *in ZPE* 30 (1978) 191-192.

YSEBAERT, J.

1973   *Propitiation, Expiation, and Redemption in Greek Biblical Terminology*, in *Mélanges Christine Mohrmann*, Utrecht - Antwerpen, 1973, pp. 1-12.

ZELLER, D.

1990   *Charis bei Philon und Paulus* (Stuttgarter Bibelstudien, 142), Stuttgart, 1990.

ZIEGLER, J.

1934 *   *Untersuchungen zur Septuaginta des Buches Isaias* (Alttestamentliche Abhandlungen 12/3), Münster, 1934.

1937   *Dulcedo Dei. Ein Beitrag zur Theologie der griechischen und lateinischen Bibel* (Alttestamentliche Abhandlungen, 13/2), Münster, 1937.

1939   *Isaias* (SVTG, 14), Göttingen, 1939.

1943   *Beiträge zum griechischen Dodekapropheton*, in *Nachrichten von der Akademie der Wissenschaften in Göttingen, Philologisch-Historische Klasse* 13 (1943) 345-412; = ID. 1971, 71-138.

1952   *Ezechiel* (SVTG, 16/1), Göttingen, 1952.

1958   *Beiträge zur Jeremias-Septuaginta* (MSU, 6), Göttingen, 1958.

1962   *Sapientia Salomonis* (SVTG, 12/1), Göttingen, 1962.

1965   *Sapientia Jesu Filii Sirach* (SVTG, 12/2), Göttingen, 1965.

1971   *Sylloge* (MSU, 10/1), Göttingen, 1971.

ZIESLER, J.A.

1983   Σῶμα *in the Septuagint*, in *NT* 25 (1983) 133-145.

ZIJDERVELD, C.

1934   Τελετή. *Bijdrage tot de kennis der religieuze terminologie in het Grieksch*, Purmerend, 1934.

ZIMMERLI, W.

1969 *   *Ezechiel*, I, 1–24 (BKAT, 13/1), Neukirchen-Vluyn, 1969; *Ezechiel*, II, 25–48 (BKAT, 13/2), 1969; = *Ezekiel* (Hermeneia), 2 vols., Philadelphia, PA, 1979/1983.

1978   *Die Seligpreisungen der Bergpredigt und das Alte Testament*, in E. BAMMEL, C. BARRETT & W. DAVIES (eds.), *Donum Gentilicium. New Testament Studies. FS David Daube*, Oxford, 1978, pp. 8-26.

ZIPOR, M.A.

1984   *1 Samuel 13:20-21 in the Light of the Ancient Versions - A Textual and Lexical Study*, in *Textus* 11 (1984) 1-50 [Hebrew, Engl. Abstract p. 141].

1991   *Notes sur les chapitres XIX à XXII du Lévitique dans la Bible d'Alexandrie*, in *ETL* 67 (1991) 328-337.

1993   *'Al Tikre' - Exegesis or Text*, in *Studies in Bible and Exegesis 3: Moshe-Gottstein - in memoriam*, Ramatgan, 1993, pp. 349-363.

1994   *Notes sur les chapitres I à XVII de la Genèse dans la Bible d'Alexandrie*, in *ETL* 70 (1994) 385-393.

ZOHARY, M.

1982   *Plants of the Bible. A Complete Handbook*, Cambridge, 1982.

ZORELL, F.

1927   *Der Gottesname "Saddai" in den alten Übersetzungen*, in *Bib* 8 (1927) 215-219.

ZUNTZ, G.

1956   *Greek Words in Talmud*, in *JSS* 1 (1956) 129-140.

1959   *Aristeas Studies II: Aristeas on the Translation of the Tora*, in *JSS* 4 (1959) 109-126.

κάβος,-ου⁺   N 0-1-0-0-0-1
2 Kgs 6,25
Hebr. loanword (קב); *corn-measure*
Cf. Tov 1979, 233; →Chantraine; Frisk

κἀγώ⁺   13-19-20-16-22-90
Gn 20,6; 30,3.30; 40,16; 42,37
crasis for καὶ ἐγώ
Cf. Wevers 1993, 722

καδημιμ   N 0-1-0-0-0-1
JgsᴬM 5,21
= קדמים *ancient, of antiquity*

καδησιμ   N M 0-1-0-0-0-1
2 Kgs 23,7
= קדשים *male temple prostitutes*

κάδιον,-ου   N2N 0-2-0-0-0-2
1 Sm 17,40.49
dim. of κάδος; *bag, pouch* 1 Sm 17,49
κάδιον ποιμενικόν *shepherd's bag* 1 Sm 17,40

κάδος,-ου⁺   N2M 0-0-1-0-0-1
Is 40,15
bucket

καθά⁺   C 71-20-3-2-16-112
Gn 7,9.16; 17,23; 19,8; 21,1
as, just as Gn 7,9
καθὰ καί *just like* Lv 9,15; *even as* 1 Mc 10,37;
καθὰ ἄν [+opt.] *as it may* Gn 19,8
neol.?
Cf. Dorival 1994, 336; Le Boulluec 1989, 362

καθαγιάζω   V 2-1-0-0-3-6
Lv 8,9; 27,26; 1 Chr 26,20; 2 Mc 1,26; 2,8
to consecrate, to dedicate (of things) Lv 8,9; *to consecrate, to sanctify* (of living creatures) Lv 27,26; neol.
Cf. Harlé 1988, 114-115

καθαίρεσις,-εως⁺   N3F 1-0-0-0-1-2
Ex 23,24; 1 Mc 3,43
decay, decayed estate, ruin (metaph.) 1 Mc 3,43
καθαιρέσει καθελεῖς (semit.) for MT הרס תהרסם
you shall utterly destroy Ex 23,24
Cf. Le Boulluec 1989, 240(Ex 23,24)

καθαιρέω⁺   V 13-21-18-17-26-95
Gn 24,18.46; 27,40; 44,11; Ex 23,24
A: *to let, put* or *take down* [τι] Gn 24,18; *to cut off* [τι] 2 Mc 12,35; *to destroy, to break* [abs.] Gn 27,40; *to break down* [τι] Lv 11,35; *to pull down* [τι] (of buildings) 1 Mc 4,38; *to destroy* [τινα] Jb 19,2
P: *to be removed from* [ἀπό τινος] Jer 13,18
τὴν πόλιν καθεῖλεν *he razed the city to the ground* Jgs 9,45; καθαιρέω ὕβριν τινός *to*

bring down sb's pride Zech 9,6; καθαιρέσει καθαιρέω *to destroy utterly* (semit.) Ex 23,24
*2 Kgs 3,25 καθῃρημένους *cast down* -◊ חרס for MT רשת *(kir-)hareseth*
Cf. Le Boulluec 1989, 240(Ex 23,24); Wevers 1990, 372(Ex 23,24); 1993, 439; →twnt

καθαίρω⁺   V 0-1-1-0-0-2
2 Sm 4,6; Is 28,27
to cleanse with [τι μετά τινος] Is 28,27; *to sift, to winnow* (grain) [τι] 2 Sm 4,6
Cf. Dorival 1994, 172(καθαιρεῖν sic); Helbing 1928, 160; Thackeray 1909, 271; →twnt
(→ἀπο-, ἐκ-, περι-)

καθάπερ⁺   C 39-9-3-9-23-83
Gn 12,4; 50,6; Ex 5,7.13.14
just as [+ind.] Gn 12,4; *id.* [ἐάν +subj.] Jgsᴬ 9,33; *id.* [+subst.] Ex 5,7
καθάπερ καί *just as* Sir 36,4; καθάπερ καὶ ὅτε [+ind.] *even as when* Ex 5,13; καθάπερ ἐνετείλατο κύριος ..., οὕτως ἐποίησαν *as the Lord commanded ..., so they did* (often as introduction of a command) Ex 7,6
Cf. Wevers 1990, 95(Ex 7,6); →mm

καθαρίζω⁺   V 56-10-19-17-23-125
Gn 35,2; Ex 20,7; 29,36.37; 30,10
A: *to purify, to cleanse* [τι] Ex 29,36; *to purge* [τι] Dt 19,13; *to purify, to acquit* [τινα] Ex 20,7; *to purge sb from* [τινα ἀπό τινος] Lv 12,7; *id.* [τινα ἔκ τινος] Ps 18,13; *to purge with* [τι ἀπό τινος] (stereotypical rendition of מן by ἀπό) Ex 30,10
M: *to purify oneself* Gn 35,2
καθαρίζω τὴν γῆν *to cleanse the land* 2 Chr 34,8; καθαρίζω ἀργύριον *to purify silver* Ps 11,7
*Is 53,10 καθαρίσαι *to cleanse, to purify* -דכא (Aram.) for MT דכא *to bruise*; *Is 57,14 καθαρίσατε *cleanse, clear* -צלל ◊ צלו (Aram.)? for MT סלו סלל *build up*
Cf. Deissmann 1897, 43-44; Dodd 1954, 82-84.95; Dorival 1994, 55.171-172; Goschen-Gottstein 1995(Is 53,10); Harlé 1988, 31.116.135; Helbing 1928, 160(Ex 30,10); Koenig 1982, 285(Is 57,14); Le Boulluec 1989, 207.302. 306-307.338-339; Lee, J. 1983, 48; Wevers 1990, 311.480.482.493; →mm; twnt
(→ἀπο-, ἐκ-, περι-)

καθαριότης,-ητος   N3F 1-2-0-2-1-6
Ex 24,10; 2 Sm 22,21.25; Ps 17(18),21.25
purity, clarity, brightness Ex 24,10
καθαριότης τῶν χειρῶν *purity of hands,*

cleanliness, innocence 2 Sm 22,21
Cf. WALTERS 1973, 58.288; WEVERS 1990, 385

καθαριόω   V 0-0-0-1-0-1
Lam 4,7
to purify; neol.

καθαρισμός,-οῦ⁺   N2M 5-1-0-5-7-18
Ex 29,36; 30,10; Lv 14,32; 15,13; Nm 14,18
purification Ex 30,10
ἡ ἡμέρα τοῦ καθαρισμοῦ *day of purification* Ex
29,36; καθαρισμῷ οὐ καθαριεῖ *he will by no
means clear* (semit.) Nm 14,18; ποιέω
καθαρισμὸν ἁμαρτίας *to purge the sin* Jb 7,21
neol.
Cf. DODD 1954, 82-84.95; LE BOULLUEC 1989, 306-307;
→TWNT

καθαρός,-ά,-όν⁺   A 90-9-15-32-14-160
Gn 7,2(bis).3(bis).8
clean (of place) Lv 4,12; *clean, pure, spotless*
Zech 3,5; *pure* Ex 30,35; *clear (of admixture),
pure* Nm 5,17; *clean* (of pers.) Lv 7,19; *free from
guilt, clear of debt, pure* Nm 8,7; *clear (of
victims)* Gn 7,2; *pure, unmixed* (of metal) Ex
25,11; *pure, honest* (of oil) Ex 27,20
καθαρὸς ἀπὸ ὅρκου *clear from an oath* Gn
24,8; ἐν καθαρᾷ καρδίᾳ *with pure heart* Gn
20,6; ἐν πάσῃ εὐλογίᾳ καθαρᾷ *with pure praise*
Tob 8,15; ἄρτος καθαρός *white bread* Jdt 10,5;
πυρόω τινὰ εἰς καθαρόν *to purge by fire* Is 1,25
*Jb 11,15 ὥσπερ ὕδωρ καθαρόν *as pure water*
-מַיִם? or -כַּמַּיִם? for MT מִמְּנּוּ *without blemish*; *Neh
2,20 καθαροί *pure* -נְקִיִּים? for MT נָקוּם *we will
arise*
Cf. DEISSMANN 1897, 24; DODD 1954, 173; DORIVAL 1994,
171-172; HARLÉ 1988, 31; LE BOULLUEC 1989, 259.280;
LUST 1997 forthcoming; WEVERS 1990, 402.404.442.622;
1993, 346; →MM; TWNT

καθαρότης,-ητος⁺   N3F 0-0-0-0-1-1
Wis 7,24
purity (metaph.)

καθάρσιος,-ος,-ον   A 0-0-0-0-1-1
4 Mc 6,29
cleansing, purifying

κάθαρσις,-εως   N3F 2-0-2-0-0-4
Lv 12,4.6; Jer 32(25),29; Ez 15,4
cleansing, purification Jer 32(25),29
αἱ ἡμέραι καθάρσεως αὐτῆς *the days of her
purification* Lv 12,4
*Ez 15,4 κάθαρσιν ἀπ' αὐτῆς *that which is
pruned of it* -◊קְצָה for MT קְצֵי קָצָה *the ends of it*
Cf. HARLÉ 1988, 134; →LSJ Suppl; LSJ RSuppl(Ez 15,4)

καθέδρα,-ας⁺   N1F 0-10-0-4-2-16
1 Sm 20,18.25bis; 1 Kgs 10,5.19
seat 1 Sm 20,25; *establishment* 2 Kgs 17,25
τὴν καθέδραν καὶ τὴν στάσιν *the sitting and
the standing* 1 Kgs 10,5
*2 Kgs 16,18 τῆς καθέδρας *the throne* -הַשַּׁבָּת for
MT הַשַּׁבָּת *the Sabbath*

καθέζομαι⁺   V 1-0-2-1-0-4
Lv 12,5; Jer 37(30),18; Ez 26,16; Jb 39,27(28)
to sit down, to remain Lv 12,5; *to remain inactive*
Ez 26,16; *to settle* Jer 37(30),18
Cf. HARLÉ 1988, 134; →LSJ RSuppl

καθεῖς⁺   M 0-0-0-0-2-2
3 Mc 5,34; 4 Mc 15,14
for καθ' εἷς; *one by one, one after another,
each individual*; neol.
→LSJ RSuppl

κάθεμα,-ατος   N3N 0-0-2-0-0-2
Is 3,19; Ez 16,11
necklace, collar

καθεύδω⁺   V 2-16-4-6-6-34
Gn 28,13; 39,10; 1 Sm 3,2.3.5
to lie down to sleep, to sleep Gn 28,13; *to sleep*
(of the dead) Ps 87(88),6
καθεύδων ὕπνῳ *fast asleep* 1 Sm 26,7
Cf. WEVERS 1993, 655; →NIDNTT; TWNT

καθηγεμών,-όνος   N3M 0-0-0-0-1-1
2 Mc 10,28
leader, guide

καθήκω⁺   V 10-1-2-0-19-32
Gn 19,31; Ex 5,13.19; 16,16.18
to belong to, to be due to [τινι] Dt 21,17; οἱ
καθήκοντες *the appropriate ones, the family*
Ex 16,16
καθήκει τινί *it is fitting, customary* Gn 19,31;
καθήκει τινί [+inf.] *it is lawful for sb to do*
2 Mc 11,36; καθήκει [+inf.] *it is proper,
convenient* Sir 10,23; ὡς καθήκει *as it is fit*
1 Sm 2,16; τὰ ἔργα τὰ καθήκοντα *ordinary,
customary tasks* Ex 5,13; τὸ καθήκόν τινος τῇ
ἡμέρᾳ *the daily rate of* Ex 5,19; τὴν καθ-
ήκουσαν δαπάνην *necessary expenses*
1 Mc 10,39; καθήκουσαι ἡμέραι *convenient
(appropriate) days* 1 Mc 12,11; πάντα ὅσα μοι
καθήκει *all my necessaries* Hos 2,7
Cf. LE BOULLUEC 1989, 108-109.184.352; WEVERS 1990,
66.251.253.592; →TWNT

καθηλόω⁺   V 0-0-0-1-0-1
Ps 118(119),120
to nail through, to penetrate; *Ps 118(119),120

καθήλωσον *nail through, penetrate (my flesh)*
-סמר (imper.) for MT סמר (pft.) *(my flesh)*
trembles?

Cf. HARL 1971=1992ᵃ, 191

κάθημαι⁺   V 18-75-38-26-23-180
Gn 18,1; 19,1.30; 21,16; 23,10
to be seated, to sit Gn 18,1; *to sit still* Ru 3,18; *to
sit doing nothing, to lie idle* Ps 126(127),2; *to
reside, to dwell* Jgs 18,7; *to settle* Gn 19,30; *to sit,
to abide, to stay* (of pers.) 1 Sm 1,23; *to sit as
judge* Ex 18,14; *to be placed, to abide, to remain*
(of things) 1 Sm 5,7; *to be placed, to be set*
Jgs 16,9; καθήμενος *sitting (down)* Dt 6,7
κάθημαι ἐπὶ τοῦ θρόνου *to sit on a throne, to
reign* 1 Kgs 1,17; οἱ καθήμενοι ἐπὶ τῆς γῆς
those who dwell upon the earth Jer 32(25),29
*1 Sm 12,2 καὶ καθήσομαι *and I will rest*
-ישבתי וישבתי for MT שיב ושבתי ◊ *and I am old;*
*2 Sm 23,10 ἐκάθητο *rested -* ישבו◊ ישב for MT
שוב◊ *returned,* see also Zech 9,12

Cf. LEE, J. 1983, 40.51; WEVERS 1995, 432; →NIDNTT; TWNT

(→ἐπι-, παρα-, προ-, συγ-)

καθημερινός,-ή,-όν⁺   A 0-0-0-0-1-1
Jdt 12,15
day by day, daily (syn. for καθ' ἡμέραν); neol.

κάθιδρος,-ος,-ον   A 0-0-1-0-0-1
Jer 8,6
sweating profusely; neol.

καθιδρύω   V 0-0-0-0-3-3
2 Mc 4,12; 3 Mc 7,20; LtJ 15
to set up, to place [τι] (of a statue of a god)
LtJ 15; *to consecrate, to dedicate* [τι] 3 Mc 7,20;
to found [τι] 2 Mc 4,12

καθιζάνω   V 0-0-0-2-0-2
Jb 12,18; Prv 18,16
to seat, to cause to sit [τινα] Prv 18,16
*Jb 12,18 καθιζάνων *he seats, he establishes*
-מושיב? for MT מוסר *bond*

καθίζω⁺   V 23-100-44-61-27-255
Gn 8,4; 21,16; 22,5; 27,19; 37,25
to set, to place [τινα] 1 Kgs 20,9; *to put into a
certain condition* [τινα εἴς τι] Jb 36,7; *to cause
to dwell, to settle, to be* or *to sit together with, to
live with* (a woman) [τινα] Ezr 10,2
to sit [abs.] Gn 21,16; *to sit (down)* (metaph.)
Is 52,2; *to sit down on* [τι] Jgsᴮ 5,17; *id.* [ἐπί
τινος] Ex 2,15; *to sit, to recline at meals*
Gn 37,25; *to sit (in a council)* Prv 31,23; *to sit
on a throne* 1 Kgs 1,46; *to reside, to be
established* (of a king) Dt 17,18

to be placed, to be set (of things) Ps 121(122),5
to reside, to abide (of pers.) Dt 21,13; *to abide*
(of things) 1 Chr 13,14; *to dwell* 1 Sm 22,5; *to
remain* 2 Sm 19,38
to rest 1 Kgs 22,1; *to run aground, to be stranded*
Gn 8,4
to let down, to spread over Ex 12,22
καθίζω εἰς βασιλέα *to be established as a king*
Neh 6,7; ἐκάθισεν κλαίων *he sat weeping*
Lam 1,1; ἐκάθισεν τὸ ἀφόδευμα εἰς τοὺς
ὀφθαλμούς μου *their dung settled* or *fell on my
eyes* Tobˢ 2,10
*Dt 25,2 καθιεῖς *you shall make sb sit, you
shall set* corr. καθίεις (from καθίημι) *you
shall make sb lie down,* cpr. MT והפילו *and he
shall make sb lie down;* *Dt 1,45 καὶ
καθίσαντες *and you sat -* ישבו ותשבו for MT ותשבו
שוב◊ *and you returned,* see also Nm 11,4; Jos 5,2;
Jgsᴮ 19,7; 1 Sm 5,11; 2 Sm 19,38; Jb 6,29;
Dnᵀʰ 11,10; *Prv 22,10 καθίσῃ *he sits -* ישבו◊ for
MT וישבת ◊שבת *it ceases*

Cf. HARL 1986ᵃ, 137(Gn 8,4); 1992, 105(Gn 8,4); LE
BOULLUEC 1989, 84-85(Ex 2,15); TREBOLLE BARRERA
1991, 51-54; WEVERS 1990, 19(Ex 2,15).180; 1993, 102;
→TWNT

(→ἐπι-, παρα-, περι-, προ-)

καθίημι⁺   V 1-0-1-0-0-2
Ex 17,11; Zech 11,13
to drop Zech 11,13; *to let down* Ex 17,11
*Dt 25,2 see καθίζω

καθίπταμαι   V 0-0-0-0-1-1
Sir 43,18
to fly down

κάθισις,-εως   N3F 0-0-2-0-0-2
Jer 30,2(49,8).25(49,30)
dwelling-place; neol.?

καθίστημι⁺   V 29-63-17-45-64-218
Gn 39,4.5; 41,33.34.41
A: *to set (down), to bring to* [τινα εἴς τι]
1 Sm 5,3; *to place* [τινα] Nm 4,19; *to appoint to
do* [τι +inf.] Nm 21,15; *to set over, to appoint
over* [τινα ἐπί τινος] Gn 39,4; *id.* [τινα ἐπί
τινα] Ex 5,14; *id.* [τινα ἐπί τι] 1 Kgs 11,28; *to
commit to, to appoint for* [τί τινι] 1 Mc 7,20; *to
establish* [τι] Sir 46,13; *to set in order, to restore*
[τι] Is 49,8; *to make, to render so and so*
[τι +pred.] Est 3,13b; *to appoint to be, to
establish sb as* [τινα +pred.] Gn 47,5; *id.* [τινα
εἴς τινα] 2 Sm 6,21; *to make sb do* [τινα
+inf.] Dt 1,15

M: *to stand (up)* Neh 13,19; *to come before, to stand in the presence of* [ἐναντίον τινός] Jos 20,3; *id.* [ἐνώπιόν τινος] 1 Sm 1,9; *to stand up* 1 Sm 30,12; *to settle (down)* 2 Chr 25,3; *to stand up against* [κατά τινος] Dt 19,16

P: *to become, to be made* [+pred.] Est 8,12x; *to be established* Ps 96(97),1

καθέστηκα *to have become, to be* Wis 10,7; οἱ καθεσταμένοι ἐπὶ πάντα Ισραηλ *the officers over all of Israel* 1 Kgs 4,7; κατέστη ἐπὶ τὴν βασιλείαν *he became king* 2 Chr 21,5; κατάστητε ἐν ταῖς περικεφαλαίαις *stand ready with your helmets* Jer 26(46),4; κατασταθήσεται ἐκ τοῦ ὀνόματος τοῦ τετελευτηκότος *it shall be named by the name of the deceased* Dt 25,6; καθεστηκὼς πρεσβύτης *someone growing old* Dt 32,25; καθεστηκὸς ὕδωρ *stagnant water* Ez 34,18

→MM

καθό⁺   C 1-0-0-0-2-3

Lv 9,5; 1 Ezr 1,48; Jdt 3,3

(according) as Lv 9,5; *because* 1 Ezr 1,48

καθοδηγέω   V 0-0-2-1-0-3

Jer 2,6; Ez 39,2; Jb 12,23

to guide [τινα] Jer 2,6; *to lead down to destruction* [τινα] Jb 12,23; neol.

κάθοδος,-ου   N2F 0-0-0-2-1-3

Eccl 6,6; 7,22; 1 Ezr 2,18

way (down), passage 1 Ezr 2,18; *cycle, recurrence* Eccl 6,6

καθόδους πολλάς *repeatedly, by many repetitions* Eccl 7,22

καθόλου⁺   D 0-0-5-2-0-7

Ez 13,3.22; 17,14; Am 3,3.4

at all Am 3,3; *entirely, at all* Dn 3,50

τὸ καθόλου μή *not at all* Ez 13,3

Cf. HAMM 1977, 329-330; ROST 1967, 119-121

καθομολογέω   V 2-0-0-0-0-2

Ex 21,8.9

M: *to betroth oneself to* [τινά τινι]

Cf. WEVERS 1990, 326-327

καθοπλίζω⁺   V 0-0-1-0-9-10

Jer 26(46),9; 2 Mc 4,40; 15,11; 3 Mc 5,23.38

A: *to equip, to arm fully* [τινα] 2 Mc 4,40; *to harnass* [τι] (anim.) 3 Mc 5,23

M: *to arm oneself fully, to put on* [τι] 4 Mc 3,12

P: *to be armed with* [τινι] Jer 26(46),9; *id.* [τινι] (metaph.) 4 Mc 11,22

καθοράω⁺   V 3-0-0-2-3-8

Ex 10,5; Nm 24,2; Dt 26,15; Jb 10,4; 39,26

to look down [abs.] Dt 26,15; *to look down upon, to see* [τι] Nm 24,2; *id.* [ἐπί τι] Jdt 6,19; *to see* [abs.] Jb 10,4; *to regard* [τι] 3 Mc 3,11

Cf. DORIVAL 1994, 444

καθόρμιον,-ου   N2N 0-0-1-0-0-1

Hos 2,15

necklace; neol.

καθότι⁺   C 29-12-10-9-8-68

Gn 26,29; 34,12; Ex 1,12.17; 10,10

as

Cf. WEVERS 1990, 5.556

καθυβρίζω   V 0-0-1-1-1-3

Jer 28(51),2; Prv 19,28; 3 Mc 2,14

to despise [τι] Prv 19,28; *to dishonour* [τι] (of a holy place) 3 Mc 2,14

*Jer 28(51),2 καθυβρίσουσιν αὐτὴν *they shall treat her contemptuously* -ה וזר ◊ירד for MT וזרוה *they shall winnow, they shall pillage her*

καθυμνέω   V 0-1-0-0-0-1

2 Chr 30,21

to sing hymns continually for sb [τινι]

καθύπερθε   D 0-0-0-0-1-1

3 Mc 4,10

above

καθυπνόω   V 0-0-0-1-0-1

Prv 24,33

to sleep

καθυστερέω   V 1-1-0-0-2-4

Ex 22,28; 1 Chr 26,27; Sir 16,13; 37,20

to be late with [τι] Ex 22,28; *to fare badly* Sir 16,13; *to come short of, to lack* [τινος] Sir 37,20

καθυφαίνω   V 1-0-0-0-1-2

Ex 28,17; Jdt 10,21

A: *to interweave in, to weave through* or *into* [τι ἔν τινι] Ex 28,17

P: *to be (inter)woven* Jdt 10,21

Cf. LE BOULLUEC 1989, 68.286

καθώς⁺   C 12-110-74-31-52-279

Gn 8,21; 18,5; 41,13; 44,2; Ex 34,1

as, just as (followed by a sentence) Gn 8,21; *id.* (followed by a word) Ex 34,1; *as, to the degree that* Nm 26,54; *(as) when* 2 Mc 1,31

καθώς ... οὕτως ... *as ... so ...* Nm 8,22

καί⁺   C 11704-20358-10700-8608-10870-62240

Gn 1,1.2(tris).3

and Gn 1,1; *id.* (stereotypical rendition of copulative -ו where δέ is expected) Gn 1,3; *and especially* 2 Chr 35,24(septimo); *and then, and so* Sir 2,6(primo); *and yet, and in spite of that, nevertheless* Ps 94(95),9; *also, likewise* Hab 2,16;

but Ct 1,5; *or* Dt 19,15(tertio)

ἐλπίδος καὶ σωτηρίας *hope of life* (expressing hendiadys) 2 Mc 3,29; τε ... καὶ ... *as well ... as ..., both ... and ...* Gn 34,28

Cf. AEJMELAEUS 1982, 1-198; BLOMQVIST 1974, 170-178; 1979, 46; DORIVAL 1994, 52; HARLÉ 1988, 56-57; MARSHALL 1954, 182-183

καινίζω   V 0-0-2-0-3-5

Is 61,4; Zph 3,17; 1 Mc 10,10; 2 Mc 4,11; Wis 7,27

to make new [τι] Wis 7,27; *to renew, to repair* [τι] Is 61,4

*Zph 3,17 καὶ καινιεῖ *and he will renew* -וחריש for MT יחריש *he will be silent*

Cf. PELLETIER 1975, 226

(→ἀνα-, ἐγ-, ἐπανα-, ἐπι-)

καινός,-ή,-όν⁺   A 3-17-20-8-10-58

Dt 20,5; 22,8; 32,17; Jos 9,13; Jgs 5,8

new Dt 20,5; τὰ καινά *new things* Is 48,6

καινοὶ θεοί *strange gods* Dt 32,17

*1 Sm 23,15 ἐν τῇ Καινῇ *in the New (Ziph)* -ב/חרשה for MT ב/חרשה *in Horesh*, see also 1 Sm 23,16.18.19

Cf. HARRISVILLE 1955, 70-72; →MM; TWNT

καινότης,-ητος⁺   N3F 0-1-1-0-0-2

1 Kgs 8,53a(13); Ez 47,12

newness; ἐπὶ καινότητος *anew* 1 Kgs 8,53a(13)

*Ez 47,12 τῆς καινότητος *of the newness, of the new products* -חֹרֶשׁ◊ for MT חֹרֶשׁ◊ *every month*

καινουργός,-οῦ   N2M 0-0-0-0-1-1

4 Mc 11,23

inventor

καίπερ⁺   C 0-0-0-1-12-13

Prv 6,8c; 2 Mc 4,34; 3 Mc 4,18; 5,32; 4 Mc 3,10

(al)though 3 Mc 5,32; *id.* [+ptc.] Prv 6,8c

καίριος,-α,-ον   A 0-0-0-1-0-1

Prv 15,23

seasonable

καιρός,-οῦ⁺   N2M 55-61-70-167-134-487

Gn 1,14; 6,13; 17,21.23.26

time Gn 17,21; *opportunity* 1 Sm 20,12; *occasion* Ex 8,28; *season* Gn 1,14; *time of prosperity* Nm 14,9; οἱ καιροί *the times, the difficulties* 1 Chr 29,30

εἰς καιρόν *in season, seasonably* Sir 40,23; πρὸς καιρόν *for a time* Eccl 10,17; κατὰ καιρόν *in time* Nm 23,23; ἐπὶ καιροῦ *in (his) time* Dt 28,12; πρὸ καιροῦ *before time, ahead of time* Sir 51,30; εἰς καιρούς *at set times* Ezr 10,14; εἰς ὥραν καὶ καιρόν *for an*

appointed season Est 10,3h; ἀπὸ καιροῦ εἰς καιρόν *from time to time* 1 Chr 9,25; ἐν καιρῷ ἑνί *at one time* 1 Chr 11,11; ἐν τῷ νῦν καιρῷ *at the present time* Gn 29,34; κατὰ τὸν καιρὸν τοῦτον *at that time, then* (of the future) Gn 18,10; κατ᾽ ἐκεῖνον τὸν καιρόν *at that time* (of the past) 2 Mc 3,5

ὁ καιρὸς τῆς ἐξοδίας τῶν βασιλέων *time of kings going out (to war)* 2 Sm 11,1; ἐν τοῖς καιροῖς *in those critical times* (mostly in bad sense) Dn 11,14; μιᾶς ὑπὸ καιρὸν ἡμέρας *within the space of one day* 2 Mc 7,20; πολλοὶ καιροὶ διῆλθον *a long time passed* 1 Mc 12,10; λαμβάνω καιρόν *to seize the opportunity, to take the occasion* Ps 74(75),3; ἐξαγοράζω καιρόν *to gain time* Dn 2,8; καιρὸς παντὸς ἀνθρώπου ἥκει *the time of every man has come before me* Gn 6,13

*Is 50,4 ἐν καιρῷ *in season* -לעת for MT לעות *to sustain*; *Ez 22,4 καιρόν *time* -עת for MT עד *to*, see also Ez 22,30

cpr. χρόνος

Cf. BARR 1969, 21-85; BURNS 1953, 20-22; DORIVAL 1994, 55.58.318; EYNIKEL-HAUSPIE 1997 forthcoming; GUILLAMAUD 1988, 359-371; HARL 1986ᵃ, 130.188; HARLÉ 1988, 188; LE BOULLUEC 1989, 157.237; LEE, J. 1983, 83; ROST 1967, 129-132; SHIPP 1979, 290-292; TRÉDÉ 1984, xi-xvi; WEVERS 1990, 130; 1993, 8.240; WILSON 1980, 177-204; →TWNT

καίτοι⁺   C 0-0-0-0-4-4

4 Mc 2,6; 5,18; 7,13; 8,16

and indeed 4 Mc 2,6; *and yet* 4 Mc 8,16

καίω⁺   V 17-3-34-25-9-88

Ex 3,2; 27,20(bis).21; 35,3

A: *to light, to kindle, to burn* [τι] Ex 27,20(primo); *to kindle* [τι] 1 Mc 12,29

P: *to be kindled, to burn* Ex 27,20(secundo); *id.* (metaph.) Dt 32,22

τοῖς καιομένοις ἐξειργάζω *to finish off (arrows) with burning (coals)* or *to complete (arrows) against the raging ones* Ps 7,14; καίω πόλιν ἐν πυρί *to burn and destroy a city, to waste with fire* (semit.?) Jer 39(32),29; καίεται πυρί *it burns with fire* (semit.?) Ex 3,2; κάμινος καιομένη *a burning furnace* Jb 41,12; καιόμενος ὁ θυμός *wrath is burning* Is 30,27

Cf. LE BOULLUEC 1989, 280; MARGOLIS 1906ᵇ=1972, 65-69

(→ἀνα-, ἀπο-, δια-, ἐγ-, ἐκ-, κατα-, περι-, προσ-, προσεκ-, συγ-, ὑπο-)

κἀκεῖ⁺   0-1-1-1-1-4

1 Kgs 19,12; Is 57,7; Ru 1,17; 3 Mc 7,19

crasis for καὶ ἐκεῖ

κἀκεῖνος   0-0-3-0-2-5

Is 57,6(bis); 66,5; Wis 18,1; 2 Mc 1,15

crasis for καὶ ἐκεῖνος

κακέω

(→ἀπο-)

κακηγορέω   V 0-0-0-0-1-1

4 Mc 9,14

to speak ill, to accuse

κακία,-ας⁺   N1F 7-45-35-23-33-143

Gn 6,5; 31,52; Ex 22,22; 23,2; 32,12

badness, wickedness Jgsᴬ 9,56; κακίαι *wicked*
actions, evil doings Gn 6,5; *sin, wicked actions*
Ex 32,12; *wickedness* Hos 9,15

evil Jgs 20,34; *hurt, damage* 1 Mc 7,23; *affliction*
1 Kgs 20,29

ἐπὶ κακία *for mischief, for evil* Gn 31,52;
ποιέω τινί κακίαν *to bring affliction to*
1 Sm 6,9; κακία κακοποιέω *to do evil*
1 Sm 12,25; κακία κακόω τινά *to afflict by ill*
treatment (semit.) Ex 22,22

*Jb 17,5 κακίας *mischief* -רָעִים for MT רֵעִים *friends*

Cf. LE BOULLUEC 1989, 322(Ex 32,12); WEVERS 1990,
525(Ex 32,12); →MM; TWNT

κακίζω   V 0-0-0-0-1-1

4 Mc 12,2

to reproach [τινα]

κακοήθεια,-ας⁺   N1F 0-0-0-1-5-6

Est 8,12f; 3 Mc 3,22; 7,3; 4 Mc 1,4; 3,4

bad disposition, malignity

Cf. SPICQ 1978ᵃ, 392-393

κακοήθης,-ης,-ες⁺   A 0-0-0-0-2-2

4 Mc 1,25; 2,16

ill-disposed, malicious

κακολογέω⁺   V 2-1-1-1-1-6

Ex 21,16(17); 22,27; 1 Sm 3,13; Ez 22,7; Prv
20,9a(20)

to revile, to abuse [τινα]

Cf. HORSLEY 1982, 88; LE BOULLUEC 1989, 218

κακόμοχθος,-ος,-ον   A 0-0-0-0-1-1

Wis 15,8

working perversely, working evil; neol.

Cf. LARCHER 1985, 862-863

κακοπάθεια,-ας⁺   N1F 0-0-1-0-3-4

Mal 1,13; 2 Mc 2,26.27; 4 Mc 9,8

misery Mal 1,13; *laborious toil, painful labour*
2 Mc 2,26; *endurance, sufferings* 4 Mc 9,8

Cf. SPICQ 1978ᵃ, 394; WALTERS 1973, 45

κακοπαθέω⁺   V 0-0-1-0-0-1

Jon 4,10

to suffer

Cf. SPICQ 1978ᵃ, 394

κακοποιέω⁺   V 5-9-3-9-3-29

Gn 31,7.29; 43,6; Lv 5,4; Nm 35,23

to do ill or *evil* Lv 5,4; *to do mischief to, to*
injure (the house of the Lord) [τι] 1 Ezr 6,32;
to hurt, to injure [τινα] Ezr 4,13

κακία κακοποιέω *to do evil* (semit.?)
1 Sm 12,25, cpr. 1 Chr 21,17

→TWNT

κακοποίησις,-εως   N3F 0-0-0-1-1-2

Ezr 4,22; 3 Mc 3,2

evil-doing; εἰς κακοποίησιν *to harm, to injure*

κακοποιός,-ός,-όν⁺   A 0-0-0-2-0-2

Prv 12,4; 24,19

bad; κακοποιοί *evil-doers* Prv 24,19

*Prv 12,4 κακοποιός *bad, evil* -מבאיש◊ for MT מבישה
◊בוש *she who brings shame*

→TWNT

κακοπραγία,-ας   N1F 0-0-0-0-1-1

Wis 5,23

wrongdoing

Cf. LARCHER 1984, 397

κακός,-ή,-όν⁺   A 17-33-91-157-86-384

Gn 19,19; 24,50; 26,29; 44,34; 48,16

bad, evil, wicked (of pers., in moral sense) Prv
3,31; *bad, evil* (of things, in moral sense)
Prv 2,12; *evil* (inclination) Prv 2,17; (τὸ) κακόν
evil Gn 24,50; τὰ κακά *sins* Jer 15,11;
reproaches, evil words Lam 3,38; κακοί *wicked*
men 1 Sm 25,39

evil, injurious, dangerous Prv 16,9; τὰ κακά *evil,*
calamity Gn 19,19; *evils* Gn 48,16; *afflictions*
Est 1,1h; κακά *troubles* Ps 87(88),4

οἱ ἐπιστάμενοι τὸ κακὸν καὶ τὸ ἀγαθόν *who*
know good and evil Nm 32,11; ἐν κακοῖς *in*
troubles Ex 5,19; εἰς κακά *for evil* Dt 29,20;
κακὰ ποιέω *to do harm* 2 Sm 12,18; λαλέω
κακὰ περί τινος *to speak evil of* 1 Kgs 22,8; ἐν
κακοῖς γίγνομαι *to be afflicted* 1 Chr 7,23;
ἐργάζομαι κακὸν εἴς τινα *to do harm to sb*
Prv 3,30; καταγράφω κατά τινος κακά *to write*
evil things against sb Jb 13,26; ἰαταὶ κακῶν
healers of diseases Jb 13,4; παράκλητορες
κακῶν *poor, miserable comforters* Jb 16,2; ὁ
σπείρων φαῦλα θερίσει κακά *he that sows*
wickedness shall reap troubles Prv 22,8; μὴ
τεκτήνῃ ἐπὶ σὸν φίλον κακά *do not devise evil*

against your friend Prv 3,29

*Mi 4,9 κακά *evil* -רַע for MT רֵעַ *roar, shouting*;
*Jb 4,12 κακόν *evil* -מָץ (late Hebr.? Aram.?)
for MT מָץ *whisper?*; *Jb 5,5 ἐκ κακῶν *out of
evil* -מ/צרים for MT מ/צנים *out of thorns?*; *Prv 13,10
κακός *a bad man* -רָע or -רָק (cpr. ῥακά Mt 5,22)
for MT רָק *but, only*; *Prv 19,6 ὁ κακός *the evil
one, the bad one* -הָרָע for MT הָרֵעַ *the friend*;
*Prv 19,27 κακάς *(of) evil* -רעה for MT דעת *of
wisdom, of knowledge*, see also Is 28,9;
*Prv 28,20 ὁ κακός *the wicked* -הרשע for MT העשיר
to enrich

Cf. Cook 1987, 36; Dhorme 1926, 44(Jb 4,12); Dodd
1954, 76; Lofthouse 1949, 264-268; Wevers 1993, 755;
→TWNT

κακοτεχνέω   V 0-0-0-0-1-1
3 Mc 7,9
to plot evil, to use base arts or *trickery for* [τι]
Cf. Milligan 1910=1980, 2

κακότεχνος,-ος,-ον   A 0-0-0-0-3-3
4 Mc 6,25; Wis 1,4; 15,4
plotting evil, treacherous Wis 1,4; *artful,
wickedly-contrived* 4 Mc 6,25

κακουργία,-ας   N1F 0-0-0-1-2-3
Ps 34(35),17; 2 Mc 3,32; 14,22
wickedness, villainy Ps 34(35),17; *treachery*
2 Mc 3,32

κακοῦργος,-ος,-ον⁺   A 0-0-0-2-2-4
Prv 21,15; Est 8,12p; Sir 11,33; 33,27
mischievous, evil Sir 33,27; (ὁ) κακοῦργος
malefactor, evil-doer Prv 21,15
Cf. Spicq 1978ᵃ, 397

κακουχέω⁺   V 0-2-0-0-0-2
1 Kgs 2,26(bis)
P: *to be afflicted*
Cf. Dorival 1994, 504

κακοφροσύνη,-ης   N1F 0-0-0-1-0-1
Prv 16,18
folly

κακόφρων,-ων,-ον   A 0-0-0-2-0-2
Prv 11,22; 19,19
ill-minded, of bad spirit, malignant
Cf. Tov 1977, 195

κακόω⁺   V 20-4-12-15-12-63
Gn 15,13; 16,6; 19,9; Ex 1,11; 5,22
A: *to do evil* [abs.] 1 Kgs 17,20; *to maltreat*
[τινα] Nm 20,15; *to afflict* [τινα] Gn 15,13; *to
hurt* [τινα] (metaph.) Jb 24,24; *to deal harshly*
[τινα] Gn 16,6; *to hurt* [τι] Ps 93(94),5
P: *to be afflicted* Ps 37(38),9; *to be in ill plight*

Jb 31,30
κακοῦντες *evil-doers* Ps 26(27),2; κακόω
ὀρφάνους *to afflict orphans* Jb 22,9
*Eccl 7,22 κακώσει *he shall afflict* -ירע for MT
ירע *he knows*, see also Hos 9,7
Cf. Dogniez 1992, 169; Dorival 1994, 504; Le
Boulluec 1989, 33.93-94.110-111.229-230; Wevers 1990,
351.352
(→προ-)

κακῶς⁺   D 4-0-3-0-8-15
Ex 22,27; Lv 19,14; 20,9(bis); Is 8,21
wrong 3 Mc 1,14; *ill* 4 Mc 12,14; *fierce* 3 Mc 1,16
κακῶς λέγω τινα *to curse* Ex 22,27; *to revile*
Lv 19,14; κακῶς ὄμνυμι *to swear falsely*
Wis 14,29; κακῶς φρονέω *to contemn, to despise*
Wis 14,30; κακῶς πάσχω *to suffer, to be afflicted*
Wis 18,19; κακῶς λαλέω περὶ τὰ ἅγια *to speak
blasphemously against the sanctuary* 1 Mc 7,42;
κακῶς ἐστιν ὑμῖν *it is evil with you* Jer 7,9; τὸ
κακῶς ἔχον *that which is sick, the sick* (of the
sheep) Ez 34,4
Cf. Wevers 1990, 355(Ex 22,27)

κάκωσις,-εως⁺   N3F 4-0-4-5-7-20
Ex 3,7.17; Nm 11,15; Dt 16,3; Is 53,4
ill-treatment Nm 11,15; *affliction* Est 1,1g;
oppression (of Israelites in Egypt) Ex 3,7;
suffering, distress Wis 3,2; ἐπὶ κακώσει *with
intent to hurt* 2 Mc 3,39
*Ps 43(44),20 κακώσεως *of the dragon* (symbol
of evil) or *of evil?* -תנין? for MT תנים *of jackals*
Cf. Dogniez 1992, 215-216(Dt 16,3); Le Boulluec 1989,
93(Ex 3,17)

καλαβώτης,-ου   N1M 1-0-0-1-0-2
Lv 11,30; Prv 30,28
gecko, spotted lizard
Cf. Harlé 1988, 131

κάλαθος,-ου   N2M 0-0-3-0-0-3
Jer 24,1.2(bis)
basket (narrow at the base)

καλαμάομαι   V 1-2-5-0-1-9
Dt 24,20; Jgs 20,45; Is 3,12; 24,13
to gather, to glean, to collect [τι] (of fruit)
Dt 24,20; *to gather up* [τινα] (metaph.)
Jgs 20,45

καλάμη,-ης⁺   N1F 2-0-11-3-2-18
Ex 5,12; 15,7; Is 1,31; 5,24; 17,6
stalk Jb 24,24; *straw (of corn)* Am 2,13; *stubble*
Ex 5,12
καλάμη ἐν ἀμητῷ *straw in harvest, harvest*
Mi 7,1; καλάμη στιππύου *tow* (the shorter, less

desirable flax fibre) Is 1,31

καλάμινος,-η,-ον   A 0-1-2-0-0-3
2 Kgs 18,21; Is 36,6; Ez 29,6
reed-like, straw-like; ἡ ῥάβδος ἡ καλαμίνη *staff
of reed*

καλαμίσκος,-ου   N2M 13-0-0-0-0-13
Ex 25,31.32(ter).33
branch of a candlestick, tube
Cf. LE BOULLUEC 1989, 262.263; WEVERS 1990,
405-407.624

κάλαμος,-ου⁺   N2M 1-0-25-4-2-32
Ex 30,23; Is 19,6; 35,7; 42,3; Ez 40,3
reed, calamus (in nature) Jb 40,21; *reed, reeds*
(coll.) Ex 30,23; *reed, measuring-rod* Ez 40,3;
reed-pen Ps 44(45),2
*Ez 42,12 καλάμου *of the measuring rod* -הקנה
for MT הנינת ?
→MM

καλέομαι
(→προ-)

καλέω⁺   V 132-140-98-53-89-512
Gn 1,5(bis).8.10(bis)
A: *to call* [τινα] Gn 3,9; *id.* [τι] Gn 1,5; *to call
to, to summon to* [τινα ἐπί τινι] Nm 25,2; *id.*
[τινα εἴς τι] 1 Kgs 12,20; *to invite* [τινα]
Ex 34,15; *to send for, to summon, to call* [τινα]
Nm 16,12; *to proclaim* [τι] 1 Kgs 20,12; *to call
by name, to name* [τινα +pred.] Ru 1,20; *id.*
[τι +pred.] Lv 23,21
P: *to be named, to be called* Gn 2,23; *to be
named after* [ἐπί τινι] Gn 48,6; *to call into
existence, to call into life* [τι] Wis 11,25; ὁ
καλούμενος *the so-called* Jos 5,3; κέκλημαι *to
be the guest* Est 5,12

καλέω ὀνόματι τινος *to invoke the name of*
Ex 34,5; καλέω τὸ ὄνομά τινος *to call the name
of* Gn 3,20; καλέω ἐπὶ τῷ ὀνόματί μου *to call
out by* or *through my name* Ex 33,19; καλέω
ὄνομά τινι *to give a name to* Gn 2,20; καλέω
τι ἐπ' ὀνόματος *to call by name* 1 Chr 6,50;
ἐκλήθην εἰς φυλήν τινος *to be reckoned to the
tribe of* 1 Chr 23,14; καλέω τὴν δίκην *to call
for judgement* Am 7,4; καλέω τινὰ εἰς τὸν
γάμον *to invite to a wedding* Tobˢ 9,5; καλέω
τινὰ εἰς εἰρήνην *to invite sb to make peace*
Jgs 21,13; ἐκλήθην ὑπὲρ τῆς διαμαρτυρίας
τινός *to be called as a witness for* 4 Mc 16,16;
μάχαιραν καλέω ἐπί τινα *to call a sword
against* Jer 32,29; ὁ καιρὸς ἡμᾶς καλεῖ ἐπί τι
the occasion invites us to 4 Mc 3,19

*Jer 26(46),19 κληθήσεται οὐαί *(Memphis)
shall be called Woe* corr.? καυθήσεται for
MT-נצתה *(Memphis) shall be laid waste, shall be
burnt*; *Hos 12,1 κεκλήσεται *is called* -נאמר for
MT נאמן *is faithful*
Cf. CERNUDA 1975, 445-455; HARL 1986ᵃ, 189(Gn 21,12);
HELBING 1928, 50-51; LARCHER 1985, 695-696(Wis 11,25);
LE BOULLUEC 1989, 335(Ex 33,19); WALTERS 1973,
245(Ex 12,16); WEVERS1990,177(Ex 12,16).551(Ex 33,19).
556(Ex 34,5); 1993, 543; →TWNT
(→ἀνα-, ἐγ-, ἐκ-, ἐπι-, μετα-, παρα-, προσ-,
προσπαρα-, συγ-)

καλλιόω   V 0-0-0-2-0-2
Ct 4,10(bis)
P: *to be beautiful*

καλλίπαις,-παιδος   A 0-0-0-0-1-1
4 Mc 16,10
blessed with beautiful children

κάλλιστος,-η,-ον
sup. of καλός

καλλίων,-ων,-ον
comp. of καλός

καλλονή,-ῆς⁺   N1F 0-0-0-2-6-8
Ps 46(47),5; 77(78),61; 1 Mc 2,12; Wis 13,3.5
beauty Wis 13,3; *lustre, pride* Ps 46(47),5;
excellence Sir 6,15

κάλλος,-ους⁺   N3N 2-2-16-9-34-63
Gn 49,21; Dt 33,17; 1 Sm 16,12; 17,42; Is 2,16
beauty Gn 49,21; *id.* (of pers.) 1 Ezr 4,18
κάλλος ὀφθαλμῶν *beautiful eyes* 1 Sm 16,12
*Ps 29(30),8 τῷ κάλλει μου *to my beauty* -להררי
for MT להררי *on my mountain*?
Cf. WEVERS 1993, 831

κάλλυνθρον,-ου   N2N 1-0-0-0-0-1
Lv 23,40
palm-frond; κάλλυνθρα φοινίκων *branches of
palm-leaves*; neol.
Cf. WALTERS 1973, 303

καλλωπίζω⁺   V 1-0-2-1-1-5
Gn 38,14; Jer 10,4; 26(46),20; Ps 143(144),12;
Jdt 10,4
M: *to adorn oneself, to make oneself a beauty*
Jdt 10,4
P: *to be beautified* Jer 10,4
δάμαλις κεκαλλωπισμένη *fair heifer*
Jer 26(46),20
Cf. HARL 1986ᵃ, 265(Gn 38,14; Jdt 10,4)

καλοκάγαθία,-ας⁺   N1F 0-0-0-0-5-5
4 Mc 1,10; 3,18; 11,22; 13,25; 15,9
the character and conduct of καλὸς κἀγαθός,

nobility of character, virtue 4 Mc 11,22; *goodness*
4 Mc 3,18
ἀποθνήσκω ὑπὲρ τῆς καλοκἀγαθίας *to die for*
the sake of virtue 4 Mc 1,10

καλός,-ή,-όν⁺   A 61-19-38-52-65-235
Gn 1,4.8.10.12.18
beautiful (mostly specified by τῷ εἴδει) Gn
12,14; *id.* (of things) Gn 27,15; *fair, shapely,*
beautiful Jdt 11,21; κάλλιστος *fairest, most*
shapely (of some parts of the body) Hos 10,11
good Gn 1,4; *good, nice* (of food) Tob 2,1;
pleasant (of words) Prv 16,24; *fine* Prv 31,11;
excellent, precious Prv 24,4; *pleasing* Prv 2,10;
κάλλιστος *most excellent* Est 8,12q
honest Tob 5,14; *(morally) good* (frequently)
Gn 2,9; τὸ καλόν *that which is morally good, the*
good Dt 6,10
(οὐ) καλόν [+inf.] *it is (not) good that* Tob 8,6;
ποιέω καλόν *to do well* Is 1,17; λαλέω καλὰ
περί τινος *to speak good concerning* Nm 10,29;
ἀνταποδίδωμι πονηρὰ ἀντὶ καλῶν *to return*
evil for good Gn 44,4; κάλλιόν τι ποιέω *to*
amend Jer 18,11; προφητεύω καλά *to prophesy*
good 1 Kgs 22,18; γήρει καλῷ *at a good old age*
Gn 15,15; τὰ ἑπτὰ ἔτη τὰ καλά *the seven good*
years Gn 41,35; ῥήματα καλά *good words,*
excellent words Jos 21,45; ὄνομα καλόν *fair*
name, good reputation Prv 22,1; καλὰς χάριτας
great favour 4 Mc 11,12; σύμβλημα καλόν
ἐστιν *it is a piece well joined* Is 41,7
*Gn 49,14 τὸ καλόν *that which is good* -חָמֵר? for
MT חֲמֹר *an ass,* cpr. Ps 118(119),20
Cf. COOK 1987, 34; DODD 1954, 126-127; DOGNIEZ 1992,
58.157(Dt 6,18).197(Dt 12,25); HARL 1986ᵃ, 88(Gn
1,4).310(Gn 49,14); TOV 1981, 107(Gn 49,14); WEVERS
1993, 828; →MM; TWNT

κάλος,-ου   N2M 2-0-0-0-0-2
Nm 3,37; 4,32
rope, cord
Cf. DORIVAL 1994, 211

κάλπη,-ης   N1F 0-0-0-0-1-1
4 Mc 3,12
pitcher; neol.
Cf. WALTERS 1973, 66

κάλυμμα,-ατος⁺   N3N 17-0-0-0-2-19
Ex 27,16; 34,33.34.35; 35,11
veil Ex 34,33; *veil, curtain* Ex 27,16; *covering*
Nm 4,8; καλύμματα *armour* 1 Mc 4,6
Cf. DORIVAL 1994, 50; LE BOULLUEC 1989, 278-279
(Ex 27,16); →TWNT

κάλυξ,-υκος   N3F 0-0-0-0-1-1
Wis 2,8
cup (of a flower); ῥόδων κάλυκες *rosebuds*

καλυπτήρ,-ῆρος   N3M 3-0-0-0-0-3
Ex 27,3; Nm 4,13.14
covering
Cf. DORIVAL 1994, 120; LE BOULLUEC 1989, 275(Ex 27,3);
WEVERS 1990, 432(Ex 27,3)

καλύπτω⁺   V 29-3-19-25-13-89
Ex 8,2; 10,5(bis); 14,28; 15,5
A: *to cover* [τι] Ex 8,2; *to cover, to flood* [τι]
Ex 14,28; *to cover, to envelop* [τι] (of a cloud)
Ex 24,15; *to cover* [τι] (of diseases) Lv 13,13; *to*
overlay with (metal) [τί τινι] Ex 27,2
to cover, to protect [τινα] Sir 23,18; *to hide, to*
conceal [τι] Jb 36,32; *to hide, to disguise* [abs.]
Neh 3,37; *id.* [τι] Ps 31(32),5; *to hide, to close,*
to make secret [τι] Dnᴸˣˣ 12,4
to cover (sins), to forgive [τι] Ps 84(85),3
M: *to shelter from, to screen from* [ἀπό τινος]
Ez 40,43
ἐκάλυψεν αὐτοὺς ἡ γῆ *they were buried*
Nm 16,33; ἡ αἰσχύνη τοῦ προσώπου μου
ἐκάλυψέν με *shame was written large on my face*
Ps 43(44),16
*Ez 44,20 καλύπτοντες καλύψουσι *they shall*
carefully cover (their heads) - כסום for MT כסם◊ *they*
shall carefully trim (the hair of their heads)
Cf. DORIVAL 1994, 120; LE BOULLUEC 1989, 123(Ex 8,2).
275(Ex 27,2); SPICQ 1982, 361; WEVERS 1990,
431(Ex 27,2); →MM; TWNT
(→ἀνα-, ἀπο-, ἐκ-, ἐπι-, κατα-, παρα-, περι-,
συγ-, ὑπο-)

κάλυψις,-εως   N3F 0-0-0-0-1-1
Sir 41,26
covering (metaph.), *concealment*

καλώδιον,-ου   N2N 0-8-0-0-0-8
Jgs 15,13.14; 16,11
dim. of κάλος; *(small) cord*
Cf. WALTERS 1973, 70

καλῶς⁺   D 3-6-7-6-14-36
Gn 26,29; 32,13; Lv 5,4; Jgsᴬ 9,16; 2 Sm 3,13
well Gn 26,29; *well, rightly* Jer 1,12; *decently*
Tobᴮᴬ 14,9; *all right* (in answers) 1 Kgs 2,18
καλῶς ἔχειν *it is good* 1 Ezr 2,16; καλῶς ποιέω
to do well Lv 5,4; καλῶς ἀκούειν *to be well*
spoken of 2 Mc 14,37; καλῶς εὖ τινα ποιέω *to*
do good to Gn 32,13; καλῶς ἔσται ὑμῖν *it shall*
be well with you 2 Kgs 25,24
*Mi 1,11 καλῶς *fairly, beautifully* -שׁפיר (Aram.?)

for MT שפיר Shaphir; *Zph 3,20 καλῶς ποιήσω I
shall do well -אטיב for MT אביא I shall bring

κάμαξ,-ᾱκος   N3M 0-0-0-0-1-1
2 Mc 5,3
pike

καμάρα,-ας⁺   N1F 0-0-1-0-0-1
Is 40,22
vault

κάμέ   3-0-0-0-1-4
Gn 27,34.38; Ex 12,32; 4 Mc 11,3
crasis for καὶ ἐμέ

καμηλοπάρδαλις,-εως/ιδος   N3F 1-0-0-0-0-1
Dt 14,5
camelopard, giraffe
Cf. MOSÈS 1970, 358

κάμηλος,-ου⁺   N2M/F 27-18-9-5-6-65
Gn 12,16; 24,10(bis).11.14
Semit. loanword (Hebr. גמל); camel Gn 12,16
*Ez 27,21 καμήλους camels -בְּכָרֹ◊ בכרים for MT
כרים/ב for (or in) lambs
Cf. CAIRD 1976, 78; TOV 1979, 220-221; →CHANTRAINE;
FRISK

καμιναία,-ας   N1F 2-0-0-0-0-2
Ex 9,8.10
furnace
Cf. LE BOULLUEC 1989, 130

κάμινος,-ου⁺   N2F 4-0-4-43-11-62
Gn 19,28; Ex 19,18; Nm 25,8; Dt 4,20; Is 48,10
furnace (general) Gn 19,28; oven (for baking)
Sir 27,5; melting furnace Prv 17,3
κάμινος σιδηρᾶ iron furnace Dt 4,20; κάμινος
δοκιμάζει τι the furnace proves Sir 31,26
*Nm 25,8 κάμινον oven or alcove? corr.?
καμάραν for MT קבה alcove, vaulted room
Cf. DOGNIEZ 1992, 139-140(Dt 4,20); DORIVAL 1994, 463

καμμύω⁺   V 0-0-3-1-0-4
Is 6,10; 29,10; 33,15; Lam 3,45
to close the eyes; καμμύω τοὺς ὀφθαλμούς to
close the eyes Is 6,10
*Lam 3,45 καμμύσαι με to close my eyes corr.?
κάμψαι με to make me bow down -שחח◊ for MT
סחי refuse, filth, cpr. Jb 9,13, or καμμύσαι to
close the eyes corr.? λικμήσαι for MT סחי◊ סחהה to
scrape off, to scatter, cpr. Ez 26,4
Cf. ALBREKTSON 1963, 157-158; →MM

κάμνω⁺   V 0-0-0-2-4-6
Jb 10,1; 17,2; 4 Mc 3,8; 7,13; Wis 4,16
to labour Wis 15,9; to be weary Jb 10,1; to be
weakened 4 Mc 7,13; καμών deceased, dead
Wis 4,16

Cf. GILBERT 1973, 199(Wis 15,9); LARCHER 1984, 340(Wis
4,16); SPICQ 1978ª, 400-402

κάμοί   0-1-0-2-0-3
Jgs^ 14,16; Jb 12,3; Dn^LXX 2,30
crasis for καὶ ἐμοί

κάμοῦ   0-0-0-0-1-1
4 Mc 5,10
crasis for καὶ ἐμοῦ

καμπή,-ῆς   N1F 0-0-0-2-0-2
Neh 3,24; 3,31
turning, corner

κάμπη,-ης   N1F 0-0-3-0-0-3
Jl 1,4; 2,25; Am 4,9
caterpillar

κάμπτω⁺   V 0-8-2-2-7-19
Jgs^ 5,27; 7,5.6; 2 Sm 22,40; 2 Kgs 1,13
A: to bend, to bow down Jgs^ 7,5; to bow down,
to bend [τινα] 2 Sm 22,40; id. [τι] Sir 7,23; to
break [τι] (metaph.) Sir 38,18; to turn [abs.]
Jgs^ 5,27
P: to bend oneself to [τινι] 4 Mc 3,4; to stoop
Jb 9,13
κάμπτω τὰ γόνατα to bend the knee (in worship)
1 Chr 29,20; κάμπτω τὸν τράχηλόν τινος to
bend one's neck, to humble Is 58,5; to bend the
neck of sb, to cause to obey Sir 7,23; ἔκαμψεν
ἐπὶ τὰ γόνατα αὐτοῦ he bent the knee 2 Kgs
1,13; ἐμοὶ κάμψει πᾶν γόνυ every knee shall
bend for me, every one shall submit to me
Is 45,23
Cf. JOBES 1991, 183-191; RENEHAN 1975, 115-116; →LSJ
RSuppl; TWNT
(→ἀνα-, δια-, κατα-, συγ-)

καμπύλος,-η,-ον   A 0-0-0-1-0-1
Prv 2,15
winding, bent, crooked (ways of dealing)

κἄν   1-0-0-0-15-16
Lv 7,16; 4 Mc 2,8.9.; 10,18; 18,14
crasis for καὶ ἐάν or καὶ ἄν

κάνθαρος,-ου   N2M 0-0-1-0-0-1
Hab 2,11
knot, beetle
Cf. LEE, J. 1969, 240; MURAOKA 1991, 205-222

κανθός,-οῦ   N2M 0-0-0-0-2-2
Tob 11,12
corner of the eye

κανοῦν,-οῦ   N2N 14-1-0-0-0-15
Gn 40,16.17(bis).18; Ex 29,3
basket of reed

κανών,-όνος⁺   N3M 0-0-1-0-2-3

Mi 7,4; Jdt 13,6; 4 Mc 7,21
rail (of the bed), (bed-)post Jdt 13,6;
(philosophic) principle 4 Mc 7,21
*Mi 7,4 ἐπὶ κανόνος *according to rule,
according to measure* -מ/מסורה for MT מ/מסוכה *of a
thornbush*

Cf. HORSLEY 1981, 44.45; →TWNT

κάπηλος,-ου   N2M 0-0-1-0-1-2
Is 1,22; Sir 26,29
retail-dealer Sir 26,29; *innkeeper, tavern-keeper* Is
1,22

Cf. DREXHAGE 1991, 28-46; SPICQ 1978ᵃ, 403-404; →TWNT

καπνίζω   V 3-0-2-2-5-12
Gn 15,17; Ex 19,18; 20,18; Is 7,4; 42,3
A: *to make smoke, to use as a fumigation*
Tobᴮᴬ 6,17; *to be black with smoke* Ex 20,18; *to
burn for smoke (for fumigation)* [τι] Tobᴮᴬ 6,8
P: *to be smoked, to smoke* Gn 15,17; *to be
wrapped up in smoke* Ex 19,18

Cf. DRESCHER 1969, 87-88

καπνός,-οῦ⁺   N2M 2-7-8-7-6-30
Ex 19,18(bis); Jos 8,20.21; Jgsᴬ 20,38
smoke

κάππαρις,-εως   N3F 0-0-0-1-0-1
Eccl 12,5
caper-plant

κάπτω   V 0-0-0-1-0-1
Dnᴸˣˣ 1,12
to gulp down

καρδία,-ας⁺   N1F 80-191-172-343-177-963
Gn 6,5; 20,5.6; 42,28; 50,21
heart (as part of the body) Tob 6,4; *heart* (as
centre and source of physical life)
Ps 103(104),15; *id.* (as centre of the whole inner
life into which God looks) 1 Sm 16,7; *heart,
mind* (as the faculty of thought or understanding) Jb 17,4; *heart, memory* Prv 3,1; *heart*
(of the will and its decisions) Jer 38,33
heart (of emotions, wishes and desires) Jb 37,1;
id. (of moral life) Ps 23,4; *heart, conscience* (as
feeling for good and evil) 1 Sm 24,6; *heart* (of
disposition) 2 Kgs 23,3
middle, midst, centre Jon 2,4; *depth* Ps 45(46),3;
heart (of a tree) Ez 17,22
ἀπὸ καρδίας *out of (their own) heart* (of false
prophets) Is 44,25, see also Ez 13,3; ἐν τῇ
καρδίᾳ αὐτοῦ *in* or *with his heart* (used with
many verbs) Gn 6,5; ἐν καρδίᾳ ἀληθίνη *with
sincere heart* Is 38,3; οἱ συντετριμμένοι τὴν
καρδίαν *the broken-hearted* Is 57,15; λαλέω εἰς

τὴν καρδίαν τινός *to speak kindly to* Gn 50,21;
λαλέω ἐπὶ τὴν καρδίαν τινός *id.* Jgs 19,3;
λέγω ἐν τῇ καρδίᾳ *to say to oneself* Dt 8,17;
ἀναβαίνει τι ἐπὶ τὴν καρδίαν τινός *to think
of something* Ez 38,10; τίθημι καρδίαν ἐπί
τινα *to pay attention to* 1 Sm 25,25; κατισχύω
τὴν καρδίαν τινός *to harden sb's heart, to
encourage* Jos 11,20; ποιέω τι ἐν καθαρᾷ
καρδίᾳ *to do with a pure heart* Gn 20,5; ποιέω
τι καρδίᾳ μεγάλη *to do generously* 2 Mc 1,3
*Ez 17,22 καρδίας αὐτῶν *of their heart* corr.?
κράδας αὐτῶν (acc. pl. of κράδη) *quivering
spray at the end of their branch* for MT ינקותיו *it
shoots*; *1 Kgs 12,33 ἀπὸ καρδίας αὐτοῦ *out of
his heart* -מ/לב׳ (= MTq) for MTˣ מ/לבד *all by
himself*; *Ez 13,3 ἀπὸ καρδίας *out of their own
hearts* -מ/לבם for MT נבלים *senseless*, cpr. Ez 13,17;
*Ps 84(85),9 πρὸς αὐτὸν καρδίαν *(their) heart
towards him* -לב לו for MT ל/כסלה *to folly*;
*Prv 15,22 ἐν δὲ καρδίαις *in the hearts* -ב/לב-
for MT ב/רב *with a multitude*, see also Prv 24,6;
*Prv 21,12 καρδίας *the hearts* -לבות for MT ל/בית
(give attention) to the house; *Eccl 9,1 καὶ
καρδία μου εἶδε *and my heart saw* -ו/לבי ראה for
MT ברר◊ ו/לבור את *and to examine*

Cf. DOGNIEZ 1992, 154-155(Dt 6,5); HARL 1986ᵃ, 61;
LARCHER 1983, 166-167(Wis 1,1).219(Wis 2,2); LE
BOULLUEC 1989, 67-68.121(Ex 7,22-23); LUST 1997
forthcoming (Ez 17,22); PIETERSMA 1990, 265-266;
WALTERS 1973, 197-198(Is 6,10).215(Ez 11,19); WEVERS
1990, 130-131(Ex 9,14).509(Ex 31,6); →TWNT

καρδιόω   V 0-0-0-2-0-2
Ct 4,9(bis)
to hearten (up), to ravish the heart of sb [τινα]
(semit.); neol.

καρόω   V 0-0-1-0-0-1
Jer 28(51),39
P: *to be intoxicated, to sleep* (of drunkenness);
*Jer 28(51),39 καρωθῶσιν *(so that) they may
swoon away* -יעלפו for MT יעלזו *(so that) they are
merry*

καρπάσινος,-η,-ον⁺   A 0-0-0-1-0-1
Est 1,6
Persian loanword (Hebr. כרפס); *made of flax*

Cf. CAIRD 1976, 79; TOV 1979, 221; →CHANTRAINE; FRISK

καρπίζω   V 0-1-0-1-0-2
Jos 5,12; Prv 8,19
M: *to enjoy the fruits of* [τι] Jos 5,12; *id.* [τινα]
Prv 8,19

κάρπιμος,-ος,-ον   A 2-0-0-0-0-2

Gn 1,11.12
fruit-bearing; ξύλον κάρπιμον *fruit-tree*

καρπόβρωτος,-ος,-ον A 1-0-0-0-0-1
Dt 20,20
with edible fruit; neol.
Cf. DOGNIEZ 1992, 242

καρπολογέω
(→ἐπι-)

καρπός,-οῦ[+] N2M 26-3-37-41-18-125
Gn 1,11.12.29; 3,2.3
fruit Lv 25,3; *offspring, fruit* (of the womb)
Gn 30,2; *fruit, profit* (of actions) Ps 103(104),13;
οἱ καρποί *fruits of the earth, corn* Gn 4,3;
products, deeds Prv 10,16
καρποὶ στόματος *words* Prv 12,14; καρποὶ
χειλέων *id.* Prv 18,20; οἱ καρποὶ τῆς συνέσεως
the fruits of understanding, knowledge Sir 37,22;
καρποὶ χειρῶν *manual labour* Prv 31,16;
καρπὸς ξυλινός *tree-fruits* 1 Mc 10,30; ποιέω
καρπόν *to bear fruit, to become fruitful* Jer 12,2
*Hos 10,12 εἰς καρπὸν ζωῆς (*gather in) for the
fruit of life* -לפי חלד for MT לפי חסר (*gather in)
according to steadfast love*, cpr. Jb 11,17;
*Hos 14,3 καρπὸν χειλέων ἡμῶν *the fruit of
our lips* פרי משפתינו- for MT שפתינו פרים (*we offer) as
bulls our lips, our prayers*, cpr. Jer 27(50),27;
*Jb 22,21 ὁ καρπός σου *your fruit, your yield*
-תְּבוּאָתְךָ for MT תְּבוּאָתֶךָ (*good) will come to you*
Cf. DOGNIEZ 1992, 164(Dt 7,13); PARADISE 1986, 195-196;
WALTERS 1973, 311(Gn 30,2); →TWNT

καρπός,-οῦ N2M 0-1-0-2-0-3
1 Sm 5,4; Ps 127(128),2; Prv 31,20
wrist, palm (of the hand) 1 Sm 5,4; *hand* Prv
31,20

καρποφορέω[+] V 0-0-1-0-2-3
Hab 3,17; Od 4,17; Wis 10,7
to bear fruit

καρποφόρος,-ος,-ον[+] A 0-0-1-2-0-3
Jer 2,21; Ps 106(107),34; 148,9
fruit-bearing, fruitful

καρπόω V 2-0-0-2-2-6
Lv 2,11; Dt 26,14; Dn^LXX 3,38; Dn^Th 3,38(23);
1 Ezr 4,52
to offer Lv 2,11; *to offer as a burnt offering*
Dt 26,14
Cf. DANIEL 1966, 165-172; HARLÉ 1988, 90(Lv 2,11)

κάρπωμα,-ατος N3N 52-4-0-1-1-58
Ex 29,25.38.41; 30,9; 40,6
rare Greek word originally meaning *offering of
yield*, in LXX mostly rendering the Hebr. אִשֶּׁה

undetermined burnt offering; *burnt offering*
Ex 29,25
ποιέω κάρπωμα *to bring a burnt offering*
Nm 15,14
Cf. DANIEL 1966, 155.169(Nm 18,9).240-244.252.254;
DORIVAL 1994, 493; HARLÉ 1988, 39-40.86; LE BOULLUEC
1989, 299-300(Ex 29,25); MONTEVECCHI 1964, 46-47;
WEVERS 1990, 477.644(Ex 40,6); →LSJ Suppl; LSJ RSuppl

κάρπωσις,-εως N3F 3-0-0-0-1-4
Lv 4,10.18; 22,22; Sir 30,19
rare Greek word originally meaning *offering of
yield*, in LXX once rendering the Hebr. אִשֶּׁה
undetermined burnt offering; *burnt offering*
Lv 4,10
ποιέω κάρπωσιν *to offer a burnt offering* Jb 42,8
Cf. MONTEVECCHI 1964, 46-47; WEVERS 1993, 110; →LSJ
RSuppl

καρπωτός,-ός,-όν A 0-2-0-0-0-2
2 Sm 13,18.19
reaching to the wrist; χιτὼν καρπωτός *a coat
with sleeves down to the wrist*

κάρταλλος,-ου N2M 2-1-1-0-1-5
Dt 26,2.4; 2 Kgs 10,7; Jer 6,9; Sir 11,30
basket with pointed bottom; neol.?
Cf. DOGNIEZ 1992, 275; LEE, J. 1983, 115-116

καρτερέω[+] V 0-0-1-1-8-10
Is 42,14; Jb 2,9; 2 Mc 7,17; 4 Mc 9,9.28
to be steadfast Sir 2,2; *to be patient, to wait*
Sir 12,15; *to wait* 2 Mc 7,17; *to endure* Is 42,14;
to bear patiently, to endure [τι] 4 Mc 9,9; *to
persevere in doing* [+ptc.] Jb 2,9
→TWNT
(→δια-, ἐγ-, προσ-)

καρτερία,-ας N1F 0-0-0-0-6-6
4 Mc 6,13; 8,26; 11,12; 15,28.30
endurance, perseverance 4 Mc 6,13; *obstinacy*
(neg.) 4 Mc 8,26; *adherence to, perseverance in*
[εἴς τι] 4 Mc 11,12
Cf. HAAS 1989, 126

καρτερός,-ά,-όν A 0-0-0-0-6-6
2 Mc 10,29; 12,11.35; 3 Mc 1,4; 4 Mc 3,12
strong (of pers.) 2 Mc 12,35; *sharp* (of fight)
2 Mc 10,29; *violent* (of winds) 4 Mc 15,32

καρτεροψυχία,-ας N1F 0-0-0-0-1-1
4 Mc 9,26
constancy of soul, steadfastness of spirit

καρτερῶς D 0-0-0-0-1-1
4 Mc 15,31
strongly; καρτερῶς ὑπέμενεν *withstood
powerfully*

καρύα,-ης   N1F 0-0-0-1-0-1
Ct 6,11
nut-bearing tree
Cf. SHIPP 1979, 305; WEVERS 1993, 728

καρύϊνος,-η,-ον   A 1-0-1-0-0-2
Gn 30,37; Jer 1,11
of almond
Cf. WALTERS 1973, 297

καρυΐσκος,-ου   N2M 2-0-0-0-0-2
Ex 25,33.34
dim. of καρύον; *almond, flower of almond*;
neol.?
Cf. LE BOULLUEC 1989, 263; WEVERS 1990, 407

κάρυον,-ου   N2N 2-0-0-0-0-2
Gn 43,11; Nm 17,23
almond
Cf. DORIVAL 1994, 362

καρυωτός,-ή,-όν   A 1-0-0-0-0-1
Ex 38,16(37,23)
almond-like
Cf. WEVERS 1990, 625; →LSJ RSuppl

κάρφος,-ους⁺   N3N 1-0-0-0-0-1
Gn 8,11
dry twig, sprig
Cf. HARL 1986ᵃ, 137

κασία,-ας   N1F 0-0-1-2-0-3
Ez 27,17; Jb 42,14; Ps 44(45),9
Semit. loanword (Hebr. קציעה); *cassia* Ps 44(45),9;
Κασία *Cassia* (girl's name) Jb 42,14
Cf. CAIRD 1976, 78; TOV 1979, 221

κασσιτέρινος,-η,-ον   A 0-0-1-0-0-1
Zech 4,10
made of tin; λίθος κασσιτέρινος *the stone
made of tin* i.e. *the plumb-stone* or *plumb-line*

κασσίτερος,-ου   N2M 1-0-3-0-1-5
Nm 31,22; Ez 22,18.20; 27,12; Sir 47,18
tin

κατά⁺   P 558-515-315-253-499-2140
Gn 1,11(ter).12(bis)
[τινος]: *down from* 2 Mc 6,10; *down upon*
3 Mc 2,22; *upon* Jgs 3,22; *id.* (metaph.)
Nm 30,13(tertio); *down into* 4 Mc 12,19; *down,
under* 3 Mc 6,7; *after* 2 Kgs 4,4; *by* (with verbs
of swearing to denote what one swears by)
Jdt 1,12; *against* Jos 24,22; *concerning* Est 3,10;
for (in hostile sense) 4 Mc 10,14
[τινα, τι]: *(downwards) to* Gn 24,62; *down into*
(metaph.) Nm 30,13(primo, secundo); *on, at* (of
place) Ex 14,16; *over, through* Ex 11,6; *at* (of
time) Ex 23,15; *every* (with word denoting time)

2 Mc 6,7; *by* (with numbers) 1 Kgs 18,4; *towards*
Gn 2,8; *in accordance with, according to, in
conformity with, corresponding to* Nm 30,7; *just
as, similarly to* Ex 25,40; *after the fashion of,
according to* Gn 1,26; *for, because of* Dt 19,15;
in relation to, concerning Gn 39,6; *during, by*
Gn 20,6; *in relation to, for, to, by* Gn 30,40
ἀριστεύω κατά τινος *to be superior to*
4 Mc 2,18; κατὰ ἀλήθειαν *truly* (κατά +abstr.
subst. periphrasis for an adverb) 4 Mc 5,18;
κατὰ τόν Νεεμιαν *of Nehemiah, by Nehemiah*
2 Mc 2,13; κατὰ ποδάς τινος *close upon one's
heels* Gn 49,19; τὰ κατά σε *by your case* or
circumstances Tob 10,9; τὰ κατά τὸν ναόν
things pertaining the temple 1 Ezr 2,16
Cf. DREW-BEAR 1972, 200-201; JOHANNESSOHN 1910, 1-82;
1926, 245-259; LE BOULLUEC 1989, 323-324; LEE, J. 1983,
35(Lv 13,23); PORTER 1966, 45-55; SHIPP 1979, 306;
WALTERS 1973, 310(Ez 27,12; 4 Mc 15,7); WEVERS 1990,
437(Ex 27,12).454(Ex 28,21).511(Ex 31,11).603.795

καταβαίνω⁺   V 69-159-58-34-29-349
Gn 11,5.7; 12,10; 15,11; 18,21
to go down, to come down Gn 43,4; *id.*
(metaph.) Ps 7,17; *to come* or *go down from* [ἔκ
τινος] Ex 32,1; *id.* [ἀπό τινος] Ex 32,15; *to
descend* (of the Lord from heaven) Ex 19,11; *to
alight, to settle on, to perch on* [ἐπί τι] (of
birds) Gn 15,11; *to go down, to descend (to a
river)* Ex 2,5; *to go down, to flow to the sea*
Jos 3,16; *to descend (to the earth)* Ex 33,9; *to go
ashore* Ez 27,29; *to come down, to drop* Is 55,10;
to come down, to precipitate, to settle, to deposit
(of dawn, manna) Nm 11,9; *to pour down* (of
hail) Is 32,19; *to go down to* [τι] Ps 103(104),8;
to go down against sb [ἐπί τινα] 2 Chr 20,16; *to
pass from ... to* [ἀπό τινος ἐπί τι] (of the
border) Nm 34,11; *to lead down* Neh 3,15; *to go
down on the degrees of the dial* [τι] (of the sun)
Is 38,8
καταβαίνω εἰς ᾅδου *to go down to Hades, to
die* Nm 16,30; καταβαίνω εἰς Αἴγυπτον *to go
down to Egypt* Gn 12,10; καταβαίνω τὸ ὄρος *to
go down the mountain* Jdt 10,10; οἱ
καταβαίνοντες εἰς τὴν θάλασσαν ἐν πλοίοις
those who sail downstream towards the sea
Ps 106(107),23; δάκρυα καταβαίνει ἐπί
σιαγόνα *tears run down the cheek* Sir 35,15
*2 Kgs 9,32 κατάβηθι μετ' ἐμοῦ *come (down)
with me* -אָתִי עִמִּי? ◊אתה0 for MT אֲתִּי מִי (*who is) with
me, who*; *Jer 28(51),14 οἱ καταβαίνοντες

those who came down -◊ירד for MT הירד *cry, shout*;
*Ez 31,18 κατάβηθι καὶ καταβιβάσθητι
descend and be brought down -והורדת רדה for MT
והורדת *and you will be brought down*, cpr.
Ez 32,18; *Ez 47,15 καταβαινούσης *that
descends* -הירד for MT הדרך *the road?*, cpr. Ez 48,1
Cf. BEWER 1953, 165(Ez 31,18); WEVERS 1990,
298(Ex 19,10).388(Ex 24,16); 1993, 728

καταβάλλω⁺   V 0-6-14-12-15-47
2 Sm 20,15; 2 Kgs 3,19.25; 6,5; 19,7
A: *to throw down* [abs.] Jb 12,14; *id.* [τι]
2 Sm 20,15; *to fell, to cut down* [τι] 2 Kgs 3,19;
to overthrow, to cast down [τινα] Jb 16,9; *to
overthrow with, to strike down with, to slay* [τινά
τινι] 1 Mc 4,33; *id.* [τινα ἐν τινι] (semit.)
2 Kgs 19,7; *to cast down, to reject* [τινα]
Ps 36(37),14; *to beat down* [τι] Sir 47,4; *to fall*
Sir 14,18
M: *to found* [τι] 2 Mc 2,13

καταβάλλομαι τρόπαιά τινος *to set down the
trophies of, to win the trophies from, to win
victories over* 2 Mc 5,6; καταβάλλω τὸ σπέρμα
αὐτῶν *to cast down their descendants*
Ps 105(106),27; καταβάλλω τι ἐκ χειρός τινος
to smite sth out of sb's hand Ez 30,22;
καταβάλλω ἔλεον *to make a humble
supplication* Bar 2,19
*Is 16,9 κατέβαλεν *threw down* -◊רמה (Aram.)
for MT רמעתי *(with) my tears*; see καταπίπτω

καταβαρύνω⁺   V 0-2-1-0-0-3
2 Sm 13,25; 14,26; Jl 2,8
M: *to weigh down upon, to grow heavy upon*
[ἐπί τινα] 2 Sm 14,26
P: *to become burdensome for* [ἐπί τινα]
(metaph.) 2 Sm 13,25
*Jl 2,8 καταβαρυνόμενοι *weighed down,
burdened* -◊כבר for MT גבר *man*

καταβάσιος,-ος,-ον   A 0-0-0-0-1-1
Wis 10,6
descending; neol.

κατάβασις,-εως⁺   N3F 0-7-2-0-3-12
Jos 8,24; 10,11; Jgs 1,16; 1 Sm 23,20
descent, precipice Mi 1,4; *falling down* (of snow)
Sir 43,18; *id.* (of hailstones) Sir 46,6
ἔργον καταβάσεως *beveled work* (temple decoration) 1 Kgs 7,16(29); ψυχὴν εἰς κατάβασιν
desire to come down 1 Sm 23,20
*Jos 8,24 ἐν τῷ ὄρει ἐπὶ τῆς καταβάσεως *on
the mountain on the descent, on the descent of
the mountain* -במורד (כהר?) for MT במדבר *in the

wilderness, cpr. 7,5; 10,11; *Jgs 1,16 ἐπὶ καταβάσεως *at the descent* -במורד for MT ערד *Arad*

καταβιάζω   V 2-0-0-0-0-2
Gn 19,3; Ex 12,33
M: *to constrain* [τινα]

καταβιβάζω⁺   V 1-2-6-1-1-11
Dt 21,4; Jos 2,18; Jgsᴬ 7,5; Jer 28(51),40; Ez
26,20
A: *to make to go down to* [τινα εἰς τι] Jgsᴬ 7,5;
to bring down [τινα] Ez 28,8; *id.* [τι] (of anim.)
Dt 21,4; *to bring down to* [τινα πρός τινα]
Ez 26,20; *to let down* [τινα] Jos 2,18
P: *to descend* Ez 31,18
*Lam 1,9 καὶ κατεβίβασεν *and she brought
down* -ותרד for MT ותרד *she fell down*

καταβιβρώσκω   V 0-0-1-2-4-7
Ez 39,4; Neh 2,3.13; Sir 36,8; Belᴸˣˣ 31-32
P: *to be devoured* Ez 39,4
καταβρωσθῆναι πυρί *to be consumed by fire*
Neh 2,13; καταβρωσθῆναι ἐν πυρί *id.* (semit.)
Neh 2,3

καταβιόω   V 0-0-1-0-0-1
Am 7,12
to spend one's life

καταβλάπτω   V 0-0-0-0-1-1
3 Mc 7,8
to hurt greatly, to inflict damage upon [τινα]

καταβλέπω   V 1-0-0-0-0-1
Gn 18,16
to look down at [ἐπί τι]; neol.

καταβοάω⁺   V 4-0-0-0-1-5
Ex 5,15; 22,22.26; Dt 24,15; 2 Mc 8,3
to cry to, to make complaint to, to complain to
[πρός τινα] Ex 22,22; *to complain of sb to sb*
[κατά τινος πρός τινα] Dt 24,15

καταβόησις,-εως   N3F 0-0-0-0-1-1
Sir 35(32),15
outcry against [ἐπί τινι]; neol.

καταβολή,-ῆς⁺   N1F 0-0-0-0-1-1
2 Mc 2,29
building, structure

καταβόσκω   V 3-0-0-0-0-3
Ex 22,4(ter)
to feed flocks upon or *in* [τι]; *to put a flock to
graze* Ex 22,4(primo); *to graze* Ex 22,4(secundo,
tertio)

κατάβρωμα,-ατος   N3N 3-0-7-0-1-11
Nm 14,9; Dt 28,26; 31,17; Ez 21,37; 29,5
that which is to be devoured, food Dt 28,26; *prey*
Ez 21,37; neol.

Cf. DANIEL 1966, 137-138; DOGNIEZ 1992, 289-290;
DORIVAL 1994, 320

κατάβρωσις,-εως   N3F 1-0-0-0-1-2
Gn 31,15; Jdt 5,24
devouring Gn 31,15; *prey* Jdt 5,24; neol.

κατάγαιος,-ος,-ον   A 1-0-0-0-1-2
Gn 6,16; PSal 8,9
under the earth PSal 8,9; κατάγαια *lower deck
of the ark, ground-floor* Gn 6,16
Cf. WALTERS 1973, 113

καταγγέλλω[+]   V 0-0-0-0-2-2
2 Mc 8,36; 9,17
to announce, to declare
Cf. GAVENTA 1983, 381

καταγέλαστος,-ος,-ον[+]   A 0-0-0-0-1-1
Wis 17,8
ridiculous, worthy to be laughed at

καταγελάω[+]   V 1-1-1-13-6-22
Gn 38,23; 2 Chr 30,10; Mi 3,7; Ps 24(25),2; Jb
5,22
A: *to laugh, to scorn at* [τινος] 2 Chr 30,10; *id.*
[τινι] Jb 39,22; *id.* [ἔν τινι] Est 4,17q; *to
laugh down, to deride* [τινα] Sir 7,11
M: *to deride to scorn* [abs.] Prv 29,9
P: *to be laughed at, to be laughed to scorn* Jb
9,23

κατάγελως,-ωτος   N3M 0-0-0-1-3-4
Ps 43(44),14; Tob[S] 8,10; 1 Mc 10,70; PSal 4,7
derision PSal 4,7; *laughing-stock* Ps 43(44),14
Cf. CAIRD 1976, 81

καταγηράσκω   V 0-0-1-0-0-1
Is 46,4
to grow old

καταγίνομαι[+]   V 3-0-0-0-1-4
Ex 10,23; Nm 5,3; Dt 9,9; Bel[LXX] 21
to dwell, to abide; neol.?
Cf. DOGNIEZ 1992, 176; LEE, J. 1983, 95(Ex 10,23)

καταγινώσκω[+]   V 1-0-0-1-2-4
Dt 25,1; Prv 28,11; Sir 14,2; 19,5
to condemn [τινος] Dt 25,1; *to damn, to curse*
[τινος] Sir 14,2; *to disapprove* Prv 28,11
→MM

κατάγνυμι[+]   V 1-1-3-0-1-6
Dt 33,11; 2 Sm 22,35; Jer 31(48),25; Hab 3,12;
Zech 2,4
to break in pieces, to shatter [τι] Dt 33,11; *to
weaken, to break down* [τι] Jdt 9,8; *id.* [τινα]
Hab 3,12
*Zech 2,4 κατέαξαν *they broke in pieces* -כפו
◊כפה or -כפא (Aram.) for MT כפי *so that*

κατάγνωσις,-εως[+]   N3F 0-0-0-0-1-1
Sir 5,14
condemnation

καταγογγύζω   V 0-0-0-0-1-1
1 Mc 11,39
to murmur against [κατά τινος]; neol.

καταγορεύω   V 1-0-0-0-0-1
Nm 14,37
to announce, to report [τι]
Cf. DORIVAL 1994, 154

καταγράφω[+]   V 3-1-1-1-4-10
Ex 17,14; 32,15; Nm 11,26; 1 Chr 9,1; 2 Chr
20,34
A: *to engrave* [ἔν τινι] 1 Mc 14,26; *to write
down* [τι] Ex 17,14; *to enroll* [τινα] Nm 11,26;
to write against [κατά τινος] 1 Ezr 2,12
P: *to be written, to be designed* Sir 48,10
καταγράφω βίβλιον *to write a book* 2 Chr
20,34
Cf. DORIVAL 1994, 89

κατάγω[+]   V 10-16-15-13-17-71
Gn 37,25.28; 39,1(bis); 42,38
to lead (down) [τινα] 3 Mc 4,9; *to lead down,
esp. into the nether world* 1 Sm 2,6; *to bring
down* [τι] Gn 43,11; *to let down* [τινα] 1 Sm
19,12; *to cause to fall* [τι] (of tears) Sir 22,19; *to
cause to flow* [τι] Ps 77(78),16; *to bring down, to
destroy* [τι] Is 26,5; *to bring down* [τινα]
(metaph.) Ps 55(56),8; *to bring to, to reduce to*
[τινα εἴς τι] Sir 48,6; *to bring into court* [τινα]
3 Mc 7,5
κατάγω τι εἰς τὴν θάλασσαν *to bring to the sea*
1 Kgs 5,23; κατάγω τινὰ ἐπὶ τὴν γῆν *to bring
down to the ground* Ob 3; κατάγω τὴν ζωήν
(τινος) εἰς τὸν τάφον *to bring sb's life to the
grave* Tob 6,15; χρυσίῳ καταγομένῳ *with gold
applied to* 1 Kgs 6,35
*Is 9,2 κατήγαγες *you conducted* -חרגלת for MT
הגרלת *you increased*; *Lam 1,13 κατήγαγεν *he
has brought* -◊ירד for MT וירדנה ררה◊ *and it
dominated, it overcame*
Cf. SPICQ 1982, 369-373

καταδαμάζω   V 0-1-0-0-0-1
Jgs[A] 14,18
to subdue [τι] (of anim.)

καταδαπανάω   V 0-0-0-0-1-1
Wis 5,13
P: *to be consumed*

καταδείκνυμι   V 1-0-4-0-0-5
Gn 4,21; Is 40,26; 41,20; 43,15; 45,18

to discover and make known, to invent [τι] Gn 4,21; *to appoint, to create* [τινα] Is 43,15; *to create, to fashion* [τι] Is 45,18

Cf. RENEHAN 1975, 117; →LSJ Suppl; LSJ RSuppl

καταδέομαι   V 1-0-1-0-0-2
Gn 42,21; Is 57,10
to plead, to entreat earnestly [τινος] Gn 42,21

καταδεσμεύω   V 0-0-0-0-2-2
Sir 7,8; 30,7
to bind up, to bandage [τι] Sir 30,7
μὴ καταδεσμεύσης δὶς ἁμαρτίαν *do not repeat your sin* Sir 7,8
neol.

κατάδεσμος,-ου   N2M 0-0-1-0-0-1
Is 1,6
bandage

καταδέχομαι⁺   V 2-0-0-0-1-3
Ex 35,5; Dt 32,29; Od 2,29
to receive, to accept

Cf. DOGNIEZ 1992, 334; WEVERS 1990, 576

καταδέω⁺ (fut. -δήσω)   V 1-1-4-0-2-8
Nm 19,15; 1 Kgs 21(20),38; Is 46,1; Ez 30,21; 34,4
to bind fast [τι] Sir 28,24; *to bind up, to bandage* [τι] Sir 27,21
καταδέομαι τοὺς ὀφθαλμοὺς τελαμῶνι *to bind one's eyes with a bandage, to blindfold* 1 Kgs 21(20),38; πᾶν σκεῦος, ὅσα οὐχὶ δεσμὸν καταδέδεται ἐπ' αὐτῷ *every vessel that has not a covering attached to it* Nm 19,15

καταδιαιρέω⁺   V 0-0-1-3-0-4
Jl 4,2; Ps 47(48),14; 54(55),10; 135(136),13
A: *to divide* [τι] Ps 54(55),10; *to observe, to analyse sth in its constituent parts* [τι] Ps 47(48),14
M: *to distribute among themselves* [τι] Jl 4,2
neol.?

καταδικάζω⁺   V 0-0-0-6-5-11
Ps 36(37),33; 93(94),21; 108(109),7; Jb 34,29; Lam 3,36
A: *to pronounce guilty, to condemn* [τινα] Lam 3,36; *to condemn with* [τινά τινι] Wis 2,20
M: *to give judgement against, to condemn* [abs.] Jb 34,29
P: *to be condemned for* [τι] Wis 17,10
καταδικάζω τὴν κεφαλήν τινι *to condemn sb's head in the eyes of, to make sb guilty in the eyes of* DnᵀʰÞ 1,10
→TWNT

καταδίκη,-ης⁺   N1F 0-0-0-0-1-1

Wis 12,27
judgement given against one, condemnation

καταδιώκω⁺   V 12-40-6-25-8-91
Gn 14,14; 31,36; 33,13; 35,5; Ex 14,4
A: *to follow hard upon, to pursue closely* (most often in hostile sense) [abs.] Ex 14,23; *id.* [ὀπίσω τινός] Gn 31,36; *to pursue* [τινα] Dt 1,44; *to search for* [τινα] Ps 22(23),6; *id.* [τι] Ps 37(38),21; *to drive hard, to overdrive* [τι] (of a cattle) Gn 33,13; *to go with* [μετά τινος] 1 Sm 30,22
P: *to flee* Mi 2,11
οἱ καταδιώκοντες *pursuers* Jos 2,16; οἱ καταδιώκοντές με *my persecutors* Ps 30(31),16
*Mi 2,11(10) κατεδιώχθητε *you run, you flee* - ◊רוץ for MT נמרץ◊מרץ *painful*; *Lam 3,11 κατεδίωξεν *he pursued* - ◊דרך (Aram.) for MT דרכי *my way*
→MM

καταδολεσχέω   V 0-0-0-1-0-1
Lam 3,20
to chatter at, to meditate with [ἐπί τινα]; *Lam 3,20 καὶ καταδολεσχήσει *and shall consider (me)* - ותשיח◊שיח for MT ותשיח◊שוח? *is bowed down (within me)*?; neol.

Cf. ALBREKTSON 1963, 143

καταδουλόω⁺   V 3-0-3-1-3-10
Gn 47,21; Ex 1,14; 6,5; Jer 15,14; Ez 29,18
M: *to cause to serve, to cause to labour* [τινα] Ex 1,14; *to oppress* [τινα] Ezr 7,24; *to enslave with* [τινά τι] Ex 6,5
κατεδουλώσατο τὴν δύναμιν αὐτοῦ δουλείᾳ μεγάλῃ ἐπὶ Τύρου *he made his army labour hard against Tyre* Ez 29,18
*Gn 47,21 κατεδουλώσατο *he made slaves* - העביד for MT העביר *he urged to pass, he removed*; *Jer 15,14 καταδουλώσω *I will enslave* - והעבדתי for MT והעברתי *I will transfer*

Cf. BARTHÉLEMY 1982, 264(Gn 47,21); DANIEL, 1966, 58-63; LE BOULLUEC 1989, 77; WEVERS 1990, 7

καταδρομή,-ῆς   N1F 0-0-0-0-1-1
2 Mc 5,3
charge, attack (by an army)

καταδυναστεία,-ας   N1F 1-0-4-0-0-5
Ex 6,7; Jer 6,6; Ez 22,12; 45,9; Am 3,9
oppression; neol.

Cf. LE BOULLUEC 1989, 77; LEE, J. 1983, 48; WEVERS 1990, 5

καταδυναστεύω⁺   V 3-4-19-2-7-35
Ex 1,13; 21,17(16); Dt 24,7; 1 Sm 12,3.4

A: *to oppress* [τινα] Ex 1,13; *to prevail against* [τινα] Hos 5,11; *id.* [ἐπί τι] 2 Chr 21,17; *to conquer* [τι] 2 Sm 8,11

P: *to be enslaved* Neh 5,5

Cf. AEJMELAEUS 1987, 83-85(Ex 21,17); DOGNIEZ 1992, 245; LE BOULLUEC 1989, 77.218(Ex 21,17); WEVERS 1990, 330-331

κατάδυσις,-εως N3F 0-1-0-0-0-1
1 Kgs 15,13

hole, hiding place; *1 Kgs 15,13 τὰς καταδύσεις αὐτῆς *her hiding places, her secret cultic places?* -מצלותה? for MT מפלצתה *her secret horrible thing, her idol?*

→SCHLEUSNER

καταδύω V 1-0-3-0-1-5
Ex 15,5; Jer 28(51),64; Am 9,3; Mi 7,19; Od 1,5

A: *to go down, to sink into* [εἰς τι] Ex 15,5; *to make to sink, to dismiss* [τι εἰς τι] Mi 7,19

M: *to go down, to sink* Jer 28(51),64

Cf. WEVERS 1990, 229

καταθαρσέω V 0-1-0-0-0-1
2 Chr 32,8

to be encouraged at [ἐπί τινι]; neol.?

καταθλάω V 0-0-1-1-0-2
Is 63,3; Ps 41(42),11

to crush in pieces, to break [τι] Ps 41(42),11; *id.* [τινα] Is 63,3; neol.

καταθύμιος,-α,-ον A 0-0-2-0-0-2
Is 44,9; Mi 7,3

according to one's mind; τὰ καταθύμια *desires* Is 44,9

καταθύμιόν τινος ἐστιν *it is the desire of* Mi 7,3

καταιγίς,-ίδος⁺ N3F 0-0-12-13-4-29
Is 5,28; 17,13; 21,1; 28,15.17

squall descending from above, hurricane, storm Ps 49(50),3

πνεῦμα καταιγίδος *stormy wind* Ps 10(11),6; καταιγὶς ὕδατος *waterflood* Ps 68(69),16

καταιδέομαι V 0-0-0-0-1-1
4 Mc 3,12

to revere, to stand in awe of [τι]

καταικίζω V 0-0-0-0-6-6
4 Mc 6,3; 7,2; 9,15; 11,1; 12,13

A: *to maltreat, to torture* [τινα] 4 Mc 9,15

P: *to be disfigured, to be tortured by* [τινι] 4 Mc 11,1

καταισχύνω⁺ V 0-5-34-27-13-79
JgsᴮB 18,7; 2 Sm 10,6; 16,21; 19,6; 2 Kgs 19,26

A: *to dishonour, to put to shame* [τινα] 2 Sm

16,21; *to disappoint* [τινα] Ps 118(119),31; *to dishonour, to violate, to rape* [τινα] (of women) Ru 2,15; *to put to shame* [τι] Jgsᴮ 18,7; *to live dishonestly* Sir 22,4

M/P: *to be ashamed* Jer 10,14; *to be ashamed of* [ἀπό τινος] Jer 31(48),13

*2 Sm 10,6 κατῃσχύνθησαν *they were ashamed* -נבושו ◊בוש(?) for MT נבאש *they had become odious;* *2 Sm 16,21 κατῄσχυνας *you have dishonoured* -הבישת for MT נבאשת *you have made yourself odious;* *Is 28,16 καταισχυνθῇ *he shall be ashamed* -יבש for MT יחיש ◊חוש *he will panic, he will be in haste;* *Jer 27(50),38 καταισχυνθήσονται *they shall be ashamed* -בושו ◊יבושו for MT יבשו ◊יבש *that they may be dried up;* *Ez 24,12 καταισχυνθήσεται *he shall become shameful* -באשה? for MT ב/אש *in fire*

Cf. HELBING 1928, 262; SCHREINER 1957, 103(Jgs 18,7)

κατακαίω⁺ V 38-15-31-7-8-99
Gn 38,24; Ex 3,2.3; 12,10; 29,14

A: *to burn completely, to destroy* [τι] Ps 45(46),10; *to burn down* [τι] 2 Kgs 23,15; *to burn up, to consume* [τι] (as an offering) Ex 12,10; *to burn* [τι] (of feet) Prv 6,28; *to burn alive* [τινα] Gn 38,24

P: *to be consumed* Ex 3,2; *to be burnt, to be scorched* (of hair) Dnᴸˣˣ 3,94

κατακαίω τι πυρί *to burn with fire* Ex 29,14; κατακαίω τι ἐν πυρί (semit.) Ex 32,20; κατακαίω τι εἰς τι *to burn to* (of bones burnt to lime) Am 2,1

Cf. MARGOLIS 1906ᵇ=1972, 68

κατακάλυμμα,-ατος N3N 9-0-2-0-0-11
Ex 26,14; 38,19; 40,19.21; Nm 3,25

covering, curtain; neol.?

Cf. DORIVAL 1994, 119-120.211; LE BOULLUEC 1989, 348; WEVERS 1990, 647

κατακαλύπτω⁺ V 10-1-12-1-2-26
Gn 38,15; Ex 26,34; 29,22; Lv 3,3.14

A: *to cover with* [τί τινι] Ex 26,34; *to cover* [τι] (of a cloud) Ez 38,9; *to cover, to flood* [τι] (of pers.) Nm 22,5; *id.* [τινα] (of water) Hab 2,14; *id.* [τινα] (of dust) Ez 26,10; *to cover* [τι] (metaph.) Jer 28(51),51

M: *to disguise* 2 Chr 18,29

ἡ κατακεκαλυμμένη *she who is covered, she who wears a veil* Susᵀʰ 32; τὸ στέαρ τὸ κατακαλύπτον τὴν κοιλίαν *the fat that covers the belly* Ex 29,22; κατακαλύπτομαι τὸ πρόσωπον *to cover one's face, to wear a veil* Gn

38,15; κατακεκαλυμμένα τὰ προστάγματα *the words are to remain hidden* Dn^LXX 12,9

Cf. DORIVAL 1994, 120; WEVERS 1990, 429(Ex 26,34)

κατακάμπτω V 0-0-0-2-2-4
Ps 37(38),7; 56(57),7; 4 Mc 11,10; Od 12,10
to bend down [τι] 4 Mc 11,10; *id.* [τινα] Ps 37(38),7; *id.* (metaph.) Ps 56(57),7

κατάκαρπος,-ος,-ον⁺ A 0-0-1-1-0-2
Hos 14,7; Ps 51(52),10
fruitful; neol.?

κατακάρπως D 0-0-1-0-0-1
Zech 2,8
fully, abundantly; neol.

κατακάρπωσις,-εως N3F 2-0-0-0-0-2
Lv 6,3.4
ashes of a burnt-sacrifice; neol.

Cf. DANIEL 1966, 169-170; HARLÉ 1988, 104

κατάκαυμα,-ατος N3N 8-0-2-0-0-10
Ex 21,25(bis); Lv 13,24(bis).25
(fiery) inflammation Lv 13,24; *burning* Nm 19,6
τὸ ὕδωρ εἰς κατάκαυμά ἐστιν *the water shall be dried up* Jer 31(48),34
*Hos 7,4 κατακαύματος *of the burning* corr. καταπαύματος *of the stopping* (of the fire) for MT ישבות *he stops* (the fire)

κατακαυχάομαι⁺ V 0-0-3-0-0-3
Jer 27(50),11.38; Zech 10,12
to boast [abs.] Jer 27(50),11
*Zech 10,12 κατακαυχήσονται *they shall boast* -יתהללו for MT יתהלכו *they shall walk* neol.

κατάκειμαι⁺ V 0-0-0-2-2-4
Prv 6,9; 23,34; Jdt 13,15; Wis 17,7
to lie down Jdt 13,15; *to be idle* Prv 6,9; *to be idle, to be ineffective* Wis 17,7

Cf. LARCHER 1985, 958-959

κατακενόω V 1-1-0-0-0-2
Gn 42,35; 2 Sm 13,9
to empty [τι] Gn 42,35; *to pour out* [τι] 2 Sm 13,9; neol.?

κατακεντέω⁺ V 0-0-2-0-1-3
Jer 28(51),4; Ez 23,47; Jdt 16,12
to pierce through, to stab, to kill [τινα]

κατακλάω⁺ V 0-0-1-0-0-1
Ez 19,12
P: *to be broken down, to be snapped off*

κατάκλειστος,-ος,-ον A 0-0-0-0-3-3
2 Mc 3,19; 3 Mc 1,18; Wis 18,4
shut up Wis 18,4; *kept inside, shut up* (of young women) 2 Mc 3,19; neol.?

Cf. LARCHER 1985, 991

κατακλείω⁺ V 0-0-1-0-4-5
Jer 39(32),3; 2 Mc 13,21; 3 Mc 3,25; Wis 17,2.15
A: *to shut up in, to enclose in* [τινα ἔν τινι] Jer 39(32),3
P: *to be shut up in* [τινι] Wis 17,2; *id.* [εἴς τι] Wis 17,15; *to be put in prison* 2 Mc 13,21

Cf. CAIRD 1976, 81

κατακληροδοτέω⁺ V 1-0-0-0-1-2
Dt 21,16; 1 Mc 3,36
to divide and leave as an inheritance [τινί τι] Dt 21,16; *to seize and parcel out* (land) [τι] 1 Mc 3,36; neol.; see κατακληρονομέω

κατακληρονομέω⁺ V 19-18-15-2-8-62
Nm 13,30; 33,54; 34,13.18; Dt 1,38
A: *to receive possession of* [τι] Dt 3,20; *to seize possession of* [τι] (with violence) Hab 1,6; *to obtain as one's assured possession* [τινα] (women) Sir 4,16; *to receive a possession among* [ἔν τινι] Jos 22,19
to give or *divide sth as possession to sb* [τί τινα] (semit.) Jer 3,18; *id.* [τί τινι] (semit.) Nm 34,18; *to give* or *divide possession to sb* [τινα] (semit.) Sir 44,21; *id.* [τινι] (semit.) Jos 14,1; *to give sb as possession* [τινα] (semit.) Jos 13,32; *to make sb heir, to give an inheritance to* [τινα] Sir 46,1
P: *to have obtained a share* Dt 19,14
ὄνομα αἰῶνος κατακληρονομήσει *he shall inherit an everlasting name* Sir 15,6
*2 Sm 7,1 κατεκληρονόμησεν αὐτόν *he gave him an inheritance* -הנחילו for MT הניח לו *he gave him rest*; *Ez 22,16 καὶ κατακληρονομήσω ἐν σοί *and I shall inherit you* -ונחלתי בך for MT ונחלת בך ◊ חללנ *you shall be profaned by you, you shall profane yourself*

Cf. DOGNIEZ 1992, 120; DORIVAL 1994, 169.186.315; HELBING 1928, 138-141; MURAOKA 1990, 43; →TWNT

κατακληρόω V 0-6-0-0-0-6
1 Sm 10,20.21(bis); 14,42(bis)
M: *to recieve by lot* [τι] 1 Sm 14,47; *to assign by the lot* [τινα] 1 Sm 14,42
P: *to be taken by lot, to be chosen* 1 Sm 10,20 neol.

κατακλίνω⁺ V 2-3-0-1-2-8
Ex 21,18; Nm 24,9; Jgs^B 5,27(bis); 1 Sm 16,11
A: *to make sb lay down* [τινα] 3 Mc 1,3
P: *to lie* or *recline* (at table), *to sit down* [abs.] 1 Sm 16,11; *id.* [ἐπί τινος] Jdt 12,15; *to lie (down)* [abs.] Nm 24,9; *to bow* Jgs^B 5,27

κατακλιθῇ δὲ ἐπὶ τὴν κοίτην *and he laid upon his bed* Ex 21,18

Cf. LEE, J. 1983, 28; MARGOLIS 1907, 247; WEVERS 1990, 331

κατάκλιτος,-ος,-ον   A 0-0-1-0-0-1
Is 3,23
flowing down; (θέριστρα) κατάκλιτα *(light summer garments) flowing down*; neol.

κατακλύζω⁺   V 0-0-5-6-2-13
Jer 29(47),2(bis); Ez 13,11.13; 38,22
A: *to overflow, to inundate* [τι] Jer 29(47)2; *to wash away* [τι or τινα] Dnᵀʰ 11,26; *to overwhelm* (metaph.) Dnᵀʰ 11,10; *to drown* [τινα] Wis 10,19
P: *to run abundantly* Ps 77(78),20; *to be drowned with the flood* Wis 10,4
ὑετὸς κατακλύζων *flooding rain* Ez 13,11.13; 38,22

κατακλυσμός,-οῦ⁺   N2M 12-0-1-3-7-23
Gn 6,17; 7,6.7.10.17
flood, deluge Gn 6,17; *flood, inundation* Sir 39,22; *flood* (metaph.) 4 Mc 15,32

Cf. HARL 1986ᵃ, 133; RÖSEL 1994, 169-170; SCHMITT 1974, 153

κατακολουθέω⁺   V 0-0-1-1-3-5
Jer 17,16; Dnᴸˣˣ 9,10; 1 Ezr 7,1; Jdt 11,6; 1 Mc 6,23
to follow after [ὀπίσω τινός] Jer 17,16; *to comply with, to obey* [τινι] Dnᴸˣˣ 9,10; *to act in conformity with, to live up to* [τινι] Jdt 11,6; *to obey, to carry out* [τινι] 1 Ezr 7,1; neol.?

→LSJ RSuppl; MM

κατακονδυλίζω   V 0-0-1-0-0-1
Am 5,11
to strike with the fist [τινα]

κατακοντίζω   V 0-0-0-1-1-2
Jb 30,14; Jdt 1,15
to shoot down with [τινά τινι] Jb 30,14; *id.* [τινα ἐν τινι] (semit.) Jdt 1,15

κατάκοπος,-ος,-ον   A 0-1-0-2-1-4
Jgsᴬ 5,26; Jb 3,17; 16,7; 2 Mc 12,36
weary, wearied; neol.

κατακόπτω⁺   V 3-6-10-1-2-22
Gn 14,5.7; Nm 14,45; Jos 10,10; 11,8
A: *to cut in pieces, to cut down, to destroy* [τι] 2 Chr 15,16; *id.* [τινα] Gn 14,5; *to cut off* [τι] Is 18,5; *to cut down with* [τινα ἐν τινι] (semit.) Jer 20,4
P: *to be slain, to be killed* 2 Mc 1,13
λίθους κατακεκομμένους *stones broken to*

pieces Is 27,9; κατακόπτω τὰς ῥομφαίας εἰς ἄροτρα *to beat swords into ploughshares* Mi 4,3
*Jgsᴮ 20,43 κατέκοπτον *they cut down* -כתתו or כרתו for MT כתרו *surrounded*; *Am 1,5 καὶ κατακόψω *and I will cut in pieces* -ורדומה or ורדמתי for MT ותומך *and the one who supports, who holds*, cpr. Hos 4,5; *Zph 1,11 τὴν κατακεκομμένην *that had been broken down* -מכתש◇שׁ◇כתש◇◇ for MT המכתש *the Mortar* (place in Jerusalem)

κατακοσμέω   V 1-0-1-0-1-3
Ex 39,5(38,28); Is 61,10; 1 Mc 4,57
to adorn, to decorate [τι] Ex 39,5 (38,28); *id.* [τινα] Is 61,10

Cf. WEVERS 1990, 635

κατακρατέω   V 0-4-8-0-18-30
1 Sm 14,42; 1 Kgs 12,24u; 2 Chr 12,1.4; Jer 8,5
A: *to prevail against* [τινος] 1 Sm 14,42; *to prevail* [abs.] Mi 1,9; *to become master of, to conquer* [τινος] 1 Mc 8,4; *to obtain* or *retain possession of* [τινος] 2 Chr 12,4; *to usurp* [τινος] 1 Mc 15,3; *to occupy* [τι] Jer 47(40),10; *to seize upon, to overcome* [τινος] (of pains) Mi 4,9; *to be master of, to rule over* [τι] 1 Ezr 4,2; *to strengthen oneself* (of pers.) 1 Kgs 12,24u; *to strengthen, to make stronger* [τινος] Na 3,14
P: *to strengthen oneself* (of pers.) Jer 8,5; *to grow strong* (of things) 2 Chr 12,1; *to be in possession of* [ὑπό τινος] 1 Mc 15,33
κατακρατεῖ τοῦ ἐννοήματος αὐτοῦ *he controls his thoughts* Sir 21,11

κατακρημνίζω⁺   V 0-1-0-0-3-4
2 Chr 25,12; 2 Mc 12,15; 14,43; 4 Mc 4,25
to throw down a precipice [τινα] 2 Chr 25,12; *to cast down, to destroy* [τι] 2 Mc 12,15

κατακρίνω⁺   V 0-0-0-2-6-8
Est 2,1; Dnᴸˣˣ 4,37a(34); Wis 4,16; PSal 4,2; Susᴸˣˣ 53
to condemn [τινα] Est 2,1
κατακρίνω τινὰ θανάτῳ *to condemn to death* Dnᴸˣˣ 4,37a; κατακρίνω τινὰ ἀποθανεῖν *id.* Susᵀʰ 41

→MM

κατακρούω   V 0-1-0-0-0-1
Jgsᴬ 16,14
to fasten with, to nail [τι ἐν τινι] (semit.)

→LSJ RSuppl

κατακρύπτω   V 1-4-7-2-1-15
Gn 35,4; Jos 10,16; 2 Kgs 7,8; 2 Chr 18,24; 22,12
A: *to hide* [τι] Gn 35,4; *id.* [abs.] Ps 55(56),7
M/P: *to hide oneself in* [εἴς τι] Jos 10,16

κατακρύψεις αὐτοὺς ἐν ἀποκρύφῳ τοῦ προσώπου σου *you shall hide them in the secret of your presence* Ps 30(31),21

κατακτάομαι V 0-1-0-0-1-2
2 Chr 28,10; 2 Mc 6,25
to get for oneself, to win [τι] 2 Mc 6,25; *to win as, to keep for* [τινα εἴς τινα] 2 Chr 28,10

κατακτείνω V 0-0-0-0-2-2
4 Mc 11,3; 12,11
to kill, to slay [τινα]

κατακυλίω V 0-2-1-0-0-3
JgsᴮB 5,27; 1 Sm 14,8; Jer 28(51),25
A: *to roll down* [τινα] Jer 28(51),25
P: *to be rolled down* JgsᴮB 5,27
*1 Sm 14,8 καὶ κατακυλισθησόμεθα πρός *and we will come down upon* -גלל for MT ◊גלה *we will show ourselves*

κατακύπτω⁺ V 0-1-0-0-0-1
2 Kgs 9,32
to look down

κατακυριεύω⁺ V 5-0-1-8-2-16
Gn 1,28; 9,1; Nm 21,24; 32,22.29
A: *to exercise complete dominion* [abs.] Ps 71(72),8; *to become master over, to become possessor of, to get dominion over* [τινος] Nm 21,24; *to be master over, to rule* [τινος] Gn 1,28; *id.* (metaph.) Ps 118(119),133
P: *to be subdued* Nm 32,22
*Ps 9,26(10,5) κατακυριεύσει *he will rule* -◊פהה? for MT יפיח *he scoffs?*; *Ps 9,31(10,10) ἐν τῷ αὐτὸν κατακυριεῦσαι *when he has mastered* -בעצמו for MT בעצומיו *by their might*
neol.
Cf. HARL 1986ᵃ, 97

καταλαλέω⁺ V 3-0-4-6-0-13
Nm 12,8; 21,5.7; Hos 7,13; Mi 3,7
to talk down, to speak ill [τινος] Ps 100(101),5; *to speak against* [πρός τινα] Nm 21,5; *id.* [τινος] Jb 19,3; *id.* [κατά τινος] Nm 12,8
*Prv 20,13 καταλαλεῖν *to speak ill* -◊שנה? (verb) *to speak again, to repeat* for MT שֵׁנָה (subst.) *sleep*
Cf. DORIVAL 1994, 55

καταλαλιά,-ᾶς⁺ N1F 0-0-0-0-1-1
Wis 1,11
evil report, slander; neol.

καταλαμβάνω⁺ V 13-31-19-20-43-126
Gn 19,19; 31,23.25; 44,4; Ex 15,9
A: *to take, lay hold of* [τι] Jgs 7,24; *to take, to overtake* [τινα] (of God) Jb 5,13; *to overtake, to befall* [τινα] (of evil) Gn 19,19; *to overtake*

[τινα] (often after a pursuit) Gn 31,23; *to reach* [τινα] (of men reaching God) Mi 6,6; *to overtake, to take hold of* [τινα] (of sin; metaph.) Ps 39(40),13; *to lay hold of, to come over, to overtake* [τινα] (of feelings; metaph.) Ps 68(69),25; *to take prisoner* [τινα] 2 Chr 25,23; *to take, to capture* [τι] (of city) 2 Sm 12,26
to comprehend, to understand [τι] Jb 34,24, cpr. Dnᴸˣˣ 1,20
to find sb doing [τινα +pred.] 1 Ezr 6,8; *to detect, to catch in the act of doing* (esp. of the detection of adultery) [τινα] Susᴸˣˣ 58, see also Jer 3,8 (double transl. of the Hebr.)
M: *to seize, to lay hold on* [τι] Prv 1,13; *to overtake, to take hold of* [τινα] (of sin) Jdt 11,11; *to take, to capture* [τι] (of city) Nm 21,32; *to occupy, to keep* [τι] 1 Mc 11,46
P: *to be taken, to be stolen* Ex 22,3; *to be detected* Ob 6; *to be convicted* Jer 3,8
καταλαμβάνω τινὰ ἐν δεσμοῖς *to take in bonds, to capture* 2 Chr 33,11; φιλίαν καταλαμβάνομαί τινι *to form friendship with* 1 Mc 10,23; καταλάβωσιν τρίβους εὐθείας *they comprehend, they understand the paths of life* Prv 2,19; κατειλημμένη ἐν ἀγῶνι θανάτου *seized by the agony of death* Est 4,17k; καταλήμψεται ὁ ἀλοητὸς τὸν τρύγητον *the threshingtime shall overtake the vintage* Lv 26,5; οἳ κατελάβοσαν τοὺς πατέρας ὑμῶν *(the prophets) who convicted your fathers* Zech 1,6
*2 Chr 9,20 χρυσίῳ κατειλημμένα *with gold, stolen?* corr.? χρυσίῳ κατακεκλεισμένα for MT זהב סגור *covered with gold, of pure gold*, cpr. 1 Kgs 6,20; *Jer 28(51),34 κατέλαβέν με *he came upon me* -ישיני? for MT יניחני *put me away*
Cf. MARGOLIS 1906ᵃ=1972, 77; →LSJ Suppl(2 Chr 9,20)

καταλάμπω⁺ V 0-0-0-0-1-1
Wis 17,19
M: *to shine with* (light) [τινι]

καταλεαίνω V 0-0-0-1-0-1
Dnᴸˣˣ 7,23
to grind down [τι]; neol.

καταλέγω⁺ V 1-0-0-0-1-2
Dt 19,16; 2 Mc 7,30
to tell, to recount [abs.] 2 Mc 7,30; *to accuse of* [τινός τι] Dt 19,16

κατάλειμμα,-ατος⁺ N3N 1-7-7-1-4-20
Gn 45,7; JgsᴮB 5,13; 1 Sm 13,15; 2 Sm 14,7; 1 Kgs 12,24y

remnant Gn 45,7; *offspring* 1 Kgs 15,4
κατάλειμμα καὶ ὄνομα *remnant and name*
2 Sm 14,7, see also Is 14,22; τὸ κατάλειμμα
τοῦ σπέρματος *the offspring of his seed* Tob[S]
13,17
Cf. HARL 1986[a], 290-291; MARGOLIS 1906[a]=1972, 77;
WEVERS 1993, 759

καταλείπω[+] V 59-70-70-27-63-289
Gn 2,24; 7,23; 14,10; 33,15; 39,12
A: *to leave* [τινα] Gn 2,24; *id.* [τι] Gn 39,12; *to
leave some of sth* [ἀπό τινος] Ex 16,20; *to
bequeath to sb* [τί τινι] Ps 48(49),11; *to forsake*
[τι] Dt 29,24; *id.* [τινα] Sir 13,4
P: *to be left, to remain* Gn 7,23; *to be left behind*
Gn 14,10; *to be left* Ex 12,10
Cf. HARL 1986[a], 136-137; HELBING 1907, 96; LE
BOULLUEC 1989, 371; WEVERS 1993, 722

κατάλειψις,-εως N3F 1-0-0-0-0-1
Gn 45,7
remnant, offspring
Cf. HARL 1986[a], 80.290-291; MARGOLIS 1906[a]=1972, 77

καταλέω V 2-0-0-1-0-3
Ex 32,20; Dt 9,21; Dn[LXX] 2,34
to grind [τι] Dn[LXX] 2,34; *id.* [τινα +pred.] (of
an offering) Ex 32,20

καταλήγω V 0-0-0-0-2-2
2 Mc 9,5; 3 Mc 6,32
to stop, to finish, to cease [τι]

κατάληψις,-εως N3F 1-0-0-0-0-1
Dt 20,19
taking, capture

καταλιθοβολέω V 2-0-0-0-0-2
Ex 17,4; Nm 14,10
to throw stones at [τινα] Ex 17,4
καταλιθοβολέω τινὰ ἐν λίθοις *to throw
stones at, to stone* (semit.) Nm 14,10
neol.
Cf. WEVERS 1990, 265

κατάλιθος,-ος,-ον A 2-0-0-0-0-2
Ex 28,17; 36,17(39,10)
set with (precious) stones; neol.
Cf. LE BOULLUEC 1989, 286; WEVERS 1990, 452

καταλιμπάνω V 1-2-0-0-0-3
Gn 39,16; 2 Sm 5,21; 1 Kgs 18,18
to leave Gn 39,16; *to forsake* 1 Kgs 18,18; see
καταλείπω
Cf. WEVERS 1993, 657

καταλλαγή,-ῆς[+] N1F 0-0-1-0-1-2
Is 9,4; 2 Mc 5,20
reconciliation 2 Mc 5,20

*Is 9,4 μετὰ καταλλαγῆς *for money, for profit*
-ב/רמים (post biblical Hebr.) for MT ב/רמים *in blood*
Cf. SEELIGMANN 1948, 50(Is 9,4); SPICQ 1978[a], 407; →MM

καταλλάσσω[+] V 0-0-1-0-3-4
Jer 31(48),39; 2 Mc 1,5; 7,33; 8,29
A: *to change oneself* Jer 31(48),39
M/P: *to become reconciled with* [τινι] 2 Mc 1,5
Cf. BREYTENBACH 1993, 60-62; SPICQ 1978[a], 407;
WALTERS 1973, 257.293; →MM

καταλογίζομαι V 0-0-1-1-1-3
Is 14,10; Dn[LXX] 5,17; Wis 5,5
to be counted Dn[LXX] 5,17; *to be counted* or
reckoned among [ἐν τινι] Is 14,10

κατάλοιπος,-ος,-ον,[+] A 3-20-55-19-0-97
Lv 5,9; Nm 3,26; Dt 3,13; Jgs[B] 7,6; 1 Sm 13,2
remnant, rest (of things) Lv 5,9; *remnant, rest* (of
people) 1 Sm 13,2; οἱ κατάλοιποι *those left
behind, the poor* Jer 52,16
*Jer 32(25),37 τὰ κατάλοιπα *the remaining, the
rest* corr.? τὰ καταλύματα? for MT נאות נוה
folds, resting places, cpr. Jer 32(25),38; *Nm 3,26
τὰ κατάλοιπα *the rest* -יתרי/מ/יתריו? for MT מיתריו
יתר[ll] *its cords*; *Mi 3,1 οἱ κατάλοιποι *the
remaining* -קצה for MT קציני ◊קצין *rulers*, see also
Mi 3,9
Cf. DORIVAL 1994, 211

καταλοχία,-ας N1F 0-1-0-0-0-1
2 Chr 31,18
register, enrollment; neol.

καταλοχισμός,-οῦ N2M 0-5-0-0-1-6
1 Chr 4,33; 5,7.17; 9,22; 2 Chr 31,17
register 1 Ezr 5,39; *registration, enumeration*
1 Chr 5,17; neol.?
Cf. HELBING 1907, 115

κατάλυμα,-ατος[+] N3N 2-5-4-0-3-14
Ex 4,24; 15,13; 1 Sm 1,18; 9,22; 2 Sm 7,6
lodging, inn Ex 4,24; *guest-room* 1 Sm 1,18;
resting-place Jer 14,8; *lodgings, habitation*
1 Mc 3,45; *lair* Jer 32(25),38
*Ez 23,21 ἐν τῷ καταλύματί σου *in your
habitation* -דריך? ◊דור for MT דדיך *your breasts*
neol.?
Cf. HUSSON 1983[a], 133-136; LE BOULLUEC 1989,
103.174-175; LEE, J. 1983, 99; →MM(1 Sm 1,18)

κατάλυσις,-εως[+] N3F 0-0-1-1-2-4
Jer 30,14(49,20); Dn[LXX] 2,22; 2 Mc 8,17; 4 Mc
11,25
dissolution, putting down 2 Mc 8,17; *feebleness,
destruction* 4 Mc 11,25
accomodation for animals Jer 30,14(49,20);

lodging, shelter, haven of refuge Dn^LXX 2,22
Cf. HUSSON 1983ᵃ, 133-136; →LSJ RSuppl

καταλύτης,-ου   N1M 0-0-0-0-1-1
Wis 5,14
lodger, guest; neol.?
→LSJ RSuppl

καταλύω⁺   V 9-10-17-5-25-66
Gn 19,2(bis); 24,23.25; 26,17
to put down, to destroy [τι] Ezr 5,12; *to take
down, to roll up* (a tent) [τι] Is 38,12; *to
dissolve, to break up, to put down* [τι]
4 Mc 1,11; *to abolish, to annul* [τι] 4 Mc 5,33;
to dismiss [τι] 2 Chr 23,8; *to put down, to
destroy* [τινα] Ps 8,3; *to deprive of* [τινα ἀπό
τινος] Ps 88(89),45; *to put an end to sth
somewhere* [τι ἔκ τινος] Jer 7,34
to lodge, to live in Gn 24,23; *id.* [τι] Jer
30,10(49,16); *to settle* Sir 43,20; *to give a rest to*
[τινα] 2 Sm 17,8; *to resort to* [πρός τι] Sir 27,9
καταλύω πόδας *to cause the feet to fail* Jer
45(38),22
*Jer 44(37),13 ἄνθρωπος παρ᾽ ᾧ κατέλυε *a
man with whom he lodged* -קפרת ◊ קפר for
MT פקרה *a sentinel*, cpr. Is 38,12; *Ez 16,8 καιρὸς
καταλυόντων *a time of resting* -עת דרים ◊ דור for
MT עת דדים *age for love*; *Ez 21,35 μὴ καταλύσῃς
stay not -תגרה אל or תעבר אל for MT תערה אל *to its
sheath*, cpr. Jer 28(51),35
Cf. BARR 1985, 71-72; CAIRD 1976, 81; DORIVAL 1994,
53-54; HARL 1986ᵃ, 64; KATZ 1946ᵃ, 319-324;
→SCHLEUSNER(Jer 44(37),13; Ez 21,35)

καταμανθάνω⁺   V 3-0-0-1-4-8
Gn 24,21; 34,1; Lv 14,36; Jb 35,5; 1 Ezr 8,41
*to observe well, to examine closely, to take great
notice of* [τινα] Gn 24,21; *to examine, to inspect*
[τι] Lv 14,36; *to gaze at, to look upon* [τινα] Sir
9,5; *id.* [τι] Sir 9,8; *to survey* [τινα] 1 Ezr 8,41

καταμαρτυρέω⁺   V 0-2-0-3-3-8
1 Kgs 20(21),10.13; Jb 15,6; Prv 25,18; Dn^LXX
6,25
to testify against [τινος] 1 Kgs 20(21),10; *id.* [τί
τινος] Prv 25,18
ψευδῆ τινὸς καταμαρτυρέω *to bear false
witness against* Sus^Th 43
Cf. HELBING 1928, 183

καταμένω⁺   V 3-2-0-0-2-7
Gn 6,3; Nm 20,1; 22,8; Jos 2,22; 7,7
to remain, to stay, to abide Nm 20,1
*Gn 6,3 καταμένῃ *shall (not) remain* -ירור for
MT ידון?, see Qumran

Cf. DORIVAL 1994, 53; ZIPOR 1994, 388(Gn 6,3)

καταμερίζω   V 4-1-0-0-2-7
Lv 25,46; Nm 32,18; 34,29; Dt 19,3; Jos 13,14
to part [τι] 3 Mc 6,31; *to distribute* (of land as a
heritage) Nm 34,29; *id.* [τι] Dt 19,3; *to distribute
to* [τινά τινι] Lv 25,46; *id.* [τινα ἔν τινι]
PSal 17,28

καταμερισμός,-οῦ   N2M 0-1-0-0-0-1
Jos 13,14
division into parts (of the land as a heritage);
neol.

καταμεστόω   V 0-0-0-0-1-1
3 Mc 5,46
to fill up with [τινι]

καταμετρέω   V 3-0-4-0-0-7
Nm 34,7.8.10; Ez 45,1; 48,14
to measure [τι] Am 7,17; *to measure out* [τι] Mi
2,4; *id.* [τί τινι] Nm 34,10; *id.* [τινι] Nm 34,7
*Ez 48,14 καταμετρηθήσεται *shall be measured*
-ימר מדר ◊ מדר for MT ימר *he shall exchange or shall
be exchanged*, see also Mi 2,4
Cf. DORIVAL 1994, 558

καταμήνια,-ων   N2N 0-0-0-1-0-1
Est 4,17w
menses of women, menstruation

καταμηνύω   V 0-0-0-0-1-1
4 Mc 4,4
to make known, to inform of [τι]

καταμίγνυμι   V 1-0-0-0-0-1
Ex 28,14
to combine, to variegate, to array with [ἔν τινι]

καταμιμνήσκομαι   V 0-0-0-0-1-1
4 Mc 13,12
to remind oneself of sth, to call to mind sth

καταμωκάομαι   V 0-1-1-0-1-3
2 Chr 30,10; Jer 45(38),19; Sir 13,7
to mock [abs.] 2 Chr 30,10; *to mock at, to laugh
to scorn* [τινος] Sir 13,7; neol.
Cf. HELBING 1928, 184

καταναγκάζω   V 0-0-0-0-1-1
1 Mc 2,15
to compel; οἱ καταναγκάζοντες τὴν ἀπο-
στασίαν *those who compel to revolt*

καταναλίσκω⁺   V 4-1-7-3-4-19
Lv 6,3; Dt 4,24; 7,22; 9,3; 1 Chr 21,26
to spend upon [τι εἴς τινα] LtJ 9; *to consume*
[abs.] Dt 4,24; *id.* [τι] Lv 6,3; *id.* [τινα] Sir
27,29
Cf. DOGNIEZ 1992, 140-141

κατανέμω   V 0-0-0-1-0-1

Ps 79(80),14
M: *to devour* [τι]
κατανίσταμαι   V 1-0-0-0-0-1
Nm 16,3
to rise up against [ἐπί τι]
κατανοέω⁺   V 7-1-4-12-6-30
Gn 3,6; 42,9; Ex 2,11; 19,21; 33,8
to understand, to comprehend Jdt 8,14; *to see, to perceive* Ex 2,11; *to look at, to gaze* Ex 19,21; *to observe, to spy out* Nm 32,8
Cf. Le BOULLUEC 1989, 331; WEVERS 1993, 39
κατανόησις,-εως   N3F 0-0-0-0-1-1
Sir 41,23
gazing
καταντάω⁺   V 0-1-0-0-4-5
2 Sm 3,29; 2 Mc 4,21.24.44; 6,14
to come to, to arrive at [εἰς τι] 2 Mc 4,21; *to come to* [πρός τι] (metaph.) 2 Mc 6,14; *to fall upon* [ἐπί τινα] (of blood-guiltiness) 2 Sm 3,29
καταντάω τι εἰς ἑαυτόν *to gain for oneself* 2 Mc 4,24
neol.?
Cf. SPICQ 1978ᵃ, 414
κατάντημα,-ατος   N3N 0-0-0-1-0-1
Ps 18(19),7
goal, end; neol.
→MM
καταντλέω   V 0-0-0-0-1-1
4 Mc 7,2
P: *to be overwhelmed* (metaph.)
κατάνυξις,-εως⁺   N3F 0-0-1-1-0-2
Is 29,10; Ps 59(60),5
astonishment, insensitivity, numbness, drowsiness
Cf. HARL 1986ᵃ, 219; 1986ᵇ=1992ᵃ, 77-95; MIQUEL 1986, 229; OTTLEY 1906, 133-134
κατανύσσω⁺   V 3-2-2-6-6-19
Gn 27,38; 34,7; Lv 10,3; 1 Kgs 20(21),27.29
P: *to be pierced to the heart, to be deeply pained* Gn 34,7; *to be pierced with sorrow, to repent* 1 Kgs 20(21),27; *to be stunned* Ps 29(30),13; neol.
Cf. HARL 1986ᵃ, 219.248; 1986ᵇ=1992ᵃ, 77-95; HARLÉ 1988, 123; OTTLEY 1906, 133-134
κατανύω   V 0-0-0-0-1-1
2 Mc 9,4
to bring to an end, to dispatch, to carry out; neol.
κατανωτίζομαι   V 0-0-0-0-1-1
Jdt 5,4
to ignore, to reject; neol.?
καταξαίνω⁺   V 0-3-0-0-0-3
Jgsᴬ 8,7.16(bis)

to flail, to tear in pieces Jgsᴬ 8,7
*Jgsᴬ 8,16 καὶ κατέξανεν *and he flailed* וירוש- for MT וירע *and he taught*
καταξηραίνω   V 0-1-1-0-1-3
Jos 2,10; Hos 13,15; Jdt 5,13
to dry up Jos 2,10
Hos 13,15 καταξηρανεῖ corr.? καταζανεῖ? (from καταξαίνω) for MT יששׂה *he shall strip, he shall plunder*
κατάξηρος,-ος,-ον   A 1-0-0-0-0-1
Nm 11,6
very dry, parched (metaph.)
κατάξιος,-α,-ον   A 0-0-0-1-0-1
Est 8,12r
worthy, fitting, suitable
καταξιόω⁺   V 0-0-0-0-5-5
2 Mc 13,12; 3 Mc 3,21; 4,11; 4 Mc 18,3; Od 14,32
to deem worthy [τινα +inf.] Od 14,32; *to deem worthy of, to bestow* [τινά τινος] 3 Mc 3,21; *to beseech* [τινα] 2 Mc 13,12
καταξύω   V 0-0-0-0-1-1
LtJ 7
to polish
καταπαίζω   V 0-1-2-0-0-3
2 Kgs 2,23; Jer 2,16; 9,4
to mock (at) [τινος] 2 Kgs 2,23; *to deceive* [κατά τινος] Jer 9,4
Cf. HELBING 1928, 184(Jer 2,16)
καταπαλαίω⁺   V 0-0-0-0-1-1
4 Mc 3,18
to throw down in wrestling (metaph.), *to overthrow*
καταπανουργεύομαι   V 0-0-0-1-0-1
Ps 82(83),4
to devise wickedly against [τι ἐπί τινα]; neol.
καταπάσσω   V 0-0-2-2-2-6
Jer 6,26; Mi 1,10; Jb 2,12; Est 4,1; 2 Mc 10,25
A: *to besprinkle with* [τί τινι] 2 Mc 10,25; *id.* [ἐν τινι] (semit.) Jer 6,26
M: *to sprinkle, to strew over oneself* [τι] Jb 2,12
καταπατέω⁺   V 0-8-25-10-10-53
Jgs 5,21; Jgsᴬ 9,27; 20,43; 1 Sm 14,48
to trample (up)on [τι] Is 28,3; *id.* [τινα] Jgsᴬ 20,43; *to oppress* Is 16,4; *to destroy* [τι] 1 Sm 17,53; *to kill* [τινα] Ps 90(91),13
to tread, to press (grapes) [τι] Jgsᴬ 9,27; *to trample, to walk, to tread* [τι] Zech 12,3
to trample under foot, to disregard [τι] Hos 5,11; *to profane* (a temple) [τι] 1 Mc 3,45

to cover [τινα] (metaph.) Ps 138(139),11
*Ps 55(56),2 κατεπάτησέν με *he trampled on me*
-שׁפני? ◊ שׁוּף for MT שׁאפני ◊ שׁאף *he sets traps for
me?*, see also Ps 55(56),3, cpr. Gn 3,15; Ps 138
(139),11

Cf. PASSONI DELL'ACQUA 1984, 1309-1310; 1986,
65-79.101-104; WALTERS 1973, 227(Is 16,9)

καταπάτημα,-ατος   N3N 0-0-8-2-1-11
Is 5,5; 7,25; 14,25; 22,5.18
trampling, treading (down) Mi 7,10; *destroying*
Lam 2,8; *profanation* Dn^LXX 8,13; neol.

Cf. PASSONI DELL'ACQUA 1984, 1312; 1986, 91-96; →LSJ
suppl(Lam 2,8)

καταπάτησις,-εως   N3F 0-1-0-0-0-1
2 Kgs 13,7
trampling; neol.

Cf. PASSONI DELL'ACQUA 1984, 1313; 1986, 97-99

κατάπαυμα,-ατος   N3N 0-0-0-0-1-1
Sir 36,12
rest

κατάπαυσις,-εως⁺   N3F 3-4-1-2-3-13
Ex 35,2; Nm 10,35(36); Dt 12,9; Jgs^A 20,43;
1 Kgs 8,56
rest 1 Kgs 8,56; *resting-place* Jdt 9,8
ἡ τῆς καταπαύσεως ἡμέρα *sabbath day* 2 Mc
15,1

Cf. DOGNIEZ 1992, 195; KHIOK-KHNG 1991, 10; LOMBARD
1971, 60-71; WALTERS 1973, 320(Ex 35,2); WEVERS
1990, 575

καταπαύω⁺   V 20-22-3-12-10-67
Gn 2,2.3; 8,22; 49,33; Ex 5,5
to put an end to, to stop [τι] 2 Chr 16,5; *to bring
to a close* [τι] 2 Mc 15,37; *to cause sth to cease
from, to turn sth back from* [τι ἀπό τινος]
Nm 25,11
to give rest to, to settle [τινα] Ex 33,14; *id.*
[τινι] 1 Chr 23,25; *to give rest from* [τινά
τινος] Ex 5,5
to cease [abs.] Jdt 6,1; *to cease doing* [+ptc.] Gn
49,33; *to cease from* [ἀπό τινος] Gn 2,2; *to rest,
to repose* Gn 8,22
*Ex 16,13 καταπαυομένης *had ceased* -שׁבת ◊ שׁבת
for MT שׁכבת ◊ שׁכב *a layer*; *2 Chr 32,22 καὶ
κατέπαυσεν αὐτούς *and he gave them rest*
-וינה להם for MT וינהלם *he guided them*; *Jb 21,34
τὸ δὲ ἐμὲ καταπαύσασθαι ἀφ'ὑμῶν *I have rest
from you* -שׁבת ◊ שׁבת for MT ותשׁובתיכם שׁוב *your replies*,
cpr. Nm 25,11; 1 Kgs 12,24

Cf. ALBREKTSON 1963(Lam 3,11); DOGNIEZ 1992, 152;
HARL 1986ª, 99; HELBING 1928, 168-170; KATZ 1946ª,

319-324(Ex 16,13; Jgs^A 18,2); LE BOULLUEC 1989, 183-184.
317; WEVERS 1990, 549; 1993, 20

καταπειράζω   V 0-0-0-0-1-1
2 Mc 13,18
to make an attempt on [τι]

καταπελματόομαι   V 0-1-0-0-0-1
Jos 9,5
P: *to be cobbled, to be clouted* (of shoes); τὰ
σανδάλια αὐτῶν παλαιὰ καὶ καταπε-
πελματωμένα *their sandals were old with
patched soles*; neol.

καταπέλτης,-ου   N1M 0-0-0-0-5-5
4 Mc 8,13; 9,26; 11,9.26; 18,20
engine of war for hurling bolts or *rounded stones,
catapult*

Cf. WALTERS 1973, 123

καταπενθέω   V 1-0-0-0-0-1
Ex 33,4
to mourn, to wail, to lament; neol.

Cf. LE BOULLUEC 1989, 329-330

καταπέτασμα,-ατος⁺   N3N 33-2-0-0-3-38
Ex 26,31.33(ter).34
curtain, veil (of the temple) 1 Kgs 6,36a; *veil* (of
the tabernacle) Ex 26,31; neol.

Cf. DORIVAL 1994, 50; HARLÉ 1988, 193; LE BOULLUEC
1989, 274.359; PELLETIER 1955, 289-307; WEVERS 1990,
427.648; →TWNT

καταπέτομαι   V 0-0-0-1-0-1
Prv 27,8
to fly down; *Prv 27,8 καταπετασθῇ (a bird)
flies down* -◊ ירד *to descend* for MT נורדת ◊ נרד *to flee*

καταπήγνυμι   V 0-1-2-0-0-3
1 Sm 31,10; Hos 5,2; 9,8(9)
to plant firmly (metaph.), *to establish* [τι] Hos
9,8(9); *to fasten, to fix* [τι] 1 Sm 31,10

καταπηδάω   V 1-1-0-0-0-2
Gn 24,64; 1 Sm 25,23
to leap down, to spring off, to dismount [ἀπό
τινος]

κατάπικρος,-ος,-ον   A 0-1-0-0-0-1
2 Sm 17,8
very bitter

καταπίνω⁺   V 10-1-10-15-5-41
Gn 41,7.24; Ex 7,12; 15,12; Nm 16,30
A: *to swallow* [τι] Jb 7,19; *to gulp, to swallow up*
[τι] Ex 7,12; *id.* [τινα] Ex 15,12; *to destroy, to
ruin completely* [τινα] Hab 1,13
M: *to gulp, to swallow up* [τι] Prv 19,28; *id.*
[τινα] Nm 16,30
P: *to be drowned* Lam 3,49; *to be consumed* Sir

23,17

*Nm 21,28 κατέπιε *devoured* -בלע for MT בעלי the
lords of

Cf. DORIVAL 1994, 409

καταπίπτω⁺   V 0-0-0-2-5-7
Ps 144(145),14; Neh 8,11; 3 Mc 2,20; 4 Mc 4,11;
Wis 7,3
to fall (down) 4 Mc 4,11; *id.* (metaph.) Ps
144(145),14; *to be cast down* (used as pass. of
καταβάλλω) 3 Mc 2,20

Cf. LARCHER 1984, 448(Wis 7,3)

καταπιστεύω⁺   V 0-0-1-0-0-1
Mi 7,5
to trust in [ἔν τινι]

Cf. HELBING 1928, 201

καταπλάσσω   V 0-0-1-1-0-2
Is 38,21; Jb 37,11
to plaster over, to apply as a plaster Is 38,21; *to
cover* Jb 37,11

καταπληγμός,-οῦ   N2M 0-0-0-0-1-1
Sir 21,4
panic, terror; neol.

Cf. SMEND 1906, 189

κατάπληξις,-εως⁺   N3F 0-0-0-1-0-1
Ezr 3,3
terror

καταπλήσσω⁺   V 0-1-0-2-7-10
Jos 5,1; Jb 7,14; 13,21; 2 Mc 3,24; 8,16
A: *to terrify* [τινα] Jb 7,14
P: *to be terror-stricken of* [τι] 4 Mc 16,17; *id.*
[τινι] 2 Mc 8,16; *to be astonished at* [ἐπί τινι]
3 Mc 5,27; *id.* [τι] 2 Mc 3,24; *to be struck with*
[τινι] 3 Mc 1,9

κατάπλους,-ου   N2M 0-0-0-0-1-1
3 Mc 4,10
voyage, trip

καταπολεμέω   V 0-1-0-0-0-1
Jos 10,25
to fight against [τινα]

Cf. HELBING 1928, 236

καταπονέω⁺   V 0-0-0-0-2-2
3 Mc 2,2.13
to bear down, to oppress [τινα]

κατάπονος,-ος,-ον   A 0-0-0-0-1-1
3 Mc 4,14
wearisome

καταποντίζω⁺   V 1-2-0-8-1-12
Ex 15,4; 2 Sm 20,19.20; Ps 54(55),10; 68(69),3
to cast or *throw into the sea* [τινα] Ex 15,4; *to
drown* [τινα] Ps 68(69),16; *to swallow up* [τινα]

(metaph.) Eccl 10,12; *to destroy, to ruin* [τι]
2 Sm 20,19

Cf. LE BOULLUEC 1989, 172-173; WEVERS 1990, 228

καταποντισμός,-οῦ   N2M 0-0-0-1-0-1
Ps 51(52),6
destruction; *Ps 51(52),6 ῥήματα κατα-
ποντισμοῦ *words that swallow up, words that
destroy* -בלע ◊דברי בלע◊ for MT 'בלעי דברי
words that confuse

→LSJ RSuppl

καταπορεύομαι   V 0-0-0-0-2-2
2 Mc 11,30; 3 Mc 4,11
to return home; neol.?

καταπραΰνω   V 0-0-0-3-1-4
Ps 82(83),2; 88(89),10; Prv 15,18; 2 Mc 13,26
to appease, to pacify [τινα] 2 Mc 13,26; *to
appease, to calm* [τι] Ps 82(83),2

καταπρίω   V 0-0-0-0-1-1
Sus^LXX 59
to saw asunder

καταπροδίδωμι   V 0-0-0-0-1-1
4 Mc 2,10
to surrender

καταπρονομεύω   V 1-1-0-0-0-2
Nm 21,1; Jgs^B 2,14
to carry off as booty; neol.

Cf. DORIVAL 1994, 186.396; LEE, J. 1983, 48

καταπτήσσω   V 0-1-0-3-1-5
Jos 2,24; Prv 28,14; 29,9; 30,30; Sir 32,18
to fear [τι] Prv 30,30; *to tremble before* [ἀπό
τινος] Jos 2,24

Cf. HELBING 1928, 26-27

κατάπτωμα,-ατος   N3N 0-0-0-1-0-1
Ps 143(144),14
falling down, gap; neol.

κατάπτωσις,-εως   N3F 0-0-0-0-1-1
3 Mc 2,14
downfall, calamity, collapse

κατάρα,-ας⁺   N1F 13-7-9-7-6-42
Gn 27,12.13; Nm 23,25; Dt 11,26.28
curse, imprecation Dt 11,26; *cursing* Ps
108(109),17

καταράομαι⁺   V 23-18-2-18-12-73
Gn 5,29; 8,21; 12,3(bis); 27,29
M: *to curse, to execrate* [τινι] 2 Kgs 2,24; *id.*
[τινα] Gn 12,3; *id.* [τι] Gn 5,29
P: *to be cursed* Nm 22,6
κατηραμένος *accursed* 2 Kgs 9,34; καταράομαί
τινα κατάραν ὀδυνηράν *to curse with a
grievous curse* 1 Kgs 2,8

*Jb 3,6(5) καταραθείη *let be cursed* -◊ ארר? for MT כמרירי ?; *Neh 10,30 κατηράσαντο αὐτούς *they called down curses upon them* -ארדוהם◊ ארר? for MT אדיריהם *their nobles*

Cf. HARLÉ 1988, 195; HELBING 1928, 71

κατάρασις,-εως N3F 1-1-1-0-0-3
Nm 23,11; Jgsᴬ 5,23; Jer 30,7(49,13)
cursing

καταράσσω V 0-0-1-5-1-7
Hos 7,6; Ps 36(37),24; 73(74),6; 101(102),11; 144(145),14
to dash down [τινα] Ps 101(102),11; *to dash down, to break in pieces* [τι] Ps 73(74),6; *to break down, to ruin* [τινα] (metaph.) Ps 144(145),14; *to make fall upon* [τι ἐπί τινα] Sir 46,6

κατάρατος,-ος,-ον A 0-0-0-0-2-2
2 Mc 12,35; 4 Mc 4,5
(ac)cursed

καταργέω⁺ V 0-0-0-4-0-4
Ezr 4,21.23; 5,5; 6,8
A: *to cause to be idle, to hinder* [τινα] Ezr 4,21
P: *to lie idle* Ezr 6,8

Cf. JOÜON 1925, 534-535

καταργυρόω V 1-0-0-0-0-1
Ex 27,17
to cover with silver

Cf. WEVERS 1990, 439

καταριθμέω⁺ V 2-1-0-0-0-3
Gn 50,3; Nm 14,29; 2 Chr 31,19
P: *to be numbered (in a census)* Nm 14,29; *to be numbered, to be accomplished* (of days required for embalming a deceased pers.) Gn 50,3; *to be reckoned among* [ἕν τινι] 2 Chr 31,19

Cf. HARL 1986ᵃ, 315

καταρ(ρ)άκτης,-ου N1M 4-2-4-1-0-11
Gn 7,11; 8,2; Lv 11,17; Dt 14,17; 2 Kgs 7,2
waterfall, cataract Ps 41(42),8; *some means of punitive restraint* (whether dungeon, stocks or other means) Jer 20,2
cormorant, a sea-bird (prob. so called from swooping down upon its prey) Lv 11,17
*Jer 36(29),26 τὸν καταρράκτην *the cistern* -הצנור for MT הצינק *the collar*

Cf. HARL 1986ᵃ, 135; WEVERS 1993, 94; →LSJ suppl(Jer 36(29),26); LSJ Rsuppl(Jer 20,2)

καταρρέω⁺ V 0-2-1-0-1-4
1 Sm 2,33; 21,14; Jer 8,13; 4 Mc 6,6
to run or *drip down* 1 Sm 21,14; *to fall off* Jer 8,13; *to stream down* 4 Mc 6,6; *to perish, to pine*

away (of the soul) 1 Sm 2,33

καταρρήγνυμι V 0-1-0-2-0-3
Jos 9,4; Ps 88(89),45; Prv 27,9
to break down Ps 88(89),45; *to rend* Jos 9,4
*Prv 27,9 καταρρήγνυται δέ *but (the soul) is broken* -קרע ומתקרעה for MT ומתק רעהו *but the sweetness of his friend?*

καταρρίπτω V 0-0-0-1-1-2
Lam 2,1; Wis 17,17
A: *to cast down* (metaph.) Lam 2,1
M: *to fall down, to tumble down* Wis 17,17

καταρρομβεύω V 1-0-0-0-0-1
Nm 32,13
to lead astray [τινα]; neol.

Cf. DORIVAL 1994, 186.536

κατάρρυτος,-ος,-ον A 0-0-0-0-1-1
2 Mc 12,16
irrigated

καταρτίζω⁺ V 0-0-0-17-0-17
Ps 8,3; 10(11),3; 16(17),5; 17(18),34; 28(29),9
M: *to create* [τι] Ps 73(74),16; *to cause (an animal) to calve, to prepare (an animal) to calve, to strengthen* [τινα] Ps 28(29),9
to adjust, to direct [τι] Ps 16(17),5; *to prepare, to make ready* [τι] Ps 39(40),7
to establish, to restore [τι] Ezr 4,12; *to finish (completely)* [τι] Ezr 5,3 *to finish* [abs.] Ezr 6,14; *to perfect* (a praise) [τι] Ps 8,3
to make good, to strengthen, to refresh [τι] Ps 67(68),10; *to restore, to protect* (a plant) [τι] Ps 79(80),16
P: *to be completed* or *finished* Ezr 4,13

Cf. SPICQ 1978ᵃ, 253.416-419; →LSJ Rsuppl

κατάρχω V 1-2-4-1-3-11
Nm 16,13; 1 Kgs 10,22a; 12,24r; Jl 2,17; Na 1,12
A: *to rule, to govern* [τινος] Nm 16,13; *id.* [ἕν τινι] Neh 9,28; *id.* [abs.] Zech 6,13
M: *to begin* [τινος] 2 Mc 4,40; *id.* [abs.] 2 Mc 1,23
κατάρχω μεθ' ὑμνῶν κραυγήν *to begin to sing hymns with loud voice* 2 Mc 12,37

Cf. CAIRD 1969=1972, 133; HELBING 1928, 114.167-168; →LSJ Rsuppl

κατασβέννυμι⁺ V 0-0-0-2-1-3
Prv 15,18a; 28,2; 4 Mc 16,4
to quench [τι] 4 Mc 16,4; *to quell, to extinguish, to appease* [τι] Prv 15,18a

κατασείω⁺ V 0-0-0-0-1-1
1 Mc 6,38
to make a sign

κατασήθω   V 0-0-0-0-2-2
Bel 14
to strew

κατασιωπάω   V 1-0-0-3-0-4
Nm 13,30; Jb 37,20; 39,17; Neh 8,11
*to make silent, to put to silence, to silence, to
reduce to silence* [τινα] Nm 13,30; *to withhold
from* [τί τινι] Jb 39,17

κατασκάπτω⁺   V 1-13-13-4-3-34
Dt 12,3; Jgsᴬ 2,2; 6,28.30.31
to destroy, to raze to the ground [τι] Dt 12,3; *to
destroy, to cast down* [τι] Jdt 3,8; *to break down*
[τι] Jl 1,17

κατασκεδάννυμι   V 1-0-0-0-0-1
Ex 24,8
to sprinkle over or *upon* [τί τινος]
Cf. HELBING 1928, 184; LE BOULLUEC 1989, 245-246

κατασκέπτομαι   V 15-10-0-4-0-29
Nm 10,33; 13,2.16.17.21
to view closely, to survey Jb 39,8; *to spy (out)* Nm
13,2; *to seek out, to provide* Nm 10,33; *to inspect,
to examine* Eccl 1,13; neol.
Cf. DORIVAL 1994, 412

κατασκευάζω⁺   V 1-1-5-1-20-28
Nm 21,27; 2 Chr 32,5; Is 40,19.28; 43,7
to make [τι] Wis 11,24; *to construct, to build*
1 Ezr 9,42; *to create* [τινα] 4 Mc 2,21; *id.* [τι]
Is 40,28
ὁμοίωμα κατεσκεύασεν αὐτόν *he made it a
similitude* Is 40,19
Cf. LARCHER 1984, 509(Wis 7,27; 9,2)

κατασκεύασμα,-ατος   N3N 0-0-0-0-2-2
Jdt 15,11; Sir 32,6
work of art Sir 32,6; κατασκευάσματα *furniture*
Jdt 15,11

κατασκευή,-ῆς   N1F 4-2-0-0-3-9
Ex 27,19; 35,24; 36,7; Nm 8,4; 1 Chr 29,19
construction Nm 8,4; *equipment* Ex 27,19;
instrument 3 Mc 5,45; *correct style* 2 Mc 15,39
Cf. LE BOULLUEC 1989, 279.350

κατασκηνόω⁺   V 5-9-16-30-6-66
Nm 14,30; 35,34(bis); Dt 33,12.28
usu. rendering שׁכן (homoeophony?); *to take up
one's quarters* or *abode* 1 Chr 23,25; *to live, to
dwell* Nm 35,34; *to live, to settle* (of birds) Ps
103(104),12; *to occupy* [τι] Ps 36(37),3; *to dwell,
to rest* [ἐπί τινι] (metaph.) Ps 15(16),9
to settle, to cause to dwell [τινα] Nm 14,30; *id.*
[τι] Neh 1,9; *to lay (down)* [τι] Ps 7,6
ἐγὼ ἡ σοφία κατεσκήνωσα βουλήν *I, wisdom,*

dwelled, lived with counsel Prv 8,12
*Ps 5,12 καὶ κατασκηνώσεις *and you shall
dwell* -שׁכן ותחם ◊ for MT וחסם ◊ סכך *and you protect?*
Cf. BARR 1985, 28-35; CAIRD 1976, 82; DORIVAL 1994, 54;
HELBING 1928, 75-80; HORSLEY 1983, 106; →LSJ Suppl(Prv
8,12); LSJ RSuppl(Ps 36(37),3; Prv 8,12); TWNT

κατασκήνωσις,-εως⁺   N3F 0-1-1-0-3-5
1 Chr 28,2; Ez 37,27; Tob 1,4; Wis 9,8
habitation (mostly of the Lord in the temple)
Tob 1,4; *building* (verbal sense, erection of a
temple for the Lord) 1 Chr 28,2
→TWNT

κατάσκιος,-ος,-ον⁺   A 0-0-4-0-1-5
Jer 2,20; Ez 20,28; Hab 3,3; Zech 1,8; Od 4,3
shady, overshadowing

κατασκοπεύω⁺   V 3-8-0-0-0-11
Gn 42,30; Ex 2,4; Dt 1,24; Jos 2,1; 2,2
to spy out Jos 2,3; *to inspect, to survey* Dt 1,24;
to watch carefully Ex 2,4; (ὁ) κατασκοπεύων *spy*
Gn 42,30

κατασκοπέω⁺   V 0-2-0-0-1-3
2 Sm 10,3; 1 Chr 19,3; 1 Mc 5,38
to spy out

κατάσκοπος,-ου⁺   N2M 6-2-0-0-2-10
Gn 42,9.11.14.16.31
spy

κατασμικρύνω   V 0-1-0-0-0-1
2 Sm 7,19
P: *to be little* or *small*

κατασοφίζομαι⁺   V 1-0-0-0-2-3
Ex 1,10; Jdt 5,11; 10,19
to deal craftily with, to outwit, to deceive [τινα];
neol.
Cf. LE BOULLUEC 1989, 37.76

κατασπαταλάω   V 0-0-1-1-0-2
Am 6,4; Prv 29,21
to live luxuriously, to be wanton; neol.

κατασπάω   V 0-16-3-1-3-23
2 Sm 11,25; 2 Kgs 10,27; 11,18; 21,3; 23,12
to pull down, to destroy [τι] 2 Sm 11,25; *to
destroy* [τινα] Belᵀʰ 28; *to tear down, to fell* [τι]
Zech 11,2; *to bring down* [τινα] (metaph.) Zph
3,6
*2 Chr 32,18 κατασπάσαι *to pull down* corr.?
κατασπεῦσαι *to hasten* for MT בהל *to terrify* or *to
hasten,* cpr. 2 Chr 26,20; 35,21
Cf. WALTERS 1973, 144-145(2 Chr 32,18)

κατασπείρω⁺   V 2-0-0-1-1-4
Lv 19,19; Dt 22,9; Jb 18,15; 3 Mc 5,26
A: *to sow* [τι] (metaph.) Jb 18,15; *to plant* [τι]

Lv 19,19

P: *to be scattered abroad, to be shed abroad* (of the rays of the sun) 3 Mc 5,26

κατασπεύδω   V 5-3-0-4-9-21

Ex 5,10.13; 9,19; 10,16; Dt 33,2

to urge, to hasten [τινα] Ex 5,13; *to hasten* [τι] Sir 43,5; *to make haste, to hasten, to speed* [abs.] Dt 33,2; *id.* (metaph.) Sir 32,10; *to hasten to do* [+inf.] Ex 9,19; κατασπεύδων *hasty* Sir 28,11; κατασπευδόμενος *hasty* Sir 28,11

*Ex 5,10 κατέσπευδον *they were urging* -יאצו for MT יצאו *they went out*

Cf. CAIRD 1969=1972, 133; DOGNIEZ 1992, 344; LE BOULLUEC 1989, 133; WALTERS 1973, 144-145.148; WEVERS 1990, 64

κατασπουδάζω   V 0-0-0-1-0-1

Jb 23,15a

P: *to take things seriously, to be troubled*

Cf. WALTERS 1973, 148

καταστασιάζω   V 1-0-0-0-0-1

Ex 38,22

to revolt

κατάστασις,-εως⁺   N3F 0-0-0-0-1-1

Wis 12,12

juridicial confrontation; τίς εἰς κατάστασίν σοι ἐλεύσεται ἔκδικος *who will stand to plead as an advocate*

Cf. LARCHER 1985, 721-722; →PREISIGKE

καταστέλλω⁺   V 0-0-0-0-2-2

2 Mc 4,31; 3 Mc 6,1

to put down (the insurrection), *to settle* (matters) [τι] 2 Mc 4,31; *to restrain from* [τινα +inf.] 3 Mc 6,1

κατάστεμα,-ατος⁺   N3N 0-0-0-0-1-1

3 Mc 5,45

state, disposition, mood, mental condition

καταστενάζω   V 1-0-3-1-1-6

Ex 2,23; Jer 22,23; Ez 9,4; 21,11; Lam 1,11

to sigh, to groan; neol.

Cf. LE BOULLUEC 1989, 87

καταστέφω   V 0-0-0-0-1-1

3 Mc 7,16

P: *to be garlanded, to be wreathed*

καταστηρίζω   V 0-0-0-1-0-1

Jb 20,7

to establish; *Jb 20,7 κατεστηρίχθαι *to be established* -גרל(?) for MT גלל *dung heap*

καταστολή,-ῆς⁺   N1F 0-0-1-0-0-1

Is 61,3

dress, garment; καταστολὴ δόξης *garment of*

glory, covering with glory

καταστραγγίζω   V 1-0-0-0-0-1

Lv 5,9

to drop, to squeeze out; neol.

καταστρατοπεδεύω   V 0-1-0-0-3-4

Jos 4,19; Jdt 3,10; 7,18; 2 Mc 4,22

to encamp, to pitch Jos 4,19; *to go to a place and take up quarters there* [εἴς τι] 2 Mc 4,22

Cf. CAIRD 1969=1972, 133; →LSJ RSuppl(2 Mc 4,22)

καταστρέφω⁺   V 6-3-12-11-10-42

Gn 13,10; 19,21.25.29; Dt 29,22

to overturn [τι] JgsᴬA 7,13; *to turn upside down* [τι] 2 Kgs 21,13; *to overthrow, to ruin* [τι] Gn 13,10; *to overthrow* [τινα] Ezr 6,12; *to undo* [τι] 3 Mc 3,23

καταστρέφω τὸν βίον *to die* 2 Mc 9,28

*Jb 11,10 καταστρέψῃ *he overthrows* -ימגר? for MT יסגיר *he arrests*

καταστροφή,-ῆς⁺   N1F 1-1-1-7-8-18

Gn 19,29; 2 Chr 22,7; Hos 8,7; Jb 8,19; 15,21

overthrow, destruction Gn 19,29; *end, conclusion* DnᴸˣˣLXX 7,28

τοῦ βίου καταστροφή *death* 3 Mc 4,4;

καταστρώννυμι⁺**/ύω**   V 1-0-0-1-8-10

Nm 14,16; Jb 12,23; Jdt 7,14.25; 12,1

to set a table, to prepare Jdt 12,1; *to extend, to enlarge* [τινα] Jb 12,23

*Nm 14,16 καὶ κατέστρωσεν αὐτούς *and he spread them* (in the wilderness) -וישטחם for MT וישחטם *and he slayed them* (in the wilderness)

Cf. DORIVAL 1994, 98.321; →MM

κατασύρω⁺   V 0-0-1-2-0-3

Jer 30,4(49,10); DnᴸˣˣLXX 11,10.26

to drag, to carry off

κατασφάζω⁺   V 0-0-2-0-9-11

Ez 16,40; Zech 11,5; 2 Mc 5,12.24; 6,9

to slaughter Zech 11,5; *to murder, to slay* Ez 16,40

κατασφαλίζομαι   V 0-0-0-0-2-2

2 Mc 1,19; 3 Mc 4,9

M: *to make sure* [τι] Mc 1,19

P: *to be made fast, to be made secure* 3 Mc 4,9

κατασφραγίζω⁺   V 0-0-0-2-1-3

Jb 9,7; 37,7; Wis 2,5

to seal up

κατάσχεσις,-εως⁺   N3F 33-11-20-2-2-68

Gn 17,8; 47,11; 48,4; Lv 25,24.25

possession Gn 17,8

*1 Chr 13,2 κατασχέσεως *possession* -מורש(?) for MT מגרש *pasture land*; *Zech 11,14 τὴν κατάσχεσιν *the possession* -האחזה for MT האחוה *the brotherhood*

Cf. HARL 1986ª, 170; HARLÉ 1988, 200; WEVERS 1993, 232

κατασχίζω   V 0-0-0-0-1-1
1 Mc 1,56
to rend asunder, to cut up, to tear up

κατατάσσω   V 0-0-1-3-0-4
Ez 44,14; Jb 7,12; 15,23; 35,10
to appoint [τινα] Ez 44,14; *to appoint over, to set over* [τι ἐπί τινα] Jb 7,12

κατατείνω   V 3-0-0-0-2-5
Lv 25,43.46.53; 4 Mc 9,13; 11,18
to stretch (for torturing) [τινα] 4 Mc 9,13; *to strain* (metaph.), *to overwork* [τινα] Lv 25,43

Cf. HARLÉ 1988, 203; LEE, J. 1983, 71

κατατέμνω   V 1-1-2-0-0-4
Lv 21,5; 1 Kgs 18,28; Is 15,2; Hos 7,14
A: *to cut, to gash* Lv 21,5
M: *to gash oneself* 1 Kgs 18,28
P: *to be cut to pieces, to be mutilated* Is 15,2
*Hos 7,14 κατετέμνοντο *they gashed themselves*
-יתגוררו *for* MT יתגודדו *they stay about as* גֵּר, *they dwell*

κατατέρπω   V 0-0-1-0-0-1
Zph 3,14
M: *to rejoice*; neol.

κατατήκω   V 0-0-1-0-0-1
Mi 4,13
to dissolve, to exterminate, to wear away, to destroy [τινα]

κατατίθημι⁺   V 0-1-0-2-3-6
1 Chr 21,27; Ps 40(41),9; Est 3,13d; Jdt 11,10; 2 Mc 4,19
A: *to place, to put down into* [τι εἴς τι] 1 Chr 21,27
M: *to spend in* [τι εἴς τι] 2 Mc 4,19; *to testify, to lodge an accusation* [τι] Ps 40(41),9
P: *to be established* Est 3,13d
κατατίθεμαί τι ἐν τῇ καρδίᾳ *to lay up in memory* Jdt 11,10; κατατίθεμαι εἰς εὐφροσύνην *to enjoy oneself* 3 Mc 5,17
→MM

κατατίλλω   V 0-0-0-0-1-1
1 Ezr 8,68
to pull off [τινος]

κατατιτρώσκω   V 0-0-0-0-1-1
4 Mc 6,6
P: *to be wounded all over, to receive deathly wounds*; neol.

κατατολμάω   V 0-0-0-0-2-2

2 Mc 3,24; 5,15
to dare, to presume, to have the boldness to [+inf.]; neol.?

Cf. MILLIGAN 1910=1980, 15

κατατοξεύω⁺   V 2-1-0-3-0-6
Ex 19,13; Nm 24,8; 2 Kgs 9,16; Ps 10(11),2; 63(64),5
to shoot [τινα]

Cf. LE BOULLUEC 1989, 201-202

κατατρέχω⁺   V 1-2-0-2-1-6
Lv 26,37; Jgsᴮ 1,6; 1 Kgs 19,20; Jb 16,10; Dnᴸˣˣ 4,24(21)
to run upon [ἐπί τινι] Jb 16,10; *id.* [ἐπί τινα] Dnᴸˣˣ 4,24(21); *to pursue* [τινα] 2 Mc 8,26; *id.* [ὀπίσω τινός] Jgsᴮ 1,6

Cf. HELBING 1928, 87; LEE, J. 1983, 83

κατατρίβω⁺   V 2-0-0-2-0-4
Dt 8,4; 29,4; Prv 5,11; Dnᴸˣˣ 7,25
to wear out [τινα] Dnᴸˣˣ 7,25; *to wear off from* [τι ἀπό τινος] Dt 8,4; *to consume* [τι] Prv 5,11

κατατρυφάω   V 0-0-0-2-0-2
Ps 36(37),4.11
to take delight in [τινος] Ps 36(37),4; *id.* [ἐπί τινι] Ps 36(37),11; neol.

Cf. HELBING 1928, 135

κατατρώγω   V 0-0-0-1-0-1
Prv 24,22e
to eat up, to devour

κατατυγχάνω   V 0-0-0-1-0-1
Jb 3,22
to be successfull, to gain; neol.

καταυγάζω⁺   V 0-0-0-0-2-2
1 Mc 6,39; Wis 17,5
to shine upon, to illuminate [τι] Wis 17,5; *to shine brightly* [abs.] 1 Mc 6,39; neol.?

Cf. LARCHER 1985, 955

καταφαίνω   V 1-0-0-0-0-1
Gn 48,17
M: *to appear, to seem*

καταφερής,-ής,-ές   A 0-1-0-0-0-1
Jos 7,5
going down; ἐπὶ τοῦ καταφεροῦς *on the steep* (ground)

καταφέρω⁺   V 3-5-5-1-2-16
Gn 37,2; Dt 1,25; 22,14; Jgsᴮ 7,4.5
A: *to bring down* [τινα] Jgsᴬ 7,4; *to bring to* [τι πρός τινα] Dt 1,25; *to bring against* [τι ἐπί τινα] Gn 37,2; *id.* [τί τινος] Dt 22,14; *to pour out* [τι] 2 Sm 14,14
P: *to flow down* Mi 1,4; *to fall, to descend* Is 28,2

ζῶν κατηνέχθη εἰς τὴν γῆν *he was brought
down to earth* (i.e. *burried*) *alive* Tobˢ 14,10

καταφεύγω⁺   V 7-2-6-2-3-20
Gn 19,20; Ex 21,14; Lv 26,25; Nm 35,25.26
to flee for refuge [abs.] Ex 21,14; *id.* [εἰς τι] Lv
26,25; *id.* [ἐπί τινα] Est 4,17k; *id.* [πρός τινα]
Ps 142(143),9; *to flee to sb* (for help) [πρός
τινα] Is 10,3

Cf. LE BOULLUEC 1989, 217-218; LEE, J. 1983, 28; SPICQ
1978ᵃ, 420-422

καταφθάνω   V 0-1-0-0-0-1
Jgsᴬ 20,42
to fall upon unawares, to overtake [τινα]

καταφθείρω⁺   V 7-7-4-2-7-27
Gn 6,12(bis).13.17; 9,11
A: *to destroy, to bring to naught* [τινα; τι] Gn
6,13
P: *to be corrupted* Gn 6,12(secundo); *to perish*
Lv 26,39

Cf. SPICQ 1978ᵃ, 423; WEVERS 1990, 284

καταφθορά,-ᾶς⁺   N1F 0-1-0-3-2-6
2 Chr 12,12; Ps 48(49),10; Est 4,17f; Dnᴸˣˣ
4,17a(14); 1 Mc 15,31
destruction, death, ruin 2 Chr 12,12; *corruption*
Sir 28,6

καταφιλέω⁺   V 4-7-0-3-6-20
Gn 31,28; 32,1; 45,15; Ex 4,27; 1 Sm 20,41
to kiss, to embrace [τινα] (between relatives)
Gn 31,28; *id.* [τινα] (in greeting) 2 Sm 14,33;
id. [τι] Sir 29,5; *to embrace each other* (metaph.)
Ps 84(85),11

Cf. SWINN 1990, 65

καταφλέγω   V 0-0-0-2-5-7
Ps 104(105),32; 105(106),18; 2 Mc 12,6; 3 Mc
2,5; 4 Mc 3,11
to burn up, to consume [τινα] Ps 105(106),18;
id. [τι] 2 Mc 12,6; *to flame* [intrans.]
Ps 104(105),32

καταφλογίζω   V 0-0-0-1-0-1
Ps 17(18),9
to burst into flame; neol.

κατάφοβος,-ος,-ον   A 0-0-0-1-0-1
Prv 29,16
fearful, fear-inspiring; *Prv 29,16 κατάφοβοι
γίνονται *they are afraid* -◊ירא *to fear* for MT יראו
◊ראה *they see*; neol.

καταφορά,-ᾶς   N1F 0-0-0-0-1-1
PSal 16,1
downwards motion

καταφράσσω   V 0-0-0-0-1-1

1 Mc 6,38
P: *to be fortified, to be covered*; neol.

καταφρονέω⁺   V 1-0-4-7-11-23
Gn 27,12; Jer 2,36; Hos 6,7; Hab 1,13; Zph 1,12
to think slightly of, to despise [τινος] Prv 13,13;
id. [ἐπί τινος] Tobᴮᴬ 4,18; *to despise, to regard
slightly* [τινα] Jdt 10,19; *to act contemptuously*
[abs.] Gn 27,12
*Jer 2,36 κατεφρόνησας *you despised* -◊זלל for
MT חזלי ◊אזל *leave?*; *Prv 25,9 καταφρόνει
despise -◊זלל חזל for MT חגל נלחה *reveal*

Cf. SPICQ 1982, 374; WEVERS 1993, 424; →TWNT

καταφρόνησις,-εως   N3F 0-0-0-0-1-1
2 Mc 3,18
contempt, disdain

→MM

καταφρονητής,-οῦ⁺   N1M 0-0-3-0-0-3
Hab 1,5; 2,5; Zph 3,4
despiser Hab 2,5
ἄνδρες καταφρονηταί *scornful men* Zph 3,4
*Hab 1,5 καταφρονηταί *despisers* -◊בגרים for MT
ב/גוים *at the nations*, cpr. 1QpHab 2,1

Cf. SPICQ 1982, 374; TALMON 1964, 131-132(Hab 1,5)

καταφυγή,-ῆς   N1F 4-1-2-15-4-26
Ex 17,15; Nm 35,27.28; Dt 19,3; 2 Sm 22,3
refuge Nm 35,27; *resource, recourse* Ps 89(90),1
καταφυγὴ σωτηρίας *a safe retreat, a sure refuge*
2 Sm 22,3
*Ex 17,15 καταφυγή μου *my resource, my
recourse* -◊נוסי נוס for MT נסי *my banner*

Cf. DOGNIEZ 1992, 232; DORIVAL 1994, 566; LE
BOULLUEC 1989, 192; WEVERS 1990, 272

καταφύτευσις,-εως   N3F 0-0-1-0-0-1
Jer 38(31),22
planting, plantation; neol.

Cf. LEE, J. 1983, 58

καταφυτεύω   V 3-2-12-4-3-24
Ex 15,17; Lv 19,23; Dt 6,11; 2 Sm 7,10; 1 Chr
17,9
to plant (trees) [τι] Lv 19,23; *id.* (places) [τι]
2 Sm 7,10; *to plant, to settle* [τινα] Ex 15,17; *to
plant* (its roots) [τι] Ps 79(80),10

Cf. LEE, J. 1983, 45.57

καταχαίρω⁺   V 0-0-0-1-0-1
Prv 1,26
to rejoice, to exult with malicious joy

καταχαλάω   V 0-1-0-0-0-1
Jos 2,15
to let down [τινα]; neol.

καταχαλκόω   V 0-1-0-0-0-1

2 Chr 4,9

to cover with bronze; θυρώματα κατα-
κεχαλκωμένα χαλκῷ *panels overlaid with bronze*

καταχέω⁺   V 1-0-0-2-1-4
Gn 39,21; Ps 88(89),46; Jb 41,15; 4 Mc 6,25
to pour down in [τι εἴς τι] 4 Mc 6,25; *to pour
over* [τί τινος] (metaph.) Gn 39,21; *id.* [ἐπί
τινος] Jb 41,15

καταχράομαι⁺   V 0-0-0-0-3-3
3 Mc 4,5; 5,22; LtJ 27
to make full use of, to apply [τινι] 3 Mc 4,5; *id.*
[τι] 3 Mc 5,22; *to misuse, to abuse* LtJ 27
Cf. HELBING 1928, 253-254

κατάχρεος,-ος,-ον   A 0-0-0-0-1-1
Wis 1,4
involved in [τινος]; neol.?

καταχρίω   V 1-0-0-0-2-3
Ex 2,3; Wis 13,14(bis)
to besmear with [τί τινι]

καταχρυσόω   V 12-4-0-0-0-16
Ex 25,11.13.28; 26,29(bis)
to gild with [τί τινι]
Cf. LE BOULLUEC 1989, 370; WEVERS 1990, 396

κατάχυσις,-εως   N3F 0-0-0-1-0-1
Jb 36,16
pouring over; *Jb 36,16 κατάχυσις *pouring over*
-מוצק קרק◊ יצק◊ for MT צוק◊ *constraint*
Cf. WALTERS 1973, 299

καταχώννυμι   V 0-0-1-0-0-1
Zech 9,15
to overwhelm [τινα]

καταχωρίζω   V 0-1-0-1-1-3
1 Chr 27,24; Est 2,23; 3 Mc 2,29
to enter (in a register), *to record* [τι] 1 Chr
27,24; *id.* [abs.] Est 2,23; *to enter, to take up*
[τινα] 3 Mc 2,29

καταψεύδομαι⁺   V 0-0-0-0-1-1
Wis 1,11
to speak falsely, to accuse falsely, to calumniate
Cf. LARCHER 1983, 192

καταψευσμός,-οῦ   N2M 0-0-0-0-1-1
Sir 26,5
slander, calumny; neol.

καταψύχω⁺   V 1-0-0-0-0-1
Gn 18,4
to cool off, to rest
Cf. HORSLEY 1987, 262; LEE, J. 1983, 50

κατεγχειρέω   V 0-0-0-0-1-1
3 Mc 1,21
to plot against; τὰ κατεγχειρούμενα *plots,*

enterprise

κατεῖπον
aor. of καταγορεύω

κατελεέω   V 0-0-0-0-1-1
4 Mc 8,10
to have compassion upon, to have mercy upon
[τινα]

κατεμβλέπω   V 1-0-0-0-0-1
Ex 3,6
to look down (before God) [ἐνώπιόν τινος]
(theological interpretation, avoiding Hebr. הביט *to
look in the face of*); neol.?
Cf. WEVERS 1990, 28

κατέναντι⁺   D/P 6-19-20-19-23-87
Gn 2,14; 4,16; 50,13; Ex 19,2; 32,5
over against, opposite, in front Ez 11,1
[τινος]: *over, against, opposite* Gn 2,14; *before,
in front of* Ex 19,2; *in the presence of* 1 Chr 8,32;
against Sir 22,18; *in the direction of* Eccl 6,8
neol.?
Cf. BLASS 1990, § 214; DORIVAL 1994, 361; SOLLAMO
1979, 29.107-108.317-318

κατεναντίον⁺   P 0-1-0-3-0-4
2 Chr 34,27; Ps 43(44),16; Dnᴸˣˣ 8,15; Neh
12,24
before, in the presence of, over against [τινος]
Cf. SOLLAMO 1979, 25.317

κατεντευκτής,-οῦ   N1M 0-0-0-1-0-1
Jb 7,20
accuser of [τινος]

κατενώπιον⁺   P 1-4-0-1-0-6
Lv 4,17; Jos 1,5; 3,7; 21,44; 23,9
[τινος]: *in front of, before* Jos 3,7; *over* Lv 4,17;
against Jos 1,5; neol.
Cf. BLASS 1990, § 214; HARLÉ 1988, 96; RINALDI 1968,
320; SOLLAMO 1979, 21.119.131; WIKENHAUSER 1910,
263-270

κατεπείγω   V 1-0-0-0-0-1
Ex 22,24
to press hard [τινα]
Cf. LE BOULLUEC 1989, 230

κατεπίθυμος,-ος,-ον⁺   A 0-0-0-0-1-1
Jdt 12,16
very eager to [τοῦ +inf.]; neol.
→LSJ RSuppl

κατεπικύπτω   V 0-0-0-1-0-1
Est 5,1d
to bow down upon [ἐπί τι]; neol.

κατεργάζομαι⁺   V 5-2-2-1-3-13
Ex 15,17; 35,33; 39,1(38,24); Nm 6,3; Dt 28,39

M: *to prepare* [τι] Ex 15,17; *to make* [τι] Nm
6,3; *to fashion, to work* [τι] Ex 35,33; *to dress* (a
vineyard) [τι] Dt 28,39; *to till* [τι] Ez 36,9; *to
level* [τι] 1 Ezr 4,4; *to weary, to oppress* [τινα]
Jgs^A 16,16; *to subdue* [τινα] Ez 34,4
P: *to be wrought* 1 Kgs 6,36
Cf. DANIEL 1966, 57-58.113; WEVERS 1990, 588(Ex 35,33);
→TWNT

κατεργασία,-ας   N1F 0-1-0-0-0-1
1 Chr 28,19
working

κάτεργον,-ου   N2N 2-0-0-0-0-2
Ex 30,16; 35,21
wages, the cost of labour
Cf. LE BOULLUEC 1989, 309.349; WEVERS 1990, 496

κατέρχομαι⁺   V 0-0-0-1-5-6
Est 3,13g; Tob 2,1; Tob^S 1,22; 2 Mc 11,29
to go down [εἴς τι] Est 3,13g; *to come back, to
return* [εἴς τι] Tob 2,1; *id.* [abs.] 2 Mc 11,29; *to
fall down upon* [ἐπί τι] Wis 11,22
Cf. BICKERMAN 1980, 57(n.67)

κατεσθίω⁺   V 30-28-70-20-13-161
Gn 31,15.38; 37,20.33; 40,17
A: *to eat, to devour* [τι] Gn 31,38; *id.* [τινα] Gn
37,20; *id.* [τι] (metaph.) Gn 31,15; *to devour, to
consume* [τινα] Lv 10,2
M: *to eat, to devour* [abs.] 2 Sm 2,26; *id.* [τι] Dt
28,39; *to devour, to consume* [τινα] 2 Kgs 1,10
Cf. DANIEL 1966, 137

κατευθικτέω   V 0-0-0-0-1-1
2 Mc 14,43
to hit exactly [τινι]; neol.

κατευθύνω⁺   V 0-15-11-31-16-73
Jgs 12,6; Jgs^A 14,6.19; 15,14
A: *to keep straight* [abs.] Ps 58(59),5; *id.* [τινα]
Ps 7,10; *to direct, to lead* [τι] 1 Chr 29,18; *id.*
[τινα] Jdt 13,18; *to guide* [τι] Zech 11,16; *to
lead to prosperity* [τι] 2 Chr 17,5
to go straight towards [εἴς τι] 1 Sm 6,12; *id.*
[ἐπί τινα] Jgs^A 14,6; *id.* [τι] 2 Sm 19,18; *to
prosper* [abs.] Ps 100(101),7; *to succeed in doing*
[τινος] Jgs 12,6; *to be right-minded to do* [+inf.]
2 Chr 30,19
P: *to prosper* Ps 139(140),12
οἱ κατευθύνοντες *the righteous, the honest* Prv
15,8; κατευθύνουσα ὁδός *direct way, honest way*
Prv 29,27

κατευλογέω⁺   V 0-0-0-0-2-2
Tob^BA 10,14; 11,17
to bless [τινα]; neol.

κατευοδόω⁺   V 0-1-0-6-1-8
Jgs^A 18,5; Ps 1,3; 36(37),7; 44(45),5; 67(68),20
A: *to give prosperity* [τινι] Ps 67(68),20; *id.*
[abs.] Jgs^A 18,5
P: *to have a prosperous journey* Ps 36(37),7; *to
prosper* Ps 44(45),5
neol.

κατευφημέω   V 0-0-0-0-1-1
3 Mc 7,13
to applaud, to extol [τινα]; neol.

κατεύχομαι   V 0-0-0-0-2-2
2 Mc 15,12; 4 Mc 12,19
to pray 4 Mc 12,19; *to pray for* [τινι] 2 Mc
15,12

κατέχω⁺   V 5-15-6-19-8-53
Gn 22,13; 24,56; 39,20; 42,19; Ex 32,13
A: *to hold* [τι] Ct 3,8; *to hold back* [τι] 1 Chr
13,9; *to withhold, to take, to lay hold on* [τινα]
2 Sm 2,21; *to withhold from* [τινα ἀπό τινος]
Ps 118(119),53; *to keep, to prevent from going
away* [τινα] Gn 24,56; *to keep, to detain*
(prisoners) [τινα] Gn 39,20; *to keep, to live with*
[τινα] Prv 18,22a
to possess [τι] Ex 32,13; *id.* [τινα] Prv 19,15; *id.*
[τινος] Ps 72(73),12; *to gain possession of* [τι]
Jos 1,11; *id.* [τινα] (metaph.) Jb 15,24
to rule, to control [τινος] 1 Mc 6,27; *to seize, to
occupy* [τινος] 2 Chr 15,8
to cling to [τινος] 1 Kgs 1,51; *to fill in, to repair*
[τι] 2 Kgs 12,13
P: *to be held* Gn 22,13; *to refrain from* [τινος]
Ru 1,13
οὐ κατέχω [+inf.] *not succeed in* 2 Mc 15,5;
ἐπὶ χεῖρα αὐτῶν κατέσχεν υἱός Ουρια *the
son of Uria made repairs next to them* Neh 3,4,
cpr. 2 Kgs 12,13
Cf. DELEKAT 1964, 172; HARL 1986ᵃ, 194-195(Gn 22,13);
1986ᶜ=1992ᵃ, 68; SPICQ 1982, 379-385; →TWNT

κατηγορέω⁺   V 0-0-0-1-5-6
Dn^LXX 6,5; 1 Mc 7,6.25; 2 Mc 4,47; 10,13
to speak against, to accuse of [τί τινος] 1 Mc
7,25; *to accuse* [τινος] Dn^LXX 6,5; *id.* [τινα]
2 Mc 10,21; τὰ κατηγορημένα *accusations,
charges* 2 Mc 4,47

κατήγορος,-ου⁺   N2M 0-0-0-1-1-2
Prv 18,17; 2 Mc 4,5
accuser

κατηφής,-ής,-ές⁺   A 0-0-0-0-1-1
Wis 17,4
sorrowful, sad

κατιόω⁺   V 0-0-0-0-1-1
Sir 12,11
to make rusty [abs.]; neol.

κατισχύω⁺   V 9-47-20-21-8-105
Gn 49,24; Ex 1,7; 7,13; 17,11(bis)
to overpower, to prevail over [τινα] Is 42,25; *id.*
[τινος] Wis 7,30; *id.* [ἐπί τινα] 2 Chr 27,5; *id.*
[ἐπί τινος] 1 Chr 5,20; *to be master of* [τι]
Dn^LXX 11,19; *to have the upper hand, to prevail*
[abs.] Ex 17,11
to strengthen, to encourage [τινα] Ex 18,23, see
also 1 Chr 22,12; *id.* [τι] Jos 11,20; *to repair* [τι]
2 Kgs 22,5; *to fortify* [τι] 2 Chr 11,12; *to feed*
[τι] Is 50,11; *to make stubborn* [τι] Dt 2,30
to be stubborn [abs.] Ex 7,13; *to establish* [τι] Sir
49,3; *to strengthen oneself* [abs.] 2 Chr 17,1; *to
grow strong* [abs.] Ex 1,7; *to be able to* [+inf.]
Wis 17,5; *to strive for, to labour to* [+inf.] Jos
23,6
*Gn 49,24 κατισχύσας *strengthening* -אביר? for
MT אבן *stone*
Cf. DOGNIEZ 1992, 127(Dt 2,30); HELBING 1928, 77.119;
JEANSONNE 1988, 77-78(Dn 12,3); WALTERS 1973, 128;
WEVERS 1990, 98(Ex 7,13).289(Ex 18,23)

κατοδυνάω   V 1-0-1-0-1-3
Ex 1,14; Ez 9,4; Tob^S 8,20
to afflict grievously, to embitter [τινα]; neol.
Cf. LE BOULLUEC 1989, 77-78; WALTERS 1973, 74-75.293;
WEVERS 1990, 6

κατοικεσία,-ας   N1F 0-0-0-1-0-1
Ps 106(107),36
dwelling, inhabiting; neol.

κατοικέω⁺   V 119-243-220-45-58-685
Gn 9,27; 11,2.31; 12,6; 13,6
A: *to settle, to dwell, to reside* [abs.] Gn 9,27; *to
remain* [abs.] Nm 32,17; *to inhabit* [τι] Gn 12,6;
to dwell in [τι] (metaph.) Mi 1,12; *to dwell with*
[τινα] Zech 2,11
P: *to have been planted, to have been settled* Is
27,10
οἱ κατοικοῦντες τὴν γῆν *the inhabitants of the
land* Nm 33,53
*2 Chr 19,8 τοὺς κατοικοῦντας *the inhabitants*
-ישב for MT שׁוּב *they returned*?, see also Hos 9,3;
11,5; *Is 16,7 κατοικοῦσιν *for the inhabitants*
-לאנשׁי for MT לאשׁישׁי *for the raisin-cakes*?, cpr. Jer
31(48),28; *Ez 45,5 πόλεις τοῦ κατοικεῖν
cities to dwell in -לשׁבת for MT עשׂרים ערים לשׁכת
twenty rooms
Cf. DORIVAL 1994, 53; HARL 1986^a, 66.148.207.211.249.

259.297.298; WALTERS 1973, 119-120.313

κατοίκησις,-εως⁺   N3F 4-4-0-0-0-8
Gn 10,30; 27,39; Ex 12,40; Nm 15,2; 2 Sm 9,12
dwelling, abode Gn 10,30; *household* 2 Sm 9,12

κατοικητήριον,-ου⁺   N2N 2-7-4-5-2-20
Ex 12,20; 15,17; 1 Kgs 8,39.43.49
dwelling-place, abode, habitation; neol.

κατοικία,-ας⁺   N1F 10-2-12-7-5-36
Ex 35,3; Lv 3,17; 7,26; 23,3.14
dwelling(-place), habitation Ex 35,3; *community
of residents, settlement* Jer 3,6
*Hos 11,7 ἐκ τῆς κατοικίας αὐτοῦ *from his
habitation* -ישׁב for MT שׁוּבב *for they return to
me*?, see also Hos 14,5; Jer 3,6.8.12; *Ps
86(87),7 ἡ κατοικία *dwelling* -מעון for MT מעין
spring
neol.?
Cf. DORIVAL 1994, 521; HORSLEY 1987, 142

κατοικίζω⁺   V 10-7-15-7-6-45
Gn 3,24; 47,6.11; Ex 2,21; Lv 23,43
A: *to settle, to establish, to cause to dwell* [τινα]
Gn 3,24; *to establish* [τι] 2 Kgs 17,32; *to people*
[τι] Is 54,3
P: *to be settled, to dwell* 1 Ezr 5,45; *to be
inhabited* Ps 92(93),1
*Ps 28(29),10 κατοικιεῖ *he shall establish* corr.
κατοικεῖ for MT ישׁב *he shall sit, he shall dwell*
Cf. LE BOULLUEC 1989, 86(Ex 2,21); WALTERS 1973,
119-120.313(Ps 28(29),10)

κατοικοδομέω   V 1-0-0-0-0-1
Gn 36,43
to build on; αἱ κατῳκοδομημέναι (sc. χῶραι)
dwelling-places, inhabited places, settlements
Cf. HARL 1986^a, 257

κάτοικος,-ου   N2M 1-1-0-1-2-5
Gn 50,11; Jos 8,20; Prv 31,23; Tob^S 13,13; 1 Mc
1,38
inhabitant

κατοικτίρω⁺   V 0-0-0-0-2-2
4 Mc 8,20; 12,2
to have mercy or *compassion on* [τινα] 4 Mc
12,2; *id.* [τι] 4 Mc 8,20

κατοινόομαι   V 0-0-1-0-0-1
Hab 2,5
to be drunk

κατόπισθεν   P 1-10-5-6-3-25
Gn 37,17; Jgs^A 18,12; 19,3; 2 Sm 2,19.27
[τινος]: *after, behind* (static) Neh 4,7; *after*
(movement) Gn 37,17

κατοπίσω   P 0-1-0-0-0-1

Jgs^A 18,22
after, behind [τινος]; neol.

κατοπτεύω V 0-0-0-1-0-1
Est 8,12d
to observe closely, to spy out [τι]

κάτοπτρον,-ου N2N 1-0-0-0-0-1
Ex 38,26(8)
mirror

κατορθόω^+ V 0-7-7-12-2-28
1 Kgs 2,35; 1 Chr 16,30; 28,7; 2 Chr 29,35; 33,16
A: *to set up, to repair, to erect* [τι] 2 Chr 33,16;
to keep straight, to direct [τι] Ps 118(119),9; *to
establish* [τι] 1 Kgs 2,35; *to go the right way, to
be upright* Prv 2,7; *to be right* Ez 18,29; *to
prosper* Prv 11,10
M: *to accomplish successfully* [τι] 2 Mc 8,36
M/P: *to be directed, to direct oneself* Ps
118(119),128
P: *to be ordered, to be accomplished successfully*
2 Chr 35,10
ἕως κατορθώσῃ ἡ ἡμέρα *until full day* Prv 4,18

κατόρθωσις,-εως N3F 0-1-0-1-1-3
2 Chr 3,17; Ps 96(97),2; Jdt 11,7
setting up Ps 96(97),2; *upholding, preservation* Jdt
11,7
*2 Chr 3,17 Κατόρθωσις *Setting up* transl. of
proper name יכין *Jachin*, cpr. 1 Kgs 7,7 Ιαχουμ

κατορύσσω V 1-2-6-0-1-10
Gn 48,7; Jos 24,32.33a; Jer 13,7; 32(25),33
to dig in order to bury sb, to bury [τινα] Gn
48,7; *id.* [τι] Jos 24,32; *to bury* [τι] (metaph.)
Tob^BA 14,6

κατορχέομαι V 0-0-1-0-0-1
Zech 12,10
*to dance in triumph over, to treat spitefully, to
mock at*; neol.

κατοχεύω V 1-0-0-0-0-1
Lv 19,19
to cross-breed with [τινά τινι] (of anim.); neol.
Cf. HARLÉ 1988, 168

κατόχιμος,-ος,-ον A 1-0-0-0-0-1
Lv 25,46
held in possession; neol.

κάτοχος,-ου N2M 0-0-1-0-1-2
Jon 2,7; Od 6,7
handle, barrier

κάτω^+ D 6-10-6-1-3-26
Ex 20,4; Dt 4,39; 5,8; 28,43(bis)
downwards, down (with verbs implying rest) Ex
20,4; *beneath* (with verbs implying motion)

2 Chr 32,30; *under (the age), younger* 1 Chr
27,23; *below, lower* (as adj.) Jos 15,19
κάτω κάτω *very low* Dt 28,43; ἕως κάτω
downwards, all the way down Ez 1,27

κατώδυνος,-ος,-ον A 0-5-0-0-0-5
Jgs^A 18,25; 1 Sm 1,10; 22,2; 30,6; 2 Kgs 4,27
in great pain or *affliction, grieved* (always in
connection with ψυχή); neol.

κάτωθεν D/P 7-0-2-0-0-9
Ex 26,24; 27,5; 28,33; 36,27(39,20).31(39,24)
below Ex 26,24; *under* [τινος] Ex 38,24
Cf. WEVERS 1990, 605(Ex 36,27)

κατώτατος,-η,-ον^+ A 0-0-0-6-1-7
Ps 62(63),10; 85(86),13; 87(88),7; 138(139),15;
Lam 3,55
lowest Ps 85(86),13; τὰ κατώτατα *the lowest
parts* Neh 4,7(13)

κατωτάτω D/P 0-0-0-0-2-2
sup. of κάτω; *at the lowest part, very low* Tob^S
4,19; *much lower than* [τινος] Tob^S 13,2

κατώτερον^+ D 1-0-0-0-0-1
Gn 35,8
comp. of κάτω; *under, below* [τινος]

καυλός,-οῦ N2M 3-0-0-0-0-3
Ex 25,31; 38,13(37,17); Nm 8,4
stem

καῦμα,-ατος^+ N3N 3-1-4-6-8-22
Gn 8,22; 31,40; Dt 32,10; 2 Sm 4,5; Is 4,6
heat Tob^S 2,9
*Prv 25,13 κατὰ καῦμα *in the heat* -בחום for MT
ביום *in the day, in the time*
Cf. MARGOLIS 1906^b=1972, 66

καῦσις,-εως^+ N3F 2-1-3-2-0-8
Ex 39,16(37); Lv 6,2; 2 Chr 13,11; Is 4,4; 40,16
burning
Cf. LE BOULLUEC 1989, 372(Ex 39,16); MARGOLIS
1906^b=1972, 66; WEVERS 1990, 640(Ex 39,16)

καυστικός,-ή,-όν A 0-0-0-0-2-2
4 Mc 6,27; 10,14
burning, scorching 4 Mc 10,14; *of burning* or *by
means of burning, fiery* 4 Mc 6,27

καύσων,-ωνος^+ N3M 0-0-8-2-4-14
Is 49,10; Jer 18,17; 28(51),1; Ez 17,10; 19,12
usu. rendering קרים or רוח קרים *east wind; burning
heat, summer heat* Sir 18,16
πνεῦμα καύσωνος *east wind* Jon 4,8; ἄνεμος
καύσων *sirocco, chamsin* Hos 13,15
neol.
Cf. MARGOLIS 1906^b=1972, 66; MORENZ 1964, 255-256

καυτήριον,-ου N2N 0-0-0-0-1-1

4 Mc 15,22
branding iron (torturing instrument)
καυχάομαι⁺ V 0-10-5-10-16-41
Jgs 7,2; 1 Sm 2,3.10(quinquies)
to boast, to pride (oneself) Jgs 7,2; *to boast in*
[ἔν τινι] 1 Sm 2,10; *id.* [ἐπί τινι] Ps 48(49),7;
to boast about [τι] Prv 27,1; *to boast that* [+inf.]
Prv 20,9; *to glory, to rejoice* Ps 31(32),11; *id.* [ἔν
τινι] Ps 149,5; *id.* [ἐπί τινι] Ps 5,12
Cf. FUCHS 1977, 321-332; SPICQ 1982, 386-394; →TWNT
(→ἐγ-, κατα-)

καύχημα,-ατος⁺ N3N 3-2-6-4-9-24
Dt 10,21; 26,19; 33,29; 1 Chr 16,27; 29,11
glory, honour (of God) Dt 10,21; *id.* (of
Babylon) Jer 28(51),41; *pride* Prv 17,6; *rejoicing*
1 Chr 16,27; neol.
Cf. DOGNIEZ 1992, 185-186; FUCHS 1977, 321-332; SPICQ
1982, 386

καύχησις,-εως⁺ N3F 0-1-7-1-1-10
1 Chr 29,13; Jer 12,13; Ez 16,12.17.39
boasting, glory, honour 1 Chr 29,13
στέφανος καυχήσεως *crown of honour, glorious
crown* Ez 16,12
Cf. FUCHS 1977, 321-332; SPICQ 1982, 386

καφουρη N 0-0-0-1-0-1
Ezr 8,27
= כפורי *bowl* (of gold), cpr. κεφφουρε/η

καψάκης,-ου N1M 0-4-0-0-1-5
1 Kgs 17,12.14.16; 19,6; Jdt 10,5
jug, jar, flask; neol.
Cf. CAIRD 1976, 81

Κεβλααμ N 0-1-0-0-0-1
2 Kgs 15,10
= קבל עם *before the people*
Cf. TOV 1973, 89

κέγχρος,-ου N2M 0-0-1-0-0-1
Ez 4,9
millet

κέδρινος,-η,-ον A 6-16-0-2-2-26
Lv 14,4.6.49.51.52
of cedar 2 Sm 7,2
ξύλον κέδρινον *cedar wood* Lv 14,4

κέδρος,-ου⁺ N2F 1-15-17-9-2-44
Nm 24,6; Jgs 9,15; 1 Kgs 5,13.24
cedar(-tree)
Cf. CAIRD 1976, 78; WALTERS 1973, 158-159

κεῖμαι⁺ V 0-2-3-2-18-25
Jos 4,6; 2 Sm 13,32; Is 9,3; 30,33; Jer 24,1
used as perf. of τίθημι: *to be laid, to lie* Is 9,3;
to be placed, to be set Est 3,13e; *to lie down*

Tobˢ 5,10; *to lie down, to be dead* 2 Sm 13,32; *to
be situated, to lie* 1 Ezr 6,22; *to lie, to be, to
stand* 1 Ezr 6,25; *to be stored* Ezr 6,1; *to be piled*
Is 30,33; *to be valid for* [τινι] 2 Mc 4,11
σημεῖον κείμενον *appointed sign* Jos 4,6
(→ἀνα-, ἀντι-, ἀπο-, δια-, ἐγ-, ἐπι-, κατα-,
παρα-, περι-, προ-, προσ-, συγ-, συνανα-,
ὑπερ-, ὑπο-)

κειρία,-ας⁺ N1F 0-0-0-1-0-1
Prv 7,16
bedsheet

κείρω⁺ V 4-9-4-4-0-21
Gn 31,19; 38,12.13; Dt 15,19; 1 Sm 25,2
A: *to cut (short)* [τι] Prv 27,25; *to shear* [τι] Gn
31,19; *to shear sheep* [abs.] 2 Sm 13,23
M: *to cut the hair* (of one's own head) [τι] 2 Sm
14,26; *to shave oneself* Mi 1,16
Cf. WALTERS 1973, 63
(→περι-)

κεκρυμμένως D 0-0-1-0-0-1
Jer 13,17
secretly; neol.

κέλευσμα,-ατος⁺ N3N 0-0-0-1-0-1
Prv 30,27
command, order

κελεύω⁺ V 0-0-0-0-29-29
1 Ezr 9,53; Jdt 2,15; 12,1; Tobᴮᴬ 8,18; 1 Mc
11,23
A: *to order, to command* [τινα +inf.] Belᴸˣˣ 14;
id. [τι +inf.] 2 Mc 2,4; *id.* [τινι +inf.] Tobᴮᴬ
8,18; *id.* [τινι] Jdt 2,15
P: *to be ordered, to be commanded* 4 Mc 9,11
Cf. DRESCHER 1969, 88-89; 1976, 313-315; PELLETIER
1982, 239
(→παρα-)

κενεών,-ῶνος N3M 0-0-0-0-2-2
2 Mc 14,44; 4 Mc 6,8
hollow between ribs and hip, flank 2 Mc 14,44;
void place, vacant space 4 Mc 6,8

κενοδοξέω⁺ V 0-0-0-0-2-2
4 Mc 5,10; 8,24
*to hold a vain opinion about, to think senselessly
about* [περί τι] 4 Mc 5,10; *to boast, to seek vain
glory by* [ἐπί τινι] 4 Mc 8,24; neol.?

κενοδοξία,-ας⁺ N1F 0-0-0-0-3-3
4 Mc 2,15; 8,19; Wis 14,14
conceit, vain glory, empty boasting

κενολογέω V 0-0-1-0-0-1
Is 8,19
to talk emptily, to speak vain words

κενόω⁺ V 0-0-2-0-0-2
Jer 14,2; 15,9
P: *to be left empty, to waste away* Jer 14,2; *to languish* (metaph.) Jer 15,9
Cf. SPICQ 1982, 395; →LSJ suppl
(→ἀπο-, ἐκ-, κατα-)

κενός,-ή,-όν⁺ A 11-9-15-29-14-78
Gn 31,42; 37,24; Ex 3,21; 5,9; 23,15
empty Gn 37,24; *bare* Jb 33,21; *vain* Ex 5,9; *without anything, empty-handed* Gn 31,42; *devoid of wit, vain, pretentious* Jgs 9,4; *worthless* Neh 5,13; *without result, without effect, without reaching its goal* Wis 1,11; *without being used, clean* 2 Sm 1,22; *of no hope* Jb 7,3
διὰ κενῆς *to no purpose, in vain* Lv 26,16; εἰς κενόν *id.* Lv 26,20; εἰς τὸ κενόν *id.* Jb 2,9b
Cf. LE BOULLUEC 1989, 95.108.341; SPICQ 1982, 395; →NIDNTT; TWNT

κενοτάφιον,-ου N2N 0-2-0-0-0-2
1 Sm 19,13.16
coffin shaped like a human being, household god, image? for MT תרפים *teraphim*

κεντέω V 0-0-0-1-0-1
Jb 6,4
to prick, to stab, to pierce [τινα]
(→ἀπο-, ἐκ-, κατα-, συγ-, συνεκ-,)

κεντρίζω
(→ἐγ-)

κέντρον,-ου⁺ N2N 0-0-2-1-3-6
Hos 5,12; 13,14; Prv 26,3; 4 Mc 14,19; Sir 38,25
goad, cattle stick Prv 26,3; *sting* (of bees) 4 Mc 14,19
*Hos 13,14 τὸ κέντρον σου *your sting* (metaph. of death) -קטבך? (Syr.) for MT קטבך *your plague, your pox* or *your sting*
Cf. BLAU 1957, 98(Hos 13,14); HORSLEY 1987, 157; MURAOKA 1986ᵇ, 133-134; →TWNT

κενῶς⁺ D 0-0-1-0-0-1
Is 49,4
in vain

κεπφόω V 0-0-0-1-0-1
Prv 7,22
P: *to be easily cajoled, to be a booby*; neol.
Cf. CAIRD 1969=1972, 133-134

κεραμεύς,-έως⁺ N3M 0-1-9-2-5-17
1 Chr 4,23; Is 29,16; 41,25(bis); 45,9
potter

κεραμικός,-ή,-όν⁺ A 0-0-0-1-0-1
DnᴸˣˣX 2,41
made of clay, earthen, of pottery

κεράμιον,-ου⁺ N2N 0-0-3-0-0-3
Is 5,10; 30,14; Jer 42(35),5
earthenware vessel, jar Is 30,14; *measure* Is 5,10
Cf. WALTERS 1973, 285.331

κέραμος,-ου⁺ N2M 0-1-0-0-0-1
2 Sm 17,28
potter's earth, potter's clay; σκεύη κεράμου *earthenware*

κεράννυμι⁺ V 0-0-2-2-4-8
Is 5,22; 19,14; Prv 9,2.5; PSal 8,14
to mingle, to mix [τι] Prv 9,2; *to mingle, to prepare* [τι] (metaph.) Is 19,14
(→συγ-)

κέρας, κέρατος⁺ N3N 17-14-17-59-16-123
Gn 22,13; Ex 27,2(bis); 29,12; 30,2
horn (of an anim.) Gn 22,13; *horn-shaped corner* (of an altar) Ex 27,2; *horn-shaped bowl* 1 Sm 16,1; *wing of an army, flank* 1 Mc 9,1; *power* (metaph.) 1 Sm 2,1
ἐκφέρω κέρατα *to grow horns* Ps 68(69),32; δίδωμι κέρας τινί *to give the upperhand to sb* 1 Mc 2,48; ὑψόω κέρας *to exalt sb* 1 Chr 25,5, cpr. 1 Sm 2,1; ἐπαίρω εἰς ὕψος τὸ κέρας *to exalt oneself, to boast* Ps 74(75),6; κέρας σωτηρίας *horn of salvation, mighty saviour* 2 Sm 22,3
*Jer 31(48),12 τὰ κέρατα αὐτοῦ *his horns* corr.? τὰ κέραμα αὐτοῦ for MT נבליהם *their vessels*
Cf. HARLÉ 1988, 72; TOV 1979, 221; →NIDNTT; TWNT

κέρασμα,-ατος N3N 0-0-1-1-0-2
Is 65,11; Ps 74(75),9
mixture Is 65,11; *drink poured out* Ps 74(75),9

κεράστης,-ου N1M 0-0-0-1-0-1
Prv 23,32
horned serpent

κερατίζω V 5-1-3-3-0-12
Ex 21,28.31.32.35; Dt 33,17
to gore [τινα] Ex 21,28; *to butt with horns* Jer 27(50),11; *to push* [τι] 1 Kgs 22,11
τοῖς κέρασιν κερατίζω *to butt with horns* Ez 34,21
*Ez 32,2 ἐκεράτιζες *you butted as with horns, you assaulted* -נגח for MT גוח, גיח *you bubbled forth* (with your nostrils?)
neol.
Cf. LEE, J. 1983, 42; →LSJ RSuppl(Ex 32,2(sic, corr. Ex 21,28); Ps 43(44),5; Ez 32,2)
(→συγ-)

κεράτινος,-η,-ον A 0-29-0-3-0-32

Jgs 3,27; 6,34; 7,8
made of horn Ps 97(98),6; ἡ κερατίνη (sc.
σάλπιγξ) *horn* Jgs 3,27
Cf. BARTHÉLEMY 1963, 60-63

κερατιστής,-οῦ   N1M 2-0-0-0-0-2
Ex 21,29.36
one that butts (said of a bull); neol.

κεραυνός,-οῦ   N2M 0-0-0-1-2-3
Jb 38,35; 2 Mc 10,30; Wis 19,13
thunderbolt, lightning

κεραυνόω   V 0-0-1-0-0-1
Is 30,30
to strike with thunderbolts, to lighten
(→συγ-)

κεράω
(→ὑπερ-)

κέρκος,-ου   N2F 2-6-0-1-0-9
Ex 4,4(bis); Jgsᴬ 15,4(ter)
tail (of anim. except for birds)

κέρκωψ,-ωπος   N3M 0-0-0-1-0-1
Prv 26,22
teller of false tales
→LSJ RSuppl

κεφάλαιον,-ου⁺   N2N 5-0-0-1-0-6
Lv 5,24; Nm 4,2; 5,7; 31,26.49
sum, capital Lv 5,24; *sum, total* Nm 31,26;
summary, main point Dnᴸˣˣ 7,1
Cf. BARR 1961, 237; DORIVAL 1994, 57; →TWNT

κεφαλαιόω⁺   V 0-0-0-0-1-1
Sir 32,8
to sum up

κεφαλή,-ῆς⁺   N1F 97-122-66-80-68-433
Gn 3,15; 8,5; 11,4; 28,11.12
head (of men and anim.) Gn 3,15; *id.* (metaph.)
Dt 28,13; *head, leader* Jgsᴬ 10,18; *person, oneself*
[τινος] Susᵀʰ 55; *top* Gn 8,5; *capital* (of a pillar)
1 Kgs 7,27; *band* or *troop of soldiers* (semit.?) Jb
1,17
κατὰ κεφαλήν *individually, a head* Ex 16,16; τῇ
κεφαλῇ *a piece* Ex 39,3; ἐπὶ τὴν κεφαλήν
τινος *upon one's responsibility* 2 Sm 1,16; κατὰ
κεφαλῆς *with the head covered* Est 6,12; κεφαλὴ
γωνίας *head of the corner, most important one*
(of a stone) Ps 117(118),22; ἄνθρακας πυρὸς
σωρεύω ἐπὶ τὴν κεφαλήν τινος *to heap burning
embers on someone's head, to cause pain to sb*
(pain leading to contrition) Prv 25,22; ἀπὸ
κεφαλῆς ἕως ποδῶν *from head to foot, from top
to toe* Lv 13,12; ἀπὸ ποδῶν ἕως κεφαλῆς Jb 2,7
*Sir 25,15(bis) κεφαλή *head* -ראש for ראש (רוש)

poison, venom (no ms evidence); cpr. Jb 20,16
Cf. CERVIN 1989, 85-112; DORIVAL 1994, 96; GRUDEM
1985, 38-59; LEVIN 1989, 85-112; MURAOKA 1990, 28;
SMEND 1906, 229; VAN ROON 1974, 278; WEVERS 1993,
449; WISSEMAN 1988, 377-384; →NIDNTT; TWNT

κεφαλίζω
(→ἀπο-)

κεφαλίς,-ίδος⁺   N3F 16-0-4-2-0-22
Ex 26,24.32.37; 27,17; 37,4(36,36)
dim. of κεφαλή; *extremity* or *capital* or *base* (of
a pillar) Ex 26,24; *roll, volume* (of a book) Ezr
6,2
Cf. GOODING 1959, 21-23.43-51.62; LE BOULLUEC 1989,
270-271.273.279.359; WEVERS 1990, 420.424.428.627.634.
638.647

κεφφουρε   N 0-1-0-0-0-1
1 Chr 28,17
= כַּף רִי (הזהב) *bowls* (of gold), cpr. καφουρη

κεφφουρη   N 0-0-0-1-0-1
Ezr 1,10
= כַּף רִי (זהב) *bowls* (of gold), cpr. καφουρη

κηδεία,-ας   N1F 0-0-0-0-2-2
2 Mc 4,49; 5,10
care for the dead, funeral
Cf. WALTERS 1973, 40

κηδεμονία,-ας   N1F 0-0-0-0-2-2
4 Mc 4,4.20
care

κηδεμών,-όνος   N3M 0-0-0-0-1-1
2 Mc 4,2
one who cares for, guardian of [τινος]

κηδεύω⁺
(→ἐγ-)

κηλιδόω   V 0-0-1-1-0-2
Jer 2,22; Dnᴸˣˣ 11,33
P: *to be stained, to be soiled*

κηλίς,-ῖδος   N3F 0-0-0-0-2-2
2 Mc 6,25; Wis 13,14
stain, spot Wis 13,14; *stain, blemish* 2 Mc 6,25

κημός,-οῦ   N2M 0-0-2-1-0-3
Ez 19,4.9; Ps 31(32),9
muzzle

κῆπος,-ου⁺   N2M 1-7-10-15-3-36
Dt 11,10; 1 Kgs 20(21),2(bis); 2 Kgs 5,26; 21,18
garden Dt 11,10; *id.* (metaph.) Ct 4,12; *orchard*
Jer 36(29),28
Cf. HARL 1991=1992ᵃ, 148-149

κηρίον,-ου⁺   N2N 0-1-2-7-1-11
1 Sm 14,27; Ez 20,6.15; Ps 18(19),11;
117(118),12

honeycomb 1 Sm 14,27; *honeycomb, delicacy, sth*
exquisite (metaph.) Ez 20,6

κηρογονία,-ας   N1F 0-0-0-0-1-1
4 Mc 14,19
formation of honeycombs; neol.

κηρός,-οῦ   N2M 0-0-2-4-1-7
Is 64,1; Mi 1,4; Ps 21(22),15; 57(58),9; 67(68),3
wax
Cf. KOENIG 1982, 66-67(Is 64,1, cpr. Ps 57(58),9)

κήρυγμα,-ατος⁺   N3N 0-1-1-1-1-4
2 Chr 30,5; Jon 3,2; Prv 9,3; 1 Ezr 9,3
proclamation 2 Chr 30,5; *message* Jon 3,2
*Prv 9,3 κηρύγματος *message* - ◊קרא? for MT קרת
town
Cf. BARR 1961, 84.143; →NIDNTT; TWNT

κῆρυξ,-υκος⁺   N3M 1-0-0-2-2-5
Gn 41,43; Dn 3,4; 4 Mc 6,4; Sir 20,15
herald Gn 41,43; *crier* Sir 20,15
Cf. BARR 1961, 287; →NIDNTT; TWNT

κηρύσσω⁺   V 3-4-14-6-5-32
Gn 41,43; Ex 32,5; 36,6; 2 Kgs 10,20; 2 Chr 20,3
to proclaim, to make proclamation [abs.] Ex 36,6;
to proclaim, to announce [τι] 2 Chr 20,3; *id.*
[τοῦ +inf.] 1 Mc 5,49
to proclaim, to preach [abs.] (of prophets) Jon
1,2; *id.* [τινί τι] Is 61,1; *id.* [τι ἐπί τινα]
Mi 3,5
ἐκήρυξεν ἔμπροσθεν αὐτοῦ κῆρυξ *a herald ran*
ahead him and announced him Gn 41,43
Cf. BARR 1961, 207-208.212; →NIDNTT; TWNT
(→ἀνα-)

κῆτος,-ους⁺   N3N 1-0-4-5-3-13
Gn 1,21; Jon 2,1(bis).2.11
sea-monster, huge fish, cetacea
Cf. HARL 1986ᵃ, 94; WEVERS 1993, 11

κίβδηλος,-ος,-ον   A 2-0-0-0-2-4
Lv 19,19; Dt 22,11; Wis 2,16; 15,9
base, false (of bronze) Wis 15,9; *not pure,*
mingled (of garments made of two materials) Lv
19,19; *hybrid, of mixed race* (of human beings)
Wis 2,16
Cf. DOGNIEZ 1992, 254; GILBERT 1973, 198(n.6)(Wis 15,9);
LARCHER 1985, 248-249(Wis 2,16)

κιβωτός,-οῦ⁺   N2F 68-147-1-1-5-222
Gn 6,14(bis).15(bis).16
chest, coffer 2 Kgs 12,10; *(Noah's) ark* Gn 6,14;
ark (of the covenant) Ex 25,10
ἡ κιβωτὸς τῆς διαθήκης *the ark of the covenant*
Jos 3,3
Cf. HARL 1986ᵃ, 130-131; 1987=1992ᵃ, 97-125; LE

BOULLUEC 1989, 80-81.254-259.375; WALTERS 1973, 126;
WEVERS 1993, 83

κίδαρις,-εως   N3F 7-0-4-0-3-14
Ex 28,4.39.40; 29,9; 36,35(39,28)
tiara, head-dress of Jewish highpriest
Cf. HARLÉ 1988, 114-115; LE BOULLUEC 1989, 292.293;
LUST 1985, 188-190(Ez 21,31); WEVERS 1990, 446.463.608

-κιδαρόω
(→ἀπο-)

κιθάρα,-ας⁺   N1F 2-1-5-19-1-28
Gn 4,21; 31,27; 2 Chr 9,11; Is 5,12; 16,11
lyre, cithara

κιθαρίζω⁺   V 0-0-1-0-0-1
Is 23,16
to play the cithara, to play the lyre
→LSJ RSuppl

κινδυνεύω⁺   V 0-0-2-2-3-7
Is 28,13; Jon 1,4; Eccl 10,9; Dnᴸˣˣ 1,10; 2 Mc
15,17
to be in danger, to run a risk [abs.] Eccl 10,9; *to*
run a risk with [τινι] Dnᴸˣˣ 1,10; *to run the risk*
of doing [+inf.] Jon 1,4
ἕως θανάτου κινδυνεύω *to be in danger of*
death Sir 34,12
Cf. DRESCHER 1969, 89-90; 1976, 315-316; WOLLENTIN
1961, 1-116
(→δια-)

κίνδυνος,-ου⁺   N2M 0-0-0-2-11-13
Ps 114(116),3; Est 4,17l; Tob 4,4; 1 Mc 11,23
danger Tob 4,4; *distress* 4 Mc 13,15
Cf. DRESCHER 1969, 89-90; WOLLENTIN 1961, 1-116

κινέω⁺   V 11-10-10-12-10-53
Gn 7,14.21(bis); 8,17.19
A: *to move, to shake* [τι] 2 Kgs 19,21; *to*
remove, to drive (away) [τινα] Bar 2,35; *to*
remove, to disturb [τι] 2 Kgs 23,18; *to move*
[abs.] Gn 11,2
M: *to move oneself* Gn 7,14
P: *to be moved, to stir* Nm 14,44; *to be removed*
Prv 17,13; *to be urged on* 4 Mc 1,33; *to move*
1 Sm 1,13; *to go* Jgsᴬ 6,18; *to move, to rise up*
Jgsᴮ 20,37; *to move away, to disappear* Ct 2,17
*Dnᴸˣˣ 11,38 κινήσει *he moves* corr.? τιμήσει
for MT יכבד *he shall honour*
Cf. DORIVAL 1994, 53; WEVERS 1993, 147; →LSJ Suppl(Gn
20,1)
(→δια-, ἐκ-, ἐπι-, μετα-)

κίνημα,-ατος   N3N 0-0-0-0-2-2
1 Mc 13,44; 4 Mc 1,35
movement 4 Mc 1,35; *uproar* 1 Mc 13,44

κίνησις,-εως⁺ N3F 0-0-0-2-3-5
Ps 43(44),15; Jb 16,5; 2 Mc 5,3; Wis 2,2; 7,24
motion, movement Jb 16,5; *movement, shaking*
Ps 43(44),15; *movement, beating* (of the heart)
Wis 2,2

κινητικός,-ή,-όν A 0-0-0-0-1-1
Wis 7,24
mobile
Cf. LARCHER 1984, 494

κιννάμωμον,-ου⁺ N2N 1-0-1-2-1-5
Ex 30,23; Jer 6,20; Prv 7,17; Ct 4,14; Sir 24,15
Semit. loanword (Hebr. קנמון); *a superior kind of
cassia, cinnamon*
Cf. CAIRD 1976, 78; LE BOULLUEC 1989, 311; TOV 1979,
221; WALTERS 1973, 82.163; →CHANTRAINE; FRISK

κινύρα,-ας N1F 0-17-0-1-4-22
1 Sm 10,5; 16,16(bis).23; 2 Sm 6,5
Semit. loanword (Hebr. כנור); *stringed instrument,
lyre*; neol.
Cf. TOV 1979, 221; WALTERS 1973, 171-173;
→CHANTRAINE; FRISK

κιρνάω V 0-0-0-1-0-1
Ps 101(102),10
to mix with [τι μετά τινος]
(→μετα-)

κισσάω⁺ V 0-0-0-1-0-1
Ps 50(51),7
*to have a strong desire to conceive (as a result of)
pleasure* [τινα]
(→ἐγ-)

κισσός,-οῦ N2M 0-0-0-0-1-1
2 Mc 6,7
ivy

κισσόφυλλον,-ου N2N 0-0-0-0-1-1
3 Mc 2,29
ivy-leaf; neol.?

κιχράω⁺ V 0-1-0-2-0-3
1 Sm 1,28; Ps 111(112),5; Prv 13,11
to lend; neol.

κίων,-ονος N3M 0-5-0-0-0-5
Jgsᴮ 16,25.26.29; 1 Kgs 15,15(bis)
pillar

κλάδος,-ου⁺ N2M 2-2-11-6-10-31
Lv 23,40(bis); Jgsᴮ 9,48.49; Is 17,6
branch, twig

κλαίω⁺ V 27-53-24-21-43-168
Gn 21,16; 27,38; 29,11; 33,4; 37,35
to cry, to weep, to wail, to lament [abs.] Gn
21,16; *to weep* or *lament for, to bewail* [τινα]
Gn 37,35; *id.* [ἐπί τινι] Nm 11,13; *id.* [τι] Lv

10,6
κλαίω κλαυθμῷ μεγάλῳ *to weep bitterly* (semit.)
2 Kgs 20,3, cpr. Gn 46,29; Jgs 21,2; 2 Sm 13,36;
Is 30,19; Jer 22,10
→NIDNTT; TWNT
(→ἀπο-)

κλάσμα,-ατος⁺ N3N 2-6-1-0-0-9
Lv 2,6; 6,14; Jgs 9,53; Jgsᴬ 19,5
fragment, morsel, piece

κλαυθμός,-οῦ⁺ N2M 3-4-16-8-9-40
Gn 45,2; 46,29; Dt 34,8; Jgs 21,2
weeping, wailing Gn 45,2
*Lam 5,13 κλαυθμόν *weeping* corr.? ἀλεσμόν
-שחון *grinding*
Cf. ALBREKTSON 1963, 203(Lam 5,13); ZIEGLER 1958,
36-37(Lam 5,13)

κλαυθμών,-ῶνος N3M 0-6-0-1-0-7
Jgs 2,1.5; 2 Sm 5,23
(place of) weeping; Κλαυθμῶν *Weeping* (proper
name of place) Jgs 2,1, see also 2,5
*2 Sm 5,23 τοῦ κλαυθμῶνος *of weeping, of the
place of weeping* -בכהם for MT בכא *balsam tree,* see
also Jgs 2,1.5; 2 Sm 5,24; Ps 83(84),7
neol.

κλάω⁺ V 0-1-1-0-1-3
Jgsᴮ 9,53; Jer 16,7; 4 Mc 9,14
A: *to break* [τι] Jgsᴮ 9,53
P: *to be disjointed* 4 Mc 9,14
→TWNT
(→ἀνα-, ἀντανα-, δια-, ἐκ-, κατα-, περι-, συγ-)

κλεῖθρον,-ου⁺ N2N 0-0-0-7-1-8
Jb 26,13; 38,10; Ct 5,5; Neh 3,3.6
bar (for closing) Neh 3,3
*Jb 26,13 κλεῖθρα *the barriers* -בריחי for MT
ב/רוח by his wind

κλείς, κλειδός⁺ N3F 0-3-0-1-1-5
Jgs 3,25; 1 Chr 9,27; Jb 31,22; Belᴸˣˣ 11
key Jgs 3,25; *collar-bone* Jb 31,22
Cf. MENESTRINA 1978ᵇ, 182

κλείω⁺ V 1-5-8-7-7-28
Gn 7,16; Jos 2,5.7; Jgsᴮ 9,51; 1 Sm 23,20
to shut, to close [abs.] Jgsᴮ 9,51; *id.* [τι] Gn 7,16;
to shut up, to close up [τι] Sir 30,18; *to shut up*
[τινα] 1 Sm 23,20; *to shut in, to enclose* [τι] Ct
4,12
Cf. CAIRD 1969=1972, 134(1 Sm 23,20)
(→ἀπο-, ἐγ-, κατα-, παρα-, συγ-)

κλέμμα,-ατος⁺ N3N 4-0-0-0-0-4
Gn 31,39(bis); Ex 22,2.3
stolen thing Ex 22,2; *theft* Gn 31,39

κλέος,-ους⁺ N3N 0-0-0-2-0-2
Jb 28,22; 30,8
report (of sth) [τινος] Jb 28,22; *fame, glory* Jb
30,8

κλέπτης,-ου⁺ N1M 2-0-8-4-3-17
Ex 22,1; Dt 24,7; Is 1,23; Jer 2,26; 30,3(49,9)
thief
Cf. BUCHANAN 1959, 169

κλέπτω⁺ V 17-5-3-4-5-34
Gn 30,33; 31,19.30.32; 40,15
to steal [abs.] Ex 20,14; *id.* [τι] Gn 30,33; *to
carry off, to kidnap, to steal* [τινα] Ex 21,17
ὁ προφήτης ὁ κλέπτων τοὺς λόγους μου παρὰ
τοῦ πλησίον αὐτοῦ *the prophet who steals my
words from his neighbour* Jer 23,30
Cf. LLEWELYN 1994, 150-151; →NIDNTT; TWNT
(→δια-)

κλεψιμαῖος,-α,-ον A 0-0-0-0-4-4
Tob 2,13(bis)
stolen; neol.

κληδονίζω V 1-2-0-0-0-3
Dt 18,10; 2 Kgs 21,6; 2 Chr 33,6
M: *to practise divination*; neol.
Cf. DOGNIEZ 1992, 50.64

κληδονισμός,-οῦ N2M 0-0-1-0-0-1
Is 2,6
observation of a sign or *omen, divination*; neol.
→LSJ Suppl; LSJ RSuppl

κληδών,-όνος N3F 1-0-0-0-0-1
Dt 18,14
omen, presage
Cf. OPPENHEIM 1954, 49-55

κλῆμα,-ατος⁺ N3N 1-0-9-1-0-11
Nm 13,23; Jer 31(48),32; Ez 15,2; 17,6.7
branch, vine-twig
→TWNT

κληματίς,-ίδος N3F 1-0-1-2-1-5
Dt 32,32; Is 18,5; Dn 3,46; Od 2,32
dim. of κλῆμα; *vine-twig* Dt 32,32; *small branch*
Is 18,5

κληροδοσία,-ας N1F 0-0-0-4-1-5
Ps 77(78),55; Eccl 7,11; DnᴸˣˣX 11,21.34; 1 Mc
10,89
distribution of land, heritage Ps 77(78),55
δίδωμί τί τινι εἰς κληροδοσίαν *to give in
possession* 1 Mc 10,89
*DnᴸˣˣX 11,34 ἐν κληροδοσίᾳ *through a
distribution of land* -◊חלק for MT בחלקלקות *in
flatteries?*
neol.

κληροδοτέω V 0-0-0-2-1-3
Ps 77(78),55; Ezr 9,12; Sir 17,11
to distribute land to, to give land as a heritage to
[τινι] Ezr 9,12; *id.* [τινα] Ps 77(78),55; *to give
for a heritage* [τί τινι] Sir 17,11; neol.
(→κατα-)

κληρονομέω⁺ V 74-42-19-19-25-179
Gn 15,3.4(bis).7.8
to inherit [abs.] Gn 21,10; *id.* [τι] Nm 27,11; *id.*
[τινος] Is 63,18; *to be an heir of, to inherit from*
[τινα] Gn 15,3; *id.* [τινα] (metaph.) Sir 19,3; *to
leave an heir behind oneself, to make sb heir*
[τινα] Prv 13,22
to acquire, to obtain (from another person) [τι]
1 Mc 2,57
to receive or *gain possession of* [τι] (with or
without violence) Gn 22,17; *to seize the
possessions of, to take possession of, to expel*
[τινα] Jgs 11,23; *to take possession of* [τι]
Dt 1,8; *to give* or *divide as possession to* [τί
τινα] Jgsᴮ 11,24; *id.* [τί τινι] Nm 34,17
κληρονομέω τὴν γῆν *to receive possession of the
land* Dt 4,1; δόξαν κληρονομέω *to inherit glory*
Prv 3,35; κληρονομέω ἄνεμον *to obtain wind, to
have nothing* Prv 11,29; κληρονομέω τὰ
μαρτύρια *to obtain the testimonies*
Ps 118(119),111; κληρονομέω ἀπώλειαν *to
share in destruction* Sir 20,25; κληρονομέω
ὀργήν *to bring wrath on oneself* Sir 39,23; ὄνομα
πονηρὸν αἰσχύνην καὶ ὄνειδος κληρο-
νομήσει *an evil name shall inherit reproach and
shame* Sir 5,15
Cf. DOGNIEZ 1992, 113; HARL 1986ᵃ, 56; 1992ᵃ=1993, 188;
HELBING 1928, 138-141; LE BOULLUEC 1989, 47;
MURAOKA 1990, 43.44; →LSJ RSuppl; TWNT
(→κατα-, συγ-, συγκατα-)

κληρονομία,-ας⁺ N1F 38-71-41-35-41-226
Gn 31,14; Ex 15,17; Nm 18,20.23; 24,18
inheritance (in secular sense) Gn 31,14;
inheritance (of Israel) Dt 32,9; *property,
possession* Jdt 16,21(25)
δίδωμί τι(να) κληρονομίαν τινί *to give
someone sth as an inheritance, as a property*
Ps 2,8; λαμβάνω τι(να) εἰς κληρονομίαν *to
receive as an inheritance, as a possession* Est
4,17m
*Mi 1,14 ἕως κληρονομίας *to the inheritance
(of)* -עד מורשת◊ ירשת for MT מורשת על *to Moreshet*;
*Mi 1,15 κληρονομία *the inheritance* -ירש◊ מורשה
for MT מרשה *Mareshah*; *Zech 4,7 τὸν λίθον τῆς

κληρονομίας *the stone of inheritance, the*
inherited stone -האבן הירשה for MT האבן הראשה *the top*
stone
Cf. DORIVAL 1994, 58.168-169; →NIDNTT; TWNT

κληρονόμος,-ου⁺   N2M 0-2-2-0-2-6
JgsᴮB 18,7; 2 Sm 14,7; Jer 8,10; Mi 1,15; Sir 23,22
heir, (designated) holder or *possessor of an estate*
→LSJ RSuppl; TWNT

κλῆρος,-ου⁺   N2M 56-61-15-16-7-155
Gn 48,6; 49,14; Ex 6,8; Lv 16,8(bis)
lot Jon 1,7; *share, portion* Dt 10,9; *that which is*
assigned by lot, office, service Neh 10,35; *plot of*
land 1 Ezr 4,56; *inheritance* Gn 48,6
ἐν κλήρῳ *by lot* Ex 6,8; βάλλω κλήρους ἐπί τι
to cast lots for Ps 21(22),19; δίδωμι τινί τι ἐν
κλήρῳ *to give by lot* Dt 3,18; ἐν ἁγίοις ὁ
κλῆρος αὐτοῦ *his place (is) among the saints, he*
shares the lot of the saints Wis 5,5
Cf. HARL 1986ᵃ, 56.303; LARCHER 1983, 235-236; →NIDNTT;
TWNT

κληρόω   V 0-1-2-0-0-3
1 Sm 14,41; Is 17,11(bis)
M: *to obtain by lot, to receive, to have* Is 17,11
P: *to be appointed by lot* 1 Sm 14,41

κληρωτί   D 0-4-0-0-0-4
Jos 21,4.5.7.8
by lot; neol.

-κλησιάζω
(→ἐκ-)

κλῆσις,-εως⁺   N3F 0-0-1-0-2-3
Jer 38(31),6; Jdt 12,10; 3 Mc 5,14
calling, call Jer 38(31),6; *invitation, meal* Jdt
12,10

κλητέον   A 0-0-0-0-3-3
LtJ 39.44.63
to be called, to be said

κλητός,-ή,-όν⁺   A 13-4-1-0-1-19
Ex 12,16; Lv 23,2.3.4.7
invited Jgsᴮ 14,11; *called out, chosen* 2 Sm 15,11;
οἱ κλητοί *the guests* 3 Mc 5,14
*Ex 12,16 (ἡ) κλητή *called out, proclaimed* - מקרא-
(ptc. pual) ◊קרא for MT מקרא *festival*, see also
Lv 23,2.3 et al.; Nm 28,25
Cf. LE BOULLUEC 1989, 148; LEE, J. 1983, 51; WALTERS
1973, 244-246.321

κλίβανος,-ου⁺   N2M 6-0-4-2-0-12
Gn 15,17; Ex 7,28; Lv 2,4; 7,9; 11,35
oven, furnace
Cf. HARLÉ 1988, 89; WALTERS 1973, 326; WEVERS 1990,
107

κλίμα,-ατος⁺   N3N 0-1-0-0-0-1
Jgsᴬ 20,2
terrestrial latitude, region

κλιμακτήρ,-ῆρος   N3M 0-0-6-0-0-6
Ez 40,22.26.31.34.37
step

κλῖμαξ,-ακος⁺   N3F 1-0-0-2-2-5
Gn 28,12; Neh 3,15; 12,37; 1 Mc 5,30; 11,59
ladder Gn 28,12; *staircase* Neh 3,15

κλίνη,-ης⁺   N1F 5-17-2-10-13-47
Gn 48,2; 49,33; Ex 7,28; Dt 3,11(bis)
that on which one lies, couch, bed (for resting)
Gn 48,2; *bier* 2 Sm 3,31
ταμίειον τῶν κλινῶν *bed-chamber* 2 Kgs 11,2
Cf. HORSLEY 1981, 6-8

κλίνω⁺   V 0-18-10-26-9-63
Jgsᴬ 9,3; 16,30; 19,8.9.11
A: *to make to slope, to tip over, to pour out* Ps
74(75),9; *to incline, to tip over* [τι] Jer
31(48),12; *to tip over, to pour out* [τι] Jb 38,37
to go down [τι] 2 Kgs 20,10; *to bow* Jgsᴬ 16,30;
to lean to [πρός τι] Zech 14,4; *to turn, to incline*
towards Jgs 9,3; *to turn to* [εἴς τι] 1 Sm 14,32
to totter, to reel Is 24,20; *to give way* Is 33,23
to decline, to come to an end, to fall Ps 45(46),7;
to lay low, to decline, to be far spent (of the day)
Jgs 19,8; *to incline to* [εἴς τι] *(of the day)*
Jgsᴬ 19,9
P: *to bow down* LtJ 26; *to turn (of the war)*
1 Sm 4,2
κλίνω ἐπὶ τὰ γόνατα *to bow on the knees* Jgsᴮ
7,5; κλῖνον τὸ οὖς σου καὶ ἄκουσον *incline*
your ear and listen 2 Kgs 19,16; τοῖχος
κεκλιμένος *bowed* or *leaning wall* Ps 61(62),4;
ἐπ᾽ ἐμὲ ἔκλινεν ἔλεος *he has given me favour*
Ezr 7,28; ἔκλιναν εἰς σὲ κακά *they plan evil*
against you Ps 20(21),12
Cf. KATZ 1946ᵃ, 322-324
(→ἀνα-, ἀπο-, ἐκ-, ἐπι-, κατα-, παρανα-, προσ-)

κλισία,-ας⁺   N1F 0-0-0-0-1-1
3 Mc 6,31
group of people eating together, company of
people sitting at meals

κλίτος,-ους   N3N 38-2-5-2-0-47
Ex 25,12(ter).14.18
side Ex 26,18
*Ex 25,12 κλίτη *sides* - ◊פעמה פעמהו for MT פעמתיו◊פעם *its*
feet?
neol.?
Cf. DORIVAL 1994, 556; HARL 1987=1992ᵃ, 119(Ex 25,12);

LE BOULLUEC 1989, 255-256.276-278; WEVERS 1990, 397

κλοιός,-οῦ N2M 2-11-6-2-2-23
Gn 41,42; Dt 28,48; Jgs^A 8,26; 1 Kgs 12,4(bis)
chain, bond Sir 6,29; *yoke* Dt 28,48; *collar* (as
ornament) Gn 41,42
*Hab 2,6 τὸν κλοιὸν αὐτοῦ *his yoke* -עולו for
MT עלי *upon him, upon himself*; *Dn^Th 8,25 τοῦ
κλοιοῦ αὐτοῦ *of his chain* -שכלו◊ שכלו for MT שכלו
שכל◊ *of his insight, cunning*, see ζυγός

-κλοιόω
(→ἐγ-)

κλοπή,-ῆς⁺ N1F 1-0-2-1-2-6
Gn 40,15; Jer 31(48),27; Hos 4,2; Prv 9,17; Wis
14,25
theft Prv 9,17
κλοπῇ ἐκλάπην *I was surely stolen* (semit.) Gn
40,15
*Jer 31(48),27 ἐν κλοπαῖς σου *among your
thefts* -בגניבותיך for MT בגנבים *among thieves*
Cf. LLEWELYN 1994, 151

κλοποφορέω V 1-0-0-0-0-1
Gn 31,26
to steal from, to rob [τινα]; *Gn 31,26
ἐκλοποφόρησας *you stole from, you robbed*
corr.? ἐκλοποφρόνησας *you had the thoughts of
a thief* for MT גנב לבב *to deceive*?; neol.
Cf. HARL 1986ᵃ, 237; MUNNICH 1986, 43-51

κλύδων,-ωνος⁺ N3M 0-0-3-1-5-9
Jon 1,4.11.12; Prv 23,34; 1 Mc 6,11
wave, billow Jon 1,4 (metaph.); *id.* 4 Mc 7,5;
flood (metaph.) 1 Mc 6,11
*Prv 23,34 ἐν πολλῷ κλύδωνι *in a great storm*
-ב/רעש? or -ב/שער? for MT ב/ראש *on top of*?

κλυδωνίζω⁺ V 0-0-1-0-0-1
Is 57,20
P: *to be disturbed, to be thrown in confusion*
(metaph.); neol.

κλύζω
(→ἀπο-, ἐκ-, ἐπι-, κατα-, περι-, συγ-)

κλώθω⁺ V 33-0-0-0-1-34
Ex 25,4; 26,1(bis).31.36
to spin, to twist by spinning; βύσσος κεκλωσμένη
fine linen spun
Cf. LE BOULLUEC 1989, 272; WEVERS 1990, 393

κλών, κλωνός N3M 0-0-0-2-1-3
Jb 18,13; 40,22; Wis 4,5
twig, spray Jb 40,22
αὐτοῦ κλῶνες ποδῶν *the twigs of his feet, his
toes* Jb 18,13

κλῶσμα,-ατος N3N 1-1-0-0-1-3
Nm 15,38; Jgs^A 16,9; Sir 6,30
thread; neol.

κλωστός,-ή,-όν A 1-0-0-0-0-1
Lv 14,6
spun

κνήμη,-ης N1F 1-1-1-3-0-6
Dt 28,35; Jgs^B 15,8; Is 47,2; Ps 146(147),10; Ct
5,15
the part between knee and ankle, leg

κνημίς,-ῖδος N3F 0-1-0-0-0-1
1 Sm 17,6
greave, legging

κνήφη,-ης N1F 1-0-0-0-0-1
Dt 28,27
itch; neol.
Cf. DOGNIEZ 1992, 64.290

κνίδη,-ης N1F 0-0-0-1-0-1
Jb 31,40
nettle

κνίζω V 0-0-1-0-0-1
Am 7,14
to scratch, to gnash
Cf. MURAOKA 1989, 212
(→ἀπο-)

κνώδαλον,-ου N2N 0-0-0-0-3-3
Wis 11,15; 16,1; 17,9
any wild creature, esp. of beasts *vermin, wild
animal, brute*

κοθωνοι N 0-0-0-1-0-1
Ezr 2,69
= כתנת *linen tunic, garment*

κοιλάς,-άδος N3F 6-36-8-5-0-55
Gn 14,8.10.17; 37,14; Lv 14,37
hollow, indentation (in a wall) Lv 14,37; *(deep)
valley* Gn 14,8
Κοιλὰς εὐλογίας *Valley of blessing* 2 Chr 20,26

κοίλασμα,-ατος N3N 0-0-1-0-0-1
Is 8,14
hollow (hollowed out as trap); neol.
→LSJ RSuppl

κοιλία,-ας⁺ 3NF 29-16-23-26-14-108
Gn 3,14; 25,23.24; 30,2; 41,21
belly Gn 3,14; *stomach* Jer 28(51),34; *womb,
uterus* Jb 1,21
ἐκ κοιλίας *from birth* Is 48,8; καρπὸν κοιλίας
fruit of the womb, child Gn 30,2; πίπτω ἐπὶ
κοιλίαν *to fall prostrate* 2 Mc 10,4
→TWNT

κοῖλος,-η,-ον A 3-1-1-0-13-18
Ex 27,8; Lv 13,32.34; Jos 9,5; Jon 1,5

hollow Ex 27,8; *depressed* Lv 13,32

ἡ κοίλη τοῦ πλοίου *the hold of the ship* Jon 1,5; τὰ κοῖλα τῶν ὑποδημάτων *boots, shoes* Jos 9,5; Κοίλη Συρία *Coelesyria* (the district between Lebanon and anti-Lebanon) 1 Ezr 2,18

Cf. WEVERS 1990, 434(Ex 27,8)

κοιλοσταθμέω   V 0-2-0-0-0-2
1 Kgs 6,9.15
to provide the ceiling of (the house) with [τί τινι]; neol.

κοιλόσταθμος,-ος,-ον   A 0-0-1-0-0-1
Hag 1,4
with curved or *hollow supports*; neol.?

→LSJ RSuppl

κοιλότης,-ητος   N3F 0-0-0-0-1-1
Wis 17,18
hollowness, hollow

κοίλωμα,-ατος   N3N 1-1-1-1-1-5
Gn 23,2; 1 Kgs 7,3(15); Ez 43,14; Ct 2,17; 2 Mc 1,19
hollow, cavity (of a cistern) 2 Mc 1,19; *fluting* (of a pillar) 1 Kgs 7,3(15), cpr. Jer 52,21; *hollow place, low-lying land, valley* Gn 23,2 see Sam. Pent.

Cf. BARTHÉLEMY 1982, 345-346(1 Kgs 7,3(15))

κοιμάω⁺   V 67-69-24-30-12-202
Gn 19,4.32.33(bis).34
M/P: *to fall asleep, to go to bed, to sleep* Gn 19,4; *to sleep* or *lie with* [μετά τινος] (of sexual intercourse) Gn 19,32; *id.* [ἔν τινι] Dt 24,12; *to sleep (a sleep)* [τι] Wis 17,13; *to fall asleep, to die* 1 Kgs 2,10; *to lie* Jgs 5,27; *to remain somewhere during the night* (of things, semit.) Ex 23,18, see also Ex 34,25; Lv 19,13; Dt 16,4; 21,23; *to lodge, to remain* Is 1,21; *to calm, to still* Eccl 2,23

κοιμάομαι μετὰ ἄρσενος κοίτην γυναικείαν *to sleep with a man as with a woman* Lv 18,22; κοιμάομαι μετὰ τῶν πατέρων *to sleep with one's fathers, to be dead* Gn 47,30

*Jer 51,33(45,3) ἐκοιμήθην *I lay down* or corr. ἐκοπώθην (see κοπόω) -יצעתי? for MT יגעתי *I am weary*; *1 Sm 9,26 καὶ ἐκοιμήθη *and he lay down* -וישכיב for MT וישכמו *and they arose early*; *Jb 21,13 ἐκοιμήθησαν *they fall asleep, they lie down* -נרחם for MT נחתו *they go down* or pre-MT? נחתת *they are terrified*; *Jb 22,11 κοιμηθέντα *lying down* -שכבת? for MT שפעת *abundance, multitude*

Cf. GEHMAN 1953, 145-148; HORSLEY 1983, 93; LARCHER

1985, 971(Wis 17,13); LE BOULLUEC 1989, 238(Ex 23,18); WALTERS 1973, 119

(→ἐπι-)

κοίμησις,-εως⁺   N3F 0-0-0-0-2-2
Sir 46,19; 48,13
sleep (of death)

κοιμίζω   V 1-10-1-2-1-15
Gn 24,11; Jgsᴬ 16,14; Jgs 16,19; 2 Sm 8,2
A: *to put to sleep, to rest* [τινα] Gn 24,11; *to harbour for the night* [τινα] 1 Kgs 3,20
P: *to be laid down* 2 Kgs 4,32
*Na 3,18 ἐκοίμισεν *he put to sleep, he put to death* -ישכיב? or -שכב? for MT ישכנו *they dwell*?

Cf. WALTERS 1973, 119; WEVERS 1993, 347

κοινῇ⁺   D 0-0-0-0-5-5
2 Mc 4,5; 9,26; Sir 18,1; 50,17; Susᵀʰ 14
in general, in its entirety Sir 18,1; *together* Sir 50,17; *in public, publicly* 2 Mc 4,5

κοινολογέομαι   V 0-0-0-0-2-2
1 Mc 14,9; 15,28
to hold discussions with, to negotiate with [τινι] 1 Mc 15,28; *id.* [abs.] 1 Mc 14,9

Cf. HELBING 1928, 246

κοινολογία,-ας   N1F 0-0-0-0-1-1
2 Mc 14,22
conference

κοινός,-ή,-όν⁺   A 0-0-0-5-15-20
Prv 1,14; 15,23; 21,9; 25,24; Est 5,1f
common Prv 1,14; *common, impure* 1 Mc 1,62; *public* Est 5,1f; τὸ κοινόν *the people* Prv 15,23

Cf. HARL 1991=1992ᵃ, 151-152; TRÉHEUX 1987, 39-46; →NIDNTT; TWNT

κοινόω⁺   V 0-0-0-0-1-1
4 Mc 7,6
to make common, to make unclean [τί τινι]

(→ἀνα-)

κοινωνέω⁺   V 0-1-0-3-9-13
2 Chr 20,35; Jb 34,8; Prv 1,11; Eccl 9,4; 2 Mc 5,20
to have in common with [τι πρός τι] Sir 13,2; *to share, to take part in* [τινος] Prv 1,11; *id.* [τινι] Wis 6,23; *to have fellowship with* [πρός τινα] Eccl 9,4; *id.* [τινι] Sir 13,1; *to enter in alliance with* [πρός τινα] 2 Chr 20,35; *to communicate with* [τινι] 3 Mc 4,11

κοινωνέω ὁδοῦ μετά τινος *to share the path with, to go the same way as sb* Jb 34,8; κοινωνέω βίου *to lead a married life* 2 Mc 14,25

Cf. HELBING 1928, 136.252; →TWNT

(→ἐπι-)
κοινωνία,-ας⁺ N1F 1-0-0-0-2-3
Lv 5,21; 3 Mc 4,6; Wis 8,18
sign of fellowship, gift, contribution Lv 5,21
κοινωνία λόγων *sharing of words, conversation*
Wis 8,18; βίου κοινωνία *partnership of*
marriage 3 Mc 4,6
Cf. HORSLEY 1983, 19; →NIDNTT; TWNT
κοινωνός,-οῦ⁺ N2M 0-1-2-2-3-8
2 Kgs 17,11; Is 1,23; Mal 2,14; Prv 28,24; Est
8,12n
accomplice [τινος] Is 1,23; (ὁ) κοινωνός
partner, friend Sir 41,19; *partner, companion in*
or of [τινος] Est 8,12n
*2 Kgs 17,11 κοινωνούς *partners, friends* חברים-
for MT רברים *(wicked) things*
Cf. HORSLEY 1983, 19; →TWNT
κοινῶς D 0-0-0-0-8-8
Tobᴮᴬ 5,14; 9,6; Tobˢ 2,2; 6,6; 8,7
together
κοιτάζω V 3-0-3-3-0-9
Lv 15,20; Dt 6,7; 11,19; Jer 40(33),12; Zph 2,14
A: *to provide a fold for, to fold (sheep)* [τινα]
Jer 40(33),12; *to cause to lie down, to cause to*
rest [τινα] Ct 1,7
M/P: *to lie (down) (for sleeping)* Dt 6,7; *to lie*
(down) on sth [ἐπί τι] Lv 15,20
Cf. DOGNIEZ 1992, 155
κοιτασία,-ας N1F 1-0-0-0-0-1
Lv 20,15
sexual intercourse; neol.
Cf. HARLÉ 1988, 177
κοίτη,-ης⁺ N1F 26-12-10-24-9-81
Gn 49,4; Ex 10,23; 21,18; Lv 15,4.5
bed Ex 10,23; *marriage-bed* Gn 49,4; *nest* (of
asps) Is 11,8; *pen, fold* (of cattle) Is 17,2; *rest* Jb
36,28a; *sexual intercourse* Lv 20,13; *ejaculation*
of seed Nm 5,20, cpr. Lv 15,16
κοίτη σπέρματος *ejaculation of seed* Lv 15,16
Cf. HARLÉ 1988, 148.174; WEVERS 1990, 157; →NIDNTT;
TWNT
κοιτών,-ῶνος⁺ N3M 1-6-2-1-5-15
Ex 7,28; Jgsᴬ 3,24; 15,1; 2 Sm 4,7; 13,10
bedroom
Cf. LE BOULLUEC 1989, 122
κόκκινος,-η,-ον⁺ A 33-5-3-2-0-43
Gn 38,28.30; Ex 25,4; 26,1.31
red, scarlet Nm 4,8; τὸ κόκκινον *scarlet thread*
or wool Gn 38,30; *scarlet garment* 2 Sm 1,24;
neol.?

Cf. LE BOULLUEC 1989, 283.347-348; LEE, J. 1983, 111;
WEVERS 1990, 393
κόκκος,-ου⁺ N2M/F 0-0-0-1-1-2
Lam 4,5; Sir 45,10
scarlet Lam 4,5; *scarlet thread* Sir 45,10
→LSJ RSuppl(Sir 45,10)
κολαβρίζω⁺ V 0-0-0-1-0-1
Jb 5,4
P: *to be derided*; neol.
κολάζω⁺ V 0-0-0-1-21-22
Dnᴸˣˣ 6,13a; 1 Ezr 8,24; 1 Mc 7,7; 2 Mc 6,14;
3 Mc 3,26
A: *to punish, to chastise* [τινα] Wis 11,8
M: *to get a person punished* [τινα] 3 Mc 7,14
P: *to be punished* 1 Ezr 8,24
→TWNT
κολακεύω⁺ V 0-0-0-1-2-3
Jb 19,17; 1 Ezr 4,31; Wis 14,17
to flatter [τινα]
Cf. SPICQ 1978ᵃ, 436-439
κολάπτω V 1-2-0-0-2-5
Ex 32,16; 1 Kgs 7,46(9).49(12); 3 Mc 2,27; Sir
45,11
A: *to carve, to engrave* [τι] 3 Mc 2,27
P: *to be carved, to be engraved* Ex 32,16; *to be*
sculptured 1 Kgs 7,49(9)
Cf. WEVERS 1990, 528
(→ἐγ-, ἐκ-)
κόλασις,-εως⁺ N3F 0-0-7-0-8-15
Jer 18,20; Ez 14,3.4.7; 18,30
chastisement, punishment Wis 11,13; *vengeance*
3 Mc 1,3; *that which brings about punishment,*
stumbling block, trap Jer 18,20, see also Ez
14,3.4.7; 18,30; 44,12; cpr. Jer 18,22
Cf. JANZEN 1973, 27(Jer 18,20); MCKANE 1986, 439(Jer
18,20); →LSJ Suppl; LSJ RSuppl
κολεός,-οῦ N2M 0-2-4-0-0-6
2 Sm 20,8; 1 Chr 21,27; Jer 29(47),6; Ez 21,8.9
sheath, scabbard
κόλλα,-ης N1F 0-0-1-0-0-1
Is 44,13
glue
κολλάω⁺ V 4-6-2-16-9-37
Dt 6,13; 10,20; 28,60; 29,19; 2 Sm 20,2
A: *to glue, to cement* [τι] Jb 38,38; *to cuase to*
cleave to, to make to clung to [τι πρός τινα] Jer
13,11(secundo)
P: *to be close to* [τινι] Jb 29,10; *to cleave to, to*
cling to [τινι] Ps 21(22),16; *id.* [εἰς τι] Ps
43(44),26; *to join oneself to, to join, to cling to,*

to associate with [πρός τινα] Dt 6,13; *id.* [εἰς τινα] 1 Kgs 11,2; *id.* [ἔν τινι] Dt 28,60; *id.* [μετά τινος] Ru 2,8; *id.* [τινος] Jb 41,8; *to be joined to (one's wife)* [πρός τινα] 1 Ezr 4,20; *to join oneself to (the Lord)* [τινι] 2 Kgs 18,6; *to become a follower* or *disciple of* [τινι] 2 Sm 20,2; *to cling to, to enter into a close relation with* [τινι] Ps 118(119),31

Cf. DOGNIEZ 1992, 58.120.156-157; HARL 1971=1992ᵃ, 191-192; HELBING 1928, 248-250; SCHWARTZ 1983, 550-555

(→ἐγ-, προσ-, συγ-)

κολλυρίζω   V 0-2-0-0-0-2
2 Sm 13,6.8
to bake; neol.

κολλύριον,-ου⁺   N2N 0-3-0-0-0-3
1 Kgs 12,24h.i.1
cake

κολλυρίς,-ίδος   N3F 0-4-0-0-0-4
2 Sm 6,19; 13,6.8.10
cake; neol.

κολοβόκερκος,-ος,-ον   A 1-0-0-0-0-1
Lv 22,23
with a docked tail; neol.
Cf. HARLÉ 1988, 186

κολοβόρριν (gen. -ινος)   A 1-0-0-0-0-1
Lv 21,18
slit-nosed, with a disfigured or *broken nose*; neol.
Cf. HARLÉ 1988, 182

κολοβόω⁺   V 0-1-0-0-0-1
2 Sm 4,12
to mutilate, to cut off [τι]

κολόκυνθα,-ης   N1F 0-0-5-0-0-5
Jon 4,6(bis).7.9.10
gourd (plant)

κόλπος,-ου⁺   N2M 11-7-5-17-1-41
Gn 16,5; Ex 4,6(ter).7
arms, bosom, breast Gn 16,5; *id.* (denoting physical closeness of a woman to a man) Dt 13,7; *id.* (denoting tender physical closeness of a man to a woman) Dt 28,56; *id.* (of a nursing woman) Ru 4,16
bottom (of chariot) 1 Kgs 22,35; *disk, bowl* Prv 19,24
*Hos 8,1 εἰς κόλπον αὐτῶν *into their bosom, into their midst* -אל חקם◊ חיקם◊ אל חך◊ חך-to *your palate, to your lips*; *Jb 23,12 ἐν δὲ κόλπῳ μου *in my bosom* -בחקי◊ חיקי for MT חקי מחקי◊ חקו *from my law*?
Cf. HORSLEY 1983, 106.107; LEE, J. 1969, 236-237;

MOLONEY 1983, 65; →LSJ Suppl(Prv 19,24); TWNT

κόλπωμα,-ατος   N3N 0-0-1-0-0-1
Ez 43,13
bosom, cavity, drain (around the altar); neol.
Cf. DIJKSTRA 1992, 28

κολυμβάω⁺
(→δια-)

κολυμβήθρα,-ας⁺   N1F 0-1-5-4-0-10
2 Kgs 18,17; Is 7,3; 22,9.11; 36,2
reservoir, cistern 2 Kgs 18,17; *pool, swimming-pool* Neh 2,14

κόμη,-ης⁺   N1F 2-0-2-3-5-12
Lv 19,27; Nm 6,5; Ez 24,23; 44,20; Jb 1,20
hair (of the head) Lv 19,27
*Jb 38,32 ἐπὶ κόμης αὐτοῦ *with his hair, with his rays?* corr. ἐπὶ κώμης αὐτοῦ? *with his quarter* -בניה◊ על בניה? for MT בק◊ על בניה *with her sons, with her little ones*

κομιδῇ   D 0-0-0-0-1-1
4 Mc 3,1
supremely, exceedingly

κομίζω⁺   V 2-0-4-2-21-29
Gn 38,20; Lv 20,17; Ez 16,52.54.58
A: *to carry off* [τι] Ezr 6,5; *to bring* [τι] 1 Ezr 9,39; *to bring to* [τί τινι] 1 Ezr 4,5
M: *to receive* [τι] Gn 38,20; *id.* [τινα] 2 Mc 7,29; *to bear* [τι] Ez 16,52; *to receive, to incur* [τι] Lv 20,17; *to take as wife* [τινα] Tobᴮᴬ 7,12
(→ἀνα-, ἀπο-, δια-, μετα-, παρα-, συγ-)

κόμμα,-ατος   N3N 0-0-0-0-1-1
1 Mc 15,6
stamp, impression of a coin

κομπέω
(→περι-)

κόμπος,-ου⁺   N2M 0-0-0-1-1-2
Est 8,12d; 3 Mc 6,5
boast, vaunt

κόνδυ,-υος   N3N 7-0-2-0-0-9
Gn 44,2.5.9.10.12
drinking-vessel, cup
Cf. CAIRD 1969=1972, 134(Gn 44,2); CUNEN 1959, 396-404; HARL 1986ᵃ, 286(Gn 44,2); LEE, J. 1983, 116; WEVERS 1993, 740

κονδυλίζω   V 0-0-2-0-0-2
Am 2,7; Mal 3,5
to strike with the fist (on the head of sb), *to oppress* [εἴς τί τινος] Am 2,7; *to maltreat, to oppress* [τινα] Mal 3,5
(→κατα-)

κονδυλισμός,-οῦ   N2M 0-0-1-0-0-1

Zph 2,8
cruel act; neol.

κονία,-ας   N1F 2-0-1-2-0-5
Dt 27,2.4; Am 2,1; Jb 28,4; 38,38
dust Jb 38,38; *plaster, lime* Dt 27,2
*Jb 28,4 ἀπὸ κονίας *because of dust, plaster*
מעם גיר- for MT מעם גר *away from human
habitation*?

κονίαμα,-ατος   N3N 0-0-0-3-0-3
Dn^LXX 5,prol.; Dn 5,5
plaster, stucco

κονιάω⁺   V 2-0-0-1-0-3
Dt 27,2.4; Prv 21,9
to plaster [τι] Dt 27,2
ἐν κεκονιαμένοις μετὰ ἀδικίας *in rooms
plastered with injustice* Prv 21,9

κονιορτός,-οῦ⁺   N2M 4-2-7-3-3-19
Ex 9,9; Dt 9,21(bis); 28,24; 2 Kgs 9,17
dust raised or *stirred up, cloud of dust* Ex 9,9;
dust Is 17,13; *powder* Ct 3,6

κόνις,-εως   N3F 0-0-0-0-2-2
3 Mc 1,18; 4,6
ashes 3 Mc 1,18; *dust* 3 Mc 4,6

κοντός,-οῦ   N2M 0-1-1-0-0-2
1 Sm 17,7; Ez 39,9
pole, shaft 1 Sm 17,7; *spear* Ez 39,9

κόνυζα,-ης   N1F 0-0-1-0-0-1
Is 55,13
fleabane, nettle

κοπάζω⁺   V 7-4-6-5-5-27
Gn 8,1.7.8.11; Nm 11,2
to have rest (from) [τινος] Jos 14,15, cpr. Jos
11,23; *to cease* (of pers.) Jgs^B 15,7; *id.* [+inf.] Ru
1,18; *to cease from* [ἀπό τινος] Ez 43,10; *to
cease* (of a plague) Nm 17,13; *to become calm,
to stay* (of water) Gn 8,1; *to be quenched* (of
fire) Nm 11,2
to cause to cease [τι] Sir 46,7; *to appease* [τι]
Sir 39,28; *to still* (the deep) [τι] Sir 43,23
ὁ βασιλεὺς ἐκόπασεν τοῦ θυμοῦ *the king's
anger was pacified* Est 2,1
*Ez 43,10 κοπάσουσιν *that they may cease*
-כלה? for MT כלם *that they may be ashamed*;
*Hos 8,10 καὶ κοπάσουσιν *and they shall cease*
חללו ויחרלו- or ?ויחלו for MT ויחלו תללו *they
began*?
Cf. HELBING 1928, 79.171; WALTERS 1973, 130-131.317;
→LSJ RSuppl

κοπανίζω   V 0-2-0-1-0-3
1 Kgs 2,46e; 5,2; Dn^LXX 7,7

to grind, to pound; neol.

κοπετός,-οῦ⁺   N2M 1-0-11-2-6-20
Gn 50,10; Is 22,12; Jer 6,26; 9,9; Jl 2,12
mourning, lamentation Is 22,12
κόπτω κοπετόν (semit.) *to mourn bitterly* Gn
50,10, see also Zech 12,10; 1 Mc 2,70; 4,39;
9,20; 13,26
Cf. HARL 1986ᵃ, 70.316-317

κοπή,-ῆς⁺   N1F 1-1-0-0-1-3
Gn 14,17; Jos 10,20; Jdt 15,7
slaughter Jos 10,20; *defeat* Gn 14,17

κοπιάω⁺   V 2-8-20-8-13-51
Dt 25,18(bis); Jos 24,13; Jgs^B 5,26; 1 Sm 6,12
to be tired, to grow or *be weary* Dt 25,18; *to work
hard, to toil, to labour* [abs.] Sir 31,3; *id.* [ἐπί
τι] Jos 24,13
κοπιῶντες *workmen* Jgs^B 5,26
*1 Sm 6,12 καὶ ἐκοπίων *and they laboured* -יגע◊
for MT וגעו נעה◊ *and they bellowed*; *1 Sm 17,39
καὶ ἐκοπίασεν *and he laboured, he tried to*
-לאה◊ וילא for MT יאל◊ ויאל *and he decided to*?;
*2 Sm 23,7 κοπιάσει *he shall labour* -יגע◊ יגע for
MT נגע◊ יגע *he shall touch*?
Cf. SPICQ 1982, 407-412; WALTERS 1973, 130-131;
→NIDNTT; TWNT

κόπος,-ου⁺   N2M 2-2-8-15-9-36
Gn 31,42; Dt 1,12; Jgs 10,16; Jer 20,18
work, labour Gn 31,42; *trouble* Ps 9,28(10,7);
trouble, difficulty 1 Mc 10,15; *suffering* Jgs 10,16;
reward for labour Sir 14,15
κόπον παρέχω τινί *to put to trouble, to cause
trouble for* Sir 29,4
*Mal 2,13 ἐκ κόπων *because of troubles* -מ/און for
MT מ/אין *without, because not*; *Jb 4,2 ἐν κόπῳ *in
weariness* -ב/תלאה for MT תלאה לאה◊ *you will be
rejected* or *you will be weary*?
Cf. DOGNIEZ 1992, 114; DRESCHER 1970, 142-145; SPICQ
1982, 404-412; →NIDNTT; TWNT

κοπόω   V 0-0-0-1-1-2
Eccl 10,15; Jdt 13,1
A: *to weary, to exhaust with physical trouble*
[τινα] Eccl 10,15
P: *to be weary* Jdt 13,1
neol.
→LSJ RSuppl

κοπρία,-ας⁺   N2N 0-2-1-8-2-13
1 Sm 2,8; 2 Kgs 9,37; Is 5,25; Ps 112(113),7; Jb
2,8
dung 2 Kgs 9,37; *dunghill* Jb 2,8; *refuse* Sir 27,4;
κοπρίαι *dung* Est 4,17k

πυλή τῆς κοπρίας *dung-gate* Neh 2,13; τὸ
τεῖχος τῆς κοπρίας *dung-wall* Neh 12,31

κόπριον,-ου⁺   N2N 0-0-1-0-2-3
Jer 32(25),33; 1 Mc 2,62; Sir 22,2
dirt, filth, dung

κόπρος,-ου⁺   N2F 5-2-3-1-0-11
Ex 29,14; Lv 4,11; 8,17; 16,27; Nm 19,5
excrement, dung

κόπτω⁺   V 9-31-39-3-9-91
Gn 23,2; 50,10; Ex 27,20; 29,40; Lv 24,2
A: *to smite, to slaughter* [τινα] Jos 10,20; *to cut*
[τι] Jer 23,29; *to cut from* [τινα ἀπό τινος] Jer
31(48),2; *to cut down, to fell* [τι] Dt 19,5; *to cut
down* [τι] Nm 13,23(24); *to cut, to block* [τινα]
Dt 25,18; *to make havoc, to destroy* 2 Sm 5,24
M: *to beat* or *strike oneself (through grief), to
mourn for* [τινα] Gn 23,2; *id.* [ἐπί τινα] 2 Sm
1,12; *to lament* [abs.] 2 Sm 3,31
P: *to be mourned for* Jer 8,2
ἔλαιον κεκομμένον *pure oil* Ex 27,20
*Jgs^Λ 20,43 ἔκοψαν *they cut down* -כרתו or - כתתו
for MT כתרו *they surrounded*?
Cf. HARL 1986ᵃ, 70.316-317; LE BOULLUEC 1989, 280;
WALTERS 1973, 341; WEVERS 1993, 843
(→ἀνα-, ἀπο-, δια-, ἐκ-, κατα-, προσ-, συγ-)

κόπωσις,-εως   N3F 0-0-0-1-0-1
Eccl 12,12
weariness; neol.

κόραξ,-ακος⁺   N3M 3-2-2-4-1-12
Gn 8,7; Lv 11,15; Dt 14,14; 1 Kgs 17,4.6
raven

κοράσιον,-ου⁺   N3N 0-5-2-11-10-28
1 Sm 9,11.12; 20,30; 25,42; 1 Kgs 12,24l
dim. of κόρη; *girl, damsel* Tobˢ 6,13; *maid, slave*
1 Sm 25,42
*1 Sm 20,30 υἱὲ κορασίων αὐτομολούντων
son of (traitorous) girls -(המרדות) בן נערת for MT
(המרדות) בן נעות *son of a perverse (rebellious)*
woman
neol.
Cf. AMUSIN 1986, 121; SPICQ 1978ᵇ, 216-218; →LSJ RSuppl

κορέω   V 1-0-0-0-0-1
Dt 31,20
to satisfy oneself
Cf. DOGNIEZ 1992, 317

κόρη,-ης⁺   N1F 1-0-1-4-4-10
Dt 32,10; Zech 2,12; Ps 16(17),8; Prv 7,2; 20,9a
pupil (of the eye), apple of the eye Prv 20,9a
κόρη ὀφθαλμοῦ *the apple of an eye* (metaph.)
Dt 32,10

Cf. DOGNIEZ 1992, 327; MCCARTHY 1981, 289-295

κόριον,-ου   N2N 3-0-0-0-0-3
Ex 16,14.31; Nm 11,7
coriander (plant)
Cf. LE BOULLUEC 1989, 56; WEVERS 1990, 249.259

κόρος,-ου⁺   N2M 2-8-1-1-1-13
Lv 27,16; Nm 11,32; 1 Kgs 2,46e(bis); 5,2
Semit. loanword (Hebr. כר); *kor* (Hebr. dry
measure of 450 litres); neol.
Cf. DORIVAL 1994, 52; HARLÉ 1988, 212; LEE, J. 1983,
116-117; TOV 1979, 232-233; WALTERS 1973, 183;
→CHANTRAINE; FRISK

κόρος,-ου   N2M 0-0-0-1-0-1
Est 8,12c
satiety, surfeit, prosperity
Cf. WALTERS 1973, 183

κορύνη,-ης   N1F 0-1-0-0-0-1
2 Sm 21,16
club, mace

κόρυς,-υθος   N3F 0-0-0-0-1-1
Wis 5,18
helmet

κορυφή,-ῆς   N1F 20-12-9-4-10-55
Gn 49,26; Ex 17,9.10; 19,20(bis)
summit, top Ex 17,9; *crown, top of the head* Dt
33,16; *extremity, point, tip* (of a finger) 4 Mc
10,7; *head* Prv 1,9
Cf. DOGNIEZ 1992, 350; DORIVAL 1994, 97

κορώνη,-ης   N1F 0-0-1-0-1-2
Jer 3,2; LtJ 53
crow, raven LtJ 53
*Jer 3,2 ὡσεὶ κορώνη *like a raven* -כְּעֹרֵב for MT
כַּעֲרָבִי *like a Nomad, like an Arab*

κόσκινον,-ου   N2N 0-0-0-0-1-1
Sir 27,4
sieve

κοσμέω⁺   V 0-1-5-3-14-23
2 Chr 3,6; Jer 4,30; Ez 16,11.13; 23,40
to set in order [τι] Sir 47,10; *to arrange, to
establish* [τι] Sir 42,21; *to prepare, to furnish (a
table)* [τι] Sir 29,26; *to order, to rule* [τι] Mi 6,9;
to adorn [τινα] Jdt 12,15; *id.* [τι] 2 Chr 3,6; *to
adorn, to embellish* [τι] (metaph.) 3 Mc 3,5; *to
dress* [τινα] LtJ 10; *to polish, to measure off*
[τι] Sir 38,28; κοσμούμενος *orderly, goodly* Sir
45,12
Cf. ROST 1967, 119-121; SPICQ 1978ᵃ, 440-445; →NIDNTT;
TWNT
(→ἀπο-, δια-, ἐγ-, ἐπι-, κατα-, περι-)

κόσμιον,-ου⁺   N2N 0-0-0-1-0-1

Eccl 12,9
ornament (in a speech), epithet
Cf. SPICQ 1978ᵃ, 442

κοσμοπλήθης,-ής,-ές   A 0-0-0-0-1-1
4 Mc 15,31
filling the world, worldwide; neol.

κοσμοποιΐα,-ας   N1F 0-0-0-0-1-1
4 Mc 14,7
creation of the world

κόσμος,-ου⁺   N2M 5-2-17-5-43-72
Gn 2,1; Ex 33,5.6; Dt 4,19; 17,3
world, universe Prv 17,6a; *world, earth* 2 Mc
3,12; *world, mankind* Wis 2,24
ornament, decoration Ex 33,5; *honour, delight*
Prv 28,17a
*Gn 2,1 ὁ κόσμος *ornamentation* - צבי or- צבאה for
MT צבאם *host, army*, see also Dt 4,19; 17,3;
Is 24,21; 40,26; Sir 50,19; *2 Sm 1,24 μετὰ
κόσμου ὑμῶν *with your ornaments* - עריכן for
MT עדנים עם *with luxury, with ornaments*
Cf. DOGNIEZ 1992, 138; HARL 1986ᵃ, 98; SCHMITT 1974,
152; →MM; NIDNTT; TWNT

κοσμοφορέω   V 0-0-0-0-1-1
4 Mc 15,31
to carry the whole living world; neol.
Cf. HARL 1987=1992ᵃ, 110

κόσυμβος,-ου   N2M 1-0-1-0-0-2
Ex 28,39; Is 3,18
tassel, fringe; neol.
Cf. LE BOULLUEC 1989, 293; WEVERS 1990, 462

κοσυμβωτός,-ός,-όν   A 1-0-0-0-0-1
Ex 28,4
tasseled, fringed; neol.
Cf. LE BOULLUEC 1989, 282-283; WEVERS 1990, 446

κοτέω
(→ἐγ-)

κοτύλη,-ης   N1F 5-0-3-0-0-8
Lv 14,10.12.15.21.24
cup, liquid measure, log

κουρά,-ᾶς   N1F 1-0-0-2-0-3
Dt 18,4; Jb 31,20; Neh 3,15
shorn wool, fleece Dt 18,4
*Neh 3,15 τῇ κουρᾷ *by the shearing* -גז for MT
גן *garden*
Cf. LEE, J. 1983, 58; WALTERS 1973, 291-292(Neh 3,15)

κουρεύς,-έως   N3M 0-1-1-0-0-2
Jgsᴬ 16,19; Ez 5,1
barber, hair-cutter

κουφίζω⁺   V 1-5-1-3-1-11
Ex 18,22; 1 Sm 6,5; 1 Kgs 12,4.9.10

A: *to lighten of sth* [ἀπό τινος] 1 Kgs 12,4; *to
unburden, to make it easier for sb* [ἀπό τινος]
Ex 18,22; *id.* [ἐπί τινα] 1 Kgs 12,24p; *to lift, to
bear* [τι] Est 5,1a; *to make light* (sins) [τι] 1 Ezr
8,84; *to lighten a ship of sth* (by throwing out the
cargo) [τι ἀπό τινος] Jon 1,5
P: *to be lightened (of his sins), to be spared* Jb
21,30
κουφίζω τὴν χεῖρα ἀπό τινος *to lighten one's
hand off sb, to lighten one's wrath weighing on sb*
1 Sm 6,5
Cf. HELBING 1928, 165
(→ἐπι-)

κοῦφος,-η,-ον   A 0-6-6-2-4-18
1 Sm 18,23; 2 Sm 1,23; 2,18; 2 Kgs 3,18; 20,10
light, nimble, swift 2 Sm 1,23; *light, slight* Wis
5,11; *easy, light* 1 Sm 18,23; *light-minded, unwise*
Sir 19,4

κούφως   D 0-0-1-0-0-1
Is 5,26
lightly, nimbly, quickly

κόφινος,-ου⁺   N2M 0-1-0-1-0-2
Jgsᴮ 6,19; Ps 80(81),7
basket

κόχλαξ,-ακος   N3M 0-1-0-0-1-2
1 Sm 14,14; 1 Mc 10,73
pebble; neol.

κραδαίνω   V 0-0-0-0-2-2
2 Mc 11,8; 3 Mc 2,22
to shake, to agitate

κράζω⁺   V 5-20-25-50-11-111
Gn 41,55; Ex 5,8; 22,22; 32,17; Nm 11,2
to cry, to say loudly Ex 5,8; *to cry to, to call to*
[πρός τινα] Gn 41,55; *id.* [τινα] Ps
118(119),146; *to cry* [τι] Jgsᴮ 18,24; *to utter
loudly* (a voice) [τι] Ps 26(27),7; *to bray* (of a
donkey) Jb 6,5
Cf. CAIRD 1976, 81; CIMOSA 1991, 108-111; HARL
1971=1992ᵃ, 189(Ps 118(119),146); LEE, J. 1983, 124.144;
RUIZ 1984, 297-312
(→ἀνα-)

κραίνω
(→παρεπι-)

κραιπαλάω   V 0-0-2-1-0-3
Is 24,20; 29,9; Ps 77(78),65
to be overpowered with wine, to become drunk

κρᾶμα,-ατος   N3N 0-0-0-1-0-1
Ct 7,3
mixed wine

κρανίον,-ου⁺   N2N 0-3-0-0-0-3

Jgs 9,53; 2 Kgs 9,35
upper part of the head, skull

κράσπεδον,-ου⁺   N2N 4-0-1-0-0-5
Nm 15,38(bis).39; Dt 22,12; Zech 8,23
fringe, tassel

Cf. DOGNIEZ 1992, 254-255; LEE, J. 1983, 51; →LSJ suppl;
LSJ RSuppl

κραταιός,-ά,-όν⁺   A 17-11-8-20-12-68
Ex 3,19; 6,1; 13,3.9.14
strong 2 Sm 22,31; *vehement* 1 Sm 14,52(51);
severe 1 Kgs 12,24g
ἐν χειρὶ κραταιᾷ *with a strong hand* Ex 13,3
and passim

Cf. LE BOULLUEC 1989, 94-95

κραταιότης,-ητος   N3F 0-0-0-1-0-1
Ps 45(46),4
power, might; neol.

κραταιόω⁺   V 0-32-0-28-3-63
Jgs 3,10; 1 Sm 4,9; 23,16; 30,6
A: *strengthen* [τινα] Jdt 13,7; *id.* [τι] 1 Sm
23,16; *to prevail against* [ἐπί τινα] 2 Sm 11,23;
id. [ὑπέρ τινα] 1 Kgs 21(20),23
P: *to strengthen oneself* 1 Sm 4,9; *to be (made)
strong* 2 Sm 3,1; *to prevail* Jgs 3,10; *to be too
strong for, to prevail against* [ὑπέρ τινα] 2 Sm
10,11; *id.* [ἐπί τινα] 2 Sm 1,23; *id.* [ὑπέρ
τινος] 2 Sm 10,12; *to be determined to* [τοῦ
+inf.] Ru 1,18; *id.* [+ inf.] 2 Chr 35,22
αἱ χεῖρες αὐτῶν ἐκραταιώθησαν *they gained
strength* Neh 2,18
neol.

Cf. ALLEN 1974, 59; PASSONI DELL'ACQUA 1982ᵃ, 192-194;
→LSJ suppl; LSJ RSuppl
(→ἐπι-)

κραταίωμα,-ατος   N3N 0-0-0-4-0-4
Ps 24(25),14; 27(28),8; 30(31),4; 42(43),2
strength Ps 27(28),8
*Ps 24(25),14 κραταίωμα *strength, support* -סעד
support or -◊יסד *basis?* for MT סוד *friendship*
neol.

→LSJ suppl(Ps 24(25),14)

κραταιῶς   D 0-2-0-1-1-4
Jgsᴬ 8,1; 1 Sm 2,16; Prv 22,3; PSal 8,15
by force 1 Sm 2,16; *severely* Prv 22,3; *sharply* Jgsᴬ
8,1

κραταίωσις,-εως   N3F 0-0-0-2-1-3
Ps 59(60),9; 67(68),36; Jdt 7,22
strength; neol.

κρατεύω
(→ἐγ-)

κρατέω⁺   V 4-23-12-59-55-153
Gn 19,16; 21,18; Dt 2,34; 3,4; Jos 18,1
A: *to be strong* Ez 22,14; *to be lord over, to be
master of, to rule over* [τινος] Jgsᴬ 7,8; *to
conquer, to prevail, to get the upper hand* [abs.]
1 Ezr 4,38; *to prevail against* [ὑπέρ τινα] 1 Chr
19,12; *to be superior to, to master* [τινος] 4 Mc
5,23; *to constrain to* [τινα +inf.] 2 Kgs 4,8
to take possession of [τινος] Dt 2,34; *id.* [ἐπί
τινι] Eccl 2,3; *to take, to apprehend* [τινα] Jgs
8,12; *to hold (in the hand)* [τι] Gn 21,18; *to
possess* [τινα] Ps 72(73),6; *to hold fast on*
[τινος] Prv 14,18; *to lean on* [τινος] 2 Sm 3,29
to strenghten, to repair [τι] (semit.) 2 Kgs 12,6,
see also Neh 3,6 (and passim in Neh)
P: *to be subdued* Jos 18,1
κρατέω τῆς χειρός τινος *to lay hold of sb* Gn
19,16
*Prv 18,21 οἱ δὲ κρατοῦντες αὐτῆς *and those
who hold it* -אחז◊ ואחזיה for MT ואהביה*and those
who love it*

Cf. HELBING 1928, 119-122; SHIPP 1979, 339-340; →NIDNTT;
TWNT
(→δια-, ἐπι-, κατα-, περι-, ὑπερ-)

κρατήρ,-ῆρος   N3M 4-0-0-3-0-7
Ex 24,6; 25,31.33.34; Prv 9,2
mixing vessel, bowl Ex 24,6; *hollow of a
candlestick* (with the form of a blossom of a
flower) Ex 25,31

Cf. LE BOULLUEC 1989, 262; WALTERS 1973, 50.286

κράτησις,-εως   N3F 0-0-0-0-1-1
Wis 6,3
might, power, conquest; neol.

Cf. HADAS-LEBEL 1979, 431; LIEBERMAN 1942, 9-10

κράτιστος,-η,-ον⁺   A 0-1-1-3-3-8
1 Sm 15,15; Am 6,2; Ps 15(16),6(bis);
22(23),5(6)
sup. of ἀγαθός; *best, most excellent* Ps 15(16),6;
noble 2 Mc 4,12

Cf. HORSLEY 1983, 11

κράτος,-ους⁺   N3N 2-2-2-14-31-51
Gn 49,24; Dt 8,17; Jgs 4,3; Is 22,21
strength, might, intensity Gn 49,24; *power* Jdt
2,12; *sovereignty* Wis 15,2
*Is 22,21 τὸ κράτος *the power* -החזקה? for MT
אחזקנו חזק◊ *I will bind firmly on him*

Cf. GILBERT 1973, 182-190(Wis 15,2); →NIDNTT; TWNT

κρατύνω   V 0-0-0-0-1-1
Wis 14,16
P: *to grow strong, to increase in strength*

κραυγάζω⁺   V 0-0-0-1-0-1
Ezr 3,13
to shout; neol.

κραυγή,-ῆς⁺   N1F 7-6-26-14-13-66
Gn 18,20.21; 19,13; Ex 3,7.9
crying, outcry Gn 18,20; *shouting* 2 Sm 6,15

κρεάγρα,-ας   N1F 3-5-1-0-0-9
Ex 27,3; 38,23(3); Nm 4,14; 1 Sm 2,13.14
flesh-hook, fork for meat; neol.

κρεανομέω   V 1-0-0-0-0-1
Lv 8,20
to divide the meat of [τινα]; neol.

κρέας, κρέως⁺   N3N 50-11-19-5-7-92
Gn 9,4; Ex 12,8.46; 16,3.8
flesh, meat Gn 9,4; τὰ κρέα *meat prepared for food* (frequently pl.) Ex 12,8
Cf. SCHARBERT 1972, 121-124.136; WEVERS 1990, 357

κρείσσων,-ων,-ον⁺   A 1-4-1-0-14-20
Ex 14,12; Jgs 8,2; Jgsᴬ 11,25; 15,2
comp. of ἀγαθός; *better* Jgsᴮ 8,2; κρεῖσσον
[+inf.] *it is better to* Prv 21,9
κρεῖσσόν τινα [+inf.] *it is better for sb to* Ex 14,12

κρεμάννυμι⁺   V 6-7-4-13-7-37
Gn 40,19.22; 41,13; Dt 21,22.23
A: *to hang up* [τι] 2 Mc 15,33; *id.* [τι ἔκ τινος]
Jdt 14,11; *id.* [τι ἔν τινι] Ps 136(137),2; *to hang* [τινα] Gn 40,22; *to hang (up)on* [τινα ἐπί τινος] Gn 40,19; *id.* [τινα ἔκ τινος] 1 Mc 1,61
P: *to be hung up, to be suspended on* (of things)
[ἐπί τι] Ct 4,4; *to be hanged* (of pers.) Est 5,14;
to be in suspense (metaph.) Dt 28,66
*Ez 17,22 καὶ κρεμάσω αὐτόν *and I will hang it* -תלה for MT ותלול (hapax) ◊ תלל, תלל *lofty*
Cf. DOGNIEZ 1992, 296-297; DANIÉLOU 1966, 53-75; HARL
1986ᶜ=1992ᵃ, 67; 1990=1992, 243; LUST 1990ᵇ, 11-14
(→ἐκ-, ἐπι-)

κρεμαστός,-ή,-όν   A 0-3-0-0-0-3
Jgsᴮ 6,2; 1 Kgs 7,6(18)(bis)
hung, suspended 1 Kgs 7,6(18); τὰ κρεμαστά
fortresses Jgsᴮ 6,2

κρημνίζω   V 0-0-0-0-1-1
2 Mc 6,10
to hurl down; neol.
(→κατα-)

κρημνός,-οῦ⁺   N2M 0-2-0-0-0-2
2 Chr 25,12(bis)
overhanging cliff, precipice

κρήνη,-ης   N1F 0-7-0-0-1-8

2 Sm 2,13(ter); 4,12; 1 Kgs 2,35e
spring, well, fountain
Cf. CLARYSSE 1994, 6-7

κρηπίς,-ῖδος   N3F 0-3-1-0-2-6
Jos 3,15; 4,18; 1 Chr 12,16; Jl 2,17; 1 Mc 9,43
foundation, base, foot (of an altar) Jl 2,17;
(river-)bank Jos 3,15
→LSJ suppl

κριθή,-ῆς⁺   N1F 5-12-10-7-1-35
Gn 26,12; Ex 9,31(bis); Lv 27,16; Dt 8,8
barley Ex 9,31; αἱ κριθαί *barley-corns, barley*
Lv 27,16
*Gn 26,12 κριθήν *barley* -שׂערים for MT שׂערים
measures (of grain)?

κρίθινος,-η,-ον⁺   A 1-4-1-0-0-6
Nm 5,15; Jgsᴬ 5,8; Jgs 7,13; 2 Kgs 4,42
made of barley Nm 5,15
*Jgsᴬ 5,8 ἄρτον κρίθινον *bread made of barley*
-לחם שׂערים for MT לחם שׂערים *war in the gates*?

κρίκος,-ου⁺   N2M 10-0-1-2-0-13
Ex 26,6(bis).11(bis); 27,10
ring, link Ex 26,6; *nose-ring* Jb 40,26
Cf. WEVERS 1990, 415.428.436.627

κρίμα,-ατος⁺   N3N 25-32-67-77-54-255
Ex 18,22; 23,6; Lv 18,4.5; 20,22
decision, judgement Lv 18,4; *decree, rule* 1 Ezr
9,4; *sentence* Ex 23,6; *law-suit, case* Ex 18,22;
judging, judgement 2 Kgs 17,26
κρίμα θανατοῦ *condemnation, death sentence*
Dt 21,22
Cf. DOGNIEZ 1992, 53-54.248(Dt 21,22); DORIVAL 1994,
379; MONSENGWO PASINYA 1973, 140-159; →LSJ suppl;
NIDNTT

κρίνον,-ου⁺   N2N 4-3-2-8-2-19
Ex 25,31.33.34; Nm 8,4; 1 Kgs 7,8(19)
lily Ct 2,16; *cup, architectural ornament* (in the
form of a lily) Ex 25,31

κρίνω⁺   V 21-58-53-75-64-271
Gn 15,14; 16,5; 18,25; 19,9; 26,21
A: *to judge, to consider, to think* [τινα +pred.]
3 Mc 2,33; *to decide to, to determine to do*
[+inf.] Jdt 2,3; *to decide that sb should* [τινα
+inf.] 3 Mc 6,30
to judge, to give a fair judgement [τινι] Gn 30,6;
id. [τινα] Ps 71(72),4; *to judge* [τινα] Dt 32,36;
id. [ἀνὰ μέσον τινῶν] Is 2,4; *id.* [τι] Ex 18,22;
to pass judgement upon, to condemn [τινα] Gn
15,14; *to condemn, to punish* [τινα] Ez 38,22; *to
plead for* [τινι] Is 1,17; *to rule* [τινα]
1 Mc 9,73; *to probe, to estimate* [τινα] Jb 7,18

M/P: *to dispute, to contend* [abs.] 2 Sm 19,10; *id.*
[πρός τινα] Jgs 21,22; *id.* [μετά τινος] Jgs^A 8,1;
id. [τινι] Jb 9,3; *to contend with, to contest with*
[πρός τινα] Sir 42,8

κεκριμένος *picked out, choosen* 2 Mc 13,15;
κρίνω τινὰ κρίσιν δίκαιαν *to judge sb with
righteous judgement, to pass a right judgement* Dt
16,18; κρίνω τινί ἐκ χειρός τινος *to give a
fair judgement for, to deliver from, to take
revenge for sb on sb* (semit.) 2 Sm 18,31;
κρίνεταί τινι *to seem good to, to decree* 1 Ezr
8,90

Cf. DORIVAL 1994, 387; HELBING 1928, 68.96.236; LEE, J.
1983, 78; MONSENGWO PASINYA 1973, 154-158; WEVERS
1993, 408; →LSJ suppl; LSJ RSuppl; NIDNTT; TWNT
(→ἀνα-, ἀνταπο-, ἀντι-, ἀπο-, δια-, ἐπι-,
κατα-, προ-, συγ-, ὑπο-)

κριός,-οῦ⁺   N2M 119-9-24-29-12-193
Gn 15,9; 22,13(bis); 30,40; 31,10
ram Gn 15,9
*Jer 32(25),34 ὥσπερ οἱ κριοί *like the rams*
-כאלי for MT כלי ?; *Ps 28(29),1 υἱοὺς κριῶν
young rams -בני אילים for MT בני אלים *sons of god*
(double translation); *Lam 1,6 ὡς κριοί *like
rams* -כאילם for MT כאילים *like stags*
Cf. HARL 1986ᵃ, 194-195; HARLÉ 1988, 44; WEVERS 1993,
493

κρίσις,-εως⁺   N3F 49-24-76-71-60-280
Gn 14,7; 18,19.25; 19,9; Ex 6,6
decision 2 Mc 14,18; *judgement* Gn 14,7; *fair
judgement, justice* Is 1,17; *interpretation*
Dn^LXX 2,36
suit, cause, case Jer 5,28; *condemnation*
Jer 33(26),11; *trial, dispute* Ex 24,14; *juridical
procedure* Ex 15,25
*Is 63,1 κρίσιν *judgement* -ריב for MT רב *great*,
see also Prv 28,2; *Prv 19,28 κρίσεις
judgements -דין? for MT און *iniquity*
Cf. DOGNIEZ 1992, 53; DORIVAL 1994, 387; LE BOULLUEC
1989, 43.112.179(Ex 15,25).196.248-249; MON-
SENGWO-PASINYA 1973, 154-156; WEVERS 1990, 240; 1993,
257

κριτήριον,-ου⁺   N2N 1-2-0-3-1-7
Ex 21,6; Jgs^B 5,10; 1 Kgs 7,44(7); Dn 7,10
judgement-seat
Cf. HORSLEY 1987, 157; WALTERS 1973, 251-252(Ex 21,6)

κριτής,-οῦ⁺   N1M 11-24-9-14-28-86
Dt 1,15.16; 16,18; 17,9.12
judge Dt 1,16; *judge, leader of the people* (in the
period before the rise of the Hebr. kingdom)

Jgs 2,16
*Dt 1,15 τοῖς κριταῖς *to your judges* -לשפטיכם for
MT לשבטיכם *for your tribes*
Cf. BICKERMAN 1980, 60(n.86-87); DOGNIEZ 1992, 114-115

κρόκη,-ης   N1F 10-0-0-0-0-10
Lv 13,48.49.51.52.53
woof(thread)

κροκόδειλος,-ου   N2M 1-0-0-0-0-1
Lv 11,29
lizard; ὁ κροκόδειλος ὁ χερσαῖος *land
crocodile, lizard*

κρόκος,-ου   N2M 0-0-0-2-0-2
Prv 7,17; Ct 4,14
Semit. loanword (Hebr. כרכם); *saffron*
Cf. ROBERT 1960, 333; 1961, 165; TOV 1979, 221;
→CHANTRAINE; FRISK

κρόμμυον,-ου   N2N 1-0-0-0-0-1
Nm 11,5
onion
Cf. WALTERS 1973, 82

κροσσός,-οῦ   N2M 3-0-0-0-0-3
Ex 28,22.29a; 36,22(39,15)
tassel, fringe; neol.
Cf. LE BOULLUEC 1989, 287-288; WALTERS 1973, 82

κροσσωτός,-ή,-όν   A 2-0-0-1-0-3
Ex 28,14(bis); Ps 44(45),14
tasseled, fringed; neol.
Cf. LE BOULLUEC 1989, 284-285; WALTERS 1973, 82

κρόταφος,-ου   N2M 0-3-0-1-1-5
Jgs^B 4,21.22; 5,26; Ps 131(132),4; PSal 4,16
temple (of the head)

κροτέω   V 0-1-6-4-0-11
2 Kgs 11,12; Ez 6,11; 21,17.19.22
to knock, to strike; κροτέω τὰς χεῖρας *to clap
the hands* Jb 27,23; κροτέω τῇ χειρί *id.* 2 Kgs
11,12; *id.* (metaph.) Ps 97(98),8; κροτέω ἐπὶ
τὴν χεῖρα *id.* Ez 21,17
(→ἐπι-, συγ-)

κρουνηδόν   D 0-0-0-0-1-1
2 Mc 14,45
like a spring, gushing; neol.

κρούω⁺   V 0-2-0-1-1-4
Jgs 19,22; Ct 5,2; Jdt 14,14
to knock [ἐπί τι] Jgs^B 19,22; *id.* [τι] Jgs^A 19,22
(→ἀνα-, ἐγ-, ἐκ-, ἐπι-, κατα-, παρα-, προσ-)

κρυβῇ   D 0-2-0-0-1-3
1 Sm 19,2; 2 Sm 12,12; 3 Mc 4,12
secretly, in secret; neol.; see κρυφῇ

κρύβω   V 0-1-0-0-1-1
2 Kgs 11,3

see κρύπτω

κρυπτός,-ή,-όν⁺   A 2-1-6-1-9-19
Dt 15,9; 29,28; 1 Kgs 6,4; Is 22,9; Jer 30,4(49,10)
hidden (archit.) 1 Kgs 6,4; secret Dt 15,9
*Ez 8,12 ἐν τῷ κοιτῶνι τῷ κρυπτῷ αὐτῶν
(dark) in their secret (room) -חשׁך◊ חשׁכתו for MT
משׂכיתו (in his room) of images
Cf. DOGNIEZ 1992, 211; →LSJ RSuppl

κρύπτω⁺   V 10-35-24-52-31-152
Gn 3,8.10; 4,14; 18,17; 31,20
A: to hide [τινα] Ex 2,12; to conceal [τι] Gn
37,26; to keep close or secret [τι] Tob 12,7; to
conceal or hide sth from sb [τί τινα] Jb 38,2; id.
[τι ἀπό τινος] Gn 18,17; to hide sb from sth (in
a safe place) [τινα ἀπό τινος] Jb 5,21; to close
(the ears) [τι] Lam 3,56; to deceive sb by doing
sth [τινά τινος] (semit.) Gn 31,20
M/P: to hide oneself from [ἀπὸ προσώπου τινός]
Gn 3,8; to be hidden from [ἀπό τινος] Ps
37(38),10
κρυπτομένη φιλία secret love Prv 27,5;
κεκρυμμένη εἴσοδος privy, secret entrance Bel^Th
12
*Hos 6,9 ἔκρυψαν they hid -חבא◊ החבאו for MT חבר
(they are) a company
Cf. BARR 1961, 38; HARL 1986ᵃ, 236(Gn 31,20); HELBING
1928, 42-43; →NIDNTT; TWNT
(→ἀπο-, ἐγ-, κατα-, συγ-, συναπο-)

κρυπτῶς   D 0-0-0-0-3-3
Tob 12,6; 1 Mc 10,79
in secret, secretly 1 Mc 10,79; in secret, apart Tob
12,6

κρυσταλλοειδής,-ής,-ές   A 0-0-0-0-1-1
Wis 19,21
like ice
Cf. LARCHER 1985, 1092

κρύσταλλος,-ου⁺   N2M 1-0-2-4-2-9
Nm 11,7; Is 54,12; Ez 1,22; Ps 147,6(17); 148,8
ice Jb 6,16; (rock-)crystal Ez 1,22
Cf. DORIVAL 1994, 149; LARCHER 1985, 931-932(Wis
16,22)

κρυφαῖος,-α,-ον⁺   A 1-0-1-1-1-4
Ex 17,16; Jer 23,24; Lam 3,10; Wis 17,3
secret Wis 17,3
ἐν κρυφαίοις in secret places Jer 23,24
*Ex 17,16 κρυφαίᾳ hidden -כסיה for MT כס יה the
throne of the Lord?
Cf. LE BOULLUEC 1989, 192; WEVERS 1990, 272

κρυφαίως   D 0-0-2-0-0-2
Jer 44(37),17; 47(40),15

secretly

κρυφῇ⁺   D 3-2-3-3-1-12
Gn 31,26; Ex 11,2; Dt 28,57; Jgs^B 4,21; 9,31
secretly, in secret Gn 31,26
ἐν κρυφῇ secretly, in secret Jgs^B 4,21

κρύφιος,-α,-ον⁺   A 0-2-0-7-3-12
Jgs 3,19; Ps 9,1; 18(19),13; 43(44),22; 45(46),1
secret Jgs 3,19
κρύφιε my good man, my friend Ru 4,1
*Ps 45(46),1 ὑπὲρ τῶν κρυφίων concerning the
secrets or hidden things -עלם◊ עלם¹ for MT על עלמות
according to Alamoth?, cpr. Ps 9,1

κρύφος,-ου   N2M 0-0-0-0-4-4
1 Mc 1,53; 2,31.36.41
hiding-place, lurking-place

-κρύφω
(→συγ-)

κτάομαι⁺   V 28-9-22-22-20-101
Gn 4,1; 12,5(bis); 25,10; 33,19
to get, to acquire, to gain [τι] Gn 12,5; id.
[τινα] Gn 4,1; to gain (direction) [τι] Prv 1,5;
to bring upon oneself, to incur [τι] Prv 3,31
to buy [τινα] Gn 39,1; id. [τι] Gn 25,10; to
provide for oneself [τι] Prv 1,14
ὁ κεκτημένος purchaser Lv 25,50; possessor
Prv 16,22; ὁ κτώμενος γυναῖκα he that gets his
wife Sir 36,24; κέκτημαί τι to have bought, to
possess, to hold Lv 27,22; ἐκτησάμην τι to have
possessed Ps 138(139),13; Ρουθ τὴν Μωαβῖτιν
τὴν γυναῖκα κέκτημαί ἐμαυτῷ εἰς γυναῖκα
I have acquired Ruth the Moabite to be my wife,
I have as wife Ruth the Moabite Ru 4,10
*Prv 3,31 μὴ κτήσῃ do not acquire -אל תקנה for
MT אל תקנא do not envy, see also Ez 8,3
Cf. HARL 1986ᵃ, 52.113.153.315; VAWTER 1980, 205-216;
WALTERS 1973, 9.220-224.339; WEVERS 1993, 51.774
(→ἐγ-, κατα-)

κτείνω   V 0-0-0-2-1-3
Prv 24,11; 25,5; 3 Mc 1,2
to kill, to slay [τινα]
(→ἀπο-, κατα-)

κτῆμα,-ατος⁺   N3N 0-0-2-5-5-12
Hos 2,17; Jl 1,11; Jb 20,29; 27,13; Prv 12,27
possession Jb 20,29; landed property, field, plot of
land Prv 23,10

κτῆνος,-ους⁺   N3N 144-23-42-31-22-262
Gn 1,25.26.28; 2,20; 3,14
(domestic) animal Ex 11,5; τὰ κτήνη cattle Gn
1,25
ἀπὸ ἀνθρώπου ἕως κτήνους from man to beast

Gn 6,7

*Gn 8,19 τὰ κτήνη the cattle -הרכש? for MT הרמש
the creeping animals

Cf. DORIVAL 1994, 58; HARLÉ 1988, 44.86; WEVERS 1990,
125.189; 1993, 175.405

κτηνοτρόφος,-ος,-ον   A 4-0-0-0-0-4
Gn 4,20; 46,32.34; Nm 32,4
appropriate for pasture, that can feed animals (of
land) Nm 32,4; κτηνοτρόφος cattle-rearer Gn
4,20; neol.?

Cf. LEE, J. 1983, 42; →LSJ RSuppl

κτηνώδης,-ης,-ες   A 0-0-0-1-0-1
Ps 72(73),22
like a beast, brutish; neol.

κτῆσις,-εως   N3F 14-5-7-8-4-38
Gn 23,4.9.18.20; 36,43
acquisition, getting Bar 3,17; acquisition, portion,
part Jb 36,33; possession Gn 23,4; property
(concrete) Gn 46,6; αἱ κτήσεις possessions,
property 2 Kgs 3,17
τὸ βιβλίον τῆς κτήσεως book of purchase Jer
39,14

Cf. HARL 1986ᵃ, 197.315; WALTERS 1973, 219-224.339;
WEVERS 1993, 774

κτίζω⁺   V 6-0-14-10-38-68
Gn 14,19.22; Ex 9,18; Lv 16,16; Dt 4,32
to found, to build (a city) [τι] 1 Ezr 4,53; to
found, to establish [τι] Lv 16,16; to make, to
create [τι] Gn 14,19; id. [τινα] Dt 4,32; to
create sb as [τινά τι] Prv 8,22; to perpetrate [τι]
Is 45,7

Cf. BARR 1961, 224; DOGNIEZ 1992, 143.324; HARL 1986ᵃ,
52.161; WALTERS 1973, 220-224.339; WEVERS 1993, 198;
→NIDNTT; TWNT

(→συγ-)

κτίσις,-εως⁺   N3F 0-0-0-0-16-16
Jdt 9,12; 16,14; Tob 8,5; Tobᴮᴬ 8,15
creation Sir 16,17; created things, creature Jdt
9,12; αἱ κτίσεις creatures Tobᴮᴬ 8,5

Cf. LARCHER 1983, 229(Wis 2,6); VANNI 1995, 288;
WALTERS 1973, 219-224.339

κτίσμα,-ατος⁺   N3N 0-0-0-0-6-6
3 Mc 5,11; Wis 9,2; 13,5; 14,11; Sir 36,14
creation Sir 38,34; creature Wis 9,2; neol.?

κτίστης,-ου⁺   N1M 0-1-0-0-7-8
2 Sm 22,32; Jdt 9,12; 2 Mc 1,24; 7,23; 13,14
creator Jdt 9,12

*2 Sm 22,32 κτίστης creator -יוצר for MT צור rock

κτύπος,-ου   N2M 0-0-0-0-1-1
Wis 17,17

crash, sound

Cf. LARCHER 1985, 977

κύαθος,-ου   N2M 3-0-1-0-0-4
Ex 25,29; 38,12(37,16); Nm 4,7; Jer 52,19
cup

Cf. LE BOULLUEC 1989, 260; WEVERS 1990, 404

κύαμος,-ου   N2M 0-1-1-0-0-2
2 Sm 17,28; Ez 4,9
bean, beans (coll.)

κυβερνάω⁺   V 0-0-0-1-3-4
Prv 12,5; Wis 10,4; 14,6; Susᵀʰ 5
to guide [τινα] Wis 10,4; to govern [τινα] Susᵀʰ
5; to devise [τι] (metaph.) Prv 12,5

(→δια-)

κυβέρνησις,-εως⁺   N3F 0-0-0-3-0-3
Prv 1,5; 11,14; 24,6
steering, direction Prv 1,5; generalship (in war)
Prv 24,6

κυβερνήτης,-ου⁺   N1M 0-0-3-1-1-5
Ez 27,8.27.28; Prv 23,34; 4 Mc 7,1
steersman, captain, pilot

→TWNT

κύβος,-ου   N2M 0-0-0-2-0-2
Jb 38,38; Est 1,6
block of stone Jb 38,38

*Est 1,6 ἐπὶ κύβοις on blocks? corr.? ἐπὶ
κύκλοις for MT על גלילי on rings

Cf. WALTERS 1973, 132(Est 1,6); →SCHLEUSNER

κυδοιμός,-οῦ   N2M 0-0-0-1-0-1
Jb 38,25
turmoil (of storm)

κῦδος,-ους   N2N 0-0-1-0-0-1
Is 14,25
glory, renown; *Is 14,25 τὸ κῦδος the glory corr.?
ὁ κύδος for MT סבל burden

κυέω
(→ἀπο-)

κύησις,-εως   N3F 0-0-0-1-0-1
Ru 4,13
pregnancy

κύθρα,-ας⁺   N1F 0-1-0-0-0-1
1 Sm 2,14
earthen pot; neol.?

κυθρόπους,-ποδος   N3M 1-0-0-0-0-1
Lv 11,35
pot, cauldron, potstand; neol.?

κυκλεύω⁺   V 0-1-0-0-0-1
2 Kgs 3,25
to compass, to surround

Cf. HORSLEY 1983, 71

κυκλέω
(→εἰσ-)
κυκλόθεν⁺   D/P 0-29-40-5-18-92
Jos 21,44; 23,1; Jgs 2,14; Jgsᴬ 8,34
from all around, round about, all around Jos
21,44; *round about* Jer 28(51),2; *round about*
[τινος] 1 Kgs 18,32

κύκλος,-ου   N2M 0-0-1-1-3-5
Jer 38(31),39; Eccl 1,6; 1 Ezr 4,34; Wis 7,19;
13,2
vault (of heaven) 1 Ezr 4,34; *circuit, cycle* Wis
7,19; *circuit, course* Eccl 1,6; see κύβος(Est 1,6)
and κύκλῳ
Cf. LARCHER 1984, 472(Wis 7,19); WALTERS 1973, 132(Est
1,6)

κυκλόω⁺   V 8-25-9-31-22-95
Gn 2,11.13; Ex 13,18; Nm 34,4.5
to encircle, to surround, to compass [τι] (in
hostile sense) Dt 2,1; *id.* [τινα] 2 Chr 21,9; *id.*
[ἐπί τινα] 2 Kgs 8,21; *id.* [τινα] (metaph.; of
pains) 2 Sm 22,6; *to go around, to circle round*
[τι] (of a name or reputation) Gn 2,11; *to
surround, to compass* [τινα] (as protection) Dt
32,10; *to encompass, to cover* [τινά τινι] Sir
45,9; *to go round* [τινα] (of boarder) Nm 34,4;
id. [abs.] Nm 34,5; *to go about* Eccl 12,5; *to lead
round, to take round, to let return* [τινα] Ex
13,18; *to move in a circle, to whirl round* Eccl
1,6; *to form a circle round* [ἐπί τινα] 2 Kgs
11,8; *to form a circle, to dance* 4 Mc 14,8
ἐκύκλωσαν ὁδὸν ἑπτὰ ἡμερῶν *they compassed
a seven days' journey* 2 Kgs 3,9; κυκλόω τινά ἐν
ψεύδει *to mislead sb, to lead sb up* or *round*
Hos 12,1
*1 Kgs 22,32 καὶ ἐκύκλωσαν αὐτόν *they
encircled* (him) ויסבו for MT ויסרו *they turned* (to
him); *Ps 90(91),4 κυκλώσει σε *he shall
surround you, he shall cover you* -יסחרך? for MT
סחרה *wall*?
Cf. DOGNIEZ 1992, 327; DORIVAL 1994, 53; WALTERS
1973, 119
(→περι-)
κύκλῳ⁺   D 62-45-72-31-24-234
Gn 23,17; 35,5; 41,48; Ex 7,24; 16,13
in a circle, round about 2 Kgs 11,8; *round about*
Gn 23,17; *around* (as adj.) 2 Mc 4,32; *round
about* [τινος] Gn 35,5
→LSJ Suppl(Jb 41,6)
κύκλωμα,-ατος   N3N 0-1-2-2-0-5
2 Chr 4,2; Ez 43,17; 48,35; Ps 139(140),10; Jb

37,12
anything round: wheel, coil Ps 139(140),10; *kerb,
rim* Ez 43,17; *circumference* 2 Chr 4,2
→LSJ Suppl(Ez 43,17); LSJ RSuppl

κύκλωσις,-εως   N3F 0-0-0-0-1-1
Sir 43,12
circle

κύκνειος,-ος,-ον   A 0-0-0-0-1-1
4 Mc 15,21
of a swan

κύκνος,-ου   N2M 2-0-0-0-0-2
Lv 11,18; Dt 14,16
swan
Cf. DOGNIEZ 1992, 206; HARLÉ 1988, 130

κυλικεῖον,-ου   N2N 0-0-0-0-1-1
1 Mc 15,32
sideboard, cup stand; neol.?
Cf. WALTERS 1973, 50.211-212

κυλίκιον,-ου   N2N 0-0-0-1-0-1
Est 1,7
small cup
Cf. CAIRD 1976, 81; WALTERS 1973, 50.221-212

κυλίω⁺   V 0-5-4-2-1-12
Jos 10,18; Jgsᴬ 7,13; 1 Sm 14,33; 2 Kgs 9,33(bis)
A: *to roll* [τι] Jos 10,18; *to throw down* [τινα]
2 Kgs 9,33
P: *to roll* Jgsᴬ 7,13
(→ἀπο-, ἐγ-, ἐπι-, κατα-)

κῦμα,-ατος⁺   N3N 1-0-8-8-10-27
Ex 15,8; Is 48,18; 51,15; Jer 5,22; 28(51),42
wave, billow
Cf. LEE, J. 1983, 33

κυμαίνω⁺   V 0-0-4-0-1-5
Is 5,30; 17,12; Jer 6,23; 26(46),7; Wis 5,10
to rise in waves, to swell Wis 5,10; *to agitate, to
roll* [τι] Jer 26(46),7

κυμάτιον,-ου   N2N 3-0-0-0-0-3
Ex 25,11.24.25
moulding
Cf. LE BOULLUEC 1989, 255; WEVERS 1990, 397

κυμβαλίζω   V 0-0-0-1-0-1
Neh 12,27
to play the cymbals

κύμβαλον,-ου⁺   N2N 0-13-0-3-4-20
1 Sm 18,6; 2 Sm 6,5; 1 Chr 13,8; 15,16.19
cymbal
Cf. SANDERS 1990, 614-618

κύμινον,-ου⁺   N2N 0-0-3-0-0-3
Is 28,25.27(bis)
Semit. loanword (Hebr. כמן); *cummin*

Cf. CAIRD 1976, 78; TOV 1979, 221; WALTERS 1973, 163; →CHANTRAINE; FRISK

κυνέω
(→προσ-)

κυνηγέω⁺   V 1-0-0-0-0-1
Gn 25,27
to hunt

κυνήγιον,-ου⁺   N2N 0-0-0-0-1-1
Sir 13,19
prey; neol.?

κυνηγός,-οῦ   N2M 2-1-0-0-0-3
Gn 10,9(bis); 1 Chr 1,10
hunter

κυνικός,-ή,-όν   A 0-1-0-0-0-1
1 Sm 25,3
currish, churlish, doglike; *1 Sm 25,3 κυνικός
doglike -◊כלב for MT כלבי *Calebite*

κυνόμυια,-ας   N1F 7-0-0-2-0-9
Ex 8,17(bis).18.20(bis)
dog-fly
Cf. LE BOULLUEC 1989, 127

κυοφορέω⁺   V 0-0-0-1-0-1
Eccl 11,5
to be pregnant

κυοφορία,-ας   N1F 0-0-0-0-2-2
4 Mc 15,6; 16,7
pregnancy, child-bearing; neol.
Cf. WALTERS 1973, 233

κυπαρίσσινος,-η,-ον   A 0-0-1-1-0-2
Ez 27,24; Neh 8,15
of cypress-wood Ez 27,24
ξύλον κυπαρίσσινον *cypress(-tree)* Neh 8,15

κυπάρισσος,-ου   N2F 0-1-8-2-2-13
2 Kgs 19,23; Is 37,24; 41,19; 55,13; 60,13
cypress 2 Kgs 19,23; *cypress-wood* Ct 1,17

κυπρίζω   V 0-0-0-2-0-2
Ct 2,13.15
to bloom; neol.

κυπρισμός,-οῦ   N2M 0-0-0-1-0-1
Ct 7,13
bloom; neol.

κύπρος,-ου   N2F 0-0-0-2-0-2
Ct 1,14; 4,13
Semit. loanword (Hebr. כפר); *camphor, henna,
Lawsonia inermis*
Cf. CAIRD 1976, 79; TOV 1979, 222; ZOHARY 1982, 190; →CHANTRAINE; FRISK

κύπτω⁺   V 5-6-3-2-2-18
Gn 43,28; Ex 4,31; 12,27; 34,8; Nm 22,31
to bend forward or *down* Ps 9,31; *to hang the*

head because of shame Bar 2,18
κύψων προσκυνέω *to bow down and worship* Ex
12,27; *to bow down and do obedience* Gn 43,28
Cf. NEIRYNCK 1977=1982, 405-417; WALTERS 1973, 97
(→ἀνα-, δια-, διεκ-, ἐγ-, εἰσ-, ἐκ-, κατα-,
κατεπι-, παρα-, προσ-, συγ-)

κυρέω
(→προσ-, συγ-)

κυρία,-ας⁺   N1F 3-2-1-2-0-8
Gn 16,4.8.9; 1 Kgs 17,17; 2 Kgs 5,3
mistress
Cf. WALTERS 1973, 40

κυριεία,-ας   N1F 0-0-1-7-3-11
Is 40,10; Dnᴸˣˣ 11,3.4; Dnᵀʰ 4,22(19); 6,27
authority, power Is 40,10; *dominion, lordship,
empire* Dnᴸˣˣ 11,3
Cf. WALTERS 1973, 40

κυριεύω⁺   V 6-11-9-16-22-64
Gn 3,16; 37,8(bis); Ex 15,9; Nm 21,18
often used with pejor. connotation: *to be
dominant, to dominate* [abs.] Ex 15,9; *id.* [τινος]
Gn 37,8(secundo); *to dominate over* (one's wife)
[τινος] Gn 3,16; *id.* (wild beasts) [τινος] Bar
3,16; *to prevail against, to have more power than*
[τινος] Dnᵀʰ 3,94; *to master, to control* [τινος]
4 Mc 1,4
*Nm 24,7 καὶ κυριεύσει ἐθνῶν *and he will
dominate over* (many) *peoples* -וזרעו בעמים *and his
arm will be over* (many) *peoples* for MT זרעו במים
and his seed shall be in (abundant) *waters*; *Is
42,19 ἀλλ' ἢ οἱ κυριεύοντες *but* (their) *rulers
כ/מלכים (ptc.) ◊מלך for MT כ/מלאכי *as my messenger*
Cf. CLARK 1976, 100-105; LE BOULLUEC 1989, 173-174(Ex
15,9); LEE, J. 1983, 113; LUST 1995, 236-237(Nm 24,7);
SPICQ 1982, 426-428; WEVERS 1990, 231(Ex 15,9)
(→κατα-)

κύριος,-α,-ον⁺   A 0-0-0-0-2-2
1 Mc 8,30; 4 Mc 1,19
valid, lawful, established 1 Mc 8,30
κυριώτατος *principal, most essential of, most
important of* 4 Mc 1,19

κύριος,-ου⁺   N2M 1903-2443-2047-1326-872-8591
Gn 2,8.15.16.18.22
Lord (designating God) Is 40,5; *master, lord*
(opp. δοῦλος) Jgs 19,11; *lord* (of husband) Gn
18,12; *id.* (of father) Gn 31,35; *my lord, sir* Gn
23,6; *owner* Ex 21,29
κύριε πάτερ *Lord father* (as terms of respect)
Sir 23,1; ὁ κύριος τῆς οἰκίας *master of the
house, head of the family* Ex 22,7; κύριος ὁ

Θεός the Lord God Gn 2,8; κύριος κύριος the Lord God (rendition of אדני יהוה) Ez 20,39
*Dn[LXX] 9,2 πρόσταγμα τῇ γῇ ordinance for the world? corr. πρόσταγμα πιπι for MT דבר יהוה word of the Lord (TH ΓΗ transcription of יהוה), cpr. λόγος κυρίου Dn[Th] 9,2; *Nm 31,3 ἔναντι κυρίου before the Lord ליהוה- for MT ויהיו and they will be, or ללצבאותbefore the Lord for MT לצבא for an army, for war; *Dt 32,4 κύριος the Lord -יהוה? for MT הוא he; *1 Sm 17,32 τοῦ κυρίου μου of my lord -אדני for MT אדם of man?
Cf. BAUDISSIN 1929, 1-602.1-316.1-710.1-228; BICKERMAN 1976, 159-160; CERFAUX 1931[a]=1954, 113-136; 1931[b]= 1954, 137-172; 1957, col.200-228; HAGEDORN 1980, 165-177; HANHART 1967, 38-64(esp. 57-63); HARL 1986[a], 47.49-52.67.169.205.265; HORSLEY 1989, 74; KILPATRICK 1968=1990, 207-212; 1973=1990, 216-222; LE BOULLUEC 1989, 41.338-339.377-378; LEE, J. 1983, 83; LLEWELYN 1992, 176(n.193); LUST 1968, 482-488; 1996, 138-145; MONTEVECCHI 1957[a], 48-49; PIETERSMA 1984, 85-101; SPICQ 1982, 415-424; SUÑOL 1965, 39-54; WALTERS 1973, 40.61.110.142.160.249.251.259.260.316; WEVERS 1990, 30.70.73.97.100.118.141.206.305.308.312.346.367.384.389. 552.557; 1993, 391; →NIDNTT; TWNT

κυρόω[+]   V 2-0-0-1-1-4
Gn 23,20; Lv 25,30; Dn[LXX] 6,10; 4 Mc 7,9
A: to confirm, to ratify [τι] Dn[LXX] 6,10; to confirm, to establish [τι] 4 Mc 7,9
P: to be confirmed Lv 25,30; to be declared as [εἴς τι] Gn 23,20

κυρτός,-ή,-όν   A 1-1-0-0-0-2
Lv 21,20; 1 Kgs 21(20),11
hump-backed

κύτος,-ους[+]   N3N 0-0-0-5-0-5
Ps 64(65),8; Dn 4,11(8); Dn[Th] 4,20(17); Dn[LXX] 4,22(19)
crown, extent (of a tree) Dn 4,11(8); depth (of the sea) Ps 64(65),8
Cf. MONTGOMERY 1938, 137

κύφω   V 0-0-0-1-0-1
Jb 22,29
to bend forward; κύφοντα ὀφθαλμοῖς with downcast eyes; see κύπτω

κυψέλη,-ης   N1F 0-0-1-0-0-1
Hag 2,16
any hollow vessel, corn-bin

κύω[+]   V 0-0-2-0-0-2
Is 59,4.13
to conceive (metaph.)

κύων, κυνός[+]   N3M/F 3-19-4-10-6-42

Ex 11,7; 22,30; Dt 23,19; Jgs 7,5
dog Ex 11,7; id. (as derogatory term for non-Jews) Ps 21(22),17; male prostitute Dt 23,19
→LSJ Suppl(Dt 23,19); LSJ RSuppl

κώδιον,-ου   N2N 0-0-0-1-1-2
Neh 3,15; Jdt 12,15
(sheep)skin
Cf. WALTERS 1973, 69-70

κώδων,-ωνος   N3M 5-1-0-0-1-7
Ex 28,33.34; 36,32.33(39,25.26)
bell

κώθων,-ωνος   N3M 0-0-0-1-1-2
Est 8,17; 3 Mc 6,31
feast, carousal, party
→LSJ Suppl; LSJ RSuppl(Est 8,17)

κωθωνίζω   V 0-0-0-1-1-2
Est 3,15; 1 Ezr 4,63
P: to drink hard, to get drunk, to drink recklessly

κωκυτός,-οῦ   N2M 0-0-0-0-1-1
3 Mc 6,32
wailing

κωλέα,-ας   N1F 0-1-0-0-0-1
1 Sm 9,24
thigh-bone with the flesh on it, ham

κῶλον,-ου[+]   N2N 5-2-1-0-0-8
Lv 26,30(bis); Nm 14,29.32.33
limb, member Lv 26,30; τὰ κῶλα dead body, corpse 1 Sm 17,46
→LSJ Suppl

κώλυμα,-ατος   N3N 0-0-0-1-0-1
Jb 13,27
hindrance, stocks

κωλυτικός,-ή,-όν   A 0-0-0-0-3-3
4 Mc 1,3.30; 2,6
hindering, controlling [τινος]

κωλύω[+]   V 3-2-4-4-20-33
Gn 23,6; Ex 36,6; Nm 11,28; 1 Sm 25,26; 2 Sm 13,13
A: to hinder [abs.] Tob[S] 8,3; to withhold, to prevent [τι] Jb 12,15; to withold from [τι ἀπό τινος] Gn 23,6; to hinder, to forbid [τινα] Nm 11,28; to hinder [+inf.] Is 28,6
P: to be hindered from, to be restrained from [+inf.] Ex 36,6; id. [τινος] 1 Ezr 6,6; id. [ἀπό τινος] Sir 20,3
ἐκ πάσης ὁδοῦ πονηρᾶς ἐκώλυσα τοὺς πόδας μου I have kept back my feet from every evil way Ps 118(119),101
Cf. ARGYLE 1956, 17; BARR 1985, 72-74; CAIRD 1976, 81; DE WAARD 1981, 554; HELBING 1928, 160-161

(→άπο-, δια-)

κωμάρχης,-ου   N1M 0-0-0-1-0-1
Est 2,3
head man of a village

κώμη,-ης⁺   N1F 2-80-5-2-8-97
Nm 21,32; 32,42; Jos 10,39; 13,30; Josᴮ 15,24(25)
village 2 Mc 8,6
αἱ κῶμαι τινός *the village of, the district of* Nm
21,32
*Josᴮ 15,24(25) καὶ αἱ κῶμαι αὐτῶν *and their
villages* וחצרם for MT וחצור *and Hazor*; *Is 32,14
αἱ κῶμαι *the villages* -בת or -בנות for MT בער
until?

-κωμάζω
(→ἐγ-)

κῶμος,-ου⁺   N2M 0-0-0-0-2-2
2 Mc 6,4; Wis 14,23
revel, carousal
Cf. SPICQ 1978ᵃ, 449-450

κωνώπιον,-ου   N2N 0-0-0-0-4-4
Jdt 10,21; 13,9.15; 16,19
canopy, bed with mosquito curtains; neol.

κώπη,-ης   N1F 0-0-1-0-0-1
Ez 27,6
handle of an oar

κωπηλάτης,-ου   N1M 0-0-6-0-0-6
Ez 27,8.9.26.27.29
rower; neol.?

κωφεύω   V 0-7-0-6-0-13
Jgs 16,2; 18,19; 2 Sm 13,20
to keep quiet, to hold one's peace Jgs 16,2; *to be
silent* Jb 13,13

κωφός,-ή,-όν⁺   A 2-0-7-2-2-13
Ex 4,11; Lv 19,14; Is 29,18; 35,5; 42,18
stereotypical rendition of חרש; *dumb, mute* Wis
10,21; *deaf* Ex 4,11; *deaf and dumb* Hab 2,18
*Is 44,11 καὶ κωφοί *and the deaf* -חרשים for MT
וחרשים *and the artisans*
Cf. HARLÉ 1988, 165; LE BOULLUEC 1989, 99

κωφόω⁺   V 0-0-0-2-0-2
Ps 38(39),3.10
P: *to become dumb*
(→άπο-)

λαβή,-ῆς   N1F 0-2-0-0-0-2
Jgs 3,22
hilt, handle

λαβίς,-ίδος   N3F 2-1-1-0-0-4
Ex 38,17(37,23); Nm 4,9; 2 Chr 4,21; Is 6,6
tongs, snuffers (to trim lamps) (mostly pl.)
Ex 38,17(37,23); *tongs* (sg.) Is 6,6
Cf. GOODING 1959, 34-35

λάβρος,-ος,-ον   A 0-0-0-3-1-4
Jb 38,25.34; Prv 28,3; 4 Mc 16,3
violent, impetuous Jb 38,25
λαβρότατος *most vehement,   most fierce*
4 Mc 16,3

λάγανον,-ου   N2N 7-2-0-0-0-9
Ex 29,2.23; Lv 2,4; 7,12; 8,26
cake; neol.?

λαγόνες,-ων   N3F 0-0-0-0-1-1
Sir 47,19
loins; παρανέκλινας τὰς λαγόνας σου
γυναικίν *you surrendered to women*

λαγχάνω⁺   V 0-0-0-0-2-2
3 Mc 6,1; Wis 8,19
to obtain (as one's portion) [τινος] Wis 8,19
λελογχὼς ἐν πρεσβείῳ τὴν ἡλικίαν *who had
attained an advanced age, who had reached old
age* 3 Mc 6,1
Cf. LARCHER 1984, 552; WALTERS 1973, 185.332
(1 Sm 14,47 v.l.)

λάθρα⁺   D 1-2-1-2-3-9
Dt 13,7; 1 Sm 18,22; 26,5; Hab 3,14; Ps 100
(101),5
secretly, in secret 1 Sm 26,5; *secretly, privately*
Dt 13,7; *without the knowledge of* [τινος]
Ps 100(101),5
Cf. SPICQ 1978ᵃ, 454-457

λαθραῖος,-ος/α,-ον   A 0-0-0-0-1-1
Wis 1,11
secret; see λάθριος

λαθραίως   D 0-1-0-0-1-2
1 Sm 24,5; 2 Mc 1,19
secretly

λάθριος,-ος/α,-ον   A 0-0-0-1-0-1
Prv 21,14
secret; see λαθραῖος

λαῖλαψ,-απος⁺   N3F 0-0-1-2-4-7
Jer 32(25),32; Jb 21,18; 38,1; Wis 5,14.23
whirlwind, hurricane Jer 32(25),32; *whirlwind (of
fire)* [τινος] Sir 48,9

λαιμαργία,-ας   N1F 0-0-0-0-1-1
4 Mc 1,27

gluttony

λακάνη,-ης   N1F 0-1-0-0-0-1
Jgsᴬ 5,25
hellenistic form for λεκάνη

λακίζω
(→περι-)

λάκκος,-ου⁺   N2M 15-13-14-31-23-96
Gn 37,20.22.24(bis).28
pit, den 1 Sm 13,6; *dungeon, prison* Gn 40,15,
see also Ex 12,29; *cistern, pit* Gn 37,20; *well,
cistern for water* Jer 6,7; *pit of death, sheol* Ps
27(28),1; *pit* (metaph.) Ps 39(40),3; *hollow place,
cavity* Jgsᴮ 15,19; cpr. βόθρος
Cf. LUST 1996ᵃ, 135; WEVERS 1990, 183; →LSJ RSuppl

λακτίζω
(→ἀπο-)

λαλέω⁺   V 360-325-229-189-86-1189
Gn 12,4; 16,13; 17,3.22.23
to speak [abs.] Gn 18,30; *to tell* [τι] Gn 24,33; *to
tell to* [τινι] Gn 12,4; *id.* [πρός τινα] Gn 16,13;
id. [πρός τι] (metaph.) Nm 20,8; *id.* [τί τινι]
Gn 28,15; *id.* [τι πρός τινα] Gn 39,19; *to
proclaim, to say* [τι] 1 Kgs 22,8; *to speak
repeatedly, to repeat (prayers)* Jb 40,27
λαλέω ῥήματα εἰς τὰ ὦτά τινος *to speak words
in the ears of sb, to communicate sth to sb
personally* Gn 20,8; λαλέω εἰς τὴν καρδίαν
τινός *to speak comfortingly to, to comfort*
2 Sm 19,8; λαλέω ἐπὶ τῷ ὀνόματί τινος *to
speak in the name of* Ex 5,23; λαλέω καλὰ περί
τινος see καλός
*Nm 16,1 καὶ ἐλάλησε *and he said* -ויקרה? or
-ויקרא for MT ויקח *and he took*; *1 Sm 14,26
λαλῶν *speaking* -דבר for MT דבש *honey*;
*Ps 21(22),8 ἐλάλησαν *they spoke* -פטרו<> (hi.,
LH) for MT יפטירו *they drew (their lips), they
made (faces at)*; *Jb 6,4 λαλεῖν -אלהᴵᴵ *to speak,
to complain* for MT אלוה *Eloah*
Cf. DORIVAL 1994, 485; LEE, J. 1983, 83.95-96; REPO
1951, 110; WEVERS 1990, 72.95.304.317.546; →TWNT
(→ἐκ-, κατα-, παρα-, προσ-, συλ-)

λάλημα,-ατος   N3N 0-1-2-0-1-4
1 Kgs 9,7; Ez 23,10; 36,3; Tobˢ 3,4
by-word

λαλητός,-ή,-όν   A 0-0-0-1-0-1
Jb 38,14
endowed with speech; neol.

λαλιά,-ᾶς⁺   N1F 0-0-1-10-11-22
Is 11,3; Ps 18(19),4; Jb 7,6; 29,23; 33,1
talk, chat Sir 5,13; *common talk, report* 2 Mc 5,5;

speech, conversation Jb 29,23; *matter, subject* Eccl 3,18; *word* Jb 7,6; *a form of speech, dialect* Ct 4,3

λαλιάν τινα ποιέω *to make sb a by-word* Sir 42,11; ἐκχέω λαλίαν *to pour out complaint* Sir 35,14

λαμβάνω⁺   V 408-428-225-72-202-1335

Gn 2,15.21.22.23; 3,6

to take [τι] Gn 2,21; *id.* [τινα] Gn 2,15; *to take* [τινος] Gn 3,6; *id.* [ἀπό τινος] Ex 12,7; *to take away, to remove* [τι] 2 Chr 16,2; *to take away* [τινα] 2 Kgs 2,5

to take by violence, to carry off as booty [τι] Jos 11,19; *to take by violence, to take captive* [τινα] Jgs 8,16; *to capture* (a city) [τι] 1 Chr 11,8; *to take up, to carry away* [τινα] (of storm) Is 41,16; *to take up, to pronounce* [τι] Mi 2,4

to take hold of, to seize [τινα] (of pains) Ex 15,14; *to attack* [τινα] (of sudden pain) 2 Mc 9,5; *to catch, to overtake* [τινα] (of sleep) Dnᴸˣˣ 4,33b

to get, to receive [τι] Lv 25,36; *id.* [abs.] Hab 1,3; *id.* [τινα] Ps 48(49),16; *to take from, to accept from* [τι παρά τινος] Gn 23,13; *to gain, to win* (virtue) [τι] Zech 6,13; *to receive (for money), to buy* [τι] Dt 2,6, cpr. Ez 29,14; Jos 11,19; *to incur* [τι] Lv 5,1; *to levy, to impose* [τι] 1 Mc 3,31

to choose, to select [τινα] Nm 8,6; *to take, to choose* 2 Mc 8,7; *to fetch, to find* [τινα] 2 Kgs 3,15; *to take as* [τινα +pred.] Lv 18,18; *to take sb for* [τινα εἰς τινα] Gn 43,18; *id.* [τινα εἰς τι] 1 Mc 14,5

λαμβάνω μάχαιραν *to draw the sword* Is 2,4; λαμβάνω τινὰ γυναῖκα *to take as one's wife* Ex 6,23; λαμβάνω τινὰ εἰς γυναῖκα *id.* Gn 12,19; λαμβάνω πεῖραν [+inf.] *to assay, to try out* Dt 28,56; λαμβάνω τὸν συλλογισμόν τινος *to take account of, to count* Ex 30,12; πρὸ ὀφθαλμῶν λαμβάνω τι *to keep in mind* 2 Mc 8,17; λαμβάνω συντέλειαν *to be finished* 1 Ezr 6,19; λαμβάνω τὴν ἐκδίκησιν *to take vengeance, to be avenged* Jer 20,10; λαμβάνω τὴν κόλασιν *to receive* or *bear punishment, to be punished* Ez 43,11; λαμβάνω πρόσωπον *to take into consideration, to show partiality* Lv 19,15; λαμβάνω καιρόν *to seize an opportunity, to take a set time* Ps 74(75),3; λαμβάνω (τῇ γλώσσῃ) *to lap* Jgs 7,5; δεξιὰς

λαμβάνω *to take right hand, to shake hands, to pledge friendship* 1 Mc 13,50; λαμβάνω ἐν γαστρί *to conceive* Gn 25,21; ἔλαβεν ἐπὶ ματαίῳ τὴν ψυχὴν αὐτοῦ *he lifted up his soul to vanity, he desired vanity* Ps 23(24),4; οὐ λαμβάνω τι *to abandon* 2 Mc 4,6; λαβών τι *with* Gn 37,24; λαβών τινα *id.* Gn 34,2; λαβόντες χρόνον *at the appointed time* 1 Ezr 9,12

*1 Chr 24,31 ἔλαβον *they received* corr. ἔβαλον for MT ויפילו *they cast (lots)*, cpr. 1 Sm 14,42; Est 3,7; Neh 11,1; *Jer 23,39 ἐγὼ λαμβάνω *I (will) take, seize* -נשׂאתי for MT נשׁיתי *I will forget*, cpr. Ez 39,26; *Zph 3,18 τίς ἔλαβεν *who took* -מי נשׂא? ◊נשׂא for MT משׂאת *the burden (of)?*; *Jb 38,14 ἦ σὺ λαβών *did you take* -תתהפש ◊תפש? for MT תתהפך ◊הפך *did it change*

Cf. HARL 1991=1992ᵃ, 152-153; HARLÉ 1988, 99.166-167; HELBING 1928, 53; LE BOULLUEC 1989, 245; MARGOLIS 1906ᵃ=1972, 71-74; →TWNT

(→ἀνα-, ἀντι-, ἀπο-, δια-, ἐκ-, ἐπι-, ἐπικατα-, κατα-, μετα-, παρα-, περι-, προ-, προκατα-, προσ-, συλ-, συμπαρα-, συμπερι-, συναντι-, ὑπο-)

λαμπάδιον,-ου   N2N 2-1-2-0-0-5

Ex 38,16(37,23)(bis); 1 Kgs 7,35; Zech 4,2.3

bowl (of a lamp), small lamp; see κρατήρ

Cf. GOODING 1959, 56-57; LE BOULLUEC 1989, 365-366; WALTERS 1973, 50-51.285-286; WEVERS 1990, 623-624

λαμπάς,-άδος⁺   N3F 2-10-4-4-3-23

Gn 15,17; Ex 20,18; Jgsᴬ 7,16.20; 15,4

torch Gn 15,17; *lamp* Jdt 10,22; *flash, lightning* (metaph., celestial burning resembling burning torches) Ex 20,18

Cf. LE BOULLUEC 1989, 211(Ex 20,18)

λαμπήνη,-ης   N1F 0-3-1-0-0-4

Jgsᴬ 5,10; 1 Sm 26,5.7; Is 66,20

covered chariot

Cf. HARL 1991=1992ᵃ, 150; →LSJ Suppl

λαμπηνικός,-ή,-όν   A 1-0-0-0-0-1

Nm 7,3

like a λαμπήνη *covered*; neol.

λαμπρός,-ά,-όν⁺   A 0-0-0-0-7-7

Tobˢ 13,13; Wis 6,12; 17,19; Sir 29,22; 30,25

bright, clear (of light) Tobˢ 13,13; *bright, radiant* (of stars) LtJ 59; *radiant* (of wisdom) Wis 6,12; *openhanded, generous* (of pers.) Sir 31,23; *joyous, cheerful* Sir 30,25; *sumptuous* Sir 29,22

Cf. LARCHER 1984, 417-418; SPICQ 1978ᵃ, 460-462; →TWNT

λαμπρότης,-ητος⁺   N3F 0-0-1-3-2-6

Is 60,3; Ps 89(90),17; 109(110),3; Dn^Th 12,3;
Bar 4,24
brightness Dn^Th 12,3; *splendour, magnificence*
Ps 89(90),17
Cf. SPICQ 1978ᵃ, 463

λαμπτήρ,-ῆρος   N3M 0-0-0-4-0-4
Prv 16,28; 20,9a; 21,4; 24,20
lantern, lamp, torch

λάμπω⁺   V 0-0-1-2-4-7
Is 9,1; Prv 4,18; Lam 4,7; Tobˢ 13,13; Bar 3,34
to give light, to shine Bar 3,34; *to shine* (metaph.)
Prv 4,18; *to be white* Lam 4,7
→TWNT
(→ἀνα-, ἐκ-, ἐπι-, κατα-)

λάμψις,-εως   N3F 0-0-0-0-1-1
Bar 4,2
shining, light (of law; metaph.); neol.?

λανθάνω⁺   V 6-2-1-3-5-17
Lv 4,13; 5,3.4.15; Nm 5,13
to escape the notice of [τινα] Lv 5,3; *id.* [ἀπό
τινος] 2 Sm 18,13; *to escape detection* [abs.]
Wis 10,8
λανθάνω ἐκ ὀφθαλμῶν τινος *to escape the
notice of sb* Lv 4,13; οὐκ ἔλαθες με
ἀγαθοποιῶν *your good deed was not hidden
from me* Tob^BA 12,13
Cf. SPICQ 1978ᵃ, 466-467
(→δια-, ἐπι-)

λάξ   D 0-0-0-0-1-1
4 Mc 6,8
with the foot

λαξευτήριον,-ου   N2N 0-0-0-1-0-1
Ps 73(74),6
stone-cutter's tool; neol.

λαξευτός,-ή,-όν⁺   A 1-0-0-0-0-1
Dt 4,49
hewn in the rock; neol.
Cf. DOGNIEZ 1992, 96.97

λαξεύω   V 7-0-3-0-1-11
Ex 34,1.4; Nm 21,20; 23,14; Dt 3,27
to hew (in stone) [τι] Ex 34,1; τὸ λελαξευ-
μένον *hewn stone, quarried rock* Nm 21,20; Λε-
λαξευμένον (proper name) Dt 3,27; neol.
Cf. DOGNIEZ 1992, 96.97; LEE, J. 1983, 48

λαογραφία,-ας   N1F 0-0-0-0-1-1
3 Mc 2,28
enrolment, census; neol.

λαός,-οῦ⁺   N2M 379-705-437-277-266-2064
Gn 14,16; 19,4; 23,7.12.13
stereotypical rendition of עם; *people (of Israel)*

(opp. other nations גוים τὰ ἔθνη) Ex 12,33; *men,
people* Gn 14,16; *people, army* Jos 10,5; *people*
(opp. priests and Levites) 1 Ezr 5,45; *a people*
Gn 25,23
*Jer 28(51),11 λαοῦ αὐτοῦ *of his people* corr.
ναοῦ αὐτοῦ for MT היכלו *of his temple*, see also
Ps 47(48),10; cpr. Jer 37(30),18; see ἔθνος;
*1 Kgs 12,28 πρὸς τὸν λαόν *to the people* -אל העם
for MT אלהם *to them*, cpr. 1 Kgs 18,40;
*1 Chr 19,6 λαός *the people* -עם for MT עם *to or
with*, see also 1 Sm 14,45; 2 Sm 1,2; 1 Chr 12,19;
2 Chr 1,14; Hos 12,1; Ps 86(87),4; *Ez 9,9 λαῶν
peoples -עמים for MT דמים *blood*, see also Ez 7,23;
*Mi 6,15(16) νόμιμα λαοῦ μου *the laws of my
people* -חקות עמי for MT חקות עמרי *the laws of Omri*
(translated twice); *Ps 27(28),8 τοῦ λαοῦ αὐτοῦ
of his people -לעמו for MT למו *for him*?
Cf. BARR 1961, 234-235; CLARYSSE 1976, 195; DOGNIEZ
1992, 237(Dt 20,1); HARL 1986ᵃ, 58-59.159-160.207.249;
1992=1993, 188; LE BOULLUEC 1989, 199; MONTEVECCHI
1979ᵇ, 51-67; ROST 1967, 112-118; SPICQ 1978ᵃ, 468-471;
VANDERSLEYEN 1973, 339-349; WEVERS 1993, 163.391;
→NIDNTT; TWAT; TWNT

λαπιστής,-οῦ   N1M 0-0-0-0-1-1
Sir 20,7
swaggerer, arrogant person; neol.

λάπτω   V 0-8-0-0-0-8
Jgs 7,5(bis).6
to lap (with the tongue) Jgs 7,7
λάπτω τῇ γλώσσῃ *to lap with the tongue* Jgs 7,5

λάρος,-ου   N2M 2-0-0-0-0-2
Lv 11,16; Dt 14,15
sea-mew, sea-gull

λάρυγξ,-υγγος⁺   N3M 0-0-0-14-1-15
Ps 5,10; 21(22),16; 68(69),4; 113,15(115,7);
118(119),103
throat Jb 6,30
λάρυγξ γλυκύς *sweet words, gentle speech*
Sir 6,5
→TWNT

λατομέω⁺   V 2-2-2-2-0-8
Ex 21,33; Dt 6,11; 1 Chr 22,2; 2 Chr 26,10;
Is 22,16
to hew out of the rock [τι] Ex 21,33; *to hew* [τι]
1 Chr 22,2; neol.?
Cf. DORIVAL 1994, 404
(→ἐκ-)

λατομητός,-ή,-όν   A 0-2-0-0-0-2
2 Kgs 12,13; 22,6
hewn; neol.?

λατόμος,-ου⁺ N2M 0-7-0-1-1-9
1 Kgs 2,35d; 5,29; 2 Kgs 12,13; 1 Chr 22,2;
2 Chr 2,1
stone-cutter; neol.?

λατρεία,-ας⁺ N1F 3-2-0-0-4-9
Ex 12,25.26; 13,5; Jos 22,27; 1 Chr 28,13
service, rite (of things; in relig. sense) Ex 12,25;
worship (of people) 1 Mc 1,43; *service, servitude*
(of works) 3 Mc 4,14
λατρεύω λατρείαν κυρίῳ *to do service to the*
Lord (semit.) Jos 22,27
Cf. Barr 1961, 103; Daniel 1966, 66-92.102-117.; Le
Boulluec 1989, 42.151; →Nidntt; Twnt

λατρευτός,-ή,-όν A 13-0-0-0-0-13
Ex 12,16; Lv 23,7.8.21.25
servile; ἔργον λατρευτόν *servile work*
(stereotypical expression); neol.
Cf. Daniel 1966, 329-334; Luciani 1984, 425-429

λατρεύω⁺ V 45-41-1-16-6-109
Ex 3,12; 4,23; 7,16.26; 8,16
stereotypical rendition of עבד in relig. contexts; *to*
serve (God) [τινι] Ex 3,12; *to use sth to serve*
(God) [τί τινι] Ex 10,26; *to serve* (gods, idols)
[τινι] Ex 20,5
*Lv 18,21 λατρεύειν *to serve* - ◊עבר for MT עברֹ◊
(hi.) *to make to go over, to devote*
cpr. λειτουργέω
Cf. Barr 1961, 103; Daniel 1966, 66-117; Harlé 1988,
162(Lv 18,21); Hilhorst 1989, 176-192; Le Boulluec
1989, 92.140; →Nidntt; Twnt

λάτρις,-ιος N3F 0-0-0-1-0-1
Jb 2,9d
hired servant, handmaid

λαύω
(→ἀπο-)

λάφυρα,-ων N2N 0-1-0-0-2-3
1 Chr 26,27; Jdt 15,7; 2 Mc 8,30
spoils

λαφυρεύω V 0-0-0-0-1-1
Jdt 15,11
to plunder, to spoil [τι]; neol.
Cf. Hanhart 1979, 106

λάχανα,-ων⁺ N2N 1-2-0-2-0-5
Gn 9,3; 1 Kgs 20(21),2bis; Ps 36(37),2; Prv 15,17
(edible) garden herbs, vegetables 1 Kgs 20(21),2
Cf. Harl 1986ᵃ, 139; Paradise 1986, 192

λαχανεία,-ας N1F 1-0-0-0-0-1
Dt 11,10
vegetable-garden, kitchen-garden; neol.?
Cf. Dogniez 1992, 188

λέαινα,-ας N1F 0-0-0-3-0-3
Jb 4,10; Dn 7,4
lioness

λεαίνω V 0-1-0-2-0-3
2 Sm 22,43; Ps 17(18),43; Jb 14,19
to polish, to wear away [τι] (of water) Jb 14,19;
to grind down, to crush [τινα] 2 Sm 22,43

λέβης,-ητος N3M 1-13-10-3-6-33
Ex 16,3; 1 Sm 2,14.15; 17,28; 1 Kgs 7,26
kettle, cauldron

λέγω⁺ V 1031-1852-732-492-503-4610
Gn 1,3.6.9.11.14
to say (often a ptc. introducing a dir. speech)
Gn 1,22; *to say that, to assert that* [+inf.]
Gn 38,22; *to say to, to speak to* [πρός τινα]
Gn 19,5; *id.* [τινι] Gn 23,3; *id.* [ἐνώπιόν
τινος] Dnᵀʰ 6,14; *id.* [ἐναντίον τινός] Ex 6,30;
to say [τι] Gn 45,9
to call so and so [τινα +pred.] 2 Mc 4,2; *to*
order, to command [abs.] Nm 32,27; *id.* [πρός
τινα] Jos 5,15; *to tell* or *command one to do*
[τινι +inf.] Ex 5,16
to mean [τι] 2 Mc 14,7; *to plead before* [ἐπί
τινος] 2 Mc 4,47
ἔγραψεν λέγων *he wrote as follows* 2 Sm 11,15;
ὁ λεγόμενος *the so-called* (by pers., cities, ...)
2 Mc 9,2; ἡ λέγουσα ἐν καρδίᾳ αὐτῆς *she that*
says in her heart, she that says to herself Zph
2,15; τὰ ὑπὸ τοῦ βασιλέως λεγόμενα
commands of the king Est 3,3; τὰ λεχθέντα ὑπό
τινος *words that have been spoken by* Jos 24,27;
λέγει ὁ νόμος *the law says* 4 Mc 2,5; λέγω *I*
mean (as interjection, without influence on the
construction) 4 Mc 1,2
*Jb 41,1 ἐπὶ τοῖς λεγομένοις *at the things said*
אל אמריו- for MT אל מראיו *by the sight of him*
Cf. Barr 1961, 212; Dorival 1994, 485; Helbing 1907,
62; 1928, 117-120; Wevers 1993, 12; →Nidntt; Twnt
(→ἀνα-, ἀντι-, ἀπο-, δια-, ἐκ-, ἐπι-, κατα-,
προσανα-, συλ-)

λεηλατέω V 0-0-0-0-1-1
2 Mc 2,21
to plunder, to spoil [τι]

λεῖμμα,-ατος⁺ N3N 0-2-0-0-0-2
2 Sm 21,2; 2 Kgs 19,4
remnant (of things) 2 Kgs 19,4; *id.* (of pers.)
2 Sm 21,2
→Twnt

λεῖος,-α,-ον⁺ A 1-1-0-3-1-6
Gn 27,11; 1 Sm 17,40; Prv 2,20; 12,13a; 26,23

smooth 1 Sm 17,40; smooth, level Prv 2,20;
smooth-skinned, without hair Gn 27,11; flat, level
4 Mc 8,2; λεῖα smoothly, gently (as adv.)
Prv 12,13a

Cf. HARL 1986ᵃ, 215

λειποτακτέω V 0-0-0-0-1-1
4 Mc 9,23
to desert one's post (in the battle) [τι]; neol.

Cf. WALTERS 1973, 32

λείπω⁺ V 0-0-0-3-4-7
Jb 4,11; Prv 11,3; 19,4; 2 Mc 4,45; 3 Mc 3,18
A: to leave (behind) [τι] Prv 11,3; to leave, to
forsake [τινα] Jb 4,11; to be wanting to sb, to be
lacking to sb [τινι] Wis 19,4
P: to be left without, to be forsaken of [τινος]
3 Mc 3,18; id. [ἀπό τινος] Prv 19,4; to be left, to
be defeated 2 Mc 4,45

Cf. SPICQ 1978ᵃ, 472-474(Wis 19,4)

(→ἀπο-, δια-, ἐγκατα-, ἐκ-, ἐλ-, κατα-, παρα-,
παρεκ-, περι-, προσκατα-, ὑπο-)

λειτουργέω⁺ V 37-30-21-3-8-99
Ex 28,35.43; 29,30; 30,20; 35,19
frequently rendition of שרת, less frequently of עבד,
to perform a religious service, to minister
Ex 28,35; to perform (the services) [τι] Nm 4,30;
to perform religious service for, to minister to
[τινι] Nm 3,6; id. (to God) [τινι] 1 Chr 15,2
to minister to, to help [τινι] 1 Kgs 1,15
λειτουργέω λειτουργίαν to minister in religious service (semit.) Nm 8,22
*2 Sm 19,19 καὶ ἐλειτούργησαν τὴν λειτουρ-
γίαν and they performed the service -העברה ועברו
for MT העברה ועברה and crossed the ford?
cpr. λατρεύω

Cf. DANIEL 1966, 66-117; DOGNIEZ 1992, 181; DORIVAL
1994, 115-117; HELBING 1928, 195-196; ROMEO 1949,
469-503; SPICQ 1978ᵃ, 475-481; →NIDNTT; TWNT

λειτούργημα,-ατος N3N 2-0-0-0-0-2
Nm 4,32; 7,9
object used in the liturgical service; neol.?

Cf. DANIEL 1966, 81-82

λειτουργήσιμος,-ος,-ον A 0-1-0-0-0-1
1 Chr 28,13
for liturgical service or use; neol.

Cf. DANIEL 1966, 88

λειτουργία,-ας⁺ N1F 19-22-1-1-4-47
Ex 37,19(38,21); Nm 4,24.27(bis).28
public, religious or liturgical service Nm 4,24;
service, ministry (of priest) Ex 37,19(38,21)

Cf. BARR 1961, 149-151; DANIEL 1966, 66-117; LE

BOULLUEC 1989, 363; NAPHTALI 1960, 175-184; ROMEO
1949, 467-503; SPICQ 1978ᵃ, 475-481; →TWNT

λειτουργικός,-ή,-όν⁺ A 5-1-0-0-0-6
Ex 31,10; 39,12(33); Nm 4,12.26; 7,5
of or for the λειτουργία, of a ministry Nm 4,12
*Ex 31,10 τὰς λειτουργικάς of a ministry -שרת
for MT השרד of corduroy, of finely worked fabric?,
see also Ex 39,12
neol.?

Cf. DANIEL 1966, 81-82; LE BOULLUEC 1989, 315-316

λειτουργός,-οῦ⁺ N2M 0-5-1-4-3-13
2 Sm 13,18; 1 Kgs 10,5; 2 Kgs 4,43; 6,15;
2 Chr 9,4
servant, minister Ezr 7,24; private servant
2 Sm 13,18; public servant 1 Kgs 10,5; neol.?

Cf. DANIEL 1966, 98.101.102.116; PONTHOT 1986, 256;
SPICQ 1978ᵃ, 475-481

λείχω⁺ V 0-2-2-1-0-5
1 Kgs 20(21),19(bis); Is 49,23; Mi 7,17; Ps 71
(72),9
to lick [τι] 1 Kgs 20(21),19
χοῦν λείχω to lick the dust, to be defeated
Ps 71(72),9; τὸν χοῦν τῶν ποδῶν τινος λείχω
to lick the dust of one's feet, to be submissive to
sb Is 49,23

Cf. CAIRD 1976, 81; WALTERS 1973, 30-31

(→ἐκ-)

λεκάνη,-ης N1F 0-3-0-0-0-3
Jgsᴮ 5,25; Jgs 6,38
dish, pot, pan

λεληθότως D 0-0-0-0-2-2
2 Mc 6,11; 8,1
secretly

λέξις,-εως N3F 0-0-0-5-3-8
Jb 36,2; 38,1; Est 1,22; 3,12; 8,9
speech Jb 36,2; manner of speech, style Sir 23,12;
expression, formulation 2 Mc 2,31; word, phrase
Sir prol.,20; language, dialect Est 1,22

λεοντηδόν D 0-0-0-0-1-1
2 Mc 11,11
like a lion; neol.

λεπίζω V 3-0-0-0-3-6
Gn 30,37(bis).38; TobᴮᴬA 3,17; 11,12
A: to peel off the husk of [τι] Gn 30,38; to remove, to scale away [τι] TobᴮᴬA 3,17; to scale off
(objects) [τι] 1 Mc 1,22
P: to peel TobᴮᴬA 11,12
λεπίζω τὰς ῥάβδους λεπίσματα λευκά to peel
off the husk of the branches, to make clear white
stripes Gn 30,37(primo)

Cf. HARL 1986ᵃ, 233
(→ἀπο-)

λεπίς,-ίδος⁺   N3F 6-0-0-0-0-6
Lv 11,9.10.12; Nm 17,3; Dt 14,9
plate Nm 17,3; λεπίδες *scales* (of anim.) Lv 11,9
Cf. SPICQ 1978ᵃ, 482-483

λέπισμα,-ατος   N3N 1-0-0-0-0-1
Gn 30,37
peel; neol.

λέπρα,-ας⁺   N1F 34-5-0-0-0-39
Lv 13,2.3.8.9.11
stereotypical rendition of צרעת; *skin disease which makes the skin scaly, leprosy?*
Cf. ANDERSEN 1980, 207-212; GRAMBERG 1960, 10-23; HARLÉ 1988, 45; HULSE 1975, 87-105; SWELLENGREBEL 1960, 69-80

λεπράω   V 3-0-0-0-0-3
Lv 22,4; Nm 12,10(bis)
to have leprosy

λεπρόν,-οῦ   N2N 0-1-0-0-0-1
2 Kgs 5,11
leprosy

λεπρόομαι   V 0-3-0-0-0-3
2 Kgs 5,1.27; 15,5
to become leprous; λελεπρωμένος *leper, leprous*; neol.?

λεπρός,-ά,-όν⁺   A 5-7-0-0-0-12
Lv 13,44.45; 14,2.3; Nm 5,2
leprous Lv 13,44; ὁ λεπρός *leper* Lv 13,45

λεπτός,-ή,-όν⁺   A 17-2-4-2-3-28
Gn 41,3.4.6.7.19
fine, small Ex 16,14; *thin* Gn 41,7; *thin, fine* (of hair or web) Lv 13,30; *fine, powdery* Ex 30,36; *lean* (of meat) Gn 41,3; *light, gentle* 1 Kgs 19,12
Cf. LE BOULLUEC 1989, 56-57.306

λεπτύνω   V 0-5-3-11-0-19
2 Sm 22,43; 2 Kgs 23,6.15; 2 Chr 23,17; 34,4
to grind to powder, to break to pieces [τι] 2 Chr 23,17; *to bite (in pieces), to crush* [τι] (of teeth) Dnᵀʰ 7,7
λεπτύνω τι εἰς τέλος see τέλος; ὡς πηλὸν ἐξόδων ἐλέπτυνα αὐτούς *I beat them fine as the mud of the street* 2 Sm 22,43
*Jer 31(48),12 λεπτυνοῦσι *they shall break to pieces* ידיקו דקפכ◊ for MT ריקו◊ יריקו *they shall empty*; *Ps 28(29),6 καὶ λεπτυνεῖ αὐτάς *and he will grind them to powder, and he will beat them fine* וירקם- דקפכ◊ for MT וירקידם רקר◊ *he makes them skip about*

λέπυρον,-ου   N2N 0-0-0-2-0-2

Ct 4,3; 6,7
rind

λέσχη,-ης   N1F 0-0-0-1-0-1
Prv 23,29
talk, gossip
Cf. WALTERS 1973, 196

λευκαθίζω   V 2-0-0-0-0-2
Lv 13,38.39
to be white (of spots on the body)
Cf. WALTERS 1973, 87.297

λευκαίνω⁺   V 1-0-3-1-0-5
Lv 13,19; Is 1,18(bis); Jl 1,7; Ps 50(51),9
A: *to make white* (metaph.), *to make pure* (sins) [τι] Is 1,18; *to grow white* Lv 13,19
P: *to be* or *become white* Ps 50(51),9
ἐλεύκανεν κλήματα αὐτῆς *its branches turned white* (cpr. MT) or *he made its branches white, he peeled its branches* Jl 1,7
(→ἐκ-)

λευκανθίζω   V 0-0-0-1-0-1
Ct 8,5
to be white; neol.; see λευκαθίζω
Cf. WALTERS 1973, 87

λεύκη,-ης   N1F 0-0-2-0-0-2
Is 41,19; Hos 4,13
white poplar

λευκός,-ή,-όν⁺   A 24-0-3-4-1-32
Gn 30,35.37(bis); 31,8(bis)
white Gn 30,35; *white, grey* (of hair) Lv 13,3; *white-skinned* (of pers.) Ct 5,10
Cf. LE BOULLUEC 1989, 56(Ex 16,14)

λευκότης,-ητος   N3F 0-0-0-0-1-1
Sir 43,18
whiteness

λευκώματα,-ων   N3N 0-0-0-0-11-11
Tobᴮᴬ 2,10; 3,17; 6,9; 11,8.12
whiteness, white films (on eyes), *leukoma*

λεχώ,-οῦς   N3F 0-0-0-0-1-1
LtJ 27
woman in childbed or *in childbirth*

λέων,-οντος⁺   N3M 6-34-47-52-22-161
Gn 49,9(bis); Nm 23,24; 24,9; Dt 33,20
lion Jgs 14,18; *a lion-hearted person* Est 4,17s
σῴζω τινὰ ἐκ στόματος λέοντος *to rescue sb from the jaws of a lion, to rescue sb from a danger* Ps 21(22),22

λεωπετρία,-ας   N1F 0-0-4-0-0-4
Ez 24,7.8; 26,4.14
smooth rock, bare rock; neol.?

λήγω   V 0-0-0-0-6-6

2 Mc 9,7.11.18; 15,24; 3 Mc 3,16
to cease from, to abate from [τινος] 2 Mc 9,7; *to stop, to cease* [abs.] 2 Mc 9,18
(→ἀπο-, κατα-)

λήθη,-ης⁺   N1F 3-0-0-1-7-11
Lv 5,15; Nm 5,27; Dt 8,19; Jb 7,21; 3 Mc 5,28
forgetfulness Wis 16,11
ποιέομαι λήθην τινός *to forget* Jb 7,21
*Nm 5,27 καὶ λήθη λάθη *and she escaped the notice of* -עלם והתעלם for MT מעל ומעל *and she has been unfaithful to*, see also Lv 5,15; cpr. Lv 4,13; 5,3
Cf. WALTERS 1973, 262.345(Lv 5,15; Nm 5,25)

λῆμμα,-ατος⁺   N3N 0-1-14-2-0-17
2 Kgs 9,25; Jer 23,33(bis).34.36
material gain, profit Hag 2,14; *burden, commission received*, esp. of *prophecy* Jer 23,33; *oracle, word of the Lord* 2 Kgs 9,25
λῆμμα λόγου κυρίου *the contents of the word of the Lord, the message of the Lord* or *an oracle, the word of the Lord* Zech 9,1

λῆμψις,-εως⁺   N3F 0-0-0-2-2-4
Prv 15,27.29a; Sir 41,21; 42,7
accepting, receiving Prv 15,27; *receipt* Prv 15,29a

ληνός,-οῦ⁺   N2F 7-3-6-6-1-23
Gn 30,38.41; Ex 22,28; Nm 18,27.30
wine-vat in which grapes are pressed, winepress Ex 22,28; *press for wine or oil* Jl 2,24; *cask, large jar* (to conserve wine) Prv 3,10; *trough, watering-place* Gn 30,38
πατέω ληνούς *to tread the grapes* Neh 13,15
Cf. DREW-BEAR 1972, 206-207; SCHNEBEL 1925, 284-286; →MM

λῆρος,-ου⁺   N2M 0-0-0-0-1-1
4 Mc 5,11
worthless finery, trash, nonsense
Cf. SPICQ 1978ª, 484-485

ληρώδης,-ης,-ες⁺   A 0-0-0-0-1-1
2 Mc 12,44
silly
Cf. SPICQ 1978ª, 484

ληστεύω   V 0-0-0-0-1-1
1 Ezr 4,23
to practise robbery, to rob, to make raids
→LSJ RSuppl

ληστήριον,-ου   N2N 0-1-0-0-0-1
2 Chr 22,1
band of robbers

ληστής,-οῦ⁺   N1M 0-0-5-0-4-9
Jer 7,11; 18,22; Ez 22,9; Hos 7,1; Ob 5

robber, brigand
Cf. BUCHANAN 1959, 171; SPICQ 1978ª, 486-492

λίαν⁺   D 2-2-4-5-9-22
Gn 1,31; 4,5; 1 Sm 11,15; 2 Sm 2,17; Jer 24,3
very [+adv.] 2 Mc 11,1; *id.* [+adj.] Gn 1,31; *extremely* [+adj.] 4 Mc 8,17; *very much, exceedingly* [+verb] Gn 4,5
*Jb 29,5 λίαν *very* -מאר for MT עמרי *with me*

λιβανόομαι   V 0-0-0-0-1-1
3 Mc 5,45
to be mixed or *mingled with frankincense*; neol.
Cf. HELBING 1907, 123

λίβανος,-ου⁺   N2M 9-0-6-3-5-23
Ex 30,34; Lv 2,1.2.15.16
Semit. loanword (Hebr. לבנה); *frankincense*
Cf. BROWN 1980, 16-21; CAIRD 1976, 78; HORSLEY 1987, 129-131; LE BOULLUEC 1989, 313; TOV 1979, 221; WALTERS 1973, 163.326; →CHANTRAINE; FRISK

λιβανωτός,-οῦ⁺   N2M/F 0-1-0-0-1-2
1 Chr 9,29; 3 Mc 5,2
frankincense
Cf. HORSLEY 1987, 129-131; WALTERS 1973, 326

λιγύριον,-ου   N2N 2-0-1-0-0-3
Ex 28,19; 36,19(39,12); Ez 28,13
stone of Liguria; neol.
Cf. LE BOULLUEC 1989, 287; WEVERS 1990, 453

λιθάζω⁺   V 0-2-0-0-0-2
2 Sm 16,6.13
to stone [τινα] 2 Sm 16,6; *id.* [abs.] 2 Sm 16,13
Cf. HELBING 1907, 118

λίθινος,-η,-ον⁺   A 14-2-3-4-1-24
Gn 35,14; Ex 24,12; 31,18; 32,15; 34,1
(made) of stone Gn 35,14; *id.* (metaph.) Ez 11,19
αἱ λίθιναι πλάκαι *the stone tables* Ex 34,1
Cf. WEVERS 1990, 527

λιθοβολέω⁺   V 17-8-2-0-0-27
Ex 8,22(26); 19,13; 21,28.29.32
A: *to stone* [τινα] Lv 20,2; *to throw stones at* [ἐπί τινα] Ez 23,47
P: *to be stoned* Ex 8,22(26)
ἐν λίθοις λιθοβοληθήσεται *he shall be stoned with stones* (semit.) Ex 19,13
neol.
Cf. DOGNIEZ 1992, 65.247
(→κατα-)

λιθοβόλον,-ου   N2N 0-0-0-0-1-1
1 Mc 6,51
machine for hurling stones, catapult

λίθος,-ου⁺   N2M 73-100-49-46-38-306

Gn 2,12; 11,3; 28,11.18.22

stone Gn 11,3; stone (thrown for stoning)
Lv 20,2; building stone, building brick 1 Kgs 6,7
λίθος κασσιτέρινος plummet of tin Zech 4,10;
λίθος πράσινος emerald Gn 2,12; λίθος
σμαραγδίτης emerald stone Est 1,6; λίθος
πάρινος Parian marble, white marble Est 1,6;
λίθος τίμιος precious stone 1 Kgs 10,2; λίθος
πολυτελής id. 1 Chr 29,2; ξύλοις καὶ λίθοις
(images of gods made of) wood and stone
(semit.) Dt 4,28, see also 28,36.64; 29,16;
Ez 20,32; (gods? or buildings? or vessels? made
of) wood and stone (semit.) Ex 7,19
*Jos 4,11 καὶ οἱ λίθοι and the stones- והאבנים
for MT והכהנים and the priests; *1 Sm 6,18 καὶ
ἕως λίθου and to the stone- ועד אבן for MT אבל
and to (the place) Abel; *Jer 18,3 ἐπὶ τῶν λίθων on the stones- האבנים על ◊ אָבֶן for MT על האבנים
◊ אָבֶן at the potter's wheel; *Jb 41,7 λίθος stone,
rock- צר for MT צַר narrow?
Cf. CARAGOUNIS 1990, 9-16.26-30; LE BOULLUEC 1989,
120.244; SPICQ 1978ᵃ, 493-495; WEVERS 1990, 381; →MM

λιθόστρωτον,-ου⁺   N2N 0-1-0-2-0-3
2 Chr 7,3; Ct 3,10; Est 1,6
pavement 2 Chr 7,13; precious pavement Ct 3,10
Cf. BENOIT 1952, 545-548; BRUNEAU 1967, 443-446; SPICQ
1978ᵃ, 496-497

λιθουργέω   V 1-0-0-0-0-1
Ex 35,33
to work in stone, to hew, to carve [τι]; neol.?

λιθουργικός,-ή,-όν   A 2-0-0-0-0-2
Ex 28,11; 31,5
of a stone-carver; τὰ λιθουργικά stone masonry,
stone carving Ex 31,5
τέχνη λιθουργική stone engraver's art Ex 28,11
Cf. LE BOULLUEC 1989, 315; WEVERS 1990, 449.508

λιθουργός,-οῦ   N2M 0-0-0-0-1-1
Sir 45,11
seal-cutter, stone-engraver, gem-engraver
→LSJ RSuppl

λιθόω
(→ἀπο-)

λιθώδης,-ης,-ες   A 0-0-0-0-1-1
Sir 32,20
stony, rocky; τὸ λιθῶδες rocky ground

λικμάω⁺   V 0-0-13-3-3-19
Is 17,13; 30,22.24; 41,16; Jer 30,27(49,32)
A: to winnow, to separate the grain from the
chaff [τι] Am 9,9; id. [abs.] Sir 5,9; to scatter like
chaff [τινα] Jer 30,27(49,32); to scatter [τι]

Is 30,22; to drive away from [τινα ἔκ τινος]
Jb 27,21
M: to scatter like chaff [τι] Wis 11,18
Cf. LABERGE 1978, 52(Is 30,22); SPICQ 1978ᵃ, 498-499;
→MM
(→ἐκ-)

λικμήτωρ,-ορος   N3M 0-0-0-1-0-1
Prv 20,26
winnower (metaph.); neol.

λικμός,-οῦ   N2M 0-0-1-0-0-1
Am 9,9
winnowing-fan, winnowing-basket; neol.

λιμαγχονέω   V 1-0-0-0-0-1
Dt 8,3
to weaken through hunger [τινα]
Cf. DOGNIEZ 1992, 66.169; LEE, J. 1983, 33

λιμήν,-ένος⁺   N3M 0-0-0-1-8-9
Ps 106(107),30; 1 Ezr 5,53; 1 Mc 14,5;
2 Mc 12,6.9
harbour 1 Ezr 5,53; haven (metaph.) Ps
106(107),30

λίμνη,-ης⁺   N1F 0-0-0-3-2-5
Ps 106(107),35; 113(114),8; Ct 7,5; 1 Mc 11,35;
2 Mc 12,16
pool Ps 106(107),35; lake 2 Mc 12,16
αἱ τοῦ ἁλὸς λίμναι saltpits 1 Mc 11,35

λιμοκτονέω   V 0-0-0-1-0-1
Prv 10,3
to let go hungry, to let starve [τινα]

λιμός,-οῦ⁺   N2M 26-13-49-12-14-114
Gn 12,10(bis); 26,1(bis); 41,27
hunger Is 5,13; famine Gn 12,10
λιμὸς ἄρτου a shortage of bread Am 8,11;
λιμὸς καὶ θάνατος famine and death Ez 7,15

λιμπάνω
(→δια-, ἐγκατα-, ἐκ-, κατα-)

λιμώσσω   V 0-0-0-2-0-2
Ps 58(59),7.15
to be famished, to be hungry; neol.

λινοκαλάμη,-ης⁺   N1F 0-1-0-0-0-1
Jos 2,6
flax-straw (used as coll.)

λίνον,-ου⁺   N2N 3-0-3-1-1-8
Ex 9,31(bis); Dt 22,11; Is 19,9; 42,3
flax Ex 9,31; linen-cloth Dt 22,11; lamp-wick
Is 42,3

λινοῦς,-ῆ,-οῦν⁺   A 11-0-4-0-1-16
Ex 28,42; Lv 6,3(bis) 13,48.52
linen Ex 28,42; τὰ λινᾶ linen-clothes Lv 13,48

λιπαίνω⁺   V 1-0-1-4-3-9

Dt 32,15; Hab 1,16; Ps 22(23),5; 140(141),5;
Prv 5,3
A: *to oil, to anoint* [τι] Ps 22(23),5; *to make fat,
to enrich* [τι] Sir 35,5
P: *to grow fat* Dt 32,15
λιπαίνω τὸν φάρυγγα *to sweeten the palate, to
please the palate, to 'French kiss'* Prv 5,3
*Hab 1,16 (ἐν αὐτοῖς) ἐλίπανε *(by them) he
has made fat* -חשמין (בהם) for MT שמן (בחמה) *(by
them) fat*

λιπαρός,-ά,-όν⁺   A 0-1-1-1-0-3
Jgs^B 3,29; Is 30,23; Neh 9,35
fat, rich, fruitful (of land) Is 30,23; *robust* (of a
pers.) Jgs^B 3,29

λίπασμα,-ατος   N3N 0-0-0-1-1-2
Neh 8,10; 1 Ezr 9,51
a fattening substance

λιποθυμέω   V 0-0-0-0-1-1
4 Mc 6,26
to fall into a swoon, to faint
Cf. WALTERS 1973, 32

λίσσομαι   V 0-0-0-1-0-1
Jb 17,2
to beg, to pray, to entreat; *Jb 17,2 λίσσομαι
κάμνων *weary I pray* -הלה אבל? (pi.) and אבל
for MT התלים לא אם *surely there are mockers*, cpr.
Ps 44(45),13 and λιτανεύω

λιτανεία,-ας   N1F 0-0-0-0-4-4
2 Mc 3,20; 10,16; 3 Mc 2,21; 5,9
prayer, entreaty 3 Mc 2,21
ποιέομαι τὴν λιτανείαν *to make supplication,
to implore* 2 Mc 3,20
neol.

λιτανεύω⁺   V 0-0-0-1-1-2
Ps 44(45),13; 2 Mc 14,15
to pray, to entreat [τινα] 2 Mc 14,15
λιτανεύω τὸ πρόσωπόν τινος *to entreat the face
of, to seek the favour of sb* for MT פנים חלה *to
soften the face of sb, to flatter sb* Ps 44(45),13

λιτός,-ή,-όν   A 0-1-0-0-0-1
Jgs^A 11,3
poor

λιχήν,-ῆνος   N3M 2-0-0-0-0-2
Lv 21,20; 22,22
a lichen-like blemish (on the skin)
Cf. HARLÉ 1988, 45; WALTERS 1973, 32

λιχνεία,-ας   N1F 0-0-0-0-1-1
3 Mc 6,36
gluttony, luxuriousness in eating

λίψ, λιβός⁺   N3M 17-24-4-2-0-47

Gn 13,14; 20,1; 24,62; 28,14; Ex 27,9
the south (in Palestina) Gn 13,14; *the west,
Libya* (in Egypt) Ex 27,9, see also 2 Chr 32,30;
33,14; Dn^Th 8,5
Cf. BOGAERT 1981, 79-85(Ex 27,9); GERLEMAN 1946^b, 14
(2 Chr 32,30; 33,14; Dn 8,5); LE BOULLUEC 1989, 276-
277.360; →MM

λοβός,-οῦ   N2M 20-0-1-0-0-21
Ex 29,13.20(bis).22; Lv 3,4
lobe, tip (of the ear) Ex 29,20; *lobe* (of the liver)
Ex 29,13
→LSJ Suppl

λογεῖον,-ου   N2N 19-0-0-0-1-20
Ex 28,15.22.29.29a(bis)
stereotypical rendition of חשן; *oracle?* Sir 45,10;
*breast-pouch, piece of cloth with a pouch
containing the means for making oracular
decisions?, oracular breastplate of the high-priest*
Ex 28,15
Cf. HARLÉ 1988, 113; LE BOULLUEC 1989, 285-286;
WALTERS 1973, 41.284; WEVERS 1990, 451

λογίζομαι⁺   V 11-9-36-27-38-121
Gn 15,6; 31,15; Lv 7,18; 17,4; 25,31
M: *to count sth to sb, to reckon sth to sb* [τι
πρός τινα] Lv 27,23; *to take into account, to
have regard for* [τι] Is 13,17
to count sb as, to account [τινα εἰς τινα]
1 Sm 1,13; *to consider as* [τι +pred.] Wis 5,4
to reckon that, to consider that [τινα +inf.]
Is 53,4; *id.* [ὅτι +ind.] 1 Mc 6,9; *to reckon upon
doing, to plan to do* [+inf.] 1 Sm 18,25
to think out, to plot (sth evil) [τι] 2 Sm 14,13; *to
think out, to devise* (sth good) [τι] Jer 36(29),11
P: *to be considered as* [+pred.] Neh 13,13; *id.*
[ὥς τινα] Gn 31,15; *to be reckoned to sb as*
[τινι εἰς τι] Gn 15,6, see also Ps 105(106),31;
to be reckoned to, to be credited to [τινι]
Nm 18,27; *to be reckoned to, to be classed
among* [τινι] 2 Sm 4,2
οὐ λογίζομαι *to be disrespected* Is 53,3
*Is 44,19 ἐλογίσατο *he considered* -חשב for MT
ישיב שוב◊ *he brings back* (to mind); *Ps 118
(119),119 ἐλογισάμην *I reckoned* -חשבתי for MT
השבת שבתה◊? *you caused to cease?*
Cf. HEIDLAND 1936, 24-102; HELBING 1928, 65-67
(→ἀνα-, δια-, ἐκ-, ἐπι-, κατα-, παρα-, προσ-,
συλ-)

λόγιον,-ου⁺   N2N 3-0-4-27-1-35
Nm 24,4.16; Dt 33,9; Is 5,24; 28,13
word, teaching, revelation (almost always of the

Lord) Ps 118(119),67

τὰ λόγια κυρίου *the sayings of the Lord* Ps 11(12)7

Cf. HARL 1971=1992ª, 189; LARCHER 1985, 907-908; MANSON 1946, 22-31; SEELIGMANN 1948, 11(n.8); WALTERS 1973, 41.47.283-284; →TWNT

λογισμός,-οῦ⁺   N2M 0-0-12-14-89-115

Is 66,18; Jer 11,19; 18,11.18; 27(50),45

reasoning, deliberation Prv 15,22; *reason, conclusion* Eccl 7,27; *thought* Ps 32(33),11; *plan* Jdt 8,14

οὐκ ἔστιν αὐτοῦ ὁ βίος ἐν λογισμῷ ζωῆς *his life is not reckoned as life* Sir 40,29; λογίζομαι λογισμόν *to devise plans* (semit.) Jer 11,19, see also Jer 18,11.18; 30(49),30; 36(29),11; Ez 38,10; Dnᵀʰ 11,24.25; cpr. 1 Mc 11,8

→TWNT

λογιστής,-οῦ   N1M 0-1-0-0-0-1

2 Chr 26,15

calculator, engineer

λόγος,-ου⁺   N2M 54-342-344-246-252-1238

Gn 4,23; 29,13; 34,18; Ex 4,28; 5,9

stereotypical rendition of דבר; *word* Gn 4,23; *word of God* Nm 11,23; *word, message, oracle* (of God) Jer 1,4; *deliberation* Jb 7,13; *question, request* 2 Sm 14,22; *word of command* Ex 4,28; *case, cause* Jb 22,4; *condition, promise* 2 Sm 3,13 *thing spoken of, matter* Ex 18,19; *event* 2 Sm 11,19; *account* 1 Mc 10,42; *accounts, treasury, revenue* 1 Mc 10,44

(some)thing (semit.) 1 Kgs 5,1(7)

λόγῳ *seemingly* 3 Mc 3,17; εἰς λόγον τινός *on account of* 2 Mc 1,14; παρὰ λόγον *illegal, without cause* 2 Mc 4,36; κατὰ λόγον *according to one's expectations, as one wishes* 3 Mc 3,14; ἐν ἔργῳ καὶ λόγῳ *in word and deed* Sir 3,8 ἔχω λόγον τινός *to take care of, to consider* Tobˢ 6,16; λόγον δίδωμι κατά τινος *to bring a charge against* 1 Sm 22,15; ἀποδίδωμι λόγον τινί *to give account to* Dnᵀʰ 6,3; λόγον ἔχω πρός τινα *to have intercourse with* Jgsᴮ 18,7; ἐρωτάω τινὰ λόγον *to ask sb a question* Jer 45(38),14; ἀμφιέννυμαι λόγους see ἀμφιέννυμαι 2 Kgs 17,9

οἱ δέκα λόγοι *the ten commandments* Ex 34,28; βιβλίον λόγων τῶν ἡμερῶν *Book of the Chronicles* 1 Kgs 14,29; ὁ παντοδύναμος λόγος *the almighty Word, hypostatic manifestation of the Lord's power* Wis 18,15

*Jb 7,13 ἰδίᾳ λόγῳ ? corr.? διὰ λόγου for

MT שׂיחי ב/שׂיחה *in my complaint, in my concern*; *Prv 26,18 λόγους *words* corr. λόγχας? *lances* for MT זקים *arrows of fire*; *2 Chr 34,24 τοὺς πάντας λόγους *all the words* -כל הדברים (see 2 Kgs 22,16) for MT כל האלות *all the curses*; *Is 10,23 λόγον *word, matter* מלה? for MT כלה *consumption*; *Mi 1,2 λόγους *words* -מלים? for MT כלם *all of them*; *Hab 3,5 λόγος *word* -דָּבָר for MT דֶּבֶר *pestilence*, see also Ps 90(91),3; *Dnᴸˣˣ 12,3 τοὺς λόγους *the words* -הדברים? for MT (=Theod.) הרבים *many*

Cf. BARR 1961, 129-140.220-222.236-237.249; DODD 1954, 115-121 and passim; DOGNIEZ 1992, 41-43.341-342; HARL 1971=1992ª, 189.244(Is 10,23); JEANSONNE 1988, 77-78(Dn 12,3); LARCHER 1984, 565; 1985, 910.1015-1016.1018-1022(Wis 18,15-16); LE BOULLUEC 1989, 58.205.346; REPO 1951, 1-204; →NIDNTT

λόγχη,-ης⁺   N1F 0-2-2-5-2-11

Jgsᴮ 5,8; 1 Sm 17,7; Ez 26,8; 39,9; Jb 16,13

spear, lance Jgsᴮ 5,8; *spear-head* 1 Sm 17,7

λοιδορέω⁺   V 7-0-0-0-1-8

Gn 49,23; Ex 17,2(bis); 21,18; Nm 20,3

A: *to revile* [τινα] Dt 33,8; *to rail at, to insult* [τινι] 2 Mc 12,14

M: *to rail at, to scoff at* [πρός τινα] Ex 17,2(primo); *id.* [τινι] Ex 17,2(secundo); *to rail at one another* Ex 21,18

*Gn 49,23 ἐλοιδόρουν *they scoffed at, they railed at* -ריב◊ for MT רבב ורבו *they shot at*

Cf. HELBING 1928, 22-23; LE BOULLUEC 1989, 188; SPICQ 1978ª, 503-505; WEVERS 1990, 263.331; 1993, 832; →TWNT (→συλ-)

λοιδορία,-ας⁺   N1F 2-0-0-2-3-7

Ex 17,7; Nm 20,24; Prv 10,18; 20,3; Sir 22,24

railing, abuse, reproach

Cf. SPICQ 1978ª, 503-505; WALTERS 1973, 151

λοίδορος,-ος,-ον⁺   A 0-0-0-3-1-4

Prv 25,24; 26,21; 27,15; Sir 23,8

railing, abusive

Cf. SPICQ 1978ª, 503-505

λοιμεύομαι   V 0-0-0-1-0-1

Prv 19,19

to be pestilent (metaph.), *to commit injury*; *Prv 19,19 λοιμεύεται *he is pestilent* -ליץ◊ חליץ for MT תצול *you effect a rescue*

neol.

λοιμός,-οῦ⁺   N2M 0-0-7-5-1-13

Is 5,14; Jer 15,21; Ez 7,21; 28,7; 30,11

plague, pest Prv 21,24; *pestilent character* Prv 19,25

*Am 4,2(3) λοιμοί *destroyers, violent robbers* -פריצים for MT ובפרצים *and (in the direction of) the breaches*

λοιμός,-ή,-όν⁺   A 0-8-3-2-2-15
1 Sm 1,16; 2,12; 10,27; 25,17.25
pestilent, pernicious, devilish Ez 18,10; *id.* (rendering בליעל) 1 Sm 1,16, see also 2,12; 10,27; 25,17.25

λοιμότης,-ητος   N3F 0-0-0-1-0-1
Est 8,12g
pestilent condition; neol.

λοιπός,-ή,-όν⁺   A 10-56-9-7-38-120
Gn 45,6; Ex 28,10; 29,12.34; 39,11(32)
remaining Gn 45,6; *remaining, other* Ex 28,10; ὁ λοιπός [+subst.] *the rest of* Ex 29,12; τὰ λοιπά *the rest* Ex 29,34; οἱ λοιποί *the others, the rest* 1 Mc 2,44
τὸ λοιπόν τινος *the rest of, the remainder of* Lv 23,22; τὸ λοιπόν ἀπό τινος *the rest of, the remainder of* Lv 2,3
Cf. LE BOULLUEC 1989, 371.372; →TWNT (sub λεῖμμα)

λουτήρ,-ῆρος   N3M 7-8-0-0-0-15
Ex 30,18.28; 31,9; 38,26(8); 38,27(40,30)
washing-tub, basin; neol.

λουτρόν,-οῦ⁺   N2N 0-0-0-2-1-3
Ct 4,2; 6,6; Sir 34,25
washing-place Ct 4,2; *bathing, washing* Sir 34,25
Cf. SPICQ 1978ᵃ, 506-510; →TWNT

λούω⁺   V 30-7-4-3-6-50
Ex 2,5; 29,4; 40,12; Lv 8,6; 11,40
A: *to wash* [τινα] Ex 29,4; *id.* [τι] Ps 6,7
M: *to wash oneself* 1 Kgs 20(21),19; *to bathe* Ex 2,5
P: *to be washed* Ct 5,12
λούσεται τὸ σῶμα αὐτοῦ ὕδατι *he will wash his body with water* Lv 14,9
Cf. HARLÉ 1988, 147; LEE, J. 1983, 36-40
(→ἀπο-)

λοφιά,-ᾶς   N1F 0-3-0-0-0-3
Jos 15,2.5; 18,19
crest of a hill, ridge

λοχάω   V 0-0-0-0-1-1
Wis 14,24
to lie in wait, to ambush
Cf. WALTERS 1973, 120
(→συλ-)

λοχεύω   V 1-0-0-1-0-2
Gn 33,13; Ps 77(78),71
to bring forth, to give birth

λοχίζω

(→ἐκ-)

λυθρώδης,-ης,-ες   A 0-0-0-0-1-1
Wis 11,6
defiled with gore, clotted; neol.

λύκος,-ου⁺   N2M 1-0-6-1-1-9
Gn 49,27; Is 11,6; 65,25; Jer 5,6; Ez 22,27
wolf
Cf. SPICQ 1978ᵃ, 511-512

λυμαίνομαι⁺   V 1-1-6-7-2-17
Ex 23,8; 2 Chr 16,10; Is 65,8.25; Jer 28(51),2
to outrage, to maltreat [τινα] Dnᵀʰ 6,23; *to harm, to injure* [abs.] 2 Chr 16,10; *to corrupt* [τι] Ex 23,8; *to cause ruin, to lay waste* [τι] Ps 79(80),14
λυμαίνομαι μήτραν *to destroy a womb* Am 1,11, cpr. Jdt 9,2; λυμαίνομαι τὰ ἀγνὰ τῆς παρθενίας *to spoil the purity of maidenhood* 4 Mc 18,8
*Prv 27,13 λυμαίνεται *he corrupts* -חבל for MT חבלתו *his pledge*
Cf. HELBING 1928, 14

λυμεών,-ῶνος   N3M 0-0-0-0-2-2
4 Mc 18,8(bis)
destroyer, corrupter

λυπέω⁺   V 3-4-13-15-30-65
Gn 4,5; 45,5; Dt 15,10; 1 Sm 29,4; 2 Sm 13,21
A: *to grieve, to vex* [τινα] 1 Ezr 1,22; *id.* [τι] Prv 25,20
M/P: *to be grieved, to be distressed, to be sorrowful* Gn 45,5; *to be grieved* or *sorrowful at sb* [ἐπί τινι] 1 Sm 29,4; *to be grieved* or *sorrowful for sth* [ἐπί τινι] Tob 13,16; *id.* [ἔν τινι] Sir 30,5; *to be grieved, to be depressed* (rendering חרה ל *it was burning to him, he was depressed*) Gn 4,5, see also Jon 4,1.4.9; Neh 5,6; λυπέω τὸ πνεῦμά τινος see πνεῦμα
Cf. HARL 1986ᵃ, 113-114; HELBING 1928, 260; SASSON 1990, 274-275(Jon 4,1.4.9.); SPICQ 1978ᵃ, 513-519
(→ἐπι-, συλ-)

λύπη,-ης⁺   N1F 6-0-6-7-30-49
Gn 3,16(bis).17; 5,29; 42,38
pain, grief, sorrow Gn 3,16(primo); λύπαι *labour pains, contractions* Gn 3,16(secundo); λυπέομαι λύπην *to be deeply grieved, depressed* (semit.) Jon 4,1; αἱ λύπαι τῶν χειρῶν *the toils of our hands* Gn 5,29
*Is 40,29 λύπην *grief* -עצבה for MT עצמה *strength*
Cf. NEYREY 1980, 155-156; SASSON 1990, 274-275(Jon 4,1); SPICQ 1978ᵃ, 513-519

λυπηρός,-ά,-όν⁺   A 1-0-0-4-1-6

Gn 34,7; Prv 14,10; 15,1; 17,22; 26,23
painful, grievous Prv 15,1; *sorrowful, sad*
Prv 14,10
λυπηρόν ἐστίν τινι *it is painful for sb*
(rendering ל חרה *it burns to*, cpr. Gn 4,5 and
λυπέω) Gn 34,7
Cf. SPICQ 1978ᵃ, 513-519; WEVERS 1993, 560

λύσις,-εως⁺   N3F 0-0-0-2-1-3
Eccl 8,1; Dnᴸˣˣ 12,8; Wis 8,8
interpretation Eccl 8,1
λύσαις αἰνίγματων *solution of riddles* Wis 8,8

λυσιτέλεια,-ας   N1F 0-0-0-0-1-1
2 Mc 2,27
advantage, benefit, interests

λυσιτελέω⁺   V 0-0-0-0-6-6
Tobᴮᴬ 3,6; Tobˢ 3,6(bis); Sir 20,10.14
to profit sb [τινι] Sir 20,10
λυσιτελεῖ τινι [+inf.] *it is profitable for sb to
do* Tob 3,6
Cf. HELBING 1928, 3

λυσιτελής,-ής,-ές   A 0-0-0-0-1-1
Sir 28,21
useful, advantageous, good

λύτρον,-ου⁺   N2N 17-0-1-2-0-20
Ex 21,30(bis); 30,12; Lv 19,20; 25,24
price of release, ransom (mostly pl.) Prv 6,35;
λύτρα *price of release, ransom* Ex 30,12
λαμβάνω λύτρα *to accept a ransom* Nm 35,31
Cf. HILL 1967, 49-66; HORSLEY 1982, 90; 1983, 72-75; LE
BOULLUEC 1989, 222; SCHENKER 1982ᵃ, 33-34; 1982, 77-80;
SPICQ 1982, 429-435; WEVERS 1990, 337.494; YSEBAERT
1973, 8-9; →TWNT

λυτρόω⁺   V 37-6-20-36-9-108
Ex 6,6; 13,13(bis).15; 15,13
M: *to release by payment of ransom, to redeem*
[τινα] Ex 6,6; id. [τι] Lv 25,25; *to deliver (life,
soul)* [τι] Ps 54(55),19; id. [τινα] Ps 58(59),2;
to atone for (sins) [τι] Dnᵀʰ 4,24
P: *to be ransomed* Lv 19,20
Cf. BEAUCHAMP 1978, 49-56; HARL 1991=1992ᵃ, 151;
HILL 1967, 53-66; HORSLEY 1983, 72-75; SPICQ 1982,
429-435
(→ἀπο-)

λυτρών,-ῶνος   N3M 0-1-0-0-0-1
2 Kgs 10,27
water-closet, latrine, outhouse; neol.

λύτρωσις,-εως⁺   N3F 4-6-1-3-1-15
Lv 25,29(bis).48; Nm 18,16; Jgsᴬ 1,15
ransoming, redemption Lv 25,48

*Jgs 1,15 λύτρωσιν ὕδατος *the ransom of water*
גאלת מים- for MT גלת מים *Gulloth-Maim*, cpr.
Jos 15,19
neol.
Cf. HILL 1967, 62; SPICQ 1982, 429-435; WALTERS 1973,
319(n.15)

λυτρωτής,-οῦ⁺   N1M 0-0-0-2-0-2
Ps 18(19),15; 77(78),35
ransomer, redeemer; neol.

λυτρωτός,-ή,-όν   A 2-0-0-0-0-2
Lv 25,31.32
redeemable; neol.

λυχνία,-ας⁺   N1F 22-6-3-0-4-35
Ex 25,31(bis).32(bis).33
stereotypical rendition of מנורה; *lampstand,
candlestick*; neol.?

λύχνος,-ου⁺   N2M 17-11-4-9-6-47
Ex 25,37(bis); 27,20; 30,7.8
stereotypical rendition of נר; *lamp*
Cf. LE BOULLUEC 1989, 365-366.372

λύω⁺   V 2-1-5-10-15-33
Gn 42,27; Ex 3,5; Jos 5,15; Is 5,27; 14,17
A: *to loose, to untie* (bounds) [τι] Jb 39,5; *to
unbind, to unfasten, to open* (a sack) [τι]
Gn 42,27; *to untie, to loose* (sandals) [τι] Ex 3,5;
to untie, to loose, to set free (the devil) [τινα]
Tobˢ 3,17; *to deliver* [τινα] Jb 5,20; *to loose*
[τινα] Ps 145(146),7; *to break down, to destroy*
[τι] 1 Ezr 1,52; *to bring to an end, to relieve*
(pains) [τι] Jb 39,2; *to weaken* [τινα]
Ps 101(102),21; *to relax, to unstring* (the sinews)
[τι] 4 Mc 7,13; *to forgive* (sins) [τι] Jb 42,9; *to
turn away* [τι] 1 Ezr 9,13
M: *to dishevel* (hair) [τι] 3 Mc 1,4
λύω νόμον *to open the book of the law, to
explain, to set forth* 1 Ezr 9,46; λύω μήτραν *to
pierce, to penetrate, to puncture the hymen, to
violate a girl's womb* Jdt 9,2, cpr. Am 1,11
Cf. BASSER 1985, 297-300; HILL 1967, 49; MOORE 1985,
191; →TWNT
(→ἀνα-, ἀπο-, δια-, ἐκ-, κατα-, παρα-, περι-,
συλ-, ὑπο-)

λῶμα,-ατος   N3N 7-0-0-0-0-7
Ex 28,33(bis).34; 36,31.32(39,24.25)
hem, border, fringe (of a robe); neol.
Cf. LEE, J. 1983, 49

λωποδυτέω   V 0-0-0-0-1-1
1 Ezr 4,24
to rob, to plunder

μά   X 0-0-0-0-1-1
4 Mc 10,15
by (part. used in asseverations, with acc. of the
deity appealed to)

μαγειρεῖον,-ου   N2N 0-0-2-0-0-2
Ez 46,23.24
cook-house, kitchen

μαγειρεύω   V 0-0-0-1-0-1
Lam 2,21
to cook, to prepare a dish; *to butcher, to
massacre* (metaph. in this particular text)

μαγείρισσα,-ας   N1F 0-1-0-0-0-1
1 Sm 8,13
cook (fem.); neol.

μάγειρος,-ου   N2M 0-2-0-1-0-3
1 Sm 9,23.24; Lam 2,20
cook, butcher
Cf. BERTHIAUME 1982, 1-141

μαγικός,-ή,-όν   A 0-0-0-0-1-1
Wis 17,7
magical; μαγικὴ τέχνη *magic*
Cf. LARCHER 1985, 958

μαγίς,-ίδος   N3F 0-2-0-0-0-2
Jgs 7,13
any kneaded mass, cake; μαγὶς ἄρτου
κριθίνου *cake of barley bread*

μάγος,-ου⁺   N2M 0-0-0-10-0-10
Dn^Th 1,20; Dn 2,2.10
wizard, enchanter, magician
→NIDNTT; TWNT

μαδαρόω   V 0-0-0-1-0-1
Neh 13,25
to make bald [τινα]; neol.
Cf. CAIRD 1976, 81

μαδάω   V 2-0-1-0-0-3
Lv 13,40.41; Ez 29,18
to lose one's hair, to become bald (of the head)
Lv 13,40; *to become bare* (by chafing) Ez 29,18
→LSJ RSuppl(Ez 29,18)

μαδων   N 0-1-0-0-0-1
2 Sm 21,20
= מרון/מדין *contention, strife*
Cf. TOV 1973, 89

μαελεθ   N M 0-0-0-2-0-2
Ps 52(53),1; 87(88),1
= מחלת *Mahalath* (unexplained musical term)

μάζα,-ης   N1F 0-0-0-0-2-2
Bel 27
lump, cake

μαζουρωθ   N 0-1-0-1-0-2

2 Kgs 23,5; Jb 38,32
= מזרות *constellation (of stars)* (Lucifer? see V.:
luciferum) Jb 38,32
*2 Kgs 23,5 καὶ τοῖς μαζουρωθ *and to the
Mazuroth?* -ולמזרות for MT ולמזלות *and to the
constellations*

μάθημα,-ατος⁺   N3N 0-0-1-0-0-1
Jer 13,21
lesson; διδάσκω τινὰ μαθήματα *to teach sb
lessons*

μαῖα,-ας⁺   N1F 9-0-0-0-0-9
Gn 35,17; 38,28; Ex 1,15.17.18
midwife

μαιμάσσω   V 0-0-1-1-0-2
Jer 4,19; Jb 38,8
to rush out (of water) Jb 38,8; *to be eager, to be
in great commotion* Jer 4,19
Cf. WALTERS 1973, 318

μαίνομαι⁺   V 0-0-2-0-3-5
Jer 32(25),16; 36(29),26; 4 Mc 8,5; 10,13; Wis
14,28
to be out of one's mind, to be mad Wis 14,28; *to
rage, to be furious* Jer 32(25),16
μαίνομαι μανίαν *to be mad with madness, to
be very mad* 4 Mc 8,5
Cf. SPICQ 1978ᵃ, 529-530; →NIDNTT; TWNT
(→ἀπο-, ἐπι-)

μαιόομαι   V 1-0-0-1-0-2
Ex 1,16; Jb 26,5
M: *to deliver (a woman)* [τινα] (said of
midwife) Ex 1,16
P: *to be brought to birth* Jb 26,5
→LSJ suppl

μακαρίζω⁺   V 2-0-4-6-12-24
Gn 30,13; Nm 24,17; Is 3,12; 9,15; Mal 3,12
A: *to bless, to pronounce happy* [τινα]
Gn 30,13; *to bless, to pronounce to be blessed*
[τι] Wis 2,16; *to bless, to make sb happy with*
[τινα ἔν τινι] Sir 45,7
P: *to be blessed* 4 Mc 16,9
*Nm 24,17 μακαρίζω *I bless him* אשרנו ◊ אשר
for MT אשורנו ◊ שור *I see him*
→TWNT

μακάριος,-α,-ον⁺   A 2-4-4-33-30-73
Gn 30,13; Dt 33,29; 1 Kgs 10,8(bis); 2 Chr 9,7
blessed, happy (of men) Gn 30,13; *blessed* (of
things) Eccl 10,17
*Is 31,9 μακάριος *blessed* -אשרי for MT אשר *who*
or *whose* (rel. part.)
Cf. LIPIŃSKI 1968, 321-367; SPICQ 1982, 436-449;

ZIMMERLI 1978, 8-26; →TWNT

μακαριότης,-ητος N3F 0-0-0-0-1-1
4 Mc 4,12
blessedness

μακαριστός,-ή,-όν A 0-0-0-3-1-4
Prv 14,21; 16,20; 29,18; 2 Mc 7,24
most blessed

μακαρίως D 0-0-0-0-1-1
4 Mc 12,1
in a blessed way, blessed

μακράν⁺ D 9-13-18-19-18-77
Gn 44,4; Ex 8,24; 33,7; Nm 9,10; Dt 13,8
far 1 Kgs 8,46; *far (off)* Ps 64(65),6; *from afar* Jb
36,3; *far from* [τινος] Sir 15,8; *id.* [ἀπό τινος]
Ex 33,7
ἕως εἰς μακράν *far off* Sir 24,32; εἰς μακράν
for a long time 2 Sm 7,19; οὐ μακράν *not far off*
Gn 44,4; *not out of reach, not unattainable* Dt
30,11
→NIDNTT

μακρόβιος,-ος,-ον⁺ A 0-0-1-0-1-2
Is 53,10; Wis 3,17
long-lived Is 53,10
μακρόβιος γίνομαι *to live long* Wis 3,17

μακροβίωσις,-εως N3F 0-0-0-0-1-1
Bar 3,14
longevity; neol.

μακροημέρευσις,-εως N3F 0-0-0-0-3-3
Sir 1,12.20; 30,22
length of days; neol.

μακροημερεύω V 4-2-0-0-1-7
Dt 5,33; 6,2; 11,9; 32,47; Jgs^A 2,7
to live long, to prolong one's days; neol.
Cf. DOGNIEZ 1992, 64.142.152; WEVERS 1995, 111

μακροήμερος,-ος,-ον A 1-0-0-0-0-1
Dt 4,40
long-lived; γίνομαι μακροήμερος *to live a
long-time*; neol.
Cf. DOGNIEZ 1992, 64.142

μακρόθεν⁺ D 9-5-9-8-7-38
Gn 21,16; 22,4; 37,18; Ex 2,4; 20,18
from afar, from a distance Ex 2,4; *at a distance*
Gn 21,16; neol.?

μακροθυμέω⁺ V 0-0-0-2-6-8
Jb 7,16; Prv 19,11; 2 Mc 6,14; Sir 2,4; 18,11
to have patience, to wait Jb 7,16; *to be patient, to
forbear* Prv 19,11; *to be patient towards* [ἐπί
τινι] Sir 18,11; *to bear patiently* [τι] Bar 4,25;
neol.
Cf. BICKERMAN 1976, 184; RIESENFELD 1963, 214-217;

WIFSTRAND 1964, 72-74; →NIDNTT; TWNT

μακροθυμία,-ας⁺ N1F 0-0-2-1-2-5
Is 57,15; Jer 15,15; Prv 25,15; 1 Mc 8,4; Sir 5,11
patience, steadfastness, endurance Is 57,15;
forbearance, patience towards people Prv 25,15
→NIDNTT; TWNT

μακρόθυμος,-ος,-ον⁺ A 2-0-3-12-4-21
Ex 34,6; Nm 14,18; Jl 2,13; Jon 4,2; Na 1,3
patient, long-suffering, slow to anger (often of the
Lord)
Cf. TOV 1977, 200; →NIDNTT; TWNT

μακρός,-ά,-όν⁺ A 3-1-3-3-6-16
Nm 9,13; Dt 12,21; 19,6; 1 Chr 17,17; Is 5,18
long (of distance) Dt 19,6; *far (away), remote,
distant* Mi 4,3; *large in size, great, long* Jb 11,9;
long (of time) Prv 28,16
ἐκ μακρῶν *from distant places* 1 Chr 17,17; ἐν
ὁδῷ μακρᾷ εἰμι *to be on a long road, to have a
long way to go* Nm 9,13
μακρότερον *farther* (adv.) Dt 12,21, see also
Wis 12,24

μακρότης,-ητος N3F 1-0-0-7-1-9
Dt 30,20; Ps 20(21),5; 22(23),6; 90(91),16;
92(93),5
length (of days, of life) [τινος] Dt 30,20; *long
time* Eccl 8,12
εἰς μακρότητα ἡμερῶν *for ever* Ps 22(23),6

μακροτονέω V 0-0-0-0-1-1
2 Mc 8,26
to persevere [+ptc.]

μακροχρονίζω V 2-0-0-0-1-3
Dt 17,20; 32,27; Od 2,27
to last a long time; neol.
Cf. DOGNIEZ 1992, 64.142.333

μακροχρόνιος,-ος,-ον⁺ A 2-0-0-0-0-2
Ex 20,12; Dt 5,16
a long time, long-lived
Cf. DOGNIEZ 1992, 142

μάκρυμμα,-ατος N3N 0-0-0-2-0-2
Ezr 9,1.11
thing put away as abominable, abomination;
neol.

μακρύνω V 0-2-4-17-4-27
Jgs 18,22; Is 6,12; 49,19; 54,2
A: *to prolong, to lengthen* [τι] Is 54,2; *to remove
to a distant time, to delay* [τι] Ps 21(22),20; *to
defer to* [+inf.] Jdt 2,13; *to keep oneself far away
from* [ἑαυτον ἀπό τινος] Ps 72(73),27
to travel far Ps 54(55),8; *to travel far from*
[τινος] Jgs 18,22; *to go far from* [ἀπό τινος]

Ps 70(71),12
P: *to be removed from* [ἀπό τινος] Ps 55(56),1;
to be far off from [ἀπό τινος] Ps 118(119),150
*Ps 119(120),5 ἐμακρύνθη *is prolonged* - ◊משׁך for
MT משׁך *Meshech*
neol.?
Cf. HELBING 1928, 165; PRIJS 1948, 27(Ps 55(56),1)

μάλα   D 0-3-0-1-7-11
2 Sm 14,5; 1 Kgs 1,43; 2 Kgs 4,14; Dn^LXX 10,21;
Tob^S 7,10
very, exceedingly 2 Mc 12,18; *indeed* 2 Sm 14,5;
however, rather Dn^LXX 10,21
εὖ μάλα *easily* 2 Mc 8,30

μάλαγμα,-ατος   N3N 0-0-2-0-1-3
Is 1,6; Ez 30,21; Wis 16,12
medicinal plaster, emollient

μαλακία,-ας⁺   N1F 5-7-2-1-0-15
Gn 42,4; 44,29; Ex 23,25; Dt 7,15; 28,61
weakliness, sickness, disease
Cf. HARL 1986ᵃ, 279; LEE, J. 1983, 66-67; WEVERS 1993,
705

μαλακίζομαι⁺   V 1-3-4-2-0-10
Gn 42,38; 2 Sm 13,5; 2 Chr 16,12(bis); Is 38,1
to be weakly, to be sick
Cf. HARL 1986ᵃ, 279; LEE, J. 1983, 66-67

μαλακός,-ή,-όν⁺   A 0-0-0-2-0-2
Prv 25,15; 26,22
soft, mild Prv 25,15; *soft, fair* Prv 26,22
Cf. LEE, J. 1983, 66-67

μαλακοψυχέω   V 0-0-0-0-1-1
4 Mc 6,17
to be faint-hearted, to be cowardly; neol.

μαλακύνω   V 0-0-0-1-0-1
Jb 23,16
to soften (the heart) [τι]

μαλακῶς   D 0-0-0-1-0-1
Jb 40,27
softly

μάλιστα⁺   D 0-0-0-0-6-6
2 Mc 8,7; 3 Mc 5,3; 4 Mc 3,10; 4,22; 12,9
sup. of μάλα; *most of all, above all, especially*
2 Mc 8,7; *exceedingly* (with verb) 4 Mc 4,22
ὡς μάλιστα *certainly, very much* 4 Mc 3,10
Cf. SKEAT 1979, 173-177

μᾶλλον⁺   D 7-0-5-11-29-52
Gn 19,9; 29,30; Nm 13,31; 14,12; Dt 9,1
comp. of μάλα; *more* [+adj.] (forming a comp.)
Prv 5,4; *more* (strengthening a comp.) Nm 13,31;
rather, the more Tob^BA 14,4
μᾶλλον ἤ *more than, rather than* Gn 19,9

μάμμη,-ης⁺   N1F 0-0-0-0-1-1
4 Mc 16,9
grandmother

μαν   N 5-0-0-0-0-5
Ex 16,31.32.33.35(bis)
= מָן *manna* see μαννα
Cf. LE BOULLUEC 1989, 56; WALTERS 1973, 173

μαναα   N F/N 0-6-10-3-0-19
2 Kgs 8,8.9; 17,3.4; 20,12
= מנחה *gift, offering*
Cf. DANIEL 1966, 201-223; LUST 1996, 135-136; WALTERS
1973, 170

μάνδρα,-ας⁺   N1F 0-5-4-3-2-14
Jgs^A 6,2; 1 Sm 13,6; 2 Sm 7,8; 1 Chr 17,7; 2 Chr
32,28
fold (of sheep) 2 Chr 32,28; *den* (of lion) Ps
9,30
*1 Sm 13,6 καὶ ἐν ταῖς μάνδραις *and in holes,
caves* (for men) -וב/חורים? ◊חר for MT ובחחים
and in thorns

μανδραγόρας,-ου   N1M 5-0-0-1-0-6
Gn 30,14(bis).15(bis).16
mandragora, mandrake
Cf. WEVERS 1993, 480

μανδύας,-ου   N1M 0-7-0-0-0-7
Jgs 3,16; 1 Sm 17,38.39; 2 Sm 10,4
Persian loanword (Hebr. מרו, מר); *woollen cloak*
Cf. CAIRD 1976, 79; WALTERS 1973, 165

μανη   N 0-0-0-4-0-4
Dn^LXX 5,prol.(bis); Dn^Th 5,25.26
= מנא *mene* (Aram. meaning *numbered*, used in
the visionary inscription *mene, tekel and parsin*)

μανθάνω⁺   V 8-1-18-10-19-56
Ex 2,4; Dt 4,10; 5,1; 14,23; 17,19
to learn 1 Chr 25,8; *to learn* [τι] Dt 5,1; *id.*
[+indir. question] Ex 2,4; *to learn of* [τινος] Prv
22,25; *to learn to* [+inf.] Dt 4,10; *to learn that,
to find out* Est 1,1n
Cf. HELBING 1928, 158; →NIDNTT; TWNT
(→κατα-)

μανία,-ας⁺   N1F 0-0-2-1-3-6
Hos 9,7.8; Ps 39(40),5; 4 Mc 8,5; 10,13
madness

μανιάκης,-ου   N1M 0-0-0-6-1-7
Dn 5,7.16.29
Persian or Gallic loanword (Aram. המניכא / המניכא);
necklace; neol.?
Cf. WALTERS 1973, 165; →CHANTRAINE; FRISK

μανιώδης,-ης,-ες   A 0-0-0-0-1-1
3 Mc 5,45

of madness, maniacal

μαννα⁺   N N 5-2-0-2-1-10
Nm 11,6.7.9; Dt 8,3.16
= מנא *manna* (Aram. for מן) Nm 11,6
*Bar 1,10 μαννα *manna* corr.? μαναα -מנחה-
cereal offering, cpr. μαν and μαναα
Cf. CAIRD 1976, 85; DOGNIEZ 1992, 169; ROCCO 1969,
273-277; TOV 1979, 231; WALTERS 1973, 169-171; →TWNT

μαντεία,-ας   N1F 3-1-9-0-1-14
Nm 23,23; Dt 18,10.14; 2 Kgs 17,17; Is 16,6
divination, prophecy, oracle Nm 23,23
μαντευόμενος μαντείαν (semit. for קסם קסמים)
one who divines divinations, diviner Dt 18,10
*Ez 21,28 ὡς μαντευόμενος μαντείαν *as one
using divination* -כְּקוֹסֵם for MT בְּקֹסֵם *as divination*
Cf. DOGNIEZ 1992, 50

μαντεῖον,-ου   N2N 1-0-1-1-0-3
Nm 22,7; Ez 21,27; Prv 16,10
oracle Prv 16,10; μαντεῖα *things attached to
divination* Nm 22,7
Cf. DORIVAL 1994, 421

μαντεύω⁺   V 1-2-9-0-0-12
Dt 18,10; 1 Sm 28,8; 2 Kgs 17,17; Jer 34(27),9;
Ez 12,24
M: *to divine, to prophesy* Dt 18,10; *to divine* [τι]
Ez 12,24
μαντευόμενος μαντείαν Is 16,6 see μαντεία
Cf. DOGNIEZ 1992, 50; →MM

μάντις,-εως⁺   N3M 0-2-3-0-0-5
Jos 13,22; 1 Sm 6,2; Jer 36(29),8; Mi 3,7; Zech
10,2
diviner, seer, prophet

μαραίνω⁺   V 0-0-0-2-2-4
Jb 15,30; 24,24; Wis 2,8; 19,21
A: *to blast* [τι] (of wind) Jb 15,30; *to waste, to
wither, to consume* [τι] (of fire) Wis 19,21
P: *to be withered* Jb 24,24
Cf. SPICQ 1978ᵃ, 531-532

μαρμάρινος,-η,-ον   A 0-0-0-1-0-1
Ct 5,15
of marble

μάρμαρος,-ου⁺   N2F 0-0-0-0-1-1
LtJ 71
marble

μαρσίππιον,-ου   N2N 0-0-1-1-1-3
Is 46,6; Prv 1,14; Sir 18,33
dim. of μάρσιππος; *small sack, purse*

μάρσιππος,-ου   N2M 18-0-1-0-0-19
Gn 42,27(bis).28; 43,12.18
sack, bag

Cf. LEE, J. 1983, 117

μαρτυρέω⁺   V 8-1-0-1-4-14
Gn 31,46.48(ter); Nm 35,30
to witness, to testify Gn 31,46; *to testify* [τι]
Dt 19,18; *to testify against* [κατά τινος]
Dt 19,15; *id.* [ἐπί τινα] 1 Mc 2,37; *id.* [κατά
τινα] Dt 31,21; *to bear witness of sth to sb* [τί
τινι] Lam 2,13; *to bear witness to* [τινι] 2 Chr
28,10
*2 Chr 28,10 μαρτυρῆσαι *testify* corr.?
ἁμαρτῆσαι for MT אשמות *guilt*
Cf. HELBING 1928, 225; →NIDNTT; TWNT
(→ἀντι-, ἀπο-, δια-, ἐκ-, ἐπι-, κατα-)

μαρτυρία,-ας⁺   N1F 3-0-0-3-6-12
Gn 31,47; Ex 20,16; Dt 5,20; Ps 18(19),8; Prv
12,19
testimony Gn 31,47; *demonstration* Sir 31,23;
evidence 4 Mc 6,32
*Prv 12,19 μαρτυρίαν *testimony* -עֵר(לָ) for MT
לָעַר *for ever*
Cf. WEVERS 1995, 93-94; →MM; NIDNTT; TWNT

μαρτύριον,-ου⁺   N2N 184-27-8-37-2-258
Gn 21,30; 31,44; Ex 16,34; 25,10.16
testimony, proof Dt 31,26; *testimony* Ex 25,10; τὰ
μαρτύρια *testimonies, the Decalogue* Ex 25,16
κιβωτὸν μαρτυρίου *the ark of testimony* Ex
25,10, cpr. 27,21
*Ex 27,21 μαρτυρίου *of testimony* -עֵד◊עֵר for
MT מוֹעֵד יִעַד *congregation* (very often in the
expression σκηνὴ τοῦ μαρτυρίου); *Hos 2,14
μαρτύριον *testimony* -עֵד◊עוּר for MT יִעַר *forest*;
*Zph 3,8 εἰς μαρτύριον *for a testimony* -לָעֵד for
MT לָעַר *for ever*, see also Am 1,11; Mi 7,18; Prv
29,14
Cf. DOGNIEZ 1992, 53.54; DORIVAL 1994, 57; HARLÉ 1988,
73; LE BOULLUEC 1989, 43.280; ROST 1967, 123-132;
WEVERS 1990, 398(Ex 25,16).442.491.500.504; →NIDNNT;
TWNT

μαρτύρομαι⁺   V 0-0-0-0-1-1
Jdt 7,28
to call to witness, to adjure, to solemnly enjoin
[τι]
Cf. HELBING 1928, 225
(→δια-)

μάρτυς,-υρος⁺   N3M 17-8-14-17-3-59
Gn 31,44.47; Ex 23,1; Lv 5,1; Nm 5,13
witness (in legal sense) Dt 17,6; *id.* (of God)
Gn 31,44
*Nm 23,18 μάρτυς *witness* -עֵד for MT עָרַי *to me*;
*Prv 12,19 μάρτυς *witness* -לָעֵד for MT לָעַר *for ever*

Cf. Spicq 1978ᵃ, 533-538; Wevers 1993, 523; →NIDNTT; TWNT

μαρυκάομαι V 2-0-0-0-0-2
Lv 11,26; Dt 14,8
to chew (the cud) [τι]; neol.

μασανα N 0-1-0-0-0-1
2 Chr 34,22
= משנה *Second Quarter*

μασάομαι⁺ V 0-0-0-1-0-1
Jb 30,4(5)
to chew
(→δια-)

Μασεκ N 1-0-0-0-0-1
Gn 15,2
= משק *inheritence*
Cf. Tov 1973, 88

μασενα N F 0-1-0-0-0-1
2 Kgs 22,14
= משנה *Second Quarter*

Μασερεμ N 0-1-0-0-0-1
1 Sm 23,14
= מצרם- for MT מצרות *stronghold*
Cf. Tov 1973, 89

μασμαρωθ N 0-0-1-0-0-1
Jer 52,19
= מזמרות- *snuffers* for MT מזרקות *bowls*

μασομελ N 0-1-0-0-0-1
Jos^B 19,27
= משמאל *in the north, on the left hand*

μάσσω
(→ἀπο-, ἐκ-)

μαστιγόω⁺ V 5-2-1-9-18-35
Ex 5,14.16; Dt 25,2.3(bis)
A: *to whip, to flog* [τινα] Ex 5,14; *to punish, to chastise* [τινα] (of God) Jer 5,3
P: *to be afflicted, to be tormented, to be mistreated* Sir 30,14
*Prv 3,12 μαστιγοῖ δέ *and he scourges* -ויכאב for MT וכאב *and like a father*
Cf. Prijs 1948, 40-41; Spicq 1978ᵃ, 539-540; →NIDNTT; TWNT

μαστίζω⁺ V 1-0-0-0-2-3
Nm 22,25; 3 Mc 2,21; Wis 5,11
to whip, to flog [τινα] Nm 22,25; *to strike, to lash* [τι] Wis 5,11
Cf. Dorival 1994, 54; Spicq 1978ᵃ, 539-540

μάστιξ,-ιγος⁺ N3F 0-5-3-11-19-38
1 Kgs 12,11.14; 24,2; 2 Chr 10,11.14
whip Prv 26,3; *scourge, plague* Jer 6,7; μάστιγες *whips, lashes* 1 Kgs 12,11

μάστιξ γλώσσης *scourge of the tongue* Jb 5,21
*Ps 72(73),4 μάστιγι *plague* -הלם◊ for MT אול/ם *their body?*
Cf. Spicq 1978ᵃ, 539-540; →LSJ Rsuppl; NIDNTT; TWNT

μαστός,-οῦ⁺ N2M 1-0-11-19-4-35
Gn 49,25; Is 28,9; 32,12; 66,11; Jer 18,14
(women's) breast Gn 49,25; *id.* (metaph.) Is 66,11
ἀποσπάω τινὰ ἀπὸ μαστοῦ *to draw from the breast, to wean* Is 28,9
*Jer 18,14 μαστοί *breasts, prominent parts?* or *fertilizing streams?* (metaph.) שדי- for MT שרי *fields?*; *Ez 16,4 τοὺς μαστούς σου *your breasts* -שדיך for MT שרך *your umbilical cord*; *Ct 1,2 μαστοί σου *your breasts* -דדי/ך◊דד for MT דדי/ך *your love*, see also Ct 1,4; 4,10; 7,13

μάταιος,-α/ος,-ον⁺ A 6-5-41-17-6-75
Ex 20,7(bis); 23,1; Lv 17,7; Dt 5,11
in profane sense: *meaningless, worthless* Mi 1,14; *vain, useless* (of human actions) Ps 59(60),13; *vain, nothing* (of pers.) Ps 61(62),10; *without ground* or *false* Ex 23,1; *foolish* Ps 93(94),11; *vain, empty* (of hope) Is 31,2
in relig. sense: *false* (of prophecies) Zph 3,13; οἱ μάταιοι or τὰ μάταια *vanities, vain gods, idols* Lv 17,7, see also 2 Chr 11,15
ἐπὶ ματαίῳ *in vain* Ex 20,7
*Is 22,2 μάταια *vain* -שוא◊? for MT תשאות שאה◊ *noise*, cpr. Is 28,29; *Hos 12,2 μάταια *vain things, idols* -שוא? for MT שד *violence*; *Ps 5,10 ματαία *vain, sinful* -און? for MT הוה◊ *destruction, disaster*
Cf. Harlé 1988, 157; Larcher 1985, 749; Le Boulluec 1989, 59.232(Ex 23,1); →LSJ Rsuppl(Lv 17,7; 2 Chr 11,15); NIDNTT; TWNT

ματαιότης,-ητος⁺ N3F 0-0-0-55-0-55
Ps 4,3; 25(26),4; 30(31),7; 37(38),13; 38(39),6
emptiness, vanity Eccl 1,2; *folly* Prv 22,8a
εἰς ματαιότητα *in vain* Ps 138(139),20; λαλέω ματαιότητας *to speak empty words* Ps 37(38),13
*Ps 39(40),5 ματαιότητας *vanities* -ריק◊? for MT רהבים *the powerful, the proud*
neol.
Cf. Bertram 1952, 26-49(esp.30-36); Harl 1992ᵃ, 24; →NIDNTT; TWNT

ματαιόφρων,-ων,-ον A 0-0-0-0-1-1
3 Mc 6,11
vain-minded, weak-minded; neol.

ματαιόω⁺ V 0-4-2-0-1-7
1 Sm 13,13; 26,21; 2 Kgs 17,15; 1 Chr 21,8; Jer

2,5

P: *to be brought to nothing* Jdt 6,4; *to be stupid*
1 Sm 26,21

μεματαίωταί σοι *it was acted foolishly by you,*
you acted foolishly 1 Sm 13,13; ματαιοῦσιν
ἑαυτοῖς ὅρασιν *they invent a vain vision for*
themselves Jer 23,16

→TWNT

ματαίως   D 0-1-0-4-0-5
1 Kgs 20(21),25; Ps 3,8; 72(73),13; 88(89),48; Jb
35,16
vainly, in vain Jb 35,16
*1 Kgs 20(21),25 ματαίως *vain* (of Achab) -ריק
for MT רק *but, indeed*; *Ps 3,8 ματαίως *without*
ground -ל/חינם? for MT לחי *(on the) cheek*

μάτην⁺   D 0-1-9-10-3-23
1 Kgs 20(21),20; Is 27,3; 28,17; 29,13; 30,4
in vain Ps 38(39),7; *in vain* or *falsely* 1 Kgs
20(21),20; *at random, without reason, without a*
cause Ps 34(35),7
εἰς μάτην *in vain, vainly* Ps 126(127),1
*Is 27,3 μάτην *in vain* -לריק? for MT לרגעים *every*
moment; *Is 29,13 μάτην δέ *in vain* -ותהו/ל for MT
ותהי ותהו *and is*; *Is 30,4 μάτην *in vain* -חנם for
MT חנס *Hanes*; *Ps 62(63),10 μάτην *in vain* -לשוא
for MT לשואה *for destruction*

μάχαιρα,-ας⁺   N1F 23-36-109-11-12-191
Gn 22,6.10; 27,40; 31,26; 34,25
alternating with ῥομφαία as stereotypical
rendition of חרב; *sword* Ez 5,2; *(short) sword,*
dagger Gn 27,40; *id.* (metaph.) Is 49,2; *sacrificial*
knife (exceptionally for מאכלת) Gn 22,6
μάχαιρα δίστομος *double-edged sword* Jgs 3,16;
μάχαιρα πετρίνη *stone knife* Jos 5,2;
παραδίδωμί τινα εἰς μάχαιραν *to deliver sb*
to the sword, to deliver sb to the death Is 65,12;
φάγεται ἡ μάχαιρα *the sword devours*
2 Sm 11,25; αἰχμαλώτιδας μαχαίρᾳ *those*
captured by the sword, prisoners of war Gn 31,26
*Jer 27(50),21 μάχαιρα *sword* -חֶרֶב for MT חֶרֶב
slaughter; *Jer 32(25),38 τῆς μαχαίρας *of the*
sword -חרב for MT חרון *of (his fierce) anger*; *Ez
26,15 μάχαιραν *the sword* -חרב for MT הרג
slaughter
Cf. DORIVAL 1994, 53.428-429; HARL 1986ᵃ, 193(Gn 22,6);
MURAOKA 1970, 499-500; WEVERS 1993, 509; →MM; TWNT

-μαχέω
(→προ-, συμ-, ὑπερ-)

μάχη,-ης⁺   N1F 2-4-1-11-15-33
Gn 13,7.8; Jos 4,13; Jgsᴬ 11,25; Jgsᴮ 20,38

battle, combat Jb 38,23; *contention, strife*
Gn 13,7; *contest, quarrel* Prv 25,8; μάχη *in battle*
Jgsᴬ 11,25
εἰς μάχην *for battle* Jos 4,13
*Jgsᴮ 20,38 τῆς μάχης *of combat* -חרב for MT הרב
multiply
→NIDNTT; TWNT

μαχητής,-οῦ   N1M 0-6-18-0-0-24
Jgsᴬ 3,29; 5,23; Jgsᴮ 12,2; 2 Sm 15,18; 24,9
fighter, warrior

-μαχίζομαι
(→δια-)

μάχιμος,-η,-ον   A 0-6-0-1-0-7
Jos 5,6; 6,3.7.9.13
quarrelsome Prv 21,19; οἱ μάχιμοι *fighting men,*
men of war Jos 5,6

μαχιρ   N 0-1-0-0-0-1
1 Kgs 5,25
= -מחיר? for MT מכלת ?
Cf. TOV 1979, 234

μαχμα   N N 0-1-0-0-0-1
2 Kgs 8,15
corr.? μαχβαρ or μακβαρ (var.) = מכבר *bed-*
cover
Cf. TOV 1979, 234

μάχομαι⁺   V 6-7-3-5-2-23
Gn 26,20.22; 31,36; Ex 21,22; Lv 24,10
to fight Gn 26,22; *to fight against* [μετά τινος]
Gn 26,20; *id.* [πρός τινα] 2 Chr 27,5; *id.* [ἔν
τινι] (semit.) Ct 1,6; *to fight, to quarrel, to*
wrangle [τινι] Gn 31,36; *to litigate with, to*
dispute with, to argue against [μετά τινος] Jgs
11,25
*Is 28,20 μάχεσθαι *to fight* -שׂתר◊? see 1QIsᵃ
משׁתריים for MT שׂרע◊ מ/השׂתרע *(too short) to stretch*
oneself
Cf. DORIVAL 1994, 387; HELBING 1928, 233; LE
BOULLUEC 1989, 84; WEVERS 1993, 515
(→ἀπο-, δια-)

μαωζιν   N 0-0-0-1-0-1
Dnᵀʰ 11,38
= מעוזים *fortresses*

μεγαλαυχέω⁺   V 0-0-2-1-2-5
Ez 16,50; Zph 3,11; Ps 9,39(10,18); 2 Mc 15,32;
Sir 48,18
to boast

μεγαλαυχία,-ας   N1F 0-0-0-0-1-1
4 Mc 2,15
boasting, arrogance

μεγαλεῖος,-α,-ον⁺   A 1-0-0-1-13-15

Dt 11,2; Ps 70(71),19; Tob^BA 11,15; 2 Mc 3,34; 7,17

in LXX almost exclusively of the Lord and his works or his service; *magnificent* 2 Mc 3,34; (τὸ) μεγαλεῖον *majesty, greatness* Sir 17,8; *mighty power* Sir 43,15; (τὰ) μεγαλεῖα *magnificent works* Dt 11,2

ἱερωσύνης μεγαλεῖον *High Priesthood* Sir 45,24

Cf. SPICQ 1978ᵃ, 543-547; WALTERS 1973, 57-58; →NIDNTT

μεγαλειότης,-ητος⁺   N3F 0-0-1-1-2-4

Jer 40(33),9; Dn^LXX 7,27; 1 Ezr 1,4; 4,40

majesty, glory; neol.

Cf. SPICQ 1978ᵃ, 543-547; WALTERS 1973, 58; →MM

μεγαλόδοξος,-ος,-ον   A 0-0-0-0-1-1

3 Mc 6,18

greatly glorious (of God)

μεγαλοδόξως   D 0-0-0-0-1-1

3 Mc 6,39

gloriously, with great glory (of God); neol.

μεγαλοκράτωρ,-ορος   N3M 0-0-0-0-1-1

3 Mc 6,2

mighty in power, of great power (of God); neol.

μεγαλομερής,-ής,-ές   A 0-0-0-0-1-1

3 Mc 5,8

magnificent, glorious (of God)

μεγαλομερῶς   D 0-0-0-0-2-2

2 Mc 4,22; 3 Mc 6,33

magnificently, with much magnificence; neol.?

μεγαλοπρέπεια,-ας⁺   N1F 0-0-0-9-1-10

Ps 8,2; 20(21),6; 28(29),4; 67(68),35; 70(71),8

magnificence, majesty

μεγαλοπρεπής,-ής,-ές⁺   A 1-0-0-0-3-4

Dt 33,26; 2 Mc 8,15; 15,13; 3 Mc 2,9

magnificent, glorious

Cf. SPICQ 1978ᵃ, 543-547; →MM

μεγαλοπρεπῶς   D 0-0-0-0-2-2

2 Mc 4,49; 4 Mc 5,24

magnificently

Cf. ROBERT 1940=1971, 257

μεγαλοπτέρυγος,-ος,-ον   A 0-0-2-0-0-2

Ez 17,3.7

with great wings; neol.

μεγαλορρημονέω⁺   V 0-0-2-3-1-6

Ez 35,13; Ob 12; Ps 34(35),26; 37(38),17; 54(55),13

to be a boaster, to boast Ob 12; *to speak proudly against* [τι εἴς τινα] Jdt 6,17; *to speak boastingly against* [ἐπί τινα] Ps 34(35),26; neol.

μεγαλορ(ρ)ημοσύνη,-ης⁺   N1F 0-1-0-0-1-2

1 Sm 2,3; Od 3,3

big talking, boasting; neol.

μεγαλορ(ρ)ήμων,-ων,-ον⁺   A 0-0-0-1-1-2

Ps 11(12),4; 3 Mc 6,4

talking big, boasting; neol.

μεγαλόσαρκος,-ος,-ον   A 0-0-1-0-0-1

Ez 16,26

great of flesh, with a great member; neol.

μεγαλοσθενής,-ής,-ές   A 0-0-0-0-1-1

3 Mc 5,13

of great strength

μεγαλοφρονέω   V 0-0-0-0-1-1

4 Mc 6,24

to be high-minded, to be confident

μεγαλόφρων,-ων,-ον   A 0-0-0-1-2-3

Prv 21,4; 4 Mc 6,5; 9,21

high-minded, generous 4 Mc 6,5; *high-minded* (in bad sense) Prv 21,4

μεγαλόψυχος,-ος,-ον   A 0-0-0-0-1-1

4 Mc 15,10

generous, magnanimous

μεγαλοψύχως   D 0-0-0-0-1-1

3 Mc 6,41

generously, magnanimously; neol.?

μεγαλύνω⁺   V 5-19-19-41-8-92

Gn 12,2; 19,19; 43,34; Nm 15,3.8

A: *to enlarge, to increase* [τι] 1 Chr 29,12; *to make great* [τι] 1 Sm 12,24; *to make great by word, to extol, to magnify* [τι] Gn 12,2; *id.* [τινα] 2 Sm 7,22

M: *to boast against* [ἐπί τινι] Jb 19,5

P: *to become powerful* Jgs^A 5,13; *to grow* 1 Sm 2,21; *to increase* Ezr 9,6; *to be made great, to be magnified* Gn 43,34; *to be magnified, to be precious* 1 Sm 26,24

μεγαλύνω εὐχήν *to honour a vow, to fulfill a vow* Nm 15,3; μεγαλύνω ἐπί τινα πτερνισμόν *to lift up the heel against* Ps 40(41),10; μεγαλύνω τὴν γλῶσσαν *to make one's tongue big, to speak big things* (with the tongue), *to boast* Ps 11(12),5

*Mi 1,10 μὴ μεγαλύνεσθε *do not exalt yourselves* -אַל תָּנְדִּילוּ? or -◊גורר (Arab.)? for MT אַל תַּגִּידוּ *do not proclaim*; *Ps 19(20),6 μεγαλυνθησόμεθα *we shall be magnified* -נגדל ◊גדלfor MT נרגל◊ נדגל *we shall set up the banner*

Cf. SPICQ 1978ᵃ, 543-547; →NIDNTT; TWNT

μεγάλωμα,-ατος   N3N 0-0-1-0-0-1

Jer 31(48),17

might; neol.

μεγαλώνυμος,-ος,-ον   A 0-0-1-0-0-1

Jer 39(32),19
with a great name
μεγάλως⁺   D 1-1-1-6-11-20
Nm 6,2; 1 Chr 29,9; Zech 11,2; Jb 4,14; 15,11
very much, exceedingly 1 Chr 29,9; *loudly,
haughtily* Jb 15,11; *honourably, becomingly, with
solemn splendour* 2 Mc 2,8
*Jb 4,14 μεγάλως *exceedingly* -רב for MT רב *the
multitude of, all;* *Jb 30,30 μεγάλως *exceedingly*
homoeophonic with מעל-? for MT מעלי *on me*
μεγαλωστί   D 0-0-0-0-1-1
1 Ezr 5,62
very much, exceedingly
μεγαλωσύνη,-ης⁺   N1F 1-5-1-13-14-34
Dt 32,3; 2 Sm 7,21.23; 1 Chr 17,19; 22,5
greatness, majesty 2 Sm 7,21; *greatness* Ps
78(79),11
δίδωμι μεγαλωσύνην τινί *to ascribe greatness
to sb* Dt 32,3 neol.
Cf. DOGNIEZ 1992, 64.322; SPICQ 1978ᵃ, 543-547
μέγας, μεγάλη, μέγα⁺   A 122-200-145-193-257-916
Gn 1,16(bis).21; 10,12; 12,2
great, big Gn 1,16; *(full-)grown* Gn 38,11; *high*
Eccl 10,6; *deep* 2 Sm 18,17(secundo); *old, adult*
Jer 38(31),34; *great, strong* (of feelings) 2 Kgs
23,26; *great, loud* Gn 27,34; *great, hard* (intensity
of plagues) Gn 12,17; *grave* (of sins) Gn 20,9;
great, mighty Jdt 16,13; *great, weighty, big,
boastful* Dn 7,11; *great, important* 1 Mc 4,25;
steadfast, lasting 1 Mc 13,37; μέγα *loud* (as adv.
with a verb) Ex 19,16; *long* (in time, id.) Tobᴮᴬ
9,4; *broadly* (id.) Prv 18,11
μέγας ὑπέρ τινα *older than sb* 1 Kgs 2,22; ὁ
ποταμὸς ὁ μέγας *the great river, the principal
river, the Euphrates* Dt 1,7; ὁ ἱερεὺς ὁ μέγας
ἀπὸ τῶν ἀδελφῶν *the highest-ranking priest
among his fellows* Lv 21,10; ἀπὸ μικροῦ ἕως
μεγάλου *from small to great, small and great,
from young to old* 1 Sm 30,19
Cf. HARLÉ 1988, 178; MCKANE 1986, 654-656(Jer
32(25),38); WEVERS 1995, 396(Dt 25,13); →TWNT
μέγεθος,-ους⁺   N3N 1-4-7-1-5-18
Ex 15,16; 1 Sm 16,7; 1 Kgs 6,23; 7,21(35); 2 Kgs
19,23
greatness Ex 15,16; *greatness, height* (of a tree)
2 Kgs 19,23; *stature* 1 Sm 16,7; *size* 1 Kgs 6,23
Cf. SPICQ 1978ᵃ, 543-547
μεγιστάν,-ᾶνος⁺   N3M 0-1-12-13-24-50
2 Chr 36,18; Is 34,12; Jer 14,3; 24,8;
25,18(49,38)

great man, noble Sir 4,7; μεγιστᾶνες *great men,
nobles* (mostly pl.) 2 Chr 36,18
*Ez 30,13 μεγιστᾶνας *great ones* -אילים for MT
אלילים *gods, images of the gods*
neol.
μέγιστος,-η,-ον⁺   A 0-0-0-3-18-21
Jb 26,3; 31,28; Est 8,12q; 2 Mc 2,19; 3,35
sup. of μέγας; *greatest, very great* Jb 26,3
μεθαρμόζω   V 0-0-0-0-1-1
Wis 19,18
to change the order of [τι]
Cf. LARCHER 1985, 1083-1084
μεθαχαβιν   V 0-1-0-0-0-1
1 Chr 21,20
= מתחבאים *hiding themselves*
Cf. TOV 1979, 234
μεθερμηνεύω⁺   V 0-0-0-0-1-1
Sir prol.,30
to translate, to interpret [τι]; neol.?
μέθη,-ης⁺   N1F 0-0-6-2-5-13
Is 28,7; Jer 28(51),57; Ez 23,33; 39,19; Jl 1,5
strong drink Prv 20,1; *drunkenness* Tobᴮᴬ 4,15
(secundo)
οἶνον εἰς μέθην μὴ πίῃς *do not drink yourself
drunk with wine, do not drink wine until you are
drunk* Tobᴮᴬ 4,15(primo)
Cf. WALTERS 1973, 248; →TWNT
μεθίστημι⁺   V 2-14-4-5-9-34
Dt 17,17; 30,17; Jos 14,8; Jgsᴬ 7,5; 9,29
A: *to change, to turn away* [τι] Jos 14,8; *to
remove* [τι] 2 Kgs 3,2; *to turn away from* [τί
τινος] Is 59,15; *id.* [τι ἀπό τινος] Am 5,23; *to
remove, to take apart* [τινα] Jgs 9,29; *to remove,
to banish* [τινα] Jgsᴬ 10,16; *to set free from, to
remove from* [τινά τινος] 1 Kgs 15,13; *to
deprive sb of sth* [τινά τινος] 3 Mc 6,24
M: *to stand by, to stand aside* 1 Kgs 18,29; *to
change, to turn away* Dt 17,17; *to turn aside*
1 Sm 6,12; *to depart* Is 54,10; *to pass over to* [εἰς
τινα] 2 Mc 11,23
μεθίστημί τινα ἀπὸ προσώπου τινός *to
remove sb from one's presence* 2 Kgs 17,23;
μεθίσθημί τινα τοῦ ζῆν *to put sb to death*
3 Mc 2,28; μεθίσταμαι ἐκ τοῦ ζῆν *to die* 3 Mc
6,12; μεθίστημί τινα τῆς χρείας *to deprive sb
of his office, to dismiss sb* 1 Mc 11,63
*2 Kgs 23,33 μετέστησεν *he removed* (him) -הסיר
for MT יאסר *he bound, he confined* (him)
Cf. DOGNIEZ 1992, 226(Dt 17,17); HELBING 1928, 165
Μεθλα   N 0-1-0-0-0-1

JgsᴮB 20,48
= -מתל for MT מתם entire
Cf. Tov 1973, 89

μεθοδεύω⁺ V 0-1-0-0-0-1
2 Sm 19,28
to deal deceitfully with sb [ἔν τινι] (semit.; aor.
with double augm.); neol.?
Cf. SPICQ 1978ᵃ, 548

μέθοδος,-ου N2F 0-0-0-1-1-2
Est 8,12n; 2 Mc 13,18
trick, ruse Est 8,12n; stratagem 2 Mc 13,18
Cf. SPICQ 1978ᵃ, 548

μεθόριον,-ου N2N 0-1-0-0-0-1
Josᴬ 19,27
border

μεθύσκω⁺ V 3-2-16-9-7-37
Gn 9,21; 43,34; Is 34,5.7; 49,26
A: to make drunk [τινα] 2 Sm 11,13; to make
drunk (metaph.), to drench [τι] Dt 32,42; to fill
with [τινά τινος] (metaph.) Lam 3,15; to give to
drink [abs.] Ps 22(23),5; to satiate [τινα] Sir
1,16; id. [τι] Jer 38(31),14; to saturate [τι] Ps
64(65),11; to water, to drench [τι] Sir 24,31
P: to be drunk Gn 9,21; id. (metaph.) Jdt 6,4; to
be filled (with food) [τινι] Hos 14,8
τὸν ποιήσαντά σε καὶ μεθύσκοντά σε ἀπὸ τῶν
ἀγαθῶν αὐτοῦ he who made you and satisfies
you with every good thing of his Sir 32,13
*Is 7,20 μεμεθυσμένῳ drunk, drenched (in
blood) -שכר for MT שכר◊ hired; *Hos 14,8
(ζήσονται καὶ) μεθυσθήσονται (they shall live
and) be satiated -(חיה◊ and) רוה for MT חיה◊ (pi.)
they shall grow
Cf. HELBING 1928, 150; →TWNT

μέθυσμα,-ατος⁺ N3N 0-5-3-0-0-8
JgsᴮB 13,4.7.14; 1 Sm 1,11.15
intoxicating drink; neol.

μέθυσος,-ος,-ον A 0-0-0-2-3-5
Prv 23,21; 26,9; 4 Mc 2,7; Sir 19,1; 26,8
drunk Sir 19,1; (ὁ) μέθυσος drunk, drunkard Prv
23,21

μεθύω⁺ V 0-4-6-2-0-12
1 Sm 1,13; 25,36; 1 Kgs 16,9; 21(20),16; Is 19,14
pass. of μεθύσκω; to be drunk 1 Sm 1,13; to be
watered, to be drenched (of a garden) Is 58,11
→TWNT

μεθωεσιμ N M 0-0-0-1-0-1
Ezr 2,62
= מתיחשים (names) registered in a genealogy

μεῖγμα,-ατος N3N 0-0-0-0-1-1

Sir 38,7
mixture, compound; neol.
Cf. WALTERS 1973, 97

μειδιάω V 0-0-0-0-1-1
Sir 21,20
to smile
(→προσ-)

μείζων,-ων,-ον⁺ A 6-5-3-3-5-22
Gn 4,13; 10,21; 25,23; 26,13; 29,16
comp. of μέγας; greater 1 Mc 6,27; elder
Gn 10,21

μειόω⁺ V 0-0-0-0-1-1
Sir 43,7
P: to become smaller, to decrease

μειράκιον,-ου N2N 0-0-0-0-4-4
2 Mc 7,25; 4 Mc 8,14; 11,24; 14,4
dim. of μεῖραξ; young man

μειρακίσκος,-ου N2M 0-0-0-0-2-2
4 Mc 8,1; 11,13
dim. of μεῖραξ; young boy

μεῖραξ,-ακος N3M 0-0-0-0-2-2
4 Mc 14,6.8
youth

μέλαθρον,-ου N2N 0-4-0-0-0-4
1 Kgs 6,5; 7,9(20)(bis).41(4)
structure
Cf. MULDER 1987, 198.238

μελαθρόω V 0-1-0-0-0-1
1 Kgs 7,42(5)
P: to be connected or fastened by beams; neol.
Cf. MULDER 1987, 238

μελάνθιον,-ου N2N 0-0-3-0-0-3
Is 28,25.27(bis)
black cummin
Cf. WALTERS 1973, 51

μελανία,-ας N1F 0-0-0-0-1-1
Sir 19,26
grief, mourning (metaph.)

μελανόομαι⁺ V 0-0-0-1-1-2
Ct 1,6; LtJ 20
to be black; neol.

μέλας,-αινα,-αν⁺ A 1-0-2-2-0-5
Lv 13,37; Zech 6,2.6; Ct 1,5; 5,11
black, dark
→TWNT

μέλει⁺ V 0-0-0-1-4-5
Jb 22,3; TobᴮA 10,5; 1 Mc 14,42.43; Wis 12,13
μέλει μοι I care TobᴮA 10,5; τί μέλει μοι
what does it matter to me Jb 22,3; μέλει μοι
περί τινος I care for, I take care of sth Wis

12,13

Cf. HELBING 1928, 112

-μελέομαι/μέλομαι

(→ἐπι-, μετα-)

μέλεος,-α,-ον   A 0-0-0-0-1-1

4 Mc 16,6

unhappy, miserable

μελετάω⁺   V 0-1-7-24-3-35

Jos 1,8; Is 16,7; 27,8; 33,18; 38,14

to care for [τινι] Is 16,7; *to meditate, to think
about* [abs.] Ps 76(77),6; *id.* [τι] Jb 6,30; *to
meditate on, to study* [ἔν τινι] Jos 1,8; *to
meditate on* [εἴς τινα] Ps 62(63),7; *id.* [τι] Jb
27,4; *to plot to* [+inf.] Is 27,8; *to heed, to pay
attention to* [τι] Prv 19,27; *to mutter, to mourn*
Is 38,14

Cf. RABIN 1954, 50(n.3)

(→ἐκ-)

μελέτη,-ης⁺   N1F 0-0-0-13-0-13

Ps 18(19),15; 38(39),4; 48(49),4; 118(119),24.77

meditation, thought Ps 18(19),15; *declamation,
discourse* Jb 37,2; *object of study* Ps 118(119),77;
study Eccl 12,12

μελέται κατά τινος *plots against sb* Lam 3,62
*Jb 33,15 μελέτη *meditation* -הגיון for MT חזיון
vision

μέλι,-ιτος⁺   N3N 21-16-11-11-7-66

Gn 43,11; Ex 3,8.17; 13,5; 16,31

honey Gn 43,11; *honey* (metaph.), *sweet words*
Prv 5,3

γῆ ῥέουσα γάλα καὶ μέλι *land of milk and
honey* (sign of fertility) Ex 3,8

μελίζω   V 1-7-1-0-0-9

Lv 1,6; Jgs 19,29; 20,6

to dismember, to cut in pieces 1 Kgs 18,23

μελιοῦσιν αὐτὸ κατὰ μέλη *they shall cut it up
into its parts* (semit.) Lv 1,6, cpr. Jgs 19,29

(→δια-, ἐκ-)

μέλισσα,-ης⁺   N1F 1-2-1-2-2-8

Dt 1,44; Jgs 14,8; Is 7,18; Ps 117(118),12

bee

μελισσών,-ῶνος   N3M 0-2-0-0-0-2

1 Sm 14,25.26

bee-house, bee-hive; neol.

μέλλω⁺   V 3-0-7-5-30-45

Gn 25,22; 43,25; Ex 4,12; Is 15,7; 28,24

*to be going to, to be about to, to be on the point
of* [+inf.] Gn 43,25; *to linger* [abs.] 4 Mc 6,23

τὴν μέλλουσαν (sc. μάχην) *the rising quarrel*
Prv 15,18

Cf. LEE, J. 1983, 29

μελον   N 0-1-0-0-0-1

2 Kgs 19,23

= מלון *retreat, place where one stays for the night*

μέλος,-ους⁺   N3N 6-1-1-0-9-17

Ex 29,17; Lv 1,6.12; 8,20(bis)

part, limb Jgs^B 19,29; τὰ μέλη *the limbs*
Lv 8,20(secundo)

κατὰ μέλη *limb by limb* Ex 29,17; μέλη ποιέω
to dismember 2 Mc 1,16

*Jb 9,28 μέλεσιν *(my) bones, (my) limbs* -עצמתי
for MT עצבתי *my sufferings*

see μελίζω

→TWNT

μέλος,-ους⁺   N3N 0-0-2-1-7-10

Ez 2,10; Mi 2,4; Job 9,28; 3 Mc 5,25; 6,32

musical part, melody Sir 32,6; *lamentation, dirge*
Ez 2,10

→LSJ suppl(Ez 2,10)

μέλπω

(→προανα-)

μελῳδέω   V 0-0-0-0-1-1

4 Mc 18,15

to sing

μελῳδία,-ας   N1F 0-0-0-0-1-1

4 Mc 15,21

chant, song

μελῳδός,-ός,-όν   A 0-0-0-0-1-1

4 Mc 10,21

singing

μέμφομαι⁺   V 0-0-0-0-3-3

2 Mc 2,7; Sir 11,7; 41,7

to blame [τινι] Sir 41,7; *id.* [abs.] Sir 11,7

Cf. HELBING 1928, 21; →NIDNTT; TWNT

(→ἀπο-)

μέμψις,-εως   N3F 0-0-0-3-1-4

Jb 33,10.23; 39,7; Wis 13,6

blame, censure Jb 39,7; *ground of charge, fault*
Jb 33,10

μέν⁺   C 19-3-4-31-165-222

Gn 18,12; 27,22; 38,23; 43,4.14

Expresses certainty, or points out that the word
or clause with which it stands is correl. to
another contrastive word or clause that is to
follow, the latter word or clause being
introduced by δέ

μὲν ... δέ ... *on the one hand, on the other hand*
Gn 27,22; μὲν γάρ ... δέ ... *for indeed ... but ...*
Jb 28,2; μὲν οὖν *then* Gn 43,4

Cf. LEE, J. 1985, 1-11

μέντοι⁺   C 0-0-0-5-0-5
Prv 5,4; 16,25.26; 22,9a; 26,12
but, however (mostly adversative)

μέντοιγε   C 0-0-0-1-0-1
Ps 38(39),7
nevertheless

μένω⁺   V 11-5-17-22-34-89
Gn 24,55; 45,9; Ex 9,28; Lv 13,5.23
to stay, to wait Jgs^A 16,2; *to tarry, to wait*
Gn 45,9; *to stay, to remain* Gn 24,55; *to lodge, to
stay, to live* 4 Mc 18,9; *to be lasting, to remain, to
stand* Lv 13,5; *to remain, to last, to continue to
live* Dn 6,27; *to remain, to be alive* Eccl 7,15; *to
adhere to, to continue in* [ἐν τινι] 2 Mc 8,1; *to
await, to expect, to tarry for* [τινα] Tob^BA 2,2; *id.*
[τι] Is 59,9
*1 Sm 20,11 καὶ μένε *and remain* corr.? καὶ
ἴωμεν for MT ונצא *and let us go*; *Jb 21,11
μένουσι *they remain, they stay* -ישליו ◊שלה for MT
ישלחו *they send*
Cf. BARR 1961, 291; MARGOLIS 1905=1972, 56-60;
WEVERS 1993, 761; →NIDNTT; TWNT
(→ἀνα-, δια-, ἐμ-, ἐπι-, κατα-, παρα-, περι-,
προσ-, συμπαρα-, ὑπο-)

μεριδάρχης,-ου   N1M 0-0-0-0-1-1
1 Mc 10,65
governor of a province; neol.?

μεριδαρχία,-ας   N1F 0-0-0-0-4-4
1 Ezr 1,5.12; 5,4; 8,28
office of the governor of a province; neol.

μερίζω⁺   V 6-7-4-8-10-35
Ex 15,9; Nm 26,53.55.56; Dt 18,8
A: *to divide, to distribute* [τι] Ex 15,9; *id.* [τι
τινι] 1 Kgs 18,6; *id.* [τινι] Neh 13,13; *to assign
a part of, to allot (an inheritance)* [τι] Nm 26,56
M: *to divide among themselves* [τι] Prv 14,18; *to
share with* [τινι] Prv 29,24; *to tear asunder*
[τινα] Jer 28(51),34
P: *to be divided, to be split up* 1 Kgs 16,21; *to be
reckoned as part of* [εἴς τι] Sir 41,9
μερίζω τι μερίδας *to divide into parts* Jos 18,6
(→ἀπο-, δια-, κατα-)

μέριμνα,-ης⁺   N1F 0-0-0-5-6-11
Ps 54(55),23; Jb 11,18; Prv 17,12; Est 1,1n;
Dn^LXX 11,26
care, thought, solicitude Prv 17,12; *ambition, plan*
Est 1,1n; *anxious mind* Jb 11,18
*Prv 17,12 μέριμνα *anxious mind* -◊ראב for MT
רב *bear*

μεριμνάω⁺   V 2-2-1-2-2-9

Ex 5,9(bis); 2 Sm 7,10; 1 Chr 17,9; Ez 16,42
to care for, to be anxious about [ὑπέρ τινος] Ps
37(38),19; *id.* [ἐν τινι] Ex 5,9(secundo); *to
meditate upon, to think about, to ponder* [τι]
Wis 12,22; *to be anxious* [abs.] 2 Sm 7,10; *to be
careful, to be concerned* [abs.] Bar 3,18; *to be
burdened with anxious care* Ez 16,42
*Ex 5,9(primo) καὶ μεριμνάτωσαν *and let them
care for (it)* -וישעו ◊שעה for MT וישעו עשה *and they
will labour (it)*
Cf. LE BOULLUEC 1989, 108(Ex 5,9); WEVERS 1990,
64(Ex 5,9); →MM; NIDNTT; TWNT

μερίς,-ίδος⁺   N3F 22-47-18-39-25-151
Gn 14,24(bis); 31,14; 33,19; 43,34
part (of a whole) Am 4,7; *part, chapter (of a
book)* Jos 18,9; *piece (of land)* 2 Kgs 3,25; *lot,
fate, condition of life* Ps 49(50),18; *party, faction?*
(in political sense) Wis 1,16; *part, share, portion*
(that which has been allotted) Ex 29,26;
inheritance, portion (of Israel, "alloted" to the
Lord) 3 Mc 6,3; *id.* (of God "allotted" to Israel)
Ps 72(73),26
*Na 3,8 μερίδα *portion* -מנה for MT מנא ?, cpr.
4QPNa 3,8 מני? or מנו?
Cf. LARCHER 1983, 208-209.235-236; →NIDNTT

μερισμός,-οῦ⁺   N2M 0-1-0-1-0-2
Jos 11,23; Ezr 6,18
division Jos 11,23; μερισμοί *subdivisions, orders*
Ezr 6,18

μεριτεύομαι   V 0-0-0-1-0-1
Jb 40,30
to divide among themselves [τι]; neol.

μέρος,-ους⁺   N3N 32-37-21-31-18-139
Gn 23,9; 47,24(bis); Ex 16,35; 25,26
part Gn 47,24; *part, piece (of land)* Gn 23,9; *the
part facing in a particular direction, side*
Ex 32,15; *border* Ex 16,35; *direction* Jos 18,19;
extremity, end (geogr.) Jos 15,2; *end (of life)*
Dn^Th 11,45; μέρος *in part* (as adv.) 3 Mc 5,17
ἐν μέρει *in turn* Jb 30,1; κατὰ μέρος *in parts,
in particular* Prv 29,11; *in pieces* 2 Mc 15,33;
μέρος μέν τι ... μέρος δέ τι ... *part of ..., part
of ...; in part ..., in part ...* Dn 2,33; ἐν ἥττονι
μέρει κεῖμαι *to weigh less, to be held in lower
esteem* 2 Mc 15,18
*Dn^Th 11,45 ἕως μέρους αὐτοῦ *to his destiny, to
his part* -קצה◊ for MT קצו◊ *to his end*, cpr. Dn 1,2;
*Ezr 4,20 μέρος *part* -חלק for MT הלך (Aram.)
tax
Cf. DORIVAL 1994, 265; HORSLEY 1983, 75; LE BOULLUEC

1989,260(Ex 25,26).270.323(Ex 32,15); LEE,J. 1972,39-42; 1983, 72-76; WEVERS 1990, 261.403.413.422.429.604.623; →LSJ Rsuppl(Ex 32,15); NIDNTT; TWNT

μεσάζω⁺   V 0-0-0-0-1-1
Wis 18,14
to be in the middle; νυκτὸς μεσαζούσης *at midnight*

μέσακλον,-ου   N2N 0-1-0-0-0-1
1 Sm 17,7
weaver's beam, beam of a loom; neol.

μεσημβρία,-ας⁺   N1F 4-6-7-6-2-25
Gn 18,1; 43,16.25; Dt 28,29; Jgs^B 5,10
midday Gn 43,16; *noontide-heat* Sir 34,16; *south* Dn^LXX 8,4; μεσημβρίας *at noon* Gn 18,1
ἐκ μεσημβρίας *afternoon* Jb 11,17
*Jgs^B 5,10 μεσημβρίας *at noon* צהרים- or -צהרות for MT צהרות *yellowish-red*
Cf. BRUZZONE 1984, 115-117

μεσημβρινός,-ή,-όν   A 0-0-1-2-1-4
Is 16,3; Ps 90(91),6; Jb 5,14; 1 Ezr 9,41
belonging to noon, at midday Ps 90(91),6; τὸ μεσημβρινόν *midday, noon* 1 Ezr 9,41

μεσθααλ   N 0-1-0-0-0-1
2 Kgs 10,22
= -מסתחל? for MT מלתחה *wardrobe*

μεσίτης,-ου⁺   N1M 0-0-0-1-0-1
Jb 9,33
mediator; neol.?
Cf. SPICQ 1978ᵃ, 549-552; →NIDNTT; TWNT

μεσόγειος,-ος,-ον⁺   A 0-0-0-0-1-1
2 Mc 8,35
inland, in the heart of a country; ἡ μεσόγειος (γῆ) *interior, inland*

μεσονύκτιον,-ου⁺   N2N 0-3-1-2-0-6
Jgs^A 16,3(bis); Jgs^B 16,3; Is 59,10; Ps 118(119),62
midnight

μεσοπόρφυρος,-ος,-ον   A 0-0-2-0-0-2
Is 3,21.24
mixed with purple, decorated with purple; neol.

μέσος,-η,-ον⁺   A 219-235-252-86-77-872
Gn 1,4(bis).6(bis).7
middle, in the middle Ex 26,28; *in the midst* Gn 15,10; (τὸ) μέσον *midst* Ex 36,30
μέσον τινός *between* Nm 2,17; μέσον τινός *in the midst of* Ex 14,27; ἀνὰ μέσον τινός *between* Jgs 15,4; ἀνὰ μέσον τινὸς καί τινος *between* Gn 32,17; διὰ μέσου *through* Am 5,17;
ἐν μέσῳ τῷ παραδείσῳ *in the middle of paradise* Gn 2,9; περὶ μέσας νύκτας *about midnight* Ex 11,4(primo); εἰς τὸ μέσον *into the*

middle or *centre* 1 Kgs 6,8; (τὸ) μέσον τινός *the middle of* Ex 11,4(secundo); ἐκ μέσου τῶν ὀδόντων *out of the midst of the teeth, from the teeth* Jb 29,17; ἦρται ἐκ τοῦ μέσου *he has been moved out of the way* Is 57,2; μένει γὰρ ὁ ἄγγελος τοῦ Θεοῦ τὴν ῥομφαίαν ἔχων πρίσαι σε μέσον *for the angel of God is standing with a sword to saw you into two* Sus^Th 59
Cf. CARAGOUNIS 1990, 50; LE BOULLUEC 1989, 88.268; LLEWELYN 1994, 207(n.36); SOLLAMO 1979, 236-239.247-257.267-269.343-346.350-351; WEVERS 1990, 163.459

μεσότης,-ητος   N3F 0-0-0-0-1-1
Wis 7,18
middle, centre, median
Cf. LARCHER 1984, 469-470

μεσόω⁺   V 2-1-1-0-2-6
Ex 12,29; 34,22; Jgs^A 7,19; Jer 15,9; Jdt 12,5
to be in or *at the middle* (of time) Jer 15,9
ἐγενήθη δὲ μεσούσης τῆς νυκτός *it happened in the middle of the night, at midnight* (semit.)
Ex 12,29; τῆς φυλακῆς τῆς μεσούσης *the middle watch* (the night was divided into three periods or watches) Jgs^A 7,19
Cf. WEVERS 1990, 183(Ex 12,29).566(Ex 34,22)

μεσσαβ   N 0-5-0-0-0-5
1 Sm 14,1.6.11.12.15
= מצב *post, outpost, station of a garrison*

Μεσσαρα   N 0-2-0-0-0-2
1 Sm 23,19; 24,23
= -מצרה for MT מצרות, מצורה *stronghold*
Cf. TOV 1973, 89

μεστός,-ή,-όν⁺   A 0-0-2-2-0-4
Ez 37,1; Na 1,10; Prv 6,34; Est 5,2a
full of [τινος]

μεστόω⁺   V 0-0-0-0-2-2
3 Mc 5,1.10
P: *to be full of, to be filled with* [τινος]
Cf. HELBING 1928, 149
(→κατα-)

μετά⁺   P 491-848-251-375-569-2534
Gn 3,6.12; 4,3; 5,4.7
[τινος]: *with*
of pers.: expressing company: *with, in company of* Gn 22,3; *(sth) in the presence of, beside* Mal 3,8
expressing relationship: *with, together with* Dt 32,43; *with* (in friendly sense) Hos 2,20; *with, against* (in hostile sense) 1 Sm 17,33; *in dealings with, to* (semit.) Jdt 8,26
of things: *accompanied by, with, in* (circum-

stances) 2 Mc 15,28; *with, by aid of, by using*
(instruments) 1 Ezr 5,57; *in return for, in*
exchange for Mi 3,11; see σύν τινι
[τι]: *after, behind, subsequent to* (temporal)
2 Mc 6,1

μετὰ τοῦτο *after this, behind* Lv 14,19; οὐκ
ἔστιν μετ' ἐμὲ ἔτι *there is none besides me*
(metaph.) Zph 2,15

*Hos 4,14(end) μετὰ πόρνης *with a harlot* -זנה עם
for MT 4,15(beginning) זנה אם *though (you) play*
the harlot, cpr. Prv 20,11; *Ps 46(47),10 μετά
with -עם for MT עם *people,* see also Ps 109(110),3
Cf. LE BOULLUEC 1989, 195-196.220.232; JOHANNESSOHN
1910, 1-82; 1926, 202-216; SOLLAMO 1979, 41-42.173.
211.226-227.242.259-260; WEVERS 1990,37.59.153.161.190.
201.278.282.289.541.571; 1993, 77.248

μεταβαίνω⁺ V 0-0-0-0-5-5
2 Mc 6,1.9.24; Wis 7,27; 19,19
to pass from one state to another, to turn into
[εἴς τι] Wis 19,19; *to pass into, to enter into*
[εἴς τι] Wis 7,27; *to depart from* [ἀπό τινος]
2 Mc 6,1; *to pass on to, to adopt* [ἐπί τι]
2 Mc 6,9

Cf. LARCHER 1984, 507-508(Wis 7,27)

μεταβάλλω⁺ V 13-2-4-5-8-32
Ex 7,17.20; 10,19; Lv 13,3.4
A: *to change, to alter* [intr.] Ex 7,17; *id.* [τι]
Ex 10,19; *to turn into, to change to* [τι +pred.]
Lv 13,10; *to turn* [+pred.] Lv 13,3; *id.* [εἴς τι]
Lv 13,17; *to come to, to turn to* [εἴς τινα] Is
60,5
M: *to turn oneself, to turn* Jos 8,21; *to change*
one's mind 4 Mc 6,24; *to turn into* [εἴς τι]
Wis 19,19

μεταβαλών τὰ νόμιμα *who abandoned the*
observance of the law 3 Mc 1,3; μεταβάλλει τὸ
πρόσωπον *his face grows pale* Is 29,22
*Is 13,8 μεταβαλοῦσιν *they will change* -פנה◊
(verb)? for MT פניהם פנה◊ (subst.) *their faces;*
*Jb 10,8 μετὰ ταῦτα μεταβαλών *subsequently*
you changed your mind -סבב אחר for MT סביב יחד
together all around?

μεταβηχας N F 0-1-0-0-0-1
1 Chr 18,8
= מ/שבחת *from Tibhath*

μεταβολή,-ῆς N1F 0-0-2-2-3-7
Is 30,32; 47,15; Est 4,17y; 8,12i; 3 Mc 5,40
modification, alteration, change Est 8,12i;
change, reversal Est 4,17y; *change, succession* (of
seasons) Wis 7,18; *exchange, traffic* Is 47,15

ἐκ μεταβολῆς *alternately, by turns, in turn*
Is 30,32

μεταβολία,-ας N1F 0-0-0-0-1-1
Sir 37,11
exchange, barter; neol.

μεταβόλος,-ου N2M 0-0-3-0-0-3
Is 23,2.3(bis)
merchant

μεταγενής,-ής,-ές A 0-0-0-0-1-1
1 Ezr 8,1
born after; μεταγενέστερός τινος *younger than*

μεταγίνομαι V 0-0-0-0-2-2
2 Mc 2,1.2
to migrate; neol.
→LSJ RSuppl

μετάγω⁺ V 0-4-0-1-6-11
1 Kgs 8,47.48; 2 Chr 6,37; 36,3; Est 8,12o
to convey from one place or person to another, to
transfer, to carry [τι εἴς τινα] Est 8,12o; *to*
carry into captivity [τινα ἕν τινι] 1 Kgs 8,48
μετάγω εἴς ἑτέραν γλῶσσαν *to transfer into*
another language, to translate Sir prol.,22

μεταδιαιτάω V 0-0-0-0-1-1
4 Mc 8,8
P: *to change one's way of life, to adopt a new*
life-style; neol.

μεταδίδωμι⁺ V 0-0-0-2-5-7
Jb 31,17; Prv 11,26; Tobᴮᴬ 7,10; 2 Mc 1,35; 8,12
to give a part to [τινι] Jb 31,17; *to share, to*
distribute, to give Prv 11,26; *to share, to give* [τί
τινι] 2 Mc 1,35; *to communicate sth with sb, to*
impart sth to sb [τί τινι] Tobᴮᴬ 7,10
Cf. HELBING 1928, 252

μεταδιώκω V 0-0-0-0-1-1
2 Mc 2,31
to pursue, to aim at [τι]

μετάθεσις,-εως⁺ N3F 0-0-0-0-1-1
2 Mc 11,24
change to [ἐπί τι]

μεταίρω⁺ V 0-2-0-2-0-4
2 Kgs 16,17; 25,11; Ps 79(80),9; Prv 22,28
to remove [τι] 2 Kgs 16,17; *to carry into exile*
[τινα] 2 Kgs 25,11

μεταίτιος,-ος,-ον A 0-0-0-1-0-1
Est 8,12e
sharing responsibility for [τινος]

μετακαλέω⁺ V 0-0-2-0-1-3
Hos 11,1.2; 1 Ezr 1,48
to call, to call back

μετακινέω⁺ V 2-1-1-1-2-7

Dt 19,14; 32,30; 2 Sm 15,20; Is 54,10; Ezr 9,11
to move away, to shift [τι] Dt 19,14; *id.* [τινα]
Dt 32,30
μετακινήσω σε μεθ' ἡμῶν τοῦ πορευθῆναι *I
shall make you wander about with us* (rendition
of hi.) 2 Sm 15,20
*Ezr 9,11 μετακινουμένη *moved, brought in
commotion* -◊ נודר or -◊ נדרד for MT נדרה ◊ נדרד
unclean
Cf. DOGNIEZ 1992, 234(Dt 19,14); ROFÉ 1988,
165-167(Dt 19,14)

μετακίνησις,-εως   N3F 0-0-0-1-0-1
Ezr 9,11
change; *Ezr 9,11 μετακινήσει *change* or
removal -◊ נודר or -◊ נדרד for MT נדרה ◊ נדרד *uncleanness*

μετακιρνάω   V 0-0-0-0-1-1
Wis 16,21
M: *to change, to transform*; neol.
Cf. LARCHER 1985, 930

μετακομίζω   V 0-0-0-0-1-1
Jdt 11,14
to convey, to bring back; neol.?

μεταλαμβάνω⁺   V 0-0-0-0-13-13
2 Mc 4,21; 11,6; 12,5.8.21
to share in [τινος] 4 Mc 8,8; *to take in exchange,
to substitute* [τι ἀντί τινος] 3 Mc 4,6; *to receive
notice of, to hear of* [τι] 2 Mc 12,5; *to receive
notice, to understand* [τι +ptc.] 2 Mc 11,6; *id.*
[τι +inf.] 2 Mc 4,21
Cf. HELBING 1928, 136

μεταλλάσσω⁺   V 0-0-0-2-10-12
Est 2,7.20; 1 Ezr 1,29; 2 Mc 4,7.37
to change, to alter [τι] Est 2,20; *to change one's
life, to die* Est 2,7; ὁ μετηλλαχώς *the dead*
2 Mc 4,37
μεταλλάσσω τὸν βίον *to exchange by leaving, to
change one's life, to die* 1 Ezr 1,29; μεταλλάσσω
τοῦτον τὸν τρόπον *id.* 2 Mc 6,31
Cf. SPICQ 1978ª, 553-554

μεταλλεύω   V 1-0-0-0-2-3
Dt 8,9; Wis 4,12; 16,25
to mine, to extract from a mine [τι] Dt 8,9; *to
exploit as if a mine, to undermine* (metaph.) Wis
4,12
Cf. DOGNIEZ 1992, 171; LARCHER 1984, 334; →LSJ RSuppl

μέταλλον,-ου   N2N 0-0-0-0-1-1
1 Mc 8,3
mine; τὰ μέταλλα *mines*

μεταμέλει   V 1-0-0-0-0-1
Ex 13,17

μεταμέλει τινί [+ptc.] *to regret, to feel sorry*;
see μετανοέω, κατανύσσω

μεταμέλεια,-ας   N1F 0-0-1-0-1-2
Hos 11,8; PSal 9,7
repentance, regret

μεταμελέομαι/μεταμέλομαι⁺   V 0-2-3-4-4-13
1 Sm 15,35; 1 Chr 21,15; Jer 20,16; Ez 14,22;
Zech 11,5
to repent, to feel regret [abs.] Ps 105(106),45; *to
be sorry for* [ἐπί τινι] 1 Chr 21,15; *id.* [ἐπί τι]
Ez 14,22; *to be sorry that* [ὅτι +ind.] 1 Sm
15,35; see μετανοέω, κατανύσσω
Cf. BARR 1961, 236-237; HARL 1991=1992ª, 158; HELBING
1928, 112; THOMPSON 1908, 1-29; WEVERS 1990, 203;
→NIDNTT; TWNT

μετάμελος,-ου   N2M 0-1-0-1-1-3
2 Kgs 3,27; Prv 11,3; 3 Mc 2,24
repentance, regret

μεταναστεύω   V 0-0-0-3-0-3
Ps 10(11),1; 51(52),7; 61(62),7
A: *to remove, to cause to flee* [τινα] Ps 51(52),7;
to flee, to depart Ps 61(62),7
M: *to flee, to depart* Ps 10(11),1
neol.

μετανίστημι   V 0-1-0-1-0-2
2 Sm 15,20(19); Ps 108(109),10
A: *to migrate from, to leave behind* [τι]
2 Sm 15,20(19)
M: *to migrate* Ps 108(109),10

μετανοέω⁺   V 0-2-14-3-5-24
1 Sm 15,29(bis); Is 46,8; Jer 4,28; 8,6
to repent [abs.] 1 Sm 15,29; *to repent of* [ἀπό
τινος] Jer 8,6; *id.* [ἐν τινι] Sir 48,15; *id.* [ἐπί
τινι] Am 7,3; *id.* [περί τινος] Jer 18,8
to reconsider Prv 24,32; *to change purpose not yet
executed* Jon 3,9
see μεταμελέομαι, κατανύσσω
Cf. BARR 1961, 236-237.252-253; HARL 1986ᵇ=1992ª, 94;
1991=1992, 158; HELBING 1928, 112; LARCHER 1984, 359;
1985, 691-692; LOEWE 1952, 261-272; MIQUEL 1986,
184-185; SPICQ 1982, 452-458; THOMPSON 1908, 1-29;
→NIDNTT; TWNT

μετάνοια,-ας⁺   N1F 0-0-0-1-6-7
Prv 14,15; Od 12,8(bis); Wis 11,23; 12,10
repentance, change of mind Wis 11,23;
afterthought Prv 14,15
Cf. BARR 1961, 236-237.253-255; HARL 1986ᵇ=1992ª,
77.92.94; HAUDEBERT 1987, 355-366; HORSLEY 1987, 160;
LARCHER 1984, 359; 1985, 691-692; MICHIELS 1965, 42-78;
MIQUEL 1986, 184-185; SPICQ 1982, 452-458; THOMPSON

1908, 1-29; Tosato 1975, 3-45; →NIDNTT; TWNT

μεταξύ⁺ D/P 0-1-0-0-3-4
Jgs^A 5,27; Wis 4,10; 16,19; 18,23
between Wis 18,23; *id.* [τινος] Jgs^A 5,27; *in the middle of* [τινος] Wis 16,19; *among* [τινος] Wis 4,10
Cf. Blass 1990, § 215

μεταπαιδεύω V 0-0-0-0-1-1
4 Mc 2,7
to re-educate, to teach to change one's nature; neol.

μεταπείθω V 0-0-0-0-1-1
4 Mc 11,25
to alter, to change (one's persuasion) [τι]

μεταπέμπω⁺ V 2-0-0-0-3-5
Gn 27,45; Nm 23,7; 2 Mc 15,31; 4 Mc 12,2.6
M: *to summon, to bring back* [τινα] Gn 27,45; *to summon* [τινα] 4 Mc 12,2

μεταπίπτω V 4-0-0-0-1-5
Lv 13,5.6.7.8; 3 Mc 3,8
used as pass. of μεταβάλλω; *to fall differently, to undergo a change* (for the better) 3 Mc 3,8; *to change for the worse, to spread* (of disease) Lv 13,5

μετασκευάζω V 0-0-1-0-0-1
Am 5,8
to refashion, to transform

μεταστρέφω⁺ V 2-3-7-7-7-26
Ex 14,5; Dt 23,6; Jgs^A 5,28; 1 Sm 10,9; 2 Chr 36,4
A: *to change, to alter* [τι] 2 Chr 36,4; *to turn back, to turn away* [τι] Jer 21,4; *to turn into, to change into* [τι εἴς τι] Dt 23,6; *to change sth for sb, to give sth to sb* [τί τινι] 1 Sm 10,9
P: *to be turned against* [ἐπί τινα] Ex 14,5; *to be turned to, to be given to* [εἴς τινα] Jer 6,12; *id.* [τινι] Lam 5,2; *to be changed into, to become* [εἴς τι] Ps 77(78),57
μετέστρεψεν τὴν βουλὴν τοῦ βασιλέως Ἀσσυρίων ἐπ' αὐτούς *he changed the opinion of the king of Assyria about them* 1 Ezr 7,15; ἐγκρυφίας οὐ μεταστρεφόμενος *a cake not turned over* Hos 7,8; μεταστρέψω ἐπὶ λαοὺς γλῶσσαν *I will change the speech of the peoples* Zph 3,9
*Jgs^A 5,28 τοὺς μεταστρέφοντας *the ones who returned* -סבב for MT תיבב *she cried out* (in Jgs^A part of doublet)
Cf. Schreiner 1957, 93(Jgs^A 5,28)

μεταστροφή,-ῆς N1F 0-2-0-0-0-2

1 Kgs 12,15; 2 Chr 10,15
turn, change (of mind)

μετασχηματίζω⁺ V 0-0-0-0-1-1
4 Mc 9,22
P: *to be changed, to be transformed*

μετατίθημι⁺ V 2-1-4-3-7-17
Gn 5,24; Dt 27,17; 1 Kgs 20(21),25; Is 29,14(bis)
A: *to change the place of, to transfer* [τινα] Gn 5,24; *to change the place of, to shift* [τι] Dt 27,17; *to remove* [τινα] Is 29,14; *to turn to* [τι εἴς τι] Est 4,17s; *to induce sb to change sb's mind* [τινα] 2 Mc 4,46; *to pervert* [τινα] 1 Kgs 20(21),25; *to turn to, to avert from* [τί τινος] 3 Mc 1,16
M: *to change loyalty to, to turn apostate from* [τινος] 2 Mc 7,24
P: *to be translated, to be taken up* Wis 4,10; *to be turned to* [εἴς τι] Sir 6,9
Cf. Larcher 1984, 330-331; Wevers 1993, 72

μετατρέπω⁺ V 0-0-0-0-4-4
4 Mc 6,5; 7,12; 15,11.18
A: *to change the mind of* [τινα] 4 Mc 15,18; *to change, to pervert* [τι] (of principles) 4 Mc 15,11
P: *to be moved in one's mind* 4 Mc 6,5

μεταφέρω⁺ V 0-1-0-0-1-2
1 Chr 13,3; 1 Ezr 4,48
to transfer, to bring over [τι]

μετάφρασις,-εως N3F 0-0-0-0-1-1
2 Mc 2,31
paraphrasing, paraphrase; neol.

μετάφρενα,-ων N2N 1-0-1-2-1-5
Dt 32,11; Is 51,23; Ps 67(68),14; 90(91),4; Od 2,11
back (part of the body)

μεταχέω V 0-0-0-0-1-1
4 Mc 1,29
to pour from one vessel into another, to transplant; neol.

μετέπειτα⁺ D 0-0-0-1-2-3
Est 3,13g; Jdt 9,5; 3 Mc 3,24
afterwards, later, thereafter

μετέρχομαι V 0-3-0-0-5-8
1 Sm 5,8(bis).9; 1 Mc 15,4; 4 Mc 10,21
to go over to [πρός τινα] 1 Sm 5,8; *to pursue, to come upon* [τινα] Wis 14,30; *to punish* [τινα] 1 Mc 15,4
Cf. Helbing 1928, 87

μετέχω⁺ V 0-0-0-2-8-10
Prv 1,18; 5,17; 1 Ezr 5,40; 8,67; 2 Mc 4,14
to partake of, to be a partaker in [τινος]

1 Ezr 5,40; *to partake with* [τινι] Prv 5,17
Cf. HELBING 1928, 136; SPICQ 1978ᵃ, 555-559

μετεωρίζω⁺   V 0-0-6-1-3-10
Ez 10,16.17(bis).19; Ob 4
M: *to mount up, to soar aloft* (of an eagle) Ob
4; *to rise up* (of the cherubim) Ez 10,16; *to rise
up against* [ἐπί τι] 3 Mc 6,5; *to be lifted, to be
raised* (of eyes) Ps 130(131),1; *to be exalted, to
be raised to a height* (of a mountain) Mi 4,1
ἐμετεωρίζετο τὴν διάνοιαν *he allowed his
spirit to soar, he was haughty* 2 Mc 5,17
Cf. SPICQ 1978ᵃ, 560-562; →MM; TWNT

μετεωρισμός,-οῦ   N2M 0-0-1-3-4-8
Jon 2,4; Ps 41(42),8; 87(88),8; 92(93),4; 2 Mc
5,21
lifting up (of mind, in pride) 2 Mc 5,21; *wave,
billow* (metaph. of sea) Ps 41(42),8, see also
Ps 87(88),8
μετεωρισμὸν ὀφθαλμῶν *lifting up of the eyes, a
haughty look* Sir 23,5
→LSJ RSuppl

μετέωρος,-ος,-ον   A 0-3-11-1-2-17
Jgs 1,15; 2 Sm 22,28; Is 2,12.13
raised from the ground, uplifted Ez 3,15; *high in
the air, towering* Is 2,13; *upper, high* Jgs 1,15;
lofty, exalted, uplifted Is 18,2; τὸ μετέωρον
eminence, high place Sir 22,18; ὁ μετέωρος
haughty one, arrogant one 2 Sm 22,28
*Jb 28,18 μετέωρα *high place?* -רוֹם for MT ראמות
corals?

μετοικεσία,-ας⁺   N1F 0-3-4-1-0-8
Jgsᴬ 18,30; 2 Kgs 24,16; 1 Chr 5,22; Ez 12,11;
Ob 20
deportation, captivity Jgsᴬ 18,30; *deported people*
Ob 20(secundo); neol.
→LSJ RSuppl

μετοικέω   V 0-1-0-0-0-1
2 Sm 15,19
to change one's dwelling place

μετοικία,-ας   N1F 0-2-2-0-0-4
1 Kgs 8,47; 1 Chr 5,41; Jer 9,10; 20,4
deportation, captivity

μετοικίζω⁺   V 0-4-4-1-1-10
Jgsᴬ 2,3; 1 Chr 5,6.26; 8,6; Jer 20,4
A: *to move to another place, to remove, to
resettle* [τινα] 1 Chr 8,6; *to remove, to drive out*
[τινα] Jgsᴬ 2,3; *to deport, to lead away captive*
[τινα] 1 Ezr 5,7
P: *to move away, to depart* Hos 10,5

μετουσία,-ας   N1F 0-0-0-0-1-1

4 Mc 2,1
participation

μετοχή,-ῆς⁺   N1F 0-0-0-1-1-2
Ps 121(122),3; PSal 14,6
sharing in, participation of [τινος] PSal 14,6
*Ps 121(122),3 ἡ μετοχή *company, partnership*
-חֶבְרָה for MT חֻבְּרָה *compacted*
Cf. CAIRD 1969=1972, 134(Ps 121(122),3); SPICQ 1978ᵃ,
555-559

μέτοχος,-ος,-ον⁺   A 0-1-1-4-1-7
Hos 4,17; Ps 44(45),8; 118(119),63; Prv 29,10;
3 Mc 3,21
companion of [τινος] Ps 44(45),8; *companion
of, being in the companionship of, partaking in
the cult of* (of idols) [τινος] Hos 4,17; *accomplice
with* [τινι] 1 Sm 20,30
ἄνδρες αἱμάτων μέτοχοι *men who participate
in bloodshed, bloodthirsty men* Prv 29,10
Cf. HORSLEY 1981, 84-85; SPICQ 1978ᵃ, 555-559

μετρέω⁺   V 2-0-1-2-1-6
Ex 16,18; Nm 35,5; Is 40,12; Ru 3,15; Dnᵀʰ 5,26
to measure
→TWNT
(→δια-, ἐκ-, κατα-)

μέτρησις,-εως   N3F 0-1-0-0-0-1
1 Kgs 7,24(38)
measuring

μετρητής,-οῦ⁺   N1M 0-2-1-0-3-6
1 Kgs 18,32; 2 Chr 4,5; Hag 2,16; 1 Ezr 8,20;
Belᴸˣˣ 3
measure (liquid measure, similar to the Hebr. בת)
Cf. HULTSCH 1882, 101.108; MONTEVECCHI 1988, 71

μετριάζω   V 0-0-0-1-0-1
Neh 2,2
to be moderate, to behave

μέτριος,-α,-ον⁺   A 0-0-0-0-2-2
Sir 31,20; PSal 5,17
moderate PSal 5,17
ἐπὶ ἐντέρῳ μετρίῳ Sir 31,20 see ἔντερον

μετρίως⁺   D 0-0-0-0-1-1
2 Mc 15,38
*neither exaggerating nor depreciating, moderately,
enough*

μέτρον,-ου⁺   N2N 9-10-40-12-3-74
Gn 18,6; Ex 16,36; 26,2.8; Lv 19,35
measure of content Gn 18,6; *measure, dimension*
Ex 26,2; *that by which sth is measured* Am 8,5;
μέτρῳ *by measure, in moderation, moderately*
Dt 2,6
ἐν μέτρῳ *id.* Jdt 7,21

*Ez 42,11 κατὰ τὰ μέτρα *according to the measures* -כמדות? for MT כמראה *like the appearance of, similar to*
Cf. LE BOULLUEC 1989, 188; ZIPOR 1991, 334; →NIDNTT; TWNT

μέτωπον,-ου⁺   N2N 2-4-2-0-1-9
Ex 28,38(bis); 1 Sm 17,49(bis); 2 Chr 26,19
forehead
→TWNT

μέχρι⁺   D/P 0-1-0-15-49-65
Jos 4,23; Ps 45(46),10; 49(50),1; 70(71),17; 104(105),19
until 3 Mc 7,4
[τινος]: *until* (of time) 1 Ezr 2,26; *as far as* (of place) 1 Ezr 3,2; *as far as* (metaph.) Jb 32,12
μέχρι τίνος (sc. χρόνου) *how long* Jb 2,9
Cf. BLASS 1990, § 216

μέχρις⁺   P 0-0-0-2-2-4
Est 5,1e; Dnᵀʰ 11,36; Jdt 5,10; Tobᴮᴬ 11,1
see μέχρι

μεχωνωθ   N 0-20-0-0-0-20
1 Kgs 7,14(27)(bis).15(28).17(30).18(32)
= מכנות *stands, bases*
Cf. WALTERS 1973, 192.334

μή   X 449-442-816-669-803-3179
Gn 3,1.3(bis).11(bis)
like its compounds, is a neg. particle, meaning *not*; while οὐ is used in sentences expressing fact, statement or objectivity, μή occurs in clauses which express will, thought or subjectivity, ἵνα μὴ ἀποθάνητε *that you will not die* Gn 3,3; placed before the verb, μή denies a whole sentence, μὴ ζηλοῦτε θάνατον ἐν πλάνῃ ζωῆς ὑμῶν *do not seek death in the error of your life* Wis 1,12; or just the word preceded by μή, ἀπὸ τῶν κτηνῶν τῶν μὴ καθαρῶν *of the unclean cattle* Gn 7,2; μὴ ... πᾶν *nothing, no* (semit. for classical μηδείς) Jgs 13,4
introduces a question to which a neg. answer is expected, μὴ δωρεὰν σέβεται Ιωβ τὸν θεόν; *surely Job does not worship God for nothing?, does Job worship God for nothing?* Jb 1,9
after verbs of fearing, μή introduces the dependent clause and looses its neg. significance although the original meaning is still understood, φοβούμενοι μὴ καὶ τὸ ζῆν ἐκλείπῃ *fearing that he would die* 3 Mc 2,23
finally, οὐ μή [+subj.] implies strong neg. in certain sentences, ὁ πιστεύων ἐπ' αὐτῷ οὐ μὴ καταισχυνθῇ *he that believes in him shall by no*

means be ashamed Is 28,16
Cf. DORIVAL 1994, 388; HORSLEY 1987, 35; KRAFT 1972, 161; MURAOKA 1990, 23-25; WALTERS 1973, 111; WEVERS 1993, 743
(→μηδαμόθεν, μηδαμῶς, μηδέ, μηδείς, μηδέποτε, μηθείς, μηθέτερος, μηκέτι, μήποτε, μήπως, μήτε, μήτι)

μηδαμόθεν   D 0-0-0-0-1-1
Wis 17,9
from no side, from nowhere

μηδαμῶς⁺   D 3-8-3-0-6-20
Gn 18,25(bis); 19,7; Jgs^ 19,23; 1 Sm 2,30
by no means, certainly not
Cf. KRAFT 1972, 168; WEVERS 1993, 261.268

μηδέ⁺   C 20-11-24-45-39-139
Gn 19,17; 21,23(bis); 22,12; 31,52
negative conjunction, continuing a preceding neg. (almost always μή or one of its compounds); *and not, but not, nor*

μηδείς, μηδεμία, μηδέν⁺   A 8-5-8-12-34-67
Gn 19,8; 22,12; Ex 16,19.29; 22,9
no (as adj.) Nm 17,5; μηδείς *nobody* Ex 16,19; *nobody at all* (in combination with another neg.) Sir 11,28; μηδέν *nothing* Gn 19,8; *nothing at all* (in combination with another neg.) Gn 22,12; *not at all, in no way* (as acc. of the inner object) 2 Mc 14,28

μηδέποτε⁺   D 0-0-0-0-4-4
3 Mc 3,16; 7,4.11; Sir 19,7
never

μηθείς
see μηδείς

μηθέτερος,-α,-ον   A 0-0-0-1-0-1
Prv 24,21
neither of the two
→LSJ Suppl

μηκέτι⁺   D 1-2-0-1-11-15
Ex 36,6; Jos 22,33; 2 Chr 16,5; Jb 40,32; Tobᴮᴬ 3,13
no more, no longer

μῆκος,-ους⁺   N3N 19-15-45-5-2-86
Gn 6,15; 12,6; 13,17; Ex 25,10.17
length Gn 6,15; *height* 2 Chr 24,13; *length (of life), duration* (metaph.) Prv 3,2; μῆκος *in length* 1 Kgs 6,20
εἰς τὸ μῆκος *lengthwise* Gn 12,6; τῷ μήκει (ὡς σταδίων τριάκοντα) (*about thirty stadia*) *long* (always with the measurement given) Dnᴸˣˣ 4,12

μηκύνω⁺   V 0-0-3-0-0-3
Is 44,14; Ez 12,25.28

to make sth grow Is 44,14; *to delay* Ez 12,25; *to linger* Ez 12,28

μῆλον,-ου N2N 1-0-1-5-0-7
Gn 30,14; Jl 1,12; Prv 25,11; Ct 2,3.5
apple, fruit Gn 30,14; *apple-tree* Ct 8,5

μῆλον,-ου N2N 0-0-0-2-0-2
Ct 4,3; 6,7
cheek

μηλωτή,-ῆς⁺ N1F 0-5-0-0-0-5
1 Kgs 19,13.19; 2 Kgs 2,8.13.14
goatskin (as mantle)
Cf. DRAGUET 1944, 99

μήν, μηνός⁺ N3M 75-82-66-47-45-315
Gn 7,11(bis); 8,4(bis).5
moon, new moon 1 Sm 20,24; *month* Gn 7,11
κατὰ μῆνα *every month* 2 Mc 6,7; μῆνα ἡμερῶν
a full month Gn 29,14, see also Nm 11,21; Jdt
3,10; cpr. Dt 21,13
*1 Sm 11,1(10,27) καὶ ἐγενήθη ὡς μετὰ μῆνα
and it happened about a month later -ויהי כמחרש
cpr. 1QSm 10,27-11,1 ויהי כמו חרש for MT
ויהי כמחריש *but he was like one made silent, like
one that held his peace?*
Cf. HARL 1986ᵃ, 79(Gn 29,14); ULRICH 1978, 69(1 Sm
10,27-11,1); WEVERS 1995, 340(Dt 21,13); →TWNT

μήν⁺ X 7-1-1-14-4-27
Gn 22,17; 42,16; Ex 22,7.10; Nm 14,23
part. used to strengthen other particles;
certainly, indeed Est 9,27
οὐ μὴν δὲ ἀλλά *nevertheless, nonetheless* Jb 2,5;
εἰ μήν see εἰ; ἦ μήν see ἦ

μηνιαῖος,-α,-ον A 10-0-0-0-0-10
Lv 27,6; Nm 3,15.22.28.34
of one month, a month old
Cf. LEE, J. 1983, 26

μηνίαμα,-ατος N3N 0-0-0-0-1-1
Sir 40,4
cause of anger or *wrath*; (hapax legomenon)
Cf. WALTERS 1973, 113

μηνιάω⁺ V 0-0-0-0-1-1
Sir 10,6
see μηνίω
Cf. HELBING 1928, 212; WALTERS 1973, 113

μῆνις,-ιος/ιδος⁺ N3F 2-0-0-0-2-4
Gn 49,7; Nm 35,21; Sir 27,30; 28,5
wrath

μήνισις,-εως N3F 0-0-0-0-1-1
PSal 2,23
wrath, anger; neol.
→LSJ RSuppl

μηνίσκος,-ου N2M 0-3-1-0-0-4
Jgs 8,21; Jgsᴮ 8,26; Is 3,18
crescent-shaped ornament, pendant
Cf. REEKMANS 1975, 748-759

μηνίω V 1-0-1-1-2-5
Lv 19,18; Jer 3,12; Ps 102(103),9; Od 12,13; Sir
28,7
to cherish wrath, to bear a grudge [abs.] Ps
102(103),9; *to bear a grudge against sb* [τινι]
Lv 19,18
Cf. HELBING 1928, 212; WALTERS 1973, 29.30.308

μηνύω⁺ V 0-0-0-0-5-5
2 Mc 3,7; 6,11; 14,37; 3 Mc 3,28; 4 Mc 4,3
A: *to make known, to inform* [abs.] 3 Mc 3,28;
id. [+inf.] 4 Mc 4,3
P: *to be mentioned* 2 Mc 3,7; *to be betrayed*
2 Mc 6,11
(→κατα-, προ-)

μήποτε⁺ C/D 30-22-2-26-37-117
Gn 3,22; 19,17; 20,2; 24,5.39
that ... not, lest (after verbs of fearing, being
concerned) Sir 11,33; *out of fear that* Gn 27,45;
(in order) that ... not Is 6,10; *whether perhaps*
(interrogative adv.) Jgs 3,24; *probably, perhaps*
(the neg. is weakened to such a degree that
μήποτε introduces sth conjectured) Jb 1,5

μήπως⁺ C 0-0-0-0-1-1
Sir 28,26
lest somehow, that not somehow

μηρία,-ων N2N 5-0-0-1-0-6
Lv 3,4.10.15; 4,9; 7,4
thigh-bones

μηρός,-οῦ⁺ N2M 17-14-3-5-2-41
Gn 24,2.9; 32,26(bis).32
thigh Gn 24,2
ἐν μηροῖς ὄρους *on the flanks of the mountain*
Jgs 19,1; ἐπί μηρόν τινος *by the side of, beside
sth* 2 Kgs 16,14; υἱοὶ ἐκπορευόμενοι ἐκ μηρῶν
αὐτοῦ *sons begotten of his loins, his offspring* Jgs
8,30; τὸ χόριον αὐτῆς τὸ ἐξελθὸν διὰ τῶν
μηρῶν αὐτῆς *the after-birth that comes out
between her thighs* Dt 28,57
→LSJ Suppl; LSJ RSuppl(Jgs 19,1)

μηρυκισμός,-οῦ N2M 11-0-0-0-0-11
Lv 11,3.4(bis).5.6
(chewing) the cud; neol.
Cf. DOGNIEZ 1992, 65.205; HARLÉ 1988, 127-128

μηρύομαι V 0-0-0-1-0-1
Prv 31,13
to wind off (of wool)

μήτε⁺   C 0-2-2-0-12-16
1 Kgs 3,26(bis); Hos 4,4(bis); 1 Mc 12,36
neg. copula; *and not, nor* (after neg.) 3 Mc 7,8;
μήτε ... μήτε ... *neither ... nor* ... 1 Kgs 3,26

μήτηρ, μητρός⁺   N3F 65-104-33-47-89-338
Gn 2,24; 3,20; 20,12; 21,21; 24,28
mother Gn 2,24; *id.* (metaph.) Tob^B 4,13;
mother, dam (of anim.) Ex 22,29; *mother-bird*
Dt 22,6; *mother* metaph. for *mother-city, capital?*
Is 50,1, see also Jer 15,10?; 27(50),12, cpr.
μητρόπολις
Cf. HORSLEY 1982, 91; →TWNT

μήτι⁺   C 0-0-0-1-0-1
Dn^LXX 2,11
neither, nor

μήτρα,-ας⁺   N1F 15-3-7-3-5-33
Gn 20,18; 29,31; 30,22; 49,25; Ex 13,2
womb Gn 49,25
ἀνοίγω τὴν μήτραν Gn 29,31 see ἀνοίγω;
διανοῖγον μήτραν Ex 13,12 see διανοίγω
*Jdt 9,2 ἔλυσαν μήτραν παρθένου *they
loosened, opened up the uterus of a virgin* (used
euphemistically of sexual intercourse) corr.?
ἔλυσαν μίτραν παρθένου *they loosened the
girdle of a virgin, they violated a virgin*
Cf. MOORE 1985, 191(Jdt 9,2); MORENZ 1964, 256

μητρόπολις,-εως   N3F 0-5-1-1-0-7
Jos 10,2; 14,15; 15,13; 21,11; 2 Sm 20,19
mother-city, metropolis, capital Jos 10,2
*Jos 14,15 μητρόπολις *the capital* -האם הגדולה? or
-הארמה הגדלה? for MT האָרם הגדל *the greatest man;*
*Jos 15,13 μητρόπολιν *mother-city, capital* -אם?
for MT אבי *my father,* see also Jos 21,11, cpr.
2 Sm 20,19

μητρῷος,-α,-ον   A 0-0-0-0-1-1
4 Mc 13,19
of a mother; γαστὴρ μητρῴα *mother's womb*

μηχανάομαι⁺   V 0-0-0-1-4-5
Est 8,12c; 3 Mc 5,5.22.28; 6,24
in a pos. sense: *to contrive, to take precautions
for* [τι] 3 Mc 5,5
in a neg. sense: *to form a design* or *plot against,
to plot against* [τινι] Est 8,12c; *to contrive
against* [τί τινι] 3 Mc 5,22
τὰ μεμηχανημένα *devices* 3 Mc 5,28

μηχανεύομαι   V 0-1-0-0-0-1
2 Chr 26,15; 3 Mc 6,22
syn. of μηχανάομαι; P: *to be invented, to be
devised*

μηχανή,-ῆς⁺   N1F 0-1-0-0-13-14

2 Chr 26,15; 1 Mc 5,30; 6,20.31.37
contrivance, device 1 Mc 6,37; *machine* or *engine*
(of war or siege) 1 Mc 5,30; *contrivance, plan*
3 Mc 4,19

μηχάνημα,-ατος   N3N 0-0-0-0-2-2
1 Mc 13,29; 4 Mc 7,4
subtle contrivance 1 Mc 13,29; *machine* or *engine*
(of war) 4 Mc 7,4
Cf. WALTERS 1973, 192-193

μία
see εἷς

μιαίνω⁺   V 56-6-45-6-16-129
Gn 34,5.13.27; 49,4; Ex 20,25
A: *to taint, to defile, to pollute* [τι] Gn 49,4; *id.*
[τι] (of sacred things) Lv 20,3; *to declare defiled,
unclean* [τινα] Lv 13,3; *to defile* (a woman)
[τινα] (in case of incest) Gn 34,5; *id.* (a
woman) [τινα] (in case of adultery) Jb 31,11
P: *to be defiled* Ex 20,25; *to be unclean* Lv 13,14
Cf. HARLÉ 1988, 31.135.176-177; →TWNT
(→ἐκ-, συμ-)

μιαιφονία,-ας   N1F 0-0-0-0-2-2
4 Mc 9,9; 10,11
pollution by murder, murder; neol.

μιαιφόνος,-ου   N2M 0-0-0-0-2-2
2 Mc 4,38; 12,6
someone polluted by murder, murderer

μίανσις,-εως   N3F 1-0-0-0-0-1
Lv 13,44
pollution; neol.

μιαρός,-ά,-όν⁺   A 0-0-0-0-11-11
2 Mc 4,19; 5,16; 7,34; 9,13; 15,32
vile (of pers.) 2 Mc 4,19; *polluted* (of things)
2 Mc 5,16

μιαροφαγέω   V 0-0-0-0-9-9
4 Mc 5,3.19.25; 8,2(bis)
to eat unclean food; neol.

μιαροφαγία,-ας   N1F 0-0-0-0-4-4
4 Mc 5,27; 6,19; 7,6; 11,25
eating of unclean food

μίασμα,-ατος⁺   N3N 1-0-2-0-4-7
Lv 7,18; Jer 39(32),34; Ez 33,31; Jdt 9,2.4
defilement (of a woman) Jdt 13,16; *pollution*
Lv 7,18
*Ez 33,31 μιασμάτων *miasmata, that which is
polluted* -בצע^II? *blemish* (cpr. Sir^Hebr 7,6) for MT
בצע^I *gain*
→DCH (sub בצע^II); TWNT

μιασμός,-οῦ⁺   N2M 0-0-0-0-2-2
1 Mc 4,43; Wis 14,26

defilement, corruption (physical or ritual)
1 Mc 4,43; *id.* (moral) Wis 14,26

Cf. GILBERT 1973, 168; LARCHER 1985, 832-834; →TWNT

μ(ε)ίγνυμι⁺   V 2-1-1-2-0-6
Gn 30,40; Ex 30,35; 2 Kgs 18,23; Is 36,8; Ps
105(106),35

A: *to mingle with* [τι εἴς τι] Gn 30,40
P: *to be mingled among, to live with* [ἔν τισι]
Ps 105(106),35; *to make an agreement with*
[τινι] 2 Kgs 18,23; *to be mixed, to be
compounded* Ex 30,35

*Prv 14,16 μίγνυται *he joins with* -מתערב for MT
מתעבר *he becomes angry?*

Cf. HELBING 1928, 250-251; WALTERS 1973, 31

(→ἀνα-, ἐπι-, κατα-, προσ-, συγκατα-, συμ-,
συνανα-)

μικρολόγος,-ος,-ον   A 0-0-0-0-1-1
Sir 14,3
*caring about petty trifles, attentive to trifles,
small-minded*

μικρός,-ά,-όν⁺   A 23-47-41-23-31-165
Gn 19,11.20(bis); 24,17.43
small, little (of things) Gn 19,20; *small* (of pers.)
Gn 19,11; *a little, a bit* (of quantity) Gn 24,17;
few Gn 47,9; *little, insignificant* Nm 16,9; *trifling,
of less importance* 4 Mc 5,19; *short* (of time)
Jb 2,9a; *young* Jer 38(31),34

μικρόν *a little while* Ex 17,4; μικροῦ *within a
little, almost* Gn 26,10; παρὰ μικρόν *id.*
Ps 72(73),2; κατὰ μικρόν *little by little* Sir 19,1;
κατὰ μικρὸν μικρόν *little by little* (semit.)
Ex 23,30; πρὸ μικροῦ *a little before, just before*
Wis 15,8; μετὰ μικρὸν ὕστερον *a little after*
4 Mc 12,7; μικρῷ [+comp.] *a little (before)*
2 Mc 9,10; ὁ μικρὸς δάκτυλος *little finger*
2 Chr 10,10

*Jos 22,19 εἰ μικρὰ ἡ γῆ *if the land is (too)
small* -אם מעט הארץ for MT אם טמאה ארץ *if the land is
unclean*; *Ez 46,22 μικρά *small* -קטנות for MT
קטרות *enclosed, adjacent?*; *Lam 4,18 μικροὺς
ἡμῶν *our little ones* -צעירינו for MT צעדינו *our steps*

Cf. OTTLEY 1906, 269; ZIEGLER 1934, 84(Is 9,13(14);
22,5.24; 33,4.19); →NIDNTT; TWNT

μικρότης,-ητος   N3F 0-2-0-0-1-3
1 Kgs 12,10.24r; PSal 14,7
smallness

μικρῶς⁺   D 0-0-0-0-1-1
2 Mc 14,8
little; οὐ μικρῶς *to a large degree*

μίλτος,-ου   N2F 0-0-1-0-1-2

Jer 22,14; Wis 13,14
red earth, vermilion

Cf. LARCHER 1985, 781

μιμέομαι⁺   V 0-0-0-0-4-4
4 Mc 9,23; 13,9; Wis 4,2; 15,9
to imitate [τι] Wis 4,2; *to imitate, to copy* [τινα]
Wis 15,9; *to follow the example of* [τινα]
4 Mc 9,23

→TWNT

μίμημα,-ατος⁺   N3N 0-0-0-0-1-1
Wis 9,8
copy

→LSJ RSuppl

μιμνήσκω⁺   V 37-15-56-82-85-275
Gn 8,1; 9,15.16; 19,29; 30,22
stereotypical rendition of זכר
M: *to remember* [τινος] Gn 8,1; *id.* [περί τινος]
TobB 4,1; *id.* [τι] Gn 9,16; *id.* [+indir. question]
Jb 4,7; *id.* [abs.] Lam 3,19
to remind sb of sth [τινι ἐπί τινι] Neh 13,29;
to consider [τι] Is 47,7; *to be mindful of* [τι]
Dt 7,18; *id.* [τινος] Dt 8,18; *id.* [ὅτι +ind.]
Dt 5,15; *to remind sb of sb* [πρός τινα περί
τινος] DnLXX 5,10; *to mention in prayer to God,
to call to God's remembrance* Is 48,1
*to proclaim, to confess with praise and adoration,
to give adoring testimony* [τινος] Ps 70(71),16; *to
believe, to obey* [τινος] Nm 15,39
to become converted, to turn about Ps 21(22),28
P: *to be remembered* Ez 18,22
οὐ μὴ μνησθήσομαι ἁμαρτιῶν αὐτῶν *I will
forget, I will forgive their sins* Jer 40(33),8; οὐ
μέμνηται ... φιλιάζειν φίλοις καὶ ἀδελφοῖς
they forget their love both to friends and brethren
1 Ezr 3,22
*Na 2,6 καὶ μνησθήσονται *they shall remind
themselves* (subject: their mighty men)? -ויזכרו
for MT יזכר *he remembers, he thinks of* (his
mighty men)?

Cf. HELBING 1928, 107-109; SPICQ 1982, 459-472; →NIDNTT;
TWNT

(→ἀνα-, ἐπι-, κατα-, προσυπο-, ὑπο-)

μισάνθρωπος,-ου   N2M 0-0-0-0-1-1
4 Mc 11,4
hater of mankind, misanthrope

μισάρετος,-ου   N2M 0-0-0-0-1-1
4 Mc 11,4
hater of virtue; neol.

μίσγω   V 0-0-2-0-0-2
Is 1,22; Hos 4,2

to mingle with [τί τινι] Is 1,22; *id.* [τι ἐπί τι]
Hos 4,2
Cf. HELBING 1928, 251; WALTERS 1973, 31
(→συμ-, συνανα-)

μισέω⁺   V 34-20-23-73-32-182
Gn 26,27; 29,31.33; 37,4.8
to hate, to abhor [τινα] Gn 26,27; *id.* [τι]
Ex 18,21; *id.* [abs.] Dt 7,10
*Prv 17,9 μισεῖ *he who hates* -שׂנא for MT שׂנה *he who repents*, cpr. Mal 2,13; Eccl 8,1
Cf. DE WAARD 1981, 559; →NIDNTT; TWNT

μισητός,-ή,-όν   A 1-0-0-3-5-9
Gn 34,30; Prv 24,24; 26,11; 30,23; Wis 14,9
hateful, hated, despicable

μίσθιος,-ου⁺   N2M 1-0-0-1-4-6
Lv 25,50; Jb 7,1; Tob^BA 5,12; Sir 7,20; 34,22
hired man, hired labourer, hireling
Cf. LEE, J. 1983, 112; →TWNT

μισθός,-οῦ⁺   N2M 18-2-18-8-31-77
Gn 15,1; 29,15; 30,18(bis).28
hire, pay, wages Sir 34(31),22; *reward, earnings*
Gn 15,1; *reward* (of the Lord presented as a
shepherd?) Is 40,10; *price* Zech 11,12
μετὰ μισθοῦ *at pay, for hire* Mi 3,11; συνάγω
τοὺς μισθούς *to earn wages* Hag 1,6;
ἀποδίδωμι τὸν μισθόν *to pay the wages*
Dt 24,15
Cf. LE BOULLUEC 1989, 227-228(Ex 22,14); PRIJS 1948,
8-9(Ex 22,14); SPICQ 1982, 473-487; WEVERS 1993, 202;
WILL 1978, 427-438; →TWNT

μισθόω⁺   V 2-10-2-3-1-18
Gn 30,16; Dt 23,5; Jgs 9,4; Jgs^A 18,4
M: *to hire* [τι] 1 Chr 19,6; *to hire, to engage for
oneself* [τινα] 2 Chr 24,12
Cf. SPICQ 1982, 486-487; →TWNT

μίσθωμα,-ατος⁺   N3N 1-0-11-1-0-13
Dt 23,19; Ez 16,31.32.33(bis)
(a whore's) price, wages, hire
Cf. MEALAND 1990, 584-586

μισθωτός,-ή,-όν⁺   A 8-0-6-2-4-20
Ex 12,45; 22,14; Lv 19,13; 22,10; 25,6
hired; mostly (ὁ) μισθωτός *hireling* Ex 12,45
δυνάμεις μισθωταί *bands of mercenaries* 1 Mc
6,29
*Is 28,1 μισθωτοί *mercenaries* -שׂכירי for MT שׂכרי
drunkards
Cf. HARLÉ 1988, 46.203; HELTZER 1988, 118-124; LE
BOULLUEC 1989, 227-228(Ex 22,14); SPICQ 1978ᵃ, 217;
WEVERS 1990, 349; →TWNT

μισοξενία,-ας   N1F 0-0-0-0-1-1

Wis 19,13
hatred of guests or *strangers*; neol.

μισοπονηρέω   V 0-0-0-0-2-2
2 Mc 4,49; 8,4
to hate the wicked or *wickedness*
(→συμ-)

μισοπονηρία,-ας   N1F 0-0-0-0-1-1
2 Mc 3,1
hatred of wickedness

μισοπόνηρος,-ος,-ον   A 0-0-0-1-0-1
Est 8,12d
hating wickedness, sin-hating

μῖσος,-ους⁺   N3N 0-2-2-8-0-12
2 Sm 13,15(bis); Jer 24,9; Ez 23,29; Ps 24(25),19
hate, hatred (felt against)

μίσυβρις,-ιος   N3M/F 0-0-0-0-1-1
3 Mc 6,9
one who hates insolence, hater of insolence; neol.

μίτρα,-ας⁺   N1F 8-0-2-0-4-14
Ex 28,37(bis); 29,6(bis); 36,35(39,28)
head-dress, tier, headband (to bind women's hair
together) Jdt 10,3; *id.* (of a bridegroom)
Is 61,10; *diadem* (of glory) Bar 5,2; *holy diadem*
(of Jewish high-priest) Ex 29,6; *crown* (of
princes) Ez 26,16
Cf. HARLÉ 1988, 73.114; LE BOULLUEC 1989, 292.293;
LEE, J. 1983, 51; MOORE 1985, 191(Jdt 9,2); RAURELL
1986, 87; WEVERS 1990, 446.461.608

μνᾶ, μνᾶς⁺   N1F 0-1-1-4-6-12
1 Kgs 10,17; Ez 45,12; Ezr 2,69(bis); Neh
7,71(70)
Semit. loanword (Hebr. מנה); *mina* (100
drachmae, weight or money)
Cf. CAIRD 1976, 78; WALTERS 1973, 163.193-194;
→CHANTRAINE; FRISK

μνεία,-ας⁺   N1F 1-0-7-2-4-14
Dt 7,18; Is 23,16; 26,8; 32,10; Jer 38(31),20
remembrance Wis 5,14; *commemoration,
memorial* 4 Mc 17,8
μιμνήσκομαι μνείᾳ *to remember surely* (semit.)
Dt 7,18; μνείαν τινὸς ποιέω *to remember sb,
to make mention of* Jb 14,13
Cf. DANIEL 1966, 230.235-236; SPICQ 1982, 459-472;
→TWNT

μνῆμα,-ατος⁺   N3N 8-4-7-1-0-20
Ex 14,11; Nm 11,34.35; 19,16.18
grave, tomb
→NIDNTT

μνημεῖον,-ου⁺   N2N 8-0-4-2-2-16
Gn 23,6(bis).9; 35,20(bis)

monument, memorial Wis 10,7; *grave, tomb* Gn 23,6

Cf. LARCHER 1984, 625; →NIDNTT

μνήμη,-ης+   N1F 0-0-0-9-8-17
Ps 29(30),5; 96(97),12; 144(145),7; Prv 1,12; 10,7
rendering זכר or זכרון; *remembrance of, memory of* [τινος] Ps 29(30),5; *remembrance, memorial* Prv 1,12

Cf. DANIEL 1966, 230.235-236; LARCHER 1984, 315(Wis 4,1); SPICQ 1982, 459-472; →TWNT

μνημονεύω+   V 1-4-1-5-15-26
Ex 13,3; 2 Sm 14,11; 2 Kgs 9,25; 1 Chr 16,12.15
always rendering זכר; *to remember, to keep in mind* [τι] Ex 13,3; *id.* [τινα] 2 Sm 14,11; *id.* [τινος] Tob 4,5; *id.* [abs.] 2 Kgs 9,25; *to remind of sth, to mention sth* [τι] Est 4,17a; *to remember sb* [τινος] 1 Mc 12,11

Cf. HELBING 1928, 109; LE BOULLUEC 1989, 156; SPICQ 1982, 452-458; →TWNT

μνημόσυνον,-ου+   N2N 22-1-6-16-30-75
Ex 3,15; 12,14; 13,9; 17,14(bis)
always rendering זכר or זכרון or אזכרה; *memorial* Ex 12,14; *memorial offering* Lv 2,2; *trace, souvenir* Wis 10,8

Cf. DANIEL 1966, 226-236; HARLÉ 1988, 40.89; LE BOULLUEC 1989, 92-93.191.284; SPICQ 1982, 459-472; →TWNT

μνημόσυνος,-η,-ον   A 0-0-0-1-0-1
Est 6,1
of record, of remembrance; γράμματα μνημόσυνα *records*

→LSJ Suppl

μνησικακέω+   V 1-0-3-1-0-5
Gn 50,15; Ez 25,12; Jl 4(3),4; Zech 7,10; Prv 21,24
to bear a grudge against sb, to bear malice against sb [τινι] Gn 50,15; *id.* [ἐπί τινι] Jl 4(3),4; *id.* [abs.] Prv 21,24; *to bear malice against sb because of sth* [τί τινος] Zech 7,10

Cf. HELBING 1928, 110

μνησίκακος,-ος,-ον+   A 0-0-0-1-0-1
Prv 12,28
bearing malice, revengeful

μνηστεύω+   V 5-0-3-0-2-10
Dt 20,7; 22,23.25.27.28
stereotypical rendition of ארש
M: *to become engaged to (a woman)* [τινα] Dt 20,7; *to betroth a woman with a man, to arrange an engagement between a man and a woman* [τινά τινι] Hos 2,21(19)

P: *to be betrothed, to be engaged* (of a woman) Dt 22,25

Cf. DOGNIEZ 1992, 239; SPICQ 1982, 488-489

μογιλάλος,-ος,-ον+   A 0-0-1-0-0-1
Is 35,6
having an impediment in one's speech; ὁ μογιλάλος *one speaking with difficulty, stammerer*; neol.

Cf. DE WAARD 1981, 557-558

μόγις+   D 0-0-0-0-1-1
3 Mc 7,6
hardly, scarcely; see μόλις

μοιχαλίς,-ίδος+   N3F 0-0-5-2-0-7
Ez 16,38; 23,45(bis); Hos 3,1; Mal 3,5
adulteress; neol.

μοιχάω+   V 0-0-9-0-1-10
Jer 3,8; 5,7; 7,9; 9,1; 23,14
P: *to commit adultery* (of a man) Jer 5,7; *id.* (of a woman) Ez 16,32; *to commit adultery with* [τινα] PSal 8,10; *to commit adultery* (metaph.), *to be unfaithful to God* Jer 3,8

→MM; TWNT

μοιχεία,-ας+   N1F 0-0-3-0-1-4
Jer 13,27; Hos 2,4; 4,2; Wis 14,26
adultery Hos 2,4; *id.* (metaph.) Jer 13,27

Cf. CARAGOUNIS 1996, 548; →TWNT

μοιχεύω+   V 6-0-5-0-1-12
Ex 20,13(14); Lv 20,10(quater)
A: *to commit adultery* (of men) Ex 20,13; *id.* (A: unusual for women) Hos 4,13; *to worship idolatrously* [τι] Jer 3,9
M: *to commit adultery with a woman* [τινα] (M: normally said of women) Lv 20,10(primo, secundo)
M/P: *to commit adultery* (of women) Sir 23,23
ὁ μοιχεύων καὶ ἡ μοιχευμένη *the adulterer and the adulteress* Lv 20,10

Cf. BOGNER 1941, 318-320; →NIDNTT; TWNT

μοιχός,-οῦ+   N2M 0-0-1-3-2-6
Is 57,3; Ps 49(50),18; Jb 24,15; Prv 6,32; Wis 3,16
adulterer

→TWNT

μόλιβος,-ου+   N2M 2-0-5-1-3-11
Ex 15,10; Nm 31,22; Jer 6,29; Ez 22,18.20
lead (metal)

μόλις+   D 0-0-0-1-7-8
Prv 11,31; 3 Mc 1,23; 5,15; Wis 9,16; Sir 21,20
syn. of μόγις, the latter is prevalent in late Greek; *hardly, scarcely* Prv 11,31; *with difficulty*

Wis 9,16

Cf. BARR 1975, 149-164(Prv 11,31); →TWNT

μολόχη-ης   N1F 0-0-0-1-0-1
Jb 24,24
mallow (plant); *Jb 24,24 ὥσπερ μολόχη like a
mallow* -מלוח/כ for MT כל/כ *like all*; neol.?

μόλυβος,-ου   N2M 0-0-1-0-0-1
Ez 27,12
lead (metal); neol.; see μόλιβος

μόλυνσις,-εως   N3F 0-0-1-0-0-1
Jer 51(44),4
defilement, pollution; neol.

μολύνω⁺   V 1-0-7-2-10-20
Gn 37,31; Is 59,3; 65,4; Jer 12,10; 23,11
A: *to stain, to soil* [τι] Gn 37,31; *to defile* [τι]
(metaph.) Sir 21,28; *to pollute (a name)* [τι]
Tob 3,15
M: *to defile oneself, to pollute oneself* 2 Mc 14,3
P: *to be defiled* Sir 13,1; *to be defiled, to be
violated, to be ravished* (of women) Zech 14,2;
to be polluted (of land) 1 Ezr 8,80
→TWNT
(→ἐμ-, συμ-)

μολυσμός,-οῦ⁺   N2M 0-0-1-0-2-3
Jer 23,15; 1 Ezr 8,80; 2 Mc 5,27
defilement, pollution (in relig. sense); neol.?
→TWNT

μονάζω⁺   V 0-0-0-1-0-1
Ps 101(102),8
to live alone; neol.

μόναρχος,-ου   N2M 0-0-0-0-1-1
3 Mc 2,2
sole ruler, monarch

μονή-ῆς⁺   N1F 0-0-0-0-1-1
1 Mc 7,38
*dwelling; μὴ δῷς αὐτοῖς μονήν do not give them
any dwelling, do not let them live any longer*
→TWNT

μόνιμος,-ος/η,-ον   A 1-0-1-0-0-2
Gn 49,26; Jer 38(31),17
fixed, stable, steady Gn 49,26; (τὸ) μόνιμον
security Jer 38(31),17

μονιός,-οῦ   N2M 0-0-0-1-0-1
Ps 79(80),14
solitary; μονιὸς ἄγριος solitary wild beast;
neol.?

Cf. BROCK 1982, 7

μονογενής,-ής,-ές⁺   A 0-2-0-3-9-14
Jgs 11,34; Ps 21(22),21; 24(25),16; 34(35),17
the only member of a kin, only-begotten, only (of

children) Jgs 11,34; *id.* (of God) Od 14,13; *alone
in its kind, one only* Wis 7,22

Cf. HARL 1960=1992ᵃ, 206-207; 1986ᵃ, 192; LARCHER
1984, 482-483; →MM; NIDNTT; TWNT

μονόζωνος,-ος,-ον   A 0-9-0-1-0-10
2 Sm 22,30; 2 Kgs 5,2; 6,23; 13,20.21
lightly armed 2 Sm 22,30; οἱ μονόζωνοι *bands
of lightly armed men* (mostly pl.) 2 Kgs 5,2; neol.

μονοήμερος,-ος,-ον   A 0-0-0-0-1-1
Wis 5,14
staying one day (of a guest)

Cf. WALTERS 1973, 300

μονόκερως,-ωτος   N3M 3-0-0-5-0-8
Nm 23,22; 24,8; Dt 33,17; Ps 21(22),22; 28(29),6
stereotypical rendition of רים, ראם, ראים; *unicorn*
Nm 23,22
*Ps 77(78),69 ὡς μονοκερώτων *as (the place) of
unicorns* -במו(א)ר-כמ for MT רמים כמו *like the
heights* or *like the high heavens* (כמרמים)?

Cf. CAIRD 1969=1972, 134-135; DOGNIEZ 1992, 350;
SCHAPER 1994, 117-136; →LSJ RSuppl

μονομαχέω   V 0-1-0-0-1-2
1 Sm 17,10; Ps 151,1
to engage in single combat

Cf. HELBING 1928, 238

μόνον⁺   D 9-7-0-6-37-59
Gn 19,8; 24,8; 27,13; 34,22.23
alone, only Gn 19,8; *only* (often with imper.)
2 Sm 20,21
οὐ μόνον ... ἀλλὰ καί *not only ... but also* Jdt
11,7

μόνορχις,-εως   N3M 1-0-0-0-0-1
Lv 21,20
with one testicle; neol.

μόνος,-η,-ον⁺   A 30-36-14-36-48-164
Gn 2,18; 3,11.17; 7,23; 21,28
alone, solitary (of men) Gn 2,18; *alone, unwed*
Ex 21,3; *alone, deserted* (of city) Lam 1,1; *alone,
only* Gn 3,11; *alone, apart, in isolation* Gn 21,28
κατὰ μόνας *apart* Gn 32,17; κυρίῳ μόνῳ *to the
Lord only* 1 Sm 7,4; σὺ κύριος ὁ θεὸς μόνος
you alone are the Lord God 2 Kgs 19,19, cpr.
2 Kgs 19,15; Ps 85(86),10; Is 37,16.20
μονώτατος *alone, without anybody* Jgs 3,20; *the
only one of all, alone* 2 Sm 17,2

Cf. DELLING 1952, 469-476

μονότροπος,-ος,-ον   A 0-0-0-1-0-1
Ps 67(68),7
living alone, solitary

Cf. HARL 1960=1992ᵃ, 207

μονοφαγία,-ας   N1F 0-0-0-0-1-1
4 Mc 1,27
eating alone, gluttony; neol.

μονοφάγος,-ος,-ον   A 0-0-0-0-1-1
4 Mc 2,7
eating alone, gluttonous

μόνωσις,-εως   N3F 0-0-0-0-1-1
PSal 4,18
solitariness, solitude

μόρον,-ου   N2N 0-0-0-0-1-1
1 Mc 6,34
mulberry

μόρος,-ου   N2M 0-0-0-0-7-7
2 Mc 9,28; 13,7; 3 Mc 3,1; 5,2.8
fate, doom, death
→NIDNTT

μορφή,-ῆς⁺   N1F 0-1-1-7-4-13
Jgs^A 8,18; Is 44,13; Jb 4,16; Dn^LXX 3,19; Dn^Th 4,36(33)
form, shape Is 44,13; *form, outward appearance* Jb 4,16; *comeliness* Tob 1,13; *countenance* Dn^Th 5,6
Cf. SPICQ 1973, 37-45; 1978, 568-573; STEENBURG 1988, 77-86; WALLACE 1966, 19-21; →NIDNTT; TWNT

μοσφαθαιμ   N 0-1-0-0-0-1
Jgs^A 5,16
= משפתים *saddlebags?*
Cf. TOV 1979, 235-236

μοσχάριον,-ου   N2N 9-0-3-0-0-12
Gn 18,7.8; Ex 24,5; 29,1.3
dim. of μόσχος; *little calf*; neol.?
Cf. HARLÉ 1988, 44.119; LEE, J. 1983, 108-109; WEVERS 1993, 248-249

μόσχευμα,-ατος   N3N 0-0-0-0-1-1
Wis 4,3
seedling, shoot taken off and planted
Cf. LARCHER 1984, 319-320

μόσχος,-ου⁺   N2M 133-55-30-15-4-237
Gn 12,16; 20,14; 21,27; 24,35; Ex 20,24
the young of cattle, calf, young bull Gn 12,16; *id.* (for sacrifice) Lv 1,5; *id.* (idolatrous object) Ex 32,8
μόσχος σιτευτός *fattened calf* Jgs^A 6,25; οἱ μόσχοι χαλκοῖ *the brazen calves* Jer 52,20
*1 Kgs 10,19 μόσχων *of calves* -עֵגֶל for MT עֵגֹל *round?*
Cf. DORIVAL 1994, 431; HARLÉ 1988, 44; LE BOULLUEC 1989, 213.222.319.341; PELLETIER 1967^b, 388-394(Ex 32,8); SCHERER 1975, 581-582; WEVERS 1990, 339.519; 1993, 172; →TWNT

μοτόω   V 0-0-1-0-0-1
Hos 6,1
to plug a wound with lint, to bind up (wounds)

μουσικός,-ή,-όν⁺   A 1-0-1-8-12-22
Gn 31,27; Ez 26,13; Dn 3,5.7
pertaining to music; (τὰ) μουσικά *music* Gn 31,27; *musical instruments* 1 Ezr 5,57; οἱ μουσικοί *musicians* Ez 26,13

μοχθέω   V 0-0-1-13-1-15
Is 62,8; Eccl 1,3; 2,11.18.19
to toil, to labour 1 Ezr 4,22
μοχθέω ὑπὸ τὸν ἥλιον *to labour under the sun* Eccl 1,3
Cf. BERTRAM 1952, 36-41

μοχθηρός,-ά,-όν   A 0-0-0-0-2-2
Sir 26,5; 27,15
causing hardships, distressing, grievous, evil Sir 26,5
ἀκοὴ μοχθηρά *grievous thing to be heard, grievous to the ear* Sir 27,15

μόχθος,-ου⁺   N2M 7-0-6-27-2-42
Ex 18,8; Lv 25,43.46.53; Nm 20,14
labour, toil Wis 10,10; *hardship, trouble* Ex 18,8; *result* or *fruit of labour* Ez 23,29
*Lam 3,65 μόχθον σου *your hardship* -תלאתך for MT תאלתך *your curse*
Cf. BERTRAM 1952, 36-41; DORIVAL 1994, 70; HARL 1984^b=1992^a, 47; 1991=1992^a, 156; SPICQ 1978^a, 574-575

μοχλεύω
(→ἀνα-)

μοχλός,-οῦ⁺   N2M 14-6-7-7-7-41
Ex 26,26.27(bis).28.29
always rendering בריח; *bar, lever* (in construction to support, to underpin, to give leverage) Ex 26,26; *bar, bolt* (of a door) Is 45,2; *bar, barrier* (of a city-entrance) 1 Sm 23,7

μυαλόομαι   V 0-0-0-1-0-1
Ps 65(66),15
to be full of marrow; neol.

μυγαλῆ,-ῆς   N1F 1-0-0-0-0-1
Lv 11,30
shrew-mouse, field-mouse

-μυελίζω
(→ἐκ-)

μυελός,-οῦ⁺   N2M 1-0-0-2-0-3
Gn 45,18; Jb 21,24; 33,24
marrow Jb 33,24; *marrow, delicious food* Gn 45,18
Cf. HARL 1986^a, 292

μυέω⁺   V 0-0-0-0-1-1

3 Mc 2,30

P: *to be initiated*

→TWNT

μυθέομαι
(→παρα-)

μυθολόγος,-ου   N2M 0-0-0-0-1-1
Bar 3,23
teller of tales, author of fables

μῦθος,-ου⁺   N2M 0-0-0-0-1-1
Sir 20,19
tale, story
Cf. BARR 1961, 220-222.229; SPICQ 1978ᵃ, 576-581;
→NIDNTT; TWNT

μυῖα,-ας   N1F 0-4-1-1-1-7
2 Kgs 1,2.3.6.16; Is 7,18
fly

μυκτήρ,-ῆρος   N3M 1-1-2-4-2-10
Nm 11,20; 2 Kgs 19,28; Ez 16,12; 23,25; Jb 40,26
nostril Nm 11,20; *nose* Ct 7,5

μυκτηρίζω⁺   V 0-3-3-8-1-15
1 Kgs 18,27; 2 Kgs 19,21; 2 Chr 36,16; Is 37,22;
Jer 20,7
A: *to turn up the nose* [abs.] Jb 22,19; *to turn up
the nose at, to sneer at, to treat with contempt*
[τινα] 1 Kgs 18,27; *id.* [τι] Prv 1,30
P: *to be mocked* Prv 12,8
Cf. HELBING 1928, 23; SPICQ 1978ᵃ, 582-583; →TWNT
(→ἐκ-)

μυκτηρισμός,-οῦ   N2M 0-0-0-6-2-8
Ps 34(35),16; 43(44),14; 78(79),4; Jb 34,7; Neh
3,36
scorn, contempt

μύλαι,-ων   N1F 0-0-1-3-1-5
Jl 1,6; Ps 57(58),7; Jb 29,17; Prv 30,14; PSal 13,3
molars, teeth

μύλος,-ου⁺   N2M 3-3-1-0-0-7
Ex 11,5; Nm 11,8; Dt 24,6; Jgsᴬ 9,53; 2 Sm 11,21
mill Ex 11,5; *millstone* Jgsᴬ 9,53; *under millstone*
Dt 24,6

μυλών,-ῶνος⁺   N2M 0-0-1-0-0-1
Jer 52,11
mill-house; οἰκία μυλῶνος *mill-house,
grinding-house*

μυξωτῆρες,-ων   N2M 0-0-1-0-0-1
Zech 4,12
small pipes or *vessel for pouring* (oil into the
lamp); neol.
→LSJ suppl

μυρεψικός,-ή,-όν   A 2-0-0-2-0-4
Ex 30,25.35; Ct 5,13; 8,2

aromatic, perfumed

μυρεψός,-οῦ   N2M 3-3-0-1-2-9
Ex 30,25.35; 38,25; 1 Sm 8,13; 1 Chr 9,30
perfumer Ex 30,25; *apothecary, druggist* Sir 38,7
→LSJ suppl

μυριάς,-άδος⁺   N3F 7-5-2-13-20-47
Gn 24,60; Ex 39,3(38,26); Lv 26,8;
Nm 10,35(36); Dt 32,30
(number of) ten thousand Ex 39,3; *myriad*
(mostly pl.) Lv 26,8; *countless thousand(s)*
(mostly pl.) Dn 7,10
Cf. DORIVAL 1994, 80

μύριοι,-αι,-α⁺   Mc 0-4-0-6-5-15
Jgs 20,10; 1 Chr 29,7(bis); Jb 42,12
ten thousand Jgs 20,10; *ten thousand,
numberless, countless* Dn 7,10; *ten thousand,
numerous* 3 Mc 3,21
μύρια τετρακισχίλια *ten and four thousand;
fourteen thousand* Jb 42,12; χιλίους πρὸς τοῖς
μυρίοις *eleven thousand men* 2 Mc 11,11
→MM

μυριοπλάσιος,-ος,-ον   A 0-0-0-1-0-1
Ps 67(68),18
ten thousand fold

μυριοπλασίως   D 0-0-0-0-1-1
Sir 23,19
ten thousand times; neol.

μυριότης,-ητος   N3F 0-0-0-0-1-1
Wis 12,22
number of ten thousand; neol.
Cf. LARCHER 1985, 736

μυρισμός,-οῦ   N2M 0-0-0-0-1-1
Jdt 16,7
anointing

μυρμηκιάω   V 1-0-0-0-0-1
Lv 22,22
to be afflicted with warts; neol.
Cf. HARLÉ 1988, 185

μυρμηκολέων,-οντος   N3M 0-0-0-1-0-1
Jb 4,11
ant-lion; neol.
Cf. DRUCE 1923, 347-364; GERHARDT 1965, 1-23

μύρμηξ,-ηκος   N3M 0-0-0-2-0-2
Prv 6,6; 30,25
ant Prv 30,25; *ant* (as a symbol of
industriousness) Prv 6,6

μυροβρεχής,-ής,-ές   A 0-0-0-0-1-1
3 Mc 4,6
wet with unguent (of the hair); neol.

μύρον,-ου⁺   N2N 1-2-5-6-2-16

Ex 30,25; 1 Chr 9,30; 2 Chr 16,14; Is 25,6; 39,2
unguent, perfume, ointment Ex 30,25
*Jer 25,10 ὀσμὴν μύρου scent of ointment
רִיחַ מֹר- for MT רֵחַיִם *handmill*
Cf. LE BOULLUEC 1989, 11; →TWNT

μυρσίνη,-ης   N1F 0-0-2-1-0-3
Is 41,19; 55,13; Neh 8,15
myrtle

μῦς, μυός⁺   N3M 1-6-0-0-0-7
Lv 11,29; 1 Sm 5,6; 6,1.5(bis)
mouse

μυσερός,-ά,-όν⁺   A 1-0-0-0-0-1
Lv 18,23
loathsome, abominable; neol.

μύσος,-ους   N3N 0-0-0-0-2-2
2 Mc 6,19.25
stain, uncleanness, defilement, pollution

μύσταξ,-ακος   N3M 0-1-0-0-0-1
2 Sm 19,25
beard on upper lip, moustache; ποιέω τὸν
μύστακα see ποιέω

μυστήριον,-ου⁺   N2N 0-0-0-17-14-31
Dn 2,18.19.27
mystery, secret rite, ceremony (mostly pl.; in relig.
sense) Wis 14,15; *mystery, secret* (in secular
sense) Tob 12,7; *secret* (in mil. sense)
2 Mc 13,21; τὰ μυστήρια *the mysteries* Dn 2,28
τὸ μυστήριον τῆς βουλῆς *secret designs* Jdt 2,2;
οὐκ ἔγνωσαν μυστήρια θεοῦ *they have not
understood the mysteries of God (God's
unfathomable purposes)* Wis 2,22
Cf. BROWN 1958, 422-427; CARAGOUNIS 1977, 22-26.
119-127; HATCH 1889, 57-58; LARCHER 1983, 264-265;
1984, 435-436; 1985, 811.827; VON SODEN 1911, 197-199;
→TWNT

μύστης,-ου   N1M 0-0-0-0-1-1
Wis 12,5
one initiated

μυστικῶς   D 0-0-0-0-1-1
3 Mc 3,10
secretly; neol.

μύστις,-ιδος   N3F 0-0-0-0-1-1
Wis 8,4
fem. of μύστης; *one who is initiated, one who is
privy to*; neol.

μυχός,-οῦ   N2M 0-0-0-0-2-2
Wis 17,4.13
deep recess, hidden nook Wis 17,4
ἐξ ᾅδου μυχῶν *the depths of Hades, the deep of
hell* Wis 17,13

Cf. LARCHER 1985, 952.970

μωκάομαι   V 0-0-1-0-0-1
Jer 28(51),18
to be ridiculed; ἔργα μεμωκημένα *works made
in mockery, objects of scorn*
(→κατα-)

μωκός,-ή,-όν   A 0-0-0-0-1-1
Sir 33,6
mocking

μώλωψ,-ωπος⁺   N3M 3-0-2-1-3-9
Gn 4,23; Ex 21,25(bis); Is 1,6; 53,5
stripe, bruise Ex 21,25
→MM; TWNT

μωμάομαι⁺   V 0-0-0-1-2-3
Prv 9,7; Wis 10,14; Sir 34,18
to censure, to find fault with, to blame [τινα]
Prv 9,7
προσφορὰ μεμωμημένη *offering made in mockery*
Sir 34,18
Cf. HELBING 1928, 21

μωμητός,-ή,-όν   A 1-0-0-0-1-2
Dt 32,5; Od 2,5
to be blamed
Cf. DOGNIEZ 1992, 323

μῶμος,-ου⁺   N2M 14-1-0-2-6-23
Lv 21,17.18.21(bis).23
ailment, infirmity Lv 21,17; *blame, reproach,
disgrace* Sir 18,15
Cf. BARTELINK 1961, 43-48; CAIRD 1976, 85; DOGNIEZ
1992, 214; LEE, J. 1983, 51; →MM; TWNT

μωραίνω⁺   V 0-1-3-0-1-5
2 Sm 24,10; Is 19,11; Jer 10,14; 28(51),17; Sir
23,14
P: *to be foolish* 2 Sm 24,10; *to become foolish*
Sir 23,14; *to be made foolish, to be turned into
foolishness, to be insane* Is 19,11
Cf. SPICQ 1982, 492

μωρεύω   V 0-0-1-0-0-1
Is 44,25
to make (sth) foolish, to turn into foolishness
[τι]; neol.

μωρία,-ας⁺   N1F 0-0-0-0-2-2
Sir 20,31; 41,15
folly
Cf. SPICQ 1982, 492-493; →TWNT

μωρός,-ά,-όν⁺   A 1-0-5-2-29-37
Dt 32,6; Is 19,11; 32,5.6(bis)
foolish, stupid (of pers.) Dt 32,6; *id.* (in relig.
sense) Jer 5,21; *id.* (of words) Is 32,6(secundo)
Cf. SPICQ 1982, 453; →TWNT

νάβλα,-ης   N1F 0-14-0-0-1-15
1 Sm 10,5; 2 Sm 6,5; 1 Kgs 10,12; 1 Chr 13,8;
15,16
Semit. loanword (Hebr. נבל); *harp, stringed
instrument*
Cf. WALTERS 1973, 163.168.171-173.328; →CHANTRAINE
(sub νάβλας); FRISK; LSJ RSuppl

ναζιρ   N 0-1-0-0-0-1
Jgs^B 13,5
= נזיר *Nazarite, consecrated by Nazarite vows*

ναζιραῖος,-α,-ον   A 0-3-0-1-1-5
Jgs^A 13,5.7; 16,17; Lam 4,7; 1 Mc 3,49
Hebr. loanword (נזיר); *Nazarite, consecrated by
Nazarite vows*; neol.
Cf. TOV 1979, 232-233; →NIDNTT; TWNT (sub Ναζωραῖος)

ναθιναῖοι,-ων   N2M 0-0-0-2-0-2
Ezr 2,43; Neh 11,3
Hebr. loanword (נתינים); *temple servants*; see
ναθινιμ and ναθινιν

ναθινιμ or **ναθινιν**   N M 0-0-0-12-0-12
Ezr 2,58.70; 7,7.24; 8,17
= נתינים/ *temple servants*; see ναθιναῖος

ναί   X 2-0-1-1-3-7
Gn 17,19; 42,21; Is 48,7; Jb 19,4; Jdt 9,12
yes (in answers) Tob^S 5,6; *certainly, indeed, yes*
(in declarations of agreement to the statements
of others) Gn 42,21; ναὶ ναί *yes, yes* (in
emphatic repetition) Jdt 9,12
Cf. WEVERS 1993, 713

ναίω   V 0-0-0-1-0-1
Jb 22,12
to inhabit, to dwell (in) [τι]

νακκαριμ   N 0-0-1-0-0-1
Am 1,1
= נקרים- for MT נקרים *sheep-raisers*

νᾶμα,-ατος   N3N 0-0-0-1-0-1
Ct 8,2
anything flowing, juice

ναός,-οῦ   N2M 0-26-23-21-48-118
1 Sm 1,9; 3,3; 2 Sm 22,7; 1 Kgs 6,5; 7,7
usual rendition of היכל; *main hall, inner shrine of
the temple* 1 Kgs 6,5; *temple* Jdt 4,2; *palace* (of
the king) Dn^Th 4,29; see also νεώς
Cf. BARR 1961, 283.286; MAY 1951, 346-347; RAHLFS
1931, 158; →TWNT

νάπη,-ης   N1F 3-1-4-0-0-8
Nm 21,20; 24,6; Dt 3,29; Jos 18,16; Is 40,12
wooded valley, vale, glen Dt 3,29; *stream-bed,
ravine* Ez 6,3
Cf. DOGNIEZ 1992, 97; SHIPP 1979, 399-400

νάρδος,-ου ^+   N2F 0-0-0-3-0-3
Ct 1,12; 4,13.14
Semit. loanword (Hebr. נרד); *nard, spikenard,
costly ointment*
Cf. CAIRD 1976, 78-79; HORSLEY 1981, 85; TOV 1979, 221;
WALTERS 1973, 163; →CHANTRAINE; FRISK; LSJ RSuppl

ναρκάω   V 3-0-0-2-0-5
Gn 32,26.33(bis); Jb 33,19; Dn^LXX 11,6
to grow numb, to stiffen
Cf. HARL 1986^a, 243; SPICQ 1978^a, 412-413; WEVERS 1993,
542.545(Gn 32,33)

νασιβ   N 0-1-0-0-0-1
1 Kgs 16,28e(22,48)
= נציב *deputy, official*

νασιφ   N M 0-1-0-0-0-1
1 Kgs 4,18(19)
= נציב *deputy, official*

ναῦλον,-ου   N2N 0-0-1-0-0-1
Jon 1,3
passage-money, fare for travel by boat; ἔδωκεν τὸ
ναῦλον αὐτοῦ *he paid his fare*
Cf. WALTERS 1973, 173.328

ναῦς, νεώς ^+   N3F 0-14-0-4-2-20
1 Sm 5,6; 1 Kgs 9,26.27; 10,11.22
ship 1 Kgs 9,26; *id.* (metaph.) 4 Mc 7,1; see
πλοῖον
Cf. MENESTRINA 1978^a, 134; TREBOLLE BARRERA 1989,
55-56(1 Sm 5,6); →LSJ Suppl(1 Sm 5,6); LSJ RSuppl(1 Sm
5,6)

ναυτικός,-ή,-όν   A 0-1-1-0-0-2
1 Kgs 9,27; Jon 1,5
seafaring 1 Kgs 9,27; ὁ ναυτικός *seaman, sailor*
Jon 1,5

Ναφεδδωρ   N 0-2-0-0-0-2
Jos 11,2; 12,23
= נפת דור *the hills of Dor*
Cf. TOV 1973, 89

Ναφετα   N 0-1-0-0-0-1
Jos 17,11
= נפת *regions*
Cf. TOV 1973, 89

νάφθα,-ης   N1F 0-0-0-2-0-2
Dn 3,46
Persian loanword (Hebr. נפט or נפטא, Aram.,
Talmudic literature, not in Dn^MT) *naphtha*; neol.;
see νεφθαι and νεφθαρ
Cf. VASOJEVIC 1984, 208-229; →CHANTRAINE; FRISK;
JASTROW (sub נפט); LSJ RSuppl

ναχαλ   N 0-0-1-0-0-1
Jer 38(31),40

= ‏נחל‎ river
Cf. SIMOTAS 1968, 117

νεάζω   V 0-0-0-0-1-1
4 Mc 5,31
to be young, to be full of youthful spirit
(→ἀνα-)

νεανίας,-ου⁺   N1M 0-12-1-4-13-30
JgsᴮB 16,26; 17,7.11; 19,3.9
young man Ru 3,10; *young man, servant* JgsᴮB
16,12; νεανίαι *children, youth* 1 Ezr 8,88

νεανικός,-ή,-όν   A 0-0-0-0-1-1
3 Mc 4,8
youthful

νεᾶνις,-ιδος⁺   N3F 9-19-0-5-3-36
Ex 2,8; Dt 22,19.20.21.24
young woman, girl, maiden Ex 2,8
*DnᵀʰTh 11,6 ἡ νεᾶνις *the maiden* -‏הַיַּלְדָּה‎ *her child*
for MT ‏הַיֹּלַדְתָּה‎ *her begetter, her mother*

νεανίσκος,-ου⁺   N2M 10-17-31-16-36-110
Gn 4,23; 14,24; 19,4; 25,27; 34,19
young man Gn 19,4; *boy, young servant* Nm
11,27; *young (cultic) servant* Ex 24,5; *young man*
(as recruit for cultic service) Am 2,11
Cf. CLARYSSE-WINNICKI 1989, 41-42; DORIVAL 1994, 86-
87; LAUNEY 1950, 859-862; LE BOULLUEC 1989, 244; VAN
'T DACK 1989, 41-42

νεβελ   N 0-2-1-0-0-3
1 Sm 1,24; 2 Sm 16,1; Hos 3,2
= ‏נבל‎ *vessel, wine-jar*
Cf. WALTERS 1973, 173; →LSJ RSuppl

νεβρός,-οῦ   N2M 0-0-0-5-0-5
Ct 2,9.17; 4,5; 7,4; 8,14
young of the deer, fawn

νεελασα   N 0-0-0-1-0-1
Jb 39,13
= ‏עלס‎ ◊ ‏נעלסה‎ *joyous*
Cf. DHORME 1926, 550; SIMOTAS 1968, 118

νεεσσαραν   N M 0-1-0-0-0-1
1 Sm 21,8
= ‏נעצר‎ *detained* (συνεχόμενος νεεσσαραν is a
transl. followed by a translit. of ‏נעצר‎)
Cf. WALTERS 1973, 316

νεζερ   N N 0-1-0-0-0-1
2 Kgs 11,12
= ‏נזר‎ *diadem, sign of consecration*

νεῖκος,-ους⁺   N3N 0-0-7-6-1-14
Jer 3,5; Ez 3,8(bis); Hos 10,11; Am 1,11
quarrel, strife Hos 10,11
*Jer 3,5 εἰς νεῖκος *for quarrel?* corr. εἰς νῖκος
until final victory or *to the end, for ever* for MT

‏לנצח‎ *for ever,* see also Am 1,11; 8,7; Zph 3,5; Jb
36,7; PSal 8,tit.; cpr. Lam 3,18
see νῖκος
Cf. WALTERS 1973, 34-36.182.282

νεκρός,-ά,-όν⁺   A 1-1-2-0-3-7
JgsᴮB 19,28; 2 Kgs 19,35; Is 37,36; Ez 32,18; Wis
13,18
dead JgsᴮB 19,28; *lifeless* Wis 15,5
Cf. GILBERT 1973, 78-81; →TWNT

νεκρός,-οῦ⁺   N2M 12-7-16-10-37-82
Gn 23,3.4.6(bis).8
dead, corpse Gn 23,3
θάπτω τὸν νεκρόν *to bury the dead* Gn 23,4
*Is 5,13 νεκρῶν (of) *dead* -‏מֵתֵי‎ for MT ‏מְתֵי‎ *men*;
*Is 14,19 ὡς νεκρός *as a corpse* -‏כנצל‎ (MH) *as
decay* for MT ‏כנצר‎ *as a branch*
Cf. DORIVAL 1994, 384; →NIDNTT; TWNT

νέμω⁺   V 5-1-10-2-2-20
Gn 36,24; 41,3.18; Ex 34,3; Nm 14,33
A: *to pasture, to tend* [τι] Gn 36,24; *id.* [τινα]
(metaph.) Hos 4,16
M/P: *to pasture, to tend* Nm 14,33; *to feed, to
graze* Gn 41,3; *id.* [τι] (cogn. acc.) Ez 34,18; *to
graze off* (grass) [τι] DnᴸˣˣLXX 4,15
(→ἀπο-, δια-, ἐν-, κατα-, προσ-)

νεογνός,-ή,-όν   A 0-0-0-0-2-2
3 Mc 1,20; 5,49
newborn

νεόκτιστος,-ος,-ον   A 0-0-0-0-1-1
Wis 11,18
newly created, newly made

νέος,-α,-ον⁺   A 44-20-9-13-39-125
Gn 9,24; 19,31.34.35.38
young (in age) Gn 37,2; *new, first* (of fruits) Lv
2,14; *new, extraordinary* Wis 19,11; νέος *child*
Prv 22,15; νέοι *young men* 2 Mc 5,13
ἐν μηνὶ τῶν νέων *in the month of the new corn*
(the month Abib) Ex 13,4
*Prv 7,10 νέων *of the young men* -◊ ‏נער‎ (cpr. 7,7)
for MT ‏נצרה‎ *guarded*
νεώτερος *younger, the youngest* (often opp. to
πρεσβύτερος) Gn 9,24; οἱ νεώτεροι *the little
ones* Jb 24,5
Cf. DORIVAL 1994, 501(Nm 28,26); LARCHER 1985,
1067(Wis 19,11); LE BOULLUEC 1989, 156(Ex 13,4);
PELLETIER 1975, 219; WEVERS 1993, 613; 1995, 266(Dt
16,1); →NIDNTT; TWNT

νεοσσιά,-ᾶς   N1F 1-0-0-0-0-1
Nm 24,22
nest; *Nm 24,22 νεοσσιά *dwelling* -‏קן‎ for MT ‏קין‎

Kain; see νεοσσός, νοσσιά
Cf. DORIVAL 1994, 455(Nm 24,22)

νεοσσός,-οῦ⁺   N2M 12-0-2-6-1-21
Lv 5,7.11; 12,6.8; 14,22
young bird, nestling, young of doves; see νεοττός,
νοσσιά
Cf. WALTERS 1973, 79-80; →MM

νεότης,-ητος⁺   N3F 7-4-17-21-15-64
Gn 8,21; 43,33; 48,15; Lv 22,13; Nm 22,30
youth Gn 8,21
ἐκ νεότητος *from youth (up)* Gn 48,15; ἀπὸ
νεότητος *id.* Jer 3,25
Cf. WEVERS 1993, 815; →NIDNTT

νεοττός,-οῦ   N2M 0-0-0-0-1-1
4 Mc 14,15
Att. form of νεοσσός; *young bird, nestling*
Cf. WALTERS 1973, 79-80

νεόφυτος,-ος,-ον⁺   A 0-0-1-3-1-5
Is 5,7; Ps 127(128),3; 143(144),12; Jb 14,9; Od
10,7
newly planted

νεόω   V 0-0-1-0-0-1
Jer 4,3
to renew, to plow up (fallow land) [τι]
(→ἀνα-)

νεοσσα   N 0-0-0-1-0-1
Jb 39,13
= נצה *falcon*

νεῦμα,-ατος   N3N 0-0-1-0-1-2
Is 3,16; 2 Mc 8,18
nod 2 Mc 8,18; *wink* (of eyes) Is 3,16

νευρά,-ᾶς   N1F 0-6-0-0-1-7
Jgs 16,7.8; Jgs^ 16,9
cord
Cf. CAIRD 1969=1972, 135

νευροκοπέω   V 3-2-0-0-0-5
Gn 49,6; Dt 21,4.6; Jos 11,6.9
to cut the sinews of, to hamstring, to hock (an
anim.) [τινα]; neol.?
Cf. LEE, J. 1983, 98; WEVERS 1995, 335

νεῦρον,-ου⁺   N2N 3-0-3-4-1-11
Gn 32,33(bis); 49,24; Is 48,4; Ez 37,6
sinew, nerve

νεύω⁺   V 0-0-0-2-0-2
Prv 4,25; 21,1
to incline or *move the head, eyes, lips* or *hand in
a motion indicating approval* or *agreement, to
incline to, to turn to, to assent to* [τι]
(→ἀνα-, δια-, ἐκ-, ἐν-, ἐπι-)

νεφέλη,-ης⁺   N1F 49-10-31-29-17-136

Gn 9,13.14(bis).16; Ex 13,21
cloud Ex 24,15; *id.* (of glory) Ex 16,10
ἐν στύλῳ νεφέλης *in a pillar of cloud* Ex 13,21
Cf. DORIVAL 1995, 265-266(Nm 14,10); →TWNT

-νεφέω
(→συν-)

νεφθαι   N 0-0-0-0-1-1
2 Mc 1,36
= נפתא? *naphtha*; see also νάφθα and νεφθαρ

νεφθαρ   N 0-0-0-0-1-1
2 Mc 1,36
= נפתא? *naphtha*; see also νάφθα and νεφθαι

νέφος,-ους⁺   N3N 0-0-0-25-1-26
Ps 103(104),3; Jb 7,9; 20,6; 22,14; 26,8
cloud
→NIDNTT; TWNT

νεφρός,-οῦ⁺   N2M 17-0-4-7-3-31
Ex 29,13.22; Lv 3,4(bis).10
stereotypical transl. of כליה; οἱ νεφροί *kidneys,
entrails* Ex 29,13; *kidneys, heart* (as seat of
emotions and affections) 1 Mc 2,24; *best* or
richest part Dt 32,14
→TWNT

νεχωθα   N 0-1-1-0-0-2
2 Kgs 20,13; Is 39,2
= נכת/ה (ketib) *treasure*?
Cf. SIMOTAS 1968, 120

νέωμα,-ατος   N3N 0-0-1-0-0-1
Jer 4,3
newly-ploughed field previously left untilled; neol.

νεώς, νεώ⁺   N2M 0-0-0-0-7-7
2 Mc 4,14; 6,2; 9,16; 10,3.5
Att. form of ναός; see ναός

νεωστί   D 0-0-0-0-1-1
Jdt 4,3
just recently, lately

νεωτερίζω   V 0-0-0-0-1-1
4 Mc 3,21
to bring in new things, to make revolution against
[πρός τι]

νεωτερικό ς,-ή,-όν⁺   A 0-0-0-0-1-1
3 Mc 4,8
youthful

νή⁺   X 2-0-0-0-0-2
Gn 42,15.16
by (part. indicating strong affirmation; with acc.
of thing by which one swears)
Cf. WEVERS 1993, 710

νήθω⁺   V 10-0-0-0-0-10
Ex 26,31; 35,25(bis).26; 36,9(39,2)

to spin; see νηστός
(→δια-)

νηκτός,-ή,-όν⁺   A 0-0-0-0-1-1
Wis 19,19
swimming, floating; see νήχω

νηπιοκτόνος,-ος,-ον   A 0-0-0-0-1-1
Wis 11,7
slaying children, killing children; neol.

νήπιος,-α/ος,-ον⁺   A 0-3-9-18-17-47
1 Sm 15,3; 22,19; 2 Kgs 8,12; Is 11,8; Jer 6,11
infant, child 1 Sm 15,3; *childish, simple, innocent*
Prv 1,32; *child* (metaph. of a nation in its early
stage of development) Hos 11,1; (τὰ) νήπια *the
infants* 2 Kgs 8,12; *(the) simple* Ps 18(19),8; (οἱ)
νήπιοι *infants* Jb 3,16
*Ps 63(64),8 νηπίων *of children* -פתאים or -פתים
simple youth for MT פתאם *suddenly*; *Jb 24,12
νηπίων *of children* -עללים for MT חללים *of the
wounded*; *Jb 31,10 τὰ δὲ νήπιά μου *and my
children* -ועולי for MT ועליה *upon her*
Cf. DUPONT 1967=1985, 583-591; LÉGASSE 1960, 321-348;
→NIDNTT; TWNT

νηπιότης,-ητος⁺   N3F 0-0-4-0-0-4
Ez 16,22.43.60; Hos 2,17
infancy

νῆσος,-ου⁺   N2F 2-0-28-3-8-41
Gn 10,5.32; Is 20,6; 23,2.6
island Is 23,2
νῆσοι τῶν ἐθνῶν *nations on the seacoasts,
costal peoples* Gn 10,5
*Jer 27(50),38 καὶ ἐν ταῖς νήσοις *and in the
isles* -ובאיים for MT ובאימים *and about frightful
visions, and about idols*?
Cf. HARL 1986ᵃ, 145(Gn 10,5); WEVERS 1993, 129(Gn
10,5)

νηστεία,-ας⁺   N1F 0-4-13-8-5-30
2 Sm 12,16; 1 Kgs 20(21),9.12; 2 Chr 20,3; Is
1,13
fast (in a relig. and ritual sense) 2 Chr 20,3
νηστεύω νηστείαν *to keep a fast, to fast* (semit.)
2 Sm 12,16
→NIDNTT; TWNT

νηστεύω⁺   V 2-12-6-3-5-28
Ex 38,26(8)(bis); Jgs 20,26; 1 Sm 7,6
to fast, to abstain from food (as relig. rite) 1 Sm
7,6; *to fast for* [ἐπί τινος] Sir 34,26; *to fast* (as
sign of grief) 2 Sm 1,12; *to fast* (as a preparation
before sth important) Is 58,4
Cf. LE BOULLUEC 1989, 368(Ex 38,26(8)); WEVERS 1990,
631(Ex 38,26(8)); →TWNT

νῆστις,-ιος/ιδος⁺   N3F 0-0-0-1-0-1
Dnᴸˣˣ 6,19
not eating, fasting
→NIDNTT; TWNT

νηστός,-ή,-όν   A 1-0-0-0-0-1
Ex 31,4
spun; neol.; see νήθω

νήθω
(→ἐκ-)

νήχω⁺   V 0-0-0-1-0-1
Jb 11,12
to swim; *Jb 11,12 νήχεται λόγοις *he swims in
words* corr.? ἐνέχεται λόγοις *caught in words,
entangled in words* for MT נבוב *empty-headed*; see
νηκτός

νικάω⁺   V 0-0-1-2-24-27
Hab 3,19; Ps 50(51),6; Prv 6,25; 1 Ezr 3,12; 4,5
to win (in a battle or contest) 1 Ezr 4,5; *to
overcome* [τινα] (in a battle or contest) 2 Mc
3,5; *to prevail, to be superior, to carry away the
victory* 1 Ezr 3,12; *to overcome* [τινα] (of
passions) Wis 18,22; *to conquer, to triumph* (the
passions) [τι] 4 Mc 3,17; *to win one's cause* (as
a legal term) Ps 50(51),6
Cf. DELEKAT 1964, 288-289(Hab 3,19); →NIDNTT; TWNT

νίκη,-ης⁺   N1F 0-1-0-1-8-10
1 Chr 29,11; Prv 22,9; 1 Ezr 4,59; 1 Mc 3,19;
2 Mc 10,28
victory
Cf. WALTERS 1973, 34-36.182; →NIDNTT; TWNT

νῖκος,-ους⁺   N3N 0-1-0-0-3-4
2 Sm 2,26; 1 Ezr 3,9; 2 Mc 10,38; 4 Mc 17,12
late form for νίκη; *victory* 1 Ezr 3,9; *prize of
victory* 4 Mc 17,12
εἰς νῖκος *until (final) victory is won* or *to the
end, for ever* 2 Sm 2,26
see νεῖκος
Cf. CAIRD 1969=1972, 136; DRIVER 1913, 128-129;
GRINDEL 1969, 499-513; HARL 1984ᵃ=1992ᵃ, 38; KRAFT
1972ᵈ, 153-156; SHIPP 1979, 403; WALTERS 1973, 32.34-
36.160.182.282; →LSJ Rsuppl; NIDNTT; TWNT

νίπτω⁺   V 15-5-0-5-1-26
Gn 18,4; 19,2; 24,32; 43,24.31
A: *to wash* (a part of the body) [τι] Gn 43,24;
to wash [τι] Lv 15,12; *to pour* [τι ἐπί τινα] Jb
20,23
M: *to wash* (a part of the body) [τι] Gn 18,4; *id.*
[τινι] Gn 24,32; *id.* [abs.] Ex 30,18
Cf. COUROYER 1984, 351-361; LEE, J. 1983, 36-38; SHIPP
1979, 404; →NIDNTT; TWNT

(→ἀπο-, περι-)

νίτρον,-ου N2N 0-0-1-0-0-1
Jer 2,22
Semit. loanword (Hebr. נתר); *washing powder,*
mineral used for making soap
Cf. CAIRD 1976, 78; TOV 1979, 221

νιφετός,-οῦ N2M 1-0-0-2-2-5
Dt 32,2; Dn 3,68; Od 2,2; 8,68
snowfall, snowstorm
Cf. DOGNIEZ 1992, 322

νοερός,-ά,-όν A 0-0-0-0-2-2
Wis 7,22.23
intelligent, perceptive, reflective, understanding
Cf. LARCHER 1984, 481-482

νοέω⁺ V 0-3-8-13-7-31
1 Sm 4,20; 2 Sm 12,19; 20,15; Is 32,6; 44,18
to perceive [ὅτι +ind.] 2 Sm 12,19; *id.* [+inf.]
2 Mc 14,30
to perceive by the mind, to comprehend, to
understand [τι] Prv 1,2; *id.* [+indir. question]
Wis 4,17; *id.* [abs.] Sir 11,7; *to propose* [+inf.]
2 Sm 20,15; *to intend* [+inf.] Jb 33,23
νοητῶς νόει *observe carefully* (semit.) Prv 23,1;
οὐκ ἐνόησεν πᾶσα ἡ νομή *the whole flock has*
failed Jer 10,21
*Jer 20,11 νοῆσαι *understand* -שכל◊ for MT כשל◊
they will stumble
Cf. DODD 1954, 108.118.122.198.211.220.237; KRISCHER
1984, 144-145; →NIDNTT; TWNT
(→ἀπο-, δια-, ἐν-, ἐπι-, κατα-, μετα-, προ-,
προσ-, συν-, ὑπο-)

νόημα,-ατος⁺ N3N 0-0-0-0-2-2
3 Mc 5,30; Bar 2,8
thought, design, plot (in bad sense)
Cf. KRISCHER 1984, 146-147; →NIDNTT; TWNT

νοήμων,-ων,-ον A 0-0-0-8-2-10
Prv 1,5; 10,5.19; 14,35; 17,2
intelligent, reflective, thougthful, discerning Prv
1,5; *wise* Dnᵀʰ 12,10
*Prv 17,12 ἀνδρὶ νοήμονι *(fall upon) a wise*
man באיש שכל- for MT שכול באיש *(let a bear) robbed*
of her cubs (meet) a man

νοητῶς D 0-0-0-1-0-1
Prv 23,1
carefully, attentively

νοθεύω V 0-0-0-0-1-1
Wis 14,24
to corrupt a marriage
Cf. LARCHER 1985, 830
(→ὑπο-)

νόθος,-η,-ον⁺ A 0-0-0-0-1-1
Wis 4,3
illegitimate (of plants)
Cf. LARCHER 1984, 320; →NIDNTT

νόθως D 0-0-0-0-1-1
3 Mc 3,17
insincerely, disingenuously

νομάς,-άδος N3M/F 0-3-0-4-1-8
1 Sm 28,24; 1 Kgs 5,3; 1 Chr 27,29; Jb 1,3; 20,17
οἱ νομάδες *the nomads* 2 Mc 12,11
often fem. adj.: *grazing* Jb 1,3; *for tending flocks*
(of dogs) Jb 30,1
*1 Sm 28,24 νομάς *grazing, free-range* (of a calf)
רבק◊ מו/רבק and מן◊ *(let loose) from bonds*? for MT
מַרְבֵּק רבק◊ *confined to the stall, fattening*
Cf. CAIRD 1969=1972, 136(1 Sm 28,24)

νομεύω
(→καταπρο-, προ-)

-νομέω
(→παρα-)

νομή,-ῆς⁺ N1F 1-3-20-9-2-35
Gn 47,4; 1 Chr 4,39.40.41; Is 49,9
pasture, pasture-land Gn 47,4; *id.* (metaph.) Jer
27(50),7; *pasture, food* Sir 13,19; *dwelling* Prv
24,15; *supply* Jb 20,17
ἐν χειρῶν νομαῖς *hand to hand fighting, in*
close combat 2 Mc 5,14
→LSJ suppl(2 Mc 5,14)

νομίζω⁺ V 0-0-0-0-15-15
2 Mc 4,32; 7,19; 8,35; 14,4; 4 Mc 2,14
to think 2 Mc 4,32; *to consider as, to suppose* [τι
+pred.] Wis 12,3
see νομιστέος
Cf. HELBING 1928, 68

νομικός,-ή,-όν⁺ A 0-0-0-0-1-1
4 Mc 5,4
learned in the law
Cf. BICKERMAN 1976, 276(n.9); →NIDNTT; TWNT

νόμιμος,-η/ος,-ον A 40-0-16-3-15-74
Gn 26,5; Ex 12,14.17.24; 27,21
conform to the law 2 Mc 4,11; (τὸ) νόμιμον
ordinance Ex 12,14; τὰ νόμιμα *the laws, the*
statutes Gn 26,5; *the customs* Jer 10,3
Cf. BLANK 1930, 277-278; DORIVAL 1994, 170-171; HARL
1986ᵃ, 54.211; LE BOULLUEC 1989, 43.147-148; WEVERS
1993, 400

νομίμως⁺ D 0-0-0-0-1-1
4 Mc 6,18
according to the rule(s) or *law, lawfully, in*
accordance with the law

νόμισμα,-ατος⁺   N3N 0-0-0-1-1-2
Ezr 8,36; 1 Mc 15,6
coin

νομιστέος,-α,-ον   A 0-0-0-0-4-4
LtJ 39.44.56.63
to be thought, to be supposed; see νομίζω

νομοθεσία,-ας⁺   N1F 0-0-0-0-3-3
2 Mc 6,23; 4 Mc 5,35; 17,16
code of laws, law, law-giving
→NIDNTT; TWNT

νομοθέσμως   D 0-0-0-1-0-1
Prv 31,28(26)
according to the law, legitimately

νομοθετέω⁺   V 2-0-0-6-2-10
Ex 24,12; Dt 17,10; Ps 24(25),8.12; 26(27),11
always transl. of ירה (hi.)
A: *to give laws to* [τινι]; *to instruct, to teach, to ordain* [τινα] Ps 24(25),8; *id.* [τινι] Ps 24(25),12; *id.* [τινά τι] Ps 118(119),33
P: *to be appointed by law to* [τινι] Dt 17,10
νομοθετῶν *law-giver* Ps 83(84),7
Cf. DODD 1954, 32-33; DOGNIEZ 1992, 43; HELBING 1928, 98; LE BOULLUEC 1989, 247-248; MONSENGWO PASINYA 1973, 131-135; →NIDNTT; TWNT

νομοθέτης,-ου⁺   N1M 0-0-0-1-0-1
Ps 9,21
law-giver; *Ps 9,21 νομοθέτην *law-giver*-מורה ירהם *teacher* for MT מורה יראם *fear*
Cf. DODD 1954, 32.33; →NIDNTT; TWNT

νόμος,-ου⁺   N2M 69-35-39-105-179-427
Ex 12,43.49; 13,9.10; 16,4
law, ordinance 2 Mc 7,2; *(the) law* Ex 12,49; *law (of God given by Moses)* Dt 33,4; *ruling, decision, precedent* Hag 2,11; *established decree, normal pattern* Jer 38(31),37; *that which is deserved* Jer 29(49),12; *the sum total of religious qualities offering protection against imminent danger* Is 33,6
ἐν τῷ βιβλίῳ τοῦ νόμου *in the book of the law* Dt 28,61
*Jer 23,27 τοῦ νόμου μου *my law* corr. τοῦ ὀνόματός μου for MT שמי *my name*; *Am 4,5 νόμον *the law*-תורה for MT תודה *thank(-offering)*; *Ps 129(130),5 τοῦ νόμου σου *of your law*-תורה for MT Ps 129(130),4 תּוּרא *that you may be revered*
Cf. BLANK 1930, 259-283; DODD 1954, 25-26.30-41; DOGNIEZ 1992, 51-52.112; DORIVAL 1994, 59.171.378-379; GASTON 1984, 39-55; LABERGE 1978, 100-101(Is 33,6); LE BOULLUEC 1989, 42.187; LIGHTSTONE 1984, 29-37;

MONSENGWO PASINYA 1973, 183; REDDITT 1983, 249-270; SEELIGMANN 1948, 79-80(Is 19,2); 104-108(Is 33,6); SEGAL 1984, 19-27; VAN RUITEN 1990, 19-20; WALTERS 1973, 183; WESTERHOLM 1986, 327-336; →NIDNTT; SCHLEUSNER(Dt 32,44); TWNT

νομός,-οῦ⁺   N2M 0-0-3-0-6-9
Is 19,2(bis); Jer 10,25; 1 Mc 10,30.38
district, province, nome
Cf. MONTEVECCHI 1988, 95-96; PASSONI DELL'ACQUA 1982ᵃ, 173-177

νομοφύλαξ,-ακος   N3M/F 0-0-0-0-1-1
4 Mc 15,32
keeper of the law, observer of the law

νοσερός,-ά,-όν   A 0-0-2-0-0-2
Jer 14,15; 16,4
sickly, sickening; ἐν θανάτῳ νοσερῷ *(they shall die) a death caused by disease*

νοσέω⁺   V 0-0-0-0-2-2
Wis 17,8(bis)
to be sick Wis 17,8(primo); *to suffer from* [τι] Wis 17,8(secundo)
→NIDNTT; TWNT

νόσος,-ου⁺   N2F 4-2-1-2-2-11
Ex 15,26; Dt 7,15; 28,59; 29,21; 2 Chr 21,15
disease
Cf. HORSLEY 1987, 248-249; →TWNT

νοσσεύω   V 0-0-3-2-1-6
Is 34,15; Jer 31(48),28; Ez 31,6; Dnᴸˣˣ 4,12.21(18)
to nest Is 34,15; *to build a nest* Ez 31,6; *to construct* [τι] (metaph.) Sir 1,15
Cf. WALTERS 1973, 80
(→ἐν-)

νοσσιά,-ᾶς⁺   N1F 4-0-5-5-3-17
Gn 6,14; Nm 24,21; Dt 22,6; 32,11; Is 10,14
nest Ps 83(84),4; *nest, dwelling* (metaph.) Nm 24,21; *lair, den* Na 2,13; *beehive* 4 Mc 14,19; *nest, compartment* Gn 6,14
*Prv 16,16 νοσσιαί (σοφίας/φρονήσεως) *the nest, the abode (of wisdom/prudence)* -קן for MT קנה and קנות *acquire, get*; see νεοσσιά, νεοσσός
Cf. WALTERS 1973, 80; WEVERS 1993, 84

νοσσίον,-ου⁺   N2N 0-0-0-1-0-1
Ps 83(84),4
nestling, young
Cf. SHIPP 1979, 404-405; WALTERS 1973, 80

νοσσοποιέω   V 0-0-1-0-0-1
Is 13,22
to make a den or *lair*; neol.
Cf. WALTERS 1973, 80

(→ἐν-)

νοσφίζω[+]   V 0-1-0-0-1-2
Jos 7,1; 2 Mc 4,32
M: *to steal, to rob* Jos 7,1; *to steal, to rob, to*
appropriate [τι] 2 Mc 4,32
Cf. SPICQ 1978[a], 584

νότος,-ου[+]   N2M 9-28-30-20-6-93
Ex 10,13(bis); 14,21; 26,20.35
south 1 Sm 30,1; *south wind* Jb 38,24; *country in*
the south Ps 125(126),4
ἄνεμος νότος *south wind* Ex 10,13
Cf. BOGAERT 1981, 79-85; DORIVAL 1994, 155.561(Nm
34,15); LE BOULLUEC 1989, 138.277; MORENZ 1964, 255-
256; WEVERS 1990, 152.220.429.434; →NIDNTT

Νουα   N 0-1-0-0-0-1
Jgs[B] 20,43
= נוחה *rest*
Cf. TOV 1973, 89

νουθεσία,-ας[+]   N1F 0-0-0-0-1-1
Wis 16,6
admonition, warning
Cf. LARCHER 1985, 898; SPICQ 1978[a], 585-588; WALTERS
1973, 136; →NIDNTT

νουθετέω[+]   V 0-1-0-7-4-12
1 Sm 3,13; Jb 4,3; 23,15; 30,1; 34,16
to admonish, to warn, to instruct [τινα] 1 Sm
3,13; *id.* [abs.] Jb 34,16
Cf. LARCHER 1985, 702; SPICQ 1978[a], 585-588; →NIDNTT

νουθέτημα,-ατος[+]   N3N 0-0-0-1-0-1
Jb 5,17
admonition, warning

νουθέτησις,-εως[+]   N3F 0-0-0-1-1-2
Prv 2,2; Jdt 8,27
admonition, warning, instruction

νουμηνία,-ας[+]   N1F 5-7-8-3-11-34
Ex 40,2.17; Nm 10,10; 28,11; 29,6
new moon, first day of the month Ex 40,2
*Ez 23,34 καὶ τὰς νουμηνίας αὐτῆς *and her*
new moon feasts -חֳרָשֶׁהּ◊ *month* for MT חֲרָשֶׂהּ ◊*and her*
potsherds?
Cf. HORSLEY 1983, 76; WALTERS 1973, 113-114

νοῦς, νοῦ[+]   N2M 1-1-4-5-18-29
Ex 7,23; Jos 14,7; Is 10,7.12; 40,13
mind Jos 14,7; *mind, attention* Ex 7,23; *mind,*
thought, opinion Is 40,13; *mind, soul, heart* 4 Mc
16,13
Cf. DODD 1954, 125.143.149.150.162.236; KRISCHER 1984,
142-144; LE BOULLUEC 1989, 121(Ex 7,23); WALTERS
1973, 130; →NIDNTT; TWNT

νυκτερεύω

(→δια-)

νυκτερινός,-ή,-όν   A 0-0-0-6-0-6
Ps 90(91),5; Jb 4,13; 20,8; 33,15; 35,10
at night, nocturnal

νυκτερίς,-ίδος   N3F 2-0-1-0-1-4
Lv 11,19; Dt 14,18; Is 2,20; LtJ 21
bat

νυκτικόραξ,-ακος   N3M 2-1-0-1-0-4
Lv 11,17; Dt 14,17; 1 Sm 26,20; Ps 101(102),7
long-eared owl or *horned owl*

νύκτωρ   D 0-0-0-0-4-4
2 Mc 12,6; 13,15; 3 Mc 1,2; Sir 38,27
by night, at night

νυμφαγωγός,-ός,-όν   A 3-1-0-0-0-4
Gn 21,22.32; 26,26; Jgs[A] 14,20
leading the bride; ὁ νυμφαγωγός *trusted friend,*
best man
Cf. CAIRD 1969=1972, 136-137; HARL 1986[a], 191

νύμφευσις,-εως   N3F 0-0-0-1-0-1
Ct 3,11
wedding; neol.

νύμφη,-ης[+]   N1F 7-3-14-13-10-47
Gn 11,31; 38,11.13.16.24
young wife Jl 1,8; *bride* Jer 7,34; *daughter-in-law*
Gn 11,31
*2 Sm 17,3 ἡ νύμφη *the bride* -הַכַּלָּה for MT הַכֹּל *the*
whole, all of it?
Cf. HARL 1986[a], 70; SHIPP 1979, 186.406; →NIDNTT; TWNT

νυμφίος,-ου[+]   N2M 0-2-7-2-3-14
Jgs[B] 15,6; 19,5; Is 61,10; 62,5; Jer 7,34
bridegroom Ps 18(19),6; *son-in-law* Jgs[B] 15,6
Cf. HORSLEY 1987, 223.226-227; →NIDNTT; TWNT

νυμφών,-ῶνος[+]   N3M 0-0-0-0-4-4
Tob 6,14.17
bridal-chamber, bride's chamber, marriage
chamber; neol.

νῦν[+]   D 92-246-107-83-173-701
Gn 2,23; 3,22; 4,11; 11,6; 12,19
now, at the present time Hos 2,9; *just now, but*
now [+aor.] Hos 5,3; *now, as things now stand*
Gn 29,32; *present* (as adj.) Gn 30,20; τὸ νῦν *the*
present (often with prep.) Ex 9,27
νῦν οὖν *so now* Gn 27,8
*Gn 18,12 ἕως τοῦ νῦν *until now* -עַד הֵנָּה or עֶרְנָה-
for MT עֶדְנָה *pleasure*; *1 Sm 28,2 νῦν *now* -עתה for
MT אתה *you*, see also 2 Sm 7,20; 1 Chr 28,9;
Dn[LXX] 8,26; *Is 18,2 νῦν *now* -בזו for MT בזאו
they divide, see also 18,7; *Ez 16,57 νῦν *now* -עתה
for MT עת *time*, see also 27,34
Cf. JEREMIAS 1939, 119-120; LAURENTIN 1964, 168-195;

WEVERS 1993, 440; →NIDNTT; TWNT

νυνί+   D 3-3-0-7-5-18
Ex 32,34; Nm 11,6; Dt 10,22; Jos 5,14; 14,12
emphatic form of νῦν; *now* [+pres.] Ex 32,34;
id. [+aor.] Jb 30,1

νύξ, νυκτός+   N3F 63-66-30-78-57-294
Gn 1,5.14.16.18; 7,4
night Gn 1,5; *id.* (point of time) Jdt 11,3; *id.*
(period) Ex 24,18; *id.* (metaph.) Mi 3,6; νυκτός
by night Ex 12,30
*Jb 18,15 ἐν νυκτὶ αὐτοῦ *in his night* -בלילו for
MT מבלי לו *nothing (remains) in it*
→NIDNTT; TWNT

νύσσω+   V 0-0-0-0-4-4
3 Mc 5,14; Sir 22,19(bis); PSal 16,4
to prick [τι] Sir 22,19; *id.* [τινα] PSal 16,4; *to
nudge* [τινα] 3 Mc 5,14
(→κατα-, ὑπο-)

νύσταγμα,-ατος   N3N 0-0-0-1-0-1
Jb 33,15
slumber; neol.
Cf. CAIRD 1969=1972, 137

νυσταγμός,-οῦ   N2M 0-0-1-2-1-4
Jer 23,31; Ps 131(132),4; Dn^LXX 4,33b(30); Sir
31,2
drowsiness, dozing Ps 131(132),4
*Jer 23,31 νυστάζοντας νυσταγμὸν ἑαυτῶν
slumbering their sleep, dozing on -◊נום for MT ◊נאם
they utter oracles?

νυστάζω+   V 0-1-4-5-2-12
2 Sm 4,6; Is 5,27; 56,10; Jer 23,31; Na 3,18
to be half asleep, to doze, to slumber Is 5,27
*Jer 23,31 νυστάζοντας see νυσταγμός

(→ἐπι-)

-νύω
(→κατα-)

νωθροκάρδιος,-ος,-ον   A 0-0-0-1-0-1
Prv 12,8
slow of mind, stupid, unintelligent; neol.

νωθρός,-ά,-όν+   A 0-0-0-1-2-3
Prv 22,29; Sir 4,29; 11,12
slothful, lazy, sluggish
Cf. SPICQ 1978ᵃ, 589-591; →TWNT

νωθρότης,-ητος   N3F 0-0-0-0-1-1
3 Mc 4,5
slugishness

νωκηδ   N M 0-1-0-0-0-1
2 Kgs 3,4
= נקד *owner of sheep*

νωτίζω
(→κατα-)

νῶτον/νῶτος,-ου+   N2N/M 5-13-17-8-5-48
Gn 9,23; 49,8; Ex 37,12.13(38,14.15); Nm 34,11
back, backside (of men) Gn 9,23; *back* (convex
side of a shield) Jb 15,26; *rim* (of a wheel) 1 Kgs
7,19; *slope* (of sea) Nm 34,11; *id.* (of land) Jos
15,8
ἐπὶ νώτου *behind* Jos 15,10; κατὰ νώτου *behind*
Ez 40,18
Cf. CAIRD 1969=1972, 137; LE BOULLUEC 1989, 360;
WEVERS 1990, 615; →LSJ RSuppl

νωτοφόρος,-ος,-ον   A 0-2-0-0-0-2
2 Chr 2,17; 34,13
carrying on the back, carrying; (οἱ) νωτοφόροι
burden-bearers, porters

ξαίνω
(→ἀπο-, δια-, κατα-)

ξανθίζω   V 3-0-0-0-0-3
Lv 13,30.31.32
to be yellow (esp. of the hair)

ξανθός,-ή,-όν   A 1-0-0-0-0-1
Lv 13,36
yellow

ξενίζω+   V 0-0-0-1-3-4
Est 3,13e; 2 Mc 9,6; 3 Mc 7,3; Sir 29,25
to entertain or *receive as a guest, to be, act* or
speak as a stranger [abs.] Sir 29,25; ξενίζων
strange, foreign Est 3,13e; *extraordinary,
astonishing* 3 Mc 7,3
Cf. SPICQ 1978ª, 596; →MM; TWNT

ξένιος,-α,-ον   A 0-2-1-1-4-8
2 Sm 8,2.6; Hos 10,6; Ezr 1,6; 1 Mc 10,36
belonging to friendship and hospitality; (τὰ)
ξένια *friendly gifts, presents* Ezr 1,6; *tribute*
2 Sm 8,2; *provisions* 1 Mc 10,36
Ζεὺς Ξένιος *Zeus who protects the rights of
hospitality* 2 Mc 6,2
Cf. DANIEL 1966, 211; SPICQ 1978ª, 596-597

ξενισμός,-οῦ+   N2M 0-0-0-1-0-1
Prv 15,17
entertainment

ξενιτεία,-ας   N1F 0-0-0-0-1-1
Wis 18,3
living abroad; neol.
Cf. LARCHER 1985, 989

ξενολογέω   V 0-0-0-0-3-3
1 Mc 4,35; 11,38; 15,3
to enlist mercenaries 1 Mc 4,35
τῶν ξένων δυνάμεων, ὧν ἐξενολόγησεν *the
foreign forces which he had raised* 1 Mc 11,38;
ξενολογέω πλῆθος δυνάμεων *to raise a
multitude of foreign soldiers* 1 Mc 15,3

ξένος,-η,-ον+   A 0-3-1-5-11-20
1 Sm 9,13; 2 Sm 12,4; 15,19; Is 18,2; Ps 68(69),9
foreign, alien, stranger (pers.) Ru 2,10;
extraordinary, strange, surprising (things) Wis
16,2; ὁ ξένος *guest* 1 Sm 9,13
ἐπὶ ξένης *abroad, in a strange land* 2 Mc 5,9
*Is 18,2 ξένον *strange* corr.? ξεστόν for MT מרט
smooth
Cf. SPICQ 1978ª, 592; →NIDNTT; TWNT

ξενοτροφέω   V 0-0-0-0-1-1
2 Mc 10,14
to maintain mercenary troops

ξενόω

(→ἀπο-, ἐπι-)

ξεστός,-ή,-όν   A 0-0-0-0-1-1
1 Mc 13,27
hewn (of stone)

ξηραίνω+   V 2-3-36-15-1-57
Gn 8,7.14; Jos 9,12; 1 Kgs 13,4; 17,7
A: *to dry* [τι] Jb 12,15; *to dry up* [τι] Ps
73(74),15
P: *to be dried up* Gn 8,7; *id.* (metaph.) Ps
21(22),16; *to be dried, to become dry* (of things)
Jos 9,12; *to be withered, to wither* Is 40,7; *to be
withered, to be incapable of motion* 1 Kgs 13,4;
to be paralysed Jl 1,11
*DnLXX 7,8 ἐξηράνθησαν *they dried up* corr.
ἐξήρθησαν (pap967) for MT אתעקרו *they were
rooted out*, cpr. Zech 10,2; *Is 44,11 ἐξηράνθησαν *they dried up* -יבשׁ◊ יבשׁ for MT יבשׁ
◊ בושׁ *they are ashamed*, see also Jl 1,11; *Is 50,2
ξηρανθήσονται *(their fish) dry up* -תיבש? for MT
תבאשׁ *(their fish) stinks*
Cf. JEANSONNE 1988, 93-94; WEVERS 1993, 104; →NIDNTT
(→ἀνα-, ἀπο-, κατα-)

ξηρασία,-ας   N1F 0-6-3-1-0-10
Jgs 6,37.39.40
drought Jgs 6,37; *dryness* Na 1,10

ξηρός,-ά,-όν+   A 11-4-15-4-8-42
Gn 1,9(bis).10; 7,22; Ex 4,9
dry Gn 1,10; *bare* Jb 24,19; ἡ ξηρά (γῆ) *dry land*
Gn 1,9; τὸ ξηρόν *dry land* (as opposed to the
sea) Ex 4,9
ἄγρωστις ξηρά *dry grass, hay* Is 9,17; χόρτος
ξηρός *id.* Is 37,27; ποιέω τὴν θάλασσαν ξηράν
to make the sea dry Ex 14,21; μαστοὶ ξηροί *dry
breasts, breasts that do not suckle* Hos 9,14
Cf. HARL 1986ª, 90(Gn 1,9); →NIDNTT

ξιφηφόρος,-ος,-ον   A 0-0-0-0-1-1
4 Mc 16,20
bearing a sword, sword in hand

ξίφος,-ους+   N3N 0-10-2-1-3-16
Jos 10,28.30.32.33.35
sword Jos 11,11
ἐν στόματι ξίφους *with the edge of the sword*
Jos 10,28
*Jb 3,14 ξίφεσιν *swords* -חרב◊ for MT חָרְבָּה *ruins*

ξυλάριον,-ου   N2N 0-1-0-0-0-1
1 Kgs 17,12
dim. of ξύλον; *small piece of wood, twig, stick*

ξύλινος,-η,-ον+   A 8-0-3-4-15-30
Lv 11,32; 15,12; 26,30; 27,30; Nm 31,20
of wood, wooden Lv 11,32; *of a tree* Lv 27,30;

growing on trees Sir 22,16; τὰ ξύλινα trees
Dt 28,42
θεοὶ ξύλινοι wooden images of gods, wooden
idols LtJ 3
Cf. CAIRD 1969=1972, 137-138(Sir 22,16)

ξυλοκόπος,-ου　　　　　　　　　N2M 1-4-0-0-0-5
Dt 29,10; Jos 9,21.23.27(bis)
wood-feller
Cf. KINDSTRAND 1983, 86-109

ξύλον,-ου⁺　　　　　　N2N 81-90-72-44-22-309
Gn 1,11.12.29; 2,9(bis)
wood, firewood Gn 22,3; timber Gn 6,14; wooden
image, idol Dt 4,28; handle Dt 19,5(tertio); shaft
(of a spear) 2 Sm 21,19; wooden collar, yoke
Lam 5,13; stocks (as instrument of punishment)
Jb 33,11; tree Gn 2,9; τὰ ξύλα wooden objects,
esp. vessels Ex 7,19
ξύλον κάρπιμον fruit-tree Gn 1,11; ξύλον
καρποφόρον id. Ps 148,9; ξύλον βρώσιμον id.
Lv 19,23; ξύλον κέδρινον cedar wood Lv 14,4;
ξύλον ἀρκεύθινον juniper wood 1 Kgs 6,31;
ξύλον τῆς ζωῆς tree of life Gn 2,9; τέκτων τῶν
ξύλων carpenter 2 Kgs 12,12; κρεμάννυμί τινα
ἐπὶ ξύλου to hang on a tree, to hang on a
gallows Gn 40,19; κατεργάζομαι τὰ ξύλα to
work up timber Ex 35,33; σπουδαῖα ξύλα choice
trees? Ez 41,25
*1 Chr 16,32 καὶ ξύλον and a tree -רעי? for MT
יעלז exult; *2 Chr 3,10 ξύλων wood - עץ? for MT
עצעצים images?; *Prv 12,4 ἐν ξύλῳ in wood - עץ?
for MT עצם bone
Cf. DANIÉLOU 1966, 53-75; DOGNIEZ 1992, 248; GARBINI
1982, 170-172(Ez 41,25); HARL 1986ᵃ, 91.131;
1986ᶜ=1992ᵃ, 67;0 HUSSON 1983ᵃ, 180-182; LARCHER 1985,
825; PARADISE 1986, 193-195; THORNTON 1972, 130-131;
WEVERS 1990, 588; →MM; NIDNTT; TWNT

ξυλοφορία,-ας　　　　　　　　　N1F 0-0-0-1-0-1
Neh 10,35
wood-bearing for offering

Cf. PELLETIER 1975, 230; WALTERS 1973, 325

ξυλοφόρος,-ου　　　　　　　　　N2M 0-0-0-1-0-1
Neh 13,31
wood-bearer, wood offerer
Cf. PELLETIER 1975, 230; WALTERS 1973, 325

ξυλόω　　　　　　　　　　　　　V 0-1-2-0-0-3
2 Chr 3,5; Jer 22,14; Ez 41,16
to make of wood or to panel with wood [τι]
2 Chr 3,5; ἐξυλωμένος panelled Jer 22,14
τὰ πλησίον ἐξυλωμένα the adjoinings were
made of wood Ez 41,16

ξυράω⁺　　　　　　　　　　V 14-8-7-0-1-30
Gn 41,14; Lv 13,33(bis).34; 14,8
A: to shave [τινα] Gn 41,14; id. [τι] Dt 21,12;
to shave the hair Mi 1,16
M: to shave (of oneself) [τι] Nm 6,9; to shave
oneself Jgsᴮ 16,22
P: to shave (of oneself) [τι] Lv 14,8; to be
shaven Jgs 16,17
ἐξυρημένοι πώγονας (men) with shaven beards
Jer 48(41),5; μετὰ τὸ ξυρήσασθαι αὐτὸν τὴν
εὐχήν after he has shaved off the hair of the
votive offering i.e. a ram Nm 6,19

ξύρησις,-εως　　　　　　　　　N3F 0-0-1-0-0-1
Is 22,12
shaving (in mourning); neol.
→MM

ξυρόν,-οῦ　　　　　　　　　　N2N 2-1-3-1-0-7
Nm 6,5; 8,7; Jgsᴬ 16,17; Is 7,20; Jer 43(36),23
razor Nm 6,5
ξυρὸν τοῦ γραμματέως penknife Jer 43(36),23

ξυστός,-ή,-όν　　　　　　　　　A 0-1-1-0-3-5
1 Chr 22,2; Am 5,11; 1 Ezr 6,8.24; Sir 22,17
polished

ξύω　　　　　　　　　　　　　V 0-0-0-2-0-2
Jb 2,8; 7,5
to scrape away
(→ἀπο-, κατα-, περι-)

ὁ, ἡ, τό⁺   19275-23273-14636-15242-16013-88439
Gn 1,1(tris).2(bis)
the art. as demonstrative pron.; ὁ μέν ... ὁ δέ ...
the one ... the other ... 4 Mc 13,11
the art. as the definite art.; *the* Gn 2,10; *his, her,
its* (expressing possession) Ex 18,24(secundo); ὁ
θεός *God* Gn 1,1
the add. of the art. making a subst.: ὁ ἀσεβής
the ungodly [art. +adj.] Prv 29,7; τὰ δέοντα *the
necessaries* [art. +ptc.] Ex 21,10; τὸ εὔξασθαι
the praying, the vowing [art. +inf.] Prv 20,25;
τοῖς σὺν αὐτῷ *to his followers* [art. +prep.]
2 Mc 8,12; ἕως τοῦ νῦν *untill now, hitherto* [art.
+adv.] Dt 12,9; ἐν τοῖς Αμαν *in the premises of
Aman* Est 7,9
the add. of the art. making a clause: ὁ
ἐπικαλύπτων *he that covers* [art. +ptc.] Prv
28,13; ὁ τὸ πολύ *he that had gathered much* Ex
16,18; τοῦ τεκεῖν *to bring forth* 1 Sm 4,19
ὁ τοῦ Ραγουηλ *the son of Raguel* Nm 10,20
Cf. BLASS 1990, §§ 249-276; DORIVAL 1994, 53-54

ὀβελίσκος,-ου⁺   N2M 0-0-0-1-1-2
Jb 41,22; 4 Mc 11,19
spit, skewer

ὀβολός,-οῦ   N2M 4-1-1-1-0-7
Ex 30,13; Lv 27,25; Nm 3,47; 18,16; 1 Sm 2,36
obole (a fifth part of a drachma), *the smallest
coin, small weight* or *coin*
Cf. DORIVAL 1994, 217

ὀγδοήκοντα⁺   MC 7-18-2-5-5-37
Gn 5,28; 16,16; 35,28; Ex 7,7(bis)
eighty

ὀγδοηκοστός,-ή,-όν   MO 0-0-0-0-1-1
2 Mc 1,9
eightieth

ὄγδοος,-η,-ον⁺   MO 16-17-3-3-6-45
Gn 17,14; 21,4; Ex 22,29; Lv 9,1; 12,3
eighth Gn 17,14
*Jer 43(36),9 τῷ ὀγδόῳ *the eighth* -השמינית for MT
החמשית *the fifth*

ὅδε⁺   R 29-118-267-10-26-450
Gn 25,24; 38,27; 43,21; 45,9; 50,18
this (demonstrative pron.), *here*

ὁδεύω⁺   V 0-0-0-0-1-1
Tob^BA 6,6
to travel, to journey
(-ἀφ-, δι-, διεξ-, ἐξ-, ἐφ-, μεθ-, παρ-, περι-,
συν-)

ὁδηγέω⁺   V 5-3-1-31-4-44
Ex 13,17; 15,13; 32,34; Nm 24,8; Dt 1,33

to guide, to lead [τινα] Ex 13,17; *id.* [τινα]
(metaph.) Eccl 2,3
*Dt 1,33 ὁδηγῶν *guiding* -◊נחה for MT ◊חנה *to
camp, to pitch tent*; *Is 63,14 ὡδήγησεν αὐτούς
(the spirit) guided them* -◊נחה תנחנו for MT
תניחנו ◊נוח (*the spirit) gave them rest*; *Ps 89(90),16 καὶ
ὁδήγησον *and guide* -◊דרך הדרך for MT הדרך והדרך
and your glorious power
Cf. DOGNIEZ 1992, 119(Dt 1,33); DORIVAL 1994, 446;
LARCHER 1984, 589; WEVERS 1995, 20(Dt 1,33); →TWNT
(→καθ-)

ὁδηγός,-οῦ⁺   N2M 0-0-0-1-4-5
Ezr 8,1; 1 Mc 4,2; 2 Mc 5,15; Wis 7,15; 18,3
leader, guide Ezr 8,1; *guide* (metaph.) Wis 18,3
Cf. LARCHER 1984, 465(Wis 7,15); →TWNT

-οδιάζω
(→εἰσ-, ἐξ-, ἐφ-)

ὁδοιπορία,-ας⁺   N1F 0-0-0-0-4-4
1 Mc 6,41; Wis 13,18; 18,3; 19,5
walking, marching 1 Mc 6,41; *journey, route* Wis
13,18
Cf. LARCHER 1985, 785.988

ὁδοιπόρος,-ου   N1M 1-3-0-1-2-7
Gn 37,25; Jgs 19,17; 2 Sm 12,4; Prv 6,11
traveller

ὁδοποιέω⁺   V 0-0-1-4-0-5
Is 62,10; Ps 67(68),5; 77(78),50; 79(80),10; Jb
30,12
to prepare a way, to build a road Ps 67(68),5; *id.*
[τι] Jb 30,12

ὁδός,-οῦ⁺   N2F 113-201-231-226-120-891
Gn 3,24; 6,12; 16,7; 18,5.19
way, road Gn 48,7; *way, path, course* (of ships)
Jb 9,26; *way* (metaph.) Is 59,8(primo); *way, path,
journey* Gn 24,42; *way of life, conduct* Gn 6,12;
way set out for sb, directive Dt 8,6; αἱ ὁδοί *way
of life, conduct* (often pl.) Zech 3,7; *towards*
[τινος] (semit.) 1 Kgs 8,44(secundo); *distance*
(of three days) [τινος] (semit.) Gn 30,36
ποιέω τὴν ὁδόν *to accomplish a journey, to
make one's way* Jgs 17,8
*1 Sm 14,5(bis) ὁδός *road* corr.? ὁδούς -שׁן *tooth,
crag* (of a rock), see also Prv 25,19; *Jer 52,24
τὴν ὁδόν *the way* corr.? τὸν οὐδόν *the treshold*,
cpr. Jer 35,4(mss); *Jer 12,4 ὁδοὺς ἡμῶν *our
ways, our behaviour* -ארחותנו for MT אחריתנו *our
future*; *Ez 9,7 τὰς ὁδούς *the ways* -חצרות? for
MT החצרות *the courts*; *Hos 2,8(secundo) τὰς
ὁδούς *the roads* -◊דרך for MT גדרה *a wall*; *Jb
28,13 ὁδὸν αὐτῆς *its way* -דרכה for MT ערכה *its*

price; *Prv 3,26 ὁδῶν σου *your ways* -מסלתיך for MT כסליך *your loins*; *Prv 22,19 τὴν ὁδόν σου *your way* -ארחתיך for MT אתה אף *even you*; *Prv 28,23 ἀνθρώπου ὁδούς *a man's ways* -ארחת אדם for MT אחרי אדם *a man afterwards*; *Ezr 8,27 εἰς τὴν ὁδὸν χαμινιμ *to the road of Chamanim* -לדרך כמנים for MT לאדרכנים *for darics* (Persian gold coins)

Cf. DORIVAL 1994, 62.185; GEHMAN 1951=1972, 100; HARL 1986ᵃ, 233; KATZ 1939, col.8(1 Sm 14,5); LARCHER 1984, 365; WEVERS 1993, 247.491; 1995, 147(Dt 8,6); →TWNT

ὁδούς,-όντος⁺   N3M 12-3-9-25-9-58
Gn 49,12; Ex 21,24(bis).27(tris)
tooth Gn 49,12
ὁδόντα ἀντὶ ὁδόντος *a tooth for a tooth* Ex 21,24; γομφιασμὸν ὁδόντων *grinding of teeth?* Am 4,6, cpr. Ez 18,2
*Ct 7,10 χείλεσίν μου καὶ ὁδοῦσιν *to my lips and teeth* -ושנים (שׁן◊) שפתי for MT ישׁנים (ישׁן◊) *lips of sleepers*

Cf. CAIRD 1968ᵇ=1972, 122(Am 4,6); 1969=1972, 138(1 Sm 13,21); KATZ 1939, col.8(1 Sm 14,5)

ὀδυνάω⁺   V 0-0-6-2-3-11
Is 21,10; 40,29; 53,4; Hag 2,14; Zech 9,5
A: *to cause pain, to grieve* [τινα] Wis 14,24
P: *to feel pain, to suffer pain* Is 53,4; *to feel pain, to feel sorry* (mentally) TobᴮᴬA 9,4
*Is 40,29 ὀδυνωμένοις *suffering* -אנן◊ for MT און *strength*; *Prv 29,21 ὀδυνηθήσεται *he shall feel sorry* -אנן◊? for MT מנון *rebel?*
→TWNT
(→κατ-, συν-)

ὀδύνη,-ης⁺   N1F 5-1-19-30-13-68
Gn 35,18; 44,31; Ex 3,7; Dt 26,14; 28,60
pain (physical) Is 30,26; *(mental) pain, grief* Gn 44,31
*Mi 1,11 ὀδύνης *grief* -רמעות? *tears* for MT עמרתו *his standing place*; *Jb 20,23 ὀδύνας *pains* -בלהת בלהה◊ *sudden terror* for MT ב/לחומו?, cpr. Jerᴹᵀ 11,19 בלחמו? εἰς τὸν ἄρτον; *Lam 1,14 ἐν χερσί μου ὀδύνας *(the Lord gave me) pains in my hands* (double transl. of בירו) read the first time as -בְּיָרִי *in my hands* and the second time as -בּרוי◊ רוה? (*pain*) for MT ירד◊ בְּיָרוֹ *in his hands?*
→TWNT

ὀδυνηρός,-ά,-όν   A 0-1-2-1-0-4
1 Kgs 2,8; Jer 14,17; 37(30),17; Lam 5,17
painful, woeful

ὀδυρμός,-οῦ⁺   N2M 0-0-1-0-1-2

Jer 38(31),15; 2 Mc 11,6
lamentation, mourning
→TWNT

ὀδύρω⁺   V 0-0-1-0-0-1
Jer 38(31),18
M: *to lament*
→TWNT
(→προσ-)

ὄζος,-ου⁺   N2M 0-0-0-0-1-1
Wis 13,13
knot (on a branch) (from which a leaf or a branch may sprout)
Cf. LARCHER 1985, 779

ὄζω⁺   V 1-0-0-0-0-1
Ex 8,10
to stink
Cf. DANIEL 1966, 335-339; →MM
(→ἐπ-, προσ-)

ὅθεν⁺   D 7-1-4-6-25-43
Gn 10,14; 13,3; 24,5; Ex 5,11; 30,36
whence, from where Gn 13,3; *from which* Jer 7,8; *from whom* Gn 10,14; *for which reason, whereupon* 2 Mc 10,13; *therefore, hence* Wis 12,23

ὀθόνιον,-ου⁺   N2N 0-1-2-0-0-3
JgsᴮB 14,13; Hos 2,7.11
linen cloth
Cf. BARTINA 1965, 27-38; SPICQ 1978ᵃ, 601-605; →MM

οἰακίζω   V 0-0-0-1-0-1
Jb 37,10
to manage, to govern

οἴαξ,-ακος   N3M 0-0-0-0-1-1
4 Mc 7,3
helm, rudder (metaph.)

οἴγω
(→ἀν-, δι-, διαν-, προσ-)

οἶδα⁺ (εἰδέναι, εἰδεῖν)   V 61-56-29-82-55-283
Gn 2,9; 3,5; 18,19; 19,33.35
pft. of εἴδω (for which ὁράω *to see*, is used); *to know* [abs.] Gn 48,19; *id.* [τι] Gn 2,9; *to know, to know about* [τινα] Ex 1,8; *to know that* [ὅτι +ind.] Gn 18,19; *id.* [ὡς +ind.] 2 Chr 2,7; *id.* [εἰ +ind.] Gn 43,7; *to know* [+indir. question] Gn 43,22; *to know how (to do), to be able to* [+inf.] Gn 25,27
*Nm 35,23 οὐκ εἰδώς *unaware* corr.? οὐκ ἰδών for MT ראות בלא ראה◊ *without seeing (him)*, see also Gn 39,3; Is 33,19; Jb 28,24; Sir 20,6; *Jb 27,12 οἴδατε *you know* corr.? εἴδετε for MT חזיתם חזה◊ *you have seen*, see also Is 26,11

see ὁράω (derived from the same root as οἶδα, sc. Ϝιδ)

Cf. DEPUYDT 1985, 36-37.42; TALMON 1961, 340-342; WALTERS 1973, 67.197-204; WEVERS 1990, 280; 1993, 256.649; →TWNT

(→προ-, συν-)

οἰκεῖος,-α,-ον⁺   A 8-4-4-1-2-19
Lv 18,6.12.13.17; 21,2
near kin, belonging to one and the same family Lv 18,12; belonging to [τινος] 2 Mc 15,12
οἱ οἰκεῖοι τοῦ σπέρματός σου the relations of your seed, your blood relatives Is 58,7; πρὸς πάντα οἰκεῖα σαρκὸς αὐτοῦ to any of his near kindred Lv 18,6

Cf. DORIVAL 1994, 75; HARLÉ 1988, 160-161; SPICQ 1978ᵇ, 216; →NIDNTT; TWNT

οἰκειότης,-ητος   N3F 1-0-0-0-0-1
Lv 20,19
kinship, intimacy

οἰκειόω   V 0-0-0-0-1-1
4 Mc 5,26
P: to be suitable for, to be convenient for [τινι]
(→ἐν-)

οἰκέτης,-ου⁺   N1M 25-3-1-8-19-56
Gn 9,25; 27,37; 44,16.33; 50,18
household slave, servant

Cf. AMUSIN 1986, 136-143.145-146; DANIEL 1966, 103.104; DOGNIEZ 1992, 355(Dt 34,5); DORIVAL 1994, 53; HARL 1986ᵃ, 68.143; HARLÉ 1988, 46.202; KRAFT 1972ᶜ, 37-38; LLEWELYN 1994, 170(n.30).173.189(n.92); SPICQ 1978ᵇ, 215-216; WEVERS 1990, 46; 1993, 342.437

οἰκετικός,-ή,-όν   A 0-0-0-0-1-1
3 Mc 2,28
suited or related to slaves

οἰκέτις,-ιδος   N3F 2-0-0-1-0-3
Ex 21,7; Lv 19,20; Prv 30,23
female household slave

Cf. AMUSIN 1986, 120-121.145-146; LE BOULLUEC 1989, 216(Ex 21,7); LEE, J. 1983, 33; VERMES 1975, 70-71; WEVERS 1990, 326(Ex 21,7)

οἰκέω⁺   V 19-23-36-47-25-150
Gn 4,16.20; 16,3; 19,30; 20,1
to inhabit [τι] Gn 24,13; to live, to dwell Gn 4,16; to be situated Dnᴸˣˣᴸˣˣ 4,37b; ἡ οἰκουμένη the (inhabited) world 2 Sm 22,16
*Is 21,12 οἴκει live, dwell -ישב for MT שבו ◊ שובו return

Cf. HELBING 1928, 73-74; →NIDNTT; TWNT

(→δι-, ἐν-, κατ-, μετ-, παρ-, συν-)

οἴκημα,-ατος⁺   N3N 0-0-1-0-2-3

Ez 16,24; Tobᴮᴬᴮᴬ 2,4; Wis 13,15
room, chamber Tobᴮᴬᴮᴬ 2,4
οἴκημα πορνικόν brothel, house of fornication Ez 16,24

οἴκησις,-εως⁺   N3F 0-2-0-0-3-5
2 Chr 17,12; 27,4; Jdt 7,14; Tobˢ 13,14; 1 Mc 13,48
house, dwelling 2 Chr 17,12; dwelling-place, habitation Jdt 7,14

οἰκητήριον,-ου⁺   N2N 0-0-0-0-1-1
2 Mc 11,2
dwelling-place, habitation

οἰκητός,-ή,-όν   A 1-0-0-0-2-3
Lv 25,29; 2 Mc 9,17; 3 Mc 4,3
inhabited 2 Mc 9,17; habitable Lv 25,29

οἰκήτωρ,-ορος⁺   N3M 0-0-0-1-1-2
Prv 2,21; Wis 12,3
inhabitant

οἰκία,-ας⁺   N1F 111-33-51-34-39-268
Gn 17,12.13; 19,3.4; 24,2
house, building Gn 17,12; house, nest (of birds) Ps 83(84),4; house (metaph.) Jb 30,23; howdah (seat on an elephant) 2 Mc 13,15
household, family 2 Sm 16,2; house, family from which one is descended 1 Chr 12,29
*Jb 20,15 ἐξ οἰκίας αὐτοῦ out of his house -מבתו or corr.? ἐκ κοιλίας αὐτοῦ out of his belly for MT מבטנו out of his belly; *Prv 14,9 οἰκίαι δέ but the houses -ובית? for MT ובין but among (the righteous)

Cf. GOLDSTEIN 1983, 465-466(2 Mc 13,15); HUSSON 1983ᵃ, 191-206; →NIDNTT; TWNT

οἰκίδιον,-ου   N2N 0-0-0-0-2-2
Tobˢ 2,4; 2 Mc 8,33
small house, outbuilding

οἰκίζω   V 0-0-0-1-2-3
Jb 22,8; Sir 10,3; 38,32
A: to settle, to cause to live [τινα] Jb 22,8
P: to be made habitable Sir 10,3
(→ἀπ-, ἐν-, κατ-, μετ-, συν-)

οἰκογενής,-ής,-ές   A 8-0-1-1-1-11
Gn 14,14; 15,2.3; 17,12.13
born in the household; ὁ οἰκογενής member of household, slave, servant Jer 2,14; prince? 1 Ezr 3,1

Cf. HARL 1986ᵃ, 68; RUNDGREN 1957, 145-152

οἰκοδομέω⁺   V 37-195-64-71-93-460
Gn 2,22; 4,17; 8,20; 10,11; 11,4
to build, to construct [τι] Gn 8,20; to build (a city) [τι] Gn 4,17; to form, to fashion [τι] Gn

2,22; *to build sth with sth* [τί τι] Dt 27,6; *to build upon* [τι] 1 Kgs 16,24; *to build sb, to restore sb* [τινα] (metaph.) Jer 40(33),7

*Is 49,17 οἰκοδομηθήσῃ *you shall be rebuilt* -בנה◊ (with 1QIsᵃ: בוניך) for MT בניך *your sons, your children*, cpr. οἰκοδομή and Ez 16,61

Cf. BICKERMAN 1980, 56(n.63); FLUSSER 1962, 140-142; LEE, J. 1983, 51; WEVERS 1993, 33; ZIPOR 1993, 361-362; →NIDNTT; TWNT

(→ἀν-, κατ-, περι-, προσαν-, συν-)

οἰκοδομή,-ῆς⁺   N1F 0-2-3-0-11-16
1 Chr 26,27; 29,1; Ez 16,61; 17,17; 40,2
building, construction 1 Chr 26,27; *house* 1 Ezr 5,70

*Ez 16,61 εἰς οἰκοδομήν *as a building* -לבנות בנה◊ *to build* for MT לבנות בת◊ *as daughters*, cpr. οἰκοδομέω and Is 49,17

→NIDNTT; TWNT

οἰκοδόμος,-ου⁺   N2M 0-5-2-1-2-10
2 Kgs 12,12; 22,6; 1 Chr 14,1; 22,15; 2 Chr 34,11
builder

→TWNT

οἰκονομέω⁺   V 0-0-0-1-2-3
Ps 111(112),5; 2 Mc 3,14; 3 Mc 3,2
to conduct, to administer (one's affairs) [τι] Ps 111(112),5; *to make* (an inventory) [τι] 2 Mc 3,14

Cf. SPICQ 1978ᵃ, 606-613; →NIDNTT

οἰκονομία,-ας⁺   N1F 0-0-2-0-0-2
Is 22,19.21
stewardship

Cf. REUMANN 1978, 482-579; 1979, 563-603; 1980, 368-430; 1981, 591-617; 1982, 115-140; SPICQ 1978ᵃ, 612-613; →NIDNTT; TWNT

οἰκονόμος,-ου⁺   N2M 0-7-3-2-3-15
1 Kgs 4,6; 16,9; 18,3; 2 Kgs 18,18.37
steward 1 Kgs 4,6; *treasurer* 1 Ezr 4,47

Cf. HORSLEY 1987, 160-161; REUMANN 1958, 339-349; SAMUEL 1966, 444-450; SPICQ 1978ᵃ, 606-611; →NIDNTT; TWNT

οἰκόπεδον,-ου   N2N 0-0-0-2-1-3
Ps 101(102),7; 108(109),10; Sir 49,13
building-site Ps 101(102),7; *building* Sir 49,13

οἶκος,-ου⁺   N2M 189-963-473-268-169-2062
Gn 7,1; 9,21.27; 12,1.15
house, any dwelling-place Gn 9,21; *big house, palace* (of the king) 2 Sm 11,8; *temple* (of Jerusalem) Is 56,7
house, family Gn 7,1; *descendants, nation* Jer 38(31),33; *id.* (for Hebr. בני *sons of*; replacing

semit.) 1 Chr 2,10; *id.* (for Hebr. עם) Lv 9,7; *property, possessions* Gn 41,40
ἐν οἴκῳ *at home* 1 Sm 19,9; οἶκος φυλακῆς *prison* Is 42,7

*Jgsᴬ 11,26 ἐν τῷ οἴκῳ *in the house* -בבית corr.? ἐν τῷ οἰκῆσαι for MT בשבת *when living*; *Lv 10,14 καὶ ὁ οἶκός σου *and your house* -ביתך וביתך for MT ובנתיך◊בת *and your daughters*, see also Jer 28(51),33; Ez 27,6; *2 Sm 3,8 εἰς τὸν οἶκον *to the house* -בית for MT ביד *in the hand*; *1 Kgs 21(20),30 τὸν οἶκον *the house* -הבית for MT העיר *the city*; *2 Kgs 12,10 ἐν τῷ οἴκῳ ἀνδρός *in the house of a man* -בבית איש for MT בבוא איש *when a man comes*; *2 Kgs 23,8 τὸν οἶκον *the house* -בית for MT במות *the high places*, see also 23,13; Mi 1,5; *Is 24,12 οἶκοι *houses* -בתי for MT יכת *is smitten*; *Jer 20,2 οἴκου ἀποτεταγμένου *the upper house* -בית מני? for MT בנימן *Benjamin*; *Mi 5,1 Βηθλεεμ οἶκος (τοῦ Εφραθα) *Bethlehem, house (of Ephrata)* double rendition of בית? for MT (אפרתה); *Jb 24,12 οἴκων ἰδίων *of their own houses* -בתיהם for MT מתים *dying*; *Prv 7,17 τὸν δὲ οἶκόν μου *my house* -אהלי *my tent* for MT אהלים *aloes*; *Ezr 7,15 εἰς οἶκον κυρίου *to the house of the Lord* -יה? for MT להיכל◊להיבלה *to bring*

Cf. BARR 1961, 283; DORIVAL 1994, 128.159.384.575; HUSSON 1983ᵃ, 211-215; STROBEL 1965, 91-100; WEVERS 1993, 257.357.453; WODKE 1977, 61.63-67; →NIDNTT; TWNT

οἰκτίρημα,-ατος   N3N 0-0-1-0-0-1
Jer 38(31),3
mercy, compassion

οἰκτιρμός,-οῦ⁺   N2M 0-4-4-22-6-36
2 Sm 24,14; 1 Kgs 8,50; 1 Chr 21,13; 2 Chr 30,9; Hos 2,21
mercy, compassion, pity (from God to humans) Sir 5,6; *id.* (from humans to humans) Zech 7,9; οἱ οἰκτιρμοί *compassionate feelings, mercies* (mostly pl.) 2 Sm 24,14

→NIDNTT; TWNT

οἰκτίρμων,-ων,-ον⁺   A 2-2-3-10-1-18
Ex 34,6; Dt 4,31; Jgsᴮ 5,30; 2 Chr 30,9; Is 63,15
merciful, compassionate (of God) Ex 34,6; *id.* (of humans) Lam 4,10; *id.* [τινι] (of humans) Ps 108(109),12

*Jgsᴮ 5,30 οἰκτίρμων οἰκτιρήσει *he will be merciful* (semit.) -רחם ירחם for MT רחמתים רחם *one or two girls*, cpr. φιλιάζω

Cf. WEVERS 1995, 84(Dt 4,31); →NIDNTT; TWNT

οἰκτίρω⁺   V 2-3-5-18-9-37
Ex 33,19(bis); Jgsᴮ 5,30; 1 Kgs 8,50; 2 Kgs 13,23

of humans: *to have pity upon, to have compassion on* [abs.] Ps 36(37),21; *id.* [τινα] Ps 102(103),13; *id.* [τι] 4 Mc 5,12
of God: *to have pity upon, to have compassion on* [abs.] Ps 76(77),10; *id.* [τινα] Is 30,18; *id.* [τι] Ps 101(102),14
οἰκτιρήσει εἰς κεφαλὴν ἀνδρός *he will be gracious to every man* JgsB 5,30, see also οἰκτίρμων
→NIDNTT; TWNT
(→κατ-)

οἴκτιστος,-η,-ον   A 0-0-0-0-1-1
2 Mc 9,28
most lamentable

οἶκτος,-ου   N2M 0-0-2-1-3-6
Jer 9,18.19; Est 3,13f; 3 Mc 1,4; 5,49
feeling of sorrow or *sympathy towards sb, pity* 3 Mc 6,22; *cry of lamentation* Jer 9,18

οἰκτρός,-ή,-όν   A 0-0-1-0-3-4
Jer 6,26; 3 Mc 5,24; 4 Mc 15,18; Wis 18,10
pitiable, lamentable (of pers.) 4 Mc 15,18; *id.* (of things) Wis 18,10
τὴν οἰκτροτάτην θεωρίαν *the most piteous spectacle* 3 Mc 5,24

οἴμμοι   I 0-2-13-2-1-18
JgsA 11,35; 1 Kgs 17,20; Jer 4,31; 15,10; 22,18
expressing a sense of horror: *alas, woe* 1 Kgs 17,20
οἴμμοι ἐγώ *woe is me* Jer 4,31
Cf. KRAFT 1972b, 161.169; WALTERS 1973, 83-84.229-230

οἰμωγή,-ῆς   N1F 0-0-0-0-1-1
3 Mc 6,32
wailing

οἰμώζω   V 0-0-0-0-1-1
4 Mc 12,14
to wail aloud, to lament

οἰνοποτέω   V 0-0-0-1-0-1
Prv 31,4
to drink wine; neol.

οἰνοπότης,-ου+   N1M 0-0-0-1-0-1
Prv 23,20
wine-drinker, tippler
→NIDNTT

οἶνος,-ου+   N2M 40-34-69-60-50-253
Gn 9,21.24; 14,18; 19,32.33
wine Gn 9,21; *id.* (for libation) Hos 9,4
ἐν οἴνων διατριβαῖς *in banquets of wine* Prv 12,11a; τὸν καρπὸν παντὸς ξύλου οἴνου καὶ ἐλαίου *the fruit of each tree, of wine and oil* Neh 10,38

*1 Sm 25,11 καὶ τὸν οἶνόν μου *and my wine* for MT מימי ואת and my water*; *Hos 3,2 οἴνου *of wine* -שׁכר◊? for MT שׁערים *barley*; *Ob 16 οἶνον *wine* -חמר for MT תמיר *continually*
Cf. WEVERS 1993, 430; →NIDNTT; TWNT

οἰνοφλυγέω   V 1-0-0-0-0-1
Dt 21,20
to be drunken; neol.
Cf. DOGNIEZ 1992, 66.247

οἰνοχοέω   V 1-0-0-1-0-2
Gn 40,13; DnLXX 5,2
to pour out wine for drinking

οἰνοχόη,-ης   N1F 0-0-0-0-1-1
Eccl 2,8
female cupbearer

οἰνοχόος,-ου   N2M 0-2-0-3-0-5
1 Kgs 10,5; 2 Chr 9,4; Neh 1,11; TobBA 1,22; Eccl 2,8
cupbearer
Cf. DRIVER 1954, 238-239

οἰνόω
(→κατ-)

οἴομαι+   V 4-0-1-9-8-22
Gn 37,7; 40,16; 41,1.17; Is 57,8
to think [+inf.] Gn 37,7; *to mean, to intend* [+inf. fut.] Jb 34,12; *to think* [ὅτι +ind.] Is 57,8; *id.* [abs.] DnLXX 2,11

οἷος, οἵα, οἷον+   R 2-1-0-6-10-19
Gn 41,19; 44,15; 1 Kgs 18,13; Jb 33,27; Est 2,1
such Gn 44,15; *of what kind* 1 Kgs 18,13; οἷος ... τοιοῦτος ... *such ... that ...* (correl. adj.) Gn 41,19

οἰστράω
(→παρ-)

οἰστρηλασία,-ας   N1F 0-0-0-0-1-1
4 Mc 2,4
mad passion, impulse; neol.

οἶστρος,-ου   N2M 0-0-0-0-2-2
4 Mc 2,3; 3,17
anything that drives someone mad, vehement desire, insane passion

οιφι   N N 5-4-1-1-0-11
Lv 5,11; 6,13; Nm 5,15; 15,4; 28,5
Eg. loanword (Hebr. איפה); *ephah, corn-measure*
Cf. CAIRD 1976, 79; SIMOTAS 1968, 122; TOV 1979, 232

οἴχομαι   V 3-3-11-4-10-31
Gn 12,4; 25,34; 31,19; 2 Chr 8,17.18
to go, to depart Gn 12,4; *to be removed, to be destroyed* Hos 10,14; *to be gone* Jer 30,1
*Jb 30,15 ᾤχετο *is gone* -תרדף *is pursued* for MT

תִּרְדֹּף *pursues*
Cf. WEVERS 1993, 164
(→ἀπ-)

οἰωνίζομαι   V 5-4-0-0-0-9
Gn 30,27; 44,5.15; Lv 19,26; Dt 18,10
to divine from omens, to augure Dt 18,10; *to
conjecture, to learn by divination* Gn 30,27
οἰωνισμῷ οἰωνιεῖται *he practises divination*
(semit.) Gn 44,15
Cf. DOGNIEZ 1992, 50; HARL 1986ᵃ, 231(Gn 30,27).287;
HARLÉ 1988, 171; WEVERS 1993, 746

οἰώνισμα,-ατος   N3N 0-1-2-0-0-3
1 Sm 15,23; Jer 14,14; 34(27),9
omen from the flight or cries of birds

οἰωνισμός,-οῦ   N2M 3-0-0-0-1-4
Gn 44,5.15; Nm 23,23; Sir 34,5
omen from the flight or cries of birds; neol.
Cf. WEVERS 1993, 742

οἰωνόβρωτος,-ος,-ον   A 0-0-0-0-2-2
2 Mc 9,15; 3 Mc 6,34
*for the birds to eat, food for the birds, to be eaten
by birds*; neol.?

οἰωνός,-οῦ   N2M 1-0-0-0-0-1
Nm 24,1
omen, token, presage (from the flight or cries of
birds)

ὀκέλλω
(→ἐξ-)

ὀκλάζω   V 0-3-0-0-0-3
1 Sm 4,19; 1 Kgs 8,54; 19,18
to crouch down, to sink down 1 Sm 4,19
ὀκλακὼς ἐπὶ τὰ γόνατα αὐτοῦ *having knelt
down upon his knees* 1 Kgs 8,54; ὀκλάζω γονύ
to bend the knee, to kneel down 1 Kgs 19,18

ὀκνέω⁺   V 1-2-0-0-7-10
Nm 22,16; Jgs 18,9; Jdt 12,13; Tob 12,6
to hesitate, to delay [+inf.] Nm 22,16
οὐδὲ πρὸς τὸν θάνατον ὤκνησεν *and he did
not shrink back from death* 4 Mc 14,4
Cf. HELBING 1928, 35; SPICQ 1978ᵃ, 614-615

ὀκνηρία,-ας   N1F 0-0-0-1-0-1
Eccl 10,18
sluggishness, laziness; neol.

ὀκνηρός,-ά,-όν⁺   A 0-0-0-12-3-15
Prv 6,6.9; 11,16; 18,8; 20,4
idle, lazy, sluggish, slothful Prv 6,6
σῖτα ὀκνηρά *the bread of idleness* Prv 31,27
Cf. SPICQ 1978ᵃ, 614-615; →TWNT

ὀκτακισχίλιοι,-αι,-α   MC 3-1-0-0-5-9
Nm 2,24; 3,28; 4,48; 1 Chr 29,7; 1 Mc 5,20

eight thousand

ὀκτακισχίλιος,-α,-ον   MC 0-0-0-0-1-1
1 Mc 15,13
eight thousand (sg. with a coll. noun)

ὀκτακόσιοι,-αι,-α   MC 3-6-0-3-4-16
Gn 5,17.19.26; 2 Sm 23,8; 24,9
eight hundred

ὀκτάπηχυς,-υς,-υ   A 0-1-0-0-0-1
1 Kgs 7,47(10)
eight cubits long; neol.?

ὀκτώ⁺   MC 12-28-11-18-14-83
Gn 5,28; 14,14; 17,12; 22,23; 46,22
eight Gn 5,28
δεκὰ καὶ ὀκτώ *eighteen* Gn 14,14
Cf. LIEBERMAN 1942, 23; →NIDNTT

ὀκτωκαίδεκα   MC 0-9-0-1-0-10
JgsᴬΛ 10,8; 20,44; Jgs 20,25; 2 Sm 8,13
eighteen

ὀκτωκαιδέκατος,-η,-ον   MO 0-10-1-3-3-17
1 Kgs 15,1; 2 Kgs 1,18a; 3,1; 22,3; 23,23
eighteenth

ὄλβος,-ου   N2M 0-0-0-0-1-1
Sir 30,15
worldly happiness, wealth, prosperity

ὀλεθρεύω⁺   V 3-6-5-0-8-22
Ex 12,23; 22,19; Nm 4,18; Jos 3,10(bis)
to destroy, to kill [abs.] Jer 2,30; *id.* [τινα] Nm
4,18; *to destroy* [τι] Jgsᴮ 6,25; ὁ ὀλεθρεύων *the
destroyer* Ex 12,23
ὀλεθρεύων ὀλεθρεύσει *he shall utterly destroy*
(semit.) Jos 3,10
neol.
Cf. DORIVAL 1994, 223-224; LEE, J. 1983, 42; →TWNT
(→ἐξ-)

ὀλεθρία,-ας   N1F 0-0-0-1-2-3
Est 8,12t; 3 Mc 4,2; 5,5
destruction, ruin; neol.
Cf. WALTERS 1973, 42

ὀλέθριος,-ος,-ον⁺   A 0-1-0-0-1-2
1 Kgs 21(20),42; Wis 18,15
doomed, destined for destruction

ὄλεθρος,-ου⁺   N2M 0-1-9-3-11-24
1 Kgs 13,34; Jer 28(51),55; 31(48),3.8.32
ruin, destruction 1 Kgs 13,34
*Jer 28(51),55 ὄλεθρον *destruction* - שֹׁאָה for MT
שְׁאוֹן *roar, rumbling noise*, see also Jer 32(25),31
→MM; NIDNTT; TWNT

ὀλεθροφόρος,-ος,-ον   A 0-0-0-0-1-1
4 Mc 8,19
destruction-bringing, fatal; neol.

ὀλέκω   V 0-0-0-3-0-3
Jb 10,16; 17,1; 32,18
A: *to destroy, to kill* [τινα] Jb 10,16
P: *to be destroyed, to die* Jb 17,1

ὀλιγόβιος,-ος,-ον   A 0-0-0-2-0-2
Jb 11,2; 14,1
short-lived

ὀλιγοποιέω   V 0-0-0-0-1-1
Sir 48,2
*to diminish the number of, to make lesser or
fewer, to decimate, to reduce (by destruction)*
[τινα]; neol.

ὀλίγος,-η,-ον⁺   A 7-8-10-25-51-101
Gn 29,20; Lv 25,52; Nm 11,32; 13,18; 26,56
little, small Prv 15,29a; *few* Gn 29,20; *little* 1 Kgs
17,10; *short* Wis 2,1; ὀλίγον *a little* Eccl 5,11; *a
little time* Lv 25,52; ὀλίγα *a little* 2 Kgs 10,18;
τὸ ὀλίγον *at least* Nm 11,32
κατ᾽ ὀλίγον *little by little* Wis 12,2; παρ᾽
ὀλίγον *almost, at the point of* Prv 5,14; μετ᾽
ὀλίγον *after a little while* Wis 15,8; πρὸ ὀλίγου
a short time before Wis 14,20

→NIDNTT; TWNT

ὀλιγοστός,-ή,-όν   A 4-2-8-2-3-19
Gn 34,30; Ex 12,4; Lv 26,22; Dt 7,7; 2 Kgs 14,26
sup. of ὀλίγος; *few in number* Ex 12,4; *small or
very small* Dn^LXX 11,23
ὀλιγοστὸς ἐν ἀριθμῷ *few in number* Gn 34,30;
ὀλιγοστὸς ἀριθμῷ *few in number* 1 Chr 16,19
Cf. DOGNIEZ 1992, 161-162(Dt 7,7)

ὀλιγότης,-ητος   N3F 0-0-0-1-0-1
Ps 101(102),24
fewness

ὀλιγοχρόνιος,-ος,-ον⁺   A 0-0-0-0-1-1
Wis 9,5
short-lived, of a few years

ὀλιγοψυχέω⁺   V 1-4-2-1-4-12
Nm 21,4; Jgs^A 8,4; 10,16; Jgs 16,16
to be disheartened, to be discouraged
Cf. DORIVAL 1994, 399; LEE, J. 1983, 76

ὀλιγοψυχία,-ας   N1F 1-0-0-1-1-3
Ex 6,9; Ps 54(55),9; PSal 16,11
discouragement, loss of heart Ex 6,9
*Ps 54(55),9 ἀπὸ ὀλιγοψυχίας *from discour-
agement* -מרוח צערה for MT מרוח סערה *from the wind
rushing*
Cf. LE BOULLUEC 1989, 113; LEE, J. 1983, 49.76; WEVERS
1990, 77

ὀλιγόψυχος,-ος,-ον⁺   A 0-0-4-2-0-6
Is 25,5; 35,4; 54,6; 57,15; Prv 14,29

discouraged, faint-hearted
→NIDNTT

ὀλιγόω   V 0-2-4-5-1-12
Jgs^B 10,16; 2 Kgs 4,3; Jl 1,10.12; Na 1,4
A: *to make few* 2 Kgs 4,3
P: *to become few* Ps 106(107),39; *to diminish, to
pass away* Jgs^B 10,16; *to be diminished, to be
shortened* (of years) Prv 10,27; *to become scarce*
(of oil) Jl 1,10; *to seem small* Neh 9,32
*Hab 3,12 ὀλιγώσεις *you will reduce* -צער◊תצער
for MT תצער *you will tread down*

ὀλιγωρέω⁺   V 0-0-0-1-1-2
Prv 3,11; PSal 3,4
to have little esteem for, to despise [τινος] Prv
3,11; *id.* [abs.] PSal 3,4
Cf. HELBING 1928, 113; →MM; NIDNTT

ὀλισθάνω   V 0-0-0-1-8-9
Prv 14,19; Sir 3,24; 9,9; 14,1; 19,16
to slip and fall (metaph.) Prv 14,19; *to cause to
fall* [τι] (metaph.) Sir 3,24
Cf. HELBING 1928, 79

ὀλίσθημα,-ατος   N3N 0-0-2-3-1-6
Jer 23,12; 45(38),22; Ps 34(35),6; 55(56),14;
114(116),8
slip, fall

ὀλίσθρημα,-ατος   N3N 0-0-0-3-0-3
Dn^Th 11,21.32.34
syn. of ὀλίσθημα

ὀλκεῖον,-ου   N2N 0-0-0-0-1-1
Jdt 15,11
basin, large bowl; neol.?

ὀλκή,-ῆς   N1F 14-7-0-0-5-26
Gn 24,22(bis); Nm 7,13.19.25
weight
Cf. LEE, J. 1983, 62-63

ὄλλυμι⁺   V 0-0-9-14-0-23
Jer 10,20; 30(49),4; 30,19(49,3); 31(48),1.15
A: *to destroy* [τινα] (of pains) Jb 18,11; *to ruin*
[τινα] (of an inquisition) Prv 13,2; *to kill* [τινα]
Jb 20,10
M: *to perish, to cease to exist* Prv 11,7; *to die* Jb
4,11
(→ἀπ-, δι-, ἐξ-, ἐξαπ-, προσαπ-, συναπ-)

ὀλοκαρπόω   V 0-0-0-0-2-2
4 Mc 18,11; Sir 45,14
P: *to be offered as a whole burnt offering*; neol.
Cf. DANIEL 1966, 172.257

ὀλοκάρπωμα,-ατος   N3N 3-0-0-0-1-4
Lv 16,24(bis); Nm 15,3; Wis 3,6
syn. of ὀλοκάρπωσις; *whole burnt offering,*

sacrifice; neol.

Cf. CAIRD 1976, 81; DANIEL 1966, 156.162.170.172. 240-258; HARLÉ 1988, 154; LEE, J. 1983, 52

ὁλοκάρπωσις,-εως   N3F 8-0-2-0-0-10
Gn 8,20; 22,2.3.6.7

syn. of ὁλοκάρπωμα; *whole burnt offering, sacrifice* Gn 8,20; *presentation of such an offering* Gn 22,3

Cf. DANIEL 1966, 240-248; HARL 1986ᵃ, 62.139; LEE, J. 1983, 52

ὁλόκαυτος,-ος,-ον   A 1-0-0-0-0-1
Lv 6,16
burnt completely; neol.

Cf. DANIEL 1966, 250-258; HARLÉ 1988, 106

ὁλοκαύτωμα,-ατος⁺   N3N 107-47-28-11-11-204
Ex 10,25; 18,12; 20,24; 24,5; 29,18

syn. of ὁλοκαύτωσις; *holocaust, (whole) burnt offering* Ex 10,25
*2 Chr 9,4 καὶ τὰ ὁλοκαυτώματα *and the burnt offerings* -ועלות for MT ועליהו *and his ascent?* neol.

Cf. CAIRD 1976, 81; DANIEL 1966, 155-164.240-258; DOGNIEZ 1992, 65; DORIVAL 1994, 106.129; HARLÉ 1988, 36

ὁλοκαύτωσις,-εως   N3F 25-48-0-9-5-87
Ex 29,25; Lv 4,34(bis); 6,2(bis)

syn. of ὁλοκαύτωμα; *holocaust, (whole) burnt offering*

Cf. DANIEL 1966, 155-163.240-258; DORIVAL 1994, 106.129; HARLÉ 1988, 36

ὁλόκληρος,-ος,-ον⁺   A 3-1-2-0-3-9
Lv 23,15; Dt 16,9; 27,6; Jos 9,2b(8,31); Ez 15,5
whole, intact, without defect (of anim.) Zech 11,16; *whole, unhewn* (of stones) Dt 27,6; *full* (of period of time) Lv 23,15; *perfect* Wis 15,3

Cf. DOGNIEZ 1992, 217.280; SPICQ 1978ᵃ, 616-617; WEVERS 1995, 270.417

ὁλολυγμός,-οῦ   N2M 0-0-2-0-0-2
Is 15,8; Zph 1,10
loud cry, wailing
Cf. CAIRD 1976, 80

ὁλολύζω⁺   V 0-0-21-0-0-21
Is 10,10; 13,6; 14,31; 15,2.3
to cry with a loud voice, to howl Is 13,6
*Is 10,10 ὁλολύξατε *howl* -הילילו ◊ ילל for MT האליל *the idol(s)*
Cf. CAIRD 1976, 80; →TWNT

ὁλοπόρφυρος,-ος,-ον   A 2-0-0-0-0-2
Nm 4,7.13
completely purple

Cf. DORIVAL 1994, 51.220

ὁλορριζεί   D 0-0-0-1-0-1
Est 3,13f
with the whole root, utterly; neol.

ὁλόρριζος,-ος,-ον   A 0-0-0-2-0-2
Jb 4,7; Prv 15,6
with the whole root (metaph.)

ὅλος,-η,-ον⁺   A 53-67-30-65-57-272
Gn 25,25; 31,35; 41,19.30.43
whole, entire, complete Nm 4,16; *whole, safe and sound* Ex 29,18; *whole* (place) Gn 31,35; *id.* (time) Ex 14,21; *all* 2 Mc 7,5; *every* 1 Sm 14,23; *entirely, fully, all of* [+adj.] Ex 28,31; *id.* [+ptc.] Jb 21,23; *altogether* [+verb] Ex 19,18; τοῖς ὅλοις *altogether* 2 Mc 6,3
δι᾽ ὅλου *continually* 1 Kgs 10,8; δι᾽ ὅλου *entirely* Ez 38,8; πᾶσαν στολὴν ἐνδεδύκει, ὅλος διὰ χρυσοῦ καὶ λίθων πολυτελῶν *he had put on all his apparel, covered all over with gold and precious stones* Est 5,1c; τοὺς κατεσθίοντας τὸν Ισραηλ ὅλῳ τῷ στόματι *those who devour Israel with open mouth* Is 9,11
Cf. SHIPP 1979, 414; WEVERS 1990, 303; →TWNT

ὁλοσφύρητος,-ος,-ον   A 0-0-0-0-1-1
Sir 50,9
of solid beaten metal; neol.

ὁλοσχερής,-ής,-ές   A 0-0-0-0-1-1
3 Mc 5,31
entire, complete, full

ὁλοσχερῶς   D 0-0-1-0-1-2
Ez 22,30; 1 Ezr 6,27
completely 1 Ezr 6,27; *perfectly* Ez 22,30

ὁλοφύρομαι   V 0-0-0-0-3-3
3 Mc 4,2; 4 Mc 16,5.12
to bewail, to wail over [τι] 3 Mc 4,2; *id.* [τινα] 4 Mc 16,12; *id.* [ἐπί τινι] 4 Mc 16,5
Cf. HELBING 1928, 73

ὄλυνθος,-ου⁺   N2M 0-0-0-1-0-1
Ct 2,13
edible fruit of the wild fig, summer or *late fig*

ὄλυρα,-ας   N1F 1-0-1-0-0-2
Ex 9,32; Ez 4,9
type of wheat (used for making bread)

ὀλυρίτης,-ου   N1M 0-1-0-0-0-1
1 Kgs 19,6
bread or *cake made of* ὄλυρα; neol.

ὁμαλίζω⁺   V 0-0-2-0-2-4
Is 28,25; 45,2; Sir 21,10; PSal 8,17
to make even, to level [τι] PSal 8,17; *to level* (mountains) [τι] Is 45,2

Cf. SCHNEBEL 1925, 105

ὁμαλισμός,-οῦ   N2M 0-0-1-0-2-3
Mi 7,12; PSal 11,4; Bar 5,7
levelling, being levelled (of mountains) PSal 11,4
φάραγγας πληροῦσθαι εἰς ὁμαλισμὸν τῆς γῆς
valleys to be filled up to become flat ground Bar
5,7
*Mi 7,12 εἰς ὁμαλισμόν *(they shall be) levelled,*
razed to the ground -◊שׁר for MT למני אשׁור *from*
Assur

ὀμβρέω
(→ἀν-, ἐξ-)

ὄμβρημα,-ατος   N3N 0-0-0-1-0-1
Ps 77(78),44
rainwater; neol.

ὄμβρος,-ου⁺   N2M 1-0-0-2-4-7
Dt 32,2; Dnᴸˣˣ 3,64(64); Dnᵀʰ 3,64(23); Od 2,2;
8,64
rainstorm
Cf. DOGNIEZ 1992, 322; →TWNT

ὁμείρομαι⁺   V 0-0-0-1-0-1
Jb 3,21
to desire, to long for [τινος]; neol.
Cf. SPICQ 1957, 194(n.1); →MM

ὅμηρος,-ου   N2M 0-0-1-0-7-8
Is 18,2; 1 Mc 1,10; 8,7; 9,53; 10,6
always pl. neutr.: ὅμηρα *hostage, group of*
hostages 1 Mc 9,53; *id.?* (Hebr. ציר *messenger?*)
Is 18,2; *(individual) hostage* 1 Mc 1,10

ὁμιλέω⁺   V 0-0-0-5-8-13
Prv 5,19; 15,12; 23,31(bis); Dnᴸˣˣ 1,19
to keep company with [τινι] Prv 5,19; *id.* [μετά
τινος] Prv 15,12; *to be conversant in, to attend*
to [ἕν τινι] Sir 11,20
to speak to, to converse with [τινι] Dnᴸˣˣ 1,19
to converse with, to have sexual intercourse with
[τινι] Jdt 12,12
Cf. ENGEL 1985, 110.160; HELBING 1928, 247; SHIPP 1979,
415; →MM

ὁμιλία,-ας⁺   N1F 1-0-0-1-2-4
Ex 21,10; Prv 7,21; 3 Mc 5,18; Wis 8,18
conversation Prv 7,21; *conference, intimacy* Wis
8,18; *conjugal rights* Ex 21,10
Cf. LARCHER 1984, 548-549; LE BOULLUEC 1989, 217(Ex
21,10); WEVERS 1990, 327; →MM

ὁμίχλη,-ης⁺   N1F 0-0-4-3-3-10
Is 29,18; Jl 2,2; Am 4,13; Zph 1,15; Ps 147,5(16)
mist, fog Ps 147,5(16); *gloom, darkness* Is 29,18

ὄμμα,-ατος⁺   N3N 0-0-0-5-5-10
Prv 6,4; 7,2; 9,18a; 10,26; 23,5

eye Prv 6,4
ἐὰν ἐπιστήσῃς τὸ σὸν ὄμμα πρὸς αὐτόν *if you*
should fix your eye upon him Prv 23,5
Cf. SHIPP 1979, 415

ὄμνυμι⁺/ύω⁺   V 64-48-34-17-25-188
Gn 21,23.24.31; 22,16; 24,7
to swear Gn 21,24; *to swear to sb* [τινι] Gn
24,7; *to swear sth to sb, to confirm sth for sb with*
an oath [τινί τινα] Gn 21,23; *id.* [τινι κατά
τινος] Ex 32,13; *to swear to give* [τί τινι] Gn
50,24; *to swear by* [τινι] Dt 32,40; *id.* [κατά
τινος] Gn 22,16; *id.* [ἕν τινι] Jgs 21,7; *to swear*
to sb that [τινι +inf. fut.] Jdt 8,9; *to swear that*
[+inf. pft.] Ex 22,7; *to swear falsely* [τι] Prv
30,9; οἱ ὀμνύμενοι *them by whom they swear*
Wis 14,31
οὐκ ὤμοσεν ἐπὶ δόλῳ τῷ πλησίον αὐτοῦ *nor*
did he swear deceitfully to his neighbour Ps
23(24),4
*Ez 6,9 ὀμώμοκα *I have sworn* -שבע◊ נשבעתי for MT
שבר◊ נשברתי *I was broken, I was crushed*
Cf. DORIVAL 1994, 514; HARL 1986ᵃ, 55; HELBING 1928,
71-72; LUST 1994, 155-164(Dt 32,40); WEVERS 1993, 310;
→NIDNTT; TWNT
(→ἐξ-)

ὁμοεθνής,-ής,-ές   A 0-0-0-0-7-7
2 Mc 4,2; 5,6; 12,5; 15,30.31
of the same people or *race*; οἱ ὁμοεθνεῖς
fellow-countrymen

ὁμοζηλία,-ας   N1F 0-0-0-0-1-1
4 Mc 13,25
common zeal for [τινος]; neol.

ὁμοθυμαδόν⁺   D 3-0-2-15-16-36
Ex 19,8; Nm 24,24; 27,21; Jer 5,5; 26(46),21
with one accord, with one mind Jb 2,11; *id.* (in
relig. sense) Jdt 4,12; *together* Jb 6,2
Cf. DORIVAL 1994, 142.455; HATCH 1889, 63-64; LE
BOULLUEC 1989, 200; SPICQ 1978ᵃ, 618-620; →TWNT

ὁμοιοπαθής,-ής,-ές⁺   A 0-0-0-0-2-2
4 Mc 12,13; Wis 7,3
with the same nature, kindred Wis 7,3; οἱ
ὁμοιοπαθεῖς *men of like feelings* 4 Mc 12,13
Cf. LARCHER 1984, 448-449(Wis 7,3)

ὅμοιος,-α,-ον⁺   A 17-16-9-23-26-91
Gn 2,20; Ex 15,11(bis); Lv 11,14.15
like, equal to, similar to [τινι] Gn 2,20; *id.*
[τινος] Jb 35,8; *id.* [εἴς τι] 4 Mc 14,14; *equal*
[abs.] Sir 44,19; τὸ ὅμοιον *the like* Sir 7,12
*Is 23,2 ὅμοιοι γεγόνασιν *they became alike*
-◊דמה for MT רמו◊דמה or רום or רמם *be silent,* see

also Is 62,7

→NIDNTT; TWNT

ὁμοιότης,-ητος⁺ N3F 2-0-0-0-2-4
Gn 1,11.12; 4 Mc 15,4; Wis 14,19
likeness, resemblance
Cf. WEVERS 1993, 6; →TWNT

ὁμοιόω⁺ V 3-0-13-14-10-40
Gn 34,15.22.23; Is 1,9; 40,18
A: *to make like (to)* [τινά τινι] Ct 1,9; *id.* [τί
τινι] Wis 13,14; *to liken, to compare* [τινά
τινι] Hos 4,5
P: *to be made like (to), to become like (to)*
[τινι] Gn 34,15; *to be like (to)* [τινι] Ps
143(144),4; *to be like* [abs.] Hos 4,6
*Ps 82(83),2 ὁμοιωθήσεται *(who) shall be
compared (to you)* -דמה◊ for MT ¹דמי רמי◊ or דום
or דמם *do (not) keep silence*
Cf. HARL 1986ª, 249(Gn 34,15); HELBING 1928, 254-255;
→TWNT
(-ἀφ-, ἐξ-)

ὁμοίωμα,-ατος⁺ N3N 12-5-17-4-3-41
Ex 20,4; Dt 4,12.15.16(bis)
expression, representation of a reality (general
sense); *likeness* Ex 20,4; *image, copy* Dt 4,16;
form, appearance Dt 4,12
*Ct 1,11 ὁμοιώματα *images* -תארי◊ *forms,
appearances* for MT תורי◊ *ornaments*
Cf. BICKERMAN 1986, 248(n.7); DOGNIEZ 1992, 137.138;
VANNI 1977, 321-345.431-470; →NIDNTT; TWNT

ὁμοίως⁺ D 0-1-2-6-13-22
1 Chr 28,16; Ez 14,10; 45,11; Ps 67(68),7; Jb
1,16
in like manner Ez 45,11; *likewise, also* 1 Chr
28,16; *alike* Wis 11,11; *like* [τινι] Prv 1,27
→NIDNTT; TWNT

ὁμοίωσις,-εως⁺ N3F 1-0-3-4-0-8
Gn 1,26; Ez 1,10; 10,22; 28,12; Ps 57(58),5
likeness, resemblance Gn 1,26
*Ez 28,12 ὁμοιώσεως *of resemblance* -תבנית◊(cpr.
8,10 Theod. and Hexaplaric text) for MT תכנית
perfect model
Cf. ALEXANDRE 1988, 175-188; HARL 1986ª, 61.95;
→NIDNTT; TWNT

ὁμολογέω⁺ V 0-0-1-2-9-12
Jer 51(44),25; Jb 40,14; Est 1,1o; 1 Ezr 4,60;
5,58
to admit [τί τινι] 4 Mc 13,5; *id.* [+inf.] 4 Mc
6,34; *to confess* [abs.] Est 1,1o; *id.* [ἐπί τινι]
(as a term in moral and relig. usage) Sir 4,26; *to
confess, to admit* [+inf.] Wis 18,13; *id.* [ὅτι

+ind.] Jb 40,14
to give thanks to [τινι] 1 Ezr 4,60
to promise, to vow Jer 51,25
Cf. HELBING 1928, 242-243; TOV 1990, 97-110; →NIDNTT;
TWNT
(-ἀνθ-, ἐξ-, καθ-, συν-)

ὁμολογία,-ας⁺ N1F 2-0-4-0-1-7
Lv 22,18; Dt 12,17; Jer 51(44),25(bis); Ez 46,12
agreement (of offerings) Lv 22,18; *voluntary
offering* (semit.) Dt 12,17; *acknowledgement,
confession* (of sin or error) Am 4,5
promise, vow Jer 51(44),25
thanksgiving 1 Ezr 9,8
Cf. DOGNIEZ 1992, 65.194; HARLÉ 1988, 185; LLEWELYN
1992, 32; TOV 1990, 99.109-110; →TWNT

ὁμόλογος,-ος,-ον A 0-0-0-0-1-1
Susᴸˣˣ 60
agreeing, confessing

ὁμολογουμένως⁺ D 0-0-0-0-3-3
4 Mc 6,31; 7,16; 16,1
confessedly, admittedly
→TWNT

ὁμολόγως D 0-0-1-0-0-1
Hos 14,5
openly, willingly, expressly; neol.?
Cf. TOV 1990, 98.109

ὁμομήτριος,-α,-ον A 2-0-0-0-0-2
Gn 43,16.29
having the same mother

ὁμονοέω⁺ V 1-0-0-2-0-3
Lv 20,5; Est 4,17s; Dnᴸˣˣ 2,43
to be of one mind with, to agree with [τινι]
Cf. HELBING 1928, 246

ὁμόνοια,-ας⁺ N1F 0-0-0-2-5-7
Ps 54(55),15; 82(83),6; 4 Mc 3,21; 13,25; Wis
10,5
concord, harmony 4 Mc 3,21
ἐν ὁμονοίᾳ *in concord* Ps 54(55),15
Cf. LARCHER 1984, 619-620; LIEBERMAN 1942, 48

ὁμοπάτριος,-α,-ον A 1-0-0-0-0-1
Lv 18,11
having the same father

ὁμορέω V 0-1-2-0-0-3
1 Chr 12,41; Jer 27(50),40; Ez 16,26
to border upon [τινι] Jer 27(50),40
οἱ ὁμοροῦντες αὐτοῖς *their neighbours* 1 Chr
12,41
Cf. HELBING 1928, 252

ὅμορος,-ος,-ον A 1-1-0-0-0-2
Nm 35,5; 2 Chr 21,16

contiguous, neighbouring (of land) Nm 35,5; id.
(of men) 2 Chr 21,6
Cf. DORIVAL 1994, 564

ὁμόσπονδος,-ος,-ον   A 0-0-0-0-1-1
3 Mc 3,7
sharing a common cup; τῷ βασιλεῖ ὁμο-
σπόνδους τοὺς ἀνθρώπους showing loyalty to
the king

ὁμοῦ⁺   D 0-0-0-1-14-15
Jb 34,29; 2 Mc 8,14; 10,15; 11,7.9
together Wis 7,11; with one accord 3 Mc 5,21;
with one blow 3 Mc 5,5
ὁμοῦ τούτῳ together with him 2 Mc 10,15; ὁμοῦ
τὸν αὐτὸν τρόπον in exactly the same way 3 Mc
4,13

ὁμόφυλος,-ος,-ον   A 0-0-0-0-2-2
2 Mc 4,10; 3 Mc 3,21
of the same race, akin; οἱ ὁμόφυλοι
fellow-countrymen

ὁμόψηφος,-ος,-ον   A 0-0-0-0-1-1
2 Mc 14,20
voting with, assenting; ὁμοψήφου γνώμης of one
mind

ὁμόψυχος,-ος,-ον   A 0-0-0-0-1-1
4 Mc 14,20
of one mind; neol.

ὀμφακίζω   V 0-0-1-0-0-1
Is 18,5
to produce or bear sour grapes; neol.

ὀμφαλός,-οῦ   N2M 0-2-1-2-0-5
Jgs 9,37; Ez 38,12; Jb 40,16; Ct 7,3
navel Ct 7,3; centre, middle Jgs 9,37

ὄμφαξ,-ακος⁺   N3F 0-0-4-2-0-6
Is 18,5; Jer 38(31),29; 38(31),30; Ez 18,2; Jb
15,33
unripe grape

ὅμως⁺   C 0-0-0-0-6-6
2 Mc 2,27; 14,18; 15,5; 4 Mc 13,27; 15,11
yet, nevertheless

ὄναγρος,-ου   N2M 0-0-0-2-1-3
Ps 103(104),11; Dnᵀʰ 5,21; Sir 13,19
wild donkey; neol.

ὀνειδίζω⁺   V 0-15-13-16-14-58
Jgs 5,18; 8,15; 1 Sm 17,10
to reproach, to revile [τινα] Jgs 8,15; id. [abs.]
Ps 73(74),10; to reproach justifiably [τινα] Prv
25,8; to reproach sb for sth [τινί τι] Wis 2,12;
to taunt, to provoke [τινα] (of the enemy
challenging Israel) Zph 2,8
ὀνειδίζουσαν φωνήν a reproachful speech 2 Mc

7,24; λαὸς ὠνείδισεν ψυχὴν αὐτοῦ εἰς
θάνατον the people reproached their soul to
death, they scorned their soul to death, they
scorned death Jgs 5,18
*Is 43,12 ὠνείδισα I have reproached corr.?
ἐνώτισα or ὠνόμασα for MT השמעתי I proclaimed;
*Sir 43,17 ὠνείδισεν γῆν reproached the earth
corr.? ὠδίνησεν γῆ the earth suffered birth pangs
for Hebr. Sirach יחיל ארצו; *Prv 20,4 ὀνειδιζό-
μενος reproaching -מחרף (ptc. חרף) for MT מ/חרף in
winter times
Cf. HELBING 1928, 21; KATZ 1956, 271(Sir 43,17); SPICQ
1978ª, 623-625; WALTERS 1973, 128(Sir 43,17); YADIN
1965, 32(Sir 43,17); →NIDNTT; TWNT

ὀνείδισμα,-ατος   N3N 0-0-1-0-0-1
Ez 36,3
insult, reproach, blame

ὀνειδισμός,-οῦ⁺   N2M 0-2-27-25-31-85
Jos 5,9; 1 Sm 25,39; Is 4,1; 37,3; 43,28
disgrace, insult (of the oppression in Egypt) Jos
5,9; id. (imposed upon Israel by Goliath) Sir
47,4; id. (imposed upon Israel by the Lord)
Jl 2,19; reproach, insult Tobˢ 3,6
*Jer 25,9 καὶ εἰς ὀνειδισμόν and (I turn
them) into a disgrace -ולחרפות for MT ולחרבת and (I
will turn them) into desolations, see also Dnᴸˣˣ
9,2
Cf. SPICQ 1978ª, 623-625; →TWNT

ὄνειδος,-ους⁺   N3N 3-3-11-22-14-53
Gn 30,23; 34,14; Lv 20,17; 1 Sm 11,2; 17,36
disgrace Gn 30,23; object of reproach Ps 21(22),7
*Prv 19,6 ὄνειδος reproach, insult -מדון conten-
tion? for MT מתן gift
Cf. SPICQ 1978ª, 623-625; →TWNT

ὄνειρος,-ου⁺   N2M 0-0-0-0-4-4
2 Mc 15,11; 4 Mc 6,5; Wis 18,17.19
dream
Cf. LARCHER 1985, 1023.

ὄνησις,-εως   N3F 0-0-1-0-0-1
Zech 8,10
profit, delight, enjoyment

ὀνίνημι⁺   V 0-0-0-0-2-2
Tobᴮᴬ 3,8; Sir 30,2
M: to have advantage [τινος] Tobᴮᴬ 3,8; to have
enjoyment in [ἐπί τινι] Sir 30,2

ὀνοκένταυρος,-ου   N2M 0-0-4-0-0-4
Is 13,22; 34,11.14(bis)
donkey-centaur, mythic creature (a centaur resembling a donkey rather than a horse); neol.

ὄνομα,-ατος⁺   N3N 257-280-174-197-137-1045

Gn 2,11.13.19.20; 3,20
name Gn 2,11; *class, genus* Gn 2,20; *name, fame*
Gn 21,23; *name, reputation* Gn 11,4; *name,
memory* Dt 25,19; *name, authority of* [τινος]
1 Sm 25,9; *name, family* Na 1,14; *name, person*
Nm 1,18
ὄνομα πονηρόν *a bad reputation* Dt 22,14;
υἱόν, ᾧ ὄνομα Εννων *a son, whose name is
Ennon* Jb 42,17c; ἐν ἑνὶ ὀνόματι θανάτου *by
the one form of death or at once, in the time
needed to pronounce the word death* Wis 18,12
*Is 42,4 ἐπὶ τῷ ὀνόματι αὐτοῦ *in his name*
corr.? ἐπὶ τῷ νόμῳ αὐτοῦ for MT לתורתו *in his
law*, see also Is 26,8; *Nm 4,27 ἐξ ὀνομάτων *by
name* -ב/מ/שמות for MT ב/משמרת/ם *in their
charge*?; *Dt 17,12 ὀνόματι *(in the) name* -שם
for MT שם *there*, see also Is 33,21; Ez 43,7; 48,35;
*Zph 1,4 ὀνόματα *name* -שם for MT שאר *remnant*;
*Ps 39(40),5 τὸ ὄνομα *the name* -שם for MT שם
(who) puts; *Ps 71(72),14 ὄνομα αὐτῶν *their
name* -שמם for MT רמם *their blood*; *Prv 27,16
ὀνόματι δέ *and by name* -ושם for MT ושמן *and oil*
Cf. HEITMÜLLER 1903, 110-111; KOENIG 1982, 232-233(Is
42,4); LARCHER 1985, 1010(Wis 18,12); SHIPP 1979, 416;
WEVERS 1993, 149.310.463; 1995, 393(Dt 25,7); →LSJ
RSuppl(Wis 18,12); NIDNTT; PREISIGKE; TWNT

ὀνομάζω⁺   V 3-3-8-1-10-25
Lv 24,16(bis); Dt 2,20; Jos 23,7; 1 Chr 12,32
A: *to name* [τι] Lv 24,26; *to give sb a name*
[τινα] Bar 4,30; *to call sb* [τινα +pred.] Dt
2,20; *to mention, to call to mind* [τι] Jer 23,36
P: *to be famous, to be known* Est 9,4; *to be
mentioned, to be remembered* Jer 3,16
εἰς Πτολεμαίδα τὴν ὀνομαζομένην ῥοδο-
φόρον *to Ptolemais, the called rose-bearing* 3 Mc
7,17; οὐ μὴ ὀνομάσω τὸ ὄνομα κυρίου *I shall
no more mention the name of the Lord* Jer 20,9
→NIDNTT; TWNT
(→ἐπ-, προσ-)

ὀνομασία,-ας   N1F 0-0-0-0-1-1
Sir 23,9
act of naming

ὀνομαστός,-ή,-όν⁺   A 3-4-10-0-4-21
Gn 6,4; Nm 16,2; Dt 26,19; 2 Sm 7,9; 1 Chr 5,24
of name, famous, renowned (of pers.) 1 Chr
11,20; *id.* (of places) Is 56,5
ἄνθρωποι ὀνομαστοί *men of renown* Gn 6,4
*Ez 39,11 τόπον ὀνομαστόν *a place of renown*
-מקום שם for MT שם מקום *a place where ...*
Cf. BARTHÉLEMY 1992, 307-309(Ez 39,11)

ὀνοματογραφία,-ας   N1F 0-0-0-0-2-2
1 Ezr 6,11; 8,48
list of names; neol.

ὄνος,-ου⁺   N2M/F 43-53-10-11-3-120
Gn 12,16; 22,3.5; 24,35; 30,43
ass, domestic ass, donkey Ex 22,3; *id.* (beast of
burden) Gn 42,26; *id.* (used to till the ground)
Is 32,20; *id.* (used for riding) Nm 22,21; *id.*
(used for riding by kings and leaders) JgsᴮB 5,10;
she-ass Ex 13,13
ὄνος ἄγριος *wild ass* Is 32,14; *id.* (metaph.) Gn
12,16
*Jer 31(48),6 ὥσπερ ὄνος ἄγριος *as a wild ass*
-כְּעָרוּר for MT כַּעֲרוֹעֵר *like Aroer?*
Cf. LE BOULLUEC 1989, 46.158; LEE, J. 1983, 140-143;
SPICQ 1982, 501-503; →TWNT

ὄντως⁺   D 1-1-2-0-1-5
Nm 22,37; 1 Kgs 12,24f; Jer 3,23; 10,19; Wis
17,13
in truth, really, certainly, indeed

ὄνυξ,-υχος   N3M 3-0-2-5-2-12
Ex 30,34; Lv 11,7; Dt 14,8; Ez 17,3.7
claw, nail DnᵀʰTh 4,33; *hoof* Lv 11,7; *onyx*
(precious stone) Jb 28,16; *aromatic material* Ex
30,34
Cf. LE BOULLUEC 1989, 313

ὀνυχίζω   V 7-1-0-0-0-8
Lv 11,3.4.7.26; Dt 14,6
M: *to pare nails* 2 Sm 19,25
ὀνυχιστῆρας ὀνυχίζον *having cleft hoofs* Lv
11,3
Cf. DOGNIEZ 1992, 205
(→περι-)

ὀνύχιον,-ου   N2N 2-0-1-0-0-3
Ex 28,20; 36,20(39,13); Ez 28,13
kind of onyx (precious stone)
→NIDNTT

ὀνυχιστήρ,-ῆρος   N3M 5-0-0-0-0-5
Lv 11,3.4.26; Dt 14,6.7
hoof; neol.

ὀξέως   D 0-0-3-0-2-5
Is 8,1.3; Jl 4,4; Wis 3,18; 16,11
quickly, swiftly
Cf. LARCHER 1983, 310

ὄξος,-ους⁺   N3N 2-0-0-3-0-5
Nm 6,3(bis); Ps 68(69),22; Ru 2,14; Prv 25,20
vinegar
Cf. SCHNEBEL 1925, 279.292; →TWNT

ὀξυγράφος,-ος,-ον   A 0-0-0-1-0-1
Ps 44(45),2

swift-writing, writing fast; neol.

ὀξύθυμος,-ος,-ον   A 0-0-0-1-0-1
Prv 14,17
quick-tempered, choleric, passionate

ὀξύνω   V 0-0-5-2-1-8
Is 44,12; Ez 21,14.15.21; Zech 2,4
A: *to sharpen, to make sharp* [τι] Prv 27,17; *id.*
[τι] (metaph.) Wis 5,20
P: *to be sharpened* Ez 21,14
*Ez 21,21 ὀξύνου *sharpen* -חתחרי◊חרר for MT
אחר◊התאחרי *go together?*; *Zech 2,4 τοῦ ὀξῦναι
to sharpen -חרר◊ for MT להחריד◊חרר *to terrify*
(→ἐπ-, παρ-)

ὀξύς,-εῖα,-ύ⁺   A 0-0-5-6-8-19
Is 5,28; 49,2; Ez 5,1; Am 2,15; Hab 1,8
sharp Jb 41,22; *sharp, passionate* (of emotions)
Prv 27,4; *sharp, quick* (of spirit, mind) Wis 8,11;
quick, swift Ps 13(14),3; *fierce* (of fire) 4 Mc
14,10
*Jb 16,10 ὀξεῖ *with the sharp (edge of the
sword)* -ב/חורפא (Aram.) for MT חרפה/ב*insolently*

ὀξύτης,-ητος   N3F 0-0-1-0-0-1
Jer 8,16
swiftness, sharpness; *Jer 8,16 φωνὴν ὀξύτητος
the sharp sound or *the sound of swiftness?* (of
approaching horses) -חרר◊? for MT נחרה*snorting*

ὀπή,-ῆς⁺   N1F 1-1-2-2-1-7
Ex 33,22; Jgsᴬ 15,11; Ob 3; Zech 14,12; Ct 5,4
hole, cleft (in a rock) Ex 33,22; *socket* (of eye)
Zech 14,12
αἱ βλέπουσαι ἐν ταῖς ὀπαῖς *the women
looking out of the windows* Eccl 12,3
Cf. LE BOULLUEC 1989, 336

ὀπηνίκα   C 0-0-0-0-2-2
Jdt 11,11; 4 Mc 2,21
since, when 4 Mc 2,21; *at which time, whenever*
Jdt 11,11

ὀπήτιον,-ου   N2N 2-0-0-0-0-2
Ex 21,6; Dt 15,17
small awl (dim. of ὅπεας *awl*); neol.
Cf. LE BOULLUEC 1989, 215

ὄπισθε(ν)⁺   D/P 2-20-7-5-7-41
Gn 18,10; Ex 14,19; Jos 6,13; 1 Sm 6,7; 12,20
behind 2 Sm 10,9
εἰς τὰ ὄπισθεν *backwards* Jer 7,24
[τινος]: *behind* Gn 18,10; *following* 2 Sm 20,2
Cf. BLASS 1990, § 215; →TWNT

ὀπίσθιος,-α,-ον   A 3-2-2-0-0-7
Ex 26,23.27; 36,26(39,19); 1 Kgs 7,13(25); 2 Chr
4,4

to the rear part, to the back Ex 26,27; τὰ
ὀπίσθια *the back parts, the hind parts* 1 Kgs
7,13

ὀπισθίως   D 0-1-0-0-0-1
1 Sm 4,18
backwards

ὀπισθότονος,-ου   N2M 1-0-0-0-1-2
Dt 32,24; Od 2,24
*disease in which the body is drawn back and
stiffens, tetanus*
Cf. DOGNIEZ 1992, 66.332-333

ὀπισθοφανής,-ής,-ές   A 1-0-0-0-0-1
Gn 9,23
facing away, looking backward; neol.

ὀπισθοφανῶς   D 1-0-0-0-0-1
Gn 9,23
backwards; neol.

ὀπίσω⁺   D/P 55-230-75-61-40-461
Gn 8,8; 14,14; 19,6.17.26
backwards Ps 49(50),17; *back* Gn 24,5; τὰ ὀπίσω
behind Jos 8,2; *back parts, hind parts* Ex 33,23;
τὸ ὀπίσω τινός *the hind end of* 2 Sm 2,23
[τινος]: *after* (place) Gn 8,8; *after* (pursuing)
Gn 14,14; *behind* Ex 26,12; *after* (time) Neh
13,19; *id.* (metaph.) Eccl 2,12
Cf. BLASS 1990, § 215; LE BOULLUEC 1989, 336(Ex 33,23);
WEVERS 1995, 189(Dt 11,4); →MM; NIDNTT; TWNT

ὀπλή,-ῆς⁺   N1F 14-0-3-1-1-19
Ex 10,26; Lv 11,3.4(bis).5
hoof

ὀπλίζω
(→ἐξ-, ἐν-, καθ-)

ὀπλίτης,-ου   N1M 1-0-0-0-0-1
Nm 32,21
heavy armed soldier, warrior

ὀπλοδοτέω   V 0-0-0-0-1-1
1 Mc 14,32
to provide with weapons, to arm [τινα]; neol.

ὀπλοθήκη,-ης   N1F 0-1-0-0-0-1
2 Chr 32,27
store for arms, armoury; neol.

ὀπλολογέω   V 0-0-0-0-2-2
2 Mc 8,27.31
to collect arms from or *of* [τινα]; neol.

ὀπλομάχος,-ος,-ον   A 0-0-2-0-0-2
Is 13,4.5
fighting with heavy arms, equipped for war

ὅπλον,-ου⁺   N2N 0-10-15-8-34-67
1 Sm 17,7; 1 Kgs 10,17(bis); 14,26.27
weapon Ps 45,10; *spear* Na 3,3; τὰ ὅπλα *arms,*

armour 1 Sm 17,7
*Jl 2,8 ἐν τοῖς ὅπλοις αὐτῶν *by their weapons*
corr.? ἐν τοῖς ὁδοῖς αὐτῶν *to their roads*;
*2 Chr 21,3 ὅπλα *weapons* -מגנות *shields* for MT
מגרנות *valuable gifts*; *Jer 28(51),12 ὅπλα
weapons -חרב◊? for MT הארבים *the ambushes*; *Prv
14,7 ὅπλα *weapons* -כלי- for MT בל י(רעת) *(you do)
not (know)*
→TWNT

ὁπλοποιέω V 0-0-0-0-1-1
Wis 5,17
to turn into weapons [τι]; neol.
Cf. LARCHER 1984, 387

ὁπλοφόρος,-ος,-ον A 0-1-0-0-0-1
2 Chr 14,7
one bearing arms

ὁποῖος,-α,-ον⁺ R 0-0-0-0-1-1
2 Mc 11,37
of what sort

ὁπόταν⁺ C 0-0-0-1-0-1
Jb 29,22
whenever

ὁπότε⁺ C 0-0-1-6-3-10
Is 16,13; Ps 3,1; 33(34),1; 55(56),1; 58(59),1
when Ps 58(59),1; *id.* (in indir. question) Jb
26,14; *id.* (in rel. clause) Tobˢ 6,14

ὅπου⁺ D 0-2-1-7-16-26
Jgsᴮ 18,10; 20,22; Is 42,22; Ru 1,16; 3,4
where Jgsᴮ 18,10; *wherever* [ἄν +subj.] Tobˢ 13,5;
whereas, since, in so far as (expressing cause)
4 Mc 14,19

ὁπτάζομαι V 1-0-0-0-0-1
Nm 14,14
P: *to be seen, to appear*; neol.?
Cf. DORIVAL 1994, 186.320

ὀπτάνω⁺ V 0-1-0-0-1-2
1 Kgs 8,8; Tobᴮᴬ 12,19
to be seen, to appear; neol.?
Cf. DORIVAL 1994, 320; →MM

ὀπτασία,-ας⁺ N1F 0-0-1-7-2-10
Mal 3,2; Est 4,17w; Dnᵀʰ 9,23; 10,1.7
appearance Sir 43,2; *act of appearing* Mal 3,2;
public appearance Est 4,17w
→NIDNTT; TWNT

ὀπτάω⁺ V 2-2-2-0-3-9
Gn 11,3; Dt 16,7; 1 Sm 2,15; 2 Chr 35,13; Is
44,16
to roast [τι] Dt 16,7; *to bake* (bricks) [τι] Gn
11,3
Cf. SHIPP 1979, 417-418; WEVERS 1995, 269(Dt 16,7)

ὀπτεύω
(→κατ-, ὑπ-)

ὀπτός,-ή,-όν⁺ A 2-0-0-0-0-2
Ex 12,8.9
roasted

ὀπώρα,-ας⁺ N1F 0-0-3-0-0-3
Jer 31(48),32; 47(40),10.12
fruit
Cf. HARL 1991=1992ᵃ, 149

ὀπωροφυλάκιον,-ου N2N 0-0-4-1-0-5
Is 1,8; 24,20; Mi 1,6; 3,12; Ps 78(79),1
hut for one who guards a garden or *orchard* Is
1,8
*Mi 1,6 εἰς ὀπωροφυλάκιον *into a hut* -ğayaya
(Arab.)? for MT לעי *into a ruin, into a heap*, see
also 3,12; Ps 78(79),1
neol.
→LSJ suppl(Mi 3,12); MM

ὅπως⁺ C 36-25-69-51-83-264
Gn 12,13; 18,19; 27,4.10.19
that, in order that [+subj.] (final clause) Gn
27,4; *id.* [ἄν +subj.] (final clause) Gn 18,19; *that*
[+conj.] (after verbs of asking) Jon 1,6

ὅραμα,-ατος⁺ N3N 8-0-6-33-1-48
Gn 15,1; 46,2; Ex 3,3; Nm 12,6; Dt 4,34
sight, spectacle Ex 3,3; *vision, dream* Gn 15,1
*Dt 26,8 καὶ ἐν ὁράμασιν *and with spectacles*
-ראה◊ ובמראה for MT ובמרא ומורא *and with terror*, see
also Dt 4,34; Jer 39(32),21
Cf. WEVERS 1995, 87.406(Dt 4,34; 26,8); →NIDNTT; TWNT

ὅρασις,-εως⁺ N3F 8-9-52-48-16-133
Gn 2,9; 24,62; 25,11; 31,49; 40,5
seeing, act of seeing LtJ 36; *sight* Gn 2,9
vision Gn 31,49; *prophetic vision* Jer 14,14;
vision, dream Dn 8,1
outward appearance, look Jl 2,4; *sight, appearance, face* Sir 11,2; *appearance* Nm 24,4
τὸ φρέαρ τῆς ὁράσεως *the well of vision* (proper
name) Gn 24,62
*Is 66,24 εἰς ὅρασιν *(they shall be) a spectacle*?
-ראה◊ for MT דראון *an abhorrence*
→TWNT

ὁρατής,-οῦ N1M 0-0-0-2-0-2
Jb 34,21; 35,13
observer of, beholder of [τινος]; neol.

ὁρατικός,-ή,-όν A 0-0-0-1-0-1
Prv 22,29
able to see, observant (of mental vision)
→LSJ RSuppl

ὁρατός,-ή,-όν⁺ A 0-2-0-2-0-4

2 Sm 23,21; 1 Chr 11,23; Jb 34,26; 37,21
to be seen, visible Jb 34,26

ἄνδρα ὁρατόν *a man to be seen, a handsome man* 2 Sm 23,21
*1 Chr 11,23 ἄνδρα ὁρατόν *a handsome man* -איש מראה? (cpr. 2 Sm 23,21) for MT מרה איש *a man of great stature*

ὁράω⁺   V 369-336-258-311-265-1539
Gn 1,4.8.9(bis).10
A: *to see, to look* [abs.] Gn 27,1; *to see, to behold* [τι] Gn 13,15; *id.* [τινα] Gn 37,29; *id.* [τι +ptc.] Jos 8,20; *id.* [τινα +ptc.] Ex 2,6; *id.* [+indir. question] Gn 18,21; *to see that* [ὅτι +ind.] Gn 26,28; *to perceive* [τι] Ex 20,18
to observe, to look at [abs.] Mi 5,4; *id.* [τι] Mi 3,7; *id.* [τινα] Zech 10,7; *to see, to visit* [τινα] 1 Sm 20,29
to witness, to experience [τι] Zph 3,15
to look to [+inf.] Gn 9,16; *to behold, to take heed* Ex 33,5; *to provide sth for sb* [τινί τι] Gn 22,8
to see visions Nm 24,3
P: *to be seen* Wis 13,1; *to appear* Gn 1,9; *to appear in a vision* Jgs 13,3
ὁ ὁρῶν,-ῶντος *seer* 2 Kgs 17,13; ὁρῶ τὸ πρόσωπόν τινος *to see sb* Gn 43,3; ἴδε *see* (frequently rendering הנה) Gn 27,6
*Lv 23,43 ἴδωσιν *(that) they may see* corr.? (with Wevers) εἴδωσιν *(that) they may know* for MT ידעו, see also 2 Kgs 10,10; Is 6,9; Sir 46,10;
*Ex 33,13 γνωστῶς ἴδω σε *knowing I see you* -ידע◊ and ראה◊? for MT ואדעך *and I know you* (double rendition in Greek?); *Dt 7,15 ἑώρακας *you have seen* -ראה◊for MT ידע◊ *you have known, you have experienced* (rendered twice: ἑώρακας and ἔγνως); *Is 26,14 ἴδωσιν *they shall see* -יחזו for MT יחיו *they shall live*; *Jer 30,16(49,22) ὄψεται *she shall look* -ראה◊ for MT יראה *she soars*; *Mi 5,3 καὶ ὄψεται *and he shall see* -וראה for MT ורעה *and he shall pasture*; *Eccl 12,5 ὄψονται *they shall look up* -ראה◊for MT יראו *they fear* see οἶδα
Cf. DORIVAL 1994, 138-139; HARL 1986ᵃ, 53.153.195.235; HARLÉ 1988, 119; LE BOULLUEC 1989, 140.265.316.331; LEE, J. 1983, 131-144; MURAOKA 1990, 36-37; WALTERS 1973, 73.197-204; WEVERS 1993, 497.521; →NIDNTT; TWNT
(→ἀφ-, δι-, εἰσ-, ἐν-, ἐφ-, καθ-, παρ-, προ-, συν-, ὑπερ-, ὑφ-)

ὀργανικός,-ή,-όν   A 0-0-0-0-1-1
2 Mc 12,15

serving as instrument, instrumental; μηχανῶν ὀργανικῶν *instruments of war*

ὄργανον,-ου⁺   N2N 0-14-2-2-10-28
2 Sm 6,5.14; 1 Chr 6,17; 15,16; 16,5
part of the body, limb 4 Mc 10,7; *instrument, engine, machine, contrivance* 2 Mc 13,5; *engine of war* 2 Mc 12,27 *musical instrument* 1 Chr 16,5
ἐν ὀργάνοις τῶν ᾠδῶν *with musical instruments* 1 Chr 5,13
*2 Sm 6,5 ἐν ὀργάνοις *with instruments* -ב/כלי for MT ב/כל *with all*, see also 6,14

ὀργή,-ῆς⁺   N1F 25-38-73-106-63-305
Gn 27,45; 39,19; Ex 4,14; 15,7; 32,10
anger, rage (of humans) Gn 27,45; *wrath, punishing destructive anger* (of God) Ps 58(59),14; αἱ ὀργαί *outbursts of anger* Ps 87(88),17
ὀργὴ θυμοῦ *fierce anger* (intensification) Nm 12,9; θυμωθεὶς ὀργῇ *greatly angered, with fierce anger* (intensification) Ex 4,14
*Ps 29(30),6 ὀργή *wrath* -רגז◊? *agitation, excitement* or נגע? *plague, stroke* for MT רגע *a moment*; *Ps 34(35),20 ἐπ᾽ ὀργήν *in anger* -רגז◊? *agitation, excitement* for MT רגע *quietness*; *Ps 54(55),22 ἀπὸ ὀργῆς *at the anger of* -חמה◊מ/חמאה for MT מ/חמאת *more than butter*
Cf. BARR 1961, 147-148; CAIRD 1976, 81; DOGNIEZ 1992, 333(Dt 32,27); DORIVAL 1994, 59; FLASHAR 1912, 261-265; GRIBOMONT-THIBAUT 1959, 86-87; LARCHER 1985, 663. 897-898; WEVERS 1990, 48; →NIDNTT; TWNT

ὀργίζω⁺   V 17-18-10-23-15-83
Gn 31,36; 40,2; 41,10; 45,24; Ex 15,14
P: *to be angry* Ex 32,22; *to be angry with* [τινι] Nm 25,3; *id.* [ἐπί τινα] 2 Kgs 19,28; *id.* [ἐπί τι] Ps 79(80),5; *id.* [ἐπί τινι] Gn 40,2; *id.* [κατά τινος] Jb 32,3; *id.* [ἐν τινι] Jgs 2,20
ὀργισθεὶς θυμῷ *being very angry* Ex 32,19
*Jgsᴬ 19,2 καὶ ὠργίσθη *and she became angry* -ותזעף? *and she became angry* or זנה◊ ותזנה¹¹ *and she felt repugnance* for MT זנה◊ ותזנה¹ *and she prostituted herself*?
Cf. HARL 1986ᵇ=1992ᵃ, 87(n.17); HELBING 1928, 211; LE BOULLUEC 1989, 175(Gn 45,24; Ex 15,14); WEVERS 1973, 768; 1990, 232(Gn 45,24; Ex 15,14); 1993, 768; →NIDNTT; TWNT
(→ἀπ-, δι-, ἐπ-, παρ-)

ὀργίλος,-η,-ον⁺   A 0-0-0-4-0-4
Ps 17(18),49; Prv 21,19; 22,24; 29,22
inclined to anger, quick-tempered

ὀργίλως⁺   D 0-0-0-0-1-1

4 Mc 8,9
angrily; διατίθημι ὀργίλως *to be angry, to be angrily disposed*

ὀρεινός,-ή,-όν⁺   A 4-17-2-1-18-42
Gn 14,10; Nm 13,29; Dt 2,37; 11,11; Jos 2,16
mountainous, of mountains Dt 11,11; ἡ ὀρεινή
(sc. χώρα) *mountain-country, hill-country* Gn
14,10

ὄρεξις,-εως⁺   N3F 0-0-0-0-8-8
4 Mc 1,33.35; Wis 14,2; 15,5; 16,2
longing, desire for [τινος] Wis 14,2; *lust* Wis
15,5; *appetite* Wis 16,2
Cf. LARCHER 1985, 789; SPICQ 1978ᵃ, 626-627; →TWNT

ὄρθιος,-α/ος,-ον   A 0-1-0-0-0-1
1 Sm 28,14
upright; *1 Sm 28,14 ὄρθιον *upright* -זקף◊ for MT
זקן *an old man*

ὀρθός,-ή,-όν⁺   A 0-2-5-16-4-27
JgsᴮB 15,5; 1 Kgs 21(20),11; Jer 38(31),9; Ez 1,7;
Mi 2,3
straight up, upright 1 Ezr 9,46; *standing* (of corn)
JgsᴮB 15,15; *upright* (opp. to humpbacked) 1 Kgs
21(20),11
straight, right Prv 4,11; *upright, just* Prv 8,6; *right,
true, correct* Prv 16,13
τὰ ὀρθά *righteousness* Mi 3,9; βλέπειν ὀρθά *to
look right on* Prv 4,25; ὀρθὰ κρῖναι *to judge
righteously* Prv 31,5
→NIDNTT; TWNT

ὀρθοτομέω⁺   V 0-0-0-2-0-2
Prv 3,6; 11,5
to cut in a straight line; ὀρθοτομέω ὁδούς *to give
the right direction, to teach correctly, to give the
right teaching* Prv 3,6, see also 11,5
Cf. SPICQ 1978ᵃ, 630; →NIDNTT

ὀρθόω⁺   V 1-0-1-2-3-7
Gn 37,7; Jer 37(30),20; Est 7,9; Ezr 6,11; 1 Ezr
1,21
P: *to be lifted up* Ezr 6,11; *to be erected* (of
sheaves) Gn 37,7; *to be upright* (of works) 1 Ezr
1,21; *to straighten oneself* LtJ 26; *to be
established* Jer 37(30),20
(→ἀν-, δι-, ἐπαν-, κατ-)

ὀρθρεύω   V 0-0-0-0-1-1
Tobᴮᴬ 9,6
to lie awake before dawn, to rise early
Cf. LEE, J. 1983, 46; TOV 1990, 119; →LSJ RSuppl

ὀρθρίζω⁺   V 9-34-4-7-11-65
Gn 19,2.27; 20,8; Ex 8,16; 9,13
to rise (up) early Gn 19,2; *to seek sb eagerly*

[πρός τινα] Wis 6,14; neol.
Cf. GEHMAN 1953, 147; HORSLEY 1981, 86; LARCHER
1984, 420; LEE, J. 1983, 46; TOV 1990, 118-125; →LSJ suppl;
LSJ RSuppl; →MM; TWNT

ὀρθρινός,-ή,-όν⁺   A 0-0-3-0-1-4
Hos 6,4; 13,3; Hag 2,14; Wis 11,22
early, of the morning; neol.
→MM

ὄρθριος,-α,-ον⁺   A 0-0-0-1-2-3
Jb 29,7; 3 Mc 5,10.23
early in the morning 3 Mc 5,10
*Jb 29,7 ὄρθριος *early in the morning* -שחר for
MT שער *gate*

ὄρθρος,-ου⁺   N2M 3-5-10-10-7-35
Gn 19,15; 32,27; Ex 19,16; Jos 6,15; Jgsᴬ 19,25
dawn, early morning Gn 19,15; *persistently* Jer
25,4
→LSJ Suppl(Jer 25,4)

ὀρθῶς⁺   D 7-1-1-2-7-18
Gn 4,7(bis); 40,16; Ex 18,17; Nm 27,7
rightly, justly, correctly
Cf. WEVERS 1993, 670

ὁρίζω⁺   V 10-5-1-3-2-21
Nm 30,3.4.5(bis).6
A: *to act as boundary* Nm 34,6; *to separate, to
determine* Prv 18,18; *to mark out sth with sth* [τί
τινι] Prv 16,30
M: *to establish, to ordain* (an ordinance) [τι]
3 Mc 6,36; *to swear* (an oath) [τι] 3 Mc 5,42
ὁρίζομαι ὁρισμῷ *to bind oneself with an
obligation* or *pledge* Nm 30,3; ὁρίζομαι
ὁρισμόν *id.* Nm 30,4
Cf. ALLEN 1970, 104-108; DORIVAL 1994, 511; SHIPP 1979,
418-420
(→ἀφ-, δι-)

ὅριον,-ου⁺   N2N 56-151-55-13-36-311
Gn 10,19; 23,17; 47,21; Ex 7,27; 10,4
boundary, limit, landmark Hos 5,10; *border* Dt
3,16; *domain of sb* [τινος] Prv 15,25; τὰ ὅρια
boundaries, bounds, frontier Nm 34,11; *territories,
region* Ex 23,18
*Jgsᴬ 2,9 ἐν ὁρίῳ *on the border* corr.? ἐν ὄρει
id. (with ms A and the pap.), see also 1 Sm 10,2;
Ez 11,10.11; Ps 77(78),54: Rahlfs changes ὄρος
into ὅριον, against the mss evidence; *Jgsᴬ 7,24
ἐν παντὶ ὁρίῳ corr.? ἐν παντὶ ὄρει (with Jgsᴮ
7,24) for MT בכל הר *throughout all the mountains*,
see also Mal 1,3
Cf. DORIVAL 1994, 331; SPICQ 1978ᵃ, 632-634(Jgsᴬ 2,9);
WEVERS 1993, 800

ὁρισμός,-οῦ⁺   N2M 12-0-0-14-1-27
Ex 8,8; Nm 30,3.4.5(bis)
decree Est 4,17o; obligation Nm 30,3; oath 2 Mc 12,25
περὶ τοῦ ὁρισμοῦ τῶν βατράχων about the agreed time concerning the frogs Ex 8,8
Cf. DORIVAL 1994, 511; LE BOULLUEC 1989, 124

-ορκέω
(→ἐπι-)

ὁρκίζω⁺   V 8-10-0-9-2-29
Gn 24,37; 50,5.6.16.25
to make sb swear [τινα] Gn 24,37; to adjure [abs.] Gn 50,16; to adjure sb by sb [τινα κατά τινος] 2 Chr 36,13; to bind by oath to do [τινα +inf.] Neh 5,12
→MM; TWNT
(→ἐξ-)

ὁρκισμός,-οῦ   N2M 3-0-0-0-2-5
Gn 21,31; 24,41; Lv 5,1; 1 Mc 6,62; Sir 36,7
swearing, taking of an oath Lv 5,1
ἀπὸ τοῦ ὁρκισμοῦ μου from the oath I made you swear or take Gn 24,41
Cf. HARL 1986ᵃ, 55; HARLÉ 1988, 99(Lv 5,1)

ὅρκος,-ου⁺   N2M 21-11-3-8-18-61
Gn 21,14.32.33; 22,19(bis)
oath Gn 21,14
ὅρκος δεσμοῦ binding oath Nm 30,14
Cf. HARL 1986ᵃ, 55; →TWNT

ὁρκωμοσία,-ας⁺   N1F 0-0-2-0-1-3
Ez 17,18.19; 1 Ezr 8,90
oath-taking, swearing
→TWNT

ὁρμάω⁺   V 2-4-4-0-6-16
Gn 31,21; Nm 17,7; Jos 4,18; 6,5; Jgsᴬ 20,37
A: to set oneself in motion, to start moving Na 3,16; to rush forward Jer 4,28; to rush impetuously (of water) Jos 4,18; to hasten to [τοῦ +inf.] 1 Sm 15,19; to rush, to hasten to [εἴς τι] Gn 31,21; id. [ἐπί τι] Nm 17,7; to hurry after [ἐπί τινα] 2 Mc 12,20; to rush at, to fall upon sb, to hurry against [ἐπί τινα] 2 Mc 12,32; to attack Jgsᴬ 20,37
Cf. DORIVAL 1994, 54.357; →TWNT
(→ἐξ-, παρ-, συνεξ-)

ὁρμή,-ῆς⁺   N1F 2-0-2-3-3-10
Nm 11,11.17; Jer 29(47),3; Ez 3,14; Prv 3,25
rushing Jer 29(47),3; onrush 3 Mc 1,23; gush, flow (of water) Prv 21,1; attack Prv 3,25; impulse Ez 3,14; impulse, inclination, desire 3 Mc 1,16; impulse, violence 3 Mc 4,5; rage, fury Nm 11,11

Cf. DORIVAL 1994, 67; →LSJ suppl(Prv 21,1); LSJ Rsuppl(Prv 21,1); TWNT

ὅρμημα,-ατος⁺   N3N 2-0-3-1-5-11
Ex 32,22; Dt 28,49; Hos 5,10; Am 1,11; Hab 3,8
sudden onrush, onset, assault, attack 1 Mc 4,8; impulsive aggression Ex 32,22; fury Hos 5,10; rush, torrent (of water) Ps 45(46),5; swoop (of eagle) Dt 28,49
Cf. DORIVAL 1994, 67; LE BOULLUEC 1989, 325(Ex 32,22); WEVERS 1990, 531(Ex 32,22); →LSJ suppl(Ps 45(46),5); LSJ Rsuppl(Ps 45(46),5); MM; TWNT

ὁρμίσκος,-ου   N2M 2-1-0-3-0-6
Gn 38,18.25; Jgsᴬ 8,26; Prv 25,11; Ct 1,10
small necklace; neol.
Cf. WEVERS 1993, 853

ὅρμος,-ου   N2M 1-0-1-0-1-3
Gn 49,13; Ez 27,11; 4 Mc 13,6
harbour Gn 49,13; wall around the harbour Ez 27,11
Cf. BARR 1985, 50-52(Ez 27,11); SHIPP 1979, 420-421

ὄρνεον,-ου⁺   N2N 10-0-8-11-9-38
Gn 6,20; 9,2.10; 15,10.11
bird
Cf. SHIPP 1979, 422-423; WEVERS 1993, 209

ὀρνίθιον,-ου   N2N 13-0-0-0-0-13
Lv 14,4.5.6(ter)
small bird

ὀρνιθοσκοπέομαι   V 1-0-0-0-0-1
Lv 19,26
to observe birds, to watch birds for omens; neol.

ὄρνις,-ιθος⁺   N3M/F 0-1-0-0-0-1
1 Kgs 5,3
bird
Cf. SHIPP 1979, 422-423

ὅρος,-ου⁺   N2M 1-0-0-1-0-2
Ex 9,5; Neh 2,6
limit (of time)
Cf. ROST 1967, 130-132

ὄρος,-ους⁺   N3N 160-177-181-87-75-680
Gn 7,19.20; 8,4.5; 10,30
mountain, hill Gn 7,19; mountainous region Am 3,9; (mountainous) desert Jos 8,24
φάραγξ ὀρέων a deep ravine or glen surrounded by mountains Zech 14,5; τὸ ὄρος τοῦ οἴκου the temple mount Jer 33(26),18
*Gn 49,26 ὀρέων of the mountains -הררי for MT הורי of my progenitors?; *Lv 19,26 ἐπὶ τῶν ὀρέων on the mountains -על הרים for MT על ה/דם with (its) blood; *Nm 33,32 τὸ ὄρος the mountain -הר for MT חר Hor (proper name), see

also 33,33; *1 Kgs 16,24 τοῦ ὄρους *the mountain* -ההר for MT העיר *the city*; *Is 31,4 τὰ ὄρη *the mountains* -ההרים for MT רעים *shepherds*; *Is 45,2 καὶ ὀρή *and mountains* -והררים (1QIs[a]) for MT והדורים *and swellings*?; *Ez 48,10 τὸ ὄρος *the mountain* -ההר for MT היה *was*; *Am 4,3 τὸ ὄρος τὸ Ρεμμαν *the mountain Remman* -ההר רמן for MT ההרמונה *into Harmon*; *Ob 19 τὸ ὄρος *the mountain* -ההר for שׂדה *the field*; *Mi 2,9 ὄρεσιν *mountains* -הררי for MT הדרי *my glory*; *Zech 1,8 τῶν ὀρέων *the hills* -ההרים? or -ההררים? for MT ההדסים *the myrtle trees*, see also 1,10.11; *Ps 74(75),7 ἀπὸ ὀρέων *from the mountains* -◊הר for MT ◊רום *lifting up*?, see also Dn[LXX] 8,11

Cf. CADELL 1967, 343-349; DORIVAL 1994, 143.435.550; SHIPP 1979, 167.228-231.424; SPICQ 1978[a], 632-634; →MM; NIDNTT; PREISIGKE; TWNT

ὀροφοιτέω V 0-0-0-0-1-1
4 Mc 14,15
to roam the mountains; neol.

ὄροφος,-ου N2M 0-0-0-0-1-1
Wis 17,2
roof

ὀρόφωμα,-ατος N3N 0-1-1-0-0-2
2 Chr 3,7; Ez 41,26
ceiling, canopy; neol.?

ὀρτυγομήτρα,-ας N1F 3-0-0-1-2-6
Ex 16,13; Nm 11,31.32; Ps 104(105),40; Wis 16,2
a bird that migrates together with quails
Cf. DORIVAL 1994, 52.297; LE BOULLUEC 1989, 183

ὄρυξ,-ῦγος N3M 1-0-0-0-0-1
Dt 14,5
kind of gazelle, sable antelope

ὀρύσσω⁺ V 13-1-7-8-8-37
Gn 21,30; 26,15.18(bis).19
to dig, to dig out [τι] Gn 21,30; *id.* [abs.] Gn 26,19; *to dig up* [τι] (metaph.) Prv 16,27
*Ps 21(22),17 ὤρυξαν *they pierced* -כארו or -כרו- ◊כרה for MT כ/ארי *like a lion*?
(→ἀν-, δι-, ἐξ-, κατ-)

ὀρφανεία,-ας N1F 0-0-1-0-0-1
Is 47,8
var. form for ὀρφανία; *state of being orphaned, bereavement, loss of children*; see ὀρφανία
Cf. WALTERS 1973, 42

ὀρφανία,-ας N1F 0-0-0-0-1-1
PSal 4,10
orphanhood; see ὀρφανεία

ὀρφανός,-ή,-όν⁺ A 13-0-13-18-10-54
Ex 22,21.23; Dt 10,18; 14,29; 16,11
always rendition of יתום; *orphaned*; (ὁ) ὀρφανός *(the) orphan* Ex 22,21
*Jb 24,19 ὀρφανῶν *of the orphans* -◊יתום for MT חם *heat*
Cf. HORSLEY 1987, 162-164; SHIPP 1979, 424; →NIDNTT; TWNT

ὀρχέομαι⁺ V 0-5-1-1-0-7
2 Sm 6,16.20.21(bis); 1 Chr 15,29
to dance 2 Sm 6,16
*2 Sm 6,20 τῶν ὀρχουμένων *of the dancers* -הרקדים for MT הריקים *of the vulgar, of the vain*?
(→κατ-)

ὅς, ἥ, ὅ⁺ R 1241-1177-897-819-752-4886
Gn 1,11.12.21.30; 2,2
who, which, what, that

ὅσιος,-α,-ον⁺ A 3-1-2-37-35-78
Dt 29,18; 32,4; 33,8; 2 Sm 22,26; Is 55,3
holy (of God) Dt 32,4; *holy, pious, devoted to God* (of humans) Ps 31(32),6; *holy, pious* (of thoughts) 2 Mc 12,45; οἱ ὅσιοι *the saints* Ps 29(30),5; (τὰ) ὅσια *the divine decrees, the holy things* Wis 6,10; *kindness, grace* Dt 29,18
οὐχ ὅσιος *ungodly* Ps 42(43),1
Cf. BARR 1961, 111; BOLKESTEIN 1936, 168.184.210; DODD 1954, 62-64; DOGNIEZ 1992, 301(Dt 29,18); DUPONT 1961=1967, 337-359(esp.342-344); LARCHER 1984, 414-415; LIFSHITZ 1962[a], 73; PRIJS 1948, 43(n.3); WEVERS 1995, 511(Dt 32,4)

ὁσιότης,-ητος⁺ N3F 1-2-0-1-5-9
Dt 9,5; 1 Sm 14,41; 1 Kgs 9,4; Prv 14,32; Od 9,75
piety, holiness Dt 9,5
*1 Sm 14,41 ὁσιότητα *holiness, symbols of truth* for MT תָמִים, originally תֻּמִּים? *Thummim*; *Prv 14,32 τῇ ἑαυτοῦ ὁσιότητι *his piety* -תֻמּוֹ for MT מותו *his death*
Cf. CAIRD 1968[b]=1972, 124; DODD 1954, 62-64; LARCHER 1984, 568-569

ὁσιόω V 0-1-0-1-1-3
2 Sm 22,26; Ps 17(18),26; Wis 6,10
P: *to be declared holy, to be holy*

ὁσίως⁺ D 0-1-0-0-1-2
1 Kgs 8,61; Wis 6,10
holily, in holiness
→TWNT

ὀσμή,-ῆς⁺ N1F 47-0-8-13-11-79
Gn 8,21; 27,27(ter); Ex 5,21
smell, odour Gn 27,27; *id.* (pleasant) Ct 7,9; *id.* (unpleasant) 2 Mc 9,9
ὀσμὴ εὐωδίας *fragrant offering* Lv 1,9 (often

used for rendering (ריח ניחוח

*Jer 25,10 ὀσμήν *scent* -ריח- for MT רחים *millstones*
Cf. DANIEL 1966, 173-199; HARLÉ 1988, 38.209; ZIEGLER
1958, 45(Jer 25,10); →NIDNTT; TWNT

ὅσος,-η,-ον⁺   R 246-158-48-71-92-615
Gn 1,31; 6,17.22; 7,5.22
as much as Prv 6,26; *as long as* Gn 25,7; *as
many as* Ex 9,19; *that* Gn 1,31; *all who* 1 Mc
10,43; *all that* Gn 6,17
ὅσῳ ... τοσούτῳ ... *the more ... the more ...* Tobˢ
2,10; ὅσον *as much as* [+numeral] Jos 3,4; *but
only* 1 Kgs 17,12; πάντα ὅσα *everything* Gn 6,22;
ὅσον χρόνον *as long as* Jos 4,14; μικρὸν ὅσον
ὅσον *in a very little while* Is 26,20

ὅσπερ, ἥπερ, ὅπερ⁺   R 0-0-0-1-4-5
Jb 6,17; 2 Mc 3,36; 4 Mc 1,12; 13,19; Wis 19,18
what exactly, which indeed

ὅσπριον,-ου   N2N 0-0-0-2-0-2
Dnᴸˣˣ 1,12.16
pulse (the edible seeds of vegetables such as
peas, beans, lentils)

ὅστις, ἥτις, ὅ τι⁺   R 53-13-13-37-19-135
Ex 9,18.24; 11,6; 20,2; 22,8
any one who, whoever Ps 63(64),4; *whichever,
whatever* Ex 22,8; *who* (as rel. pron.) Ex 9,18

ὁστισοῦν, ἡτισοῦν, ὁτιοῦν   R 1-0-0-0-3-4
Dt 24,10; 2 Mc 5,10; 14,3; 3 Mc 7,7
whatever

ὀστοῦν,-οῦ⁺   N2N 11-29-32-40-17-129
Gn 2,23(bis); 29,14; 50,25; Ex 12,10
bone Gn 2,23; τὰ ὀστᾶ *the bones* (indicating a
dead pers.) Gn 50,25
καὶ εἰσῆλθεν τρόμος εἰς τὰ ὀστᾶ μου *and
trembling penetrated my bones* or *trembling took
hold of my bones* (indicating the inner part of
the body) Hab 3,16
Cf. DORIVAL 1994, 140; →NIDNTT

ὀστράκινος,-η,-ον⁺   A 6-0-5-8-0-19
Lv 6,21; 11,33; 14,5.50; 15,12
earthen, made of clay
→NIDNTT

ὅστρακον,-ου⁺   N2N 0-0-1-14-1-16
Is 30,14; Ps 21(22),16; Jb 2,8; Prv 26,23; Dnᴸˣˣ
2,35
earthenware Dn 2,35; *potsherd* Jb 2,8
→MM; NIDNTT

ὀστρακώδης,-ης,-ες   A 0-1-0-0-0-1
Jgsᴮ 1,35
full of potsherds

ὀσφραίνομαι   V 5-4-1-2-4-16

Gn 8,21; 27,27; Ex 30,38; Lv 26,31; Dt 4,28
to smell, to catch the scent of [τι] Gn 27,27; *id.*
[τινος] Lv 26,31; *id.* [ἔν τινι] Ex 30,38; *id.*
[abs.] Dt 4,28; *to get scent of* [τινος] (metaph.)
Jb 39,25
Cf. DANIEL 1966, 334-339; SCHREINER 1957, 60(JgsᴬA
15,14)

ὀσφρασία,-ας   N1F 0-0-1-0-0-1
Hos 14,7
scent, odour; neol.

ὀσφύς,-ύος⁺   N3F 9-11-30-9-7-66
Gn 35,11; 37,34; Ex 12,11; 28,42; Lv 3,9
waist, loins Gn 37,34; *id.* (as the place of
reproductive organs) Gn 35,11
*Is 15,4 ἡ ὀσφύς *the loins* -חלצי (subst. st.cstr. pl.)
for MT חלצי (part.) *equipped for war*?
Cf. HARLÉ 1988, 92; →TWNT

ὅταν⁺   C 55-13-61-49-32-210
Gn 38,9; 40,14; Ex 1,16; 3,21; 11,1
contr. of ὅτε ἄν; conj. with (often) indefinite
significance; *when*

ὅτε⁺   C 22-27-18-31-75-173
Gn 2,4; 11,10; 12,4; 24,30; 25,20
when Lv 26,45; *during the time when, while* Zech
7,7; *when* (as a substitute for a rel. pron. after a
noun denoting time) Gn 11,10
ἀφ' ὅτε [+ind.] *after that* Ezr 5,12; ἕως ὅτε
[+ind.] *until that* Dnᴸˣˣ 7,9; ἐγένετο ὅτε
[+ind.] *and (it came about that) when* 1 Sm 5,4

ὅτι⁺   C 518-1188-767-936-632-4041
Gn 1,4.8.10.12.18
that (introduces a clause which explains what is
meant by a word in the preceding clause) Jdt
8,8; *that* (introduces a clause after verbs that
denote a mental or sense perception) Ps
93(94),11; *that* (introduces a clause after verbs
of believing, hoping) Jdt 6,9; *that* (introduces a
clause after verbs of saying) Jdt 11,8; *that*
(introduces direct speech after verbs of saying;
remains untranslated) Gn 48,1
*with regard to the fact that, in consideration of
the fact that* Ru 2,13; *so that* 1 Sm 20,1; *because,
since* Jer 38(31),15; *for* Jgsᴮ 14,3; *that* (indicating
a circumstance which calls for explanation) Hab
2,18
τί ὅτι *why* Ex 1,18
Cf. AEJMELAEUS 1985=1993, 17-36; 1990=1993, 37-48;
PRÉAUX 1931, 414-415; TRÉBOLLE BARRERA 1989,
109-111

ὀτρύνω   V 0-0-0-0-1-1

3 Mc 5,46
to urge on sb to [τινα ἐπί τι]
(→ἐπ-)

οὗ⁺ D 54-13-20-8-20-115
Gn 2,11; 13,3.4.14; 19,27
where Gn 2,11; *where* (after a noun that denotes locality) Gn 13,3; *where, to which* Jos 1,9

οὐ⁺ X 630-305-651-493-451-2530
Gn 2,5.17.18; 3,1.3
Οὐ -like its compounds- is a neg. part. meaning *not.* Οὐ is used in sentences expressing fact, statement or objectivity. Οὐ placed before a verb can deny a whole sentence, οὐ μέμνησαι τῶν λόγων *you do not remember the words* Tob^BA 6,16; or just the word preceded by it, αὐτοὶ παρεζήλωσάν με ἐπ' οὐ θεῷ *they have provoked me to jealousy with that which is not God* Dt 32,21; οὐ introduces a question to which an affirm. answer is expected, οὐ μή [+subj.] expresses a strong prohibition, οὐ μὴ φάγητε ἀπὸ παντὸς ξύλου τοῦ ἐν τῷ παραδείσῳ *you shall not eat of any tree in the garden* Gn 3,1; οὐ μόνον ... ἀλλὰ καί ... *not only ... but also ...* Jdt 11,7; πᾶς ... οὐκ *nobody, no* (semit. for class. οὐδείς) Ex 12,43
*Gn 4,15 οὐχ οὕτως *not so* -לא כן for MT לכן *therefore*, see also 30,15; *Gn 26,32 οὐχ *not* -לא for MT לו *to him*; *Mi 2,4 οὐκ *not* -אין for MT איך *how*
Cf. CONYBEARE 1905=1988, 79-80; SHIPP 1979, 424-425
(→οὐδαμοῦ, οὐδαμῶς, οὐδέ, οὐδείς, οὐδέποτε, οὐδέπω, οὐθείς, οὐκ, οὐκέτι, οὔπω, οὔτε, οὐχ, οὐχί)

οὐαί⁺ I 1-4-50-4-7-66
Nm 21,29; 1 Sm 4,7.8; 1 Kgs 12,24m; 13,30
exclamation of pain or grief or horror; *ah!, woe!, alas!* [+nom.] Am 5,18; *id.* [+voc.] 1 Kgs 12,24m; *id.* [+dat.] Nm 21,29; *id.* [ἐπί τινι] Jer 10,19; *id.* [ἐπί τινα] Jer 22,18; *id.* [ἐπί τι] Jer 31(48),1; *woe* (as subst.) Ez 2,10
οὐαὶ οὐαί *id.* (doubled for emphasis) Am 5,16
*Jer 28(51),2 οὐαί *woe* -הוי for MT היו *they were*; *Na 3,17 οὐαὶ αὐτοῖς *woe to them* -אוים? for MT אים *where are they*; *Zph 3,18 οὐαί *woe* -הוי for MT היו *they are*?
Cf. KRAFT 1972^b, 161.170-172; LOWE 1967, 34-39; SPICQ 1982, 446-449; →NIDNTT

οὐδαμοῦ D 0-1-0-3-0-4
1 Kgs 2,36; Jb 19,7; 21,9; Prv 23,5
nowhere at all

οὐδαμῶς⁺ D 0-0-0-0-7-7
2 Mc 9,7.18; 11,4; 3 Mc 1,11; 2,24
no way, by no means

οὐδέ⁺ C 105-74-192-107-136-614
Gn 3,3; 21,26(bis); 39,9; 45,6
negative conjunction continuing a preceding negation almost always with οὐ; *and not, nor* Ps 15(16),10; *not even* 2 Sm 13,30

οὐδείς, οὐδεμία, οὐδέν⁺ A 43-31-37-58-101-270
Gn 19,31; 20,9; 23,6; 30,31; 31,32
not one, no one, none Gn 19,31; *nothing* Gn 30,31; *no* [+subst.] Jb 15,3
*Mi 2,11 οὐδενός *no one* -לא־איש or- לא יש for MT לי־איש *if a man*; *Jb 42,2 οὐθέν *nothing* -מומה for MT מזמה *a plan*
Cf. BICKERMAN 1976, 159; HORSLEY 1987, 164-165

-ουδενέω
(→ἐξ-)

οὐδενόω
(→ἐξ-)

οὐδέποτε⁺ D 1-1-0-0-2-4
Ex 10,6; 1 Kgs 1,6; 2 Mc 6,16; Wis 15,17
never (ever)

οὐδέπω⁺ D 1-0-0-0-0-1
Ex 9,30
not yet

οὐθείς, οὐθέν⁺
see οὐδείς

-ουθενέω
(→ἐξ-)

-ουθενόω
(→ἐξ-)

οὐκ⁺ X 572-920-790-741-534-3557
Gn 2,5.25; 4,7; 9,11(bis)
see οὐ

οὐκέτι⁺ D 8-3-74-12-15-112
Ex 5,7.10; 9,28; 10,29; 11,6
no more, no longer, no further Ex 5,7
*Jb 14,10 οὐκέτι ἐστίν *he is no more* -איננו for MT איו *where is he?*

οὐλή,-ῆς N1F 7-0-0-0-0-7
Lv 13,2.10(bis).19.23
scar, mark

οὖν⁺ C 80-16-2-47-115-260
Gn 6,14; 8,21; 12.12.13; 16,2
so, therefore, consequently, accordingly, then Gn 12,12; *so, therefore* (in commands) Gn 6,14; *so* (introducing a summary) Ex 5,16; *then* Gn 19,9; *in reply, in turn* Ex 8,6
Cf. NAUCK 1958, 134-135; WEVERS 1993, 112.270

οὕπερ   D 0-0-0-0-1-1
2 Mc 4,38
where (as rel. adv.)

οὕπω⁺   D 3-0-1-1-3-8
Gn 15,16; 18,12; 29,7; Is 7,17; Eccl 4,3
not yet Gn 15,16; *not, not at all* Is 7,17
*Gn 18,12 οὕπω *not yet* -אַחֲרֵי בְלֹתִי? for MT אַחֲרֵי בְלֹתִי
now that I am withered
Cf. HARL 1986ᵃ, 175

οὐρά,-ᾶς⁺   N1F 2-0-3-2-0-7
Dt 28,13.44; Is 9,13.14; 19,15
tail Jb 40,17
κεφαλὴν καὶ οὐράν *head and tail* (social
categories) Is 9,13, cpr. 19,15; Dt 28,13.44
Cf. DOGNIEZ 1992, 286

οὐραγέω   V 0-1-0-0-1-2
Jos 6,9; Sir 32,11
to be the rear guard, to bring up the rear Jos 6,9;
to lag behind Sir 32,11; neol.?

οὐραγία,-ας   N1F 1-1-0-0-0-2
Dt 25,18; Jos 10,19
rear guard; neol.?
Cf. DOGNIEZ 1992, 274; WEVERS 1995, 398

οὐράνιος,-ος,-ον⁺   A 0-0-0-1-7-8
Dnᵀʰ 4,26(23); 1 Ezr 6,14; 2 Mc 7,34; 9,10; 3 Mc
6,18
heavenly, dwelling in heaven 1 Ezr 6,14; *of
heaven, in heaven* 2 Mc 9,10
→TWNT

οὐρανόθεν⁺   D 0-0-0-0-1-1
4 Mc 4,10
from heaven
→NIDNTT

οὐρανός,-οῦ⁺   N2M 106-97-108-234-137-682
Gn 1,1.8.9(bis).14
heaven Gn 1,1; *sky* Dt 4,11; *heaven* (as abode of
the divine) Is 66,1; *heaven* (periphrasis for God)
Jb 22,26; οἱ οὐρανοί *the heavens* Ps 96(97),6
ὑπὸ τὸν οὐρανόν *under heaven, on earth* Eccl
1,13
Cf. ALEXANDRE 1988, 111-112; DODD 1954, 20.23;
HORSLEY 1983, 50; KATZ 1950, 141-149; 1956,
267-273(esp.268); TORM 1934, 48-50; WEVERS 1995,
81.182; →NIDNTT; TWNT

οὐρέω   V 0-5-0-0-0-5
1 Sm 25,22.34; 1 Kgs 12,24m(14,10); 20(21),21;
2 Kgs 9,8
to urinate; οὐρῶν πρὸς τοῖχον *one urinating
against the wall, male*

οὔριος,-α,-ον   A 0-0-1-0-0-1

Is 59,5
with a fair wind; (ᾠὸν) οὔριον *wind-egg* (i.e. a
sterile and unimpregnated egg, producing no
chick)

οὖρον,-ου   N2N 0-1-1-0-0-2
2 Kgs 18,27; Is 36,12
urine

οὖς, ὠτός⁺   N3N 27-36-50-53-24-190
Gn 20,8; 23,13.16; 35,4; 50,4
ear Ex 29,20
εἰσέρχομαι εἰς τὰ ὦτά τινος *to come to one's
ears* Ps 17(18),7; ἐν τοῖς ὠσί τινος *in
someone's hearing* Dt 5,1; τοῖς ὠσὶ βαρέως
ἀκούω *to be hard of hearing, to comprehend
slowly* Is 6,10; δὸς εἰς τὰ ὦτα Ἰησοῖ *speak in
the ears of Joshua, recite (this) in the hearing of
Joshua* Ex 17,14
Cf. SHIPP 1979, 425; →TWNT

οὐσία,-ας⁺   N1F 0-0-0-0-2-2
Tobᴮᴬ 14,13; 3 Mc 3,28
property, estate
Cf. HAMM 1977, 416-417(Dn 3,96(30)); →NIDNTT

οὐσιάζω
(→ἐνεξ-, ἐξ-)

οὔτε⁺   C 21-2-14-15-71-123
Ex 20,17(quinquies)
neg. conjunction; *and not, nor* Dnᴸˣˣ 2,43
οὔτε ... οὔτε ... *neither ... nor ...* Sir 42,21

οὗτος, αὕτη, τοῦτο⁺   R 1104-1099-929-526-753-4411
Gn 2,4.11.13.14(bis)
this Gn 2,4; *this* (referring to the pers. who has
just been mentioned) 1 Sm 1,2; *id.* (referring to
that which has just been mentioned) Gn 2,13;
this (referring to the pers. who is about to be
mentioned) Ex 6,26; *id.* (referring to that which
is about to be mentioned) 2 Mc 1,24; *this, the
present* (of time) Jer 51,6; *this* (referring to sth
very close; of place) Ex 4,17
*Gn 18,10 τοῦτον *this* -הזה for MT היה *life*; *Jer
23,10 τούτων *of these* -אלה for MT אָלָה *curse*; *Ez
47,13 ταῦτα *this* -זה for MT נה (= גיא?) *valley*;
*Zech 14,17 καὶ οὗτοι *and these* -ואלה for MT
ולא *and not*; *Ps 143(144),13 εἰς τοῦτο *to the
other* -אל־זה for MT אל־זן *to (another) kind?*; *Jb
19,26 ταῦτα *these things* -אלה for MT אלוה *God*,
see also Jb 27,22
Cf. HARL 1986ᵃ, 173.175

οὕτω(ς)⁺   D 137-193-234-124-164-852
Gn 1,6.9.11.15.20
so, in this way (referring to what precedes) Is

53,7; *id.* (referring to what follows) 1 Kgs 13,9; *so much, accordingly* Hos 4,7; *such a thing, such a person* Gn 29,26; *so* (as adj.) Gn 15,5
*Is 57,20 οὕτως *so* -כזה for MT כים *as the sea*

οὐχ   X 70-86-78-110-92-436
Gn 2,20; 4,15; 5,24; 8,7.9
see οὐ

οὐχί⁺   X 33-72-32-33-30-200
Gn 18,15; 19,2; 23,15; 40,8; 42,10
emphatic form of οὐ
Cf. WALTERS 1973, 309-310

ὀφείλημα,-ατος⁺   N3N 2-0-0-0-2-4
Dt 24,10(bis); 1 Ezr 3,20; 1 Mc 15,8
debt
→NIDNTT; TWNT

ὀφείλω⁺   V 4-1-3-5-11-24
Ex 16,3; Nm 14,2; 20,3; Dt 15,2; 2 Kgs 5,3
A: *to owe, to have to pay for* [τί τινι] Dt 15,2; *id.* [τι] 1 Mc 10,43; *id.* [τι] (metaph.) Jb 6,20; *to be obligated to, to be bound to* [+inf.] 4 Mc 11,15; *to deserve to* [+inf.] Wis 12,15
εἰ ὄφελον [+hist. tense] *would I ...* (expressing an unfulfilled wish) Jb 14,13; εἰ ὄφελον [+subj.] *id.* (expressing an unfulfilled wish) Jb 30,24; ὄφελον [+hist. tense] *id.* (unfulfilled wish) Ex 16,3; ὄφελον [+subj.] *id.* (unfulfilled wish) Ps 118(119),5; ὄφελον *id.* (as adv.) 2 Kgs 5,3; ὁ ὀφείλων *debtor* Is 24,2
P: *to be due* or *liable to* [τινι] Wis 12,20; *to be deserved* 3 Mc 7,10
Cf. HARL 1992ᵃ=1992ᵇ, 235(Jer 15,10); LE BOULLUEC 1989, 180; →NIDNTT; TWNT

ὄφελος,-ους⁺   N3N 0-0-0-1-0-1
Jb 15,3
profit, benefit, good
Cf. KRAFT 1972ᵇ, 161.172

-οφθαλμέω
(→ἀντ-)

ὀφθαλμός,-οῦ⁺   N2M 88-158-140-174-118-678
Gn 3,5.6.7; 13,10.14
eye Gn 3,5
ὀφθαλμοῖς κατ᾽ ὀφθαλμούς *face to face* Nm 14,14; ἀδύνατος τοῖς ὀφθαλμοῖς *of weak eyes, blind* Tobˢ 5,10; ἐν ὀφθαλμοῖς (frequent rendition of semiprepos. such as בעיני, semit.) *in (your) eyes* 1 Sm 1,18; cpr. κατ᾽ ὀφθαλμούς, πρὸ ὀφθαλμῶν
*1 Sm 2,29 ἀναιδεῖ ὀφθαλμῷ see ἀναιδής; *Ez 7,13 ὀφθαλμῷ *eye* -עין for MT עונו *his iniquity*; *Zph 3,7 ἐξ ὀφθαλμῶν αὐτῆς *from her*

eyes, from her face מעיניה for MT מעונה *from her dwelling*; *Prv 15,15 οἱ ὀφθαλμοί *the eyes* -עני for MT עני *the poor*; *Lam 3,63 ἐπὶ ὀφθαλμοὺς αὐτῶν *upon their eyes* -מעיניהם for MT מנגינתם *their mockering song*
Cf. SCHENKEL 1978, 13-17; SHIPP 1979, 426-427; SOLLAMO 1979, 123-155; →MM; NIDNTT; TWNT

ὀφθαλμοφανῶς   D 0-0-0-1-0-1
Est 8,13
visibly; neol.

ὀφιόδηκτος,-ος,-ον   A 0-0-0-0-1-1
Sir 12,13
bitten by a snake; neol.

ὀφιομάχης,-ου   N1M 1-0-0-0-0-1
Lv 11,22
one who fights with snakes; neol.
Cf. HARLÉ 1988, 130

ὄφις,-εως⁺   N3M 18-1-9-7-5-40
Gn 3,1(bis).2.4.13
snake, serpent Gn 3,1; *id.* (of brass) Nm 21,9
Cf. LE BOULLUEC 1989, 36.101; TOV 1979, 221; →NIDNTT; TWNT

ὄφλησις,-εως   N3F 0-0-0-0-1-1
Bar 3,8
penalty, punishment; neol.
Cf. WAMBACQ 1957, 374

ὀφρύς,-ύος⁺   N3F 1-0-0-0-0-1
Lv 14,9
eyebrow

ὀχεία,-ας   N1F 0-0-0-0-1-1
Sir 33,6
impregnating, covering (of a male horse)

ὀχεύω
(→κατ-)

ὀχθίζω
(→προσ-)

ὀχλαγωγέω   V 0-0-1-0-0-1
Am 7,16
to draw a crowd, to stir up [ἐπί τινα]; neol.?

ὀχλέω⁺   V 0-0-0-0-3-3
Tobᴮᴬ 6,8(bis); 3 Mc 5,41
A: *to disturb, to trouble* [τινα] Tobᴮᴬ 6,8 (primo); *to cause tumult* 3 Mc 5,41
P: *to be troubled* Tobᴮᴬ 6,8(secundo)
Cf. HELBING 1928, 99
(→ἐν-, παρεν-)

ὄχλος,-ου⁺   N2M 1-5-9-15-25-55
Nm 20,20; Jos 6,13(bis); 2 Sm 15,22; 1 Kgs 21(20),13
crowd, host, multitude Nm 20,20; *army, troop*

1 Mc 1,17; *population* (as distinct from the Jews) Bel^LXX 30; οἱ ὄχλοι *the peoples* (syn. of λαοί and ἔθνη) Dn^LXX 3,4
*Jer 39(32),24 ὄχλος *crowd* corr.? ὁ χοῦς *the soil heaped up, rampart* for MT סללות *ramparts*
Cf. JOÜON 1937, 618-619; ROST 1967, 112-118; →NIDNTT; TWNT

ὀχυρός,-ά,-όν⁺   A 5-19-17-7-16-64
Ex 1,11; Nm 13,28; 32,36; Dt 3,5; 28,52
strong, firm, lasting, fortified Ex 1,11; *strong, secure* Is 17,3
Cf. DORIVAL 1994, 62

ὀχυρόω   V 0-2-1-0-14-17
Jos 6,1; 2 Chr 11,11; Jer 28(51),53; 1 Mc 1,62; 4,61
A: *to fortify* [τι] Sir 48,17; *to lock, to secure* [τι] LtJ 17
P: *to be fortified, to be secured, to be besieged* Jos 6,1; *id.* (metaph.) 4 Mc 13,7
(→προσ-)

ὀχύρωμα,-ατος⁺   N3N 4-7-15-12-35-73
Gn 39,20(bis); 40,14; 41,14; Jos^A 19,29
stronghold, fortress 2 Sm 22,2; *prison* Gn 39,20; *fortress* (metaph.) Prv 10,29
*Dn^Th 11,43 ἐν τοῖς ὀχυρώμασιν αὐτῶν *in their strongholds* -ב/מצוריו for MT ב/מצעריו *in his steps*
Cf. HARL 1986ᵃ, 269; LEE, J. 1983, 68; WEVERS 1993, 660; →TWNT

ὀχυρωμάτιον,-ου   N2N 0-0-0-0-1-1
1 Mc 16,15
small fortification; neol.

ὀχύρωσις,-εως   N3F 0-0-0-0-2-2
1 Mc 10,11; 14,10
fortifying, process of fortification; neol.?

ὀψάριον,-ου⁺   N2N 0-0-0-0-1-1
Tob^S 2,2
dim. of ὄψον; ὀψάρια *foodstuff, victuals, food*
Cf. KALLITSUNAKIS 1926, 96-106; SHIPP 1979, 427; →LSJ RSuppl; NIDNTT

ὀψέ⁺   D 2-0-2-0-0-4
Gn 24,11; Ex 30,8; Is 5,11; Jer 2,23

late in the day, in the evening
Cf. WEVERS 1993, 347; →NIDNTT

ὀψία,-ας⁺   N1F 0-0-0-0-1-1
Jdt 13,1
the latter part of the day, evening

ὀψίζω   V 0-0-0-0-1-1
Sir 36,27
to come at night, to come late
→LSJ Suppl; LSJ RSuppl

ὄψιμος,-ος,-ον⁺   A 2-0-4-1-0-7
Ex 9,32; Dt 11,14; Jer 5,24; Hos 6,3; Jl 2,23
far on in time, late Ex 9,32
ὑετὸς ὄψιμος *late rain* (in spring) Dt 11,14
Cf. DOGNIEZ 1992, 189; →NIDNTT

ὄψις,-εως⁺   N3F 24-2-9-7-17-59
Gn 24,16; 26,7; 29,17; 39,6; 41,21
outward appearance, aspect (of pers.) Gn 24,16; *id.* (of things) Lv 13,3; *face* (of pers.) Ct 2,14; *countenance* 2 Mc 3,16; *face* (of the earth) Ex 10,5; *sight* Wis 3,4; αἱ ὄψεις *the eyes* Tob^BA 14,2
ὑπὸ τὴν ὄψιν *under the notice, under the eyes* Est 8,12i, see also 2 Mc 3,36; 12,42
Cf. BRUNSCHWIG 1973, 24-39; LE BOULLUEC 1989, 136(Ex 10,5); WALTERS 1973, 67(Nm 10,31)

ὄψον,-ου   N2N 0-0-0-0-2-2
Tob^BA 2,2; 7,8
food; ὄψα *varied dishes*
Cf. KALLITSUNAKIS 1926, 96-106; SHIPP 1979, 428; →MM

ὀψοποίημα,-ατος   N3N 0-0-0-0-1-1
Jdt 12,1
food, meat (dressed); neol.

ὄψος,-ους   N3N 1-0-0-0-0-1
Nm 11,22
fish (coll. sg.); neol.
Cf. DORIVAL 1994, 293

ὀψώνιον,-ου⁺   N2N 0-0-0-0-3-3
1 Ezr 4,56; 1 Mc 3,28; 14,32
pay, wages 1 Mc 3,28; *provisions* 1 Mc 14,32
Cf. CARAGOUNIS 1974, 41-42; HORSLEY 1982, 93; LAUNEY 1950, 726; SHIPP 1979, 429; SPICQ 1978ᵃ, 635-638; →NIDNTT; TWNT

παγγέωργος,-ος,-ον   A 0-0-0-0-1-1
4 Mc 1,29
master-gardener (metaph.); neol.

παγετός,-οῦ   N2M 1-0-1-0-2-4
Gn 31,40; Jer 43(36),30; Sir 3,15; Bar 2,25
frost

παγιδεύω⁺   V 0-1-0-1-0-2
1 Sm 28,9; Eccl 9,12
to spread a snare for, to entrap [τινα]; neol.
→MM; TWNT

παγίς,-ίδος⁺   N3F 0-1-13-37-13-64
Jos 23,13; Is 8,14; 24,17.18; 42,22
trap, snare Jb 18,8; *id.* (metaph.) Tob 14,10
*Prv 21,6 παγίδας *snares* -מוקשי for MT מבקשי
they who seek
Cf. BARR 1985, 52-53; CAIRD 1976, 81; DE WAARD 1981,
555; LIEBERMAN 1942, 45; STÄHLIN 1930, 98-104; →TWNT

παγκρατής,-ής,-ές   A 0-0-0-0-1-1
2 Mc 3,22
all-powerful

πάγος,-ου⁺   N2M 1-0-2-3-1-7
Ex 16,14; Na 3,17; Zech 14,6; Jb 37,10; Dnᴸˣˣ
3,69
frost
Cf. SHIPP 1979, 429; WEVERS 1990, 249

παθεινός,-ή,-όν   A 0-0-0-1-0-1
Jb 29,25
suffering, mournful; neol.?
-παθέω
(→συμ-)

παθοκράτεια,-ας   N1F 0-0-0-0-2-2
4 Mc 13,5.16
mastery over passion; neol.

παθοκρατέομαι   V 0-0-0-0-1-1
4 Mc 7,20
to be governed by passion, to be slave to one's passions, emotions; neol.

πάθος,-ους⁺   N3N 0-0-0-2-62-64
Jb 30,31; Prv 25,20; 4 Mc 1,1.3.4
misfortune, calamity, trouble Prv 25,20; *mourning* Jb 30,31; *emotion, passion, lust* 4 Mc 1,1; *propensity* 4 Mc 1,35
→NIDNTT; TWNT

παιάν,-ᾶνος   N3M 0-0-0-0-1-1
2 Mc 15,25
paean, battle-cry

παιγνία,-ας   N1F 0-1-1-0-0-2
Jgsᴮ 16,27; Jer 30(49),10
game, amusement Jgsᴮ 16,27; *insolence* Jer 30(49),10

Cf. HARL 1984ᵇ=1992ᵃ, 49

παίγνιον,-ου   N2N 0-0-1-0-2-3
Hab 1,10; Wis 12,26; 15,12
plaything, toy Hab 1,10; *child's game, playful gesture* Wis 12,26
Cf. GILBERT 1973, 214-215; LARCHER 1985, 741.874

παιδάριον,-ου⁺   N2N 8- 188-3-12-23-234
Gn 22,5.12; 33,14; 37,30; 42,22
little boy, child Gn 22,5; *young man* Tob 6,3; *servant* 1 Sm 25,8
παιδαρίων καὶ κορασίων *of young boys and girls* Zech 8,5; ἐκ παιδαρίου *from childhood* Jer 31(48),11
Cf. SCHOLL 1983, 9-12.15; SPICQ 1978ᵇ, 220-224; STANTON
1988, 476-477; WEVERS 1993, 567; →MM

παιδεία,-ας⁺   N1F 1-0-16-35-58-110
Dt 11,2; Is 26,16; 50,4.5(4); 53,5
teaching, instruction, correction, discipline Dt 11,2; *mental culture, learning* (result of teaching) Sir prol.,29; *education, training* Wis 2,12; *chastisement* Prv 22,15
*Ps 2,12 παιδείας *correction* corr. παιδός *lad* for MT בר (Aram.) *son*; *Ez 13,9 ἐν παιδείᾳ *in chastisement* -יסר◊ for MT בסוד/בסר *in secret*, see also Am 3,7; *Hab 1,12 παιδείαν αὐτοῦ *his chastisement* -יסר◊ for MT יסדתו *you have established him*; *Ps 17(18),36 ἡ παιδεία σου *your chastisement* -וענתך for MT וענותך¹¹ענה◊ *your gentleness*, cpr. 2 Sm 22,36
Cf. DOGNIEZ 1992, 186; LARCHER 1983, 175.243.281; PRIJS
1948, XVI(Ps 2,12).64(Is 50,4); →MM; NIDNTT; TWNT

παιδευτής,-οῦ⁺   N1M 0-0-1-0-4-5
Hos 5,2; 4 Mc 5,34; 9,6; Sir 37,19; PSal 8,29
teacher, instructor 4 Mc 5,34; *corrector* Hos 5,2
Cf. SPICQ 1978ᵃ, 641

παιδεύω⁺   V 9-10-14-25-30-88
Lv 26,18.23.28; Dt 4,36; 8,5
A: *to bring up, to rear* [τινα] Est 2,7; *to teach, to instruct* [τινα] Dt 4,36; *to correct, to discipline, to chastise, to punish* [τινα] Lv 26,18
P: *to be instructed* Prv 10,4a; *to be discreet* Tobᴮᴬ 4,14
*Ez 28,3 ἐπαίδευσάν σε *they have instructed you* -עממוך◊ *they have loaded* (with their instruction) for MT עממוך ?, cpr. 2 Chr 10,11; *Ps 89(90),10 παιδευθησόμεθα *we shall be chastened* -ענה◊ for MT נעפה *and we fly away*; *Prv 22,3 παιδεύεται *he is instructed* -יוסר for MT יסתר *he hides*
Cf. BERTRAM 1932, 33-51; DOGNIEZ 1992, 170-171.327;
HARL 1992ᵃ=1993, 193; HARLÉ 1988, 207; WEVERS 1995,

88.356; →NIDNTT; TWNT

(→ἐκ-, μετα-)

παιδίον,-ου⁺ N2N 58-16-17-6-72-169
Gn 17,12; 21,7.8.12.14
dim. of παῖς little, young child, infant (of newborns) Gn 17,12; child Nm 14,3; (own) child Is 49,15; foal (young of anim.) Gn 32,16
ἐκ παιδίου from childhood Is 46,3
*Is 66,12 τὰ παιδία αὐτῶν their sucklings -יונקיהם for MT ינקתם you shall suck them
Cf. SCHOLL 1983, 12-13.15; SPICQ 1978ᵇ, 221-222; STANTON 1988, 468-471; WEVERS 1993, 303.548.567

παιδίσκη,-ης⁺ N1F 53-8-6-9-22-98
Gn 12,16; 16,1.2.3.5
young woman Gn 34,4; female slave, servant-girl, maid Gn 12,16
Cf. AMUSIN 1986, 117-119.145-146; HEINEN 1984, 1287-1295; LLEWELYN 1994, 166; SCHOLL 1983, 8-9.15; SHIPP 79, 430; SPICQ 1978ᵇ, 220-224; STANTON 1988, 471.472(Jdt 11,5).473-474; WEVERS 1993, 217; →MM

παιδοποιέω V 0-0-0-0-1-1
2 Mc 14,25
M: to beget children

παιδοποιία,-ας N1F 0-0-0-0-1-1
4 Mc 17,6
child-bearing

παίζω⁺ V 3-8-5-2-3-21
Gn 21,9; 26,8; Ex 32,6; Jgs 16,25
to play Zech 8,5; to play with [μετά τινος] Gn 21,9; id. [ἔν τινι] Jb 40,29(26); to dance and sing Ex 32,6; to play an instrument Jer 37(30),19; to play amorously with [μετά τινος] Gn 26,8; to jest, to mock Jer 15,17
Cf. HARL 1984ᵇ=1992ª, 45.46.49; 1986ª, 189.210; WEVERS 1993, 402; →TWNT

(→ἐγκατα-, ἐκ-, ἐμ-, κατα-, προσ-, συμ-)

παῖς, παιδός⁺ N3M/F 126-184-39-47-74-470
Gn 9,25.26.27; 12,16; 14,15
child (in relation to parents) Prv 29,15; slave, servant Gn 9,25; courtier, attendant 1 Sm 22,17; servant (of humans in relation to God) Is 41,8; girl, young lady Gn 24,28; girl, slave, maid Ru 2,6; παῖδες children Prv 4,1
ἐκ παιδός from childhood, from youth Gn 46,34
*Gn 26,18 οἱ παῖδες the servants -עברי- (Sam. Pent.) for MT בימי in the days of; *Gn 47,21 εἰς παῖδας for servants -ל/עברים for MT ל/ערים into the cities; *Jos 7,7 διεβίβασεν ὁ παῖς σου your servant brought over -עברד העביר for MT העברת העביר you surely brought over; *Jer 47(40),9 τῶν

παίδων of the servants of -מעברי- מעבור for MT to serve, see also 2 Kgs 25,24; *Prv 1,4 παιδὶ δὲ νέῳ but to a young child, but to a little child double translation of MT נער young man
Cf. AMUSIN 1986, 132-136.145-146; DANIEL 1966, 103.104; HARL 1986ª, 68.143.200; HEINEN 1984, 1287-1295; KATZ 1956, 268-269; LARCHER 1983, 245-246; LE BOULLUEC 1989, 109; SCHOLL 1983, 7-8.15; SPICQ 1978ᵇ, 220-224; STANTON 1988, 475-476; WEVERS 1990, 46; 1993, 319.567; 1995, 173.357; →NIDNTT; TWNT

παίω⁺ V 2-11-5-7-1-26
Ex 12,13; Nm 22,28; Jos 20,9; Jgsᴬ 14,19; 1 Sm 13,4
to strike, to hit [τινα] 2 Sm 14,6; to strike, to wound [τινα] 2 Sm 20,10; to smite sb with (plagues) [τινά τι] Is 14,6; to strike [abs.] Ex 12,13

παλάθη,-ης N1F 0-5-1-0-1-7
1 Sm 25,18; 30,12; 2 Kgs 4,42; 20,7; 1 Chr 12,41
cake of dried fruit

πάλαι⁺ D 0-0-3-1-4-8
Is 37,26; 48,5.7; Est 3,13g; 3 Mc 4,1
long ago Wis 11,14; before Is 37,26; for a long time Est 3,13g; old (as adj.) Wis 12,3
Cf. LARCHER 1985, 670; →NIDNTT; TWNT

παλαιός,-ά,-όν⁺ A 7-4-2-9-2-24
Lv 25,22(ter); 26,10(bis)
old Lv 25,22; aged (of pers.) Jb 15,10; ancient, traditional Est 8,12g
διὰ τὴν ἐκ τῶν παλαιῶν χρόνων πρὸς τὸν ἄνδρα γνῶσιν because of (their) long acquaintance with the man 2 Mc 6,21
*1 Sm 7,12 τῆς παλαιᾶς of the old -ישׁן for MT השׁן Shen
→NIDNTT; TWNT

παλαιόω⁺ V 2-2-4-14-6-28
Lv 13,11; Dt 29,4; Jos 9,5.13; Is 50,9
A: to make old [τι] Lam 3,4; to enjoy a long time of [τι] Is 65,22; to wear out [τι] Jb 32,15
P: to wax old, to grow old, to become old Jb 21,7; to decay through lapse of time Ez 47,12; to fail Ps 48(49),15; to become chronic, lingering (of a disease) Lv 13,11; to be worn out Jb 14,18
*Dnᴸˣˣ 11,33 παλαιωθήσονται ἐν αὐτῇ they will become old in it -בלה בה for MT בלהבה by flame
Cf. CAIRD 1976, 82; →NIDNTT; TWNT

(→κατα-)

παλαιστής,-ού N1F 1-2-3-1-0-7
Ex 25,25; 1 Kgs 7,12(26); 2 Chr 4,5; Ez 40,5.43
a palm's-breadth, four inches (later form for

class. παλαστή, a measure of length equivalent
to four fingers or 77-78 mm)

παλαίστρα,-ας   N1F 0-0-0-0-1-1
2 Mc 4,14
place for exercise, wrestling-school (pars pro toto
for gymnasion)

παλαίω[+]   V 2-1-0-1-0-4
Gn 32,25.26; Jgs^ 20,33; Est 1,1e
to wrestle, to struggle (with) [abs.] Est 1,1e; *id.*
[μετά τινος] Gn 32,25

παλαίωμα,-ατος   N3N 0-0-0-3-0-3
Jb 36,28; 37,18.21
antiquity, relic of ancient times; neol.
Cf. CAIRD 1969=1972, 138

παλαίωσις,-εως   N3F 0-0-1-0-0-1
Na 2,1
decay

πάλιν[+]   D 16-7-11-13-41-88
Gn 8,10.12; 26,18; 29,33; 30,31
back Ps 70(71),20; *again, once more* Gn 8,10; *on
the other hand, in turn* Wis 13,8; *in so far as* Wis
14,1
*Jgs^B 20,39 πάλιν corr. πλήν (Jgs^ 20,39) for
MT אך *but*; *Jer 43(36),15 πάλιν *again* -שב for MT
שב *sit down*
Cf. LARCHER 1985, 770.787; LE BOULLUEC 1989, 97;
WEVERS 1990, 34; →MM

παλλακή,-ῆς   N1F 5-41-0-6-2-54
Gn 22,24; 25,6; 35,22; 36,12; 46,20
concubine (homoeophonic with פלגש)
Cf. TOV 1979, 221; WALTERS 1973, 165-166;
→CHANTRAINE; FRISK

παλλακίς,-ίδος   N3F 0-0-0-1-0-1
Jb 19,17
concubine (homoeophonic with פלגש)
Cf. TOV 1979, 221; WALTERS 1973, 165-166

πάλλω   V 0-0-0-2-0-2
Ezr 9,3.5
M: *to tremble, to quiver*

παμβασιλεύς,-έως   N3M 0-0-0-0-1-1
Sir 50,15
absolute monarch, universal king

παμβότανον,-ου[+]   N2N 0-0-0-1-0-1
Jb 5,25
all the herbage, grass; neol.

παμμελής,-ής,-ές   A 0-0-0-0-1-1
3 Mc 7,16
in all kinds of melodies; neol.

παμμιαρός,-ός,-όν   A 0-0-0-0-1-1
4 Mc 10,17

totally or *utterly abominable*

παμμ(ε)ιγής,-ής,-ές   A 0-0-0-0-2-2
2 Mc 3,21; 12,13
mixed of all sorts

παμπληθής,-ής,-ές[+]   A 0-0-0-0-1-1
2 Mc 10,24
*of vast size, very numerous, multitudinous, with
the whole crowd*

παμποίκιλος,-ος,-ον   A 0-0-0-0-1-1
4 Mc 15,11
various, many

παμπόνηρος,-ος,-ον   A 0-0-0-0-1-1
2 Mc 14,27
thoroughly depraved; ὁ παμπόνηρος *scoundrel,
depraved man*

πάμφυλος,-ος,-ον   A 0-0-0-0-3-3
2 Mc 8,9; 12,27; 4 Mc 4,11
of all nationalities, of all tribes 2 Mc 8,9; *open to
all nationalities* 4 Mc 4,11

πανάγιος,-ος,-ον[+]   A 0-0-0-0-2-2
4 Mc 7,4; 14,7
all-holy; neol.

πάνδεινος,-ος,-ον   A 0-0-0-0-2-2
4 Mc 3,15; 4,7
terrible

πανδημεί   D 1-0-0-0-0-1
Dt 13,17
altogether, completely
Cf. DANIEL 1966, 264.265.268; DOGNIEZ 1992, 202

πάνδημος,-ος,-ον   A 0-0-0-0-1-1
2 Mc 3,18
of the whole community, general, common

πανεθνεί   D 0-0-0-0-1-1
Wis 19,8
with the whole nation, with all their hosts; neol.?

πανεπίσκοπος,-ος,-ον   A 0-0-0-0-1-1
Wis 7,23
all-surveying, all-controlling; neol.
Cf. LARCHER 1984, 490-491

πανηγυρίζω   V 0-0-1-0-0-1
Is 66,10
*to celebrate a relig. festival, to observe a holy day,
to rejoice*
Cf. HELBING 1928, 259

πανήγυρις,-εως[+]   N3F 0-0-4-0-0-4
Ez 46,11; Hos 2,13; 9,5; Am 5,21
general assembly, public festival (with religious
character)
Cf. ROST 1967, 130-132; SPICQ 1978[a], 643

πανηγυρισμός,-οῦ   N2M 0-0-0-0-1-1

Wis 15,12

celebration of a feast; neol.

Cf. GILBERT 1973, 215-218; LARCHER 1985, 874-875

πανθήρ,-ῆρος N3M 0-0-2-0-0-2

Hos 5,14; 13,7

panther

πανόδυρτος,-ος,-ον A 0-0-0-0-2-2

3 Mc 4,2; 6,32

most lamentable; neol.

πανοικία,-ας N1F 3-1-0-1-1-6

Gn 50,8.22; Ex 1,1; Jgs^A 18,21; Est 8,12r

whole household

Cf. HARL 1986^a, 316; LE BOULLUEC 1989, 73

πανοπλία,-ας⁺ N1F 0-1-0-1-9-11

2 Sm 2,21; Jb 39,20; Jdt 14,3; 1 Mc 13,29(bis)

suit of armour, complete armour 2 Sm 2,21; *id.*

(metaph.) Wis 5,17

→NIDNTT

πανούργευμα,-ατος N3N 0-0-0-0-3-3

Jdt 11,8; Sir 1,6; 42,18

great deeds

Cf. CAIRD 1969=1972, 138-139

πανουργεύομαι V 0-1-0-0-0-1

1 Sm 23,22

to be clever or *cunning*; neol.

(→κατα-)

πανουργία,-ας⁺ N1F 1-1-0-2-4-8

Nm 24,22; Jos 9,4; Prv 1,4; 8,5; Sir 19,23

craftiness Jos 9,4; *prudence* Sir 19,23; *subtlety* Prv

1,4

*Nm 24,22 πανουργίας *prudence* -ערמה for MT

ער מה *until*

→NIDNTT; TWNT

πανοῦργος,-ος,-ον⁺ A 0-0-0-14-5-19

Jb 5,12; Prv 12,16; 13,1.16; 14,8

crafty Jb 5,12; *prudent, wise* Prv 12,16

*Prv 14,24 πανοῦργος *a prudent man* -ערם? for

MT עשרם *their riches*

Cf. CAIRD 1969=1972, 138-139; →NIDNTT; TWNT

πάνσοφος,-ος,-ον A 0-0-0-0-3-3

4 Mc 1,12; 2,19; 13,19

all-wise (of God) 4 Mc 1,12; *most wise* (of men)

4 Mc 2,19

πανταχῆ⁺ D 0-0-1-0-2-3

Is 24,11; 2 Mc 8,7; Wis 2,9

everywhere

Cf. LARCHER 1983, 234

πανταχόθεν⁺ D 0-0-0-0-2-2

4 Mc 13,1; 15,32

from every side 4 Mc 15,32; *from every side,*

universally 4 Mc 13,1

πανταχοῦ⁺ D 0-0-1-0-0-1

Is 42,22

everywhere

παντελής,-ής,-ές⁺ A 0-0-0-0-1-1

3 Mc 7,16

complete

παντελῶς⁺ D 0-0-0-0-5-5

2 Mc 3,12.31; 7,40; 11,1; 14,46

quite, utterly

παντεπόπτης,-ου N1M 0-0-0-0-1-1

2 Mc 9,5

the all-seeing

παντευχία,-ας N1F 0-0-0-0-1-1

4 Mc 3,12

complete armour

πάντη⁺ D 0-0-0-0-2-2

3 Mc 4,1; Sir 50,22

in every way and everywhere

παντοδαπός,-ή,-όν A 0-0-0-1-0-1

Jb 40,21

of every kind

παντοδύναμος,-ος,-ον A 0-0-0-0-3-3

Wis 7,23; 11,17; 18,15

all-powerful; neol.

Cf. LARCHER 1984, 490

πάντοθεν⁺ D 0-1-2-0-8-11

2 Sm 24,14; Jer 20,9; 31(48),31; 2 Mc 13,5; 3 Mc

3,25

from all directions, on all sides 2 Sm 24,14

*Jer 20,9 πάντοθεν *totally* -כליל for MT כלכל

holding

παντοῖος,-α,-ον A 0-0-0-1-4-5

Dn^LXX 2,6; 2 Mc 5,3; 3 Mc 5,22; 7,16; 4 Mc 1,34

of all kinds

παντοκράτωρ,-ορος⁺ N3M 0-10-124-16-31-181

2 Sm 5,10; 7,8.25.27; 1 Kgs 19,10

all-mighty 1 Chr 29,12

κύριος παντοκράτωρ *the Lord Almighty* 2 Sm

5,10; θεὸς παντοκράτωρ *Almighty God* Jer 3,19

neol.?

Cf. DODD 1954, 19; HORSLEY 1983, 118; MONTEVECCHI

1957^b, 403-413; TOV 1976^b, 541; →MM; NIDNTT; TWNT

πάντοτε⁺ D 0-0-0-0-2-2

Wis 11,21; 19,18

always, at all times

Cf. SHIPP 1979, 438-439

παντοτρόφος,-ος,-ον A 0-0-0-0-1-1

Wis 16,25

all-nourishing; neol.

παντοφαγία,-ας   N1F 0-0-0-0-1-1
4 Mc 1,27
*eating of strange meat, indiscriminate eating,
eating all kinds of food indiscriminately*; neol.

πάντως⁺   D 0-0-0-0-3-3
2 Mc 3,13; 3 Mc 1,15; Tob^BA 14,8
surely, by all means 2 Mc 3,13; *perhaps* 3 Mc
1,15
Cf. LEE, G.M. 1970, 137-138

πάνυ⁺   D 0-0-0-0-4-4
2 Mc 9,6; 12,43; 13,8; 15,17
very, quite 2 Mc 9,6
λόγοις πάνυ καλοῖς *with very good words*
(periphrastic sup.) 2 Mc 15,17

πανυπέρτατος,-η,-ον   A 0-0-0-0-1-1
3 Mc 1,20
highest of all

πάππος,-ου   N2M 0-0-0-0-1-1
Sir prol.,7
grandfather

πάπυρος,-ου   N2M/F 0-0-1-2-0-3
Is 19,6; Jb 8,11; 40,21
papyrus

παρά⁺   P 225-158-97-204-195-879
Gn 13,18; 18,14; 19,1.24; 21,30
[τινος]: *from (the side of)* Jb 21,2; *from* (to
denote the one who originates or directs) Ps
117(118),23; *from* (to denote the point from
which an action originates) Jdt 12,15; *out of the
hand of, given by* (God) Ex 4,20
οἱ παρὰ τοῦ βασιλέως *the king's officers* 1 Mc
2,15; οἱ παρ' αὐτῆς *her friends* Sus 33
[τινι]: *beside, near* 2 Sm 10,8; *in the sight of* Jb
9,2; *with sb, before sb* Ex 33,16
[τι] or [τινα]: *beside, near, by* Gn 19,1; *in
comparison to* Dn 7,7; *instead of, rather than* Ps
44(45),8; *because of* Gn 29,20
παρὰ μικρόν *almost* Ps 72(73),2; παρ' ὀλίγον
id. Ps 72(73),2; παρὰ βραχύ *id.* Ps 93(94),17
Cf. JOHANNESSOHN 1910, 1-82; 1926, 226-235; WEVERS
1993, 683; →NIDNTT; TWNT

παραβαίνω⁺   V 16-7-11-4-29-67
Ex 32,8; Lv 26,40; Nm 5,12.19.20
to deviate from the way (metaph.), *to apostatise*
Dt 11,16; *to transgress, to break* [abs.] Lv 26,40;
id. [τι] Nm 14,41; *to transgress against* (God)
[τινα] 3 Mc 7,10; *id.* [ἔν τινι] Is 66,24; *to
deviate from* [ἀπό τινος] Dt 9,16; *id.* [ἔκ τινος]
Ex 32,8
παραβαίνων ἀπὸ τῆς κλίνης *one who sins*

against his marriage bed, one who breaks wedlock
Sir 23,18
*Ps 118(119),119 παραβαίνοντας *sinners,
transgressors* -סוג סנים for MT סנים סוג *oxide of
lead*
Cf. DODD 1954, 79; HELBING 1928, 85; WEVERS 1995, 166;
→NIDNTT; TWNT

παραβάλλω⁺   V 0-1-0-8-1-10
Jgs^A 19,21; Prv 2,2(bis); 4,20; 5,1
A: *to throw to* (as fodder) [τινι] Jgs^A 19,21; *to
throw aside, to let fall* Ru 2,16 παραβάλλω
οὖς/καρδίαν ἐπί/εἰς τι *to incline one's ear/
heart to, to be attentive to* Prv 2,2; 5,1.13; 22,17
M: *to risk* [τι] 2 Mc 14,38

παραβασιλεύω   V 0-0-0-0-1-1
3 Mc 6,24
*to reign as if one was king at the side of the king,
to govern badly*; neol.

παράβασις,-εως⁺   N3F 0-0-0-1-2-3
Ps 100(101),3; 2 Mc 15,10; Wis 14,31
transgression Ps 100(101),3; *breach* (of an oath)
2 Mc 15,10
Cf. WALTERS 1973, 137; →NIDNTT; TWNT

παραβιάζομαι   V 2-3-2-0-0-7
Gn 19,9; Dt 1,43; 1 Sm 28,23; 2 Kgs 2,17; 5,16
to act in defiance of orders Dt 1,43; *to urge*
[τινα] 1 Sm 28,23; *to press, to constrain* [τινα]
Gn 19,9; *to try very hard* Jon 1,13; neol.
Cf. CAIRD 1969=1972, 139; DOGNIEZ 1992, 64.121;
WEVERS 1995, 26

παραβιβάζω   V 0-2-0-1-0-3
2 Sm 12,13; 24,10; Dn^Th 11,20
to remove, to put aside [τι] 2 Sm 12,13; *to pass
over, to usurp* Dn^Th 11,20

παραβλέπω⁺   V 0-0-0-3-1-4
Jb 20,9; 28,7; Ct 1,6; Sir 38,9
to observe, to watch Jb 20,9; *to look unfavourably upon, to despise* [τινα] Ct 1,6; *to be
negligent* Sir 38,9
Cf. WALTERS 1973, 264

παραβολή,-ῆς⁺   N1F 8-5-13-8-12-46
Nm 23,7.18; 24,3.15.20
stereotypical rendition of משל; *proverb* Ez 17,2;
byword Wis 5,4; *poem, figurative discourse* Nm
23,7; *taunt, mocking speech* Mi 2,4
Cf. DOGNIEZ 1992, 291-292; DORIVAL 1994, 135; HATCH
1889, 64-71; LARCHER 1984, 361; SIDER 1981, 457-458;
WACKERNAGEL 1913=1969, 1239-1244; WALTERS 1973,
143; →NIDNTT; TWNT

παραγγέλλω⁺   V 0-8-3-3-9-23

Jos 6,7; Jgs^A 4,10; 1 Sm 10,17; 15,4; 23,8
to order, to charge [τινί] Jos 6,7; *to command
sb to do sth* [τινί τι] 2 Mc 5,25; *to declare* Jer
26,14; *to proclaim, to issue* [τι] Ezr 1,1; *to
summon* [τινι] (as mil. term) 1 Sm 10,17; *to
summon against* [τινι ἐπί τινα] (as mil. term)
Jer 27(50),29

Cf. SPICQ 1978ᵃ, 647-649; →NIDNTT; TWNT

παράγγελμα,-ατος   N3N 0-1-0-0-0-1
1 Sm 22,14
command

παραγίνομαι⁺   V 27-80-5-11-55-178
Gn 14,13; 26,32; 32,21; 35,9; 45,19
to be beside, to be near Jgs 6,5; *to be present at*
[ἐπί τι] 1 Sm 20,29
to come, to appear 1 Mc 4,46; *to come near, to
arrive* Est 6,14; *to come* Gn 14,13; *to come to, to
arrive at* [εἰς τι] Gn 50,10; *id.* [ἐπί τι] Jos 11,5;
id. [πρός τινα] Gn 50,16; *id.* [τινι] Is 62,11; *to
come against* [εἰς τινα] Jer 30,8
to arrive, to come up 1 Sm 20,24; *to come to pass*
Jos 21,45
οἱ παρεγένοντο ἐπὶ τὴν συμμαχίαν αὐτοῦ
the allies who joined him Jdt 7,1

Cf. HELBING 1928, 315

παράγω⁺   V 0-4-0-5-5-14
1 Sm 16,9.10; 20,36; 2 Sm 15,18; Ps 128(129),8
to bring [τι] 1 Ezr 5,54; *id.* [τινα] 4 Mc 11,17;
to divert one's course, to send aside [τι] 1 Sm
20,36; *to remove* [τι] Eccl 11,10; *to bring in, to
introduce* [τινα] 1 Sm 16,9; *to pass by* Ps
128(129),8
*Ezr 9,2 παρήχθη *passed (among)* or free
rendition - ◊עבר? for MT ערב ◊ *mixed itself*

παράδειγμα,-ατος   N3N 2-4-4-0-2-12
Ex 25,9(bis); 1 Chr 28,11.12.18
model, plan, pattern Ex 25,9; *example* Na 3,6

Cf. BARR 1961, 151-156; LE BOULLUEC 1989, 253

παραδειγματίζω⁺   V 1-0-2-2-1-6
Nm 25,4; Jer 13,22; Ez 28,17; Est 4,17q; Dn^LXX
2,5
A: *to punish publicly as an example way, to put
to open shame* [τινα] Nm 25,4; *to show, to
reveal, to disclose* [τι] PSal 2,12
P: *to be put to open shame, to be exposed to
shame* Jer 13,22

Cf. HARL 1984ᵇ=1992ᵃ, 58; SPICQ 1978ᵃ, 650; →NIDNTT;
TWNT

παραδειγματισμός,-οῦ   N2M 0-0-0-0-2-2
3 Mc 4,11; 7,14

*making an example of, pointing out to public
shame*

παραδείκνυμι   V 1-0-2-0-2-5
Ex 27,8; Ez 22,2; Hos 13,4; Bel^LXX 8.9
to reveal, to make manifest

παράδεισος,-ου⁺   N2M 15-1-8-3-18-45
Gn 2,8.9.10.15.16
Persian loanword (Hebr. פרדס); *garden, orchard*
Nm 24,6; *paradise, garden of Eden* Gn 2,8

Cf. CAIRD 1976, 79; HARL 1986ᵃ, 101; 1991=1992ᵃ,
148-149; HUSSON 1988, 64-73; LEE, J. 1983, 53-56;
→NIDNTT; TWNT

παραδέχομαι⁺   V 1-0-0-1-1-3
Ex 23,1; Prv 3,12; 3 Mc 7,12
to receive in a friendly way, to accept, to love
[τινα] Prv 3,12; *to receive, to allow, to permit*
[τι] Ex 23,1; *to accept, to admit, to acknowledge*
[τι] 3 Mc 7,12

παραδίδωμι⁺   V 31-101-52-42-51-277
Gn 14,20; 27,20; Ex 21,13; 23,31; Lv 26,25
to give, to hand over [τι] 1 Ezr 8,56; *to give* [τι]
Gn 27,20; *to hand over, to deliver into the hands
of sb, to give up* [τινα] Gn 14,20; *id.* [τι] Nu
32,4
παραδίδωμι εἰς τὰς χεῖράς τινος *to deliver
into one's hands* Ex 21,13
*Ps 62(63),11 παραδοθήσονται *they will be
given over to (the sword)* - ◊נגר? *they will be cut
(by the sword)* for MT יגירו◊(hi.)? *they shall throw
down,* cpr. Jer^MT 18,21; Ez^MT 35,5

Cf. BERÉNYI 1984, 510-517; DOGNIEZ 1992, 113; LABERGE
1978, 99(Is 33,6); SPICQ 1982, 504-515; WALTERS 1973,
129.238.257; WEVERS 1993, 199; →NIDNTT

παραδοξάζω   V 4-0-0-0-3-7
Ex 8,18; 9,4; 11,7; Dt 28,59; 2 Mc 3,30
to treat with distinction [τι] 2 Mc 3,30; *to
distinguish, to mark off* [τι] Ex 8,18; *id.* [ἀνὰ
μέσον] Ex 9,4; *to make extraordinary* [τι] Dt
28,59

Cf. DOGNIEZ 1992, 65.295; LE BOULLUEC 1989,
34-35.127.129.143; WEVERS 1995, 454(Dt 28,59)

παράδοξος,-ος,-ον⁺   A 0-0-0-0-8-8
Jdt 13,13; 2 Mc 9,24; 3 Mc 6,33; 4 Mc 2,14
contrary to expectation, unexpected 2 Mc 9,24;
strange Jdt 13,13; *unexpected, wonderful,
marvellous* Wis 16,17

Cf. DREW-BEAR 1972, 87-88; ROBERT 1940=1971, 250-252

παραδόξως   D 0-0-0-0-1-1
4 Mc 4,14
unexpectedly, astonishingly; neol.?

παράδοσις,-εως+   N3F 0-0-2-0-0-2
Jer 39(32),4; 41(34),2
delivery (of pers.) Jer 39(32),4; surrender,
capitulation (of a city) Jer 41(34),2
→NIDNTT

παραδρομή,-ῆς   N1F 0-0-0-1-1-2
Ct 7,6; 2 Mc 3,28
train, retinue 2 Mc 3,28; corridor, gallery Ct 7,6

παραζεύγνυμι   V 0-0-0-0-1-1
Jdt 10,17
to associate sb with sb [τινά τινι]

παραζηλόω+   V 2-1-0-4-3-10
Dt 32,21(bis); 1 Kgs 14,22; Ps 36(37),1.7
A: to provoke to jealousy, to make jealous [τινα]
1 Kgs 14,22; to make sb jealous with sth [τινα
ἐπί τινι] Dt 32,21
M: to fret, to be vexed Ps 36(37),1
Cf. DOGNIEZ 1992, 64.331-332; HELBING 1928, 80

παραζώνη,-ης   N1F 0-1-0-0-0-1
2 Sm 18,11
belt; neol.

παραθαλάσσιος,-ος/α,-ον+   A 0-1-2-0-3-6
2 Chr 8,17; Jer 29(47),7; Ez 25,9; 1 Mc 7,1; 11,8
near the sea, by the seaside 2 Chr 8,17
ἐπί τὰς παραθαλασσίους against the regions on
the seacoast Jer 29(47),7
*Ez 25,9 πόλεως παραθαλασσίας of the city by
the sea-side -קרית ימה‎(ו) for MT‎q קריתמה‎(ו)
Kiriathaim
Cf. HORSLEY 1987, 165

παραθαρσύνω+   V 0-0-0-0-1-1
4 Mc 13,8
to embolden, to encourage [τινα]

παράθεμα,-ατος   N3N 3-0-0-0-0-3
Ex 38,24(bis)(4.5); 39,9(38,30)
sth put alongside sth, an appendage; neol.
Cf. LE BOULLUEC 1988, 368; LEE, J. 1983, 52; WEVERS
1990, 629

παραθερμαίνω   V 1-0-0-0-0-1
Dt 19,6
to warm; παρατεθέρμανται they are heated in
anger, they are in hot anger
Cf. WEVERS 1995, 310

παράθεσις,-εως   N3F 0-2-0-2-4-8
2 Kgs 6,23; 2 Chr 11,11; Prv 6,8; 15,17; 1 Mc
6,53
what is set aside, (stored) provisions Prv 6,8;
what is set before sb, dinner, dish 2 Kgs 6,23

παραθήκη,-ης+   N1F 2-0-0-0-1-3
Lv 5,21.23; Tob^S 10,13

deposit
Cf. HORSLEY 1982, 85; KIESSLING 1956, 71-77; PRIJS 1948,
2; SPICQ 1978^a, 651-655

παραθλίβω   V 0-1-0-0-0-1
2 Kgs 6,32
to press close, to hold, to detain [τινα]; neol.

παραίνεσις,-εως   N3F 0-0-0-0-1-1
Wis 8,9
comfort, counsel, encouragement, exhortation
Cf. LARCHER 1984, 537

παραινέω+   V 0-0-0-0-4-4
2 Mc 7,25.26; 3 Mc 5,17; 7,12
to exhort, to urge 2 Mc 7,25; to recommend, to
approve, to praise 3 Mc 7,12

παραιρέω   V 1-0-0-0-0-1
Nm 11,25
M: to draw off from, to remove from [ἀπό τινος]

παραιτέομαι+   V 0-3-0-2-3-8
1 Sm 20,6(bis).28; Est 4,8; 7,7
to ask from [ἀπό τινος] 1 Sm 20,6; to entreat
[τινα] Est 4,8; to ask pardon for [τι] 3 Mc 6,27;
to get excused from [πρός τι] 4 Mc 11,2; to shun,
to avoid [τι] 2 Mc 2,31
Cf. HORSLEY 1983, 78; →NIDNTT

παραίτιος,-ος,-ον   A 0-0-0-0-1-1
2 Mc 11,19
sharing, being partly to blame for sth [τινος]

παρακαθεύδω   V 0-0-0-0-1-1
Jdt 10,20
to sleep beside, to guard [τινι]; neol.

παρακάθημαι+   V 0-0-0-1-0-1
Est 1,14
to sit beside [τινι]

παρακαθίζω+   V 0-0-0-1-0-1
Jb 2,13
to sit down beside [τινι] (intrans.)

παρακαθίστημι+   V 0-0-0-0-1-1
2 Mc 12,3
P: to be equipped for sea (of ships)

παρακαλέω+   V 9-17-34-31-48-139
Gn 24,67; 37,35(bis); 38,12; 50,21
A: to invite to, to summon to, to call to [τινα
εἴς τι] Ex 15,13; to exhort, to encourage [τινα]
Dt 3,28; to strengthen [τι] Jb 4,3; to excite, to
tempt [τινα] Dt 13,7; to persuade [τινα]
1 Sm 22,4; to comfort, to console [τινα] Gn
37,35; to console one another Is 35,4; to try to
console or conciliate, to propose peace to [τινα]
2 Mc 13,23; to soothe [τι] Sir 30,23; to beseech,
to entreat [τινα] 4 Mc 4,11; to beseech strongly

[τινα] 2 Mc 6,12; *to entreat for sth* [τι] Is 33,7
P: *to be comforted* Gn 24,67; *to relent* Dt 32,36;
id. [περί τινος] Jgsᴬ 21,6; *id.* [πρός τινα] Jgsᴮ
21,6; *to regret, to repent* 1 Sm 15,11; *id.* [ἐπί
τινι] 2 Sm 24,16
μάταια παρεκάλουν *they have given vain
comfort* Zech 10,2
*1 Sm 22,4 καὶ παρεκάλεσεν *and he consoled,
he comforted* -ינחם/ו ◊נחם for MT נחום/ינחם ◊נחה *and he
led them,* see also Is 57,18; *Is 57,5 οἱ
παρακαλοῦντες ἐπί *those who comfort* -◊נחם for
MT ◊חמם *those who burn with lust;* *Ez 24,22
παρακληθήσεσθε *you shall be counseled* -תיעשו
◊ישע (Aram.)? for MT תעשו ◊עטה *you shall cover;*
*Ez 24,23 παρακαλέσετε *you shall comfort* נחמתם
◊נחם for MT נהמתם ◊נהם *you shall groan*

Cf. Barr 1961, 232.236; Bjerkelund 1967, 88-92;
Dogniez 1992, 59.65.201.337; Harl 1971=1992ᵃ, 192;
1986ᵃ, 205; 1991=1992, 158; 1992=1993, 198; Helbing
1928, 100-101; Le Boulluec 1989, 175; Lee, J. 1983, 83;
Nestle 1900, 170-171; →Nidntt; Twnt

παρακάλυμμα,-ατος N3N 0-0-0-0-1-1
Wis 17,3
curtain, screen, veil (metaph.: sth that hides)

παρακαλύπτω⁺ V 0-0-2-0-0-2
Is 44,8; Ez 22,26
A: *to hide* [τι] Ez 22,26
M: *to hide oneself* Is 44,8

παρακαταθήκη,-ης⁺ N1F 2-0-0-0-4-6
Ex 22,7.10; Tobᴮᴬ 10,13; 2 Mc 3,10.15;
deposit

Cf. Horsley 1982, 85; Le Boulluec 1989, 226; Prijs
1948, 2-3

παρακατατίθημι V 0-0-2-0-2-4
Jer 47(40),7; 48(41),10; 2 Mc 3,15; 9,25
M: *to entrust sb to, to commit sb to* [τινά τινι]
Jer 47(40),7; οἱ παρακαταθέμενοι *depositors*
2 Mc 3,15

παράκειμαι⁺ V 0-0-0-0-10-10
Jdt 3,2.3; 2 Mc 4,41; 9,25; 12,16
to lie before Sir 30,18; *to be at hand, to be
available* 2 Mc 4,41; *to be adjacent* 2 Mc 9,25; *to
be set before* [τινα] (of food) Sir 31,16; *to press
on, to urge* [τινι] 3 Mc 7,3; *to lie prostrate* (as
sign of abs. subjection) Jdt 3,3

παρακελεύω⁺ V 0-0-0-1-1-2
Prv 9,16; 4 Mc 5,2
A: *to command* [τινι] 4 Mc 5,2
M: *to exhort* [τινι] Prv 9,16

παρακλείω V 0-0-0-0-1-1

2 Mc 4,34
to shut up, to incarcerate [τινα]

παράκλησις,-εως⁺ N3F 0-0-9-2-5-16
Is 28,29; 30,7; 57,18; 66,11; Jer 16,7
exhortation, encouragement 1 Mc 10,24; *comfort,
consolation* Jb 21,2

Cf. Ziegler 1934, 146-147(Is 28,29; 30,7)

παρακλητικός,-ή,-όν A 0-0-1-0-0-1
Zech 1,13
comforting

παρακλήτωρ,-ορος N3M 0-0-0-1-0-1
Jb 16,2
comforter; neol.

παρακμάζω V 0-0-0-0-1-1
Sir 42,9
to pass one's prime

παράκοιτος,-ου N2F 0-0-0-3-0-3
Dnᵀʰ 5,2.3.23
wife

παρακολουθέω V 0-0-0-0-2-2
2 Mc 8,11; 9,27
to follow closely upon [ἐπί τινι] 2 Mc 8,11; *to
adhere to* [τινι] 2 Mc 9,27

παρακομίζω V 0-0-0-0-7-7
2 Mc 4,19(bis).20.23; 9,8
A: *to carry, to bear* [τι] 2 Mc 4,19
M: *to bring home* [τι] 2 Mc 9,29
P: *to be carried away* 2 Mc 9,8

παρακούω⁺ V 0-0-1-4-3-8
Is 65,12; Est 3,3.8; 4,14; 7,4
to pay no attention to, to take no heed of [τινος]
Tob 3,4; *id.* [τι] Est 3,3; *to disobey* [τινος]
1 Ezr 4,11

Cf. Helbing 1928, 156; →Nidntt

παρακρούω V 1-0-0-0-0-1
Gn 31,7
M: *to deceive, to mislead, to cheat* [τινα]

παρακύπτω⁺ V 1-3-0-2-2-8
Gn 26,8; Jgsᴮ 5,28; 1 Kgs 6,4; 1 Chr 15,29; Prv
7,6
A: *to look through* [διά τινος] Gn 26,8; *to look
into* [εἴς τι] Prv 7,6
M: *to incline inwards* (of windows) 1 Kgs 6,4

Cf. Neirynck 1977=1982, 401-440; →Twnt

παραλαλέω V 0-0-0-1-0-1
Ps 43(44),17
*to talk at random, to prattle, to babble, to
chatter, to talk nonsense*

παραλαμβάνω⁺ V 9-4-4-10-16-43
Gn 22,3; 31,23; 45,18; 47,2; Nm 22,41

A: *to take sb along* Gn 22,3; *to receive* [τι] 1 Ezr 8,59; *to inherit* [τι] Jer 30(49),17(secundo); *to succeed (to)* [τινι] Jer 30(49),17(primo)

M/P: *to be induced to* [+inf.] Nm 23,20

Cf. LEE, J. 1983, 28-29; →NIDNTT

παραλείπω⁺   V 0-0-0-0-4-4

1 Ezr 8,7; 3 Mc 1,19.20; PSal 8,13

to neglect, to leave [τινα] 3 Mc 1,20; *to forget* [τι] 3 Mc 1,19; *to leave untold, to omit* [τι] 1 Ezr 8,7; Παραλειπομένων α' *Matters omitted, first part* 1 Chr tit., see also 2 Chr tit.

παραλία,-ας   N1F 1-2-2-0-8-13

Dt 1,7; Jos 9,1; Jgsᴮ 5,17; Is 8,23; Ez 25,16

sea-coast, seaboard, seashore

παράλιος,-ος/α,-ον⁺   A 2-2-0-1-0-5

Gn 49,13; Dt 33,19; Jos 11,3(bis)(2.3); Jb 6,3

near the sea, by the sea

παραλλαγή,-ῆς⁺   N1F 0-1-0-0-0-1

2 Kgs 9,20

frenzy, madness

παράλλαξις,-εως   N3F 0-0-0-1-0-1

Dnᵀʰ 12,11

change

παραλλάσσω⁺   V 0-1-0-4-1-6

1 Kgs 5,1(7); Prv 4,15; Est 3,13e; Dnᵀʰ 6,16; Ezr 1,9

to change [τι] Est 3,13e; *to pass by, to pass away* Prv 4,15; τὰ παρηλλαγμένα *strange things, extraordinary things, peculiar things* Ezr 1,9

τὸ τῆς χρόας παρηλλαγμένον *the changing of his colour, changed colour* 2 Mc 3,16; οὐ παραλλάσσουσιν λόγον *they omit nothing* (semit., see λόγος) 1 Kgs 5,1(7)

παραλογίζομαι⁺   V 2-8-0-2-2-14

Gn 29,25; 31,41; Jos 9,22; Jgsᴬ 16,10.13

to deceive [τι] Est 8,12f; *to calculate fraudulently, to reckon fraudulently* [τι] Gn 31,41; *to defraud* [τινα] Gn 29,25

*2 Sm 21,5 ὃς παρελογίσατο *who deceived* -רמה? for MT רמה *who planned, who devised*

→NIDNTT

παραλογισμός,-οῦ   N2M 0-0-0-2-3-5

Est 8,12f.n; 2 Mc 1,13; PSal 4,10.22

deception, trick

παράλυσις,-εως   N3F 0-0-1-0-0-1

Ez 21,15

destruction

παραλύω⁺   V 4-2-10-0-8-24

Gn 4,15; 19,11; Lv 13,45; Dt 32,36; 2 Sm 8,4

A: *to disband* [τι] 2 Sm 8,4; *to weaken, to*

disable, to enfeeble [τινα] Jdt 16,6; *id.* [τι] Ez 25,9; *to bring down* (the proud) [τι] Is 23,9; *to pay* (penalty) [τι] Gn 4,15

P: *to be loosed* (of garments) Lv 13,45; *to be weakened, to be feeble* (of limbs) Jer 6,24; *to be paralysed* Wis 17,14; *to be exhausted* Gn 19,11

Cf. CAIRD 1969=1972, 139; HARL 1986ᵃ, 116-117.180-181; →NIDNTT

παραμένω⁺   V 1-0-0-2-6-9

Gn 44,33; Prv 12,7; Dnᵀʰ 11,17; Jdt 12,7.9

to remain, to stay, to abide (of pers.) Jdt 12,9; *id.* (of things) Prv 12,7; *to remain with* [τινι] (of slaves) Gn 44,33

Cf. HORSLEY 1987, 98-99; SAMUEL 1965, 221-311; SCHOLL 1990, 120; →MM; NIDNTT

παραμυθέομαι⁺   V 0-0-0-0-1-1

2 Mc 15,9

to comfort [τινα]

Cf. BARR 1961, 232-233; SPICQ 1978ᵃ, 658-663; →NIDNTT; TWNT

παραμυθία,-ας⁺   N1F 0-0-0-1-1-2

Est 8,12e; Wis 19,12

exhortation Est 8,12e; *consolation, comfort* Wis 19,12

Cf. HORSLEY 1983, 79; 1987, 166; SPICQ 1978ᵃ, 658-663; →NIDNTT; TWNT

παραμύθιον,-ου⁺   N2N 0-0-0-0-1-1

Wis 3,18

comfort

Cf. HORSLEY 1987, 14; SPICQ 1978ᵃ, 658-663

παραναγινώσκω   V 0-0-0-0-2-2

2 Mc 8,23; 3 Mc 1,12

to read publicly [τι]

παρανακλίνω   V 0-0-0-0-1-1

Sir 47,19

to bend; παρανέκλινας τὰς λαγόνας σου γυναιξίν *you gave your sides to women, you gave your embraces to women*

παραναλίσκω   V 1-0-0-0-0-1

Nm 17,27

P: *to be consumed, to be lost to no purpose*; neol.?

παρανομέω⁺   V 0-0-0-6-5-11

Ps 25(26),4; 70(71),4; 74(75),5(bis); 118(119),51

to transgress the law, to act unlawfully

→NIDNTT

παρανομία,-ας⁺   N1F 0-0-0-3-8-11

Ps 36(37),7; Prv 5,22; 10,26; 4 Mc 2,11; 4,19

lawlessness, iniquity, transgression of the law

Cf. DODD 1954, 79; →TWNT

παράνομος,-ος,-ον⁺   A 1-9-0-36-27-73
Dt 13,14; Jgs 19,22; Jgsᴮ 20,13; 2 Sm 16,7
lawless, against the law, wicked Dt 13,14;
unlawful, of transgression Ps 40(41),9
ὁ παράνομος *the transgressor, the treacherous*
Prv 2,22
Cf. DODD 1954, 79; DOGNIEZ 1992, 202; →TWNT

παρανόμως   D 0-0-0-2-0-2
Jb 34,20; Prv 21,27
unlawfully, wickedly

παραξιφίς,-ίδος   N3F 0-1-0-0-0-1
2 Sm 5,8
knife worn beside the sword, dagger; *2 Sm 5,8
ἐν παραξιφίδι *with a dagger* -בצנה/ב *with a shield*
for MT בצנור/ב *by the canal;* neol.

παράπαν   D 0-1-8-0-0-9
1 Kgs 11,10; Jer 7,4; Ez 20,9.14.15
τὸ παράπαν *completely, absolutely* Zph 3,6;
(not) at all [+neg.] 1 Kgs 11,10

παραπέμπω   V 0-0-0-1-1-2
Est 3,13d; 3 Mc 1,26
to give up, to omit, to neglect [τι] Est 3,13d; *to
dismiss, to ignore* 3 Mc 1,26

παραπέτασμα,-ατος   N3N 0-0-1-0-0-1
Am 2,8
curtain
Cf. PELLETIER 1955, 292-294; 1984, 404.405.406

παραπηδάω   V 0-0-0-0-1-1
4 Mc 11,1
to leap forward

παραπικραίνω⁺   V 1-2-24-15-1-43
Dt 31,27; 1 Kgs 13,21.26; Jer 39(32),29; 51(44),3
often rendition of the verbs מרה ,מרד ,סרד (*to rebel*),
which are mistakingly associated with מר (*bitter*);
to provoke [abs.] Ez 2,5; *id.* [τινα] Ps 5,11; *id.*
[τι] Lam 1,18; *to rebel against* [τι] 1 Kgs 13,26;
to be disobedient to, to be rebellious towards [τι]
Dt 31,27
*Hos 10,5 καθὼς παρεπίκραναν αὐτόν *as they
rebelled against him* -מריו/כ/מרה for MT כמריו *its
(idolatrous) priests,* see χωμαριμ
Cf. DOGNIEZ 1992, 58.64.319; GRIBOMONT-THIBAUT 1959,
87-89; HELBING 1928, 101-103; WALTERS 1973,
149.150-154.319; →NIDNTT; TWNT

παραπικρασμός,-οῦ⁺   N2M 0-0-0-1-0-1
Ps 94(95),8
rebellion, provocation (rendering Hebr. מריבה
Meribah); neol.
Cf. GRIBOMONT-THIBAUT 1959, 87-89; WALTERS 1973,
151.153.181-182; →NIDNTT

παραπίπτω⁺   V 0-0-5-1-2-8
Ez 14,13; 15,8; 18,24; 20,27; 22,4
to fall beside, to be neglected Est 6,10; *to fall
away, to commit apostasy* Ez 14,13
Cf. LARCHER 1984, 413-414; →NIDNTT

παράπληκτος,-ος,-ον   A 1-0-0-0-0-1
Dt 28,34
mad

παραπληξία,-ας   N1F 1-0-0-0-0-1
Dt 28,28
madness, frenzy, derangement
Cf. DOGNIEZ 1992, 68.290

παράπλους,-ου   N2M 0-0-0-0-1-1
3 Mc 4,11
coasting, aimless voyage

παραπομπή,-ῆς   N1F 0-0-0-0-1-1
1 Mc 9,37
escort, procession, train

παραπορεύομαι⁺   V 10-15-4-7-2-38
Gn 32,22; 37,28; Ex 2,5; 30,13.14
to go by, to pass by, to walk by Gn 37,28; *to cross*
[τι] Dt 2,13; *to pass by* (metaph.) Gn 32,22; *to
pass away, to wither* (of flower) Zph 2,2; *to
transgress* [τι] 2 Chr 24,20
παραπορεύωνται τὴν ἐπίσκεψιν *those who
passed the survey, those who are registered* Ex
30,13, cpr. 30,14; παραπορευομένους ὁδόν
those who travel the roads Jb 21,29; neol.?
Cf. HELBING 1928, 87; LEE, J. 1983, 92

παράπτωμα,-ατος⁺   N3N 0-0-10-7-5-22
Ez 3,20; 14,11.13; 15,8; 18,22
transgression, trespass; neol.?
Cf. DODD 1954, 79; →NIDNTT

παράπτωσις,-εως⁺   N3F 0-0-1-0-0-1
Jer 22,21
transgression, trespass; *Jer 22,21 ἐν τῇ
παραπτώσει σου *in (the times of) your sin*
-בשלותך/ב (Aram.)? for MT בשלותיך/ב *in (the times of)
your prosperity,* cpr. Dn 6,5; Ezr 4,22; 6,9

παραριθμέω   V 0-0-0-0-1-1
Tobˢ 9,5
to check, to count over [τι]; neol.?
→NIDNTT

παραρρέω⁺   V 0-0-1-1-0-2
Is 44,4; Prv 3,21
to flow by (of water) Is 44,4; *to be careless, to
neglect* (of pers.) Prv 3,21

παραρριπτέω   V 0-0-0-1-0-1
Ps 83(84),11
P: *to be thrown down* or *aside;* neol.; see

παραρρίπτω

παραρρίπτω   V 0-1-0-0-1-2
1 Sm 2,36; 2 Mc 1,16
to throw, to toss [τι] 2 Mc 1,16; *to admit* [τινα]
1 Sm 2,36

παράρρυμα,-ατος   N3N 1-0-0-0-0-1
Ex 35,11
curtain-like covering, sth stretched over
Cf. WEVERS 1990, 578

παράστημον,-ου   N2N 0-0-0-0-1-1
3 Mc 2,29
emblem, insignia

παρασιωπάω   V 6-2-4-7-1-20
Gn 24,21; 34,5; Nm 30,5.8.12
A: *to pass over in silence, to omit mention of* [τι]
1 Sm 23,9; *id.* [τινος] Ps 38(39),13; *id.* [ἀπό
τινος] Ps 27,1; *to turn a blind eye to* [ἕν τινι]
Am 6,12(13); *to keep silence* Gn 34,5; *to hold
one's peace at sb* [τινι] Nm 30,8
P: *to be passed over in silence, to be ignored* Prv
12,2
Cf. HARL 1986ᵃ, 80; HELBING 1928, 166; WALTERS 1973,
259(Prv 12,2)

παρασκευάζω⁺   V 0-1-6-4-5-16
1 Sm 24,4; Is 26,7; Jer 6,4; 12,5; 26(46),9
A: *to prepare* [τινα] Tobˢ 8,19; *id.* [τι] Jer
26(46),9; *to superintend* [τι] 2 Mc 2,27; *to stir up*
(conflicts) [τι] Prv 15,18
M: *to prepare for oneself* [τι] Prv 29,5; *to prepare
oneself, to make preparation* Jdt 5,1; *to make
preparation, to relieve oneself* (euph.) 1 Sm 24,4
τὰ παρασκευαζόμενα *things prepared as food*
Belᴸˣˣ 8
→NIDNTT

παρασκευή,-ῆς⁺   N1F 0-0-0-0-3-3
Jdt 2,17; 4,5; 2 Mc 15,21
preparation, provision Jdt 2,17; *what is prepared,
equipment* 2 Mc 15,21
→NIDNTT

παράστασις,-ιδος⁺   N3F 0-0-0-0-1-1
1 Mc 15,32
exhibition, display

παραστήκω   V 0-1-0-0-0-1
Jgsᴬ 3,19
to stand near [τινι]; neol.; see παρίστημι

παρασυμβάλλω   V 0-0-0-2-0-2
Ps 48(49),13.21
P: *to be compared to, to be likened with* [τινι];
neol.

παράταξις,-εως⁺   N3F 5-35-5-2-13-60

Nm 31,5.14.21.27.28
marshalling, line of battle, battle array Nm 31,14;
army 1 Sm 17,10; *place of battle* Jgs 6,26

παρατάσσω   V 10-51-10-4-4-79
Gn 14,8; Ex 17,9.10; Nm 1,45; 21,23
A: *to draw up in battle-order, to set up the army
in array against* [τινι] Ex 17,9
M: *to set oneself in array against* [abs.] Nm 1,45;
id. [τινι] Gn 14,8; *id.* [ἐπί τινα] Ps 26(27),3;
id. [πρός τινα] Jgsᴮ 1,3; *id.* [μετά τινος] Jgsᴮ
5,20; *to set in order, to decree* Zech 1,6
παρατάξασθαι πόλεμον *to set up the army in
array for battle* Jgsᴬ 20,22
*Zech 8,15 παρατέταγμαι *I am prepared* -חשבתי?
for MT שבתי *I returned, I reconsidered*
Cf. HELBING 1928, 236

παρατείνω⁺   V 2-1-1-1-2-7
Gn 49,13; Nm 23,28; 2 Sm 2,29; Ez 27,13; Ps
35(36),11
to extend Gn 49,13; *to spread oneself* Jdt 7,3; *to
extend* [τι] (metaph.) Ps 35(36),11
ὅλην τὴν παρατείνουσαν (sc. ἡμέραν) *all the
lengthening day, throughout the whole morning*
(homoeophonic with בתרון?) 2 Sm 2,29
*Ez 27,13 καὶ τὰ παρατείνοντα *and the
adjacent coasts* -משך◊ for MT מֶשֶׁךְ *Meshech*
Cf. BARR 1985, 54-55(2 Sm 2,29); CAIRD 1976, 85;
→LSJ suppl(2 Sm 2,29)

παρατηρέω⁺   V 0-0-0-3-3-6
Ps 36(37),12; 129(130),3; Dnᵀʰ 6,12; Susᵀʰ 12.15
A: *to watch closely* Susᵀʰ 15; *to watch for* [τινα]
Susᵀʰ 16; *to mark* [τι] Ps 129(130),3
M: *to watch for* [τινα] Ps 36(37),12
Cf. ENGEL 1985, 156; →NIDNTT

παρατίθημι⁺   V 10-9-0-2-25-46
Gn 18,8; 24,33; 30,38; 43,31.32
A: *to place beside, to put* [τι] Lv 6,3; *to set
before, to serve* (food) [τι] Gn 43,31; *id.* [τινι]
Gn 18,8; *id.* [τί τινι] Gn 24,33; *to lay, to put*
[τι] Gn 30,38; *to store up* [τι] 1 Mc 1,35; *to set
before, to expose, to communicate* (words) [τινί
τι] Ex 19,7
M: *to entrust, to leave in trust* (money) [τι] Tob
1,14; *to set before, to expose, to communicate*
[τι] Dt 4,44; *to entrust sb to the care of sb* [τινά
τινι] Tob 10,13
P: *to be entrusted to* [τινι] Lv 5,23
παρέθετο αὐτὸν εἰς φυλακήν *he put him in
prison* 2 Chr 16,10
Cf. LE BOULLUEC 1989, 214

παρατρέχω   V 0-14-0-0-2-16
1 Sm 22,17; 2 Sm 15,1; 1 Kgs 1,5; 14,27.28
to run by, to pass, to slip away 3 Mc 5,15; *to run,*
to accompany 2 Sm 15,1; οἱ παρατρέχοντες
bodyguard 1 Kgs 14,27
ὡς ἀγγελία παρατρέχουσα *like an (oral)*
message passing by (with its messenger) Wis 5,9
Cf. LARCHER 1984, 371

παραυτίκα⁺   D 0-0-0-1-1-2
Ps 69(70),4; Tob^BA 4,14
immediately

παραφέρω⁺   V 0-2-0-1-0-3
Jgs^A 6,5; 1 Sm 21,14; Ezr 10,7
A: *to bring, to transport* [τι] Jgs^A 6,5
P: *to move, to behave like a madman* 1 Sm 21,14
παρήνεγκαν φωνήν *they made proclamations*
(semit.) Ezr 10,7
Cf. SPICQ 1978ᵃ, 666-667

παραφρονέω⁺   V 0-0-1-0-0-1
Zech 7,11
to be beside oneself, to be deranged

παραφρόνησις,-εως   N3F 0-0-1-0-0-1
Zech 12,4
derangement, insanity

παράφρων,-ων,-ον   A 0-0-0-0-1-1
Wis 5,20
insane, senseless

παραφυάς,-άδος⁺   N3F 0-0-3-1-1-5
Ez 31,3.6.8; Ps 79(80),12; 4 Mc 1,28
shoot Ps 79(80),12; *offshoot* (metaph.) 4 Mc 1,28

παραχρῆμα⁺   D 2-1-3-3-11-20
Nm 6,9; 12,4; 2 Sm 3,12; Is 29,5; 30,13
immediately
Cf. WALTERS 1973, 260(Jb 40,12)

παραχωρέω   V 0-0-0-0-2-2
2 Mc 2,28; 8,11
to concede [τινι] 2 Mc 2,28; *to deliver, to hand*
over [τινα] 2 Mc 8,11

παρδάλεος,-ος,-ον   A 0-0-0-0-1-1
4 Mc 9,28
like a leopard; οἱ παρδάλεοι θῆρες *leopard-like*
beasts (metaph. of men)

πάρδαλις,-εως⁺   N3F 0-0-5-3-1-9
Is 11,6; Jer 5,6; 13,23; Hos 13,7; Hab 1,8
leopard, panther

παρεδρεύω⁺   V 0-0-0-2-0-2
Prv 1,21; 8,3
to sit beside, to wait on

πάρεδρος,-ος,-ον⁺   A 0-0-0-0-2-2
Wis 6,14; 9,4

sitting by [τινος]
Cf. LARCHER 1984, 421.570-572

παρεῖδον
aor. of παροράω

πάρειμι (εἶναι)⁺   V 2-6-7-10-36-61
Nm 22,20; Dt 32,35; Jgs^A 19,3; 1 Sm 9,6; 2 Sm
5,23
to be present 2 Sm 13,35; *to be by, to be near sb*
[τινι] 2 Sm 5,23; *to have come* Nm 22,20; *to*
have come at [τινι] 1 Chr 14,14; *id.* [πρός
τινα] 1 Ezr 6,3; *id.* [εἰς τι] 1 Mc 11,63; *to be*
present so as to help sb, to stand by sb [τινι]
4 Mc 6,27; *to arrive* (of letters, circumstances)
Est 9,1; *to be near* Jl 2,1; *to be ready, to be at*
hand [τινι] Dt 32,35
παρόν [+inf.] *being possible* 4 Mc 8,26;
πάρεστίν τί μοι *sth is at my disposal, I have*
sth Wis 11,21; κατὰ τὸ παρόν *for the moment*
3 Mc 3,11; ἐπὶ τοῦ παρόντος *for the present, for*
the moment 2 Mc 6,26
*Jgs^A 19,3 καὶ παρῆν *and he had come* -ושמה
and (was) there for MT וישמח *and he was pleased*;
*Hab 3,2 ἐν τῷ παρεῖναι *when (the time)*
comes near -בְּ/קְרֹב for MT בְּ/קֶרֶב *in the midst of*
→NIDNTT

πάρειμι (ἰέναι)⁺   V 0-0-0-2-0-2
Prv 9,15; 15,10
to pass by

παρεισπορεύομαι   V 0-0-0-0-1-1
2 Mc 8,1
to infiltrate; neol.
Cf. CAIRD 1969=1972, 139

παρεκλείπω   V 0-0-0-0-1-1
Jdt 11,12
to fail; neol.

παρεκτείνω   V 0-0-1-1-0-2
Ez 47,19; Prv 23,4
A: *to extend to* [ἐπί τι] Ez 47,19
M: *to measure oneself with, to compare oneself*
with [τινι] Prv 23,4

παρέλκυσις,-εως   N3F 0-0-0-1-0-1
Jb 25,3
retraction, delay, respite; neol.

παρέλκω   V 0-0-0-0-4-4
Sir 4,1.3; 29,5.8
to draw aside, to put off [τι] Sir 4,1; *to keep*
waiting [τινα] Sir 29,8; *to prolong* [τι] Sir 29,5

παρεμβάλλω⁺   V 89-54-1-3-51-198
Gn 32,2; 33,18; Ex 14,9; 15,27; 17,1
A: *to encamp, to pitch camp, to set up (a more*

or less fortified) camp Gn 32,2; *to pitch (the tabernacle)* [τι] Nm 1,51; *to gather together, to muster (troops)* [τινα] 1 Mc 10,77

M: *to insert oneself, to interpose oneself, to interrupt* Sir 11,8

Cf. HARL 1986ᵃ, 64.239; WEVERS 1995, 367(Dt 23,10); →NIDNTT

παρεμβολή,-ῆς⁺   N1F 109-121-8-4-86-328
Gn 32,2.3(bis).8.9

encampment, camp Gn 32,2; *army* Ex 14,19; *detachment, company* Jdt 7,7

Παρεμβολαί proper name of place Gn 32,3

*1 Sm 14,16 παρεμβολή *camp* -מחנה for MT המון *tumult;* *1 Sm 29,4 παρεμβολῆς *camp* -מחנה for MT מלחמה *war*

Cf. HARL 1986ᵃ, 64.239; LE BOULLUEC 1989, 188; ROST 1967, 122-129; WEVERS 1993, 843; →MM; NIDNTT

παρεμπίπτω   V 0-0-0-0-1-1
Wis 7,25

to creep in, to enter into, to intrude [εἴς τι]

παρενοχλέω⁺   V 0-4-2-7-3-16
Jgs 14,17; Jgsᴬ 16,16; 1 Sm 28,15; Jer 26(46),27
to trouble, to annoy [τινι] Jgsᴬ 14,17; *id.* [τινα] Jgsᴮ 14,17

Cf. HELBING 1928, 99-100; HORSLEY 1987, 166-167

πάρεξ   D/P 0-5-5-4-1-15
Jgsᴮ 8,26; 1 Sm 20,39; 21,10; 1 Kgs 3,18; 12,20
only 1 Sm 20,39; *furthermore, besides* Ez 15,4
[τινος]: *beside, in addition to* Jgsᴮ 8,26; *except* Ru 4,4; *without* Eccl 2,25

Cf. BLASS 1990, § 216; →LSJ suppl(sub πάρεκ); LSJ RSuppl(sub πάρεκ)

παρεξίστημι   V 0-0-1-0-0-1
Hos 9,7

P: *to be deranged, to go mad*

παρεπιδείκνυμι   V 0-0-0-0-1-1
2 Mc 15,10

to point out at the same time [τι]; neol.

παρεπίδημος,-ος,-ον⁺   A 1-0-0-1-0-2
Gn 23,4; Ps 38(39),13

sojourner settled in a district only for a time; neol.?

Cf. BITTER 1982, 20; HARL 1986ᵃ, 197; ORRIEUX 1985, 92-123; SPICQ 1978ᵃ, 671; WEVERS 1993, 332; →MM; NIDNTT

πάρεργος,-ος,-ον   A 0-0-0-0-1-1
2 Mc 15,19

incidental; οὐ πάρεργος ἀγωνία *no small, no inconsiderable* or *insignificant anxiety*

παρέρχομαι⁺   V 44-45-17-32-19-157

Gn 18,3.5; 30,32; 32,32; 41,53
to go by, to pass by Gn 30,32; *id.* [τι] Ex 12,23; *id.* [τινα] Dt 2,8; *to pass (of time)* Gn 41,53; *to pass over, to give in to, to surrender* 2 Kgs 3,10; *to pass away* Ps 56(57),2; *to pass by* (metaph.), *to pass without heeding* [τινα] Gn 18,3; *to rush by* Is 28,17; *to reject, to neglect* [τι] Jdt 11,10; *to transgress* [τι] Dt 17,2; *id.* [ἀπό τινος] Jb 23,12; *to pass unnoticed, to escape* [τινα] Sir 14,14; *to go, to depart (from)* Gn 18,5; *to omit* [τι] 1 Mc 2,22; *to come* 1 Kgs 18,29; *to go over* [τι] Jdt 2,24

τὰ παρεληλυθότα *the past* Sir 42,19; ἀπ' ἐμαυτοῦ παρῆλθον *I have come of my own accord* 4 Mc 11,3

*2 Sm 23,4 παρῆλθεν *he passed on* -עבר for MT עבות *clouds;* *Jb 14,16 παρέλθῃ *it shall pass (unnoticed)* -תעבור for MT תשמור *you shall keep watch;* *Prv 27,13 παρῆλθεν *he has passed by* -עבר for MT ערב *he gave surety for;* *Dnᴸˣˣ 12,1 παρελεύσεται *he shall pass by* -יעבר for MT יעמד *he shall stand up*

Cf. HELBING 1928, 86; LE BOULLUEC 1989, 48.89.150; WALTERS 1973, 249; WEVERS 1990, 360; 1995, 278; →NIDNTT

παρέχω⁺   V 0-0-2-5-8-15
Is 7,13(bis); Ps 29(30),8; Jb 34,29; Est 3,13b
A: *to provide* [τι] Jb 34,29; *to afford, to cause, to bring (forth)* [τι] Wis 17,12; *to maintain, to render in a certain position* [τι +pred.] Est 3,13g; *to give as* [τι +pred.] Wis 18,3
M: *to maintain* [τι] Est 8,12h; *to render in a certain position* [τι +pred.] Est 3,13b; *to grant sth to sth* [τί τινι] 3 Mc 6,28

παρέχω ἀγῶνά τινι *to contend with* Is 7,13; παρέσχον κόπον τοῖς βοηθήσασιν αὐτοῖς *they objected to those who helped them* Sir 29,4

Cf. BLOMQVIST 1979, 28; HELBING 1928, 56; →MM

παρηγορέω   V 0-0-0-0-1-1
4 Mc 12,2

to persuade, to counsel, to exhort

παρηγορία,-ας⁺   N1F 0-0-0-0-2-2
4 Mc 5,12; 6,1

benevolence 4 Mc 5,12; *exhortation* 4 Mc 6,1

παρθενεύω
(→δια-)

παρθενία,-ας⁺   N1F 0-0-1-0-3-4
Jer 3,4; 4 Mc 18,8; Sir 15,2; 42,10

virginity 4 Mc 18,8; *maidenhood, youth* Jer 3,4

Cf. SPICQ 1982, 519

παρθένια,-ων N2N 5-4-0-0-0-9

Dt 22,14.15.17(bis).20

signs pertaining to virginity, virginity; neol.

Cf. DOGNIEZ 1992, 65.255

παρθενικός,-ή,-όν A 0-0-1-1-0-2

Jl 1,8; Est 2,3

of or *for a maiden*; ἐπὶ τὸν ἄνδρα αὐτῆς τὸν παρθενικόν *for her husband of her youth* Jl 1,8; κοράσια παρθενικά *young maidens* Est 2,3

παρθένος,-ου⁺ N2F 16-10-17-12-12-67

Gn 24,14.16(bis).43.55

virgin Jgs 19,24; *virgin* (as adj.) Lv 21,3; *young woman* Ez 9,6; *a girl of marriageable age* Gn 24,14

Cf. DODD 1976, 301-305; DOGNIEZ 1992, 257; DUBARLE 1978, 370-371; FORD 1966, 293-299; GESE 1971, 88; HARL 1986ᵃ, 200; HORSLEY 1987, 222-226; SEELIGMAN 1948, 118-119(Is 7,14); SPICQ 1982, 519-521; WEGNER 1992, 106-115; →NIDNTT; TWNT

-παρθενόω

(→ἀπο-)

παρίημι⁺ V 3-2-4-0-9-18

Ex 14,12; Nm 13,20(21); Dt 32,36; 1 Sm 2,5; 2 Sm 4,1

A: *to let go* [τινα] Jdt 12,12; *to leave alone* [τινα] Ex 14,12; *to leave undone, to neglect, to forsake* [τι] 1 Sm 2,5; *to pass over* [τι] Ps 137(138),8

P: *to be neglected, to be poor* (of land) Nm 13,20(21); *to be weakened* (of people) Dt 32,36; *to be faint* (of hands) Sir 2,12; *to be negligent, to be careless* Sir 4,29; *to be disregarded* Mal 2,9

παρήσει τὰς χεῖρας αὐτῆς *she will lose the strength of her hands* Jer 4,31

Cf. WEVERS 1990, 215

πάρινος,-η,-ον A 0-0-0-2-0-2

Est 1,6(bis)

of marble; neol.?

→LSJ Suppl(sub Πάρινα); LSJ RSuppl

πάριος,-α,-ον A 0-1-0-0-0-1

1 Chr 29,2

of (the island) Paros; λίθον πάριον *Parian marble*

παρίστημι⁺ V 24-23-8-18-20-93

Gn 18,8; 40,4; 45,1(bis); Ex 9,31

to set by or *near* [τι παρά τινα] 1 Sm 5,2; *id.* [τινά τινι] 1 Mc 6,35; *to bring in* [τινα] Sir 23,22

to place [τινα] 1 Kgs 12,32; *to show* Ps 49(50),21; *to be present with sb* [μετά τινος] Nm

1,5

to preside over [ἐπί τινος] Nm 7,2

to attend on [τινι] Prv 22,29; *to prepare for* [τινα εἴς τι] 1 Mc 6,34; *to make sb such, to render sb* [τινα +pred.] 2 Mc 8,21

to stand by or *beside, to help* [abs.] Ex 19,17; *id.* [τινι] Gn 18,8; *id.* [πρός τινα] 2 Kgs 5,25; *id.* [ἐπί τινος] Nm 23,3; *to make a stand* Ex 18,23; *to stand* 1 Kgs 12,6

to approach, to come near (in hostile sense) Ps 2,2

ὁ παρεστηκώς *the one attending, the assistant* Nm 11,28; ἔναντι τῶν παρεστηκότων *against the adversaries* Sir 51,2; παρέστη πάση ὁδῷ οὐκ ἀγαθῇ *he gives* or *presents himself to every evil way* Ps 35(36),5; ἡ κριθὴ παρεστηκυῖα *the barley was in the ear, the barley was ready for harvest* Ex 9,31

*Hos 9,13 παρέστησαν τὰ τέκνα αὐτῶν *they proffered* or *gave their children* -שתו לה בניתם for MT שתולה ב/נוה *it was planted in a meadow*; *Jb 37,20 παρέστηκεν *he may stand* -◊עמר for MT אמר *he says*

Cf. DANIEL 1966, 95.96; DOGNIEZ 1992, 181.243; HELBING 1928, 59.315; LE BOULLUEC 1989, 248; LEE, J. 1983, 56-57; WALTERS 1973, 226-227; WEVERS 1990, 141.289.303.387. 556; →NIDNTT; TWNT

παροδεύω⁺ V 0-0-0-1-0-5-6

Ez 36,34; Wis 1,8; 2,7; 5,14; 6,22

to pass by Ez 36,34; *to pass by, to disregard* [τινα] Wis 1,8; *id.* [τι] Wis 6,22; *to pass away* Wis 5,14

Cf. HELBING 1928, 87; LARCHER 1983, 187

πάροδος,-ου N2M 0-1-2-0-0-3

2 Sm 12,4; Ez 16,15.25

passer-by, traveller

Cf. THACKERAY 1923, 26-28

πάροδος,-ου⁺ N2F 1-1-0-0-3-5

Gn 38,14; 2 Kgs 25,24; Wis 2,5; 17,9

trajectory Wis 2,5; *way, narrow road* Gn 38,14

*2 Kgs 25,24 πάροδον *going by, incursion* -◊עבר for MT ◊עבר *servants, officials*

Cf. LARCHER 1983, 225(Wis 2,5)

παροικεσία,-ας N1F 0-0-2-0-0-2

Ez 20,38; Zech 9,12

sojourning in a foreign land, temporary stay as alien resident Ez 20,38

*Zech 9,12 παροικεσίας σου *of your sojourning in a foreign land, of your exile* -מגוריך for MT מגיר *I declare*; neol.

παροικέω⁺ V 21-22-8-12-9-72
Gn 12,10; 17,8; 19,9; 20,1; 21,23
to dwell beside, to live near Prv 3,29; *to live with*
[παρά τινι] Jgs 17,11; *id.* [μετά τινος] 2 Chr
15,9; *to inhabit, to live* Sus^LXX 28
to inhabit as a πάροικος [abs.] Gn 12,10; *id.*
[τι] Gn 17,8; *id.* [ἔν τινι] Gn 20,1; *id.* [παρά
τι] Jgs^A 5,17(secundo); *id.* [τινι] Jgs^B 5,17; *to
sojourn among sb* [ἔν τινι] Gn 24,37; *to sojourn
in* [τινι] (metaph. of the soul) Ps 93(94),17
*Hos 10,5 παροικήσουσιν *they shall dwell near*
-◊גורי for MT גור^III *they shall tremble*, see also Ez
21,17; Ps 30(31),14
Cf. BITTER 1982, 23-26; HARL 1986ª, 66.148.155.169.197.
211.221.259.297-298; HELBING 1928, 74.316; LEE, J. 1983,
49.61; WEVERS 1993, 169; →NIDNTT; TWNT

παροίκησις,-εως N3F 2-0-0-0-1-3
Gn 28,4; 36,7; Sir 21,28
neighbourhood Sir 21,28; *sojourning, living as a*
πάροικος Gn 28,4
Cf. HARL 1986ª, 66.221; LEE, J. 1983, 49

παροικία,-ας⁺ N1F 0-0-1-7-12-20
*sojourning in a foreign country, a stay in a foreign
place* Ezr 8,35; *id.* (metaph.) Ps 118(119),54;
foreign country Jdt 5,9
*Hab 3,16 παροικίας μου *of my sojourning*
-גור for MT ◊גור *who attacks us*
Cf. LARCHER 1985, 1063-1064; →NIDNTT; TWNT

πάροικος,-ος,-ον⁺ A 16-3-3-3-7-32
Gn 15,13; 23,4; Ex 2,22; 12,45; 18,3
foreign, alien Gn 15,13; (ὁ) πάροικος *sojourner*
(of Israelites in a foreign country) Gn 23,4; *id.*
(of a foreigner in Israel) 2 Sm 1,13
*1 Chr 5,10 πρὸς τοὺς παροίκους *against the
sojourners* -עם ה/גרים for MT עם ההגראים *against the*
Hagarites
cpr. προσήλυτος
Cf. BITTER 1982, 16-31; HARL 1986ª, 66.197; LE
BOULLUEC 1989, 51.86.87.149; LEE, J. 1983, 49.60-61.145;
WALTERS 1973, 34.173; WEVERS 1995, 248(Dt
14,21).367(Dt 23,8); →NIDNTT; TWNT

παροιμία,-ας⁺ N1F 0-0-0-2-5-7
Prv 1,1; 26,7; Sir 6,35; 8,8; 18,29
proverb Sir 6,35
Παροιμίαι *Proverbs* Prv tit.
Cf. HATCH 1889, 64-71; →NIDNTT; TWNT

παροιμιάζω V 0-0-0-0-1-1
4 Mc 18,16
to utter proverbs; τὸν Σαλωμῶντα ἐπαροι-
μίαζεν *he mentioned, quoted the proverbs of*

Solomon
παροινέω V 0-0-1-0-0-1
Is 41,12
to behave ill at wine, to insult, to rage against
[εἴς τινα]

παροιστράω V 0-0-3-0-0-3
Ez 2,6; Hos 4,16(bis)
to rage madly, to be provoked, to be incited (of
anim. by e.g. a goad); neol.

παροξύνω⁺ V 15-2-15-15-5-52
Nm 14,11.23; 15,30; 16,30; 20,24
A: *to provoke* (to wrath), *to irritate* [τινα] Nm
14,11; *to provoke* [τι] Ps 73(74),10; *to provoke
sb with* [τινα ἐπί τινι] Dt 32,16; *id.* [τινα ἐν
τινι] Ps 105(106),29; *to sharpen* (a sword) [τι]
Dt 32,41
P: *to be provoked at* [abs.] Dt 1,34; *id.* [ἐπί
τινι] Dt 9,19; *id.* [διά τι] Dt 32,19; *id.* [ἐν
τινι] Ezr 9,14; *to be sharp* (of mountains) Is
5,25
Cf. BRUZZONE 1982, 147-155; DOGNIEZ 1992, 119; HARL
1991=1992ª, 135; HELBING 1928, 211; WEVERS 1995,
167.502.518; →NIDNTT; TWNT

παροξυσμός,-οῦ⁺ N2M 1-0-1-0-0-2
Dt 29,27; Jer 39(32),37
irritation, sharp disagreement
Cf. BRUZZONE 1982, 147-155; →NIDNTT

παρόρασις,-εως N3F 0-0-0-0-1-1
2 Mc 5,17
*turning away and withholding of grace as a
(temporary) punishment, oversight, neglect*; neol.
Cf. WALTERS 1973, 263

παροράω⁺ V 5-1-1-3-9-19
Lv 5,21(bis); Nm 5,6(bis).12
A: *to overlook* [τι] Jb 11,11; *id.* [τινα] Is 57,11;
to disregard, to despise [τι] Sir 32,18
P: *to be overlooked* 1 Kgs 10,3
*Nm 5,12 παρίδη *she despises* -◊עלם for MT
◊עמל *act perfidiously*
Cf. LARCHER 1985, 691; WALTERS 1973, 262-264

παροργίζω⁺ V 4-23-13-7-10-57
Dt 4,25; 31,29; 32,21(bis); Jgs^A 2,12
to provoke to anger [τινα] Dt 4,25; *id.* Ez 32,9
*Ez 16,54 ἐν τῷ σε παροργίσαι με *in your
provoking me to anger* corr.?, ἐν τῷ σε
παρηγορεῦσαι for MT ב/נחמ/ך *in your being a
consolation, when you become a consolation*, see
Syh
→NIDNTT

παρόργισμα,-ατος N3N 0-3-0-0-0-3

1 Kgs 16,33; 20(21),22; 2 Chr 35,19c
provocation, cause of anger; neol.

παροργισμός,-οῦ⁺   N2M 0-3-1-2-1-7
1 Kgs 15,30; 2 Kgs 19,3; 23,26; Jer 21,5; Neh
9,18
provocation, anger; neol.

παρορμάω   V 0-0-0-0-2-2
2 Mc 15,17; 4 Mc 12,6
to urge on, to stimulate, to stir up [τινα ἐπί τι]

παρουσία,-ας⁺   N1F 0-0-0-0-4-4
Jdt 10,18; 2 Mc 8,12; 15,21; 3 Mc 3,17
presence Jdt 10,18; *coming* 2 Mc 8,12; *solemn
visit of a king* 3 Mc 3,17
Cf. HORSLEY 1987, 167-168; LLEWELYN 1994, 60.71; SPICQ
1978ᵃ, 673-675; →MM; NIDNTT; TWNT

παρρησία,-ας⁺   N1F 1-0-0-5-6-12
Lv 26,13; Jb 27,10; Prv 1,20; 10,10; 13,5
confidence Jb 27,10; *freedom of action* Sir 25,25;
boldness Wis 5,1; *boldness of speech* 4 Mc 10,5
μετὰ παρρησίας *openly* Lv 26,13; *with boldness*
1 Mc 4,18; *plainly, confidently* 3 Mc 4,1
Cf. LARCHER 1984, 355; MIQUEL 1986, 204; VAN UNNIK
1962, 1-19; →NIDNTT; TWNT

παρρησιάζομαι⁺   V 0-0-0-4-1-5
Ps 11(12),6; 93(94),1; Jb 22,26; Prv 20,9; Sir 6,11
to speak freely, openly Ps 93(94),1; *to declare
boldly* Prv 20,9
παρρησιάσομαι ἐν αὐτῷ *I will deal openly with
him* Ps 11(12),6
→NIDNTT; TWNT

παρωθέω   V 0-0-0-0-1-1
2 Mc 4,11
to set aside [τι]

παρωμίς,-ίδος   N3F 1-0-0-0-0-1
Ex 28,14
shoulder-strap; neol.
Cf. LE BOULLUEC 1989, 285

πᾶς, πᾶσα, πᾶν⁺   A 1596-1689-1118-1129-1301-6833
Gn 1,21(bis).25.26(bis)
every (in sg.) Gn 1,21; *all* (in pl.) Gn 1,25; *all,
the whole* (in sg.) Gn 1,26(primo)
πᾶσα σάρξ *all flesh, everyone* (semit.) Is 40,5; οὐ
πᾶς *not any, none* Ps 142(143),2; διὰ παντός
continually Ex 27,20; ἐν παντί *in every way* or
respect Sir 18,27; τὸ πᾶν *the universe* Sir 42,17
*Jb 29,8 πάντες *all* corr.? στάντες for MT קמו
they stood up, they rose; *Ez 3,9 διὰ παντός
always -תמיר? for MT שמיר *adamant*; *Am 6,2
πάντες *all of them* -כלנה ◊כל for MT כלנה *Calneh*;
*Am 8,6 καὶ ἀπὸ παντός *and from every kind*

-כל/מ/ו for MT מפל/ו *and the refuse* (of wheat); *Jb
19,27 πάντα *all, the whole* -כלילה? for MT כליתי *my
reins, my heart*; *Prv 14,7 πάντα *all things* - כל?
for MT לך *go, leave*; *Lam 2,22 πάντας *all (of
them)* -כל/ם for MT כלהם כלם *destroyed them*
Cf. SHIPP 1979, 443.289.414; →NIDNTT; TWNT

πάσσαλος,-ου   N2M 10-14-3-0-3-30
Ex 27,19; 37,18(38,20); 38,21(20)(bis); 39,8
(38,31)(bis)
peg Ez 15,3; *pin, tent-peg* Ex 27,19; *pin, trowel*
Dt 23,14
Cf. DOGNIEZ 1992, 261

πάσσω   V 2-1-0-2-2-7
Ex 9,8.10; 2 Sm 16,13; Ps 147,5; Est 1,6
A: *to scatter* [τι] Ps 147,5; *to besprinkle with*
[τινι] 2 Sm 16,13
M: *to sprinkle with, to scatter on* [τί τινι] 3 Mc
1,18
κύκλῳ ῥόδα πεπασμένα *roses scattered* (i.e.
worked) *round about* Est 1,6
(→κατα-, προσ-)

παστός,-οῦ   N2M 0-0-1-1-3-5
Jl 2,16; Ps 18(19),6; 1 Mc 1,27; 3 Mc 1,19; 4,6
bridal chamber; neol.?
Cf. DREW-BEAR 1972, 88; VATIN 1970, 211-228

παστοφόριον,-ου   N2N 0-5-5-0-4-14
1 Chr 9,26; 23,28; 26,16; 28,12; 2 Chr 31,11
chamber (in the temple) Ez 40,17
*1 Chr 26,16 παστοφορίου *of the chamber* -לשכת
for MT שלכת *of Shallecheth* (or לכת/ש *that leads to*);
*Is 22,15 εἰς τὸ παστοφόριον *to the chamber*
-אל הלשכה? for MT אל הסכן *to the steward*
neol.?
Cf. HUSSON 1983ᵃ, 221-223; PASSONI DELL'ACQUA 1981,
171-211

πασχα⁺   N N 21-4-1-3-14-43
Ex 12,11.21.27.43.48
Aram. loanword (פסחא); *Passover, Paschal feast*
Ex 12,11; *Paschal lamb* Ex 12,21
Cf. DORIVAL 1994, 271.496-497; GUÉRAUD 1979, 113-114;
LE BOULLUEC 1989, 48-51; LEE, J. 1983, 16.30.52; TOV
1979, 231.232; WALTERS 1973, 169-171.247-249;
→CHANTRAINE; NIDNTT; TWNT

πάσχω⁺   V 0-0-3-2-14-19
Ez 16,5; Am 6,6; Zech 11,5; Est 9,26; Dnᴸˣˣ
11,17
to suffer [τι] Est 9,26; *to suffer punishment* Wis
12,27; *to grieve over* [ἐπί τινι] Am 6,6
κακῶς πάσχουσιν *they are badly off, they are in
a terrible plight* Wis 18,19

→NIDNTT; TWNT

πατάσσω⁺   V 71-256-51-24-32-434
Gn 8,21; 14,15; 19,11; 32,12; 37,21
usual translation of נכה; *to strike, to smite* [τι] Ex
7,20; *to smite, to slay* [τινα] Gn 8,21; *to smite*
(with the tongue) [τινα ἔν τινι] Jer 18,18; *to*
afflict [τινά τινι] Dt 28,28
πατάξαι τὸ δόρυ εἰς Δαυιδ *to smite David*
with the spear 1 Sm 19,10
see τύπτω

Cf. WALTERS 1973, 127; →NIDNTT; TWNT

παταχρον/παταχρος,-ου   N2N/M 0-0-2-0-0-2
Is 8,21; 37,38
Aram. loanword (פתכרא); *idol*

Cf. LEE, J. 1983, 16; O'CALLAGHAN 1980, 585; WALTERS
1973, 173-175.255

πατέω⁺   V 1-1-11-4-2-19
Dt 11,24; JgsᴮB 9,27; Is 1,12; 16,10; 25,10
to set foot on, to walk on [τι] Jb 28,8; *id.* [ἐπί
τι] Am 2,7; *to tread* (grapes) [τι] Jgsᴮ 9,27; *to*
trample [τινα] Is 26,6
πάντα τὸν τόπον, οὗ ἐὰν πατήσῃ τὸ ἴχνος τοῦ
ποδὸς ὑμῶν *each place on which you set your*
foot Dt 11,24
→NIDNTT; TWNT

(-ἐμπερι-, κατα-, περι-, συμ-)

πάτημα,-ατος   N3N 0-1-1-0-0-2
2 Kgs 19,26; Ez 34,19
that which is trodden

πατήρ, πατρός⁺   N3M 367- 566-133-117-268-1451
Gn 2,24; 4,20; 9,18.22(bis)
father Gn 2,24; *father* (as the prototype of a
group) Gn 17,4; *father* (as an honorary title of
respectful address) 2 Kgs 2,12; *God, father* Dt
32,6; *father, originator* Jb 38,28
*1 Chr 4,11 πατήρ *father of* -אבי for MT אחי
brother of; *Is 17,11 ὥσπερ πατήρ *as father* -כ/אב
for MT כאב *sorrow*
→NIDNTT; TWNT

πατητός,-ή,-όν   A 0-0-1-0-0-1
Is 63,2
trodden upon; neol.

πατράδελφος,-ου   N2M 0-5-0-0-0-5
Jgs 10,1; 2 Sm 23,9.24; 1 Chr 27,32
father's brother, uncle; neol.

πατριά,-ᾶς⁺   N1F 62-72-4-23-20-181
Ex 6,14.15.17.19.25
paternal lineage Ex 6,14; *people, nation* 1 Chr
16,28
κατὰ πατριάν *concerning the paternal*

inheritance Dt 18,8
*1 Chr 11,25 τὴν πατριάν *family* -משפחת for MT
משמעת *body-guard*

Cf. LE BOULLUEC 1989, 114; WEVERS 1995, 297(Dt 18,8);
→MM; NIDNTT; TWNT

πατριάρχης,-ου⁺   N1M 0-5-0-0-2-7
1 Chr 24,31; 27,22; 2 Chr 19,8; 23,20; 26,12
chief, chief of families 1 Chr 24,31; *chief of tribes*
1 Chr 27,22; *patriarch* 4 Mc 7,19
→MM

πατρικός,-ή,-όν   A 4-5-0-0-4-13
Gn 50,8; Lv 22,13; 25,41; Nm 36,8; Jos 6,25
of one's father Gn 50,8; *of one's father's tribe*
Nm 36,8
ἐν τοῖς πατρικοῖς *in one's father's house* Sir
42,10

πάτριος,-α,-ον   A 0-0-0-0-19-19
2 Mc 6,1; 7,2.8.21.24
derived from one's fathers, of the fathers 2 Mc
6,1; *of one's father* Sir prol.,10

πατρίς,-ίδος⁺   N3F 0-0-3-3-17-23
Jer 22,10; 26(46),16; Ez 23,15; Est 2,10.20
fatherland, homeland, native land Jer 22,10;
kindred Est 2,10

πατρῷος,-α,-ον⁺   A 0-0-0-1-8-9
Prv 27,10; 2 Mc 4,15; 5,10; 6,6; 12,39
of one's father Prv 27,10; *of their fathers* 2 Mc
6,1
→TWNT

παῦλα,-ης   N1F 0-0-0-0-1-1
2 Mc 4,6
cessation, end of [τινος]

παῦσις,-εως   N3F 0-0-1-0-0-1
Jer 31(48),2
stopping, ceasing; neol.

παύω⁺   V 17-5-27-13-16-78
Gn 11,8; 18,33; 24,14.19.22
A: *to cause to cease* [τι] Dt 32,26; *to cause sb to*
cease [τινά τινι] Jb 6,26; *to keep from* [τι ἀπό
τινος] Ps 33(34),14; *to quell* (a conflict) [τι] Prv
18,18
M: *to cease* Ex 9,29; *to leave off* [+ptc.] Gn
11,8; *to cease from* [τινος] Ex 32,12; *id.* [ἀπό
τινος] Ps 36(37),8; *id.* [τοῦ +inf.] Ex 9,28
ἐπαύσατο ῥήμασιν *he ceased speaking* Jb 31,40
*Is 26,10 πέπαυται *he has ceased, he is put*
down -נוחה or -חנה for MT יחן *let be favoured*; *Jb
6,7 παύσασθαι *to cease* -רגוע *to become calm* for
MT נגוע *to touch*; *Jb 6,26 παύσει *will cause to*
cease -תחשו *be quiet, be silent* for MT תחשבו *you*

think; *Prv 30,1 παύομαι *I cease* -אכלה for MT אֻכָל *Ucal*

Cf. HARL 1990=1992ª, 142.158; HELBING 1928, 168; LE
BOULLUEC 1989, 134; LEE, J. 1983, 34; WEVERS 1990,
139.515.525

(→ἀνα-, δια-, διανα-, ἐπανα-, κατα-,
προσανα-, συνανα-)

πάχνη,-ης   N1F 0-0-0-6-4-10
Ps 77(78),47; 118(119),83; Jb 38,24.29; Dn^LXX
3,70
frost, hoarfrost

πάχος,-ου   N3N 1-7-1-2-1-12
Nm 24,8; 1 Kgs 7,3.9.12.33(15.20.26.46)
thickness 1 Kgs 7,3

ἐν τῷ πάχει τῆς γῆς *in the clay ground* 1 Kgs
7,33; ξύλων πάχη *logs of wood, clubs* 2 Mc 4,41;
τὰ πάχη αὐτῶν ἐκμυελιεῖ *he shall suck their*
fatness, he shall drain them of their strength Nm
24,8

παχύνω⁺   V 1-1-2-1-1-6
Dt 32,15; 2 Sm 22,12; Is 6,10; 34,6; Eccl 12,5
A: *to make thick* or *dense* 2 Sm 22,12
P: *to grow fat* Dt 32,15; *to be glutted with* [ἀπό
τινος] Is 34,6; *to be made gross* Is 6,10
→TWNT

παχύς,-εῖα,-ύ   A 0-3-2-1-2-8
1 Kgs 12,10.24r; 2 Chr 10,10; Is 28,1; Ez 34,3
thick 1 Kgs 12,10; *fat* Ps 143(144),14; *fertile* Is
28,1; *precious, rich* (of ointment) Jdt 10,3
ὕδωρ παχύ *marsh-water* 2 Mc 1,20

πεδάω⁺   V 0-0-0-13-1-14
Ps 67(68),7; 68(69),34; 78(79),11; 89(90),12;
101(102),21
A: *to bind* [τινα] Dn^Th 3,20
P: *to be bound (in fetters)* Jb 36,8; *to be tied by,*
to be fettered in [ἐν τινι] (metaph.) Ps
89(90),12
πεπεδημένους *fettered ones, prisoners* Ps
67(68),7
*Ps 89(90),12 καὶ τοὺς πεπεδημένους (ἐν
σοφίᾳ) *and those that are tied by (wisdom),*
fettered in (wisdom) (metaph.) corr.? καὶ τοὺς
πεπαιδευμένους for MT ונבא read as בין ◊ ונבוני
and those that are instructed

πέδη,-ης⁺   N1F 0-6-1-3-7-17
Jgs 16,21; 2 Sm 3,34; 2 Kgs 25,7; 2 Chr 33,11
fetter, shackle

πεδήτης,-ου   N1M 0-0-0-0-1-1
Wis 17,2
fettered one, prisoner

πεδίλον,-ου   N2N 0-0-1-0-1-2
Hab 3,5; Od 4,5
sandal

Cf. BOUSFIELD 1929-30, 397-399; WALTERS 1973, 134-135;
ZIEGLER 1943=1971, 113-115

πεδ(ε)ινός,-ή,-όν⁺   A 2-13-6-0-3-24
Dt 4,43; 11,11; Jos 9,1; 10,40; 11,16
flat, level, plain Dt 4,43
ἡ πεδινή (sc. γῆ) *the plain* Jos 15,33
*Is 13,2 ἐπ᾽ ὄρους πεδινοῦ *on a low mountain,*
on a humble mountain cpr. 3,17 -על הר נשפה
◊שפי/שפה (Aram.) for MT על הר נשפה *on a bare*
mountain, cpr. Is^MT 3,17

Cf. SEELIGMANN 1948, 50(Is 13,2); →NIDNTT

πεδίον,-ου⁺   N2N 43-22-48-18-43-174
Gn 4,8(bis); 11,2; 14,17; 24,63
level place, plain, field Gn 4,8; *piece of land used*
for pasture or tillage Lv 25,12
*Gn 35,27 πόλιν τοῦ πεδίου *town of the plain*
-קרית ערבה? for MT קרית הארבע *Kiriath-arba* (cpr.
Gn 23,2 ἐκ πόλει Αρβοκ); *Jos 17,5 πεδίον
plain -שרה? for MT עשרה *a tenth*; *Ez 26,10 ἐκ
πεδίου *from the plain* -מ/בקעה? for MT מבקעה
breached, opened by breaches; *Ps 103(104),16
τὰ ξύλα τοῦ πεδίου *the trees of the field* -עצי שרי
for MT עצי יהוה *the trees of the Lord* via עצי שרי *the*
trees of Shaddai

Cf. LEE, J. 1983, 58; WALTERS 1973, 134-135(Hab 3,5 var.)

πεζικός,-ή,-όν   A 0-0-0-0-3-3
1 Mc 15,38; 16,5; 3 Mc 1,1
on foot; δυνάμεις πεζικαί *host of footmen,*
foot-soldiers, infantry

πεζομαχία,-ας   N1F 0-0-0-0-1-1
4 Mc 17,24
land battle

πεζός,-ή,-όν   A 2-11-0-0-18-31
Ex 12,37; Nm 11,21; Jgs^A 5,15; Jgs 20,2
on foot, walking (of foot-soldiers) Jgs 20,2;
πεζοί *foot-soldiers, infantry* Ex 12,37; πεζῇ *on*
foot 2 Sm 15,17

πειθαρχέω⁺   V 0-0-0-1-2-3
Dn^LXX 7,27; 1 Ezr 8,90; Sir 33,29
to obey [τινι] 1 Ezr 8,90; *id.* [abs.] Sir 33,29
Cf. HELBING 1928, 204; SPICQ 1978ª, 676-678; →TWNT

πείθω⁺   V 6-24-60-42-52-184
Lv 25,18.19; Dt 28,52; 32,37; 33,12
A: *to persuade* [τινα] 1 Sm 24,8; *to exhort, to*
encourage [τινα +inf.] 4 Mc 16,24
M/P: *to listen to, to obey* 4 Mc 12,5; *id.* [τινι]
Tob^S 10,7; *to consent* Est 4,4; *to believe* [τι]

Tob^BA 14,4

πέποιθα to trust, to rely on [abs.] Ru 2,12; id.
[τι] 2 Kgs 18,19; to trust that [ὅτι +ind.] Jb
31,21; to trust in [ἐπί τι] 2 Chr 32,10; id. [ἐπί
τινα] 2 Kgs 18,21; id. [ἐπί τινι] Dt 28,52; id.
[τινι] 2 Kgs 18,20; id. [ἐν τινι] Jdt 2,5;
πεποιθώς being confident Lv 25,18

Cf. HELBING 1928, 203; SPICQ 1982, 534-547; →NIDNTT;
TWNT

(→ἀνα-, μετα-, συμ-)

πεινάω⁺ V 2-6-20-13-12-53
Gn 41,55; Dt 25,18; Jgs 8,4; Jgs^A 8,5
to be hungry Gn 41,55
*Jer 38(31),12 οὐ πεινάσουσιν they shall not be
hungry - רעב◊ for MT ראב◊ they shall not grieve, be
anxious, see also 38(31),25

→NIDNTT; TWNT

πεῖρα,-ας⁺ N1F 2-0-0-0-4-6
Dt 28,56; 33,8; 2 Mc 8,9; 4 Mc 8,2; Wis 18,20
attempt, trial 4 Mc 8,2; experience Wis 18,20
πεῖραν λαμβάνω [+inf.] to attempt, to venture
Dt 28,56; πειράζω τινὰ ἐν πείρᾳ to lead sb
into temptation, to tempt sb Dt 33,8; πεῖραν ἔχω
ἔν τινι to have experience 2 Mc 8,9

Cf. SPICQ 1982, 548-559

πειρασμός,-οῦ⁺ N2M 6-0-0-1-7-14
Ex 17,7; Dt 4,34; 6,16; 7,19; 9,22
test, trial Dt 4,34; temptation Sir 44,20; disaster,
plague Dt 7,19; Πειρασμός (proper name) Ex
17,7; neol.

Cf. BERTRAM 1952, 41-45; DOGNIEZ 1992, 58.65.98.144.
157.179; HATCH 1889, 71-72; KORN 1937, 1-88; SPICQ
1982, 548-559; WEVERS 1990, 267; →NIDNTT; TWNT

πειρατεύω V 2-0-0-0-0-2
Gn 49,19(bis)
to attack, to raid (as a pirate); neol.

Cf. KORN 1937, 8-18

πειρατήριον,-ου N2N 1-0-0-4-0-5
Gn 49,19; Ps 17(18),30; Jb 7,1; 10,17; 19,12
trial, test Jb 7,1; gang of pirates, gang of raiders
Gn 49,19

Cf. KORN 1937, 8-18

πειρατής,-οῦ N1M 0-0-1-2-0-3
Hos 6,9; Jb 16,9; 25,3
pirate, raider; neol.?

Cf. KORN 1937, 8-18

πειράω⁺/πειράζω⁺ V 10-12-1-13-26-62
Gn 22,1; Ex 15,25; 16,4; 17,2.7
A: to test, to put to the test [τινα] Ps 25(26),2;
id. [τινα] (pers. put God to the test) Ex 17,2;

id. [τινα] (God puts pers. to the test) Gn 22,1;
to prove [τι] Eccl 7,23; to try, to attempt [+inf.]
Dt 4,34; to experience [τι] Wis 12,26
M: to be used to 1 Sm 17,39
*Ps 34(35),16 ἐπείρασάν με they put me to the
test - בחנני for MT ב/חנפי with mockers?

Cf. BERTRAM 1952, 41-45; DOGNIEZ 1992, 347; HATCH
1889, 71-72; HELBING 1928, 143; KORN 1937, 1-88;
LARCHER 1983, 271; LYONNET 1958, 27-36; SHIPP 1979,
444; SPICQ 1982, 548-559; WALTERS 1973, 130; →NIDNTT;
TWNT

(→ἀπο-, δια-, ἐκ-, κατα-)

-πειρέω
(→ἐμ-)

-πείρω
(→ἀνα-, δια-)

πέλαγος,-ους⁺ N3N 0-0-0-0-2-2
2 Mc 5,21; 4 Mc 7,1
sea, open sea

πέλας⁺ D 0-0-0-1-0-1
Prv 27,2
near; ὁ πέλας neighbour

πελειόομαι V 0-0-0-1-0-1
Lam 5,10
to become pale, to become blackened; neol.

πέλειος,-α,-ον A 0-0-0-1-0-1
Prv 23,29
pale

Cf. WALTERS 1973, 56-57

πελεκάω V 0-1-0-0-0-1
1 Kgs 6,1b(5,32)
to hew, to cut (stones or wood) [τι]

πελεκάν,-ᾶνος N3M 2-0-0-1-0-3
Lv 11,18; Dt 14,18; Ps 101(102),7
pelican

πελεκητός,-ή,-όν A 0-1-0-0-0-1
1 Kgs 10,22
hewn

πέλεκυς,-εως N3M 0-1-1-1-1-4
1 Kgs 6,7; Jer 22,7; Ps 73(74),6; LtJ 13
double-edged axe 1 Kgs 6,7; battle axe Jer 22,7

πέλμα,-ατος N3N 0-0-0-1-0-1
Est 4,17d
sole (of foot)

πελματόομαι
(→κατα-)

πελταστής,-οῦ N1M 0-2-0-0-0-2
2 Chr 14,7; 17,17
one who bears a light shield, one who is lightly
armed

πέλτη,-ης   N1F 0-0-5-0-0-5
Ez 23,24; 27,10; 38,4.5; 39,9
(light) shield

πέλυξ,-υκος   N3M 0-0-2-0-0-2
Jer 23,29; Ez 9,2
axe; neol.

πέμμα,-ατος   N3N 0-0-12-0-0-12
Ez 45,24(ter); 46,5(bis)
pastry, cake Hos 3,1
*Ez 45,24 πέμμα *cake* - אפה◊ *to bake* for MT איפה
ephah, see also Ez 46,5.7.11, cpr. οιφι
Cf. SIMOTAS 1968, 122

πέμπτος,-η,-ον⁺   Mo 9-21-14-4-15-63
Gn 1,23; 30,17; 47,24; Ex 13,18; Lv 5,24
fifth Gn 1,23
(τῇ) πέμπτῃ τοῦ μηνός (sc. ἡμέρᾳ) *on the fifth
day of the month* Ez 1,1; (τῇ) πέμπτῃ καὶ
εἰκάδι (sc. ἡμέρᾳ) *on the twenty fifth day* Neh
6,15
*Ex 13,18 πέμπτη *fifth* -חמישי for MT חמשים *in
battle array* (army in five parts)
Cf. LE BOULLUEC 1989, 160

-πεμπτόω
(→ἀπο-)

πέμπω⁺   V 1-0-0-4-17-22
Gn 27,42; Est 8,5; Ezr 4,14; 5,17; Neh 2,5
to send [τινα] Gn 27,42; *id.* [τι] 1 Ezr 2,20
→NIDNTT
(→δια-, εἰσ-, ἐκ-, ἐπι-, μετα-, παρα-, προ-,
συμπρο-)

πένης,-ητος⁺   N3M 5-4-11-51-8-79
Ex 23,3.6; Dt 15,11; 24,14.15
poor man Ex 23,3; *poor* (as adj.) Dt 15,11, cpr.
πενιχρός, πραΰς, πτωχός, ταπεινός
Cf. HATCH 1889, 73-77; SHIPP 1979, 446-447; TRENCH
1890, 128-130; →NIDNTT; TWNT

πενθερά,-ᾶς⁺   N1F 1-0-1-11-0-13
Dt 27,23; Mi 7,6; Ru 1,14; 2,11.18
mother-in-law
Cf. DOGNIEZ 1992, 283; HORSLEY 1983, 37

πενθερός,-οῦ⁺   N2M 2-3-0-0-7-12
Gn 38,13.25; Jgsᴬ 1,16; 1 Sm 4,19.21
father-in-law Gn 38,13
τίμα τοὺς πενθερούς σου *honour your father
and mother in law* Tobᴮᴬ 10,12
Cf. HARL 1991=1992ᵃ, 150.151

πενθέω⁺   V 5-9-26-10-16-66
Gn 23,2; 37,34.35; 50,3; Nm 14,39
A: *to mourn for* [τινα] Gn 37,34; *id.* [τι] Sir
51,19; *id.* [ἐπί τινα] 2 Sm 13,37; *id.* [ἐπί τινι]

2 Sm 14,2; *id.* [ὑπέρ τινος] 1 Ezr 9,2; *id.* [ἐπί
τινος] Is 66,10; *to mourn, to be sad* Gn 23,2
*Jer 38(31),21 πενθοῦσα *mourning* -אבלה? for MT
אלה *these*
Cf. HARL 1986ᵃ, 70; HELBING 1928, 73; →NIDNTT; TWNT
(→κατα-)

πενθικός,-ή,-όν⁺   A 1-1-0-0-0-2
Ex 33,4; 2 Sm 14,2
pertaining to mourning (of garments, etc.); neol.
Cf. LE BOULLUEC 1989, 329-330

πένθος,-ους⁺   N3N 8-2-12-9-23-54
Gn 27,41; 35,8; 50,4.10.11
grief, sorrow, mourning Est 4,3; *mourning for the
dead* Gn 27,41
ἐν χερσὶν ἔχοντες τὰ πένθη *while they were in
the midst of their mourning* Wis 19,3; ἄρτος
πένθους *bread of mourning, bread presented to
mourners* Hos 9,4; αἱ ἡμέραι πένθους
κλαυθμοῦ Μωυσῆ *the days of weeping*, (i.e.) *of
mourning for Moses* (semit.) Dt 34,8
Cf. HARL 1986ᵃ, 70.317; 1986ᵇ=1992ᵃ, 77; MIQUEL 1986,
219-220; WEVERS 1995, 560(Dt 34,8); →NIDNTT; TWNT

πενία,-ας   N1F 0-0-0-9-4-13
Jb 36,8; Prv 6,11; 10,4.15; 13,18
poverty

πενιχρός,-ά,-όν   A 1-0-0-2-0-3
Ex 22,24; Prv 28,15; 29,7
poor
Cf. HORSLEY 1983, 80

πένομαι   V 5-0-0-1-0-6
Ex 30,15; Lv 14,21; 25,25.35; Dt 24,12
to be poor

πενταετηρικός,-ή,-όν   A 0-0-0-0-1-1
2 Mc 4,18
held every five years, quinquennial; neol.

πενταετής,-ής,-ές   A 2-0-0-0-0-2
Lv 27,5.6
five years old

πεντάκις⁺   MD 0-1-0-0-0-1
2 Kgs 13,19
five times

πεντακισχίλιοι,-αι,-α⁺   Mc 0-5-0-3-12-20
Jgsᴮ 20,45; 1 Kgs 5,12; 1 Chr 5,21; 29,7; 2 Chr
35,9
five thousand

πεντακισχίλιος,-α,-ον⁺   Mc 0-0-0-0-1-1
1 Mc 4,28
five thousand (sg. with a coll. noun)

πεντακόσιοι,-αι,-α⁺   Mc 26-6-16-4-11-63
Gn 5,30.32; 11,11; Ex 30,23.24

five hundred

πεντακόσιος,-α,-ον⁺   MC 0-0-0-0-1-1
1 Mc 6,35
five hundred (sg. with a coll. noun)

πεντάπηχυς,-υς,-υ   A 0-1-0-0-0-1
1 Chr 11,23
five cubits high (of a pers.)

πενταπλασίως   D 1-0-0-0-0-1
Gn 43,34
five times as much, five times over

πενταπλοῦς,-ῆ,-οῦν   A 0-1-0-0-0-1
1 Kgs 6,31
five-fold; neol.?

πέντε⁺   MC 93-99-45-16-25-278
Gn 5,6.10.11.15.17
five

πεντεκαίδεκα   MC 4-3-1-0-0-8
Ex 27,14; 37(38),12.13; Lv 27,7; Jgsᴬ 8,10
fifteen

πεντεκαιδέκατος,-η,-ον⁺   MO 7-6-2-4-3-22
Ex 16,1; Lv 23,6.34.39; Nm 28,17
fifteenth

πεντεκαιεικοσαετή ς,-ής,-ές   A 7-0-0-0-0-7
Nm 4,23.30.35.39.43
twenty-five years old

πεντήκοντα⁺   MC 56-47-17-24-20-164
Gn 5,31; 6,15; 7,24; 8,3; 9,28
fifty

πεντηκονταετή ς,-ής,-ές   A 7-0-0-0-0-7
Nm 4,23.30.35.39.43
fifty years old

πεντηκόνταρχος,-ου⁺   N2M 3-8-1-0-1-13
Ex 18,21.25; Dt 1,15; 2 Kgs 1,9(bis)
leader of a company of fifty men, lieutenant

πεντηκοστός,-ή,-όν   MO 2-2-0-0-8-12
Lv 25,10.11; 2 Kgs 15,23.27; Tobᴮᴬ 2,1
fiftieth Lv 25,10

πεντηκοστήν *Pentecost* 2 Mc 12,32
Cf. PELLETIER 1975, 224; →NIDNTT; TWNT

πέπειρος,-ος,-ον⁺   A 1-0-0-0-0-1
Gn 40,10
ripe

πεποίθησις,-εως⁺   N3F 0-1-0-0-0-1
2 Kgs 18,19
confidence; neol.
Cf. SPICQ 1978ᵃ, 534-547; →NIDNTT

πεποιθότως   D 0-0-1-0-0-1
Zech 14,11
confidently, securely; neol.; see πείθω

πέπων,-ονος   N3M 1-0-0-0-0-1

Nm 11,5
kind of gourd or *melon*

περαίνω   V 0-1-1-0-1-3
1 Sm 12,21; Hab 2,5; 3 Mc 4,11
to finish, to achieve [τι] 3 Mc 4,11; *to accomplish one's purpose* [τι] 1 Sm 12,21
(→συμ-)

πέρα(ν)⁺   P 24-52-7-15-9-107
Gn 50,10.11; Nm 21,11.13; 27,12
beyond [τινος] Gn 50,10
τὸ πέραν τινός *the other side of sth* Nm 21,13; *the opposite side to sb* Jos 22,11
*Jgs 11,29 εἰς τὸ πέραν *to the other side* -(ל)עֲבַר? for MT עָבַר *he went over to, he passed on to*, cpr. 1 Sm 30,10; Jer 48(41),10; *Jer 52,8 ἐν τῷ πέραν *beyond, on the other side of* -ב/עבר for MT ב/ערבת *in the plains of*
Cf. BLASS 1990, § 184; WALTERS 1973, 70-71; →NIDNTT

πέρας,-ατος⁺   N3N 0-0-18-31-11-60
Jer 18,7.9; 28(51),13; Ez 7,2(bis)
limit, end, boundary Est 3,13b; *end, conclusion, perfection* 1 Ezr 9,17; *at last?* Jer 18,7, see also 18,9
*Zph 3,10 ἐκ περάτων ποταμῶν *from the remotest reaches of the rivers* corr.? πέραν τῶν ποταμῶν for MT מעבר לנהרי *from beyond the rivers*; *Ps 7,7 ἐν τοῖς πέρασι *to the boundaries* -בְּעֶבְרֵי? for MT בְּעֶבְרֹות *in rage* (of the Lord against the enemy)
Cf. WALTERS 1973, 70-71.292

περασμός,-οῦ   N2M 0-0-0-3-0-3
Eccl 4,8.16; 12,12
finishing, end; neol.

περάτης,-ου   N1M 1-0-0-0-0-1
Gn 14,13
wanderer, migrant; neol.
Cf. HARL 1986ᵃ, 159; LEE, J. 1983, 52; WEVERS 1993, 193

περάω
(→δια-, ἐκ-)

πέρδιξ,-ικος   N3F 0-0-1-0-1-2
Jer 17,11; Sir 11,30
partridge

περί⁺   P 242- 118-79-100-313-852
Gn 12,17.20; 15,12; 17,20; 19,21
[τινος]: *about, concerning* Gn 19,21; *because of* Gn 12,17; *in the interest of* Gn 20,7; *for* (always with ἁμαρτία and a verb of atoning) Nm 8,8 τὰ περὶ τῆς ἁμαρτίας *the sin-offering* Lv 6,23 [τι, τινα]: *about, near* (time) Gn 15,12; *around, about, near* (place) Dt 20,19; *around* (a part of

the body) Gn 24,47

οἱ περὶ τὸν Νεεμιαν *Nehemiah and his company* 2 Mc 1,33

[τινι]: *round* Prv 1,9

*Jb 41,4 δι' αὐτόν *because of him* -בְּרִי/ל? for MT בְּרִי √ *his limbs*

Cf. JOHANNESSOHN 1910, 1-82; 1926, 219-226; WEVERS 1993, 390; →NIDNTT; TWNT

περιαγκωνίζω   V 0-0-0-0-1-1
4 Mc 6,3
to tie the hands behind the back; neol.

περιάγω⁺   V 0-0-5-0-2-7
Is 28,27; Ez 37,2; 46,21; 47,2; Am 2,10
to lead round or *about* [τινα] Am 2,10; *id.* [abs.]
2 Mc 4,38; *to lead sb round about sth* 2 Mc 6,10;
to go round or *about* [intr.] Is 28,27

Cf. HELBING 1928, 87

περιαιρέω⁺   V 33-11-5-6-4-59
Gn 38,14.19; 41,42; Ex 8,4.7
A: *to take away* [τι] Lv 3,4; *to take away from, to remove from* [τι ἀπό τινος] Ex 8,4; *to make void, to cancel (a vow)* Nm 30,13
M: *to take off* (garments) [τι] Gn 38,14; *to take off from* [τι ἀπό τινος] Gn 41,42; *to remove* (strange gods) [τινα] Jos 24,14

Cf. DORIVAL 1994, 515; SPICQ 1978ᵃ, 679-680

περιαντλέω   V 0-0-0-0-1-1
4 Mc 15,32
P: *to be drenched, to be sunk in, to be submerged, to be overwhelmed* (metaph.); neol.

περιάπτω⁺   V 0-0-0-0-1-1
3 Mc 3,7
to fasten with; καὶ οὐ τῷ τυχόντι περιῆψαν ψόγῳ *and they cast no small contempt upon them*

περιάργυρος,-ος,-ον   A 0-0-0-0-7-7
LtJ 7.38.50.54.57
overlaid with silver, silver-plated

περιαργυρόω   V 7-0-1-1-0-9
Ex 27,11; 37,15(bis).17.18
A: *to plate with silver* [τι] Ex 38,18(36,34)
P: *to be overlaid with silver* Ex 27,11; *to be covered with silver* Ps 67(68),14

Cf. WEVERS 1990, 437.616.626

περιαστράπτω⁺   V 0-0-0-0-1-1
4 Mc 4,10
to flash around; neol.

περιβάλλω⁺   V 5-13-20-19-14-71
Gn 24,65; 28,20; 38,14; Lv 13,45; Dt 22,12
A: *to throw around* or *over, to put on* [τι] Ru

3,9; *to cover* [τινα] Jgsᴮ 4,19; *to cover sb with sth* [τινά τινι] Jgsᴮ 4,18; *to clothe* [τινα] 2 Chr 28,15; *to clothe sb with sth* [τινά τι] Zech 3,5 *to cover sth with sth* [τί τινι] Jdt 4,12; *to cast over* [τι ἐπί τινα] Ez 32,3; *to throw up (a mound) around* (a city) [τι ἐπί τι] Ez 4,2; *to encompass* Jb 23,9; *to involve in* [τινά τινι] Est 8,12e
M: *to throw round* or *over oneself, to put on* [τι] Gn 24,65; *to put around* [περί τι] Lv 13,45; *to clothe oneself with* [τι] Lam 4,5; *to embrace* [τι] Jb 24,8
P: *to be clothed in* [τι] 1 Ezr 3,6

Cf. HELBING 1928, 46-47; WEVERS 1993, 455

περιβιόω   V 0-0-0-0-1-1
3 Mc 5,18
to survive, to remain alive; neol.

περίβλεπτος,-ος,-ον   A 0-0-0-1-0-1
Prv 31,23
respected, admired, distinguished

περιβλέπω⁺   V 2-2-0-1-6-11
Gn 19,17; Ex 2,12; Jos 8,20; 1 Kgs 21(20)40; Jb 7,8
A: *to look round about towards* [εἴς τι] Gn 19,17
M: *to look around* [abs.] Ex 2,12; *to look around towards* [πρός τι] Bar 4,36; *to look about for* [τινα] Tobᴮᴬ 11,5; *to keep looking at* [τι] Tobˢ 10,7

*1 Kgs 21(20),40 περιεβλέψατο *he looked around* -שָׁעָה? for MT עָשָׂה *he was busy*

περίβλημα,-ατος   N3N 1-0-0-0-0-1
Nm 31,20
garment

Cf. DORIVAL 1994, 524; LEE, J. 1983, 84

περιβόητος,-ος,-ον⁺   A 0-0-0-0-1-1
2 Mc 2,22
widely famed, renowned

περιβόλαιον,-ου⁺   N2N 2-1-5-3-0-11
Ex 22,26; Dt 22,12; Jgsᴬ 8,26; Is 50,3; 59,17
covering, wrap, cloak Ex 22,26; *covering* (metaph.) Jer 15,12

Cf. WEVERS 1990, 354

περιβολή,-ῆς   N1F 1-0-0-1-3-5
Gn 49,11; Dnᴸˣˣ 7,9; 2 Mc 3,26; Sir 11,4; 50,11
covering Sir 11,4; *robe, cloak* Gn 49,11

Cf. WEVERS 1993, 827

περίβολος,-ου   N2M 0-0-3-1-6-10
Is 54,12; Ez 40,5; 42,20; Dnᴸˣˣ 3,1; 1 Mc 14,48
enclosing wall (of the temple) Ez 40,5; *walled*

place, enclosure Dn^LXX 3,1

περιγίνομαι⁺   V 0-1-0-0-1-2
1 Chr 28,19; 4 Mc 13,3
to be superior to, to master [τινος] 4 Mc 13,3; *to be left to, to be given to* [τινι] 1 Chr 28,19
Cf. HELBING 1928, 177

περιδειπνέω   V 0-1-0-0-0-1
2 Sm 3,35
to invite sb to eat a περίδειπνον [τινα]; neol.

περίδειπνον,-ου   N2N 0-0-0-0-1-1
LtJ 31
feast (a dinner given in honour of a dead person for the relatives and friends nine days after the burial)

περιδέξιον,-ου   N2N 2-0-1-0-0-3
Ex 35,22; Nm 31,50; Is 3,20
armlet, bracelet (for the right arm)
Cf. DORIVAL 1994, 531; LE BOULLUEC 1989, 349; LEE, J. 1983, 84; WEVERS 1990, 584

περιδιπλόω   V 0-0-0-0-1-1
Jdt 10,5
to wrap round, to pack up, to double-wrap (for travel) [τι]

περιδύω   V 0-0-0-0-1-1
4 Mc 6,2
to strip [τινα]

περίειμι (περιεῖναι)   V 0-0-0-3-3-6
Jb 27,3.15; 31,21; 2 Mc 7,24; 14,10
to survive sb [τινος] Jb 27,15; *to be alive, to live* 2 Mc 7,24; *to remain in sb* [τινι] Jb 27,3; *to remain* 3 Mc 5,18; *to be superior* Jb 31,21

περίειμι (περιέναι)   V 0-0-0-0-1-1
Wis 8,18
to go around

περιεκτικός,-ή,-όν   A 0-0-0-0-1-1
4 Mc 1,20
comprehensive
περιεκτικώταται *most comprehensive*

περιεργάζομαι   V 0-0-0-0-1-1
Sir 3,23
to meddle with, to do sth unnecessary [ἔν τινι]
Cf. HORSLEY 1983, 26

περιεργία,-ας   N1F 0-0-0-0-1-1
Sir 41,24
meddling

περιέρχομαι⁺   V 0-11-2-2-1-16
Jos 6,7.11.15; 15,10; 16,6
to go round, to go about Jos 6,7; *to go round, to come round* (of a border) Jos 15,10; *to compass* [τι] Jb 1,7; *to come about* (of a speech) 2 Sm

14,20

*Ez 3,15 περιῆλθον *I walked around* -אָסֵב for MT
אָבִיב *Abib*
Cf. HELBING 1928, 87

περιέχω⁺   V 0-10-3-10-11-34
2 Sm 22,5; 1 Kgs 6,15.20.21.22
A: *to compass* [τι] 1 Kgs 6,15; *id.* [τινα] Jb 30,18; *to encompass, to surround* [τινα] (in hostile sense) Ps 21(22),13; *to encircle* [τινα] 4 Mc 8,4; *to compass, to come upon, to befall, to seize* [τινα] 2 Sm 22,5
to embrace, to include [τι] 4 Mc 1,2; *to enwrap* [τι] Wis 18,14; *to contain* [τι] (of a letter) 1 Mc 15,2
P: *to be in a siege* Ez 6,12
πολλὴν ἐπιστήμην περιεῖχεν *he had very great skill* 1 Ezr 8,7; ἐκστάσει περιειχόμην *I was seized with dismay* Dn^LXX 7,28

περίζωμα,-ατος   N3N 1-0-7-2-0-10
Gn 3,7; Jer 13,1.2.4.6
girdle Jer 13,1; *apron, skirt* Ru 3,15; neol.?
Cf. HARL 1986ᵃ, 68.107-108; LEE, J. 1983, 95; WEVERS 1993, 40

περιζώννυμι⁺/ύω⁺   V 1-15-11-11-5-43
Ex 12,11; Jgs 3,16; Jgsᴬ 18,11.16
A: *to gird sb with sth* [τινά τι] Sir 45,7; *id.* [τινά τι] (metaph.) Ps 17(18),33
M: *to gird oneself, to put on a garment* [abs.] Jl 1,13; *to gird oneself, to arm oneself* [abs.] 1 Mc 3,58; *to gird oneself with* [τι] Jgsᴬ 18,11; *id.* [ἔν τινι] 1 Chr 15,27; *id.* [τι] (metaph.) Ps 64(65),13; *to gird oneself about* (the loins) *with sth* [τί τι] 2 Kgs 1,8; *to gird* (the loins) [τι] Jer 1,17; *to gird* (the loins) *with* [τί τινι] Dn^LXX 10,5
P: *to be (well-)girded* (of loins) Ex 12,11
Cf. HELBING 1928, 47-48; →LSJ Suppl; LSJ RSuppl

περίθεμα,-ατος   N3N 2-1-0-0-0-3
Nm 17,3.4; Jgsᴮ 8,26
cover, wrapping; neol.
Cf. DORIVAL 1994, 355

περιίπταμαι   V 0-0-0-0-1-1
4 Mc 14,17
to fly over and around, to flutter around

περιίστημι⁺   V 0-3-0-0-3-6
Jos 6,3; 1 Sm 4,15(16); 2 Sm 13,31; Jdt 5,22; 2 Mc 14,9
M: *to place* or *set round* [τινά τινι] Jos 6,3; *to stand round (about)* [τινι] 1 Sm 4,15; *id.* [τι] Jdt 5,22

P: *to be pressed on every side, to be sorely tried* (of a nation) 2 Mc 14,9

ἄνθρωπον τυφλὸν εἰς ὅρασιν οὐ μὴ περιστήσωσιν *they cannot restore a blind man to his sight, sight cannot be restored to a blind man* LtJ 36

περικαθαίρω⁺   V 1-1-0-0-1-3
Dt 18,10; Jos 5,4; 4 Mc 1,29
to purge, to purify [τινα] Dt 18,10; *to weed* (as a task of a husbandman) 4 Mc 1,29
Cf. DOGNIEZ 1992, 65; LE DÉAUT 1981, 184-185; WEVERS 1995, 298(Dt 18,10); →MM

περικαθαρίζω   V 2-0-1-0-0-3
Lv 19,23; Dt 30,6; Is 6,7
to clean away [τι] Lv 19,23; *to cleanse* [τι] Dt 30,6
Cf. DOGNIEZ 1992, 59.307; LE DÉAUT 1981, 184-185; WALTERS 1973, 117; WEVERS 1995, 480(Dt 30,6)

περικάθαρμα,-ατος⁺   N3N 0-0-0-1-0-1
Prv 21,18
expiation, ransom; neol.
Cf. LE DÉAUT 1981, 184-185; SPICQ 1978ᵃ, 681-682; WALTERS 1973, 330; →MM

περικάθημαι   V 0-3-0-0-5-8
Jgsᴮ 9,31; 1 Kgs 15,27; 2 Kgs 6,25; 1 Mc 5,3; 6,24
to besiege (a city) [τι] Jgsᴮ 9,31; *id.* [abs.] 1 Mc 11,22; *to besiege, to lay siege to* [ἐπί τι] 2 Kgs 6,25
Cf. HELBING 1928, 88

περικαθίζω⁺   V 2-12-0-0-4-18
Dt 20,12.19; Jos 10,5.31.34
to camp around, to besiege [τι] Dt 20,12; *id.* [περί τι] Dt 20,19; *id.* [ἐπί τι] Jgsᴬ 9,50; *id.* [ἐπί τινα] 1 Mc 6,19
Cf. DOGNIEZ 1992, 66.240; HELBING 1928, 88

περικαίω   V 0-0-0-0-1-1
4 Mc 16,3
to burn, to inflame, to excite [τινα]

περικαλύπτω⁺   V 1-3-0-0-0-4
Ex 28,20; 1 Kgs 7,5(17).28(42); 8,7
A: *to cover* [τι] 1 Kgs 7,5
P: *to be embedded, to be set in* [τινι] Ex 28,20

περικατάλημπτος,-ος,-ον   A 0-0-0-0-1-1
2 Mc 14,41
surrounded on every side; neol.

περίκειμαι⁺   V 0-0-0-0-3-3
4 Mc 12,2; LtJ 23.57
to lie around, to encompass (of bounds) 4 Mc 12,2; *to wear* [τι] LtJ 23

→MM

περικείρω   V 0-0-2-0-0-2
Jer 9,25; 32(25),23
to shear all round; περικειρόμενον τὰ κατὰ πρόσωπον *one who shaves his face round about* Jer 9,25, see also 32(25),23

περικεφαλαία,-ας⁺   N1F 0-4-5-0-1-10
1 Sm 17,5.38.49; 2 Chr 26,14; Is 59,17
helmet; neol.?

περικλάω   V 0-0-0-0-3-3
4 Mc 7,5; 10,6; Wis 4,5
to twist round, to bend [τι] 4 Mc 10,6; *to break off* Wis 4,5; *to break* [τι] (metaph.) 4 Mc 7,5
Cf. LARCHER 1984, 322

περικλύζομαι   V 0-0-0-0-2-2
Jdt 10,3; Tobᴮᴬ 6,2
to wash oneself, to bathe oneself Tobᴮᴬ 6,2; *to wash* (the body) [τι] Jdt 10,3

περικνημίς,-ῖδος   N3F 0-0-0-1-0-1
Dnᵀʰ 3,21
covering of the leg, gaiter; neol.

περικομπέω   V 0-0-0-0-1-1
Wis 17,4
to sound all around, to echo, to reverberate [τινα]; neol.
Cf. LARCHER 1985, 993

περικοσμέω   V 0-0-0-1-0-1
Ps 143(144),12
to be decorated or *adorned round about* (of girls); neol.

περικρατέω   V 0-0-0-0-5-5
4 Mc 1,9; 2,2; 7,17.22; 14,11
to control [τινος] 4 Mc 1,9; *to be superior to* [τινος] 4 Mc 14,11
Cf. HELBING 1928, 122

περικυκλόω⁺   V 4-5-2-5-1-17
Gn 19,4; Ex 36,20(39,13); Nm 21,4; 32,38; Jos 6,13
A: *to compass, to encircle* [τι] Gn 19,4; *id.* [τινα] Jos 7,9; *to come round about* [τινα] (metaph.) Ps 17(18),6
P: *to be surrounded with walls* (of cities, houses) Nm 32,38
περικεκυκλωμένα χρυσίῳ καὶ συνδεδεμένα χρυσίῳ *precious stones set in gold and held in place by gold* Ex 36,20
Cf. DORIVAL 1994, 53; LE BOULLUEC 1989, 355; WALTERS 1973, 294; WEVERS 1990, 454

περικύκλῳ   D 3-7-11-3-2-26
Ex 28,33; Dt 6,14; 13,8; Josᴬ 19,8; Jgs 2,12

round about Ex 28,33; round about, on every side
of [τινος] Ez 28,23

περιλακίζω V 0-0-0-0-1-1
4 Mc 10,8
P: to be rent round about, to be torn all over, to
hang in strips; neol.

περιλαμβάνω V 3-3-1-6-1-14
Gn 29,13; 33,4; 48,10; Jgs 16,29
to embrace [τινα] Gn 29,13; to put one's arms
around [τι] Jgs 16,29; to compass, to surround
[τι] Ps 47(48),13
περιέλαβεν τὰς χεῖρας αὐτοῦ he folded his
hands together Eccl 4,5

περιλείπομαι V 0-0-0-0-4-4
2 Mc 1,31; 8,14; 4 Mc 12,6; 13,18
to remain over 2 Mc 1,31; to survive 4 Mc 13,18
Cf. SPICQ 1978ᵃ, 683

περίλημψις,-εως N3F 0-0-0-1-0-1
Eccl 3,5
embracing; neol.

περίλοιπος,-ος,-ον A 0-0-1-1-0-2
Am 5,15; Ps 20(21),13
remaining, surviving; τοὺς περιλοίπους τοῦ
Ιωσηφ the remnant of Joseph Am 5,15
*Ps 20(21),13 τοῖς περιλοίποις the remaining,
surviving - ◊יתר for MT מיתר bowstring

περίλυπος,-ος,-ον⁺ A 1-0-0-4-3-8
Gn 4,6; Ps 41(42),6.12; 42(43),5; Dnᴸˣˣ 2,12
very sad, deeply grieved
Cf. LUST 1993, 99-100

περιλύω V 0-0-0-0-1-1
4 Mc 10,7
to dismember; περιλύσαντες τὰ ὄργανα they
dismembered the body; neol.

περιμένω⁺ V 1-0-0-0-1-2
Gn 49,18; Wis 8,12
to wait for [τινα] Wis 8,12; id. [τι] Gn 49,18

περίμετρον,-ου N2N 0-1-0-0-2-3
1 Kgs 7,3(15); 3 Mc 4,11; Sir 50,3
circumference, circuit 1 Kgs 7,3; abundance Sir
50,3

περινίπτομαι V 0-0-0-0-1-1
Tobˢ 6,2
to wash oneself; neol.

περιξύω V 0-0-0-0-1-1
Wis 13,11
to scrape off or away (the bark) [τι]
Cf. LARCHER 1985, 778

περιοδεύω V 0-1-5-0-0-6
2 Sm 24,8; Zech 1,10.11; 6,7(bis)

to travel around [τι] Zech 1,10; id. [ἔν τινι] 2
Sm 24,8; neol.?
Cf. HELBING 1928, 88

περίοδος,-ου N2F 0-1-0-0-0-1
Jos 6,16
journey around, circuit

περιοικοδομέω V 0-0-3-1-0-4
Jer 52,4; Ez 26,8; 39,11; Jb 19,8
A: to build a wall round about sth, to enclose by
building [τι] Jer 52,4; id. [abs.] Ez 26,8
P: to be fenced Jb 19,8

περίοικος,-ος,-ον⁺ A 3-5-1-0-0-9
Gn 19,25.29; Dt 1,7; Jgsᴮ 1,27(quater)
dwelling round; ἡ περίοικος (χώρα) country
round about Gn 19,25; ὁ περίοικος region
round about 1 Kgs 7,33(46); τὰ περίοικα
territories Jgsᴮ 1,27; οἱ περίοικοι neighbours Dt
1,7

περιονυχίζω V 1-0-0-0-0-1
Dt 21,12
to trim sb's nails (of a woman) [τινα]; neol.

περιουσιασμός,-οῦ N2M 0-0-0-2-0-2
Ps 134(135),4; Eccl 2,8
wealth, treasure Ps 134(135),4; abundance,
superfluity Eccl 2,8; neol.

περιούσιος,-ος,-ον⁺ A 5-0-0-0-0-5
Ex 19,5; 23,22; Dt 7,6; 14,2; 26,18
above and beyond, peculiar, special; neol.
Cf. DODD 1954, 167; DOGNIEZ 1992, 65.161.204; LE
BOULLUEC 1989, 199; WALTERS 1973, 221; WEVERS 1990,
294

περιοχή,-ῆς⁺ N1F 0-13-8-4-0-25
1 Sm 22,4.5; 2 Sm 5,7.9.17
fortified enclosure 1 Sm 22,4; wall of
circumvallation Ez 4,2; hemming Ez 12,13; siege
Zech 12,2
*Ob 1 περιοχήν besieging army corr.? περίοχου
one who rides around, a messenger for MT ציר a
messenger; *Ps 140(141),3 περιοχῆς fortification
-נצרה? for MT נצרה keep watch
→LSJ Suppl; LSJ RSuppl

περιπαθῶς D 0-0-0-0-1-1
4 Mc 8,2
in violent rage, passionately; neol.

περιπατέω⁺ V 3-5-2-19-11-40
Gn 3,8.10; Ex 21,19; Jgs 21,24
to walk up and down Sir 38,32; to walk Gn 3,8;
id. (metaph.) Jb 20,25
Cf. LUCIANI 1973, 472-473

περίπατος,-ου N2M 0-0-5-2-1-8

Ez 42,4.5.10.11.12

walk Ez 42,4; *(public) walk, walk in public* Prv
23,31; *digression* 2 Mc 2,30; *range* Jb 41,24

περιπίπτω⁺ V 0-1-0-3-5-9
2 Sm 1,6; Prv 11,5; Ru 2,3; Dnᴸˣˣ 2,9; 2 Mc 6,13
to fall on the side 2 Mc 9,7; *to encounter* [τινι]
Prv 11,5; *to incur* (punishment) [τινι] 2 Mc
6,13

περιέπεσεν περιπτώματι τῇ μερίδι τοῦ ἀγροῦ
Βοος *she happened by chance to come upon a
portion of the land of Boaz* Ru 2,3; περιπτώματι περιέπεσον ἐν τῷ ὄρει τῷ Γελβουε *I
happened accidentally to be upon mount Gelbue*
2 Sm 1,6

Cf. HELBING 1928, 316; SPICQ 1978ᵃ, 684-685; →MM

περιπλέκω⁺ V 0-0-2-2-4-8
Ez 17,7; Na 1,10; Ps 49(50),19; 118(119),61;
3 Mc 2,22

A: *to bind up* 4 Mc 1,29; *to embrace* (metaph.),
to enframe [τι] Ps 49(50),19

M/P: *to entangle* [τινι] Ps 118(119),61; *to be
twisted* Na 1,10; *to bend oneself* Ez 17,7; *to
embrace* 3 Mc 5,49; *to wear sth around sth* [τινί
τι] 3 Mc 4,8

περιποιέω⁺ V 6-10-5-5-5-31
Gn 12,12; 31,18; 36,6; Ex 1,16; 22,17

A: *to keep alive, to preserve* [τινα] Ex 22,17)
M: *to procure* [τι] Prv 6,32; *to save* [τι] 1 Chr
29,3; *to obtain, to acquire, to gain for oneself* [τι]
Gn 31,18; *to save the life of* [τινα] Gn 12,12; *to
bring about* [τινί τι] 2 Mc 15,21

Cf. LE BOULLUEC 1989, 229; SPICQ 1978ᵃ, 687-688;
WALTERS 1973, 249; WEVERS 1990, 350; 1993, 505.592

περιποίησις,-εως⁺ N3F 0-1-2-0-0-3
2 Chr 14,12; Hag 2,9; Mal 3,17

keeping safe, preservation, saving 2 Chr 14,12;
gaining possession of Hag 2,9; *possession,
property* Mal 3,17

Cf. SPICQ 1978ᵃ, 689

περιπόλιον,-ου N2N 0-0-0-0-2-2
1 Mc 11,4.61

surrounding fortification

περιπορεύομαι V 0-1-0-0-0-1
Jos 15,3

to go round [τι]

περιπόρφυρος,-ος,-ον A 0-0-1-0-0-1
Is 3,21

edged with purple; τὰ περιπόρφυρα *garments
with a purple border, purple trimmed garments*

περίπτερος,-ος,-ον A 0-0-1-2-0-3

Am 3,15; Ct 8,6(bis)

encircled by a colonnade Am 3,15
(τὰ) περίπτερα (πυρός) *sparks (of fire)* Ct 8,6

περίπτωμα,-ατος N3N 0-1-0-1-0-2
2 Sm 1,6; Ru 2,3

circumstance, sudden event, sudden happening

περιρραίνω⁺ V 6-0-0-0-0-6
Lv 14,7.51; Nm 8,7; 19,18.19

to sprinkle [τι] Nm 19,21; *to sprinkle sb with sth*
[τινά τι] Nm 8,7; *to sprinkle upon* [ἐπί τι] Lv
14,51; *id.* [ἐπί τινα] Lv 14,7

Cf. DORIVAL 1994, 124.384

περιρραντίζω V 2-0-0-0-0-2
Nm 19,13.20

P: *to be sprinkled*; neol.

Cf. DORIVAL 1994, 382.384

περιρρέω V 0-0-0-0-1-1
4 Mc 9,20

to run round, to be scattered round [περί τι]

περιρρήγνυω⁺ V 0-0-0-0-1-1
2 Mc 4,38

M: *to rend, to tear off* [τι]

περισιαλόω V 1-0-0-0-0-1
Ex 36,13(39,6)

P: *to be embroidered about, to be set around
with*; neol.

Cf. LE BOULLUEC 1989, 354; WEVERS 1990, 600

περισκελής,-ής,-ές A 4-0-1-0-1-6
Ex 28,42; 36,35; Lv 6,3; 16,4; Ez 44,18

around the leg; τὰ περισκελή *underpants,
leggings*

περισκυθίζω V 0-0-0-0-1-1
2 Mc 7,4

to scalp in the Scythian way

περισπασμός,-οῦ N2M 0-0-0-8-2-10
Eccl 1,13; 2,23.26; 3,10; 4,8

stereotypical rendition of ענין; *preoccupation*;
neol.?

Cf. BERTRAM 1952, 41-45; CAIRD 1969=1972, 139-140;
KORN 1937, 6-8; →LSJ Rsuppl

περισπάω⁺ V 0-1-0-3-1-5
2 Sm 6,6; Eccl 1,13; 3,10; 5,19; Sir 41,2

A: *to draw away, to shake sth out of its place*
[τι] 2 Sm 6,6; *to divert, to occupy* [τινα] Eccl
5,19

P: *to be distracted, to be engaged, to be troubled*
Eccl 1,13

Cf. CAIRD 1969=1972, 140

περισπόρια,-ων N2N 0-65-0-0-0-65
Jos 21,2.3.8.11.34

country round about, open country surrounding a city; neol.

Cf. CAIRD 1969=1972, 140

περισσεία,-ας⁺   N1F 0-0-0-12-0-12
Eccl 1,3; 2,11.13(bis); 3,9
stereotypical rendition of ◊יתר in Eccl; *gain, advantage* Eccl 1,3; *surplus* Eccl 2,13; *abundance* Eccl 5,8; neol.
→NIDNTT

περίσσευμα,-ατος⁺   N3N 0-0-0-1-0-1
Eccl 2,15
abundance; ἐκ περισσεύματος λαλεῖ *he speaks from abundance, he speaks out of the abundance (of the heart)*, cpr. Mt 12,34; Lk 6,45

περισσεύω⁺   V 0-2-0-1-6-9
1 Sm 2,33.36; Eccl 3,19; Tob^BA 4,16; 1 Mc 3,30
to survive 1 Sm 2,36; *to be more than enough for, to remain over for* [τινι] Tob^BA 4,16; *to abound in* [τινι] Sir 11,12; *id.* [ἔν τινι] Sir 10,27; *to be superior to, to be better than* [παρά τινα] Eccl 3,19; *to be more lavish than* [ὑπέρ τινα] 1 Mc 3,30; *to act superior towards, to be overbearing* [ἐπί τινι] Sir 33,30

περισσός,-ή,-όν⁺   A 2-4-4-11-5-26
Ex 10,5; Nm 4,26; Jgs^B 21,7.16; 1 Sm 30,9
superfluous, useless 2 Mc 12,44; *remaining* Ez 48,15; *excellent* Dn^Th 5,12; οἱ περισσοί *the rest, those who remain* Jgs^B 21,7; περισσόν (as adv.) *furthermore, moreover* Eccl 2,15; περισσά (as adv.) *very, excessively, over-* Eccl 7,16; τὸ περισσόν τινος *the rest of, abundance of* Ex 10,5; ἐκ περισσοῦ *exceedingly* Dn^Th 3,22; τί περισσὸν τῷ ἀνθρώπῳ; *what advantage has a man?* Eccl 6,11
*Nm 4,26 τὰ περισσά *the rest, the remainder* -◊יתר^י for MT ◊יתר^II *the cords*, cpr. Nm 3,26
περισσότερος *greater, more* Dn^Th 4,36
Cf. DORIVAL 1994, 211

περισσῶς⁺   D 0-0-0-5-1-6
Ps 30(31),24; Dn^Th 7,7(bis).19; 8,9
exceedingly, beyond measure, in excess, very

περίστασις,-εως   N3F 0-0-1-0-1-2
Ez 26,8; 2 Mc 4,16
difficult position, crisis, calamity 2 Mc 4,16
περίστασιν ὅπλων *surrounding of weapons, warlike works* Ez 26,8
Cf. CORNILL 1886, 340(Ez 26,8)

περιστέλλω⁺   V 0-0-2-0-4-6
Is 58,8; Ez 29,5; Tob 12,13; Sir 38,16
A: *to bury* [τινα] Tob 12,13; *to wrap up, to*

cover [τινα] (metaph.) Is 58,8; *to cover with* [τι ἔν τινι] PSal 16,10
P: *to be buried* Ez 29,5

περιστερά,-ᾶς⁺   N1F 16-1-8-10-1-36
Gn 8,8.9.10.11.12
pigeon, dove

περιστήθιον,-ου   N2N 1-0-0-0-0-1
Ex 28,4
breast-band; neol.
Cf. LE BOULLUEC 1989, 282

περιστολή,-ῆς   N1F 1-0-0-0-2-3
Ex 33,6; Sir 45,7; PSal 13,8
adornment, robe Ex 33,6; *id.* (metaph.) Sir 45,7
ἐν περιστολῇ *secretly?* PSal 13,8
Cf. HOLM-NIELSEN 1977, 90(PSal 13,8)

περιστόμιον,-ου   N2N 4-0-1-2-0-7
Ex 28,32(bis); 36,30(39,23)(bis); Ez 39,11
collar (of a garment) Jb 30,18; *edge, outlet* (of a valley) Ez 39,11
*Jb 15,27 περιστόμιον *collar* -◊פים for MT פימה *fat*
Cf. WEVERS 1990, 459

περιστρέφω   V 3-0-0-0-0-3
Gn 37,7; Nm 36,7.9
M: *to turn round, to gather in a circle* Gn 37,7
P: *to be diverted, to be removed* Nm 36,7

περιστροφή,-ῆς   N1F 0-0-0-0-1-1
Sir 50,5
turning round, parade, procession; ἐν περιστροφῇ λαοῦ *amidst the people, surrounded by the people*

περίστυλον,-ου   N2N 0-0-7-0-2-9
Ez 40,17(bis).18; 42,3.5
peristyle, colonnade round a temple or *round the court of a house* Ez 40,17; *colonnade, gallery* 3 Mc 5,23

περισύρω   V 1-0-0-0-1-2
Gn 30,37; 2 Mc 7,7
to tear away [τι]; neol.?

περισχίζω⁺   V 0-0-2-0-0-2
Ez 47,15; 48,1
to divide, to draw a line

περιτειχίζω⁺   V 0-0-1-0-1-2
Hos 10,14; 1 Mc 13,33
to fence with [τί τινι] 1 Mc 13,33
τὰ περιτετειχισμένα *strong places* Hos 10,14

περίτειχος,-ους   N3N 0-1-1-0-0-2
2 Kgs 25,1; Is 26,1
surrounding wall; neol.

περιτέμνω⁺   V 21-7-3-1-7-39
Gn 17,10.11.12.13.14

A: *to circumcise* [τινα] Gn 17,27; *id.* [τι] Gn 17,23
M: *to circumcise* [τι] Gn 34,24; *id.* [τι] (metaph.) Dt 10,16
P: *to be circumcised* Gn 17,10
Cf. HARL 1986ᵃ, 170; HORSLEY 1983, 81; LEE, J. 1983, 111

περιτίθημι⁺ V 11-0-13-17-12-53
Gn 24,47; 27,16; 41,42(bis); Ex 29,9
A: *to put sth on sb* [τινί τι] Gn 24,47; *to put sth on sth* [τι ἐπί τι] Gn 27,16; *to put sth about sth* [τι περί τι] Gn 41,42; *to put sth around sb* [τι ἐπί τινι] Ru 3,3; *to invest sb with sth* [τινά τινι] Jb 39,19; *to surround sth with sth* [τί τινι] Jb 38,10; *to compass sb with sth* [τί τινι] (metaph.) Jb 13,26; *to set up* [τι] Ex 40,8; *to assign to, to ascribe* [τί τινι] Nm 27,7
M: *to put round oneself, to put on* [τι] Lv 16,4; *id.* [τι] (metaph.) Wis 5,18; *to put sth on sth* [τι περί τι] Jer 13,1; *to put sth around sth* [τι ἐπί τινι] Jb 31,36; *to put about* [τι] Jdt 10,4
*Ez 27,3 περιέθηκα *I put on, I crowned (myself)* -כלל for MT כליל *perfect*, cpr. 27,4
Cf. DANIEL 1966, 261(Ez 27,3); DORIVAL 1994, 482; HELBING 1928, 316-318; WEVERS 1990, 573.644

περιτομή,-ῆς⁺ N1F 3-0-1-0-0-4
Gn 17,13; Ex 4,25.26; Jer 11,16
circumcision Gn 17,13
*Jer 11,16 περιτομῆς *of its circumcision* -מול◊ for MT המולה *of a great noise?*

περιτρέπω⁺ V 0-0-0-0-1-1
Wis 5,23
to overturn [τι]

περιτρέχω⁺ V 0-0-2-0-0-2
Jer 5,1; Am 8,12
to run about

περιφανῶς D 0-0-0-0-1-1
4 Mc 8,2
notably, manifestly, evidently

περιφέρεια,-ας N1F 0-0-0-2-0-2
Eccl 9,3; 10,13
madness, error
Cf. CAIRD 1969=1972, 140

περιφερής,-ής,-ές A 0-0-1-0-1-2
Ez 41,10; 2 Mc 13,5
revolving, round 2 Mc 13,5; τὸ περιφερές *circumference* Ez 41,10

περιφέρω⁺ V 0-1-0-2-1-4
Jos 24,33a; Prv 10,24; Eccl 7,7; 2 Mc 7,27
A: *to carry about* [τι] Jos 24,33a; *id.* [τινα] (being pregnant) 2 Mc 7,27; *to turn round, to*

make dizzy, to turn mad [τινα] Eccl 7,7
P: *to be made dizzy, to be troubled* Prv 10,24

περιφορά,-ᾶς N1F 0-0-0-3-0-3
Eccl 2,2.12; 7,25
madness
Cf. CAIRD 1969=1972, 140-141

περιφράσσω V 0-1-0-1-4-6
1 Kgs 10,22a; Jb 1,10; 2 Mc 1,34; 12,13; Sir 28,24
to fortify, to enclose [τι]

περιφρονέω⁺ V 0-0-0-0-3-3
4 Mc 6,9; 7,16; 14,1
to despise [τινος]
Cf. HELBING 1928, 190; SPICQ 1978ᵃ, 691

περίφρων,-ων,-ον A 0-0-0-0-1-1
4 Mc 8,28
despising [τινος]
Cf. SPICQ 1978ᵃ, 690

περιφυτεύω V 0-0-0-0-1-1
4 Mc 2,21
to plant round about, to implant [τι] (metaph.)

περιχαλάω V 0-0-0-0-1-1
4 Mc 7,13
P: *to be relaxed*; neol.

περιχαλκόω V 1-0-0-0-0-1
Ex 27,6
to plate with brass or *copper* [τι]; neol.?
Cf. LE BOULLUEC 1978, 275; LEE, J. 1983, 45

περιχαρακόω V 0-0-1-1-0-2
Jer 52,4; Prv 4,8
to surround with a stockade (metaph.), *to secure* [τι] Prv 4,8; *to besiege* [τι] Jer 52,4

περιχαρής,-ής,-ές⁺ A 0-0-0-2-1-3
Jb 3,22; 29,22; 3 Mc 5,44
exceedingly glad, very joyful

περιχέω V 0-1-1-0-4-6
2 Chr 29,22; Jon 2,6; Jdt 13,2; 2 Mc 3,17.27
A: *to pour round* [τί τινι] 2 Chr 29,22
P: *to be poured around, to be enveloped* [τινι] Jon 2,6
περιεκέχυτο περὶ τὸν ἄνδρα δέος τι *the man was compassed with terror* 2 Mc 3,17; ἦν περικεχυμένος αὐτῷ ὁ οἶνος *he was overflowing, filled (i.e. drunk) with wine* Jdt 13,2

περίχρυσος,-ος,-ον A 0-0-0-0-7-7
LtJ 7.38.50.54.57
gilded, gold-plated

περιχρυσόω V 0-1-2-0-0-3
1 Kgs 10,18; Is 30,22; 40,19
to gild all over, to cover with gold [τι]

περίχωρος,-ος,-ον⁺ A 9-3-0-9-1-22
Gn 13,10.11.12; 19,17.28
round about, neighbouring Gn 19,28
ἡ περίχωρος (γῆ) *the country round about, neighbourhood* Gn 13,10; οἱ περίχωροι *neighbouring people* Gn 13,12; τὰ περίχωρα *country round about* Dt 3,4
Cf. DOGNIEZ 1992, 129; WEVERS 1993, 179

περίψημα,-ατος⁺ N3N 0-0-0-0-2-2
Tob 5,19
ransom; neol.
Cf. SPICQ 1978[a], 681-682; →MM

περιψύχω V 0-0-0-0-1-1
Sir 30,7
to refresh, to cherish, to pamper [τινα]; neol.

περκάζω V 0-0-1-0-1-2
Am 9,13; Sir 51,15
to turn dark (of grapes beginning to ripen)

πέσσω V 8-2-5-0-0-15
Gn 19,3; Ex 12,39; 16,23(bis); Lv 2,4
to bake Gn 19,3; πεσσούσας *bakers, cooks* 1 Sm 8,13

πετάζω
(→ἐκ-)

πέταλον,-ου⁺ N2N 5-2-0-0-0-7
Ex 28,36; 29,6; 36,10.37(39,3.30); Lv 8,9
leaf, thin plate (of metal)
Cf. LE BOULLUEC 1989, 291.295; WEVERS 1990, 468.598.608

πέταμαι⁺ V 1-0-2-0-0-3
Dt 4,17; Is 60,8; Ez 32,10
to fly (of birds) Dt 4,17; *to fly, to move in the air with speed* (of sword) Ez 32,10

πετάννυμι V 0-1-1-5-0-7
2 Sm 22,11; Hab 1,8; Ps 17(18),11(bis); 54(55),7
P: *to be spread all over* Jb 26,11; *to fly* 2 Sm 22,11
(→ἀνα-, δια-, κατα-)
Cf. COOK 1994, 472

πέτασος,-ου N2M 0-0-0-0-1-1
2 Mc 4,12
petasus, broad-brimmed felt hat (worn by the ἔφηβοι, as badge of the palaestra); τοὺς κρατίστους τῶν ἐφήβων ὑποτάσσων ὑπὸ πέτασον ἤγαγεν *he made the noblest of the young men wear the petasus*

πετεινός,-ή,-όν⁺ A 34-7-27-19-11-98
Gn 1,20.21.22.26.28
able to fly, winged Gn 6,20; τὸ πετεινόν *winged creature, bird* Gn 1,20
Cf. SHIPP 1979, 55-56; WALTERS 1973, 135

πέτευρον,-ου N2N 0-0-0-1-0-1
Prv 9,18
tight-rope?
Cf. CAIRD 1969=1972, 141

πέτομαι⁺ V 1-0-9-7-0-17
Gn 1,20; Is 6,2; 11,14; 14,29; 30,6
to fly (of anim.) Gn 1,20; *to fly, to move in the air with speed* (of arrows, sickles) Ps 90(91),5; *to flee* Jb 20,8
(→ἐκ-)

πέτρα,-ας⁺ N1F 13-30-31-26-7-107
Ex 17,6(bis); 33,21.22; Nm 20,8
rock Ex 17,6; *hollow rock, cave* 1 Sm 13,6; *stone* (as material) Is 5,28
*Jer 31(48),28 ἐν πέτραις στόματι βοθύνου *in the caves at the mouth of a gorge* corr.? ἐν τῷ πέραν στόματος βοθύνου for MT ב/עברי פי פחת *on the side of the mouth of a gorge*; *Hab 2,1 πέτραν *rock* -צור◊ for MT מצור *rampart, wall* (1QpHab 6,13 מצורי); *Jb 22,24 ἐν πέτρᾳ *on a rock* -ב/צר for MT בצר *ore, gold dust*; *Ps 103(104),12 τῶν πετρῶν *(among) the rocks* -סעפים סעיף◊[l] *(cleft* cpr. Jgs[B] 15,8.11; Is 2,21; 57,5) for MT[k] עפאים or for MT[q] עפים *(among) the branches*
Cf. CARAGOUNIS 1990, 9-16.26-30; WALTERS 1973, 71(Jer 31(48),28); →NIDNTT; TWNT

πέτρινος,-η,-ον A 0-4-0-0-0-4
Jos 5,2.3; 21,42d; 24,31a
of stone, of rock

πετροβόλος,-ος,-ον A 0-1-2-1-1-5
1 Sm 14,14; Ez 13,11.13; Jb 41,20; Wis 5,22
throwing stones; (ὁ) πετροβόλος *engine of war, engine for throwing stones* Jb 41,20
λίθους πετροβόλους *stones hurled as from a sling* (of hailstones) Ez 13,11

πέτρος,-ου⁺ N2M 0-0-0-0-2-2
2 Mc 1,16; 4,41
stone

πεύκη,-ης N1F 0-0-1-0-0-1
Is 60,13
pine

πεύκινος,-η,-ον A 0-8-0-0-0-8
1 Kgs 5,22; 6,15.32.34; 9,11
of pine

πέψις,-εως N3F 0-0-1-0-0-1
Hos 7,4
cooking

πηγή,-ῆς N1F 22-20-12-30-15-99
Gn 2,6; 7,11; 8,2; 14,7; 16,7

spring, fountain Gn 2,6; *id.* (metaph. as origin of sth) Ps 35(36),10

*Jos^B 19,29 καὶ ἕως πηγῆς *and to the source* ועד עין *for MT* ועד עיר *and to the town*; *Ez 25,9 ἐπάνω πηγῆς *above the source* -על מעין/ב *for MT* בעל מעון *Baal-Meon* (proper name); *Prv 4,21 αἱ πηγαί σου *your fountains* -עיניך עין ◊ *(source) for* MT עיניך עין ◊ *(eye) your eyes*

Cf. ALEXANDRE 1988, 231(Gn 2,6); CAIRD 1976, 82; COOK 1994, 473; HARL 1986ᵃ, 65.100(Gn 2,6); SHIPP 1979, 449-453; →NIDNTT; TWNT

πῆγμα,-ατος   N3N 0-1-0-0-1-2
Jos 3,16; 4 Mc 9,21
solid mass Jos 3,16
τὸ τῶν ὀστέων πῆγμα *bodily frame* 4 Mc 9,21

πήγνυμι⁺   V 8-9-4-8-12-41
Gn 26,25; 31,25; 35,16; Ex 15,8(bis)
A: *to pitch* (a tent) [τι] Gn 26,25; *to establish* [τι] Is 42,5; *to fix, to fasten* [τι] Jgs^B 4,21; *to fix with* [τί τινι] Jgs^B 16,14; *to be firm* (of a heart) Jb 41,16
P: *to be fixed* Ezr 6,11; *to be congealed, to be frozen* Ex 15,8; *to be compacted* Wis 7,2; *to cleave to* [ἐπί τι] Lam 4,8
βέλος πεπηγὸς ἐν μηρῷ σαρκός *an arrow that stuck in the fleshy thigh* Sir 19,12

Cf. LE BOULLUEC 1989, 173.331.368-369; WEVERS 1990, 230.544.631

(→ἐμ-, κατα-)

πηδαλιουχέω   V 0-0-0-0-1-1
4 Mc 7,1
to steer (a ship) [τι] (metaph.); neol.

πηδάω⁺   V 1-0-0-1-0-2
Lv 11,21; Ct 2,8
to leap
(→ἀνα-, ἀπο-, εἰσ-, ἐκ-, ἐμ-, κατα-, παρα-)

πηδύω
(→ἀνα-)

πηλίκος,-η,-ον⁺   A 0-0-2-0-1-3
Zech 2,6(bis); 4 Mc 15,22
how great, how long

πήλινος,-α,-ον⁺   A 0-0-0-4-1-5
Jb 4,19; 13,12; Dn^LXX 2,41.43; Bel^LXX 7
of clay

πηλός,-οῦ⁺   N2M 2-1-1-12-10-7-32
Gn 11,3; Ex 1,14; 2 Sm 22,43; Is 14,23; 29,16
clay, earth Gn 11,3; *mud* 2 Sm 22,43

Cf. LE BOULLUEC 1989, 77(Ex 1,14)

πηλουργός,-οῦ   N2M 0-0-0-0-1-1
Wis 15,7

one who works in clay, craftsman; neol.

πῆξις,-εως   N3F 0-0-0-0-1-1
Sir 41,20
fixity, stiffness (of elbow; from reclining too long, or from relentless eating)

πήρα,-ας⁺   N1F 0-0-0-0-3-3
Jdt 10,5; 13,10.15
leather pouch, bag

πηρόω   V 0-0-0-0-1-1
4 Mc 18,21
to blind (the eyes) [τι]

πῆχυς,-εως⁺   N3M 51-68-103-12-11-245
Gn 6,15(ter).16; 7,20
arm Prv 31,19; *cubit* (measure of length) Gn 6,15

πιάζω⁺   V 0-0-0-1-1-2
Ct 2,15; Sir 23,21
to seize, to arrest [τινα] (of pers.) Sir 23,21; *to catch* [τινα] (of anim.) Ct 2,15

Cf. SHIPP 1979, 454

(→ἀπο-)

πιαίνω   V 0-0-4-3-1-8
Is 58,11(bis); Ez 17,8.10; Ps 19(20),4
A: *to make fat, to enrich* [τι] Prv 15,30; *to cherish, to honour* [τι] Ps 19(20),4
P: *to be enriched* Ps 64(65),13; *to thrive* Ez 17,8

πιέζω⁺   V 0-0-1-0-0-1
Mi 6,15
to press tight, to squeeze (the olive) [τι]

Cf. HORSLEY 1983, 82

(→ἐκ-)

πίθηκος,-ου⁺   N2M 0-1-0-0-0-1
2 Chr 9,21
monkey

πίθος,-ου⁺   N2M 0-0-0-1-0-1
Prv 23,27
jar, vessel, cash

Cf. SCHNEBEL 1925, 285-286

πικραίνω⁺   V 1-0-4-4-4-13
Ex 16,20; Is 14,9; Jer 39(32),32; 40(33),9; 44(37),15
A: *to make* (tears) *bitter* [τι] (of weeping) Sir 38,17; *to embitter, to irritate* [τινα] Jb 27,2; *to irritate, to provoke* [τινα] Jer 39(32),32; *to grieve, to anger* [τινα] 1 Mc 3,7
P: *to be embittered* [ἐπί τινι] Ex 16,20; *id.* [ἐν τινι] Ru 1,20; *id.* [τινι] Tob^S 5,14; *id.* [ἐπί τινα] 1 Ezr 4,31; *id.* [περί τινος] Jer 40(33),9
ἐπικράνθη μοι *it grieved me* Ru 1,13

Cf. HELBING 1928, 212; LE BOULLUEC 1989, 25; WALTERS

1973,150

(→ἐκ-, παρα-)

πικρασμός,-οῦ N2M 0-0-0-1-0-1
Est 4,17o
bitterness, bitter feeling; neol.

πικρία,-ας⁺ N1F 5-0-8-9-7-29
Ex 15,23; Nm 33,8.9; Dt 29,17; 32,32
bitterness (of taste) Dt 32,32; *id.* (of temper) Jb
21,25; Πικρία (proper name) Ex 15,23
*Ez 28,24 πικρίας *of bitterness* -◊ממרר for MT
ממאיר *malignant, pricking*; *Ps 9,28(10,7) καὶ
πικρίας *and of bitterness*-ומררות for MT ומרמות
and of deceit cpr. Rom 3,14
Cf. DORIVAL 1944, 123; LE BOULLUEC 1989, 178;
WALTERS 1973, 151

πικρίς,-ίδος N3F 2-0-0-0-0-2
Ex 12,8; Nm 9,11
bitter herb
Cf. LE BOULLUEC 1989, 146

πικρός,-ά,-όν⁺ A 2-4-10-4-15-35
Gn 27,34; Ex 15,23; Jgsᴮ 18,25; 1 Sm 15,32; 2
Sm 2,26
bitter (to drink) Ex 15,23; *id.* (metaph.) Gn
27,34; *embittered, angry* (of people) Jgsᴮ 18,25;
Πικρά (proper name) Ru 1,20
*Jer 20,8 ὅτι πικρῷ λόγῳ μου *for in the
bitterness of my speech, for with bitter speech*
כי מר דברי-? *for* MT כי מרי ארבר *for whenever I
speak*; *Ps 63(64),4 πρᾶγμα πικρόν *a painful
matter, a bitter thing*, cpr. πρᾶγμα
Cf. DORIVAL 1994, 123

πικρῶς⁺ D 0-0-3-1-5-9
Is 22,4; 33,7; Jer 27(50),21; Dnᴸˣˣ 2,15; 2 Mc
7,39
bitterly Is 22,4; *harshly* Dnᴸˣˣ 2,15
πικρῶς φέρω *to take grievously, to be grieved*
2 Mc 7,39
*Jer 27(50),21 πικρῶς *bitterly, harshly* -◊ממרר for
MT מרתים *Merathaim*

πίμπλημι⁺ V 16-17-35-36-12-116
Gn 6,11.13; 21,19; 24,16; 26,15
A: *to fill* [τι] Gn 24,16; *to fill sth with sth* [τί
τινος] Gn 21,19
P: *to be filled with, to be full of* [τινος] Gn 6,11;
to be satisfied with [τινος] Ex 16,12; *to be filled
with, to be satisfied* [ἔν τινι] Ps 64(65),5
*Jer 30,23(49,28) καὶ πλήσατε *fill* corr.? καὶ
πλήξατε? *strike* for MT ושררו *and destroy*; *Prv
15,4 πλησθήσεται *it shall be filled with* -◊שבע for
MT שבר *it breaks*

Cf. HELBING 1928, 144

(→ἐμ-)

πίμπρημι

(→ἐμ-, προσ-)

πίννινος,-ου N2M 0-0-0-1-0-1
Est 1,6
of a mollusk; πίννινος λίθος *a mollusk stone*
i.e. *pearl*

πίνω⁺ V 56-73-78-49-41-297
Gn 9,21; 24,14(ter).18
to drink [abs.] Gn 24,14; *id.* [τι] Ex 7,18; *id.*
[τινος] Nm 20,19; *id.* [ἔκ τινος] Gn 9,21; *id.*
[ἀπό τινος] Jer 28(51),7
*Is 5,12 πίνουσιν *they drink* -שתו for MT משתיהם
their feasts, cpr. Dnᴸˣˣ 1,5; *Is 19,5 πίονται
they shall drink -◊שתה for MT ◊נשת *they shall fail*
Cf. HELBING 1928, 133-135

(→ἐκ-, κατα-, συμ-)

πιότης,-τητος⁺ N3F 2-4-2-4-0-12
Gn 27,28.39; Jgs 9,9; 1 Kgs 13,3
oil (of an olive) Jgs 9,9; *fat* (fat ashes on the
altar) 1 Kgs 13,3; *fatness, abundance* (of the
earth) Gn 27,28
υἱοὶ τῆς πιότητος *sons of the oil* (lit.), *anointed
ones*? Zech 4,14

πιπράσκω⁺ V 12-4-6-2-8-32
Gn 31,15; Ex 22,2; Lv 25,23.34.39
to sell [τινα] (as a slave) Gn 31,15; *id.* [τι] Lv
25,23

πίπτω⁺ V 29- 117-123-69-86-424
Gn 17,3.17; 44,14; 49,17; Ex 9,19
to fall 2 Chr 6,13; *id.* (metaph.) Jer 27(50),32; *to
fall down* (of pers.) Jgs 19,26; *to fall* (of hail) Ex
9,19; *to fall* (in battle) Ex 32,28; *to fall, to
collapse* (of edifice) Jos 6,5; *to perish* Jb 24,23;
to fall upon, to come over 1 Sm 26,12; *to fall to*
[τινι] 1 Chr 26,14; *to fall out* Ru 3,18
πίπτω ἐπὶ πρόσωπον *to fall upon the face* (act
of cultic adoration) Gn 17,3; κατὰ τὴν δύναμιν
τὴν πεσοῦσαν *according to the army that was
destroyed* 1 Kgs 21(20),25
*Ez 13,10 πεσεῖται *it shall fall* -נפל◊ חפל for MT
הפל◊ (שפל) *whitewash*, see also 13,15; 22,28;
*Ps 57(58),9 ἐπέπεσε *it has fallen* -נפל◊ for MT נפל
untimely birth; *Dnᴸˣˣ 11,14 καὶ ἀνοικο-
δομήσει τὰ πεπτωκότα *and he shall rebuild the
ruins* -ויבנה פרוצי for MT ובני פריצי *and the sons of
robbers, the lawless*, see ἀνοικοδομέω
Cf. HUSSON 1983ᵃ, 200-203; SPICQ 1978ᵃ, 692-694

(→ἀνα-, ἀντι-, ἀπο-, δια-, ἐκ-, ἐμ-, ἐπι-, κατα-,

μετα-, παρα-, παρεμ-, περι-, προ-, προσ-, συμ-,
ὑπο-)

πίσσα,-ης   N1F 0-0-2-2-3-7
Is 34,9(bis); Dn 3,46; Sir 13,1
pitch, resin

πιστεύω⁺   V 15-5-8-21-39-88
Gn 15,6; 42,20; 45,26; Ex 4,1.5
stereotypical rendition of אמן (mostly hi.)
A: *to trust, to put faith in, to believe in* [τινι]
Gn 15,6; *id.* [ἔν τινι] Ps 77(78),22; *id.* [ἐπί
τινα] Wis 12,2; *to believe* [abs.] Ex 4,31; *to
believe that* [+inf.] Nm 20,12; *id.* [ὅτι+ind.]
Tobˢ 10,8; *to admit the reality of* [τι] Hab 1,5; *to
commit sth to sb or sth* [τί τινι] Wis 14,5
P: *to be believed* Gn 42,20
Cf. BARR 1961, 172-175; DODD 1954, 66-70.198-200;
HELBING 1928, 200-201; LARCHER 1985, 703-704; LE
BOULLUEC 1989, 97; →NIDNTT; TWNT
(→ἐμ-, κατα-)

πίστις,-εως⁺   N3F 1-11-10-11-26-59
Dt 32,20; 1 Sm 21,3; 26,23; 2 Kgs 12,16; 22,7
stereotypical rendition of derivatives of אמן; *faith*
Dt 32,20; *faithfulness* Ps 32(33),4; *honesty* Prv
12,22
Cf. BARR 1961, 172-175.191-193.198-203; BARTH 1982,
110-126; DODD 1954, 66-70.198-200; HATCH 1889, 83-88;
LARCHER 1983, 304-305; LEE, J. 1983, 51; LINDSAY 1993,
103-118; LÜHRMANN 1973, 19-38; SPICQ 1978ᵃ, 700; VAN
DAALEN 1982, 523-527(Hab 2,4); →NIDNTT; TWNT

πιστοποιέω   V 0-0-0-0-2-2
4 Mc 7,9; 18,17
to make credible [τι] 4 Mc 7,9; *to confirm the
query of sb* [τινα] 4 Mc 18,17

πιστός,-ή,-όν⁺   A 4-9-10-23-29-75
Nm 12,7; Dt 7,9; 28,59; 32,4; 1 Sm 2,35
stereotypical rendition of אמן (mostly niphal);
trustworthy, worthy of credit (of pers.) 2 Mc 1,2;
reliable (of pers.) Tobˢ 5,3; *faithful* (of heart)
Neh 9,8; *trustworthy, sure* 1 Sm 25,28; *lasting* Dt
28,59; *dependable, unfailing, plentiful* Is 33,16
πιστά *trustworthiness, bona fide* Hos 5,9
*2 Sm 23,1 πιστός *faithful* - ◊נאמן for MT נאם *word,
saying*; *Prv 17,7 χείλη πιστά *faithful lips,
faithful words* - שׂפת ישׁר? for MT שׂפת יתר *fine words*
Cf. BARR 1961, 166.172-174; DOGNIEZ 1992, 163.295;
HORSLEY 1982, 94; LARCHER 1983, 290-291.304-305;
LIEBERMAN 1942, 75.76; →NIDNTT; TWNT

πιστόω⁺   V 0-8-0-3-4-15
2 Sm 7,16.25; 1 Kgs 1,36; 8,26; 1 Chr 17,14
A: *to confirm* [τι] 2 Sm 7,25; *id.* [abs.] 1 Kgs

1,36; *to establish* [τινα] 1 Chr 17,14
P: *to be steadfast, to show oneself faithful* Ps
77(78),37; *to be faithful* Sir 27,17; *to be made
sure* 2 Sm 7,16
Cf. DODD 1954, 68-69

πιστῶς⁺   D 0-1-0-0-0-1
2 Kgs 16,2
faithfully

πίτυρον,-ου   N2N 0-0-0-0-1-1
LtJ 42
bran, husks of corn

πίτυς,-υος   N3F 0-0-2-0-0-2
Ez 31,8; Zech 11,2
pine tree

πίων,-ων,-ον⁺   A 3-1-5-9-2-20
Gn 49,15.20; Nm 13,20; 1 Chr 4,40; Is 5,1
fat (of anim.) Ps 21(22),13; *id.* (of pers.) Ps
21(22),30; *id.* (of bread) Gn 49,20; *id.* (of oil) Ps
91(92),11; *rich, fertile* (of soil) Gn 49,15; *good*
(of pasture) 1 Chr 4,40; *made plump, fattened*
(of sacrificial anim.) Mi 6,7

πλαγιάζω   V 0-0-2-0-0-2
Is 29,21; Ez 14,5
to lead astray [τινα]

πλάγιος,-α,-ον   A 14-3-0-1-2-20
Gn 6,16; Ex 25,32; 26,13; Lv 1,11; 26,21
on the side, private Susᵀʰ 18; *treacherous, crooked*
Lv 26,21; τὰ πλάγια *flanks* Ex 26,13
ἐκ πλαγίων *alongside* Ru 2,14
Cf. HARLÉ 1988, 207(Lv 26,21.23.24.27.28.40.41); SHIPP
1979, 457

πλανάω⁺   V 10-6-53-24-33-126
Gn 21,14; 37,15; Ex 14,3; 23,4; Dt 4,19
A: *to make to wander, to lead astray* [τινα] Dt
27,18; *to make sb err from the right way* [τινα
ἀπό τινος] Dt 13,6; *to mislead, to deceive*
[τινα] Jgsᴮ 16,13; *to deal deceitfully with* [μετά
τινος] 2 Kgs 4,28
P: *to wander* (of people in the desert) Gn 21,14;
to go astray Ex 23,4; *id.* (as a symbol for straying
from the right way) Wis 13,6; *to be seduced* Sir
9,8
πλανῶνται τῇ καρδίᾳ *their minds are going
astray* Ps 94(95),10
*Is 17,11 πλανηθήσῃ *you erred, you went astray*
- ◊שׂגה for MT תשׂגשׂי ◊שׂגא *you make (them) grow*,
see also Jb 12,23, cpr. Dt 27,18; Jb 6,24; 19,4;
*Is 30,20 οἱ πλανῶντές σε *those who cause you
to err* - ◊מרה (hi.)? *those who are rebellious* for MT
מוריך *your teachers*; *Is 41,10 μὴ πλανῶ *I do not*

deceive -◊תעה? for MT שעה◊ אל תשתע *do not be afraid, do not look about in terror;* *Is 64,4 ἐπλανήθημεν *we have erred* -נמשע? for MT נושע *we were saved,* cpr. Ez 33,12; *Ez 44,13 ἐν τῇ πλανήσει, ᾗ ἐπλανήθησαν *for the error in which they erred* -תעה for MT אשר עשו התעבותם *of the abominations that they have committed;* *Hos 8,6 πλανῶν *erring* -◊שבב, שוב for MT שבבים *splinters?* or *going up in flames?* (hapax)

Cf. BARTHÉLEMY 1960, 343-348(Hos 8,6); COOK 1994, 470; DODD 1954, 79; DOGNIEZ 1992, 49.59.138.200; →NIDNTT; TWNT

(→ἀπο-)

πλάνη,-ης⁺   N1F 0-0-2-1-3-6
Jer 23,17; Ez 33,10; Prv 14,8; Tob^BA 5,14; Wis 1,12
error, deceit

Cf. DODD 1954, 79; HORSLEY 1982, 94; LARCHER 1983, 195-196; →MM; NIDNTT; TWNT

πλάνησις,-εως   N3F 0-0-8-0-3-11
Is 19,14; 22,5; 30,10.28; 32,6
error Is 19,14; *deception* Is 30,28
*Ez 44,13 ἐν τῇ πλανήσει, ᾗ ἐπλανήθησαν see πλανάω

πλανήτης,-ου⁺   N1M 0-0-1-0-0-1
Hos 9,17
wanderer

πλανῆτις,-ιδος   N3F 0-0-0-1-0-1
Jb 2,9d
wanderer

πλάνος,-ου⁺   N2M 0-0-1-1-0-2
Jer 23,32; Jb 19,4
error

πλάξ, πλακός⁺   N3F 30-3-0-0-0-33
Ex 31,18(bis); 32,15(bis).16
flat stone, tablet, table (the tablets of the law)
Cf. SHIPP 1979, 458

πλάσμα,-ατος⁺   N3N 0-0-2-2-1-5
Is 29,16; Hab 2,18; Ps 102(103),14; Jb 40,19; Jdt 8,29
that which is formed, molded, handiwork, creature Hab 2,18; *creation* (of God) Jb 40,19; *frame* Ps 102(103),14; *disposition* Jdt 8,29
→MM

πλάσσω⁺   V 5-2-22-15-8-52
Gn 2,7.8.15.19; Ex 32,4
A: *to form, to mold* Gn 2,7
M: *to devise* 1 Kgs 12,33
*Hab 1,12 ἔπλασεν *he has formed* -יצר◊ for MT צור *rock;* *Prv 24,12 ὁ πλάσας *he that formed* -יצר-

for MT נצר *he that guarded*
Cf. HARL 1986ª, 100; HELBING 1928, 56; WEVERS 1993, 24; →MM

(→ἀνα-, ἐμ-, κατα-)

πλάστιγξ,-ιγγος   N3F 0-0-0-0-2-2
2 Mc 9,8; Wis 11,22
scale, balance

πλάτανος,-ου   N2F 1-0-0-0-1-2
Gn 30,37; Sir 24,14
plane-tree

πλατεῖα,-ας⁺   N1F 0-1-0-0-0-1
2 Chr 32,6; Dn^Th 9,25
square; neol.
Cf. SHIPP 1979, 459

πλάτος,-ους⁺   N3N 9-12-23-7-7-58
Gn 6,15; 13,17; 32,26(bis).33
measurement from side to side, breadth, width Ex 26,16; *broad part* Gn 32,26; *broad place* Neh 8,1; τὸ πλάτος *the breadth, in breadth* Gn 6,15; πλάτος *id.* 1 Kgs 6,20
τὰ πλάτη τῆς γῆς *the breadth of the earth, the whole earth, wide area* Hab 1,6; πλάτος καρδίας *width of knowledge* 1 Kgs 2,35a
Cf. WEVERS 1990, 421; 1993, 541

πλατύνω⁺   V 6-1-6-7-4-24
Gn 9,27; 26,22; 28,14; Ex 34,24; Dt 11,16
A: *to make wide, to enlarge* [τι] Is 54,2; *id.* [τι] (metaph.) Hab 2,5; *to open wide, to enlarge over* [ἐπί τινα] (of mouth) 1 Sm 2,1; *to open* (the heart) [τι] Ps 118(119),32; *to make room for* [τινι] Gn 9,27; *id.* [τι] Ps 17(18),37
P: *to grow fat* Dt 32,15; *to spread abroad* Gn 28,14; *to be puffed up* (of heart) Dt 11,16; *to spread far* Ez 31,5
*Jer 2,24 ἐπλάτυνεν *she extended (her ways)* -◊פרץ for MT פרה (פרא) *wild ass,* cpr. Gn 28,14 (פרץ); *Prv 24,28 μηδὲ πλατύνου σοῖς χείλεσιν *neither exaggerate with your lips* or πλατύνου *widen, make spacious* -חפת◊ פתה^II for MT פתית◊ פתה^I *deceive*
Cf. DOGNIEZ 1992, 189(Dt 11,16); HARL 1971=1992ª, 192; 1986ª, 143(Gn 9,27).213; 1992ª, 12; WEVERS 1993, 125; →LSJ Suppl(Prv 24,28)

(→δια-, ἐμ-)

πλατύς,-εῖα,-ύ⁺   A 3-8-19-26-10-66
Gn 19,2; 34,10.21; Jgs^B 18,10; 1 Chr 4,40
wide, broad Neh 3,8; *spread over a wide space, spacious* Gn 34,10; *great* Neh 4,13; *broad* (metaph.) Ps 118(119),96; ἡ πλατεῖα (sc. ὁδός) *wide (street)* Gn 19,2

Cf. WEVERS 1993, 562

πλατυσμός,-οῦ⁺ N2M 0-2-0-3-1-6
2 Sm 22,20.37; Ps 17(18),20; 117(118),5;
118(119),45
broad space; neol.

πλειστάκις D 0-0-0-1-0-1
Eccl 7,22
mostly, very often

πλεῖστος,-η,-ον⁺ A 0-4-2-0-10-16
Jos 5,6; 1 Chr 12,30; 2 Chr 25,9; 30,18; Is 7,22
sup. of πολύς; *most* 1 Ezr 2,6; *greatest* 2 Chr
30,18; *very great, considerable great* 3 Mc 3,16;
πλεῖστον *most* Is 7,22; οἱ πλειστοί *the most,
the greatest part* Jos 5,6
πλειστὴν ἤ *more than* 3 Mc 7,21

πλείων,-ων,-ον/πλέον⁺ A 15-12-10-6-47-90
Gn 46,29; Ex 1,12; 23,2(bis); Lv 15,25
comp. of πολύς; *more, more numerous* Ex 1,12;
τὸ πλεῖον *the greater part* Ps 89(90),10
ἐπὶ πλεῖον *exceedingly, thoroughly* Ps
122(123),4; πολὺ πλέον *much better, best* 4 Mc
1,8; μετὰ πλειόνων *with the multitude* Ex 23,2

πλέκω⁺ V 1-0-1-0-0-2
Ex 28,14; Is 28,5
P: *to be wreathed, to be braided, to be woven*
(-ἐμ-, περι-, συμ-, συμπροσ-)

πλεονάζω⁺ V 10-5-2-3-7-27
Ex 16,18.23; 26,12(bis); Nm 3,46
*to be more than enough, to be present in
abundance* 2 Chr 24,11; *to abound* Sir 23,3; *to
multiply, to increase* [abs.] 1 Chr 4,27; *id.* [τινα]
Jer 37(30),19; *to make to increase* [τι]
Nm 26,54; *to bring abundantly* [τι] 2 Chr 31,5;
to exceed in number [παρά τινα] Nm 3,46; *id.*
[abs.] Nm 3,48; *to have too much* [abs.] Ex
16,18; *to be lengthy* 2 Mc 2,32; τὸ πλεονάζον
excess Ex 16,23; ὁ πλεονάζων λόγῳ *he that is
abundant in word* Sir 20,8; ἐπλεόνασεν ὁ
δρυμὸς τοῦ καταφαγεῖν ὑπὲρ οὓς κατέφαγεν
ἡ μάχαιρα *the wood consumed more men than
the sword consumed* 2 Sm 18,8
*Prv 15,6 ἐν πλεοναζούσῃ *in abounding* -ברבות
for MT בית *the house*
Cf. HELBING 1928, 79; LEE, J. 1983, 84
(-ὑπερ-)

πλεονάκις D 0-0-1-3-6-10
Is 42,20; Ps 105(106),43; 128(129),1.2; Tob^BA 1,6
many times, often

πλεόνασμα,-ατος N3N 1-0-0-0-0-1
Nm 31,32

superfluity; neol.?
Cf. DORIVAL 1994, 152; LEE, J. 1983, 99

πλεονασμός,-οῦ N2M 1-0-4-1-0-6
Lv 25,37; Ez 18,8.13.17; 22,12
usury, unjust gains

πλεοναστός,-ή,-όν A 1-0-0-0-1-2
Dt 30,5; 1 Mc 4,35
numerous; neol.

πλεονεκτέω⁺ V 0-1-2-0-0-3
Jgs^B 4,11; Ez 22,27; Hab 2,9
to be greedy, to be grasping, to be covetous Ez
22,27
*Jgs^B 4,11 πλεονεκτούντων *of the greedy* -בצע◊
for MT בצענים *in Zaanannim*

πλεονέκτης,-ου⁺ N1M 0-0-0-0-1-1
Sir 14,9
greedy person, covetous man

πλεονεξία,-ας⁺ N1F 0-1-4-1-2-8
Jgs^A 5,19; Is 28,8; Jer 22,17; Ez 22,27; Hab 2,9
covetousness, greed
Cf. SPICQ 1978ᵃ, 704-706

πλευρά,-ᾶς⁺ N1F 3-11-7-3-4-28
Gn 2,21.22; Nm 33,55; 2 Sm 2,16; 13,34
rib Gn 2,21; *side* (of a pers.) Nm 33,55; *id.* (of a
mountain) 2 Sm 13,34; *side chamber* Ez 41,5; αἱ
πλευραί *body* 1 Kgs 8,19
*2 Sm 21,14 ἐν τῇ πλευρᾷ *at the side of, beside*
-בצלע צלחה◊ for MT בְּצֶלְע צלחה‖ *at Zelah*
Cf. WALTERS 1973, 292(n.73)

πλευρόν,-οῦ N2N 2-1-10-5-2-20
Ex 27,7; 30,4; 1 Kgs 6,16; Ez 4,4.6
side (of things) Ex 27,7; *id.* (of pers.) Ez 4,4
*Dn^LXX 10,16 τὸ πλευρόν *side* -צר◊ for MT ציר◊
pain

πλέω⁺ V 0-0-2-0-4-6
Is 42,10; Jon 1,3; 1 Ezr 4,23; 1 Mc 13,29; 4 Mc
7,3
to sail, to travel by boat, to go by sea Jon 1,3; *to
sail on* [τι] Sir 43,24; *id.* [εἴς τι] 1 Ezr 4,23
Cf. SHIPP 1979, 460
(-εἰσ-)

πληγή,-ῆς⁺ N1F 18-23-24-6-26-97
Ex 11,1; 12,13; 33,5; Lv 26,21; Nm 11,33
blow, stroke Dt 25,2; *wound* 1 Kgs 22,35; *blow,
stroke of misfortune* Jgs 11,33; *plague* (the ten
plagues of Egypt) Ex 11,1; *misfortune* Is 53,10
*Ex 33,5 πληγή *plague* -נגע for MT רגע *moment*;
*Mi 1,11 πληγήν *blow, stroke* -מכה◊ for MT מכם
from you (rendered twice in LXX: ἐξ ὑμῶν
πληγήν)

Cf. DORIVAL 1994, 59.61; LE BOULLUEC 1989, 35-36.141; →NIDNTT; TWNT

πλῆθος,-ους⁺   N3N 24-57-61-46-100-288
Gn 16,10; 17,4; 27,28; 30,30; 32,13
quantity, number Jos 11,4; *multitude, great number* Gn 16,10; *multitude, horde* 2 Mc 2,21; *the people, the mass* Wis 6,2; *multitude of* (persons) [τινος] Gn 17,4; *abundance of things* [τινος] Gn 27,28; *richess* Mi 4,13
εἰς πλῆθος *in great number* 1 Kgs 1,19; πλῆθος φέρει ὁ λαός *the people bring more than enough* Ex 36,5
*Ez 32,6 ἀπὸ τοῦ πλήθους σου *because of your multitude* -מרבך for MT מדמך *with your blood*; *Zech 9,10 πλῆθος *multitude* -רב? for MT דבר *he shall command*
Cf. LE BOULLUEC 1989, 145; ROST 1967, 112-118

πληθύνω⁺   V 52-23-46-46-38-205
Gn 1,22(bis).28; 3,16(bis)
mostly rendering forms of רבה
A: *to multiply* [τι] Gn 3,16; *id.* [τινα] Gn 17,2; *id.* [intrans.] Ex 1,20; *to increase* [τι] Nm 33,54; *to swarm with* [τινι] 3 Mc 5,41; *to increase with, to fill with* [τί τι] Ez 27,15
P: *to increase, to grow, to be multiplied* Gn 1,22; *to be filled with* [τινος] Lam 1,1; *to enrich with* [(ἔν) τινι] Jdt 5,9; *to be fulfilled* Gn 38,12; *to be satisfied with* [ἀπό τινος] Ps 4,8
Φαραω πληθύνοντα ἅρμασιν *Pharao, with his multitude of chariots* 3 Mc 6,4
Cf. HARL 1986ᵃ, 57; HELBING 1928, 148-149; LE BOULLUEC 1989, 74-75; →TWNT
(→ἐμ-)

πληθύς,-ύος   N3F 0-0-0-0-1-1
3 Mc 4,17
crowd

πληκτίζομαι
(→δια-)

πλημμέλεια,-ας⁺   N1F 25-8-0-9-6-48
Lv 5,15.16.18.25; 6,10
trespass, sin Lv 6,10; *offering for sin* or *error* Lv 5,15; *lie, deceit* Sir 41,18
Cf.DANIEL1966,301.302.304.305.307-308.313-316.321-323. 325-327.341-361; DODD 1954, 76.79; DORIVAL 1994, 50; WEVERS 1993, 713; →NIDNTT; TWNT

πλημμελέω   V 14-7-2-4-7-34
Lv 4,13.22.27; 5,3.6
to offend, to commit sin, to trespass
Cf. DANIEL 1966, 302.314.315.321-323.341-361; DODD 1954, 76.79; HELBING 1928, 217

πλημμέλημα,-ατος   N3N 2-0-1-0-0-3
Nm 5,8(bis); Jer 2,5
trespass, mistake, transgression Jer 2,5; *compensation* or *restitution for transgression* Nm 5,8
Cf. DANIEL 1966, 304.322.341-361; DODD 1954, 76.79

πλημμέλησις,-εως   N3F 1-0-0-1-0-2
Lv 5,19; Ezr 10,19
mistake, transgression; neol.

πλήμμυρα,-ας⁺   N1F 0-0-0-1-0-1
Jb 40,23
flood
Cf. WALTERS 1973, 84.297

πλήν⁺   D/C 64-93-26-33-32-248
Gn 9,4; 39,6.9; 41,40
but, anyway Gn 9,4; *only* Gn 41,40; *surely, no doubt* Zph 3,7; *but, nevertheless* Hos 12,9; *however* 2 Mc 6,17
Cf. BLOMQVIST 1969, 92-100; DORIVAL 1994, 478; THRALL 1962, 20-24; WEVERS 1990, 110.111.308

πλήν⁺   P 64-93-26-33-32-248
Gn 14,24; 39,6.9; 41,40
[τινος]: *except* Gn 14,24; *besides, in addition to* Dt 18,8
Cf. BLASS 1990, § 216; DORIVAL 1994, 499; JOHANNESSOHN 1926, 342-344; WEVERS 1993, 201

πλήρης,-ης,-ες⁺   A 39-20-24-23-16-122
Gn 25,8; 27,27; 35,29; 41,7.22
full Gn 41,7; *full of* [τινος] Ex 9,8; *abundant* Gn 27,27; *complete, full, in full* Ru 2,12
πλήρης εἰμὶ ὁλοκαυτωμάτων *I have enough of whole burnt offerings* Is 1,11; πλήρης ἡμερῶν *full of days* Gn 25,8; σμύρναν πλήρη *choice myrrh* Ct 5,5, see also 5,13
*Ezr 4,20 πλήρεις *abundant* -מלא for MT בלו *tax*
Cf. HARL 1986ᵃ, 207(Gn 25,8); WEVERS 1990, 127.260; →MM

πληροφορέω⁺   V 0-0-0-1-0-1
Eccl 8,11
P: *to be fully bent on, to be set to (e.g. do evil)* [+inf.]
Cf. SPICQ 1978ᵃ, 708; →MM

πληρόω⁺   V 15-21-18-27-31-112
Gn 1,22.28; 9,1.7; 25,24
A: *to fill* [τι] Gn 1,22; *to fulfil, to perform* [τι] 1 Kgs 1,14; *to make full, to complete* (a period of time) [τι] Nm 6,13; *to fill sb with* [τινά τινος] Ps 15(16),11; *to satisfy* [τι] Ps 126 (127),5; *to overflow* Jos 3,15; *to complete, to finish, to bring to an end* [τι] 1 Mc 4,19
P: *to be filled with, to be full of, to be satisfied*

with [ἀπό τινος] Eccl 1,8; *id.* [τινι] Jdt 2,8; *to be made full, to be fulfilled* Gn 25,24

ἐπληρώσατε τὰς χεῖρας ὑμῶν κυρίῳ *you have filled your hands, you ordained yourselves for the service of the Lord* (of priests) Ex 32,29; πεπληρωμένος τῆς τέχνης *accomplished in art* 1 Kgs 7,2; πληρώσει πτώματα *he shall increase the number of corpses* Ps 109(110),6

Cf. HELBING 1928, 144-148; LARCHER 1983, 183; LE BOULLUEC 1989, 44(Ex 32,29); LEE, J. 1983, 51; VAN ROON 1974, 228-232; WEVERS 1990, 535; →NIDNTT; TWNT

(→ἀνα-, ἐκ-, ἐπι-, προσανα-)

πλήρωμα,-ατος⁺ N3N 0-1-5-9-0-15
1 Chr 16,32; Jer 8,16; 29(47),2; Ez 12,19; 19,7
that which fills, content Eccl 4,6; *fullness* 1 Chr 16,32

πληρώματα ὑδάτων *contents of water, pools of water* Ct 5,12

Cf. DODD 1954, 134; VAN ROON 1974, 229-232; →NIDNTT; TWNT

πλήρωσις,-εως N3F 2-1-4-1-1-9
Ex 35,27; Dt 33,16; 1 Chr 29,2; Jer 4,12; 5,24
filling Jdt 8,31; *fullness* Dt 33,16; *fulfilment* (of time) Ez 5,2; *completion, accomplishment* Jer 4,12; *setting* (for stones) Ex 35,27

*Jer 5,24 πληρώσεως *fulfilment* -שָׁבֻעָה? for MT שְׁבֻעוֹת *weeks*

Cf. LE BOULLUEC 1989, 351

πλησιάζω V 0-0-0-0-1-1
2 Mc 6,4
to have sexual intercourse with [τινι]

Cf. HELBING 1928, 30

πλησίον⁺ D 61-37-42-28-56-224
Gn 11,3.7; 26,31; Ex 2,13; 11,2
near 4 Mc 8,4; *near, adjacent, adjoining* (as adj.) Jdt 7,13; (ὁ) πλησίον *neighbour* Gn 11,3; ἡ πλησίον (sc. γυνή) *neighbour* Jer 9,19; ἡ πλησίον *fellow, companion* Ct 1,9

*Jgs^A 4,11 καὶ οἱ πλησίον *and the companions* -וחברי for MT וחבר *and Heber*; *1 Sm 28,16 τοῦ πλησίον σου *your fellow* -רע/ך for MT ער/ך *your enemy?*

πλησιέστερον *nearer* 4 Mc 12,2

Cf. WEVERS 1990, 162.534.555

πλησίος,-α,-ον A 0-0-0-1-0-1
Ct 5,1
near, close to; πλησίοι *friends*

πλησμονή,-ῆς⁺ N1F 6-0-11-6-5-28
Gn 41,30; Ex 16,3.8; Lv 25,19; 26,5
in pos. sense: *satiety* Ps 77(78),25; *repletion,*

surfeit (of food) Ex 16,3; *satisfaction* (of feelings) Is 55,2; *abundance, plenty* Gn 41,30
in pejor. sense: *surfeit, excess* Is 1,14

*Is 65,15 εἰς πλησμονήν *to satiety?* -לשבעה for MT לשבועה/ל *as an oath, as a curse;* *Ps 105(106),15 πλησμονήν *abundance* -רוזה? for MT רזון *emaciation*

Cf. HORSLEY 1987, 28

πλήσσω⁺ V 8-9-4-3-2-26
Ex 9,31.32; 16,3; 22,1; Nm 25,14
A: *to pierce, to sting* [τινα] (of bees) 4 Mc 14,19
P: *to be hit physically, to be wounded* Zech 13,6; *to be smitten, ruined* (of fruits) Ex 9,31; *to be smitten* (metaph. by God) Ex 16,3; *to be shot* Prv 7,23

Cf. DREW-BEAR 1972, 90; LE BOULLUEC 1989, 180-181; TOD 1939, 59-60; WEVERS 1990, 141(Ex 9,32)

(→ἐκ-, κατα-)

πλινθεία,-ας N1F 5-0-0-0-0-5
Ex 1,14; 5,8.14.18.19
brick-making; neol.

Cf. LEE, J. 1983, 47

πλινθεῖον,-ου N2N 0-2-0-0-0-2
2 Sm 12,31; 1 Kgs 2,46h
brickworks, brick factory

Cf. WALTERS 1973, 47.285

πλινθεύω V 1-0-0-0-0-1
Gn 11,3
to make bricks

πλίνθος,-ου N2F 4-0-6-0-1-11
Gn 11,3(bis); Ex 5,16; 24,10; Is 9,9
brick Gn 11,3

*Is 24,23 πλίνθος *brick* -לְבֵנָה for MT לְבָנָה *moon;* *Mi 7,11 πλίνθου *of a brick* -לבנה for MT ל/בנות *to build*

Cf. LE BOULLUEC 1989, 246; WEVERS 1990, 67.385

πλινθουργία,-ας N1F 1-0-0-0-0-1
Ex 5,7
brick-making; neol.

πλοῖον,-ου⁺ N2N 2-7-17-5-11-42
Gn 49,13; Dt 28,68; Jgs 5,17; 2 Chr 8,18
ship; see ναῦς

πλόκαμος,-ου⁺ N2M 0-0-0-0-1-1
3 Mc 1,4
braid, lock of hair

πλοκή,-ῆς⁺ N1F 1-0-0-0-0-1
Ex 28,14
twining, twisting, wreathing, braiding

Cf. LE BOULLUEC 1989, 282

πλόκιον,-ου N2N 0-0-0-1-0-1

Ct 7,6
curl, lock of hair

πλοῦς, πλοῦ   N2M 0-0-0-0-1-1
Wis 14,1
sailing, voyage

πλούσιος,-α,-ον⁺   A 1-4-7-19-25-56
Gn 13,2; 1 Sm 2,10; 2 Sm 12,1.2.4
rich Ru 3,10; *rich in* [τινι] Gn 13,2
*Is 5,14 πλούσιοι *riches* -שָׁאוֹן? אוֹן◊? *wealth for*
MT שָׁאוֹנָהּ *her uproar;* *Ps 9,29(10,8) πλουσίων
rich -עֲשֵׁרִים for MT חֲצֵרִים *villages;* *Ps 33(34),11
πλούσιοι *rich* -כְּבִרִים for MT כְּפִירִים *young lions*
πλουσιώτερον *richer* Wis 8,5

πλουτέω⁺   V 2-0-3-6-3-14
Gn 30,43; Ex 30,15; Jer 5,27; Hos 12,9; Zech
11,5
to be rich Gn 30,43
*Prv 31,28 ἐπλούτησαν *they grow rich* -יַעְשִׁרוּ for
MT יְאַשְּׁרוּהָ *they praise her*
Cf. WEVERS 1993, 495

πλουτίζω⁺   V 1-1-1-5-5-13
Gn 14,23; 1 Sm 2,7; Ez 27,33; Ps 64(65),10; Jb
15,29
A: *to enrich* [abs.] 1 Sm 2,7; *id.* [τινα] Gn 14,23;
id. [τι] Ps 64(65),10
P: *to grow rich* Jb 15,29

πλοῦτος,-ου/ους⁺   N2M/3N 2-12-15-47-24-100
Gn 31,16; Dt 33,19; 1 Sm 2,10; 1 Kgs 3,11.13
wealth, riches Gn 31,16
*Is 29,2 καὶ τὸ πλοῦτος *and the riches* -וְאָנָה אוֹן◊
or הוּן◊ for MT וַאֲנִיָּה *and lamentation;* *Is 32,18
πλούτου *wealth* -שָׁאֲנָן? אוֹן◊? for שַׁאֲנוֹת *quiet;* *Ps
36(37),3 τῷ πλούτῳ αὐτῆς *with its wealth* -הֲמוֹנָהּ?
for MT אֱמוּנָה *security*
→NIDNTT; TWNT

-πλόω
(→ἐπι-, δι-)

πλύνω⁺   V 47-2-1-2-0-52
Gn 49,11; Ex 19,10.14; 29,17; Lv 1,9
*to wash, to cleanse by agitating or rubbing in
water* Ex 19,10; *to wash out* [τι] Lv 13,55; *to
cleanse sb, to free sb from* [τινα ἀπό τινος]
Ps 50(51),4; *to cleanse sb, to free sb* [τινα] Ps
50(51),9
πόα πλυνόντων *cleaners' lye* (potassium
hydroxide or sodium hydroxide) Mal 3,2
see λούω, νίπτω
Cf. LEE, J. 1983, 36-37
(→ἀπο-, ἐκ-)

πλωτός,-ῆΥός,-όν   A 0-0-0-1-1-2

Jb 40,31; 2 Mc 5,21
floating Jb 40,31; *navigable* 2 Mc 5,21

πνεῦμα,-ατος⁺   N3N 29-68-109-108-68-382
Gn 1,2; 6,3.17; 7,15; 8,1
mostly rendering רוּחַ; *wind* Ex 15,10; *the
breathing out of air, blowing, breath* Jb 8,2;
breath, (life-)spirit, soul (that which gives life to
the body) Jgs 15,19; *spirit* (to denote the
immaterial part of the human personality) Wis
15,11; *spirit* (as seat of feelings and will) 1 Kgs
20,5; *spirit, spiritual being* Nm 16,22; *(evil) spirit*
Jgs 9,23; *spirit* (of God) Gn 1,2
πνεῦμα ζωῆς *breath of life* Gn 6,17; διὰ
πνεύματος τοῦ θυμοῦ *by the breath of anger* Ex
15,8; λυπέω τὸ πνεῦμά τινος *to grieve the spirit
of sb, to grieve sb, to cause pain to sb* 2 Sm 13,21
*Jb 7,15 πνεύματος *(from my) spirit* corr.?
πνίγματος for MT מַחֲנָק *strangulation;* *Is 11,3
πνεῦμα *spirit* -רוּחַ (subst.) for MT וַהֲרִיחוֹ (hi.)
and his delight
cpr. πνοή
Cf. ALEXANDRE 1988, 83-85(Gn 1,2); GOODWIN 1881, 73-
86; HARL 1971=1992ᵃ, 187; 1984ᵃ=1992ᵃ, 40; 1986ᵃ, 60-61.
87.101; HILL 1967, 217-226; HORSLEY 1987, 38; JEAN-
SONNE 1988, 73(Dn 10,8); LARCHER 1983, 175-176.183-
186; 1984, 480.491-493.602-603.641; 1985, 700.872-873;
SCHARBERT 1972, 124-125; →NIDNTT; TNWNT

πνευματοφορέομαι   V 0-0-1-0-0-1
Jer 2,24
to be borne as by the wind, to be blown about;
neol.

πνευματοφόρος,-ος,-ον⁺   A 0-0-2-0-0-2
Hos 9,7; Zph 3,4
*he who has the spirit, a bearer of the spirit,
spiritual (man);* neol.

πνεύμων,-ονος   N3M 0-2-0-0-0-2
1 Kgs 22,34; 2 Chr 18,33
the lungs

πνέω⁺   V 0-0-1-1-4-6
Is 40,24; Ps 147,7(18); 2 Mc 9,7; Sir 43,16.20
to blow (of wind) Sir 43,16; *to blow, to send out*
(a wind) [τι] Ps 147,7; *to breathe* [τι] 2 Mc 9,7
(→ἀνα-, ἀπο-, δια-, ἐμ-)

πνιγμός,-οῦ   N2M 0-0-0-0-1-1
Sir 51,4
choking, suffocation; ἀπὸ πνιγμοῦ πυρᾶς *from
choking fire*

πνίγω⁺   V 0-2-0-0-0-2
1 Sm 16,14.15
to choke [τινα]

(→ἀπο-)

πνοή,-ῆς⁺   N1F 2-2-4-13-5-26
Gn 2,7; 7,22; 2 Sm 22,16; 1 Kgs 15,29; Is 38,16
wind Jb 37,10; *blow, blast* 2 Sm 22,16; *breath*
Wis 2,2; *opening, gap* (in a wall) Neh 6,1
πνοὴν ζωῆς *breath of life* Gn 2,7; ἐν ἐσχάτῃ
πνοῇ *at his last gasp* 2 Mc 3,31; πᾶσα πνοή
everything that breathes Ps 150,6
cpr. πνεῦμα
Cf. ALEXANDRE 1988, 239-242; HARL 1986ᵃ, 60.101; →LSJ
suppl

πόα,-ας   N1F 0-0-2-1-0-3
Jer 2,22; Mal 3,2; Prv 27,25
grass, herb Prv 27,25; *kind of grass with cleansing*
properties, lye (extracted from this grass) Jer 2,22

ποδάγρα,-ας   N1F 0-0-0-0-1-1
4 Mc 11,10
trap for the feet, clamp

ποδήρης,-ης,-ες⁺   A 5-0-4-0-3-12
Ex 25,7; 28,4.31; 29,5; 35,9
full-length, reaching to the feet Ex 28,31
ὁ ποδήρης *robe reaching to the feet* Sir 27,8; εἰς
τὴν ἐπωμίδα καὶ τὸν ποδήρη *on the breast-*
plate and the full-length robe (often in this
combination) Ex 25,7
Cf. LE BOULLUEC 1989, 252.282.295

ποδίζω
(→ἀνα-, ἐμ-, συμ-)

ποδιστήρ,-ῆρος   N3M 0-1-0-0-0-1
2 Chr 4,16
tripod or *footbath*
→LSJ RSuppl

-ποδοστατέω
(→ἐμ-)

ποθεινός,-ἡ/ός,-όν   A 0-0-0-1-2-3
Prv 6,8b; 4 Mc 13,26; 15,1
desired, eligible (of pers.) Prv 6,8b; *fervent* (of
friendship) 4 Mc 13,26; *dear* 4 Mc 15,1

πόθεν⁺   D 4-15-9-7-13-48
Gn 16,8; 29,4; 42,7; Nm 11,13; Jos 9,8
whence, from what place Gn 16,8; *whence, out of*
what 2 Kgs 6,27; *how* Prv 22,27; *wherefore* Nm
11,13

ποθέω⁺   V 0-0-0-2-5-7
Prv 7,15; Est 3,13b; Wis 4,2; 6,11; 8,8
to desire, to long for [τι]
(→ἐπι-, κατα-)

ποιέω⁺   V 850- 941-576-490-533-3390
Gn 1,1.7.11.12.16
to make [τι] Gn 3,7; *to make sth into sth* [τί τι]

Lv 24,5; *to create* (a position) [τινα] Gn 41,34;
to build [τι] Gn 13,4; *to create* [τινα] Gn 1,21;
id. [τι] Gn 1,1; *to produce, to bear, to yield* [τι]
Gn 41,47; *to cause, to bring about* [τι] 2 Mc 1,4;
to do, to execute, to carry out [τι] Ex 24,3; *to*
execute, to perform [τι] Ex 13,5; *to commit* [τι]
Dt 22,8; *to execute, to work, to show* (kindness)
[τι] Gn 47,29
to make ready, to prepare [τι] Gn 19,3; *to*
prepare, to give as food [τι] Gn 18,8; *to keep, to*
celebrate [τι] Ex 23,15
to observe [τι] Ex 31,16; *to sacrifice* [τινα] Ex
29,36; *to spend* [τι] (a period of time) Prv 13,23
to make sb sth [τινα +pred.] Gn 27,37; *id.*
[τινα εἴς τινα] Gn 12,2; *to appoint* [τινα]
1 Sm 12,6; *to make sth into sth* [τι +pred.] Nm
6,17
to do, to act [abs.] Gn 29,28; *to do* [τι] Gn 3,13;
to do sth to sb [τί τινι] Gn 26,10; *id.* [τί τινα]
Nm 24,14; *to do to* [τινα] Dt 22,3; *id.* [τι] Dt
3,21; *to do with* [τι] Ex 22,29; *to do with, to deal*
with [μετά τινος] Jgs 9,19; *to do for* [τί τινι]
Hos 10,3; *to cause to* [+inf.] Ex 23,33
ποιέω τὸν μύστακα *to trim the moustache* 2 Sm
19,25; τάδε ποιήσαι μοι κύριος *the Lord may*
do so to me (wording of the oath) Ru 1,17; Σὺ
νῦν οὕτως ποιεῖς βασιλέα ἐπὶ Ισραηλ; *is this*
the way you reign as king over Israel?
1 Kgs 20(21),7; διάστημα ποιεῖτε ἀνὰ μέσον
ποίμνης καὶ ποίμνης *put a distance between*
drove and drove Gn 32,17
*Is 32,10 μνείαν ποιήσασθε *remember* - זכר for
MT תרגזנה *you will be troubled*; *Is 41,29(28) οἱ
ποιοῦντες ὑμᾶς *your makers* - עשיכם for MT מעשיהם
their works; *Jer 7,29 τὴν ποιοῦσαν ταῦτα *that*
does these things - עבר דנה (Aram.?) for MT עברתו
his wrath; *Jer 30,2(49,8) ἐποίησεν *he*
commited - עשה for MT עשו *Esau*; *Ez 23,44
ποιῆσαι *to work* - לעשות for MT אשת *the women of*;
*Zph 3,20 καλῶς ποιήσω *I shall deal well* - אטיב
for MT אביא *I shall bring*; *Jb 29,4 ὅτε
ἐπισκοπὴν ἐποιεῖτο *when he took care* - בסוך for
MT בסוד *when the intimacy*; *Jb 30,24 ποιήσει *he*
shall do - יעשה for MT שוע *he cries out*; *Prv 20,11
ὁ ποιῶν αὐτά *he that makes them* - עשהם for MT
שניהם *the two of them*; *Eccl 8,11 ἀπὸ τῶν
ποιούντων *on the part of those who do* - מעשי for
MT מעשה *a work*
Cf. DOGNIEZ 1992, 32.115.187.198; DORIVAL 1994, 496;
HARL 1971=1992ᵃ, 188-189.192; 1981=1992ᵃ, 36; 1986ᵃ,

86.174; HELBING 1928, 3-8.54-56; LE BOULLUEC 1989, 301;
LEE, J. 1983, 51; WALTERS 1973, 274; WEVERS 1990, 502;
1993, 1.150.183.437.488.547.690.700.809
(→ἀνα-, ἀντι-, ἀπο-, ἐκ-, ἐμ-, περι-, προσ-,
συμ-)

ποίημα,-ατος⁺   N3N 0-3-1-25-0-29
JgsᴮB 13,12; 1 Sm 8,8; 19,4; Is 29,16; Ps 63(64),10
work Ps 142(143),5; *deed, act* 1 Sm 8,8

ποίησις,-εως⁺   N3F 4-1-1-2-3-11
Ex 28,8; 32,35; 36,12(39,5); Lv 8,7; 2 Kgs 16,10
fabrication, creation Ex 28,8; *work* Ps 18(19),2;
performing, fulfilling (of the law) Sir 19,20
Cf. LE BOULLUEC 1989, 286.328; WEVERS 1990, 448

ποιητής,-οῦ⁺   N1M 0-0-0-0-1-1
1 Mc 2,67
one who does sth, doer; τοὺς ποιητὰς τοῦ
νόμου *the observers of the law, those who
observe the law*

ποικιλία,-ας⁺   N1F 3-2-1-0-5-11
Ex 27,16; 35,35; 36,15(39,8); Jgs 5,30
embroidery Ex 27,16; *variety, diversity* Jgs 5,30
Cf. LE BOULLUEC 1989, 279.355; WEVERS 1990, 591

ποικίλλω   V 0-0-0-2-0-2
Ps 44(45),10.14
P: *to be dressed* or *adorned with embroidery*

ποίκιλμα,-ατος   N3N 0-0-3-0-0-3
Jer 13,23; Ez 23,15; 27,16
colourful embroidered work Ez 23,15; *spottedness,
coloured spot* Jer 13,23

ποικίλος,-η,-ον⁺   A 10-3-7-0-6-26
Gn 30,37.39.40; 31,8(bis)
many coloured, variegated 1 Chr 29,2; *spotted* Gn
30,37; *spotted, speckled* (of sheep) Gn 30,39;
piebald (of a horse) Zech 1,8; *wrought in various
colours, embroidered, beautiful* (of clothes) Gn
37,3; *manifold, various* 3 Mc 1,21
Cf. HARL 1986ᵃ, 232.233.259

ποικιλτής,-οῦ⁺   N1M 6-0-0-0-1-7
Ex 26,36; 28,6.15.35(39); 36,36(39,29)
embroiderer
Cf. LE BOULLUEC 1989, 279.282.283

ποικιλτικός,-ή,-όν   A 1-0-0-1-0-2
Ex 37,21(38,23); Jb 38,36
embroidered, related to embroidery; neol.

ποικιλτός,-ή,-όν   A 1-1-0-0-0-2
Ex 35,35; Jgsᴮ 5,30
embroidered

ποικίλως   D 0-0-0-1-1-2
Est 1,6; 4 Mc 16,3
variously

ποιμαίνω⁺   V 6-7-20-18-3-54
Gn 30,31.36; 37,2.13; Ex 2,16
stereotypical transl. of the verb רעה; *to herd, to
tend* [τινα] Gn 30,31; *to tend flocks* [abs.] Gn
37,13; *to guide, to govern, to rule* [τινα] 2 Sm
5,2; *id.* [τι] Prv 9,12a; *to keep* [τινα] Prv 29,3;
to keep up [τι] Prv 28,7; *to protect, to care for,
to nurture* [τινα] Ps 22,1; *to look after devotedly,
to nurture* [τι] Zech 11,17
*Jer 3,15 ποιμαίνοντες *tending* -◊רעה◊for MT רעה
knowledge; *Jer 6,18 καὶ οἱ ποιμαίνοντες *and
those who herd, and the shepherds* -ורעי for MT
ידעו ורעי◊ *and know,* (see ποίμνιον) cpr. Hos
13,5; *Ps 2,9 ποιμανεῖς αὐτούς *you shall tend
them* -רעם◊ for MT תרעם◊ רעם◊ *you shall break
them;* *Prv 22,11 ποιμαίνει *he tends, he rules
-רעה for MT רע *a friend*
→NIDNTT; TWNT

ποιμενικός,-ή,-όν⁺   A 0-1-1-0-0-2
1 Sm 17,40; Zech 11,15
of a shepherd

ποιμήν,-ένος⁺   N3M 16-5-53-4-3-81
Gn 4,2; 13,7(bis).8(bis)
stereotypical transl. of the subst. רעה; *shepherd*
Gn 4,2; *leader, ruler* (metaph.) Na 3,18
*Is 32,14 ποιμένων *of shepherds* corr.?
ποιμνίων for MT ערדים (1QIsᵃ ל/ערדים) *of flocks,
for the flocks;* *Gn 29,8 τοὺς ποιμένας *the
shepherds* -הרעים (Sam.Pent.) for MT הערדים *the
flocks;* *Gn 38,12 ὁ ποιμὴν αὐτοῦ *his shepherd
-רעהו◊ רעה◊ for MT רע/הו *his friend,* cpr. Gn
38,20; Jer 3,1; *Zech 13,7 ἐπὶ τοὺς ποιμένας
against the shepherds -על הרעים? for MT על הצערים
against the little ones; *Jb 24,2 σὺν ποιμένι
with its shepherd -ורעו for MT וירעו *and they
herded*
Cf. CAIRD 1969=1972, 141; →SCHLEUSNER(Zech 13,7)

ποίμνη,-ης⁺   N1F 2-0-0-0-0-2
Gn 32,17(bis)
flock

ποίμνιον,-ου⁺   N2N 11-25-25-8-5-74
Gn 29,2(bis).3; 30,40; 31,4
flock (of sheep) Gn 29,2; *id.* (of goats) 1 Kgs
21(20),27; *id.* (metaph. for the people of Israel)
Jer 13,17; *head of flock* 1 Sm 25,2(secundo)
*Jer 6,18 τὰ ποίμνια *the flocks* -עדר? for MT ערה
congregation, see also ποιμαίνω; *Ez 13,5
ποίμνια *flocks* -עדר for MT גדר *wall*
Cf. DELCOR 1974, 7-14; DOGNIEZ 1992, 164; →NIDNTT;
TWNT

ποῖος,-α,-ον⁺   R 2-7-8-8-16-41
Dt 4,7.8; Jgsᴬ 9,2; 1 Sm 9,18; 2 Sm 15,2
mostly used in direct questions: *what kind of*
[+subst.] Dt 4,7; *what, which* Jgsᴬ 9,2; *id.*
[+subst.] 2 Sm 15,2; *what* (used in indir.
question) Eccl 11,6
*Is 45,9 ποῖον *what* -אי for MT הוי *woe*

πόκος,-ου   N2M 0-15-0-1-0-16
Jgs 6,37(bis).38(bis)
wool, fleece

-πολάζω
(→ἐπι-)

-πολάω
(→ἐμ-)

πολεμέω⁺   V 9-114-24-18-60-225
Ex 14,14.25; 17,8.16; Nm 21,1
A: *to fight, to make war* [abs.] Ex 14,14; *to fight
with, to make war upon* [τινι] Jgsᴬ 11,25; *id.*
[τινα] Ex 14,25; *id.* [τι] (a city or place) Jgsᴮ
1,8; *id.* [ἐπί τινα] Ex 17,16; *id.* [ἐπί τι] (a city
or place) 1 Kgs 21(20),1; *id.* [πρός τινα] Nm
21,1; *id.* [ἐν τινι] Jgsᴬ 1,1; *id.* [μετά τινος] Jgsᴬ
5,20; *to fight* [τι] (cogn. acc.) 2 Chr 32,8; *to fight
against with sth* [ἐν τινι] 1 Mc 3,12
M: *to fight, to make war* Jos 11,23
*Jgsᴬ 5,14 ἐπολέμει *he fought* -ירד? (5,13 *he
went down to fight*) no equivalent in MT 5,14;
*2 Chr 15,6 καὶ πολεμήσει *and he shall wage
war* -וְכִתּתּוּ (*and shall crush*) for MT וְכֻתְתּוּ *and they
were crushed to pieces*
Cf. HELBING 1928, 233-235; SCHREINER 1957, 51(Jgsᴬ
5,14)
(→ἀντι-, ἐκ-, κατα-, συμ-, συνεκ-)

πολεμικός,-ή,-όν   A 1-8-4-0-5-18
Dt 1,41; Jgsᴬ 18,11.16.17; 1 Sm 8,12
of war, for war Dt 1,41; *skilled in war, warlike*
2 Chr 26,13
ἰσχύων εἰς τὰ πολεμικά *strong for war* Jer
31(48),14

πολέμιος,-α,-ον   A 0-1-0-2-38-41
1 Chr 18,10; Est 9,16; Ezr 8,31; 1 Ezr 4,4; Jdt
15,4
hostile, inimical 1 Chr 18,10; οἱ πολέμιοι *the
enemy* 1 Ezr 4,4; τὰ πολέμια *warring activities*
Est 9,16; ἡ πολεμία *the enemy* Is 27,4

πολεμιστής,-οῦ   N1M 8-24-11-0-9-52
Nm 31,27.28.32.42.49
warrior Nm 31,27; *id.* (mostly used in opp. with
another subst.) Nm 31,28
Cf. DORIVAL 1994, 59

πόλεμος,-ου⁺   N2M 40- 165-34-37-116-392
Gn 14,2.8; Ex 1,10; 13,17; 15,3
war Gn 14,2; *battle, fight* 1 Kgs 22,34
ἁγιάζω πόλεμον *to declare a holy war* (semit.)
Jl 3(4),9; συντρίβω πόλεμον see συντρίβω

πολεμοτροφέω   V 0-0-0-0-3-3
2 Mc 10,14.15; 14,6
to maintain war with [πρός τινα] 2 Mc 10,14; *to
keep up war, to keep up the feud* 2 Mc 10,15;
neol.

πολιά,-ᾶς⁺   N1F 0-4-2-2-9-17
Jgsᴬ 8,32; 1 Kgs 2,6.9; 2,35o; Is 47,2
greyness of hair, grey hairs Prv 20,29; *old age* Sir
6,18
πολιὰ ἀγαθή see ἀγαθός
*Is 47,2 τὰς πολιάς *the gray hairs* -שׂיבה? for MT
שׂבל *robe, hem of skirt*

πολιορκέω   V 0-12-9-3-4-28
Jos 10,29.31.34; Jgsᴬ 2,18; 9,31
to besiege [τι] Jos 10,31; *id.* [ἐπί τι] 2 Kgs 16,5;
id. [τινα] Jgsᴬ 2,18; *to harass* [abs.] 1 Ezr 5,69
*Jb 17,7 πεπολιόρκημαι *I have been hard
pressed* -◊צור *to be enclosed, besieged* for MT יצרי
my limbs
(→ἐκ-)

πολιορκία,-ας⁺   N1F 0-0-1-1-4-6
Jer 19,9; Prv 1,27; 1 Ezr 2,17; 2 Mc 10,18.19
siege 1 Ezr 2,17; *distress, tribulation, anguish* Prv
1,27

πολιός,-ά,-όν   A 1-0-0-0-0-1
Lv 19,32
grey; ἀπὸ προσώπου πολιοῦ *in presence of an
old person*
Cf. SHIPP 1979, 468.579

πόλις,-εως⁺   N3F 210- 667-308-144-247-1576
Gn 4,17(bis); 10,11.12; 11,4
city, town Gn 4,17; *id.* (meton.) Hos 6,8
πόλις ἡ ἁγία see ἅγιος
*Jgsᴮ 8,32 πόλει *city* corr. πολιᾷ for MT שׂיבה *old
age;* *Dnᴸˣˣ 11,13 πόλεως *of the city* corr.?
πολλούς (double transl.) for MT רב *great;* *Gn
14,5 τῇ πόλει *(in) the city* -קרית ◊קריה for MT
קריתים *(in) Kiriathaim,* cpr. Am 2,2; *Jos 7,3 τὴν
πόλιν *the city* -העיר for MT העי *Ai,* see also Jos
8,18.28; *Jos 19,13 ἐπὶ πόλιν *to the city* -עירה
for MT עתה *to Et* (proper noun); *1 Sm 22,5
πόλει *city* -עיר for MT יער *wood,* see also Is 22,8;
*2 Kgs 23,16 πόλει *city* -עיר for MT הר *hill,* see
also 2 Chr 21,11; Is 66,20; *Jer 31(48),34 αἱ
πόλεις αὐτῶν *their cities* -עריהם for MT עד יחץ *as*

far as Jahaz; *Jer 44(37),4 τῆς πόλεως *of the city*
-העיר for MT העם *the people*; *Ez 16,7 εἰς πόλεις
πόλεων *into the great cities* -ערים בערי for MT
עריים בערי *with the highest adornment*; *Ez 25,9
πόλεως παραθαλασσίας *of the city by the sea
side* -ימח קרית (Aram.) for MT קריתמה *Kiriath(ai)m*;
*Ez 45,5 πόλεις *cities* -ערים for MT עשרים *twenty*;
*Mi 1,11 τὰς πόλεις αὐτῆς *her cities* -עריה for
MT עריה *nakedness*; *Jb 6,10 πόλις *city* -עיר for
MT עוד *yet*, see also Mi 6,9(10); *Jb 6,20 ἐπὶ
πόλεσιν *in cities* -ערימה for MT עריה *there*, see also
Mi 7,12

Cf. DORIVAL 1994, 412.542.566.569; WALTERS 1973, 294

πολιτεία,-ας⁺   N1F 0-0-0-0-8-8
2 Mc 4,11; 8,17; 13,14; 3 Mc 3,21.23
citizenship 3 Mc 3,21; *daily life, mode of life*
2 Mc 4,11; *polity, nation* 2 Mc 8,17

Cf. SHIPP 1979, 468-469; SPICQ 1978ᵃ, 710-720

πολίτευμα,-ατος⁺   N3N 0-0-0-0-1-1
2 Mc 12,7
body of citizens

Cf. SPICQ 1978ᵃ, 710-720

πολιτεύω⁺   V 0-0-0-1-7-8
Est 8,12p; 2 Mc 6,1; 11,25; 3 Mc 3,4; 4 Mc 2,8
M: *to live, to lead one's life as a citizen*

Cf. SPICQ 1978ᵃ, 710-720

(-ἀντι-, ἐκ-)

πολίτης,-ου⁺   N1M 1-0-3-3-10-17
Gn 23,11; Jer 36(29),23; 38(31),34; Zech 13,7;
Prv 11,9
countryman, citizen

Cf. SPICQ 1978ᵃ, 710-720

πολλάκις⁺   D 0-0-0-3-9-12
Jb 4,2; 31,31; Est 8,12e; Tobˢ 1,6; 5,6
often, many times

πολλαχόθεν   D 0-0-0-0-1-1
4 Mc 1,7
in many ways, by many examples

πολλαχῶς   D 0-0-1-0-1-2
Ez 16,26; 3 Mc 1,25
in many ways

πολλοστός,-ή,-όν   A 0-1-0-1-0-2
2 Sm 23,20; Prv 5,19
late form for πολύς; *great* (metaph. for pers.)
Prv 5,19
ἀνὴρ πολλοστὸς ἔργοις *a man abundant in
deeds, valiant man* 2 Sm 23,20

πολυάνδριος,-ος,-ον   A 0-0-7-0-3-10
Jer 2,23; 19,2.6(bis); Ez 39,11
full of men 4 Mc 15,20; τὸ πολυάνδριον

common burial place Jer 2,23

Cf. BRUCE 1979, 21-22; WALTERS 1973, 51.179.286.330

πολύγονος,-ος,-ον   A 0-0-0-0-2-2
4 Mc 15,5; Wis 4,3
fertile, prolific

Cf. LARCHER 1984, 319

πολύδακρυς (gen. -υος)   A 0-0-0-0-1-1
3 Mc 5,25
tearful

πολυέλεος,-ος,-ον   A 2-0-2-5-2-11
Ex 34,6; Nm 14,18; Jl 2,13; Jon 4,2; Ps 85(86),5
very merciful; neol.

πολυετής,-ής,-ές   A 0-0-0-0-1-1
Wis 4,16
prolonged, long many years

πολυημερεύω   V 1-0-0-0-0-1
Dt 11,21
to attain length of days, to be long-lived; neol.

πολυήμερος,-ος,-ον   A 3-0-0-1-0-4
Dt 22,7; 25,15; 30,18; Dnᴸˣˣ 4,27(24)
of many days, long-lived Dt 22,7
πολυήμερος γίνομαι *to live many days, to live
a long life* Dt 25,15

Cf. DOGNIEZ 1992, 142.251

πολύθρηνος,-ος,-ον   A 0-0-0-0-1-1
4 Mc 16,10
much-wailing, full of sorrows; neol.

πολυκέφαλος,-ος,-ον   A 0-0-0-0-1-1
4 Mc 7,14
many-headed

πολυλογία,-ας⁺   N1F 0-0-0-1-0-1
Prv 10,19
talkativeness, multitude of words

πολυμερής,-ής,-ές   A 0-0-0-0-1-1
Wis 7,22
manifold

πολυοδία,-ας   N1F 0-0-1-0-0-1
Is 57,10
a long journey; neol.

Cf. TOV 1977, 194

πολύορκος,-ος,-ον   A 0-0-0-0-2-2
Sir 23,11; 27,14
frequently swearing, given to oaths Sir 23,11; ὁ
πολύορκος *frequent swearer of oaths* Sir 27,14

πολυοχλία,-ας   N1F 0-0-0-2-1-3
Jb 31,34; 39,7; Bar 4,34
great multitude, crowd of people; neol.?

πολύπαις,-παιδος   N3F 0-0-0-0-1-1
4 Mc 16,10
who has many children; neol.

πολυπειρία,-ας   N1F 0-0-0-0-2-2
Wis 8,8; Sir 25,6
*great experience, extensive experience, many
experiences*
πολύπειρος,-ος,-ον   A 0-0-0-0-3-3
Sir 21,22; 34,9; 36,20
very experienced, much-experienced
πολυπλασιάζω   V 3-0-0-0-0-3
Dt 4,1; 8,1; 11,8
P: *to be multiplied, to become numerous* (of
pers.); neol.
πολυπλάσιος,-α,-ον   A 0-0-0-0-1-1
2 Mc 9,16
many times over; neol.
πολυπλήθεια,-ας⁺   N1F 0-0-0-0-1-1
2 Mc 8,16
great multitude, large crowd
πολυπληθέω   V 3-0-0-0-0-3
Ex 5,5; Lv 11,42; Dt 7,7
to multiply, to become numerous Ex 5,5
ὁ πολυπληθεῖ ποσίν *which abounds with feet,
which has many feet* Lv 11,42
πολυπληθύνω   V 1-0-0-0-0-1
Ex 32,13
to multiply, to make numerous [τινα]
πολύπλοκος,-ος,-ον   A 0-0-0-2-2-4
Jb 5,13; Est 8,12n; 4 Mc 14,13; 15,24
complex 4 Mc 14,13; *ingenious, crafty* 4 Mc
15,24; ὁ πολύπλοκος *crafty person, schemer* Jb
5,13
πολυπραγμονέω   V 0-0-0-0-1-1
2 Mc 2,30
to be interested in, to inquire closely into [ἔν
τινι] (in pos. sense)
πολυρήμων,-ων,-ον   A 0-0-0-1-0-1
Jb 8,2
wordy, talking (too) much; neol.
πολύς, πολλή, πολύ⁺   A 61-107-142-241-271-822
Gn 6,1; 13,6; 15,1.14; 17,5
many, numerous Gn 6,1; *great, populous* Gn
18,18; *much* Gn 15,14; *abundant* Prv 6,8;
abundant in [ἔν τινι] 1 Sm 2,5; *great* (of size)
Gn 41,29; *great, high* (of worth, value) Gn 15,1;
long (of time) Jb 12,12; *long, large, wide* (of
distance) Jos 9,13; πολύ *widely* Est 8,12k;
greatly, very much, strongly Dnᵀʰ 6,15; τὸ πολύ
much (as adv.) Ex 16,17; πολλοί *many* Ps 3,2;
οἱ πολλοί *the majority, most (people)* 2 Mc 1,36
πολλῷ μᾶλλον *much more* Sir prol.,14; ἐπὶ
πολύ *more than once, often* Is 55,7; *very, much*

Neh 3,33; μετ' οὐ πολύ *a little after* 1 Ezr 3,22;
πολὺ νῦν *it is enough* 2 Sm 24,16
ἔτι ἐστὶν ἡμέρα πολλή *it is still broad daylight*
Gn 29,7; ἀετὸς πολὺς ὄνυξιν *an eagle with
great talons* Ez 17,7; ἡ βόμβησις ἡ μεγάλη ἡ
πολλὴ αὕτη *this very great multitude* Bar 2,29;
μὴ πολὺς ἴσθι πρὸς ἀλλοτρίαν *be not intimate
with a strange woman* Prv 5,20
*Dnᴸˣˣ 11,10 ἐπὶ πολύ *for much?* corr.? ἐπὶ
πόλιν *against the town* for MT עד מעוז *to the
fortified town*; *Is 14,11 ἡ πολλή *great, much*
-המון? *(multitude)* for MT המית *sound*; *Jer 3,3
πολλούς *many* -רבב◊ for MT רבבים *showers*; *Hab
2,13 πολλά *many* -ב/רי? ◊ רי for MT ברי *for
Cf. DORIVAL 1994, 477; JEANSONNE 1988, 75-76(Dn 11,10)
πολυτελής,-ής,-ές⁺   A 0-1-1-8-5-15
1 Chr 29,2; Is 28,16; Jb 31,24; Prv 1,13; 3,15
very expensive, costly Wis 2,7; *valuable* Prv 1,13
λίθος πολυτελής *precious stone* Jb 31,24, see
also 1 Chr 29,2; Is 28,16; Prv 3,15; 8,11; 31,10;
Dnᴸˣˣ 11,38; 1 Ezr 6,9; Jdt 10,21; Est 5,1c; Sir
45,11; 50,9
Cf. LABERGE 1978, 10(Is 28,16); SEELIGMANN 1948, 36(Is
28,16); SPICQ 1978ᵃ, 721-722; ZIEGLER 1934, 67(Is 28,16)
πολυτόκος,-ος,-ον   A 0-0-0-1-0-1
Ps 143(144),13
prolific, giving many births
πολυτρόπος,-ος,-ον   A 0-0-0-0-3-3
4 Mc 1,25; 3,21; 14,11
various, manifold, multiform, variegated
πολύφροντις (gen. -ιδος)   A 0-0-0-0-1-1
Wis 9,15
full of thoughts, full of cares; neol.
Cf. LARCHER 1984, 597
πολυχρονίζω   V 1-0-0-0-0-1
Dt 4,26
to live long, to live many years [τι]; neol.
Cf. DOGNIEZ 1992, 64.142
πολυχρόνιος,-ος,-ον   A 1-0-0-1-4-6
Gn 26,8; Jb 32,9; 4 Mc 17,12; Wis 2,10; 4,8
long-lived Jb 32,9; *everlasting, eternal* 4 Mc 17,12
γίγνομαι πολυχρόνιος (ἐκεῖ) *to stay, to live
a long time* Gn 26,8
Cf. HARL 1986ᵃ, 211; LARCHER 1983, 237(Wis 2,10)
πολυωρέω   V 1-0-0-2-0-3
Dt 30,9; Ps 11(12),9; 137(138),3
to treat with much care, to care for greatly [τινα]
Cf. DOGNIEZ 1992, 307; HELBING 1928, 113
πόμα,-ατος⁺   N3N 0-0-0-2-3-5
Ps 101(102),10; Dnᵀʰ 1,16; 3 Mc 5,2.45; 4 Mc

3,16
drink

πομπεύω   V 0-0-0-0-2-2
2 Mc 6,7; Wis 4,2
to parade, to walk in a procession

πονέω[+]   V 1-6-4-3-5-19
Gn 49,15; 1 Sm 22,8; 23,21; 1 Kgs 15,23; 1 Chr
10,3
to toil, to labour Gn 49,15; *to suffer, to be
wounded* 1 Chr 10,3; *to suffer from, to be pained
in* [τι] 1 Kgs 15,23; *to be troubled* Jer 28(51),29;
to be distressed, to be afflicted Jdt 16,7; *to feel
sorry for, to be grieved for* [περί τινος] 1 Sm
22,8
Cf. SHIPP 1979, 470-471
(→δια-, κατα-, συμ-)

πονηρεύομαι[+]   V 6-4-6-15-5-36
Gn 19,7; 37,18; Ex 22,7.10; Dt 15,9
to act wickedly Gn 19,7; *to act wickedly towards*
[ἔν τινι] 1 Chr 16,22; *id.* [κατά τινος] Sus[Th]
43; *to intend maliciously* [+inf.] Dt 19,19; *id.*
[τοῦ +inf.] Gn 37,18
πονηρεύσηται ὁ ὀφθαλμός σου τῷ ἀδελφῷ *your
eye shall be evil toward your brother, you shall be
unfavourably disposed towards your brother* Dt
15,9
*Jer 2,33 σὺ ἐπονηρεύσω *you acted wickedly*
-אֶת־הָרֵעוֹת for MT אֶת־הָרָעוֹת *the evil ones, the wicked
women;* *Eccl 7,22 πονηρεύσεται *he shall act
wickedly towards sb* -רֵעַ◊רֵעֲעֹ for MT ידע *it knows*
Cf. HELBING 1928, 14; LE BOULLUEC 1989, 226; WEVERS
1995, 259(Dt 15,9).317(Dt 19,19)

πονηρία,-ας[+]   N1F 3-9-19-18-22-71
Ex 10,10; 32,12; Dt 31,21; Jgs[B] 9,56; Jgs[A] 11,27
wickedness, vice, evil Ex 10,10; πονηρίαι
iniquities Jer 39(32),32
Cf. DOGNIEZ 1992, 59.138; HATCH 1889, 77-82; LE
BOULLUEC 1989, 137.322; →NIDNTT; TWNT

πονηρός,-ά,-όν[+]   A 68-94-78-65-76-381
Gn 2,9.17; 3,5.22; 6,5
evil (of things) Gn 2,9; *evil, wicked* (of pers.)
Nm 14,27; *evil, ferocious* (of anim.) Gn 37,20;
bad 2 Kgs 2,19; *severe* Gn 12,17; τὰ πονηρά
wicked thoughts, evil deeds Gn 6,5; *evil things,
immorality* Hab 1,13; ὁ πονηρός *the evil man* Dt
13,6
ὄνομα πονηρόν *bad name* Sir 5,15
*Hos 3,1 πονηρά *evil* -רֵעַ for MT רֵעַ *friend, lover;*
*Hos 12,2 πονηρὸν πνεῦμα *evil spirit* -רָעָה ר חַ for
MT רֵעָה רוּחַ *(Ephraim) herds the wind,* cpr. Is

56,11; *Mi 2,9 πονηρὰ ἐπιτηδεύματα *evil
practices* -עֲלִילָה for MT עֹלְלֵיהָ *their children;* *Jb
34,17 (τὸν ὀλλύντα) τοὺς πονηρούς *(the one
who destroys) the evil* -שֹׂנְאִים (יַחְבֹּל?) for
MT וְאָם (יַחְבֹּשׁ) *(will he lock up,) and will ...?*
Cf. DODD 1954, 76.79; DOGNIEZ 1992, 200; DORIVAL
1994, 154; HATCH 1889, 77-82; WEVERS 1995, 80; →NIDNTT;
TWNT

πόνος,-ου[+]   N2M 5-4-22-22-40-93
Gn 34,25; 41,51; Ex 2,11; Nm 23,21; Dt 28,33
toil, labour Jdt 5,11; *result of such labour,
product* Dt 28,33; *pain, affliction* Gn 34,25; *pain,
distress, grief* 1 Sm 15,23; πόνοι *labour pains,
contractions* Jb 2,9b
κόπος καὶ πόνος *pain and grief* Ps 9,28(10,7);
ἀγαθῶν πόνων *virtuous labours* Wis 3,15
Cf. DODD 1954, 77; DORIVAL 1994, 137.440; LARCHER
1983, 307; LE BOULLUEC 1989, 83; SPICQ 1982, 560-563;
WALTERS 1973, 180-181; WEVERS 1993, 520.571.700; 1995,
441

ποντίζω
(→κατα-)

ποντόβροχος,-ος,-ον   A 0-0-0-0-1-1
3 Mc 6,4
drowned in the sea; σὺν τῇ ὑπερηφάνῳ στρατιᾷ
ποντοβρόχους *overwhelmed with his proud army;*
neol.

ποντοπορέω   V 0-0-0-1-0-1
Prv 30,19
to pass through the sea (of ship)

πόντος,-ου[+]   N2M 1-0-0-0-1-2
Ex 15,5; Od 1,5
the open sea
Cf. WEVERS 1990, 229

πορεία,-ας[+]   N1F 1-0-10-6-15-32
Nm 33,2; Is 3,16; 8,11; Jer 10,23; 18,15
journey, trip Nm 33,2; *manner of walking, gait* Is
3,16; *going* Ps 67(68),25; *course, way* Wis 5,11;
step Prv 4,27b
*Prv 26,7 πορείαν *motion* -פסח◊ *to limp* for MT
פִּסֵּחַ *lame*
Cf. DORIVAL 1994, 544; LARCHER 1983, 276; →MM

πορεῖον,-ου   N2N 1-0-0-0-0-1
Gn 45,17
conveyance, wagon, cart; *Gn 45,17 τὰ πορεῖα
ὑμῶν corr.? φορεῖα ὑμῶν *beasts of burden* for
MT בְּעִירְכֶם *your animals*
Cf. HARL 1986[a], 291-292; WALTERS 1973, 51; WEVERS
1993, 764

πόρευσις,-εως   N3F 1-0-0-0-0-1

Gn 33,14
journey; *Gn 33,14 τῆς πορεύσεως *of the journey*
-מחלך? or -התליכה? ◊ הלך for MT המלאכה*property*
Cf. HARL 1986ª, 80.246-247; WEVERS 1993, 553

πορευτός,-ή,-όν A 0-0-0-1-1-2
Est 3,13b; 2 Mc 5,21
passable, safe for travel

πορεύω⁺ V 179- 581-202-137-164-1263
Gn 2,14; 3,14; 8,3.5; 9,23
M: *to go, to walk, to march* Gn 11,31; *to march
through* [τι] Dt 1,19; *to come, to proceed from
sth to sth* [ἀπό τινος ἐπί τι] (of borders) Jos
16,8; *to go forth, to flow* (of water) Gn 2,14; *to
go, to crawl* (of serpent) Gn 3,14; *to grow, to
develop, to spread* (of branches) Hos 14,7; *to
advance* (of shadow) 2 Kgs 20,9; *to walk after, to
seek* [ὀπίσω τινός] Jgs 2,12; *to walk, to conduct
oneself* Prv 28,6; *to go about in a certain state
and manner* [+pred.] Mi 1,8; *to pass away and
cease to exist* Hos 6,4; *to function, to work*
Mi 2,7
Cf. BANKS 1987, 305; DORIVAL 1994, 89; HARL 1986ª,
78.80.254; LEE, J. 1983, 85.128; LUCIANI 1973, 471-472;
WALTERS 1973, 61.62.134; WEVERS 1990, 36.121.149.150.
185.266.549; 1993, 344.627
(→δια-, εἰσ-, ἐκ-, ἐκπερι-, ἐμ-, ἐπι-, κατα-,
παρα-, παρεισ-, περι-, προ-, προσ-, συμ-,
συνεκ-)

πορθέω⁺ V 0-0-0-0-2-2
4 Mc 4,23; 11,4
to destroy, to subdue, to plunder [τινα]
Cf. SPICQ 1978ª, 723-724
(→ἐκ-)

πορίζω⁺ V 0-0-0-0-1-1
Wis 15,12
to make profit
Cf. LARCHER 1985, 875

πορισμός,-οῦ⁺ N2M 0-0-0-0-2-2
Wis 13,19; 14,2
means of livelihood, gaining, gain; neol.?
Cf. HORSLEY 1987, 169; LARCHER 1985, 785

πορνεία,-ας⁺ N1F 2-1-40-0-7-50
Gn 38,24; Nm 14,33; 2 Kgs 9,22; Is 47,10; 57,9
whoredom, fornication Gn 38,24; *sexual urges*
Tob 8,7; *unfaithfulness and apostasy* (in relation
to God) Hos 4,12
*Is 47,10 ἡ πορνεία σου *your unfaithfulness*
corr. ἡ πονηρία σου *your wickedness* -רעתך
Is 57,9
Cf. CARAGOUNIS 1996, 548-554; LARCHER 1985, 805-807;

SEELIGMANN 1948, 974(Is 47,10; 57,9); →NIDNTT; TWNT

πορνεῖον,-ου N2N 0-0-3-0-0-3
Ez 16,25.31.39
brothel, house of harlotry

πορνεύω⁺ V 1-2-13-2-0-18
Dt 23,18; Jgsᴬ 2,15; 1 Chr 5,25; Jer 3,6.7
to prostitute oneself Dt 23,18; *to act unfaithfully,
to act idolatry* [ὀπίσω τινος] 1 Chr 5,25; *id.*
[abs.] (of men and women) Hos 4,10
*Jgsᴬ 2,15 ἐπόρνευον *they acted unfaithfully*
corr. ἐπορεύοντο for MT יצאו *they marched out*,
cpr. Jgsᴮ 2,15
Cf. WEVERS 1995, 372(Dt 23,18)
(→ἐκ-)

πόρνη,-ης⁺ N1F 10-12-15-3-4-44
Gn 34,31; 38,15.21(bis).22
harlot, prostitute Gn 34,31; *id.* (metaph.) Is 1,21
*Prv 5,3 πόρνης *of a whore* -זנה? for MT זרה
foreign, strange
Cf. WALTERS 1973, 214.294; WEVERS 1995, 372

πορνικός,-ή,-όν A 0-0-1-1-0-2
Ez 16,24; Prv 7,10
of or for a harlot

πορνοκόπος,-ου N2M 0-0-0-1-0-1
Prv 23,21
*one who has commerce with prostitutes,
fornicator, whoremonger*

πόρνος,-ου⁺ N2M 0-0-0-0-2-2
Sir 23,17(bis)
fornicator, whoremonger; ἄνθρωπος πόρνος *id.*

πορπάω
(→ἐμ-, συμ-)

πόρπη,-ης N1F 0-0-0-0-3-3
1 Mc 10,89; 11,58; 14,44
brooch, pin; see συμπορπάω

πορπόω
(→ἐμ-)

πόρρω⁺ D 0-1-8-4-4-17
2 Chr 26,15; Is 17,13; 22,3; 29,13; 65,5
far off, far away, from a distance 2 Chr 26,15; *far
from* [τινος] 3 Mc 4,16; *id.* [ἀπό τινος] Jb 5,4
Cf. WALTERS 1973, 292

πόρρωθεν⁺ D 0-1-11-3-1-16
2 Kgs 20,14; Is 10,3; 13,5; 33,13.17
from a distance, from afar 2 Kgs 20,14; οἱ
πόρρωθεν *those who were at a distance* Is 33,13

πορφύρα,-ας⁺ N1F 22-3-2-9-13-49
Ex 25,4; 26,1.31.36; 27,16
purple
Cf. WEVERS 1990, 392-393

πορφυρίς,-ίδος   N3F 0-1-0-0-0-1
Jgsᴮ 8,26
purple garment
πορφυρίων,-ωνος   N3M 2-0-0-0-0-2
Lv 11,18; Dt 14,18
purple coat, flaming
Cf. HARLÉ 1988, 130
πορφυρούς,-ᾶ,-οῦν⁺   A 1-1-0-3-1-6
Nm 4,14; Jgsᴬ 8,26; Ct 3,10; Est 1,6; 8,15
purple
ποσάκις⁺   D 0-2-0-1-2-5
1 Kgs 22,16; 2 Chr 18,15; Ps 77(78),40; 3 Mc
5,37; Sir 20,17
how many times, how often
ποσαπλῶς   D 0-0-0-1-0-1
Ps 62(63),2
how many times, how often; *Ps 62(63),2
ποσαπλῶς *how many times, how often* -כַּמָּה for
MT כָּמַהּ *(my flesh) longs for*
ποσαχῶς   D 0-0-0-0-2-2
Sir 10,31(bis)
in how many ways, how much more
πόσις,-εως   N3F 0-0-0-2-0-2
Dn 1,10
drink, beverage
πόσος,-η,-ον⁺   R 1-1-1-3-10-16
Gn 47,8; 2 Sm 19,35; Ez 27,33; Ps 118(119),84;
Jb 13,23
how many (with noun in pl.) Gn 47,8; *how great,
how much* (with noun in sg.) Tobˢ 12,2; πόσῳ
[+comp.] *how much* Wis 13,3
ποταμός,-οῦ⁺   N2M 48-34-76-57-36-251
Gn 2,10.13.14(bis); 15,18
river, stream Gn 2,10
ποταμὸς πυρός *stream of fire* (connected with
judgement) Dn 7,10
Cf. WEVERS 1993, 215(Gn 15,18).607(Gn 36,37).674(Gn
41,2)
ποταπός,-ή,-όν⁺   A 0-0-0-0-1-1
Susᴸˣˣ 54
of what sort or kind, which; neol.?
Cf. SPICQ 1978ᵃ, 725-726
ποτε⁺   X 1-4-1-4-14-24
Dt 1,46; Jos 5,4(bis); 22,28; 2 Sm 11,25
ever, at any time Dt 1,46; ποτὲ μέν ..., ποτὲ δέ
... *at one time ..., at another ...* Wis 16,18-19
πότε⁺   D 2-5-7-31-2-47
Gn 30,30; Ex 8,5; Jgsᴬ 5,13; 1 Sm 1,14; 2 Sm
2,26
when? Gn 30,30

ἕως πότε *how long* 1 Sm 1,14
πότερον⁺   X 0-0-0-12-0-12
Jb 4,6.12; 7,1.12; 13,7
introducing a dir. double question, rendering the
Hebr. interrogative part. /ה prefixed to the first
word of the question exclusively in Job;
(untranslatable, rendered by inversion in the
English language) Jb 4,6; πότερον ... ἤ ...
whether ... or ... Jb 7,12
πότημα,-ατος   N3N 0-0-1-0-0-1
Jer 28(51),39
drink, potion
ποτήριον,-ου⁺   N2N 5-3-15-9-1-33
Gn 40,11(ter).13.21
cup Gn 40,11; *id.* (metaph.) Lam 2,13; *content of
a cup* Jer 16,7
*Lam 2,13 ποτήριον *cup* -כוס or -כיס for MT כים
as the sea
Cf. WALTERS 1973, 211
ποτίζω⁺   V 28-7-15-11-6-67
Gn 2,6.10; 13,10; 19,32.33
A: *to give sb to drink* [τινα] (of pers.) Gn 21,19;
id. [τινα] (of anim.) Gn 29,2; *to give sb sth to
drink* [τινά τι] Gn 19,32; *id.* [τινά τινι]
3 Mc 5,2; *id.* [τινα ἀπό τινος] Ct 8,2; *id.* [τινά
τι] (metaph.) Sir 15,3; *id.* [τινά τινι]
(metaph.) Is 29,10
to water [τι] (of plants) Ez 17,7; *to irrigate* [τι]
(of fields, lands) Gn 13,10; *to fill with water* [τι]
Jl 4,18
P: *to be drenched* Ez 32,6
ποτίζωσιν τοῖς ποσίν *they water it by stamping
their feet, they irrigate by foot* Dt 11,10
Cf. DOGNIEZ 1992, 188; HELBING 1928, 49; LEE, J. 1983,
118-119; OLESON 1984, 99(Dt 11,10); SPICQ 1982, 566-569;
WEVERS 1995, 192-193(Dt 11,10); ~LSJ suppl; LSJ RSuppl;
MM; PREISIGKE
ποτιστήριον,-ου   N2N 2-0-0-0-0-2
Gn 24,20; 30,38
drinking-trough for cattle, watering trough; neol.
Cf. WEVERS 1993, 352.492
ποτόν,-οῦ⁺   N2N 1-0-0-2-3-6
Lv 11,34; Jb 15,16; Ezr 3,7; 1 Ezr 5,53; 4 Mc
3,14
drink, draught 4 Mc 3,14
βρώματα καὶ ποτά *meat and drink* Ezr 3,7
πότος,-ου⁺   N2M 2-13-1-15-7-38
Gn 19,3; 40,20; Jgs 14,10.12
drinking, drinking-party (most often etymological
rendering of מִשְׁתֶּה, a word derived from שׁתה *to*

drink, but meaning *feast*)

Cf. GEHMAN 1953, 145-148; WEVERS 1993, 266.301.672

που⁺   X 0-1-0-1-1-3

1 Kgs 10,12; 2 Mc 5,27; Prv 31,21

anywhere 1 Kgs 10,12; *about* (with numerals)
2 Mc 5,27

ποῦ⁺   D 13-29-39-25-19-125

Gn 3,9; 4,9; 16,8; 18,9; 19,5

where? Gn 3,9; *where, to which place?* (with verb
of motion) Gn 16,8

πούς, ποδός⁺   N3M 55-66-49-93-38-301

Gn 8,9; 18,4; 19,2; 24,32(bis)

foot Gn 8,9; *footstep, track* 2 Kgs 3,9; *step* Gn
33,14; *leg* (of a piece of furniture) Ex 25,26;
wheel (of a chariot) Jgs^B 5,28; *pattering* (of rain)
1 Kgs 18,41; *foot* (euph. for *bottom, anus*) Jgs^B
3,24

κατὰ πόδας *on the heels, close behind, in close
pursuit* Gn 49,19; παρὰ πόδας *present before
them, yawning before them* 3 Mc 5,8; ἐπὶ τῷ
ποδί μου *at my passing, wherever I go* (semit.)
Gn 30,30

Cf. HARL 1986ᵃ, 231; WEVERS 1993, 488.553.830

πρᾶγμα,-ατος⁺   N3N 16-10-6-28-66-126

Gn 19,22; 21,26; 44,15; Ex 1,18; Lv 5,2

deed, action, thing Gn 19,22; *undertaking,
occupation, task* Eccl 3,1; *thing, matter* Nm 22,8;
thing, object Nm 31,23; τὰ πράγματα *affairs,
interests* Est 3,13e; *state-affairs, public affairs*
Est 3,13f; *business* Prv 16,20

τὸν ἐπὶ τῶν πραγμάτων *the administrator, the
treasurer* 2 Mc 3,7

Ῥῆμα and πρᾶγμα are often confused in the
LXX; both occur as rendering of the Hebr. רבד
which means both *word* and *matter, thing*; *Nm
22,8 πράγματα *matter* corr.? ῥήματα *words* for
MT רבד (יתבשה), see also Dt 17,10; Ps 63(64),4; Est
3,15; *Ps 90(91),6 ἀπὸ πράγματος *of the thing
-רְּבַ ,מ* for MT רֶבָּ ,מִ *of the plague*; *Est 7,5 τὸ
πρᾶγμα *thing* -אתלמ (Aram.) for MT אולמ *filled
him*; *Dn^LXX 2,48 πραγμάτων *service, administration* -אחדירבע for MT מרינת *the province of*

Cf. DORIVAL 1994, 392.422; LE BOULLUEC 1989, 78;
WEVERS 1982, 129; 1993, 279.312.746; 1995, 283(Dt 17,10)

πραγματεία,-ας⁺   N1F 0-6-0-1-1-8

1 Kgs 7,19(33); 9,1; 10,22a; 1 Chr 28,21; Dn^LXX
6,4

work, occupation 1 Kgs 7,19; *treatment, narration
of facts* 2 Mc 2,31; αἱ πραγματεῖαι *affairs*
Dn^LXX 6,4

Cf. SPICQ 1978ᵃ, 727

πραγματεύω⁺   V 0-1-0-1-0-2

1 Kgs 10,22a(9,19); Dn^LXX 8,27

to be engaged in [τι]

Cf. SPICQ 1978ᵃ, 727

(→συμ-)

πραγματικός,-οῦ   N2M 0-0-0-0-1-1

1 Ezr 8,22

official; πραγματικοῖς τοῦ ἱεροῦ τούτου *to the
ministers of this temple*

Cf. BICKERMAN 1980, 59

πράκτωρ,-ορος⁺   N3M 0-0-1-0-0-1

Is 3,12

exactor

Cf. SPICQ 1978ᵃ, 730; →NIDNTT; TWNT

πρᾶξις,-εως⁺   N3F 0-4-0-3-13-20

2 Chr 12,15; 13,22; 27,7; 28,26; Jb 24,5

act, action, deed 2 Chr 12,15; *business* Sir 38,24;
αἱ πράξεις *occupation, doings, pursuits* Prv
13,13a

ἡ τῶν διαφόρων πρᾶξις *the collecting of the
revenue* 2 Mc 4,28

Cf. LLEWELYN 1992, 90-92; →NIDNTT; TWNT

πρᾶος,-ος,-ον⁺   A 0-0-0-0-1-1

2 Mc 15,12

gentle, meek

Cf. WALTERS 1973, 71

πρασιά,-ᾶς⁺   N1F 0-0-0-0-1-1

Sir 24,31

garden-plot, garden-bed

Cf. HARL 1991=1992ᵃ, 148; MILLIGAN 1910=1980, 62;
ORLINSKY 1936, 134-135(n.6-7)

πράσινος,-ος,-ον   A 1-0-0-0-0-1

Gn 2,12

leek-green, light green; ὁ λίθος ὁ πράσινος *the
green stone* prob. *emerald*

Cf. SHIPP 1979, 473; WEVERS 1993, 28

πρᾶσις,-εως   N3F 10-2-1-4-4-21

Gn 42,1; Lv 25,14.25.27.28

sale, (act of) selling Dt 18,8; *transaction*
Lv 25,25; *market* Gn 42,1; *wares* Neh 13,16

ἀνὰ μέσον πράσεως καὶ ἀγορασμοῦ *between
selling and buying* Sir 27,2

*2 Kgs 12,6 τῆς πράσεως αὐτῶν *of their trade
-◊ורכמ for MT ורכמ ◊נכר? *his friend?* or ורכמ ◊רכמ
his trader?, see also 2 Kgs 12,8

Cf. HARL 1986ᵃ, 279(Gn 42,1); WEVERS 1993, 704

πράσον,-ου   N2N 1-0-0-0-0-1

Nm 11,5

leek

πράσσω⁺ V 1-1-1-19-19-41
Gn 31,28; Jos 1,7; Is 57,10; Jb 5,27; 7,20
to affect, to accomplish, to do [τι] Prv 13,10; *to do* [abs.] Susᵀʰ 23; *to act* [abs.] Gn 31,28; *to earn, to win* [τι] Dnᵀʰ 11,20; *to exact payment* 1 Mc 10,35
εὖ πράττειν *to be well off, to fare well* 2 Mc 9,19
Cf. SHIPP 1979, 461-468.473; WALTERS 1973, 191; WEVERS 1993, 510; →NIDNTT; TWNT
(→δια-, προ-)

-πρατίζομαι
(→ἀπο-)

πρατός,-ή,-όν A 0-0-0-0-1-1
2 Mc 11,3
for sale

πράττω
see πράσσω
(→ἀντι-)

πραΰθυμος,-ος,-ον A 0-0-0-2-0-2
Prv 14,30; 16,19
of gentle mind, sensitive, meek, of quiet spirit;
neol.

πραΰνω V 0-0-0-2-0-2
Ps 93(94),13; Prv 18,14
to soothe, to calm [τι] Prv 18,14; *to give rest to sb from sth* [τινι ἀπό τινος] Ps 93(94),13
(→κατα-)

πραΰς, πραεῖα, πραΰ⁺ A 1-0-4-10-1-16
Nm 12,3; Is 26,6; Jl 4,11; Zph 3,12; Zech 9,9
mild, gentle, humble, meek (of pers. mostly in relig. context) Nm 12,3; *modest, unassuming* (of eschatological king-saviour) Zech 9,9; *soft, gentle, quiet* (of sound) Dnᴸˣˣ 4,19
*Jl 4,11 πραΰς *meek* - ◊נוח for MT הנחת ◊נחת*bring down*
Cf. DORIVAL 1994, 80.301; HATCH 1889, 73-77; HEATER 1982, 118(Jb 36,15); SPICQ 1982, 570-582(esp.576-578); →NIDNTT; TWNT

πραΰτης/πραότης,-ητος⁺ N3F 0-0-0-4-6-10
Ps 44(45),5; 89(90),10; 131(132),1; Est 5,1e; Sir 1,27
mildness, gentleness, humility, meekness (relig. quality)
Cf. HORSLEY 1987, 169-170; SPICQ 1982, 570-582; →NIDNTT; TWNT

πρεπόντως D 0-0-0-0-1-1
2 Mc 15,12
fitly, meetly, gracefully; λαλιὰν προϊέμενον πρεπόντως *well-spoken*

πρέπω⁺ V 0-0-0-3-7-10
Ps 32(33),1; 64(65),2; 92(93),5; 1 Mc 12,11; 3 Mc 3,20
to be fitting; usu. impers. verb in 3rd pers.:
ἔπρεπεν *it was fitting, it was proper, it was right* 3 Mc 3,20
πρέπον ἐστίν *it is fitting* 1 Mc 12,11; πρέπει τινί *it is fitting for sb, it becomes to sb* Ps 32(33),1
→NIDNTT

πρεσβεία,-ας⁺ N1F 0-0-0-0-1-1
2 Mc 4,11
embassy; τοῦ ποιησαμένου τὴν πρεσβείαν *who went as ambassador*
Cf. SPICQ 1978ᵃ, 738-742

πρεσβεῖον,-ου N2N 1-0-0-1-2-4
Gn 43,33; Ps 70(71),18; 3 Mc 6,1; Susᵀʰ 50
privilege of age Gn 43,33; *status of an elder* Susᵀʰ 50; *old age* Ps 70(71),18
Cf. ENGEL 1985, 168-169; WALTERS 1973, 53-54; →NIDNTT

πρεσβευτής,-οῦ N1M 0-1-0-0-5-6
2 Chr 32,31; 1 Mc 13,21; 14,21.22.40
ambassador
Cf. SPICQ 1978ᵃ, 738-742

πρέσβυς,-εως N3M 3-0-7-1-4-15
Nm 21,21; 22,5; Dt 2,26; Is 13,8; 21,2
ambassador Nm 21,21; *old man* 4 Mc 7,10
*Is 13,8 οἱ πρέσβεις *the messengers* -◊צירᴵᴵ for MT צירים ◊צירᴵᴵᴵ *pangs, convulsions*, cpr. Is 21,2; 63,9
Cf. DORIVAL 1994, 57.102.407; →NIDNTT; PREISIGKE; TWNT

πρεσβύτατος,-ος,-ον A 0-0-0-0-1-1
4 Mc 9,11
sup., derived from πρέσβυς; *oldest*

πρεσβύτερος,-α,-ον⁺ A 38-70-30-14-54-206
Gn 18,11.12; 19,4.31(bis)
comp., derived from πρέσβυς; *older, old* Gn 18,11; *older* (in comparison with νεώτερος) Gn 19,31; *elder, official* (mostly pl.) Ps 106(107),32; ὁ πρεσβύτερος *old man* Prv 20,29; οἱ πρεσβύτεροι *the elders* Gn 50,7; *officials, members of councils* (syn. of γερουσία) Ex 24,1 ἀπὸ νεανίσκου ἕως πρεσβυτέρου *from young to old, both young and old* Gn 19,4
Cf. BICKERMAN 1980, 48; ENGEL 1985, 88.116.167-168; HORSLEY 1983, 138; LEE, J. 1983, 61; WALTERS 1973, 53-54; WEVERS 1990, 35.571; 1993, 283.342; →NIDNTT; PREISIGKE; TWNT

πρεσβύτης,-ου⁺ N1M 4-18-5-6-16-49
Gn 25,8; Nm 10,31; Dt 28,50; 32,25; Jos 6,21

old man Gn 25,8; *old* (as adj.) 1 Sm 2,22;
ambassador, spokesman 2 Chr 32,31
ἔση ἐν ὑμῖν πρεσβύτης *you will be for us sb
with experience, sb who has seen it all* Nm 10,31
Cf. DORIVAL 1994, 102.282.283(Nm 10,31); →NIDNTT; TWNT

πρεσβῦτις,-ιδος⁺   N3F 0-0-0-0-1-1
4 Mc 16,14
old women

πρήθω⁺   V 3-0-0-0-0-3
Nm 5,21.22.27
to swell out [τι]
Cf. SHIPP 1979, 473

πρηνής,-ής,-ές⁺   A 0-0-0-0-4-4
3 Mc 5,43.50; 6,23; Wis 4,19
forward, to the ground, prostrate (of pers.)
3 Mc 5,50; *level to the ground* (of the
destruction of the temple) 3 Mc 5,43

πρίαμαι   V 5-0-0-1-0-6
Gn 42,2.3.10; 43,2.20
to buy, to purchase [τι]
(→ἐκ-)

πρίζω⁺   V 0-0-1-0-1-2
Am 1,3; Susᵀʰ 59
*to cut with a saw, to thresh with sledges of iron,
to torture* [τινα] (war-crime)
Cf. ENGEL 1985, 20.25.123.127; HAMM 1969, 257;
HORSLEY 1987, 170

πρίν⁺   C 4-8-15-1-26-54
Gn 27,4; 29,26; Ex 1,19; Nm 11,33; Jos 2,8
before [+inf.] (of time) Gn 27,4; *id.* [+subj.]
Sir 11,7; *id.* [+opt.] 4 Mc 5,6
πρὶν ἤ [+subst.] *before* Gn 29,26; πρὶν ἤ
[+inf.] *before* Nm 11,33
Cf. AMIGUES 1980, 210; WEVERS 1990, 9

πρίν   D 0-0-0-0-4-4
3 Mc 5,28; 6,4.31.34
formerly, before 3 Mc 5,28
τὸ πρίν *before* 3 Mc 6,31

πρίν⁺   P 0-0-0-0-2-2
Susᴸˣˣ 35a; Susᵀʰ 42
before [τινος]

πρῖνος,-ου   N2F 0-0-0-0-2-2
Sus 58
oak-tree
Cf. ENGEL 1985, 20-25.123.127

πριστηροειδής,-ής,-ές   A 0-0-1-0-0-1
Is 41,15
like a saw, saw-shaped; neol.

πρίω
(→δια-, ἐκ-, κατα-)

πρίων,-ονος   N3M 0-2-2-0-1-5
2 Sm 12,31; 1 Chr 20,3; Is 10,15; Am 1,3; Jdt 3,9
saw Is 10,15; *serrated mountain ridge* Jdt 3,9
ἔθηκεν ἐν τῷ πρίονι *he assigned (them) to
work with saws* or *he put (them) under the saw,
he tortured (them)* 2 Sm 12,31, cpr. διέπρισε
πρίοσι *he sawed (them) with saws* 1 Chr 20,3
Cf. SHIPP 1979, 473

πρό⁺   P 74-10-57-48-62-251
Gn 2,5(bis); 11,4; 13,10; 19,4
[τινος]: *before, in front of* (of place) 2 Mc 12,27;
before (of time) 2 Mc 15,36
πρὸ τοῦ [+inf.] *before* Gn 2,5; πρὸ βραχέως *a
little ago* 4 Mc 9,5; πρὸ ὀλίγου *id.* Wis 14,20;
πρὸ μικροῦ *id.* Wis 15,8; πρὸ προσώπου τινός
before sb Ex 23,20; πρὸ δύο ἐτῶν τοῦ σεισμοῦ
two years before the earthquake Am 1,1
Cf. ALEXANDRE 1988, 229(Gn 2,5); JOHANNESSOHN 1910,
1-82; 1926, 184-198; LE BOULLUEC 1989, 189(Ex 17,6);
SOLLAMO 1979, 321-324; WEVERS 1990, 266(Ex 17,6);
1993, 22(Gn 2,5).148.149(Gn 11,4); →NIDNTT; TWNT

προάγω⁺   V 0-0-0-3-10-13
Prv 4,27b; 6,8c; Est 2,21; Jdt 10,22; 1 Mc 10,77
A: *to go before sb, to lead* [τινα] 2 Mc 10,1; *to
lead, to guide* [τι] Prv 4,27b; *to go before, to
precede* [τινος] Jdt 10,22; *to move forward, to
advance* [abs.] 1 Mc 10,77; *to promote, to
advance* [τινα] Sir 20,27
P: *to be pressed forward* 2 Mc 5,18; *to move
forward* 3 Mc 3,16; *to be led on* Wis 19,11; *to be
induced* Sir prol.,12
Cf. HELBING 1928, 187; →TWNT

προαγωνίζομαι   V 0-0-0-0-1-1
4 Mc 17,13
to fight before

προαδικέω⁺   V 0-0-0-0-1-1
Wis 18,2
P: *to be previously wronged*

προαίρεσις,-εως⁺   N3F 0-1-2-10-2-15
Jgsᴬ 5,2; Jer 8,5; 14,14; Eccl 1,14.17
choice, inclination Jgsᴬ 5,2; *policy* 2 Mc 9,27
Cf. BERTRAM 1952, 47-48; →PREISIGKE

προαιρέω⁺   V 4-0-1-2-7-14
Gn 34,8; Dt 7,6.7; 10,15; Is 7,15
A: *to take out* [τι] Jdt 13,15
M: *to prefer, to choose* [τινα] Gn 34,8; *id.* [τι]
Prv 1,29; *id.* [+inf.] Prv 21,25
*Is 7,15 προελέσθαι *choose* corr.? προέσθαι
reject for MT מאוס *reject*

προαλής,-ής,-ές   A 0-0-0-0-1-1

Sir 30,8
rash, precipitous
προαναμέλπω V 0-0-0-0-1-1
Wis 18,9
to sing first [τι]; neol.
προανατάσσω V 0-0-0-1-0-1
Ps 136(137),6
M: *to set before oneself, to prefer* [τι]; neol.
προανατέλλω V 0-0-1-0-0-1
Ez 17,9
to sprout afresh; τὰ προανατέλλοντα αὐτῆς *her early shoots*
προαπαγγέλλω V 0-0-1-0-0-1
Ez 33,9
to forewarn sb of sth [τινί τι]
προαποδείκνυμι V 0-0-0-0-1-1
3 Mc 2,25
P: *to be previously defined* or *mentioned*
προαποθνήσκω V 0-0-0-0-1-1
4 Mc 13,18
to die before or *first;* τοὺς προαποθανόντας ἡμῶν ἀδελφούς *our brothers who are already dead*
προασπίζω V 0-0-0-0-3-3
4 Mc 6,21; 9,15; 14,15
to defend [τινος] 4 Mc 9,15; *id.* [τι] 4 Mc 6,21
προάστειον,-ου N2N 2-0-0-0-0-2
Nm 35,2.7
pasture lands surrounding the town, area outside the wall of the city
Cf. CAIRD 1969=1972, 140.141; HUSSON 1967, 187-200
προβαίνω⁺ V 4-6-0-1-7-18
Gn 18,11; 24,1; 26,13; Ex 19,19; Jos 13,1
to advance, to make progress Gn 26,13; *to grow on, to wax* Ex 19,19; *to increase in greatness, to increase in honour* Jdt 16,23; *to advance, to pass* (of time) Jgsᴮ 19,11
προβεβηκότος τὴν ἡλικίαν *advanced in age* 2 Mc 4,40; προβεβηκὼς ταῖς ἡμέραις *advanced in days* Jos 23,1; προβεβηκότες ἡμερῶν *advanced in days* Gn 18,11
Cf. WEVERS 1993, 251
προβάλλω⁺ V 0-6-1-2-2-11
Jgs 14,12.13.16
A: *to put forth* [τι] Prv 26,18; *to bring (arms) into combat position, to advance* [τι] Jer 26(46),4; *to thrust out* [τι] 2 Mc 7,10; *to tear out* [τι] 2 Mc 14,46
M: *to confront sb with a problem, to question* Prv 22,21

προβάλλω πρόβλημα *to propound a riddle* (semit.) Jgsᴬ 14,12; προβάλλομαι πρόβλημα *id.* (semit.) Jgsᴮ 14,12
Cf. SPICQ 1978ᵃ, 743-744
προβασανίζω V 0-0-0-0-2-2
4 Mc 8,5; 10,16
to torture earlier [τινα]; neol.?
προβασκάνιον,-ου N2N 0-0-0-0-1-1
LtJ 69
amulet, charm, phylactery; ἐν σικυηράτῳ προβασκάνιον *a scarecrow in a garden of cucumbers;* neol.
Cf. MILLIGAN 1910=1980, 133
προβατικός,-ή,-όν⁺ A 0-0-0-3-0-3
Neh 3,1.32; 12,39
pertaining to sheep; ἡ πύλη ἡ προβατική *the sheep-gate*
πρόβατον,-ου⁺ N2N 144-35-78-24-15-296
Gn 4,2.4; 12,16; 13,5; 20,14
mostly pl.; sheep Gn 4,2; *sheep* (to be slaughtered) Ps 43(44),23; *sheep* (as sacrificial anim.) Gn 4,4; *sheep, wool of sheep (for clothing)* Prv 27,26; *sheep* (metaph. for people) Mi 7,14
*Jer 10,20 τὰ πρόβατά μου *my sheep* צאני for MT יצאני *they have left me*
Cf. DORIVAL 1994, 539; LE BOULLUEC 1989, 144; WEVERS 1993, 172.313.518.532.798; →NIDNTT; TWNT
προβιβάζω⁺ V 2-0-0-0-0-2
Ex 35,34; Dt 6,7
to teach Ex 35,34; *id.* [τί τινα] Dt 6,7
Cf. CAIRD 1969=1972, 141; DOGNIEZ 1992, 43.155; HELBING 1928, 39; LE BOULLUEC 1989, 352; SPICQ 1978ᵃ, 745; WEVERS 1990, 589; →MM
προβλέπω⁺ V 0-0-0-1-0-1
Ps 36(37),13
to foresee; neol.
→MM
πρόβλημα,-ατος N3N 0-15-1-3-0-19
Jgsᴬ 14,12(bis); Jgsᴮ 14,12; Jgs 14,13
riddle
προβλής,-ῆτος N3M/F 0-0-0-0-1-1
4 Mc 13,6
jutting out
προγίνομαι⁺ V 0-0-0-0-3-3
2 Mc 14,3; 15,8; Wis 19,13
to happen before, to become before, to be before, to be done before
προγεγονώς *former*
Cf. LARCHER 1985, 1070-1071
προγινώσκω⁺ V 0-0-0-0-3-3

Wis 6,13; 8,8; 18,6
A: *to foresee* [τι] Wis 8,8
P: *to make oneself known in advance* Wis 6,13;
to be made known in advance to [τινι] Wis 18,6
Cf. LARCHER 1984, 420.533; 1985, 998; →MM; NIDNTT;
TWNT

πρόγνωσις,-εως⁺   N3F 0-0-0-0-2-2
Jdt 9,6; 11,19
foreknowledge; neol.
→NIDNTT

προγονικός,-ή,-όν   A 0-0-0-0-2-2
2 Mc 8,17; 14,7
ancestral; neol.?

πρόγονοι,-ων   N2M 0-0-0-2-9-11
Est 4,17m; 8,12q; 2 Mc 8,19; 11,25; 3 Mc 5,31
ancestors

προγράφω⁺   V 0-0-0-1-1-2
Dnᴸˣˣ 3,3; 1 Mc 10,36
P: *to be enrolled* 1 Mc 10,36; οἱ προγεγραμ-
μένοι *the aforementioned; the aforenamed*
Dnᴸˣˣ 3,3
→NIDNTT; TWNT

πρόδηλος,-ος,-ον⁺   A 0-0-0-0-3-3
Jdt 8,29; 2 Mc 3,17; 14,39
perfectly clear, manifest

προδηλόω⁺   V 0-0-0-0-1-1
3 Mc 4,14
to explaine beforehand; προδεδηλωμένην *which
has already been explained*
→MM

προδίδωμι⁺   V 0-1-0-0-2-3
2 Kgs 6,11; 2 Mc 7,37; 4 Mc 4,1
to offer up [τι] 2 Mc 7,37; *to betray* [τινα]
2 Kgs 6,11; *id.* [τι] 4 Mc 4,1

προδοσία,-ας   N1F 0-0-0-0-2-2
Wis 17,11.14
abandonment, betrayal, treason
Cf. LARCHER 1985, 966

προδότης,-ου⁺   N1M 0-0-0-0-4-4
2 Mc 5,15; 10,13.22; 3 Mc 3,24
betrayer, traitor

πρόδρομος,-ου⁺   N2M 1-0-1-0-1-3
Nm 13,20; Is 28,4; Wis 12,8
forerunner, herald
Cf. DORIVAL 1994, 54.500; LARCHER 1985, 713; →NIDNTT;
TWNT

προεῖδον
aor. of προοράω

προεκφέρω   V 1-0-0-0-0-1
Gn 38,28

to put forth first
Cf. WEVERS 1993, 647

προεξαποστέλλω   V 0-0-0-0-1-1
2 Mc 12,21
to send out beforehand [τινα]; neol.?

προέρχομαι⁺   V 2-0-0-1-6-9
Gn 33,3.14; Prv 8,24; Jdt 2,19; 15,13
to go before [ἔμπροσθέν τινος] Gn 33,3; *id.*
[τινος] Jdt 2,19; *id.* [πρό τινος] Sir 32,10; *to
come out, to proceed* 2 Mc 4,34; *to come forth*
Prv 8,24; *to advance to, to reach* [ἐπί τι]
(metaph.) 3 Mc 2,26
Cf. HELBING 1928, 187; WEVERS 1993, 547.552; →NIDNTT

προετοιμάζω⁺   V 0-0-1-0-1-2
Is 28,24(23); Wis 9,8
to prepare beforehand [τι]
→NIDNTT

προηγέομαι⁺   V 1-0-0-1-11-13
Dt 20,9; Prv 17,14; 1 Ezr 5,8.9; 8,28
to go before, to precede [τινος] Prv 17,14; *to
prefer* [+inf.] 2 Mc 10,12; οἱ προηγούμενοι
leaders Dt 20,9
Cf. HELBING 1928, 119

προηγορέω   V 0-0-0-0-1-1
2 Mc 4,48
to speak for sb, to be spokesmen for sb [περί
τινος]

προήγορος,-ου   N2M 0-0-0-0-2-2
2 Mc 7,2.4
one who speaks on behalf of others, defender;
neol.

προήκω   V 0-0-0-0-1-1
4 Mc 5,4
to have advanced; τὴν ἡλικίαν προήκων
advanced in age

προθερίζω   V 0-1-0-0-0-1
Jgsᴬ 15,5
to reap first [τι]; τὰ προτεθερισμένα *that which
had already been reaped*; neol.

πρόθεσις,-εως⁺   N3F 3-8-0-0-7-18
Ex 39,17(36); 40,4.23; 1 Sm 21,7; 1 Chr 9,32
setting forth, putting out, offering 2 Chr 29,18;
plan, purpose 2 Mc 3,8
τοὺς ἄρτους τῆς προθέσεως *the loaves laid
before, the bread of presentation, show-bread*
1 Sm 21,7, cpr. ἐνώπιος, πρόσωπον
Cf. DANIEL 1966, 146-153; LE BOULLUEC 1989, 372.373;
WEVERS 1990, 405.640.649

προθυμέομαι   V 0-8-0-0-3-11
1 Chr 29,5.6.9(bis).14

to be willing 1 Mc 1,13; *to be eager, to be zealous*
[+inf.] 1 Chr 29,5; *to do willingly* [τι]
1 Chr 29,17

προθυμία,-ας⁺   N1F 0-0-0-0-1-1
Sir 45,23
willingness, eagerness
Cf. SPICQ 1978ᵃ, 746-751; →TWNT

πρόθυμος,-ος,-ον⁺   A 0-2-1-0-3-6
1 Chr 28,21; 2 Chr 29,31; Hab 1,8; 2 Mc 4,14;
15,9
ready 1 Chr 28,21; *eager* Hab 1,8; τὸ πρόθυμον
desire 3 Mc 5,26
Cf. SPICQ 1978ᵃ, 746-751; →TWNT

προθύμως⁺   D 0-1-0-0-6-7
2 Chr 29,34; Tobᴮᴬ 7,7; Tobˢ 7,8; 2 Mc 6,28;
11,7
willingly 2 Mc 6,28; *zealously* 2 Chr 29,34
Cf. SPICQ 1978ᵃ, 746-751

πρόθυρον,-ου⁺   N2N 1-4-19-0-0-24
Gn 19,6; Jgs 19,27; 1 Sm 5,4; 1 Kgs 7,36(50)
doorway, porch
Cf. HUSSON 1983ᵃ, 237; LUST 1996 forthcoming; WEVERS
1993, 268(Gn 19,6)

προίημι⁺   V 1-0-0-7-3-11
Ex 3,19; Jb 7,19; 27,6; Prv 1,23; 5,9
M: *to bring forth, to utter* [τι] Prv 1,23; *to let go*
[abs.] Jb 27,6; *id.* [τινα] Jb 7,19; *to give away to*
[τί τινι] Prv 5,9; *to deliver up to* [τί τινι]
4 Mc 18,3; *to abandon* [τινα] Prv 30,32; *to
permit* [+inf.] Ex 3,19
λαλιὰν προϊέμενον πρεπόντως *well-spoken*
2 Mc 15,12

πρόιμος,-ος,-ον⁺   A 1-0-7-0-0-8
Dt 11,14; Is 58,8; Jer 5,24; 24,2; Hos 6,3
early Hos 9,10; πρόιμον *morning* Is 58,8
πρόιμος ὑετός *early rain, autumnal rainfall* Jer
5,24
Cf. DOGNIEZ 1992, 189; WALTERS 1973, 75

προΐστημι⁺   V 0-1-2-2-3-8
2 Sm 13,17; Is 43,24; Am 6,10; Prv 23,5; 26,17
M: *to be at the head of, to rule* [τινος]
1 Mc 5,19; *to stand before* [τινος] (to protect)
4 Mc 11,27; *to stand before* [τινος] (metaph.)
Is 43,24
ὁ προεστηκώς *the superior, the master* (said of
God) Prv 23,5; ὁ προεστηκώς τινος *the
caretaker of, the intendant of* 2 Sm 13,17
*Prv 26,17 ὁ προεστώς *the one who stands up
for, mouthpiece* -ערב◊ⁱ for MT ערב◊ⁱⁱ *one who
meddles in* ...

Cf. HELBING 1928, 187; HORSLEY 1987, 82; →NIDNTT; TWNT

προκαθηγέομαι   V 0-0-0-0-1-1
1 Ezr 6,11
to guide, to have influence; οἱ προκαθηγού-
μενοι *leaders, persons of influence, principal
men*; neol.

προκάθημαι⁺   V 0-0-0-0-4-4
1 Ezr 1,30; 5,60; 9,4.45
to sit in the place of honour 1 Ezr 9,45;
προκαθήμενοι *residing, appointed* 1 Ezr 9,4; οἱ
προκαθήμενοι *chief men* 1 Ezr 1,30

προκαθίζω   V 0-0-0-0-1-1
4 Mc 5,1
to sit in public, to sit in judgement

προκακόω   V 0-0-0-0-1-1
4 Mc 17,22
P: *to be afflicted before, to be ill treated before*;
neol.

προκαλέω⁺   V 0-0-0-0-1-1
2 Mc 8,11
M: *to invite*

προκαταλαμβάνω   V 0-25-0-2-14-41
Jgs 1,12.13; 3,28
A: *to overtake, to surprise* [τινα] 3 Mc 2,20
M: *to take first, to capture first* [τι] 2 Kgs 12,18;
id. [τινα] 1 Mc 6,27; *to occupy in advance* [τι]
Jgsᴬ 3,28; *to capture, to occupy* [τινα] 2 Sm 8,4
προκατελάβοντο φυλακὰς οἱ ὀφθαλμοί μου
*my eyes have anticipated the watchers, my eyes
stayed awake* Ps 76(77),5
→SCHLEUSNER(Ps 76(77),5)

προκατασκευάζω   V 0-0-0-0-1-1
Sir prol.,35
to prepare in advance [τινα]

προκατασκιρρόομαι   V 0-0-0-0-1-1
3 Mc 4,1
to be hardened beforehand; τῆς προκατεσκιρω-
μένης ... ἀπεχθείας *the inveterate hatred*; neol.

πρόκειμαι⁺   V 5-0-0-3-3-11
Ex 10,10; 38(37),9; 39,17(36); Lv 24,7; Nm 4,7
to lie before, to be present 4 Mc 15,2; *to be set
before* [τινι] Lv 24,7; *to be set out* Est 1,7; *to be
published* Est 10,3l; *to be attached to* [τινι] Ex
10,10; τὸ προκείμενον *the business that lays
before, the business at hand* 3 Mc 5,46
τοὺς ἄρτους τοὺς προκειμένους *the show-bread*
Ex 39,17(36), cpr. 25,30 and ἐνώπιος
*Est 1,8 οὐ κατὰ προκείμενον νόμον *not
according to the prescribed law* -אין כרת אנס for MT
אין כ/רת אנס *according to the law, without restraint*

Cf. DANIEL 1966, 148.149.159; HARLÉ 1988, 194; WEVERS 1990, 150.405.622.640

προκοπή,-ῆς   N1F 0-0-0-0-2-2
2 Mc 8,8; Sir 51,17
progress, success
Cf. HORSLEY 1987, 36; SPICQ 1978ᵃ, 752-755; →NIDNTT

πρόκρημνος,-ος,-ον   A 0-0-0-0-1-1
4 Mc 7,5
beetling, overhanging; neol.

προκρίνω⁺   V 0-0-0-0-1-1
Wis 7,8
to prefer sth to sth [τί τινος]
Cf. HELBING 1928, 188

προλαμβάνω⁺   V 0-0-0-0-1-1
Wis 17,16
P: *to be overtaken, to be surprised*
→NIDNTT

προλέγω⁺   V 0-0-1-0-12-13
Is 41,26; 1 Ezr 6,31; 2 Mc 2,32; 3,7.28
to foretell Is 41,26; προειρημένος *aforesaid, aforementioned* 2 Mc 3,7; καθὼς προειρήκαμεν *as we have said before, as we already said* 3 Mc 6,35

προλήνιον,-ου   N2N 0-0-1-0-1-2
Is 5,2; Od 10,2
vat fronting a wine press

πρόλοβος,-ου   N2M 1-0-0-0-0-1
Lv 1,16
crop (of a bird)

πρόλογος,-ου   N2M 0-0-0-0-1-1
Sir prol.,tit.
prologue, introduction

προμαχέω   V 0-0-0-0-1-1
Wis 18,21
to fight as the champion of sb, to act as the champion of sb
Cf. LARCHER 1985, 1028

προμαχών,-ῶνος   N3M 0-0-3-0-2-5
Jer 5,10; 40(33),4; Ez 4,2; Tob 13,17
outer fortification, bulwark, rampart

προμηνύω   V 0-0-0-0-1-1
Wis 18,19
to indicate beforehand, to foreshow, to predict, to presage, to forebode [τι]

προνοέω⁺   V 0-0-0-3-6-9
Prv 3,4; Dnᴸˣˣ 11,37(bis); 1 Ezr 2,24; 2 Mc 14,9
A: *to care for, to take thought for* [τινος] Wis 13,16; *id.* [περί τινος] Wis 6,7
M: *to be careful for* [τινος] 2 Mc 14,19; *id.* [ἐπί τινα] (semit.) Dnᴸˣˣ 11, 37; *to take care*

1 Ezr 2,24
προνοοῦ καλά *provide good (repute)* Prv 3,4
Cf. HELBING 1928, 111-112; →NIDNTT

πρόνοια,-ας⁺   N1F 0-0-0-1-8-9
Dnᴸˣˣ 6,19; 2 Mc 4,6; 3 Mc 4,21; 5,30; 4 Mc 9,24
attention (of men) 2 Mc 4,6; *providence* (of God) 3 Mc 4,21
ὁ θεὸς ... πρόνοιαν ποιούμενος *God taking care of, paying attention to* Dnᴸˣˣ 6,19
Cf. HORSLEY 1983, 143-144; LARCHER 1985, 791-792; →NIDNTT; TWNT

προνομεύω   V 9-8-17-0-9-43
Nm 24,17; 31,9(bis).32.53
to plunder, to spoil, to capture [τινα] Nm 24,17; *to plunder, to spoil* [τι] Nm 31,9
Cf. DOGNIEZ 1992, 66.128.244; DORIVAL 1994, 59.396.521; HELBING 1928, 103; WEVERS 1995, 47

προνομή,-ῆς   N1F 6-6-23-4-6-45
Nm 31,11.12.32; Dt 20,14; 21,10
plunder, booty Dt 21,11; *(act of) plundering* 1 Ezr 8,74; *captivity, slavery* (of people) Jdt 9,4
προνομεύσεις τὴν προνομὴν αὐτῶν *you shall take them captive* (semit.) Dt 21,10; προνομεύσει τὴν προνομὴν αὐτῆς *he shall carry off its wealth, he shall plunder it* (semit.) Ez 29,19
Cf. CAIRD 1969=1972, 142; DOGNIEZ 1992, 128.240.244; DORIVAL 1994, 396.521

προνουμηνία,-ας   N1F 0-0-0-0-1-1
Jdt 8,6
eve of the new moon; neol.

προοδηγός,-οῦ   N2M 0-0-0-0-1-1
2 Mc 12,36
one who goes before to show the way, leader; neol.

πρόοιδα⁺   V 0-0-0-0-2-2
4 Mc 4,25; Wis 19,1
to know beforehand

προοίμιον,-ου   N2N 0-0-0-3-0-3
Jb 25,2; 27,1; 29,1
poem, parable Jb 27,1, see also 29,1
*Jb 25,2 τί γὰρ προοίμιον *what is the parable?* -הַמָּשֵׁל (מה) *for* MT הַמְשֵׁל *the domination*
Cf. DORIVAL 1994, 135

προοράω⁺   V 1-0-0-2-0-3
Gn 37,18; Ps 15(16),8; 138(139),3
A: *to foresee* [τι] Ps 138(139),3; *to see beforehand* [τινα] Gn 37,18
M: *to see before one, to have before one's eyes* [τινα ἐνώπιόν τινος] Ps 15(16),8

Cf. ALLEN 1970, 104-108; MILLIGAN 1910=1980, 15;
→NIDNTT; TWNT

πρόπαππος,-ου   N2M 1-0-0-0-0-1
Ex 10,6
great-grandfather

προπάτωρ,-ορος⁺   N3M 0-0-0-0-1-1
3 Mc 2,21
forefather

προπέμπω⁺   V 0-0-0-0-5-5
1 Ezr 4,47; Jdt 10,15; 1 Mc 12,4; 2 Mc 6,23; Wis
19,2
to send on one's way [τινα] *1 Ezr 4,47; to
conduct, to accompany, to escort* [τινα]
Jdt 10,15
προπέμπειν εἰς τὸν ᾅδην *to dispatch to Hades*
2 Mc 6,23

προπετής,-ής,-ές⁺   A 0-0-0-2-1-3
Prv 10,14; 13,3; Sir 9,18
rash, hasty, reckless, thoughtless
Cf. SPICQ 1978ᵃ, 756-757

προπίπτω   V 0-0-0-2-5-7
Ps 21(22),30; 71(72),9; Jdt 13,2; 2 Mc 12,39.42
to fall forward Jdt 13,2; *to fall, to bow down* Ps
21(22),30; *to fall (in battle), to die* 2 Mc 12,39

προπομπή,-ῆς   N1F 0-0-0-0-1-1
1 Ezr 8,51
escort

προπορεύω⁺   V 19-6-1-6-2-34
Gn 32,17.18.20.21; Ex 14,19
M: *to go (on) before* [abs.] Gn 32,20; *id.* [τινος]
Gn 32,18; *id.* [ἔμπροσθέν τινος] Gn 32,17; *id.*
[πρὸ προσώπου τινός] Ex 32,34; *id.* [ἐναντίον
τινός] Jos 6,13; *id.* [κατὰ πρόσωπόν τινος]
Gn 32,22; *to proceed, to advance* Jos 10,13
*Jos 6,13 προεπορεύοντο *they went on before*
-הולכים for MT היבלים *of rams horns*
Cf. DORIVAL 1994, 53.283.543; HELBING 1928, 188

προπράσσω   V 0-0-0-0-2-2
1 Ezr 1,31; 3 Mc 6,27
to do ahead of time; τὰ προπεπραγμένα *things
done previously*

προπτύω   V 0-0-0-0-1-1
2 Mc 6,20
to spit forth or *out*; neol.

πρόπτωσις,-εως   N3F 0-0-0-0-2-2
2 Mc 3,21; 13,12
prostration, lying prostrate (in supplication,
entreaty); neol.?

πρόπυλον,-ου   N2N 0-0-2-0-0-2
Am 9,1; Zph 1,9

gateway, entrance
Cf. LUST 1996 forthcoming

πρός⁺   P 962-1595-288-287-206-3338
Gn 2,19.22.24; 3,16; 4,7
[τινος]: *towards* (time) Gn 24,63; *id.* (place) Jos
15,8; *before, in the presence of* Lam 1,9; *at* Gn
28,11
ἀπὸ πρὸς κεφαλῆς αὐτοῦ *from near his head,
which lies at his head* 1 Sm 26,11; καταγελώ-
μενοι πρὸς ἀπάντων *being mocked of all men*
4 Mc 6,20
[τινι]: *near, at, by* Gn 14,13; *near, towards* Gn
15,17; *in addition to* (with numerals) 2 Mc 4,8
οἱ πρὸς ταῖς χρείαις *the officers* Jdt 12,10,
cpr. 2 Mc 6,21; 3 Mc 5,14
[τι, τινα]: *to, towards* (with verbs of speaking,
asking, praying) 2 Kgs 1,2; *to* (with verbs of
motion) Am 7,10; *towards, facing* (with subst. of
place) Zech 14,4; *towards* (with subst. of time)
Zech 14,7; *to* (expressing purpose, destiny) 3 Mc
2,9; *for, for the purpose of* [+inf.] Jer 34,10;
about to [+inf.] Ex 1,16; *to, towards, with, before*
(denoting a friendly relationship) 4 Mc 15,24;
towards, against (denoting a hostile relationship)
Hos 12,3; *with reference to* Ex 4,16; *in
comparison with* Sir 25,19; *by* 2 Kgs 23,3
τὸ πρὸς πρωί *towards the forenoon, towards the
early morning* Ps 45(46),6
Cf. JOHANNESSOHN 1910, 1-82; 1926, 259-271; →NIDNTT;
TWNT

πρός⁺   D 0-0-0-1-1-2
Ct 1,16; Sir 29,25
besides
→LSJ Suppl; LSJ RSuppl

προσάββατον,-ου⁺   N2N 0-0-0-1-1-2
Ps 92(93),1; Jdt 8,6
eve of the sabbath; neol.

προσαγγέλλω   V 0-0-0-0-6-6
Jdt 10,18; 2 Mc 3,6; 9,24; 10,21; 13,21
to announce, to report [τι] 2 Mc 9,24; *id.* [τί
τινι] 2 Mc 13,21; *id.* [τινι περί τινος] Jdt
10,18; *id.* [περί τινος] 2 Mc 3,6
Cf. BICKERMAN 1980, 162

προσαγορεύω⁺   V 1-0-0-0-6-7
Dt 23,7; 1 Mc 14,40; 2 Mc 1,36; 4,7; 10,9
A: *to call* [τι +pred.] Wis 14,22
P: *to be called* [+pred.] 1 Mc 14,40
προσαγορεύω εἰρηνικά τινι *to wish peace to
sb, to greet sb* Dt 23,7

προσάγω⁺   V 81-43-17-6-27-174

Gn 27,25(bis); 48,9; Ex 3,4; 14,10

A: *to bring to* or *upon* [τί τινι] Lv 1,2; *id.* [τι πρός τινα] Lv 14,2; *to bring* [τι] Tob 12,12; *to bring sb to sb* [τινά τινι] Gn 48,9; *id.* [τινα πρός τινα] Nm 25,6; *to bring sb* [τινα] Jos 7,16; *to bring sb to* or *before* [τινα πρός τι] Ex 21,6(primo); *to bring sb to* or *near* [τινα ἐπί τι] Ex 21,6(secundo); *to offer* [τι] Lv 7,8; *id.* [τινα] Lv 14,12; *to draw near, to approach* Jos 3,9; *id.* [πρός τινα] 1 Kgs 18,21; *to draw near to* [+inf.] Ex 3,4

M: *to bring near* [τινα] Nm 16,10; *to bring sb forward to* [τινα +inf.] Lv 7,35; *to resort to* [πρός τινα] Sus^Th 4

προσῆγον εἰς πόλεμον *they drew near to war* 1 Sm 7,10; προσηγαγόμην ὑμᾶς πρὸς ἐμαυτόν *I brought you near to myself* Ex 19,4, cpr. 28,1; Nm 16,5.9

*1 Sm 13,6 προσάγειν *draw near* -נגש for MT נגש *they were hard pressed*; *Prv 24,15 προσαγάγῃς *bring* -קרב for MT תארב *lie in wait*

Cf. DORIVAL 1994, 53.254.491; HELBING 1928, 289; LE BOULLUEC 1989, 89.164; WEVERS 1990, 213; →TWNT

προσαιτέω⁺ V 0-0-0-1-0-1
Jb 27,14
to beg

προσαναβαίνω⁺ V 1-7-0-0-2-10
Ex 19,23; Jos 11,17; 15,3.6.7
to go up Ex 19,23; *to climb, to ascend* [τι] Jdt 13,10; *to go on up, to continue on, to proceed* (of borders) Jos 15,6

προσανάβασις,-εως N3F 0-1-0-0-0-1
Jos 15,3
ascent, approach

προσαναλέγω V 0-0-0-0-1-1
2 Mc 8,19
M: *to rehearse (besides), to relate* [τι]; neol.

προσαναπαύω V 0-0-0-0-1-1
Wis 8,16
M: *to find rest with* [τινι]; neol.?

προσαναπληρόω⁺ V 0-0-0-0-1-1
Wis 19,4
to fulfil, to fill up (a punishment) [τι]
Cf. LARCHER 1985, 1052

προσανατρέπω V 0-0-0-0-1-1
Sir 13,23
to overthrow (further), to overturn [τινα]; neol.

προσαναφέρω V 0-0-0-0-3-3
Jdt 11,18; Tob^BA 12,15; 2 Mc 11,36
to report; neol.

προσανοικοδομέω V 0-0-0-0-1-1
Sir 3,14
P: *to be built up (credit)* (metaph.); neol.
Cf. CAIRD 1969=1972, 142; KILPATRICK 1943, 147-148

προσαξιόω V 0-0-0-0-1-1
3 Mc 7,10
to petition of sb, to request of sb [τινα]; neol.?

προσαποθνῄσκω V 1-0-0-0-0-1
Ex 21,29
to die also; neol.

προσαπόλλυμι V 0-0-0-0-1-1
2 Mc 13,4
to put to death [τινα]

προσαποστέλλω V 0-0-0-0-1-1
2 Mc 11,14
to send off

προσαπωθέω V 0-0-0-0-1-1
Sir 13,21
P: *to be pushed away*; neol.

προσαρτίως D 0-0-0-0-1-1
3 Mc 1,19
recently; neol.

προσβαίνω⁺ V 0-0-0-0-5-5
1 Ezr 4,53(bis); 8,1; Jdt 4,7; 7,10
to ascend, to approach

προσβάλλω V 0-0-0-1-7-8
Dn^Th 7,2; 2 Mc 10,17.28.35; 12,10
to strike, to blow violently upon [εἴς τι] (of wind) Dn^Th 7,2; *to attack* [τινι] 2 Mc 10,17; *id.* [abs.] 2 Mc 10,28
προσβάλλω ἀλάστορά τινι *to bring an avenger upon sb* 4 Mc 11,23
Cf. HELBING 1928, 289-290

πρόσβασις,-εως N3F 0-1-0-0-3-4
Jos 15,7; Jdt 4,7; 2 Mc 4,13; 3 Mc 1,26
approach, ascending Jdt 4,7; *means of access* (metaph.), *occasion, opportunity* 2 Mc 4,13

προσβλητός,-ή,-όν A 0-0-1-0-0-1
Jer 10,9
attached, overlaid (of silver); neol.

προσβολή,-ῆς N1F 0-0-0-0-2-2
2 Mc 5,3; 15,19
assault, attack

προσγελάω V 0-0-0-0-3-3
1 Ezr 4,31; Sir 13,6.11
to smile upon [τινι] 1 Ezr 4,31; *id.* [abs.] Sir 13,11
Cf. HELBING 1928, 290

προσγίνομαι V 3-0-0-0-0-3
Lv 18,26; 20,2; Nm 15,14

to attach oneself to sb [ἔν τινι] (of the alien residing among the Israelites)

προσγράφω V 0-0-0-0-1-1
1 Ezr 6,31
to specify in writing; τῶν προσγεγραμμένων *of the written specifications*

προσδεκτός,-ή,-όν⁺ A 0-0-0-2-1-3
Prv 11,20; 16,15; Wis 9,12
acceptable Wis 9,12; *acceptable to, in favour with* [τινι] Prv 11,20; neol.
→TWNT

προσδέομαι⁺ V 0-0-0-1-4-5
Prv 12,9; Sir 4,3; 11,12; 13,3; 42,21
to need in addition, to be needy [τινος] Prv 12,9; *id.* [abs.] Sir 4,3; *to beg* Sir 13,3
Cf. HELBING 1928, 173

προσδέχομαι⁺ V 6-2-14-14-12-48
Gn 32,21; Ex 10,17; 22,10; 36,3; Lv 26,43
to receive, to take up, to welcome [τινα] 1 Chr 12,19; *to receive* [τι] Ex 36,3; *to take* (food) [τι] Jb 33,20; *to accept* [τι] Gn 32,21; *to agree, to consent* Ex 22,10; *to bear with, to endure, to pardon* [τι] Ex 10,17; *to admit* [τι] Lv 26,43; *to undertake, to attempt* [+inf.] Dnᴸˣˣ 7,25; *to expect, to wait for* [τι] Jb 2,9a; *id.* [τινα] Ru 1,13; *to look to* [+inf.] Wis 14,29
*Is 45,4 προσδέξομαί σε *I will accept you* -אקהך for MT אכנך *I will name you;* *Ps 54(55),9 προσεδεχόμην *I waited for* -אחילה for MT אחישה *I would hasten;* *Ps 103(104),11 προσδέξονται *they shall hope* -ישברו for MT ישברו *they shall break*
Cf. LE BOULLUEC 1989, 139; WEVERS 1990, 154.593; 1993, 539; →NIDNTT; TWNT

προσδέω⁺ V 0-0-0-0-2-2
4 Mc 9,26; Sir 18,32
A: *to bind sb to* [τινά τινι] 4 Mc 9,26; *to be tied to* [τινι] (metaph.) Sir 18,32

προσδίδωμι⁺ V 1-0-2-0-1-4
Gn 29,33; Ez 16,33.34; TobᴮᴬA 2,12
to give in addition [τι]
Cf. WEVERS 1993, 472

προσδοκάω⁺ V 1-0-0-4-8-13
Dt 32,2; Ps 68(69),21; 103(104),27; 118(119),166; Lam 2,16
to expect, to look for [τι] Wis 12,22; *to wait upon* [πρός τινα] Ps 103(104),27; *to expect* [τινα +inf.] 2 Mc 12,44
*Ps 68(69),21 προσεδόκησεν *expected* -שברה for MT שברה *broke, have broken*
Cf. DOGNIEZ 1992, 321(Dt 32,2); HARL 1992ᵃ= 1993, 185-

186(Dt 32,2); →NIDNTT; TWNT

προσδοκία,-ας⁺ N1F 1-0-1-1-6-9
Gn 49,10; Is 66,9; Ps 118(119),116; 2 Mc 3,21; 3 Mc 5,41
expectation Ps 118(119),116; *expectation in fear, anxiety* 2 Mc 3,21
*Gn 49,10 προσδοκία *expectation* (in hope or in fear) -קוה for MT יקהת ◊יקה *obedience;* *Is 66,9 προσδοκίαν *expectation* -◊שבר for MT אשביר ◊שבר *I cause to travail, I open the womb*
Cf. HARL 1992ᵃ=1993, 186(Gn 49,10); MONSENGWO PASINYA 1980, 365(Gn 49,10); WEVERS 1993, 826(Gn 49,10); →NIDNTT; TWNT

προσεγγίζω⁺ V 6-6-1-2-1-16
Gn 33,6.7(bis); Lv 2,8; Nm 8,19
to bring near [τι] JgsᴬA 5,25; *to draw near, to approach* [abs.] Gn 33,6; *id.* [τινι] DnᴸˣˣA 9,21; *id.* [πρός τι] Lv 2,8; *id.* [πρός τινα] 2 Sm 20,17
προσεγγίσαι εἰς πόλεμον *to draw near to battle* JgsᴬA 20,23
→TWNT

προσεδρεία,-ας N1F 0-0-0-0-1-1
3 Mc 4,15
close attention, diligence

προσεδρεύω⁺ V 0-0-0-0-1-1
1 Mc 11,40
to insist, to press sore upon [τινι]

προσεῖδον
aor. of προσοράω

πρόσειμι⁺ V 0-0-0-0-4-4
4 Mc 6,13; 14,16.19(bis)
to go up to [τινι] 4 Mc 6,13; ὁ προσιών *the intruder* 4 Mc 14,16

προσεῖπον
aor. of προσλέγω

προσεκκαίω V 1-0-0-0-0-1
Nm 21,30
to ignite further [τι]; *Nm 21,30 προσεξέκαυσαν *they ignited further* -◊נפח *to set aflame, to ignite* for MT נֹפַח *Nophah* (geogr. name); neol.?
Cf. ALTHANN 1985, 568-571; DORIVAL 1994, 411; PRIJS 1948, 52

προσεμβριμάομαι V 0-0-0-0-1-1
Sir 13,3
to continue to be indignant, to scream to prove oneself right or *to prove to be the wronged one;* neol.

προσεμπίμπρημι V 1-0-0-0-0-1
Ex 22,5

to burn through [τι]; neol.

προσενέχομαι V 0-0-0-0-1-1
2 Mc 5,18
to be held by, to be in the grip of, to be involved in [τινι]; neol.

προσεξηγέομαι V 0-0-0-0-1-1
2 Mc 15,11
to relate, to recount [τι]; neol.

προσεπικατατείνω V 0-0-0-0-1-1
4 Mc 9,19
to strain still more; neol.

προσεπιτιμάω V 0-0-0-0-1-1
Sir 13,22
to further criticize or *censure* [τινι]; neol.?

προσερυθριάω V 0-0-0-0-1-1
Tobˢ 2,14
to colour up, to redden against [πρός τινα]; neol.

προσέρχομαι⁺ V 47-18-6-16-26-113
Gn 29,10; 42,24; 43,19; Ex 12,48(bis)
to come to, to go to [τινι] Lv 19,33; *id.* [πρός τινα] Gn 42,24; *to come, to approach, to draw near* [abs.] Gn 29,10; *to come near to* (of man and woman in sexual relations) [τινι] Ex 19,15; *to approach, to draw nigh to* [εἰς τι] Nm 18,22; *id.* [πρός τι] Lv 9,7; *to go up to* [ἐπί τι] 2 Mc 13,26
προσέλθωσιν εἰς κρίσιν *they came forward to judgement* Dt 25,1; μὴ προσέλθῃς μοι περὶ αὐτῶν *do not approach me for them, do not intercede with me for them* Jer 7,16
often used in cultic sense: *to draw near (to offer gifts)* Lv 21,17; *to approach (the Lord)* [ἐναντίον τινί] Ex 16,9; ἐὰν δέ τις προσέλθῃ πρὸς ὑμᾶς προσήλυτος ποιῆσαι τὸ πάσχα *if any proselyte shall come to you to keep the passover* Ex 12,48, see προσήλυτος
*2 Chr 24,27 προσῆλθον *they came near* -◊קרב- for MT ורב/ו *and the many*?; *Ps 63(64),7 προσελεύσεται *he shall come near* -וְקָרֵב- for MT וְקֶרֶב *and the intestines, the inner parts (of man or woman), the thoughts*; *Dnᴸˣˣ 9,22 καὶ προσῆλθε *and he came near* -ויבא- for MT ויבן *and he made to understand*
Cf. EDWARDS 1987, 65-67; HELBING 1928, 290; LE BOULLUEC 1989, 51.154; LEE, J. 1983, 91; ROST 1967, 119-121; WEVERS 1990, 193; →NIDNTT; PREISIGKE; TWNT

προσέτι D 0-1-0-1-2-4
2 Sm 16,11; Jb 36,16; 2 Mc 12,14; 4 Mc 14,1
still more, more than that

προσευχή,-ῆς⁺ N1F 0-20-9-42-44-115
2 Sm 7,27; 1 Kgs 8,29.38.45.54
prayer 2 Sm 7,27; *vow* Ps 64(65),3
*Is 60,7 καὶ ὁ οἶκος τῆς προσευχῆς μου *and my house of prayer* -תפארתי ובית for MT תפלתי ובית *and my glorious house*; *Hab 3,16 προσευχῆς *of the prayer* -צלו (Aram.) *prayer* for MT צללו *they quiver* (of lips)
neol.?
Cf. CIMOSA 1991, 98-102; HORSLEY 1983, 121; 1987, 201.219.220; LEE, J. 1983, 46; →NIDNTT; PREISIGKE; TWNT

προσεύχομαι⁺ V 3-41-19-19-25-107
Gn 20,7.17; Ex 10,17; Jgsᴮ 13,8; 1 Sm 1,10
to pray [abs.] 1 Kgs 8,33; *to pray to* [πρός τινα] Gn 20,17; *id.* [ἔν τινι] Is 45,14; *to pray for* [περί τινος] Gn 20,7; *id.* [ὑπέρ τινος] 1 Sm 1,27; *id.* [εἰς τι] Ezr 6,10; *to pray to sb for sb* [πρός τινι περί τινος] Jer 36(29),7
Cf. CIMOSA 1985, 29-31.39-40; 1991, 94-96; HELBING 1928, 224-225; →NIDNTT; TWNT

προσεχόντως D 0-0-0-1-0-1
Prv 31,25(26)
attentively, carefully, heedfully

προσέχω⁺ V 25-3-15-47-30-120
Gn 4,5; 24,6; 34,3; Ex 9,21; 10,28
to pay attention, to give heed [abs.] Jb 29,21; *to turn one's attention* or *mind to, to regard, to follow* [τινι] 1 Ezr 1,26; *id.* [εἰς τι] Ex 9,21; *id.* [τι] Ex 34,11; *id.* [ἐπί τινι] Gn 4,5; *id.* [ἐπί τινος] Sir 16,24; *id.* [τινος] Neh 9,34; *id.* [κατά τινος] Jb 1,8; *id.* [ἔν τινι] Sir 1,29
to beware of [ἀπό τινος] Lv 22,2
to be attached to [τινι] Gn 34,3
προσέχον *attentive* (of ears) Ps 129(130),2; τὰ προσέχοντα *bases* 1 Kgs 7,17; πρόσεχε σεαυτῷ *be careful for yourself* Gn 24,6; προσέχω τὸν νοῦν *to pay attention to* Jb 7,17; προσέχω τῇ καρδίᾳ *id.* Dt 32,46
*1 Kgs 7,17(30) τὰ προσέχοντα corr.? τὰ προέχοντα -סרני ᴵᴵ *princes* for MT סרני ᴵ *axles*
Cf. DOGNIEZ 1992, 58.122.135.197.211; HELBING 1928, 290-295; LE BOULLUEC 1989, 340; WALTERS 1973, 83; WEVERS 1990, 135.159.299; 1993, 53.344.558; 1995, 27.381

προσηκόντως D 0-0-0-0-1-1
4 Mc 6,33
properly, suitably

προσήκω⁺ V 0-0-0-0-3-3
1 Ezr 5,50; 2 Mc 3,6; 4 Mc 4,3
to belong to [τινι] 4 Mc 4,3; *id.* [πρός τι] 2 Mc 3,6

προσῆκον ἦν *it was fitting, it was meet* 1 Ezr 5,50

προσηλόω⁺   V 0-0-0-0-1-1
3 Mc 4,9
P: *to be fastened* (metaph. of pers.)

προσηλυτεύω   V 0-0-1-0-0-1
Ez 14,7
to live among (as an immigrant); neol.

προσήλυτος,-ου⁺   N2M 64-7-11-2-1-85
Ex 12,48.49; 20,10; 22,20(bis)
always transl. of גר; *one who has come near (to live as an immigrant); immigrant, resident alien, stranger, (proselyte?)* Ez 22,7; *Jewish immigrant in Israel coming from abroad* Nm 9,14; *Jewish immigrant in Egypt* Ex 22,20; neol.; cpr. πάροικος
Cf. ALLEN 1894, 264-275; BITTER 1982, 16-30.296.332; DORIVAL 1994, 158.274.333; LE BOULLUEC 1989, 51-52.87.154; LEE, J. 1980ᵇ, 112(n.27); LOADER 1973, 270-277; MURAOKA 1986ᵃ, 260-261; TOV 1976ᵇ, 537-539; WEVERS 1995, 248; →NIDNTT; TWNT

προσημαίνω   V 0-0-0-0-3-3
2 Mc 4,23; 3 Mc 5,13.47
P: *to be announced, to be mentioned beforehand* 3 Mc 5,13; ὁ προσημαινόμενος *the aforesaid* 2 Mc 4,23

προσημειόω   V 0-0-0-0-1-1
4 Mc 15,19
M: *to forebode, to forecast, to presage, to indicate*; neol.

προσηνής,-ής,-ές   A 0-0-0-1-0-1
Prv 25,25
agreeable

πρόσθεμα,-ατος   N3N 1-0-1-0-0-2
Lv 19,25; Ez 41,7
something added, increase

πρόσθεσις,-εως⁺   N3F 0-0-1-0-0-1
Ez 47,13
addition, increase; *Ez 47,13 πρόσθεσις σχοινίσματος *addition of a part* - ◊יסף and - חבל for MT יוֹסֵף חֲבָלִים *Joseph: two parts* (of land)
→NIDNTT

προσθλίβω   V 1-0-0-0-0-1
Nm 22,25
to press, to squeeze against [πρός τι]; neol.
Cf. DORIVAL 1994, 56.427

προσκαθίστημι   V 0-1-0-0-0-1
JgsᴬᴬA 14,11
to appoint to [τινά τινι]; neol.

πρόσκαιρος,-ος,-ον⁺   A 0-0-0-0-3-3
4 Mc 15,2.8.23
temporary, for a time 4 Mc 15,2; *present* 4 Mc 15,23; neol.
→NIDNTT

προσκαίω   V 0-0-1-0-0-1
Ez 24,11
P: *to be burnt thoroughly*

προσκαλέω⁺   V 3-1-3-5-12-24
Gn 28,1; Ex 3,18; 5,3; 1 Sm 26,14; Jl 3,5
M: *to call on* [τινα] Ex 5,3; *to summon* [τι] Ps 49(50),4; *to call to oneself, to invite, to summon* [τινα] Gn 28,1; *to invite to perform a certain task* [τινα] Jl 3,5; *to call for* [τι] Am 5,8
P: *to be called* Est 8,1
*Ex 3,18 προσκέκληται -◊קרא (Sam. Pent.) *he has called on* for MT קרה *he has encountered (us)*
Cf. LE BOULLUEC 1989, 94; WEVERS 1990, 36; 1993, 444; →NIDNTT; TWNT

προσκαρτερέω⁺   V 1-0-0-0-2-3
Nm 13,20; Tobˢ 5,8; Susᵀʰ 6
to persevere Nm 13,20; *to spend much time in* [ἔν τινι] Susᵀʰ 6
Cf. DORIVAL 1994, 311; SPICQ 1978ᵃ, 758; →NIDNTT

προσκαταλείπω   V 1-0-0-0-0-1
Ex 36,7
to leave behind, to leave over
Cf. WEVERS 1990, 596

πρόσκαυμα,-ατος   N3N 0-0-2-0-0-2
Jl 2,6; Na 2,11
marks of burning; πρόσκαυμα χύτρας *soot on the outside of a pot*

πρόσκειμαι⁺   V 16-2-4-1-1-24
Lv 16,29; 17,3.8.10.12
to lie near, to be adjacent to [τινι] Nm 21,15; *to be joined to, to abide among* [ἔν τινι] Lv 16,29; *id.* [πρός τινα] Lv 22,18; *id.* [τινι] Tobˢ 1,8; *to belong to* [πρός τινα] Ez 37,19; *id.* [ἐπί τινα] Ez 37,16; *to be attached* Dt 1,36; *to keep close to, to adhere to* [τινι] Dt 4,4; *id.* [πρός τινα] Is 56,3
Cf. DOGNIEZ 1992, 120; DORIVAL 1994, 334; HELBING 1928, 295-296

προσκεφάλαιον,-ου⁺   N2N 0-0-2-0-1-3
Ez 13,18.20; 1 Ezr 3,8
pillow Ez 13,18; *treasure-chamber* 1 Ezr 3,8
Cf. HILHORST 1982, 161-163

προσκήνιον,-ου   N2N 0-0-0-0-1-1
Jdt 10,22
space before the tent, outer area; neol.

πρόσκλησις,-εως⁺   N3F 0-0-0-0-1-1
2 Mc 4,14
summons; μετὰ τὴν τοῦ δίσκου πρόσκλησιν
*after the calling of the gong, as soon as the gong
had sounded*
Cf. CAIRD 1969=1972, 142

προσκλίνω⁺   V 0-0-0-0-1-1
2 Mc 14,24
P: *to be attached to, to incline towards* [τινι]

προσκολλάω⁺   V 7-3-1-5-2-18
Gn 2,24; Lv 19,31; Nm 36,7.9; Dt 11,22
A: *to cause to stick to* [τινα πρός τι] Ez 29,4;
to attach sth to sb [τι εἴς τινα] Dt 28,21
M: *to stick to, to cleave to* [πρός τι] 2 Sm 23,10;
to attach oneself to, to cleave to [τινι] Lv 19,31;
id. [ἔν τινι] Nm 36,7; *id.* [πρός τινα] (of rel.
between man and wife) Gn 2,24; *id.* [μετά
τινος] Ru 2,21; *id.* [ὀπίσω τινός] Jgsᴬ 20,45; *to
cleave, to be faithfully devoted to* [τινι] Jos 23,8
Cf. DOGNIEZ 1992, 120.156.288; HELBING 1928, 248;
→NIDNTT; TWNT

πρόσκομμα,-ατος⁺   N3N 2-0-3-0-6-11
Ex 23,33; 34,12; Is 8,14; 29,21; Jer 3,3
stumbling Sir 34,16; *obstacle* Ex 23,33; *offence*
Sir 17,25
ξύλον προσκόμματος *stumbling-block* Sir 31,7
*Jer 3,3 πρόσκομμα *stumbling-block* -מוקש for MT
מלקוש *spring rain*
Cf. LE BOULLUEC 1989, 38-39.242; →NIDNTT; TWNT

προσκόπτω⁺   V 0-1-2-6-8-17
Jgsᴬ 20,32; Is 3,5; Jer 13,16; Ps 90(91),12; Prv
3,23
to strike sth against sth [τι πρός τι] Ps
90(91),12; *to stumble* Jgsᴬ 20,32; *to offend* [abs.]
Sir 31,17; *id.* [πρός τινα] Is 3,5
→NIDNTT; TWNT

προσκρούω⁺   V 0-0-0-1-2-3
Jb 40,23; 2 Mc 13,19; Sir 13,2
to knock against, to strike against Sir 13,2; *to
rush up into* [εἴς τι] (of a river) Jb 40,23

προσκυνέω⁺   V 46-74-28-55-26-229
Gn 18,2; 19,1; 22,5; 23,7.12
*to fall down and worship, to do reverence to, to
do obeisance to, to prostrate oneself before, to
salute* [abs.] Gn 18,2; *id.* [τινι] (to pers.) Gn
27,29; *to fall down and worship* [τινι] (to God)
Gn 24,26; *id.* [τινι] (to idols) Ps 96(97),7; *id.*
[τινα] (to pers.) Gn 37,9; *id.* [τινα] (to God)
Jgsᴬ 7,15; *id.* [τι] Gn 37,7; *to bow down, to beg,
to plead, to implore* Ex 11,8

Cf. ALTINK 1984, 189; CIMOSA 1985, 53-65.66-68;
DOGNIEZ 1992, 49.138.156; HARL 1986ᵃ, 62.67.193;
HELBING 1928, 296-298; HORST 1932, 16-32; JOBES 1991,
186-187; WEVERS 1990, 165.278.372.379; 1993, 245.319.
617.706.813; 1995, 76.407; →NIDNTT; TWNT

προσκύνησις,-εως   N3F 0-0-0-0-2-2
3 Mc 3,7; Sir 50,21
act of worship, obeisance
→NIDNTT

προσκύπτω   V 0-0-0-0-1-1
2 Mc 7,27
to stoop over to, to lean over to [τινι]

προσκυρέω   V 0-0-0-0-1-1
1 Mc 10,39
to adjoin, to belong to [τινι]

προσλαλέω⁺   V 1-0-0-0-1-2
Ex 4,16; Wis 13,17
to speak to [τινι] Wis 13,17; *to speak for sb to
sb* [τινι πρός τινα] Ex 4,16
Cf. LARCHER 1985, 784

προσλαμβάνω⁺   V 0-1-0-4-3-8
1 Sm 12,22; Ps 17(18),17; 26(27),10; 64(65),5;
72(73),24
A: *to increase* [τι] Wis 17,10
M: *to take, to draw* (out of sth) [τινα] Ps
17(18),17; *to take along with as companion*
[τινα] 2 Mc 8,1; *to accept* or *receive in one's
society* [τινα] 2 Mc 10,15
Cf. SPICQ 1982, 583-588; →NIDNTT; TWNT

προσλέγω⁺   V 0-1-0-1-1-3
Jgsᴮ 17,2; Prv 7,13; 2 Mc 7,8
aor. is always προσεῖπον; *to speak, to say* Jgsᴮ
17,2; *to speak to, to say to* [τινι] Prv 7,13

προσλογίζομαι   V 1-1-0-1-2-5
Lv 27,18; Jos 13,3; Ps 87(88),5; Sir 7,16; Bar
3,11
M: *to reckon, to calculate* [τι] Lv 27,18; *id.*
[τινα] Sir 7,16
P: *to be reckoned* Jos 13,3

προσμαρτυρέω   V 0-0-0-0-1-1
3 Mc 5,19
to confirm, to bear additional witness [τινι]

προσμείγνυμι   V 0-0-0-1-1-2
Prv 14,13; 2 Mc 15,20
A: *to unite, to come close, to approach* 2 Mc
15,20
M: *to mingle with* [ἔν τινι] (metaph.) Prv 14,13
Cf. HELBING 1928, 251

προσμειδιάω   V 0-0-0-0-1-1
4 Mc 8,4

to smile at [τινι]; neol.

προσμένω⁺   V 0-1-0-0-3-4
Jgs^A 3,25; Tob^S 2,2; 3 Mc 7,17; Wis 3,9
to wait Jgs^A 3,25; *to abide with* [τινι] Wis 3,9; *to wait for* [τινα] Tob^S 2,2
→NIDNTT

προσνέμω   V 0-0-0-0-1-1
4 Mc 6,33
to attribute to [τί τινι]

προσνοέω   V 1-2-1-3-2-9
Nm 23,9; Jgs 3,26; Is 63,5; Jb 20,9
to observe, to notice, to pay attention to [abs.] Is 63,5, see also 59,16; *id.* [τινα] Nm 23,9; *id.* [τινι] Jgs 3,26
Cf. LEE, J. 1983, 84

πρόσοδος,-ου   N2F 0-0-0-1-6-7
Prv 28,16; 2 Mc 3,3; 4,8; 9,16; 14,3
going to, approach 2 Mc 14,3; *revenue, fund* 2 Mc 4,8; πρόσοδοι *revenues* 2 Mc 3,3
*Prv 28,16 προσόδων *revenues* -תבואות or -תנובות for MT תבונות *wisdom, understanding*

προσοδύρομαι   V 0-0-0-0-1-1
Wis 19,3
to lament at [τινι]; neol.

προσόζω   V 0-0-0-1-0-1
Ps 37(38),6
to smell, to stink

προσοίγω   V 1-0-0-0-0-1
Gn 19,6
to shut [τι]; neol.
Cf. HARL 1986ᵃ, 179; WEVERS 1993, 268

προσονομάζω⁺   V 0-0-0-0-1-1
2 Mc 6,2
to call by name [τι +pred.]

προσοράω   V 0-0-0-1-1-2
Jb 6,15; Wis 17,9
to look at, to behold [τινα] Jb 6,15; *id.* [τι] Wis 17,9

προσοχή,-ῆς   N1F 0-0-0-0-4-4
Wis 6,18; 12,20; Sir prol.,16; 11,18
attention, care

προσοχθίζω⁺   V 12-1-1-3-4-21
Gn 27,46; Lv 18,25.28(bis); 20,22
A: *to be irritated by, to be provoked at* [τινι] Lv 18,25; *id.* [ἔν τινι] Nm 21,5; *id.* [ἀπό τινος] Nm 22,3; *to be angry, to be offended, to be provoked* [abs.] Ez 36,31; *to be irritated by, to be weary of* [τινι] Gn 27,46
P: *to be treated with contempt, to be assailed, reviled* 2 Sm 1,21

neol.
Cf. DOGNIEZ 1992, 65.168; DORIVAL 1994, 400; HARL 1986ᵃ, 80.221; HELBING 1928, 266-267; WEVERS 1993, 442

προσόχθισμα,-ατος   N3N 1-6-0-0-3-10
Dt 7,26; 1 Kgs 11,33; 16,32; 18,29; 2 Kgs 23,13
offence, provocation, idol, object of anger; neol.
Cf. DOGNIEZ 1992, 24.64.168

προσοχυρόω   V 0-0-0-0-2-2
1 Mc 13,48.52
to strengthen further, to strengthen more, to fortify [τι]; neol.

πρόσοψις,-εως⁺   N3F 0-0-0-4-1-5
Dn^LXX 2,31(bis); Dn^Th 2,31; Dn^LXX 7,20; 2 Mc 6,18
appearance, aspect

προσπαίζω   V 0-0-0-1-1-2
Jb 21,11; Sir 8,4
to make fun of [τινι] Sir 8,4; *to play* Jb 21,11

προσπαρακαλέω   V 0-0-0-0-1-1
2 Mc 12,31
to enjoin, to exhort [+inf.]

προσπάσσω   V 0-0-0-0-1-1
Tob^BA 11,11
to sprinkle on [τι ἐπί τι]; neol.

προσπίπτω⁺   V 2-0-0-5-16-23
Gn 33,4; Ex 4,25; Ps 94(95),6; Prv 25,8.20
to fall upon [ἐπί τι] Gn 33,4; *id.* [ἐπί τι] (metaph.) Sir 25,21; *to fall (down) before* or *at* [πρός τι] Ex 4,25; *id.* [τινι] Jdt 14,7; *id.* [ἐπί τι] 2 Mc 10,26; *to come to* [πρός τινα] 1 Ezr 8,8; *to reach* [τινι] 2 Mc 5,11; *to become known* 3 Mc 3,25; *to befall* [ἔν τινι] Prv 25,20; τὰ προσπίπτοντα *what happens, the circumstances* 1 Ezr 2,19; ὁ τὰ προσπίπτοντα (sc. κατα-γράφων) *reporter, recorder* 1 Ezr 2,13; μὴ πρόσπιπτε εἰς μάχην *do not get into a quarrel* Prv 25,8
Cf. HELBING 1928, 298-300; MOULTON 1910, 298-299 (1 Ezr 2,13); THACKERAY 1909, 161(1 Ezr 2,13)

προσποιέω⁺   V 0-1-0-1-2-4
1 Sm 21,14; Jb 19,14; Sir 31,30; Sus^LXX 10/11
A: *to add on, to produce further* [τι] Sir 31,30
M: *to pretend, to feign* 1 Sm 21,14; *to conceal sth from sb* [τί τινι] Sus^LXX 10/11; *to take notice of* [τινα] Jb 19,14

προσπορεύομαι⁺   V 12-2-0-1-2-17
Ex 24,14; 28,43; 30,20; 36,2; 38,27
to go to [τινι] Ex 24,14; *id.* [πρός τινα] Lv 19,34; *to approach, to advance to* [πρός τι] Ex 28,43; *to come near, to advance* [abs.] Nm 1,51

to turn to, to apply oneself to [πρός τι] Neh 10,29; *to approach, to have sexual intercourse with* [τινι] Tob^BA 6,18; *to attach oneself to, to associate with* [τινι] Sir 12,14

Cf. HELBING 1928, 300; LEE, J. 1983, 89-91(Ex 24,14; 36,2); WEVERS 1995, 320

προσπυρόω   V 0-0-0-0-1-1
2 Mc 14,11

to inflame, to incense still more [τινα]; neol.

προσραίνω   V 2-0-0-0-0-2
Lv 4,6; 8,30

to sprinkle around Lv 4,6; *to sprinkle on* [ἐπί τινα]

προσσιελίζω   V 1-0-0-0-0-1
Lv 15,8

to spit upon [ἐπί τινα]; neol.

προσταγή,-ῆς   N1F 0-0-0-1-0-1
Dn^LXX 3,95

ordinance, command; neol.

Cf. LLEWELYN 1994, 84

πρόσταγμα,-ατος⁺   N3N 31-33-29-39-34-166
Gn 24,50; 26,5; 47,26; Ex 18,16.20
ordinance, command Gn 24,50

*Prv 14,27 πρόσταγμα *command* -תורה for MT
ירא *fear*

Cf. BLANK 1930, 266-267; DODD 1954, 27.29.32; DOGNIEZ 1992, 53; DORIVAL 1994, 275; LE BOULLUEC 1989, 43.207; MONSENGWO PASINYA 1973, 147-150; WEVERS 1993, 400; 1995, 206.254; →NIDNTT; TWNT

προσταράσσω   V 0-0-0-0-1-1
Sir 4,3

to trouble further [τι]; neol.

προστάς,-άδος   N3F 0-2-0-0-0-2
Jgs^B 3,22; Jgs^A 3,23
porch, portico; neol.?

Cf. HUSSON 1983^a, 238-241

προστάσσω⁺   V 12-3-7-13-39-74
Gn 47,11; 50,2; Ex 36,6; Lv 10,1; 14,4
to command, to prescribe [abs.] Gn 47,11; *id.* [τινι] Gn 50,2; *id.* [τι] 3 Mc 5,3; *id.* [+inf.] Dt 18,20
ὡς προσέταξεν τὸν λόγον *as he gave the command* 2 Chr 31,5

Cf. HELBING 1928, 208; PELLETIER 1982, 236-242; WEVERS 1990, 595; →NIDNTT; TWNT

προστατέω   V 0-0-0-0-1-1
1 Mc 14,47

to rule, to be in charge of [τινος]

προστάτης,-ου⁺   N1M 0-5-0-0-3-8
1 Chr 27,31; 29,6; 2 Chr 8,10; 24,11(bis)

head, chief 1 Chr 29,6; *superintendent* 1 Chr 27,31; *officer* 2 Chr 8,10; *governor* (of a place) 1 Ezr 2,8

Cf. HORSLEY 1987, 242.244

προστίθημι⁺   V 75-100-36-50-45-306
Gn 4,2.12; 8,12.21(bis)

A: *to put* [τι] Lv 19,14; *to put sb with sb* [τινα μετά τινος] 1 Sm 15,6

to add, to increase [abs.] Sir 18,6; *to add to* [ἐπί τινι] 2 Chr 28,13; *id.* [ἐπί τι] Nm 32,14; *id.* [πρός τι] Dt 4,2; *id.* [τινι] Dt 1,11; *id.* [ἐπί τινα] Ps 113(114),22; *to add sb to sb* [τινά τινι] Gn 30,24; *to join sb to sb* [τινα πρός τινα] (through death, semit.) 2 Kgs 22,20; *to add sth to sth* [τι ἐπί τι] Lv 5,16; *id.* [τι ἐπί τινι] Sir 3,27

to bring upon [τί τινι] Lv 26,21; *id.* [τι ἐπί τινα] Neh 13,18; *to spend more money* Ex 30,15; *to advance beyond* [παρά τινα] Eccl 2,9 *to continue, to repeat* (semit.) Gn 25,1; *id.* [+inf.] (semit.) Gn 4,2

M: *to add to, to increase* Ez 23,14; *to continue, to repeat* Nm 11,25; *to attach oneself to sb* Dt 23,16

P: *to be added to, to be joined to* [πρός τινα] (through death, semit.) Gn 25,8; *id.* [εἴς τι] Nm 36,3; *to be imposed upon* [τινι] 1 Ezr 7,6; *to be joined with, to associate with* [πρός τινα] Nm 18,4; *id.* [μετά τινος] Ex 23,2; *id.* [ἐπί τινος] Est 9,27; *id.* [τινι] Dn^Th 4,36; *to be repeated* Ex 11,6

μὴ προστίθεσθε καρδίαν *set not your heart upon it* Ps 61(62),11; προσέθετο λαλῆσαι *he spoke again* (semit.) Is 7,10; μὴ προσθῇς ἔτι λαλῆσαι *do not speak any more* (semit.) Dt 3,26

*Zech 14,17 προστεθήσονται *they shall be added* -נגשׁם ◊נגשׁ (*to add*) for MT הַגֶּשֶׁם *the rain*; *Ps 68(69),27 προσέθηκαν *they have added* -יספו or -ספחו ◊ספח for MT יספרו *they tell*; *Jb 32,13 προσθέμενοι *we have added* -יספנו for MT ידפנו ◊נדף *he will scatter us*?

Cf. DOGNIEZ 1992, 226; DORIVAL 1994, 366; GEHMAN 1953, 144-145; 1974, 229-232; HARL 1984^a=1992^a, 39; 1986^a, 70.78.113.207.315; HELBING 1928, 300-302; WEVERS 1990, 62.159.216.359; 1995, 64(Dt 3,26).229(Dt 13,5); →NIDNTT; TWNT

πρόστιμον,-ου⁺   N2N 0-0-0-0-1-1
2 Mc 7,36
penalty, fine

προστρέχω⁺   V 3-0-0-1-2-6
Gn 18,2; 33,4; Nm 11,27; Prv 18,10; Tob^BA 11,9
to run forth Nm 11,27; *to run to* [τινι] Tob^BA
11,10
Cf. HELBING 1928, 302; →TWNT

προσυπομιμνήσκω   V 0-0-0-0-1-1
2 Mc 15,9
to recall, to bear in mind [τινά τι]; neol.?
Cf. HELBING 1928, 49

προσυστέλλομαι   V 0-0-0-0-1-1
3 Mc 2,29
to be reduced to a former state; neol.

προσυψόω   V 0-0-0-0-1-1
1 Mc 12,36
to raise higher [τι]; neol.

πρόσφατος,-ος,-ον⁺   A 2-0-0-2-2-6
Nm 6,3; Dt 32,17; Ps 80(81),10; Eccl 1,9; Od
2,17
new Eccl 1,9; *new, recent* Dt 32,17; *fresh* (of
fruit) Nm 6,3
Cf. DOGNIEZ 1992, 49.330; →TWNT

προσφάτως⁺   D 1-0-1-0-3-5
Dt 24,5; Ez 11,3; Jdt 4,3.5; 2 Mc 14,36
recently, newly
→TWNT

προσφέρω⁺   V 109-11-8-7-26-161
Gn 4,7; 27,31; 43,26; Ex 29,3; 32,6
A: *to bring to* or *upon, to offer* Gn 4,7; *id.* [τί
τινι] Gn 27,31; *id.* [τι] Ex 29,3; *id.* [τι πρός
τινα] Lv 2,8(secundo); *to approach to* [τί τινι]
4 Mc 11,19; *to use for* [τι πρός τι] Prv 6,8b
M: *to bring, to bestow* [τι] Sir prol.,30; *to bring*
[τινα] LtJ 40; *to report to* [τινι +inf.] 3 Mc
4,17; *to take* (food) Wis 16,21
Cf. DANIEL 1966, 122.151.167; DORIVAL 1994,
53.248.249-250.332.353.491; HARL 1986ᵃ, 115; HELBING
1928, 302; LARCHER 1985, 930; WEVERS 1990, 594; →TWNT

προσφιλής,-ής,-ές⁺   A 0-0-0-1-2-3
Est 5,1b; Sir 4,7; 20,13
beloved (of pers.) Sir 4,7; *cheerful* Est 5,1b
Cf. WALTERS 1973, 46

προσφορά,-ᾶς⁺   N1F 0-1-0-4-11-16
1 Kgs 7,34(48); Ps 39(40),7; Dn 3,38; Dn^LXX
4,37b(34)
presenting, offering 1 Kgs 7,34(48); *gift, offering*
Ps 39(40),7
Cf. DANIEL 1966, 122.129.130.151.152.173.219-222;
WEVERS 1990, 405; →NIDNTT; TWNT

προσφύω   V 0-0-0-1-0-1
Dn^LXX 7,20

to grow upon or *to*

προσφωνέω⁺   V 0-0-0-0-4-4
1 Ezr 2,16; 6,6.21; 2 Mc 15,15
A: *to speak to* [τινι] 1 Ezr 2,16; *to speak* [τι]
2 Mc 15,15
P: *to be signified* 1 Ezr 6,6

προσχαίρω⁺   V 0-0-0-1-0-1
Prv 8,30
to rejoice at [τινι]; neol.

προσχέω   V 17-5-1-0-0-23
Ex 24,6; 29,16.21(20); Lv 1,5.11
to pour, to pour out
Cf. WEVERS 1990, 382; 1995, 222

προσχράομαι   V 0-0-0-1-0-1
Est 8,12r
to put to use [τινι]
Cf. HELBING 1928, 253

πρόσχωμα,-ατος   N3N 0-2-0-1-0-3
2 Sm 20,15; 2 Kgs 19,32; Dn^Th 11,15
mound (raised for attacking a city)

προσχωρέω   V 0-2-1-0-1-4
1 Chr 12,20.21; Jer 21,9; 1 Mc 10,26
to go over to, to side with, to desert to [τινι]
1 Chr 12,21; *id.* [πρός τινα] 1 Chr 12,20
Cf. HELBING 1928, 302

προσωθέω   V 0-0-0-0-1-1
2 Mc 13,6
to push to [τινα εἴς τι]

προσωπεῖον,-ου   N2N 0-0-0-0-1-1
4 Mc 15,15
mask

πρόσωπον,-ου⁺   N2N 215-342-308-249-183-1297
Gn 2,6.7; 3,8.19; 4,5
face Gn 3,19; *countenance, expression* Gn 4,5
face, surface Gn 2,6; *face, front* (of pot) Jer
1,13; *foremost part* or *line of hostile army, front*
Hab 1,9; *mouth* (of well) 2 Sm 17,19; *form* (of
speech) 2 Sm 14,20; *person* Mal 1,8; *the presence
of* [τινος] Gn 27,30
ἐκ τοῦ ἑνὸς προσώπου *from one side* (semit.)
Ex 25,37; κατὰ πρόσωπον *on* (his) *forehead* Lv
13,41; *personally* Dt 7,10
often used as part of an expression rendering
semiprepositions with פנים (semit.): ἐπὶ
πρόσωπόν τινος *in front of* Ex 16,14; ἀπὸ
προσώπου τινός *from* (the face of) Ex 14,25; *on
account of, because of* Hos 10,15; *confronted by*
Na 1,6; κατὰ πρόσωπόν τινος *facing, fronting,
in front of* Gn 33,18; πρό προσώπου τινός
before sb Ex 33,2; κατὰ πρόσωπόν τινος *against*

sb Dt 7,24

πρόσωπον κατὰ πρόσωπον λαλέω *to speak face to face* Dt 5,4; μὴ ἀποστρέψῃς τὸ πρόσωπόν σου *do not reject my prayer* 1 Kgs 2,20, cpr. Mi 3,4; ἄρτοι τοῦ προσώπου *the bread placed before (the Lord)* 1 Sm 21,7, cpr. ἐνώπιος, πρόθεσις; οὐ θαυμάζει πρόσωπον *he does not show favour, he is not partial* Dt 10,17, cpr. Gn 32,21; Lv 19,15; Dt 28,50; ἠλλοίωσεν τὸ πρόσωπον *he changed countenance* 1 Sm 21,14

*JgsᴮB 20,2 κατὰ πρόσωπον *before* -פני for MT פנות *chiefs?*; *Jer 47(40),9 ἀπὸ προσώπου τῶν παίδων *before the servants, because of the servants* -מעברי for MT מעבר *to serve*, cpr. 2 Kgs 25,24

Cf. DANIEL 1966, 150.152; DOGNIEZ 1992, 55-56.163.184.318; GHIRON-BISTAGNE 1983, 155-174; HARL 1984ᵃ=1992ᵃ, 39; 1986ᵃ, 54.241; LE BOULLUEC 1989, 264; LEE, J. 1983, 51; SOLLAMO 1979, 13-122; VAN ROMPAY 1976, 569-575; →NIDNTT, TWNT

προτάσσω⁺ V 0-0-0-0-1-1
2 Mc 8,36
P: *to be ordained, to be fixed, to be determined* (of laws)

προτείνω⁺ V 0-0-0-0-7-7
2 Mc 3,20; 7,10; 14,33.34; 15,12
to hold up, to stretch forth (hands) [τι]

προτείχισμα,-ατος N3N 0-3-4-2-0-9
2 Sm 20,15; 1 Kgs 20(21),23; 2 Chr 32,5; Jer 52,7; Ez 40,5
advanced fortification, outwork, wall 2 Sm 20,15
*Ez 48,15 προτείχισμα *outwork, wall* -חל for MT חל *profane*, see also Ez 42,20
neol.

προτέρημα,-ατος N3N 0-2-0-0-0-2
Jgs 4,9
advantage gained, success; neol.?

πρότερον D 3-3-5-1-12-24
Gn 26,1; Lv 5,8; Dt 2,12; 1 Kgs 13,6; 1 Chr 9,2
before, earlier Lv 5,8; *formerly, in earlier times* Gn 26,1
→NIDNTT

πρότερος,-α,-ον⁺ A 24-12-13-5-35-89
Gn 13,3; 28,19; 38,28; 40,13; Ex 10,14
former, earlier Dt 4,32; *before* [τινος] (time) Sir 1,4; *first in time, at the start* 1 Mc 8,24; *before* [τινος] (place) Ex 23,28; *before, in front of* [τινος] (place) Ex 33,19; *first, ahead of* [τινος] (place) Nm 10,33; *superior* Wis 7,29; τὸ πρότερον *before* Gn 13,3

Cf. DORIVAL 1994, 540; LE BOULLUEC 1989, 334-335; WEVERS 1990, 153.540

προτίθημι⁺ V 4-0-0-4-4-12
Ex 29,23; 40,4.23; Lv 24,8; Ps 53(54),5
A: *to set forth, to set before* [τι] Ex 40,4
M: *id.* [τι] (metaph.) Ps 100(101),3; *to aim for, to put first* [τινα] Ps 53(54),5; *to propose* [+inf.] 3 Mc 2,27
P: *to be set before* Ex 29,23; *to be uttered* Prv 29,24

Cf. DANIEL 1966, 153; PELLETIER 1960, 967; →TWNT

προτιμάω V 0-0-0-0-2-2
2 Mc 15,2; 4 Mc 1,15
A: *to prefer* [τι] 4 Mc 1,15
P: *to be honoured above others* 2 Mc 15,2

προτομή,-ῆς N1F 0-1-0-0-1-2
1 Kgs 10,19; 2 Mc 15,35
head and face of a decapitated person 2 Mc 15,35; *head in relief* (in archit.) 1 Kgs 10,19

Cf. DREW-BEAR 1972, 215-216

προτρέπω⁺ V 0-0-0-0-5-5
2 Mc 11,7; 4 Mc 12,7; 15,12; 16,13; Wis 14,18
M: *to encourage* [τινα] 4 Mc 12,7; *to exhort* [τινα] 2 Mc 11,7

Cf. SPICQ 1978ᵃ, 762-764

προτρέχω⁺ V 0-1-0-0-3-4
1 Sm 8,11; Tob 11,3; 1 Mc 16,21
to run before, to run ahead [τινος] 1 Sm 8,11; *id.* [ἔμπροσθέν τινος] TobᴮA 11,3; *id.* [abs.] 1 Mc 16,21

Cf. HELBING 1928, 188; →TWNT

προϋπάρχω⁺ V 0-0-0-1-0-1
Jb 42,17b
to be before, to exist before

προϋποτάσσω V 0-0-0-0-1-1
3 Mc 1,2
P: *to be assigned to, to be committed to* [τινι]; neol.

προϋφίσταμαι V 0-0-0-0-1-1
Wis 19,7
M: *to be previously present*; neol.

προφαίνω V 0-0-0-0-2-2
2 Mc 3,26; 4 Mc 4,10
to appear 4 Mc 4,10; *to appear before* [τινι] 2 Mc 3,26

προφανῶς D 0-0-0-0-1-1
Sir 51,13
in a conspicuous or *extraordinary fashion*

προφασίζομαι V 0-1-0-2-0-3
2 Kgs 5,7; Ps 140(141),4; Prv 22,13

to allege a pretext, to make excuses [abs.] Prv
22,13; *id.* [τινα] 2 Kgs 5,7
προφασίζεσθαι προφάσεις *to employ pretexts*
Ps 140(141),4

πρόφασις,-εως⁺   N3F 0-0-1-5-0-6
Hos 10,4; Ps 140(141),4; Prv 18,1; Dn^Th 6,5(bis)
pretext Dn^Th 6,5

*Hos 10,4 προφάσεις *pretexts* -עֶלֹות (Aram., see
Dn^Th 6,5) for MT אֱלֹות *curses;* *Prv 18,1 προφάσεις *excuses* -תַאֲנָה for MT תֹּאֲוָה *desire*
     Cf. Spicq 1978ᵃ, 765-767

προφασιστικός,-ή,-όν   A 2-0-0-0-0-2
Dt 22,14.17
reproachfully accusing, falsely accusing; neol.
     Cf. Caird 1969=1972, 143; Dogniez 1992, 64.66.255;
     Wevers 1995, 354

προφέρω⁺   V 0-0-0-1-5-6
Prv 10,13; Tob^BA 9,5; 3 Mc 1,12; 5,39; 7,4
A: *to bring out, to produce* [τι] Prv 10,13
M: *to plead, to insist* 3 Mc 1,12; *to urge* [+inf.]
3 Mc 7,4

προφητεία,-ας⁺   N1F 0-2-1-2-9-14
2 Chr 15,8; 32,32; Jer 23,31; Dn^LXX 11,14; Neh
6,12
prophecy 2 Chr 15,8; *gift of prophecy* Sir 24,33
ὁ νόμος καὶ αἱ προφητεῖαι καὶ τὰ λοιπὰ
τῶν βιβλίων *the Law, the Prophecies and the
rest of the books* Sir prol.,24
→NIDNTT; TWNT

προφητεύω⁺   V 3-18-88-1-7-117
Nm 11,25.26.27; 1 Sm 10,5.6
stereotype transl. of נבא; *to prophesy* [abs.] Nm
11,25; *id.* [τι] Wis 14,28; *id.* [τί τινι] 1 Kgs
22,18; *id.* [τινι] Jer 14,16; *id.* [περί τινος]
2 Chr 18,7; *id.* [τι περί τινος] 2 Chr 18,17
     Cf. Larcher 1985, 839; →NIDNTT; TWNT

προφήτης,-ου⁺   N1M 15- 138-106-22-47-328
Gn 20,7; Ex 7,1; Nm 11,29; 12,6; Dt 13,2
almost always transl. of נביא; *prophet, spokesman
of God* Ex 7,1; τῶν προφητῶν *of (the books of)
the prophets* Sir prol.,9
     Cf. Dogniez 1992, 50.199; Fascher 1927, 1-228;
     Larcher 1984, 509-512; Lipiński 1975, 556; Vawter
     1985, 206-219; →NIDNTT; TWNT

προφῆτις,-ιδος⁺   N3F 1-4-1-0-0-6
Ex 15,20; Jgs 4,4; 2 Kgs 22,14; 2 Chr 34,22
fem. of προφήτης; *prophetess*
→NIDNTT; TWNT

προφθάνω⁺   V 0-4-1-12-3-20
1 Sm 20,25; 2 Sm 22,6.19; 2 Kgs 19,32; Jon 4,2

to outrun [τινα] 1 Mc 10,23; *to come upon, to
prevent* [τινα] 2 Sm 22,6; *to take advantage of*
[τινα] Sir 19,27; *to approach, to come near to*
[τι] Ps 94(95),2; *to extend in front* [τι] Ps
67(68),32; *to act with foresight* or *in anticipation*
Jon 4,2

*1 Sm 20,25 καὶ προέφθασε *and he prevented?*
-ויקרם for MT ויקם *and he rose up* or *and he stood*
     Cf. Helbing 1928, 104-105

προφυλακή,-ῆς   N1F 3-0-3-3-3-12
Ex 12,42(bis); Nm 32,17; Ez 26,8; 38,7
advance guard, sentry-party, outpost Nm 32,17;
vigil, watch Ex 12,42; *guarding, serving as sentries*
Ezr 14,16
     Cf. Dorival 1994, 71; Le Boulluec 1989, 154(Ex 12,42);
     Wevers 1990, 190(Ex 12,42)

προφύλαξ,-ακος   N3M 0-0-0-2-1-3
Neh 4,3; 7,3; 1 Mc 12,27
sentinel, advance guard

προφυλάσσω⁺   V 0-1-0-0-0-1
2 Sm 22,24
M: *to guard oneself against, to keep oneself from*
[ἀπό τινος]
     Cf. Helbing 1928, 30

προχαλάω   V 0-0-0-0-1-1
4 Mc 10,19
P: *to be loosed beforehand, to be extended, to be
put out* (of tongue); neol.

προχειρίζω⁺   V 1-1-0-1-3-6
Ex 4,13; Jos 3,12; Dn^LXX 3,22; 2 Mc 3,7; 8,9
M: *to choose, to select* [τινα] Jos 3,12; *to
appoint* [τινα] Ex 4,13
P: *to be appointed* Dn^LXX 3,22
     Cf. Spicq 1978ᵃ, 768-770; →NIDNTT; TWNT

πρόχειρος,-ος,-ον   A 0-0-0-1-0-1
Prv 11,3
at hand, speedy

προχώρημα,-ατος   N3N 0-0-1-0-0-1
Ez 32,6
excrement; neol.

πρύτανις,-εως   N3M 0-0-0-0-1-1
Wis 13,2
master, lord
     Cf. Gilbert 1973, 7.17-19; Larcher 1985, 758-759;
     Robert 1960, 316-324

πρώην   D 0-1-0-0-0-1
Jos 8,5
the day before yesterday, in the past

πρωί⁺   D 68-63-27-26-10-194
Gn 1,5.8.13.19.23

in Rahlfs always without dieresis; *in the morning,
early* Gn 24,54; *morning* (as subst.) Gn 1,5; τὸ
πρωί *early* Gn 19,27; *in the morning* 1 Chr 16,40
εἰς τὸ πρωί *until morning* Ex 16,19; πρωὶ πρωί
every morning (semit.) Ex 16,21
*Lv 24,4 ἕως τὸ πρωί *until morning* עד בקר
(=Sam. Pent.) for MT תמיד*always*; *1 Sm 11,5 τὸ
πρωί *early morning* -הַבֹּקֶר for MT הַבָּקָר *the oxen,* see
also 2 Chr 35,12; *2 Kgs 16,15 εἰς τὸ πρωί *in
the morning* -לַבֹּקֶר for MT לְבַקֵּר *to inquire;*
*Jer 31(48),33 πρωί *in the morning* השׁבכם? for MT
השׁבתי *I have stopped*

Cf. DOGNIEZ 1992, 189; HARL 1986ᵃ, 88; LE BOULLUEC
1989, 185; WALTERS 1973, 93.292.300-301

πρωία,-ας⁺   N1F 0-1-0-8-2-11
2 Sm 23,4; Ps 64(65),9; 72(73),14; 100(101),8;
129(130),6
in Rahlfs always without dieresis; *early morning*
Cf. WALTERS 1973, 93.300-301

πρωίθεν⁺   D 2-3-0-2-3-10
Ex 18,13.14; 2 Sm 2,27; 24,15; 1 Kgs 18,26
in Rahlfs always without dieresis; *from the
morning* (always in combination with ἀπό or ἐκ)
Cf. WALTERS 1973, 93

πρωινός,-ή,-όν⁺   A 4-3-2-1-2-12
Gn 49,27; Ex 29,41; Lv 9,17; Nm 28,23; 1 Sm
11,11
in Rahlfs always without dieresis; *early, belonging
to the morning, morning* Ex 29,41; τὸ πρωινόν
in the morning Gn 49,27; neol.?
Cf. LEE, J. 1983, 110; SHIPP 1979, 427-428.475; WALTERS
1973, 75-76.93

πρωρεύς,-έως   N3M 0-0-2-0-0-2
Ez 27,29; Jon 1,6
officer in command at the bow (of a ship)
Cf. WALTERS 1973, 69

πρωταγωνιστής,-οῦ   N1M 0-0-0-0-2-2
1 Mc 9,11; 2 Mc 15,30
protagonist, leader, foremost fighter

πρώταρχος,-ος,-ον   A 0-0-0-0-1-1
2 Mc 10,11
primal; στρατηγὸν πρώταρχον *supreme governor*

πρωτεύω⁺   V 0-0-0-1-2-3
Est 5,11; 2 Mc 6,18; 13,15
to take precedence, to have the first place Est
5,11; *to be the first among* [τινος] 2 Mc 13,15
Cf. HORSLEY 1982, 96; 1987, 172

πρωτοβαθρέω   V 0-0-0-1-0-1
Est 3,1
to assume the first seat among [τινος]; neol.

πρωτοβολέω   V 0-0-1-0-0-1
Ez 47,12
to bring forth new fruit; neol.

πρωτογένημα,-ατος   N3N 9-1-2-2-3-17
Ex 23,16.19; 34,26; Lv 2,14(bis)
feast of the first-fruits Lv 23,19; τὰ πρωτο-
γενήματα *first-fruits* Ex 23,16
Cf. DORIVAL 1994, 500-501; HARLÉ 1988, 190; WALTERS
1973, 115-117.162

πρωτογενής,-ής,-ές   A 1-0-0-1-0-2
Ex 13,2; Prv 31,2
first-born; see πρωτόγονος, πρωτότοκος
Cf. LE BOULLUEC 1989, 155; WEVERS 1990, 195

πρωτόγονος,-ος,-ον   A 0-0-1-0-1-2
Mi 7,1; Sir 36,11
first-born; πρωτόγονος *first-born* (as subst.) Sir
36,11; τὰ πρωτόγονα *first-fruits* Mi 7,1; see
πρωτογενής, πρωτότοκος

πρωτοκλίσια,-ων   N2N 0-0-0-0-1-1
2 Mc 4,21
festival on a king's proclamation (read
πρωτοκλήσια); neol.
Cf. WALTERS 1973, 48-49; →NIDNTT; TWNT

πρωτοκουρία,-ας   N1F 0-0-0-0-2-2
Tob 1,6
first-shearing; neol.

πρωτολογία,-ας   N1F 0-0-0-1-0-1
Prv 18,17
prosecutor's part (right of speaking first in a
law-court)

πρῶτον   D 1-0-2-0-6-9
1 Ki 2,16; Is 8,23; 11,14; Tobᴮᴬ 4,12; 2 Mc 14,8
first

πρωτόπλαστος,-ος,-ον   A 0-0-0-0-2-2
Wis 7,1; 10,1
first-formed, first-created; neol.
Cf. LARCHER 1984, 444

πρῶτος,-η,-ον⁺   A 45-59-26-46-47-223
Gn 8,5.13; 32,18.20; 33,2
first (order) Ex 34,1; *first* (time) Gn 8,13; *former*
Ezr 3,12; *found in front, foremost* (place) Jl 2,20;
first, foremost, important (degree) Ez 27,22; ἡ
πρώτη *the first day* Gn 8,5
ἐν πρώτοις *first, at first, in the beginning* Gn
33,2; *among the first, among the important ones*
1 Sm 9,22
*1 Chr 27,33 πρῶτος *first, main, chief* (friend)
-הארכי read as ἀρχι-? (ἀρχιεταῖρος in L) for MT
(רע) הארכי *the Archite (the friend of)*; *Dnᴸˣˣ 10,21
τὰ πρῶτα *the first* -הרישׁנים or הראשׁנים for MT הרשׁום

that which is prescribed
→NIDNTT; TWNT

πρωτοστάτης,-ου⁺   N1M 0-0-0-1-0-1
Jb 15,24
*one who stands first, one who stands in the first
rank*
Cf. HORSLEY 1987, 244

πρωτοτοκεύω   V 1-0-0-0-0-1
Dt 21,16
*to invest with the privilege of primogeniture, to
treat as first-born*; neol.
Cf. DOGNIEZ 1992, 64.246; LEE, J. 1983, 52; WALTERS
1973, 52

πρωτοτοκέω   V 0-2-1-0-0-3
1 Sm 6,7.10; Jer 4,31
to bring forth her first child Jer 4,31; *to calve for
the first time* 1 Sm 6,7; neol.
Cf. WALTERS 1973, 52-53

πρωτοτόκια,-ων⁺   N2N 6-1-0-0-0-7
Gn 25,31.32.33.34; 27,36
*the birthright of the first-born, right of
primogeniture*; neol.
Cf. WALTERS 1973, 52.287; →TWNT

πρωτότοκος,-ος,-ον⁺   A 75-42-4-7-5-133
Gn 4,4; 10,15; 22,21; 25,13.25
most frequently transl. of בכר; *first-born* (of pers.)
Gn 10,15; *id.* (of anim.) Gn 4,4; *first-born* (of
Israel in a transferred sense, expressing a close
relationship to the Lord) Ex 4,22; *highest in
rank, chief* (of Israel's king) Ps 88(89),28; τὰ
πρωτότοκα *the first-born* (as well of pers. as of
anim.) Nm 18,15
*1 Chr 8,38 πρωτότοκος αὐτοῦ *his first-born*
-בְּכֹרוֹ for MT בִּכְרוֹ *Bocheru*, see also 9,44;
*1 Chr 26,6 τοῦ πρωτοτόκου Ρωσαι *of his first-
born Rosai* transl.? for MT הממשלים *chiefs* followed by translit. of its syn. ראשי (not in MT)
heads (of)
neol.; see πρωτογενής, πρωτόγονος
Cf. DOGNIEZ 1992, 213; FREY 1930, 385-390; HARL 1986ª,
57.210; LE BOULLUEC 1989, 155.231; MICHAELIS 1954ᵇ,
313-320; SPICQ 1978ª, 771-773; WALTERS 1973, 52-53.126;
→NIDNTT; TWNT

πταῖσμα,-ατος   N3N 0-1-0-0-0-1
1 Sm 6,4
mistake, error, fault, offence

πταίω   V 1-11-0-0-3-15
Dt 7,25; 1 Sm 4,2.3.10; 7,10
to cause to fall [τινα] 1 Sm 4,3; *to fall* 1 Sm 4,2;
to stumble, to fall Dt 7,25; *to be defeated* 2 Mc

14,17; *to fail* Sir 2,8
Cf. DOGNIEZ 1992, 167; HELBING 1928, 79; →NIDNTT;
TWNT

πταρμός,-οῦ   N2M 0-0-0-1-0-1
Jb 41,10
sneezing

πτέρνα,-ης⁺   N1F 3-3-2-3-1-12
Gn 3,15; 25,26; 49,17; Jos 23,13; Jgsᴬ 5,22
heel Gn 3,15; *hoof* Gn 49,17; *footstep* Ct 1,8

πτερνίζω   V 1-0-6-0-0-7
Gn 27,36; Jer 9,3; Hos 12,4; Mal 3,8(bis)
to go behind the back of sb to deceive, to outwit
(metaph. meaning of *to bite the heel of sb*; from
wrestling) Jer 9,3; *id.* [τινα] Gn 27,36
*Mal 3,8 εἰ πτερνιεῖ *does one go behind the
back of, does one deceive* -יעקב עקב◊ for MT היקבע
◊קבע *does one rob*, see also Mal 3,9
Cf. CAIRD 1969=1972, 143-144; HARL 1984ª=1992ª, 42;
1986ª, 80.218-219; MURAOKA 1986ª, 265-268; →LSJ RSuppl

πτερνισμός,-οῦ   N2M 0-1-0-1-0-2
2 Kgs 10,19; Ps 40(41),10
*going-behind-the back, deception, cunning
treachery* 2 Kgs 10,19
ἐμεγάλυνεν ἐπ' ἐμὲ πτερνισμόν *he magnified
his going-behind-the back against me, he gave me
a grave stab in the back, he dealt treacherously
with me* Ps 40(41),10
neol.
Cf. CAIRD 1969=1972, 143-144

πτερόν,-οῦ   N2N 1-0-0-6-0-7
Lv 1,16; Dn 7,4(bis)
feather Lv 1,16; *wing* Dn 7,4

πτεροφυέω⁺   V 0-0-1-0-0-1
Is 40,31
to put forth new feathers, to grow feathers

πτερόω
(→ἀνα-)

πτερύγιον,-ου⁺   N2N 8-9-0-1-0-18
Ex 36(39),26; Lv 11,9.10.12; Nm 15,38
wing 1 Kgs 6,24; *fin* Lv 11,9; *end, projecture* Ex
36,26; *border, flap* (of a garment) Nm 15,38
Cf. WEVERS 1990, 605; →NIDNTT

πτέρυξ,-υγος⁺   N3F 6-20-31-19-2-78
Ex 19,4; 25,20(bis); 38,8(37,9); Lv 1,17
wing Ex 19,4; *id.* (metaph. for the rays of the
sun) Mal 3,20; *id.* (metaph. of the wind) 2 Sm
22,11; *end, farthest edge, extremity* (of the earth)
Is 11,12
→LSJ Suppl; LSJ RSuppl; NIDNTT

πτερύσσομαι   V 0-0-2-0-0-2

πτερωτός,-ή/ός,-όν⁺   411   πυκνός,-ή,-όν⁺

Ez 1,23; 3,13
to flutter, to flap the wings; neol.

πτερωτός,-ή/ός,-όν⁺   A 2-0-1-3-0-6
Gn 1,21; Dt 4,17; Ez 1,7; Ps 77(78),27; 148,10
with wings, winged Gn 1,21; τὰ πτερωτά *winged*
creatures, birds Prv 1,17
*Ez 1,7 καὶ πτερωτοί *and (their feet were)*
winged -◊כנף for MT ככף *like the foot*

πτήσσω   V 1-1-0-1-3-6
Dt 1,29; 2 Kgs 19,26; Jb 38,17; 1 Mc 12,28;
3 Mc 6,13
to cower in fear Dt 1,29; *to cower for, to fear* [τι]
3 Mc 6,13
Cf. DOGNIEZ 1992, 118; HELBING 1928, 26
(→κατα-)

πτίλος,-η,-ον   A 1-0-0-0-0-1
Lv 21,20
suffering from disease of the eyelids, inflamed,
infected (of the eyelids); neol.

πτοέω⁺   V 2-6-20-4-5-37
Ex 19,16; Dt 31,6; Jos 7,5; 1 Chr 22,13; 28,20
A: *to terrify, to scare, to dismay* [τινα] Prv 13,3
P: *to tremble* Hab 3,7; *to be terrified, to tremble*
Ex 19,16; *to tremble at* [τι] Is 31,4; *to tremble, to*
be useless (of a bow) Jer 28(51),56
*Ez 2,5 πτοηθῶσιν *they tremble* -◊רחל (Aram.)
for MT ◊חרל *they do not (listen)*, see also 2,7
Cf. HELBING 1928, 27; LE BOULLUEC 1989, 202

πτοή,-ῆς   N1F 0-0-0-0-2-2
1 Mc 3,25; 3 Mc 6,17
fear, terror; neol.

πτόησις,-εως⁺   N3F 0-0-0-1-0-1
Prv 3,25
terrifying, intimidation, alarm

πτύελος,-ου   N2M 0-0-0-2-0-2
Jb 7,19; 30,10
saliva, spittle

πτύσσω
(→ἀνα-)

πτύξις,-εως   N3F 0-0-0-1-0-1
Jb 41,5
fold (of clothing)

πτυχή,-ῆς   N1F 0-2-0-0-0-2
1 Kgs 6,34(bis)
panel (of a door)

πτύω⁺   V 1-0-0-0-1-2
Nm 12,14; Sir 28,12
to spit
(→ἀπο-, ἐμ-, προ-)

πτῶμα,-ατος⁺   N3N 0-2-4-10-7-23

Jgs 14,8; Is 8,14; 30,13.14
fall Jdt 8,19; *disaster, misfortune* Is 8,14; *fallen*
body, corpse, carcass Jgs 14,8
*Jb 15,23 εἰς πτῶμα *to be a carcass* -ב/איר or
-ב/פיר for MT ב/ירו *in his hand?*; *Jb 33,17 ἀπὸ
πτώματος *from a fall* -מ/שבר for MT מ/גבר *from*
man
Cf. HORSLEY 1987, 8; →NIDNTT

πτῶσις,-εως⁺   N3F 1-1-17-2-16-37
Ex 30,12; Jgsᴮ 20,39; Is 17,1; 51,17.22
falling, fall Jgsᴮ 20,39; *destruction, calamity* Ex
30,12
→NIDNTT

πτωχεία,-ας⁺   N1F 1-1-1-9-7-19
Dt 8,9; 1 Chr 22,14; Is 48,10; Ps 30(31),11;
43(44),25
(extreme) poverty Dt 8,9; *low estate* 1 Chr 22,14
→LSJ Suppl; NIDNTT; TWNT

πτωχεύω⁺   V 0-3-0-3-2-8
Jgs 6,6; Jgsᴬ 14,15; Ps 33(34),11; 78(79),8
to become poor or *impoverished*
→NIDNTT; TWNT

πτωχίζω⁺   V 0-1-0-0-1-2
1 Sm 2,7; Od 3,7
to make poor; neol.

πτωχός,-ή,-όν⁺   A 5-4-21-62-32-124
Ex 23,11; Lv 19,10.15; 23,22; Dt 24,19
materially poor, needy Ex 23,11
*Is 25,3 πτωχός *poor* -עני? for MT עז *strong*
Cf. HARL 1960=1992ᵃ, 205; HATCH 1889, 73-77; LIAÑO
1966, 117-167; NÚÑEZ 1966, 193-205; SHIPP 1979, 446;
→NIDNTT; TWNT

πύγαργος,-ου   N2M 1-0-0-0-0-1
Dt 14,5
white-rump (kind of antilope)

πυγμή,-ῆς⁺   N1F 1-0-1-0-0-2
Ex 21,18; Is 58,4
fist
→NIDNTT; TWNT

πυθμήν,-ένος   N3M 4-0-0-2-0-6
Gn 40,10.12; 41,5.22; Prv 14,12
stem, stalk Gn 40,10; *depth, bottom* Prv 14,12

πυκάζω   V 0-0-1-2-1-4
Hos 14,9; Ps 117(118),27; Jb 15,32; 3 Mc 4,5
A: *to overshadow, to protect* Hos 14,9; *to deck*
with branches or *garlands* Ps 117(118),27; *to be*
thick, to flourish (of branches) Jb 15,32
P: *to be covered* 3 Mc 4,5

πυκνός,-ή,-όν⁺   A 0-0-0-0-3-3
3 Mc 1,28; 4,10; 4 Mc 12,12

incessant 3 Mc 1,28; *compact, strong, thick* 3 Mc 4,10; *rapid* 4 Mc 12,12

πυκνότερον D 0-0-0-1-3-4
Est 8,12c; 2 Mc 8,8; 3 Mc 4,12; 7,3
often, frequently

πύλη,-ης⁺ N1F 23-88-153-76-33-373
Gn 19,1; 28,17; 34,20.24; 38,14
gate (of a town) Gn 19,1; *id.* (of a camp) Ex 32,26; *id.* (of a prison) Ps 106(107),16; *door* Ex 27,16; *gate* (consisting of two wings, doors) 1 Sm 21,14; *gate, gate-house, gateway* Ez 8,3; *opening, entrance* (of a womb) Jb 3,10; *gate* (metaph.) Ps 117(118),19; αἱ πύλαι *gates* Gn 38,14
ἐν πύλαις *in the gates, in a public place* Prv 22,22
*Ez 40,32 τὴν πύλην *the gate* -השער or corr. τὴν αὐλήν for MT החצר *the court*, see also 42,1; *2 Kgs 7,10 πρὸς τὴν πύλην *towards the gate* -אל שער for MT אל שער *to the gatekeeper*, see also 2 Sm 18,26; 1 Chr 9,18.24.26.; 26,1.12; 2 Chr 23,4; *Dnᴸˣˣ 8,2 τῇ πύλῃ (by) *the gate* -אבולא (Aram.) for MT אובל *river, canal*, see also 8,3.6
→NIDNTT; TWNT

πυλών,-ῶνος⁺ N3M 1-14-7-0-8-30
Gn 43,19; Jgsᴬ 18,16.17; 19,26; 1 Kgs 6,8
porch Gn 43,19; *porch, gate* Jgsᴬ 18,16
Cf. HARL 1986ᵃ, 284; HUSSON 1983ᵃ, 244; LEE, J. 1983, 108; →TWNT

πυλωρός,-οῦ N2M 0-13-0-17-0-30
1 Chr 9,17.21; 15,18.23.24
gate-keeper, warder, porter Neh 7,1; *doorkeeper* (for the ark) 1 Chr 15,23
*Neh 12,25 τοὺς πυλωρούς *the doorkeepers* -השערים for MT השערים *the gates*, see also 12,30; Jb 38,17

πυνθάνομαι⁺ V 1-2-0-3-7-13
Gn 25,22; 2 Chr 31,9; 32,31; Est 3,13c; 6,4
to inquire, to ask, to inform 2 Mc 3,9; *to inquire of, to learn from* [τινος] 2 Chr 31,9; *id.* [παρά τινος] Gn 25,22
Cf. HELBING 1928, 158-159

πυξίον,-ου N2N 1-0-2-1-0-4
Ex 24,12; Is 30,8; Hab 2,2; Ct 5,14
tablet (in class. Greek always of (box-)wood, in the LXX also of stone, of ivory) Ct 5,14
τὰ πυξία τὰ λίθινα *the tablets of stone* Ex 24,12
Cf. LE BOULLUEC 1989, 247

πύξος,-ου N2F 0-0-1-0-0-1
Is 41,19

boxwood tree

πῦρ,-ός⁺ N3N 107-83-146-100-104-540
Gn 11,3; 15,17; 19,24; 22,6.7
fire 4 Mc 15,15; *id.* (of a furnace) Gn 11,3; *offering by fire* 1 Sm 2,28; *(destructive punishing) fire* Am 1,4; *fire* (as punishment of the individual at the end of his life) 4 Mc 12,12; *fire* (accompanying the Lord's presence) Ex 3,2
εἰμι πῦρ *to be a fire, to act like fire* Ob 18; ἰσόπεδον πυρὶ καὶ δόρατι θήσεσθαι *to level with fire and sword* 3 Mc 5,43, see also Est 8,12x
*Nm 21,30 πῦρ ἐπί *a fire against* -על אש or עד-אש fire (spread) to* for MT אשר עד *which is in the neighbourhood of*; *Jer 6,23 ὡς πῦρ *as a fire* -כאש for MT כאיש *as a man* (as a man of war, as a warrior), see also Jer 27(50),42; Mi 6,10; *Am 4,10 ἐν πυρί *in fire* -בְּאֵשׁ for MT בְּאָשׁ *stench*; *Ps 57(58),9 ἐπέπεσε πῦρ *fire has fallen* -נפל אש for MT נפל אשת *miscarriage, aborted child of a woman*
Cf. DORIVAL 1994, 410-411(Nm 21,30); LE BOULLUEC 1989, 134.249; WALTERS 1973, 124-125; →NIDNTT; TWNT

πυρά,-ᾶς⁺ N1F 0-0-0-0-8-8
Jdt 7,5; 1 Mc 12,28; 2 Mc 1,22; 7,5; 10,36
pile of burning material, burning mass Jdt 7,5; *pyre* 4 Mc 17,1
→NIDNTT

πυραμίς,-ίδος N3F 0-0-0-0-1-1
1 Mc 13,28
pyramid

πυργόβαρις,-εως N3F 0-0-0-1-1-2
Ps 121(122),7; PSal 8,19
citadel, fortress; neol.
Cf. MUNNICH 1983, 78-80; WALTERS 1973, 186; WEBER 1950, 20-32; WILL 1987ᵇ, 253-259

πύργος,-ου⁺ N2M 4-28-12-16-27-87
Gn 11,4.5.8; 35,16; Jgsᴬ 8,9
tower (of a city) Gn 11,4; *tower* (in a vineyard) Is 5,2; οἱ πύργοι *city walls with their towers* Jdt 7,5
Cf. SHIPP 1979, 477-479; SPICQ 1978ᵃ, 774-779; →TWNT

πυρεῖον,-ου N2N 17-3-0-0-1-21
Ex 27,3; 38,22.23.24(1.3.4); Lv 10,1
censer
Cf. DORIVAL 1994, 49; WEVERS 1990, 432.629

πυρετός,-οῦ⁺ N2M 1-0-0-0-0-1
Dt 28,22
fever
→NIDNTT

-πυρίζω

(→ἐμ-)

πυρίκαυστος,-ος,-ον   A 0-0-3-0-0-3
Is 1,7; 9,4; 64,10
burned with fire
Cf. WALTERS 1973, 124

πύρινος,-η,-ον⁺   A 0-0-2-0-1-3
Ez 28,14.16; Sir 48,9
fiery

πυριφλεγής,-ής,-ές   A 0-0-0-0-2-2
3 Mc 3,29; Wis 18,3
flaming with fire
Cf. WALTERS 1973, 125

πυροβόλον,-ου   N2N 0-0-0-0-1-1
1 Mc 6,51
instrument for casting fire, fire-throwing catapult
Cf. WALTERS 1973, 125-126

πυρόπνους,-ους,-ουν   A 0-0-0-0-1-1
3 Mc 6,34
fire-breathing, fiery; neol.
Cf. WALTERS 1973, 125-126

πυρός,-οῦ⁺   N2M 6-12-6-7-6-37
Gn 30,14; Ex 9,32; 29,2; 34,22; Dt 8,8
wheat
Cf. CADELL 1973, 329-338; WALTERS 1973, 124-125

πυροφόρος,-ου   N2M 0-0-1-0-0-1
Ob 18
bearer of sacrificial fire, survivor?
Cf. WALTERS 1973, 125

πυρόω⁺   V 0-1-4-15-9-29
2 Sm 22,31; Is 1,25; Jer 9,6; Zech 13,9(bis)
A: to burn [τι] 4 Mc 9,17; to make red hot, to
cause to glow, to heat thoroughly [τι]
4 Mc 11,19; to try in the fire, to purge [τινα] Jdt
8,27; id. [τι] Ps 25(26),2
P: to be tried by fire (of metals) Jb 22,25; id.
(metaph.) 2 Sm 22,31; to be inflamed, to be
aflame 2 Mc 4,38
πυρώσαντες λίθους striking fire out of flints
2 Mc 10,3
→NIDNTT; TWNT
(→δια-, ἐκ-, προσ-)

πύρπνοος,-ος,-ον   A 0-0-0-0-1-1
Wis 11,18
fire-breathing
Cf. WALTERS 1973, 124.126.315

πυρπολέω   V 0-0-0-0-1-1
4 Mc 7,4
P: to be consumed by fire

πυρράκης,-ου   N1M 1-2-0-0-0-3
Gn 25,25; 1 Sm 16,12; 17,42

red or ruddy person; neol.?
Cf. HARL 1986ᵃ, 209; LEE, J. 1983, 109

πυρρίζω   V 5-0-0-0-0-5
Lv 13,19.42.43.49; 14,37
to be red, to be inflamed (of wounds, skin
diseases)
Cf. HARLÉ 1988, 137
(→ὑπο-)

πυρρός,-ά,-όν   A 2-2-3-1-0-8
Gn 25,30; Nm 19,2; 2 Kgs 3,22; 5,17; Zech 1,8
red Gn 25,30; with red hair (of pers.) Ct 5,10;
tawny (of anim.) Nm 19,2
Cf. DANIEL 1966, 173-174; SHIPP 1979, 480.559-560;
→NIDNTT; TWNT

πυρσεύω   V 0-0-0-2-0-2
Jb 20,10; Prv 16,28
to kindle, to ignite [τι] Prv 16,28; id. [τι] (of a
feeling) Jb 20,10

πυρσός,-οῦ   N2M 0-2-0-0-0-2
Jgsᴬ 20,38.40
signal-fire

πυρφόρον,-ου   N2N 0-0-0-1-0-1
Jb 41,21
flaming weapon, javelin with combustibles tied to
it
Cf. WALTERS 1973, 124-125

πυρώδης,-ης,-ες   A 0-0-0-0-1-1
Sir 43,4
fiery

πύρωσις,-εως⁺   N3F 0-0-1-1-0-2
Am 4,9; Prv 27,21
testing, proving by fire Prv 27,21; fever, inflammation, rust (disease of cereal plants) Am
4,9
→LSJ Suppl; NIDNTT; TWNT

πώγων,-ωνος   N3M 5-5-4-3-2-19
Lv 13,29.30; 14,9; 19,27; 21,5
beard

πωλέω⁺   V 3-0-6-3-4-16
Gn 41,56; 42,6; Ex 21,8; Is 24,2; Ez 7,12
to sell

πῶλος,-ου⁺   N2M 3-4-1-1-0-9
Gn 32,16; 49,11(bis); Jgs 10,4
colt of a horse Jgs 10,4; foal of an ass Gn 32,16
→TWNT

πώποτε⁺   D 0-1-0-0-4-5
1 Sm 25,28; Jdt 12,20; Susᵀʰ 27; Bel 7
ever; always with neg. part.: never

πωρόω⁺   V 0-0-0-1-0-1
Jb 17,7

to become dim (of eyes)

πῶς⁺   X 0-5-1-1-0-7
2 Sm 14,15; 16,12; 1 Kgs 18,5; 21(20),31; 2 Kgs
19,4

always in combination with εἰ or ἐάν: *somehow,
in some way*

πῶς⁺   D 17-22-29-31-30-129
Gn 39,9; 43,27; 44,8.34; Ex 6,12

how Gn 39,9; *how, with what right* (to denote
disapproval or rejection) Jer 2,23; *how*
(rhetorical question) Jb 25,4; *how!* (in
exclamation) Zph 2,15

*2 Sm 11,11 πῶς *how* - חיך - or - איך for MT חיך *your
life*

Cf. BAUER 1957=1972, 27-39

ραβδίζω⁺ V 0-2-0-1-0-3
Jgs 6,11; Ru 2,17
to thresh (by beating with a rod)
→MM; TWNT

ράβδος,-ου⁺ N2F 56-8-32-18-0-121
Gn 30,37(bis).38(bis).39
rod, staff Gn 30,37; *ruler's rod, sceptre* Ps
44(45),7; *rod* (for punishment) Prv 23,13; *id.* (for
punishment and instruction) Prv 22,15;
shepherd's staff or *crook* Ps 22(23),4; *goad, stick*
Sir 33,25; *stick for divination* Ez 21,26; *pen* (for
writing) Jgsᴮ 5,14; *young shoot, rod* Is 11,1
ράβδος χειρῶν *handstaff* Ez 39,9
*Gn 47,31 τῆς ράβδου *rod* -הַמַּטֶּה for MT הַמִּטָּה *bed*;
*Na 1,13 τὴν ράβδον αὐτοῦ *his rod* -מֹטֵהוּ? מטהו
for MT מֹשׁוּ ◊מוֹט *his yoke*; *Ps 73(74),2 ράβδος *rod*
-שֵׁבֶט for MT שֵׁבֶט *tribe* (of your inheritance)
Cf. LE BOULLUEC 1989, 218; WEVERS 1993, 533; →NIDNTT;
TWNT

ραγάς,-άδος N3F 0-0-1-0-0-1
Is 7,19
crevice, ravine; *Is 7,19 ραγάδα *ravines* -נחלים for
MT נחלים *watering-place*?

ράγμα,-ατος N3N 0-0-1-0-0-1
Am 6,11
crack, fissure, rent; neol.

ράδαμνος,-ου N2M 0-0-0-4-0-4
Jb 8,16; 14,7; 15,32; 40,22
shoot, twig, branch

ράδιος,-α,-ον A 0-0-0-0-2-2
2 Mc 2,26; 4,17
easy 2 Mc 2,26
ἀσεβεῖν ... οὐ ράδιον *to act ungodly ... is not a
light matter* 2 Mc 4,17

ραθμ N 0-1-0-0-0-1
1 Kgs 19,4
= רתם; *broom-shrub, broom-tree*

ραθυμέω⁺ V 1-0-0-0-3-4
Gn 42,1; Jdt 1,16; 2 Mc 6,4; Sir 32,11
to take one's ease Jdt 1,16; *to be remiss, to be
indolent* Gn 42,1; *to dally, to delay* Sir 32,11; *to
dally with* [μετά τινος] 2 Mc 6,4
Cf. HARL 1986ᵃ, 278-279; TOV 1979, 225

ραθυμία,-ας N1F 0-0-0-0-1-1
3 Mc 4,8
ease, relaxation, amusement
Cf. WALTERS 1973, 72

ραίνω⁺ V 11-0-2-0-0-13
Ex 29,21; Lv 4,17; 5,9; 8,11; 14,16
to sprinkle [abs.] Ex 29,21; *id.* [τι] Lv 16,15; *id.*

[τι] (metaph.) Is 45,8
→TWNT
(→δια-, περι-, προσ-)

ράκος,-ους⁺ N3N 0-0-2-1-0-3
Is 64,5; Jer 45(38),11; Est 4,17w
rag

ρακώδης,-ης,-ες A 0-0-0-1-0-1
Prv 23,21
ragged; neol.?
Cf. CAIRD 1976, 82

ράμμα,-ατος N3N 0-1-0-0-0-1
Jgsᴬ 16,12
thread

ράμνος,-ου N2F 0-5-0-1-1-7
Jgs 9,14.15(bis)
name of various prickly shrubs: bramble, thorn

ρανίς,-ίδος N3F 0-0-0-0-1-1
Wis 11,22
drop

ραντίζω⁺ V 1-1-0-1-0-3
Lv 6,20; 2 Kgs 9,33; Ps 50(51),9
A: *to sprinkle with, to purify* [τινά τινι] Ps
50(51),9
P: *to be sprinkled* 2 Kgs 9,33
neol.
Cf. DODD 1954, 84; →NIDNTT; TWNT
(→ἐπι-, περι-)

ραντισμός,-οῦ⁺ N2M 5-0-0-0-0-5
Nm 19,9.13.20.21(bis)
sprinkling; neol.
→MM; NIDNTT; TWNT

ραντός,-ή,-όν A 7-0-0-0-0-7
Gn 30,32.33.35(bis).39
sprinkled, speckled, spotted
Cf. HARL 1986ᵃ, 232-233; →MM

ραπίζω⁺ V 0-1-1-0-1-3
Jgsᴮ 16,25; Hos 11,4; 1 Ezr 4,30
to strike, to thrash [τινα] Jgsᴮ 16,25
ραπίζω ἐπὶ τὰς σιαγόνας τινός *to smite sb on
the cheeks, to slap in the face* Hos 11,4; ραπίζω
τινὰ τῇ ἀριστερᾷ *to strike sb with the left hand*
1 Ezr 4,30
→MM

ράπισμα,-ατος⁺ N3N 0-0-1-0-0-1
Is 50,6
stroke, blow (with the palm of the hand); neol.
→MM

ραπτός,-ή,-όν A 0-0-1-0-0-1
Ez 16,16
patched, stitched, of needle-work

ράπτω   V 1-0-0-2-0-3
Gn 3,7; Jb 16,15; Eccl 3,7
to sew [abs.] Eccl 3,7; *to sew together* [τι] Gn
3,7; *to sew sth on sth* [τι ἐπί τινος] Jb 16,15
Cf. CAIRD 1976, 82
(→συρ-, ὑπο-)

ράσσω⁺   V 0-0-4-3-2-9
Is 9,10; 13,16; Jer 23,33.39; Dnᴸˣˣ 8,10
to strike, to dash, to throw down [τι] Jdt 9,8; *to
overthrow* [τινα] Is 9,10; *to strike, to beat* [τινα]
Wis 4,19
Cf. LARCHER 1984, 348

ραφιδευτής,-οῦ   N1M 1-0-0-0-0-1
Ex 27,16
stitcher, embroiderer; neol.
Cf. LE BOULLUEC 1989, 279; WEVERS 1990, 430.439

ραφιδευτός,-ή,-όν   A 1-0-0-0-0-1
Ex 37,21
patched, stitched; τὰ ραφιδευτά *needle-works*
Cf. LE BOULLUEC 1989, 363; WEVERS 1990, 619

ράχις,-ιος   N3F 0-1-0-1-0-2
1 Sm 5,4; Jb 40,18
backbone Jb 40,18
*1 Sm 5,4 πλὴν ἡ ράχις (רק rendered twice:
semantic rendition followed by a word
homoeophonic with רק) *only the backbone* for
MT רק *only*
Cf. CAIRD 1976, 74; WELLHAUSEN 1871, 59(1 Sm 5,4)

ρέγχω   V 0-0-2-0-0-2
Jon 1,5.6
to snore

ρεμβασμός,-οῦ   N2M 0-0-0-0-1-1
Wis 4,12
whirling, turning (metaph.); neol.
Cf. LARCHER 1984, 333-334

ρεμβεύω   V 0-0-1-0-0-1
Is 23,16
to roam, to rove, to wander; neol.; see ρέμβομαι
Cf. WALTERS 1973, 294

ρέμβομαι   V 0-0-0-1-0-1
Prv 7,12
to roam, to rove, to wander; see ρεμβεύω
Cf. WALTERS 1973, 294

Ρεμμων   N 0-0-1-0-0-1
Zech 14,10
= ראמה *it will rise*
Cf. TOV 1973, 89

ρεῦμα,-ατος   N3N 0-0-0-0-1-1
Sir 39,13
stream

ρέω⁺   V 20-1-9-9-2-41
Ex 3,8.17; 13,5; 33,3; Lv 15,3
to flow, to run, to stream Jb 38,30; *id.* (metaph.)
Jb 36,28; *to flow out* Ct 4,16; *to let run, to
overflow with* [τι] Ex 3,8; *to let run, to let stream*
[τι] Prv 3,20; *to have a discharge of blood*
Lv 15,25 (iterum)
ρέων γόνον *he who has a discharge of semen* Lv
15,3; ρέουσα αἵματι *she who has a discharge of
blood* Lv 15,19
Cf. WEVERS 1995, 435; →NIDNTT
(→ἀπο-, δια-, ἐκ-, ἐπι-, κατα-, παρα-, περι-,
ὑπεκ-)

ρῆγμα,-ατος⁺   N3N 0-5-0-0-0-5
1 Kgs 11,30.31; 12,24ο(bis); 2 Kgs 2,12
piece (torn off sth)
Cf. CAIRD 1976, 82

ρήγνυμι/ρήσσω⁺   V 4-10-13-11-2-40
Gn 7,11; Ex 14,16; 28,32; Nm 16,31; Jos 9,13
A: *to break* [τι] Jb 17,11; *to rend* [τι] Ex 28,32;
to split, to divide [τι] Ex 14,16; *to rend from, to
withdraw from* [τι ἔκ τινος] 1 Kgs 11,31; *to let
break loose, to vent* [τι] Jb 15,13; *to cause to
break or burst forth* [τι] Jb 28,10; *to hatch*
(eggs) [τι] Is 59,5
P: *to burst, to cleave asunder* Nm 16,31; *to be
broken up* 2 Kgs 25,4; *to burst or break forth*
Gn 7,11
ρῆξον καὶ βόησον *break into shouting and cry
aloud* Is 54,1; ρήγνυμι εὐφροσύνην *to burst into
joy* (metaph.) Is 49,13; ρήγνυμι φωνήν *to let
loose the voice, to break into lowing* (of an ox) Jb
6,5
Cf. LARCHER 1984, 348; →LSJ suppl(Jb 15,13)
(→ἀνα-, ἀπο-, δια-, ἐκ-, κατα-, περι-)

ρῆμα,-ατος⁺   N3N 164-186-32-113-53-548
Gn 15,1(bis); 18,14.25; 19,21
that which is said or *spoken, word, saying* Gn
20,8; *word (of God), commandment, order,
direction* Dt 1,26; *subject of speech, matter, thing*
(semit.?) Gn 15,1; *object, thing* (semit.) Dt 17,1;
τὰ ρήματα *words, speech* Ps 18(19),5
τὰ ρήματα τοῦ νόμου *the content of the law* Dt
28,58; τὸ ρῆμά τινος *the matter of sb* or *sth,
what concerns sb* or *sth* 1 Sm 10,2; ρῆμα
γογγυσμοῦ *murmuring speech* Is 58,9; πολὺς ἐν
ρήμασι γίγνομαι *to be profuse in words, to be
talkative* Jb 11,3
*Jer 18,20 ρήματα *words* -שיחה for MT שוחה *pit*
Cf. BARR 1961, 130; DOGNIEZ 1992, 22.41-43.

117.123-124.222.223.231; HARL 1986ᵃ, 53.162-163; LE
BOULLUEC 1989, 150.196.234; REPO 1951, 1-204; WEVERS
1993, 565; 1995, 99(Dt 5,5); →NIDNTT

ῥῆσις,-εως⁺   N3F 0-0-0-9-0-9
Prv 1,6.23; 2,1; 4,5.20
saying, speech, words Prv 1,6; *report, declaration*
Ezr 5,7; *expression, utterance* Prv 1,23

ῥητίνη,-ης   N1F 2-0-4-0-0-6
Gn 37,25; 43,11; Jer 8,22; 26(46),11; 28(51),8
resin (of the mastix or terebinth)
Cf. WALTERS 1973, 66

ῥητορεύω
(→ἀντι-)

ῥητός,-ή,-όν   A 2-0-0-0-0-2
Ex 9,4; 22,8
having been said, having been agreed upon Ex
9,4; *above mentioned* Ex 22,8
Cf. BARR 1961, 137-138; HARL 1984ᵃ=1992ᵃ, 40; LE
BOULLUEC 1989, 129-130.226; PRIJS 1948, 4-5

Ρηχαβ   N 0-2-0-0-0-2
= רכב *chariot*
Cf. TOV 1973, 89

ῥῖγος,-ους   N3N 1-0-0-1-0-2
Dt 28,22; DnᴸˣˣX 3,67
frost, cold DnᴸˣˣX 3,67; *shivering, chill* Dt 28,22
Cf. DOGNIEZ 1992, 288(Dt 28,22); WEVERS 1995, 435;
→PREISIGKE

ῥίζα,-ης⁺   N1F 1-1-18-23-19-62
Dt 29,17; 2 Kgs 19,30; Is 5,24; 11,1(bis)
root Jb 30,4; *id.* (metaph.) Dt 29,17; *root, stock,
family* Tob 5,14; *root, basic source, point* Jb
19,28; *root, origin* (metaph.) Sir 1,6; *shoot, scion*
Is 11,1
ἐκ ῥιζῶν *to its roots, root and branch, utterly* Jb
31,12; εἰς ῥίζας τῶν ποδῶν μου *to the sole of
my feet* Jb 13,27; ἡ ῥίζα τοῦ ὄρους *foot of the
hill* Jdt 6,13; βάλλω ῥίζαν *to take root* Jb 5,3;
δίδωμι ῥίζαν *id.* Wis 4,3; διαδίδωμι εἰς
ῥίζαν *id.* Sir 23,25
→LSJ Suppl; MM; TWNT

ῥιζόω⁺   V 0-0-2-1-3-6
Is 40,24; Jer 12,2; Ps 47(48),3; Sir 3,28; 24,12
A: *to take* or *strike root in* [ἔν τινι] Sir 3,28; *id.*
(metaph.) Ps 47(48),3; *id.* [ἔν τινι] (metaph.)
Sir 24,12
P: *to take root* Jer 12,2; *id.* [εἴς τι] Is 40,24
→MM
(→ἐκ-)

ῥίζωμα,-ατος   N3N 0-0-0-2-0-2
Ps 51(52),7; Jb 36,30

root, stem Ps 51(52),7
τὰ ῥιζώματα τῆς θαλάσσης *the bottom of the
sea* Jb 36,30

ῥιπίζω⁺   V 0-0-0-1-0-1
DnᴸˣˣX 2,35
to blow up [τι]

ῥιπιστός,-ή,-όν   A 0-0-1-0-0-1
Jer 22,14
ventilated, breezy; neol.

ῥίπτω⁺   V 16-30-22-19-25-112
Gn 21,15; 37,20.24; Ex 1,22; 4,3
to throw, to cast [τινα] Gn 37,20; *id.* [τι] Jgs
9,53; *to cast away* [τι] Ex 32,19; *to cast down*
[τι] Ex 7,10; *to cast down, to thrust down* [τι]
Zech 5,8; *to cast away, to reject* [τινα] Wis
11,14; *to bring, to throw sth before sb* [τι
ἐνώπιόν τινος] DnᵀʰTh 9,18; ρεριμμένος
prostrate, lying on the ground JgsᴮB 4,22
ῥίπτω ἑαυτόν *to prostrate oneself* 2 Mc 3,15; *to
throw* or *hurl oneself* 4 Mc 12,19; ῥίπτω τι or
τινὰ ὀπίσω σώματός μου *to reject* Neh 9,26
*Jer 27(50),30 ῥιφήσονται *they shall be cast
down* -ירמו (Aram.) for MT ירמו *they shall be
destroyed*
Cf. SPICQ 1978ᵃ, 780; →NIDNTT; TWNT
(→ἀπο-, δια-, ἐπι-, ἐκ-, κατα-, παρα-, ὑπο-)

ῥίς, ῥινός⁺   N3F 0-0-1-6-2-9
Is 37,29; Ps 113,14(115,6); Jb 27,3; 40,24.25
nose, snout Jb 40,24; αἱ ῥίνες *nostrils* Jb 27,3

ῥόα,-ας   N1F 5-5-7-6-1-24
Ex 28,33; 36,31(39,24); Nm 13,23; 20,5; Dt 8,8
pomegranate-tree Ex 28,33; *pomegranate* Nm
13,23; *knob shaped like a pomegranate*
1 Kgs 7,6(18)
*Ez 19,10 ἐν ῥόα *on a pomegranate* -ברמן for MT
ברמך *in your blood*
Cf. CAIRD 1969=1972, 144-145; WEVERS 1990, 460

ῥόαξ,-ακος   N3M 0-0-1-0-0-1
Ez 40,40
stream, drain; *Ez 40,40 ῥόακος *drain* -מרוצה for
MT מחוצה *outside*; neol.

ῥόδον,-ου⁺   N2N 0-0-0-1-4-5
Est 1,6; Wis 2,8; Sir 24,14; 39,13; 50,8
rose Wis 2,8
*Est 1,6 ῥόδα *roses* -(ו)רד (Aram.)? for MT (ו)רד
mother-of-pearl, precious pavement
→SCHLEUSNER

ῥοδοφόρος,-ος,-ον   A 0-0-0-0-1-1
3 Mc 7,17
bearing roses; ῥοδοφόρος *Rose-bearing* (epithet

of Ptolemais)

ῥοιζέω   V 0-0-0-1-0-1
Ct 4,15
to babble, to ripple, to flow with a purl (of water)

ῥοῖζος,-ου⁺   N2M 0-0-1-0-3-4
Ez 47,5; 2 Mc 9,7; Wis 5,11; Bel^Th 36
élan, rush Wis 5,11; *rushing, motion, rush, swing*
2 Mc 9,7; *id.* (metaph.) Bel^Th 36

ῥοῖσκος,-ου   N2M 6-2-0-0-1-9
Ex 28,33(bis).34; 36,31.32(39,24.25)
(small) pomegranate Ex 36,31(39,24); *tassel
shaped like a pomegranate* Ex 28,34; neol.
Cf. CAIRD 1969=1972, 144-145; WALTERS 1973, 92;
WEVERS 1990, 460

ῥομφαία,-ας⁺   N1F 5-101-87-30-36-259
Gn 3,24; Ex 5,21; 32,27; Nm 22,23; 31,8
sword Gn 3,24
ἐν ῥομφαίᾳ καὶ ἐν λιμῷ *by war and by famine*
Jer 51(44)18
*2 Kgs 3,23 τῆς ῥομφαίας *of the sword* -חֶרֶב for
MT הָחֳרֵב (inf. hoph.) *to fight*; *Ez 29,10
ῥομφαίαν *sword* -חֶרֶב for MT חֹרֶב *desolation,* see
also Hag 1,11; Ps 9,7
Cf. HARL 1991=1992ᵃ, 161; →TWNT

ῥόπαλον,-ου   N2N 0-0-0-1-0-1
Prv 25,18
club (weapon)

ῥοπή,-ῆς⁺   N1F 0-1-1-1-4-7
Jos 13,22; Is 40,15; Prv 16,11; 3 Mc 5,49; Wis
11,22
turn of the scale, poise (of the balance), weight
Prv 16,11; *small additional weight, make-weight,
casting weight* Wis 11,22; *weight, decisive
influence* Sir 1,22; *turn of events, decisive
moment, crisis* Jos 13,22; *moment* Wis 18,12
Cf. DORIVAL 1994, 427; LARCHER 1985, 688.1011; TOV
1978, 55

ῥοποπώλης,-ου   N1M 0-0-0-2-0-2
Neh 3,31.32
dealer in petty wares, huckster, haggler; neol.

ῥοῦς, ῥοῦ   N2M 0-0-0-0-1-1
Sir 4,26
flow of water, current, stream, course; ῥοῦς
ποταμοῦ *course of a river*

ῥοῶν,-ῶνος   N3M 0-0-1-0-0-1
Zech 12,11
pomegranate-orchard; neol.

Ροως   N 0-2-0-0-0-2
2 Sm 15,32; 16,1
= ראשׁ *summit*

Cf. TOV 1973, 89

ῥύδην   D 0-0-0-0-1-1
2 Mc 3,25
violently, furiously, fiercely; φερόμενος ῥύδην
moving, running furiously

ῥυθμίζω   V 0-0-1-0-0-1
Is 44,13
to arrange, to fit, to put in order
(→δια-)

ῥυθμός,-οῦ   N2M 1-1-0-1-2-5
Ex 28,15; 2 Kgs 16,10; Ct 7,2; Wis 17,17; 19,18
measured motion, rhythm Wis 17,17; *rhythm,
tune* Wis 19,18; *proportion, form, shape*
2 Kgs 16,10
ῥυθμοὶ μηρῶν *the shapely contours (lines) of
your thighs* Ct 7,2
Cf. LARCHER 1985, 977.1085; LE BOULLUEC 1989, 286;
RENEHAN 1975, 177; WEVERS 1990, 451

ῥύμη,-ης⁺   N1F 0-0-1-0-2-3
Is 15,3; Tob^BA 13,18; Sir 9,7
street Tob^BA 13,18; *narrow street* Is 15,3
Cf. SHIPP 1979, 486

ῥύομαι⁺   V 7-20-36-97-35-195
Gn 48,16; Ex 2,17.19; 5,23; 6,6
to rescue, to save, to deliver, to preserve [abs.]
Jgs^B 18,28; *to save oneself* Prv 6,31; *id.* [τινα]
Ex 2,17; *id.* [τι] Ex 12,27; *to deliver out of* [τινα
ἔκ τινος] Ex 6,6; *to deliver from* [τινα ἔκ
τινος] Gn 48,16; *id.* [τινα ἀπό τινος] Ex 2,19;
to spare [τι] 2 Kgs 23,18; *to redress* [τι] LtJ 53;
ὁ ῥυόμενος *deliverer* Is 59,20
ῥύομαί τινα ἐκ χειρός τινος *to rescue sb out
of the hands of* Jos 22,31
Cf. HARL 1991=1992ᵃ, 151; LE BOULLUEC 1989, 85-86.90;
WEVERS 1990, 225; →NIDNTT; TWNT

ῥυπαρός,-ά,-όν⁺   A 0-0-2-0-0-2
Zech 3,3.4
filthy, dirty
Cf. SPICQ 1978ᵃ, 784-785

ῥύπος,-ου⁺   N2M 0-0-1-3-0-4
Is 4,4; Jb 9,31; 11,15; 14,4
filth, dirt Is 4,4; *uncleanness, defilement* Jb 11,15
Cf. SPICQ 1978ᵃ, 784-785; →NIDNTT

ῥύσις,-εως⁺   N3F 17-0-0-1-0-18
Lv 15,2(bis).3(ter)
issue of blood, flow Lv 15,19; *discharge* or *issue
of seed* Lv 15,2; *course* Jb 38,25
Cf. WEVERS 1995, 368(Dt 23,11)

ῥύσις,-εως   N3F 0-0-0-0-1-1
Sir 51,9

deliverance; neol.

Cf. DOGNIEZ 1992, 261

ῥύστης,-ου   N1M 0-0-0-4-1-5
Ps 17(18),3.49; 69(70),6; 143(144),2; 3 Mc 7,23
saviour, deliverer; neol.

ῥωγολογέομαι
(→ἐπι-)

Ρωκεϊμ   N 0-0-0-1-0-1
Neh 3,8
= רקחים *perfumers*
Cf. Tov 1973, 89

ῥωμαλέος,-α,-ον   A 0-0-0-0-1-1
2 Mc 12,27

strong (of body)

ῥώμη,-ης   N1F 0-0-0-1-2-3
Prv 6,8c; 2 Mc 3,26; 3 Mc 2,4
bodily strength, physical power

ῥώννυμι⁺   V 0-0-0-10-0-10
2 Mc 9,20; 11,21.28.33; 3 Mc 1,4
P: *to fare well, to be in good health* (of pers.)
2 Mc 9,20; *to favour* [τινι] (of things) 3 Mc 1,4
(→ἐπι-)

ῥώξ, ῥωγός   N3M 1-0-2-0-0-3
Lv 19,10; Is 17,6; 65,8
grape Lv 19,10; *berry* Is 17,6

Cf. SHIPP 1978, 481

σαβαχα N 0-2-0-0-0-2

2 Kgs 25,17(bis)

= שׂבכה lattice-work

σαβαωθ⁺ N M 0-6-53-0-3-62

Jos 6,17; 1 Sm 1,3.11.20; 15,2

= צבאות Sabaoth (used as a title of God)

Cf. DODD 1954, 16-17; TALSHIR 1987, 57-75

σαββατίζω⁺ V 5-2-0-0-2-9

Ex 16,30; Lv 23,32; 26,34.35(bis)

Hebr. loanword (שׁבת); to keep sabbath, to rest
Ex 16,30; to enjoy a sabbatical year Lv 26,34
σαββατίζω τὰ σάββατα to keep sabbath (semit.)
Lv 23,32; τὴν γῆν τὰ σάββατα αὐτῆς
σαββατίσαι that the land keeps its sabbath by
resting untilled 2 Chr 36,21

neol.

Cf. BICKERMAN 1976, 183(n.43); TOV 1977, 199

σάββατον,-ου⁺ N2N 41-15-33-20-21-130

Ex 16,23.25.26.29; 20,8

Hebr. loanword (שׁבת / שׁבתון); sabbath 2 Kgs 4,23;
τὰ σάββατα = שׁבתא (Aram.) sabbath (pl.
indicating a category) Ex 16,23; τὰ σάββατα
sabbaths (pl. for more than one) Neh 10,34
σάββατα σαββάτων special sabbath, holy
sabbath Lv 16,31; σάββατον κατὰ σάββατον
every sabbath 1 Chr 9,32; τετράδι σαββάτων on
the fourth day of the week Ps 93(94),1, see also
Ps 23(24),1; 47(48),1; φυλάττω τὰ σάββατα to
keep sabbath Ex 31,13; ἁγιάζω τὴν ἡμέραν τῶν
σαββάτων to sanctify the (day of) sabbath, to
keep the sabbath day holy Jer 17,22; σαββατίζω
τὰ σάββατα Lv 23,32 see σαββατίζω

*Am 6,3 σαββάτων Sabbaths -שַׁבָּת? for MT שֶׁבֶת
inaction? or end?

neol.

Cf. HARLÉ 1988, 43.155; LE BOULLUEC 1989, 57.186; LEE,
J. 1983, 16.30.52; MATEOS 1990, 36; PELLETIER 1972,
436-447; 1975, 221-224; SCHWYZER 1935, 1-16; TOV 1979,
231; WALTERS 1973, 159-161.171-173.179-180; →NIDNTT;
TWNT

σαβεκ N 1-0-0-0-0-1

Gn 22,13

= סבך thicket

Cf. HARL 1986ª, 195

σαβι N 0-0-0-3-0-3

Dnᵀʰ 11,16.41.45

= צבי beauty

Cf. JEANSONNE 1988, 108

σαγή-ῆς N1F 0-0-0-0-1-1

2 Mc 3,25

armour, harness

σαγήνη,-ης⁺ N1F 0-0-6-1-0-7

Is 19,8; Ez 26,5.14; 47,10; Hab 1,15

(large) drag-net Hab 1,15; net (metaph.; to
ensnare men) Eccl 7,26

βάλλω σαγήνας to cast nets Is 19,8

σάγμα,-ατος N3N 1-0-0-0-0-1

Gn 31,34

pack-saddle, saddle-bag

Cf. LEE, J. 1983, 45.84

Σαδαιεμ N 0-1-0-0-0-1

1 Sm 24,3

= צורי היעלים the rocks of the wild goats

Cf. TOV 1973, 89

σαδημωθ N 0-1-0-0-0-1

2 Kgs 23,4

= שׁרמות (pl. of שׁרמה) fields, terraces

Cf. WALTERS 1973, 320

σαδηρωθ N N 0-2-0-0-0-2

2 Kgs 11,8.15

= שׁררות (pl. of שׁררה to be understood as
connected with סׄרׄרׅ֧ם?) ranks?

Cf. MULDER 1987, 207-208; SIMOTAS 1968, 132

σαθρός,-ά,-όν A 0-0-0-1-1-2

Jb 41,19; Wis 14,1

rotten (of wood) Jb 41,19; fragile Wis 14,1

Cf. LARCHER 1985, 788

σαθρόω V 0-1-0-0-0-1

Jgsᴬ 10,8

to make feeble, to weaken [τινα]; neol.

σάκκος,-ου⁺ N2M 5-13-20-12-13-63

Gn 37,34; 42,25.35(bis); Lv 11,32

Semit. loanword (Hebr. שק); coarse cloth of hair,
sackcloth Is 50,3; sackcloth (as sign of mourning)
Gn 37,34; sack, bag Gn 42,25

σάκκον ἔχοντι καὶ σποδόν wearing sackcloth
and ashes Est 4,2

Cf. CAIRD 1976, 78; HARL 1986ª, 263.281-282; TOV 1979,
221; WALTERS 1973, 163; WEVERS 1993, 629;
→CHANTRAINE; FRISK; TWNT

σαλαμιν N 0-1-0-0-0-1

Jos 22,29

= שׁלמים peace often used in the expression
זבחי שׁלמים peace-offerings (in Jos 22,29 MT has זבח
without שׁלמים)

Cf. DANIEL 1966, 217

σαλεύω⁺ V 0-7-12-41-19-79

Jgs 5,5; 2 Sm 22,37; 2 Kgs 17,20; 21,8

A: to cause to rock [τινα] Sir 29,17; to shake
(the head) [τι] Ps 108(109),25; to shake, to

afflict [τινα] 2 Kgs 17,20; *to stir up* [τινα] Sir 28,14

P: *to be driven to and fro* (by the wind) Wis 4,4; *to be shaken, to be moved* (of the sea) Ps 97(98),7; *to be shaken* (of mountains) Jgs 5,5; *to be shaken, to tremble* Zech 12,2; *to slip* (of steps) Ps 16(17),5; *to totter* 2 Sm 22,37; *to stagger* Ps 106(107),27; *to tremble* (from fear) Eccl 12,3; *to be moved, to waver, to change one's mind* Jb 41,15; *to be shaken, to be in sore distress* Sir 13,21; *to wander* Ps 108(109),10; *to be (re)moved* Dnᵀʰ 4,14

σαλεύω τὸν πόδα ἀπὸ τῆς γῆς *to remove one's foot from the land* 2 Kgs 21,8 et al.; βοοζύγιον σαλευόμενον *an ox-yoke rubbing and chafing the neck, a hard yoke* Sir 26,7; σαλεύσει αὐτοὺς ἐκ θεμελίων *he shall shake them to their foundations, he shall eradicate them from their foundations* Wis 4,19

*Hab 2,16 σαλεύθητι καὶ σείσθητι *shake and quake* -והרעל (cpr. 1QpHab 11,9, see σείω) for MT והערל *be uncircumcised*

Cf. HELBING 1928, 320; TALMON 1964, 131; →NIDNTT; TWNT

(→δια-)

σάλος,-ου⁺   N2M 0-0-2-5-2-9
Jon 1,15; Zech 9,14; Ps 54(55),23; 65(66),9; 88(89),10

rolling swell, surge Jon 1,15; *restlessness, perplexity* Sir 40,4; *tribulation* Lam 1,8

ἐν σάλῳ ἀπειλῆς *with a whirling menace* Zech 9,14; οὐ δώσει σάλον τῷ δικαίῳ *he shall not allow the righteous to be moved* Ps 54(55),23; μὴ δῷς εἰς σάλον τὸν πόδα σου *let not your foot be moved* Ps 120(121),3, see also Ps 65(66),9

*Ps 88(89),10 τὸν σάλον *the surge* -שאון for MT שוא *to lift*

→NIDNTT

σάλπιγξ,-ιγγος⁺   N3F 13-29-22-19-17-100
Ex 19,13.16.19; 20,18; Lv 23,24

(war-)trumpet Ex 19,13; *trumpet-call* Zph 1,16; *trumpeter* 2 Kgs 11,14

Cf. HARLÉ 1988, 43; LE BOULLUEC 1989, 211; PELLETIER 1975, 231; →NIDNTT; TWNT

σαλπίζω⁺   V 10-37-9-2-11-69
Nm 10,3.4.5.6(bis)

to sound the trumpet, to trumpet Jos 6,9; *to sound* (with trumpets) Nm 10,3; *to sound* (of people) 1 Ezr 5,62

σαλπίζω σημασίαν *to sound an alarm* Nm 10,5; σαλπίζω σημασίᾳ *id.* Nm 10,7

→NIDNTT

σαμβύκη,-ης   N1F 0-0-0-5-0-5
Dn 3,5; Dnᵀʰ 3,7.10.15

oriental loanword (Hebr. סבכא or שבכא); *triangular musical instrument with strings*

Cf. CAIRD 1976, 78; KOLARI 1947, 1-103; MITCHELL 1965, 24-25; WALTERS 1973, 163; →CHANTRAINE; FRISK

σανδάλιον,-ου⁺   N2N 0-1-1-0-2-4
Jos 9,5; Is 20,2; Jdt 10,4; 16,9

sandal

σανίδωμα,-ατος   N3N 0-0-0-0-1-1
3 Mc 4,10

planking, planks, deck

σανιδωτός,-ή,-όν   A 1-0-0-0-0-1
Ex 27,8

planked, boarded over; neol.?

Cf. LE BOULLUEC 1989, 276; LEE, J. 1983, 45.112

σανίς,-ίδος⁺   N3F 0-1-0-1-0-2
2 Kgs 12,10; Ct 8,9

plank Ct 8,9; *lid* (of a box) 2 Kgs 12,10

Cf. SPICQ 1978ᵃ, 786

σαπρία,-ας   N1F 0-0-1-6-3-10
Jl 2,20; Jb 2,9c; 7,5; 8,16; 17,14

decay, decayed matter Jl 2,20

*Jb 8,16 ἐκ σαπρίας αὐτοῦ *out of his corruption* corr. ἐκ πρασίας αὐτοῦ *out of his garden-plot* for MT גנתו על over his garden neol.

Cf. ORLINSKI 1935, 134-135

σαπρίζω   V 0-0-0-1-0-1
Eccl 10,1

to make rotten or *stinking* [τι]

σάπφειρος,-ου⁺   N2F 3-0-5-4-2-14
Ex 24,10; 28,18; 36,18(39,11); Is 54,11; Ez 1,26

Semit. loanword (Hebr. ספיר); *sapphire* Ex 24,10

*Ez 9,2 σαπφείρου *sapphire* -ספיר for MT ספר *writer*

Cf. CAIRD 1976, 78; LIEBERMAN 1942, 58; TOV 1979, 221; WALTERS 1973, 163; WEVERS 1990, 453; →CHANTRAINE; FRISK

σαράβαρα,-ων   N2N 0-0-0-3-0-3
Dnᵀʰ 3,21; Dn 3,94(27)

sandal

Cf. SHIPP 1979, 491; WALTERS 1973, 176

σάρδιον,-ου⁺   N2N 4-0-1-2-0-7
Ex 25,7; 28,17; 35,9; 36,17(39,10); Ez 28,13

the Sardion stone, sardius Ex 28,17

λιθοὺς σαρδίου *sardius stones* Ex 25,7, see also

35,9

Cf. Le Boulluec 1989, 287; Wevers 1990, 394

σαρκίζω

(→ἐκ-)

σάρκινος,-η,-ον⁺   A 0-1-2-2-0-5

2 Chr 32,8; Ez 11,19; 36,26; Prv 24,22c;
Est 4,17p

of flesh (metaph.), *weak* 2 Chr 32,8; *mortal* (of
pers.) Est 4,17p

καρδίαν σαρκίνην *a heart of flesh, a heart
capable of feeling* Ez 11,19

Cf. Spicq 1982, 601-602

σαρκοφαγέω   V 0-0-0-0-1-1

4 Mc 5,26

to eat flesh

σαρκοφαγία,-ας   N1F 0-0-0-0-2-2

4 Mc 5,8.14

eating flesh

σάρξ, σαρκός⁺   N3F 58-15-40-51-51-215

Gn 2,21.23(bis).24; 6,3

stereotypical rendition of בשר; *flesh, meat* (food
for men) Dn 10,3; *flesh* (of the human body,
distinguished from the spirit or life-giving
breath) Gn 2,21; *body* Ex 30,32; *male member,
penis* Ez 23,20; *living being* Gn 8,17; σάρκες
portions of meat, meat Gn 40,19; *body* 2 Mc 9,9
πᾶσα σάρξ *everybody, all mankind* Gn 6,12; εἰς
σάρκα μίαν *to one body* (said of a married
couple) Gn 2,24; σάρξ καὶ αἷμα *flesh and
blood, human being* (in contrast to God)
Sir 17,31; τῶν τῆς σαρκὸς παθῶν *the weakness
of the flesh* 4 Mc 7,18; σάρξ ἡμῶν ἐστιν *he is
our flesh, he is our relative* Gn 37,27

*Nm 16,22 θεὸς τῶν πνευμάτων καὶ πάσης
σαρκός *god of the spirits and of all flesh*
אלהי הרוחת לכל בשר MT for בשר- וכל הרוחת אלהי-*god
of the spirits of all flesh*, see also Nm 27,16;
*Hos 9,12 σάρξ μου *my flesh* בשרי- for MT בשורי/ב
when I depart; *Mi 3,3 ὡς σάρκας *like meat* כשאר-
for MT כאשר *as, like*; *Ps 27(28),7 ἡ σάρξ μου *my
body* בשרי? for MT ומשירי *and with my song*
see κρέας, σῶμα, χρώς

Cf. Barr 1961, 35.37.159(n.1); Harl 1986ᵃ, 60-61.
105.106.130; Lys 1983, 47-70; 1986, 163-204; Scharbert
1972, 121-124. 136; Spicq 1982, 591-602; Tov 1976ᵇ,
543-544; →Nidntt; twnt

σάσσω

(→ἀπο-, ἐπι-)

σαταν⁺   N 0-2-0-0-0-2

1 Kgs 11,14.14(25)

Hebr. loanword (שטן); *enemy, adversary*

→Chantraine; nidntt; twnt

σατανᾶς,-ᾶ⁺   N1M 0-0-0-0-1-1

Sir 21,27

see σαταν

σάτον,-ου⁺   N2N 0-0-2-0-0-2

Hag 2,16(bis)

Hebr. loanword (סאתא); *measure* (1/30 of a
κόρος); neol.

Cf. Walters 1973, 327-328

σατραπεία,-ας   N1F 0-2-0-2-2-6

Jos 13,3; Jgs 3,3; Est 8,9.12b

satrapy, province of a satrap (properly one of the
originally twenty divisions of the Persian empire,
ruled by a σατράπης) Est 8,9; *id.* (in Jos and Jgs
the term is used - for MT סרני - of the five
divisions of Philistia each ruled by a Philistine
lord) Jos 13,3

σατράπης,-ου   N1M 0-23-0-15-6-44

Jgs 5,3; Jgsᴬ 16,5.8.18

governor (one of the five lords of the Philistines,
originally a governor over the satrapy in the
Persian empire) Jgs 5,3; *id.* (in opp. to
βασιλεῖς) 1 Kgs 21(20),24

*Est 1,3 οἱ ἄρχοντες τῶν σατραπῶν *the
governors of the satraps* corr.? οἱ ἄρχοντες τῶν
σατραπείων for MT שרי המדינות *the governors of
the satrapies*, see also Est 9,3

Cf. Petit 1988, 59-65

σατραπία,-ας   N1F 0-1-0-0-0-1

Jgsᴬ 16,18

see σατραπεία

σαύρα,-ας   N1F 1-0-0-0-0-1

Lv 11,30

lizard

σαυτοῦ,-ῆς,-οῦ   R 1-14-3-0-1-19

see σεαυτοῦ

σαφέω

(→δια-)

σαφής,-ής,-ές   A 0-0-0-0-5-5

2 Mc 12,40; 4 Mc 3,6; Wis 7,22; Sus 48

clear, plain Wis 7,22; *clear, manifest* 4 Mc 3,6;
τὸ σαφές *the plain truth* Sus 48

σαφφωθ   N N 0-1-1-0-0-2

2 Sm 17,29; Jer 52,19

= שפות *curds?* 2 Sm 17,29

*Jer 52,19 σαφφωθ *curds?* שפות- for MT ספים *bowls*

Cf. Simotas 1968, 135(Jer 52,19)

σαφῶς⁺   D 2-0-1-0-2-5

Dt 13,15; 27,8; Hab 2,2; 2 Mc 4,33; 3 Mc 4,19

clearly Dt 13,15; *plainly* Dt 27,8; *undoubtedly*
3 Mc 4,19

σαχωλ N M 0-0-0-1-0-1
Ezr 8,18
= שכל *prudence*; ἀνὴρ σαχωλ *a man of discretion*

σβέννυμι⁺ V 3-5-14-14-9-45
Lv 6,2.5.6; 2 Sm 14,7; 21,17
A: *to quench, to put out* [τι] 2 Sm 14,7; *to
quench* (a feeling) Ct 8,7; *to extinguish* (glory)
[τι] Est 4,17o
P: *to be quenched, to be put out* Lv 6,2; *to be
quenched, to be quelled* Jb 4,10; *to be
extinguished* (of a name) Prv 10,7; *to die* Ez 32,7
*Jb 30,8 ἐσβεσμένον *extinguished* (of name and
fame) - נכהו ◊כהה or -נכבה ◊כבה for MT נכאו ◊נכא
or נכה *cut of*; *Jb 34,26 ἔσβεσεν δέ *and he
extinguished* -רעך◊ ורער for MT 34,25 וירכאו? *and
they are crushed*
Cf. SPICQ 1978ᵃ, 789-790(n.7); →NIDNTT; TWNT
(→ἀπο-, κατα-)

σβεστικός-ή,-όν A 0-0-0-0-1-1
Wis 19,20
able to quench, quenching

σεαυτοῦ,-ῆς,-οῦ⁺ R 72-31-46-31-38-218
Gn 6,14.19.21(bis); 8,17
occurs also in dat. and in acc.; *of yourself*
Cf. WEVERS 1990, 564.568

σέβασμα,-ατος⁺ N3N 0-0-0-0-3-3
Wis 14,20; 15,17; Belᵀʰ 27
an object of awe or *worship, an idol*; neol.
Cf. GILBERT 1973, 156-157; LARCHER 1985, 820; →NIDNTT

σέβω⁺ V 0-3-3-5-15-26
Jos 4,24; 22,25; 24,33b; Is 29,13; 66,14
A: *to worship, to revere* (God) [τινα] 4 Mc 5,24
M: *to worship, to revere* (God) [τινα] Jos 4,24;
id. (gods) [τινα] Jos 24,33b; *id.* (creatures)
[τινα] Wis 15,18; *id.* (idols) [τι] Belᵀʰ 5
Cf. DODD 1954, 77; →NIDNTT; TWNT

σειρά,-ᾶς⁺ N1F 0-4-0-1-0-5
Jgs 16,13; Jgsᴮ 16,14.19; Prv 5,22
cord, rope, chain (metaph.) Prv 5,22; *locks of
hair* Jgs 16,13
→MM

σειρήν,-ῆνος N3F 0-0-5-1-0-6
Is 13,21; 34,13; 43,20; Jer 27(50),39; Mi 1,8
siren, demon of the dead living in the desert
(used to translate words rendered as ostrich (or
desert-owl) and jackal) Is 13,21
θυγατέρων σειρήνων *of the daughters of sirens*
(semit.) Mi 1,8

Cf. KAUPEL 1935, 161; →LSJ RSuppl

σειρήνιος,-ος,-ον A 0-0-0-0-1-1
4 Mc 15,21
of a siren

σειρομάστης,-ου N1M 1-2-1-0-0-4
Nm 25,7; 1 Kgs 18,28; 2 Kgs 11,10; Jl 4,10
barbed lance; neol.?
Cf. CONYBEARE 1905=1988, 273; DORIVAL 1994, 463;
HARL 1991=1992ᵃ, 161; WALTERS 1973, 36

σεῖσμα,-ατος N3N 0-0-0-0-1-1
Sir 27,4
shaking (of a sieve); neol.?

σεισμός,-οῦ⁺ N2M 0-0-12-2-1-15
Is 15,5; 29,6; Jer 10,22; 23,19; 29(47),3
vibrating, whirring Jb 41,21; *earthquake* Est 1,1d;
rattling (of wheels) Na 3,2; *shock* 4 Mc 17,3;
earthquake (metaph.) Jer 23,19
*Is 15,5 καὶ σεισμός *and earthquake, tempest*
-וסערה? for MT יעערו *they raise?*
→LSJ Suppl; LSJ RSuppl

σείω⁺ V 0-3-26-5-3-37
Jgs 5,4; 2 Sm 22,8; Is 10,13; 13,13
A: *to shake, to quake* [τι] Hag 2,6; *to shake* (a
city) [τι] Is 10,13; *to agitate, to disturb* [τινα]
Is 14,16
P: *to shake* 1 Ezr 4,36; *to shake, to quake* (of an
earthquake) Jgs 5,4; *to stagger* (from
drunkenness) Is 28,7
*Is 17,4 σεισθήσεται *shall be shaken* -ירגזה ◊רגז
for MT ירזה *will grow lean*; *Am 1,14 καὶ
σεισθήσεται *and shall be shaken* -וסער for MT
בסער *with a storm*, cpr. Hab 3,14; *Hab 2,16 καὶ
σείσθητι *and quake* -ורעל◊ רעל (cpr. 1QHab
11,9) for MT והערל *and be uncircumcised*, see
σαλεύω
Cf. DE WAARD 1981, 553; TALMON 1964, 131
(→ἀπο-, δια-, ἐν-, ἐπι-, κατα-, συσ-)

σελήνη,-ης⁺ N1F 3-3-11-15-9-41
Gn 37,9; Dt 4,19; 17,3; Jos 10,12.13
moon Gn 37,9
σελήνη πλήρης *full moon* Sir 50,6
Cf. SHIPP 1979, 494-496

σελίς,-ίδος N3F 0-0-1-0-0-1
Jer 43(36),23
column of writing (of a papyrus-roll)
Cf. LEWIS 1974, 79-83.

σεμίδαλις,-εως⁺ N3F 47-8-5-0-6-66
Gn 18,6; Ex 29,2.40; Lv 2,1.2
the finest wheaten flour (as a meal) Gn 18,6; *id.*
(as an offering) Lv 5,13

Cf. BATTAGLIA 1989, 66-67; DANIEL 1966, 204.207.
208.214.217.222.232.257; DORIVAL 1994, 257-258

σεμνολογέω   V 0-0-0-0-1-1
4 Mc 7,9
to speak solemnly about, to speak in honour of
[τι]; neol.?

σεμνός,-ή,-όν⁺   A 0-0-0-3-6-9
Prv 6,8a; 8,6; 15,26; 2 Mc 6,11.28
solemn, sacred 2 Mc 6,11; *reverend* 2 Mc 8,15;
worthy of respect, held in honour, august
Prv 6,8a; *majestic* 4 Mc 17,5
σεμνὰ λέγω *to speak solemnly* Prv 8,6; τὸ
σεμνὸν γήρως στόμα *the pure mouth of (my) old
age* 4 Mc 5,36
Cf. DRESCHER 1969, 92-93; SPICQ 1978ᵃ, 791-795; →NIDNTT

σεμνότης,-ητος⁺   N3F 0-0-0-0-1-1
2 Mc 3,12
majesty, dignity, augustness
Cf. SPICQ 1978ᵃ, 791-795; →NIDNTT

σεμνῶς⁺   D 0-0-0-0-1-1
4 Mc 1,17
with due reverence

σεραφιν   N 0-0-2-0-0-2
Is 6,2.6
= שְׂרָפִים *Seraphs*

σερσερωθ   N 0-1-0-0-0-1
2 Chr 3,16
= שַׁרְשְׁרוֹת *chains*

σευτλίον,-ου   N2N 0-0-1-0-0-1
Is 51,20
beet

σήθω
(→κατα-)

σηκός,-οῦ⁺   N2M 0-0-0-0-1-1
2 Mc 14,33
sacred enclosure, shrine, temple

σημαία,-ας   N1F 0-0-1-0-0-1
Is 30,17
military standard, ensign; neol.?

σημαίνω⁺   V 2-4-5-11-4-26
Ex 18,20; Nm 10,9; Jos 6,8; Jgs 7,21
A: *to show to* [τί τινι] Ex 18,20; *to make
known to* [τί τινι] DnᴸˣˣX 2,15; *to give a sign to
sb* [τινι] Zech 10,8; *to bid sb to do, to
command sb to do* [τινι +inf.] 1 Ezr 2,2; *to
sound* (of trumpets) Jos 6,8; *to sound an alarm*
Jgs 7,21
P: *to be signified, to be noted* (of things)
2 Mc 2,1; *to be signified, to be shown* (of pers.)
1 Ezr 8,48

σημαίνω σάλπιγξι *to sound with trumpets*
Nm 10,9; σημαίνει ποδί *he makes a sign with
his foot* Prv 6,13; ὁ λαὸς ἐσήμαινον φωνὴν
μεγάλην *the people shouted with a loud voice*
Ezr 3,11; περὶ τῶν δι' αὐτοῦ σημαινομένων
about its contents 2 Mc 11,17
Cf. DORIVAL 1994, 166; WEVERS 1990, 286; →TWNT
(→ἐπι-, προ-, ὑπο-)

σημασία,-ας   N1F 18-2-0-2-3-25
Lv 13,2.6.7.8; 14,56
signal Lv 25,10; *mark* (of a disease) Lv 13,2;
shouting (of pers.) 1 Chr 15,28
ἡμέρα σημασίας *a day for blowing the trumpets*
Nm 29,1; σαλπίζω σημασίαν *to sound an
alarm* Nm 10,5; σημασία σαλπίζω *id.* Nm 10,6;
ταῖς σάλπιγξιν τῶν σημασιῶν *on the trumpets
of the signals, on the trumpets for giving signs*
(indicating a kind of trumpet), *on alarm
trumpets* 1 Mc 4,40
Cf. DORIVAL 1994, 166; HARLÉ 1988, 135(Lv 13,2).198;
WALTERS 1973, 178.328-329(Lv 25,10-13)

σημεῖον,-ου⁺   N2N 44-13-29-17-17-120
Gn 1,14; 4,15; 9,12.13.17
sign, calendar marks Gn 1,14; *sign, token* Ex 4,8;
sign, miracle, wonder Dt 7,19; *(warning-)sign*
Nm 17,25; *mark* Gn 4,15; *signal* Is 33,23;
standard, flag Jer 28(51),12
τὸ σημεῖον (τῆς) διαθήκης *the sign of (the)
convenant* Gn 9,12
*Jos 2,18 τὸ σημεῖον *the sign* -אות for MT את
(nota accusativi); *Jer 31(48),9 σημεῖα *signs,
monuments* -ציון ? for MT ציי ?
Cf. DOGNIEZ 1992, 144; DORIVAL 1994, 166; HARL 1986ᵃ,
92(Gn 1,14); LARCHER 1984, 533-534.641; LE BOULLUEC
1989, 34; MERKELBACH 1970, 245-246; ROST 1967, 130-
132; SPICQ 1978ᵃ, 796-801; YOUTIE 1970, 105-116;
→NIDNTT; TWNT

σημειόω⁺   V 0-0-0-1-0-1
Ps 4,7
P: *to be manifested*
(→προ-)

σημείωσις,-εως⁺   N3F 0-0-0-1-1-2
Ps 59(60),6; PSal 4,2
sign, token, signal Ps 59(60),6; *appearance*
PSal 4,2

σήμερον⁺   D 102-121-11-20-36-290
Gn 4,14; 19,37.38; 21,26; 22,14
today Gn 4,14
ἕως τῆς σήμερον ἡμέρας *till today* Gn 19,38
*JgsᴮB 6,17 σήμερον *today* corr. σημεῖον for MT

אוֹת *a sign*, cpr. Jgs^ 6,17
→NIDNTT; TWNT

σήπη,-ης   N1F 0-0-0-0-1-1
Sir 19,3
decay, putrefaction; neol.

σήπω⁺   V 0-0-1-5-2-8
Ez 17,9; Ps 37(38),6; Jb 16,7; 19,20; 33,21
A: *to consume* [τινα] Jb 40,12
P: *to rot, to decay, to be consumed* Jb 33,21; *to
be blighted* Ez 17,9; σεσηπότα *worn out person*
Jb 16,7
*Jb 19,20 ἐσάπησαν *rotted away* -רקבה for MT רבקה
clung to
→TWNT

σής, σητός⁺   N3M 0-0-4-5-1-10
Is 33,1; 50,9; 51,8; Mi 7,4; Jb 4,19
moth Is 33,1
ὡς σὴς καταφάγεται ὑμᾶς *as the moth shall
devour you* (as a sign of man's frailty) Is 50,9
*Jb 32,22 ἐμὲ σῆτες (ἔδονται) *moths (will eat)
me* -עשׁ◊ for MT עשׂני עשׂה◊ *my maker*
Cf. CAIRD 1976, 78; DE WAARD 1981, 554; TOV 1979, 221;
→CHANTRAINE; FRISK; TWNT

σητόβρωτος,-ος,-ον⁺   A 0-0-0-1-0-1
Jb 13,28
eaten by moths; neol.
→TWNT

σῆψις,-εως   N3F 0-0-1-0-0-1
Is 14,11
decay, putrefaction

σθένος,-ους   N3N 0-0-0-3-2-5
Jb 4,10; 16,15; 26,14; 3 Mc 2,2; PSal 17,14
strength

σθένω   V 0-0-0-0-1-1
3 Mc 3,8
to be able to [+inf.]

σιαγόνιον,-ου   N2N 1-0-0-0-0-1
Dt 18,3
cheek; τά σιαγόνια *the fleshy parts around the
jaw*

σιαγών,-όνος⁺   N3F 0-17-4-7-1-29
Jgs 15,14.15.16
jaw, jaw-bone, cheek

σιαλόω
(→περι-)

σιγάω⁺   V 1-0-1-7-11-20
Ex 14,14; Am 6,10; Ps 31(32),3; 38(39),3;
49(50),21
to be silent, to keep silence, to say nothing
1 Ezr 3,24; *to keep silence* Ex 14,14; *to be still*

(of waves) Ps 106(107),29
ἐσίγησεν κλαίουσα *she stopped weeping*
Tob^S 5,23
Cf. KRISCHER 1981, 93-107

σιγή,-ῆς⁺   N1F 0-0-0-0-2-2
3 Mc 3,23; Wis 18,14
silence Wis 18,14; σιγῇ *in silence, refraining
from words* (in opp. to λόγῳ) 3 Mc 3,23

σιγηρός,-ά,-όν   A 0-0-0-0-1-1
Sir 26,14
silent (of a pers.)

σιδήριον,-ου   N2N 1-2-0-1-0-4
Dt 19,5; 2 Kgs 6,5.6; Eccl 10,10
axe-head, iron blade

σιδηρόδεσμος,-ος,-ον   A 0-0-0-0-1-1
3 Mc 4,9
with bonds of iron, unyielding; σιδηροδέσμοις
ἀνάγκαις *under the constraint of iron bonds*;
neol.

σίδηρος,-ου⁺   N2M 7-22-9-26-10-74
Gn 4,22; Nm 31,22; 35,16; Dt 8,9; 20,19
iron Gn 4,22; *iron tool* Dt 20,19; *razor*
Jgs^B 16,17; *sword* Jdt 6,6; *irons, fetters*
Ps 106(107),10
τέκτων σιδήρου *smith* 1 Sm 13,19

σιδηροῦς,-ᾶ,-οῦν⁺   A 5-9-9-21-8-52
Lv 26,19; Dt 3,11; 4,20; 28,23.48
made of iron, iron Dt 28,48; *of iron, hard*
(metaph.) Is 48,4
σκέλη σιδηρᾶ *iron legs* (of an image)
Dn^LXX 2,33; ἐν ῥάβδῳ σιδηρᾷ *with an iron rod,
mercilessly* Ps 2,9; ἀπὸ τῆς ῥίζης τῆς σιδηρᾶς *of
the iron root, of the strength of iron* Dn^Th 2,41

σιελίζω
(→προσ-)

σίελον/σίελος,-ου   N2N/M 0-1-1-0-0-2
1 Sm 21,14; Is 40,15
spittle 1 Sm 21,14
*Is 40,15 ὡς σίελος *as spittle* -כרק for MT כדק *like
fine dust*
Cf. WALTERS 1973, 330(Is 40,15)

σικερα⁺   N N 6-4-6-0-0-16
Lv 10,9; Nm 6,3(bis); 28,7; Dt 14,26
Semit. loanword (Hebr. שֵׁכָר); *fermented liquor,
strong drink*; neol.
Cf. CAIRD 1976, 78; DOGNIEZ 1992, 208; DORIVAL 1994,
244; HARLÉ 1988, 125; THACKERAY 1909, 33; WALTERS
1973, 169-170.247-248; →CHANTRAINE

σίκλος,-ου   N2M 47-21-6-0-2-76
Ex 30,23.24; 39,1(bis).2(38,24.25)

Semit. loanword (Hebr. שֶׁקֶל); *shekel* (unit of weight) Ex 30,23; *coin* 1 Mc 10,40; *silver coin* Dt 22,19

*1 Sm 13,21 τρεῖς σίκλοι εἰς τὸν ὀδόντα *three shekel for sharpening?* -שֶׁקֶל לְשֵׁן שָׁלֹשׁ for MT שָׁלֹשׁ קִלְּשׁוֹן *three pronged forks?*

Cf. BEWER 1942, 45-46; CAIRD 1976, 78; DORIVAL 1994, 216-217; HARLÉ 1988, 102; TOV 1979, 221; WALTERS 1973, 164-165; →CHANTRAINE (sub σίγλος); FRISK (sub σίγλος)

σικυήρατον,-ου N2N 0-0-1-0-1-2
Is 1,8; LtJ 69
cucumber-bed; neol.?

σίκυς,-υος N3M 1-0-0-0-0-1
Nm 11,5
cucumber

Cf. DORIVAL 1994, 288; TOV 1979, 221; →CHANTRAINE (sub σικύα); FRISK (sub σικύα)

σινδών,-όνος⁺ N3F 0-3-0-1-0-4
Jgs 14,12; Jgsᴬ 14,13; Prv 31,24
Semit. loanword (Hebr. סָדִין); *fine linen* Prv 31,24; *linen sheet or garment* Jgs 14,12

Cf. CAIRD 1976, 82; CONYBEARE 1905=1988, 233; LUCCHESI 1978ᵃ, 141-142; TOV 1979, 221; →CHANTRAINE; FRISK

σιρομάστης,-ου N1M 0-1-0-0-0-1
Jgsᴬ 5,8
see σειρομάστης

σιρώνων N 0-1-0-0-0-1
Jgsᴬ 8,26
= שַׂהֲרֹנִים *crescents* (jewels)
Cf. WALTERS 1973, 162

σισόη,-ης N1F 1-0-0-0-0-1
Lv 19,27
curl of hair; neol.
Cf. ZIPOR 1991, 330.333

σιτευτός,-ή,-όν⁺ A 0-3-1-0-0-4
Jgsᴬ 6,25.28; 1 Kgs 5,3; Jer 26(46),21
fed, fatted

σιτέω V 0-0-0-1-1-2
Prv 4,17; 2 Mc 5,27
M: *to feed on* [τι]
(-ἐν-)

σιτίζω
(-ἐπι-)

σιτίον,-ου⁺ N2N 0-0-0-1-0-1
Prv 30,22
mostly pl.: *food, bread, victuals*

σιτοβολών,-ῶνος N3M 1-0-0-0-0-1
Gn 41,56

place for storing agricultural produce, granary; neol.?

Cf. HARL 1986ᵃ, 277; HUSSON 1983ᵃ, 23-254; 1991, 123; LEE, J. 1983, 107

σιτοδεία,-ας N1F 1-0-0-1-0-2
Lv 26,26; Neh 9,15
want of food, famine Neh 9,15
σιτοδείᾳ ἄρτων *by dearth of bread, by famine* Lv 26,26

σιτοδοσία,-ας N1F 2-0-0-0-0-2
Gn 42,19.33
distribution or *allowance of grain;* τὸν ἀγορασμὸν τῆς σιτοδοσίας *the allowance of grain you bought;* neol.?
Cf. HARL 1986ᵃ, 280

σιτομετρέω V 2-0-0-0-0-2
Gn 47,12.14
to deal out portions of grain, to measure out grain; neol.?
Cf. HARL 1986ᵃ, 298; LAUNEY 1950, 726-727; LEE, J. 1983, 98

σῖτον/σῖτος,-ου⁺ N2N/M 23-9-18-26-4-80
Gn 27,28.37; 41,35.49; 42,2
grain Gn 27,28; τὰ σῖτα *bread* Prv 31,27; *food* Jb 3,24
ῥαβδίζων σῖτον *threshing* or *one who threshes wheat* Jgsᴮ 6,11

Cf. BATTAGLIA 1989, 41-43; DANIEL 1966, 132.133.135; →MM

σιτοποιός,-οῦ N2M 1-0-0-0-0-1
Gn 40,17
miller, baker
Cf. BATTAGLIA 1989, 201-203

σιφωνίζω
(-ἐκ-)

σιωπάω⁺ V 3-7-9-10-7-36
Nm 30,15(bis); Dt 27,9; Jgsᴬ 18,9; Jgsᴮ 3,19
to keep silence, to say nothing Nm 30,15; *to be silent, to say nothing* Dt 27,9; *to be silent, to stop rumbling* (of stomach) Jb 30,27
ἐσιώπησεν τοῦ λαλεῖν *he held his tongue* 1 Ezr 4,41

*Jb 18,3 σεσιωπήκαμεν *we have been silent* - רִדְמֹם for MT נִטְמִינוּ *we are stupid*
Cf. HARL 1986ᵇ=1992ᵃ, 81; KRISCHER 1981, 93-107
(-ἀπο-, κατα-, παρα-)

σιωπή,-ῆς⁺ N1F 0-0-1-0-1-2
Am 8,3; Sir 41,21
silence

σιώπησις,-εως N3F 0-0-0-3-0-3

Ct 4,1.3; 6,7
covering, veil; neol.
Cf. BLAKENEY 1944, 138

σκάζω
(→ἐπι-)

σκάλλω   V 0-0-0-1-0-1
Ps 76(77),7
to search, to probe

σκαμβός,-ή,-όν   A 0-0-0-1-0-1
Ps 100(101),4
crooked, bent; καρδία σκαμβή *perverse heart*

σκανδαλίζω⁺   V 0-0-0-0-4-4
Sir 9,5; 23,8; 32,15; PSal 16,7
A: *to cause sb to stumble* [τινα] PSal 16,7
P: *to be entrapped in* [ἔν τινι] Sir 9,5; *to take
offence at* [ἔν τινι] Sir 32,15
Cf. HARL 1992ᵃ=1992ᵇ, 234; LINDBLOM 1921, 22-24;
MOULTON 1914-15,331-332; STÄHLIN 1930, 108-128; →MM;
NIDNTT; TWNT

σκάνδαλον,-ου⁺   N2N 1-6-1-7-8-23
Lv 19,14; Jos 23,13; Jgs 2,3; Jgsᴬ 8,27
trap, snare Jdt 5,1; *id.* (metaph.) Jos 23,13;
temptation to sin Wis 14,11; *offence* 1 Sm 25,31;
stumbling-block Sir 27,23
*Ps 48(49),14 σκάνδαλον *offence* -כשל for MT כסל
fate
neol.
Cf. LARCHER 1985, 804; LINDBLOM 1921, 8-14; MOULTON
1914-15, 331-332; STÄHLIN 1930, 23-92.141-146; →MM;
NIDNTT; TWNT

σκάπτω⁺   V 0-0-1-0-1-2
Is 5,6; Od 10,6
to dig, to spade [τι]
Cf. SCHNEBEL 1925, 39.246
(→ἀνα-, κατα-)

σκαρίζω
(→ἀπο-)

σκάφη,-ης⁺   N1F 0-0-0-0-2-2
Bel 33
bowl
Cf. WALTERS 1973, 83; →MM

σκάφος,-ους   N3N 0-0-0-0-2-2
2 Mc 12,3.6
boat

σκεδάννυμι
(→ἀπο-, δια-, κατα-)

σκελίζω   V 0-0-1-0-0-1
Jer 10,18
to overthrow, to upset [τινα]; neol.
Cf. LEE, J. 1969, 240-241; →LSJ suppl

(→ὑπο-)

σκέλος,-ους⁺   N3N 1-2-4-3-1-11
Lv 11,21; 1 Sm 17,6; 2 Sm 22,37; Ez 1,7; 16,25
leg

σκεπάζω⁺   V 9-3-6-7-16-41
Ex 2,2; 12,13.27; 33,22; 40,3
A: *to cover, to hide, to shelter* [τινα] Ex 2,2; *to
draw over* [ἐπί τινος] Nm 9,20; *id.* [ἐπί τινα]
Ex 33,22; *id.* [τι] Ex 12,27; *to protect, to shelter*
[τινα] Ex 12,13; *to watch over, to protect* [τινα]
Dt 32,11
M/P: *to shelter oneself* Ps 60(61),5
*1 Sm 23,26 σκεπαζόμενος *covering himself,
hiding* -נחפה or -חפף for MT נחפז *hurrying*
Cf. DOGNIEZ 1992, 201.327-328; HARL 1992ᵃ=1993, 193;
LE BOULLUEC 1989, 49.80.147.151.336; LEE, J. 1983,
50.76-77; WALTERS 1973, 249

(→ἐπι-)

σκέπαρνον,-ου⁺   N2N 0-1-1-0-0-2
1 Chr 20,3; Is 44,12
(carpenter's) axe

σκέπασις,-εως   N3F 1-0-0-0-0-1
Dt 33,27
shelter, protection; neol.
Cf. DOGNIEZ 1992, 64.353; WALTERS 1973, 342-343

σκεπαστής,-οῦ   N1M 2-0-0-1-5-8
Ex 15,2; Dt 32,38; Ps 70(71),6; Jdt 9,11; 3 Mc
6,9
protector, defender; neol.
Cf. DOGNIEZ 1992, 65.338

σκεπεινός,-ή,-όν   A 0-0-0-1-0-1
Neh 4,7
sheltered; ἐν τοῖς σκεπεινοῖς *in the
lurking-places*

σκέπη,-ης⁺   N1F 2-3-12-12-12-41
Gn 19,8; Ex 26,7; Jgsᴬ 5,8; 9,15; 1 Sm 25,20
covering Ex 26,7; *shelter* Jb 24,8; *protection*
Jgsᴬ 5,8; *covert* 1 Sm 25,20
ὑπὸ τὴν σκέπην τῶν δοκῶν *under the shelter of
my roof* Gn 19,8
*Sir 6,14 σκέπη *tent* -אהל for Sirᴴᵉᵇʳ אהב *friend*
Cf. LE BOULLUEC 1989, 267.348; LLELEWYN 1994, 101;
WEVERS 1990, 415

σκέπτομαι⁺   V 2-0-1-0-1-4
Gn 41,33; Ex 18,21; Zech 11,13; Belᴸˣˣ 17
used as aor. and fut. for σκοπέω; *to look (out)
for, to search out, to select* [τινα] Gn 41,33; *to
watch out, to take care* [+indir. question]
Belᴸˣˣ 17
*Zech 11,13 σκέψομαι *I will observe* -אראה for

MT אדד *splendor*
Cf. LEE, J. 1983, 51; WEVERS 1990, 287
(→ἐπι-, κατα-, συν-)

σκευάζω   V 0-0-0-0-2-2
3 Mc 5,31; Sir 49,1
A: *to prepare, to furnish* (a meal) [τι] 3 Mc 5,31
P: *to be prepared* Sir 49,1
(→ἀπο-, δια-, ἐπι-, κατα-, μετα-, παρα-, προ-)

σκευασία,-ας   N1F 0-0-0-1-0-1
Eccl 10,1
preparation of sth [τινος]

σκεῦος,-ους[+]   N3N 82-114-35-35-50-316
Gn 24,53; 27,3; 31,37(bis); 45,20
vessel Lv 15,12; *thing* Gn 24,53; *equipment*
Gn 27,3; σκεύη *attributes* Ex 25,9; *outfit* Dt 22,5;
τὰ σκεύη *train* (of the army) 1 Sm 30,24
σκεύη τῆς τραπέζης *table-furniture* Ex 38,12;
σκεύη λειτουργικά *liturgical vessels* Nm 4,26;
σκεύη πολεμικά *weapons of war* Dt 1,41; τὸ
παιδάριον τὸ αἶρον τὰ σκεύη *the young man
who bears the armour* Jgs[B] 9,54; οἱ τροχοὶ καὶ
τὰ σκεύη τῶν βοῶν *the wheels and the harness
of the oxen* 2 Sm 24,22; ἐνέβαλον εἰς τὰ σκεύη
αὐτῶν *they put into their store* Jos 7,11
Cf. DOGNIEZ 1992, 250; HOLLEAUX 1942, 24; LE
BOULLUEC 1989, 95; LEE, J. 1983, 39; WEVERS 1990,
637-638; →TWNT

σκηνή,-ῆς[+]   N1F 283-69-20-26-36-434
Gn 4,20; 12,8; 13,3.5; 18,1
tent Gn 4,20; *booth* (for cattle) Gn 33,17
(primo); *tabernacle* Ex 26,13
σκηνὴ τοῦ μαρτυρίου *tent* or *tabernacle of
testimony* Ex 29,4; ἐν τῇ ἑορτῇ τῶν σκηνῶν *at
the feast of tabernacles* 2 Chr 8,13; Σκηναί
Booths Gn 33,17(secundo)
*Nm 24,6 σκηναί *tents* -אֹהָלִים for MT אֲהָלִים *aloes*;
*Ps 41(42),5 σκηνῆς *of a booth* -סֹךְ for MT סָךְ ?
Cf. BARR 1985, 28-35; CAIRD 1976, 82; DE WAARD 1981,
559-560; HARL 1986ª, 66; LE BOULLUEC 1989, 267.269.
280; MICHAELIS 1954ª, 40-43; PELLETIER 1975, 225;
WEVERS 1990, 396.415.641.644; →NIDNTT; TWNT

σκηνοπηγία,-ας[+]   N1F 2-0-3-0-4-9
Dt 16,16; 31,10; Zech 14,16.18.19
booth-making 2 Mc 1,9
ἐν τῇ ἑορτῇ τῆς σκηνοπηγίας *at the feast of
tabernacles* Dt 16,16
Cf. DOGNIEZ 1992, 65.219; →MM

σκῆνος,-ους[+]   N3N 0-0-0-0-1-1
Wis 9,15
tent (metaph.), *body* (dwelling place of the soul)

Cf. LARCHER 1984, 596-597; →MM; NIDNTT; TWNT

σκηνόω[+]   V 1-3-0-0-0-4
Gn 13,12; Jgs[B] 5,17(bis); 8,11
to pitch one's tent Gn 13,12; *to live in a tent*
Jgs[B] 8,11
Cf. BARR 1985, 28-35; CAIRD 1976, 82; DE WAARD 1981,
559-560; →NIDNTT; TWNT
(→ἀπο-, κατα-)

σκήνωμα,-ατος[+]   N3N 1-32-8-30-9-80
Dt 33,18; Jos 3,14; Jgs[A] 7,8; Jgs 19,9
tent, hut Dt 33,18; *tabernacle* Ps 25(26),8;
dwelling, habitation Jgs 19,9; σκηνώματα *feast of
Tabernacles* 2 Mc 10,6
σκήνωμα τοῦ μαρτυρίου *tabernacle of the
testimony* 1 Kgs 8,4
*2 Sm 7,23 καὶ σκηνώματα *tabernacles* -אֹהָלִים
for MT ואלהיו *and his gods*
Cf. BARR 1985, 28-35; CAIRD 1976, 82; HORSLEY 1987,
172; →MM

σκήνωσις,-εως   N3F 0-0-0-0-1-1
2 Mc 14,35
dwelling; neol.

σκῆπτρον,-ου[+]   N2N 0-22-3-1-6-32
Jgs[A] 5,14; 1 Sm 2,28; 9,21(bis); 10,19
staff, stick 1 Sm 14,27; *sceptre* Wis 6,21
*1 Sm 2,28 σκήπτρων *staffs* -שבטי (first meaning
of שבט) for MT שבטי *tribes* (second meaning of שבט),
see also 1 Sm 9,21; 10,19.20.21; 15,17; 1 Kgs
11,31.32.35.36; 12,20.21.24u(bis)

σκιά,-ᾶς[+]   N1F 0-8-12-28-6-54
Jgs 9,36; Jgs[B] 9,15; 2 Kgs 20,9.10
shade, shadow Jb 15,29; *shadow* (as protection)
Jgs[B] 9,15; *shadow* (on a sun-dial) 2 Kgs 20,9;
shadow (as a sign of instability) 1 Chr 29,15
*Ps 22(23),4 ἐν μέσῳ σκιᾶς θανάτου *in the
midst of the shadow of death* -צל מות for MT צלמות
darkness, see also Is 9,1; Jer 13,16; Ps 43(44),20;
106(107),10.14; Jb 24,17; 28,3
Cf. BARR 1989, 50-54; →NIDNTT; TWNT

σκιαγράφος,-ου   N2M 0-0-0-0-1-1
Wis 15,4
*painter of shadows, scene-painter, producer of
illusion*; neol.
Cf. LARCHER 1985, 855-856

σκιάδιον,-ου   N2N 0-0-1-0-0-1
Is 66,20
fabric roof or *sunshade, tilt* (on a carriage)

σκιάζω   V 6-2-2-3-3-16
Ex 38,8(37,9); Nm 9,18.22; 10,36(34); 24,6
to overshadow Nm 9,18; *to overshadow, to cover*

Ex 38,8(37,9); *to shade, to shelter from* [ἀπό τινος] Jon 4,6

νάπαι σκιάζουσαι *shady valleys* Nm 24,6

*2 Sm 20,6 καὶ σκιάσει *and he shall overshadow, and he shall blind (the eyes)*? or *and he shall escape (from our sight)*? -צלל◊ והצל for MT והציל◊ נצל *and he shall snatch away (our eyes)*?, cpr. Jon 4,6; *Jb 36,28 ἐσκίασεν (νέφη) *(clouds) overshadowed* -יצלו for MT יזלו *pour down*

Cf. DRIVER 1962, 134-135(2 Sm 20,6); LE BOULLUEC 1989, 364; LEE, J. 1983, 50

(→ἐπι-, συ-)

σκιρρόω

(→προ-, κατα-)

σκιρτάω⁺ V 1-0-3-2-1-7

Gn 25,22; Jer 27(50),11; Jl 1,17; Mal 3,20; Ps 113(114),4

to leap, to bound, to skip (as a sign of joy) Jer 27(50),11; *id.* (of the movements of a child in the womb) Gn 25,22

*Jl 1,17 ἐσκίρτησαν *they shook their chains* -עכשו or -עכסו for MT עבשו *they shriveled*

Cf. WEVERS 1993, 391; →TWNT

(→δια-)

σκληρία,-ας N1F 0-0-0-1-0-1

Eccl 7,25

hardness; neol.

σκληροκαρδία,-ας⁺ N1F 1-0-1-0-1-3

Dt 10,16; Jer 4,4; Sir 16,10

hardness of heart; neol.

Cf. DOGNIEZ 1992, 58.183-184; LEE, J. 1983, 52; SPICQ 1982, 606-610; →NIDNTT

σκληροκάρδιος,-ος,-ον A 0-0-1-1-0-2

Ez 3,7; Prv 17,20

hard-hearted, stubborn; neol.

Cf. SPICQ 1982, 606-610

σκληρός,-ά,-όν⁺ A 14-12-12-11-10-59

Gn 21,11.12; 42,7.30; 45,5

most often with a neg. connotation; *hard* (of work) Ex 1,14; *hard, difficult* 1 Sm 1,15; *hard to accept* (of words) Gn 21,11; *stiff* Dt 31,27; *harsh* (of sound) Zph 1,14; *sharp* (of wind) Prv 27,16; *severe* (of battle) 2 Sm 2,17; *thick* (of darkness) Is 5,30; *stubborn* (of pers.) Nm 16,26, see also Gn 49,3; *hard, hardened* (of pers.) Jb 9,4

*Is 8,12 σκληρόν *hard* -קשה for MT קשר *conspiracy*; *Zph 1,14 σκληρά (τέτακται) *(is made) harsh* -(שם) צרה for MT (שם) צרח *cries (there)*; *Jb 22,21 γενοῦ δὴ σκληρός *be hard* (translating Jb 9,4)

-◊קשה for MT ◊סכם *agree with him*

Cf. HARL 1986ᵃ, 307(Gn 49,3); HEATER 1982, 74(Jb 22,21); SEELIGMANN 1948, 106(Is 8,12); SHIPP 1979, 503; SPICQ 1982, 606-610; →NIDNTT; SCHLEUSNER

σκληρότης,-ητος⁺ N3F 1-1-2-0-0-4

Dt 9,27; 2 Sm 22,6; Is 4,6; 28,27

hardness (of pers.) Dt 9,27; *id.* (of weather) Is 4,6; *hard treatment* Is 28,27

σκληρότητες θανάτου *agonies of death* 2 Sm 22,6

Cf. SPICQ 1982, 606-610; →NIDNTT

σκληροτράχηλος,-ος,-ον⁺ A 5-0-0-1-2-8

Ex 33,3.5; 34,9; Dt 9,6.13

stiff-necked (metaph.), *obstinate*; neol.

Cf. DOGNIEZ 1992, 65.176; LE BOULLUEC 1989, 329; SPICQ 1982, 606-610; →MM; NIDNTT

σκληρύνω⁺ V 17-8-4-5-4-38

Gn 49,7; Ex 4,21; 7.3.22; 8,15

A: *to harden, to make heavy* [τι] 2 Chr 10,4; *to harden* (one's heart) [τι] (said of pers.) Ps 94(95),8; *id.* (said of God) Ex 4,21; *to stiffen* (the neck) [τι] 2 Chr 36,13

P: *to be hardened* (of feelings) Gn 49,7; *to become stubborn* Sir 30,12; *to be sharp* (of words) 2 Sm 19,44; *to be withered* Ps 89(90),6

ἐσκλήρυνεν Φαραω ἐξαποστεῖλαι ἡμᾶς *Pharao hardened (his heart) so as not to send us away, Pharao refused to send us away* Ex 13,15; ἐσκλήρυνας τοῦ αἰτήσασθαι *you hardened in asking, you asked a hard thing* 2 Kgs 2,10

Cf. DOGNIEZ 1992, 127; LE BOULLUEC 1989, 38; SPICQ 1982, 606-610; WEVERS 1990, 98.201-202; →NIDNTT

(→ἀπο-)

σκληρῶς D 1-2-1-0-2-6

Gn 35,17; 1 Sm 20,7.10; Is 22,3; 3 Mc 4,19

hardly, with difficulty Gn 35,17; *harshly, roughly* 1 Sm 20,7; *fiercely, severely* 3 Mc 4,19

*Is 22,3 σκληρῶς *tightly* -קשה for MT קשת *bow*

σκνίψ, σκνιπός/σκνιφός N3M 5-0-0-1-1-7

Ex 8,12.13(bis).14(bis)

small fly, gnat

Cf. LE BOULLUEC 1989, 125

σκολιάζω V 0-0-0-3-0-3

Prv 10,8; 14,2; 17,16a

to be crooked, to be perverse Prv 10,8

ὁ σκολιάζων τοῦ μαθεῖν *he who turns aside from instruction* Prv 17,16a

-σκολιεύομαι

(→ἐν-)

σκολιός,-ά,-όν⁺ A 1-0-3-14-4-22

Dt 32,5; Is 27,1; 42,16; Hos 9,8; Ps 77(78),8
crooked, bent Wis 13,13; *crooked, winding* (of
paths) Prv 2,15; *unjust, unrighteous, rebellious*
Dt 32,5; *unscrupulous, dishonest* Prv 16,28;
σκολιόν τι *sth wrong* Jb 4,18

ὄφιν σκολιόν *crooked serpent* (said of δράκων)
Is 27,1; παγὶς σκολιά *twisted trap* Hos 9,8

Cf. LARCHER 1978, 171; SPICQ 1978ᵃ, 218-220; →TWNT

σκολιότης,-ητος⁺   N3F 0-0-1-0-0-1
Ez 16,5
dishonesty, perversity
Cf. HARL 1991=1992ᵃ, 159

σκολιῶς   D 0-0-1-0-0-1
Jer 6,28
perversely

σκόλοψ,-οπος⁺   N3M 1-0-2-0-1-4
Nm 33,55; Ez 28,24; Hos 2,8; Sir 43,19
thorn Hos 2,8

σκολόπων ἄκρα *sharp peaks* Sir 43,19; σκόλοπες
ἐν τοῖς ὀφθαλμοῖς ὑμῶν *(they shall be) thorns*
or *splinters in your eyes* Nm 33,55

→MM; NIDNTT; TWNT

σκόπελον,-ου   N2N 0-1-0-0-0-1
2 Kgs 23,17
mound; neol.

σκοπεύω⁺   V 1-1-1-4-0-7
Ex 33,8; 1 Sm 4,13; Na 2,2; Jb 39,29; Prv 5,21
to keep watch, to watch closely [abs.] Ex 33,8; *id.*
[τι] 1 Sm 4,13; *id.* [τινα] Prv 15,3; *id.* [εἴς τι]
Prv 5,21

πύργος τοῦ Λιβάνου σκοπεύων πρόσωπον
Δαμασκοῦ *the tower of Lebanon looking toward*
Damascus Ct 7,5

(→ἀπο-, κατα-)

σκοπέω⁺   V 0-0-0-1-1-2
Est 8,12g; 2 Mc 4,5
to observe, to watch closely [τι]
(→ἀπο-, ἐπι-, κατα-)

σκοπή,-ῆς   N1F 0-0-0-0-1-1
Sir 37,14
watch-tower

σκοπιά,-ᾶς   N1F 2-6-4-0-1-13
Nm 23,14; 33,52; Jgsᴮ 10,17; Jgsᴬ 11,29(bis)
height, hilltop, lookout Nm 23,14; *out-look point,*
watch-tower 1 Kgs 15,22; *high place* Nm 33,52;
watch, guard duty Sir 40,6
Cf. DORIVAL 1994, 554

σκοπός,-οῦ⁺   N2M 1-11-10-2-3-27
Lv 26,1; 1 Sm 14,16; 2 Sm 13,34(bis); 18,24
lookout, watcher, watchman, sentry 1 Sm 14,16;

target, mark Wis 5,12; *object on which one fixes*
the eye Lv 26,1

*Hos 9,10 ὡς σκοπὸν ἐν συκῇ *like a watchman*
in a fig-tree interprets MT כבכורה בתאנה *like the first*
fruit on the fig-tree, see also Na 3,12(10), cpr.
Jerᴹᵀ 1,11 מקל שקד (blossoming trees are like
watchmen announcing spring)

Cf. HARL 1961=1992ᵃ, 215-233; HARLÉ 1988, 204
(Lv 26,1); →TWNT

σκορακίζω
(→ἀπο-)

σκορακισμός,-οῦ   N2M 0-0-0-0-1-1
Sir 41,21
contemptuous behaviour; neol.

σκόρδον,-ου   N2N 1-0-0-0-0-1
Nm 11,5
garlic
Cf. SHIPP 1979, 504

σκορπίδιον,-ου   N2N 0-0-0-0-1-1
1 Mc 6,51
dim. of σκορπίος; *device for firing* or *shooting*
arrows (resembling the uplifted tail of a
scorpion); neol.?

σκορπίζω⁺   V 0-1-3-5-15-24
2 Sm 22,15; Ez 5,12; Hab 3,10; Mal 2,3; Ps 17
(18),15

A: *to scatter, to disperse* [abs.] Jb 39,15; *id.* [τι]
2 Sm 22,15; *id.* [τινα] Jdt 7,32

P: *to be dispersed, to disperse* Ezr 14,13; *to be*
scattered Zech 11,16

*Hab 3,10 σκορπίζων *dispersing* -זרם (verb) for
MT זֶרֶם *heavy rain*

→TWNT; NIDNTT

(→δια-)

σκορπίος,-ου⁺   N2M 1-5-1-0-3-10
Dt 8,15; 1 Kgs 12,11(24).14; 2 Chr 10,11.14
scorpion

→TWNT

σκορπισμός,-οῦ⁺   N2M 0-0-0-0-1-1
PSal 17,18
scattering; neol.

σκοτάζω   V 0-0-2-4-0-6
Ez 31,15; Mi 6,14; Ps 104(105),28; Eccl 12,3;
Lam 4,8

to become dark, to remain in darkness Eccl 12,3;
to grow dark, to become dark, to sadden
Ez 31,15; *to become black* Lam 4,8

*Mi 6,14 καὶ σκοτάσει *and there shall be*
darkness -ויחשך ⟨חשך⟩ (verb) for MT וישחך ⟨ישח⟩ *your*
dung (subst.)

neol.

(→συ-)

σκοτεινός,-ή,-όν⁺   A 1-1-4-9-0-15

Gn 15,12; 2 Kgs 5,24; Is 45,3.19; 48,16

dark Jb 15,23; *gloomy* Gn 15,12; *dark, obscure*
(of speech) Prv 1,6; *secret* Dn^LXX 2,22

θησαυρούς σκοτεινούς *treasures that lie in*
darkness Is 45,3; εἰς γῆν σκοτεινήν *to a land of*
darkness Jb 10,21

*2 Kgs 5,24 εἰς τὸ σκοτεινόν *to the darkness,*
to a secret place - אל האפל for MT אל העפל *to the hill*

→NIDNTT; TWNT

σκοτία,-ας⁺   N1F 0-0-2-1-0-3

Is 16,3; Mi 3,6; Jb 28,3

darkness; neol.?

→TWNT

σκοτίζω⁺   V 0-0-1-4-1-6

Is 13,10; Ps 68(69),24; 73(74),20; 138(139),12;
Eccl 12,2

P: *to be darkened* Ps 138(139),12; *to be dark*
Is 13,10; *to be blinded* Ps 68(69),24

οἱ ἐσκοτισμένοι (sc. τόποι) *dark places* Ps 73
(74),20

→NIDNTT; TWNT

σκοτομήνη,-ης   N1F 0-0-0-1-0-1

Ps 10(11),2

dark, moonless night; neol.

Cf. WALTERS 1973, 114

σκότος,-ους⁺   N3N 11-7-29-54-19-120

Gn 1,2.4.5.18; Ex 10,21

darkness Gn 1,2

*2 Sm 1,9 σκότος δεινόν *dreadful darkness* corr.
σκοτόδινος for MT שבץ *dizziness, vertigo*;
*2 Sm 22,12 σκότος ὑδάτων *darkness of waters*
◊חשרת◊ חשרת מים for MT חשכת מים- *a*
gathering of water; *Ps 54(55),6 σκότος *darkness*
(of death) -צלמות? for MT פלצות *shuddering*

Cf. LE BOULLUEC 1989, 167-168(Ex 14,20); SHIPP 1979,
504-505; WALTERS 1973, 36(2 Sm 1,9); →NIDNTT; TWNT

σκοτόω⁺   V 0-1-2-2-1-6

Jgs^B 4,21; Jer 8,21; 14,2; Jb 3,9; 30,30

A: *to darken* [τι] Sir 25,17

P: *to be in darkness* Jer 14,2; *to suffer from*
vertigo Jgs^B 4,21; *to be blackened* Jb 30,30; *to be*
saddened Jer 8,21

σκοτωθείη τὰ ἄστρα *the stars are darkened*
Jb 3,9

Cf. SHIPP 1979, 504-505; →TWNT

σκυβαλίζω   V 0-0-0-0-1-1

Sir 26,28

M: *to suffer contempt*; neol.?

σκύβαλον,-ου⁺   N2N 0-0-0-0-1-1

Sir 27,4

filth; neol.?

Cf. SPICQ 1978ᵃ, 802-804; →TWNT

σκυθίζω

(→ἀπο-, περι-)

σκυθρωπάζω   V 0-0-2-5-0-7

Jer 19,8; 27(50),13; Ps 34(35),14; 37(38),7;
41(42),10

to look angry or *sullen, to be of a sad*
countenance

σκυθρωπός,-ή/ός,-όν⁺   A 1-0-0-1-1-3

Gn 40,7; Dn^Th 1,10; Sir 25,23

sad, sullen

→TWNT

σκυθρωπῶς   D 0-0-0-0-1-1

3 Mc 5,34

sullenly

σκυλεία,-ας   N1F 0-0-0-0-1-1

1 Mc 4,23

act of despoiling, plundering; neol.

σκυλεύω   V 2-8-12-0-8-30

Ex 3,22; 12,36; 1 Chr 10,8; 2 Chr 14,12.13

to strip, to plunder, to spoil [τινα] Ex 3,22; *id.*
[τι] 2 Chr 14(13),13

Cf. LE BOULLUEC 1989, 95; WEVERS 1990, 39.187

σκυλμός,-οῦ   N2M 0-0-0-0-3-3

3 Mc 3,25; 4,6; 7,5

vexation, cruel treatment; neol.?

Cf. PASSONI DELL'ACQUA 1974, 197-202

σκῦλον,-ου⁺   N2N 10-45-17-7-28-107

Ex 15,9; Nm 31,11.12.26.27

σκῦλα *spoils, booty* Ex 15,9

*1 Sm 23,3 εἰς τὰ σκῦλα *after the spoil* (to go
after the spoil) corr.? εἰς τὰ κοῖλα for
hypothetical original Hebr. אל מערות? *to the caves*
(MT has מערכות *battle lines*)

Cf. DHORME 1910, 207-208(1 Sm 23,3)

σκύμνος,-ου   N2M 5-2-15-6-1-29

Gn 49,9(bis); Nm 23,24; 24,9; Dt 33,22

cub, whelp (esp. of a lion)

σκυτάλη,-ης   N1F 2-2-0-0-0-4

Ex 30,4.5; 2 Sm 3,29; 1 Kgs 12,24b

pole Ex 30,4; *staff, crutch* 2 Sm 3,29

*1 Kgs 12,24b ἄρχοντα σκυτάλης - פלך◊ ל/שׂר פלך
head of the staff or *head of the tribe*? for
hypothetical Hebr. פלך◊ ל/שׂר פלך^II *head of the*
district, cpr. Neh 3,9.12

see ἀναφορεύς, διωστήρ

Cf. DEBUS 1967, 57(1 Kgs 12,24b); GOODING 1959, 23.33; McCARTER 1984, 118(2 Sm 3,29); LE BOULLUEC 1989, 256.305

σκώληξ,-ηκος⁺   N3M 3-0-3-7-6-19
Ex 16,20.24; Dt 28,39; Is 14,11; 66,24
worm Ex 16,20; *woodworm* Prv 12,4; *worm in decayed matter* 2 Mc 9,9
Cf. HORSLEY 1983, 83; →TWNT

σκῶλον,-ου   N2N 2-3-1-0-0-6
Ex 10,7;   Dt 7,16;   Jgs^B 8,27;   Jgs^A 11,35; 2 Chr 28,23
thorn, prickle (metaph.) Ex 10,7; *sharpened stake* (driven into ground), *hindrance, obstacle* Is 57,14
σκῶλον ἐν ὀφθαλμοῖς *a thorn in the eye* Jgs^A 11,35
Cf. CAIRD 1969=1972, 145; LE BOULLUEC 1989, 38-39.137; SCHREINER 1957, 120(Jgs^A 11,35); WALTERS 1973, 76

σκώπτω   V 0-0-0-0-1-1
Sir 10,10
to mock

σμαραγδίτης,-ου   N1M 0-0-0-1-0-1
Est 1,6
emerald; σμαραγδίτης λίθος *emerald(-stone)*

σμάραγδος,-ου⁺   N2F 6-0-1-0-4-11
Ex 28,9.17; 35,12a(12).27; 36,13(39,6)
emerald (bright-green, transparent precious stone)
Cf. LE BOULLUEC 1989, 354; WEVERS 1990, 394.453; →NIDNTT

σμῆγμα,-ατος⁺   N3N 0-0-0-3-1-4
Est 2,3.9.12; Sus^Th 17
soap, unguent, salve

σμικρύνω   V 0-2-2-4-4-12
1 Chr 16,19;   17,17;   Jer 36(29),6;   Hos 4,3; Ps 88(89),46
A: *to diminish the number of* [τινα] Ps 106(107),38; *to reduce, to lessen* [τι] Sir 17,25; *to make short* [τι] Ps 88(89),46
P: *to be diminished* Hos 4,3; *to be diminished in number, to be small* Jer 36(29),6; *to be treated as insignificant* 1 Chr 17,17
(→κατα-)

σμῖλαξ,-ακος   N3F 0-0-2-0-0-2
Jer 26(46),14; Na 1,10
bindweed

σμιρίτης,-ου   N1M 0-0-0-1-0-1
Jb 41,7
emery-powder; σμιρίτης λίθος *smyrite stone*

σμύρνα,-ης⁺   N1F 1-0-0-8-1-10
Ex 30,23; Ps 44(45),9; Ct 3,6; 4,6.14
myrrh
Cf. CAIRD 1976, 78; LE BOULLUEC 1989, 311; →CHANTRAINE (sub σμύρνη); FRISK (sub σμύρνη); MM; NIDNTT; TWNT

σμύρνινος,-η,-ον   A 0-0-0-1-0-1
Est 2,12
made of myrrh, of myrrh; neol.

σοβέω
(→ἀπο-, ἐκ-)

σοομ   A 0-1-0-0-0-1
1 Chr 29,2
= שהם *carnelian*

Σορ   N 0-0-1-0-0-1
Jer 21,13
= צור *rock*
Cf. TOV 1973, 89

σορός,-οῦ⁺   N2M 1-0-0-1-0-2
Gn 50,26; Jb 21,32
coffin
Cf. HARL 1986ᵃ, 318; 1987=1992ᵃ, 100

σός, σή, σόν⁺   A 9-13-5-80-27-134
Gn 14,23; 20,7; 21,13; 30,27; 31,32
your, yours, of you Gn 14,23; τὰ σά *your property, your own* Gn 31,32
τὸ κρίμα μου καὶ τὸ σόν *my judgement and yours* Sir 38,22
→MM

σοφία,-ας⁺   N1F 8-19-10-113-104-254
Ex 31,3; 35,26.31.33.35
cleverness, skill Jb 38,36; *(speculative) wisdom* Is 29,14; *wisdom* (as an advantage given to a certain pers.) Jer 9,22; *wisdom* (which God imparts to those who are close to him) 1 Kgs 5,9; *wisdom* (of God) Ps 50(51),8; *wisdom* (hypostatized and personified as the divine agent in creation) Wis 7,21
ἀρχὴ σοφίας φόβος θεοῦ *fear of the Lord is the beginning of wisdom* Prv 1,7
Cf. CAIRD 1969=1972, 145-146; DODD 1954, 130-131.217-218.242; LARCHER 1983, 173; LE BOULLUEC 1989, 350; WEVERS 1990, 507; →LSJ RSuppl; NIDNTT; TWNT

σοφίζω⁺   V 0-3-0-8-10-21
1 Sm 3,8; 1 Kgs 5,11(bis); Ps 18(19),8; 104(105),22
A: *to make wise, to instruct* [τινα] Ps 18(19),8; *id.* [τινά τι] Ps 118(119),98
M: *to be wise, to gain wisdom* 1 Kgs 5,11; *to become aware that* [ὅτι +ind.] 1 Sm 3,8; *to*

display one's wisdom, to play the wise man
Sir 7,5; to devise cleverly Sir 10,26
P: to be made wise Prv 16,17
Cf. HELBING 1928, 40; →MM
(→κατα-)

σοφιστής,-οῦ   N1M 1-0-0-8-0-9
Ex 7,11; Dnᴸˣˣ 1,20; 2,14.18.24
wise man, diviner, sophist (in pejor. sense)
Cf. LE BOULLUEC 1989, 36-37

σοφός,-ή,-όν⁺   A 12-17-17-117-37-200
Gn 41,8; Ex 28,3; 35,10.25; 36,1
skilled, skillful, clever 1 Chr 22,15; clever,
prudent, wise Jb 32,9; learned, wise Gn 41,8; wise
man, scholar Eccl 12,11; wise (said of God)
Sir 1,8; wise (said of sophists; in pejor. sense)
Dn 2,12; cleverly devised, wise (of things)
1 Ezr 3,5
Cf. DOGNIEZ 1992, 114.134; KILPATRICK 1947, 63-64;
LARCHER 1984, 342.465.466

σοφόω   V 0-0-0-1-0-1
Ps 145(146),8
to give wisdom to, to make wise [τινα]; neol.

σοφῶς   D 0-0-1-1-0-2
Is 40,20; Prv 31,28
wisely

σπάδων,-οντος   N3M 1-0-1-0-0-2
Gn 37,36; Is 39,7
eunuch; neol.?
Cf. GUYOT 1980, 42; HARL 1986ᵃ, 263; WEVERS 1993, 630

σπαίρω   V 0-0-0-0-1-1
4 Mc 15,15
to quiver

σπανίζω   V 0-1-0-2-1-4
2 Kgs 14,26; Jb 14,11; Dnᴸˣˣ 9,24; Jdt 11,12
A: to be scarce, to be wanting Dnᴸˣˣ 9,24
P: to be exhausted, to be wanting (of water)
Jb 14,11; to be in want 2 Kgs 14,26

σπάνιον   D 0-0-0-1-0-1
Prv 25,17
seldom

σπάνις,-εως   N3F 0-0-0-0-1-1
Jdt 8,9
lack, scarcity

σπαράσσω⁺   V 0-1-1-1-1-4
2 Sm 22,8; Jer 4,19; Dnᴸˣˣ 8,7; 3 Mc 4,6
A: to rend asunder [τινα] Dnᴸˣˣ 8,7
P: to be torn asunder 2 Sm 22,8; to be torn (of
the heart) Jer 4,19; to be scarred (of people)
3 Mc 4,6

σπάργανον,-ου   N2N 0-0-1-0-1-2

Ez 16,4; Wis 7,4
swaddling band

σπαργανόω⁺   V 0-0-1-1-0-2
Ez 16,4; Jb 38,9
to swathe [τινα] Ez 16,4; id. [τι] (metaph.)
Jb 38,9

σπαρτίον,-ου   N2N 1-2-3-4-0-10
Gn 14,23; Jos 2,18; Jgsᴮ 16,12; Is 34,11;
Jer 52,21
string, cord Gn 14,23; measuring cord Jb 38,5

σπασμός,-οῦ   N2M 0-0-0-0-1-1
2 Mc 5,2
convulsion, spasm; μαχαιρῶν σπασμούς drawing
of swords

σπαταλάω⁺   V 0-0-1-0-1-2
Ez 16,49; Sir 21,15
to give oneself to pleasure Ez 16,49; ὁ σπαταλῶν
the wanton one Sir 21,15; neol.?
→MM
(→κατα-)

σπατάλη,-ης   N1F 0-0-0-0-1-1
Sir 27,13
wantonness; neol.

σπάω⁺   V 2-23-3-1-4-33
Nm 22,23.31; Jos 5,13; Jgs 8,10
A: to draw (a sword) [τι] Nm 22,23; to draw in
(air) [τι] Wis 7,3
M: to draw (a sword) [τι] Jgs 8,10
(→ἀνα-, ἀπο-, δια-, εἰσ-, ἐκ-, ἐπι-, κατα-,
περι-, συ-)

σπεῖρα,-ας⁺   N1F 0-0-0-0-4-4
Jdt 14,11; 2 Mc 8,23; 12,20.22
tactical unit, division
→MM

σπειρηδόν   D 0-0-0-0-2-2
2 Mc 5,2; 12,20
by cohorts, in troops; neol.?

σπείρω⁺   V 22-4-23-9-4-62
Gn 1,11.12.29; 26,12; 47,19
to sow (seed) [τι] Gn 1,11; id. (a land, a field)
[τι] Gn 47,23; id. [abs.] Sir 7,3; to scatter [τι]
Nm 17,2; to scatter, to disperse [τινα] Zech 10,9
ὁ σπείρων φαῦλα θερίσει κακά he who sows
wickedness shall reap troubles Prv 22,8
Cf. HARL 1986ᵃ, 211; PARADISE 1986, 193; WEVERS 1990,
530; →NIDNTT; TWNT
(→δια-, κατα-)

σπένδω⁺   V 6-2-9-1-2-20
Gn 35,14; Ex 25,29; 30,9; 38,12(37,16); Nm 4,7
A: to pour out as an offering [τί τινι]

4 Mc 3,16; *to offer drink-offerings* Ex 25,29
M: *to offer to sb* [τί τινι] Dnᵀʰ 2,46
σπένδω σπονδήν *to offer a libation* (semit.)
Gn 35,14; σπείσεις σπονδήν σικερα κυρίῳ *you
poured strong drink as a drink-offering to the
Lord* Nm 28,7
→NIDNTT; TWNT

σπέρμα,-ατος⁺   N3N 113-27-51-36-53-280
Gn 1,11(bis).12(bis).29
seed (of plants) Gn 47,19; *seed-time, time of
sowing* Gn 8,22; *the male seed, semen* Lv 18,21;
seed, offspring (of men) Gn 9,9; *id.* (of anim.)
Gn 3,15; σπέρματα *descendants, children,
posterity* 4 Mc 18,1; *crops* 1 Sm 8,15
κοιτὴ σπέρματος *emission of seed, intercourse*
Lv 15,16; σπείρων σπέρμα *yielding seed?*
(semit.) Gn 1,11; σπέρμα σπόριμον *seed for
sowing* (semit.) Lv 11,37
*Jer 27(50),16 σπέρμα *seed* -זרע for MT זורע
sower; *Ez 31,17 σπέρμα *seed* -זרע for MT זרוע?
arm?, see also 1 Sm 2,31; Is 17,5; 33,2;
Dnᵀʰ 11,6.31; *Nm 21,30 καὶ τὸ σπέρμα αὐτῶν
and their seed -ונינם וניב *and their offspring* or
ונירם ניירᴵᴵ *and their fields tilled for the first time*
for MT ונירם ירהδ *we shot them*
Cf. HARL 1986ª, 45.47-48.56-57.91.109.162.184; HARLÉ
1988, 131.162; MARTIN 1965, 425-427(Gn 3,15); PARADISE
1986, 192-193; TALMON 1960, 153.175; →LSJ Suppl; NIDNTT;
TWNT

σπερματίζω   V 2-0-0-0-0-2
Ex 9,31; Lv 12,2
A: *to go to seed, to seed* (of plants) Ex 9,31
P: *to conceive, to become pregnant* Lv 12,2
neol.
Cf. HARLÉ 1988, 133; LEE, J. 1983, 50
(→ἐκ-)

σπερματισμός,-οῦ   N2M 1-0-0-0-0-1
Lv 18,23
insemination
Cf. HARLÉ 1988, 163

σπεύδω⁺   V 10-26-6-9-15-66
Gn 18,6(bis); 19,22; 24,18.20
to hasten, to be hasty Gn 18,6; *to make haste
with, to make haste to* [+inf.] Est 8,14; *to seek
eagerly, to strive after* [τι] Is 16,5; *to hasten, to
shorten* [τι] Sir 36,7
to be troubled, to be frightened Ex 15,15, see also
Jgs 20,41; 1 Sm 28,21
*Jer 4,6 σπεύσατε *hasten* -האיצו ◊אוץ? for MT העיזו
◊עוז *flee;* *Ez 30,9 σπεύδοντες *hastening* -אצים?

◊אוץ or בצים בוצ◊ (Arab.) for MT צים/ב *in ships;*
*Mi 4,1 καὶ σπεύσουσι *and they shall hasten*
-ומהרו for MT ונהרו *and they shall stream* (towards
it), see also Jer 38(31),20
Cf. LE BOULLUEC 1989, 175; WALTERS 1973, 144-148.318
(→ἐπι-, κατα-)

σπήλαιον,-ου⁺   N2N 15-23-12-2-3-55
Gn 19,30; 23,9.11.17(bis)
cave Gn 19,30; *cave, place of refuge* Is 33,16; *den*
Jer 7,11
*Jer 12,9 σπήλαιον *hiding place* -עיט ◊ġāṭa
(Arab.) for MT עיט *bird of prey;* *Jer 27(50),26 ὡς
σπήλαιον *as a cave* -כ/מערה for MT כמו ערמים *like
heaps of grain;* *Hab 2,15 τὰ σπήλαια αὐτῶν
their caves -מערותיהם for MT מעוריהם ◊ערה *nakedness?,*
cpr. 1QpHab 9,3 מוערד◊ מערידם *their meetings, their
feasts?*
Cf. CAIRD 1969=1972, 146; DRIVER 1955, 139(Jer 12,9);
EMERTON 1969, 185-188

σπιθαμή,-ῆς⁺   N1F 4-3-2-0-0-9
Ex 28,16(bis); 36,16(bis)(39,9(bis)); Jgsᴬ 3,16
span (space between thumb and little finger)

σπιλόω⁺   V 0-0-0-0-1-1
Wis 15,4
P: *to be spotted* or *stained;* neol.
Cf. LARCHER 1985, 856

σπινθήρ,-ῆρος   N3M 0-0-2-0-6-8
Is 1,31; Ez 1,7; Wis 2,2; 3,7; 11,18
spark, cpr. Ct (ed. sexta) 8,6: σπίνθραξ

σπλάγχνον,-ου⁺   N2N 0-0-1-2-14-17
Jer 28(51),13; Prv 12,10; 26,22; 2 Mc 9,5.6
mostly in pl.: *inward parts, entrails* 4 Mc 10,8;
body (in opp. to πνεῦμα) Bar 2,17; *seat of
feelings, affections* Prv 12,10; *love, yearning*
Wis 10,5
*Jer 28(51),13 εἰς τὰ σπλάγχνα σου *towards
your inward parts* -במעיך for MT בצעך *your share*
Cf. HORSLEY 1983, 84; LARCHER 1984, 621; MACLAURIN
1971, 42-45; SPICQ 1978ª, 812-815; →TWNT

σπλαγχνίζω⁺   V 0-0-0-0-1-1
2 Mc 6,8
to share in the sacrifices; neol.
Cf. SPICQ 1978ª, 812-815; →NIDNTT; TWNT
(→ἐπι-)

σπλαγχνισμός,-οῦ   N2M 0-0-0-0-3-3
2 Mc 6,7.21; 7,42
the eating of internal organs of a sacrificial victim
or *pagan sacrifices;* neol.

σπλαγχνοφάγος,-ος,-ον   A 0-0-0-0-1-1
Wis 12,5

eating internal organs of a sacrificial victim; neol.
Cf. LARCHER 1985, 707

σποδιά,-ᾶς   N1F 4-0-0-0-0-4
Lv 4,12(bis); Nm 19,10.17
ashes, heap of ashes
Cf. DANIEL 1966, 170

σποδοειδής,-ής,-ές   A 3-0-0-0-0-3
Gn 30,39; 31,10.12
ashen, ash-coloured

σποδόομαι   V 0-0-0-0-1-1
Jdt 4,11
to cast ashes upon one's head, to strew one's head with ashes [τι]

σποδός,-οῦ⁺   N2F 3-1-8-12-14-38
Gn 18,27;   Lv 1,16;   Nm 19,9;   2 Sm 13,19;
Is 44,20
ashes Lv 1,16; *id.* (metaph.) Is 44,20; *ashes*
(used in a ceremony of mourning) 2 Sm 13,19
ἐγώ εἰμι γῆ καὶ σποδός *I am earth and ashes*
(as a designation for sth transitory) Gn 18,27
Cf. DANIEL 1966, 170

σπονδεῖον,-ου   N2N 3-1-0-0-4-8
Ex 25,29;   38,12(37,16);   Nm 4,7;   1 Chr 28,17;
1 Ezr 2,9
cup or *bowl from which the* σπονδή *was poured*
Cf. LE BOULLUEC 1989, 260

σπονδή,-ῆς   N1F 43-4-13-5-3-68
Gn 35,14; Ex 29,40.41; 30,9; Lv 23,13
drink-offering, libation

σπόνδυλα,-ων   N2N 0-0-0-0-1-1
4 Mc 10,8
spine, vertebra (later form of σφόνδυλος)

σπονδυλίζομαι
(→ἐκ-)

σπορά,-ᾶς⁺   N1F 0-1-0-0-1-2
2 Kgs 19,29; 1 Mc 10,30
sowing 2 Kgs 19,29; *seed* 1 Mc 10,30
Cf. DODD 1954, 232; WALTERS 1973, 213; →TWNT

σπόριμος,-ος,-ον⁺   A 3-0-0-0-0-3
Gn 1,29(bis); Lv 11,37
fit for sowing, bearing seed
Cf. HARL 1986ᵃ, 97; HARLÉ 1988, 131; →TWNT

σπόρος,-ου⁺   N2M 5-0-3-2-1-11
Ex 34,21; Lv 26,5.20; 27,16; Dt 11,10
seed-time Ex 34,21; *seed* Lv 26,20
χλόην σπόρου *crops of the field* Sir 40,22
Cf. LE BOULLUEC 1989, 342; WALTERS 1973, 227; →NIDNTT

σπουδάζω⁺   V 0-0-1-7-3-11
Is 21,3; Jb 4,5; 21,6; 22,10; 23,15
to make haste to do [+inf.] Jdt 13,1; *to make*

haste to sth [εἴς τι] Jb 31,5; *to pay serious attention to* [περί τινος] Eccl 8,2; *to trouble, to disturb* [τινα] Jb 22,10; *to be upset, to be alarmed, to be frightened, to be anxious* (semit.?)
Jb 4,5
Cf. GEHMAN 1951=1972, 89; SPICQ 1978ᵃ, 817-818;
WALTERS 1973, 144.148; →MM; TWNT
(→ἐπι-, κατα-)

σπουδαῖος,-α,-ον⁺   A 0-0-1-0-0-1
Ez 41,25
worth serious attention, excellent
Cf. SPICQ 1978ᵃ, 822-824; →NIDNTT

σπουδαιότης,-ητος   N3F 0-0-0-0-1-1
3 Mc 1,9
earnestness, care displayed

σπουδαίως⁺   D 0-0-0-0-1-1
Wis 2,6
earnestly, ardently
Cf. SPICQ 1978ᵃ, 821

σπουδή,-ῆς⁺   N1F 3-2-4-9-15-33
Ex 12,11.33; Dt 16,3; Jgsᴮ 5,22; 1 Sm 21,9
haste, hurry Ex 12,11; *zeal, diligence, effort*
Wis 14,17; *anxiety, fright* (semit.) Jer 8,15;
σπουδῇ *with speed* Ex 12,33
*Jgsᴮ 5,22 σπουδῇ -מהר⟨⟩ *quickly* for MT מרהרות
from the galloping
Cf. SPICQ 1978ᵃ, 816-825; WALTERS 1973, 145-146.148;
WEVERS 1990, 174.186; →NIDNTT; TWNT

σταγών,-όνος⁺   N3F 0-0-2-4-3-9
Is 40,15; Mi 2,11; Ps 64(65),11; 71(72),6; Jb
36,27
drop of water Is 40,15; *raindrop* Jb 36,27; *drop of blood* 4 Mc 10,8

στάδιον,-ου⁺   N2N 0-0-0-1-7-8
Dnᴸˣˣ 4,12(9); 2 Mc 11,5; 12,9.10.16
stade (as a standard of length the stadium
differed from place to place, the representative
- Olympic - stadium was c. 192 m) Dnᴸˣˣ
4,12(9); *walk* Susᴸˣˣ 37
→LSJ RSuppl

στάζω⁺   V 1-6-3-7-1-18
Ex 9,33; Jgsᴬ 5,4; Jgsᴮ 5,4(bis); Jgsᴮ 6,38
to drop, to trickle [abs.] Ex 9,33; *to stream, to pour down* (metaph., of divine anger)
2 Chr 12,7; *to drop, to let fall, to shed drop by drop* (water) [τι] Jgs 5,4; *id.* (myrrh) [τι] Ct 5,5;
to fall (of drops) Ps 71(72),6; *to fall to pieces* (of a house) Eccl 10,18
στάζοι μου ὁ ὀφθαλμός *let my eye weep*
Jb 16,20(21)

Cf. HELBING 1928, 91; WEVERS 1990, 142; →LSJ suppl
(→ἀπο-)

σταθμάω V 0-1-0-0-0-1
1 Kgs 6,23
P: *to be measured*

στάθμιον,-ου N2N 6-1-4-4-1-16
Lv 19,35.36; 27,25; Dt 25,13(bis)
(standard) weight Lv 19,35; *weight, small stone*
(for balance, for scales) Lv 19,35; *plummet*
2 Kgs 21,13
ζυγὸν σταθμίων *pair of scales* Ez 5,1
Cf. WEVERS 1995, 396

σταθμός,-οῦ⁺ N2M 10-24-8-5-7-54
Gn 43,21; Ex 12,7.22.23; 21,6
lodge, rest station Jer 9,1(2); *stage* (of a journey)
Nm 33,1; *post, doorpost* Ex 12,7; *door* 2 Kgs
12,10; *balance, scales* Is 40,12; *weight* Gn 43,21;
id. (metaph.) Sir 16,25; *(standard) measure*
Is 28,17
οὐκ ἔστιν σταθμὸς τῆς καλλονῆς αὐτοῦ *his*
excellence cannot be weighed Sir 6,15
Cf. DORIVAL 1994, 167; HARLÉ 1988, 208; LARCHER 1985,
684-686; LAUNEY 1950, 695-712; LLEWELYN 1994, 4

σταῖς, σταιτός N3N 2-1-1-0-0-4
Ex 12,34.39; 2 Sm 13,8; Jer 7,18
flour of spelt mixed and made into dough, dough
Cf. WEVERS 1990, 186

στακτή,-ῆς N1F 3-2-2-2-1-10
Gn 37,25; 43,11; Ex 30,34; 1 Kgs 10,25; 2 Chr
9,24
oil of myrrh Gn 37,25
Cf. LE BOULLUEC 1989, 313; MONTGOMERY 1938, 137

σταλαγμός,-οῦ N2M 0-0-0-0-1-1
4 Mc 9,20
dropping, dripping

σταλάζω V 0-0-1-0-0-1
Mi 2,11
to drop, to drip; neol.
(→ἀπο-)

στάμνος,-ου⁺ N2M 1-3-0-0-1-5
Ex 16,33; 1 Kgs 12,24h.i.l; Bel^LXX 33
jar, pot
Cf. LE BOULLUEC 1989, 188; WEVERS 1990, 260

στασιάζω⁺ V 0-0-0-0-3-3
Jdt 7,15; 2 Mc 4,30; 14,6
to rebel, to stir sedition
(→κατα-)

στάσιμος,-η,-ον A 0-0-0-0-1-1
Sir 26,17
steady; ἐπὶ ἡλικίᾳ στασίμῃ *at a ripe age*

στάσις,-εως⁺ N3F 1-11-3-11-4-30
Dt 28,65; Jos 10,13; Jgs 9,6; 1 Kgs 10,5
standing (of pers.) 1 Kgs 10,5; *rest* Dt 28,65;
position, post 2 Chr 35,15; *posture* 3 Mc 1,23;
position, array (of heavenly bodies) Neh 9,6;
military position Na 3,11; *place, foundation*
2 Chr 23,13; *statute, decree* Dn^Th 6,8; *rebellion,*
sedition Prv 17,14
στάσιν ποδῶν *place for the feet, place for people*
1 Chr 28,2, see also 1 Mc 10,72; ὁ λαὸς ἐν τῇ
στάσει αὐτοῦ *the people stood in their place, the*
people replaced them Neh 8,7
*Ez 1,28 στάσις *position, array* corr. ὅρασις for
MT מראה *appearance*; *Jgs 9,6 τῆς στάσεως *of the*
military post, of the garrison? -המצב? for MT מצב
erected? (see also εὑρετός); *Neh 9,6 στάσιν
αὐτῶν *their array* -נצבם for MT צבא/ם *their host*
Cf. CAIRD 1969=1972, 146(Jgs 9,6); DORIVAL 1994, 343;
SOISALON-SOININEN 1951, 81(Jgs 9,6); SPICQ 1978ᵃ,
826-828; →LSJ RSuppl(Jgs 9,6); NIDNTT; TWNT

-στατέω
(→ἀπο-, ἐπι-, προ-)

-στατόω
(→ἀνα-)

σταυρόω⁺ V 0-0-0-2-0-2
Est 7,9; 8,12r
to crucify
→NIDNTT; TWNT

σταφίς,-ίδος N3F 1-3-1-0-0-5
Nm 6,3; 1 Sm 25,18; 2 Sm 16,1; 1 Chr 12,41;
Hos 3,1
dried grape, raisin

σταφυλή,-ῆς⁺ N1F 12-3-6-1-9-31
Gn 40,10.11; 49,11; Lv 25,5; Nm 6,3
(bunch of) grapes Gn 40,10
*Ez 36,8 ὑμῶν τὴν σταφυλήν *your grapes* -ענביכם
for MT ענפכם *your branches*

στάχυς,-υος⁺ N3M 12-3-2-2-0-19
Gn 41,5.6.7(bis).22
ear of corn Gn 41,5; *corn* Jgs 15,5
Cf. CAIRD 1969=1972, 146-147(Jgs^B 12,6); WEVERS 1990,
343(Ex 22,5)

στέαρ, στέατος N3N 64-11-10-7-7-99
Gn 4,4; Ex 23,18; 29,13(bis).22
hard fat Ex 29,22; *(animal) fat* Gn 4,4; *(dough*
made from) flour of spelt? (syn. of σταῖς;
rendering Hebr. חלב *fat, the finest part*) Hos 7,4,
cpr. Ps 80(81),17
*Jb 21,24 στέατος *fat* -חלב for MT חלב *milk*, see
also Is 55,1

στεατόομαι   V 0-0-1-0-0-1
Ez 39,18
to be fatted; neol.

στεγάζω   V 0-1-0-4-0-5
2 Chr 34,11; Ps 103(104),3; Neh 2,8; 3,3.6
to roof, to cover with a roof

στέγη,-ης+   N1F 1-0-1-0-2-4
Gn 8,13; Ez 40,43; 1 Ezr 6,4; 4 Mc 17,3
covering, roof (of the ark) Gn 8,13; roof
1 Ezr 6,4; shelter, roof Ez 40,43

στεγνός,-ή,-όν   A 0-0-0-1-0-1
Prv 31,27
waterproof, watertight; στεγναὶ διατριβαὶ
οἴκων αὐτῆς the ways of her household are
careful

στέγω+   V 0-0-0-0-1-1
Sir 8,17
to cover, to conceal, to keep secret [τι]
Cf. SPICQ 1978ᵃ, 829-830; →TWNT

στεῖρα, (gen. -ας)+   A 5-5-3-2-2-17
Gn 11,30; 25,21; 29,31; Ex 23,26; Dt 7,14
sterile, incapable of bearing children, barren (only
fem. forms of the adj.)

στειρόω   V 0-0-0-0-1-1
Sir 42,10
to prove barren, to be childless; neol.

στέλεχος,-ους   N3N 3-0-4-3-1-11
Gn 49,21; Ex 15,27; Nm 33,9; Jer 17,8; Ez 19,11
stem, trunk Ex 15,27; id. (metaph.) Gn 49,21;
branch Jer 17,8; pillar, column (of smoke) Ct 3,6
*Gn 49,21 στέλεχος branch -עלה? (cpr. Jer 17,8)
for MT לה אַ doe; *Jb 29,18 ὥσπερ στέλεχος
φοίνικος as the stem of a palm-tree -כ/נחל? for
MT כ/חול like sand or כ/חולᴵᴵ like the phoenix, see
φοῖνιξ

στέλλω+   V 0-0-1-1-5-7
Mal 2,5; Prv 31,25(26); 2 Mc 5,1; 3 Mc 1,19;
4,11
M: to journey, to go 3 Mc 4,11; to keep away
from, to stand aloof from [ἀπό τινος] Mal 2,5;
to prepare for oneself [τι] Wis 14,1; to obtain, to
acquire Wis 7,14
P: to be introduced (into a new family), to be
married 3 Mc 1,19
τάξιν ἐστείλατο τῇ γλώσσῃ αὐτῆς she
controlled her tongue Prv 31,25
→TWNT
(→ἀνα-, ἀνταπο-, ἀπο-, δια-, ἐπ-, ἐξ-, κατα-,
περι-, προ-, προσ-, συ-, ὑπο-)

στέμφυλον,-ου   N2N 1-0-0-0-0-1

Nm 6,4
mass of pressed grapes
Cf. SHIPP 1979, 517

στεναγμός,-οῦ+   N2M 3-2-6-11-6-28
Gn 3,16; Ex 2,24; 6,5; Jgs 2,18
sighing, groaning Gn 3,16
*Ez 24,17 στεναγμός sigh -אנק (subst.) for MT
האנק sigh (verb imper.)
Cf. HARL 1986ᵃ, 109(Gn 3,16); LE BOULLUEC 1989, 87;
WEVERS 1993, 45; →NIDNTT; TWNT

στενάζω+   V 0-0-13-7-7-27
Is 19,8(bis); 21,2; 24,7; 30,15
to sigh, to groan Tobˢ 3,1; to bemoan, to lament
over [τινα] Na 3,7
*Ez 26,16 στενάζουσιν they shall groan corr.
στυγνάζουσιν for MT שממו they shall be
appalled, see also Jb 18,20, cpr. Ez 28,19; see
στυγνάζω; *Is 21,2 στενάζω I will groan -אנחתי
for MT אנחתה her sighing? cpr. 30,15
Cf. HELBING 1928, 73; WALTERS 1973, 131-132(Ez 26,16);
→NIDNTT; TWNT
(→ἀνα-, κατα-)

στενακτός,-ή,-όν   A 0-0-1-0-0-1
Ez 5,15
to be mourned

στενός,-ή,-όν+   A 1-7-5-3-3-19
Nm 22,26; 1 Sm 23,14.19; 24,1.23
narrow, strait (of place) Nm 22,26; short (of
time) Jer 37(30),7; scant (of water) Is 30,20;
close, constricting Is 8,22; hard 1 Chr 21,13;
severe Jb 18,11; τὰ στενά narrow passes, places
difficult to approach 1 Sm 23,14; narrows, straits
Jb 24,11; anguish Bar 3,1
στενά μοι πάντοθεν σφόδρα ἐστίν I am in
straits on every side 2 Sm 24,14, see also Susᵀʰ 22
*1 Sm 24,23 εἰς τὴν Μεσσαρα στενήν to
Messara, the narrow place translit. of מצורה-על?
(reading ר for ד) followed by a transl. of מצורה
narrow, place difficult to approach, stronghold for
MT המצורה על to the stronghold, cpr. 1 Sm 23,14.
19
→TWNT

στενότης,-ητος   N3F 0-0-0-0-1-1
2 Mc 12,21
narrowness, straitness; διὰ τὴν πάντων τῶν
τόπων στενότητα because of the narrow
approaches on all sides

στενοχωρέω+   V 0-2-2-0-1-5
Jos 17,15; Jgsᴮ 16,16; Is 28,20; 49,19; 4 Mc 11,11
A: to press closely [τινα] Jgsᴮ 16,16; to be

narrow Is 49,19; *to be too little for* [τινα]
Jos 17,15
P: *to be straitened, to be in straits, to be cramped*
Is 28,20
τὸ πνεῦμα στενοχωρούμενος *not being able to
breathe freely, in a grievous strait for breath, his
breath confined* 4 Mc 11,11
→TWNT

στενοχωρία,-ας⁺   N1F 3-0-3-2-5-13
Dt 28,53.55.57; Is 8,22.23
distress, difficulty
→TWNT

στενόω
(→ἀπο-)

στένω   V 2-0-0-4-0-6
Gn 4,12.14; Jb 10,1; 30,28; Prv 28,28
to moan, to sigh, to groan, to lament Gn 4,12
*Jb 10,1 στένων *lamenting* -נהי for MT בחיי *in my
life, of my life*

στενῶς   D 0-1-0-0-0-1
1 Sm 13,6
*presenting a threat, offering difficulties, in
difficulties, in a strait*

στέργω⁺   V 0-0-0-0-1-1
Sir 27,17
to love [τινα]
Cf. MURAOKA 1990, 50
(→ἀπο-)

στερεός,-ά,-όν⁺   A 5-1-8-1-1-16
Ex 38,13.16(37,17.23); Nm 8,4(bis); Dt 32,13
solid Ex 38,13; *severe* Jer 15,18; *strong* Ps
34(35),10; *mighty* 1 Sm 4,8
*Is 17,5 στερεᾷ *sound, strong* -רפה◊for MT רפאים
Rephaim
Cf. LE BOULLUEC 1989, 365; WEVERS 1990, 624; →TWNT

στερεόω⁺   V 0-2-11-8-13-34
1 Sm 2,1; 6,18; Is 42,5; 44,24; 45,12
A: *to make firm* or *solid, to fix* [τι] Jer 10,4; *to
strenghten* [τι] Ps 74(75),3; *id.* [τινα] Sir 45,8;
to establish [τι] Ps 92(93),1; *to confirm* [τι]
Sir 3,2; *to fortify* [τι] Sir 50,1; *to lay on* [τι]
Sir 39,28; *to make hard* [τι] (metaph.) Jer 5,3
P: *to be established* Ps 32(33),6; *to be fortified*
1 Sm 6,18; *to be severe* Jer 52,6
ἐστερεώθησαν ὑπὲρ ἐμέ *they were stronger than
I* Ps 17(18),18; ἐπὶ θυγατρὶ ἀδιατρέπτῳ
στερέωσον φυλακήν *keep a strict watch over
your headstrong daughter* Sir 26,10, see also
42,11; καὶ ἐστερέωσεν τὸν πόλεμον *he
continued the battle fiercely* 1 Mc 10,50

*1 Sm 2,1 ἐστερεώθη *(my heart) is established,
is strong* -עצם◊ for MT עלץ *exults*; *Is 51,6
ἐστερεώθη *it appeared solid* -מלא◊? for MT נמלחו
they are dispersed in fragments; *Am 4,13
στερεῶν *establishing* -יוצב for MT יוצר *forming*
→TWNT

στερέω⁺   V 3-0-0-5-11-19
Gn 30,2; 48,11; Nm 24,11; Ps 20(21),3; 77(78),30
A: *to deprive sb of sth* [τινά τινος] Nm 24,11;
id. [τινά τι] Gn 30,2; *to cause sth to be lacking
from* [τί τινος] Jb 22,7
P: *to be deprived of* [τινος] Gn 48,11; *to loose*
[τινος] 2 Mc 13,10
τὸ ζῆν ἐστερήθης *you were deprived of life, you
died* 3 Mc 5,32
Cf. HELBING 1928, 44
(→ἀπο-)

στερέωμα,-ατος⁺   N3N 11-0-5-9-5-30
Gn 1,6.7(ter).8
firmness Ps 72(73),4; *strength* (metaph.)
Ps 17(18),3; *solid part, strength* (of an army)
1 Mc 9,14; *foundation, firm place* 1 Ezr 8,78;
confirmation, ratification (of a letter) Est 9,29;
firmament Gn 1,6; *dome, firmament, sky*
Ex 24,10, see also Ez 1,22.23.25; 10,1
Cf. HARL 1986ᵃ, 89; WEVERS 1990, 385; 1993, 3; →MM;
TWNT

στερέωσις,-εως   N3F 0-0-0-0-1-1
Sir 28,10
obstinacy (of conflict); neol.

στερίσκω   V 0-0-0-1-0-1
Eccl 4,8
to deprive sth of sth [τι ἀπό τινος]
Cf. HELBING 1928, 45

στέρνον,-ου   N2N 0-0-0-0-1-1
Sir 26,18
chest, breast

στεφάνη,-ης   N1F 7-0-1-0-0-8
Ex 25,25(bis).27; 27,3; 30,3
rim, moulding
Cf. DOGNIEZ 1992, 251; LE BOULLUEC 1989, 260.275.305;
WEVERS 1990, 397.403.432

στεφανηφορέω   V 0-0-0-0-1-1
Wis 4,2
to wear a wreath or *crown*
Cf. LARCHER 1984, 317

στέφανος,-ου⁺   N2M 0-2-13-14-21-50
2 Sm 12,30; 1 Chr 20,2; Is 22,18.21; 28,1
most often translation of עטרה; *crown, sign of
distinction* Is 22,21; *royal crown* (as distinguished

from the priestly κίδαρις? Ez 21,31)
Ps 20(21),4; *garland* (sign of joy) Jdt 3,7; *crown,
reward* (metaph.) Prv 17,6; *sign of distinction*
(metaph. of old age) Prv 16,31; οἱ στέφανοι
crown taxes 1 Mc 10,29

*Is 22,18 τὸν στέφανον *the crown* -צנוף for MT
צנוף (inf.) *wind around*; *Ps 64(65),12 τὸν
στέφανον *the crown* -עטרת (subst.) for MT עטרת
(verb) *you crown*

Cf. DELCOR 1967ª, 161-163; DE TROYER 1997
forthcoming; HORSLEY 1982, 50; LUST 1985, 188-190
(Ez 21,31); MONSENGWO PASINYA 1980, 369-375; →NIDNTT;
TWNT

στεφανόω⁺   V 0-0-0-4-4-8
Ps 5,13; 8,6; 102(103),4; Ct 3,11; Jdt 15,13
A: *to crown* (athletes in contests) [τινα]
4 Mc 17,15; *to crown* [τινα] (of the nuptial
crown) Ct 3,11; *to crown* [τινα] (metaph.)
Ps 5,13
M: *to crown oneself with* [τι] Jdt 15,13
→NIDNTT; TWNT

στέφος,-ους   N3N 0-0-0-0-1-1
3 Mc 4,8
garland, wreath

στέφω   V 0-0-0-0-1-1
Wis 2,8
M: *to crown oneself*
Cf. LARCHER 1983, 232
(→κατα-)

στηθοδεσμίς,-ίδος   N3F 0-0-1-0-0-1
Jer 2,32
breast-band, girdle; neol.

στῆθος,-ους⁺   N3N 4-0-0-5-0-9
Gn 3,14; Ex 28,29.30(bis); Jb 39,20
breast Ex 28,29; στήθη *breast* Prv 6,10
Cf. LE BOULLUEC 1989, 288

στηθύνιον,-ου   N2N 12-0-0-0-0-12
Ex 29,26.27; Lv 7,30.31.34
dim. of στῆθος; *breast* (as part of a victim)

στήκω⁺   V 0-1-0-0-0-1
Jgsᴮ 16,26
to stand; neol.
→TWNT

στήλη,-ης⁺   N1F 22-14-5-0-4-45
Gn 19,26; 28,18.22; 31,13.45
pillar 3 Mc 2,27; *cultic pillar* (used in the cult of
pagan gods) Gn 19,26; *pillar* (to the Lord) Is
19,19; *gravestone* Gn 35,20
*2 Chr 33,3 στήλας *cultic pillars* -מצבות for MT
מזבחות *altars*

Cf. DANIEL 1966, 39-40; HARL 1986ª, 62; HARLÉ 1988,
208(Lv 26,30); WEVERS 1990, 372-373; 1993, 453.585

στηλογραφία,-ας   N1F 0-0-0-6-0-6
Ps 15(16),1; 55(56),1; 56(57),1; 57(58),1;
58(59),1
inscription or *title* (of certain Psalms)

στηλόω   V 0-8-0-1-0-9
Jgsᴬ 18,16.17; 2 Sm 1,19; 18,17.18
A: *to set up as a* στήλη *or pillar, monument, to
erect, to set up* [τι] 2 Sm 18,17; *to set up* [τινα]
(metaph.) Lam 3,12
P: *to take one's place, to stand* Jgsᴬ 18,16
*2 Sm 1,19 στήλωσον *set up a monument* -◊יצב
for MT צבי *glory, elite*

στήμων,-ονος   N3M 10-0-0-0-0-10
Lv 13,48.49.51.52.53
warp

στῆρ, στῆτος   N3N 0-0-0-0-1-1
Belᵀʰ 27
contr. of στέαρ; *fat*

στήριγμα,-ατος   N3N 0-2-4-3-9-18
2 Sm 20,19; 2 Kgs 25,11; Ez 4,16; 5,16; 7,11
support, provision (of bread) Ps 104(105),16, cpr.
Ps 71(72),16; *support, staff* Ez 7,11; *support,
helper* Tob 8,6
*2 Kgs 25,11 τὸ λοιπὸν τοῦ στηρίγματος *the
rest of the solid (citizens)* -יתר האמון for MT
יתר ההמון *the rest of the multitude*, cpr. Jerᴹᵀ 52,15
Cf. CAIRD 1969=1972, 147(2 Sm 20,19; 2 Kgs 25,11)

στηρίζω⁺   V 5-7-17-9-17-55
Gn 27,37; 28,12; Ex 17,12(bis); Lv 13,55
A: *to support, to strengthen* [τι] Ex 17,12(primo);
id. [τινα] Gn 27,37; *to strengthen* [τι] Jgs 19,5;
to establish [τι] Prv 15,25; *to lean sth upon sth*
[τι ἐπί τι] Jer 17,5; *to continue* [τι] Sir 40,19
M: *to establish* Is 59,16
P: *to be fixed* Gn 28,12; *to be fixed, to be present*
Lv 13,55; *to be established* 1 Sm 26,19; *to be held
up, to be supported* Sir 13,21; *to stay on* [ἐπί τι]
2 Kgs 18,21; *to be steadfast* Sir 5,10
τὰ ἐστηριγμένα *the pillars* 2 Kgs 18,16; στηριῶ
τοὺς ὀφθαλμούς μου ἐπ' αὐτοὺς *I will fix my
eyes on them* (semit.) Am 9,4; στηριῶ τὸ
πρόσωπόν μου ἐφ' ὑμᾶς *I will set my face on you*
(to denote firmness of purpose; semit.) Jer 3,12
Cf. BARR 1961, 166-170; HARL 1986ª, 219(Gn 27,37);
SPICQ 1982, 611-615; TURNER 1978, 481-482(Prv 16,30;
27,20a; Am 9,4; Jer 24,6); →LSJ RSuppl; TWNT
(→ἀντι-, ἐπι-, κατα-, ὑπο-)

στιβαρός,-ά,-όν⁺   A 0-0-1-0-0-1

Ez 3,6
harsh, bulky, thick, heavy

στιβαρῶς   D 0-0-1-0-0-1
Hab 2,6
heavily

στίβι,-ιος   N3N 0-0-1-0-0-1
Jer 4,30
stibium, powdered antimony used for eyepainting;
neol.
Cf. WALTERS 1973, 104.305-306

στιβίζομαι   V 0-0-1-0-0-1
Ez 23,40
to paint with black paint [τι]
Cf. WALTERS 1973, 305

στίγμα,-ατος⁺   N3N 0-0-0-1-0-1
Ct 1,11
stud, mark, ornament
→NIDNTT; TWNT

στιγμή,-ῆς⁺   N1F 0-0-1-0-1-2
Is 29,5; 2 Mc 9,11
(a brief) *moment* Is 29,5
κατὰ στιγμὴν ἐπιτεινόμενος *increasing every*
moment 2 Mc 9,11

στικτός,-ή,-όν   A 1-0-0-0-0-1
Lv 19,28
pricked, tattooed
Cf. JONES 1987, 144

στιλβόω   V 0-0-0-1-0-1
Ps 7,13
to polish, to furbish (a sword) [τι]; neol.

στίλβω⁺   V 0-0-3-2-4-9
Ez 21,33; 40,3; Na 3,3; Dnᵀʰ 10,6; Ezr 8,27
to glitter, to gleam 1 Ezr 8,56; *to shine* 1 Mc 6,39
→TWNT

στίλβωσις,-εως   N3F 0-0-2-0-0-2
Ez 21,15.20
gleam, shining; neol.

στιμίζομαι   V 0-1-0-0-0-1
2 Kgs 9,30
see στιβίζομαι

στιππύινος,-η,-ον   A 2-0-0-0-0-2
Lv 13,47.59
made of tow; neol.?
Cf. HARLÉ 1988, 140; WALTERS 1973, 78-79

στιππύον,-ου   N2N 0-3-1-2-1-7
Jgs 15,14; Jgsᴮ 16,9; Is 1,31; Dnᴸˣˣ 3,46
the coarse fibre of flax or *hemp, tow, oakum;*
neol.?
Cf. WALTERS 1973, 78-79.296

στιχίζω   V 0-0-1-0-0-1

Ez 42,3
P: *to be arranged in a row;* neol.
Cf. BARTHÉLEMY 1990, 259

στίχος,-ου   N2M 11-10-0-0-.-21
Ex 28,17(bis).18.19.20
row, file
Cf. BARTHÉLEMY 1990, 259

στοά,-ᾶς⁺   N1F 0-1-3-0-0-4
1 Kgs 6,33; Ez 40,18; 42,3.5
portico, covered colonnade
Cf. DOWNEY 1937, 194-211

στοιβάζω   V 1-3-0-1-0-5
Lv 6,5; Jos 2,6; 1 Kgs 18,33(bis); Ct 2,5
to pile, to heap up [τι] Lv 6,5; *to overwhelm*
[τινα] Ct 2,5; neol.
Cf. LEE, J. 1983, 41
(→ἐπι-)

στοιβή,-ῆς   N1F 0-1-1-1-0-3
Jgsᴬ 15,5; Is 55,13; Ru 3,7
broom-bush Is 55,13; *heap* Jgsᴬ 15,5

στοιχεῖα,-ων⁺   N2N 0-0-0-0-3-3
4 Mc 12,13; Wis 7,17; 19,18
elemental substances, (four basic) *elements*
Cf. LARCHER 1984, 468-469; 1985, 759; SHIPP 1979, 518;
→NIDNTT

στοιχείωσις,-εως   N3F 0-0-0-0-1-1
2 Mc 7,22
elementary exposition, fashion of the elements;
neol.

στοιχέω⁺   V 0-0-0-1-0-1
Eccl 11,6
to prosper, to go on to sprout
Cf. HORSLEY 1982, 97; →NIDNTT; TWNT

στολή,-ῆς⁺   N1F 42-17-13-9-18-99
Gn 27,15; 35,2; 41,14.42; 45,22
often coll. sg. rendering בגדים; *raiment, garment,*
clothing Gn 27,15
στολὴν ἱματίων *change of raiment* Jgs 14,13
*Ex 33,5 τὰς στολὰς (τῶν δοξῶν) ὑμῶν *your*
*garments -*מעלי/ך for MT מ/עלי/ך *off from you;*
*Is 9,4 στολήν *vestment -*נשא◊ ?שאון for MT סאון
boot (Accad. loanword); *Ez 10,2 τὴν στολήν
*garment -*בגדים? for MT בדים *linen;* *Jb 30,13 μου
τὴν στολήν *my garment -*מעילי for MT יעילו *they*
rise up
see περιβολή
Cf. GOODING 1959, 89-91(Ex 39,13); HARL 1986ᵃ, 69.309;
LE BOULLUEC 1989, 281.300.330; WEVERS 1990, 444-445.
581.645; 1993, 425; →LSJ suppl(Ex 33,5); SCHLEUSNER
(Is 9,4); TWNT

στολίζω   V 0-0-0-7-5-12
Est 4,4; 6,9.11; 8,15; Dn^LXX 5,7
A: *to clothe* [τινα] Est 4,4; *to dress sb with sth*
[τινά τι] Dn^LXX 5,7
M: *to clothe oneself* Jdt 10,3
P: *to be dressed with, to wear* [τι] Est 8,15; *to be
in full dress* 1 Ezr 1,2
Cf. HELBING 1928, 47

στολισμός,-οῦ   N2M 0-1-1-0-1-3
2 Chr 9,4; Ez 42,14; Sir 19,30
clothing, outfit; neol.

στολιστής,-οῦ   N1M 0-1-0-0-0-1
2 Kgs 10,22
*who had charge of the sacred vestments, the
keeper of the sacred robes*; neol.

στόλος,-ου   N2M 0-0-0-0-4-4
1 Mc 1,17; 2 Mc 12,9; 14,1; 3 Mc 7,17
fleet, navy 2 Mc 12,9; *equipment*, esp. *gear for
military force* 1 Mc 1,17

στόμα,-ατος^+   N3N 49-93-84-185-78-489
Gn 4,11; 8,11; 24,57; 29,2.3
stereotypical rendering of פה; *mouth* (human)
Gn 8,11; *id.* (of anim.) Nm 22,28; *mouth as an
organ of speech* Gn 41,40; *mouth, entrance* (of a
well) Gn 29,3; *id.* (of a cave) Jos 10,18; *id.* (of a
den) Dn 6,18; *mouth, fissure* Gn 4,11; *edge* (of
a sword) Jos 6,21; *person* Gn 24,57
στόμα λέοντος *jaws of a lion* Ps 21(22),22;
στόμα κατὰ στόμα λαλήσω αὐτῷ *I shall speak
to him face to face* Nm 12,8; οὗ ἔπλησεν τὴν
Ιερουσαλημ στόμα εἰς στόμα *he filled
Jerusalem with it from one end to the other*
(semit.) 2 Kgs 21,16, see also Ezr 9,11
*Jgs 14,8 ἐν τῷ στόματι *in the mouth* corr. ἐν
τῷ σώματι for MT בגויה גויה *in the body, in the
carcass*, see also 14,9, cpr. Ez 3,3
Cf. HARL 1984^a=1992^a, 39.40; LEE, J. 1983, 51; WEVERS
1993, 371; →TWNT

στόμωμα,-ατος   N3N 0-0-0-0-1-1
Sir 31,26
steel

στοργή,-ῆς   N1F 0-0-0-0-4-4
3 Mc 5,32; 4 Mc 14,13.14.17
love, affection

στοχάζομαι   V 1-0-0-0-3-4
Dt 19,3; 2 Mc 14,8; Wis 13,9; Sir 9,14
to reckon, to calculate [τι] (of a distance)
Dt 19,3; *to guess at* [τινα] Sir 9,14; *to have
regard for* [τινος] 2 Mc 14,8
Cf. DOGNIEZ 1992, 232; GILBERT 1973, 8.33-35; HELBING

1928, 143; LARCHER 1985, 770-771

στοχαστής,-οῦ   N1M 0-0-1-0-0-1
Is 3,2
conjecturer, diviner; neol.

στραγγαλάω^+   V 0-0-0-0-2-2
Tob 2,3
P: *to be strangled*

στραγγαλιά,-ᾶς   N1F 0-0-1-1-0-2
Is 58,6; Ps 124(125),5
(intricate) knot

στραγγαλίς,-ίδος   N3F 0-1-0-0-0-1
Jgs^B 8,26
*chain (some kind of ornament in the shape of a
knot)*

στραγγαλώδης,-ης,-ες   A 0-0-0-1-0-1
Prv 8,8
knotted, tortuous; neol.

στραγγίζω   V 1-0-0-0-0-1
Lv 1,15
to squeeze out [τι]; neol.
(→κατα-)

στρατεία,-ας^+   N1F 0-0-0-0-1-1
4 Mc 9,24
expedition, fight
Cf. WALTERS 1973, 42-43; →NIDNTT; TWNT

στράτευμα,-ατος^+   N3N 0-0-0-0-7-7
Jdt 11,8; 1 Mc 9,34; 2 Mc 5,24; 8,21; 12,38
expedition, campaign Jdt 11,8; *army, host*
1 Mc 9,34; στρατεύματα *troops* 4 Mc 5,1
→NIDNTT; TWNT

στρατεύω^+   V 0-3-1-0-4-8
Jgs 19,8; 2 Sm 15,28; Is 29,7; 1 Ezr 4,6
A: *to be a soldier, to serve in the army* Jgs^B 19,8
M/P: *to be a soldier, to serve in the army*
2 Sm 15,28; *to advance with an army, to wage
war* 2 Mc 15,17; *to fight against* [ἐπί τινα]
Is 29,7
ἱερὰν καὶ εὐγενῆ στρατείαν στρατεύσασθε
περὶ τῆς εὐσεβείας *wage a holy and honourable
war on behalf of righteousness* 4 Mc 9,24
→NIDNTT; TWNT
(→ἐκ-, ἐπι-)

στρατηγέω   V 0-0-0-0-2-2
2 Mc 10,32; 14,31
to command

στρατήγημα,-ατος   N3N 0-0-0-0-1-1
2 Mc 14,29
stratagem, trick

στρατηγία,-ας   N1F 0-1-0-0-0-1
1 Kgs 2,35

military command
στρατηγός,-οΰ⁺   N2M 0-5-7-15-32-59
1 Sm 29,3.4; 1 Chr 11,6; 12,20; 2 Chr 32,21
captain, commander, general 1 Sm 29,3; *governor*
2 Mc 12,2
*Ez 32,30 στρατηγοὶ Ασσουρ *the commanders
of Assur* -אשר סרני? for MT צרני אשר *the Sidonians,
who*
Cf. DELCOR 1967ᵃ, 155-156; PETIT 1988, 59-65; →NIDNTT;
TWNT

στρατιά,-ᾶς⁺   N1F 5-18-5-1-13-42
Ex 14,4.9.17; Nm 10,28; Dt 20,9
army Ex 14,4; *host, company, band* (of heavenly
elements) 2 Chr 33,3
*Jer 7,18 τῇ στρατιᾷ τοῦ οὐρανοῦ *to the host
of heaven*? -השמים צבא- or -השמים לממלכת for MT
השמים למלכת *to the queen of heaven*
Cf. WALTERS 1973, 37.42-43.285; WEVERS 1990, 210;
→NIDNTT; TWNT

στρατιώτης,-ου⁺   N1M 0-0-0-0-6-6
2 Mc 5,12; 14,39; 3 Mc 3,12; 4 Mc 3,7.12
soldier
Cf. LAUNEY 1949, 25-26.29-30; →NIDNTT; TWNT

στρατιῶτις,-ιδος   N3F 0-0-0-0-1-1
4 Mc 16,14
soldier (fem. of στρατιώτης)

στρατοκῆρυξ,-υκος   N3M 0-1-0-0-0-1
1 Kgs 22,36
herald of the army; *1 Kgs 22,36 στρατοκῆρυξ
the herald of the camp -במחנה הרונה? for MT
במחנה הרנה *a shout (went through) the camp*; neol.?

στρατοπεδεία,-ας   N1F 0-1-0-0-1-2
Jos 4,3; 2 Mc 13,14
(military) camp

στρατοπεδεύω   V 7-0-0-1-2-10
Gn 12,9; Ex 13,20; 14,2(bis).10
to encamp Gn 12,9; *to march out to camp*
Dt 1,40
Cf. DOGNIEZ 1992, 66.121; LE BOULLUEC 1989, 164;
WEVERS 1990, 205.214; 1995, 23-24
(→ἀνα-, ἐπι-, κατα-)

στρατόπεδον,-ου⁺   N2N 0-0-2-0-5-7
Jer 41(34),1; 48(41),12; 2 Mc 8,12; 9,9; 3 Mc
6,17
army

στρατός,-οῦ   N2M 0-0-0-0-4-4
2 Mc 8,35; 4 Mc 3,8; 4,5.11
army

στρέβλη,-ης   N1F 0-0-0-0-9-9
4 Mc 7,4.14; 8,11.24; 9,22

rack, instrument of torture 4 Mc 7,14; *torture,
punishment* Sir 33,27

στρεβλός,-ή,-όν⁺   A 0-1-0-2-1-4
2 Sm 22,27; Ps 17(18),27; 77(78),57; Sir 36,20
crooked Ps 77(78),57; *perverse, stubbornly
contrary* 2 Sm 22,27

στρεβλόω⁺   V 0-1-0-0-5-6
2 Sm 22,27; 3 Mc 4,14; 4 Mc 9,17; 12,3.11
A: *to twist* [τινα] 4 Mc 9,17; *to torture* [τινα]
4 Mc 12,11
P: *to be tortured* 3 Mc 4,14; *to be perverted*
2 Sm 22,27
(→ἀπο-)

στρεβλωτήριον,-ου   N2N 0-0-0-0-1-1
4 Mc 8,13
rack; neol.

στρέμμα,-ατος   N3N 0-1-0-0-0-1
Jgsᴮ 16,9
that which is twisted, thread

στρεπτός,-ή,-όν   A 6-3-0-1-0-10
Ex 25,11.24.25; 30,3.4
plaited, twisted Ex 25,11; (τὸ) στρεπτόν *braid*
Dt 22,12; *moulding, capital (of a pillar)* (archit.
term) 1 Kgs 7,27
Cf. LE BOULLUEC 1989, 255.259.305; WEVERS 1990, 397

στρέφω⁺   V 3-6-9-18-7-43
Gn 3,24; Ex 4,17; 7,15; Jgsᴮ 7,13; 1 Sm 10,6
A: *to turn into, to change into* [τι εἰς τι]
Ezr 23,2; *id.* [τι ἐν τινι] Ps 40(41),4; *to turn,
to bring* (the night) [τι] Jb 34,25; *to turn, to turn
back, to convert* (the heart of sb) [τι]
1 Kgs 18,37
M/P: *to turn* (of pers.) 1 Sm 14,47; *id.* (of doors)
1 Kgs 6,34; *to be turned up* Jb 28,5; *to be turned
upside down, to be overthrown* Prv 12,7; *to be
turned into, to change into* [εἰς τι] Ex 4,17; *to
turn away* 1 Kgs 2,15; *to turn about* Gn 3,24; *to
roll* Jgsᴮ 7,13; *to compass* 1 Ezr 4,34
ὁ Ιορδάνης ἐστράφη εἰς τὰ ὀπίσω *the Jordan
was turned back, returned* Ps 113(114),3; ὀργὴ
στρεφομένη *a whirlwind of anger* Jer 37(30),23
Cf. HOLLADAY 1958, 20-33; LE BOULLUEC 1989, 101.120;
→TWNT
(→ἀνα-, ἀπο-, δια-, ἐκ-, ἐπανα-, ἐπι-, κατα-,
μετα-, περι-, συ-, συνανα-, ὑπο-)

στρῆνος,-ους⁺   N3N 0-1-0-0-0-1
2 Kgs 19,28
insolence, arrogance

στρίφνος,-ου   N2M 0-0-0-1-0-1
Jb 20,18

hard or tough meat; neol.

στροβέω   V 0-0-0-4-0-4
Jb 9,34; 13,11; 15,23(24); 33,7
to distract, to distress [τινα] Jb 9,34

στρογγύλος,-η,-ον   A 0-3-0-0-0-3
1 Kgs 7,10(23).21(35); 2 Chr 4,2
round, circular

στρουθίον,-ου⁺   N2N 0-0-1-9-4-14
Jer 8,7; Ps 10(11),1; 83(84),4; 101(102),8;
103(104),17
dim. of στρουθός; sparrow Tob 2,10; ostrich
Lam 4,3

στρουθός,-οῦ⁺   N2M 2-0-4-2-0-8
Lv 11,16; Dt 14,15; Is 34,13; 43,20; Jer 10,22
sparrow Is 34,13; ostrich Lv 11,16

στροφεύς,-έως   N3M 0-2-0-0-0-2
1 Kgs 6,34; 1 Chr 22,3
hinge

στροφή,-ῆς   N1F 0-0-0-1-3-4
Prv 1,3; Wis 8,8; Sir 39,2; PSal 12,2
turning (metaph.), subtlety, literary craft (of
words)
Cf. LARCHER 1984, 532-533

στρόφιγξ,-ιγγος   N3M 0-0-0-1-0-1
Prv 26,14
hinge

στρόφος,-ου   N2M 0-0-0-0-1-1
Sir 31,20
inward disorder, twisting of the bowels, colic

στροφωτός,-ή,-όν   A 0-0-1-0-0-1
Ez 41,24
turning on pivots (of doors); neol.

στρῶμα,-ατος   N3N 0-0-0-1-0-1
Prv 22,27
bed, mattress

στρωμνή,-ῆς   N1F 1-0-2-6-2-11
Gn 49,4; Ez 27,7; Am 6,4; Ps 6,7; 62(63),7
bed Gn 49,4; bedding, covering Est 1,6

στρωννύω⁺   V 0-0-3-4-2-9
Is 14,11; Ez 23,41; 28,7; Jb 17,13; Prv 7,16
to spread [τι] Jdt 12,15; to spread a bed, to
make up (a bed) [τι] Ez 23,41; id. [abs.]
Tobˢ 7,16; to lay low, to bring down [τι] Ez 28,7
(-δια-, κατα-, ὑπο-)

στυγέω   V 0-0-0-0-2-2
2 Mc 5,8; 3 Mc 2,31
A: to abhor [τι] 3 Mc 2,31
P: to be hated 2 Mc 5,8

στυγνάζω⁺   V 0-0-3-0-0-3
Ez 27,35; 28,19; 32,10

to be horrified by sb or sth, to be appalled at sb
or sth [ἐπί τινα]; neol.; see στενάζω
Cf. WALTERS 1973, 131-132

στυγνός,-ή,-όν⁺   A 0-0-1-1-1-3
Is 57,17; DnᴸˣˣX 2,12; Wis 17,5
gloomy, sullen (of pers.) DnᴸˣX 2,12; gloomy,
horrible (of night) Wis 17,5
Cf. LARCHER 1985, 955

στῦλος,-ου⁺   N2M 72-45-9-12-9-147
Ex 13,21(bis).22(bis); 14,19
pillar Ex 37,15(38,17); pillar, column (of a cloud,
of a fire) Ex 13,21; pole, post, frame Ex 26,15
Cf. GOODING 1959, 20.41-42.74-75

στυράκινος,-η,-ον   A 1-0-0-0-0-1
Gn 30,37
made of the wood, of the storax tree; ῥάβδον
στυρακίνην rod of a storax tree; neol.

στύφω
(-ἀπο-)

σύ⁺   R 2486-1996-2225-2488-1497-10692
Gn 1,10.11(bis).14(tris)
acc. σέ, σε; gen. σοῦ, σου; dat. σοί, σοι; you
Gn 3,11; συ you (nom. in contrast with other
pers.) Ps 101,27; σου of you (as substitute for
the possessive adj.) Gn 3,10

συγγελάω   V 0-0-0-0-1-1
Sir 30,10
to laugh with sb [τινι]

συγγένεια,-ας⁺   N1F 22-13-1-4-5-45
Gn 12,1; 50,8; Ex 6,14.16.19
kinship, kindred Nm 1,2; kindred, kinsfolk, family
Gn 12,1
ἐν συγγενείᾳ τινός in kinship with, in con-
nection to sth Wis 8,17
Cf. DES PLACES 1964ᵃ, 1-223; DORIVAL 1994, 192;
LARCHER 1984, 546(Wis 8,17); SPICQ 1982, 616-622;
WEVERS 1993, 842; -TWNT

συγγενής,-ής,-ές⁺   A 3-1-1-0-19-24
Lv 18,14; 20,20; 25,45; 2 Sm 3,39; Ez 22,6
of the same kin, related, akin to Lv 18,14; (ὁ)
συγγενής kinsman, relative 2 Mc 11,35; (king's)
cousin (title bestowed at the Hellenistic courts
as a mark of honour) 1 Ezr 3,7; οἱ συγγενεῖς
kinsmen, kinsfolk Ez 22,6
προσώπου συγγενοῦς of a kinsman Sir 41,22;
*2 Sm 3,39 συγγενής kinsman רד- for MT רך
soft, powerless; *Ez 22,6 πρὸς τοὺς συγγενεῖς
αὐτοῦ with his kinsmen לזרעו- for MT לזרעו
according to his power
Cf. SPICQ 1978ᵃ, 836-839; 1982, 616-622; WALTERS 1973,

270-271(2 Sm 3,39); →TWNT

συγγίνομαι   V 2-0-0-0-3-5

Gn 19,5; 39,10; Jdt 12,16; SusTh 11.39

to have sexual intercourse with sb [τινι]
SusTh 11; *id.* [μετά τινος] Jdt 12,16

Cf. HARL 1986^a, 70.179; HELBING 1928, 310; WEVERS
1993, 268

συγγινώσκω⁺   V 0-0-0-0-2-2

2 Mc 14,31; 4 Mc 8,22

to be conscious, to know [ὅτι +ind.] 2 Mc 14,31;
to forgive [τινι] 4 Mc 8,22

συγγνώμη,-ης⁺   N1F 0-0-0-0-2-2

Sir prol.,18; 3,13

concession, pardon; συγγνώμην ἔχω *to pardon,
to be considerate*

Cf. CARAGOUNIS 1996, 554-559; METZLER 1991, 1-352

συγγνωμονέω⁺   V 0-0-0-0-1-1

4 Mc 5,13

to pardon sb for sth [τινι ἐπί τινι]; neol.

συγγνωστός,-ός/ή,-όν   A 0-0-0-0-2-2

Wis 6,6; 13,8

to be excused, pardonable (of pers.)

συγγραφεύς,-έως   N3M 0-0-0-0-1-1

2 Mc 2,28

author

συγγραφή,-ῆς   N1F 0-0-1-1-4-6

Is 58,6; Jb 31,35; Tob 7,14; 1 Mc 13,42

writing, document, contract Is 58,6

ἐν ταῖς συγγραφαῖς καὶ συναλλάγμασιν
1 Mc 13,42 see συνάλλαγμα

Cf. SCHÜRER 1890, 259

συγγράφω   V 0-0-0-0-1-1

Sir prol.,12

to write down sth [τι]

συγγυμνασία,-ας   N1F 0-0-0-0-1-1

Wis 8,18

shared training, training together; neol.

συγκάθημαι⁺   V 0-0-0-1-0-1

Ps 100(101),6

to dwell with [μετά τινος]

Cf. HELBING 1928, 310

συγκαθίζω⁺   V 3-0-1-0-2-6

Gn 15,11;   Ex 18,13;   Nm 22,27;   Jer 16,8;
1 Ezr 9,6

to sit together 1 Ezr 9,6; *to sit together with*
[τινι] Gn 15,11; *id.* [μετά τινος] Jer 16,8; *to sit
down, to lay down* Nm 22,27

*Gn 15,11 συνεκάθισεν αὐτοῖς *he sat with
them* -וישב אתם/ישב for MT וישב אתם/נשב*he
drove them away*

Cf. DORIVAL 1994, 428; HARL 1986^a, 165; HELBING 1928,
310; →TWNT

συγκαθυφαίνω   V 0-0-1-0-0-1

Is 3,23

P: *to be interwoven*; neol.

συγκαίω   V 1-0-4-4-0-9

Gn 31,40; Is 5,11.24; 9,18; Jon 4,8

A: *to burn (up)* [τι] Prv 24,22e; *id.* [τινα]
Ps 120(121),6; *to burn, to blaze* (of wind)
Jon 4,8; *to inflame* [τινα] (said of wine) Is 5,11
P: *to be consumed, to be parched* Gn 31,40

Cf. MARGOLIS 1906^b=1972, 68-69

συγκαλέω⁺   V 1-5-2-1-4-13

Ex 7,11; Jos 9,22; 10,24; 22,1; 23,2

to call together, to convoke [τινα] Ex 7,11; *to
invite* Prv 9,3

→TWNT

συγκάλυμμα,-ατος   N3N 2-0-0-0-0-2

Dt 23,1; 27,20

covering, protection (skirt of the father's cloak);
neol.

Cf. DOGNIEZ 1992, 258; WEVERS 1995, 363

συγκαλύπτω⁺   V 3-11-2-1-2-19

Gn 9,23; Ex 26,13; Nm 4,14; Jgs^A 4,18.19

A: *to cover* Gn 9,23

M: *to disguise oneself* 1 Kgs 22,30

P: *to be muffled up* Sus^{LXX} 39

συγκαλύπτον *covering* Ex 26,13

συγκάμπτω⁺   V 0-2-0-2-0-4

Jgs^A 5,27; 2 Kgs 4,35; Ps 68(69),11.24

to cause to bend [τι] Ps 68(69),24; *to bend down*
[intrans.] 2 Kgs 4,35

*Ps 68(69),11 συνέκαμψα *I bent down*
(metaph.) -אכפה for MT אבכה *I wept*

→TWNT

συγκαταβαίνω⁺   V 0-0-0-3-1-4

Ps 48(49),18; Dn 3,49; Wis 10,14

to go down with, to descend with [τινι] Ps
48(49),18; *id.* [ἅμα τινί] Dn 3,49

συγκαταγηράσκω   V 0-0-0-0-2-2

Tob 8,7

to grow old with [τινι] Tob^{BA} 8,7; *to grow old
together* [abs.] Tob^S 8,7

συγκατακληρονομέομαι   V 1-0-0-0-0-1

Nm 32,30

*to inherit with, to receive a common inheritance
with sb* [ἔν τινι]; neol.

Cf. DORIVAL 1994, 169.540

συγκαταμίγνυμι   V 0-1-0-0-0-1

Jos 23,12

P: *to become mingled with* [τινι]

συγκατατίθημι⁺   V 2-0-0-0-1-3
Ex 23,1.32; Susᵀʰ 20
M: *to agree with, to consent to* [τινι] Ex 23,1; *to
make a covenant with* [τινι] Ex 23,32
Cf. HELBING 1928, 310; LE BOULLUEC 1989, 232.242; →MM

συγκαταφέρω   V 0-0-1-0-0-1
Is 30,30
to bear down together; συγκαταφερομένη βίᾳ
gushing down violently (of rain and hail)

συγκατεσθίω   V 0-0-1-0-0-1
Is 9,17
to consume, to devour together [τι]; neol.

σύγκειμαι⁺   V 0-1-0-0-1-2
1 Sm 22,8; Sir 43,26
to conspire against sb [ἐπί τινα] 1 Sm 22,8; *to
be composed, to consist* Sir 43,26

συγκεντέω   V 0-0-0-0-1-1
2 Mc 12,23
to pierce, to put to the sword [τινα]

συγκεράννυμι⁺   V 0-0-0-1-1-2
Dnᴸˣˣ 2,43; 2 Mc 15,39
P: *to be mingled with, to be mixed with* [τινι]

συγκερατίζομαι   V 0-0-0-2-0-2
Dn 11,40
to fight with the horns on the side of sb [τινι]
Dnᴸˣˣ 11,40; *id.* [μετά τινος] Dnᵀʰ 11,40; neol.

συγκεραυνόω   V 0-0-0-0-1-1
2 Mc 1,16
to strike with or *as with a thunderbolt* [τινα];
neol.

συγκλασμός,-οῦ   N2M 0-0-1-0-0-1
Jl 1,7
breaking, breakage; neol.

συγκλάω⁺   V 0-0-3-4-1-8
Is 45,2; Jer 27(50),23; Ez 29,7; Ps 45(46),10;
74(75),11
to break, to crush [τι] Ps 45(46),10; *to burst, to
shatter* [τι] Is 45,2
*Ez 29,7 συνέκλασας *you crushed* -מער◊המערת
(hi.) for MT העמרת◊עמר (hi.) *you made stand*

σύγκλεισμα,-ατος   N3N 0-4-0-0-0-4
1 Kgs 7,16(29).21(35).22(36); 2 Kgs 16,17
rim; neol.

συγκλεισμός,-οῦ⁺   N2M 0-2-6-1-1-10
2 Sm 5,24; 22,46; Ez 4,3.7.8
closed place, refuge, hiding-place 2 Sm 22,46;
hole (of a snake) Mi 7,17; *shutting up, siege* Ez
4,3; *hardness* (of the heart) Hos 13,8; *clashing
together* 2 Sm 5,24; *massiveness* (of gold) Jb

28,15
→LSJ Suppl; LSJ RSuppl(2 Sm 22,46; Mi 7,17)

συγκλειστός,-ή,-όν   A 0-3-0-0-0-3
1 Kgs 7,15(28)(bis).36(50)
shut up 1 Kgs 7,36(50)
ἔργον συγκλειστόν *rim* 1 Kgs 7,15(28)
→LSJ Suppl

συγκλείω⁺   V 4-9-9-8-14-44
Gn 16,2; 20,18(bis); Ex 14,3; Jos 6,1
A: *to shut up, to confine* [τινα] Ps 30(31),9; *to
shut, to close* [τι] Gn 20,18; *to shut in* [τινα] Ex
14,3; *to shut up, to encircle* (a city) [τι] Jos 6,1;
to besiege [τι] Ez 4,3; *to restrain sb from sth*
[τινά τινος] Gn 16,2; *to hedge in sb* [κατά
τινος] Jb 3,23; *to consign sb to sth* [τινα εἰς
τι] Ps 77(78),50; *to complete* [τι] 1 Kgs 11,27
P: *to be closed* Mal 1,10; *to be shut in together*
1 Ezr 9,16; *to be straitened* Prv 4,12
ὁ συγκλείων *smith* 2 Kgs 24,14; ὑπὸ τῆς ὥρας
συγκλειόμενοι *obliged by lack of time* 2 Mc
8,25; σκεύη χρυσίῳ συγκεκλεισμένα *vessels
overlaid with* (a plate of) *gold* 1 Kgs 10,21
Cf. GEHMAN 1966=1972, 107; →TWNT

συγκληρονομέω   V 0-0-0-0-1-1
Sir 22,23
to be joint heir, to be heir with; neol.
Cf. HORSLEY 1982, 97; →TWNT

σύγκλητος,-ος,-ον   A 1-0-0-0-0-1
Nm 16,2
called together, summoned; σύγκλητοι βουλῆς
chosen councillors
Cf. DORIVAL 1994, 345

συγκλύζω   V 0-0-1-1-1-3
Is 43,2; Ct 8,7; Wis 5,22
to wash over, to overwhelm [τινα] (of rivers);
neol.

σύγκοιτος,-ου   N2F 0-0-1-0-0-1
Mi 7,5
bedfellow (of wife)

συγκολλάω   V 0-0-0-0-1-1
Sir 22,9
to glue together [τι]

συγκομίζω⁺   V 0-0-0-1-0-1
Jb 5,26
to collect
Cf. MILLIGAN 1910=1980, 62; →MM

συγκόπτω⁺   V 3-4-3-2-1-13
Gn 34,30; Ex 30,36; Dt 9,21; 2 Kgs 10,32; 16,17
to cut in pieces, to cut asunder [τι] Ps
128(129),4; *to hew down, to destroy* [τινα]

Gn 34,30; *to beat small* [τι] Ex 30,36; *to cut short* 2 Kgs 10,32; *to cut off* [τι] 2 Kgs 16,17; *to beat sth into sth* [τι εἰς τι] Jl 4,10

σύγκρασις,-εως⁺   N3F 0-0-1-0-0-1
Ez 22,19
mixture

σύγκριμα,-ατος   N3N 0-1-0-15-3-19
Jgsᴬ 18,9; Dnᴸˣˣ 5,7(ter).8
composition, concert Sir 32,5; *interpretation* Dnᵀʰ 5,26; *decree, judgement* 1 Mc 1,57; *excuse, rationalization* Sir 32,17

συγκρίνω⁺   V 8-0-0-3-3-14
Gn 40,8.16.22; 41,12.13
A: *to interpret* (dreams) [τι] Gn 40,8; *to decide* Nm 15,34
P: *to be compared with* [τινι] Wis 7,29; *to be compared* Wis 15,18; *to measure oneself with sb* [τινι] 1 Mc 10,71
Cf. HARL 1986ᵃ, 270; LEE, J. 1983, 78; →NIDNTT; TWNT

σύγκρισις,-εως   N3F 12-3-0-33-1-49
Gn 40,12.18; Nm 9,3; 29,6.11
comparison Wis 7,8; *interpretation* Gn 40,12; *decision, ruling* Nm 9,3; (usual) *pattern, manner* Jgsᴬ 18,7
Cf. DORIVAL 1994, 271; HARL 1986ᵃ, 270; LEE, J. 1983, 78

συγκροτέω   V 1-0-0-1-0-2
Nm 24,10; Dnᵀʰ 5,6
M: *to knock together* (of trembling knees) Dnᵀʰ 5,6
συνεκρότησεν ταῖς χερσὶν αὐτοῦ *he clapped his hands* Nm 24,10
Cf. DORIVAL 1994, 439

συγκρουσμός,-οῦ   N2M 0-0-0-0-1-1
1 Mc 6,41
collision, clashing together, rattling (of arms); neol.

συγκρύπτω   V 0-0-0-0-1-1
2 Mc 14,30
M: *to conceal oneself from sb, to withdraw from sb* [τινα]

συγκρύφω   V 0-0-0-0-1-1
Sir 19,27
to cover, to hide [τι]; neol.; see συγκρύπτω

συγκτίζω   V 0-0-0-0-1-1
Sir 1,14
P: *to be created along with* [μετά τινος]
Cf. HELBING 1928, 311

συγκύπτω⁺   V 0-0-0-1-2-3
Jb 9,27; Sir 12,11; 19,26
to bend down Jb 9,27; συγκεκυφώς *bent* (as sign

of grief) Sir 19,26; *bent, humbly* Sir 12,11

συγκυρέω   V 3-0-0-0-1-4
Nm 21,25; 35,4; Dt 2,37; 1 Mc 11,34
to belong to, to be adjacent to [τινι] Nm 21,25; *to be contiguous with, to border on* [τινος] Dt 2,37
τὰ συγκυροῦντα τῶν πόλεων *the suburbs of the cities* Nm 35,4
Cf. DOGNIEZ 1992, 65.129; DORIVAL 1994, 408; HELBING 1928, 308; LEE, J. 1983, 78-81

συγχαίρω⁺   V 1-0-0-0-0-1
Gn 21,6
to rejoice with sb [τινι]; see χαίρω
Cf. WALTERS 1973, 105; WEVERS 1993, 300; →TWNT

συγχέω⁺   V 2-3-6-0-6-17
Gn 11,7.9; 1 Sm 7,10; 1 Kgs 8,35; 20,21(43)
A: *to confound* [τι] Gn 11,7; *to demolish* [τι] Am 3,15
P: *to be thrown into confusion* Na 2,5; *to be confounded, to be troubled, to be amazed* (of pers.) 1 Sm 7,10; *to be confounded, to be shaken* (of the earth) Jl 2,10
Cf. HARL 1986ᵃ, 149

συγχρονίζω   V 0-0-0-0-1-1
Sir prol.,28
to spend time, to continue; neol.

σύγχυσις,-εως⁺   N3F 1-3-0-0-0-4
Gn 11,9; 1 Sm 5,6.11; 14,20
confusion 1 Sm 14,20
σύγχυσις θανάτου μεγάλη *a great confusion caused by death, a great tumult caused by death, a deathly panic* 1 Sm 5,6; Σύγχυσις (proper noun; of Babel) Gn 11,9
Cf. HARL 1986ᵃ, 149

συγχωρέω⁺   V 0-0-0-0-6-6
2 Mc 2,31; 11,15.18.24.35
to grant, to agree 2 Mc 11,15; *to grant to sb* [τινι] 2 Mc 11,35; συγχωρητέον *it must be conceded, it must be allowed* or *granted* 2 Mc 2,31

συζεύγνυμι⁺   V 0-0-2-0-0-2
Ez 1,11.23
P: *to be joined*
→NIDNTT

συζώννυμι   V 1-0-0-0-1-2
Lv 8,7; 1 Mc 3,3
A: *to gird sb* [τινα] Lv 8,7
M: *to gird up* (one's armour) [τι] 1 Mc 3,3

συκάμινον,-ου   N2N 0-0-1-0-0-1
Am 7,14

Semit. loanword? (Hebr. שׁקמה, שׁקמים); *mulberry*
Cf. CAIRD 1976, 78; TOV 1979, 221; WALTERS 1973,
163.326; →CHANTRAINE; FRISK; LSJ suppl; LSJ Rsuppl

συκάμινος,-ου⁺ N2F 0-4-1-1-0-6
1 Kgs 10,27; 1 Chr 27,28; 2 Chr 1,15; 9,27; Is 9,9
Semit. loanword? (Hebr. שׁקמה, שׁקמים); *mulberry*
tree, sycamore tree
Cf. CAIRD 1976, 78; TOV 1979, 221; WALTERS 1973,
163.326; →CHANTRAINE; FRISK; LSJ suppl; LSJ Rsuppl;
NIDNTT; TWNT

συκῆ,-ῆς⁺ N1F 4-7-13-4-2-30
Gn 3,7; Nm 13,23; 20,5; Dt 8,8; Jgs^ 9,10
fig tree
→NIDNTT; TWNT

σῦκον,-ου⁺ N2N 0-1-10-1-1-13
2 Kgs 20,7; Is 28,4; 38,21; Jer 8,13; 24,1
fig

συκοφαντέω⁺ V 2-0-0-7-0-9
Gn 43,18; Lv 19,11; Ps 118(119),122; Jb 35,9;
Prv 14,31
to slander, to denounce, to inform against, to
bear false witness against [τινα] Gn 43,18; *to*
slander, to harass, to oppress [τινα] Prv 14,31
Cf. CARAGOUNIS 1974, 49-51; HARL 1986ª, 284(Gn 43,18);
HARLÉ 1988, 165(Lv 19,11); HATCH 1889, 89-91; WALTERS
1973, 184-185; →MM

συκοφάντης,-ου N1M 0-0-0-2-0-2
Ps 71(72),4; Prv 28,16
denouncer, false accuser Ps 71(72),4; *oppressor*
Prv 28,16
Cf. WALTERS 1973, 184-185

συκοφαντία,-ας N1F 0-0-1-4-0-5
Am 2,8; Ps 118(119),134; Eccl 4,1; 5,7; 7,7
false accusation Ps 118(119),134; *oppression* Eccl
4,1; *extortion?* Am 2,8
Cf. NESTLÉ 1904, 271-272; WALTERS 1973, 184-185

συκών,-ῶνος N3M 0-0-2-0-0-2
Jer 5,17; Am 4,9
fig yard; neol.

συλάω⁺ V 0-0-0-0-1-1
LtJ 17
to spoil [τινα]
Cf. SPICQ 1978ª, 840-841; 1982, 623-626; →NIDNTT

συλλαλέω⁺ V 1-0-2-1-0-4
Ex 34,35; Is 7,6; Jer 18,20; Prv 6,22
to talk with [τινι] Ex 34,35
*Jer 18,20 συνελάλησαν *they spoke (words*
against) -רברו? for MT כרו *they have dug (a pit*
for), cpr. 18,22 and see λόγος
neol.

Cf. LEE, J. 1983, 95-96

συλλαμβάνω⁺ V 23-28-25-15-27-118
Gn 4,1.17.25; 16,4; 19,36
A: *to lay hold of, to arrest* [τινα] (of pers.)
1 Kgs 13,4; *to take, to catch* [τινα] (of anim.)
Jgs 15,4; *to take, to capture* [τι] 2 Kgs 14,7; *to*
conceive [abs.] Gn 4,1; *id.* [τινα] Ct 3,4; *id.* [τι]
(metaph.) Ps 7,15
P: *to be taken* (from earth) Jb 22,16
συλλήμψεται μεθ' ἑαυτοῦ *he shall take with*
himself Ex 12,4
*Ct 8,2 τῆς συλλαβούσης με *of her who*
conceived me - ◊ילדfor MT ◊למד*she teaches me?,*
cpr. Ct 3,4 (הורתי)
Cf. HELBING 1928, 310; MARGOLIS 1906ª=1972, 78-79;
→NIDNTT; TWNT

συλλέγω⁺ V 17-7-1-14-3-42
Gn 31,46(bis); Ex 5,11; 16,4.16
A: *to collect, to gather* [abs.] Ex 16,16; *id.* [τι]
Gn 31,46; *to glean* Ru 2,3
P: *to gather, to come together* Jgs^ 11,3
→NIDNTT

σύλλημψις,-εως⁺ N3F 0-0-4-1-0-5
Jer 18,22; 20,17; 41,3(34,3); Hos 9,11; Jb 18,10
capture [τινος] Jer 18,22; *conception, pregnancy*
Hos 9,11
Cf. MARGOLIS 1906ª=1972, 78-79

συλλογή,-ῆς N1F 0-1-0-0-0-1
1 Sm 17,40
gathering, collection, store

συλλογίζομαι⁺ V 4-0-1-0-0-5
Lv 25,27.50.52; Nm 23,9; Is 43,18
M: *to calculate* [τι] Lv 25,27; *to reckon with, to*
consider [τι] Is 43,18
P: *to be reckoned among* [ἔν τισι] Nm 23,9
Cf. SPICQ 1982, 627-628

συλλογισμός,-οῦ N2M 1-0-0-0-1-2
Ex 30,12; Wis 4,20
reckoning, calculation Wis 4,20
ἐὰν λάβῃς τὸν συλλογισμόν *if you take on a*
calculation, if you compute Ex 30,12
Cf. WEVERS 1990, 494; →LSJ suppl; LSJ Rsuppl

συλλοιδορέω V 0-0-1-0-0-1
Jer 36(29),27
to join in reviling [τινα]; neol.
Cf. HELBING 1928, 22

συλλοχάω V 0-0-0-0-1-1
1 Mc 4,28
to gather, to recruit (soldiers) [τινα]; neol.
Cf. WALTERS 1973, 120

συλλοχισμός,-οῦ   N2M 0-1-0-0-0-1
1 Chr 9,1
muster-roll, enrollment, census-list; neol.?
συλλύω   V 0-0-0-0-3-3
1 Mc 13,47; 2 Mc 11,14; 13,23
M: *to agree to (certain conditions)* [ἐπί τινι]
2 Mc 11,14
P: *to come to a settlement with* [τινι] 1 Mc
13,47
συλλυπέω⁺   V 0-0-1-1-0-2
Is 51,19; Ps 68(69),21
M: *to share in grief with, to sympathize with*
[τινι] Is 51,19; *to sympathize* [abs.] Ps 68(69),21
→TWNT
συμβαίνω⁺   V 10-1-3-6-31-51
Gn 41,13; 42,4.29.38; 44,29
to happen to, to befall [τινι] Gn 42,4;
συμβαίνει [+inf.] *it happens that, it comes to
pass that* Gn 41,13
τὰ συμβάντα αὐτοῖς *what happened to them* Gn
42,29
Cf. HELBING 1928, 303; WEVERS 1990, 388
συμβάλλω⁺   V 0-1-2-0-6-9
2 Chr 25,19; Is 46,6; Jer 50(43),3; 1 Mc 4,34;
2 Mc 8,23
A: *to compare with* [τί τινι] Sir 22,1; *to join
battle with* [τινι] 1 Mc 4,34; *to set up sb against
sb* [τινα πρός τινα] Jer 50(43),3
M: *to be profitable for* [τινι] Wis 5,8; *to
contribute* [τι] Is 46,6
ἵνα τί συμβάλλεις ἐν κακίᾳ; *why should you
stir in evil?, why should you provoke trouble?*
(semit.) 2 Chr 25,19
Cf. HELBING 1928, 307-308
συμβασταζω   V 0-0-0-2-0-2
Jb 28,16.19
P: *to be compared with* [τινι]; neol.
συμβιβάζω⁺   V 5-1-2-2-0-10
Ex 4,12.15; 18,16; Lv 10,11; Dt 4,9
to teach, to instruct, to advise [τί τινα] Ex 4,12;
id. [τινα] Dt 4,9; *to guide* [τινα] Ps 31,8
Cf. DODD 1954, 30; DOGNIEZ 1992, 43.136; HARLÉ 1988,
125; HELBING 1928, 39; LE BOULLUEC 1989, 99; WEVERS
1990, 284; →TWNT
συμβιόω   V 0-0-0-0-1-1
Sir 13,5
to live with [τινα]
συμβίωσις,-εως   N3F 0-0-0-0-3-3
Wis 8,3.9.16
living with, shared life; neol.?

Cf. LARCHER 1984, 522
συμβιωτής,-οῦ   N1M 0-0-0-0-3-3
Bel 2; Bel^LXX 30
companion, confidant; neol.?
Cf. POLAND 1931, 1075-1082
σύμβλημα,-ατος   N3N 0-0-1-0-0-1
Is 41,7
juncture, seam; neol.
σύμβλησις,-εως   N3F 1-0-0-0-0-1
Ex 26,24
juncture, seam; neol.
Cf. LE BOULLUEC 1989, 271
συμβοηθός,-ός,-όν   A 0-1-0-0-0-1
1 Kgs 21(20),16
assisting; (ὁ) συμβοηθός *helper*; neol.
συμβολή,-ῆς   N1F 7-0-1-1-1-10
Ex 26,4(bis).5.10; 28,32
juncture, connection, coupling Ex 26,4; *expense,
contribution* Sir 18,32; συμβολαί *subscription,
contribution* (to festival or shared meal) Prv
23,20
Cf. LE BOULLUEC 1989, 266; WEVERS 1990, 413.459.604
συμβολοκοπέω   V 1-0-0-0-2-3
Dt 21,20; Sir 9,9; 18,33
to share in meals or *parties, to revel*; neol.
Cf. DOGNIEZ 1992, 66.247; HELBING 1928, 312;
KINDSTRAND 1983, 98.108-109
σύμβολον,-ου   N2N 0-0-1-0-2-3
Hos 4,12; Wis 2,9; 16,6
token Wis 2,9; *sign, seal* Wis 16,6
Cf. LARCHER 1983, 234; 1985, 898-899
συμβόσκομαι   V 0-0-1-0-0-1
Is 11,6
to feed with, to graze with [μετά τινος]; neol.
Cf. HELBING 1928, 310
συμβουλευτής,-οῦ   N1M 0-0-0-0-1-1
1 Ezr 8,11
adviser, counsellor
συμβουλεύω⁺   V 2-14-5-2-10-33
Ex 18,19; Nm 24,14; Jos 15,18; 2 Sm 17,11(bis)
A: *to advise, to counsel* [τινι] Ex 18,19; *id.* [τι]
1 Kgs 12,9; *id.* [τινί τι] Nm 24,14; *id.* [τινι
+inf.] 4 Mc 8,29; *id.* [+inf.] 4 Mc 8,5; *to advise,
to give advice* [abs.] 2 Sm 17,11
M: *to counsel sb* [τινι] Jos 15,18; *to take
counsel* Is 40,14; *to consult, to deliberate* 1 Kgs
12,8
συμβουλεύων εἰς ἑαυτόν *one who counsels for
himself* Sir 37,7
*Is 33,19 συνεβουλεύσαντο *they took counsel*

יעץ ◊ נועַע for MT נוֹעַז ◊ יעז *presumptuous?*
Cf. HELBING 1928, 303-304; →NIDNTT

συμβουλία,-ας⁺   N1F 0-2-0-2-5-9
1 Kgs 1,12; 2 Chr 25,16; Ps 118(119),24; Prv
12,15; Tob^BA 4,18
advice, counsel
→NIDNTT

συμβούλιον,-ου⁺   N2N 0-0-0-0-1-1
4 Mc 17,17
council; neol.?
→NIDNTT

σύμβουλος,-ου⁺   N2M 0-8-5-5-10-28
2 Sm 8,18; 15,12; 1 Kgs 2,46h; 1 Chr 27,32.33
adviser, counsellor 2 Sm 15,12; *councillor* Ezr
7,14
θαυμαστὸν σύμβουλον *honourable counsellor* Is
3,3
Cf. PÉPIN 1987, 53-74; →MM; NIDNTT

συμβραβεύω   V 0-0-0-0-1-1
1 Ezr 9,14
to be assessor with, to become fellow arbitrator;
neol.

συμμαχέω⁺   V 0-2-0-0-9-11
Jos 1,14; 1 Chr 12,22; 1 Mc 8,25.27; 10,47
to be confederated with [τινι] 1 Mc 10,47; *to
fight on the side of* [τινι] Jos 1,14; *to help, to
succour* 1 Mc 8,25
Cf. HELBING 1928, 312

συμμαχία,-ας   N1F 0-0-1-0-15-16
Is 16,4; Jdt 3,6; 7,1; 1 Mc 8,17.20
alliance, confederacy 1 Mc 8,17; *allies* Jdt 3,6;
help 3 Mc 3,14
Cf. LAUNEY 1949, 36-42

σύμμαχος,-ου   N2M 0-0-0-0-14-14
1 Mc 8,20.24.28.31; 9,60
ally
Cf. LAUNEY 1949, 36-42

συμμειγής,-ής,-ές   A 0-0-0-2-0-2
Dn 2,43
mingled with

συμμείγνυμι⁺   V 0-0-0-3-3-6
Prv 11,15; 20,1; Dn^Th 11,6; 2 Mc 3,7; 13,3
A: *to mingle with, to converse with* [τινι] 2 Mc
3,7; *to meet* [τινι] Prv 11,15; *to come near to*
[τινι] Ex 14,20; *to come near to* (in hostile
sense), *to join battle* [τινι] 2 Mc 15,26
P: *to be commingled with* [τινι] Prv 20,1; *to
associate* Dn^Th 11,6
*Prv 11,15 συμμείξῃ *he meets* -ערב◊^II for MT ערב^i
he stands bail for

Cf. HELBING 1928, 250

συμμετέχω   V 0-0-0-0-1-1
2 Mc 5,20
to take part in, to partake of [τινος]

συμμετρία,-ας   N1F 0-0-0-0-1-1
PSal 5,16
due proportion

σύμμετρος,-ος,-ον   A 0-0-1-0-0-1
Jer 22,14
well-proportioned, suitable, symmetrical

συμμιαίνω   V 0-0-0-0-1-1
Bar 3,11
P: *to be defiled with* [τινι]; neol.

συμμίγνυμι⁺   V 1-0-0-0-0-1
Ex 14,20
see συμμείγνυμι
Cf. HELBING 1928, 250

σύμμικτος,-ος,-ον   A 0-0-13-0-2-15
Jer 27(50),37; 32(25),20.24; Ez 27,16.17
mixed, consolidated PSal 17,15; ὁ σύμμικτος
market of mixed goods Ez 27,17; *army of several
nationalities* Jdt 1,16; οἱ σύμμικτοι *soldiers of
several nationalities* Jer 32(25),20
*Ez 27,16 τοῦ συμμίκτου σου *of your mixing,
trading* -מערבך for MT מעשׂיך *your works*; *Na 3,17
ὁ σύμμικτός σου *your mixed crowd, your people
of bastards* -ממזריך for MT מנזריך *your courtiers?*

σύμμιξις,-εως   N3F 0-2-0-0-0-2
2 Kgs 14,14; 2 Chr 25,24
commingling; *2 Kgs 14,14 τοὺς υἱοὺς τῶν
συμμίξεων *children of mixed marriages* -ערב^II
foreigners for MT ערב◊ בני התערבות *sons of pledges,
hostages,* see also 2 Chr 25,24
Cf. CAIRD 1969=1972, 149; →LSJ RSuppl (sub υἱός);
NIDOTT (sub בן)

συμμίσγω   V 0-0-0-0-3-3
1 Mc 11,22; 2 Mc 14,14.16
to meet [τινι] 2 Mc 14,14; *to speak with* [τινι]
1 Mc 11,22

συμμισοπονηρέω   V 0-0-0-0-1-1
2 Mc 4,36
to feel common hatred of what is bad; neol.

συμμολύνω   V 0-0-0-1-0-1
Dn^LXX 1,8
M: *to defile oneself;* neol.?

συμπάθεια,-ας   N1F 0-0-0-0-7-7
4 Mc 6,13; 14,13.14.18.20
sympathy

συμπαθέω⁺   V 0-0-0-0-1-1
4 Mc 5,25

to sympathize with, to feel for [τινι]
Cf. HELBING 1928, 312; SPICQ 1978ᵃ, 842-843; →NIDNTT;
TWNT

συμπαθής,-ής,-ές⁺   A 0-0-0-0-2-2
4 Mc 13,23; 15,4
sympathetic to [τινι] 4 Mc 15,4; *sympathetic,
strong* 4 Mc 13,23
Cf. SPICQ 1978ᵃ, 842-843; →TWNT

συμπαθῶς   D 0-0-0-0-1-1
4 Mc 13,23
συμπαθέστερον *more sympathetically* (comp.)

συμπαίζω   V 0-0-0-0-1-1
Sir 30,9
to play with [τινι]

συμπαραγίνομαι⁺   V 0-0-0-1-0-1
Ps 82(83),9
to come together with [μετά τινος]
Cf. HELBING 1928, 311

συμπαραλαμβάνω⁺   V 1-0-0-1-2-4
Gn 19,17; Jb 1,4; 3 Mc 1,1; PSal 13,5
A: *to take along with* [τινα] Jb 1,4
P: *to be overtaken together with someone else*
PSal 13,5
Cf. MARGOLIS 1906ᵃ=1972, 79

συμπαραμένω⁺   V 0-0-0-1-0-1
Ps 71(72),5
to continue as long as [τινι]; *Ps 71(72),5
συμπαραμενεῖ *he shall continue as long as -*יָרִיךְ
for MT יִרָאוּךְ *they shall fear you*

συμπάρειμι⁺   V 0-0-0-1-2-3
Prv 8,27; Tobᴮᴬ 12,12; Wis 9,10
to be present with [τινι]

συμπαρίστημι   V 0-0-0-1-0-1
Ps 93(94),16
M: *to stand up for sb against sb* [τινι ἐπί τινα]

σύμπας,-πασα,-παν⁺   A 0-0-4-6-5-15
Is 11,9; Ez 7,14; 27,13; Na 1,5; Ps 38(39),6
the whole of 2 Mc 7,38; τὰ σύμπαντα *all
together, all at once* Ps 38(39),6; *all things*
Ps 118(119),91; ἡ σύμπασα (γῆ) *the whole world*
Jb 2,2
*Ez 27,13 ἡ σύμπασα *the whole world,
completeness, totality -*תֵּבֵל for MT תֻּבַל Tubal; *Jb
25,2 σύμπασαν *the whole -*שָׁלֹם for MT שָׁלוֹם (עֹשֶׂה)
(he makes) peace

συμπατέω   V 0-4-1-6-0-11
2 Kgs 7,17.20; 9,33; 14,9; Na 3,14
to tread down [τι] 2 Kgs 14,9; *to trample on*
[τινα] 2 Kgs 7,17; *id.* [τινα] (of horses)
2 Kgs 9,33

συμπείθω   V 0-0-0-0-2-2
2 Mc 13,26; 3 Mc 7,3
to persuade, to convince 2 Mc 13,26; *to persuade
sb to* [τινα εἰς τι] 3 Mc 7,3

συμπεραίνω   V 0-0-1-0-0-1
Hab 2,10
to finish off completely, to destroy completely
[τινα]

συμπεριλαμβάνω⁺   V 0-0-1-0-0-1
Ez 5,3
to wrap
Cf. MARGOLIS 1906ᵃ=1972, 79

συμπεριφέρω   V 0-0-0-2-3-5
Prv 5,19; 11,29; 2 Mc 9,27; 3 Mc 3,20; Sir 25,1
M: *to go around with, to live* [τινι] Sir 25,1; *id.*
[ἔν τινι] Prv 5,19; *to accommodate to* [τινι]
3 Mc 3,20; *to treat, to deal with* [τινι] 2 Mc
9,27
Cf. HELBING 1928, 309

συμπίνω⁺   V 0-0-0-1-0-1
Est 7,1
to drink with [τινι]

συμπίπτω⁺   V 2-6-5-0-2-15
Gn 4,5.6; 1 Sm 1,18; 17,32; 2 Sm 5,18
to fall together, to meet, to meet violently 2 Sm
5,18; *to fall* Is 3,5; *to fall in, to collapse* Ez 30,4;
to collapse (of a person's mental state) 1 Mc
6,10; *to fall, to be distorted* Gn 4,5; *to become
extinct* Is 64,10
→MM (sub συνπίπτω)

συμπλεκτός,-ός,-όν   A 1-0-0-0-0-1
Ex 36,30(39,23)
plaited, woven together; neol.

συμπλέκω   V 4-0-4-4-0-12
Ex 28,22; 36(39),12.22.28; Ez 24,17
A: *to plot* [τι] Ps 57(58),3
P: *to be woven, to be plaited, to be twined
together* Ex 28,22; *to be entangled with* [τινι]
(metaph.) Prv 20,3; *to embrace* [μετά τινος]
(see μετά) Hos 4,14; *to collide, to clash together*
Na 2,5; *to be joined to* [πρός τι] Zech 14,13
ἔργον ὑφαντὸν εἰς ἄλληλα συμπεπλεγμένον
καθ' ἑαυτό *a work woven by mutual twisting of
the parts into one another* Ex 36,12
Cf. HELBING 1928, 308

συμπλήρωσις,-εως   N3F 0-1-0-1-1-3
2 Chr 36,21; Dnᵀʰ 9,2; 1 Ezr 1,55
fulfilment, completion; neol.?

συμπλοκή,-ῆς⁺   N1F 0-1-0-0-0-1
1 Kgs 16,28d(22,47)

*mingling (of male and female) in sexual
intercourse*
Cf. DION 1981, 45

συμποδίζω V 1-0-2-8-1-12
Gn 22,9; Hos 11,3; Zech 13,3; Ps 17(18),40;
19(20),9
A: *to tie the feet of sb, to bind sb hand and foot*
[τινα] Gn 22,9; *to bind the feet together* (of a
child, using swaddling clothes, with educational
purposes)? Hos 11,3; *to bind the feet together of
sb, to hinder* [τινα] (in order to stop a child
from walking off)? Zech 13,3; *to hinder, to
enchain* [τινα] Ps 17(18),40
P: *to be restrained, to be impeded* Prv 20,11
Cf. HARL 1986ᵃ, 193; 1986ᶜ=1992ᵃ, 62-65(Gn 22,9);
MURAOKA 1991,211-212(Hos 11,3); →LSJ suppl(Zech 13,3)

συμποιέω V 0-0-0-0-1-1
1 Ezr 6,27
to help, to assist, to cooperate with [τινι]

συμπολεμέω V 0-2-0-0-0-2
Jos 10,14.42
to join in war with, to fight on the side of [τινι]

συμπονέω V 0-0-0-0-1-1
Sir 37,5
to suffer with, to labour with [τινι]

συμπορεύομαι⁺ V 9-4-1-4-8-26
Gn 13,5; 14,24; 18,16; Ex 33,16; 34,9
to come, to go along with [τινι] Jos 10,24; *id.*
[μετά τινος] Gn 13,5; *to come together* Dt 31,11
συμπορευόμενοι οἱ υἱοὶ αὐτοῦ πρὸς
ἀλλήλους *his sons coming together with each
other, visiting one another* Jb 1,4
Cf. HELBING 1928, 304-305; LEE, J. 1983, 85; WEVERS
1990, 550

συμπορπάομαι V 1-0-0-0-0-1
Ex 36,13(39,6)
to be fastened or *pinned together*; neol.
Cf. LE BOULLUEC 1989, 354

συμποσία,-ας⁺ N1F 0-0-0-0-4-4
3 Mc 5,15.16.17; 7,20
banquet 3 Mc 5,16
τὸν τῆς συμποσίας καιρόν *dinner time*
3 Mc 5,15

συμπόσιον,-ου⁺ N2N 0-0-0-2-8-10
Est 4,17x; 7,7; 1 Mc 16,16; 2 Mc 2,27; 3 Mc 4,16
drinking party, symposium Sir 31,31; *banquet* Est
4,17x; *party* or *group of people, guests* 3 Mc 5,36

συμπότης,-ου N1M 0-0-0-0-1-1
3 Mc 2,25
drinking companion, boon companion

συμπραγματεύομαι V 0-0-0-0-1-1
3 Mc 3,10
to associate in business, to do business together;
neol.?

συμπροπέμπω V 2-0-0-0-0-2
Gn 12,20; 18,16
*to join in sending forward, to join in escorting, to
accompany* [τινα]

συμπρόσειμι V 0-0-0-2-0-2
Ps 93(94),20; Eccl 8,15
to be present with as a support [τινι]; neol.?
→LSJ RSuppl

συμπροσπλέκομαι V 0-0-0-1-0-1
Dnᵀʰ 11,10
to contend or *struggle hard*; neol.

σύμπτωμα,-ατος N3N 0-2-0-2-0-4
1 Sm 6,9; 20,26; Ps 90(91),6; Prv 27,9
chance event, mishap Ps 90(91),6; *sign,
indication, symptom* 1 Sm 6,9
*Prv 27,9 συμπτωμάτων *by mishaps* -מעצבה *by
pain* for MT מעצת *from the counsel*
Cf. HANHART 1994, 88

συμφερόντως D 0-0-0-0-1-1
4 Mc 1,17
profitably

συμφέρω⁺ V 1-0-1-3-6-11
Dt 23,7; Jer 33(26),14; Prv 19,10; 31,19; Est 3,8
to be profitable to [τινι] Sir 37,28; τὸ συμφέρον
common good, interests of the people 2 Mc 11,15;
τὰ συμφέροντα *the useful, profitable works* Prv
31,19; συμφέροντα *benefits* Dt 23,7
συμφέρει τινί *it suits, it fits* Prv 19,10;
συμφέρει τινί [+inf.] *it is expedient for sb to
do sth* Est 3,8
Cf. WEVERS 1995, 366(Dt 23,7); →MM; TWNT

συμφεύγω V 0-0-0-0-4-4
1 Mc 10,84; 2 Mc 10,18.32; 12,6
to flee together, to take refuge

σύμφημι⁺ V 0-0-0-1-1-2
Dnᴸˣˣ 2,9; Susᴸˣˣ 38
*to talk together with, to talk in a conspiring way
with* [τινι] Susᴸˣˣ 38; *to agree, to conspire* Dnᴸˣˣ
2,9
Cf. ENGEL 1985, 110-111

συμφλέγω V 0-0-1-0-0-1
Is 42,25
to burn to ashes, to consume with fire [τινα]

συμφλογίζω V 0-0-0-0-1-1
2 Mc 6,11
P: *to be burnt together*; neol.

συμφορά,-ᾶς⁺   N1F 0-0-0-1-8-9
Est 8,12e; 2 Mc 6,12.16; 9,6; 14,14
misfortune, calamity
→TWNT

συμφοράζω   V 0-0-1-0-0-1
Is 13,8
to wail; neol.

σύμφορον,-ου⁺   N2N 0-0-0-0-1-1
2 Mc 4,5
the good, welfare
→TWNT

συμφράσσω   V 0-0-1-0-0-1
Is 27,12
to fence in, to hem in; *Is 27,12 συμφράξει *he shall fence in* -סבש? *he shall imprison* for MT יחבש *he will start threshing*

συμφρονέω   V 0-0-0-0-1-1
3 Mc 3,2
to agree with, to be of the same opinion as [τινι]

συμφρύγω   V 0-0-0-1-1-2
Ps 101(102),4; 4 Mc 3,11
to burn up, to parch [τι] Ps 101(102),4; *id.* [τινα] 4 Mc 3,11

συμφύρω   V 0-0-1-0-2-3
Hos 4,14; Sir 12,14; PSal 8,9
M: *to mingle with* [μετά τινος] (of sexual intercourse) Hos 4,14; *to get involved in* [ἐν τινι] Sir 12,14
Cf. MURAOKA 1983, 52

σύμφυτος,-ος,-ον⁺   A 0-0-2-0-1-3
Am 9,13; Zech 11,2; 3 Mc 3,22
innate 3 Mc 3,22; *thickly wooded* Am 9,13
δρυμὸς σύμφυτος *thicket* Zech 11,2
Cf. SPICQ 1978ᵃ, 844-846

συμφύω⁺   V 0-0-0-0-1-1
Wis 13,13
to grow up with [τινι]
Cf. SPICQ 1978ᵃ, 844-847

συμφωνέω⁺   V 1-1-1-0-1-4
Gn 14,3; 2 Kgs 12,9; Is 7,2; 4 Mc 14,6
to agree, to consent 2 Kgs 12,9; *to agree, to be of one mind* 4 Mc 14,6; *to meet* Gn 14,3
Cf. SPICQ 1978ᵃ, 847-850; WEVERS 1993, 187; →TWNT

συμφωνία,-ας⁺   N1F 0-0-0-5-1-6
Dn 3,5; Dnᵀʰ 3,7.10.15
bagpipe? (musical instrument) Dn 3,5; *harmony* 4 Mc 14,3
Cf. BARRY 1904, 180-190; MOORE 1905, 166-175; SPICQ 1978ᵃ, 847-850; →TWNT

σύμφωνος,-ος,-ον⁺   A 0-0-0-1-2-3

Eccl 7,14; 4 Mc 7,7; 14,7
in harmony, harmonious 4 Mc 14,7; *corresponding with* [τινι] Eccl 7,14
ὦ σύμφωνε νόμου *man in harmony with the law* 4 Mc 7,7
Cf. SPICQ 1978ᵃ, 847-850; →TWNT

συμφώνως   D 0-0-0-0-1-1
4 Mc 14,6
in harmony with, harmoniously with [τινι]

συμψάω   V 0-0-3-0-0-3
Jer 22,19; 30,14(49,20); 31(48),33
P: *to be swept away*

σύν⁺   P 53-24-22-57-77-233
Ex 6,26; 7,4(bis); 10,9(bis)
[τινι]: *with, in the company of* Ex 10,9; *together with* Ex 12,9; *with* (of sth that belongs to sth) Lv 1,16; *with* (of circumstance) Ex 6,26; *with* (denoting instrument) Ex 36,10; *with* (of manner) Ex 7,4; *besides, in addition to* 3 Mc 1,22; see also μετά τινος
*Dt 33,2 σύν *with* -אתה for MT אתה *he came*; *Mi 7,13 σύν *with* -עם for MT על *on account of*; *Jb 39,25 σύν *with* -עם for MT רעם *thunder*; *Eccl 1,14 σύν *with* -את for MT את nota acc., see also 2,17.18; 3,11; 4,1 et al.; *Dnᵀʰ 9,26 σύν *with* -עם for MT עם *people*
Cf. JOHANNESSOHN 1910, 1-82; 1926, 202-216; MURAOKA 1991, 205; VOIGT 1989, 36-37.46(n.103); WEVERS 1990, 473.598; →TWNT

συναγελάζομαι   V 0-0-0-0-1-1
4 Mc 18,23
to be gathered together; neol.?

σύναγμα,-ατος   N3N 0-0-0-1-0-1
Eccl 12,11
collection

συνάγω⁺   V 50-87-105-65-70-377
Gn 1,9(bis); 6,21; 29,3.7
A: *to bring together, to gather* [τινα] Gn 29,22; *to gather, to assemble* (a council) [τινα] Ex 3,16; *to gather* (anim.) [τινα] Gn 29,3; *id.* [τι] Gn 1,9; *to glean* [τι] Ru 2,2; *to collect* (money) [τι] 2 Kgs 22,4; *to gather, to pick up* [τινα] Dt 30,3; *to receive, to invite, to take care of* [τινα] Mi 4,6; *to lead sb* (to marry her) [τινα] 2 Sm 11,27, see also Jgs 19,18; *to lead into one's house, to take care of* (anim.) [τινα] Dt 22,2
M/P: *to assemble, to gather* Gn 49,1; *to be wrapped together* (of tow) Sir 21,9
συνάγονται εἰς πόλεμον *they gather for war, they are drafted for war* 1 Sm 13,5; συνήχθησαν

ἐπ' ἐμὲ μάστιγες *I was thoroughly lashed* Ps 34(35),15; συνάγαγε τὰς χεῖράς σου *withdraw your hands* 1 Sm 14,19; ἐν νεότητι οὐ συναγείοχας, καὶ πῶς ἂν εὕροις ἐν τῷ γήρᾳ σου; *if you have not gathered in your youth, how will you find anything in your old age?* Sir 25,3; συναχθήσῃ εἰς τὸν τάφον σου *you will be gathered to your grave, you will be burried* 2 Kgs 22,20

*DnᴸˣˣX 12,12 καὶ συνάξει *and he shall collect* corr.? συνάψει for MT ויגיע *and he reaches to, and he lives until;* *Jgsᴬ 7,22 συνηγμένη *gathered* -◇צבר? *heap up* or -◇צרדה? *bound together, gathered* for MT צררתה *towards Zererah;* *2 Sm 3,34 καὶ συνήχθη *and they came together, and they assembled* -◇אסף? for MT ויספ ויסף? *they added to, they (wept) even more,* see also 2 Sm 6,1; *1 Kgs 7,10(23) συνηγμένοι *collected ends, circumference?* -◇קוהᴵᴵ (verb) for MT קוה *measuring line;* *Is 29,7 καὶ ... οἱ συνηγμένοι *and those who were gathered* -◇ממערתה? יערˉ◇ for MT ומצרתה *and her stronghold;* *Ez 13,5 καὶ συνήγαγον ποίμνια *and they gathered flocks* -◇ותחררו עדר? for MT ותגדרו גדר *and they built a wall;* *Zech 2,10 συνάξω *I will gather, I will invite* -◇כנשתי? for MT פרשתי *I have spread (you);* *Ps 15(16),4 (οὐ μὴ) συναγάγω *I will (not) bring together, assemble* -◇אסף◇for MT אסיך נסך◇ *I will pour out*

Cf. LE BOULLUEC 1989, 133(Ex 9,19-21); ROST 1967, 108-111.118-121; →MM; NIDNTT; TWNT

συναγωγή,-ῆς⁺   N1F 136-24-23-21-24-228

Gn 1,9(bis); 28,3; 35,11; 48,4

collection, pile Jb 8,17; *harvest* Ex 34,22; *place of collecting* Gn 1,9; *gathering (of people), company* 1 Mc 7,12; *gang, band* Ps 21(22),17; *congregation, assembly, host* Ex 12,3; *multitude* Ez 38,4; *local congregation* Sir 4,7; *synagogue, house of meeting* Susᴸˣˣ 28

συναγωγαὶ ἐθνῶν *gatherings of people* Gn 28,3; συναγωγὴ μελισσῶν *swarm of bees* Jgsᴮ 14,8; συναγωγὴ ταύρων *crowd of bulls* Ps 67(68),31 *Zech 9,12 τῆς συναγωγῆς *of the assembly* -◇קוהᴵᴵ for MT התקוה קוהᴵ *of hope;* *Ps 15(16),4 τὰς συναγωγὰς αὐτῶν *their assemblies* -◇אסף◇for MT נסכיהם *their libations;* see συνάγω; *Ps 61(62),9 συναγωγὴ λαοῦ *assembly of the people* -◇ערת עם for MT עת עם *time, o people;* *Dnᴸˣˣ 8,25 συναγωγήν *gathering* -◇אסף◇for MT אפסᴸᴸ◇*without*

Cf. BARR 1961, 119-127; DOGNIEZ 1992, 136; HARL 1986ᵃ,

90(Gn 1,9); HORSLEY 1983, 43; 1987, 202.220; KATZ 1950, 146; 1960, 162; PERI 1989, 245-251; ROST 1967, 111-118.122-129.134-138; WEVERS 1991, 52; 1993, 581; →MM; NIDNTT; TWNT

συνᾴδω   V 0-0-2-0-0-2

Hos 7,2(bis)

to be in accord with, to agree with; *Hos 7,2(bis) συνᾴδωσιν ὡς συνᾴδοντες τῇ καρδίᾳ αὐτῶν *they agree as men in harmony with each other, they are in full harmony* -◇זמר? for MT יאמרו ללבבם *they say in their heart*

συναθροίζω⁺   V 3-20-3-1-6-33

Ex 35,1; Nm 16,11; Dt 1,41; Jos 22,12; Jgsᴬ 12,4

to gather [τινα] Ex 35,1; *to gather, to draft (an army)* [τινα] 1 Kgs 21(20),1

συναθροίζονται εἰς πόλεμον *they gather to war, they are levied to war* 1 Sm 4,1

Cf. ROST 1967, 108-111.119-121

συναινέω⁺   V 0-0-0-0-2-2

3 Mc 5,21; 6,41

to approve 3 Mc 5,21; *to concede to, to grant for* [τινι] 3 Mc 6,41

Cf. HELBING 1928, 17

συνακολουθέω⁺   V 0-0-0-0-2-2

2 Mc 2,4.6

to follow, to go with, to accompany [τινι] 2 Mc 2,4; *id.* [abs.] 2 Mc 2,6

→NIDNTT; TWNT

συναλγέω   V 0-0-0-0-1-1

Sir 37,12

to share in suffering with sb [τινι]

συνάλλαγμα,-ατος⁺   N3N 0-0-1-0-2-3

Is 58,6; 1 Mc 13,42; PSal 4,4

covenant, contract PSal 4,4

συναλλάγματα *dealings, transactions, bargains* Is 58,6; συγγραφαὶ καὶ συναλλάγματα *documents and treaties* 1 Mc 13,42

Cf. SCHÜRER 1890, 259

συναλοάω   V 0-0-0-1-0-1

Dnᴸˣˣ 2,45

to grind to powder; neol.?

συναναβαίνω⁺   V 7-2-0-0-3-12

Gn 50,7.9.14; Ex 12,38; 24,2

to go up together Gn 50,14; *to go up with* [τινι] Gn 50,7; *id.* [μετά τινος] Ex 24,2

Cf. HELBING 1928, 307; →TWNT

συνανάκειμαι⁺   V 0-0-0-0-1-1

3 Mc 5,39

to recline together; neol.

συναναμείγνυμι⁺   V 0-0-1-0-0-1

Hos 7,8
P: *to be mixed up together with, to be mixed
among* [ἔν τινι]; see συναναμίσγω
→TWNT

συνανάμιξις,-εως   N3F 0-0-0-1-0-1
Dn^Th 11,23
combination with another, league [πρός τινα];
neol.

συναναμίσγω   V 0-0-1-0-0-1
Ez 20,18
P: *to have fellowship with* [ἔν τινι]; neol.; see
συναναμείγνυμαι

συναναπαύομαι⁺   V 0-0-1-0-0-1
Is 11,6
to lie down with [τινι]; neol.

συναναστρέφω⁺   V 1-0-0-0-2-3
Gn 30,8; Sir 41,5; Bar 3,38
M/P: *to live among* [ἔν τινι] Bar 3,38; *to live in*
[τινι] Sir 41,5; *to share the family circle with* or
to wrestle with? [τινι] Gn 30,8
Cf. CAIRD 1969=1972, 147(Gn 30,8); HARL 1986ᵃ, 229;
HELBING 1928, 309

συναναστροφή,-ῆς   N1F 0-0-0-0-4-4
3 Mc 2,31.33; 3,5; Wis 8,16
living with, intercourse, intimate companionship
Wis 8,16; *association* 3 Mc 2,31; *shared conduct*
or *way of life* 3 Mc 3,5; neol.
Cf. LARCHER 1984, 544

συναναφέρω   V 2-1-0-0-0-3
Gn 50,25; Ex 13,19; 2 Sm 6,18
to carry up with [τι μετά τινος] Gn 50,25; *to
offer up* [τι] 2 Sm 6,18

συναναφύρω⁺   V 0-0-1-0-0-1
Ez 22,6
P: *to be mixed up with, to conspire in* [ἔν τινι];
neol.

συναντάω⁺   V 15-8-6-22-10-61
Gn 32,2.18; 46,28; Ex 4,24.27
A: in pos. sense: *to meet together* Ps 84(85),11;
to meet [τινι] Gn 32,2; *id.* [ἐνώπιόν τινος]
2 Sm 18,9; *to rally to* [πρός τινα] Jdt 1,6; *to
come upon* [τινι] Dt 22,6
in hostile sense: *to fall upon, to run upon* [ἔν
τινι] Jgsᴮ 15,12; *to befall, to happen to* [τινι]
Ex 5,3; *id.* [ἐπί τινα] Jgsᴮ 20,41; *to come
against sb* [τινι] (of projectiles) Jb 41,18
M: in pos. sense: *to meet with* [τινι] Prv 12,23
in hostile sense: *to come upon, to befall, to
happen to* [τινι] Dt 31,29; *to come against*
[τινι] Is 8,14

συναντᾶν εἰς πόλεμον πρός Ισραηλ *to wage
war against Israel* Jos 11,20
*Gn 46,28 συναντῆσαι *to present (himself to
him), to meet* -לתראות? (Sam. Pent.) for MT להורת
to instruct?
Cf. HARL 1986ᵃ, 297(Gn 46,28); HELBING 1928, 229-230;
LE BOULLUEC 1989, 35.107; LEE, J. 1983, 84; WEVERS
1993, 529; →MM

συναντή,-ῆς   N1F 0-3-0-0-0-3
1 Kgs 18,16; 2 Kgs 2,15; 5,26
meeting; εἰς συναντήν τινι *to meet sb* 1 Kgs
18,16; εἰς συναντήν τινος *to meet sb* 2 Kgs
2,15

συνάντημα,-ατος   N3N 1-1-0-7-0-9
Ex 9,14; 1 Kgs 8,37; Eccl 2,14.15; 3,19
event, fate Eccl 2,14; *plague, adversity* Ex 9,14;
neol.
Cf. HANHART 1994, 88; LE BOULLUEC 1989, 35.132; →MM

συνάντησις,-εως⁺   N3F 27-31-3-2-17-80
Gn 14,17; 18,2; 19,1; 24,17.65
meeting Nm 23,3
εἰς συνάντησιν αὐτῷ *to meet him* (mostly used
in this expression rendering לקראת) Gn 14,17; εἰς
συνάντησίν τινος *to meet sb* Gn 24,17

συναντιλαμβάνομαι⁺   V 2-0-0-1-0-3
Ex 18,22; Nm 11,17; Ps 88(89),22
to assist in supporting [τι] Nm 11,17; *to help*
[τινι] Ex 18,22; neol.?
Cf. HORSLEY 1983, 84; MARGOLIS 1906ᵃ=1972, 79; →MM

συναπάγω⁺   V 1-0-0-0-0-1
Ex 14,6
*to lead sb away with oneself, to take sb with
oneself* [τινα μεθ᾽ ἑαυτοῦ]

συναποθνήσκω⁺   V 0-0-0-0-1-1
Sir 19,10
to die together with [τινι]
Cf. SPICQ 1978ᵃ, 852-853; →NIDNTT

συναποκρύπτω   V 0-0-0-0-1-1
LtJ 48
P: *to be hidden with sth* [μετά τινος]; neol.

συναπόλλυμι⁺   V 4-0-0-3-3-10
Gn 18,23; 19,15; Nm 16,26; Dt 29,18; Ps
25(26),9
A: *to destroy sb together with sb* [τινα μετά
τινος] Gn 18,23
P: *to perish together* Nm 16,26; *id.* [τινι] Gn
19,15
*Ps 25(26),9 μὴ συναπολέσῃς *do not destroy*
-◊סֵפֶה? or -◊סוּף? for MT אַל־תֶּאֱסֹף *do not gather*
Cf. HELBING 1928, 311

συναποστέλλω⁺   V 2-0-0-0-1-3

Ex 33,2.12; 1 Ezr 5,2

to send as a companion [τινα] Ex 33,2; *to send sb with sb* [τινα μετά τινος] Ex 33,12

Cf. LE BOULLUEC 1989, 329; WEVERS 1990, 547

συνάπτω   V 10-24-4-2-16-56

Ex 26,6.9.10.11(bis)

to join together Ex 26,10; *id.* [τι] Ex 26,11; *to join sth to sth* [τί τινι] Ex 26,6; *id.* [τι πρός τι] Ex 29,5

to border upon [τινι] Jos 19,26; *id.* [ἐπί τι] Jos 17,10; *to reach, to extend to* [ἕως τινός] Sir 35,16; *id.* [τι] Is 15,8; *to reach to, to touch* Neh 3,19; *to press closely on* [τινι] 2 Sm 1,6

to join (in battle), to attack [τινι] JgsᴮB 20,20; *id.* [πρός τινα] JgsᴮB 20,30; *id.* [τι] 1 Mc 15,14; *to form (an alliance)* [τι] 2 Kgs 10,34; *to come together* Is 16,8

συνάπτω εἰς πόλεμον *to join in battle* 1 Mc 7,43; μὴ συνάψητε πρὸς αὐτοὺς πόλεμον *don't engage in war against them* Dt 2,5; συνῆψεν ὁ πόλεμος *the battle was joined* 1 Mc 9,47

Cf. HELBING 1928, 305-306; LE BOULLUEC 1989, 268; WEVERS 1990, 417

συναριθμέω⁺   V 1-0-0-0-0-1

Ex 12,4

M: *to make a reckoning, to reckon, to compute*

Cf. WALTERS 1973, 61.105; WEVERS 1992, 230

συναρπάζω⁺   V 0-0-0-1-3-4

Prv 6,25; 2 Mc 3,27; 4,41; 4 Mc 5,4

A: *to catch up, to take up* [τινα] 2 Mc 3,27; *id.* [τι] 2 Mc 4,41

P: *to be taken by force* 4 Mc 5,4; *to be captivated* (metaph.) Prv 6,25

συναρχία,-ας   N1F 0-0-0-1-0-1

Est 3,13d

common government, shared rule, dominion

συνασπίζω   V 0-0-0-0-1-1

3 Mc 3,10

to stand in close array (for battle), *to protect, to support*

→LSJ Suppl; LSJ RSuppl

συναυλίζομαι⁺   V 0-0-0-1-0-1

Prv 22,24

to have dealings with, to associate with, to have social intercourse [τινι]

συναύξω⁺   V 0-0-0-0-2-2

2 Mc 4,4; 4 Mc 13,27

to increase [τι]

συναφίστημι   V 0-0-0-0-1-1

Tobᴮᴬ 1,5

M: *to rebel with, to revolt in coalition with*

σύναψις,-εως   N3F 0-2-0-0-0-2

1 Kgs 16,20; 2 Kgs 10,34

alliance

συνδάκνω   V 0-0-0-0-1-1

Tobᴮᴬ 11,12

M: *to smart, to feel great pain*

συνδειπνέω   V 1-0-0-1-0-2

Gn 43,32; Prv 23,6

to dine with [τινι] Prv 23,6; *id.* [μετά τινος] Gn 43,32

σύνδειπνος,-ος,-ον   A 0-0-0-0-1-1

Sir 9,16

companion at table

σύνδεσμος,-ου⁺   N2M 0-4-3-3-0-10

1 Kgs 14,24; 2 Kgs 11,14(bis); 12,21; Is 58,6

that which binds together, texture of skin Jb 41,7; *ligaments, joints* Dnᵀʰ 5,6; *band, fetter* (metaph.) Is 58,9; *difficulty, problem* Dnᵀʰ 5,12; *conspiracy* 2 Kgs 11,14

*1 Kgs 14,24 σύνδεσμος *conspiracy* -קשר for MT קדש *temple prostitute*

Cf. DION 1981, 41-48(1 Kgs 14,24); →NIDNTT; TWNT

συνδέω⁺   V 3-1-2-1-1-8

Ex 14,25; 28,20; 36,20(39,13); Jgsᴬ 15,4; Ez 3,26

A: *to fasten sth to sth, to bind together* [τι πρός τι] Jgsᴬ 15,4; *to bind* [τι] Ez 3,26; *to bind up* [τι] (metaph.) Sir 33(36),4

P: *to be bound (together) with* [τινι] Jb 17,3; *to be joined in prayer closely together* Zph 2,1

*Ex 14,25 καὶ συνέδησεν *and he bound together, and he blocked* -אסר◊ יאסר for MT ויסר *and he removed*

Cf. HELBING 1928, 309-310; LE BOULLUEC 1989, 169

συνδιώκω   V 0-0-0-0-1-1

2 Mc 8,25

to pursue sb [τινα]

σύνδουλος,-ου⁺   N2M 0-0-0-8-0-8

Ezr 4,7.9.17.23; 5,3

fellow-servant

συνδρομή,-ῆς⁺   N1F 0-0-0-0-2-2

Jdt 10,18; 3 Mc 3,8

tumultuous concourse (of people)

συνδυάζω   V 0-0-0-1-0-1

Ps 140(141),4

to be joined with sb, to be in collusion [μετά τινος]

Cf. HELBING 1928, 312

συνεγγίζω   V 0-0-0-0-4-4

2 Mc 10,25.27; 11,5; Sir 35,17
to draw near [abs.] Sir 35,17; *to draw near to*
[τινι] 2 Mc 10,27

σύνεγγυς   D/P 1-0-0-0-5-6
Dt 3,29; Tobˢ 11,15; Sir 14,24; 26,12; 51,6
nearby Sir 26,12; *near, next to* [τινος] Dt 3,29

συνεγείρω⁺   V 1-0-1-0-1-3
Ex 23,5; Is 14,9; 4 Mc 2,14
A: *to help to raise up* [τι] Ex 23,5; *to gather up*
[τι] 4 Mc 2,14
P: *to raise up together against sb* [τινι] Is 14,9
Cf. LE BOULLUEC 1989, 233(Ex 23,5); WEVERS 1990,
360(Ex 23,5)

συνεδρεύω   V 0-0-0-0-4-4
Sir 11,9; 23,14; 42,12; Susᴸˣˣ 28
to sit in council, to deliberate [abs.] Susᴸˣˣ 28; *to
sit in the midst of, among* [ἐν μέσῳ τινός] Sir
42,12; *id.* [ἀνὰ μέσον τινός] Sir 23,14

συνεδρία,-ας   N1F 0-0-0-0-3-3
Jdt 6,1.17; 11,9
council
Cf. DELCOR 1967ª, 157-161; WALTERS 1973, 43

συνεδριάζω   V 0-0-0-1-0-1
Prv 3,32
to sit among, to meet in council [ἐν τινι]; neol.

συνέδριον,-ου⁺   N2N 0-0-1-9-2-12
Jer 15,17; Ps 25(26),4; Prv 11,13; 15,22; 22,10
council, assembly
Cf. DELCOR 1967ª, 157-161; NESTLÉ 1895, 289; ROST 1967,
112-118; →NIDNTT; TWNT

σύνεδρος,-ου⁺   N2M 0-2-0-0-1-3
Jgsᴮ 5,10; 4 Mc 5,1
member of a council

συνεθίζω   V 0-0-0-0-3-3
Sir 23,9.13.15
A: *to accustom* (one's mouth) *to sth* [τι] Sir
23,13; *id.* [τινι] Sir 23,9
P: *to become accustomed to* [τινι] Sir 23,15
Cf. HELBING 1928, 40

συνείδησις,-εως⁺   N3F 0-0-0-1-1-2
Eccl 10,20; Wis 17,10
inner consciousness Eccl 10,20; *moral conscience,
consciousness of right- or wrongdoing* Wis 17,10
Cf. DUPONT 1948, 119-153; HORSLEY 1983, 85; LARCHER
1985, 964-965; SPICQ 1978ª, 854-858; →MM; NIDNTT; TWNT

συνεῖδον
aor. of συνοράω

σύνειμι⁺   V 0-0-1-1-3-5
Jer 3,20; Prv 5,19; 2 Mc 9,4; 1 Ezr 6,2; 8,50

to be with [abs.] 1 Ezr 6,2; *id.* [τινι] 1 Ezr 8,50;
to follow sb [τινι] (metaph.) 2 Mc 9,4
τὸν συνόντα αὐτῇ *her husband* Jer 3,20

συνεῖπον   V 0-0-0-1-1-2
Dnᴸˣˣ 2,9; Susᴸˣˣ 38
aor. of σύμφημι

συνεισέρχομαι⁺   V 1-0-0-2-2-5
Ex 21,3; Jb 22,4; Est 2,13; 1 Mc 12,48; Sir 39,2
to enter together with [τινι] Est 2,13; *id.* [μετά
τινος] Ex 21,3; *to enter in* [ἔν τινι] (metaph.)
Sir 39,2
Cf. HELBING 1928, 308; WEVERS 1990, 323

συνεκκεντέω   V 0-0-0-0-1-1
2 Mc 5,26
to pierce through at once [τινα]; neol.

συνεκπολεμέω   V 2-0-0-0-1-3
Dt 1,30; 20,4; Wis 5,20
to fight with sb on behalf of sb [τινι μετά
τινος] Dt 1,30; *id.* [τινι ἐπί τινα] Wis 5,20;
neol.
Cf. DOGNIEZ 1992, 66.118; HELBING 1928, 311

συνεκπορεύομαι⁺   V 0-2-0-0-0-2
Jgsᴬ 11,3; Jgsᴮ 13,25
to go out together with, to accompany [τινι];
neol.?
Cf. HELBING 1928, 304

συνεκτρέφω   V 0-1-0-0-0-1
2 Chr 10,8
P: *to be raised with, to grow up with* [μετά τινος]
Cf. HELBING 1928, 311

συνεκτρίβω   V 0-0-0-0-1-1
Wis 11,19
to destroy utterly together or *altogether* [τινα];
neol.

συνέκτροφος,-ος,-ον   A 0-0-0-0-1-1
1 Mc 1,6
reared together with, brought up with; neol.

συνελαύνω⁺   V 0-0-0-0-3-3
2 Mc 4,26.42; 5,5
A: *to drive* [τινα] 2 Mc 4,42
P: *to be driven to* [εἰς τι] 2 Mc 4,26

συνέλευσις,-εως⁺   N3F 0-3-0-0-0-3
Jgsᴮ 9,46.49(bis)
gathering, meeting of people, stronghold

συνέλκω   V 0-0-0-1-0-1
Ps 27(28),3
to draw together, to associate with [τι μετά
τινος]
Cf. HELBING 1928, 311

συνεξέρχομαι⁺   V 0-0-0-1-1-2

Prv 22,10; Jdt 2,20
to go along with, to come with [τινι] Jdt 2,20;
id. [τινι] (metaph.) Prv 22,10

συνεξορμάω V 0-0-0-0-1-1
1 Ezr 8,11
to depart together

συνεπακολουθέω V 2-0-0-0-0-2
Nm 32,11.12
to follow along, to accompany [ὀπίσω τινός]
Cf. DORIVAL 1994, 536

συνεπισκοπέω V 3-0-0-0-0-3
Nm 1,49; 2,33; 26,62
A: *to muster* [τινα] Nm 1,49
P: *to be numbered among, to be enumerated
along with in the census* [ἔν τινι] Nm 2,33; *id.*
[ἐν μέσῳ τινός] Nm 26,62;
Cf. DORIVAL 1994, 200

συνεπίσταμαι V 0-0-0-2-0-2
Jb 9,35; 19,27
to know very well, to be conscious of [abs.] Jb
9,35; *id.* [τι] Jb 19,27

συνεπισχύω V 0-1-0-1-0-2
2 Chr 32,3; Est 8,12s
to join in helping, to assist [τινι]

συνεπιτίθημι⁺ V 2-0-3-1-1-7
Nm 12,11; Dt 32,27; Ob 13; Zech 1,15(bis)
M: *to join in attacking* Dt 32,27; *id.* [τινι] Ps
3,7; *id.* [ἐπί τινα] Ob 13; *to lay sth to the
charge of sb* [τί τινι] Nm 12,11
Cf. DOGNIEZ 1992, 65.333-334(Dt 32,27); →MM

συνέπομαι⁺ V 0-0-0-0-3-3
2 Mc 15,2; 3 Mc 5,48; 6,21
to follow, to accompany [τινι] 2 Mc 15,2; *id.*
[abs.] 3 Mc 5,48

συνεργέω⁺ V 0-0-0-0-2-2
1 Ezr 7,2; 1 Mc 12,1
to assist [τινι] 1 Ezr 7,2
ὁ καιρὸς αὐτῷ συνεργεῖ *the time is favourable
for him, the time is propitious for him* 1 Mc 12,1
Cf. HELBING 1928, 312; →NIDNTT; TWNT

συνεργός,-ός,-όν⁺ A 0-0-0-0-2-2
2 Mc 8,7; 14,5
helping, furthering [τινος] 2 Mc 14,5; *id.* [πρός
τι] 2 Mc 8,7
→NIDNTT; TWNT

συνερίζω V 0-0-0-0-1-1
2 Mc 8,30
to contend on the side of, together with [τινι];
neol.

συνέρχομαι⁺ V 1-2-3-4-13-23

Ex 32,26; Jos 9,2; 11,5; Jer 3,18; Ez 33,30
to go together (with), to go in company (of) [abs.]
Jos 11,5; *id.* [μετά τινος] Prv 23,35; *id.* [τινι]
Tobˢ 11,4; *id.* [τινι] (metaph.) Wis 7,2; *to come
together (with), to assemble (to)* [abs.] Jos 9,2; *id.*
[πρός τινα] Ex 32,26; *id.* [ἐπί τι] Jer 3,18; *id.*
[εἴς τι] Zech 8,21; *to unite with* [τινι] Jb 6,29
Cf. HELBING 1928, 308; ROST 1967, 118-121; →NIDNTT

συνεσθίω⁺ V 2-1-0-1-0-4
Gn 43,32; Ex 18,12; 2 Sm 12,17; Ps 100(101),5
to eat together with [τί τινι] 2 Sm 12,17; *id.* [τι
μετά τινος] Gn 43,32
*Ps 100(101),5 συνήσθιον *I have eaten with*
-אֹכַל for MT אוּכָל *I will endure*
Cf. HELBING 1928, 311; WEVERS 1990, 281; →TWNT

σύνεσις,-εως⁺ N3F 6-12-14-53-43-128
Ex 31,3.6; 35,31.35; Dt 4,6
faculty of comprehension, intelligence Dt 4,6;
understanding Ex 31,3
Cf. DOGNIEZ 1992, 134.357; WEVERS 1990, 507.590;
→TWNT

συνεταιρίς,-ίδος N3F 0-4-0-0-0-4
Jgs 11,37.38
companion

συνέταιρος,-ου N2M 0-2-0-3-4-9
JgsᴬLXX 15,2.6; DnLXX 2,17; 3,25; 5,6
companion

συνετίζω⁺ V 0-0-0-16-0-16
Ps 15(16),7; 31(32),8; 118(119),27.34.73
to cause to understand, to instruct [τινα] Neh
8,7; *id.* [τινά τι] Dn 8,16; neol.
Cf. HELBING 1928, 39

συνετός,-ή,-όν⁺ A 5-4-12-15-17-53
Gn 41,33.39; Ex 31,6; Dt 1,13.15
intelligent, wise, prudent (of men) Gn 41,33; *wise*
(of words) Prv 23,9
παντὶ συνετῷ καρδίᾳ *everyone understanding
of heart, everyone innately intelligent* Ex 31,6
*2 Kgs 11,9 ὁ συνετός *the wise* החכם for MT הכהן
the priest; *Is 32,8 συνετά *wise things* נבונות for בין
for MT נדיבות *noble things*
Cf. WEVERS 1990, 509; →TWNT

συνετῶς D 0-0-1-1-0-2
Is 29,16; Ps 46(47),8
wisely, with understanding

συνευδοκέω⁺ V 0-0-0-0-3-3
1 Mc 1,57; 2 Mc 11,24.35
to consent to, to agree to [τινι] 1 Mc 1,57; *to
give one's consent, to approve* 2 Mc 11,35; neol.?

συνευφραίνομαι⁺ V 0-0-0-1-0-1

Prv 5,18
to rejoice together with [μετά τινος]; neol.
Cf. HELBING 1928, 311

συνέχω⁺   V 6-15-6-15-8-50
Gn 8,2; Ex 26,3; 28,7; 36,11.28(39,4.21)
A: *to confine* [τι] Jb 34,14; *to enclose* [τι] 1 Kgs
6,10; *to detain, to hold fast, to arrest* [τινα]
1 Sm 23,8
to shut up [τι] (metaph.) Ps 76(77),10; *to close*
[τι] Ps 68(69),16; *to keep shut* (the mouth) [τι]
Is 52,15
to hold [τι] Jer 2,13; *to hold together* [τι] Wis
1,7; *to keep under control* [τι] Mi 7,18
to hinder, to hold back [τι] Dt 11,17; *to get hold
of, to press hard* [τι] (of a city) 2 Mc 9,2; *to
fasten* Ex 28,7
M: *to keep oneself close* 1 Chr 12,1
P: *to be straitened* 2 Kgs 14,26; *to be constrained
to* [+inf.] 1 Sm 14,6; *to be enclosed* 1 Kgs 6,15;
to be detained 1 Sm 21,8; *to be restrained, to be
withheld* 2 Sm 24,21; *to be occupied, to go about*
Wis 17,19; *to be distressed, to be afflicted by*
[τινι] Jer 23,9; *to be absorbed with, to be
oppressed by* [τινι] Wis 17,10; *to be fastened* Ex
36,28
ὁ συνέχων σῖτον *one who hoards corn* Prv
11,26; μηδὲ συνέχου ἀγκάλαις τῆς μὴ ἰδίας
*don't (let yourself) be held in the arms of one
who is not your wife* Prv 5,20
Cf. LARCHER 1983, 184-186; 1985, 964.979-980; SPICQ
1989, 859-863; WEVERS 1990, 413; →LSJ suppl(Is 52,15);
TWNT

συνζυγής,-οῦς   N3M 0-0-0-0-1-1
3 Mc 4,8
husband; neol.

συνήθεια,-ας⁺   N1F 0-0-0-0-4-4
4 Mc 2,13; 6,13; 13,22.27
daily companionship 4 Mc 13,22; *acquaintance,
intimacy* 4 Mc 2,13
Cf. LLEWELYN 1994, 76

συνήθης,-ης,-ες   A 0-0-0-0-1-1
2 Mc 3,31
intimate; ὁ συνήθης *intimate, friend*

συνῆλιξ,-ικος   N3N 0-0-0-1-0-1
Dnᵀʰ 1,10
of equal age

συνηχέω   V 0-0-0-0-1-1
3 Mc 6,17
to resound, to re-echo

συνθέλω   V 1-0-0-0-0-1

Dt 13,9
to have the same wish as, to consent with [τινι]

σύνθεσις,-εως⁺   N3F 13-1-1-0-1-16
Ex 30,32.37; 31,11; 35,19.28
compounding, composition (of spices and
incense) Ex 30,32; *set, collection, whole* Is 3,20;
τὰς συνθέσεις *ingredients* (for a compound) Ex
35,28
Cf. LE BOULLUEC 1989, 351; WEVERS 1990, 491.501.586;
→LSJ suppl

σύνθετος,-ος,-ον   A 1-0-0-0-0-1
Ex 30,7
compounded, mixed
Cf. LE BOULLUEC 1989, 306; WEVERS 1990, 491

συνθήκη,-ης   N1F 0-0-2-3-9-14
Is 28,15; 30,1; Dn 11,6; Dnᴸˣˣ 11,17
agreement, pact, covenant (based on an accord
between two parties, in opp. to διαθήκη where
in most of the cases one party imposes upon the
other)
Cf. JAUBERT 1963, 311-315; PENNA 1965, 149-180; SPICQ
1953, 286-287; WEVERS 1993, 86

σύνθημα,-ατος   N3N 0-1-0-0-2-3
Jgsᴬ 12,6; 2 Mc 8,23; 13,15
watchword

συνθλάω⁺   V 0-2-1-5-0-8
Jgsᴬ 5,26; 9,53; Mi 3,3; Ps 57(58),7; 67(68),22
to crush, to dash in pieces [τι] Jgsᴬ 9,53; *id.*
[τινα] Ps 109(110),5

συνθλίβω⁺   V 0-0-0-1-1-2
Eccl 12,6; Sir 31,14
M: *to collide with* [τινι] Sir 31,14
P: *to be pressed together* Eccl 12,6

συνίημι⁺   V 5-15-16-74-7-117
Ex 35,35; 36,1; Dt 29,8; 32,7.29
to understand, to have understanding [abs.] Ezr
8,15; *to do intelligently* [τι] Dt 29,8; *to
understand* [ὅτι +ind.] 2 Sm 12,19; *id.* [+inf.]
Ex 35,35; *to understand, to take notice of* [τινα]
Is 1,3; *to consider* [τι] Dt 32,7; *to be wise, to be
prudent* Jos 1,7; *to think on* [ἐπί τινα] Jb 31,1;
to be aware of, to take notice of [τινος] Ps 5,2;
id. [εἰς τι] Ps 27(28),5; *to hear* [abs.] Jb 36,4; *to
discern between* [ἀνὰ μέσον τινὸς καί τινος]
1 Kgs 3,9
ταῦτα σύνετε *keep this firmly in your mind, take
your stand upon this truth* 2 Chr 20,17
*Is 59,15 τοῦ συνιέναι *from understanding* -משכל
for MT ממשתולל *plundered*; *Ps 48(49),13 συνῆκεν
he understands -יבין for MT ילין *he stays overnight*

Cf. DOGNIEZ 1992, 299; GEHMAN 1974, 233-234; HARL 1991=1992ᵃ, 155; HELBING 1928, 158; WEVERS 1990, 590.592; →NIDNTT; TWNT

συνίστημι⁺ V 8-0-0-9-27-44
Gn 40,4; Ex 7,19; 32,1; Lv 15,3(bis)
A: *to associate* or *join sb to sb* [τινά τινι] 2 Mc 8,9; *to introduce, to commend sb to sb* [τινά τινι] 1 Mc 12,43; *to place sb in the care* or *control of sb* [τινά τινι] Gn 40,4
to appoint sb [τινα] Nm 27,23; *to establish* [τινα] 2 Mc 14,15; *to convict* [τινα] Susᵀʰ 61
to contrive [τι] Jb 28,23; *to frame, to set* [τι] Ps 140(141),9; *to bring about, to cause to occur* [τί τινι] Prv 6,14
M: *to join, to muster* (a force) [τι] 1 Mc 2,44; *to array oneself for battle, to sustain* (a siege) [τι] 1 Ezr 2,17; *to hold, to organize* [τι] Ps 117(118),27; *to set up, to erect* [τι] 2 Mc 4,9; *to establish* [τι] Ps 106(107),36; *to fix, to appoint* [τι] 3 Mc 6,38; *to unite, to take a stand* Nm 16,3; *to be blocked* Lv 15,3; *to stand* Ps 38(39),2
P: *to be commended* Wis 7,14
συνέστηκα *to be* 3 Mc 4,18; συνεστήσατο πρὸς αὐτὸν πόλεμον *he joined in battle with him* 1 Ezr 1,27; δρόμον ἄτακτον συνίσταντο *they ran in a disorderly manner* 3 Mc 1,19; τοιούτων συνεστηκότων *at this juncture* 2 Mc 4,30; συνεστηκὸς ὕδωρ *accumulating water, standing water in a body* Ex 7,19
Cf. DREW-BEAR 1972, 221-222; HARLÉ 1988, 146; HELBING 1928, 306; LE BOULLUEC 1989, 120; LEE, J. 1990, 1-15; MILLIGAN 1910=1980, 7; ROST 1967, 108-111; WEVERS 1993, 664; →MM; TWNT

συνίστωρ,-ορος N3M 0-0-0-1-0-1
Jb 16,19
one who knows, a witness; συνίστωρ μου *one who knows me thoroughly*

συννεφέω V 1-0-0-0-0-1
Gn 9,14
to let clouds gather [τι]; neol.
Cf. HARL 1986ᵃ, 141

συννεφής,-ής,-ές A 1-0-0-0-0-1
Dt 33,28
clouded over, cloudy

συννοέω V 0-0-0-0-3-3
2 Mc 5,6; 11,13; 14,3
to comprehend, to understand

σύννους,-ους,-ουν A 0-0-0-0-1-1
1 Ezr 8,68
deep in thought, gloomy

σύννυμφος,-ου N2F 0-0-0-2-0-2
Ru 1,15(bis)
husband's brother's wife, sister-in-law, the wives of two brothers (in their relation to one another); neol.

συνοδεύω⁺ V 0-0-0-0-2-2
Tobˢ 5,17; Wis 6,23
to travel in company with [τινι] Tobˢ 5,17; *to have fellowship with* [τινι] Wis 6,23
Cf. LARCHER 1984, 438

συνοδία,-ας⁺ N1F 0-0-0-3-0-3
Neh 7,5(bis).64
caravan, company of travellers; neol.
Cf. CAIRD 1969=1972, 148; →MM

σύνοδος,-ου⁺ N2F 1-1-1-0-0-3
Dt 33,14; 1 Kgs 15,13; Jer 9,1
meeting 1 Kgs 15,13; *assembly, conspiracy* Jer 9,1; *conjunction* (of months) Dt 33,14

συνοδυνάομαι V 0-0-0-0-1-1
Sir 30,10
to suffer (pain) together; neol.

σύνοιδα⁺ V 1-0-0-1-0-2
Lv 5,1; Jb 27,6
to know Lv 5,1
σύνοιδα ἐμαυτῷ *I am conscious of*
→MM; NIDNTT; TWNT

συνοικέω⁺ V 4-1-1-0-8-14
Gn 20,3; Dt 22,13; 24,1; 25,5; Jgsᴬ 14,20
to live together with [τινι] (of a woman with a man) Jgsᴬ 14,20; *id.* [τινι] (metaph.) Wis 7,28; *to be married with* [τινι] Gn 20,3; *id.* [μετά τινος] 1 Ezr 8,67; συνῳκηκυῖα *married* Sir 42,9
Cf. DOGNIEZ 1992, 272; HELBING 1928, 306-307; HORSLEY 1983, 85

συνοίκησις,-εως N3F 0-0-0-0-1-1
Tobˢ 7,14
cohabitation in marriage

συνοικίζω V 2-0-0-0-5-7
Dt 21,13; 22,22; 1 Ezr 8,81.89; 9,7
A: *to allow to live with, to give in marriage* [τινά τινι] 1 Ezr 8,81; *to take in marriage* [τινα] 1 Ezr 8,89
P: *to be bound in marriage* Dt 21,13; *to be populated* (of a city) Sir 16,4
Cf. BICKERMAN 1980, 51(n.29); HELBING 1928, 307; WALTERS 1973, 119-120

συνοικοδομέω⁺ V 0-0-0-0-1-1
1 Ezr 5,65
to build together with [τινι]; neol.?
→NIDNTT

συνολκή,-ῆς   N1F 0-0-0-0-1-1
Wis 15,15
drawing (air), inhaling; neol.
Cf. GILBERT 1973, 237-238; LARCHER 1985, 880

σύνολος,-ος,-ον⁺   A 0-0-0-1-7-8
Est 8,12x; 3 Mc 3,29; 4,3.11; 7,8
τὸ σύνολον *without exception, in every case* (as
adv.) Est 8,12x; *at all* (as adv.; after a neg.) Sir
9,9

συνομολογέω   V 0-0-0-0-1-1
4 Mc 13,1
P: *to be agreed*

συνοράω⁺   V 0-0-0-1-15-16
Dn^LXX 3,14; 1 Mc 4,21(bis); 2 Mc 2,24; 4,4
to see, to perceive [τι] 2 Mc 4,4; *id.* [τινα +ptc.]
2 Mc 7,20; *id.* [ὅτι +ind.] 2 Mc 5,17; *to see, to
consider* [τι] 2 Mc 2,24; *to survey* [τι] 2 Mc
15,21
*Dn^LXX 3,14 συνιδών *seeing* ◊עין for MT ענה *he
answered*

συνούλωσις,-εως   N3F 0-0-1-0-0-1
Jer 40(33),6
complete scar forming, healing of a wound; neol.

συνουσιασμός,-οῦ   N2M 0-0-0-0-2-2
4 Mc 2,3; Sir 23,6
sexual intercourse; neol.

συνοχή,-ῆς⁺   N1F 0-2-2-1-0-5
Jgs 2,3; Jer 52,5; Mi 4,14; Jb 30,3
siege Mi 4,14; *distress* Jb 30,3
*Jgs 2,3 συνοχάς *distress, afflictions* -צרים for MT
צרים *sides*
Cf. CAIRD 1969=1972, 148; →TWNT

συνταγή,-ῆς   N1F 0-1-0-1-1-3
Jgs^A 20,38; Ezr 10,14; PSal 4,5
assignation PSal 4,5; *preplanned signal* Jgs^A 20,38
εἰς καιροὺς ἀπὸ συνταγῶν *at appointed times*
Ezr 10,14
Cf. ROST 1967, 130-132

σύνταγμα,-ατος   N3N 0-0-0-1-1-2
Jb 15,8; 2 Mc 2,23
book, treatise 2 Mc 2,23; *body of doctrine* Jb 15,8

σύνταξις,-εως⁺   N3F 7-1-1-0-5-14
Ex 5,8.11.14.18; 37,19(38,21)
array, army (of soldiers) 1 Mc 4,35; *composition,
story, book* 2 Mc 15,38; *ordinance, arrangement*
Ex 37,19
rate Ex 5,8; *portion* Jer 52,34; *assigned tax or
duty, tribute, contribution* 2 Mc 9,16
Cf. BICKERMAN 1980, 53; GOODING 1959, 82-85; LE
BOULLUEC 1989, 64.108.362; WEVERS 1990, 66.617; →TWNT

συνταράσσω⁺   V 1-1-2-13-1-18
Ex 14,24; 2 Sm 22,8; Is 10,33; Hos 11,8; Ps
17(18),15
A: *to trouble, to confound* [τινα] Ps 17(18),15;
to bring into disarray [τι] Ex 14,24
P: *to be troubled* (of people) 1 Mc 3,6; *to be
troubled as well* Dn^Th 5,9; *to be confounded* (of
foundations) 2 Sm 22,8; *to be excited* (of
feelings) Hos 11,8
Cf. WEVERS 1990, 222

συντάσσω⁺   V 82-9-12-7-15-125
Gn 18,19; 26,11; Ex 1,17.22; 5,6
A: *to order, to appoint* [abs.] Ex 9,12; *to order sb*
[τινι] Gn 18,19; *id.* [πρός τινα] Nm 15,23; *id.*
[τινα] 2 Mc 9,4; *to appoint, to prescribe sth* [τι]
Ex 16,16; *to order sth to sb* [τί τινι] Ex 19,7; *to
give sb a charge to someone else* [τινι πρός
τινα] Ex 6,13; *to ordain, to prescribe, to order to
do* [+inf.] Ex 35,29
M: *to appoint* [τι] Sus^Th 14
P: *to be drawn up in order of battle* Jdt 2,16
οἱ λοιποὶ οἱ τούτοις συντασσόμενοι *the rest
that were in commission with them* 1 Ezr 2,12
*Jb 25,5 συντάσσει *he appoints* -יער◊ for MT ער
even
Cf. HARLÉ 1988, 117; HELBING 1928, 207-208; LE
BOULLUEC 1989, 131.316.346.362; PELLETIER 1982,
236-242; WEVERS 1990, 9.130.187.512.617; →TWNT

συντέλεια,-ας⁺   N1F 2-10-19-35-20-86
Ex 23,16; Dt 11,12; Jos 4,8; Jgs 20,40
consummation, accomplishment 1 Ezr 2,1;
completion (of an activity) Ex 23,16; *completion,
end* (of time) Dt 11,12; *perfection* Sir 45,8;
conclusion, sum Sir 43,27; *destruction* 2 Kgs
13,17; *profit, (unjust) gain* 1 Sm 8,3
ἐπὶ συντελείας *perfectly* Sir 43,7; λαμβάνω
συντέλειαν *to finish* 1 Ezr 6,19; ποιέω τινὰ
εἰς συντέλειαν *to make an end of* Ez 20,17;
περὶ συντελείας *about the termination of his
year's contract* Sir 37,11
*Am 1,14 συντελείας αὐτῆς *of her end, of her
destruction* -סופה/ה for MT סופה *of the whirlwind*, see
also Na 1,3; *Am 8,8 συντέλεια *destruction* -כלה
◊כלה for MT כל/ה ◊כל *all of it*, see also Am 9,5;
Hab 1,9.15; *Hab 3,19 εἰς συντέλειαν *to the
end? perfectly?* -כלה/◊ for MT אילות/כ *like (the feet
of) a deer*; *Jb 30,2 συντέλεια *completion, end,
full term of life?* -כלה for MT כלח *maturity, old age?*
Cf. CAIRD 1969=1972, 148-149; DANIEL 1966, 263; HARL
1971=1992ᵃ, 189; KATZ 1960, 162; LE BOULLUEC 1989,

237; WAANDERS 1983, 186.293.294; →NIDNTT; PREISIGKE; TWNT

συντελέω⁺   V 27-57-48-34-50-216

Gn 2,1.2; 6,16; 17,22; 18,21

A: *to finish (off), to accomplish* [abs.] 2 Chr 24,14; *id.* [τι] Gn 2,2; *to finish, to leave off* [+inf.] Gn 43,2; *id.* [+ptc.] Gn 17,22; *to bring to accomplishment, to fulfill* [τι] Jer 41,8; *to end* [τι] Jdt 2,4; *to make an end to* [τι] Lv 23,39; *to continue till the end* Dt 31,1; *to consume* [τινα] 1 Sm 15,18; *to kill* [τινα] Tobˢ 8,19; *id.* [ἐπί τινα] 2 Sm 21,5

M: *to finish (off), to accomplish* [τι] Gn 44,5; *to perpetrate* [abs.] Gn 18,21

P: *to have come to an end, to be over* Dt 34,8; *to be accomplished* Gn 2,1; *to be fulfilled* Sir 34(31),8; *to be completely formed* Is 18,5; *to occur, to happen* Tobˢ 14,9

συντετελεσμέ νον *perfect* Ez 16,14

*Gn 49,5 συνετέλεσαν *they accomplished* -כְּלִי for MT כְּלִי *tools;* *1 Sm 20,34 συνετέλεσεν *he accomplished* -◊כלה for MT הכלם *he disgraced or hurt;* *2 Chr 30,22 συνετέλεσαν *they accomplished* or *completed* -יכלו for MT יאכלו *they ate,* see also Jer 15,16; *Jer 6,11 συνετέλεσα *did destroy* -◊כלה for MT הכיל כלו◊ *to hold in,* see also Ez 23,32

Cf. DANIEL 1966, 260; DOGNIEZ 1992, 312.332; HARL 1986ᵃ, 177; 1990=1992ᵃ, 244; →NIDNTT; TWNT

συντέμνω⁺   V 0-0-3-3-1-7

Is 10,22.23; 28,22; Dnᴸˣˣ 5,26-28; Dnᵀʰ 9,24

A: *to cut short* [τι] Is 10,22; *to summarize* [τι] 2 Mc 10,10

P: *to be shortened, to be completed* Dnᵀʰ 9,26; *to run short (of time)* Dnᵀʰ 9,24

Cf. HARL 1990=1992ᵃ, 244; →MM

συντηρέω⁺   V 0-0-1-7-30-38

Ez 18,19; Prv 15,4; Dnᴸˣˣ 3,23.30; 4,26(23)

to keep or *preserve closely* [τινα] Tob 1,11; *id.* [τι] Prv 15,4; *to keep close, to treasure up in one's memory* [τι] Sir 39,2; *to observe strictly* [τι] Sir 2,15

ἄνθρωπος ἀνθρώπῳ συντηρεῖ ὀργήν *man cherished anger against another* Sir 28,3

→TWNT

συντίθημι⁺   V 0-2-0-1-8-11

1 Sm 22,13; 1 Kgs 16,28c(22,44); Dnᵀʰ 2,9; Tobˢ 9,5; 1 Mc 9,70

A: *to place, to put, to lay together* [τι] Tobˢ 9,5

M: *to make an agreement* 1 Kgs 16,28c; *to make (an agreement) with sb* [πρός τινα] 1 Mc 9,70; *id.* [τινι] 1 Mc 15,27; *to agree* Susᴸˣˣ 19; *to agree to do* [+inf.] Dnᵀʰ 2,9; *to conspire against* [κατά τινος] 1 Sm 22,13

Cf. HELBING 1928, 310

συντίμησις,-εως   N3F 3-3-0-0-0-6

Lv 27,4.18; Nm 18,16; 2 Kgs 12,5(bis)

valuation, assessment; neol.?

Cf. LEE, J. 1983, 96

σύντομος,-ος,-ον⁺   A 0-0-0-0-3-3

2 Mc 2,31; 4 Mc 14,10; Wis 14,14

concise (of language) 2 Mc 2,31; *stringent* 4 Mc 14,10; *speedy* Wis 14,14

Cf. LARCHER 1985, 809

συντόμως⁺   D 0-0-0-2-1-3

Prv 13,23; 23,28; 3 Mc 5,25

suddenly Prv 13,23; *quickly, speedily* 3 Mc 5,25

συντρέφω   V 0-0-0-1-2-3

Dnᴸˣˣ 1,10; 4 Mc 13,21.24

P: *to be reared together, to be brought up together*

συντρέχω⁺   V 0-0-0-1-6-7

Ps 49(50),18; Jdt 6,16; 13,13; 14,3; 15,12

to run together Jdt 6,16; *to run along with* [τινι] Ps 49(50),18

συντριβή,-ῆς⁺   N1F 0-0-10-11-1-22

Is 13,6; 65,14; Jer 4,6; 6,1; 27(50),22

crushing, breaking Ez 21,11; *bruise* Na 3,19; *breaking (of the spirit), anguish, vexation* Is 65,14; *destruction, ruin* Prv 6,15

*Hos 13,13 ἐν συντριβῇ *in the destruction* -ב/שבר? for MT ב/משבר *at the mouth of the womb*

συντρίβω⁺   V 28-27-76-63-42-236

Gn 19,9; 49,24; Ex 9,25; 12,10.46

A: *to crush, to break (in pieces)* [τι] Ex 9,25; *to break through (a door)* [τι] Gn 19,9; *to beat to a pulp, to annihilate (enemies)* [τινα] Ex 15,7; *to tear (an anim.)* [τινα] 1 Kgs 13,28; *to shatter, to crush* [τι] (metaph.) Lv 26,19

P: *to be broken* 1 Sm 4,18; *to get wounded* Ex 22,9; *to be wrecked (of ships)* 2 Chr 20,37; *to be bruised* Zech 11,16

συντετριμμέ νον *with broken members* Lv 22,22; συντρίβω πόλεμον *to make an end to war* Ex 15,3

*Gn 49,24 συνετρίβη *which are broken* -תשבר for MT תשב *she abides;* *2 Kgs 23,15 καὶ συνέτριψεν *he broke in pieces* -וישבר for MT וישרף *and he burned;* *Jer 13,17 συνετρίβη *it is broken, it is bruised* -נשבר for MT נשבה *it is taken captive;*

*Jer 23,9 (ἀνὴρ) συντετριμμένος *a broken (man)* - שבור for MT שכור *drunk*; *Jb 38,11 ἐν σεαυτῇ συντριβήσεται *it shall be destroyed within thee* - ישבר בגוך for MT בגאן ישית *it shall stop proud?*; *Prv 6,16 συντρίβεται *he is broken* - ישבר for MT שבע *seven*; *Prv 26,10 συντρίβεται *it is brought to nothing* - שבר for MT שכר *hiring*

Cf. HARL 1986ᵇ=1992ᵃ, 94; LE BOULLUEC 1989, 172; WEVERS 1990, 228; →TWNT

σύντριμμα,-ατος⁺   N3N 4-0-18-9-4-35
Lv 21,19(bis); 24,20(bis); Is 15,5
fracture Lv 21,19; *wound* Ps 146(147),3; *affliction, ruin* Ps 13(14),3

*Is 28,12 σύντριμμα *affliction* - גרע◊ for MT מרגעה *refreshing*; *Am 9,9 σύντριμμα *crushed grain* - צרר◊ for MT צרור *pebble*

Cf. WEVERS 1990, 334; →MM; TWNT

συντριμμός,-οῦ   N2M 0-1-4-0-0-5
2 Sm 22,5; Jer 4,20; Am 5,9; Mi 2,8; Zph 1,10
ruin Am 5,9; *crushing* Zph 1,10
συντριμμοὶ θανάτου *troubles of death* 2 Sm 22,5

*Mi 2,8 συντριμμὸν πολέμου *crushing of war, end of war* - שבר מלחמה for MT שובי מלחמה *those returning from war?*

σύντριψις,-εως   N3F 0-1-0-0-0-1
Jos 10,10
ruin, destruction; neol.

συντροφία,-ας   N1F 0-0-0-0-2-2
3 Mc 5,32; 4 Mc 13,22
common education 4 Mc 13,22; *familiarity* 3 Mc 5,32

σύντροφος,-ου⁺   N2M 0-3-0-0-1-4
1 Kgs 12,24r(bis).24s; 2 Mc 9,29
one who has been brought up with one, comrade
Cf. HORSLEY 1983, 37.38

συντροχάζω   V 0-0-0-1-0-1
Eccl 12,6
to run together; neol.

συντυγχάνω⁺   V 0-0-0-0-1-1
2 Mc 8,14
to meet

συνυφαίνω   V 3-0-0-0-0-3
Ex 28,32; 36,10.17(39,3.10)
to interweave, to weave together
Cf. HELBING 1928, 311; LE BOULLUEC 1989, 68.353; WEVERS 1990, 459.598.602

συνυφή,-ῆς   N1F 1-0-0-0-0-1
Ex 36,27(39,20)
sth woven of the same stuff (as the main piece)

Cf. LE BOULLUEC 1989, 356; →LSJ suppl

συνωμότης,-ου   N1M 1-0-0-0-0-1
Gn 14,13
ally, confederate

συνωρίς,-ίδος   N3F 0-0-1-0-0-1
Is 21,9
pair, team (of horses)

σύριγμα,-ατος   N3N 0-0-1-0-0-1
Jer 18,16
hissing
Cf. CAIRD 1976, 82

συριγμός,-οῦ   N2M 0-0-3-0-1-4
Jer 19,8; 25,9; 32(25),18; Wis 17,9
hissing (of a snake) Wis 17,9; *id.* (metaph. of a city) Jer 19,8
Cf. CAIRD 1976, 82; LARCHER 1985, 961

σύριγξ,-ιγγος   N3F 0-0-0-5-0-5
Dn 3,5; Dnᵀʰ 3,7.10.15
pipe
Cf. DORIVAL 1994, 277

συρίζω   V 0-1-8-3-1-13
1 Kgs 9,8; Is 5,26; 7,18; Jer 19,8; 26(46),22
to make a whistling, hissing sound, to hiss (as sign of astonishment) 1 Kgs 9,8; *to hiss* Is 5,26; *to whistle* (of mind) Wis 17,17; *to hiss at sb* [τινα] Jb 27,23

*Jer 26(46),22 ὡς ὄφεως συρίζοντος *like (the voice) of a hissing serpent* - ילל כנחש? for MT כנחש ילך *(the voice) goes like that of a serpent* or συρίζοντος *hissing* corr. σύροντος *crawling* for MT ילך *goes*, cpr. Dt 32,24, see σύρω
Cf. CAIRD 1976, 82
(→ἀπο-, δια-, ἐκ-)

συρισμός,-οῦ   N2M 0-3-1-0-0-4
Jgs 5,16; 2 Chr 29,8; Mi 6,16
hissing 2 Chr 29,8; *bleating* (of flocks) Jgs 5,16; neol.
Cf. WALTERS 1973, 279

συρράπτω   V 0-0-1-1-0-2
Ez 13,18; Jb 14,12
A: *to sew* [τι] Ez 13,18
P: *to be composed, not to be decomposed, to keep together* Jb 14,12

σύρω⁺   V 1-1-4-0-2-8
Dt 32,24; 2 Sm 17,13; Is 3,16; 28,2; 30,28
to draw [τι] 2 Sm 17,13; *to trail along* [τι] Is 3,16; *to draw, to drag, to trail* [τινα] 4 Mc 6,1; *to sweep away* [τι] (of water) Is 28,2; *to crawl* (of anim.) Dt 32,24, cpr. Jer 26(46),22, see συρίζω; *to flow, to rush* (of water) Is 30,28

(→ἀνα-, ἀπο-, ἐκ-, κατα-, περι-, συσ-)

σῦς, συός   N3M 0-0-0-1-0-1
Ps 79(80),14
wild swine, boar; see ὗς

συσκήνιος,-ου   N2M 1-0-0-0-0-1
Ex 16,16
*one who lives in the same tent, tentmate, fellow
lodger;* neol.
Cf. WEVERS 1990, 251

σύσκηνος,-ου   N2M 1-0-0-0-0-1
Ex 3,22
tentmate, fellow lodger
Cf. LAUNEY 1950, 1002-1004; LE BOULLUEC 1989, 95

συσκιάζω   V 2-0-1-0-0-3
Ex 25,20; Nm 4,5; Hos 4,13
to (over)shadow
Cf. WEVERS 1990, 400

σύσκιος,-ος,-ον   A 0-1-1-1-0-3
1 Kgs 14,23; Ez 6,13; Ct 1,16
shady

συσκοτάζω   V 0-1-10-0-0-11
1 Kgs 18,45; Jer 4,28; 13,16; Ez 30,18; 32,7
to make dark [τι] Ez 32,7; *to grow quite dark*
1 Kgs 18,45
ἡμέραν εἰς νύκτα συσκοτάζων *he who darkens
the day into night* Am 5,8

συσπάω⁺   V 0-0-0-1-0-1
Lam 5,10
P: to be shrivelled up
Cf. CAIRD 1969=1972, 149

συσσεισμός,-οῦ   N2M 0-6-2-0-1-9
1 Kgs 19,11(bis).12; 2 Kgs 2,1.11
earthquake 1 Kgs 19,11; *commotion of air,
whirlwind* 2 Kgs 2,1; *upheaval, commotion* Jer
23,19
*1 Chr 14,15 τοῦ συσσεισμοῦ *of the tempest*
-הסעה (cpr. Ps 54(55),9) or -הסערה for MT הצערה *of
the marching (of the Lord)*, cpr. 2 Sm 5,24
neol.
Cf. ALLEN 1974, 113(1 Chr 14,15)

συσσείω   V 0-0-1-4-1-6
Hag 2,7; Ps 28(29),8(bis); 59(60),4; Jb 4,14
to shake [τι] Ps 28(29),8; *id.* [τινα] Hag 2,7; *to
make to shake* [τι] Jb 4,14

σύσσημον,-ου⁺   N2N 0-2-3-0-0-5
Jgsᴮ 20,38.40; Is 5,26; 49,22; 62,10
signal

συσσύρω   V 0-0-0-0-1-1
2 Mc 5,16
to pull down, to pull about; neol.

σύστασις,-εως⁺   N3F 1-0-0-0-2-3
Gn 49,6; 3 Mc 2,9; Wis 7,17
association of men, conspiracy Gn 49,6;
composition, structure 3 Mc 2,9
Cf. LARCHER 1984, 468(Wis 7,17); ROST 1967, 112-118

συστέλλω⁺   V 0-2-0-0-5-7
Jgsᴮ 8,28; 11,33; 1 Mc 3,6; 5,3; 2 Mc 6,12
A: to humiliate, to humble [τινα] 1 Mc 5,3
P: to be discouraged 2 Mc 6,12; *to be subdued*
Jgsᴮ 8,28; *to shrink (for fear), to cower* 1 Mc 3,6;
to be contracted, to be shut Sir 4,31
τῇ ὁράσει καὶ τῷ προσώπῳ συνεστάλη *his eyes
and countenance fell* 3 Mc 5,33

σύστεμα,-ατος   N3N 0-1-2-0-2-5
1 Chr 11,16; Jer 28(51),32; Ez 31,4; 2 Mc 8,5;
3 Mc 3,9
community 3 Mc 3,9; *band, garrison, company*
1 Chr 11,16; *(water) system* Jer 28(51),32;
canalization system Ez 31,4; see σύστημα

σύστημα,-ατος   N3N 1-1-0-0-2-4
Gn 1,10; 2 Sm 23,15; 2 Mc 15,12; 3 Mc 7,3
community 2 Mc 15,12; *band, garrison*
2 Sm 23,15; *gathering* (of water) Gn 1,10; see
σύστεμα
Cf. ALEXANDRE 1988, 188; DREW-BEAR 1972, 222-223;
HARL 1986ª, 90; WEVERS 1993, 6

σύστρεμμα,-ατος   N3N 1-5-0-1-0-7
Nm 32,14; 2 Sm 4,2; 15,12; 1 Kgs 11,14(24);
2 Kgs 14,19
body of men, crowd Nm 32,14; *band, company*
2 Sm 4,2; *conspiracy* 2 Kgs 14,19
Cf. DORIVAL 1994, 100

συστρέφω⁺   V 1-14-4-1-4-24
Gn 43,30; Jgsᴮ 11,3; 12,4; 2 Sm 15,31; 1 Kgs 16,9
A: to tie up, wrap up [τι] Prv 30,4; *to turn* [τι]
Sir 38,29; *to gather* [τινα] Jgsᴮ 12,4; *to conspire
against* [ἐπί τινα] 1 Kgs 16,9; *to amass wealth*
[abs.] Mi 1,7
M: to move to and fro Ez 1,13; *to whirl around
as with a sling* Jer 23,19; *to form in a compact
body* (of soldiers) 1 Mc 12,50; *to gather* [πρός
τινα] Jgsᴮ 11,3; *to conspire* 1 Kgs 16,16; *to
conspire against* [ἐπί τινα] 2 Kgs 10,9; *to
conspire with* [μετά τινος] 2 Sm 15,31
συνεστρέφετο τὰ ἔντερα αὐτοῦ *his bowels
contracted, he was overcome with affection* Gn
43,30; ἡ συστροφὴ αὐτοῦ, ἥν συνεστράφη *the
conspiracy in which he was engaged* (semit.)
2 Kgs 15,15

*Ez 13,20 ὑμεῖς συστρέφετε *you tie up*
-מצררות? אתנה for MT אתנהמצרדרות*you hunt*, cpr.
Ez 13,21 and συστροφή
Cf. DORIVAL 1994, 357

συστροφή,-ῆς⁺   N1F 0-2-5-1-3-11
JgsᴬA 14,8; 2 Kgs 15,15; Jer 4,16; Ez 13,21; Hos
4,19
band 3 Mc 5,41; *assembly* 1 Mc 14,44; *conspiracy*
2 Kgs 15,15; *swarm (of bees)* JgsᴬA 14,8
συστροφὴ πνεύματος *whirlwind* Sir 43,17
*Jer 4,16 συστροφαί *bands (of enemies)* צרים-?
for MT נצרים *guards*?; *Ez 13,21 εἰς συστροφήν
as a disorderly band? -◊צררד? for MT למצורה*as a*
prey; cpr. Ez 13,20 and συστρέφω
Cf. ROST 1967, 122-129

συσφίγγω   V 3-1-0-0-0-4
Ex 36,28(39,21); Lv 8,7; Dt 15,7; 1 Kgs 18,46
to bind close together, to fasten [τι] Ex 36,28; *to*
gird up [τι] 1 Kgs 18,46; *to close up, to shut, to*
clench [τι] Dt 15,7; neol.?
→LSJ Suppl(Dt 15,7)

συχνός,-ή,-όν   A 0-0-0-0-1-1
2 Mc 5,9
frequent, much

σφαγή,-ῆς⁺   N1F 0-0-15-5-4-24
Is 34,2.6; 53,7; 65,12; Jer 12,3
slaughter Ps 43(44),23; *destruction* Jb 21,20
→TWNT

σφαγιάζω   V 0-0-0-0-2-2
4 Mc 13,12; 16,20
to slay, to sacrifice [τινα]

σφάγιον,-ου⁺   N2N 1-0-4-0-0-5
Lv 22,23; Ez 21,15.20.33; Am 5,25
victim, offering Am 5,25
σφάγια ῥομφαίας *they are delivered as victims*
of the sword or *they are delivered to the sword*
Ez 21,20
Cf. DANIEL 1966, 251; HARLÉ 1988, 186

σφάζω⁺   V 51-11-16-3-3-84
Gn 22,10; 37,31; 43,16; Ex 12,6; 21,37
to slay, to slaughter anim. [τινα] Gn 37,31; *to*
slay, to kill (men) [τινα] Gn 22,10; *to offer* [τι]
Ex 34,25
Cf. HARLÉ 1988, 86; SHIPP 1979, 525; →TWNT
(→ἀπο-, κατα-)

σφαιρωτήρ,-ῆρος   N3M 7-0-0-0-0-7
Gn 14,23; Ex 25,31.33.34.35
thong, latchet Gn 14,23; *ornamental ball, knob*
Ex 25,31; neol.?

Cf. HARLÉ 1986ᵃ, 161; LE BOULLUEC 1989, 262.263;
MASSON 1986, 231-252; WALTERS 1973, 68-69(Gn 14,23);
→LSJ Suppl

σφακελίζω   V 2-0-0-0-0-2
Lv 26,16; Dt 28,32
to be infected, to be gangrenous
Cf. DOGNIEZ 1992, 65.66.291

σφαλερός,-ά,-όν   A 0-0-0-1-0-1
Prv 5,6
slippery

σφάλλω⁺   V 1-1-1-2-5-10
Dt 32,35; 2 Sm 22,46; Am 5,2; Jb 18,7; 21,10
A: *to cause to stumble* Jb 18,7; *to fall* Am 5,2
P: *to fall, to sin, to err* 1 Ezr 4,27; *to slip, to be*
tripped up Dt 32,35
*2 Sm 22,46 καὶ σφαλοῦσιν ἐκ *and they shall*
stumble out (of) ויחרגו/מ *they came trembling out*
(of) for MT ויחגרו *and they girded themselves*?,
cpr. Ps 17(18),47; *Jb 21,10 οὐκ ἔσφαλε *she*
does not stumble -לא תכשל for MT לא תשכל *she does*
not miscarry, cpr. Jb 18,7 (ותכשילהו- for MT
ותשליכהו?)
(→δια-)

σφάλμα,-ατος   N3N 0-0-0-1-0-1
Prv 29,25
stumble, false step

σφενδονάω   V 0-2-0-0-0-2
1 Sm 17,49; 25,29
to sling, to throw [τι] 1 Sm 17,49; *id.* [τι]
(metaph.) 1 Sm 25,29
Cf. WALTERS 1973, 313

σφενδόνη,-ης   N1F 0-3-1-1-3-8
1 Sm 17,40; 25,29; 2 Chr 26,14; Zech 9,15; Prv
26,8
sling 1 Sm 17,40; *bullet, stone (thrown by a sling)*
1 Mc 6,51

σφενδονήτης,-ου   N1M 0-4-0-0-2-6
Jgs 20,16; 2 Kgs 3,25; 1 Chr 12,2; Jdt 6,12
slinger
Cf. WALTERS 1973, 312-313

σφηκία,-ας   N1F 2-0-0-0-0-2
Ex 23,28; Dt 7,20
hornet, wasp
Cf. LE BOULLUEC 1989, 241

σφηκιά,-ᾶς   N1F 0-1-0-0-0-1
Jos 24,12
wasps' nest

σφήν, σφηνός   N3M 0-0-0-0-2-2
4 Mc 8,13; 11,10
wedge

σφηνόω   V 0-3-0-1-0-4
Jgs 3,23; Jgsᴮ 3,24; Neh 7,3
to close, to lock, to shut

σφήξ, σφηκός   N3M/F 0-0-0-0-1-1
Wis 12,8
wasp

σφιγγία,-ας   N1F 0-0-0-0-1-1
Sir 11,18
restraint, constriction, miserliness; neol.

σφίγγω   V 0-1-0-1-0-2
2 Kgs 12,11; Prv 5,22
A: *to tie up in a bundle* [τι] 2 Kgs 12,11
P: *to be bound in* [τινι] Prv 5,22
(→συ-)

σφόδρα⁺   D 75-137-46-62-94-414
Gn 7,18.19; 12,14; 13,2.13
very (much), exceedingly Gn 7,18
*Gn 7,19 σφόδρα σφόδρα *exceedingly* (semit.),
see also 17,6; 30,43; Ex 1,7

σφοδρός,-ά,-όν⁺   A 2-0-0-1-1-4
Ex 10,19; 15,10; Neh 9,11; Wis 18,5
mighty, strong

σφοδρῶς⁺   D 1-1-0-0-5-7
Gn 7,19; Jos 3,16; 4 Mc 5,32; 6,11; 13,22
very much Gn 7,19
σφοδρότερον *much more* 4 Mc 5,32

σφόνδυλος,-ου   N2M 1-0-0-0-0-1
Lv 5,8
cervical vertebra; see σπόνδυλα

σφραγίζω⁺   V 1-2-7-17-7-34
Dt 32,34; 1 Kgs 20(21),8; 2 Kgs 22,4; Is 8,16;
29,11
A: *to (en)close with a seal, to seal* [τι] Dt 32,34;
to authenticate a document with a seal [τι]
Jer 39(32),11; *to set an end* or *limit to* [τι]
Dnᵀʰ 9,24(primo); *to seal up* [τι] (in order to
keep it secret) Jb 14,17
M: *to (en)close with a seal, to seal* [τι] (in the
case of a closed building, so that it cannot be
opened) Belᴸˣˣ 14; *to authenticate a document
with a seal* [τι] 1 Kgs 20(21),8; *to seal oneself* Is
8,16, see also Jb 24,16
*2 Kgs 22,4 καὶ σφράγισον *and seal* -םתח for
MT םתיו *and complete*?
(→ἐναπο-, ἐπι-, κατα-)

σφραγίς,-ῖδος⁺   N3F 7-1-1-2-17-28
Ex 28,11.21.36; 35,22; 36,13(39,6)
seal, signet
Cf. WEVERS 1990, 449.454.603

σφῦρα,-ης   N1F 0-4-3-1-1-9

Jgs 4,21; Jgsᴮ 5,26; 1 Kgs 6,7; Is 41,7
hammer

σφυροκοπέω⁺   V 0-1-0-0-0-1
Jgsᴮ 5,26
to beat with a hammer; neol.?
Cf. KINDSTRAND 1983, 86-109(-κοπεω)

σφυροκόπος,-ος,-ον   A 1-0-0-0-0-1
Gn 4,22
*hammer-wielding, one who beats with the
hammer*; neol.
Cf. KINDSTRAND 1983, 86-109(-κοπος)

σχάζω   V 0-0-1-0-0-1
Am 3,5
P: *to relax, to spring up, to lack force* (of a trap)
(→ὑπο-)

σχεδία,-ας   N1F 0-2-0-0-4-6
1 Kgs 5,23; 2 Chr 2,15; 1 Ezr 5,53; Wis 14,5.6
raft, float 1 Kgs 5,23; Σχεδια *Schedia* (toponym)
3 Mc 4,11
Cf. HARL 1987=1992ᵃ, 108.109.123; LARCHER 1985, 796

σχεδιάζω   V 0-0-0-0-1-1
Bar 1,19
to act carelessly

σχεδόν⁺   D 0-0-0-0-3-3
2 Mc 5,2; 3 Mc 5,14.45
almost

σχετλιάζω   V 0-0-0-0-2-2
4 Mc 3,12; 4,7
to utter indignant complaints, to be indignant

σχέτλιος,-α,-ον   A 0-0-0-0-1-1
2 Mc 15,5
merciless, abominable, wicked

σχῆμα,-ατος⁺   N3N 0-0-1-0-0-1
Is 3,17
(bodily) form or *appearance*; κύριος ἀπο-
καλύψει τὸ σχῆμα αὐτοῦ *the Lord will let the
public see through the appearances?*
→NIDNTT; TWNT

σχηματίζω
(→μετα-)

σχίδαξ,-ακος   N3F 0-4-0-0-0-4
1 Kgs 18,33(bis).34.38
cleft wood; neol.
Cf. WALTERS 1973, 334-335

σχίζα,-ης   N1F 0-9-0-0-1-10
1 Sm 20,20.21(bis).22.36
lath, shaft, arrow
Cf. WALTERS 1973, 194-195.335

σχίζω⁺   V 2-1-4-1-4-12
Gn 22,3; Ex 14,21; 1 Sm 6,14; Is 36,22; 37,1

A: *to split, to cleave* (wood) [τι] Gn 22,3; *to
part, to separate, to divide* [τι] Ex 14,21; *to tear*
(garments) [τι] Is 36,22; *to split, to cleave
asunder* [τι] Zech 14,4; *to cut in two* [τινα] Sus
55
P: *to be divided, to part* (of soldiers in a battle
field) 1 Mc 6,45
Cf. WEVERS 1990, 220; →NIDNTT; TWNT
(→ἀνα-, ἀπο-, δια-, κατα-, περι-)

σχῖνος,-ου   N2F 0-0-0-0-2-2
Sus 54
mastic tree

σχισμή,-ῆς[+]   N1F 0-0-3-0-1-4
Is 2,19.21; Jon 2,6; Od 6,6
cleft; neol.

σχιστός,-ή,-όν   A 0-0-1-0-0-1
Is 19,9
split; λίνον σχιστόν *fine flax*

σχοινίον,-ου[+]   N2N 0-4-13-8-3-28
2 Sm 8,2; 17,13; 1 Kgs 21(20),31.32; Is 3,24
rope, cord 2 Sm 17,13; *measuring line, land
measure* 2 Sm 8,2; *measuring line, portion* Ps
15(16),6; *cord, girdle* LtJ 42; *snare* Jb 18,10

σχοίνισμα,-ατος[+]   N3N 1-6-5-1-1-14
Dt 32,9; Jos 17,14; 19,29; 2 Sm 8,2(bis)
piece of land measured out by the σχοινίον,
portion, allotment Dt 32,9; *long narrow area,
border, coast* Zph 2,5; *line* 2 Sm 8,2; Σχοίνισμα
(proper noun) Zech 11,7.14; neol.; see
πρόσθεσις
Cf. DOGNIEZ 1992, 65.66.129.326

σχοινισμός,-οῦ   N2M 0-1-0-0-0-1
Jos 17,5
allotment; neol.?

σχοῖνος,-ου   N2M 0-0-4-1-0-5
Jer 8,8; 18,15; Jl 4,18; Mi 6,5; Ps 138(139),3
pen, stylus (for writing) Jer 8,8; *reed, measure*
(of length) Jer 18,15; *bed (of rushes)* Ps
138(139),3
*Mi 6,5 ἀπὸ τῶν σχοίνων *from the reeds*, transl.
of proper noun in MT השטים מן *from Shittim*, see
also Jl 4,18
LSJ suppl(Ps 138(139),3)

σχολάζω[+]   V 2-0-0-1-0-3
Ex 5,8.17; Ps 45(46),11
to have nothing to do Ex 5,8; *to cease acting, to
linger* Ps 45(46),11
Cf. LE BOULLUEC 1989, 108

σχολαστής,-οῦ   N1M 1-0-0-0-0-1
Ex 5,17

one who has nothing to do, man of leisure; neol.
Cf. LE BOULLUEC 1989, 108.109

σχολή,-ῆς[+]   N1F 1-0-0-1-1-3
Gn 33,14; Prv 28,19; Sir 38,24
leisure Sir 38,24; *idleness* Prv 28,19
κατὰ σχολὴν τῆς πορεύσεως *according to the
ease of the journey* (see πόρευσις) Gn 33,14
Cf. HORSLEY 1981, 129

σώζω[+]   V 10-100-92-110-51-363
Gn 19,17(ter).20.22
A: *to save (from death), to keep alive* [τινα]
Gn 47,25; *id.* [abs.] 1 Sm 14,6; *to save, to
preserve* [τι] Zech 12,7
P: *to save oneself, to escape* Gn 19,20; *to be
saved, to attain salvation* Prv 11,31
σώσατε τὰς ψυχὰς ὑμῶν *save your lives* Jer 31,6,
see also Gn 19,17; 1 Sm 19,11
*1 Sm 14,47 ἐσῴζετο *he was victorious*
-יושיע? ◊ישע for MT ירשיע *he put (them) to worse*;
*Lam 2,13 τίς σώσει (σε) *who shall save (you)*
-מי יושע for MT מה אשוה *what can I liken (to you)*
or τίς σώσει *who shall save* corr. τί ἰσώσω for
MT מה אשוה *what can I liken (to you)*
Cf. GEHMAN 1974, 234-240; HARL 1986ª, 181; SPICQ 1982,
629-636; →NIDNTT; TWNT
(→ἀνα-, δια-)

σῶμα,-ατος[+]   N3N 30-16-5-30-55-136
Gn 15,11; 34,29; 36,6; 47,12.18
body Lv 14,9; *dead body, corpse* Gn 15,11; *body,
self, person* Gn 47,18; *flesh* (meton.), *penis*
Lv 15,3; σώματα *slaves* Gn 36,6, see also 34,29
κατὰ σῶμα *per person, a head* Gn 47,12; ὀπίσω
σώματος αὐτῶν *behind their backs* Neh 9,26, see
also Ez 23,35
*Jb 13,12 σῶμα *body* -גף◊ or -◊גו for MT גב◊
shield, defence?; *Prv 3,8 σώματι *body* -שאר or
-בשר for MT שר *navel* (pars pro toto); *Prv 25,20
σώματι *the body* -בשר◊ for MT בשרים/ב *in Songs*
Cf. BARR 1961, 35-37; GROBEL 1954, 52-59; HARL 1986ª,
60.68.250.299; HARLÉ 1988, 146(Lv 15,2); HORSLEY 1987,
38.39; LEE, J. 1983, 84; LYS 1983, 47-70; 1986, 163-204;
SCHOLL 1983, 13-15; SPICQ 1978[b], 224-225; STANTON 1988,
473-474; WEVERS 1993, 572-573.592.795; ZIESLER 1983,
133-145; →NIDNTT; TWNT

σωματικός,-ή,-όν[+]   A 0-0-0-0-2-2
4 Mc 1,32; 3,1
belonging to the body, of the body
Cf. HORSLEY 1983, 86; SPICQ 1978ª, 866; →TWNT

σωματοποιέω   V 0-0-1-0-0-1
Ez 34,4

to revive, to refresh [τινα]

σωματοφύλαξ,-ακος   N3M 0-0-0-0-3-3
1 Ezr 3,4; Jdt 12,7; 3 Mc 2,23
body-guard
Cf. MOOREN 1977, 28-36; →LSJ RSuppl

σῶος,-ος,-ον/σῷος,-ος,-ον   A 0-0-0-0-6-6
2 Mc 3,15.22; 12,24; 3 Mc 2,7; BelᵀʰX 17
safe, unharmed 2 Mc 12,24; *safe, intact* (of
deposits) 2 Mc 3,15; *whole, intact, undamaged*
(of seals) BelᵀʰX 17

σωρεύω⁺   V 0-0-0-1-1-2
Prv 25,22; Jdt 15,11
to heap sth upon sth [τι ἐπί τι] Prv 25,22; *id.*
[τι ἐπί τινος] Jdt 15,11
→TWNT

σωρηδόν   D 0-0-0-0-1-1
Wis 18,23
by heaps, in heaps; neol.?

σωρηκ   N 0-0-0-0-1-1
Od 10,2
= שֹׂרֵק *choice grapes*

σωρηχ   N 0-0-1-0-0-1
Is 5,2
= שֹׂרֵק, see σωρηκ

σωρός,-οῦ   N2M 0-8-0-0-1-9
Jos 7,26; 8,29; 2 Sm 18,17; 2 Chr 31,6(bis)
heap, pile

σωτήρ,-ῆρος⁺   N3M 1-6-7-12-15-41
Dt 32,15; Jgs 3,9.15
saviour, deliverer Neh 9,27; *Saviour* (God)
Dt 32,15
Cf. HAERENS 1948, 57-68; HOLTZMANN 1912, 270-271;
LARCHER 1985, 901; LAUNEY 1950, 914-919; MERKELBACH
1971, 14; NOCK 1972, 720-735; SPICQ 1978ᵃ, 629-641;
→NIDNTT; TWNT

σωτηρία,-ας⁺   N1F 6-29-24-50-51-160
Gn 26,31; 28,21; 44,17; 49,18; Ex 14,13
deliverance, salvation (of God) Gn 49,18; *saving*
2 Mc 12,25

μετὰ σωτηρίας *in safety* Gn 26,31
Cf. DANIEL 1966, 275-277; HAERENS 1948, 57-64;
LARCHER 1984, 358.439; SPICQ 1982, 629-636; WEVERS
1993, 414; →NIDNTT; TWNT

σωτήριον,-ου⁺   N2N 55-14-23-36-7-135
Gn 41,16; Ex 20,24; 24,5; 29,28; 32,6
deliverance, salvation Ps 41(40),6; *answer of*
safety Gn 41,16; *peace-offering* Lv 6,5; τὰ
σωτήρια *peace-offering* Ex 20,24
θυσία σωτηρίου *peace-offering* Ex 24,5;
σωτηρία ἀγαγεῖν *to keep a festival of*
deliverance 3 Mc 6,30; Σωτήριον (proper noun)
Is 60,18
Cf. BROCKINGTON 1954, 80-86; DANIEL 1966,
275-287.289.295-297; HARLÉ 1988, 37.91; LAUNEY 1950,
914-919; LE BOULLUEC 1989, 244; ROST 1967, 130-132;
WEVERS 1993, 414; →NIDNTT; TWNT

σωτήριος,-ος,-ον⁺   A 0-0-0-0-5-5
3 Mc 6,31; 7,18; 4 Mc 12,6; 15,26; Wis 1,14
bringing safety, of deliverance
Cf. DANIEL 1966, 275-277; SPICQ 1982, 642-643; →NIDNTT;
TWNT

σωφερ   N 0-1-0-0-0-1
1 Chr 15,28
= שׁוֹפָר *ram's horn*

σωφρόνως⁺   D 0-0-0-0-1-1
Wis 9,11
wisely, prudently
Cf. LARCHER 1984, 589; SPICQ 1978ᵃ, 867-874; →NIDNTT

σωφροσύνη,-ης⁺   N1F 0-0-0-1-8-9
Est 3,13c; 2 Mc 4,37; 4 Mc 1,3.6.18
soundness of judgement, prudence Est 3,13c;
moderation, self-control, temperance Wis 8,7
Cf. BIRD 1940, 259-263; SPICQ 1978ᵃ, 867-874; →NIDNTT

σώφρων,-ων,-ον⁺   A 0-0-0-0-8-8
4 Mc 1,35; 2,2.16.18.23
temperate, wise
Cf. SPICQ 1978ᵃ, 867-875; →NIDNTT; TWNT

τάγμα,-ατος⁺   N3N 11-4-0-0-0-15
Nm 2,2.3.10.18.25
division, group, rank, troop (mil.)
Cf. DORIVAL 1994, 163-164.202; →TWNT

ταινία,-ας   N1F 0-0-1-0-0-1
Ez 27,5
board, strip (of wood)

τακτικός,-ή,-όν   A 0-0-0-4-0-4
Dn^Th 6,3.5.6.7
fit for ordering or *arranging;* ὁ τακτικός *one of the three chief administrators set by Darius over his 120 satraps*

τακτός,-ή,-όν⁺   A 0-0-0-1-0-1
Jb 12,5
appointed (of time)

ταλαιπωρέω⁺   V 0-0-14-2-1-17
Is 33,1; Jer 4,13.20(bis); 9,18
to endure distress, to suffer misery Ps 37(38),7; *id.* (metaph.) Hos 10,2; *to be in ruin* Jer 10,20; *to trouble, to afflict* [τινα] Ps 16(17),9
Cf. SPICQ 1978ᵃ, 875; →NIDNTT

ταλαιπωρία,-ας⁺   N1F 0-0-19-8-2-29
Is 47,11; 59,7; 60,18; Jer 4,20; 6,7
distress, wretchedness, misery Jb 30,3; *distressful state* 2 Mc 6,9; *shameful fate* 3 Mc 4,12
*Jer 28(51),35 αἱ ταλαιπωρίαι μου *my troubles* -שברי for MT שארי *my flesh;* *Jl 1,15 ταλαιπωρίας *trouble* -שדד◊ for MT שׁדי *Mighty;* *Ps 31(32),4 εἰς ταλαιπωρίαν *to my misery* -לשׁרי for MT לשׁדי *my dainty?*
Cf. SPICQ 1978ᵃ, 875; →NIDNTT

ταλαίπωρος,-ος,-ον⁺   A 0-1-1-1-9-12
Jgs^A 5,27; Is 33,1; Ps 136(137),8; Tob^S 7,6; Tob^BA 13,12
suffering, distressed, wretched, miserable Jgs^A 5,27; *disastrous* 4 Mc 16,7
Cf. SPICQ 1978ᵃ, 876; →NIDNTT

τάλαντον,-ου⁺   N2N 7-33-1-6-27-74
Ex 25,39; 39,1.2.4(bis)(38,24.25.27(bis)
talent
→MM

τάλας,-αινα,-αν   A 0-0-1-0-3-4
Is 6,5; 4 Mc 8,17; 12,4; Wis 15,14
wretched, suffering

ταμίας,-ου   N1M 0-0-1-0-0-1
Is 22,15
steward, treasurer

ταμιεῖον,-ου⁺   N2N 4-18-3-13-9-47
Gn 43,30; Ex 7,28; Dt 28,8; 32,25; Jgs^A 16,9
magazine, storehouse Prv 3,10; *chamber* Gn

43,30; *innermost, hidden, secret room* Ex 7,28; *innermost part* (metaph.) Prv 26,22
Cf. BARR 1985, 18(Ez 28,16); DOGNIEZ 1992, 286; HARL 1986ᵃ, 285; HUSSON 1983ᵃ, 141.151-154.275-276; LE BOULLUEC 1989, 122; ROSÉN 1963, 63; WEVERS 1990, 107

ταμιεύω   V 0-0-0-1-1-2
Prv 29,11; 4 Mc 12,12
M: *to store up, to reserve* [τινα] (metaph.) 4 Mc 12,12; *to deliver, to administer, to distribute* Prv 29,11

τανύω   V 0-0-0-1-1-2
Jb 9,8; Sir 43,12
to strech out [τι] Jb 9,8; *to string* (a bow) [τι] Sir 43,12
Cf. SHIPP 1979, 528

τάξις,-εως⁺   N3F 1-2-1-7-9-20
Nm 1,52; Jgs^A 5,20; 1 Kgs 7,23(37); Hab 3,11; Ps 109(110),4
order, class Nm 1,52
post or *place in the line (of battle)* Jgs^A 5,20; *appointed place* Jb 38,12; *appointed time* or *place* Jb 28,23
army, band 2 Mc 10,36
good order, regularity Jb 16,3; *order, disposition* 1 Kgs 7,23(37)
order, ordinance Jb 36,28a; *limit* Jb 28,3
form, nature, appearance 2 Mc 1,19; *nature* Ps 109(110),4
Cf. DORIVAL 1994, 163.343

ταπεινός,-ή,-όν⁺   A 8-5-20-19-18-70
Lv 13,3.4.20.21.25
qualification of men and women, without connotation of moral inferiority: lowly, of no account 1 Sm 18,23 *often in a good sense of men and women favoured by the Lord: lowly, humble* Jb 5,11; *oppressed, afflicted* Jdt 9,11
deep below Lv 13,3; *lower, low-lying* (geogr.) Jgs 1,15
τὰ ταπεινά *the low country* Jos 11,16; *the places below, underneath* Ps 112(113),6
*Is 58,4 ταπεινόν *the poor* -רשׁ for MT רשׁע *wicked*
see also πραΰς, πένης, πτωχός
Cf. COSTE 1953; HARL 1960=1992ᵃ, 205; HATCH 1889, 73-77; LEIVESTAD 1966, 36-47; REHRL 1961, 228; SPICQ 1978ᵃ, 878-880; →NIDNTT; TWNT

ταπεινότης,-ητος   N3F 0-0-0-0-1-1
Sir 13,20
humility, abasement

ταπεινοφρονέω⁺   V 0-0-0-1-0-1
Ps 130(131),2

to be lowly in mind, to be humble-minded; neol.
→NIDNTT

ταπεινόφρων,-ων,-ον⁺　　　　　A 0-0-0-1-0-1
Prv 29,23
lowly in mind, humble; neol.
→NIDNTT; TWNT

ταπεινόω⁺　　　　　　　V 15-37-37-68-21-178
Gn 15,13; 16,9; 31,50; 34,2; Ex 1,12
A: *to bow* (the head) [τι] Sir 4,7; *to bring low, to abase, to confound, to overthrow* (pride) [τι] Is 13,11; *to bring down* (the body) [τι] Est 4,17k; *to bring down, to humble, to lower* (the eyes) [τι] (metaph.) 2 Sm 22,28; *to bring low* (a tree) [τι] (metaph.) Ez 17,24; *to humble* [τινα] Gn 15,13; *to violate* [τινα] Gn 34,2
P: *to be lowered, to be levelled* Is 40,4; *to be humbled* Ps 50(51),19
ταπεινώσατε τὰς ψυχὰς ὑμῶν *humble your souls, discipline yourselves, fast* Lv 16,29
*Jgs^A 5,13 ταπείνωσόν μοι *humble (them) before me, make (them) low before me* -◊רדד? *to subdue* for MT ירד ◊ירד *(the people of the Lord) went down for me*; *Is 3,8 ἐταπεινώθη *it has been brought low* -◊ענה for MT עני? (עיני 1QIsa) *eyes*; *Is 3,17 καὶ ταπεινώσει *and he will humble* -◊שפל? for MT ושפח *he will lay bare*; *Ps 38(39),3 ἐταπεινώθην *I was humbled* -רממתי? *I was brought to silence* for MT רומיה *silence*; *Ps 87(88),16 ἐταπεινώθην *I am brought low* -מך◊ מך- or - מכר for MT אמי/ך *your terrors*; *Jb 22,23 ταπεινώσῃς σεαυτόν *you humble yourself* -תענה for MT תבנה *you will be rebuilt, you will be rehabilitated*
Cf. DORIVAL 1994, 504-505; SPICQ 1978ᵃ, 878-880; →NIDNTT; TWNT

ταπείνωσις,-εως⁺　　　　N3F 5-4-3-17-13-42
Gn 16,11; 29,32; 31,42; 41,52; Dt 26,7
humiliation, abasement (as an experience) Is 53,8; *humiliation, humility, low estate, low condition* (as a state of being) Gn 16,11
*2 Sm 16,12 ἐν τῇ ταπεινώσει μου *on my humilation* -עני/ב for MTᵍ עיני/ב *with my eye* or MTᵏ עוני/ב *on my guilt*; *Ps 21(22),22 τὴν ταπείνωσίν μου *my humiliation* -(ת)עני-י for MT עניתני *you answered me*
Cf. HARL 1971=1992ᵃ, 199-200; McCARTHY 1981, 81-85; SPICQ 1978ᵃ, 878-880; →NIDNTT; TWNT

ταράσσω⁺　　　　　　　V 7-8-23-60-23-121
Gn 19,16; 40,6; 41,8; 42,28; 43,30
A: *to trouble* [τινα] Jgs^B 11,35; *to stir up* (water

of the sea) [τι] Is 51,15; *to pervert* [τι] Jb 34,10
P: *to be troubled* Gn 19,16; *to be inwardly moved* Jdt 14,19; *to be moved; to be stirred* (of water) Is 24,14; *to be in commotion* Jer 4,24; *to be troubled* (of earth; describing an earthquake) 2 Sm 22,8; *to be vexed* (of parts of the body) Ps 6,3; *to disturb, to muddy* (water) Hos 6,8
*1 Chr 29,11 ταράσσεται *he is troubled, is stirred up* -מתנשאה (Aram.)? נשא◊ (Ezr 4,19) for MT נשא◊ והמתנשא *and you are exalted*
Cf. ALLEN 1974, 130; HELBING 1928, 27; SPICQ 1978ᵃ, 881-885; →NIDNTT

ταραχή,-ῆς⁺　　　　　　N1F 0-1-9-6-11-27
Jgs^B 11,35; Is 22,5; 24,19; 52,12; Jer 14,19
trouble, anxiety Sir 40,4; *disturbance, tumult, rebellion* 3 Mc 3,24; *vexation* Ps 30(31),21; *cause of upheaval* Hos 5,12; ταραχαί *tumults, troubles* Prv 6,14
→NIDNTT

τάραχος,-ου⁺　　　　　　N2M 0-2-0-2-1-5
Jgs^B 11,35; 1 Sm 5,9; Est 1,1d.g; Wis 14,25
see ταραχή
Cf. SPICQ 1978ᵃ, 881-885; →NIDNTT

ταραχώδης,-ης,-ες　　　　A 0-0-0-1-1-2
Ps 90(91),3; Wis 17,9
terrifying, dreadful

ταριχεύω　　　　　　　V 0-0-0-0-1-1
LtJ 27
to salt, to add salt

ταρσός,-οῦ　　　　　　N2M 0-0-0-0-1-1
Wis 5,11
wing, pinion

τάρταρος,-ου　　　　　N2M/F 0-0-0-3-0-3
Jb 40,20; 41,24; Prv 30,16
place of imprisonment Prv 30,16; *deep place* Jb 40,20; *lowest place of the deep* Jb 41,24

τάσσω⁺/τάττω　　　　　V 4-17-33-14-18-86
Gn 3,24; Ex 8,5.8; 29,43; Jgs^A 18,21
A: *to station* [τινα] Gn 3,24; *to post sb before, to set sb before* [τινά τινι] 2 Kgs 10,24; *to set* [τι] Jer 7,30; *to set sth before sb* [τί τινι] Jgs^A 18,31; *to set up* [τι] Jer 11,13; *to set sb against sb* [τι πρός τινα] Jgs^A 20,36; *to set, to put* (a feeling) [τι] 2 Mc 8,27
to appoint (a time) Ex 8,5; *to appoint* [τι] 2 Chr 31,2; *to appoint sb over* [τινα ἐπί τι(να)] 2 Sm 7,11
to appoint sb as [τινα +pred.] 1 Sm 22,7; *to make sth as* [τι +pred.] Jer 5,22; *id.* [τι εἴς τι] 2 Kgs 10,27

M: *to appoint* [τι] 2 Mc 3,14; *to give order to* [τινι] Ex 29,43; *to ordain, to prescribe* Ex 8,8
P: *to be set in array* Ct 6,4; *to be well ordered* Sir 10,1; *to be appointed* 2 Mc 6,21

ἔταξεν τὰ αἵματα πολέμου ἐν εἰρήνῃ *he ordered blood in peace, he shed blood in times of peace* 1 Kgs 2,5; ἔταξαν ὀσμὴν εὐωδίας *they offered a sweet-smelling savour* Ez 20,28; συνοχὴν ἔταξεν ἐφ' ἡμᾶς *he has laid siege against us* Mi 4,14; ἔταξεν Αζαηλ τὸ πρόσωπον αὐτοῦ ἀναβῆναι ἐπὶ Ιερουσαλημ *Azael set his face to go against Jerusalem* 2 Kgs 12,18, see also Dnᵀʰᵇ 11,17

*Jgsᴬ 20,30 καὶ ἔταξεν *and Israel stationed* -◇יער? (and influence of παρετάξαντο?) for MT עלה◇ ויעלו *they went up*; *Zech 10,4 ἔταξε *he set* -יתור? תור◇ *he explored* for MT יתד *tent-peg*; *Ct 2,4 τάξατε *set* -רגלו (verb.) for MT דגל/ו (subst. +suffix) *his signal, his intention*

Cf. CAPPELLUS 1775, 593(Zech 10,4); HELBING 1928, 59; LE BOULLUEC 1989, 123.303; ROST 1967, 119-121; WEVERS 1990, 109.112.486; →NIDNTT; TWNT

ταυρηδόν D 0-0-0-0-1-1
4 Mc 15,19
like a bull; θεωροῦσα ταυρηδόν *looking boldly*

ταῦρος,-ου⁺ N2M 18-2-6-5-8-39
Gn 32,16; 49,6; Ex 21,28(ter)
bull, ox Gn 32,16; *id.* (as sacrificial anim.) Is 1,11
*Is 5,17 ὡς ταῦροι *as bulls* -כאבירים *as strong ones, as bulls* for MT כדברם◇ דְּבָרִי *as their pasture*
Cf. TOV 1979, 221; →CHANTRAINE; FRISK

ταφή,-ῆς⁺ N1F 3-1-5-2-3-14
Gn 50,3; Dt 21,23; 34,6; 2 Chr 26,23; Is 53,9
burial Dt 21,23; *mode of burial* Jer 22,19; *burial place* 2 Chr 26,23; *sepulchre, grave* Dt 34,6; *mummy-wrapping, embalming* Gn 50,3
*Is 57,2 ἡ ταφὴ αὐτοῦ *his burial* -נוחו *his rest* for MT ינוחו *they rest*
Cf. WEVERS 1993, 893; →MM; NIDNTT

τάφος,-ου⁺ N2M 3-27-4-10-20-64
Gn 23,4.20; 47,30; Jgs 8,32
grave, tomb Gn 23,4
*Ps 48(49),12 οἱ τάφοι αὐτῶν *their grave* -קברם for MT קרבם *their insides*; *Ps 67(68),7 τάφοις *tombs* -צריחים? for MT צחיחה *a dry land*; *Jb 6,10 τάφος *rest* -◇נוח for MT נחמתי *consolation*
→NIDNTT

τάφρος,-ου N2F 0-0-1-0-0-1
Mi 5,5
ditch, trench

τάχα⁺ D 0-0-0-0-2-2
Wis 13,6; 14,19
perhaps
Cf. DRESCHER 1969, 96-97; LARCHER 1985, 768.819; LEE, G. 1970, 137-138

ταχέως⁺ D 0-5-3-3-20-31
Jgs 9,48; 2 Sm 17,18.21; 2 Kgs 1,11
quickly, without delay, soon Jgs 9,48; *too quickly, too easily, hastily* Prv 25,8; τάχιον *quicker, sooner* Wis 13,9; *quickly, soon* 1 Mc 2,40
ὡς τάχιστα *as quickly as possible* 3 Mc 1,8

ταχινός,-ή,-όν⁺ A 0-0-2-1-3-6
Is 59,7; Hab 1,6; Prv 1,16; Wis 13,2; Sir 11,22
quick, swift Prv 1,16; *speedy* Hab 1,6; *soon* Sir 18,26; ταχινὸν ἀέρα *strong winds* Wis 13,2
Cf. LARCHER 1985, 756; →MM

τάχος,-ους⁺ N3N 8-10-2-5-10-35
Ex 32,7; Nm 17,11; Dt 7,4.22; 9,12
course (of night) Wis 18,14; τὸ τάχος *quickly* (as adv.) Ex 32,7; τάχος *id.* (as adv.) 1 Kgs 22,9
ἐν τάχει *in speed, speedily, swiftly* Dt 11,17; διὰ τάχους *id.* Ps 6,11; ἕως τάχους *id.* Ps 147,4; τῷ τάχει *id.* 1 Chr 12,9
*Ez 29,5 ἐν τάχει *quickly* -במהרת for MT המדברה *into the wilderness*
Cf. DORIVAL 1994, 358; LARCHER 1985, 1014-1015

ταχύνω V 4-6-0-4-4-18
Gn 18,7; 41,32; 45,13; Ex 2,18; Jgs 13,10
to send quickly [τι] Sir 43,13; *to be quick, to make haste, to hurry* Gn 18,7
Cf. WALTERS 1973, 147

ταχύς,-εῖα,-ύ⁺ A 2-4-12-12-18-48
Gn 27,20; Ex 32,8; Jgs 2,17; Jgsᴮ 9,54
swift 1 Ezr 4,34; *quick, soon* Sir 21,22; *hasty* Prv 12,19; *hasty in* [ἔν τινι] Ezr 7,6; ταχύ *quickly, at a rapid rate* Gn 27,20; *without delay, quickly, at once* Is 13,22
τὴν ταχίστην (ὁδόν) *in great haste, as soon as possible, without delay* 1 Mc 11,22
Cf. WALTERS 1973, 147.274

τε⁺ C 56-3-2-62-154-277
Gn 2,25; 3,8; 13,17; 20,11; 27,3
and Prv 1,3
ἐάν τε *if* (τε as enclitic part.) Lv 3,1; τε ... καί ... *both ... and ...* Gn 2,25; τε ... δέ ... *id.* Gn 41,13; ἐάν τε γάρ ... μήτε ... *for if ... neither ...* Gn 31,52
Cf. BLOMQVIST 1974, 170-178; WEVERS 1990, 135.300.312.342

τέγος,-ους⁺ N3N 0-0-0-0-1-1

LtJ 9
roof; ταῖς ἐπὶ τοῦ τέγους πόρναις to the
harlots on the roof (possibly referring to
temple-harlots)
Cf. CHARLES 1913=1963, 601

τείνω V 0-2-4-2-1-9
1 Chr 5,18; 8,40; Jer 27(50),14; 28(51),3(bis)
to stretch out, to spread [τι] Prv 7,16; to draw (a
bow) [τι] 1 Chr 5,18
τείνω τὰς χεῖρας to reach out the hands 3 Mc
5,25, see also Ez 30,22

τειχήρης,-ης,-ες A 2-8-1-0-0-11
Nm 13,19; Dt 9,1; Jos 19,35; 1 Kgs 4,13
walled, fortified
Cf. DOGNIEZ 1992, 174

τειχίζω V 4-2-3-0-2-11
Lv 25,29; Nm 13,28; 32,17; Dt 1,28; 1 Sm 27,8
A: to wall in, to fortify [τι] Jdt 4,5
P: to be fortified, to be walled Lv 25,29
*1 Sm 27,8 τετειχισμέ νων fortified -◊שור for MT
שורה the way to Shur (double transl.)
Cf. DORIVAL 1994, 62

τειχιστή ς,-οῦ N1M 0-2-0-0-0-2
2 Kgs 12,13; 22,6
builder, mason; neol.

τεῖχος,-ους⁺ N3N 10-39-45-50-49-193
Ex 14,22(bis).29(bis); 15,8
city-wall Lv 25,30; wall (around sth) Neh 3,15;
outer wall, fortification (of a temple) 1 Mc 9,54;
wall (metaph.) Ex 14,22
Cf. WALTERS 1973, 186; WEVERS 1990, 221; →NIDNTT

τεκμήριον,-ου⁺ N2N 0-0-0-0-3-3
3 Mc 3,24; Wis 5,11; 19,13
sign, token Wis 5,11; proof 3 Mc 3,24
→NIDNTT

τέκνον,-ου⁺ N2N 47-40-61-24-142-314
Gn 3,16; 17,16; 22,7.8; 27,13
child (son or daughter) Gn 3,16; my son, my
child (voc. as affectionate address to a son) Gn
22,7; descendant Prv 17,6; young (of anim.)
2 Chr 35,7; inhabitant (of a city) Bar 4,19; child
(metaph.) Hos 10,9
*1 Sm 6,7 τῶν τέκνων the young (of anim.) -◊עול
or -על for MT על yoke
see also παῖς, υἱός
Cf. SHIPP 1979, 530; STANTON 1988, 463-480; WEVERS
1995, 343(Dt 21,17).352(Dt 22,7); →NIDNTT

τεκνοποιέω V 3-0-4-0-0-7
Gn 11,30; 16,2; 30,3; Is 65,23; Jer 12,2
A: to bear children (of women) Gn 11,30; to

beget (children) [τι] (of men) Jer 36(29),6; to
beget children (of men and women) Is 65,23; to
obtain children by, to have children by sb else [ἔκ
τινος] Gn 16,2; to beget [τι] (metaph.) Jer
38(31),8
M: to get children through, to have children by sb
else Gn 30,3
*Jer 12,2 ἐτεκνοποίησαν they obtained children
-ילדו for MT ילכו they went
Cf. SHIPP 1979, 530

τεκνοφόνος,-ος,-ον A 0-0-0-0-1-1
Wis 14,23
child-murdering; neol.
Cf. LARCHER 1985, 827

τεκταί νω V 0-0-1-9-3-13
Ez 21,36; Ps 128(129),3; Prv 3,29; 6,14.18
A: to work, to contrive or to scheme in order to
get (silver) [τι] Bar 3,18; to devise, to plan, to
scheme [τι] Ez 21,36; id. [abs.] Ps 128(129),3
M: to devise, to plan, to scheme [τι] Prv 3,29

τεκτονικό ς,-ή,-όν A 1-0-0-0-0-1
Ex 31,5
of carpentry
Cf. WEVERS 1990, 508

τέκτων,-ονος⁺ N3M 0-13-9-3-5-30
1 Sm 13,19; 2 Sm 5,11(bis); 1 Kgs 7,2(14); 2 Kgs
12,12
carpenter 2 Kgs 22,6; craftsman, workman Is
44,12
τέκτων σιδήρου smith 1 Sm 13,19; τέκτων
ξύλων carpenter 2 Sm 5,11; τέκτων λίθων
stone-mason 2 Sm 5,11; τέκτων χαλκοῦ worker
in brass 1 Kgs 7,2
→NIDNTT

τελαμών,-ῶνος N3M 0-2-0-0-0-2
1 Kgs 21(20),38.41
bandage
→LSJ Suppl; LSJ RSuppl

τέλειος-α,-ον⁺ A 3-9-1-4-2-19
Gn 6,9; Ex 12,5; Dt 18,13; Jgsᴮ 20,26; 21,4
perfect, entire, without spot or blemish (of
sacrificial victims) Ex 12,5; perfect (in his kind;
of pers.) Gn 6,9; perfect, complete, expert 1 Chr
25,8; complete Jer 13,19; absolute Ps 138(139),22
Cf. DANIEL 1966, 287-288.295-296; WEVERS 1993, 81;
→NIDNTT; TWNT

τελειότης,-ητος⁺ N3F 0-4-0-0-2-6
Jgs 9,16; 9,19; Wis 6,15
completeness, perfection Wis 6,15
ἐν τελειότητι in whole-ness, in integrity, in

sincerity Jgs 9,16

Cf. DANIEL 1966, 295-296; WAANDERS 1983, 217; →NIDNTT; TWNT

τελειόω⁺ V 9-2-1-3-6-21

Ex 29,9.29.33.35; Lv 4,5

A: *to finish, to accomplish* [τι] 2 Chr 8,16; *to complete, to bring to its fullness* [τι] Ez 27,11
P: *to be perfect* 2 Sm 22,26; *to be consecrated to, to be initiated into* [τινι] Nm 25,3
τελειόω τὰς χεῖρας *to validate the hands, to consecrate* (semit.) Ex 29,9

Cf. DORIVAL 1994, 174.264.459(Nm 25,3); HARLÉ 1988, 178(Lv 21,10); LE BOULLUEC 1989, 44.295; DU PLESSIS 1959, 70-72; WEVERS 1990, 463.469; →NIDNTT; TWNT

τελείως⁺ D 0-0-0-0-4-4

Jdt 11,6; 2 Mc 12,42; 3 Mc 3,26; 7,22
perfectly, wholly, fully

Cf. WAANDERS 1983, 213-214

τελείωσις,-εως⁺ N3F 12-1-1-0-3-17

Ex 29,22.26.27.31.34

completion 2 Mc 2,9; *accomplishment, fulfilment* Jdt 10,9; *perfection* Sir 34,8; *maturity* Jer 2,2; *accomplishment, validation* Ex 29,22

Cf. DANIEL 1966, 287-288.296-297; WAANDERS 1983, 222; WEVERS 1990, 474.476.481; →NIDNTT; TWNT

τέλεος,-α,-ον A 0-0-0-0-1-1

3 Mc 1,22

syn. of τέλειος; τέλεον *to an extremity, completely, entirely*

τελεσιουργέω V 0-0-0-1-0-1

Prv 19,7

to accomplish fully, to perfect [τι]

τελεσφορέω⁺ V 0-0-0-0-1-1

4 Mc 13,20

to be perfected, to be brought to perfection

τελεσφόρος,-ος,-ον A 1-0-0-0-0-1

Dt 23,18

being in charge, having a ritual task; τελεσφόρος *person with a sacral duty, temple-prostitute*

Cf. DOGNIEZ 1992, 65.262; WAANDERS 1983, 193-194.294

τελετή,-ῆς N1F 0-1-1-0-4-6

1 Kgs 15,12; Am 7,9; 3 Mc 2,30; Wis 12,4; 14,15
cultic rite, ritual Wis 14,15; *(pagan) sanctuary* Am 7,9

Cf. LARCHER 1985, 706-707.811; ZIJDERVELD 1934, 81-83

τελευταῖος,-α,-ον⁺ A 0-0-0-4-1-5

Prv 14,12.13; 16,25; 20,9b(21); 3 Mc 5,49
last 3 Mc 5,49; *in the end* Prv 14,13; τὰ τελευταῖα *the last parts, ends* Prv 14,12

τελευτάω⁺ V 39-9-10-15-20-93

Gn 6,17; 25,32; 30,1; 44,31; 50,16
to die
→NIDNTT

τελευτή,-ῆς⁺ N1F 3-6-0-1-17-27

Gn 27,2; Dt 31,29; 33,1; Jos 1,1; Jgsᴬ 1,1
end of life, death

WEVERS 1993, 419; →NIDNTT

τελέω⁺ V 2-0-1-11-10-24

Nm 25,3.5; Hos 4,14; Ps 105(106),28; Ru 2,21
A: *to finish* [τι] Ru 2,21; *to come to an end, to be fulfilled* [intrans.] Ru 3,18
P: *to be finished* Ezr 5,16; *to be perfected* (of youth) Wis 4,16; *to be fulfilled* Ezr 1,1
to be consecrated to, to be initiated into the mysteries of [τινι] Nm 25,3
περὶ πραγμάτων ἀναγκαίων ὑπομνηματισμοὺς τελέσοντα *who reminds him of some matters which required attention* 2 Mc 4,23

Cf. DORIVAL 1994, 459; DU PLESSIS 1959, 70-72; WAANDERS 1983, 1-354; →NIDNTT; TWNT

τελίσκω V 1-0-0-0-0-1

Dt 23,18

to initiate; (ὁ) τελισκόμενος *sb who is initiated, an initiate,* cpr. τελεσφόρος; neol.?

Cf. DOGNIEZ 1992, 65.262; WAANDERS 1983, 194

τέλος,-ους⁺ N3N 11-16-9-101-28-165

Gn 46,4; Lv 27,23; Nm 17,28; 31,28.37
end Jgs 11,39; *conclusion* Eccl 12,13; *completion* 3 Mc 1,26; *totality* Lv 27,33
tax, tribute Nm 31,28
τὸ τέλος *in the end, finally* 2 Mc 5,7
most often used adverbially; adverbial expression of totality: τοῦ ἐπὶ τέλος ἀγαγεῖν *to bring to an end, to accomplish* 1 Chr 29,19; εἰς τέλος *utterly, completely* Nm 17,28 (cpr. νῖκος); μέχρι τέλους *to the end, utterly* Wis 16,5; διὰ τέλους *continually* Est 3,13g; ἐλέπτυνεν αὐτοὺς εἰς τέλος *he reduced them to powder* Dnᵀʰ 2,34; ἕως εἰς τὸ τέλος ἐξέλιπεν *they failed completely, the waters were cut off completely* Jos 3,16
prepositional phrases of time: ἀπὸ τέλους (τεσσαράκοντα ἐτῶν) *from the end of (fourty years), after (fourty years)* 2 Sm 15,7; μετὰ τὸ τέλος *after* 2 Kgs 8,3; διὰ τέλους ἐτῶν *after some years* 2 Chr 18,2
Ps, headers of Psalms (55 times) εἰς τὸ τέλος? for ever or to the end -לנצח? for MT למנצח/ל to the (choir-)leader?

Cf. ACKROYD 1969, 126; DELEKAT 1964, 287-290; DORIVAL 1994, 364.527; DU PLESSIS 1959, 56-67; HARL

1961=1992ᵃ, 215-233; 1984ᵃ=1992ᵃ, 38; WAANDERS 1983, 1-354; →NIDNTT; TWNT

τελωνέω							V 0-0-0-0-2-2
1 Mc 13,39(bis)
P: *to be assessed* or/and *to be paid*
→NIDNTT

τέμνος,-ους							N3N 0-0-3-0-8-11
Ez 6,4.6; Hos 8,14; 1 Mc 1,47; 5,43
shrine, sacred precinct
Cf. BARR 1961, 286-287

τέμνω							V 3-1-1-4-4-13
Ex 36,10(39,3); Lv 25,3.4; 2 Kgs 6,4; Is 5,6
to cut, to cleave [τι] Ex 36,10; *to cut* (wood)
[τι] 2 Kgs 6,4; *to cut off* [τι] 4 Mc 9,17; *to hew*
(stones) [τι] Dn 2,34; *to prune, to trim* (vine)
[τι] Lv 25,3
→TWNT

τένων,-οντος							N3M 0-0-0-0-1-1
4 Mc 9,28
sinew

τέρας,-ατος⁺							N3N 16-4-11-10-8-49
Ex 4,21; 7,3.9; 11,9.10
portentous sign, wonder
Cf. DOGNIEZ 1992, 144; FERNANDEZ MARCOS 1980ᵃ,
27-39; LE BOULLUEC 1989, 34; →NIDNTT; TWNT

τερατεύομαι							V 0-0-0-0-1-1
3 Mc 1,14
to talk marvels, to talk strangely

τερατοποιός,-ός,-όν							A 0-0-0-0-2-2
2 Mc 15,21; 3 Mc 6,32
working wonders; neol.

τερατοσκόπος,-ου							N2M 1-0-1-0-0-2
Dt 18,11; Zech 3,8
observer of τέρατα
Cf. DOGNIEZ 1992, 50; LEE, J. 1983, 33; →NIDNTT

τερέβινθος,-ου							N2F 0-0-2-0-0-2
Is 1,30; 6,13
see τερέμινθος

τερέμινθος,-ου							N2F 3-4-0-0-1-8
Gn 14,6; 35,4; 43,11; Jos 17,9; 24,26
terebinth tree Gn 14,6; *fruit from terebinth tree,
pistachio-nut* Gn 43,11; see τερέβινθος

τέρετρον,-ου							N2N 0-0-1-0-0-1
Is 44,12
gimlet, awl

τέρμα,-ατος⁺							N3N 0-1-0-0-1-2
1 Kgs 7,32(47); Wis 12,27
end, limit 1 Kgs 7,32(47); *culmination, uttermost
point* (of penalty) Wis 12,27

τερπνός,-ή,-όν⁺							A 0-0-0-2-0-2

Ps 80(81),3; 132(133),1
delightful, pleasant

τερπνότης,-ητος							N3F 0-0-0-2-0-2
Ps 15(16),11; 26(27),4
delight, pleasure; neol.

τέρπω							V 0-0-1-6-5-12
Zech 2,14; Ps 34(35),9; 64(65),9; 67(68),4;
118(119),14
A: *to delight, to cheer* [τινα] Sir 26,13; *to cause
to rejoice* [τι] Ps 64(65), 9
M/P: *to be delighted, to be (made) happy, to
have pleasure* Ps 67(68), 3
Cf. HELBING 1928, 259

τέρψις,-εως							N3F 0-1-1-0-3-5
1 Kgs 8,28; Zph 3,17; 1 Mc 3,45; 3 Mc 4,6; Wis
8,18
delight, enjoyment, joy

τεσσαράκοντα⁺							Mc 57-44-9-24-17-151
Gn 5,13; 7,4(bis).12(bis)
forty
→NIDNTT

τεσσαρακοστός,-ή,-όν							Mο 2-3-0-0-10-15
Nm 33,38; Dt 1,3; Jos 14,10; 1 Kgs 6,1; 1 Chr
26,31
fortieth

τέσσαρες,-ες,-α⁺							Mc 56-67-64-37-23-247
Gn 2,10; 11,16; 14,9; 31,41; 47,24
four
→NIDNTT; TWNT

τεσσαρεσκαιδέκατος,-η,-ον⁺							Mο 8-6-3-9-3-29
Gn 14,5; Ex 12,6.18; Lv 23,5; Nm 9,3
fourteenth

τεταγμένως							D 0-0-0-0-1-1
1 Mc 6,40
in orderly manner

τέταρτος,-η,-ον⁺							Mο 21-37-18-24-6-106
Gn 1,19; 2,14; 15,16; Ex 20,5; 28,20
fourth Gn 1,19; *to the fourth generation* 2 Kgs
10,30; τέταρτον *fourth part* 1 Sm 9,8
*Jos 15,7 τὸ τέταρτον *the fourth part* -רבע for
MT רברה *to Debir*; *Jgs 14,15 τῇ τετάρτῃ *the
fourth* -הרביעי for MT השביעי *the seventh*
→TWNT

τετράγωνος,-ος,-ον⁺							A 5-1-4-0-0-10
Gn 6,14; Ex 27,1; 28,16; 30,2; 36,16(39,9)
square
Cf. HARL 1986ᵃ, 131; 1987=1992ᵃ, 104; WEVERS 1993, 83

τετράδραχμον,-ου							N2N 0-0-0-1-0-1
Jb 42,11
coin of four drachmas, tetradrachm

→LSJ RSuppl

τετραίνω   V 0-2-1-2-0-5
2 Kgs 12,10; 18,21; Is 44,12; Jb 40,24; Prv 23,27
to bore, to drill [τι] 2 Kgs 12,10; *to pierce* [τι]
2 Kgs 18,21

τετρακισμύριοι,-αι,-α   MC 0-1-0-0-0-1
Jos 4,13
four times ten thousand, forty thousand

τετρακισχίλιοι,-αι,-α⁺   MC 0-1-6-1-1-9
1 Chr 12,27; Ez 48,16(bis).30.32
four times thousand, four thousand
→NIDNTT

τετρακόσιοι,-αι,-α⁺   MC 22-28-0-7-10-67
Gn 11,13; 15,13; 23,15.16; 32,7
four hundred
→NIDNTT

τετρακοσιοστός,-ή,-όν   MO 0-1-0-0-0-1
1 Kgs 6,1
four hundredth

τετραμερής,-ής,-ές   A 0-0-0-0-1-1
2 Mc 8,21
quadripartite

τετράμηνος,-ος,-ον⁺   A 0-2-0-0-0-2
Jgsᴬ 19,2; 20,47
four months long, lasting four months

τετράπεδος,-ος,-ον⁺   A 0-1-1-0-0-2
2 Chr 34,11; Jer 52,4
four-sided, four-faced; neol.?

τετραπλῶς   D 0-1-0-0-0-1
1 Kgs 6,33
in a four-fold way; *1 Kgs 6,33 τετραπλῶς *in a
four-fold way* -רְבָעוֹת for MT רְבִיעִית *a fourth part*
Cf. SPICQ 1978ᵃ, 886-887

τετράποδος,-ος,-ον   A 0-0-0-0-1-1
1 Mc 10,11
late form of τετράπεδος

τετράπους (gen.: -ποδος)⁺   A 15-0-2-6-3-26
Gn 1,24; 34,23; Ex 8,12.13.14
four-footed Jb 41,17; τὸ τετράπουν *quadruped*
(often pl.) Gn 34,23
Cf. WEVERS 1993, 13

τετράς,-άδος⁺   N3F 0-0-8-1-1-10
Jer 52,31; Hag 1,15; 2,10.18.20
fourth day (of the month) Hag 1,15; *id.* (of the
week; see σάββατον) Ps 93(94),tit.; *fourth* (as
adj.) Zech 8,19

τετράστιχος,-ος,-ον   A 2-0-0-0-1-3
Ex 28,17; 36,17(39,10); Wis 18,24
arranged in four rows; neol.

τέφρα,-ας   N1F 0-0-0-0-6-6

Tob 6,17; 8,2; Wis 2,3
ashes

τεχνάζω   V 0-0-1-0-0-1
Is 46,5
M: *to contrive*

τεχνάομαι   V 0-0-0-0-1-1
Wis 13,11
to craft, to shape craftily

τέχνη,-ης⁺   N1F 2-2-0-1-5-10
Ex 28,11; 30,25; 1 Kgs 7,2(14); 1 Chr 28,21;
Dnᴸˣˣ 1,17
art, craft
→NIDNTT

τεχνίτης,-ου⁺   N1M 1-2-3-1-5-12
Dt 27,15; 1 Chr 22,15; 29,5; Jer 10,9; 24,1
artificer, craftsman, skilled workman

τεχνῖτις,-ιδος   N3F 0-0-0-0-3-3
Wis 7,21; 8,6; 14,2
craftswoman, artisan (metaph.); neol.?

τηγανίζω⁺   V 0-0-0-0-1-1
2 Mc 7,5
to fry in the τήγανον; neol.?

τήγανον,-ου   N2N 3-4-1-0-5-13
Lv 2,5; 6,14; 7,9; 2 Sm 6,19; 13,9
frying-pan, saucepan
Cf. SHIPP 1979, 527

τηκτός,-ή,-όν   A 0-0-0-0-1-1
Wis 19,21
capable of being melted

τήκω⁺   V 5-4-13-13-16-51
Ex 15,15; 16,21; Lv 26,39; Dt 28,65; 32,24
A: *to melt* [τι] Ps 147,7; *to melt, to waste* (the
flesh) [τι] (said of the smith near his furnance)
Sir 38,28; *to consume* (the flesh) [τι] (as
torture) 4 Mc 15,15; *to cause to melt and
disappear, to bring to naught* [τι] Na 1,6; *to
waste away* [intrans.] Jb 7,5
M/P: *to melt* Ex 16,21; *to thaw* (of snow and the
like) Wis 16,22; *to be dissolved* (of the earth) Ps
74(75),4; *to be consumed* (of bonds) Jgsᴮ 15,14;
to melt away, to dissolve in fear (of people) Ex
15,15; *to fail* (of ideas) Jos 5,1
τηκομένην ψυχήν *a wasting soul, a soul without
courage* Dt 28,65
*Is 24,23 καὶ τακήσεται *and* (brick) *shall decay*
-פוּר◊ (*to destroy*) for MT וחפרה *and* (the moon)
shall be abashed, see πλίνθος; *Jer 6,29 οὐκ
ἐτάκησαν (*their wickednesses*) *are not melted
away* -נתק◊ לא נתקו? נתק◊ לא נתקו for MT (*the wicked*)
are not removed

Cf. BARR 1985, 43-44; MARGOLIS 1907, 246-247.248; TOV 1979, 225; WEVERS 1990, 233(Ex 15,15)

τηλαύγημα,-ατος   N3N 1-0-0-0-0-1
Lv 13,23
bright spot, whitened place, whiteness (of leprosy); neol.

τηλαυγής,-ής,-ές⁺   A 4-0-0-2-0-6
Lv 13,2.4.19.24; Ps 18(19),9
conspicuous, bright Lv 13,2; *id.* (metaph.) Ps 18(19),9; *far-shining, far seen* Jb 37,21

τηλαύγησις,-εως   N3F 0-0-0-1-0-1
Ps 17(18),13
brightness, splendour (shining from afar); neol.

τηλικοῦτος,-αύτη,-οῦτο⁺   R 0-0-0-0-3-3
2 Mc 12,3; 3 Mc 3,9; 4 Mc 16,4
such 2 Mc 12,3; *so great* 3 Mc 3,9; *so strong* 4 Mc 16,4

τηρέω⁺   V 2-1-1-23-10-37
Gn 3,15(bis); 1 Sm 15,11; Jer 20,10; Prv 2,11
to guard, to keep, to take care of [τινα] Prv 2,11; *id.* [τι] Ct 7,14; *id.* [abs.] Ezr 8,29; *to keep, to keep a watch over, to guard* (a city) [τι] 1 Mc 4,61; *to keep watch* [abs.] 1 Ezr 4,11; *to keep sb* [τινα +pred.] Wis 10,5; *to protect sb from* [τινα ἀπό τινος] Prv 7,5
to observe [τι] (of the eyes) Prv 23,26; *to observe, to notice* [τινα] Dnᴸˣˣ 6,12; *to watch (carefully)* [τι] Jer 20,10
to await (a time) [τι] Jdt 12,16
to observe, to keep, to fulfil (an engagement) [τι] Tobᴮᴬ 14,9; *to mind* [τι] Prv 15,32
οἱ τηροῦντες *watchmen* Ct 3,3; *keepers* Ct 8,11
*Gn 3,15 τηρήσει *he will lie in wait, he will watch* corr.? τειρήσει *he will bruise, he will break* for MT שׁוּף◊? or τηρήσει *he will be in wait* -שָׁאַף◊ (*to pant after*) for MT שׁוּף ◊ *he will bruise*
Cf. ALEXANDRE 1988, 316(Gn 3,15); →MM; NIDNTT; TWNT

τήρησις,-εως⁺   N3F 0-0-0-0-5-5
1 Mc 5,18; 2 Mc 3,40; 3 Mc 5,44; Wis 6,18; Sir 32,23
guarding, keeping 1 Mc 5,18; *keeping of sth, preservation of sth* [τινος] 2 Mc 3,40; *observation of sth* [τινος] Wis 6,18(19)
→NIDNTT; TWNT

τιάρα,-ας   N1F 0-0-1-2-0-3
Ez 23,15; Dn 3,21
tiara, kind of headdress

τίθημι⁺   V 66-146-136-138-72-558
Gn 1,17; 2,8.15; 3,15; 4,15
A: *to set, to put* [τι] Gn 30,41; *to place* [τινα]

Jos 4,3; *to set, to plant* [τι] Jos 2,18; *to lay* [τι] Jgsᴮ 9,24
to lay (stones) [τι] 1 Ezr 6,8; *to construct, to make* (streets) [τι] 1 Kgs 21(20),34
to set, to draw (a border, boundary) Ex 23,31
to establish, to institute [τι] Ex 34,10; *to make a decree, to ordain* [τι] Ezr 4,21
to give (the name) [τί τινος] Jgsᴮ 8,31
to make sb (as) [τινα +pred.] Gn 17,5; *id.* [τινα εἰς τινα] Gn 17,6; *to make sth* (as) [τι +pred.] Lv 26,31; *id.* [τι εἰς τι] Zph 2,13; *to turn into* [τι εἰς τι] Jdt 1,14
M: *to set, to put, to place* [τι] Gn 1,17; *to place* [τινα] Is 27,4
to show, to bestow [τι] Jb 10,12; *to lay* (a reproach) [τι] 1 Sm 11,2
to appoint to [τί τινι] 2 Sm 7,10; *id.* [τινι] Gn 47,26; *to entrust sth to sb* [τι ἔν τινι] Ps 104(105),27
to appoint sb [τινα] 2 Chr 32,6; *to set sb* (on a throne) [τινα] 1 Kgs 2,24; *to put sb in* (prison) [τινα ἔν τινι] Gn 41,10
to establish, to institute [τι] Gn 17,2; *to appoint* (a law) [τι] Ps 77(78), 5
to make for sb a name [τινί τι] 1 Chr 17,21
to make sb (as) [τινα +pred.] 1 Sm 28,2; *id.* [τινα εἰς τι] Zph 3,19; *id.* [τινα εἰς τινα] Jdt 5,11; *to make sth* (as) [τι +pred.] Jb 11,13
ἐπ᾿ ἐμὲ ἔθετο πᾶς Ισραηλ τὸ πρόσωπον αὐτοῦ εἰς βασιλέα *all Israel looked to me as (their next) king* 1 Kgs 2,15; ἔθηκας τὸν οἶκον ... ὡς ἡ ἡμέρα αὕτη *you have made the temple as it is today* Bar 2,26
*Is 50,4 ἔθηκε *he put, he stablished (me)* -עלה (causal) *to bring up, to place?* for MT יעיר עורר◊ *he lights up;* *Ez 14,8 καὶ θήσομαι αὐτόν *and I will put him, I will turn him into* -והשׁמתיהו for MT והשׁמתיהו(uncertain hi.) *id.?;* *Hos 13,1 καὶ ἔθετο αὐτά *and he put them, and he established them* -וישׂם for MT ויאשׁם אשׁם◊ *and he incurred guilt;* *Hab 3,4 καὶ ἔθετο *and he puts, and he makes* -ושׁם שׂים◊ for MT ושׁם *and there;* *Neh 5,10 ἐθήκαμεν *we put (to them), we gave (them)* -נשׁא◊ or -שׁים for MT נשׁים נשׁה◊ *we gave loan (to them)* see κεῖμαι
Cf. CAIRD 1976, 82; HELBING 1928, 57; WEVERS 1993, 183; →MM; NIDNTT; TWNT

τιθηνέω   V 0-0-0-1-2-3
Lam 4,5; 3 Mc 3,15; Sir 30,9
to nurse, to bring up [τινα] Lam 4,5; *to foster, to*

cherish [τινα] (metaph.) 3 Mc 3,15

τιθηνία,-ας   N1F 0-0-0-0-1-1
4 Mc 16,7
nursing; neol.

τιθηνός,-ός,-όν   A 1-3-1-1-1-7
Nm 11,12; 2 Sm 4,4; 2 Kgs 10,1.5; Is 49,23
stereotypical translation of אֹמֵן; *nursing*; ἡ
τιθηνός *nurse* 2 Sm 4,4; ὁ τιθηνός *one who
takes care, foster-father* 2 Kgs 10,1; *one who
takes care* Is 49,23
Cf. DORIVAL 1994, 78.290

τίκτω+   V 101-72-44-19-8-244
Gn 3,16; 4,1.2.17.20
to bring forth [τινα] (said of women) Gn 3,16;
id. [abs.] 1 Sm 4,19; *id.* [τινα] (of anim.) Gn
30,39; *to generate, to produce* [τι] Jb 38,28
Cf. LE BOULLUEC 1989, 78-79(Ex 1,16.19).115; WALTERS
1973, 116; WEVERS 1990, 9; →NIDNTT
(→ἀνα-, ἀπο-, ἐκ-)

τίλλω+   V 0-0-1-2-1-4
Is 18,7; Dn^LXX 7,4; Ezr 9,3; PSal 13,3
A: *to pluck hair* Ezr 9,5; *to tear* [τι] PSal 13,3
P: *to be plucked* Dn^LXX 7,4; *to be peeled* Is 18,7
Cf. SPICQ 1978ᵃ, 888-889
(→δια-, ἐκ-, κατα-)

τιμάω+   V 12-0-2-14-20-48
Ex 20,12; Lv 19,32; 27,8(bis).12
A: *to honour* [τινα] Wis 14,15; *id.* (parents)
[τινα] Ex 20,12; *id.* (the Lord) [τινα] Prv 3,9;
id. [τι] Prv 6,8c
M: *to value* [τινα] Lv 27,8
*Prv 25,2 τιμᾷ (the glory of a king) honours -הֹקֵר
◊ יקר for MT חֵקֶר ◊ הֹקֵר (it is the glory of the king) to
search out, see also Prv 25,27
Cf. DORIVAL 1994, 424.449(Nm 22,17; 24,11)
(→ἐπι-, προ-, προσεπι-, ὑπερ-)

τιμή,-ῆς+   N1F 25-2-6-28-16-77
Gn 20,16; 44,2; Ex 28,2.40; 34,20
honour Est 1,20; *mark of honour* Sir 45,12
value, price (money) Gn 44,2; *valuation* Lv 27,2;
2 Chr 1,16; *taxes, customs, tribute* 1 Mc 10,29;
τιμαί *honours* 2 Mc 4,15
τιμαῖς αὐτοῦ *with honours due to him* Sir 38,1;
τιμὴν δίδωμι *to pay a price* Ex 34,20, see also
Nm 20,19; τιμὰς λαμβάνοντες *taking bribes* Ez
22,25; εἰς τιμὴν καὶ δόξαν *for honour and
glory* Ex 28,2
*2 Chr 1,16 ἡ τιμή *the charge* (of importing)
-מִקְרָא ◊ יקר (Aram.)? *honour, price* for MT קֹוֵה ◊ מִקְרָא
collection

Cf. DRIVER 1954, 240; HARL 1986ᵃ, 187(Gn 20,16); LE
BOULLUEC 1989, 281.341(Ex 34,20); WEVERS 1993, 741;
→MM; NIDNTT; TWNT

τίμημα,-ατος   N3N 1-0-0-0-0-1
Lv 27,27
valuation, price

τίμιος,-α,-ον+   A 0-16-2-17-7-42
1 Sm 3,1; 2 Sm 12,30; 1 Kgs 6,1a(5,31); 7,46(9).
47(10)
held in honour, noble Ezr 4,10; *of high price,
costly, precious* (often said of stones) 2 Sm
12,30; *precious, dear* (said of pers.) Prv 6,26;
precious (metaph.) 1 Sm 3,1; *honourable* 4 Mc
5,35
*Hos 11,7 τὰ τίμια αὐτοῦ *his precious things*
-◊יקר for MT יקראהו ◊ קרא *they call him*; *Prv 20,6
τίμιον *precious* -יקר for MT יקרא ◊ קרא *he proclaims*

τιμογραφέω   V 0-1-0-0-0-1
2 Kgs 23,35
to tax by assessment [τι]; neol.?
→LSJ RSuppl

τιμόω
(→ἐν-)

τιμωρέω+   V 0-1-2-1-7-11
Jgs^A 5,14; Ez 5,17; 14,15; Prv 22,3; 2 Mc 7,7
A: *to take vengeance on, to punish* [τινα] 4 Mc
9,24
M: *to take vengeance on, to punish* [τινα] Wis
12,20
P: *to be punished* Prv 22,3
*Jgs^A 5,14 ἐτιμωρήσατο αὐτούς (Ephraim)
punished them -◊שֹׁרֶשׁ (Aram.) *to castigate* for MT
שֹׁרֶשׁ (Ephraim is) *their root*?
Cf. HELBING 1928, 36-37

τιμωρητής,-οῦ+   N1M 0-0-0-0-1-1
2 Mc 4,16
avenger; neol.

τιμωρία,-ας+   N1F 0-0-1-3-11-15
Jer 38(31),21; Prv 19,29; 24,22; Dn^LXX 2,18;
1 Ezr 8,24
retribution, punishment 1 Ezr 8,24; *help* Dn^LXX
2,18
*Jer 38(31),21 τιμωρίαν *retaliation* or *help* for
MT תַמְרוּרִים *signposts* (due to homoeophony)
Cf. CAIRD 1976, 86; HARL 1991=1992ᵃ, 158

τίναγμα,-ατος   N3N 0-0-0-1-0-1
Jb 28,26
shake, quake; neol.?
→LSJ RSuppl

τινάσσω

(→ἀπο-, ἐκ-, ἐν-)
-τιννύω
(→ἀπο-)
τίνω⁺   V 0-0-0-4-0-4
Prv 20,9c(22); 24,22.29; 27,12
A: *to pay, to undergo* [τι] Prv 27,12
M: *to avenge oneself on* [τινα] Prv 20,9c
Cf. HELBING 1928, 37
(→ἀνταπο-, ἀπο-, ἐκ-)
τίς, τίς, τί⁺   R 204-400-294-383-249-1530
Gn 2,19; 3,1.11.13; 4,6
who (dir. question) Gn 3,11; *id.* (indir. question)
Gn 43,22; *what* (dir. question) Gn 4,10; *id.*
(indir. question) Ex 2,4; *who, what sort of person*
Ex 3,11; *what, what sort of thing* Ex 16,15; *how*
(in an exclamation) 2 Sm 6,20
τί ὅτι *why* Gn 40,7; ἵνα τί *wherefore* Gn
31,26; τίς δώσει *would that* (semit.) Sir 22,27
Cf. LEE, J. 1983, 11
τις, τις, τι⁺   R 72-16-23-57-151-319
Gn 6,5; 13,16; 14,13; 18,30.32
anyone, someone Gn 13,16; *a certain* Gn 38,1;
anything, something Ex 19,12; *some, any, a*
certain (as adj.) 1 Kgs 3,5; *some kind of* 2 Mc
3,17; τινες *some, a number, certain* Gn 27,44;
some of [+partitive gen.] Gn 14,13
πᾶς τις *everyone* Gn 6,5; βραχύ τι *(only) a little*
2 Sm 16,1
Cf. HORSLEY 1989, 71
τιτάν,-ᾶνος   N3M 0-2-0-0-1-3
2 Sm 5,18.22; Jdt 16,6
titan, giant
τιτρώσκω⁺   V 3-1-1-11-3-19
Nm 31,19; Dt 1,44; 7,21; 1 Kgs 22,34; Jer 9,7
A: *to wound* [τινα] Dt 1,44; *to pierce through*
(walls) [τι] 2 Mc 3,16
P: *to be wounded* (metaph., in the heart) Ct 5,8;
to be slain Nm 31,19
Cf. DORIVAL 1994, 57.524
(→κατα-)
τλάω
(→ἀνα-)
τμητός,-ή,-όν   A 1-0-0-0-0-1
Ex 20,25
cut, dressed (of stones)
τοι⁺   X 0-0-0-0-8-8
4 Mc 2,17; 4,11; 5,1; 6,8.11
enclitic part. emphasizing the reliability of a
statement; γέ τοι *whence, therefore, then*
τοιγαροῦν⁺   C 0-0-1-4-6-11

Is 5,26; Jb 22,10; 24,22; Prv 1,26.31
therefore, for that reason Is 5,26; *also* 2 Mc 7,23
τοίνυν⁺   C 0-2-4-2-12-20
1 Chr 28,10; 2 Chr 28,23; Is 3,10; 5,13; 27,4
hence, so, indeed
τοῖος,-α,-ον   R 0-0-0-1-0-1
Ezr 5,3
such (referring to what follows)
τοιόσδε,-άδε,-όνδε⁺   R 0-0-0-0-2-2
2 Mc 11,27; 15,12
such as this (referring to what follows)
τοιοῦτος,-αύτη,-οῦτο(ν)⁺   R 10-6-15-19-32-82
Gn 39,11; 41,19.38; Ex 9,18.24
such (a), like this Gn 41,38; *certain* Gn 39,11
ἥτις τοιαύτη *such as* (τοιοῦτος after a rel.
pron. is due to Semit. influence) Ex 9,18
*Ez 31,8 τοιαῦται *as this* -כמוהו for MT עממהו
overshadowed him
τοῖχος,-ου⁺   N2M 6-31-29-7-10-83
Ex 30,3; Lv 5,9; 14,37(bis).39
wall Lv 14,37; *side* Ex 30,3
Cf. WEVERS 1990, 489; →NIDNTT
τοκάς,-άδος   N3F 0-1-0-0-0-1
1 Kgs 2,46i
breeding stock
τοκετός,-οῦ⁺   N2M 1-0-0-2-1-4
Gn 35,16; Jb 39,1.2; Sir 23,14
childbirth, delivery Gn 35,16; *bringing forth* (of
anim.) Jb 39,1; *birth, being born* Sir 23,14
τοκίζω
(→ἐκ-)
τόκος,-ου⁺   N2M 6-1-7-4-1-19
Ex 22,24; Lv 25,36.37; Dt 23,20(bis)
childbirth Hos 9,11
interest Ex 22,24; *usury, financial oppression*
(homoeophonic? with תך) Ps 71(72),14, see also
Ps 54(55),12; Jer 9,5
*Jer 9,5 (... ἐπιστρέψαι.) τόκος ἐπὶ τόκῳ *(... to
return.) usury upon usury* - (שׁב) תּׂךְ בְּתׂךְ *to return*
oppression upon oppression for MT שׁבְתּךָ בְּתוֹךְ *your*
dwelling is in the midst of ...
Cf. BARR 1985, 15-20; CAIRD 1969=1972, 149(Ps
71(72),14); 1976, 86; MCKANE 1986, 201(Jer 9,5); TOV
1979, 86; WEVERS 1990, 354; 1995, 373; →LSJ RSuppl; MM
τόλμα,-ης⁺   N1F 0-0-0-2-3-5
Jb 21,27; 39,20; Jdt 16,10; 2 Mc 8,18; 3 Mc 6,34
courage, daring 2 Mc 8,18; *boldness, recklessness*
3 Mc 6,34
τολμάω⁺   V 0-0-0-3-4-7
Jb 15,12; Est 1,18; 7,5; Jdt 14,13; 2 Mc 4,2

to dare [τι] Jb 15,12; *id.* [+inf.] Est 1,18; *to be bold to do* [+inf.] Jdt 14,13

→NIDNTT; TWNT

(→κατα-)

τολμηρός,-ά,-όν⁺   A 0-0-0-0-3-3
Sir 8,15; 19,2.3

bold, daring, audacious

→NIDNTT; TWNT

τολύπη,-ης   N1F 0-1-0-0-0-1
2 Kgs 4,39

gourd, pumpkin

τομή,-ῆς   N1F 0-0-0-2-0-2
Jb 15,32(31); Ct 2,12

pruning Ct 2,12

*Jb 15,32(31) ἡ τομὴ αὐτοῦ *his vine shoot* -זמורתו
for MT זמורתו *his exchange value*

τομίς,-ίδος   N3F 0-0-0-1-0-1
Prv 30,14

knife

τόμος,-ου   N2M 0-0-1-0-1-2
Is 8,1; 1 Ezr 6,22

scroll, volume

Cf. LIEBERMAN 1950, 206(n.30)

τόνος,-ου⁺   N2M 0-0-0-0-1-1
4 Mc 7,13

sinew

τόξευμα,-ατος   N3N 1-1-8-2-1-13
Gn 49,23; 2 Kgs 9,16; Is 7,24; 13,18; 21,15

arrow

τοξεύω   V 0-7-1-0-0-8
2 Sm 11,20.24(bis); 2 Kgs 13,17(bis)

to shoot (with bow and arrow) 2 Sm 11,20; οἱ τοξεύοντες *the archers* 2 Sm 11,24

(→κατα-)

τοξικός,-ή,-όν   A 0-1-0-0-0-1
JgsᴮB 5,28

of or *for the bow*; ἐκτὸς τοῦ τοξικοῦ *out of the loophole*

τόξον,-ου⁺   N2N 7-20-23-21-7-78
Gn 9,13.14.16; 21,16; 27,3

bow Gn 27,3; *bow in the clouds, rainbow* Gn 9,13; τόξα *bow and arrows* 2 Kgs 13,18

τοξότης,-ου⁺   N1M 1-6-1-0-2-10
Gn 21,20; 1 Sm 31,3; 1 Chr 10,3; 2 Chr 14,7; 17,17

archer Gn 21,20

ἱππεῖς τοξότας *archers on horseback, archer-cavalry* Jdt 2,15

*2 Chr 22,5 οἱ τοξόται *the archers* -הרמים for MT
הרמים *the Arameans*

τοπάζιον,-ου⁺   N2N 2-0-1-2-0-5
Ex 28,17; 36,17(39,10); Ez 28,13; Ps 118(119),127; Jb 28,19

topaz (a yellow stone of some kind)

Cf. DRESCHER 1969, 97-98; LIEBERMAN 1942, 57.58; WALTERS 1973, 90; WEVERS 1990, 453; →NIDNTT

τοπάρχης,-ου   N1M 1-1-1-7-5-15
Gn 41,34; 2 Kgs 18,24; Is 36,9; Est 3,13a; Dnᴸˣˣ 3,2

regional commander, governor, officer in charge of a τόπος *or* τοπαρχία

Cf. CONYBEARE 1905=1988, 124; HARL 1986ᵃ, 274; LEE, J. 1983, 98.145.147; PETIT 1988, 59-65

τοπαρχία,-ας   N1F 0-0-0-0-1-1
1 Mc 11,28

district (governed by a τοπάρχης)

τοπίζω

(→ἐκ-)

τόπος,-ου⁺   N2M 147-142-94-91-139-613
Gn 12,6; 13,3.4.14; 18,24

place Ex 24,10; *place (for camels)* Gn 24,31; *toilet area* Dt 23,13; *place (locality)* Gn 12,6; *place, position* Jb 28,12

occasion, opportunity 1 Mc 9,45

ἐν τῷ τόπῳ τινός *in the place of* Lv 13,19, see also Ezr 9,8; εἰς τὸν ἅγιον τόπον *to the holy land* 2 Mc 2,18

*2 Chr 34,6 καὶ τοῖς τόποις αὐτῶν *in their places* -בדבותיהם? for MTᵏ בדר בתים or MTᵠ בהר בתים *in their desolated places*; *Jer 10,20 τόπος *place* -מקום for MT מקים ◊ קום *setting up*; *Jer 30,2(49,8) ὁ τόπος αὐτῶν *their place* -מקומו *his place* for MT העמיקו *get down low*; *Ps 83(84),7 τόπον *to the place* -מעון for MT מעין *source*; *Prv 28,12 ἐν δὲ τόποις *but in the places* -וברב/מקום for MT ובקום *and when (the wicked) stand up*, see also Prv 28,28

Cf. WEVERS 1995, 269(Dt 23,13); →TWNT

τορευτός,-ή,-όν   A 3-1-1-2-0-7
Ex 25,18.31.36; 1 Kgs 10,22; Jer 10,9(5)

carved, worked in relief 1 Kgs 10,22; *forged, worked in relief* (of metals) Jer 10,9

Cf. LE BOULLUEC 1989, 257.262; MILNE 1941, 392-394; WALTERS 1973, 132

τόσος,-η,-ον   R 0-0-0-0-2-2
Sir 11,11; 13,9

so much more

τοσοῦτος,-αύτη,-οῦτον⁺   R 2-0-0-2-21-25
Ex 1,12; Nm 15,5; Est 8,12g.l; Tobˢ 2,10

so much Nm 15,5; *so great, such* Wis 12,20; *so many* 4 Mc 5,7 καθότι ... τοσούτῳ [+comp.] *as much as ... so much the more* Ex 1,12

Cf. DORIVAL 1994, 332; WEVERS 1990, 6

τότε⁺   D 21-61-24-113-74-293
Gn 12,6; 13,7; 24,41; 49,4; Ex 12,44
at that time, then (past) Gn 12,6; *then* (fut.) Gn 24,41; *then* (pres.) Is 28,25; *then, next* Gn 49,4; *that ... then* (as adj.) 4 Mc 18,20
ἀπὸ τότε *from then* (sometimes after a prep.) Ezr 5,16
*Eccl 8,12 ἀπὸ τότε *from that time on* -מאז for MT מאת *a hundred (times)*; *Dn^LXX 11,45 τότε *then* -אָרֵין? (Aram.) for MT אפדן *palace*

Cf. BOGAERT 1984, 197-224; POHLMANN 1970, 49

τραγέλαφος,-ου   N2M 1-0-0-1-0-2
Dt 14,5; Jb 39,1
goat-deer (kind of wild goat)

τράγος,-ου⁺   N2M 18-0w-12-2-36
Gn 30,35; 31,10.12; 32,15; Nm 7,17
he-goat Gn 30,35; *id.* (as sacrificial anim.) Nm 7,17

τρανός,-ή,-όν   A 0-0-1-0-2-3
Is 35,6; Wis 7,22; 10,21
clear, articulate Wis 10,21; *clear* Wis 7,22
*Is 35,6 τρανή *clear* for MT חרן *shout* (due to homoeophony?)

Cf. BARR 1985, 60-61; CAIRD 1976, 86; DE WAARD 1981, 557; SHIPP 1979, 536-537

τράπεζα,-ης⁺   N1F 18-25-13-17-13-86
Ex 25,23.27.28.30; 26,35
table Ex 25,23; *dining-table* 1 Sm 20,24; *meal, food* 1 Kgs 2,7; *paten, tray, dish*? 1 Mc 4,49

Cf. DRESCHER 1969, 98-100; HORSLEY 1982, 37; 1983, 69; LEFEBVRE 1991, 317; →NIDNTT; TWNT

τραῦμα,-ατος⁺   N3N 3-1-3-4-7-18
Gn 4,23; Ex 21,25(bis); Jgs^A 15,19; Is 1,6
wound, hurt Ex 21,25
*Jgs^A 15,19 τὸ τραῦμα *the wound* -מכתש (Aram.) for MT מכתש *tooth*?

Cf. WEVERS 1990, 334; 1993, 65(Gn 4,23)

τραυματίας,-ου   N1M 11-21-37-7-12-88
Gn 34,27; Nm 19,16.18; 23,24; 31,8
always rendition of חלל; *wounded man* 2 Mc 4,42; *casualty* (of war, wounded or dead) 1 Mc 1,18; *corpse of one slain* 1 Kgs 11,15; *one fatally wounded* Dt 21,1

Cf. DOGNIEZ 1992, 242; DORIVAL 1994, 57.384.441; HARL 1986ª, 250

τραυματίζω⁺   V 0-1-7-1-1-10
1 Sm 31,3; Is 53,5; Jer 8,23; Ez 28,16.23

to wound [τινα]

τραχηλιάω   V 0-0-0-1-0-1
Jb 15,25
to stiffen or *arch one's neck, to be haughty* (metaph.)

τράχηλος,-ου⁺   N2M 11-10-23-21-20-85
Gn 27,16.40; 33,4; 41,42; 45,14
neck Gn 27,16; *id.* (around which a necklace is put) Gn 41,42; *id.* (on which a yoke is laid) Gn 27,40; *id.* (of anim.) Jgs 8,21
ἐπιπίπτω ἐπὶ τὸν τράχηλόν τινος *to embrace sb* Gn 45,14; προσπίπτω ἐπὶ τὸν τράχηλόν τινος *to embrace sb* Gn 33,4; κάμπτω τὸν τράχηλόν τινος *to bow down sb's neck, to make sb obedient* Sir 7,23

Cf. DOGNIEZ 1992, 353(Dt 33,29)

τραχύς,-εῖα,-ύ⁺   A 1-1-2-0-3-7
Dt 21,4; 2 Sm 17,8; Is 40,4; Jer 2,25; Sir 6,20
rough, uneven (of valley) Dt 21,4; *rough* (of roads) Jer 2,25; *harsh, unpleasant* Sir 6,20; *rough, savage* (of anim.) 2 Sm 17,8

Cf. DOGNIEZ 1992, 243

τραχύτης,-ητος   N3F 0-0-0-0-1-1
3 Mc 1,23
ruggedness, formidable disturbance, confusion, uproar

τρεῖς,τρεῖς,τρία⁺   Mc 88-149-40-60-39-376
Gn 5,31.32; 6,10; 7,13; 9,19
three Gn 5,31
*Jon 3,4 τρεῖς *three* corr.? τεσσαράκοντα *forty* (confusion of γ =*three* and ν =*forty*, or confusion influenced by τρεῖς in 3.3?) for MT ארבעים *forty*

Cf. WALTERS 1973, 33.36.103.315; →NIDNTT; TWNT

τρέμω⁺   V 2-1-3-4-3-13
Gn 4,12.14; 1 Sm 15,32; Is 66,2.5
to tremble, to shake Jer 4,24; *to tremble at* [τι] Is 66,2; *to tremble, to fear* Gn 4,12; *to tremble of fear, to stand in awe* Dn^Th 5,19
*1 Sm 15,32 τρέμων *trembling* -מערנית for MT מערנת *cheerfully*?

Cf. HARL 1986ª, 115; HELBING 1928, 27

τρέπω⁺   V 2-0-0-0-15-17
Ex 17,13; Nm 14,45; Jdt 15,3; 2 Mc 3,24; 4,37
A: *to turn, to charge, to shift* [τι] 4 Mc 7,3
M: *to turn to, to turn in the direction of* [πρός τι] 3 Mc 5,3; *to turn to* [εἴς τι] 4 Mc 1,12; *to rout, to put, to flight* [τινα] Ex 17,13
P: *to be turned to* [εἴς τινα] Sir 37,2; *id.* [εἴς τι] Sir 39,27; *id.* [ἐπί τι] 2 Mc 9,2; *to be moved*

to [ἐπί τι] 2 Mc 4,37; *to be turned into, to be changed in* [εἴς τι] 2 Mc 8,5
ἐτράπησαν εἰς φυγήν *they fled away* Jdt 15,3
Cf. DORIVAL 1994, 68; LE BOULLUEC 1989, 191
(→ἀνα-, ἀπο-, δια-, ἐκ-, ἐν-, ἐπι-, μετα-, περι-, προσανα-)

τρέφω⁺ V 5-1-3-4-12-25
Gn 6,19.20; 48,15; Nm 6,5; Dt 32,18
A: *to feed, to nourish* [τινα] Gn 48,15; *id.* [τινα] (metaph.) Bar 4,11; *to rear, to bring up, to educate* (an anim.) [τινα] Is 7,21; *to let grow* [τι] Nm 6,5
M: *to grow up* Is 33,18
*Is 33,18 τοὺς τρεφομένους *those that are growing up* -גדל◊ for MT המגדלים *the towers*
Cf. DEMONT 1978, 358-384; HARL 1986^a, 165(Gn 15,15); SPICQ 1978^a, 890-893
(→ἀνα-, δια-, ἐκ-, ἐπισυ-, συν-, συνεκ-)

τρέχω⁺ V 7-33-8-14-7-69
Gn 18,7; 24,20.28.29; 29,12
to run Gn 18,7; *id.* (metaph.) Jb 15,26; *to run swiftly, to spread quickly* Ps 147,4(15)
*Jer 8,6 ὁ τρέχων ἀπὸ τοῦ δρόμου αὐτοῦ *the runner from his course* -שב ממרוצתו *returns from his course* for MT^k שב במרוצותם or MT^q שב במרוצתם *they turn to their own course*; *Ps 61(62),5 ἔδραμον *they ran* -רוץ◊ ירצו for MT רצה◊ ירצו *they take pleasure*; *Jb 41,14 τρέχει *runs* (metaph.) -רוץ◊? for MT דוץ◊ *leaps, exults*
→NIDNTT; TWNT
(→ἀνα-, ἀπο-, δια-, εἰσ-, ἐκ-, ἐπι-, κατα-, παρα-, περι-, προ-, προσ-, συν-)

τριακάς,-άδος N3F 0-0-0-0-1-1
2 Mc 11,30
thirtieth day (of a month)

τριάκοντα⁺ Mc 63-79-7-22-13-184
Gn 5,3.5.16; 6,15
thirty Gn 6,15
τριάκοντα χιλιάδας *thirty thousand* 1 Mc 10,36

τριακονταετής,-ής,-ές N3N 0-1-0-0-0-1
1 Chr 23,3
thirty years old

τριακόσιοι,-αι,-α⁺ Mc 14-37-0-22-17-90
Gn 5,23; 6,15; 9,28; 11,13.15
three hundred

τριακοστός,-ή,-όν Mo 0-10-2-2-2-16
1 Kgs 16,23; 2 Kgs 13,10; 15,8.13.17
thirtieth

τρίβολος,-ου⁺ N2M 1-1-1-1-0-4
Gn 3,18; 2 Sm 12,31; Hos 10,8; Prv 22,5
tribulus terrestris, thistle, caltrops (growing on ruins) Gn 3,18; οἱ τρίβολοι *harrows, a threshing-machine* 2 Sm 12,31
→LSJ RSuppl(2 Sm 12,31); NIDNTT

τρίβος,-ου⁺ N3F/M 1-7-15-35-12-70
Gn 49,17; Jgs^A 5,6; Jgs^B 5,20; 1 Sm 6,12; 2 Sm 20,12
path (on land) Gn 49,17; *id.* (on sea) Ps 8,9; *path, track* (of a ship) Prv 30,19; *path* (metaph., way of living) Ps 24(25),4; αἱ τρίβοι *paths, behaviour* Wis 2,15

τρίβω V 1-0-2-1-0-4
Nm 11,8; Is 38,21; Jer 7,18; Prv 15,19
A: *to crush, to grind* [τι] Nm 11,8; *to knead* [τι] Jer 7,18
P: *to be worn smooth* (of paths) Prv 15,19
Cf. WALTERS 1973, 96
(→ἀπο-, δια-, ἐκ-, ἐνδια-, κατα-, συν-, συνεκ-)

τριετής,-ής,-ές⁺ A 0-1-1-0-2-4
2 Chr 31,16; Is 15,5; 2 Mc 4,23; 14,1
of three years 2 Mc 4,23; *three years old* 2 Chr 31,16

τριετίζω V 3-1-0-0-0-4
Gn 15,9(ter); 1 Sm 1,24
to be three years old, to become three years old, to live three years; τριετίζων *three-year-old*; neol.
Cf. HARL 1986^a, 163

τριημερία,-ας N1F 0-0-1-0-0-1
Am 4,4
period of three days; neol.

τριήρης,-ους N3F 0-0-0-0-1-1
2 Mc 4,20
trireme (a fast battle ship having three rows of oars on either side)

τρικυμία,-ας N1F 0-0-0-0-1-1
4 Mc 7,2
the third of three waves, sea storm; ταῖς τῶν βασάνων τρικυμίαις *by the swelling waves of tortures*

τριμερίζω V 1-0-0-0-0-1
Dt 19,3
to divide into three parts, to apportion in thirds [τι]; neol.
Cf. DOGNIEZ 1992, 64.232; WALTERS 1973, 121

τρίμηνος,-ος,-ον⁺ A 1-4-0-0-0-5
Gn 38,24; 2 Kgs 23,31; 24,8; 2 Chr 36,2.9
of three months; τρίμηνον *period of three months*

τριόδους (gen. -οντος)　　　　A 0-1-0-0-0-1
1 Sm 2,13
with three teeth, three-pronged

τριπλασίως　　　　D 0-0-0-0-1-1
Sir 43,4
three times over

τριπλούς,-ῆ,-οῦν　　　　A 0-0-1-0-0-1
Ez 42,6
triple, threefold

τρίς⁺　　　　MD 0-5-0-6-2-13
1 Sm 20,41; 1 Kgs 17,21; 2 Kgs 13,18.19.25
three times, trice
Cf. WALTERS 1978, 33.36.314-315; →NIDNTT

τρισάθλιος,-α,-ον　　　　A 0-0-0-0-1-1
4 Mc 16,6
thrice-unhappy, thrice-wretched

τρισαλιτήριος,-ος,-ον　　　　A 0-0-0-1-2-3
Est 8,12p; 2 Mc 8,34; 15,3
thrice-sinful, thoroughly evil; neol.

τρισκαίδεκα　　　　MC 1-4-0-0-0-5
Nm 29,14; 1 Kgs 7,38(1); 1 Chr 6,45.47; 26,11
thirteen
Cf. WALTERS 1973, 33

τρισκαιδέκατος,-η,-ον　　　　MO 1-2-2-5-3-13
Gn 14,4; 1 Chr 24,13; 25,20; Jer 1,2; 25,3
thirteenth; neol.?
Cf. WALTERS 1973, 33

τρισμύριοι,-αι,-α　　　　MC 0-0-0-1-0-1
Est 1,7
thrice ten thousand, thirty thousand

τρισσεύω　　　　V 0-3-0-0-0-3
1 Sm 20,19.20; 1 Kgs 18,34
to do for the third time 1 Kgs 18,34; *to do thrice*
or *to do on the third day, on the day after
tomorrow* 1 Sm 20,20
Cf. WALTERS 1973, 120-121(1 Sm 20,20)

τρισσός,-ή,-όν　　　　A 0-1-3-0-0-4
2 Kgs 11,10; Ez 23,15.23; 42,3
threefold Ez 42,3; *third in rank, important* (of
pers.; semit.) Ez 23,15, see also 23,23
*2 Kgs 11,10 τοὺς τρισσούς *the third in rank*
-השלשים for MT השלשים *the shields*
Cf. GEHMAN 1966=1972, 105; WALTERS 1973, 314

τρισσόω　　　　V 0-1-0-0-0-1
1 Kgs 18,34
to do for the third time; neol.
Cf. WALTERS 1973, 120-121

τρισσῶς　　　　D 0-3-2-1-0-6
1 Sm 20,12; 1 Kgs 7,41(4); 7,42(5); Ez 16,30;
41,16

threefoldly, three times Prv 22,20; *in three rows*?
1 Kgs 7,41(4)
*Ez 16,30 τρισσῶς *threefoldly* -שלשית for MT שלטת
domineering

τριστάτης,-ου　　　　N1M 2-7-0-0-1-10
Ex 14,7; 15,4; 2 Kgs 7,2.17.19
always rendition of שלישׁ⁗ *knight, officer?*,
interpreted as a derivation of שלוש *three*; *third
man, officer* Ex 14,7; *officer attending on the king*
2 Kgs 7,2; neol.
Cf. LE BOULLUEC 1989, 55-56; VERVENNE 1987, 356;
WEVERS 1990, 211; →LSJ Suppl; LSJ RSuppl

τρισχίλιοι,-αι,-α⁺　　　　MC 5-12-0-4-16-37
Ex 32,28; 39,3(38,26); Nm 1,46; 2,32; 4,44
three thousand

τρισχίλιος,-ος,-ον　　　　MC 0-0-0-0-1-1
1 Mc 10,77
three thousand (sg. with a coll. noun)

τριταῖος,-α,-ον　　　　A 0-2-0-0-0-2
1 Sm 9,20; 30,13
on the third day, after three days, three days ago

τρίτος,-η,-ον⁺　　　　MO 50-74-10-20-25-179
Gn 1,13; 2,14; 22,4; 31,2.5
third Gn 1,13; *a third set of* [+pl.] 1 Sm 19,21;
τρίτον *a third time* Nm 22,32; τὸ τρίτον *the
third part* Nm 15,6; τρίτη *the day before
yesterday* (referring to the past) Ex 36,29(39,12)
γλῶσσα τρίτη *slanderer's tongue* Sir 28,14
*2 Sm 23,8 τοῦ τρίτου *of the third* -השלשה for MT
הַשָּׁלִשִׁי *(of) the third men, (of) the officers*?
Cf. SHIPP 1979, 214.537; VERVENNE 1987, 356; WALTERS
1973, 314; →NIDNTT

τρίχαπτος,-ος,-ον　　　　A 0-0-2-0-0-2
Ez 16,10.13
plated or *woven of hair*; (τὸ) τρίχαπτον *fine veil
of hair*

τρίχινος,-η,-ον⁺　　　　A 1-0-1-0-0-2
Ex 26,7; Zech 13,4
made of hair
Cf. WEVERS 1990, 416

τρίχωμα,-ατος　　　　N3N 0-0-1-3-1-5
Ez 24,17; Ct 4,1; 6,5; Dnᴸˣˣ 7,9; 1 Ezr 8,68
hair, head of hair

τριώροφος,-ος,-ον　　　　A 1-1-1-0-0-3
Gn 6,16; 1 Kgs 6,8; Ez 41,7
having three stories, of three stories; τὰ τριώροφα
the third-storey rooms

τρομέω　　　　V 0-0-0-0-1-1
1 Mc 2,24
to tremble (with anger)

Cf. HELBING 1928, 27

τρόμος,-ου⁺   N2M 5-0-8-7-10-30
Gn 9,2; Ex 15,15.16; Dt 2,25; 11,25
trembling, quaking Sir 16,19; *trembling, quivering*
(from fear) Gn 9,2; *trembling, falling* (of water)
Jb 38,34
*Is 63,19(64,1) τρόμος λήμψεται *trembling will
take hold -יָרֵעַ*? for MT ירדת *you come down*, see
also 64,2
Cf. WALTERS 1973, 145; WEVERS 1990, 233-234

τρόπαιον,-ου   N2N 0-0-0-0-2-2
2 Mc 5,6; 15,6
trophy

τροπή,-ῆς⁺   N1F 2-1-1-1-6-11
Ex 32,18; Dt 33,14; 1 Kgs 22,35; Jer
30,27(49,32); Jb 38,33
change, movements (of the skies) Jb 38,33; *rout,
(military) reversal, retreating* Ex 32,18; τροπαί
turnings of the sun, solar cycle Wis 7,18
ἡλίου τροπαί *turnings of the sun, solar cycle* Dt
33,14
Cf. LARCHER 1984, 470-471; LE BOULLUEC 1989, 324;
TOV 1978, 55; WEVERS 1990, 529; 1995, 547(Dt 33,14)

-τροπιάζω
(→ἀπο-)

τρόπις,-ιος   N3F 0-0-0-0-1-1
Wis 5,10
ship's keel

τρόπος,-ου⁺   N2M 68-44-65-14-53-244
Gn 26,29; Ex 2,14; 13,11; 14,13; 16,34
way, manner Prv 9,11; *method* Est 8,12o; *way of
life, conduct* 1 Sm 25,33; *condition, custom* 2 Mc
15,12; *nature* 4 Mc 2,8
τρόπον τινός *as, like* (mostly with anim.) Jb
4,19; ὃν τρόπον *as* (frequently in LXX) Gn
26,29; καθ' ὃν τρόπον *just as* 2 Mc 6,20; κατὰ
πάντα τρόπον *in every way* 3 Mc 3,24; κατὰ
μηδένα τρόπον *by no means* 3 Mc 4,13
Cf. DORIVAL 1994, 366(Nm 18,7); LE BOULLUEC 1989,
165(Ex 14,13)

τροπόω   V 0-15-0-2-12-29
Jos 11,6; Jgsᴮ 4,23; Jgsᴬ 20,35.36.39(bis)
A: *to cause to turn away, to put to flight* [τινα]
Jgsᴮ 4,23
M: *id.* [τινα] 2 Sm 8,1
P: *to be put to flight* Jos 11,6; *to reach a turning
point* (of war) 1 Kgs 22,35
neol.
→LSJ Suppl(1 Kgs 22,35); LSJ RSuppl; PREISIGKE

τροφεία,-ας   N1F 0-0-0-0-1-1

4 Mc 15,13
service as wet-nurse; neol.

τροφεύω   V 1-0-0-0-1-2
Ex 2,7; Bar 4,8
to serve as a wet-nurse, to nurse Ex 2,7; *id.*
[τινα] (metaph. of God) Bar 4,8; neol.

τροφή,-ῆς⁺   N1F 1-2-0-12-18-33
Gn 49,27; Jgsᴮ 8,5; 2 Chr 11,23; Ps 64(65),10;
103(104),27
food Gn 49,27; *provisions* (of the army) 1 Mc
1,35
Cf. CAIRD 1976, 82

τροφός,-οῦ⁺   N2F 1-2-1-0-0-4
Gn 35,8; 2 Kgs 11,2; 2 Chr 22,11; Is 49,23
nurse
Cf. HORSLEY 1982, 8

τροφοφορέω⁺   V 2-0-0-0-1-3
Dt 1,31(bis); 2 Mc 7,27
to bring nourishment, to nurse [τινα]; neol.
Cf. DOGNIEZ 1992, 64.118; MOUSSY 1969, 74; WEVERS
1995, 18

τροχάζω
(→συν-)

τροχαντήρ,-ῆρος   N3M 0-0-0-0-1-1
4 Mc 8,13
bone-crusher (instrument of torture); neol.

τροχιά,-ᾶς⁺   N1F 0-0-0-6-0-6
Prv 2,15; 4,11.26.27b; 5,6
wheel-track, course, path Prv 2,15; *id.* (metaph.)
Prv 5,6

τροχιαῖος,-α,-ον   A 0-0-0-0-1-1
4 Mc 11,10
worked by a wheel; περὶ τροχιαῖον σφῆνα *over
a rolling wedge*; neol.

τροχίζω   V 0-0-0-0-1-1
4 Mc 5,3
P: *to be broken on the wheel, to be tortured*

τροχίσκος,-ου   N2M 0-0-1-0-0-1
Ez 16,12
dim. of τροχός; *ear-ring*

τροχός,-οῦ⁺   N2M 0-6-35-5-12-58
2 Sm 24,22; 1 Kgs 7,17.18.19(bis)(30.32(bis).33)
wheel (of a chariot) Sir 33,5; *id.* (of an
agricultural implement) 2 Sm 24,22; *potter's
wheel* Sir 38,29; *wheel of torture* 4 Mc 15,22

τρυβλίον,-ου⁺   N2N 17-1-0-0-1-19
Ex 25,29; 38,12(37,16); Nm 4,7; 7,13.19
cup, dish
Cf. LE BOULLUEC 1989, 260; WALTERS 1973, 95

τρυγάω⁺   V 3-3-5-3-1-15

Lv 25,11; Dt 24,21; 28,30; Jgs 9,27
to gather in [τι] Lv 25,11; *to gather grapes* Jer
6,9; *to gather off, to reap off* [τι] Dt 24,21; *to
reap* (sins) [τι] (metaph.) Hos 10,13; *to reap, to
gather* [abs.] (metaph.) Hos 10,12
→NIDNTT
(→ἀπο-, ἐκ-, ἐπανα-)

τρυγητής,-οῦ N1M 0-0-3-0-1-4
Jer 30,3(49,9); 31(48),32; Ob 5; Sir 33,17
gatherer of grapes; neol.?

τρύγητος,-ου/τρυγητός,-οῦ N2M 2-4-8-0-1-15
Lv 26,5(bis); Jgs 8,2; 1 Sm 8,12
gathering of fruit, vintage, harvest Lv 26,5; *crop* Jl
1,11
*1 Sm 13,21 ὁ τρύγητος *the time of harvest*
-הבצירה or -הקצירה for MT הפצירה *the sharpening*
Cf. WALTERS 1973, 95.226-227; ZIPOR 1984, 40.141

τρυγίας,-ου N1M 0-0-0-1-0-1
Ps 74(75),9
lees of wine, dregs

τρυγών,-όνος+ N3F/M 11-0-1-3-0-15
Gn 15,9; Lv 1,14; 5,7.11; 12,6
turtledove
Cf. SHIPP 1979, 540; WEVERS 1993, 208; →LSJ RSuppl

τρυμαλιά,-ᾶς+ N1F 0-3-3-0-0-6
JgsᴮB 6,2; 15,8.11; Jer 13,4; 16,16
hole (in the rock); neol.?

τρυπάω+ V 2-0-1-1-0-4
Ex 21,6; Dt 15,17; Hag 1,6; Jb 40,26
to pierce [τι] Ex 21,6
δεσμὸν τετρυπημένον *a bag full of holes* Hag
1,6

τρυφάω+ V 0-0-1-1-1-3
Is 66,11; Neh 9,25; Sir 14,4
to delight oneself, to riot, to revel
(→ἐν-, κατα-)

τρυφερεύομαι V 0-0-0-1-0-1
Est 5,1a
to be delicate, to be dainty; neol.

τρυφερός,-ά,-όν+ A 2-0-5-0-3-10
Dt 28,54.56; Is 47,1.8; 58,13
delicate (used to a comfortable lifestyle, not
prepared for a rough one) Dt 28,54; *joyous,
delightful* (of Sabbath) Is 58,13

τρυφερότης,-ητος N3F 1-0-0-0-0-1
Dt 28,56
delicacy, daintiness

τρυφή,-ῆς+ N1F 3-0-9-8-5-25
Gn 3,23.24; 49,20; Jer 28(51),34; Ez 28,13
dainty Gn 49,20; *luxury* Mi 2,9; *delight* Prv 4,9

ὁ παράδεισος τῆς τρυφῆς *the garden of delight*
Gn 3,23
*Ps 138(139),11 ἐν τῇ τρυφῇ μου *in my luxury*
בְּעָרְנִי for MT בַּעֲרֵנִי *around me*
Cf. HARL 1986ᵃ, 101; HUSSON 1988, 64-73; JACOBSON
1976, 204; LARCHER 1985, 1067

τρύφημα,-ατος N3N 0-0-0-0-1-1
Sir 31,3
the object in which one takes pleasure or *pride*

τρύχω V 0-0-0-0-2-2
Wis 11,11; 14,15
P: *to be tormented, to be vexed* (of pers.)
Cf. LARCHER 1985, 666

τρώγλη,-ης N1F 0-2-4-1-0-7
1 Sm 14,11; 2 Kgs 12,10; Is 2,19.21; 7,19
hole (in a chest) 2 Kgs 12,10; *hole* (of an asp) Is
11,8; *cave, cavern* (in a rock) Jb 30,6

τρώγω+
(→ἐκ-, κατα-)

τυγχάνω+ V 1-0-0-6-22-29
Dt 19,5; Jb 3,21; 7,2; 17,1(2); Prv 30,23
to happen to be, to be Tobᴮᴬ 5,14; *id.* [+ptc.]
Tobˢ 5,14
to overtake [τινι] (of night) Tobˢ 6,1; *light on,
to hit upon* [τινος] Dt 19,5
to meet [τινος] Prv 30,23; *to find* [τινος] 1 Mc
11,42; *id.* [τι] 2 Mc 5,8; *to obtain* [τινος] Jb
3,21; *to grasp* [τινος] Jb 7,2
οὐ τῷ τυχόντι *not the common* or *ordinary one*
3 Mc 3,7
Cf. HELBING 1928, 141-142; →MM; TWNT
(→ἀπο-, ἐν-, ἐπι-, κατα-, συν-)

τυλόω V 1-0-0-0-0-1
Dt 8,4
P: *to become calloused*
Cf. DOGNIEZ 1992, 170

τυμπανίζω+ V 0-1-0-0-0-1
1 Sm 21,14
*to pound as if on a drum, to drum with the
hands*; *1 Sm 21,14 ἐτυμπάνιζεν *he drummed*
-יתף for MT יתו *he made marks*; neol.
Cf. GEHMAN 1948, 241-243
(→ἀπο-)

τυμπανίστρια,-ας N1F 0-0-0-1-0-1
Ps 67(68),26
(female) drum-player

τύμπανον,-ου N2N 3-6-3-3-6-21
Gn 31,27; Ex 15,20(bis); Jgs 11,34
Semit. loanword (Hebr. תף); *tambourine, timbrel*
Gn 31,27; *instrument of torture, rack* 2 Mc 6,19

Cf. CAIRD 1976, 78; TOV 1979, 221; WEVERS 1990, 236;
→CHANTRAINE; FRISK; LSJ RSuppl

τύπος,-ου⁺ N2M 1-0-1-0-2-4
Ex 25,40; Am 5,26; 3 Mc 3,30; 4 Mc 6,19
*figure worked out in relief, that which is formed,
image, statue, idol* Am 5,26; *archetype, pattern,
model* Ex 25,40; *content, text* (of a letter) 3 Mc
3,30; *example, pattern* (in moral life) 4 Mc 6,19
Cf. BARR 1961, 154-155; HORSLEY 1981, 77-78; 1987, 41;
LE BOULLUEC 1989, 265; LEE, E. 1961, 169-171;
LLEWELYN 1994, 24; SPICQ 1978ᵃ, 894-897; →NIDNTT; TWNT

τυπόω V 0-0-0-0-2-2
Wis 13,13; Sir 38,30
to form, to model [τι]
Cf. LARCHER 1985, 780
(→ἀνα-, δια-, ἐκ-)

τύπτω⁺ V 8-18-3-6-6-41
Ex 2,11.13; 7,17.27; 21,15
A: *to beat, to strike, to smite* [τινα] Ex 2,11; *id.*
[abs.] Ex 7,17; *to smite* [τι] 1 Sm 27,9; *to afflict
with* [τί τινι] Ex 7,27
to beat, to strike (a coin) [τι] Prv 25,4; *to smite*
(of a smith) Is 41,7
P: *to receive blows* 4 Mc 6,10
*1 Sm 1,8 τύπτει σε *he smites you* -יכך for MT
ירע *it is afflicted*; *Dnᴸˣˣ 11,20 τύπτων *putting
down* -נגע or -נגש for MT נוגש *an exactor*
Cf. WEVERS 1990, 100.106; →TWNT

τυραννέω V 0-0-0-1-3-4
Prv 28,15; 4 Mc 5,38; Wis 10,14; 16,4
to rule as a tyrant, to tyrannize [abs.] Wis 16,4; *to
rule over, to tyrannize over* [τινος] Prv 28,15
Cf. LARCHER 1984, 637; 1985, 895

τυραννικός,-ή,-όν A 0-0-0-0-2-2
3 Mc 3,8; 4 Mc 5,27
befitting a tyrant, tyrannical, despotic

τυραννίς,-ίδος⁺ N3F 0-0-0-1-6-7
Est 1,18; 4 Mc 1,11; 8,15; 9,30; 11,24
tyranny, despotic conduct Wis 14,21; *princess* Est
1,18
Cf. LARCHER 1985, 823

τύραννος,-ου⁺ N2M 0-0-1-7-56-64
Hab 1,10; Jb 2,11; 42,17e; Prv 8,16; Est 9,3
tyran 4 Mc 10,16; *king, sovereign* Jb 2,11; *prince*
Est 9,3

τυρός,-οῦ N2M 0-0-0-1-0-1
Jb 10,10
cheese

τυρόω V 0-0-0-4-0-4
Ps 67(68),16.17; 118(119),70; Jb 10,10
A: *to curdle, to make into cheese* [τι] (metaph.)
Jb 10,10
P: *to be curdled* (metaph.) Ps 67(68),16

τυφλός,-ή,-όν⁺ A 7-3-12-2-1-25
Ex 4,11; Lv 19,14; 21,18; 22,22; Dt 15,21
blind Ex 4,11; *id.* (mental or spiritual blindness)
Ps 145(146),8
→NIDNTT; TWNT

τυφλόω⁺ V 0-0-1-0-1-2
Is 42,19; Tobˢ 7,6
to be blind (of mental or spiritual blindness)
→TWNT
(→ἀπο-, ἐκ-)

τῦφος,-ου⁺ N2M 0-0-0-0-1-1
3 Mc 3,18
arrogance, pride
Cf. SPICQ 1978ᵃ, 898

τύχη,-ης⁺ N1F 1-0-1-0-0-2
Gn 30,11; Is 65,11
(good) fortune Is 65,11
ἐν τύχῃ *happily, by chance* Gn 30,11
Cf. HANHART 1994, 88; WEVERS 1993, 478

ὕαινα,-ης⁺   N1F 0-0-1-0-1-2
Jer 12,9; Sir 13,18
hyena

ὑακίνθινος,-η,-ον⁺   A 22-0-2-0-2-26
Ex 25,5; 26,4.14; 28,31; 35,7
hyacinth-coloured, blue
Cf. DORIVAL 1994, 38.51.220; WEVERS 1990, 392.393;
→NIDNTT

ὑάκινθος,-ου⁺   N2M 24-3-5-0-2-34
Ex 25,4; 26,1.31.36; 27,16
a hyacinth-coloured cloth
Cf. DORIVAL 1994, 51.220; WEVERS 1990, 392

ὕαλος,-ου⁺   N2M 0-0-0-1-0-1
Jb 28,17
a kind of crystalline stone

ὑβρίζω⁺   V 0-1-3-0-2-6
2 Sm 19,44; Is 13,3; 23,12; Jer 31(48),29; 2 Mc
14,42
A: *to boast, to be proud* Is 13,3; *to insult* [τινα]
2 Sm 19,44
P: *to be abused, to be insulted, to suffer outrages*
2 Mc 14,42
ὕβρισε λίαν ὕβριν αὐτοῦ *he became very
haughty* Jer 31(48),29
Cf. HELBING 1928, 23; →NIDNTT; TWNT
(→ἐξ-, καθ-)

ὕβρις,-εως⁺   N3F 1-0-32-16-13-62
Lv 26,19; Is 9,8; 10,33; 13,11(bis)
insolence, pride, arrogance Est 4,17d; *shame,
insult, mistreatment* Sir 10,8; *hardship* 3 Mc 3,25
ἡ ὕβρις τῆς ἰσχύος αὐτῆς *hybris* i.e. *haughty
behaviour (on account) of her strength* Ez 33,28
*Mi 6,10 ὕβρεως *(of) pride* -זדון for MT רזון
emaciation; *Prv 14,10 ὕβρει *(with) pride* -זֵד for
MT זָר *stranger*
Cf. BERTRAM 1964, 29-38; →NIDNTT; TWNT

ὑβριστής,-οῦ⁺   N1M 0-0-3-5-2-10
Is 2,12; 16,6; Jer 28(51),2; Jb 40,11; Prv 6,17
a haughty, insolent man Jb 40,11; *haughty,
insolent* (as adj.) Is 16,6
*Prv 27,13 ὑβριστής *a haughty man* -זֵד for MT
זָר *a stranger*
→NIDNTT; TWNT

ὑβριστικός,-ή,-όν   A 0-0-0-1-0-1
Prv 20,1
full of violence, relating to insolence (metaph. of
wine)

ὑβρίστρια,-ας   N1F 0-0-1-0-0-1
Jer 27(50),31
an insolent, haughty woman; neol.

ὑγιάζω   V 3-2-4-1-0-10
Lv 13,18.24.37; Jos 5,8; 2 Kgs 20,7
A: *to heal, to restore to health* [τινα] Hos 6,2;
id. [τι] Ez 47,8; *to recover* [intrans.] 2 Kgs 20,7
P: *to be healed, to recover* Lv 13,18
Cf. LEE, J. 1983, 50

ὑγιαίνω⁺   V 6-4-0-2-37-49
Gn 29,6(bis); 37,14; 43,27.28
to be well, to be in good health
Cf. HARL 1986ᵃ, 67.225; →NIDNTT; TWNT

ὑγίεια,-ας⁺   N1F 2-0-2-2-8-14
Gn 42,15.16; Is 9,5; Ez 47,12; Prv 6,8b
health Gn 42,15
μετὰ ὑγιείας *in safety* Tobᴮᴬ 8,21
Cf. SHIPP 1979, 544

ὑγιής,-ής,-ές⁺   A 4-1-1-0-3-9
Lv 13,10.15(bis).16; Jos 10,21
healthy, sound, safe (of people) Jos 10,21; *sound*
(of flesh) Lv 13,15; *sound* (of heart) Sir 17,28
→NIDNTT; TWNT

ὑγιῶς   D 0-0-0-1-0-1
Prv 31,8
soundly, fairly

ὑγραίνω   V 0-0-0-1-0-1
Jb 24,8
P: *to be wet*

ὑγρασία,-ας   N1F 0-0-3-0-0-3
Jer 31(48),18; Ez 7,17; 21,12
moisture Jer 31(48),18; *moisture, urine* (euph.)
Ez 7,17
→LSJ suppl(Ez 7,17; 21,12); LSJ RSuppl

ὑγρός,-ά,-όν⁺   A 0-4-0-1-1-6
Jgs 16,7.8; Jb 8,16
moist

ὑδραγωγός,-οῦ   N2M 0-2-2-0-1-5
2 Kgs 18,17; 20,20; Is 36,2; 41,18; Sir 24,30
aqueduct, conduit

ὑδρεύω   V 6-5-0-1-1-13
Gn 24,11.19.20.43.44
M: *to draw* or *carry water*

ὑδρία,-ας⁺   N1F 9-12-0-1-0-22
Gn 24,14.15.16.17.18
jar, pitcher

ὑδρίσκη,-ης   N1F 0-1-0-0-0-1
2 Kgs 2,20
dim. of ὑδρία; *small jar*

ὑδροποτέω⁺   V 0-0-0-1-0-1
Dnᴸˣˣ 1,12
to drink water

ὑδροφόρος,-ου   N2M 1-3-0-0-0-4

Dt 29,10; Jos 9,21.27(bis)
water carrier, person who draws or carries water

ὕδωρ, ὕδατος⁺   N3N 214-112-158-118-73-675
Gn 1,2.6(ter).7
water Gn 1,2; *(spring-)water* Gn 24,13;
(drinking-)water Gn 21,14; τὰ ὕδατα *waters,
rivers* Nm 24,6

τέκνα ὑδάτων *children of the waters, fishes* Hos
11,10
*Ex 14,27 τὸ ὕδωρ *the water* -חמים? for MT הים *the
sea*; *1 Kgs 18,44 ὕδωρ *water* -מים for MT ים/מ
from the sea, see also Is 24,14; Hos 11,10; Am
8,12; Na 3,8; Zech 9,10; *Jer 2,24 ἐφ' ὕδατα
over the waters -למי/ל ◊ מים for MT למד *used to*?; *Ez
30,16 ὕδατα *waters* -מים for MT יומם *by day*; *Hos
6,8 ὕδωρ *water* -מים for MT דם/מ *with blood*; *Na
1,12 κατάρχων ὑδάτων πολλῶν *ruler of many
waters* -רבים מים משל for MT רבים (וכן שלמים אם *though
they are prosperous and many*?; *Jb 11,15 ὥσπερ
ὕδωρ καθαρόν *as pure water* -ממים or -כמים? for
MT ממום *without blemish*

Cf. DORIVAL 1994, 388; →NIDNTT; TWNT

ὕειος,-α,-ον   A 0-0-3-0-6-9
Is 65,4; 66,3.17; 1 Mc 1,47; 2 Mc 6,18
of pigs Is 65,4; τὰ ὕεια *the pigs* 4 Mc 5,6

ὑετίζω   V 0-0-1-1-0-2
Jer 14,22; Jb 38,26
to cause rain, to bring rain; neol.

ὑετός,-οῦ⁺   N2M 13-17-23-18-12-83
Gn 7,4.12; 8,2; Ex 9,29.33
rain

Cf. WALTERS 1973, 201.336(Jb 28,24); →NIDNTT

υἱός,-οῦ⁺   N2M 1283-2277-435-698-497-5190
Gn 4,17.25.26; 5,4.7
male child, son Gn 4,17; *id.* (of anim.) Sir 38,25;
descendant Nm 16,7; *accepted* or *adopted son* Ex
2,10; *son, pupil, follower* (of a spiritual father)
Prv 3,11; *member* (of a community) Gn 6,4;
years old [+numeral] (semit.) Gn 11,10; υἱέ *son*
(an author's address to the reader) Prv 7,24
υἱοὶ ἀνθρώπων *sons of men, men* (also sg.) Wis
9,6; υἱοὶ τῶν συμμίξεων *sons of pledges,
hostages* 2 Chr 25,24, see σύμμιξις
*Gn 36,2 υἱός *son* -בן (Sam.Pent.) for MT בת
daughter, see also 36,14.39; *Gn 37,4 τῶν υἱῶν
αὐτοῦ *(more than) his sons* -בניו (Sam.Pent.) for
MT אחיו *(more than) his brothers*; *Gn 49,22 υἱός
μου νεώτατος *my youngest son* -צעירי בני
(Sam.Pent.) for MT צערה בנות *daughters* or
branches of a fruit tree?; *2 Sm 23,27 ἐκ τῶν

υἱῶν *from the sons (of)* -בני/מ for MT מבני
Mebunnai; *Jer 26(46),25 τὸν υἱὸν αὐτῆς *her
son* -נה/מ/? *from her* or -בנה? *her son* for MT גא/מ *of
No, of Thebes*; *Ez 27,4 υἱοί σου *your sons* בניך
◊ בן for MT בניך *your builders*; *Ez 27,32 οἱ υἱοὶ
αὐτῶν *their sons* בניהם ◊ בן for MT ניהם/בי? *in
their wailing*; *Prv 11,19 υἱός *son* -בן for MT כן
yes, so; *Prv 23,24 υἱῷ *in a son* -ילד for MT יולד
he who begets, father; *Neh 3,2 υἱῶν *of the sons
בני* בן ◊ for MT בנה *they built*

Cf. CAIRD 1969=1972, 149(2 Kgs 14,14); CARAGOUNIS
1996ᵇ forthcoming; DOGNIEZ 1992, 203(Dt 14,1); DORIVAL
1994, 53-54.62; GEHMAN 1951= 1972, 100; LARCHER 1983,
252-254; 1984, 363-364; 1985, 731; WEVERS 1995, 513(Dt
32,8).534(Dt 32,43); ZIPOR 1993, 357.361-362; →LSJ RSuppl;
NIDNTT; TWNT

ὑλακτέω   V 0-0-1-0-0-1
Is 56,10
to bark

ὕλη,-ης⁺   N1F 0-0-1-2-5-8
Is 10,17; Jb 19,29; 38,40; 2 Mc 2,24; 4 Mc 1,29
wood Is 10,17; αἱ ὗλαι *woods* Jb 38,40; *matter,
stuff* Wis 15,13; *material* (metaph.) 4 Mc 1,29
ὕλη ἄμορφος *formless matter* (out of which the
world is created) Wis 11,17

Cf. LARCHER 1985, 676-680(Wis 11,17); SHIPP 1979,
545-547; WALTERS 1973, 295-296

ὑλίζω
(→δι-)

ὑλοτόμος,-ος,-ον   A 0-0-0-0-1-1
Wis 13,11
cutting wood; ὑλοτόμος τέκτων *carpenter*

ὑλώδης,-ης,-ες   A 0-0-0-1-0-1
Jb 29,5
wooded or *full of matter, stuff*; *Jb 29,5 ἤμην
ὑλώδης λίαν *I lived in abundance*? -עמרי/שׁ
there is enough in store with me? for MT עמרי שׁרי
the Almighty (was) with me

ὑμεῖς⁺   R 1227-668-994-176-270-3335
Gn 1,29(bis); 3,5; 9,2(bis)
pl. of συ; acc. ὑμᾶς; gen. ὑμῶν; dat. ὑμῖν; *you*

ὑμέναιος,-ου⁺   N2M 0-0-0-0-1-1
3 Mc 4,6
οἱ ὑμέναιοι *wedding hymn, bridal song*

ὑμέτερος,-α,-ον⁺   A 1-0-1-1-2-5
Gn 9,5; Am 6,2; Prv 1,26; Tobˢ 8,21; Bar 4,24
your, yours, belonging to you (pl.) Tobˢ 8,21;
your, incumbent upon you Prv 1,26

ὑμνέω⁺   V 0-5-4-79-46-134
Jgsᴮ 16,24; 1 Chr 16,9; 2 Chr 23,13; 29,30(bis)

A: *to sing of, to sing praise of* [τι] Tobˢ 12,6; *to sing hymns to* [τινι] 1 Chr 16,9; *id.* [τινα] Jgsᴮ 16,24; *id.* [abs.] 2 Chr 29,30; *to sing* [τι] 2 Chr 23,13

P: *to be sung* Prv 1,20

Cf. HELBING 1928, 69; LEDOGAR 1967, 29-56; →NIDNTT; TWNT

(→ἐξ-, καθ-)

ὕμνησις,-εως N3F 0-0-0-2-0-2

Ps 70(71),6; 117(118),14

singing in praise, (act of) praising; neol.

→NIDNTT

ὑμνητός,-ή,-όν A 0-0-0-3-0-3

Dnᴸˣˣ 3,54; Dn 3,56

worthy of praise, to be praised

ὑμνογράφος,-ου N2M 0-0-0-0-1-1

4 Mc 18,15

hymn-writer, psalmist; neol.

ὕμνος,-ου⁺ N2M 0-1-1-14-17-33

2 Chr 7,6; Is 42,10; Ps 6,1; 39(40),4; 53(54),1

hymn, praise Neh 12,46

ἐν ὕμνοις Δαυιδ *with the hymns of David* 2 Chr 7,6

Cf. LEDOGAR 1967, 29-56; →NIDNTT; TWNT

ὑμνῳδέω V 0-1-0-0-0-1

1 Chr 25,6

to sing hymns

Cf. BICKERMAN 1980, 61

ὑπαγορεύω V 0-0-0-0-1-1

1 Ezr 6,29

to define, to designate

ὑπάγω⁺ V 1-0-0-0-5-6

Ex 14,21; Tobˢ 8,21; 10,11.12; 12,5

A: *to carry back, to draw off* Ex 14,21; *to go away* Tobˢ 8,21

P: *to be moved* 4 Mc 4,13

Cf. LE BOULLUEC 1989, 168; LEE, J. 1983, 127.144; WEVERS 1990, 220; →TWNT

ὕπαιθρος,-ος,-ον A 0-0-0-1-1-2

Prv 21,9; 2 Mc 15,19

under the sky, in the open air Prv 21,9

ἐν ὑπαίθρῳ *in the open air* 2 Mc 15,19

ὑπακοή,-ῆς⁺ N1F 0-1-0-0-0-1

2 Sm 22,36

response

Cf. SPICQ 1982, 243-245; →MM

ὑπακούω⁺ V 17-4-9-22-7-59

Gn 16,2; 22,18; 26,5; 27,13; 39,10

to listen, to give ear [abs.] Prv 1,24; *id.* [τινος] Gn 16,2; *id.* [τι] Dt 21,18

to obey, to follow, to be obedient [τινι] Ps 17(18),45; *id.* [τινος] Prv 17,4; *id.* [τι] Prv 29,12; *id.* [ἐπί τινι] Gn 41,40

to hear, to grant [τινι] Jb 5,1

to answer Ct 5,6

*Jb 38,34 ὑπακούσεταί σου *will it listen to you* -חענך for MT תכסך *will it cover you*

Cf. HELBING 1928, 155-156; LEE, J. 1983, 34; SPICQ 1982, 238-243; →MM; TWNT

ὕπανδρος,-ος,-ον⁺ A 0-0-0-2-2-4

Prv 6,24.29; Sir 9,9; 41,23

married (of a woman) Sir 9,9

*Prv 6,24 γυναικὸς ὑπάνδρου *a married woman* -אשת רע for MT רע אשת *a bad woman* neol.?

→MM

ὑπαντάω⁺ V 0-0-0-1-5-6

Dnᴸˣˣ 10,14; Tobᴮᴬ 7,1; Wis 6,16; Sir 9,3; 12,17

to meet [τινι] Tobᴮᴬ 7,1; *to come upon* [τινι] Dnᴸˣˣ 10,14

Cf. HELBING 1928, 230; LARCHER 1984, 424; →NIDNTT

ὑπάντησις,-εως⁺ N3F 0-1-0-0-0-1

Jgsᴮ 11,34

coming to meet; neol.

→NIDNTT

ὕπαρ, ὕπαρος N3N 0-0-0-0-1-1

2 Mc 15,11

sort of vision

Cf. HERMANN 1918, 284-286

ὕπαρξις,-εως⁺ N3F 0-1-1-9-2-13

2 Chr 35,7; Jer 9,9; Ps 77(78),48; Prv 8,21; 13,11

substance, property 2 Chr 35,7; *existence* Prv 8,21; neol.?

→MM; NIDNTT

ὑπάρχω⁺ V 23-12-23-49-50-157

Gn 12,5; 13,6; 14,16; 24,59; 25,5

to be present, to be there, to be at some one's disposal Gn 42,13; *to exist* Ps 145(146),2; *to remain* 2 Chr 20,33; *to be (copula)* 4 Mc 4,12; *to belong to, to fall to* [τινι] 1 Sm 9,7; τὰ ὑπάρχοντα *the possessions, the goods* Gn 12,5

*Gn 24,59 τὰ ὑπάρχοντα *the goods* -מקנתה for MT מנקתה *nurse*; *Jb 20,20 τοῖς ὑπάρχουσιν *to (his) possessions* -בשובו for MT בבטנו *in his belly*

Cf. HARL 1986ᵃ, 204.206.279; →NIDNTT; TWNT

ὑπασπιστής,-οῦ N1M 0-0-0-0-2-2

4 Mc 3,12; 9,11

shield-bearer, guard

ὕπατος,-ου N2M 0-0-0-5-2-7

Dn 3,2; Dnᵀʰ 3,3; Dnᴸˣˣ 3,94; Dnᵀʰ 6,8

highest official Dn 3,2; *consul* (title of the Romans) 1 Mc 15,16

ὑπείκω⁺   V 0-0-0-0-1-1
4 Mc 6,35
to yield to, to give way to [τινι]

ὑπεκρέω   V 0-0-0-0-1-1
3 Mc 5,34
to slink away

ὑπεναντίος,-α,-ον⁺   A 9-4-7-5-18-43
Gn 22,17; 24,60; Ex 1,10; 15,7; 23,27
opposing; ὁ ὑπεναντίος *the enemy* Ps 73(74),10; οἱ ὑπεναντίοι *id.* Gn 22,17

ὑπεξαιρέω   V 1-0-0-0-0-1
Gn 39,9
P: *to be removed, to be taken away*

ὑπέρ⁺   P 7-110-63-130-117-427
Gn 48,22; Ex 1,9; Dt 24,16(bis); 25,3
[τινος]: *over, above* Dt 28,23; *in defence of, on behalf of* Jgs^B 6,31; *for, instead of, in the name of* Jdt 8,12; *for* Dt 24,16; *because of* 1 Sm 4,21; *for, on account of* Jb 24,5; *concerning* 1 Sm 21,3
[τι] or [τινα]: *over, beyond* Is 57,9; *above* 1 Sm 10,23; *above, exceeding, beyond* (indicating measure) Dt 25,3; *than* (with a comp.) Sir 24,20; *above, more than, upwards of* (with number) Eccl 7,19; *above, more than* Ps 86(87),2
Cf. JOHANNESSOHN 1910, 1-82; 1926, 216-219; →NIDNTT; TWNT

ὑπεράγαν⁺   D 0-0-0-0-1-1
2 Mc 10,34
beyond measure, exceedingly; neol.?

ὑπεραγόντως   D 0-0-0-0-1-1
2 Mc 7,20
exceedingly; neol.?

ὑπεράγω   V 0-0-0-0-3-3
1 Mc 6,43; Sir 33,23; 36,22
to be pre-eminent Sir 33,23; *to be higher* 1 Mc 6,43
Cf. HELBING 1928, 190

ὑπεραινετός,-ός,-όν   A 0-0-0-2-2-4
Dn 3,52; Od 8,52.54
to be praised exceedingly; neol.

ὑπεραίρω⁺   V 0-1-0-3-2-6
2 Chr 32,23; Ps 37(38),5; 71(72),16; Prv 31,29; 2 Mc 5,23
A: *to rise above* [τι] Ps 37(38),5; *to surpass* [τινα] Prv 31,29
P: *to be exalted above* [ὑπέρ τι] Ps 71(72),16; *to be exalted* (of pers.) 2 Chr 32,23; *to be exalted above* or *to lord over* [τινι] (of pers.) 2 Mc 5,23

Cf. HELBING 1928, 190

ὑπεράλλομαι   V 0-0-0-0-1-1
Sir 38,33
to leap to a high place, to leap into prominence (metaph.)

ὑπεράνω⁺   D/P 2-0-9-8-3-22
Dt 26,19; 28,1; Is 2,2; Ez 8,2; 10,19
beyond, from now on (of time) Hag 2,15; *above* [τινος] Is 2,2; neol.?
Cf. BLASS 1990, § 215; HORSLEY 1983, 87; →MM

ὑπεράνωθεν   D/P 0-0-1-1-0-2
Ez 1,25; Ps 77(78),23
from above Ps 77(78),23; *id.* [τινος] Ez 1,25
Cf. BLASS 1990, § 215

ὑπέραρσις,-εως   N3F 0-0-1-0-0-1
Ez 47,11
high water mark; *Ez 47,11 τῇ ὑπεράρσει αὐτοῦ *its high water* -נבהו for MT גבאיו *its pools*
Cf. CAIRD 1969=1972, 149-150; LSJ suppl; LSJ RSuppl

ὑπερασπίζω⁺   V 2-2-6-4-8-22
Gn 15,1; Dt 33,29; 2 Kgs 19,34; 20,6; Is 31,5
to shield [τινος] Gn 15,1; *to defend as with a shield* [ὑπέρ τινος] 2 Kgs 19,34; *to protect* [τι] Prv 2,7; *to defend against* [τινι] 4 Mc 7,8; *to cover sb with sth* [τινός τινι] Prv 4,9; neol.?
Cf. HARL 1986ᵃ, 163; HELBING 1928, 188-189

ὑπερασπισμός,-οῦ⁺   N2M 0-1-0-2-1-4
2 Sm 22,36; Ps 17(18),36; Lam 3,65; Sir 34,16
covering with a shield, protection 2 Sm 22,36; *covering* (metaph.) Lam 3,65; neol.

ὑπερασπιστής,-οῦ⁺   N1M 0-2-0-17-1-20
2 Sm 22,3.31; Ps 17(18),3.31; 26(27),1
one who holds a shield over, protector 2 Sm 22,3
*Ps 70(71),3 ὑπερασπιστήν *protecting* -מעוז for MT מעון *dwelling place*
neol.
Cf. TALMON 1964, 124-125(Ps 70(71),3)

ὑπερασπίστρια,-ας   N1F 0-0-0-0-1-1
4 Mc 15,29
one who holds a shield, protector (a woman); neol.

ὑπερβαίνω⁺   V 0-4-3-5-4-16
1 Sm 5,5(bis); 2 Sm 18,23; 22,30; Jer 5,22
to step over [τι] 1 Sm 5,5; *to get over, to leap over, to jump over* [τι] 2 Sm 22,30; *to cross* [τι] Prv 9,18b
to pass, to go beyond [τινα] Jb 9,11; *to pass over, to intentionally overlook* (sins) [τι] Mi 7,18
to outrun [τινα] 2 Sm 18,23
to exceed (time) Jb 14,5; *to pass over* (a bound)

[τι] Jb 24,2; *to exceed sb in sth* [τινά τινι]
3 Mc 6,24

οὐδὲ ὑπερέβην πατρικὸν οἶκον *I did not go
beyond my father's house, I did not stray from my
father's house* 4 Mc 18,7

ὑπερβαλλόντως⁺   D 0-0-0-1-0-1
Jb 15,11

exceedingly; *Jb 15,11 ὑπερβαλλόντως *exceedingly* -טעם לא *without taste* for MT עם לאט *gently
with*

ὑπερβάλλω⁺   V 0-0-0-0-6-6
2 Mc 4,13.24; 7,42; 3 Mc 2,23; Sir 5,7
A: *to surpass* [ὑπέρ τι] Sir 25,11; *to outbid*
[τινα] 2 Mc 4,24
M: *to postpone, to wait out* Sir 5,7
ὑπερβάλλων *exceeding* 2 Mc 4,13
Cf. HELBING 1928, 190; LLEWELYN 1994, 199(n.6); →TWNT

ὑπερβολή,-ῆς⁺   N1F 0-0-0-0-1-1
4 Mc 3,18

excess; καθ' ὑπερβολήν *to an extraordinary
degree, beyond measure*
→TWNT

ὑπερδυναμόω   V 0-0-0-1-0-1
Ps 64(65),4
to overcome, to overpower [τινα]; neol.

ὑπερεῖδον⁺   V 12-0-1-6-12-31
Gn 42,21; Lv 20,4; 26,40.43.44
aor. of ὑπεροράω
Cf. DOGNIEZ 1992, 132; WALTERS 1973, 263-264

ὑπερείδω   V 0-0-0-2-0-2
Jb 8,15; Prv 9,1
to prop up [τι] Jb 8,15
*Prv 9,1 ὑπήρεισε *he placed under as support*
-הציב ◊ נצב for MT חצבה *she has hewn*
Cf. CAIRD 1969=1972, 150

ὑπερεκχέω⁺   V 0-0-2-1-0-3
Jl 2,24; 4,13; Prv 5,16
to flow out, to spill Prv 5,16; *to overflow* Jl 2,24;
neol.

ὑπερένδοξος,-ος,-ον   A 0-0-0-2-2-4
Dn 3,53; Od 8,53.56
exceedingly glorious; neol.

ὑπερέχω⁺   V 5-3-0-2-3-13
Gn 25,23; 39,9; 41,40; Ex 26,13; Lv 25,27
to rise above, to excel, to surpass [τινος] Gn
41,40
to be highly placed (of pers.) Jgs^B 5,25; *to reign
over, to rule over, to dominate* [τινος] Gn 25,23;
id. [τι] Dn^Th 7,23
to exceed, to excel [abs.] Sir 43,30; *id.* [τινα]

Dn^LXX 5,11; *to be better than* [τινος] Sir 33,7
to be left over to, to remain over for [τινι] Lv
25,27
Cf. CAIRD 1976, 82; HARL 1986ª, 275; HELBING 1928, 189;
WEVERS 1993, 653; →TWNT

ὑπερηφανεύω   V 0-0-0-4-3-7
Ps 9,23(10,2); Jb 22,29; Dn^Th 5,20; Neh 9,16;
Tob^BA 4,13
M: *to behave arrogantly*; neol.

ὑπερηφανέω⁺   V 0-0-0-1-1-2
Neh 9,10; 4 Mc 5,21
A: *to be arrogant to* [ἐπί τινα] Neh 9,10
P: *to be despised* 4 Mc 5,21

ὑπερηφανία,-ας⁺   N1F 4-0-7-16-31-58
Ex 18,21; Lv 26,19; Nm 15,30; Dt 17,12; Is 16,6
arrogance, pride Ex 18,21; *splendour,
magnificence* Est 4,17w
*Ps 73(74),3 τὰς ὑπερηφανίας *the pride* -◊נשא for
MT משאות *desolation*
Cf. DOGNIEZ 1992, 231; DORIVAL 1994, 344; LE
BOULLUEC 1989, 197; SPICQ 1982, 644-648; WEVERS 1990,
287; →NIDNTT; TWNT

ὑπερήφανος,-ος,-ον⁺   A 0-0-5-16-20-41
Is 1,25; 2,12; 13,11; 29,20; Zph 3,6
arrogant, proud, haughty (of pers.) Est 4,17d; *id.*
(of things) 4 Mc 9,30; *sumptuous, splendid* Est
4,17k
*Zph 3,6 ὑπερηφάνους *the proud* -גאים for MT
גוים *nations*
Cf. SPICQ 1982, 648-649; →MM; NIDNTT; TWNT

ὑπερηφάνως   D 0-0-0-0-3-3
1 Mc 7,34.47; 2 Mc 9,4
proudly
Cf. SCHOONHEIM 1966, 235-246

ὑπέρθυρον,-ου   N2N 0-0-1-0-0-1
Is 6,4
lintel (of door or gate)

ὑπερισχύω   V 1-2-0-2-10-15
Gn 49,26; Jos 17,18; 2 Sm 24,4; Dn^Th 3,22; 11,23
to prevail, to be strong 1 Ezr 3,5; *to prevail
against* [πρός τινα, εἰς τινα] 2 Sm 24,4; *to be
stronger than* [τινος] Jos 17,18; *id.* [ἐπί τινι]
Gn 49,26; *to overpower* [τινος] Dn^Th 11,23
Cf. HELBING 1928, 189-190

ὑπέρκειμαι   V 0-0-1-1-0-2
Ez 16,47; Prv 31,29
to excel, to exceed [τινα]; neol.?

ὑπερκεράω   V 0-0-0-0-2-2
Jdt 15,5; 1 Mc 7,46
to outflank, to attack the wings of (mil. term)

[τινα]; neol.?

ὑπερκρατέω V 0-1-0-0-0-1
1 Kgs 16,22
to overpower [τινα]; neol.

ὑπερμαχέω V 0-0-0-0-1-1
1 Mc 16,3
to defend, to fight on behalf of [ὑπέρ τινος]
Cf. HELBING 1928, 191

ὑπέρμαχος,-ος,-ον⁺ A 0-0-0-0-4-4
2 Mc 8,36; 14,34; Wis 10,20; 16,17
defending, fighting for, vindicating [τινος] Wis
10,20; ὁ ὑπέρμαχος *defender* 2 Mc 14,34

ὑπερμεγέθης,-ης,-ες A 0-1-0-1-0-2
1 Chr 20,6; Dnᴸˣˣ 4,37a(34)
immensely great, of extraordinary size

ὑπερμήκης,-ης,-ες A 1-0-0-0-0-1
Nm 13,32
very long, very tall (of men)

ὑπέρογκος,-ος,-ον⁺ A 3-1-0-3-0-7
Ex 18,22.26; Dt 30,11; 2 Sm 13,2; Lam 1,9
puffed up, swollen Dnᵀʰ 11,36; *burdensome, dif-*
ficult 2 Sm 13,2; *important, difficult* Ex 18,22;
excessive Dt 30,11
*Lam 1,9 ὑπέρογκα *exaggerated, immoderate*
-פלאים (subst.) *wonderful things* for MT פלאים (adv.)
in an astonishing manner
Cf. DOGNIEZ 1992, 308

ὕπερον,-ου N2N 0-0-0-1-0-1
Prv 23,31
pestle

ὑπερόρασις,-εως N3F 1-0-0-0-0-1
Nm 22,30
contempt, disdain or *taking no notice*; neol.; see
ὑπεροράω
Cf. WALTERS 1973, 264

ὑπεροράω⁺ V 2-1-3-1-4-11
Lv 26,37; Dt 22,4; Jos 1,5; Is 58,7; Ez 7,19
A: *to disregard* [τινα] Lv 26,37; *id.* [τι] Ps
54(55),2; *id.* [ἀπό τινος] Is 58,7; *id.* [abs.] Ps
9,22(10,1); *to neglect* [τι] Sir 38,16; *to despise, to*
disdain [τι] 4 Mc 9,6
P: *to be despised* Ez 7,19
ὑπερεωραμένη *disdained, despised* Na 3,11
*Lv 26,40 ὑπερεῖδόν με *they disregarded me*
-עלם? for MT מעל *they committed treachery*
against me, cpr. Nm 5,12; 31,16; *Nm 22,30
ὑπεριδοῦσα (*I was*) *disregarding* -סכל *I was*
acting foolishly for MT הסכנתי סכן *I was*
accustomed to
Cf. DORIVAL 1994, 106.236; HARLÉ 1988, 209.210;

HELBING 1928, 190; SPICQ 1978ᵃ, 899-900; WALTERS 1973,
262-264.301

ὑπεροχή,-ῆς⁺ N1F 0-0-1-0-4-5
Jer 52,22; 2 Mc 3,11; 6,23; 13,6; 15,13
height Jer 52,22; *excess* 2 Mc 13,6; *dignity* 2 Mc
3,11
→TWNT

ὑπέροψις,-εως N3F 1-0-0-0-0-1
Lv 20,4
taking no notice; neol.
Cf. WALTERS 1973, 264

ὑπερπλεονάζω⁺ V 0-0-0-0-1-1
PSal 5,16
to abound exceedingly; neol.
→NIDNTT

ὑπερτήκω V 0-0-0-0-1-1
4 Mc 7,12
M/P: *to melt completely, to waste away*; neol.

ὑπερτίθημι⁺ V 0-0-0-1-0-1
Prv 15,22
M: *to put off, to defer* [τι]

ὑπερτιμάω V 0-0-0-0-1-1
4 Mc 8,5
to honour greatly [τινα]; neol.

ὑπερυμνητός,-ός,-όν A 0-0-0-3-3-6
Dn 3,53; Dnᵀʰ 3,55; Od 8,53.55
highly praised, highly extolled; neol.

ὑπερυψόω⁺ V 0-0-0-74-36-110
Ps 36(37),35; 96(97),9; Dnᴸˣˣ 3,52(bis).54
A: *to exalt exceedingly, to raise to the loftiest*
height [τινα] Dnᴸˣˣ 3,57
M: *to raise oneself, to rise* Ps 36(37),35
P: *to be exalted* Dnᴸˣˣ 3,52; *to be exalted above*
[ὑπέρ τινα] Ps 96(97),9
neol.
→NIDNTT; TWNT

ὑπερφερής,-ής,-ές A 0-0-0-2-0-2
Dn 2,31
excellent, surpassing; neol.

ὑπερφέρω V 0-0-0-3-1-4
Dnᴸˣˣ 7,7.20; Dnᵀʰ 7,24; 1 Ezr 8,72
to be surpassing, to be excessive 1 Ezr 8,72; *to*
surpass [τι] Dnᴸˣˣ 7,20; *id.* [τινα] Dnᵀʰ 7,24

ὑπέρφοβος,-ος,-ον A 0-0-0-1-0-1
Dnᴸˣˣ 7,19
exceedingly terrifying

ὑπερφρονέω⁺ V 0-0-0-0-3-3
4 Mc 13,1; 14,11; 16,2
to despise [τινος]
Cf. HELBING 1928, 190

ὑπερφωνέω   V 0-0-0-0-1-1
Jdt 15,14
to sing loudly [τι]; neol.

ὑπερχαρής,-ής,-ές   A 0-0-0-1-1-2
Est 5,9; 3 Mc 7,20
overjoyed; neol.?

ὑπερχέω   V 0-0-0-1-0-1
Lam 3,54
P: *to overflow*

ὑπέρχομαι   V 0-0-0-0-1-1
3 Mc 4,6
to enter, to retire to [τι]
Cf. HELBING 1928, 88

ὑπερῷον,-ου⁺   N2N 0-17-4-4-3-28
Jgs 3,20.23.24
the upper part of the house, attic Jgs 3,20;
upstairs room (in a gate) 2 Sm 19,1

ὑπερῷος,-α,-ον⁺   A 0-0-1-0-0-1
Ez 42,5
upper; neol.?

ὑπεύθυνος,-ος,-ον   A 0-0-0-1-0-1
Prv 1,23
subject to [τινι]

ὑπευλαβέομαι   V 0-0-0-0-1-1
2 Mc 14,18
to be cautious of, to shrink from [+inf.]; neol.
→LSJ RSuppl

ὑπέχω⁺   V 0-0-0-2-2-4
Ps 88(89),51; Lam 5,7; 2 Mc 4,48; PSal 16,13
A: *to bear* [τι] Ps 88(89),51; *to undergo, to suffer*
[τι] 2 Mc 4,48
M: *to take sth upon oneself, to take on* [τι] PSal
16,13

ὑπήκοος,-ος,-ον⁺   A 1-1-0-3-0-5
Dt 20,11; Jos 17,13; Prv 4,3; 13,1; 21,28
obedient Prv 21,28; *obedient to* [τινι] Prv 4,3;
subject to [τινος] Dt 20,11
ἐποίησαν ὑπηκόους *they made subject, they
subjected* Jos 17,13

ὑπηρεσία,-ας⁺   N1F 0-0-0-1-2-3
Jb 1,3; Wis 13,11; 15,7
service Wis 13,11; *domestic personnel* (coll.) Jb
1,3
Cf. LARCHER 1985, 778; →PREISIGKE

ὑπηρετέω⁺   V 0-0-0-0-5-5
Wis 16,21.24.25; 19,6; Sir 39,4
to serve, to render service Sir 39,4; *to serve to*
[τινι] Wis 16,21
Cf. HILHORST 1989, 179-181; LARCHER 1985, 930-931.934;
→NIDNTT; TWNT

ὑπηρέτης,-ου⁺   N1M 0-0-1-3-1-5
Is 32,5; Prv 14,35; Dn 3,46; Wis 6,4
servant, subordinate officer
Cf. KUPISZEWSKI & MODRZEJEWSKI 1957-1958, 141-166;
SPICQ 1978ᵃ, 901-906; →NIDNTT; TWNT

ὑπισχνέομαι⁺   V 0-0-0-0-4-4
2 Mc 4,9; 8,11; 12,11; Wis 17,8
to promise to do [+inf.]
Cf. LARCHER 1985, 959

-ὑπνιάζω
(→ἐν-)

ὑπνίζω
(→ἐξ-)

ὕπνος,-ου⁺   N2M 13-6-6-19-19-63
Gn 20,3.6; 28,16; 31,10.11
sleep, slumber Gn 28,16
ὕπνον αἰώνιον *an everlasting sleep* (for the
sleep of death) Jer 28(51),39; ἐν ὕπνῳ *in sleep,
in a dream* Gn 20,3; καθ᾽ ὕπνον *id.* Gn 20,6
Cf. DORIVAL 1994, 70.302.445(Nm 12,6; 24,4.16); →NIDNTT;
TWNT

ὑπνόω⁺   V 1-3-5-11-4-24
Gn 2,21; JgsᴬA 19,4; 1 Sm 26,12; 1 Kgs 19,5; Jer
14,9
to sleep Jgsᴬ 19,4; *id.* (euph. for dying) Jer
28(51),39; *to cause to sleep* Gn 2,21
Cf. HARL 1986ᵃ, 105(Gn 2,21); SHIPP 1979, 547-548;
→TWNT
(→ἐξ-, καθ-)

ὑπνώδης,-ης,-ες   A 0-0-0-1-0-1
Prv 23,21
drowsy; (ὁ) ὑπνώδης *drowsy person, sluggard*

ὑπό⁺   P 61-42-43-140-212-498
Gn 9,2; 16,9; 18,4.8; 19,8
[τινος]: *by* (accompanied with a pass. verbform)
Gn 26,29; *from* Ps 73(74),22; *under, in*
(indicating reason) Jb 30,4; *under* Jb 8,16
[τι, τινα] *under* (with verb of motion) 1 Mc
6,46; *under* (place) Gn 18,8; *under, at the foot of*
Ex 24,4; *under* (in geogr. sense) Dt 3,17; *beyond*
Ex 3,1
about (time) Jos 5,2; *little before* Jon 4,10; *in the
course of, during* 3 Mc 7,12
under (as subordination) 1 Ezr 3,1; *under, in the
hand of* 2 Mc 3,6
under (reason) Ex 23,5
ὑπὸ τὸν οὐρανόν *under heaven, on earth* Ex
17,14; ὑπὸ τὴν ὄψιν *under (our) notice* Est
8,12i; ὑπὸ χεῖρας *in (your) hands* Gn 9,2; ὑπὸ
τὴν σκιάν *in the shadow* Bar 1,12; ὑπὸ

διαθήκην (θεοῦ) *under (God's) covenant* 2 Mc
7,36; ὑπὸ φόρον *under tribute* 1 Mc 8,2; ὑπὸ
καιρόν *within the space of one day* 2 Mc 7,20;
ὑφ᾽ ἕν *at one stroke* Wis 12,9

Cf. DORIVAL 1994, 56; JOHANNESSOHN 1910, 1-82; 1926,
174-184; →NIDNTT

ὑποβάλλω⁺ V 0-0-0-0-1-1
1 Ezr 2,14
M: *to lay a foundation for* [τι]

ὑποβλέπω V 0-1-0-0-1-2
1 Sm 18,9; Sir 37,10
M: *to look askance at, to eye angrily, to look
suspiciously at* [τινα]

ὑπόγειος,-ος,-ον A 0-0-1-0-0-1
Jer 45(38),11
underground; *Jer 45(38),11 τὴν ὑπόγειον *the
underground (part)* (of the house of the king)
תחת האריץ‎ for MT האוצר תחת‎ *under the storehouse*

Cf. WALTERS 1973, 113

ὑπογραμμός,-οῦ⁺ N2M 0-0-0-0-1-1
2 Mc 2,28
outline; neol.

Cf. LEE, E. 1962, 172-173; →NIDNTT

ὑπογράφω V 0-0-0-1-9-10
Est 8,12a; 1 Ezr 2,12.19; 1 Mc 8,25.27
A: *to write below* 3 Mc 2,30
P: *to be indicated to, to be suggested to* [τινι]
1 Mc 8,25; *to be subscribed, to be copied below*
1 Ezr 2,12
τὴν ὑπογεγραμμένην ἐπιστολήν *the following
letter* 2 Mc 9,18

→NIDNTT

ὑπόγυος,-ος,-ον A 0-0-0-0-1-1
2 Mc 12,31
close at hand, approaching

ὑπόδειγμα,-ατος⁺ N3N 0-0-1-0-4-5
Ez 42,15; 2 Mc 6,28.31; 4 Mc 17,23; Sir 44,16
pattern, plan (of a house) Ez 42,15; *example* Sir
44,16

Cf. BARR 1961, 152-154; HURST 1983, 156-165; LEE, E.
1962, 167-169; SPICQ 1978ᵃ, 907-909; →NIDNTT; TWNT

ὑποδείκνυμι⁺/ύω⁺ V 0-3-1-20-36-60
1 Chr 28,18; 2 Chr 15,3; 20,2; Jer 38(31),19; Est
1,1n
to show [τί τινι] 1 Chr 28,18; *to show to, to
declare to* [τινι] 2 Chr 20,2; id. [τί τινι] Tob
7,10; *to show forth* [τι] Tobᴮᴬ 12,6; id. [τί τινι]
Tobˢ 12,6; *to teach* [abs.] 2 Chr 15,3; *to inform
sb concerning sb* [τινι περί τινος] Tob 1,19; *to
discover* [τι] Est 2,10

ὑποδέχομαι⁺ V 0-0-0-0-5-5
Jdt 13,13; Tobᴮᴬ 7,7; Tobˢ 7,8; 1 Mc 16,15; 4 Mc
13,17
to receive, to welcome [τινα] Jdt 13,13; *to
entertain* [τινα] Tobᴮᴬ 7,7

ὑποδέω⁺ V 0-1-1-0-0-2
2 Chr 28,15; Ez 16,10
to put on shoes on sb [τινα] 2 Chr 28,15; *to put
on sth as shoes on sb* [τινά τι] Ez 16,10

ὑπόδημα,-ατος⁺ N3N 7-5-6-6-2-26
Gn 14,23; Ex 3,5; 12,11; Dt 25,9.10
shoe, footwear Gn 14,23
*1 Sm 12,3 ὑπόδημα *shoes* נעלים‎ for MT אעלים‎
I may hide

Cf. WALTERS 1973, 162.177

ὑποδύτης,-ου N1M 10-0-0-0-0-10
Ex 28,31.33(bis).34; 36,29(39,22)
undergarment; neol.?

Cf. LE BOULLUEC 1989, 290; →PREISIGKE

ὑποδύω⁺ V 0-0-0-0-1-1
Jdt 6,13
to go down below sth [ὑποκάτω τινός]

ὑποζύγιον,-ου⁺ N2N 14-12-1-1-1-29
Gn 36,24; Ex 4,20; 9,3; 20,10.17
draught animal, beast of burden, ass, mule or
horse

Cf. LE BOULLUEC 1989, 46.101; LEE, J. 1983, 140-144;
WEVERS 1993, 601

ὑποζώννυμι⁺ V 0-0-0-0-2-2
2 Mc 3,19; PSal 17,22
A: *to gird sb with* [τινά τι] (metaph.) PSal 17,22
P: *to be girded with* [τι] 2 Mc 3,19

ὑπόθεμα,-ατος N3N 1-0-0-0-0-1
Ex 25,38
dish placed under a cup; neol.?

Cf. LE BOULLUEC 1989, 264

ὑπόθεσις,-εως N3F 0-0-0-0-1-1
4 Mc 1,12
general theory, doctrine

ὑποκαίω V 0-0-3-2-1-6
Jer 1,13; Ez 24,5; Am 4,2; Dnᴸˣˣ 3,25.46
A: *to set fire underneath, to heat from below* [τι]
Ez 24,5
P: *to be heated from underneath* Dnᴸˣˣ 3,25
*Am 4,2 εἰς λέβητας ὑποκαιομένους *in boiling
caldrons* -דור בסירות ◊דור‎? *stack of logs in circles,
pyre* (cpr. Ez 24,5), and -סיר◊‎ *jar, caldron* for MT
בסירות דוגה‎ *fisher's hook* ◊דוג‎ *to fish* and ◊סירה‎ *angle,
hook*

Cf. MARGOLIS 1906ᵇ=1972, 69; →SCHLEUSNER

ὑποκαλύπτω V 2-0-0-0-0-2
Ex 26,12(bis)
to fold over, to drape over [τι]; neol.
Cf. LE BOULLUEC 1989, 268; WEVERS 1990, 419

ὑποκάτω⁺ D/P 17-26-26-18-5-92
Gn 1,7.9(bis); 6,17; 7,19
below Dt 28,13; *id.* (as adj.) 1 Kgs 6,6
[τινος]: *below, under* Gn 1,7; *under, below,
down at* Ps 8,7; *under, at the foot of* (a hill) Jdt
6,13; *at the base of, close to* 1 Sm 7,11; *under* (in
geogr. sense) Jdt 6,11
Cf. BLASS 1990, § 215

ὑποκάτωθεν⁺ D/P 1-10-12-4-1-28
Dt 9,14; Jgs^A 7,8; 1 Kgs 6,8; 7,11.16
from beneath Jb 18,16; *below* (as adj.) Ez 42,5;
from under [τινος] Dt 9,14
Cf. BLASS 1990, § 215

ὑπόκειμαι⁺ V 0-0-0-1-3-4
Jb 16,4; 1 Ezr 8,8; 1 Mc 12,7; PSal 16,8
to be given below (in the text) 1 Ezr 8,8; *to be,
to exist* Jb 16,4; *to be subject to, to be liable to*
[ἀπό τινος] PSal 16,8
Cf. HOLM-NIELSEN 1977, 96(PSal 16,8)

ὑποκρίνω⁺ V 0-0-0-0-10-10
2 Mc 5,25; 6,21.24; 4 Mc 6,15.17
M: *to play the actor, to feign, to pretend* [τι]
2 Mc 5,25; *id.* [+inf.] 4 Mc 6,15; *to be a
hypocrite* Sir 1,29
Cf. SPICQ 1982, 650-653; →NIDNTT; TWNT

ὑπόκρισις,-εως⁺ N3F 0-0-0-0-2-2
2 Mc 6,25; PSal 4,6
hypocrisy, dissimulation 2 Mc 6,25; *wickedness*
PSal 4,6
Cf. HATCH 1889, 91-93; SPICQ 1982, 653-656; →NIDNTT;
TWNT

ὑποκριτής,-οῦ⁺ N1M 0-0-0-2-0-2
Jb 34,30; 36,13
hypocrite, impious person
Cf. ARGYLE 1963-1964, 113-114; HATCH 1889, 91-93;
SPICQ 1982, 655-657; →NIDNTT; TWNT

ὑπολαμβάνω⁺ V 0-1-1-36-13-51
2 Chr 25,8; Jer 44(37),9; Ps 16(17),12; 29(30),2;
47(48),10
to lift up [τινα] Ps 29(30),2
to take up what is said, to reply, to answer Jb 2,4
to take up a notion, to suppose, to think 4 Mc
5,18; *id.* [ὅτι +ind.] Tob 6,18; *id.* [+inf.] Jb
20,2; *to ponder, to think about* [τι] Ps 47(48),10;
to think to [+inf.] 1 Mc 1,16; *to hold as* [τινα
+pred.] Wis 12,24

to take up to, to undertake to [+inf.] 2 Chr 25,8
*Ps 16(17),12 ὑπέλαβόν με *they took me up,
they thought of me* -◊ רמה (pi.) *they likened me,
they thought of me* for MT רמינו *his likeness*, cpr.
Ps 47(48),10
→NIDNTT; TWNT

ὑπόλειμμα,-ατος⁺ N3N 0-2-4-1-1-8
1 Sm 9,24; 2 Kgs 21,14; Mi 4,7; 5,6.7
remnant 2 Kgs 21,14; *remainder, residue* Mal
2,15
→NIDNTT

ὑπολείπω⁺ V 18-38-22-8-6-92
Gn 27,36; 30,36; 32,25; 44,20; 45,7
A: *to leave for* [τί τινι] Gn 27,36; *to leave to*
[εἴς τι] 2 Kgs 25,12
M: *to leave behind* [τινα] Gn 50,8; *to leave* [τι]
Ob 5; *id.* [τινα] Zph 3,12; *id.* [τινος] Ex 10,24;
to leave for [τινί τι] Jdt 8,7; *to leave, to spare*
[τι] Ex 10,12; *to reserve* [τι] 2 Sm 8,4; *to leave
behind, to save* [ἔν τινι] 2 Sm 17,12
P: *to be left* 1 Kgs 17,17; *to be left behind, to
remain* Jgs 21,7; *to be left, to be spared* Ex 10,15
Cf. WEVERS 1990, 363.418; →NIDNTT

ὑπόλημψις,-εως N3F 0-0-0-0-1-1
Sir 3,24
prejudice, assumption, speculation
Cf. CAIRD 1969=1972, 150-151

ὑπολήνιον,-ου⁺ N2N 0-0-4-0-0-4
Is 16,10; Jl 4,13; Hag 2,16; Zech 14,10
vessel or *vat placed under the winepress* (to
receive the wine); neol.

ὑπόλοιπος,-ος,-ον A 0-0-1-0-0-1
Is 11,11
remaining, surviving

ὑπόλυσις,-εως N3F 0-0-1-0-0-1
Na 2,11
loosening, weakening (of knees); neol.

ὑπολύω⁺ V 2-0-1-2-0-5
Dt 25,9.10; Is 20,2; Ru 4,7.8
A: *to untie* (sandals) *from under* (one's feet) [τι
ἀπό τινος] Dt 25,9
M: *id.* [τι] Ru 4,7

ὑπομαστίδιον,-ου N2N 0-0-0-0-1-1
3 Mc 3,27
suckling; neol.

ὑπομένω⁺ V 1-3-13-39-30-86
Nm 22,19; Jos 19,48a; Jgs^B 3,25; 2 Kgs 6,33; Is
40,31
to remain (of pers.) Jb 17,13; *id.* (of sit.) Jb 3,9;
to remain, to stand firm (of things) Jb 8,15

to tarry, to wait Jgs^B 3,25; *to wait for* [τινα]
Tob^BA 5,7; *id.* [τι] Ps 105(106),13; *id.* [εἴς τι] Ps
129(130),5
to wait patiently Zech 6,14; *to wait (up)on*
[τινα] Sir 36,15; *id.* [τινι] Ps 32(33),20; *to wait
upon, to hope* [ἐπί τινι] Mi 7,7
to endure patiently Jb 6,11; *to endure* [τι] 4 Mc
5,23; *to endure, to forbear* [+inf.] 1 Ezr 2,15; *to
continue* [τοῦ +inf.] Jos 19,48a
πᾶν δὲ σκότος αὐτῷ ὑπομείναι *let all darkness
be waiting you* Jb 20,26
*Na 1,7 τοῖς ὑπομένουσιν αὐτόν *to them that
wait on him* -למקויו for MT למעוז *as a stronghold*;
*Jb 7,3 ὑπέμεινα *I have endured* -תוחלתי for
MT הנחלתי *I have inherited*; *Jb 22,21 ἐὰν
ὑπομείνῃς *if you can endure* -אם תשלם for MT
עמו ושלם *with Him and be at peace*; *Jb 41,3 καὶ
ὑπομενεῖ *and shall stand firm* or *and shall
remain safe* -וישלם for MT וַאֲשַׁלֵּם *and I shall repay*?
Cf. HELBING 1928, 103-104; MARGOLIS 1905=1972, 63-64;
SPICQ 1982, 658-664; →LSJ RSuppl(Lam 3,21); LSJ RSuppl;
NIDNTT; TWNT

ὑπομιμνήσκω⁺   V 0-1-0-0-3-4
1 Kgs 4,3; 4 Mc 18,14; Wis 12,2; 18,22
to remind sb of sth [τινά τι] 4 Mc 18,14; *to call
to mind* [τι] Wis 18,22; (ὁ) ὑπομιμνήσκων
recorder (a pers.) 1 Kgs 4,3
→NIDNTT

ὑπόμνημα,-ατος   N3N 0-1-0-1-0-2
2 Sm 8,16; Ezr 6,2
record
Cf. BICKERMAN 1980, 47(n.6).112-113; LLEWELYN 1992,
122; 1994, 33

ὑπομνηματίζομαι   V 0-0-0-0-1-1
1 Ezr 6,22
P: *to be recorded*; neol.?

ὑπομνηματισμός,-οῦ   N2M 0-0-0-1-3-4
Ezr 4,15; 1 Ezr 2,17; 2 Mc 2,13; 4,23
remembrance, remembering 2 Mc 4,23; *record*
Ezr 4,15; οἱ ὑπομνηματισμοί *archives,
chronicles* 1 Ezr 2,17; *commentaries, memoirs*
2 Mc 2,13; neol.?

ὑπομνηματογράφος,-ου   N2M 0-2-2-0-0-4
1 Chr 18,15; 2 Chr 34,8; Is 36,3.22
recorder; neol.?

ὑπόμνησις,-εως⁺   N3F 0-0-0-0-2-2
2 Mc 6,17; Wis 16,11
reminder 2 Mc 6,17
εἰς ὑπόμνησιν ἐνεκεντρίζοντο *their memory
was jogged, they had their memory jogged* Wis

16,11
Cf. HORSLEY 1982, 73; →NIDNTT

ὑπομονή,-ῆς⁺   N1F 0-1-2-6-16-25
1 Chr 29,15; Jer 14,8; 17,13; Ps 9,19; 38(39),8
staying, tarrying (here on earth) 1 Chr 29,15;
endurance, perseverance 4 Mc 1,11; *hope,
expectation* Ps 9,19
Cf. MARGOLIS 1905=1972, 64; MIQUEL 1986, 263;
NIKIPROWETZKY 1976, 114-115; SPICQ 1982, 658-665;
→LSJ suppl(1 Chr 29,15; Jer 14,8); LSJ RSuppl; NIDNTT;
TWNT

ὑπονοέω⁺   V 0-0-0-1-4-5
Dn^Th 7,25; Jdt 14,14; Tob 8,16; Sir 23,21
to expect, to suspect Tob 8,16; *to think, to
suppose that* [+inf.] Jdt 14,14; *to think to, to
devise* [τοῦ +inf.] Dn^Th 7,25
→TWNT

ὑπονόημα,-ατος   N3N 0-0-0-0-1-1
Sir 25,7
supposition, consideration

ὑπονοθεύω   V 0-0-0-0-3-3
2 Mc 4,7.26(bis)
to procure by corruption, to labour underhand
[τι] 2 Mc 4,7; *to undermine* [τινα] 2 Mc 4,26;
neol.

ὑπόνοια,-ας⁺   N1F 0-0-0-3-1-4
Dn^LXX 4,19(16).33b(30); 5,6; Sir 3,24
suspicion, conjecture
→TWNT

ὑπονύσσω   V 0-0-1-0-0-1
Is 58,3
to prod, to goad [τινα]

ὑποπίπτω⁺   V 0-0-0-1-3-4
Prv 15,1; 1 Ezr 8,18; Jdt 16,6; Sus^LXX 52
to fall Jdt 16,6; *to belong to* [τινι] 1 Ezr 8,18; *to
happen to, to befall* [τινι] Sus^LXX 52
ἀπόκρισις ὑποπίπτουσα *a submissive answer*
Prv 15,1
Cf. ENGEL 1985, 119-120

ὑποπόδιον,-ου⁺   N2N 0-0-1-3-0-4
Is 66,1; Ps 98(99),5; 109(110),1; Lam 2,1
footstool

ὑποπτεύω⁺   V 0-0-0-1-1-2
Ps 118(119),39; Sir 9,13
to view with apprehension or *anxiety* [τι]

ὕποπτος,-ος,-ον   A 0-0-0-0-2-2
2 Mc 3,32; 12,4
suspecting, viewing with suspicion (of pers.) 2 Mc
3,32; *suspected, subject to suspicion* 2 Mc 12,4

ὑποπυρρίζω   V 1-0-0-0-0-1

Lv 13,24
to become red; neol.?

ὑπορράπτω   V 0-0-0-0-1-1
Sir 50,1
to mend [τι]

ὑπορρίπτω   V 0-0-0-0-1-1
4 Mc 6,25
to cast, to throw down [τινα]; neol.?

ὑποσημαίνω   V 0-0-0-0-1-1
1 Ezr 6,6
P: *to be indicated concerning, to send word about*
[περί τινος]

ὑποσκελίζω   V 0-0-1-6-0-7
Jer 23,12; Ps 16(17),13; 36(37),31; 139(140),5;
Prv 10,8
to trip up, to overthrow [τινα] Jer 23,12; *id.* [τι]
(metaph.) Ps 36(37),31
Cf. LEE, J. 1969, 240-241

ὑποσκέλισμα,-ατος   N3N 0-0-0-1-0-1
Prv 24,17
fall brought by tripping up, stumble; neol.

ὑπόστασις,-εως⁺   N3F 2-5-6-7-3-23
Dt 1,12; 11,6; Jgs 6,4; 1 Sm 13,21
supporting, firm stratum, place to stand Ps
68(69),3; *foundation* Na 2,8; *plan, outline* Ez
43,11; *station of soldiers, camp* 1 Sm 13,23
substance, support Jgs 6,4; *possession?* Jb 22,20,
see also Jer 10,17; *inheritance* Wis 16,21
protection, recourse Ps 38(39),8
(actual) existence Ps 38(39),6(primo); *coming
into existence, origin* Ps 138(139),15
expectation, hope Ru 1,12, see also Ps
38(39),6(secundo); Ez 19,5
being of God Jer 23,22
resisitance, rebellious attitude Dt 1,12
Cf. DÖRRIE 1955, 38.39.40.41.44.45-46.47.79; DOGNIEZ
1992, 58(Dt 1,12).65.114.187; HATCH 1889, 88-89;
LARCHER 1985, 927-929(Wis 16,21); PERLITT 1990,
299-311(Dt 1,12); SPICQ 1978ᵃ, 910-912; TOV 1981, 67(Jer
10,17); WITT 1933, 319-343; ZIEGLER 1937, 12-16(Wis
16,12); →MM; NIDNTT; PREISIGKE; TWNT

ὑποστέλλω⁺   V 2-0-2-1-1-6
Ex 23,21; Dt 1,17; Hab 2,4; Hag 1,10; Jb 13,8
M: *to draw back, to give way to, to shrink before*
Dt 1,17; *to draw back* Hab 2,4; *to hold back* [τι]
Hag 1,10
*Ex 23,21 ὑποστείληταί σε *he gives way to you,
he shrinks before you -ךינפ אשׂי*? (see Jb 13,8) for
MT םכעשׁפל אשׂי *he pardons your transgression*
Cf. DOGNIEZ 1992, 115.231; LE BOULLUEC 1989, 239;

WEVERS 1995, 11; →PREISIGKE

ὑπόστημα,-ατος   N3N 0-1-1-0-0-2
2 Sm 23,14; Jer 23,18
station of soldiers, camp 2 Sm 23,14; *id.*
(metaph.) Jer 23,18

ὑποστήριγμα,-ατος   N3N 0-3-1-1-0-5
1 Kgs 2,35e; 7,11(24); 10,12; Jer 5,10; Dnᵀʰ 11,7
undergirding support; neol.

ὑποστηρίζω   V 0-0-0-2-0-2
Ps 36(37),17; 144(145),14
to undergird, to support [τινα]; neol.

ὑποστρέφω⁺   V 4-5-0-3-5-17
Gn 8,7.9; 43,10; Ex 32,31; Jos 2,23
to return, to turn back

ὑποστρώννυμι⁺   V 0-0-2-0-2-4
Is 58,5; Ez 27,30; 4 Mc 9,19; Sir 4,27
A: *to spread sth under sb* [τί τινι] 4 Mc 9,19
M: *to spread under oneself* [τι] Is 58,5
μὴ ὑποστρώσῃς ἀνθρώπῳ μωρῷ σεαυτόν *do not
spread yourself out for a fool, do not subject
yourself to a fool* Sir 4,27

ὑποσχάζω   V 0-0-0-0-1-1
Sir 12,17
to cause to collapse; ὑποσχάσει πτέρναν σου *he
will cause your heel to collapse, he will trip you
up*; neol.

ὑπόσχεσις,-εως   N3F 0-0-0-0-2-2
4 Mc 15,2; Wis 12,21
promise

ὑποτάσσω⁺   V 0-4-1-15-9-29
1 Kgs 10,15; 1 Chr 22,18; 29,24; 2 Chr 9,14; Hag
2,18
A: *to put* or *place under* [τι] Ps 8,7; *to put in
place* [τι] Hag 2,18; *to subdue* [τινα] Wis 18,22;
to subdue sb under [τινα ὑπό τινα] Ps
17(18),48
M/P: *to be subjected (to the Lord), to submit (to
the Lord)* [τινι] (as a virtue) Ps 61(62),2, see
also Ps 36(37),7; 61(62),6; 2 Mc 9,12; *to be
subjected, to be subdued* (of political subjects)
1 Kgs 10,15; *to be subjected to* [τινι] 1 Chr
29,24; *to submit oneself* 2 Mc 13,23
Cf. HELBING 1928, 318; SPICQ 1978ᵃ, 913-916; →NIDNTT;
TWNT

ὑποτίθημι⁺   V 7-0-1-0-5-13
Gn 28,18; 47,29; 49,15; Ex 17,12; 26,12
A: *to put sth (below) under* [τι] Gn 28,18; *id.*
[τι ὑπό τι] Gn 47,29; *id.* [τι ὑπό τινα] Ex
17,12; *to thrust sb from beneath, to make a
venture, to hazard* [τινι] 1 Mc 6,46; *to subject to*

[τι εἴς τι] Gn 49,15; *to let hang down* [τι] Ex 26,12

M: *to suggest* [abs.] 2 Mc 6,8; *id.* [τινι] Jer 43(36),25

ὑπέθηκεν ἑαυτῷ τὸ ξίφος *he fell upon his sword* 2 Mc 14,41

Cf. HELBING 1928, 318-319; LE BOULLUEC 1989, 268

ὑποτίτθιος,-ος,-ον   A 0-0-1-0-0-1
Hos 14,1

under the breast; τὰ ὑποτίτθια *children at the breast, nurslings;* neol.?

ὑπουργός,-ός,-όν   A 0-1-0-0-0-1
Jos 1,1

helpful; ὁ ὑπουργός *the helper, the assistant, the minister*

Cf. DANIEL 1966, 97(n.18)

ὑποφαίνω   V 0-0-0-0-2-2
2 Mc 10,35; 13,17

to begin to break, to break gradually; ὑποφαινούσης τῆς ἡμέρας *at dawn, at daybreak*

ὑπόφαυσις,-εως   N3F 0-0-1-0-0-1
Ez 41,16

narrow opening (giving light); neol.

ὑποφέρω⁺   V 0-1-2-9-8-20
1 Kgs 8,64; Am 7,10; Mi 7,9; Ps 54(55),13; 68(69),8

to bear [τι] 1 Kgs 8,64; *to endure* [τι] Jb 2,10; *id.* [τινα] Prv 18,14; *to bear up, to endure* [abs.] Jb 31,23

ὑπόφρικος,-ος,-ον   A 0-0-0-0-1-1
3 Mc 6,20

shuddering a little, seized by a light shudder; neol.

ὑποχείριος,-ος,-ον   A 3-4-2-0-7-16
Gn 14,20; Nm 21,2.3; Jos 6,2; 9,25

in one's hands, in one's authority Nm 21,2; *id.* [τινι] Jos 9,25; ὁ ὑποχείριος *dependant* Is 58,3

Cf. WEVERS 1993, 199

ὑποχόνδριον,-ου   N2N 0-1-0-0-0-1
1 Sm 31,3

soft part of the body below the cartilage and above the navel, part under the ribs, belly (always pl.); *1 Sm 31,3 εἰς τὰ ὑποχόνδρια *in the belly* -אל המתנים? *at the loins* for MT מחמורים ?

ὑπόχρεως,-ως,-ων   A 0-1-1-0-0-2
1 Sm 22,2; Is 50,1

indebted; (ὁ) ὑπόχρεως *debtor*

Cf. LLEWELYN 1994, 219(n.99)

ὑποχυτήρ,-ῆρος   N3M 0-0-1-0-0-1
Jer 52,19

vessel for pouring (oil into a lamp); neol.

ὑποχωρέω⁺   V 0-1-0-0-1-2
Jgsᴮ 20,37; Sir 13,9

to retreat, to withdraw, to go back

ὑποψία,-ας⁺   N1F 0-0-0-0-1-1
2 Mc 4,34

suspicion

ὑπτιάζω   V 0-0-0-1-0-1
Jb 11,13

to stretch out [τι]

ὕπτιος,-α,-ον   A 0-0-0-1-0-1
Jb 14,19

flowing calmly, flowing without turbulence (of water)

ὑπώπιον,-ου   N2N 0-0-0-1-0-1
Prv 20,30

a blow in the face, black eye, bruise

ὗς, ὑός⁺   N3M/F 2-3-0-1-0-6
Lv 11,7; Dt 14,8; 2 Sm 17,8; 1 Kgs 20(21),19; 22,38

wild swine; see σῦς

Cf. SHIPP 1979, 209-210

ὕσσωπος,-ου⁺   N2F/M 8-1-0-1-0-10
Ex 12,22; Lv 14,4.6.49.51

Semit. loanword (Hebr. אזוב); *hyssop*

Cf. CAIRD 1976, 78; TOV 1979, 221; →CHANTRAINE; FRISK

ὑστερέω⁺   V 2-0-1-10-7-20
Nm 9,7.13; Hab 2,3; Ps 22(23),1; 38(39),5

A: *to be behind schedule, to be late in arriving* Hab 2,3; *to postpone* [+inf.] Nm 9,7; *to lag behind, to be inferior to* Ps 38(39),5

to lack, to be wanting Neh 9,21; *to want* [τινι] Sir 11,12

to be wanting, to be missed (of things) Eccl 9,8
to be missing, to fail sb [τινα] Ps 22(23),1; *id.* [abs.] Eccl 10,3; *to withdraw oneself from* [ἀπό τινος] Sir 7,34

M: *to be behind* Sir 11,11; *to be wanting* [τι] Ct 7,3

Cf. DORIVAL 1994, 128(Nm 9,7.13); HELBING 1928, 173-176; SPICQ 1982, 666-669; →NIDNTT; TWNT
(→ἀφ-, καθ-)

ὑστέρημα,-ατος⁺   N3N 0-6-0-3-0-9
Jgs 18,10; 19,19.20

shortcoming, deficiency; neol.

Cf. SPICQ 1982, 669-670; →NIDNTT; TWNT

ὑστεροβουλία,-ας   N1F 0-0-0-1-0-1
Prv 31,3

deliberation after the facts, remorse, wisdom after the events, hindsight; *Prv 31,3 εἰς ὑστερο-βουλίαν *to have remorse* -מַלְכִין *thoughts, counsel* for MT מַלְכִין kings; neol.

ὕστερον D 0-0-5-3-7-15
Jer 27(50),17; 36(29),2; 38(31),19(bis); 47(40),1
afterward(s), later
Cf. SPICQ 1982, 670; →NIDNTT

ὕστερος,-α,-ον⁺ A 0-1-0-0-4-5
1 Chr 29,29; 3 Mc 5,49; Wis 19,11; PSal 2,28;
LtJ 71
latter, later (opp. to πρότερος) 1 Chr 29,29
ἐφ' ὑστέρῳ *later, in the end* Wis 19,11; ἐξ
ὑστέρου *later, afterwards* LtJ 71
ὕστατος *last, final* 3 Mc 5,49
Cf. SPICQ 1982, 670; →NIDNTT

ὑφαίνω⁺ V 3-10-1-0-0-14
Ex 35,35; 37(38),21; Lv 19,19; Jgs 16,13
to weave [τι] Ex 35,35; *id.* [abs.] 2 Chr 2,13; οἱ
ὑφαίνοντες *the weavers* 1 Sm 17,7
Cf. LE BOULLUEC 1989, 68; SHIPP 1979, 548
(→δι-, καθ-, συγκαθ-, συν-)

ὑφαιρέω V 0-0-0-3-1-4
Jb 21,18; 27,20; Eccl 2,10; LtJ 9
A: *to take away (from under)* [τι] Eccl 2,10
M: *to take away from, to filch away* [τι] LtJ 9;
to take up [τι] Jb 21,18

ὑφάντης,-ου N1M 4-0-0-0-0-4
Ex 26,1; 28,32; 37,3.5(36,35.37)
weaver
Cf. LE BOULLUEC 1989, 68.266

ὑφαντός,-ή,-όν⁺ A 9-0-0-0-0-9
Ex 26,31; 28,6; 35,35; 36,10.12(39,3.5)
woven
Cf. LE BOULLUEC 1989, 68.266.272.354

ὑφάπτω V 0-0-0-0-3-3
2 Mc 8,33; 12,9; 14,41
to set fire to [τι] 2 Mc 12,9; *to burn* [τινα] 2 Mc
8,33

ὕφασμα,-ατος N3N 4-2-0-1-0-7
Ex 28,8.17; 36,17.28(39,10.21); Jgs 16,14
woven cloth
Cf. LE BOULLUEC 1989, 68.283

ὑφίστημι⁺ V 1-4-7-7-8-27
Nm 22,26; Jos 7,12; Jgsᴮ 9,15; 1 Sm 30,10; 2 Sm
2,23
M: *to place for, to set up for* [τί τινι] Zech 9,8
to stand Nm 22,26; *to stand still* 2 Sm 2,23; *to
remain behind* 1 Sm 30,10; *to stand under, to
take refuge* [ἐν τινι] Jgsᴮ 9,15
to stand ground, to withstand, to resist Jos 7,12;
id. [τι] Jdt 6,3; *id.* [τινα] 1 Mc 5,40; *to endure*
[τι] Prv 13,8; *id.* [abs.] Ez 22,14; *to bear, to*

stand [τινα] Prv 27,4
Cf. DÖRRIE 1955, 40-41; HELBING 1928, 88; →NIDNTT;
TWNT

ὑφοράω V 0-0-0-0-2-2
2 Mc 7,24; 3 Mc 3,23
M: *to suspect*
Cf. LEE, J. 1969, 242

ὑψαυχενέω V 0-0-0-0-2-2
2 Mc 15,6; 3 Mc 3,19
to carry the neck high, to show off [abs.] 2 Mc
15,6; *to show off against, to lift the head against*
[τινι] 3 Mc 3,19; neol.

ὑψηλοκάρδιος,-ος,-ον A 0-0-0-1-0-1
Prv 16,5
high-hearted, proud; neol.

ὑψηλός,-ή,-όν⁺ A 24-67-63-35-28-217
Gn 7,19.20; 12,6; 22,2; Ex 6,1
cultic high place 1 Kgs 3,2
high, lofty Gn 7,19; *high, elevated, fortified* Neh
9,25; *high* (of pers.) 1 Sm 9,2; *high, proud,
haughty* 1 Sm 2,3; *upraised, mighty* Ex 6,1; *loud*
Prv 9,3; *sublime* Prv 10,21; τὰ ὑψηλά *cultic high
places* (outside the Pentateuch frequently
stereotypical rendition of בָּמָה) 1 Kgs 3,2
ὑψηλῷ τραχήλῳ *with outstretched neck, haughtily*
Is 3,16
*Gn 12,6 τὴν ὑψηλήν *high* -מָרוֹם? or -מָרֵת? (cpr. Is
45,14) for MT מוֹרֶה *Moreh*, see also Dt 11,30; cpr.
Gn 22,2; *Is 10,34 σὺν τοῖς ὑψηλοῖς *with its
mighty ones*? -בָּאֲרִירִיו for MT בָּאַדִּיר *by a mighty one*
ὑψηλότερος *higher* Dnᵀʰ 8,3; *the highest*
(comparison between two without gen.) Dnᴸˣˣ
8,3(secundo)
Cf. DANIEL 1966, 35-37.45-48.50-52.249.379; DOGNIEZ
1992, 98; HARL 1986ᵃ, 192.195; 1990=1992ᵃ, 138; LE
BOULLUEC 1989, 111.163; ROST 1967, 130-132; →NIDNTT

ὕψιστος,-η,-ον⁺ A 6-1-4-61-68-140
Gn 14,18.19.20.22; Nm 24,16
highest, loftiest (of places) Sir 26,16; *Most High*
(of the Lord) Gn 14,18; *highest, most high* (of
things) Sir 47,8
Cf. DODD 1954, 11-13; HAHNHART 1992, 348-349; 1994,
89; HARL 1986ᵃ, 52.160-161; HORSLEY 1981, 25-28;
KRAABEL 1969, 81-93; MUNNICH 1995, 147-148; SIMON
1972, 372-385; →NIDNTT; TWNT

ὕψος,-ους⁺ N3N 10-35-33-25-25-128
Gn 6,15; Ex 25,10.23; 27,1.14
height (of sth) Gn 6,15; *high place* 2 Sm 1,19;
height, summit 2 Kgs 19,23; *height* (opp. to
βάθος) Is 7,11

exaltation 2 Chr 32,26; *majesty* Is 35,2;
haughtiness Is 10,12
(τὰ) ὕψη *(the) heights* Jgs 5,18
ἐξ ὕψους *from above* 2 Sm 22,17; ἀδικίαν εἰς
τὸ ὕψος ἐλάλησαν *they have uttered
unrighteousness loftily* Ps 72(73),8; ἐν τῷ ὕψει
τῶν ἡμερῶν μου *at the height of my days, in my
best years* Is 38,10
*Is 38,10 ἐν τῷ ὕψει *in the summit* (of age)
-רום/ב? for MT ב/רמי *in the silence?*; *Jer 6,2 τὸ
ὕψος *the exaltation, the pride* -רום for MT Iרמיתי
have likened?; *Ez 43,13 τὸ ὕψος *the height* -גבה
for MT גב *mound?*; *Am 5,7 εἰς ὕψος *on a high
level* -למעלה? for MT ללענה *to wormwood*
Cf. DANIEL 1966, 35-37.50-52; →NIDNTT; TWNT

ὑψόω⁺   V 15-19-47-87-31-199
Gn 7,17.20.24; 19,13; 24,35
A: *to lift high, to raise up* [τι] Ezr 9,9; *to set sb
upon sth* [τινα ἐν τινι] Ps 26(27),5; *to take up*
[τι] 2 Kgs 2,13
to raise, to lift up (the voice) [τι] Gn 39,15; *to
raise* (a song) [τι] Ezr 3,12
to set on high [τινα] (metaph.) 2 Sm 22,49; *to
elevate, to exalt* [τινα] Ex 15,2; *id.* [τι] Tobᴮᴬ
12,6
M: *to rise* Jb 39,27
P: *to be lifted up* Gn 7,17; *to be exalted* Dt 8,14
*Dnᴸˣˣ 12,1 ὑψωθήσεται *shall be exalted* corr.?
σωθήσεται (=Dnᵀʰ 12,1) for MT ימלט *shall be
delivered*; *Nm 32,35 καὶ ὕψωσαν αὐτάς *they
raised them up* -גבה◊ for MT ויגבהה *and Jogbehah*;

*Is 19,13 ὑψώθησαν *they are lifted up* -נשא for
MT נשא *they are deluded*; *Jer 38(31),35 ἐὰν
ὑψωθῇ *if (the sky) should be raised* -ירמו אם for
MT אם ימרו *if (the sky) should be measured*; *Mi
6,12 ὑψώθη *has been exalted* רום◊ for MT רמיה
deceit; *Hab 2,19 ὑψώθητι *be exalted* -רומם or
-רום◊ רומי for MT דומם *silent*, cpr. Ps 130(131),2;
*Ps 36(37),20 καὶ ὑψωθῆναι *and to be exalted*
-כ/רום for MT כרים *pastures*; *Ps 60(61),3 ὑψωσάς
με *you lifted me* -תרוממני for MT ממני ירום *higher
than I*; *Ps 63(64),8 καὶ ὑψωθήσεται ὁ θεός
and God shall be exalted רום◊ ויָרם אלהים for MT
רמהו ויר/ם אלהים *and God will shoot them*
Cf. ALLEN 1974, 42.49(1 Chr 17,17); →NIDNTT; TWNT
(→ἀν-, ἐξ-, προσ-, ὑπερ-)

ὕψωμα,-ατος⁺   N3N 0-0-0-1-3-4
Jb 24,24; Jdt 10,8; 13,4; 15,9
exaltation Jdt 10,8
*Jb 24,24 τὸ ὕψωμα αὐτοῦ *his exaltation* -רומו?
for MT רומו *they exalted themselves*
neol.
Cf. DANIEL 1966, 51.52; →NIDNTT; TWNT

ὕψωσις,-εως   N3F 0-0-0-1-0-1
Ps 149,6
lifting up high, exaltation; neol.

ὕω   V 2-0-0-0-0-2
Ex 9,18; 16,4
to cause to rain (hailstones) [τι] Ex 9,18; *id.*
(bread) [τι] (metaph.) Ex 16,4
Cf. LE BOULLUEC 1989, 181; LEE, J. 1983, 122-124; SHIPP
1979, 176

φαζ N 0-0-0-1-0-1
Ct 5,11
= ᵱ refined gold

φαιδρός,-ά,-όν A 0-0-0-0-1-1
4 Mc 13,13
of cheerful countenance, cheerful

φαίνω⁺ V 11-5-5-15-30-66
Gn 1,15.17; 21,11; 30,37; 35,22
A: to give light, to shine [abs.] Gn 1,15; id. [τι]
Ez 32,8
M: to appear (of pers.) Tobˢ 6,17; id. Gn 30,37
to seem to [τινι] Neh 4,1; to seem Gn 21,11; to
appear to be [+inf.] 4 Mc 1,32
ἂν φαίνηταί σοι if it seems good to you 1 Ezr
2,16
→NIDNTT; TWNT
(→ἀνα-, ἀπο-, δια-, ἐκ-, ἐμ-, ἐπι-, κατα-, προ-,
ὑπο-)

φαιός,-ά,-όν A 3-0-0-0-0-3
Gn 30,32.33.35
gray
Cf. HARL 1986ᵃ, 231

φακός,-οῦ N2M 1-8-1-0-0-10
Gn 25,34; 1 Sm 10,1; 26,11.12.16
lentil Gn 25,34; gourd-like container (bottle
shaped like a gourd; homoeophonic with ᵱ also
in 2 Kgs 9,1.3) 1 Sm 10,1
Cf. BARR 1985, 62-63; CAIRD 1976, 82; TOV 1979, 221;
WALTERS 1973, 195-196

φάλαγξ,-αγγος N3F 0-0-0-0-5-5
1 Mc 6,35.38.45; 9,12; 10,82
rank, battle, line, phalanx

φαλακρός,-ά,-όν A 1-1-1-0-0-3
Lv 13,40; 2 Kgs 2,23; Ez 29,18
bald Lv 13,40; (ὁ) φαλακρός bald man, bald
head 2 Kgs 2,23

φαλάκρωμα,-ατος N3N 5-0-5-0-0-10
Lv 13,42(bis).43; 21,5; Dt 14,1
baldness, bald head; neol.
Cf. DOGNIEZ 1992, 65.203; HARLÉ 1988, 139; WEVERS
1995, 240

φανερός,-ά,-όν⁺ A 2-0-3-4-10-19
Gn 42,16; Dt 29,28; Is 8,16; 33,9; 64,1
clear Gn 42,16; clear, evident, apparent Prv 14,4;
known, revealed Dt 29,28; manifest (of pers.) Is
8,16; manifest, bare (of land) Is 33,9
Cf. DODD 1954, 237; →NIDNTT; TWNT

φανερόω⁺ V 0-0-1-0-0-1
Jer 40(33),6
to reveal to sb to do [τινι +inf.]

→NIDNTT; TWNT

φανερῶς⁺ D 0-0-0-0-1-1
2 Mc 3,28
manifestly
→NIDNTT

-φανίζω
(→ἐμ-)

φαντάζω⁺ V 0-0-0-0-2-2
Wis 6,16; Sir 34,5
M: to appear
→NIDNTT; TWNT

φαντασία,-ας⁺ N1F 0-0-4-0-2-6
Hab 2,18.19; 3,10; Zech 10,1; Od 4,10
appearance Hab 2,18; vision Wis 18,17; sign
(from God) Zech 10,1
*Hab 2,18 φαντασία appearance -מראה for MT
מורה teacher, see also 2,19; 3,10
Cf. BICKERMAN 1980, 181; SHIPP 1979, 552

φαντασιοκοπέω V 0-0-0-0-1-1
Sir 4,30
to play a role, to act in pretence; neol.

φάντασμα,-ατος⁺ N3N 0-0-0-0-1-1
Wis 17,14
apparition, delusion
Cf. LARCHER 1985, 971; →NIDNTT; TWNT

φάραγξ,-αγγος⁺ N3F 17-22-34-5-8-86
Gn 14,3; 26,17.19; Nm 13,23.24
ravine Gn 14,3; valley Jos 13,9
Cf. DOGNIEZ 1992, 97.128.243; WALTERS 1973, 187.189;
→MM

φαρασιν N 0-1-0-0-0-1
1 Chr 14,11
= פרצים Perasim (proper name)

φαρες N 0-0-0-4-0-4
DnᴸˣˣX 5,prol.(bis); DnᵀʰTh 5,25.28
= פרס half-mina (unit of measurement)

φαρέτρα,-ας N1F 1-0-5-3-1-10
Gn 27,3; Is 22,6; 49,2; Jer 28(51),11.12
quiver (for arrows)

φαρμακεία,-ας⁺ N1F 4-0-2-0-2-8
Ex 7,11.22; 8,3.14; Is 47,9
sorcery, magic
Cf. WEVERS 1990, 97; →NIDNTT

φαρμακεύω⁺ V 0-1-0-1-1-3
2 Chr 33,6; Ps 57(58),6; 2 Mc 10,13
M: to practise magic 2 Chr 33,6
P: to be mixed with poison Ps 57(58),6
φαρμακεύσας ἑαυτόν he who poisoned himself
2 Mc 10,13

φάρμακον,-ου⁺ N2N 0-1-3-0-8-12

2 Kgs 9,22; Mi 5,11; Na 3,4(bis); Tobˢ 2,10
medicament Tobˢ 2,10; *poison* Wis 1,14; *magical*
potion Mi 5,11; *medicine* (metaph.) Sir 6,16
Cf. LARCHER 1983, 203; →NIDNTT

φαρμακός,-οῦ⁺   N2M/F 5-0-2-6-0-13
Ex 7,11; 9,11(bis); 22,17; Dt 18,10
mixer of magical potions, sorcerer, magician Ex
7,11; *id.* (fem.) Mal 3,5
Cf. DOGNIEZ 1992, 50; LE BOULLUEC 1989, 36; WALTERS
1973, 95-96; WEVERS 1990, 98; 1995, 299; →NIDNTT

φαρουρμι   N 0-1-0-0-0-1
2 Kgs 23,11
= פרורים *courts*
Cf. TOV 1973, 89

φάρυγξ,-υγγος   N3M 0-1-1-5-2-9
1 Sm 17,35; Jer 2,25; Prv 5,3; 8,7; 24,13
throat

φασεκ   N N 0-6-1-0-0-7
2 Chr 30,1.2.5.15.17
= פסח *Passover*
Cf. WALTERS 1973, 169-170.248-249

φασεχ   N N 0-12-0-0-0-12
2 Chr 35,1(bis).6.7.8
= פסח *Passover*
Cf. WALTERS 1973, 249

-φασίζομαι
(→προ-)

φάσις,-εως⁺   N3F 0-0-0-0-1-1
Susᵀʰ 55
judgement, sentence

φάσκω⁺   V 1-0-0-0-4-5
Gn 26,20; 2 Mc 14,27.32; 3 Mc 3,7; Belᴸˣˣ 8
to say, to assert [+inf.]

φάσμα,-ατος   N3N 1-0-1-1-1-4
Nm 16,30; Is 28,7; Jb 20,8; Wis 17,4
apparition, delusion Jb 20,8; *phantom* Wis 17,4
*Nm 16,30 ἐν φάσματι δείξει *he shall show by*
a sign from heaven, he shall perform a miracle
-יִרְאֶה בָּרָא֒ for MT יִבְרָא בְּרִיאָה ראה֒ *he shall*
create a creation, he shall create something new,
see also Is 28,7
Cf. DORIVAL 1994, 94; LARCHER 1985, 953-954

φάτνη,-ης⁺   N1F 0-1-3-3-1-8
2 Chr 32,28; Is 1,3; Jl 1,17; Hab 3,17; Jb 6,5
manger Prv 14,4; *stall* 2 Chr 32,28
*Jl 1,17 ἐπὶ ταῖς φάτναις αὐτῶν *at their*
mangers -ברפתיהם for MT מגרפתיהם *their shovels*
→TWNT

φατνόω   V 0-1-1-0-0-2
1 Kgs 7,40(3); Ez 41,16

to roof [τι] 1 Kgs 7,40(3)
*Ez 41,16 πεφατνωμένα *ceiled* -ספונים for MT ספים
thresholds

φάτνωμα,-ατος⁺   N3N 0-0-3-1-1-5
Ez 41,20; Am 8,3; Zph 2,14; Ct 1,17; 2 Mc 1,16
coffered ceiling Ez 41,20; φατνώματα *rafters* Ct
1,17
*Am 8,3 τὰ φατνώματα *ceilings* -שדרות? for MT
שירות *songs*

φαυλίζω   V 2-1-5-5-3-16
Gn 25,34; Nm 15,31; 2 Sm 12,9; Is 33,19; 37,22
to despise, to consider worthless [τι] Gn 25,34;
id. [τινα] Jdt 11,2
Cf. HELBING 1928, 15
(→ἐκ-)

φαύλισμα,-ατος   N3N 0-0-1-0-0-1
Zph 3,11
contemptible act; neol.

φαυλισμός,-οῦ   N2M 0-0-3-0-0-3
Is 28,11; 51,7; Hos 7,16
contempt, contemptibility; neol.

φαυλίστριος,-α,-ον   A 0-0-1-0-0-1
Zph 2,15
showing contempt, contemptuous; neol.

φαῦλος,-η,-ον⁺   A 0-0-0-8-2-10
Jb 6,3.25; 9,23; Prv 5,3; 13,6
worthless (of pers.) Jb 9,23; *evil* 3 Mc 3,22; *vain*
Jb 6,3
*Prv 16,21 φαύλους *evil* -נבל◇ for MT נבון
intelligent
→NIDNTT

φαυλότης,-ητος   N3F 0-0-0-0-1-1
Wis 4,12
meanness, worthlessness

φαῦσις,-εως   N3F 2-0-0-1-1-4
Gn 1,14.15; Ps 73(74),16; Jdt 13,13
light Ps 73(74),16; *illumination* Gn 1,14; neol.
Cf. HARL 1986ᵃ, 92

-φαύσκω
(→δια-, ἐπι-)

φέγγος,-ους⁺   N3N 0-2-13-4-5-24
2 Sm 22,13; 23,4; Ez 1,4(bis).13
light, splendour, lustre Ez 10,4; *light* (of the day)
Jb 3,4; *id.* (of the stars) Jl 2,10

φείδομαι⁺   V 12-10-29-26-18-95
Gn 19,16; 20,6; 22,12.16; 45,20
to spare [τινος] Jb 20,13; *id.* [ἐπί τινι] Jer
27(50),14; *id.* [ἐπί τινα] 2 Sm 21,7; *id.* [ἀπό
τινος] 1 Sm 15,3; *id.* [περί τινος] 2 Sm 12,6;
id. [abs.] Jb 6,10

to have pity on [τινος] Ex 2,6; *id.* [ὑπέρ τινος]
Jon 4,10; *id.* [ἐπί τινα] Jdt 2,11

to refrain [τινος] Prv 10,19; *to restrain, to stop*
[τινος] 2 Sm 18,16; *to refrain* [τι] Jb 30,10; *id.*
[abs.] Prv 24,11; *to forbear to* [+inf.] Prv 17,27
μὴ φείσησθε τοῖς ὀφθαλμοῖς τῶν σκευῶν ὑμῶν
let your eyes not spare your property (lit.), *do not
take care of your property* Gn 45,20, see also Ez
9,5; ἀτὰρ οὖν οὐδὲ ἐγὼ φείσομαι τῷ στόματί
μου *then neither will I restrain my mouth* Jb 7,11
*Eccl 2,25 φείσεται *he shall be sparing* יחוס for
MT יחוש *he can enjoy himself*

Cf. DE WAARD 1979, 522; HARL 1986ᵃ, 292; HELBING
1928, 161-164; LARCHER 1983, 191; LE BOULLUEC 1989,
81-82

φειδώ,-οῦς   N3F 0-0-0-1-2-3
Est 3,13f; Wis 12,18; PSal 5,13
sparing Est 3,13f
μετὰ φειδοῦς *with forbearing, with fairness, with
gentleness* Wis 12,18

Cf. LARCHER 1985, 729

φειδωλός,-ή/ός,-όν   A 0-0-0-0-1-1
4 Mc 2,9
sparing, thrifty

φελεθθι   N M 0-3-0-0-0-3
1 Kgs 1,38.44; 1 Chr 18,17
= פלתי *Peletite*

Φελλανι   N 0-1-0-0-0-1
1 Sm 21,3
= פלני *a certain person* (as part of the expression
פלני ואלמוני, cpr. 2 Kgs 6,8; Ruᴹᵀ 4,1)

Cf. TOV 1973, 89

φελμουνι   N 0-0-0-2-0-2
Dn 8,13
= פלמוני *a certain person*

Cf. TOV 1973, 89

Φερεζαίων   N 1-1-0-0-0-2
Dt 3,5; 1 Sm 6,18
= פרזי *unwalled*

Cf. TOV 1973, 89

φερνή,-ῆς   N1F 3-1-0-0-1-5
Gn 34,12; Ex 22,15.16; Jos 16,10; 2 Mc 1,14
dowry 2 Mc 1,14; *bridal price* Gn 34,12

Cf. BICKERMAN 1956=1976, 210-211.213; HARL 1974,
246.256; 1986ᵃ, 249; LE BOULLUEC 1989, 228; LLEWELYN
1992, 2.16

φερνίζω   V 1-0-0-0-0-1
Ex 22,15
to pay the bridal price, to obtain as wife [τινα]

Cf. WEVERS 1990, 349

φέρω⁺   V 69-76-45-55-45-290
Gn 4,3.4; 27,4.7.13

A: *to bear* [τινα] Gn 36,7; *id.* [τι] Ex 28,30; *to
carry, to carry away* [τινα] Is 64,5; *to bring* [τι]
Gn 4,3; *to bring, to offer* (an anim.) [τινα] Lv
5,7; *id.* [τι] Jgsᴬ 6,18; *to bear, to produce* (fruit)
[τι] Hag 2,19; *to bear, to endure* [τι] Dt 1,12; *to
bear, to lead* [τινα] Nm 11,14; *to lead, to direct,
to incline sb to do* [τινα +inf.] Ex 35,29; *to
stretch, to extend* Jos 15,2

M: *to give to sb* [τί τινι] Sir 47,6; *to fling* 2 Mc
3,25

P: *to be carried, to be moved* Jb 17,1; *to be
shaken* (of leaves) Lv 26,36; *to gush out* 2 Mc
14,45

φέρετε ἑαυτοῖς βουλήν *deliberate among
yourselves* 2 Sm 16,20; μὴ βαρέως φέρε *be not
indignant* Gn 31,35; καταιγὶς φερομένη *rushing
storm* Is 28,15
*Gn 49,3 φέρεσθαι *to endure* -נשׂא for MT שׂאת
dignity

Cf. BICKERMAN 1980, 178(n.118); DORIVAL 1994, 53.325;
WEVERS 1990, 584; →TWNT

(→ἀνα-, ἀπο-, δια-, εἰσ-, ἐκ-, ἐμ-, ἐπεισ-, ἐπι-,
κατα-, μετα-, παρα-, περι-, προ-, προεκ-,
προσ-, προσανα-, συγκατα-, συμ-, συμπερι-,
συνανα-, ὑπερ-, ὑπο-)

φεύγω⁺   V 26-101-46-13-64-250
Gn 14,10(bis); 39,12.13.15

to flee Gn 14,10; *to have recourse to, to take
refuge in* [εἰς τινα] Is 20,6; *to flee* [τι] Wis 1,5;
id. [τινα] Is 27,1; *to shun* [τι] (in moral sense)
4 Mc 8,19; *to escape* [τι] Wis 16,15; *to vanish,
to disappear from* [ἀπό τινος] Ps 67(68),2
*1 Chr 21,12 φεύγειν σε *your fleeing* -נסכה for
MT נספה *swept away*; *Is 10,18 ὡς ὁ φεύγων *he
that flees* -נוס for MT כמסס *as the wasting away*
(*of a sick man*); *Is 31,9 ὁ φεύγων *he that flees*
-נוס for MT נסס ◊ מנס *from the standard*; *Jer 4,6
φεύγετε *flee* -נס֫ל for MT נֵס *a signal*, see also 4,21;
*Jer 26(46),15 ἔφυγεν ὁ ᵀἈπις *Apis fled* -נס חף
for MT נסחף *he was swept away*; *Am 6,5 οὐχ ὡς
φεύγοντα *not as fleeing* -בלי שׂור *without receding*
for MT כלי שׂיר *musical instruments*

Cf. HELBING 1928, 27-29; LEE, J. 1983, 28; WALTERS 1973,
256; WEVERS 1990, 222; →NIDNTT

(→ἀπο-, δια-, ἐκ-, κατα-, συμ-)

φευκτός,-ή,-όν   A 0-0-0-0-1-1
Wis 17,9
avoidable, that can be avoided

φήμη,-ης⁺   N1F 0-0-0-1-3-4
Prv 15,30; 2 Mc 4,39; 3 Mc 3,2; 4 Mc 4,22
report, news

φημί⁺   V 7-4-26-5-31-73
Gn 24,47; Ex 2,6; Nm 24,3(bis).4
A: *to say, to affirm, to assert* Gn 24,47; *id.*
[+inf.] Est 10,31; *to say, to declare* Nm 24,3
M: *to say* [+inf.] Jb 24,25
Cf. DORIVAL 1994, 445; →NIDNTT

-φημίζω
(→ἐπι-)

φθάνω⁺   V 0-5-0-16-6-27
Jgs^B 20,34.42; 2 Sm 20,13; 1 Kgs 12,18; 2 Chr
28,9
to forestall, to come before, to precede [τινα]
Wis 6,13; *id.* [τι] Wis 16,28; *to be the first to do*
[+inf.] 1 Kgs 12,18
to overtake [ἐπί τινα] Jgs^B 20,34; *id.* [πρός
τινα] Eccl 8,14
to reach [εἰς τι] Dn^Th 6,25; *id.* [τινι] Tob 5,19;
id. [ἕως τινός] Dn^Th 4,11; *id.* [ἕως τινός] (of
time) Dn^Th 7,13; *to arrive* Ct 2,12
ἐὰν φθάσῃ τελευτῆσαι *when he dies before his
time* Wis 4,7
Cf. CARAGOUNIS 1989, 12-15.20-23; HELBING 1928,
104-105; LARCHER 1984, 325.419-420; →TWNT
(→κατα-, προ-)

φθάρμα,-ατος   N3N 1-0-0-0-0-1
Lv 22,25
corrupted thing or *act*; neol.
Cf. HARLÉ 1988, 186

φθαρτός,-ή,-όν⁺   A 0-0-1-0-3-4
Is 54,17; 2 Mc 7,16; Wis 9,15; 14,8
perishable, corruptible
Cf. LARCHER 1985, 801; →TWNT

φθέγγομαι⁺   V 0-1-5-5-4-15
Jgs^A 5,11(10); Jer 9,16; 28(51),14; Am 1,2; Na
2,8
to speak Wis 8,12; *to utter* [τι] Jb 13,7; *to utter
sounds* (of anim.) Na 2,8
(→ἀπο-)

φθέγμα,-ατος   N3N 0-0-0-1-1-2
Jb 6,26; Wis 1,11
sound Jb 6,26; *utterance, saying* Wis 1,11

φθειρίζω   V 0-0-2-0-0-2
Jer 50(43),12(bis)
to pick the lice off [τι]

φθείρω⁺   V 4-1-6-7-2-20
Gn 6,11; Ex 10,15; Lv 19,27; Dt 34,7; 1 Chr 20,1
A: *to destroy, to mar* [τι] Lv 19,27; *to destroy, to*

ravage [τι] 1 Chr 20,1; *to corrupt* [τινα] 4 Mc
18,8; *to seduce* [τινα] Ez 16,52; *to punish by
destroying* [τι] Jer 13,9
P: *to be morally corrupted* Gn 6,11
*Ex 10,15 ἐφθάρη *it was destroyed* -חשׁת for MT
חשׁך *it was darkened*; *Jb 15,32 φθαρήσεται *it
shall wither* -תמל for MT תמלא *it shall be completed*
Cf. LE BOULLUEC 1989, 138; WEVERS 1990, 153; →NIDNTT;
TWNT
(→δια-, κατα-)

φθίνω⁺   V 0-0-0-1-0-1
Jb 31,26
to wane (of the moon)

φθόγγος,-ου⁺   N2M 0-0-0-1-1-2
Ps 18(19),5; Wis 19,18
sound, tone Wis 19,18; *voice* Ps 18(19),5
Cf. LARCHER 1985, 1084

φθονερός,-ά,-όν   A 0-0-0-0-1-1
Sir 14,10
envious

φθονέω⁺   V 0-0-0-0-2-2
Tob^BA 4,7.16
to be envious
→NIDNTT

φθόνος,-ου⁺   N2M 0-0-0-0-4-4
1 Mc 8,16; 3 Mc 6,7; Wis 2,24; 6,23
envy 1 Mc 8,16; *envious fool play* Wis 2,24
Cf. SPICQ 1978ᵃ, 919-921; →NIDNTT

φθορά,-ᾶς⁺   N1F 1-0-3-3-4-11
Ex 18,18; Is 24,3; Jon 2,7; Mi 2,10; Ps
102(103),4
destruction, ruin, decay Is 24,3; *depravity,
corruption* (in physical and moral sense) Ex
18,18
Cf. LE BOULLUEC 1989, 196; WEVERS 1990, 284; →NIDNTT;
TWNT

φθορεύς,-έως   N3M 0-0-0-0-1-1
4 Mc 18,8
corruptor; neol.

φιάλη,-ης⁺   N1F 17-9-3-4-2-35
Ex 27,3; 38,23(38,3); Nm 4,14; 7,13.19
shallow bowl, cup
Cf. HARL 1991=1992ᵃ, 148; WEVERS 1990, 432.472.629;
→MM

φιλάγαθος,-ος,-ον⁺   A 0-0-0-0-1-1
Wis 7,22
loving goodness; neol.
Cf. SPICQ 1982, 671-673; →NIDNTT

φιλαδελφία,-ας⁺   N1F 0-0-0-0-3-3
4 Mc 13,23.26; 14,1

brotherly love
→MM; NIDNTT

φιλάδελφος,-ος,-ον⁺ A 0-0-0-0-3-3
2 Mc 15,14; 4 Mc 13,21; 15,10
loving one's brother and/or sister 4 Mc 13,21;
loving one's fellow-countrymen 2 Mc 15,14
Cf. HORSLEY 1983, 87; →NIDNTT

φιλαμαρτήμων,-ων,-ον A 0-0-0-1-0-1
Prv 17,19
loving sin; neol.

φιλανθρωπέω V 0-0-0-0-1-1
2 Mc 13,23
to treat kindly, to deal kindly with [τινα]; neol.?
Cf. HELBING 1928, 11

φιλανθρωπία,-ας⁺ N1F 0-0-0-1-4-5
Est 8,12l; 2 Mc 6,22; 14,9; 3 Mc 3,15.18
philantropy Est 8,21l; *clemence* 2 Mc 14,9
Cf. BELL 1949, 31-37; HORSLEY 1981, 87; HUNGER 1963,
1-20; LE DÉAUT 1964, 255-294; PELLETIER 1979, 14-15;
SPICQ 1978ᵃ, 922-927; →MM; NIDNTT; TWNT

φιλάνθρωπος,-ος,-ον⁺ A 0-0-0-0-6-6
1 Ezr 8,10; 2 Mc 4,11; 4 Mc 5,12; Wis 1,6; 7,23
kindly, appealing to human feeling 4 Mc 5,12;
merciful (of pers.) Wis 12,19; τὰ φιλάνθρωπα
the privileges 2 Mc 4,11
Cf. HORSLEY 1981,88; LARCHER 1983, 179; 1984, 489;
PELLETIER 1980, 397-403; →NIDNTT

φιλανθρώπως⁺ D 0-0-0-0-2-2
2 Mc 9,27; 3 Mc 3,20
with kindness
Cf. SPICQ 1978ᵃ, 922-927; →TWNT

φιλαργυρέω⁺ V 0-0-0-0-1-1
2 Mc 10,20
to love money
Cf. SPICQ 1978ᵃ, 928-929

φιλαργυρία,-ας⁺ N1F 0-0-0-0-1-1
4 Mc 1,26
love of money
Cf. SPICQ 1978ᵃ, 928-929; →NIDNTT

φιλάργυρος,-ος,-ον⁺ A 0-0-0-0-1-1
4 Mc 2,8
loving money, fond of money
Cf. SPICQ 1978ᵃ, 53-56.928-929; →NIDNTT

φιλαρχία,-ας N1F 0-0-0-0-1-1
4 Mc 2,15
love of power, lust for power, ambition

φιλελεήμων,-ων,-ον A 0-0-0-0-1-1
TobᴮᴬA 14,9
merciful; neol.

φιλεχθρέω V 0-0-0-1-0-1

Prv 3,30
*to exercise enmity against, to be ready to quarrel
with* [πρός τινα]; neol.

φιλέω⁺ V 12-1-3-12-5-33
Gn 27,4.9.14.26.27
to love [τινα] Est 10,3; *to kiss* [τινα] (between
parents and children) Gn 27,26; *id.* [τινα]
(between a whore and a man) Prv 7,13; *to like,
to be fond of* [τι] Prv 21,17; *to kiss* [τι] Est
4,17d; *to love to do, to like to do* [+inf.] Is 56,10
*Jer 22,22 τῶν φιλούντων σε *of those who love
you* - רֵעַיִךְ for MT רָעָתֵךְ *your depravity*
Cf. BARR 1987, 3-18; HORSLEY 1983, 15; JOLY 1968,
49-51; PAESLACK 1954, 51-99; SHIPP 1979, 126-127;
STEINMÜLLER 1951, 404-413; SWINN 1990, 49-81; →NIDNTT;
TWNT
(→κατα-)

φιλӗκοΐα,-ας N1F 0-0-0-0-1-1
4 Mc 15,21
fondness for listening to

φίλημα,-ατος⁺ N3N 0-0-0-2-0-2
Prv 27,6; Ct 1,2
kiss
Cf. KLASSEN 1993, 122-135; →NIDNTT; TWNT

φιλία,-ας⁺ N1F 0-0-0-9-27-36
Prv 5,19(bis); 7,18; 10,12; 15,17
friendship Sir 22,20; *affection, tenderness* (in the
family) 4 Mc 2,11; *love* (of lovers in erotic
sense) Prv 7,18; *love* (towards God) Wis 7,14;
treaty of friendship 2 Mc 4,11
Cf. BARR 1987, 3-18; LARCHER 1984, 547; PAESLACK 1954,
74-82; SWINN 1990, 51; →NIDNTT

φιλιάζω V 0-4-0-0-2-6
Jgsᴬ 5,30; Jgsᴮ 14,20; 2 Chr 19,2; 20,37; 1 Ezr
3,22
*to be friends with, to act friendly towards, to act
as a friend to* [τινι]
*Jgsᴬ 5,30 φιλιάζων φίλοις *he will be friendly
towards his friends* - רחם for MT רחמתים רחם *one or
two girls*, cpr. οἰκτίρμων
neol.?
Cf. HELBING 1928, 213

φιλογέωργος,-ος,-ον A 0-1-0-0-0-1
2 Chr 26,10
fond of husbandry, fond of agriculture

φιλογύναιος,-ος,-ον A 0-1-0-0-0-1
1 Kgs 11,1
fond of women

φιλοδοξία,-ας N1F 0-0-0-1-1-2
Est 4,17d; 4 Mc 1,26

love of honour or *glory* or *fame*; neol.?
Cf. LLEWELYN 1994, 237

φιλόκοσμος,-ος,-ον   A 0-0-0-0-1-1
LtJ 8
fond of adornment; neol.?

φιλομαθέω   V 0-0-0-0-2-2
Sir prol.,5.34
to love learning, to be fond of learning; neol.?

φιλομαθής,-ής,-ές   A 0-0-0-0-1-1
Sir prol.,13
loving learning, fond of learning, eager for knowledge

φιλομήτωρ (gen.: -ορος)   A 0-0-0-0-1-1
4 Mc 15,10
loving one's mother; neol.

φιλονεικέω   V 0-0-0-1-0-1
Prv 10,12
to love argument or *strife, to be contentious*
Cf. WALTERS 1973, 34.35

φιλονεικία,-ας⁺   N1F 0-0-0-0-3-3
2 Mc 4,4; 4 Mc 1,26; 8,26
contentiousness 4 Mc 1,26; *dispute, strife* 2 Mc 4,4
→NIDNTT

φιλόνεικος,-ος,-ον⁺   A 0-0-1-0-0-1
Ez 3,7
contentious, stubborn
Cf. WALTERS 1973, 35; →NIDNTT

φιλοπολίτης,-ου   N1M 0-0-0-0-1-1
2 Mc 14,37
lover of one's countrymen, lover of one's fellow-citizens, patriot; neol.

φιλοπονέω⁺   V 0-0-0-0-1-1
Sir prol.,20
P: *to be lovingly worked through*

φιλοπονία,-ας   N1F 0-0-0-0-1-1
Sir prol.,30
love of labour, industry

φίλος,-η,-ον⁺   A 2-5-7-62-111-187
Ex 33,11; Dt 13,7; Jgs^A 5,30; Jgs^B 14,20; 15,2
beloved 4 Mc 5,34; (ὁ) φίλος *(the) friend* Ex 33,11; *courtier* Est 6,9; φίλοι *associates* 1 Mc 2,39
τῶν πρώτων φίλων *among the Friends of the First Rank* (privileged member of the royal court) 1 Mc 10,65
*Jgs^A 5,30 φίλοις see φιλιάζω
Cf. BICKERMAN 1938, 40-50; BOGAERT 1984, 223-224; HORSLEY 1987, 17.18; LARCHER 1984, 508-509; LE BOHEC 1985, 93-124; PAESLACK 1954, 82-99; SPICQ 1978ᵃ,

936-939.940-943; SWINN 1990, 56; →NIDNTT; TWNT

φιλοσοφέω   V 0-0-0-0-4-4
4 Mc 5,7.11; 7,21; 8,1
to be philosopher 4 Mc 5,7; *to learn the philosophy of* [τι] 4 Mc 5,11; *to practise philosophical reasoning* 4 Mc 8,1
→NIDNTT
(→ἀντι-)

φιλοσοφία,-ας⁺   N1F 0-0-0-0-5-5
4 Mc 1,1; 5,11.22; 7,9.21
philosophy 4 Mc 5,11; *philosophical exposition* 4 Mc 1,1
Cf. KLAUCK 1989, 686; →NIDNTT; TWNT

φιλόσοφος,-ου⁺   N2M 0-0-0-1-3-4
Dn^LXX 1,20; 4 Mc 1,1; 5,35; 7,7
philosopher Dn^LXX 1,20
φιλόσοφος,-ος,-ον *loving wisdom* 4 Mc 5,35; φιλοσοφώτατος *most philosophical* 4 Mc 1,1
→NIDNTT; TWNT

φιλοστοργία,-ας⁺   N1F 0-0-0-0-3-3
2 Mc 6,20; 4 Mc 15,6.9
tender love, strong affection
Cf. HORSLEY 1982, 101-103; 1983, 41-42; SPICQ 1978ᵃ, 944-948

φιλόστοργος,-ος,-ον⁺   A 0-0-0-0-1-1
4 Mc 15,13
loving dearly, yearning
Cf. SPICQ 1978ᵃ, 944-948; →NIDNTT

φιλοστόργως   D 0-0-0-0-1-1
2 Mc 9,21
kindly

φιλοτεκνία,-ας   N1F 0-0-0-0-5-5
4 Mc 14,13; 15,11.23.25; 16,3
love of one's children, parental love, mother-love; neol.

φιλότεκνος,-ος,-ον⁺   A 0-0-0-0-3-3
4 Mc 15,4.5.6
loving one's children
→NIDNTT

φιλοτιμία,-ας⁺   N1F 0-0-0-0-1-1
Wis 14,18
love of honour, ambition
Cf. LARCHER 1985, 818

φιλότιμος,-ος,-ον   A 0-0-0-0-2-2
3 Mc 4,15; Wis 18,3
glorious, worthy of emulation Wis 18,3; *intense, zealous* 3 Mc 4,15
Cf. LARCHER 1985, 989

φιλοτίμως   D 0-0-0-0-2-2
2 Mc 2,21; Sus^Th 12

honourably 2 Mc 2,21; *diligently, intensely* SusTh 12

φιλοφρονέω V 0-0-0-0-1-1
2 Mc 2,25
to be of a friendly disposition towards, to be of a kindly mind towards [εἴς τι]

φιλοφρόνως⁺ D 0-0-0-0-2-2
2 Mc 3,9; 4 Mc 8,5
in a friendly manner, hospitably, honourably 2 Mc 3,9; *obligingly, benevolently* 4 Mc 8,5; neol.
Cf. WALTERS 1973, 310; →NIDNTT

φιλόψυχος,-ος,-ον A 0-0-0-0-1-1
Wis 11,26
loving human beings, loving men
Cf. LARCHER 1985, 697

φίλτρον,-ου N2N 0-0-0-0-3-3
4 Mc 13,19.27; 15,13
τὰ φίλτρα *love, affection*

φιμός,-οῦ N2M 0-0-1-1-1-3
Is 37,29; Jb 30,28; Sir 20,29
muzzle (metaph.) Jb 30,28; *bridle* Is 37,29

φιμόω⁺ V 1-0-0-0-2-3
Dt 25,4; 4 Mc 1,35; Sus^{LXX} 60
A: *to muzzle* (an ox) [τινα] Dt 25,4; *to gag* [τινα] Sus^{LXX} 60
P: *to be inhibited* 4 Mc 1,35

φλεγμαίνω V 0-0-2-0-0-2
Is 1,6; Na 3,19
to inflame, to become purulent

φλεγμονή,-ῆς N1F 0-0-0-0-1-1
4 Mc 3,17
heat, passion, fire (of strong feelings)

φλέγω⁺ V 2-0-3-3-4-12
Ex 24,17; Dt 32,22; Jer 20,9; 23,29; Mal 3,19
to set on fire [τι] Dt 32,22; *to burn, to consume* [τινα] Mal 3,19; *to burn* [intrans.] Ex 24,17
P: *to be burned, to burn* Wis 16,22; *to be roasted* 4 Mc 15,14; *to be set on fire* (metaph. of pers.) Prv 29,1
Cf. LE BOULLUEC 1989, 249; LEE, J. 1983, 50; WEVERS 1990, 389
(→δια-, ἐκ-, κατα-, συμ-)

φλέψ, φλεβός⁺ N3F 0-0-1-0-0-1
Hos 13,15
vein

φλιά,-ᾶς N1F 5-3-4-0-0-12
Ex 12,7.22.23; Dt 6,9; 11,20
doorpost Dt 6,9; *lintel* Ex 12,7
Cf. DOGNIEZ 1992, 155; SHIPP 1979, 556; →LSJ suppl; LSJ RSuppl

φλογίζω⁺ V 2-0-0-2-3-7
Ex 9,24; Nm 21,14; Ps 96(97),3; DnTh 3,94(27); 1 Mc 3,5
to set on fire [τι] Nm 21,14; *to burn up, to consume* [τινα] Ps 96(97),3; *to burn* [intrans.] Ex 9,24
Cf. DORIVAL 1994, 402-403; LE BOULLUEC 1989, 134; LEE, J. 1983, 49-50; WEVERS 1990, 136
(→κατα-, συμ-)

φλόγινος,-η,-ον A 1-0-0-0-0-1
Gn 3,24
burning, flaming

φλοιός,-οῦ N2M 0-0-0-0-1-1
Wis 13,11
bark
Cf. LARCHER 1985, 778

φλόξ, φλογός⁺ N3F 4-8-16-19-14-61
Gn 15,17; 19,28; Ex 3,2; Nm 21,28; Jgs 3,22(bis)
flame Ex 3,2; *light, shine* Wis 10,17; *blade* (of a flashing sword) Jgs 3,22
*Gn 15,17 φλόξ *flame* -להט for MT עלטה *darkness*
Cf. CAIRD 1969=1972, 151; HARL 1986ᵃ, 166; LARCHER 1985, 955; WALTERS 1973, 322-323; WEVERS 1990, 25; →LSJ RSuppl(Jgs 3,22)

φλύαρος,-ος,-ον⁺ A 0-0-0-0-1-1
4 Mc 5,11
trifling, talkative, nonsensical
Cf. SPICQ 1978ᵃ, 949

φλυκτίς,-ίδος N3F 2-0-0-0-0-2
Ex 9,9.10
blister, pustule
Cf. CONYBEARE 1905=1988, 180; LE BOULLUEC 1989, 131; WEVERS 1990, 128

φοβερίζω V 0-0-0-5-0-5
DnTh 4,5(2); Ezr 10,3; Neh 6,9.14.19
to terrify, to scare, to alarm [τινα]; neol.

φοβερισμός,-οῦ N2M 0-0-0-1-0-1
Ps 87(88),17
terror, terrifying deed; neol.

φοβεροειδής,-ής,-ές A 0-0-0-0-1-1
3 Mc 6,18
terrible to behold, terrible of form; neol.

φοβερός,-ά,-όν⁺ A 5-2-2-24-7-40
Gn 28,17; Dt 1,19; 2,7; 8,15; 10,17
fearful, terrible (of God) Dt 10,17; *id.* (of things) Is 21,1; *terrible, horrifying* (of desert) Dt 1,19; *dreadful* (of pers.) Wis 10,16
Cf. DOGNIEZ 1992, 166.184; →NIDNTT

φοβερῶς D 0-0-0-1-1-2
Ps 138(139),14; 3 Mc 5,45

fearfully Ps 138(139),14; *frightening* 3 Mc 5,45

φοβέω+   V 77-94-78-107-104-460
Gn 3,10; 15,1; 18,15; 19,30; 20,2
M/P: *to fear* [τινα] Nm 21,34; *id.* [τι] 2 Kgs
25,24; *id.* [abs.] (*as feeling of shame*) Gn 3,10; *to
fear, to be afraid* [abs.] Dt 1,21; *to fear to do, to
be afraid of doing* [+inf.] Gn 19,30; *to be afraid
of* [ἀπό τινος] Dt 1,29; *to fear for* [περί τινος]
Jos 9,24

to reverence [τινα] Lv 19,3; *id.* [τι] Prv 30,1; *id.*
[ἀπό τινος] Lv 19,30

ὁ φοβούμενος *one who respects* Ex 9,20; οἱ
φοβούμενοι *the religious men* 2 Chr 5,6
*Is 33,7(tertio) φοβηθήσονται *they shall fear*
corr.? βοήσονται *they shall cry out* for MT צעקו;
*Ex 20,18 φοβηθέντες *fearing* -◊ירא *to be afraid*
for MT וירא ◊ראה *and he saw*; *Jgs^A 14,11 ἐν τῷ
φοβεῖσθαι αὐτούς *in their fearing* -ביראתם for MT
כראותם *at their seeing, when they saw,* see also
1 Kgs 19,3; Jer 17,3(MT^k-MT^q); Ez 18,14; Mi 6,9;
Jb 37,24(secundo); *Dn^LXX 11,12 οὐ μὴ φοβηθῇ
he shall not fear -◊זוע for MT יעוז לא *he shall not
prevail*

Cf. DODD 1954, 77; HELBING 1928, 29-30; WEVERS 1990,
134.315; →NIDNTT; TWNT
(→ἐκ-)

φόβητρον,-ου+   N2N 0-0-1-0-0-1
Is 19,17
terror, terrible sight

φόβος,-ου+   N2M 12-6-38-75-68-199
Gn 9,2; 15,12; 31,42.53; 35,5
fear Gn 9,2; *terror* Gn 15,12; *scruple, reverence*
Ps 35(36),2
*Jb 39,19 φόβον *terror* corr.? φόβην *mane* for
MT רעמה*mane*; *Is 33,3(secundo) ἀπὸ τοῦ φόβου
σου *for fear of you* -ממוראך for MT מרוממתך *for
lifting yourself up*; *Jer 37(30),6 φόβου *fear* -◊ירא
for MT ראיתי *I have seen*; *Ez 38,21 φόβον *fear*
-חרדה for MT חרב הרי *my mountains, a sword?*;
*Dn^LXX 11,31 φόβου *fear* -◊זוע for MT מעוז
fortress; *2 Chr 26,5 ἐν φόβῳ *in fearing* -ביראת for
MT בראת *in seeing*

Cf. HARL 1986^a, 52.186.238; WALTERS 1973, 146; WEVERS
1990, 233.374; →NIDNTT; TWNT

φοιβάω   V 1-0-0-0-0-1
Dt 14,1
to seek oracular ecstasy

Cf. DOGNIEZ 1992, 65.203; WEVERS 1995, 240

φοινικοῦς,-ῆ,-οῦν   A 0-0-1-0-0-1
Is 1,18

purple

φοῖνιξ,-ικος+   N3M 4-15-13-6-4-42
Ex 15,27; Lv 23,40; Nm 33,9; Dt 34,3; Jgs 1,16
date-palm Ex 15,27; *date* (*fruit of a date-palm*)
2 Sm 16,2; *id.* (*ornament*) Ez 41,25

φονευτής,-οῦ+   N1M 11-4-1-1-0-17
Nm 35,11.16(bis).17(bis)
slayer, murderer, killer; neol.

Cf. WEVERS 1995, 91

φονεύω+   V 19-18-2-7-8-54
Ex 20,15(13); 21,13; Nm 35,6.12.19
to murder, to kill [abs.] Ex 20,15; *id.* [τινα] Dt
4,42; *to destroy* [τι] 1 Kgs 21(20),40

Cf. WEVERS 1990, 329

φονή,-ῆς+   N1F 0-0-0-0-1-1
Wis 12,5
blood shed by slaying, murder

Cf. DODD 1954, 174; →NIDNTT

φονοκτονέω   V 2-0-0-1-0-3
Nm 35,33(bis); Ps 105(106),38
to defile with murder [τι]; neol.

φονοκτονία,-ας   N1F 0-0-0-0-1-1
1 Mc 1,24
murder, deed of murder, massacre; neol.

φόνος,-ου+   N2M 9-0-5-3-7-24
Ex 5,3; 17,13; 22,1; Lv 26,7; Nm 21,24
murder Ex 5,3; *massacre, slaughter* (*by the
sword*) Ex 17,13
*Jb 21,22 φόνους *murders* -רמים for MT רמים *the
exalted*

Cf. DOGNIEZ 1992, 288; LE BOULLUEC 1989, 35.107;
WEVERS 1990, 60.270.341; →LSJ Suppl; LSJ RSuppl

φονώδης,-ης,-ες   A 0-0-0-0-1-1
4 Mc 10,17
murderous, bloodthirsty
-φοράζω
(→συμ-)

φορβεά,-ας   N1F 0-0-0-1-0-1
Jb 40,25
halter

Cf. WALTERS 1973, 60-61.288-289

φορεῖον,-ου   N2N 0-0-0-1-2-3
Ct 3,9; 2 Mc 3,27; 9,8
litter, sedan-chair; neol.

Cf. WALTERS 1973, 51

φορεύς,-έως   N3M 3-0-0-0-0-3
Ex 27,6.7(bis)
carrying-pole

Cf. LE BOULLUEC 1989, 276

φορέω+   V 0-0-0-4-2-6

Prv 3,16a; 16,23.26; Est 4,17w; Sir 11,5
to wear [τι] Est 4,17w; *to carry* [τι] Prv 3,16a
→TWNT
(→δια-)

φορθομμιν N 0-0-0-1-0-1
Dnᵀʰ 1,3
= פרתמים *nobles*

φορολογέω V 0-1-0-0-1-2
2 Chr 36,4a; 1 Ezr 2,22
A: *to levy tribute* 1 Ezr 2,22
P: *to be subject to tribute, to pay tribute* 2 Chr
36,4a

φορολόγητος,-ος,-ον A 1-0-0-0-0-1
Dt 20,11
tributary to, paying tribute to [τινι]; neol.
Cf. DOGNIEZ 1992, 64.66.240

φορολογία,-ας N1F 0-0-0-0-4-4
1 Ezr 2,15; 6,28; 8,22; 1 Mc 1,29
levying tribute 1 Ezr 8,22; *tribute* 1 Ezr 2,15;
neol.?

φορολόγος,-ου N2M 0-0-0-6-0-6
Jb 3,18; 39,7; Ezr 4,7.18.23
tax-gatherer, tribute-collector; neol.?

φόρος,-ου⁺ N2M 0-25-0-6-13-44
Jos 19,48a; Jgsᴬ 1,28.29.30.31
tribute 2 Sm 20,24; *levy* 1 Kgs 5,27; *paying of
tribute* Jos 19,48a
*1 Kgs 10,15 τῶν φόρων *the tributes (of)* מענשי-
for MT מאנשי *from the men of*
Cf. BICKERMAN 1980, 58-59; DANIEL 1966, 222; LLEWELYN
1994, 127(n.60); →NIDNTT; TWNT

φορτίζω⁺ V 0-0-1-0-0-1
Ez 16,33
to load [τινα]
→NIDNTT; TWNT

φορτίον,-ου⁺ N2N 0-3-1-2-2-8
Jgsᴬ 9,48.49; 2 Sm 19,36; Is 46,1; Ps 37(38),5
burden, load, freight Sir 33,25; *burden* (metaph.)
2 Sm 19,36
→NIDNTT; TWNT

φραγμός,-οῦ⁺ N2M 3-3-5-8-3-22
Gn 38,29; Nm 22,24(bis); 1 Kgs 10,22a(9,15)
fence Nm 22,24; *hedge* Na 3,17; *barrier* Gn 38,29
*Mi 4,14 φραγμῷ *hedge* - גדר◊for MT גדוד*troop of
warriors*
Cf. HARL 1986ᵃ, 267; →NIDNTT

φράζω⁺ V 0-0-0-3-0-3
Jb 6,24; 12,8; Dnᴸˣˣ 2,4
to show to, to explain to [τινι] Jb 6,24; *id.* [τί
τινι] Dnᴸˣˣ 2,4

φραζων N 0-1-0-0-0-1
Jgsᴬ 5,7
= פרזון *rustics*

φράσσω⁺ V 0-0-1-5-0-6
Hos 2,8; Jb 38,8; Prv 21,13; 25,26; Ct 7,3
A: *to stop* [τι] Prv 21,13; *to shut up with* [τί
τινι] Jb 38,8; *to hedge up, to build a hedge
along* [τι] Hos 2,8
P: *to be set about with* [ἔν τινι] Ct 7,3; *to be
shut (up)* (metaph.) Dnᴸˣˣ 8,26
→NIDNTT
(→ἀνα-, ἀπο-, ἐμ-, κατα-, περι-, συμ-)

φρέαρ,-ατος⁺ N3N 42-2-6-5-2-57
Gn 14,10(bis); 16,14(bis); 21,14
(artificial) well Gn 21,19; *pit* Gn 14,10
*Nm 21,18(secundo) ἀπὸ φρέατος *from the well*
-מבאר for MT ממדבר*from the desert*; *Jer 48(41),9
φρέαρ μέγα τοῦτό ἐστιν *this is the great pit*
-(א)בור גדל הו for MT ב/יר גדליהו *by the hand of
Gedaliah*
Cf. CLARYSSE 1994, 6-7; SHIPP 1979, 449-450

φρενόω V 0-0-0-0-1-1
2 Mc 11,4
P: *to be puffed up, to be elated*

φρήν, φρενός⁺ N3F 0-0-0-10-2-12
Prv 6,32; 7,7; 9,4; 11,12; 12,11
heart 3 Mc 5,47; *mind* 3 Mc 4,16; (αἱ) φρένες
(the) understanding, (the) reason Prv 6,32
ἐνδεὴς φρενῶν *a senseless man* Prv 18,2
→MM; TWNT

φρικασμός,-οῦ N2M 0-0-0-0-1-1
2 Mc 3,17
trembling (in fear); neol.

φρίκη,-ης⁺ N1F 0-0-1-1-0-2
Am 1,11; Jb 4,14
shivering fear Jb 4,14; *shivering anger* Am 1,11
Cf. PRIJS 1948, 49

φρικτός,-ή,-όν A 0-0-3-0-1-4
Jer 5,30; 18,13; 23,14; Wis 8,15
to be shocked at, awful, horrible (of pers.) Wis
8,15; *id.* (of things) Jer 5,30
Cf. LARCHER 1984, 542

φρικτῶς D 0-0-0-0-1-1
Wis 6,5
awfully, horribly; neol.
Cf. LARCHER 1984, 408

φρικώδης,-ης,-ες A 0-0-1-0-0-1
Hos 6,10
causing shuddering horror

φρίττω⁺ V 0-0-1-2-4-7

Jer 2,12; Jb 4,15; Dnᵀʰ 7,15; Jdt 16,10; 4 Mc 14,9
to shudder 4 Mc 14,9; *to quiver* Jb 4,15; *to quake
at* [τι] Jdt 16,10
Cf. HELBING 1928, 35

φρονέω⁺   V 1-0-4-3-8-16
Dt 32,29; Is 44,18.28; 56,10; Zech 9,2
to be wise, to have understanding Ps 93(94),8; *id.*
[+inf.] Dt 32,29; *to think* [abs.] 4 Mc 6,17; *id.*
[τι] 2 Mc 9,12; *to think of* [περί τινος] Wis 1,1;
id. [ὑπέρ τινος] 2 Mc 14,8
μεῖζον ἐφρόνησαν *they thought arrogantly, they
became arrogant* Est 8,12c; φρονεῖν τὰ ἡμῶν *to
take our part* 1 Mc 10,20, see also Est 8,12b
*Is 44,28 φρονεῖν *to be wise* -◊ידע *to know* for
MT רעי *my shepherd*
Cf. LARCHER 1983, 165; →NIDNTT; TWNT
(→κατα-, παρα-, περι-, συμ-, ὑπερ-)

φρόνημα,-ατος⁺   N3N 0-0-0-0-2-2
2 Mc 7,21; 13,9
thinking, mind
→NIDNTT; TWNT

φρόνησις,-εως⁺   N3F 0-14-4-23-21-62
Jos 5,1; 1 Sm 2,10; 1 Kgs 2,35a.35b(bis)
wisdom, insight, intelligence
→NIDNTT; TWNT

φρόνιμος,-ος,-ον⁺   A 3-4-2-16-13-38
Gn 3,1; 41,33.39; 1 Kgs 2,46a; 3,12
wise, prudent 1 Kgs 2,46a; *clever* Gn 3,1;
understanding 1 Kgs 3,12; *wise, enlightened* 4 Mc
7,17
μὴ ἴσθι φρόνιμος παρὰ σεαυτῷ *rely not on
your own wisdom* Prv 3,7
Cf. HARL 1986ᵃ, 107; →NIDNTT; TWNT

φροντίζω⁺   V 0-1-0-4-10-15
1 Sm 9,5; Ps 39(40),18; Jb 3,25; 23,15; Prv 31,21
to consider, to ponder [τι] Wis 8,17; *to take
thought for, to give heed to, to take care of*
[τινος] Jb 23,15; *id.* [περί τινος] 1 Sm 9,5; *to
consider* [abs.] Sir 8,13; *to aim at, to provide* [τι]
2 Mc 2,25; see φροντιστέος
Cf. HELBING 1928, 111; SPICQ 1978ᵃ, 950-952

φροντίς,-ίδος   N3F 0-0-0-2-6-8
Jb 11,18; 15,20; 4 Mc 16,8; Wis 5,15; 6,17
care Jb 11,18; *care for, anxiety of* [τινος] 4 Mc
16,8
Cf. LARCHER 1984, 382

φροντιστέος,-α,-ον   A 0-0-0-0-1-1
2 Mc 2,29
one must take heed; see φροντίζω

φρουρά,-ᾶς⁺   N1F 0-4-0-0-8-12

2 Sm 8,6.14; 1 Chr 18,6.13; 1 Mc 6,50
garrison

φρουρέω⁺   V 0-0-0-0-2-2
1 Ezr 4,56; Wis 17,15
A: *to set garrison in, to keep* (a city) [τι] 1 Ezr
4,56
P: *to be kept in custody, to be guarded, to be
warded* Wis 17,15
Cf. LARCHER 1985, 974; →NIDNTT

φρούριον,-ου   N2N 0-0-0-0-3-3
2 Mc 10,32.33; 13,19
fort, fortress

φρουρόω   V 0-0-0-0-1-1
Jdt 3,6
to set garrison in, to guard [τι]; neol.

φρύαγμα,-ατος   N3N 0-0-5-0-1-6
Jer 12,5; Ez 7,24; 24,21; Hos 4,18; Zech 11,3
snorting (of horses) 3 Mc 6,16; *insolence* Zech
11,3; *pride* Ez 7,24
*Hos 4,18 ἐκ φρυάγματος αὐτῶν *through their
insolence* -◊גאון מ/גאנה or -◊גואן מ/גו(י)ת/נוהג for MT
מגניה *her shields*

φρυάττω⁺   V 0-0-0-1-2-3
Ps 2,1; 2 Mc 7,34; 3 Mc 2,2
A: *to rage* Ps 2,1
P: *to be wanton* 3 Mc 2,2; *to be uplifted with, to
be puffed up with* [τινι] 2 Mc 7,34
→MM

φρύγανον,-ου⁺   N2N 0-0-5-1-0-6
Is 40,24; 41,2; 47,14; Jer 13,24; Hos 10,7
dry stick (easy to manipulate) Is 40,24;
brushwood Jb 30,7
→MM

φρύγιον,-ου   N2N 0-0-0-1-0-1
Ps 101(102),4
firewood; neol.

φρύγω   V 2-0-0-0-0-2
Lv 2,14; 23,14
P: *to be parched*
(→συμ-)

φυγαδευτήριον,-ου   N2N 7-9-0-0-2-18
Nm 35,6.11.12.13.15
(*city of*) *refuge* Nm 35,6; *place of refuge* 1 Mc
1,53; neol.

φυγαδεύω⁺   V 0-0-0-1-5-6
Ps 54(55),8; 1 Mc 2,43; 2 Mc 5,5; 9,4; 10,15
to banish [τινα] 2 Mc 9,4; *to flee away* [abs.] Ps
54(55),8; *to flee away for* [ἀπό τινος] 1 Mc 2,43;
to flee (in)to [εἰς τι] 2 Mc 5,5; *id.* [τι] 2 Mc
14,14

φυγάδιον,-ου   N2N 1-0-0-2-0-3
Nm 35,15(14); Ezr 4,15.19
place of refuge; neol.
Cf. WALTERS 1973, 43

φυγάς,-άδος   N3M 1-0-1-1-6-9
Ex 23,27; Is 16,4; Prv 28,17; 2 Mc 4,26; 5,7
fugitive (of an outcast or runaway) Is 16,4; *id.*
(of a routed enemy) Ex 23,27
Cf. WEVERS 1990, 374

φυγή,-ῆς⁺   N1F 0-1-6-2-3-12
2 Sm 18,3; Is 52,12; Jer 26(46),5; 30,30(49,24);
32(25),35
flight 2 Sm 18,3
ἐτράπησαν εἰς φυγήν *they were put to flight,*
they fled away Jdt 15,3, see also Jer 30,30(49,24)
*Na 3,9 τῆς φυγῆς *flight* -◊פלט for MT פוט *Put*
(proper name)
→NIDNTT

φυή,-ῆς   N1F 0-0-0-4-0-4
Dnᵀʰ 4,15(12).23(20).26(23); Neh 4,1
stump (of roots) Dnᵀʰ 4,15(12); *height, original*
form Neh 4,1

φῦκος,-ους   N3N 0-0-0-0-1-1
Wis 13,14
orchil, rouge
Cf. GILBERT 1973, 89-90; LARCHER 1985, 781

φύλαγμα,-ατος   N3N 4-0-2-0-2-8
Lv 8,35; 22,9; Nm 4,31; Dt 11,1; Zph 1,12
observance, obligation, commandment Lv 8,35
*Zph 1,12 τὰ φυλάγματα αὐτῶν *their things*
committed -◊שמר for MT שמריהם ◊שמר *their dregs*
neol.

φυλακή,-ῆς⁺   N1F 34-30-27-18-12-121
Gn 40,3.4.7; 41,10; 42,17
guarding, guard Nm 1,53; *watch* (as a division of
time during which a watch was kept) Ex 14,24;
id. (as group or division of personnel) Nm
8,26(secundo); *keeping* (the law) 4 Mc 13,13;
task, responsibility Nm 3,7; *place of guarding,*
prison Jgsᴬ 16,25; *precaution, preservation* Sir
34,16
ἐν φυλακῇ *in ward, under guard* Gn 40,3;
φυλάσσω φυλακάς *to keep the charge* 1 Chr
23,32
*Ez 23,24 φυλακήν *a watch* -◊שמר for MT ישימו
they will set; *Ps 76(77),5 φυλακάς *watches* -שמרות
for MT שמרות *eyelids*; *Jb 35,10 φυλακάς *watches*
-שמרות for MT זמרות *songs*
Cf. CONYBEARE 1905=1988, 194; WEVERS 1990, 170; →MM;
NIDNTT; TWNT

φυλακίζω⁺   V 0-0-0-0-1-1
Wis 18,4
P: *to be imprisoned*; neol.

φυλάκισσα,-ας   N1F 0-0-0-1-0-1
Ct 1,6
keeper (fem.); neol.

φύλαξ,-ακος⁺   N3M 1-4-2-9-0-16
Gn 4,9; 2 Sm 22,3.47(bis); 23,3
watcher, guard, sentinel Ct 5,7; *keeper* Gn 4,9

φυλάρχης,-ου   N1M 0-0-0-0-1-1
2 Mc 8,32
chief of a tribe; neol.?

φύλαρχος,-ου⁺   N2M 1-0-0-0-4-5
Dt 31,28; 1 Ezr 7,8; 8,54.58.92
chief of a tribe Dt 31,28; *chief priest* 1 Ezr 8,54

φυλάσσω⁺/φυλάττω   V 114-110-69-130-41-464
Gn 2,15; 3,24; 18,19; 26,5; 30,31
A: *to keep watch, to guard* [τι] 2 Sm 15,16; *to*
guard [τινα] 1 Sm 26,15; *to watch over sb* [ἐπί
τινα] Jos 10,18; *to keep the charge of* [τι] Nm
3,10; *to keep sb from* [τινα ἔκ τινος] Ps
139(140),5; *to preserve sb from* [τινα ἀπό τινος]
Ps 120(121),7
to watch [τι] Ps 55(56),7
to observe [τι] Dt 16,1; *to keep, to maintain* [τι]
Gn 26,5
M: *to keep watch, to guard* [τι] Jgs 2,22; *to*
beware of [τι] 2 Sm 20,10; *id.* [ἀπό τινος] Jgs
13,13
to observe [abs.] Jos 1,7; *id.* [τι] Jgs 13,14; *to*
preserve, to maintain [τι] Ex 13,10; *to preserve,*
to cherish [τι] Jon 2,9; *to be careful, to give heed*
[+inf.] Ex 23,15; *id.* [τοῦ +inf.] Jos 23,11
φύλαξαι σεαυτόν *take heed* Gn 31,24;
φυλάξουσιν οἱ Λευῖται αὐτοὶ τὴν φυλακὴν
τῆς σκηνῆς τοῦ μαρτυρίου *the Levites*
themselves shall keep the guard of the tabernacle
of witness Nm 1,53; φυλάξουσιν τὰς φυλακὰς
αὐτοῦ *they shall keep his charges* Nm 3,7;
φυλασσόμενος λαλήσει *speaking cautiously* Prv
21,28
*1 Sm 29,11 φυλάσσειν *to guard* -לשמר for MT
לשוב *to return*; *Is 60,21 φυλάσσων *guarding* -נצר
for MT נצר *sprout*; *1 Chr 26,10 φυλάσσοντες
keeping -שמרי for MT שמרי *Shimri*
Cf. DOGNIEZ 1992, 45.134; DORIVAL 1994, 430; HELBING
1929, 30-32; WALTERS 1973, 61.62; WEVERS 1990,
294.310.364.512; 1995, 97; →NIDNTT; TWNT
(→δια-, προ-)

φυλή,-ῆς⁺   N1F 139-189-47-25-44-444

Gn 10,5.18.20.31.32
tribe Gn 10,18; *nation, people* Gn 12,3
*Ru 3,11 φυλή *tribe* corr. πύλη for MT שַׁעַר *gate*,
see also 4,10; *Nm 25,5 ταῖς φυλαῖς *the tribes*
-שִׁבְטֵי for MT שֹׁפְטֵי *the judges*, see also Mi 4,14;
*Am 3,12 φυλῆς *of a tribe* -מַטֶּה for MT מִטָּה *bed*;
*Hag 1,1 ἐκ φυλῆς *of the tribe* פַחַת-for MT מִמְמְשֶׁפַחַת
governor, see also 1,12.14; 2,2.21
Cf. BICKERMAN 1980, 162(n.22); DORIVAL 1994, 360(Nm
17,3); WEVERS 1990, 12; →NIDNTT; TWNT

-φυλλίζω
(→ἐπι-)

φύλλον,-ου⁺   N2N 3-0-5-11-2-21
Gn 3,7; 8,11; Lv 26,36; Is 1,30; 34,4
leaf
→NIDNTT

φῦλον,-ου   N2N 0-0-0-0-2-2
3 Mc 4,14; 5,5
race, nation

φύραμα,-ατος⁺   N3N 4-0-0-0-0-4
Ex 7,28; 12,34; Nm 15,20.21
that which is kneaded, dough
Cf. LE BOULLUEC 1989, 122.152; WEVERS 1990, 107.186;
→NIDNTT

φύρασις,-εως   N3F 0-0-1-0-0-1
Hos 7,4
mixing, kneading; neol.

φυράω   V 10-3-0-0-0-13
Gn 18,6; Ex 29,2.40; Lv 2,4.5
to mix, to knead [τι]

φύρδην   D 0-0-0-0-1-1
2 Mc 4,41
with confusion

φυρμός,-οῦ   N2M 0-0-1-0-1-2
Ez 7,23; PSal 2,13
disorder PSal 2,13
*Ez 7,23 (ποιήσουσι) φυρμόν (*they shall make*)
disorder -עֲשׂוּ הָבָתוּק *they shall do slaughter* for MT
עֲשֵׂה הָרַתּוּק *make the chain?*
neol.

φύρω   V 0-1-3-3-1-8
2 Sm 20,12; Is 14,19; Ez 16,6.22; Jb 7,5
P: *to be steeped, to be soaked with* [ἕν τινι] Is
14,19; *to be weltering in* [ἕν τινι] 2 Sm 20,12; *to
be steeped with* [ἕν τινι] (metaph.) Jb 30,14
(→ἐκ-, συμ-, συνανα-)

φυσάω   V 0-0-1-0-3-4
Is 54,16; Wis 11,18; Sir 28,12; 43,4
to blow [τι] Is 54,16; *to blow on* [εἴς τι] Sir
28,12; *to breathe* [τι] Wis 11,18

Cf. LARCHER 1985, 681
(→ἀπο-, ἐκ-, ἐμ-)

φυσητήρ,-ῆρος   N3M 0-0-1-1-0-2
Jer 6,29; Jb 32,19
bellows

-φυσιόω
(→ἐμ-)

φύσις,-εως⁺   N3F 0-0-0-0-12-12
3 Mc 3,29; 4 Mc 1,20; 5,8.9.25
nature, natural condition Wis 13,1; *nature,
natural disposition* Wis 7,20; *creature* 3 Mc 3,29
Cf. LARCHER 1984, 473; 1985, 750-751; SHIPP 1979, 560;
→NIDNTT; TWNT

φυτεία,-ας⁺   N1F 0-1-2-0-1-4
2 Kgs 19,29; Ez 17,7; Mi 1,6; PSal 14,4
planting 2 Kgs 19,29; *plantation* Ez 17,7
→NIDNTT

φύτευμα,-ατος   N3N 0-0-3-0-0-3
Is 17,10; 60,21; 61,3
something planted Is 60,21; *planting* (metaph.) Is
61,3
→NIDNTT

φυτεύω⁺   V 7-1-21-13-8-50
Gn 2,8; 9,20; 21,33; Dt 16,21; 20,6
A: *to plant* [τι] Gn 2,8; *id.* [abs.] Eccl 3,2; *id.*
[τι] (metaph.) Ps 93(94),9; *id.* [τινα] (metaph.)
Sir 10,15; *to plant sth for sb* [τί τινα] Jer 2,21;
to beget, to engender 4 Mc 13,19
P: *to be firmly fastened* (of nails) Eccl 12,11; *to
be planted* (metaph.) Ps 91(92),14
Cf. LEE, J. 1983, 57-58; →NIDNTT
(→ἐπι-, κατα-, περι-)

φυτός,-ή,-ον   A 0-0-1-0-0-1
Ez 17,5
fruitful

φυτόν,-οῦ⁺   N2N 1-1-2-4-9-17
Gn 22,13; 1 Kgs 19,5; Ez 31,4; 34,29; DnᴸˣˣX 11,7
plant Ez 31,4; *plant, bush, thicket* Gn 22,13;
shoot Dnᴸˣˣ 11,7; *tree* 1 Kgs 19,5; *id.* (metaph.)
4 Mc 1,28
Cf. HARL 1986ª, 48.195; 1986ª=1992ª, 67; SHIPP 1979,
561-562

φύω⁺   V 2-0-2-6-5-15
Ex 10,5; Dt 29,17; Is 37,31; Ez 37,8; Prv 11,30
A: *to spring up, to put forth shoots* (of roots) Dt
29,17; *to grow* Sir 14,18
M: *to grow* Ex 10,5
τὰ φυόμενα *things growing, plants* Dn 3,76;
φυήσουσιν ῥίζαν *they shall take root* Is 37,31
*Ct 5,13 φύουσαι *to bring forth, to grow* -מִגְדְּלוֹת?

◊גדל for MT מִגְדָּלוֹת *towers?*
(→ἀνα-, ἐπι-, προσ-, συμ-)

φωνέω⁺   V 0-1-8-4-11-24
1 Chr 15,16; Is 8,19(bis); 19,3; 29,4
to sound (of instruments) 1 Chr 15,16
to speak Ps 113,15(115,7); *to shout* 1 Ezr 4,41; *to sing aloud* 1 Ezr 5,58; *to call, to summon* [τινα] Tob^BA 5,9; *to call upon* [τινα] 4 Mc 15,21; *to call to* [+inf.] 3 Mc 1,23
to utter (of anim.) Jer 17,11
→TWNT
(→ἀνα-, ἀντι-, δια-, ἐκ-, ἐπι-, προσ-, συμ-, ὑπερ-)

φωνή,-ῆς⁺   N1F 117-111-175-143-87-633
Gn 3,8.10.17; 4,10.23
sound, tone Ex 19,16; *sound* Lv 26,36; *noise* Jgs 5,11; *voice* Gn 3,8; *cry* (of anim.) Jb 4,10; *report, rumour* Gn 45,16; *language* 4 Mc 16,15
φωνῇ *with a voice, audibly* Ex 19,19; φωνὰς καὶ χάλαζαν *thunderings and hail* Ex 9,23
*Is 28,28 φωνή *the voice of* -◊המה for MT המם *one drives (a cartwheel)*; Ez 35,12 τῆς φωνῆς *the voice of* -קול for MT כל *all*, see also Jb 38,7
Cf. CONYBEARE 1905=1988, 181; DODD 1954, 176; LE BOULLUEC 1989, 97.133.323; WEVERS 1990, 44.136.285.300.304.315.353.371.380.529; →NIDNTT; TWNT

φωράω   V 0-0-0-1-1-2
Prv 26,19; 3 Mc 3,29
P: *to be discovered, to be detected*

φῶς, φωτός⁺   N3N 12-7-57-59-41-176
Gn 1,3(bis).4(bis).5
light Gn 1,3; *day-light* 2 Kgs 7,9; *light* (metaph.) Hos 10,12; *illumination* Ex 27,20
*Is 26,9 διότι φῶς *because light* -כי כאור for MT כי כאשר *for when*; *Jer 10,13 φῶς *light* -אור for MT רוח *wind*, see also 28(51),16; *Ez 42,7 καὶ φῶς *and light* -ואור for MT וגדר *and a wall*, see also

42,10.12; *Jb 22,11 τὸ φῶς *light* -אור for MT או *or*
Cf. DODD 1954, 107.133-136.167.183-187.199.211; HORSLEY 1981, 98-99; LE BOULLUEC 1989, 280; SPICQ 1982, 678-691; →NIDNTT; TWNT

φωστήρ,-ῆρος⁺   N3M 4-0-0-1-4-9
Gn 1,14.16(ter); Dn^LXX 12,3
luminary Gn 1,14; *light, splendour* 1 Ezr 8,76; neol.
Cf. DODD 1954, 139-140; HARL 1986ᵃ, 92; SPICQ 1982, 692-693; →MM; NIDNTT; TWNT

φωταγωγέω   V 0-0-0-0-1-1
4 Mc 17,5
to guide with a light, to light the path of sb [τινα]; neol.

φωτεινός,-ή,-όν⁺   A 0-0-0-0-2-2
Sir 17,31; 23,19
shining, bright; φωτεινότερος *brighter*
→NIDNTT; TWNT

φωτίζω⁺   V 3-6-5-17-9-40
Ex 38,13(37,17); Nm 4,9; 8,2; Jgs^A 13,8.23
to shine, to give light Ex 38,13(37,17); *to illuminate for, to enlighten for* [τινί τι] Neh 9,12; *to enlighten, to instruct, to teach* [τινα] Jgs^A 13,8; *id.* [τί τινα] Jgs^A 13,23; *to lighten* [τι] Ps 17(18),29; *to provide light for* [τινι] Mi 7,8
*Hos 10,12 φωτίσατε ἑαυτοῖς *light yourselves* -נירו לכם for MT נירו לכם *till for you (the fallow)*
Cf. BROCK 1992, 317-318; DODD 1954, 107.187; HARL 1990=1992ᵃ, 261; HELBING 1928, 40; KLEIN 1962, 50-61; SMITH 1967, 443-445; SPICQ 1982, 691-692; WEVERS 1990, 623; →NIDNTT; TWNT
(→δια-)

φωτισμός,-οῦ⁺   N2M 0-0-0-6-0-6
Ps 26(27),1; 43(44),4; 77(78),14; 89(90),8; 138(139),11
light Jb 3,9; *id.* (metaph.) Ps 26(27),1
Cf. SPICQ 1982, 695-696; →MM; NIDNTT; TWNT

χαβραθα N 2-0-0-0-0-2
Gn 35,16; 48,7
= כברת *a good stretch* (distance)
Cf. HARL 1986ᵃ, 253.303; TOV 1973, 88; VOGT 1975, 30-
36; WEVERS 1993, 583

χαιρετίζω V 0-0-0-0-3-3
Tob 7,1; Tobˢ 5,10
to greet, to salute [τινα]; neol.?

χαίρω⁺ V 3-7-21-9-47-87
Gn 45,16; Ex 4,14.31; 1 Sm 19,5; 1 Kgs
2,46a(4,20)
to rejoice, to be glad Gn 45,16; *to rejoice at, to
take pleasure in* [τινι] Prv 6,16; *id.* [ἐπί τινα]
2 Kgs 20,13; *id.* [ἐπί τινι] Tobᴮᴬ 13,16; *id.* [ἐν
τινι] Tobˢ 13,16; *to please* [τινι] Tobˢ 5,10;
χαίροντες *glad, joyful* 1 Kgs 8,66; χαίρετε
welcome Tobˢ 7,1
χαρήσεται ἐν ἑαυτῷ *he will rejoice within
himself* Ex 4,14; (Βασιλεῖ Δαρείῳ) χαίρειν
greetings (to king Darius) 1 Ezr 6,8, see also
1 Ezr 8,9; Est 8,12b; passim in 1 Mc, 2 Mc and
3 Mc
*Ex 4,31 καὶ ἐχάρη *and they rejoiced* -וישמחו for
MT וישמעו *and they heard*, see also 2 Kgs 20,13;
*Jer 38(31),13(bis) χαρήσονται *shall rejoice
-יחדו ◊חרה for MT יַחְדֵּו *simultaneously*; *Prv 6,16
χαίρει *he rejoices* -שש ◊שישו for MT שש *six*
Cf. BICKERMAN 1976, 120-125; 1980, 136-137; HELBING
1928, 258; LE BOULLUEC 1989, 105; LLEWELYN 1994, 35;
WALTERS 1973, 105; →NIDNTT; TWNT
(→ἐπι-, κατα-, προσ-, συγ-)

χάλαζα,-ης⁺ N1F 19-2-5-6-6-38
Ex 9,18.19.22.23(bis)
hail
Cf. SHIPP 1979, 564; →NIDNTT

χαλαστόν,-οῦ N2N 0-2-0-0-0-2
2 Chr 3,5.16
festoon, chain (in archit. as ornament); neol.

χαλάω⁺ V 1-0-3-0-0-4
Ex 36,28(39,21); Is 33,23; 57,4; Jer 45(38),6
A: *to loosen* [τι] Is 57,4; *to let down* [τινα] (lit.)
Jer 45(38),6
P: *to be loosed from* [ἀπό τινος] Ex 36,28(39,21)
Cf. SHIPP 1979, 564-565
(→κατα-, περι-, προ-)

χαλβάνη,-ης N1F 1-0-0-0-1-2
Ex 30,34; Sir 24,15
Semit. loanword (Hebr. חלבנה); *the resinous
extract of the galbanum plant, galbanum*
Cf. CAIRD 1976, 78; LE BOULLUEC 1989, 313; TOV 1979,

221; →CHANTRAINE; FRISK

χαλεπαίνω V 0-0-0-0-2-2
4 Mc 9,10; 16,22
to be angry 4 Mc 16,22; *to be embittered towards*
[κατά τινος] 4 Mc 9,10

χαλεπός,-ή,-όν⁺ A 0-0-1-0-10-11
Is 18,2; 2 Mc 4,4.16; 6,3; 4 Mc 8,1
difficult 4 Mc 16,8; *grievous* Wis 3,19; *cruel,
harsh* Is 18,2; τὸ χαλεπόν *the danger* 2 Mc 4,4
χαλεπώτερος *harder, more difficult to bear* Sir
3,21
Cf. LARCHER 1983, 311; SPICQ 1978ᵃ, 955-956; →NIDNTT

χαλινός,-οῦ⁺ N2M 0-1-3-2-1-7
2 Kgs 19,28; Is 37,29; Hab 3,14; Zech 14,20; Ps
31(32),9
bit, bridle 2 Kgs 19,28; *bridle, restraint* Jb 30,11
*Zech 14,20 τὸν χαλινόν *the bridle* -צלא◊
(Aram., Arab.) *leather* for MT מצלות צלל◊*bells*, cpr.
Hab 3,14
Cf. MARGOLIS 1911, 314(Hab 3,14; Zech 14,20)

χάλιξ,-ικος⁺ N3M/F 0-0-0-2-0-2
Jb 8,17; 21,33
small stone, pebble

χαλκεῖον,-ου N2N 0-2-0-1-1-4
1 Sm 2,14; 2 Chr 35,13; Jb 41,23; 1 Ezr 1,13
copper vessel, copper cauldron; see χαλκίον
Cf. WALTERS 1973, 48; →PREISIGKE

χαλκεῖος,-α,-ον A 0-1-0-5-2-8
Jgsᴮ 16,21; Jb 6,12; 20,24; 40,18; 41,7
brazen, of brass, bronze
Cf. CONYBEARE 1905=1988, 48

χαλκεύς,-έως⁺ N3M 1-1-2-2-1-7
Gn 4,22; 2 Chr 24,12; Is 41,7; 54,16; Jb 32,19
coppersmith, smith, metal-worker Gn 4,22
*Jb 32,19 χαλκέως *of a coppersmith* -חרשים חרש◊
for MT חרשים חרש◊ *new*
Cf. SPICQ 1978ᵃ, 957-958; →NIDNTT; PREISIGKE

χαλκεύω V 0-1-0-0-0-1
1 Sm 13,20
to forge [τι]

χαλκίον,-ου⁺ N2N 0-1-0-0-0-1
1 Sm 2,14
see χαλκεῖον
Cf. CAIRD 1976, 82; WALTERS 1973, 48; →LSJ RSuppl;
NIDNTT

χαλκοπλάστης,-ου N1M 0-0-0-0-1-1
Wis 15,9
bronze-worker, copperdraper; neol.

χαλκός,-οῦ⁺ N2M 12-23-11-12-4-62
Gn 4,22; Ex 25,3; 27,2.6; 31,4

copper, brass Gn 4,22; *money* LtJ 34

χαλκοῦς,-ῆ,-οῦν⁺   A 31-37-15-11-9-103
Ex 26,11.37; 27,3.4(bis)
made of copper, of brass, brazen

χαλκόω
(→κατα-, περι-)

χαμαί⁺   D 0-0-0-6-2-8
Jb 1,20; Dnᴸˣˣ 2,46; 8,11.12.18
on the ground Jdt 14,18; *to the ground* Jb 1,20

χαμαιλέων,-οντος   N3M 1-0-1-0-0-2
Lv 11,30; Zph 2,14
chameleon

χαμαιπετής,-ής,-ές   A 0-0-0-0-1-1
1 Ezr 8,88
lying (flat) on the ground

χαμανιμ   N 0-0-0-1-0-1
Ezr 8,27

= כמנים ?; *Ezr 8,27 εἰς τὴν ὁδὸν χαμανιμ *on
the road to Chamanim?* -כמנים- לדרך corr. (εἰς τὴν
ὁδὸν) δραχμῶν *worth drachmas* -לדרכמנים for
MT לאדרכנים *worth darics?*
Cf. HANHART 1993, 124; WILLIAMSON 1977, 123-125

χάος,-ους   N3N 0-0-2-0-0-2
Mi 1,6; Zech 14,4
gaping abyss, chasm (homoeophonic with גיא?
valley)
Cf. CAIRD 1976, 86; WALTERS 1973, 189

χαρά,-ᾶς⁺   N1F 0-1-12-9-26-48
1 Chr 29,22; Is 39,2; 55,12(bis); 66,10
joy, delight
Cf. LARCHER 1984, 545; SPICQ 1978ᵃ, 959; →NIDNTT; TWNT

χαραδριός,-οῦ   N2M 2-0-0-0-0-2
Lv 11,19; Dt 14,18
plover

χαρακοβολία,-ας   N1F 0-0-1-0-0-1
Ez 17,17
*throwing up a mound, erection of a palisade,
bulwark, stockade*; neol.

χαρακόω⁺   V 0-0-2-0-0-2
Is 5,2; Jer 39(32),2
to fence in with stakes Is 5,2; *to raise a barricade
against, to besiege* [ἐπί τι] Jer 39(32),2
(→περι-)

χαρακτήρ,-ῆρος⁺   N3M 1-0-0-0-2-3
Lv 13,28; 2 Mc 4,10; 4 Mc 15,4
mark Lv 13,28; *character, nature* 2 Mc 4,10
→NIDNTT; TWNT

χαράκωσις,-εως⁺   N3F 1-0-0-0-0-1
Dt 20,20
palisade, bulwark, stockade

Cf. DOGNIEZ 1992, 64

χάραξ,-ακος⁺   N3M/F 1-3-8-1-2-15
Dt 20,19; 1 Kgs 12,24f; 21(20),12(bis); Is 29,3
palisade, bulwark, stockade Dt 20,19
*Ez 21,27 χάρακα *mound* homoeophonic? with
MT כרים *battering rams*
Cf. CAIRD 1976, 86; DOGNIEZ 1992, 242; →NIDNTT

χαράσσω   V 0-1-0-0-2-3
2 Kgs 17,11; 3 Mc 2,29; Sir 50,27
A: *to provoke* [τοῦ +inf.] 2 Kgs 17,11; *to
engrave, to write* [τι] Sir 50,27
P: *to be stamped, to be branded* 3 Mc 2,29
Cf. CAIRD 1969=1972, 151(1 Kgs 15,27); →NIDNTT

χαρίεις,-εσσα,-εν   A 0-0-0-0-1-1
4 Mc 8,3
beautiful, attractive

χαρίζω⁺   V 0-0-0-1-11-12
Est 8,7; 2 Mc 1,35; 3,31.33; 4,32
to give freely [τί τινι] Est 8,7; *id.* [τι] Sir 12,3;
to favour [abs.] 4 Mc 5,7
Cf. HARL 1991=1992ᵃ, 152-153; →NIDNTT; TWNT

χάρις,-ιτος⁺   N3F 26-12-5-37-84-164
Gn 6,8; 18,3; 30,27; 32,6; 33,8
frequently rendition of חן; *grace, favour, kindness*
(often of the Lord's kindness received
gratuitously) Gn 6,8; *graciousness, attractiveness*
Eccl 10,12; *grace, beauty, elegance* Sir 7,19;
gratitude 3 Mc 5,20
χάριν τίνος *why?, wherefore?* 2 Chr 7,21;
ἐποίησεν ἡμᾶς ἐν χάριτι ἐνώπιόν τινος *he
brought us into favour with sb* 1 Ezr 8,77; εὗρον
χάριν ἐναντίον σου *I found favour with you,
you were kind to me* Gn 18,3
Cf. DODD 1954, 61; LARCHER 1983, 293-294;
MONTGOMERY 1939, 97-102; SPICQ 1978ᵃ, 960-966;
WEVERS 1993, 80; ZELLER 1990, 26-32; →NIDNTT; TWNT

χαριστήριον,-ου   N2N 0-0-0-0-1-1
2 Mc 12,45
gracious reward, thank-offering

χαριτόω⁺   V 0-0-0-0-1-1
Sir 18,17
P: *to be favoured, to be gracious, to be justified*;
neol.
Cf. CAMBE 1963, 194; →MM; NIDNTT; TWNT

χαρμονή,-ῆς   N1F 0-0-1-3-1-5
Jer 38(31),13; Jb 3,7; 20,5; 40,20; 3 Mc 6,31
joy, delight

χαρμοσύνη,-ης   N1F 1-1-2-0-3-7
Lv 22,29; 1 Sm 18,6; Jer 31(48),33; 40(33),11;
Jdt 8,6

joyfulness, delight Lv 22,29; *day of rejoicing, joyful day* Jdt 8,6

Cf. HARLÉ 1988, 187

χαροπός,-ῆ/ός,-όν   A 1-0-0-0-0-1
Gn 49,12
amber

Cf. HARL 1986ᵃ, 309; MAXWELL-STUART 1981, 61; WEVERS 1993, 827

χαρσιθ   N F 0-0-1-0-0-1
Jer 19,2

= חרסית *potsherd*; πύλης τῆς χαρσιθ *Charsith Gate, Potsherd Gate*

Cf. SIMOTAS 1968, 145-146

χαρτηρία,-ας   N1F 0-0-0-0-1-1
3 Mc 4,20
stock of papyrus, paper; neol.

χάρτης,-ου⁺   N1M 0-0-1-0-0-1
Jer 43(36),23
papyrus roll

χαρτίον,-ου   N2N 0-0-13-0-0-13
Jer 43(36),2.4.6.14(bis)
dim. of χάρτης; *papyrus roll*

χάσκω   V 1-0-1-0-2-4
Gn 4,11; Ez 2,8; 1 Ezr 4,19.31

to open (the mouth) [τι] Ez 2,8; *to gape, to open* (the mouth) *widely* [τι] 1 Ezr 4,19; *id.* [τι] (metaph.) Gn 4,11

(→ἀνα-, ἐγ-)

χάσμα,-ατος⁺   N3N 0-1-0-0-0-1
2 Sm 18,17
(yawning) chasm, gulf

χαῦνος,-η/ος,-ον   A 0-0-0-0-1-1
Wis 2,3
thin, soft (of air)

χαυών,-ῶνος   N3M 0-0-2-0-0-2
Jer 7,18; 51(44),19

Hebr. loanword (כַּוָּן); *cake*; neol.

→CHANTRAINE

χεῖλος,-ους⁺   N3N 19-18-22-95-22-176
Gn 11,1.6.9; 22,17; 41,3

lip Nm 30,7; *language* (semit.; metaph.) Gn 11,9; *rim* (of a cup) 2 Chr 4,5; *edge* (of a curtain) Ex 26,4; *border* (of skin) Ex 26,10; *shore, bank* (of the sea) Gn 22,17; *id.* (of a river) Gn 41,3

*Jer 3,21 ἐκ χειλέων *of the lips* -שפתים על for MT שפים על ◇ שפיים על *on the trails, on the bare heights?*, see also Jer 7,29

Cf. CONYBEARE 1905=1988, 290; GEHMAN 1951=1972, 100-101; HARL 1984ᵃ=1992ᵃ, 40; WEVERS 1993, 147.150

χειμάζω⁺   V 0-0-0-1-0-1

Prv 26,10
P: *to suffer grievously*

χείμαρρος/ους,-ου⁺   N2M 18-46-8-17-12-101
Gn 32,24; Lv 11,9.10; 23,40; Nm 21,14

torrent, brook (with abundant water in winter)

Cf. CAIRD 1969=1972, 151; DOGNIEZ 1992, 96.128

χειμερινός,-ή,-όν⁺   A 0-0-2-2-1-5
Jer 43(36),22; Zech 10,1; Prv 27,15; Ezr 10,13; 1 Ezr 9,11

pertaining to winter, winter-

χειμέριος,-ος,-ον   A 0-0-0-0-1-1
Wis 16,29
wintry

χειμών,-ῶνος⁺   N3M 0-0-0-4-3-7
Jb 37,6(bis); Ct 2,11; Ezr 10,9; 1 Ezr 9,6

heavy rain, storm Ezr 10,9; *id.* (metaph.) 4 Mc 15,32

*Sir 21,8 χειμῶνα *winter* corr.? χῶμα *mound*

Cf. SPICQ 1978ᵃ, 305-306

χείρ, χειρός⁺   N3F 367-628-349-370-229-1943
Gn 3,22; 4,11; 5,29; 8,9; 9,2

hand Gn 3,22; *forefoot* (of anim.) Lv 11,27; *arm* Gn 24,22

hand, power, control Gn 41,35; *rule, dominion* 2 Sm 8,3; *power* (of iron) Jb 5,20; *hand, power* (of God) Ezr 7,6

signpost (monument with pointing hand) Ez 21,24

axle-tree 1 Kgs 7,18(32); *space* 1 Kgs 7,21; *handle* Ct 5,5(secundo)

rendition of Hebr. semi-prep. with יד: διὰ χειρός τινος *by the hand of, by* (instrumental, semit.) Ez 30,10; ἐκ χειρός τινος *from the hand of, from* Gn 9,5; ἐν χειρί τινος *by the hand of, by* (instrumental, semit.) Jos 21,2; ἐπὶ χεῖρά τινος *next to* Neh 3,4

κατὰ χεῖράς σου *according to your will* Sir 25,26; χεῖρας σιδηρᾶς *iron claws* (instrument of torture) 4 Mc 8,13; ἀνέστακεν αὐτῷ χεῖρα *he raised a hand for him, he set up help for him* 1 Sm 15,12; παραδίδωμί σε εἰς χεῖρας ὧν μισεῖς *I will deliver you into the hands of those whom you hate* Ez 23,28; ἐν ταῖς χερσίν σου *in your hands* (indicating power) Gn 16,6; οὐκ ἐν ἀληθείᾳ χειρός *not in truth of hand* 1 Chr 12,18; παραδώσει αὐτὸν εἰς χεῖρας πτώσεως αὐτοῦ *she will give him over to his own ruin* Sir 4,19; ἀνὰ χεῖρα αὐτοῦ παρῆγον *they passed by him* (semit.) 2 Sm 15,18

*Dt 2,36 εἰς τὰς χεῖρας ἡμῶν *in our hands*

בירׄ(י)נו (Sam. Pent.) for MT לפנינו *before us*; *Jer
2,34 ἐν ταῖς χερσίν σου *on your hands* -בכפיך
for MT בכנפיך *on your wings, on your skirts*; *Jer
30,3(49,9) χεῖρα αὐτῶν *their hand* -יד/ם for MT
רי/ם *their need, that which is required by them*;
*Jer 30,4(49,10) διὰ χεῖρα *by the hand, by the*
arm -זרוע for MT זרע *offspring*; *Ez 21,17 ἐπὶ τὴν
χεῖρά σου *(clap) your hands* יד/ך for MT ירך *the*
thigh; *Hos 11,6 ἐν ταῖς χερσὶν αὐτοῦ *with his*
hands -בד/יריו for MT בריו *his parts?*; *Ps 57(58),11
τὰς χεῖρας αὐτοῦ *his hands* -כפיו for MT פעמיו
his feet; *Ps 73(74),3 τὰς χεῖράς σου *your hands*
-כפיך for MT פעמיך *your feet*; *Jb 33,7 (οὐ)δὲ ἡ
χείρ μου *and my hand* -וכפי for MT ואכפי *and*
my burden

Cf. DELCOR 1967ᵇ, 230-240; GEHMAN 1951=1972, 100;
1966=1972, 105; LE BOULLUEC 1989, 44.94-95.
112-113.117-118.163-164; LUST 1994, 163; SOLLAMO 1979,
156-221; WEVERS 1993, 221.291; →LSJ suppl(2 Sm 8,3; 1
Chr 18,3; Ez 21,24); NIDNTT; TWNT

χειραγωγέω⁺   V 0-1-0-0-1-2
Jgsᴬ 16,26; Tobˢ 11,16
to lead by the hand [τινα]; neol.
Cf. SPICQ 1978ᵃ, 967; →TWNT

-χειρέω
(→ἐγ-, ἐπι-)

χειρίζω   V 0-0-0-1-0-1
Est 8,12e
to handle, to administer [τι]; neol.?
(→προ-)

χείριστος,-η,-ον   A 0-0-1-0-5-6
Est 3,13e; 2 Mc 5,23; 9,28; 13,9; 3 Mc 3,1
sup. of κακός; *worst*

χειρίστως   D 0-0-0-0-1-1
2 Mc 7,39
in a worse way

χειρόγραφον,-ου⁺   N2N 0-0-0-0-6-6
Tob 9,5; Tobᴮᴬ 5,3; Tobˢ 5,3(bis)
handwritten document, certificate of indebtedness,
bond; neol.?
Cf. DEISSMANN 1927, 332-334; MEGAS 1928, 305-320;
SPICQ 1978ᵃ, 968-970; →LAMPE; MM; PREISIGKE; TWNT

χειρονομία,-ας   N1F 0-0-0-0-1-1
3 Mc 1,5
hand-to-hand encounter

χειροπέδη,-ης   N1F 0-0-4-3-1-8
Is 45,14; Jer 47(40),1.4; Na 3,10; Ps 149,8
handcuff; neol.?

χειροποίητος,-ος,-ον⁺   A 2-0-8-3-3-16
Lv 26,1.30; Is 2,18; 10,11; 16,12

made by hands, artificial (of idols) Jdt 8,18; τὰ
χειροποίητα *the idols* Is 19,1
→TWNT

χειροτονία,-ας   N1F 0-0-1-0-0-1
Is 58,9
stretching forth of the hand(s), extension of the
hand(s)
Cf. TOV 1977, 193

χειρόω   V 0-0-0-3-3-6
Jb 3,8; 13,15; 30,24; 2 Mc 4,34.42
M: *to subdue, to overpower* [τινα] Jb 13,15; *to*
attack (an anim.) [τινα] Jb 3,8; *to kill* [τινα]
2 Mc 4,42

χείρων,-ων,-ον⁺   A 0-1-0-0-3-4
1 Sm 17,43; 3 Mc 5,20; Wis 15,18; 17,6
comp. of κακός; *worse*

χελεθθι   N M 0-1-0-0-0-1
2 Sm 8,18
= כרתי? *Cheretites, Cretans?*; see χερεθθι

χελιδών,-όνος   N3F 0-0-2-0-2-4
Is 38,14; Jer 8,7; Od 11,14; LtJ 21
swallow

χελύνιον,-ου   N2N 1-0-0-0-0-1
Dt 34,7
jaw; *Dt 34,7 τὰ χελύνια αὐτοῦ *his jaws* -לחי/ו
for MT לחה *his power, his vital strength*
Cf. DOGNIEZ 1992, 356

χελώνη,-ης   N1F 0-0-1-0-0-1
Hos 12,12
hillock, mound
Cf. DRIVER 1954, 238-239

χελωνίς,-ίδος   N3F 0-0-0-0-1-1
Jdt 14,15
threshold; neol.

χερεθ   N F 0-0-1-0-0-1
Jer 44(37),16
= (ה)כרת? (MH) *excommunication?* for MT
(ה)חניות ◊חנות *vaulted rooms, cells?*

χερεθθι   N M 0-3-0-0-0-3
1 Kgs 1,38.44; 1 Chr 18,17
= כרתי *Cheretites, Cretans?*; see χελεθθι

χερουβ⁺   N M/N 4-7-6-0-0-17
Ex 25,19(bis); 38,7(37,8)(bis); 1 Kgs 6,24
= כרוב *cherub*

χερουβιμ/ιν⁺   N M/N 12-25-22-5-2-66
Gn 3,24; Ex 25,18.19.20(bis)
pl. of χερουβ
Cf. WEVERS 1990, 412.611; →NIDNTT; TWNT

χερσαῖος,-α,-ον   A 1-0-0-0-1-2
Lv 11,29; Wis 19,19

accustomed or suited to dry land Lv 11,29;
χερσαῖα land animals Wis 19,19
Cf. LARCHER 1985, 1089

χέρσος,-ος,-ον   A 0-0-6-0-2-8
Is 5,6; 7,23.24.25; Hos 10,4
dry, barren Is 7,24; (ἡ) χέρσος barren land Is 5,6
Cf. SHIPP 1979, 569

χερσόω⁺   V 0-0-2-1-1-4
Jer 2,31; Na 1,10; Prv 24,31; Wis 4,19
P: to be left dry and barren Jer 2,31; id.
(metaph.) Prv 24,31

χεττιιν   N 0-1-0-0-0-1
2 Kgs 23,7
= -כתים? or -כתנים? linen garments for MT בָּתִים
houses?
Cf. SIMOTAS 1968, 147-148

χέω⁺   V 0-0-6-3-1-10
Jer 7,20; Ez 20,33.34; Hos 4,2; Jl 2,2
A: to pour, to shed [τι] Sir 43,19; id. [τινα]
(metaph.) Mal 3,3
P: to be poured forth with [τινι] Jb 29,6; to be
spread out Jb 38,38; id. (metaph.) Hos 4,2
(→ἀπο-, δια-, ἐγ-, ἐκ-, ἐπι-, κατα-, μετα-,
περι-, προσ-, ὑπερ-)

χήλη,-ης   N1F 2-0-0-0-0-2
Lv 11,3; Dt 14,6
hoof, cloven hoof

χήρα,-ας⁺   N1F 18-7-18-13-13-69
Gn 38,11; Ex 22,21.23; Lv 21,14; 22,13
widow Gn 38,11
γυναικὸς χήρας of the widow 1 Kgs 11,26; τῷ
ὀρφανῷ καὶ τῇ χήρᾳ for the orphan and for the
widow (frequent) Dt 24,19
Cf. WALTERS 1973, 182; →NIDNTT; TWNT

χηρεία,-ας⁺   N1F 0-0-3-0-0-3
Is 47,9; 54,4; Mi 1,16
widowhood
Cf. ZIEGLER 1943=1971, 112(Mi 1,16)

χήρευσις,-εως   N3F 2-0-0-0-4-6
Gn 38,14.19; Jdt 8,5.6; 10,3
widowhood; neol.

χηρεύω⁺   V 0-1-1-0-1-3
2 Sm 13,20; Jer 28(51),5; Jdt 8,4
to be deprived or forsaken Jer 28(51),5; to be
widowed, to live in widowhood Jdt 8,4

χθιζός,-ή,-όν   A 0-0-0-1-0-1
Jb 8,9
of yesterday

χίδρον,-ου   N2N 3-0-0-0-0-3
Lv 2,14.16; 23,14

groat, hulled kernel
Cf. WALTERS 1973, 98.303

χιλιαρχία,-ας   N1F 1-0-0-0-1-2
Nm 31,48; 1 Mc 5,13
unit of a thousand soldiers, unit under the
command of a χιλίαρχος Nm 31,48; a
thousand 1 Mc 5,13

χιλίαρχος,-ου⁺   N2M 8-14-3-0-4-29
Ex 18,21.25; Nm 1,16; 31,14.48
captain over a thousand men Ex 18,21
*Jos 22,14 χιλίαρχοι captains of a thousand
אַלֻּפֵי(ל) for MT אַלְפֵי(ל) to the clans
→NIDNTT

χιλιάς,-άδος⁺   N3F 73-202-35-6-24-340
Gn 24,60; Ex 12,37; 20,6; 34,7; Nm 1,21
a thousand, one thousand
→NIDNTT; TWNT

χίλιοι,-αι,-α⁺   Mc 14-44-8-36-27-129
Gn 20,14.16; Ex 39,2.5.6(38,25.28.29)
a thousand, one thousand
→NIDNTT

χιλιοπλασίως   D 1-0-0-0-0-1
Dt 1,11
a thousandfold more, a thousand times over;
neol.

χίλιος,-α,-ον   Mc 0-2-0-0-2-4
1 Kgs 3,4; 2 Chr 1,6; 1 Mc 4,1; 10,79
always followed by a coll. sg.; a thousand, of
thousand

χίμαιρα,-ας   N1F 3-0-0-0-0-3
Lv 4,28.29; 5,6
young she-goat

χίμαρος,-ου⁺   N2M 48-2-0-5-1-56
Lv 4,23.24; 9,3.15; 10,16
young he-goat Lv 4,23
*Neh 5,18 χίμαρος goat - צָפִיר for MT צִפֳּרִים fowls
Cf. SHIPP 1979, 569-570; →SCHLEUSNER(Neh 5,18)

χιονόομαι   V 0-0-0-1-0-1
Ps 67(68),15
P: to be snowed upon; neol.
Cf. CAIRD 1969=1972, 151-152; SHIPP 1979, 570

χιτών,-ῶνος⁺   N3M 21-4-3-2-5-35
Gn 3,21; 37,3.23.31(bis)
Semit. loanword (Hebr. כֻּתֹּנֶת); tunic, shirt
(garment worn next to the skin; by women) Gn
3,21; id. (id.; by men) Jdt 14,19; id. (id.; by
priests) Lv 6,3
Cf. DODD 1954, 182.191-193; HARL 1986ᵃ, 69.111; HARLÉ
1988, 113; LE BOULLUEC 1989, 295; LEVIN 1969, 66-75;
TOV 1979, 221; WALTERS 1973, 163.172; →CHANTRAINE;

FRISK

χιών,-όνος⁺ N3F 2-3-3-13-6-27
Ex 4,6; Nm 12,10; 2 Sm 23,20; 2 Kgs 5,27; 1 Chr
11,22
snow
Cf. SHIPP 1979, 570; →NIDNTT

χλαῖνα,-ης N1F 0-0-0-1-0-1
Prv 31,22
upper-garment

χλαμύς,-ύδος⁺ N3F 0-0-0-0-1-1
2 Mc 12,35
cloak, coat

χλευάζω⁺ V 0-0-0-0-3-3
2 Mc 7,27; 4 Mc 5,22; Wis 11,14
to scoff, to mock at, to treat scornfully [τινα]
2 Mc 7,27; *id.* [τι] 4 Mc 5,22
Cf. HELBING 1928, 23; HORSLEY 1982, 104

χλεύασμα,-ατος N3N 0-0-0-1-0-1
Jb 12,4
object of mockery; neol.

χλευασμός,-οῦ N2M 0-0-1-1-0-2
Jer 20,8; Ps 78(79),4
object of mockery
Cf. CAIRD 1976, 82; HARL 1984ᵇ=1992ᵃ, 48.57.58

χλιδών,-ῶνος N3M 1-2-1-0-2-6
Nm 31,50; 2 Sm 1,10; 8,7; Is 3,20; Jdt 10,4
bracelet, anklet

χλόη-ης N1F 0-2-0-9-3-14
2 Sm 23,4; 2 Kgs 19,26; Ps 22(23),2; 36(37),2;
89(90),5
young green growth Jb 38,27; *tender grass* 2 Kgs
19,26

χλοηφόρος,-ος,-ον A 0-0-0-0-1-1
Wis 19,7
green-growing
Cf. LARCHER 1985, 1060

χλωρίζω V 2-0-0-0-0-2
Lv 13,49; 14,37
to be greenish; neol.

χλωρός,-ά,-όν⁺ A 7-1-5-2-0-15
Gn 1,30; 2,5; 30,37(bis); Ex 10,15
(light) green (of plants) Gn 1,30; τὰ χλωρά *green
herbs, herbage* Nm 22,4
Cf. LEE, J. 1983, 58-59

χλωρότης,-ητος N3F 0-0-0-1-0-1
Ps 67(68),14
pale (green-)yellow, yellowness (of gold); neol.
→LSJ RSuppl

χνοῦς,-οῦ⁺ N2M 0-0-5-2-1-8
Is 5,24; 17,13; 29,5; 41,15; Hos 13,3

dust Ps 1,4; *chaff* Hos 13,3
*Is 5,24 χνοῦς *chaff* -מץ for MT פח *smell of decay*
Cf. LARCHER 1984, 378; →LSJ suppl(Is 5,24)

χοεύς,-έως N3M 0-1-0-0-0-1
1 Kgs 7,24(38)
chous (liquid measure of volume; rendering
Hebr. בת *bath*); cpr. χοῖνιξ and χοῦς

χοθωνωθ N 0-0-0-2-0-2
Neh 7,70(69).72(71)
= כתנות *garments*

χοῖνιξ,-ικος⁺ N3F 0-0-3-0-0-3
Ez 45,10.11(bis)
choenix, a quart (a dry measure; rendering Hebr.
בת *bath*); cpr. χοεύς and χοῦς
Cf. SHIPP 1979, 573

χοιρογρύλλιος,-ου N2M 2-0-0-2-0-4
Lv 11,6; Dt 14,7; Ps 103(104),18; Prv 30,26
rabbit, coney; neol.
Cf. HARLÉ 1988, 128; PIETERSMA 1990, 267-268

χολάω
(→ἐκ-)

χολέρα,-ας N1F 1-0-0-0-2-3
Nm 11,20; Sir 31,20; 37,30
cholera, nausea, dysentery

χολή,-ῆς⁺ N1F 2-0-2-6-15-25
Dt 29,17; 32,32; Jer 8,14; 9,14; Ps 68(69),22
gall bladder Tob 6,4; *gall* (metaph.) Dt 29,17
Cf. DOGNIEZ 1992, 301; →NIDNTT

χόλος,-ου N2M 0-0-0-1-3-4
Eccl 5,16; 3 Mc 5,1.30; Wis 18,22
gall, bitter anger, wrath

χονδρίτης,-ου N1M 1-0-0-0-0-1
Gn 40,16
cake of coarse grain; neol.
Cf. CONYBEARE 1905=1988, 120; HARL 1986ᵃ, 271;
WEVERS 1993, 670

χορδή,-ῆς⁺ N1F 0-0-1-1-0-2
Na 3,8; Ps 150,4
string (of musical instrument made of guts); ἐν
χορδαῖς *with string instruments* Ps 150,4
*Na 3,8 χορδήν *string* -מן for MT מִצֹּא (better)
than No or *(better) than Thebes*

χορεία,-ας N1F 0-0-0-0-1-1
Jdt 15,13
choral dance

χορεύω⁺ V 0-7-0-0-1-8
Jgs 21,21; 21,23; 1 Sm 18,6
to dance a round or *choral dance* 4 Mc 14,8; *to
dance* Jgs 21,21

χορηγέω⁺ V 0-3-0-1-14-18

1 Kgs 4,7(bis); 5,1(5,7); Dnᴸˣˣ 4,12(9); Jdt 12,2
A: *to defray the charges* 2 Mc 9,16; *to provide for*
[τινι] 1 Kgs 4,7(primo); *to supply, to provide*
[abs.] 1 Kgs 4,7(secundo); *to provide sb with sth*
[τινί τι] 1 Mc 14,10; *to give to* [τί τινι] Sir
1,10; *to give* [τι] Sir 39,33
P: *to be provided for* 3 Mc 6,40
Cf. Helbing 1928, 193-194; Lefebvre 1991, 316
(→ἐπι-)

χορηγία,-ας   N1F 0-0-0-2-5-7
Ezr 5,3.9; 1 Ezr 4,54.55; 2 Mc 4,14
expense, charges 1 Ezr 4,54; *abundant supply,*
abundance 3 Mc 5,2; *spectacle at public expense*
2 Mc 4,14; *furniture* (of the temple) Ezr 5,3
Cf. Mowinckel 1965, 134; Robert 1937, 290(2 Mc 4,14);
Wilhelm 1932, 46(2 Mc 4,14); →LSJ suppl(Ezr 5,3); LSJ
RSuppl(Ezr 5,3)

χορηγός,-οῦ   N2M 0-0-0-0-1-1
2 Mc 1,25
one who defrays the costs, sponsor and manager

χόριον,-ου   N2N 1-0-0-0-0-1
Dt 28,57
placenta, afterbirth
Cf. Dogniez 1992, 294

χορός,-οῦ⁺   N2M 2-10-0-5-7-24
Ex 15,20; 32,19; Jgsᴬ 9,27; 11,34; 21,21
dance Ex 15,20; *band of dancers* 1 Sm 10,5
*2 Sm 6,13 χοροί *choirs, bands* -צערים (ptc. of
צער)? *those processing* for MT צערים (pl. of subst.
צער) *steps*
Cf. Perpillou-Thomas 1989, 153-155

χορτάζω⁺   V 0-0-1-12-1-14
Jer 5,7; Ps 16(17),14.15; 36(37),19; 58(59),16
A: *to feed, to fatten* [τι] Jb 38,27; *to satisfy with*
[τινά τινος] Ps 131(132),15; *id.* [τινά τι] Ps
80(81),17; *id.* [τινά τινος] (metaph.) Lam 3,15
P: *to be full of fruit* (of trees) Ps 103(104),16; *to*
be filled with [τινος] (metaph.) Tobˢ 12,9; *to be*
satisfied Ps 16(17),15; *to be satisfied with* [τινος]
Ps 16(17),14; *id.* [ἀπό τινος] Ps 103(104),13
Cf. Helbing 1928, 50.149; →NIDNTT

χορτασία,-ας   N1F 0-0-0-1-0-1
Prv 24,15
being fed, satiety, fullness; neol.

χόρτασμα,-ατος⁺   N3N 5-2-0-0-3-10
Gn 24,25.32; 42,27; 43,24; Dt 11,15
fodder, forage (for anim.); neol.?
Cf. Lee, J. 1983, 100; →LSJ RSuppl; NIDNTT

χορτομανέω   V 0-0-0-1-0-1
Prv 24,31

to run to grass, to grow rank, to be covered, to be
covered with grass; neol.

χόρτος,-ου⁺   N2M 8-1-15-25-2-51
Gn 1,11.12.29.30; 2,5
grass, herb Prv 19,12; *grass, hay* (as fodder) Ps
105(106),20; *hay, stubble* (for MT עמיר) Jer 9,21,
cpr. Is 10,17; 32,13 (for MT שמיר *thorns*)
λάχανα χόρτου *vegetables of hay* for MT ירק עשׂב
green grass Gn 9,3, cpr. Ps 36(37),2
Cf. Harl 1986ᵃ, 91.97.110.139; Paradise 1986, 192;
Rösel 1994, 195(Gn 9,3); Schnebel 1925, 211-218;
→NIDNTT

χορτώδης,-ης,-ες   A 0-0-0-0-1-1
2 Mc 5,27
of grass, grass-like; neol.

χοῦς, χοός⁺   N2/3M 5-11-9-16-2-43
Gn 2,7; Lv 14,41.42.45; Dt 28,24
dust
Cf. Alexandre 1988, 236-237; Harl 1986ᵃ, 101; Rösel
1994, 61; →NIDNTT

χοῦς, χοός   N2/3M 1-0-0-0-0-1
Lv 19,36
chous (liquid measure, rendering Hebr. בת *bath*);
cpr. χοεύς and χοῖνιξ
Cf. Zipor 1991, 334; →LSJ RSuppl

χόω   V 0-0-0-0-2-2
Tob 8,18
to fill up (with earth) [τι]

χράω⁺   V 7-1-3-27-18-56
Gn 12,16; 16,6; 19,8; 26,29; 34,31
A: *to use sb or sth* [τινι] Jdt 3,2; *id.* [abs.] Jdt
3,3; *to use for, to apply for* [τί τινι] 4 Mc 13,13
M: *to use* Est 1,19; *id.* [τινι] Gn 16,6; *id.* [ἔν
τινι] 3 Mc 4,20; *id.* [ἐπί τινι] LtJ 58; *to treat*
[τινι] Gn 12,16; *to deal* [abs.] Jb 34,20
P: *to be used* Jer 13,7
ἄλλως χράομαι *to use differently, to change* Est
1,19, see also 9,27; ἵνα ἑαυτῇ χρήσηται *so that*
she will abuse herself Sir 26,10
(→κατα-, παρα-, προσ-)
Cf. Helbing 1928, 253; Wevers 1990, 163.187

χρεία,-ας⁺   N1F 0-1-3-6-45-55
2 Chr 2,15; Is 13,17; Jer 22,28; 31(48),38; Ps
15(16),2
need 2 Chr 2,15; *need of* [τινος] Tobˢ 5,12; *what*
is necessary, needful thing Sir 29,3; *use* Sir 39,26;
office, duty, service LtJ 59; *occupation, business*
1 Mc 11,63; (αἱ) χρεῖαι *affairs, business* 1 Mc
10,37; *services* Sir 38,1
χρείαν ἔχω *I need* Tobˢ 5,7; οἱ πρὸς ταῖς

χρείαις the officers on duty Jdt 12,10
*Ps 15(16),2 οὐ χρείαν ἔχεις (of my goods)
you have no need -בל אליך (my goods) are nothing
for you for MT בל עליך not above you, not apart
from you
→NIDNTT

χρεμετίζω   V 0-0-2-0-1-3
Jer 5,8; 38(31),7; Sir 33,6
to neigh, to whinny (of horses) Sir 33,6; id.
(metaph.) Jer 38(31),7

χρεμετισμός,-οῦ   N2M 0-0-4-0-0-4
Jer 8,6.16; 13,27; Am 6,7
neighing, whinnying Jer 8,16; id. (metaph.) Jer
13,27
*Jer 8,6 ἐν χρεμετισμῷ αὐτοῦ in his neighing
-במצהלה? (cpr. Jer 13,27) for MT במלחמה in battle

χρεοκοπέω   V 0-0-0-0-1-1
4 Mc 2,8
M: to cut down the debt [τι]

χρέος,-ους   N3N 2-1-0-0-1-4
Dt 15,2.3; 1 Sm 2,20; Wis 15,8
debt Dt 15,3
ἀντὶ τοῦ χρέους τινός in return for 1 Sm 2,20;
τὸ τῆς ψυχῆς ἀπαιτηθεὶς χρέος the soul which
was lent is demanded, end of life, death Wis 15,8
Cf. DOGNIEZ 1992, 210; LARCHER 1985, 865-866

χρεοφειλέτης,-ου⁺   N1M 0-0-0-2-0-2
Jb 31,37; Prv 29,13
debtor
Cf. WALTERS 1973, 32.33

χρή (impers.)⁺   V 0-0-0-1-0-1
Prv 25,27
it is necessary [+inf.]
→NIDNTT

χρῄζω⁺   V 0-1-0-0-0-1
JgsᴮB 11,7
to want, to have need, to desire
→NIDNTT

χρῆμα,-ατος⁺   N3N 0-3-0-7-31-41
Jos 22,8; 2 Chr 1,11.12; Jb 6,20; 27,17
τὰ χρήματα goods, wealth, means Jos 22,8;
means Sir 34,20; money 2 Mc 3,7
Cf. BICKERMAN 1980, 163; →NIDNTT; TWNT

χρηματίζω⁺   V 0-1-8-1-0-10
1 Kgs 18,27; Jer 32(25),30(bis); 33(26),2(bis)
to deal with [τινι] Jb 40,8; to be engaged in
business 1 Kgs 18,27
to give a response, to declare (of an oracle of the
Lord) Jer 33(26),2; to speak, to prophesy [τι] Jer
36(29),23

Cf. BICKERMAN 1986, 139-144; HELBING 1928, 245;
→NIDNTT; TWNT

χρηματισμός,-οῦ⁺   N2M 0-0-0-1-2-3
Prv 31,1; 2 Mc 2,4; 11,17
oracular response, divine statement 2 Mc 2,4;
public written document, petition 2 Mc 11,17;
neol.?
Cf. HORSLEY 1987, 176; →NIDNTT; TWNT

χρηματιστήριον,-ου   N2N 0-0-0-0-1-1
1 Ezr 3,14
seat of judgement; neol.
Cf. BARR 1961, 136

χρησιμεύω   V 0-0-0-0-2-2
Wis 4,3; Sir 13,4
to be useful

χρήσιμος,-η,-ον⁺   A 1-0-3-1-10-15
Gn 37,26; Ez 15,4; Zech 6,10.14; Prv 17,17
useful Ez 15,4; id. (of pers.) Prv 17,17;
χρήσιμον (unjust) gain Gn 37,26
*Zech 6,10 παρὰ τῶν χρησίμων αὐτῆς from its
useful men -מאת טוביה from its good ones for MT
מאת טוביה from Tobiah, see also 6,14
χρησιμώτερος more useful, more profitable Tobᴮˢ
3,10
Cf. WAANDERS 1983, 186; WEVERS 1993, 624-625

χρῆσις,-εως⁺   N3F 0-1-0-0-4-5
1 Sm 1,28; Tobˢ 1,13; Wis 15,7.15; Sir 18,8
use Wis 15,7; usefulness, profit Sir 18,8; loan
1 Sm 1,28

χρησμολογέω   V 0-0-1-0-0-1
Jer 45(38),4
to prophesy [τι]

χρηστεύομαι⁺   V 0-0-0-0-1-1
PSal 9,6
to be kind to, to be merciful towards [τινι];
neol.
Cf. SPICQ 1978ᵃ, 975; →NIDNTT; TWNT

χρηστοήθεια,-ας   N1F 0-0-0-0-1-1
Sir 37,11
goodness of heart, generosity of spirit

χρηστός,-ή,-όν⁺   A 0-0-10-20-11-41
Jer 24,2.3(bis).5; 40(33),11
good Ps 51(52),11; fine (of metals) 1 Ezr 8,56;
good, precious (of stones) Ez 27,22; good, tasty,
sweet (of fruits) Jer 24,2; kind, good (of pers.) Jb
31,31; good, bountiful (of pers.) 1 Mc 6,11; good,
merciful (of God) Ps 24(25),8
Cf. GRIBOMONT-THIBAUT 1959, 75-77; SPICQ 1978ᵃ,
971-973; ZIEGLER 1937, 18-54; →NIDNTT; TWNT

χρηστότης,-ητος⁺   N3F 0-0-0-17-9-26

Ps 13(14),1.3; 20(21),4; 24(25),7; 30(31),20
goodness, kindness, generosity Est 8,12c;
goodness, uprightness, what is right Ps 36(37),3;
goodness, mercy (of God) 1 Ezr 5,58

Cf. SPICQ 1947, 321-324; 1978ᵃ, 971-976; STACHOWIAK
1957, 3-7; →NIDNTT; TWNT

χρηστῶς   D 0-0-0-0-1-1
Wis 8,1
well

χρῖσις,-εως   N3F 14-0-0-0-1-15
Ex 29,21; 30,31; 31,11; 35,28; 38,25
anointing Ex 29,21
*Lv 7,35 χρῖσις *anointing* -משחה‖ for MT משחה‖
part, portion

Cf. HARLÉ 1988, 112; WALTERS 1973, 98; →NIDNTT

χρῖσμα,-ατος⁺   N3N 7-0-0-2-1-10
Ex 29,7; 30,25(bis); 35,12a(12).19
anointing Ex 29,7; *coating, glazing* Sir 38,30

Cf. WALTERS 1973, 98; →NIDNTT, TWNT

χριστός,-ή,-όν   A 5-21-3-13-8-50
Lv 4,5.16; 6,15; 21,10.12
anointed Lv 4,5; *id.* (of the Messiah) PSal 18,tit.,
see also 17,32; 18,5.7; *id.* (of the kings of Israel)
1 Sm 24,7; οἱ χριστοί *the anointed ones* (of the
prophets) Ps 104(105),15
τοῦ ἐλαίου τοῦ χριστοῦ *of the anointing oil* Lv
21,10
*Am 4,13 χριστὸν αὐτοῦ *his anointed one* -משיחו
for MT שׂחו מה *what (is) his thought*

Cf. DE JONGE 1966, 134-137; GROSART 1890, 275-276;
HARLÉ 1988, 179; →NIDNTT; TWNT

χρίω⁺   V 26-37-7-4-5-79
Ex 28,41; 29,2.7.29.36
to anoint [τι] Ex 30,26; *id.* [τινα] Ex 28,41; *to
anoint sb to be* [τινα εἰς τινα] 1 Sm 9,16; *to
coat, to paint* [τι] Jer 22,14
*Ez 43,3 τοῦ χρῖσαι *to anoint* -משׁח◊ למשחת for
MT לשׁחת *to destroy*; *Hos 8,10 τοῦ χρίειν *from
anointing* -מ/משׁח for MT מ/משׂא *under the burden*

Cf. HELBING 1928, 63; →NIDNTT; TWNT

(-δια-, ἐγ-, κατα-)

χρόα,-ας⁺   N1F 1-0-0-0-2-3
Ex 4,7; 2 Mc 3,16; Wis 13,14
colour of the skin, complexion Ex 4,7; *colour of
the face* (of idols) Wis 13,14

Cf. LE BOULLUEC 1989, 97

χρονίζω⁺   V 5-3-3-6-10-27
Gn 32,5; 34,19; Ex 32,1; Dt 4,25; 23,22
to spend a long time, to dwell a long time Dt
4,25; *to take time, to tarry, to linger* Gn 32,4; *to

delay [abs.] Ps 69(70),6; *id.* [+inf.] Ex 32,1; *id.*
[τοῦ +inf.] Gn 34,19; *to delay beyond* [ἀπό
τινος] 2 Sm 20,5
*Prv 31,21 ὅταν χρονίζῃ *when he tarries* corr.?
ὅταν χιονίζῃ *when it snows* for MT משׁלג *because
of snow*

Cf. WEVERS 1990, 517(Ex 32,1); 1993, 530; 1995, 80(Dt
4,25); →NIDNTT

(-ἐγ-, συγ-)

χρονίσκος,-ου   N2M 0-0-0-0-1-1
2 Mc 11,1
a short time; neol.

χρόνος,-ου⁺   N2M 7-3-23-41-67-141
Gn 26,1.15; Ex 14,13; Dt 12,19; 22,19
time Dt 22,19; *a stretch of time, period* Dt 12,19;
lifetime Is 23,15; *age* Jb 32,6; *delay* Wis 12,20;
time, duration Jb 10,20; οἱ χρόνοι *chronicles*
1 Ezr 1,40
χρόνον μικρόν *a little while* Jb 2,9a; εἰς τὸν
μετέπειτα χρόνον *hereafter* Est 3,13g; εἰς τὸν
αἰῶνα χρόνον *for ever* Ex 14,13; εἰς χρόνον
πολύν *for a long time* Is 34,10; διὰ χρόνου *after
a long time* Is 30,27; ἐν τῷ χρόνῳ τινός *in the
time of* Gn 26,15; χρόνον τινά ... χρόνον δέ *at
one time ... at another time* Prv 7,12; ὅσον
χρόνον *so long* Jos 4,14
*Is 51,8 χρόνον *time* -עת for MT עשׁ *a moth*; *Jb
12,5 εἰς χρόνον *at time* -לעתות for MT לעשׁתות
thoughts?; *Jb 14,11 χρόνῳ *in (length of) time*
-ים⁺ for MT ים *sea, lake*, cpr. Is 54,9
cpr. καιρός

Cf. BARR 1962, 5-174; DES PLACES 1964ᵇ, 112-117;
EYNIKEL-HAUSPIE 1997 forthcoming; LEE, J. 1983, 83;
WALTERS 1973, 160.245.325; WEVERS 1990, 216; →NIDNTT;
TWNT

χρυσαυγέω   V 0-0-0-1-0-1
Jb 37,22
to shine like gold; neol.

χρυσίον,-ου⁺   N2N 65-88-33-49-58-293
Gn 2,11.12; 13,2; 24,35; 44,8
Semit. loanword (Hebr. חרוץ); *gold* Gn 2,11;
golden ornament Ex 32,24
ἀργύριον καὶ χρυσίον *silver and gold, money*
Dt 17,17

Cf. TOV 1979, 221; →CHANTRAINE; FRISK; NIDNTT

χρυσοειδής,-ής,-ές   A 0-0-0-0-1-1
1 Ezr 8,56
gold-like

χρυσόλιθος,-ου⁺   N2M 2-0-1-0-0-3
Ex 28,20; 36(39),20; Ez 28,13

chrysolite; neol.
→LSJ RSuppl; NIDNTT

χρυσός,-οῦ⁺   N2M 0-2-1-7-6-16
JgsᴬA 8,26; 1 Kgs 10,2; Is 60,9; Jb 3,15; 41,22
Semit. loanword (Hebr. חרוץ); *gold*
Cf. BICKERMAN 1980, 12-13; LEE, J. 1983, 63-65; TOV
1979, 221; →CHANTRAINE; FRISK; LSJ RSuppl; NIDNTT

χρυσουργός,-οῦ   N2M 0-0-0-0-1-1
Wis 15,9
gold-worker, goldsmith; neol.

χρυσοῦς,-ῆ,-οῦν/-εος,-α,-ον⁺ A 52-62-10-56-36-216
Gn 24,22.53; 37,28; 41,42; 45,22
golden
Cf. LEE, J. 1983, 63-65; WEVERS 1990, 260; →NIDNTT

χρυσοῦς,-οῦ⁺   N2M 15-1-0-0-0-16
Gn 24,22; 37,28; Nm 7,14.20.26
a gold coin Gn 37,28; *piece of gold, golden coin*
(used as a measure of weight) Nm 7,14
Cf. DORIVAL 1994, 258

χρυσοφορέω   V 0-0-0-0-1-1
1 Mc 14,43
to wear gold, to wear golden ornaments

χρυσοχάλινος,-ος,-ον   A 0-0-0-0-2-2
1 Ezr 3,6; 2 Mc 10,29
with golden bridles

χρυσοχόος,-ου⁺   N2M 0-0-5-0-1-6
Is 40,19; 46,6; Jer 10,9.14; 28(51),17
smelter of gold, goldsmith

χρυσόω⁺   V 3-4-0-0-0-7
Ex 25,11; 26,32.37; 2 Kgs 18,16; 2 Chr 3,7
to gild [τι] Ex 25,11
ἐχρύσωσε χρυσίῳ *he gilded with gold* (semit.)
2 Chr 3,9 and passim
→NIDNTT
(→κατα-, περι-)

χρύσωμα,-ατος⁺   N3N 0-0-0-0-7-7
1 Ezr 3,6; 8,56; 1 Mc 11,58(bis); 15,32
golden cup 1 Ezr 3,6; *golden vessel* 2 Mc 4,32

χρῶμα,-ατος⁺   N3N 2-0-0-1-1-4
Ex 34,29.30; Est 5,1d; Wis 15,4
complexion Ex 34,29; *colour* Wis 15,4
Cf. LE BOULLUEC 1989, 345; WALTERS 1973, 137

χρώς, χρωτός⁺   N3M 15-0-0-0-0-15
Ex 28,42; Lv 13,2(bis).3(bis)
skin Ex 28,42; *flesh* Lv 13,2
Cf. WALTERS 1973, 137

χυδαῖος,-α,-ον   A 1-0-0-0-0-1
Ex 1,7
numerous; neol.?
Cf. LE BOULLUEC 1989, 74-75; WEVERS 1990, 3

χυλός,-οῦ   N2M 0-0-0-0-1-1
4 Mc 6,25
juice of plants

χύμα,-ατος   N3N 0-1-0-0-1-2
1 Kgs 5,9; 2 Mc 2,24
confused mass 2 Mc 2,24; *largeness, overflow* (of
heart) 1 Kgs 5,9

χύννω
(→ἀπο-, συγ-)

χυτός,-ή,-όν   A 0-1-0-1-0-2
2 Chr 4,2; Jb 40,18
cast, melted

χύτρα,-ας   N1F 1-2-3-0-1-7
Nm 11,8; Jgs 6,19; Jl 2,6; Mi 3,3
earthen pot

χυτρόκαυλος,-ου   N2M 0-4-0-0-0-4
1 Kgs 7,24(38)(ter); 7,29(43)
laver, basin; neol.

χωθαρ   N N 0-3-0-0-0-3
2 Kgs 25,17(ter)
= כתרת *capital* (of pillar)
Cf. SIMOTAS 1968, 149

χωθαρεθ   N F 0-3-0-0-0-3
2 Chr 4,12(bis).13
= כתרות (Hebr. pl.) *capital* (of pillar)

χωλαίνω   V 0-2-0-1-0-3
2 Sm 4,4; 1 Kgs 18,21; Ps 17(18),46
A: *to walk lamely, to halt, to be irresolute, to
vacillate* (metaph.) 1 Kgs 18,21
P: *to become lame, to be made lame* 2 Sm 4,4
*Ps 17(18),46 καὶ ἐχώλαναν *and they went
lamely, they limped* -ויחגרו (Aram. and MH) for
MT ויחרגו *they came out trembling*

χωλός,-ή,-όν⁺   A 2-5-4-1-0-12
Lv 21,18; Dt 15,21; 2 Sm 5,6.8(bis)
lame
Cf. WALTERS 1973, 290(n.60)(Prv 26,7); →NIDNTT

χῶμα,-ατος   N3N 3-1-3-6-0-13
Ex 8,12.13(bis); Jos 8,28; Is 25,2
earth thrown up, mound (thrown up against the
walls of cities in order to take them) Ez 21,27;
sepulchral mound Jb 17,16; *heap of rubbish, ruin*
Jos 8,28; *dust of the earth* Ex 8,12
Cf. LE BOULLUEC 1989, 37-38.125; SHIPP 1979, 576;
WALTERS 1973, 196

χωμαριμ   N M 0-1-0-0-0-1
2 Kgs 23,5
= כמרים (pl.) *idolatrous priests*, cpr. Hos 10,5 (see
παραπικραίνω) and Zph 1,4
Cf. SIMOTAS 1968, 149-150

χωματίζω   V 0-1-0-0-0-1
Jos 11,13
to embank or *fortify with earthen mounds* or
dykes [τι]; neol.?

χώνευμα,-ατος⁺   N3N 1-1-3-0-0-5
Dt 9,12; 2 Kgs 17,16; Jer 10,3; Hos 13,2; Hab
2,18
molten work, molten image; neol.?

χώνευσις,-εως   N3F 1-1-0-0-0-2
Ex 39,4(38,27); 2 Chr 4,3
smelting, casting (of metal); neol.?

χωνευτήριον,-ου   N2N 0-1-3-0-1-5
1 Kgs 8,51; Zech 11,13(bis); Mal 3,2; Wis 3,6
smelting-furnace Wis 3,6
*Zech 11,13 εἰς τὸ χωνευτήριον *in the
smelting-furnace* -◊צור⁻ᴵᴵᴵ *to melt* for MT אל היוצר
◊יצר? *to the potter* or *to the smelter*
neol.

χωνευτής,-οῦ   N1M 0-1-0-0-0-1
Jgsᴬ 17,4
smelter, caster of metal; neol.

χωνευτός,-ή,-όν⁺   A 6-16-3-4-0-29
Ex 32,4; 34,17; Lv 19,4; Nm 33,52; Dt 9,16
formed of cast metal, molten Ex 32,4; τὸ
χωνευτόν *the molten image* Jgs 18,20; neol.
→LSJ Suppl

χωνεύω   V 5-6-9-0-1-21
Ex 26,37; 38(37),3; 38,10(37,13).18.20
to cast, to form by casting [τι] 2 Chr 4,3; *to
smelt, to cast* [τι] Ez 22,22; *to smelt* or *to collect*
[τι] 2 Kgs 22,9; neol.?

χώννυμι
(→κατα-)

χώρα,-ας⁺   N1F 15-16-59-71-86-247
Gn 10,20.31; 11,28.31; 15,7
place, spot Ex 14,27; *town* Jer 4,29; *spot, location*
(on a human body) Lv 13,23; *land, country* Gn
11,28; *territory* 1 Kgs 18,10; *the (open) country*
1 Ezr 5,45; *field, cultivated land* Sir 43,3; *region,
district* Gn 41,57
*Gn 11,28 ἐν τῇ χώρᾳ *in the land*
homoeophonic with MT אור *Ur*, see also Gn 15,7;
*Am 3,9 χώραις *to the countries* -◊ארמה? for MT
◊ארמון *to the strongholds*, see also Am 3,10.11; Mi
5,4
Cf. SHIPP 1979, 577-578; TREBOLLE BARRERA 1989,
57(1 Sm 5,6); WEVERS 1990, 223(Ex 14,27); 1993, 158

χωρέω⁺   V 1-3-0-0-6-10
Gn 13,6; 1 Kgs 7,24(38); 18,32; 2 Chr 4,5; 2 Mc
3,40
to have room for [τινα] Gn 13,6; *id.* [τι] 4 Mc
7,6; *to penetrate* Wis 7,23; *to turn out* 2 Mc 3,40;
to contain, to hold [τι] (often used with
measures) 1 Kgs 7,24
Cf. LARCHER 1984, 491(Wis 7,23); →NIDNTT
(→ἀνα-, ἀπο-, ἐκ-, ἐπι-, παρα-, προσ-, συγ-,
ὑπο-)

χωρίζω⁺   V 1-4-1-5-12-23
Lv 13,46; Jgs 4,11; Jgsᴮ 6,18; 1 Chr 12,9
A: *to remove* [τι] 1 Ezr 8,66; *to separate from*
[τινά τινος] 1 Ezr 8,54; *to remove from the teat*
[τινά τινος] 3 Mc 5,50; *to separate from* [ἀπό
τινος] Wis 1,3
P: *to be separated* 2 Ezr 9,1; *to be separated from*
[ἀπό τινος] 1 Chr 12,9; *to remove from* [ἀπό
τινος] Jgs 4,11; *id.* [τινος] 1 Ezr 5,39; *to depart*
2 Mc 5,21
κεχωρισμένος *separated, apart* Lv 13,46
Cf. HELBING 1928, 164; →NIDNTT
(→ἀπο-, δια-, κατα-)

χωρίον,-ου⁺   N2N 0-2-0-0-4-6
1 Chr 27,27(bis); 2 Mc 11,5; 12,7.21
place 4 Mc 15,20; *village* 2 Mc 11,5; *field* for MT
כרם *vineyard* (due to homoeophony?) 1 Chr 27,27
Cf. CAIRD 1976, 86; SHIPP 1979, 577-578

χωρίς⁺   P 7-4-0-1-8-20
Gn 26,1; 46,26; 47,22.26; Lv 9,17
[τινος]: *without* 4 Mc 2,8; *different from,
otherwise than* Gn 26,1; *except* Gn 47,26; *besides*
Gn 46,26
Cf. BLASS 1990, § 216

χωρισμός,-οῦ⁺   N2M 2-0-0-0-1-3
Lv 12,2; 18,19; 3 Mc 3,4
separation; τοῦ χωρισμοῦ τῆς ἀφέδρου *of the
menstrual discharge* Lv 12,2, cpr. 18,19;
χωρισμὸν ἐποίουν ἐπὶ τῷ κατὰ τὰς τροφάς
*they held themselves apart in the matter of food,
they stayed away from certain food* 3 Mc 3,4
→LSJ Suppl; LSJ RSuppl

χωροβατέω   V 0-3-0-0-0-3
Jos 18,8(bis).9
to explore, to survey, to measure sth by steps [τι];
neol.?

ψαλίς,-ίδος　　　　　　　　　　　N3F 4-0-0-0-0-4
Ex 27,10.11; 30,4; 37,6(36,38)
band, ring; ψαλίδες *rings*
Cf. LE BOULLUEC 1989, 277; SHIPP 1979, 579;
TAILLARDAT 1978, 1-11; →LSJ RSuppl; SCHLEUSNER

ψάλλω[+]　　　　　　　　　　　V 0-11-0-45-3-59
Jgs 5,3; 1 Sm 16,16(bis).17
to play on a stringed instrument 1 Sm 16,23; *to
sing to sb with* (the accompaniment of a harp)
[τινι ἕν τινι] Ps 97(98),5; *to sing with* (the
accompaniment of a harp) [ἕν τινι] 1 Sm
16,16; *to sing to sb with the accompaniment of a
harp* [τινι] Jgs 5,3; *to praise* [τι] Ps 20(21),14
*Ps 68(69),13 καὶ εἰς ἐμὲ ἔψαλλον *and they
sang to me* ונגנו בי- for MT ונגינות *and the songs*
Cf. HELBING 1928, 69-70; →NIDNTT; TWNT
(→ἐπι-)

ψαλμός,-οῦ[+]　　　　　　　　　N2M 0-2-3-75-12-92
1 Sm 16,18; 2 Sm 23,1; Is 66,20; Am 5,23; Zech
6,14
song of praise, psalm 2 Sm 23,1; *music made
with an instrument* (harp) Am 5,23
*Zech 6,14 εἰς ψαλμόν *for a psalm* -זמרה? for
MT זכרון *memorial*
→NIDNTT; TWNT

ψαλτήριον,-ου　　　　　　　　　N2N 1-0-4-16-4-25
Gn 4,21; Is 5,12; 38,20; Ez 26,13; 33,32
stringed musical instrument, lyre, harp
→LSJ RSuppl

ψάλτης,-ου　　　　　　　　　　　N1M 0-0-0-0-1-1
1 Ezr 5,41
harpist or *psalm-singer, cantor*
→LSJ RSuppl

ψαλτός,-ή,-όν　　　　　　　　　　A 0-0-0-1-0-1
Ps 118(119),54
sung as psalms, sung to the harp; neol.

ψαλῳδέω　　　　　　　　　　　　V 0-1-0-0-0-1
2 Chr 5,13
to sing psalms, to sing to the harp; neol.

ψαλῳδός,-οῦ　　　　　　　　　　N2M 0-10-0-0-3-13
1 Chr 6,18; 9,33; 13,8; 15,16.19
psalm-singer; neol.

ψάμμος,-ου　　　　　　　　　　　N2M 0-0-0-0-2-2
Od 12,9; Wis 7,9
sand

ψαμμωτός,-ή,-όν　　　　　　　　A 0-0-0-0-1-1
Sir 22,17
(made) of stucco or *plaster*

ψαρός,-ά,-όν　　　　　　　　　　A 0-0-3-0-0-3
Zech 1,8; 6,3.7

dapple-grey (of horses)
Cf. SHIPP 1979, 579

ψαύω　　　　　　　　　　　　　　V 0-0-0-0-1-1
4 Mc 17,1
to touch [τινος]

ψάω
(→συμ-)

ψεκάς,-άδος　　　　　　　　　　N3F 0-0-0-2-0-2
Jb 24,8; Ct 5,2
drop (of rain)
→NIDNTT

ψέλιον,-ου　　　　　　　　　　　N2N 4-0-3-1-1-9
Gn 24,22.30.47; Nm 31,50; Is 3,20
armlet Gn 24,22; *clasp* Jb 40,26
Cf. TAILLARDAT 1978, 1-11; →LSJ RSuppl

ψελλίζω　　　　　　　　　　　　V 0-0-2-0-0-2
Is 29,24; 32,4
to stammer, to speak inarticulately

ψευδής,-ής,-ές[+]　　　　　　　　A 2-9-44-31-23-109
Ex 20,16; Dt 5,20; Jgs 16,10; Jgs 16,13
lying, false (of pers.) Prv 21,28; *false* Ex 20,16;
untrue Tob 3,6; *vain* Ps 32(33),17; (ὁ) ψευδής
liar Prv 28,6; ψευδῆ *false things, lies* Jgs 16,10
ἄνθρωπος ψευδής *liar* Sir 20,26
Cf. DODD 1954, 79; →NIDNTT; TWNT

ψευδοθύριον,-ου　　　　　　　　N2N 0-0-0-0-1-1
Bel[LXX] 21
secret door; neol.

ψευδοθυρίς,-ίδος　　　　　　　　N3F 0-0-0-0-1-1
Bel[LXX] 15
secret door; neol.

ψευδολογέω　　　　　　　　　　V 0-0-0-1-0-1
Dn[LXX] 11,27
to speak falsely, to lie

ψευδομαρτυρέω[+]　　　　　　　V 2-0-0-0-1-3
Ex 20,16; Dt 5,20; Sus[Th] 62
*to be a false witness against, to bear false witness
against* [κατά τινος] Sus[Th] 62; *id.* [τι κατά
τινος] Ex 20,16
Cf. LE BOULLUEC 1989, 210; →NIDNTT; TWNT

ψευδομάρτυς,-υρος[+]　　　　　　N3M 0-0-0-0-1-1
Sus[LXX] 60
false witness
Cf. CORSSEN 1918, 106-114; →NIDNTT; TWNT

ψευδοπροφήτης,-ου[+]　　　　　　N1M 0-0-10-0-0-10
Jer 6,13; 33(26),7.8.11.16
false prophet; neol.
Cf. CORSSEN 1918, 106-114; REILING 1971, 147-156;
VAWTER 1985, 218-219; →NIDNTT; TWNT

ψεῦδος,-ους[+]　　　　　　　　　N3N 0-0-20-10-10-40

Is 28,15(bis).17; 30,12; 44,20

lie

Cf. Dodd 1954, 79; →NIDNTT; TWNT

ψεύδω⁺ V 4-3-6-14-11-38

Lv 5,21.22; 19,11; Dt 33,29; Jos 24,27

M: *to lie* [abs.] Lv 19,11; *to speak falsely to* [τινα] Dt 33,29; *id.* [τινι] Ps 17(18),45; *to lie against sth* [εἴς τι] Sus 55; *id.* [ἐναντίον τινός] Jb 31,28; *id.* [κατά τινος] Bel^Th 11

to deal falsely with [τι] Lv 5,21; *to lie concerning* [περί τινος] Lv 5,22; *to belie, to deny* [τι] Jb 6,10; *to deny* [τινα] Jb 8,18

to disappoint [τινα] Hos 9,2; *to disappoint, to fail* [abs.] Hab 3,17

P: *to be deceived* Wis 12,24

Cf. Helbing 1928, 105-106; →NIDNTT; TWNT

(→δια-, κατα-)

ψεύστης,-ου⁺ N1M 0-0-0-2-2-4

Ps 115,2(116,11); Prv 19,22; Sir 15,8; 25,2

liar

→NIDNTT; TWNT

ψηλαφάω⁺ V 5-2-5-3-0-15

Gn 27,12.21.22; Dt 28,29(bis)

A: *to grope* [abs.] Dt 28,29; *to feel, to touch* [τινα] Gn 27,12; *id.* [τι] Jgs^B 16,26; *id.* [abs.] Ps 113,15(115,7); *to search out* [τι] Zech 3,9

P: *to be grasped after* Na 3,1

Zech 9,13 καὶ ψηλαφήσω σε and I will handle you - ומשתיך◊ששמ for MT ושמתיך *and I will put you*

ψηλάφησις,-εως N3F 0-0-0-0-1-1

Wis 15,15

feeling, touching, handling

ψηλαφητός,-ή,-όν A 1-0-0-0-0-1

Ex 10,21

that can be felt; ψηλαφητὸν σκότος *profound darkness, dense darkness*

Cf. Le Boulluec 1989, 139

ψήφισμα,-ατος N3N 0-0-0-2-4-6

Est 3,7; 9,24; 2 Mc 6,8; 10,8; 12,4

decree 2 Mc 6,8; *proposal, decree passed by casting the lot* Est 3,7

ψηφολογέω V 0-0-0-0-2-2

Tob 13,17

to pave with mosaic [τι]; neol.

ψῆφος,-ου⁺ N2M 1-0-0-2-2-5

Ex 4,25; Eccl 7,25; Lam 3,16; 4 Mc 15,26; Sir 18,10

pebble, gravel Lam 3,16; *grain* (of sand) Sir 18,10; *sharp stone* (used as a knife) Ex 4,25; *pebble used in voting, vote* 4 Mc 15,26; *account*

Eccl 7,25

→TWNT

ψιθυρίζω V 0-1-0-1-1-3

2 Sm 12,19; Ps 40(41),8; Sir 21,28

to whisper 2 Sm 12,19; *to whisper against, to spread gossip* or *slander* Ps 40(41),8

(→δια-)

ψιθυρισμός,-οῦ⁺ N2M 0-0-0-1-0-1

Eccl 10,11

whistle (of a snake-charmer); neol.

ψίθυρος,-ος,-ον A 0-0-0-0-6-6

Sir 5,14; 28,13; PSal 12,1.3.4

slanderous PSal 12,1; (ὁ) ψίθυρος *whisperer* Sir 5,14

ψιλή,-ῆς N1F 0-1-0-0-0-1

Jos 7,21

mantle?; neol.

→SCHLEUSNER

ψιλόω V 0-0-1-0-0-1

Ez 44,20

to strip bare, to pluck off [τι]

ψόα,-ας N1F 1-3-0-0-0-4

Lv 3,9; 2 Sm 2,23; 3,27; 20,10

muscles of the pelvis or *loins; see* ψύα

ψογίζω V 0-0-0-0-2-2

1 Mc 11,5.11

to censure, to criticize [τινα]; neol.

Cf. Helbing 1928, 21

ψόγος,-ου N2M 1-0-1-1-2-5

Gn 37,2; Jer 20,10; Ps 30(31),14; 3 Mc 2,27; 3,7

fault, censure

ψοφέω V 0-0-1-0-0-1

Ez 6,11

to make a noise, to stamp (one's foot)

(→ἐπι-)

ψόφος,-ου⁺ N2M 0-0-1-0-0-1

Mi 1,13

sound, noise

ψύα,-ας N1F 0-0-0-1-0-1

Ps 37(38),8

muscles of the pelvis or *loins; see* ψόα

ψυγμός,-οῦ N2M 1-0-3-0-0-4

Nm 11,32; Ez 26,5.14; 47,10

drying, place for drying; neol.?

Cf. Caird 1969=1972, 152; Dorival 1994, 298(Nm 11,32)

ψυκτήρ,-ῆρος N3M 0-0-0-2-0-2

Ezr 1,9(bis)

container for cooling wine

ψύλλος,-ου N2M 0-1-0-0-0-1

1 Sm 24,15

flea; neol.

Cf. SHIPP 1979, 555.584

ψυχαγωγία,-ας   N1F 0-0-0-0-1-1
2 Mc 2,25
amusement, delight

ψυχή,-ῆς[+]   N1F 200-127-154-271-224-976
Gn 1,20.21.24.30; 2,7
life Ex 4,19; *soul* Wis 16,14; *id.* (as centre of the
inner life of pers.) Prv 25,25; *id.* (as centre of
life that transcends the earthly life) 4 Mc 15,4;
conscious self, personality Nm 6,6; *person,
individual* Ex 12,16; *soul, self* (substitute for
reflexive pron.; semit.) Hos 9,4; *corpse* (semit.)
Ez 44,25; ψυχῇ *for the sake of life itself* Dt 16,8
εἰς ψυχήν *so as to die* Gn 37,21; περὶ ψυχῆς *a
matter of life and death* 1 Mc 12,51; ἀπὸ τῆς
ψυχῆς τινος *at the expense of one's life* or
vitality Sir 14,4; ψυχὴ ζῶσῃ *living being, living
creature* Gn 1,20
*Jb 24,7 ψυχῆς *of them?* corr.? ἐν ψύχει
(ψῦχος) for MT בקרה *in the cold*; *Is 21,4 ἡ ψυχή
μου *my soul* -נפשי for MT נשף *twilight*

Cf. ALEXANDRE 1988, 147-148; BRATSIOTIS 1966, 58-89;
DOGNIEZ 1992, 32.197.266; GOODWIN 1881, 73-86; HARL
1984[b]=1992[a], 43-44; 1986[a], 60-61.94.153; HORSLEY 1987,
38.39.144; LARCHER 1985, 870-873.913-914; LE BOULLUEC
1989, 74.148.235; LEE, J. 1969, 235; LYS 1966, 181-228;
MURAOKA 1990, 42-43; ORLINSKY 1962, 119-151;
PIETERSMA 1990, 265-266; ROBERT & ROBERT 1962,
138-139; SCHARBERT 1972, 121-143; →LSJ suppl; NIDNTT;
TWNT

ψυχικός,-ή,-όν[+]   A 0-0-0-0-1-1
4 Mc 1,32
belonging to the soul, mental
→NIDNTT; TWNT

ψυχικῶς   D 0-0-0-0-2-2
2 Mc 4,37; 14,24
heartily, from the heart; neol.

ψῦχος,-ους[+]   N3N 1-0-1-6-2-10

Gn 8,22; Zech 14,6; Ps 147,6(147,17); Jb 37,9;
Dn 3,67
cold, cold weather Gn 8,22
*Zech 14,6 καὶ ψῦχος *and cold* -וְקָרוּת for MT
יְקָרוּת *the glorious ones*

ψυχουλκέομαι   V 0-0-0-0-1-1
3 Mc 5,25
to draw the last breath; neol.

ψυχρός,-ά,-όν[+]   A 0-0-0-1-2-3
Prv 25,25; 4 Mc 11,26; Sir 43,20
cold

Cf. HORSLEY 1983, 144.145; →NIDNTT

ψύχω[+]   V 1-2-3-0-0-6
Nm 11,32; 2 Sm 17,19; 2 Kgs 19,24; Jer 6,7(bis)
to cool, to refresh [τι] Nm 11,32; *to cool* [τι] Jer
6,7; *to seek the cold air* 2 Kgs 19,24; *to dry* [τι]
2 Sm 17,19

(→ἀνα-, ἀπο-, ἐκ-, κατα-, περι-)

ψωμίζω[+]   V 5-1-5-8-4-23
Nm 11,4.18; Dt 8,3.16; 32,13
to feed sb with sth [τινά τι] Nm 11,4; *id.* [τινά
τι] (metaph.) Is 58,14; *id.* [τινα ἔκ τινος] Ps
80(81),17; *to feed sb with morsels* [τινα] 2 Sm
13,5

Cf. DOGNIEZ 1992, 169.328; HARL 1991=1992[a], 138-139;
HELBING 1928, 49-50; WEVERS 1995, 145

ψωμός,-οῦ   N2M 0-3-0-9-0-12
Jgs[B] 19,5; 1 Sm 28,22; 1 Kgs 17,11; Ps 147,6
(147,17); Jb 22,7
morsel, bit
Cf. SHIPP 1979, 583

ψώρα,-ης   N1F 3-0-0-0-0-3
Lv 21,20; 26,16; Dt 28,27
itch, mange, scab

ψωραγριάω   V 1-0-0-0-0-1
Lv 22,22
to have malignant itch, to suffer from mange;
neol.

ὦ⁺   I 3-4-25-11-48-91

Gn 27,20; Nm 24,23(bis); 2 Kgs 3,10; 6,5

Followed by a voc. expressing a mode of
address, it remains untranslated Gn 27,20; *o, ho*
Nm 24,23; *o, ho* [+gen.] Tobˢ 7,6; followed by
a nom. it is often used as a rendition of Hebr.
הוֹי *woe, alas* Na 3,1

*Jer 6,6 ὦ (πόλις ψευδής) *o (false city), woe
(false city)* -הוֹי for MT היא *this (is the city ...)*

Cf. KRAFT 1972, 161.173-175; WALTERS 1973, 228-236

ᾧα,-ας   N1F 2-0-0-1-0-3

Ex 28,32; 36,30(39,23); Ps 132(133),2
border, collar (of a garment)

Cf. SHIPP 1979, 584

ὧδε⁺   D 24-42-12-7-4-89

Gn 15,14.16; 19,12; 22,5; 31,37
hither Gn 15,14; *here* Nm 23,29

Cf. LEE, J. 1983, 81-82

ᾠδή,-ῆς⁺   N1F 7-14-4-47-16-88

Ex 15,1; Dt 31,19(bis).21.22
song, ode (to God) Ex 15,1; *song of praise, joyful
song* Am 8,10

Cf. WEVERS 1990, 227; →NIDNTT

ὠδίν,-ῖνος⁺   N3F 2-3-15-9-7-36

Ex 15,14; Dt 2,25; 1 Sm 4,19; 2 Sm 22,6; 2 Kgs
19,3
labour-pain Is 26,17; mostly pl.: ὠδῖνες *pangs of
childbirth* 1 Sm 4,19; *pangs* (metaph.) Ex 15,14
*2 Sm 22,6 ὠδῖνες (θανάτου) *pangs (of death)*
-חֶבְלֵי◊ חֶבֶל◊? *labour-pains* for MT חבלי *bonds,
cords (of death)*, cpr. Ps 17(18),5; 114(115),3,
see θάνατος; *Ez 7,4(7) ὠδίνων *pangs* -הרה◊? for
MT הרים *mountains*

Cf. BOGAERT 1986, 33(Ez 7,4(7)); DOGNIEZ 1992, 125-126;
WALTERS 1973, 293(Jer 22,23); →NIDNTT; SCHLEUSNER;
TWNT

ὠδίνω⁺   V 0-0-13-3-6-22

Is 23,4; 26,17; 26,18; 45,10; 51,2
*to have the pains of childbirth, to suffer the pains
of childbirth* Sir 19,11; *to be in labour with*
[τινα] Ct 8,5
to be in labour with [τι] (metaph.) Ps 7(8),15; *to
be in labour* (metaph. of the earth) Is 66,8; *to be
in pain* (metaph. of a people) Hab 3,10

Cf. KATZ 1956, 271(Sir 43,17); WALTERS 1973, 128(Sir
43,17); →NIDNTT; TWNT

ᾠδός,-οῦ   N2M 0-4-0-0-0-4

1 Kgs 10,12; 2 Kgs 11,14; 2 Chr 9,11; 23,13
singer 1 Kgs 10,12
*2 Kgs 11,14 καὶ οἱ ᾠδοί *and the singers* -וְהַשָּׂרִים

for MT וְהַשָּׂרִים *and the captains*, see also 2 Chr
23,13

Cf. BICKERMAN 1980, 61

ὠθέω⁺   V 2-0-2-3-0-7

Nm 35,20.22; Is 30,22; Jer 41(34),11; Ps 61(62),4
to thurst, to shove [τινα] Nm 35,20
καὶ ἔωσαν αὐτοὺς εἰς παῖδας καὶ παιδίσκας
*and they gave them over to be men-servants and
maid-servants* Jer 41(34),11; ὦσας αὐτὸν εἰς
τέλος *you drove him to the end* Jb 14,20;
φραγμῷ ὠσμένῳ *with a broken edge* Ps 61(62),4
*Is 30,22 ὤσεις *you shall thrust forth* -תמאס? *you
shall refuse* for MT תאמר *you shall say*

(→ἀπ-, δι-, ἐξ-, παρα-, προσ-)

ὠμία,-ας   N1F 0-13-0-0-0-13

1 Sm 9,2; 10,23; 1 Kgs 6,8; 7,17.20(30.34)
shoulder 1 Sm 9,2; *side, angle, corner* (of
building or part of a building) 1 Kgs 6,8;
shoulder-piece (to support a sacred vessel) 1 Kgs
7,17; neol.

→LSJ RSuppl

ὠμόλινον,-ου   N2N 0-0-0-0-1-1

Sir 40,4
flax, raw rough cloth, cloth made of raw flax

ὦμος,-ου⁺   N2M 13-9-17-3-7-49

Gn 21,14; 24,15.45; 49,15; Ex 12,34
shoulder Gn 21,14; *id.* (in a dress) Ex 28,12
*Jer 38(31),21 εἰς τοὺς ὤμους *to the shoulders*
corr. εἰς τοὺς οἴμους *to the roads* for MT למסלה
to the road; *Is 10,27 (ἀπὸ) τῶν ὤμων *(from) the
shoulders* -שכם◊ for MT שמן *fatness, oil*?; *Mal 2,3
τὸν ὦμον *the shoulder* -זרוע *the arm* for MT זרע
offspring

Cf. WEVERS 1990, 449

ὠμός,-ή,-όν   A 1-0-0-0-4-5

Ex 12,9; 2 Mc 4,25; 7,27; 4 Mc 9,30; 18,20
raw (of food) Ex 12,9; *cruel* (of pers.) 2 Mc
4,25; *cruel, barbarous* (of things) 4 Mc 18,20
ὠμότατε τύραννε *most cruel tyrant, most
ruthless of tyrants* 4 Mc 9,30

ὠμότης,-ητος   N3F 0-0-0-0-4-4

2 Mc 12,5; 3 Mc 5,20; 6,24; 7,5
cruelty, savagery, fierceness

ὠμοτοκέω   V 0-0-0-1-0-1

Jb 21,10
to miscarry; neol.

ὠμόφρων,-ων,-ον   A 0-0-0-0-1-1

4 Mc 9,15
savage-minded, cruel-minded

φόν,-οῦ⁺   N2N 2-0-3-2-0-7

Dt 22,6(bis); Is 10,14; 59,5(bis)
egg

ὥρα,-ας⁺   N1F 14-10-3-30-17-74
Gn 18,10.14; 29,7; Ex 9,18; 10,4
fitting time, season Gn 29,7; *season* (one of the
four seasons) 1 Ezr 9,11; *time, moment* Ex 9,18;
springtime Is 52,7; *fruit, product* Dt 33,13
εἰς ὥρας *next year* or *in due time, hereafter* Gn
18,10; πᾶσαν ὥραν *hour after hour, every hour,
constantly* Ex 18,22; αὐτῇ τῇ ὥρᾳ *at that very
time, at once, instantly* Dnᵀʰ 3,6
*1 Sm 25,6 εἰς ὥρας *in due time* -◊ חיה *life, time*
(cpr. Gn 18,10.14) for MT לחי (= לאחי?) *to my
brother?*; *Dnᴸˣˣ 11,45 ὥρα *time* -עת for MT ער *to,
towards*
Cf. DOGNIEZ 1992, 189.349; DORIVAL 1994, 55; HARL
1986ᵃ, 175; 1991=1992ᵃ, 149; LE BOULLUEC 1989, 157;
ROST 1967, 129-132; WEVERS 1990, 133; 1993, 250; 1995,
547(Dt 33,13); →LSJ suppl(1 Sm 25,6); LSJ Rsuppl(1 Sm
25,6); NIDNTT; TWNT

ὡραΐζω   V 0-0-0-0-1-1
Sir 25,1
P: *to be made beautiful, to be beautified, to enjoy
beauty, to take delight*

ὡραΐοομαι   V 0-1-0-3-0-4
2 Sm 1,26; Ct 1,10; 7,2.7
to be beautiful; neol.

ὡραῖος,-α,-ον⁺   A 6-4-4-9-13-36
Gn 2,9; 3,6; 26,7; 29,17; 39,6
beautiful (of things) Gn 2,9; *well-formed* Sir
26,18; *beautiful, graceful* (of pers.) Gn 29,17; *ripe*
(of fruit) Lv 23,40; *proper* Sir 15,9; τὰ ὡραῖα
the beauty Jb 18,13
Cf. HARL 1991=1992ᵃ, 149; SHIPP 1979, 585; →NIDNTT

ὡραιότης,-ητος   N1F 0-0-1-5-0-6
Ez 16,14; Ps 44(45),4; 49(50),2.11; 67(68),13
beauty Ps 44(45),4; *ripeness* Ps 49(50),11
Cf. DANIEL 1966, 261

ὡραϊσμός,-οῦ   N2M 0-0-1-0-0-1
Jer 4,30
elegance, adornment; neol.

ὥριμος,-ος,-ον⁺   A 0-0-1-1-0-2
Jer 28(51),33; Jb 5,26
in season Jer 28(51),33; *ripe* Jb 5,26

ὥρυμα,-ατος   N3N 0-0-1-0-0-1
Ez 19,7
roaring; neol.

ὡρύομαι⁺   V 0-2-5-3-2-12
Jgs 14,5; Jer 2,15; Ez 22,25; Hos 11,10
to roar (of lions) Jgsᴮ 14,5; *id.* (of wild anim.)

Wis 17,18; *to howl, to roar* (of pers.) Ps 37(38),9
Cf. SHIPP 1979, 586

(→ἐπ-)

ὡς⁺   C/D/I 151-379-599-394-520-2043
Gn 3,5.22; 6,4; 9,3; 10,9
as conjunction: like Gn 3,22; *as, like* (comp.
clause) Is 26,17; *when* (temporal clause) Gn
27,30; *so that* (consecutive clause) Wis 5,12; *that*
(object clause) 1 Sm 13,11
ὡς ... οὕτως ... *as ... so ...* Is 53,7
as adv.: about, nearly [+numeral] 1 Sm 13,15; *as
... possible* [+sup.] Ps 22(23),5
as interjection: how (exclamation) Ps 8,2
Cf. MURAOKA 1964, 51-72

ὧς   D 1-0-4-3-2-10
Lv 26,44; Ez 16,47; Am 4,9.10.11
so, thus Eccl 9,2
οὐδ' ὧς *not even so* Lv 26,44

ὡσανεί   C 0-0-0-1-0-1
Est 1,1i
as it were

ὡσαύτως⁺   D 11-5-4-4-16-40
Ex 7,11.22; 8,3.14; 30,32
in like manner, just so Ex 7,11; *in return* Lv
24,19

ὡσεί⁺   C/D 44-28-17-81-10-180
Gn 19,28; 21,16; 24,55; 25,25; 34,31
as if, like Gn 19,28; *about* [+numeral] Gn 24,55

ὥσπερ⁺   C/D 33-11-41-137-41-263
Gn 37,9; 38,11; 41,2.18.22
like, as, even as Gn 37,9; *as it were* 4 Mc 6,16

ὥστε⁺   C/D 62-27-13-26-54-182
Gn 1,15.17; 9,15; 15,7; 23,8
for this reason, therefore, so [+imper.] (introducing an independent clause) 4 Mc 11,16; *so
that* [+inf.] Gn 1,15; *id.* [sine verbo] Lv 27,2; *for
the purpose of, in order that* [+inf.] Jb 6,23
ὥστε λίαν *very, exceedingly* 2 Sm 2,17
Cf. MURAOKA 1973, 205-219

-ωτίζομαι
(→ἐν-)

ὠτίον,-ου⁺   N2N 1-8-3-2-3-17
Dt 15,17; 1 Sm 9,15; 20,2.13; 22,8
dim. of οὖς; *ear* (usu. syn. of οὖς) Dt 15,17; *(a
small) handle* Ps 17(18),45

ὠτότμητος,-ος,-ον   A 2-0-0-0-0-2
Lv 21,18; 22,23
with ears chopped off or *cut off*; neol.

ὠφέλεια,-ας⁺   N1F 0-1-4-3-5-13
2 Sm 18,22; Is 30,5; Jer 23,32; 26(46),11;

37(30),13

help Jer 26(46),11; *profit* 2 Sm 18,22; *gain made in war, spoil, booty* 2 Mc 8,20

*Jer 26(46),11 ὠφέλεια *help* -תועלת ◊ יעל? for MT עלה ◊ תעלה *healing*, see also 37(30),13

ὠφελέω⁺   V 0-0-14-3-10-27

Is 30,5.6.7; 44,9; 47,12

to be of use, to benefit Hab 2,18; *to benefit, to profit* [τινα] Prv 10,2; *id.* [τινι] Sir 34,25; *to be good* Prv 25,13; *to do good to* [τινα] Sir 38,21;

to help [τινα] Tob^BA 2,10; *to have advantages* Ps 88(89),23; *to gain* [τι] Sir 34,23

Cf. HARL 1992ᵃ=1992ᵇ, 235(Jer 15,10); HELBING 1928, 1-2

ὠφέλημα,-ατος   N3N 0-0-1-0-0-1

Jer 16,19

benefit, use

ὤχρα,-ας   N1F 1-0-0-0-0-1

Dt 28,22

yellow ochre, mildew

Cf. DOGNIEZ 1992, 288